TELEVISION

The Critical View

SEVENTH EDITION

Edited by
HORACE NEWCOMB
University of Georgia

New York   Oxford
OXFORD UNIVERSITY PRESS
2007

Oxford University Press, Inc., publishes works that further Oxford University's
objective of excellence in research, scholarship, and education.

Oxford   New York
Auckland   Cape Town   Dar es Salaam   Hong Kong   Karachi
Kuala Lumpur   Madrid   Melbourne   Mexico City   Nairobi
New Delhi   Shanghai   Taipei   Toronto

With offices in
Argentina   Austria   Brazil   Chile   Czech Republic   France   Greece
Guatemala   Hungary   Italy   Japan   Poland   Portugal   Singapore
South Korea   Switzerland   Thailand   Turkey   Ukraine   Vietnam

Published by Oxford University Press, Inc.
198 Madison Avenue, New York, New York, 10016
http://www.oup.com

Library of Congress Cataloging-in-Publication Data

Television : the critical view / edited by Horace Newcomb. — 7th ed.
    p.   cm.
ISBN-13: 978-0-19-530116-8 (alk. paper)
ISBN-10: 0-19-530116-1 (alk. paper)
1. Television broadcasting—United States.   I. Newcomb, Horace.

PN1992.3.U5T42   2006
91.45'0973—dc27
                                        2005050881

Printing number: 9 8 7 6 5 4 3 2 1

Printed in the United States of America
on acid-free paper

For my colleagues in the Grady College
of Journalism and Mass Communication
at the University of Georgia

CONTENTS

PREFACE TO THE SEVENTH EDITION

In the summer of 2005 I participated in a workshop dealing with the premise that "television, as the medium of shared experience, is dead or dying." The invitation to the workshop went on to describe television, as most of us now know it, as an invention or device variously—almost randomly—placed in home or other setting, providing a substantial if not enormous number of offerings and perhaps "personally programmed" with digital video recorders or other means.

This description of "the medium," as we once referred to it, follows tendencies outlined in the introduction to the previous edition of this collection entitled "Television and the Present Climate of Criticism." I have not revised that introductory essay for this volume because I consider the current conditions to indicate the continuation of those tendencies, and also because the larger contexts of television remain in a process of change. As essays in this collection suggest, many of the "foundational" notions related to the analysis and criticism of television emerged from the study of other media and were grounded in questions common to fields such as sociology or political science on one side, on literary and film study on the other. Increasingly, there have been advances that now approach various aspects of television in terms created specifically for that purpose. These include attempts to define the aesthetic properties, the narrative strategies, the generic formations, the modes of production, the varieties of reception, the industrial practices, the economic and policy contexts, and other factors that may have been discovered, invented, understood only in terms of this device, this institution, this experience.

We must inquire, however, whether any approach or merged set of approaches, any set of questions or methods, any examples, interviews, observations, or other body of evidence can "keep up" with changes and developments in television. On the other hand, we can suggest that despite any sense of "change," the basic questions of expression, representation, rhetoric, ideology, culture, society, or effects remain in place. And yet another approach would posit that every instance requires the formulation of questions specific to itself. Even this most focused analytic strategy would, of course, acknowledge and apply important work done previously, work on which any serious study would build.

That the questions and approaches, the objects and examples, the processes and effects, the evidence and the arguments continue to spread across so many aspects of social and cultural experience indicates both the difficulty and the necessity of our attempts to understand many of them. The point of this collection has never been to discover, define, or determine "the right way" to examine television. Indeed, such an attempt would undermine the very notion of "criticism" or "analysis" or "study" as best understood.

This edition presents a wider range of problems and of attempts to address them than previous ones. As suggested, this results in part from changes in industrial, technological, economic, and political circumstances. But it is also a result of experimentation within those contexts, of distinct efforts to tell stories, transmit information, educate, and inspire. And it is the result as well of a growing body of scholarship, constructed on previous work and recognized within educational institutions and professional organizations as significant efforts to understand television, no matter what its current configuration.

H. N.
Athens, Georgia

PREFACE TO THE FIRST EDITION

The essays in this collection were selected because they view television in broad rather than narrow perspectives. Newspaper columns have not been included. This is not to say that newspaper criticism is excluded by definition from a breadth of vision, but simply that the pieces included here all develop their point of view in the single essay rather than over a period of time, as is the case with the columnist.

The essays in the first section all deal with specific program types. They serve as excellent models for practical television criticism because they show us that there is a great deal of difference between watching television and "seeing" it. They are, of course, involved with critical interpretation and assertion. Other analyses of the same programs may be offered by other critics, and the audience, as critic, must learn to make its own decisions. These essays will help in that learning process.

The second section is comprised of essays that attempt to go beyond the specific meanings of specific programs or program types. They suggest that television has meaning in the culture because it is not an isolated, unique entity. These writers want to know what television means, for its producers, its audiences, its culture.

The essays in the final section are concerned with what television is. They seek to define television in terms of itself, to determine how it is like and how it is different from other media.

All the essays are seeking connections, trying to place television in its own proper, enlarged critical climate. Consequently, many of them use similar examples, ask similar questions, and rest on shared assumptions. Some of the connections are obvious. Others will occur to the reader using the book. In this way the reader too becomes a critic and the printed comments may serve to stimulate a new beginning, a new and richer viewpoint regarding television.

I would like to express my thanks to John Wright of Oxford University Press for his initial interest and continued support for this book. His suggestions have strengthened it throughout. A special note of thanks must go to all my friends and colleagues who have made suggestions about the book and who, in some cases, have offered their own fine work for inclusion. Thanks, too, goes to my family for the supportive world in which I work.

H. N.
Baltimore
November 1975

TELEVISION

Television and the Present Climate of Criticism

The purpose of this collection has always been the same, to contribute to what Moses Hadas many years ago referred to as the "climate of criticism." In defining that concept he admonished "all who take education seriously in its larger sense" to "talk and write about television as they do about books." Earlier editions of the collection struggled with the fact that this was hardly the case, the realization that television was rarely considered a prominent, significant, or special contributor to culture and society. It was seen as neither conduit for nor commentator on the aesthetic, political, or moral lives of citizens—except in the most negative manner. When television was "seriously" thought of by anyone who would take education seriously in its large sense, it was most often figured as intruder, complicator, as rogue or polluter. Many of these attempts to understand the medium must now be seen as incomplete, partial, narrow definitions supporting one narrow perspective or another.

This is not to say that television should have been warmly and naively welcomed into society and home. Many aspects of the medium (less than fifty years old in its basic forms) were and are troublesome, threatening, oppressive, repressive, and obnoxious. So, too, are many books. The issue—the problem for criticism, for this collection and others, for teachers and students in classrooms—has been the development of vocabularies sufficient to consider all these matters. A second purpose of this anthology has been to explore the development of that vocabulary from the perspective of the "humanities," broadly defined. That is to say, because television was early on considered as a social problem, many approaches and considerable terminology had already been developed to deal with the medium by the time scholars, critics, and thinkers who had traditionally focused their attention on books turned to this newer medium. Those first approaches, terms, and analytical paradigms were drawn largely from the realms of social psychology and sociology and had little use for strategies that would look closely at television as an expressive form.

This aspect of the "climate" of television criticism is the one that has altered most perceptibly in recent years, years encompassing previous editions of *Television: The Critical View* and now affording work for the present volume. And while this feature has changed, many others implied in Hadas's comments have remained essentially the same. This introduction focuses on the differences and similarities that can be marked in the present critical climate.

The most prominent change in our understanding and approach to television has occurred within academic settings. "Television studies" is now an established area of concern in many universities. While the concept, the term, and the designation are constantly under discussion and revision, it is clear that from this academic perspective, Hadas's admonition is taken quite seriously. Interestingly enough, however, the development of television studies has modified our basic notions of what the medium is, what "humanities approaches" consist of, and what the role of "academic" discourse surrounding television (or any other subject) has to do with "education in its larger sense."

Television studies as an academic enterprise developed from four major backgrounds. In the United States the first of these was grounded in literary studies that redirected critical analysis toward the study of popular entertainment forms: novels, material culture, magazines, radio programs, and so on. The study of popular films was also important in this enterprise but developed through a somewhat different route, to be discussed below. The choice to examine these "inferior" or "unappreciated" forms was motivated by a number of concerns. Philosophically, scholars in this movement often felt the works they wished to examine were more indicative of larger cultural preferences, expressive of a more "democratic" relationship between works and audiences than the "elite" works selected, archived, and taught as the traditional canon of humanistically valued forms of expression.

Politically, these same impulses suggested that it was important to study these works precisely because their exclusion from canonical systems also excluded their audiences, devalued large numbers of citizens, or saddled them with inferior intellectual or aesthetic judgment. It is not coincidental that the study of popular entertainment developed momentum at the end of the 1960s, when many cultural categories were under question and when these questions made their way into educational institutions as questions concerning curricula, canonical content, and the value of "traditions."

For the most part, though these early studies were politically motivated, presented as part of far larger political movements and actions, they did not offer systematic ideological analyses of the works they examined. Their agenda was broadly cultural, examining popular forms for their contribution to ongoing discussions about various "meanings" within expressive culture. They did, however, open questions of how we might study nontraditional forms of cultural expression; games, events, designs, fashion. And it is necessary to remember that many of these analyses were carried out prior to the intense concern with theories of how meanings might be systematically imposed through cultural codes, social strategies, industrial organization, or other more embedded and socially grounded influences on expression. These early studies of popular culture were, rather, one of the final applications of critical analysis rooted in what is referred to in traditional literary studies as the New Criticism. And in this linkage they represent the extension of New Critical questions to "profane" culture thus contributing, in my view, to a radical modification and appropriation of that form of analysis. What remains of New Critical approaches, an immensely valuable contribution, is the close attention to textual detail, even when this "close analysis" is exercised in the examination of social constructs, cultural patterns, behaviors, and artifacts that far exceed earlier notions of "texts."

The second major influence on television studies emerged in Europe, its primary sources for American students coming from Great Britain. Cultural studies, developing from the work of Raymond Williams, Richard Hoggart, and Stuart Hall, had already begun to examine similar artifacts, television among them, as American popular culture scholars, but had done so within a far more formidable analytical tradition. Where American approaches had acknowledged something about "politics" in their work, the British scholars systematically explored "ideology."

This work was profoundly influenced by continental Marxism and structural anthropology, two varying but in early stages almost equally powerful forms of "structuralism." While Marxist theory analyzed structures grounded in the economic determination of social categories, structural anthropology searched for (and presumably in) "mental structures" that crossed specific social, geographic, and cultural boundaries. The argument that much of human experience, from "texts" to forms of social organization and action, was informed, ordered, and directed by "deeper" structures was immensely powerful. It allowed scholars and critics to bundle vast amounts of discrete artifacts and events into significant and manageable "patterns." The patterns, the formulas, the genres, the classes—of citizens or of texts—were the items to be analyzed. Complexities of contemporary life were thus more easily handled, described, and written about.

Work done at the Centre for Contemporary Cultural Studies at the University of Birmingham struggled with these varied and mixed approaches, sorted through theories and methods, and offered a number of powerful models for research on a number of topics. One of the primary syntheses accomplished centered on the work of Antonio Gramsci and the application of notions of hegemony to the study of contemporary culture. Mass media generally and television specifically occupied central positions of inquiry in these efforts.

When these approaches reached American universities, they reached into work already primed for more systematic analysis, and television studies, among other topics, eagerly appropriated some of the models, techniques, and styles of analysis. These American appropriations also distorted, in the view of some scholars and critics, the critical analysis of ideology that undergirded British work.

They did mesh well, however, with a third influence on the developing field of television studies. This work maintained the ideological focus and drew on the tradition of critical sociology associated with the Frankfurt School of sociological analysis. In the United States analysis of television carried out in departments of sociology and philosophy was most involved with these sources. Academic critics working from this tradition were able to critique what they perceived to be a central weakness in the earlier "popular culture" approach, its reliance on a naive notion of "liberal pluralism" central to many expressive forms. The arrival of "British cultural studies" required and enabled some scholars working within that earlier tradition to sharpen their own critiques, to recognize weaknesses and gaps in their work, and to move to a more complex perspective on television and other aspects of popular expressive culture. Generally, the arrival and conflicted acceptance of cultural studies approaches in the United States overlaps heavily with the development of television studies, and ongoing debates have developed around the varying emphases on and definitions of ideology.

A fourth influence on television studies emerged from the growing body of film studies in the United States and abroad. Unlike television, film had been accepted, in some quarters since its earliest days, as a "fine art." In popular general discussion, many of the same issues and concerns that would occupy critics of television—crass commercialism, "debased" moral attitudes, direct influence on viewer behavior, ideological agendas—were central to discussions of movies. Still, some early popular, and much academic, discussion of film took on a far more appreciative tone. And at times film occupied a decidedly noble position within public discourse. Put another way, the "climate of criticism" for film has, throughout its history, been more favorable than that surrounding television. In its most recent stages, film criticism, both for the general reader and for the academic community, developed sophisticated and complex forms and styles of analysis widely accepted as legitimate.

Even in these discussions, however, much of the work focused historically on its own canonical topics: films produced in Europe or other parts of the world, experimental or lyrical personal films created by individual artists in all countries, and early popular film that had taken on a valued status because of the announced "declines" (formal, social, aesthetic) that followed. Categories of analysis were often quite close to those used for formal analysis of literary works by New Critics, but moved quickly to the appropriation and development of various forms of structuralism. And perhaps even more significantly, film studies explored an extraordinary range of applications of psychoanalytic theory to its objects.

The study of popular American film, the "Hollywood film," came later, and with considerable opposition. But much of the recognition of the particular value of these works came from European critics and filmmakers who saw in Hollywood a form of personal and cultural expression with its own powerful creative techniques, its own intrinsic values. Gradually, the study of popular American film was accepted in the United States as a legitimate enterprise. At times this work was related to the broader study of popular culture, but because of the history of film studies, it remained, for the most part, separate.

When these approaches were infused by the same European theories of structuralism, Marxism, and cultural studies, another wave of work emerged and, slowly at first, then more swiftly, film scholars turned their attention to television. In some cases this involved the straightforward application of film theory to the newer medium. And in many instances it also involved the modification or rejection of those theories because of the many significant differences between the two media.

Operating throughout this history, crossing all these influences, and so widespread as to be an influence on almost every field of study in the humanities and elsewhere, was and is feminist theory. I list it as a separate force because it exceeds television studies even while it is now central to that topic.

The recognition of gendered distinctions has been central to television studies in two ways. First, as in many other fields, it has called into question the theoretical base of many approaches, from considerations of form to the organization of labor in the creation of television texts. Second, and more problematic, television itself has been defined at times as a "feminine" medium. This designation rises on the one hand from the economic-social fact of television's "address" to women through its base in advertiser-supported, consumer-targeted content. On the other hand, it emerges from arguments that the form of television (again in advertiser-supported commercial systems such as American television), with its demand for open, unending narrative strategies, relates somehow to feminine experience. Discussion of such questions continues. Within either formulation, feminist theorists have been among the most active and perceptive in the study of television and all theoretical positions must take note of these approaches to the medium.

None of these influences, however, should be taken as fully definitive, fully encompassing the study of television. For one thing, their application to television was merely part of larger discussions of their usefulness in studying an array of cultural artifacts: literary, cinematic, pictorial, social. And they were applied to "high" as well as "low" or "popular" forms and behaviors.

Moreover, no sooner than one influence was fully absorbed, others were layered upon it. Much of the discussion in what might be termed the "theory wars" in the academic life of the seventies and eighties had to do with ways in which varying methods and systematic approaches might be applied in varying contexts, or might be combined for more powerful forms of analysis. These ongoing intellectual discussions and struggles are not conducted merely over the utility of methods and theories. They are also directed by more profound questions of epistemology, of how we know what we know. And they are legitimate attempts to come to terms with the role of expressive forms in the social and political lives of citizens as individuals and members of social groups. They are attempts to contribute to social and cultural improvement, to understand the role of expressive media in constructing or altering forms of inequality and oppression. Despite attempts to present these ongoing discussions as mere tempests in small teapots, or as the corrupt agenda of "radicals" in universities, these sometimes fierce exchanges, these often arcane presentations of ideas, have most often been good faith attempts to recognize and understand how social life, now dependent on mass media, on popular forms of expression and entertainment, on the far-reaching lines of information afforded by new technologies, can best be taught and understood, learned, and used by all citizens.

Thus it is that various forms of structuralism have been challenged by what have now been defined as "post-structuralist" assumptions. From these perspectives the very notions of "unified" or "coherent" patterns of meaning, of social organization, or of individual psychology are called into question. How can invariant meanings be established by individuals who are themselves constructed of multiple and conflicting psychological, social, and cultural influences? How can mass audiences "receive" coherent meanings from ambiguous and conflicted texts, be they television programs, canonically approved "high culture," films, or rock and roll? And if these varying, conflicting, multiple, unstable artifacts and users are constantly engaged in the process of "constructing" their own social meanings and behaviors, how can any coherent ideological effects be determined?

Added to post-structuralist problems are those suggested by a related category, "postmodernism." Here the issues of instability and potential incoherence are taken in still other directions, in some cases to still greater levels of challenge.

For some critics, commentators, and scholars the notion of postmodernism means simply that all citizens are now both creator and critic, making up their own individual or group culture from the massive resources of our "cultural archives." In this view the mixing of style and fashion, image and ideology, meaning and significance, are evidence of a new, liberated consciousness. For others, however, the consequences of postmodernism are far more significant, more dire. The very possibility of meaningful discourse, about politics and ideology, categories of thought and social organization, about any sense of "shared culture," seems either impossible or now requires new forms of analysis, argument, and expression. This is especially the case if, as some arguments would have it, there is no longer any way to establish the "real" in human experience, if all has dissolved into "representation."

Most important for our concerns here, television has often been seen as both cause and effect, source and symptom, agent and evidence of these newer social and cultural developments. This is especially the case when "television" is defined as or by "American commercial television." And because the form of American commercial television is shared throughout the world, either through the export of programming or through the collapse of various forms of public service broadcasting in the face of an advancing privatization of investment, "television" in any context often means "American TV."

American TV is defined most fundamentally in these discussions by its commercialism. And commercialism results in, indeed demanded, continuous programming flow, organized programming strategies matched to other forms of social organization, and the constant attempts to enforce existing power relationships. Thus, television secures conventional and dominant formations of race, class, gender, age, ethnicity, region, and style. So long as the fundamental purpose of the medium can be defined as the delivery of audiences to advertisers, or perhaps more significantly as uniting the world within an equation of television, consumerism, and "reality," using all possible strategies to accomplish this end, civilization itself must be thought of as sliding into the postmodern condition exemplified by television. This concern, fear, pessimistic conclusion has been heightened in recent years by vast changes in the technological and economic contexts of television. As we have moved, in American and world television, from a few central network presentations to the vast proliferation of televisual options, the postmodern model has taken on ever-increasing power.

Again, however, our very notion of a "climate of criticism" should alert us to the fact that climates are changeable, always unstable, never the same in two places at once. The field of television studies is neither closely bounded nor fixed. Questions implied by this brief survey of the winds that have crossed the field in the past ten years remain unsettled, unanswered. In many cases they are in constant states of reconsideration. Keeping this background in mind, then, I will now suggest some of the most pressing categories of questions that define the field at the present moment. These are, in some cases, the questions that have directed the reorganization of this collection, changing its format from that of previous editions. It is necessary in examining these questions to remember that none of the issues discussed above has "gone away." Rather, new problems, new issues, are woven into others. Some of them are refined and some approaches are made stronger. Others are seen as less helpful and partially discarded. Still others are applied under new conditions, in response to changes in television itself. In all cases, criticism works with both the wisdom and the burden of its own pasts carried into the present. Moreover, it is equally important to remember that while questions may be grouped in patterns, answers remain more diverse. Even when several essays are presented here as focused on similar questions, their approaches and techniques for understanding and answering those questions may differ widely.

Early television criticism focused on definitions of the television "text," its forms and conventions, and the meanings of these patterns. Often the analysis was conducted as a form of genre study, and the question of meanings circulated between individual instances of a genre—programs or series—and the larger group to which the instance belonged. Meaning was discovered in both the generic pattern and at the level of "plot" or "story."

Another wave of critical discussion focused on issues of ideology, and here meaning, significance and effect were discovered at the level of structure and organization. Clearly, genre remains central in such inquiry, but the primary shift was from meaning residing *in* genre and individual instance to the ways in which these patterns reorganized and reinforced existing social meanings.

This critical discussion of television and ideology continues to offer some of the most prominent questions for television studies, questions that inform many of the essays in this collection and are somehow, directly or indirectly, addressed by all of them. In one sense this merely indicates that television analysis and criticism are part of a much larger critical enterprise, for the centrality of ideological issues is now common to almost all humanistic discourse. The remaining problem is, what are the unique features of television that demand critical explication? Early explorations of television from this perspective often viewed television as little more than an "ideology machine," churning out replications of the most oppressive and repressive aspects of contemporary American society. Some of this work was grounded in film study and could not escape more widespread notions that television is merely a degenerate cinematic form. Other versions were far more sophisticated and sought to define television's specific economic, social, aesthetic, and cultural characteristics in order to show that it contributed to, rather than replaced, other forms of ideological discourse.

These views of television as ideologically monolithic, however, were quickly displaced by some of these same attempts. As the medium was analyzed and described more precisely and from different perspectives, the question shifted. Instead of asking, How does television perform this monolithic ideological function? questions came to center on whether or not television was so unified in its forms and effects. One way to formulate the problem at this moment is to grant that the medium (like all others) is varied and conflicted, but to ask whether or not it is more "open" or "closed," more rigid or flexible as a form of ideological expression. Even more precisely, we must seek to determine the circumstances in which either condition will define the case. Clearly, this means that all the questions of form, genre, content—broadly defined as the aesthetic questions—must still come into play. Many of the questions focused on these topics are addressed by essays in part 3 of this collection, essays that focus on specific programs or program types. As some of these essays indicate, the questions must be examined in far richer contexts than in many early studies.

Defining contexts is the problem at the center of the second major focus of contemporary television criticism, and various attempts to establish these contexts now occupy a far more prominent place in television studies than in earlier periods. Again, these developments led to the reorganization of this collection. Major contributions to this area of concern came from the introduction of cultural studies approaches to our critical repertoire, for the reinsertion of expressive forms into social context lies at the heart of this enterprise.

The two most significant contextual categories in contemporary television studies are broadly defined as the context of "production" and the context of "reception." Part 2 of the current collection focuses on various forms of production studies. The essays variously examine industrial, technological, and creative contexts of television production both social and industrial. They involve broad applications of technique and design within television program types and present case studies of the production of specific television programs.

Essays in part 4 focus on the reception context. Here the studies are also informed by serious disagreements over the limits of audiences' interpretive power. Are meanings constructed in the process of "receiving" television? If so, are audiences able to "subvert" those meanings that interpretive critics might find repressive or regressive? In what instances is such power exercised? What other social factors might direct or limit this process of meaning making? These questions have become central to the current discussions of this medium and others. Here, too, are interesting examples of other kinds of interactions with television, especially those involving variations in national political and cultural contexts.

In this edition, however, another version of context is given its own prominence. Part 1 provides a selection of essays focused on the histories of television. The term must be plural because historical analysis has ranged from case studies of particular programs to policy debates, from studies of individual careers to concerns about industrial strategies. The body of work from which these essays were drawn has become one of the richest in television studies, as more and more scholars recognize that easily received notions of television history demand more precise examination. These essays open new doors for students as well as other scholars.

The final section of the collection offers essays that attempt larger overviews of the entire medium of television. Some focus on aesthetic concerns, some on social. Many see the necessity of avoiding such easy dichotomies and seek various forms of synthesis. It is in this section that a clearer distinction between earlier approaches and later ones emerges. Newer essays, more focused on television's social and technological proliferation, and informed by notions of post-structuralism and postmodernism, ask decidedly different questions from those presented in earlier editions of this collection. But the newer questions could not have been formulated without the older ones, and the resonances among these explanations are telling.

As stated above, almost all these developments in the burgeoning field of television studies have taken place within academic settings. There, it is now commonplace for television to be taken as seriously as books by scholars and critics in various fields. This has not been the case, however, in writing offered to more general audiences. There the best writing about television remains essentially personal, individualized, subjective. While occasionally interesting, the commentary is most often repetitive, familiar, unwilling to consider the possibility that television presents itself in terms distinctive and definable. Questions remain much the same as over the past decades. Answers to those questions that might be available from academic approaches to television are overlooked or ignored. In worst cases, writers for general readers look on in bemused and thinly veiled contempt at the academic critics. The implication is that no one should take television *this* seriously.

There remains, then, another step, another stage in the history of television criticism. In that stage the serious histories, the detailed analyses, the studies of television reception that now remain, in every sense of the word, "academic" approaches to television will be shared more widely with all audiences. This book is an attempt to assist in taking that next step. And it must be stated here that there are problems with presenting some academic criticism to general audiences. Academic critics and scholars bear responsibility for making their work clear, powerful, accessible, usable. But an equal responsibility is borne by editors and writers for more generally distributed publications. One part of that responsibility rests in taking the academic work more seriously, learning from its insights, its hard historical work, its detailed case studies. Another part of the responsibility is grounded in the very lack of opportunity for anyone to write seriously about television for the public. Too many newspapers relegate television criticism to small columns in back pages. Too few magazines print television commentary of any sort other than the contemptuous or satirical.

There is no doubt that we are closer now to Hadas's preferred state of television commentary. For one thing, more and more students have the opportunity to make television studies a part of their general education. These opportunities do not replace their experiences with books, as some might fear. Rather, with books as their tutors, they learn to see television more clearly, more critically. And perhaps these students will come to demand more powerfully and precisely informed commentary about television in their wider experience as citizens.

More to the point, perhaps some of these students, the present users of this collection, will come to write the sort of criticism—the informed, precise, exploratory, and explanatory criticism—that has been missing from our shared experiences of this medium in other times. Hadas's concern, finally, was with the making of critics, not merely with the making of criticism. That, too, is the primary purpose of this collection.

PART 1

History

The increasing interest in television history may be driven in part by the sense that an "era" has ended. Many commentators, critics, and scholars, as well as many industry practitioners, see the current contexts of television as profoundly different from what they were just a few short years ago. The changes may be said to have begun with the wide adoption of cable television technologies, the first means by which a substantial increase in the number of television "channels" came into the home. As other technologies, distribution arrangements, and alternative recording devices have led to still more choices, terms such as "post-network television" have come to be increasingly applied. This term or something similar implies a substantial shift of some sort and encourages a look at what went before.

This sense that television has "a past" is intensified when researchers, scholars, and archivists begin to explore the physical artifacts of the earlier period. "Television history" has become a subfield in media studies, dependent on close examination of collections of television programs and of the "paper records" of corporations, networks, production companies, trade publications, and individuals. While much of television's early programming history has been lost or destroyed, substantial amounts remain for review and analysis. One need only note the commercial application of this historical record, the "boxed sets" of digital video collections, to acknowledge a popular as well as scholarly interest in television history. Programs once dismissed as banal, throwaway culture, evoke nostalgic responses and become icons to be revered.

The essays in this section take more precisely disciplined rather than nostalgic approaches to television's earlier periods (though at times they, too, call up powerful memories). Their aim is to improve our knowledge of the past, to make us more careful in our generalizations, to correct previous misconceptions—all with the goal of understanding how things were as we attempt to think critically about how they might be now and in the future.

Mark Alvey's essay, "'Too Many Kids and Old Ladies': Quality Demographics and 1960s US Television," is a project that "corrects the record." It presents clear and convincing evidence that events often cited as a moment of great change—the increased attention to demographics by television programmers—were in fact part of an ongoing process with years of precedent. Relying on meticulous readings of corporate records and trade publications, Alvey also demonstrates the importance of looking beyond programming itself (or recollections and descriptions of programming) to understand industry practices. Even more important, he challenges notions of causality grounded in "great man" approaches to history. Given the relentless reliance on demographics as currency in contemporary television practices, this essay shows the significance of discerning accurate historical contexts.

"Negotiating Civil Rights in Prime Time: A Production and Reception History of CBS's *East Side/West Side*" by Aniko Bodroghkozy continues the author's exploration of 1960s television begun in *Groove Tube: Sixties Television and the Youth Rebellion*. *East Side/West Side* holds almost mythic presence in television history, despite the fact that few critics or commentators have seen much of it. One of the first television series to include an African American character as a regular, continuing cast member, the series is noted for dealing with volatile social issues, race relations among them. Bodroghkozy looks closely at episodes of the series, but also at the struggles between producers and network executives and among viewers. In her analysis the program, like so many others, becomes a site revealing far more than the content of plots or the roles of characters. It becomes the negotiating ground on which social and cultural stances are put into play. Here, too, the past is prologue to continuing examples available in today's television schedules.

Marsha Cassidy and Mimi White use the lives and careers of two women prominent in early television to consider several topics—local television in relation to national television, urban experience in relation to regional experience, and importantly, how these factors and these careers relate to the development of "daytime television" as a gendered, feminine arena for information and entertainment. Ruth Lyons, based in Cincinnati, emerged as a major "star" in regional radio and television. Arlene Francis was seen at times as the embodiment of urban cosmopolitanism. Cassidy and White discuss the two as embodiments of two "taste cultures," which might be related in some ways to Alvey's discussion of demographics, but which figure in the much larger arena of television's ongoing struggle to "place" viewers in gender-specific categories.

A similar "problem" for the "medium" emerges in Susan Murray's discussion of an "alternative form of masculinity" prominent in the early days of television, "Ethnic Masculinity and Early Television's Vaudeo Star." Drawn from vaudeville and shaped by Jewish ethnicity, early television comedians such as Milton Berle and Jack Benny dominated the medium with, in Murray's terms, "a flexible yet historically defined and culturally determined gender identity." But by the late 1950s and early 1960s these comedians and their programs—often comedy-variety shows built from older forms of comedy that might include skits such as Berle's "drag" performances—were in decline. The end of this period was caused by influences from financial concerns (the programs were expensive), from "aesthetic" concerns (they were seen as repetitious), and from social concerns (they were thought by some to be too risqué). In any case, in this example we once again see the difficulties faced by a medium in search of an identity that will move it to the mainstream of American consumer culture.

Nathan Godfried's study, "Identity, Power, and Local Television: African Americans, Organized Labor and UHF-TV in Chicago, 1962–1968," reveals a struggle of a very different kind, focused on the competition over the license for ultrahigh frequency Channel 38. On one side of the contest was the Chicagoland TV Company, seeking a television station that would provide programming primarily for Chicago's African American community. The opposition was found in the Chicago Federation of Labor, seeking to highlight the role of organized labor. As Godfried says, "[T]he debate between the two reveals much about how African-American community activists and conservative trade union officials perceived a role for television in modern society." Change the names and identities of the groups, and similar struggles continue today. Godfried's analysis of documents, local newspapers, and trade publications should serve as a model for how others can pursue this type of historical research.

Taken together these essays make it quite clear that the roles perceived "for television in modern society" were anything but simple, anything but easily determined. That the roles remain contested today speaks to the need for the kinds of historical analysis found here.

"Too Many Kids and Old Ladies"
Quality Demographics and 1960s U.S. Television

Mark Alvey

It has become something of a historical truism that the US television industry, and consequently its programming, underwent significant changes in 1970.
According to the standard account, after two decades of battling for the largest
possible Nielsen audience, "demographic thinking" suddenly took hold at the
networks. Executives were paying attention to *who* was watching as well as *how
many*. The quest for younger, more affluent viewers led to a "purge" of CBS
programmes dear to rural and older audiences, and sparked a trend towards
"quality" programming and more socially relevant themes. The story of this
sea change in attitude rivals that of the quiz show scandals and the demise of
live drama as a mythic benchmark in the annals of US television.

Les Brown's *Televi$ion: The Business Behind the Box* is the essential account
of the 1970 shift.[1] Cited in virtually all subsequent chronicles of the period,
Brown's book has been the primary force in determining the way the history has
been presented, with its images of radical rethinking and sudden change inspired
by the personal vision of a few executives. Sheer ratings success, reported Brown,
"was becoming irrelevant." The television networks were "suddenly . . . on the
make for the youth audience." Leading the charge at NBC was the network's
vice president of research Paul Klein, "the apostle of the demographic
approach," who saw it as his "mission" to redefine the gauge of success in terms
of audience composition rather than headcount. Likewise, according to Brown's
account, the changes at CBS were largely the work of one man, network president Robert Wood, who proposed in 1970 that the network "de-ruralize" its
schedule and "begin to divest itself of the aging programs" like the Jackie Gleason and Red Skelton comedy–variety shows, which were deficient in attracting
younger audiences, "as but the first stage in a thorough re-ordering of program
priorities leading to a rejuvenation of CBS."[2] A year later Wood dumped all of
his network's core rural-themed shows, such as *The Beverly Hillbillies* and *Mayberry RFD,* some of which were still drawing respectable Nielsen ratings.

Brown's book is an immensely valuable inside look at this particular moment
in US television history, and makes no pretence of being anything more. But it

Mark Alvey, "'Too Many Kids and Old Ladies': Quality Demographics and 1960s U.S.
Television." From *Screen,* Vol. 45, No. 1 (Spring 2004), pp. 21–39. Copyright © 2004,
Oxford University Press.

has come to be taken as the accepted version of these events, and subsequent accounts have invoked its facts and repeated its inflections with no probing of historical context. Jane Feuer's introduction to her *MTM: Quality Television* contains a typical account: "The crucial change that began to occur around 1970 was a de-emphasis on numbers and a greater emphasis on 'demographics,' i.e., directing television shows toward specific audience groups," whereas "during the 1960s the emphasis in ratings was on numbers alone."[3] Muriel Cantor provides a similar reading: "Before 1970, the commercial value of a network television program was judged simply in terms of the percentage of households and the share a particular program attracted."[4] In *Up the Tube*, Sally Bedell reports that "network television roiled through a sea change in 1970," with the push for "quality demographics" and "relevant' programming."[5] Todd Gitlin's discussion of the events describes the changes at CBS as "Bob Wood's great shift of 1970–71," and declares that "his successes changed the tone and texture of television comedy."[6] There are occasional hints in the literature of a larger context—Bedell notes that ABC had carved out its niche as a younger audience network early on, but "nobody paid much attention,"[7] and Brown and others admit that *sponsors* were becoming increasingly concerned with audience composition, albeit in the *late* 1960s—but the "sea change" scenario has become the standard account of the networks' embracing of upscale demographics. Similar versions of the tale—all based on Brown's—are told in various broadcast surveys, network histories and critical works.[8]

The network quest for "quality demographics" is generally linked, either as a direct cause or a parallel development, with an upgrading of the aesthetic and ideological nature of prime time, whereby programming experienced a "renaissance" of sophistication and social significance. A typical (albeit entertainingly overstated) account holds that US television in the late 1960s appeared to have been "frozen in Jell-O the day Ike left the White House," while shows with more contemporary sensibilities and/or more overt political discourse, like *The Mary Tyler Moore Show* and *All in the Family*, heralded a kind of renaissance; "it was again worth our while to watch TV."[9] The notion of a post-wasteland rebirth of quality and relevance is invoked in numerous renderings of this transition, with varying degrees of explicitness and critique. Significantly, the advent of this programming not only marked a perceived new era of quality for the medium itself, but helped advance the progress of television studies as a legitimate academic pursuit, providing a body of self-consciously political or reflexively modernist texts that academics could embrace and analyze without embarrassment. Critic Horace Newcomb points to this influence in an article on the development of scholarly television criticism, citing the early-1970s "renaissance" as a factor in the growth of academic television criticism during the same period. "The MTM shows, the Lear shows, *M*A*S*H*, and other works convinced many viewers, critics among them, that there was something here that had to be taken seriously," Newcomb writes. "There was something here that could be lived with, in the sense that critics must always live with the objects of their concern, with a degree of affection, comfort, enlightenment."[10]

While US prime time in the 1960s was much more diverse, interesting and aesthetically rich than typical historical accounts allow, it is true that CBS built its ratings leadership during the decade on a core foundation of situation comedies, many of which had rural settings and themes: *The Beverly Hillbillies*, an absurdist farce about a backwoods family transplanted to the wealthy LA enclave of Beverly Hills; *Petticoat Junction*, centring on the humorous happenings at a small rural hotel; *The Andy Griffith Show*, a warm-hearted comedy about a small southern town and its sometimes eccentric inhabitants; *Gomer Pyle, USMC*, in which a good-hearted gas station attendant from that same southern town joins the US Marines, and so on. It is also true that with the arrival of shows like *All in the Family*, depicting a blue-collar bigot's confrontations with social change,[11] *The Mary Tyler Moore Show*, notable for its depiction of a single working woman, and *M*A*S*H*, an antiwar critique played out in a Korean War combat hospital, the tenor of the prime-time schedule in the 1970s was very different from that of even a few years before (although admittedly in some respects, such as a handful of shows surviving from the 1950s, it looked much the same). The fact is, US television's fictional programming caught up with its news reporting, dramatizing the various social revolutions of the decade—the Civil Rights movement, black radicalism, women's liberation, youth unrest, opposition to the Vietnam War, and so on. Which is not to say that all of the efforts were as smart and successful as the handful of classics on which the critics tend to reflect—the first wave of self-consciously "relevant" programmes were often unfortunate graftings of contemporary topics onto Hollywood melodramatics (*The Storefront Lawyers*, *The Young Rebels*, *The Interns*), and few lasted more than one season.[12]

While there are multiple implications that could be pursued in the accepted account of how US television rode the transition from the 1960s to the 1970s, the year 1970 looms large in the literature as a pivotal moment in terms of both how the networks measured their audience and the impact of that reassessment and that is the central focus of this essay. As with many "overnight" shifts, this one had been in the works for some time. The "crucial change" did not *begin* in 1970 but rather *culminated* then, capping more than a decade of research and rhetoric. Explicit concern for composition and indeed "quality" of audience rather than sheer size had been developing throughout the 1960s. The events of 1970–71 did not constitute the abrupt, radical rethinking that critics and historians have depicted, but were a continuation of practices (and propaganda) that had been established years earlier. And the concrete impact of this supposed realignment of priorities is far from straightforward—indeed, it has arguably more hype than substance. This essay will amplify these arguments and document that context, charting the rise of "demographic thinking" in the 1960s. The discussion will be framed largely by the contest between CBS and NBC—partly in order to focus the argument within the given space limits, and partly to "track" the framework set by Brown et al.—a function of the fact that the demographic battle was largely waged between those two networks, ABC by the mid 1960s having set its sights on the "young family" audience. Examining the uses to which these data were put, particularly their relevance to programme scheduling and retention, provides a broader and more detailed account of the real impact of demographics on programming, and highlights a number of ironies and ambiguities that arose from the emergent, and by no means uniform, exploitation of the demographic approach. Establishing the context for demographic-influenced practices in the 1960s as a foundation for the more familiar developments of the 1970s also suggests certain implications for the historiographical and critical arguments that generally permeate the standard historical accounts.

NBC: For Those Who Think Young

The case of NBC is worth considering in some detail. According to the standard account, NBC led the way in promoting the demographic makeup of its audience as a measure of programming value. Demographic thinking was largely the brainchild of Paul Klein, who sought to "alter the rules" of the ratings game, in Brown's words, and whose "push for demographics was timed to diminish the importance of CBS's dominance in the ratings by the old standard of circulation."[13] The broad outline of this scenario is correct—Klein did indeed flaunt his network's demographic superiority at every opportunity, citing it as the criterion for leadership—but the journalistic focus on those few months in 1970 inevitably ignores essential institutional background and historical context. In fact, this sort of strategic redefinition of success was being employed by NBC at least as early as 1953, and was a staple of that network's prime-time promotion by 1963. Klein (who joined the network in 1961) was clearly a loyal adherent of the strategy but he did not suddenly launch it in 1970; rather, by that time it was an established NBC practice.

"Research Bulletins" and "Research Highlights," released by the NBC Research Department throughout the 1950s and 1960s to analyze and promote the merits of NBC programming for sponsors and affiliates, are a revealing resource in tracing the trajectory of demographic thinking.[14] As these documents confirm, throughout the 1950s the network's primary goal was to garner the largest possible audience for its prime-time programming. The prime-time ratings Bulletins from this era emphasized one thing—mass circulation—touting NBC's "improving competitive position" vis-à-vis CBS, its victories on certain nights or time slots, the Nielsen scores of specials, and so on. Significantly, the Reports during this period cited the numbers from either Nielsen, Arbitron or Trendex, whichever would present the network or the particular programme in the best possible light.[15] In an interesting contrast to the network's later partiality towards urban viewers, several 1953 and 1954 Bulletins chided CBS for basing its leadership claims on Trendex, which measured only nine eastern cities and Chicago and was therefore not viewed as representative of national audience size. (Four years later the Bulletins were trumpeting NBC as the number one network, based on the Trendex reports.)[16]

Notably, as indicated, as early as 1953 NBC was already taking notice of audience composition—and, explicitly, audience "quality"—for its *daytime* programming. One Bulletin analyzed the "audience quality" of the video-kindergarten *Ding-Dong School* along lines that would be familiar to a later generation of executives, touting the show's appeal to younger, better-educated, higher-income families.[17] Likewise, a series of Bulletins on the daytime audience from February 1956 begins with the following prescient paragraph:

> Most advertisers know *how many people* or homes a program reaches but few are aware of the *kind of people* in the audience. The quality of a program's audience is particularly important since it tells the advertiser if he is reaching the *prospects and customers* for his product.[18]

Admittedly, as far as the prime-time schedule was concerned, the largest audience share was still the network's primary goal in the 1950s, and it remained the main focus of the Research Bulletins into the early 1960s. Nevertheless, the major ratings services were offering demographic breakdowns of the audience by the late 1950s,[19] and as the new decade dawned there were early hints that the networks were gaining a growing appreciation of reaching the "right" audience in prime time as well. For example, a 1960 NBC Bulletin sketched Arbitron's breakdown of the prime-time viewing audience by age (which was drawn rather broadly: children twelve and under, teens thirteen to seventeen, men eighteen and over, women eighteen and over).[20] A practical indication of the emerging importance of audience composition came in spring 1961, when Chevrolet pulled its sponsorship (and strong product identification) from NBC's musical variety hour, *The Dinah Shore Chevy Show*, because it attracted older and wealthier viewers who tended to purchase more expensive cars than Chevy's solid blue-collar models.[21] The carmaker retained the same Sunday timeslot for the following season, throwing its support behind the entire hour of the popular Western series *Bonanza*, which at that time had a younger family appeal, and continuing its full sponsorship of the family comedy *My Three Sons* on ABC, and a "participation buy" in *Route 66* on CBS (that is, purchasing one half-hour of the hour-long drama). Chevrolet's television advertising choices at this juncture are worth considering for a moment, as the firm was following two distinct sponsorship strategies, one of which was on the wane in the industry, the other on the rise. Its full sponsorship of *Bonanza* and *My Three Sons* followed the one-show–one-sponsor model established in radio, while its underwriting of one half of *Route 66* was consistent with the growing trend towards various forms of multiple sponsorship. Already by 1960 fully half of prime-time programmes were supported by more than one sponsor, and many advertisers, like Chevy, were buying "participations" or commercial minutes in more than one show. The trend was partly a response to increasing programme costs, which made it progressively more difficult for one sponsor to underwrite an entire weekly programme according to the traditional model, and, more compelling by most accounts, a function of sponsors' efforts to "spread costs over a multiplicity of shows in order to gain reach and circulation" as *Variety* put it.[22] "Participating sponsorship" or "scatter buying" of ads was aimed principally at reaching the greatest number of viewers and/or increasing the odds of having some exposure in a "hit" show, but obviously the approach could also be used to target specific audiences, as Chevrolet was attempting to do with both its single sponsorships and participation buys. Still, although targeted advertising was on the rise, the rhetoric of NBC's prime-time Bulletins around this time maintained a general emphasis on gross ratings, using selective statistics to justify calling itself "the #1 television network," and boasting "the largest national audience."[23]

In 1963, however, a pronounced emphasis on "quality" of audience began to appear in the NBC Bulletins for nighttime programming. A January Report noted that "advertisers know they ring doorbells to sell to people and not to homes," and stressed that ratings figures alone did not give an accurate picture of "an actual competitive situation." An April "Highlights" touted the strength of the psychiatry drama *Eleventh Hour,* which tied with the ABC Sunday movie as the top programme among female viewers aged eighteen to thirty-nine (according to Arbitron), and argued that the show's Nielsen "slant" towards "the younger, middle and upper income, better-educated parents," made it a "real 'find' for the advertiser." By November the network was broadening its claims, calling itself "the leading network for upper income, upper educated young adults."[24] The latter claim was based on a study from the National Testing Institute (the source of TvQ), which featured demographic categories that would become standard Nielsen equipment by the end of the decade (age, education and income of head of household). The NBC Report, subtitled "which network is really first—a look behind the average ratings," clearly anticipates the sort of strategic claims NBC would be making in spring 1970. The Report pointed out that overall ratings leader CBS actually *trailed* NBC according to this measurement, leading instead in the lower-educated, lower-income, age fifty-five or older homes. Whatever strength CBS and ABC had in the young, affluent, upper-educated homes, the Report claimed, was caused by children in those homes controlling the dial (for example, the stone-age cartoon *The Flintstones* rated well in such households, but its audience was only 40% adult).

At about this time NBC also began promoting the aesthetic quality of its programming, and its consequent ability to attract a more desirable audience segment. The 19 November Highlights just cited pointed out that

> NBC's schedule is composed largely of dramas and anthologies. Over half of NBC's schedule contains programming which varies week to week. This kind of programming, while not producing consistent top ten ratings, does recruit the biggest audience from the important discriminating upper part of the socio-economic scale.

The piece went on to deride what it called the "low-end" situation comedies on CBS (including *The Beverly Hillbillies* and *Petticoat Junction*), whose homes rating for upper-slant groups was distorted by their "kiddie" viewers. A subsequent Bulletin continued the argument, suggesting that NBC's programmes garnered the more desirable audience slant due to its programming of "anthologies and anthology-type programs" (which included *Walt Disney's Wonderful World of Color, Espionage, The Richard Boone Show, Kraft Suspense Theater, Chrysler Theatre, Monday Night at the Movies* and *Saturday Night at the Movies*). This Report explicitly expressed the notion of the "quality" of audience in its title. CBS's ratings successes in prime time, the Report pointed out, were due to "old-slanted" programmes, or sitcoms that attracted children and older viewers. Likewise, a series of December Bulletins emphasized NBC's leadership among younger, more affluent, better-educated adults, charging that CBS's homes lead was won by its strength with older viewers—and proclaiming NBC "the young adult network."[25]

One particularly revealing Report pointed out the young-adult leadership of certain NBC shows compared to more highly rated CBS shows—such as *Dr Kildare* vs *Rawhide*, *Mr Novak* vs *What's My Line*, *The Lieutenant* vs *I've Got a Secret*, *The Richard Boone Show* vs *Danny Thomas*, *Saturday Night at the Movies* vs *Ed Sullivan*, *Kraft Suspense Theater* vs *Petticoat Junction*—in each case arguing a demographic advantage for shows that were running deficits in overall ratings.[26] Similarly, a January 1964 Bulletin boasted that the addition of the political satire show *That Was the Week That Was* (*TW3*) to the NBC schedule would be a certain enhancement of "the network's position as the young adult, upper income network." This American incarnation of the British hit, the Report argued, was the ideal vehicle for "reaching a quality audience composed largely of young, college educated, upper income family homes." And indeed—based on the November special cited—the better the skew the higher the rating, with roughly a twenty-two average audience rating in all the "right" categories (household income, household size, age of housewife, education of head of household, occupation of head of household), versus a sixteen for the nation.[27] Interestingly enough, a subsequent Report on the performance of the series' January 1964 debut ignored the show's audience slant in favour of its ratings, highlighting an impressive thirty-six share. However, the Report's title did allude to the show's demographics with a pointed comparison to the rural slant of CBS's ratings blockbuster, dubbing *TW3* "the urban *Beverly Hillbillies*."[28]

The NBC Research Bulletins and Highlights continued in the same vein throughout the mid 1960s, with regular claims of being the "number one network among young adults," "the leading network among the better marketing groups," the "preferred network among college-educated adults," and/or the leading network in the top-ten young adult programmes.[29] In addition to age, education and income as "quality" factors, by mid decade the significance of region was given a more pronounced emphasis, with NBC boasting of its slant towards the "best marketing targets"—upper-income urban families—and its ratings in "affluent urban areas," and generously recommending that "advertisers of commercial fertilizer would be better off on another network."[30]

These Reports demonstrate that NBC was indeed paying attention to demographics, and promoting the ability of certain programmes or programme types to attract more upscale viewers. One has to read between the lines, however—and read the fall schedules over several years—to discern the real purpose of this data and its apparent influence on programming. In short, its purpose was rhetorical and its influence negligible. More than anything these Reports underline the fact that for NBC circa 1963, the value of demographics rested largely in its usefulness in a post-facto defence of low-rated programmes, rather than as a proactive tool in programme decisions. Despite the network's crowing about its young adult advantage, leadership with the "right" viewers was not enough to save most of these programmes. The supposedly prized anthologies of *Boone, Espionage* and *DuPont* were canceled at the end of the season, as were *Lieutenant* and *Eleventh Hour* (*Boone, Espionage* and *Lieutenant* after only one season). *TW3*, despite being impeccably upscale, not to mention critically acclaimed, was also canceled at the end of its first full season. Given the fate of these shows, it is reasonable to infer that *Dr Kildare*'s survival was due less to its young adult viewers than to the fact that it was in the top twenty Nielsen winners (outrating *Rawhide*, we should note) for the season. Likewise, while *Saturday Night at the Movies* may have been able to boast superior delivery of younger women, it also earned a respectable 21.4 share—significantly higher than many of the other upper-slant programmes that the NBC Bulletins were promoting.

Countless examples of these demographic comparisons appear in the NBC Bulletins from 1963 through to the tumultuous days of 1970. NBC not only trumpeted its own demographic leadership, but also made certain to highlight the older slant of CBS, and ABC's dominance in the children and teen audience. Yet clearly, in practice, NBC's self-proclaimed status as the "young adult network" did not signify a change in programming philosophy as much as an emergent, statistically grounded, rhetorical strategy by which to defend programmes whose average audience share was below par. In the early 1960s, as in the early 1970s, when NBC could not post a victory by traditional measurements, it highlighted those aspects of the data where it *could* claim an advantage. In another prescient move, at the end of the 1964–65 season, NBC claimed a three-network tie for homes reached, and pointed out that it was "the only network that cared to speak at any length about the number and kind of viewers in its audience." NBC's "superiority in quality audience," the Report charged, was "the only real ratings difference between the three networks"—much the same claim it would make in 1970.[31]

It is instructive to note that while CBS was NBC's most frequent target in (selective) demographic comparisons, the near-absurdities of NBC's ballyhoo played out in much the same fashion on the ABC front. For example, a 1965 Report attempted to deflate ABC's ratings victories by emphasizing that the third-ranked network's only real strength was in its share of children and teenagers. Similarly, in early 1966 another NBC Report derided ABC's camp superhero entry *Batman* because of its almost exclusive appeal to kids; yet several NBC Reports in the autumn of the same year boasted that its frenetic made-for-television pop group vehicle *The Monkees* was the most popular prime-time show among viewers under eighteen.[32]

The largely situational, expedient and rhetorical value of NBC's "young adult" argument is further underscored by the fact that NBC continued to stress its "mass" successes whenever and however it could. With claims ranging from television's "most-viewed programmes" (seven of the top ten "entertainment" shows for one semi-monthly Nielsen report), dominance in the top ten programmes (for one week, due to two specials), leadership in "reach" (with the top five shows that fulfilled "the primary objective of most advertisers—greatest possible reach"), to outright Nielsen victory (for example, in homes-per-minute, or the first Nielsen results of the season)—the NBC Reports would marshal evidence that could be spun favourably by considering selective criteria or time frames.[33]

One aspect of NBC's superiority that did not need to be embellished was its leadership in colour programming, which gave it an undeniable edge in attracting more desirable demographics. "The peacock network" increasingly touted the advantages of colour programming in reaching "upper" homes as colour sets became more widespread and its menu of colour programming grew. A 1964 Report entitled "A New Look at the Color TV Set Owner" noted that colour set owners represented "an 'elite' group among the general population": they were wealthier, better-educated, professional/managerial—and heavier television viewers—than owners of monochrome receivers. A March 1965 Bulletin reported that while the first wave of colour set buyers tended to be older, upper-income people, the more recent owners were "larger, younger, upper-income families," and a subsequent profile of colour set owners noted that both current owners and prospective buyers were not only younger ("centering in the prime-earning 35–49 age group") and in higher income and education brackets, but also more urban. A December Report cited a Brand Ratings Index study that correlated colour set ownership with heavier spending patterns on household products, convenience food, travel and "status symbols," as well as more "venturesome" buying habits (such as trying modern products).[34]

By 1965 about 6% of total "television homes" owned colour sets, and, not surprisingly, colour shows attracted significantly higher ratings in "colour homes" than in homes with black-and-white sets, which translated into a small but significant enhancement to overall ratings for colour shows, and thus for NBC.[35] While there is no question that the primary motivation driving the shift to colour was the sale of colour sets by the network's parent company, RCA, and the desire to capture more of the mass audience through the novelty of "tint-ups" as colour receivers were adopted more widely, NBC's move towards an all-colour prime-time schedule carried obvious, if ancillary, demographic benefits. With NBC the first to go "all colour" in 1965, it was the primary beneficiary of that segment of "homes" leadership as well as the demographic benefits that accompanied colour shows, and the network played up those benefits in its propaganda. As one Bulletin put it, sponsors of NBC's colour shows could reach both the "class" (colour owners) and "mass" (black and white) audience.[36]

Ultimately, even with its promotion of the colour advantage, at mid decade NBC's attention to demographics was largely a defensive strategy, an attempt to provide more favourable shadings for its numbers. From a programming standpoint, the size and not the quality of the audience was still the primary force in determining a show's survival. Yet if NBC's substantive employment of its demographic data was largely rhetorical during the early 1960s, nevertheless it is clear that by mid decade "demographic thinking" had begun to take hold in the industry. As *Variety*'s George Rosen observed in early 1965:

"This year as never before Madison Ave advertisers and tv analysts are scrutinizing audience composition and demographic data."[37]

And the quest for the upper audience slant did begin to exert a more active influence on programming as the decade wore on. Although demographics were not an apparent factor in selecting or developing programming, as they ostensibly would become in the early 1970s, by 1967 they began to play a role in the retention of programmes with marginal audience share (twenty-eight to thirty-one). In a 1967 article in *Television* magazine on programmes in this "vast grey belt," recently-installed vice-president Klein observed that "quality" of audience was the most important criterion for evaluating such shows. "A quality audience—lots of young adult buyers—provides a high level that may make it worth holding onto a program despite low overall ratings," Klein suggested, citing this as a key factor in *Star Trek*'s renewal. As Klein told *TV Guide* in a later interview, *Star Trek* was retained "because it delivers a quality, salable audience"—particularly "upper-income, better-educated males." There was a limit to the power of demographics of course, and Klein pointed to *The Rogues* (a family of aristocratic jewel thieves headed by Charles Boyer and David Niven) as an example of a programme that delivered a quality audience but did not rate well enough to avoid cancellation. *Tarzan,* on the other hand, was dropped despite an acceptable homes rating because, in Klein's words, "it hadn't been delivering the right kind of people. Too many kids and old ladies." (This despite an NBC Highlights just a few weeks earlier that glowingly dubbed *Tarzan* an "all-family program.")[38]

Klein argued that "a 16 share on *Saturday Night At The Movies,* we found, is better than a 30 audience on *Petticoat Junction,*" but in fact, Klein and company retained no programmes that posted less than a twenty-eight share at the end of the 1966–67 season—and the comparison was curiously moot, since at this time NBC's Saturday feature film package had been earning a thirty-five share or better—far from "grey-belt."[39] The reality was that for all of the research department's rhetoric, NBC's sales department could not sell a show based on demographics alone. An upscale shading certainly helped, but as one industry observer noted, the cases of advertisers deliberately buying into third-place competitors in a time slot were rare, no matter what the audience composition.[40]

While the use of demographic data to determine the fate of marginal shows constitutes a more concrete factor in programming decisions, it also reinforces their status as largely a post-facto measure rather than an active development or scheduling tool, one that allowed NBC—as it did in 1964, and would again in 1970—to declare victory over CBS on its own terms. As the 1960s wound down, the network was still using demographics largely to put a "young adult" spin on its lineup. While the network was proactive in adding some youth-oriented shows like the rapid-fire topical satire *Laugh-In* and the globetrotting espionage drama *I Spy* to its schedule, it was a far from wholesale infusion of hipness. Indeed, the NBC Reports expressed no embarrassment over the fact that its top-rated shows nationally—*Bonanza, The Virginian, Disney's Wonderful World of Color*—some of which had been on the schedule since the late 1950s, were also among the highest rated for older viewers. In fact, Klein's research department was quick to herald the fact that the long-running *Bonanza* was soundly beating CBS's musical–comedy satire *Smothers Brothers Comedy Hour* in overall ratings—despite the fact that *Smothers* was among the very top shows in the educated/affluent/professional audience segment.[41] Adding irony to ambiguity, when CBS canceled the seventh-ranked *Red Skelton* comedy–variety show in the spring of 1970, NBC—which had knocked the show as "old-slant" two years earlier[42]—promptly picked it up for the autumn schedule. All of which further illustrates the degree to which NBC's pointed celebration of young adult viewership was more talk than action. But if NBC's efforts were less than a full-scale campaign for the quality audience, that is not to say that its demographic push and rhetoric had no direct effect on programming. It did, just as it would in 1970, at CBS.

Quo Vadis CBS: Class or Corn?

That question—directed at the medium in general, not just CBS—was posed by *Variety* in June 1963. The upcoming season was posited as the most ambitious in years, particularly in the area of serious dramatic series and star-powered musical–variety shows, and a pivotal year for US television. The success or failure of these "classier" offerings, the reporter predicted, would determine "the IQ level of future network seasons."[43] The "class or corn" question was a particularly pointed one for CBS, at which network president James Aubrey was simultaneously programming the period's most ambitious dramas (for example, the issue-oriented courtroom drama *The Defenders* or the peripatetic social problem drama *Route 66*) and its most defiantly lowbrow—and highest-rated—rural farces (such as *Beverly Hillbillies* or *Petticoat Junction*) in the prime-time schedule. It was a tightrope walk between retaining the network's "Tiffany" image and maintaining ratings dominance, and the balance, in most observers' eyes, was already tilting towards "corn."

Of course the facts of network life at this time dictated that television executives spent more time reading the Nielsen Reports than pondering the artistic trajectory of the medium. It is clear that the mass ratings constituted CBS's central goal in the early 1960s, and that sponsors were largely willing to stick with success in those terms. Certainly the network was not averse to exploiting the prestige of its own quality or anthology-style shows like *The Defenders, East Side, West Side* and *The Great Adventure,* which it could boast about in trade ads, before Senate subcommittees and in stockholder meetings. And demographics were an emerging if ancillary benefit; for example, as early as 1962 sales material for *The Defenders* contrasted the show's adult audience segment with that of the competition.[44] But *The Defenders* was an exception—a happy coincidence of critical acclaim, prominent awards, upslant demographics, and Nielsen scores high enough for a four-year run. Minus the ratings, shows like *East Side, West Side* (the struggles of a New York social worker) and *Great Adventure* (an anthology of colourful tales from US history) did not stand a chance. CBS took the accolades when it could get them, but such shows were retained only as long as the prestige could be combined with respectable ratings. The exceptions were high-prestige documentary series like *Eyewitness* and *CBS Reports,* which survived by virtue of their value for "balance" and public service, as well as the aura of class and seriousness they brought to the network.[45] CBS was certainly aware of the young/urban/upscale audience these shows attracted, but these viewers were a by-product rather than a target market—the target was the largest possible audience. Looking back a few months after his dismissal as network president, James Aubrey explained his approach in very simple terms: "I felt that we had an obligation to reach the vast majority of most of the people. Unfortunately, the people began to indicate through the ratings service a preference for certain particular shows. We made an effort to continue purposeful drama on television, but we found out that people just don't want an anthology. They would rather tune in on *Lucy.*"[46] Or *The Beverly Hillbillies,* as the case may be. In short, Aubrey and company did not look at the nuances of audience segment but rather the mass, and, following those cues, continued to give the people what they ostensibly "preferred."

There is no doubt that the blockbuster ratings of *The Beverly Hillbillies* and other CBS hits were what kept the network's stock high during Aubrey's tenure. CBS's ratings were so superior in 1964 that CBS was essentially blind-selling its prime-time schedule, locking sponsors into a time slot to be filled later by a programme which, according to a CBS representative, "Mr Aubrey will select."[47] Although chief programmer Mike Dann was less high-handed in his methods after the autocratic Aubrey's departure in 1965, CBS's ratings leadership continued, as did its quest for "the vast majority of most of the people." Meanwhile, as I have shown, its major competitor's emphasis ostensibly was shifting. Witness the trade advertisements of the two rivals: while a CBS advertisement in *Variety* in January 1965 boasted of the presence of eleven CBS titles in the top fifteen prime-time shows, an NBC advertisement a few weeks later staked a claim for NBC as the best choice for viewers in the eighteen-to-forty-nine age group.[48] Obviously each network was highlighting an existing strength. CBS touted its top-rated shows, while NBC downplayed gross ratings and stressed audience composition. Still, the changes were not far off. NBC's barrage of comparative demographic ballyhoo may have been constructed, rhetorical and post facto, but the network made the most of it. As historians have told us, CBS began to take heed—but some time earlier than we have been led to believe.

CBS took its first serious moves in translating demographic concerns into programming action during the 1966–67 season. The familiar version of CBS's demographic transformation relates that the network took a hard look at itself in 1970–71, largely due to NBC broadsides about the aging of its audience, canceling *Petticoat Junction,* the *Red Skelton* and *Jackie Gleason* comedy–variety hours in 1970, and a host of rural-oriented programmes a year later. Since these moves were carried out under the guidance of a newly arrived CBS television president Wood, it is easy to see why credit for them might be laid at his feet. But as at NBC, the changes of 1970 and 1971 at CBS were not "the first stage in a thorough reordering of priorities," as Brown asserts, but in fact a culmination of sorts. Aubrey, Dann, et al. had certainly been reading the comparative rhetoric from NBC since the early years of the decade, and watched major sponsors shift their advertising dollars from older-slanted shows to ones with younger and/or broader appeal, and by 1966 CBS was overtly reconsidering its bias towards older audiences on a broader scale, and translating its findings into action. In the middle of the 1966 season, in a clear foreshadowing of its "rural purge" of 1970 and 1971, the network announced the cancellation of five programmes—the long-running Western *Gunsmoke*, the game shows *What's My Line, I've Got a Secret* and *To Tell the Truth*, and the hidden-camera ambush *Candid Camera*—that, in *Variety*'s words, "were judged to be performing poorly in the 18–34 age group." While the overall ratings for these shows were also in decline, *TV Guide* called the move a symptom of "the current network rage for entertainment of known young-adult appeal."[49]

CBS programmer Dann recalled in an interview several years later that his network was indeed following NBC's lead in looking at the demographics of its programmes at this time. *Gunsmoke*'s ratings in 1966 would have been acceptable by traditional measures, Dann suggested, but in light of NBC's demographic comparisons, a decision was made that Marshall Dillon and company were setting the bias too far in favour of the old, and the series was canceled. However, not long after the cancellation was announced, the twelve-year-old Western was reinstated through the intervention of CBS chairman William Paley, in a new time period. In its new berth in the schedule, *Gunsmoke* jumped back to fourth place in the Nielsens, and, notably, although it was a popular show among the over-fifty set, it also attained virtually the same young-adult profile as *Star Trek*.[50]

The example of *Gunsmoke* illustrates a rather obvious but key point: hit shows—shows that earned large overall ratings—inevitably captured a decent share of the upscale demographic into the bargain. This should not be overlooked, especially in the context of changing ad-buying patterns. Multiple sponsorship continued to increase as the dominant model during the decade, and by 1970 participation sponsorship and scatter buying covered well over 90% of prime time.[51] As noted earlier, advertisers used this strategy chiefly to achieve circulation, but it could also be used for demographic targeting. Interestingly, the one sacrifice that came with participation sponsorship was the loss of a close association between a product and a show—most clearly exemplified by sponsor-identified anthology dramas like *Chrysler Theater* or *The Alcoa Hour*, but also clearly a factor in popular dramas like *Bonanza* ("brought to you by Chevrolet") and *Alfred Hitchcock Presents* (sponsored exclusively by Lincoln—Mercury in the early 1960s). Somewhat ironically, as demographic consciousness developed, attempts by sponsors to maintain prestige or goodwill associations with individual shows largely faded, but it was a sacrifice they seemed willing to make. A "buy" in a show like *Gunsmoke* hit a broad audience that also included a significant upscale segment. In Dann's view, *Gunsmoke*'s rebirth "broke a great myth about its demographics, and ended up breaking the back of *Laugh-In*."[52] The programme also gained revitalized ratings and remained in the top ten for the next six seasons. The three quiz shows and *Candid Camera* were not as fortunate, however, and their cancellation was final.

The impact of demographics (and NBC's rhetoric) on CBS programming in 1966–67 was not only one of negative moves. As at NBC, demographics were a factor in the survival or decline of "grey-belt" shows, the espionage thriller *Mission Impossible* being a notable CBS entry whose survival was aided by its "quality audience." Toeing the traditional company line, CBS director of audience measurement Arnold Becker argued that "there are an awful lot of people who put exaggerated importance on young audiences," but in the next breath admitted that "given equal amounts of audience, we would rather have them younger."[53] Of course the implicit corollary was that, given *unequal* audience shares, they would rather have the larger.

In addition to rescuing marginal raters, demographic thinking was exerting a discernible influence in programme development at CBS. In sketching the 1967 season for *Television* magazine, Dann announced a trend towards "reality comedy," taking a direct swipe at some of the fantasy–escapist sitcoms in which his network had specialized during the Aubrey years (for example, *The Munsters*, *Gilligan's Island*, *My Favorite Martian*). In the new season's lineup, he declared, "Nobody disappears, nobody is marooned on an island, nobody is from another planet." Dann drew particular attention to two new sitcoms for which CBS had high hopes, *He and She* and *Good Morning World*, both of which centred on young characters in urban settings.[54] In addition, with an aging Garry Moore variety hour dying opposite NBC's *Bonanza*, Dann and his Los Angeles programming lieutenant, Perry Lafferty, decided to counter-programme with *The Smothers Brothers Comedy Hour*, which combined contemporary music with pointed social satire, in an explicit effort to attract the younger (fifteen-to-thirty) audience with the comedy duo's "irreverence."[55] Happily for the programmers, the show also proved to be an unqualified ratings success.

The rural comedies (along with *Gunsmoke* and Lucille Ball) were still entrenched in the CBS schedule, of course, and not surprisingly, since they were also entrenched at the upper end of the Nielsens. But it is clear that CBS was rethinking its bias, and that NBC's incessant demographic comparisons were beginning to make themselves felt. Sweeping aside the faltering game shows, and (temporarily) *Gunsmoke*, the first of the CBS programming "purges" was underway in the winter of 1966–67, more than two years before Robert Wood joined the network's executive ranks, and long before the allegedly radical changes of 1970. Like his counterpart at NBC, Wood would not be charting a daring new direction as the decade began, but embracing an existing strategy.

And CBS's renaissance of sophistication under Wood was not without its own ironies. Although Dann and company were actively scheduling programmes that promised attractive demographics, they still managed to hang on to the "mass," and to dominate the Nielsens. As for CBS's elimination of its rural programmes in 1971, the operation might better be described as a pruning than a purge. Of the shows canceled, only *Mayberry RFD* (an updated version of *The Andy Griffith Show*, minus star Griffith) and *Hee-Haw* (a kind of countrified *Laugh-In*) even ranked in the top twenty (fifteenth and sixteenth, respectively); the others were largely played out as ratings winners. While the decision to jettison those two fairly strong bucolic comedies and retain an even lower-ranked *Mary Tyler Moore Show* does attest to significant changes in network ideology, it is also, of course, wholly consistent with the well-established practice of giving upslant programmes a chance. At the same time, the continued presence of the highly-rated *Here's Lucy* (Lucille Ball's second post–*I Love Lucy* sitcom) and the venerable *Gunsmoke* attest to the continued importance of the mass ratings. *All in the Family,* revered for its audacity and topicality, also had the good fortune to become a mass-audience blockbuster, so we will never know if its demographics (or "relevance") would have ensured its longevity in the case of marginal or poor ratings—the same goes for *Mary Tyler Moore* and *M*A*S*H* and any number of other such "quality" shows. When the dust of the 1970 rural purge and ratings wars had settled, the most concrete impact of demographics was still primarily felt in deciding the fates of those shows in the "grey belt." If there is happy medium between quality of audience and size, there can be little doubt that quality demographics *and* big ratings were the happiest compromise of all.

The Pursuit of Quality: Contexts and Continuities

Of course Brown's claim that "bulk circulation, which once had been all-important to the networks, was becoming irrelevant" was an overstatement, perhaps a product of dramatic (journalistic) licence.[56] As the 1970s wore on, mass ratings maintained considerable importance, and made for some rather interesting programming juxtapositions in terms of audience slant as well as style. Controversial sitcoms from producer Norman Lear shared the Nielsen top ten with *Gunsmoke*. Old-skewed, high-rated shows like *Here's Lucy* and *Barnaby Jones* (a geriatric detective) held their own with the hipper but equally popular *Sonny and Cher* and *Flip Wilson* comedy–variety shows, and all prospered. By the late 1970s CBS had no trouble living with both the prestige of *M*A*S*H* and the redneck appeal of *The Dukes of Hazzard* (southern good-old-boy Robin Hoods in a souped-up Dodge Charger), each a top ten Nielsen winner. What I am suggesting, of course, is that the gross Nielsen rating numbers were still paramount, and demographic data continued to provide post-facto shadings for programme decisions and sponsor targeting, just as they had ten years earlier.

None of this is meant to diminish the importance of the events of 1970–71, but to emphasize that the developments that led up to them are equally, if not more, important, and that the whole subject of demographics and its place and effect on television during the 1960s and 1970s (and the 1950s, 1980s and 1990s) needs to be documented more fully and carefully. The CBS–NBC contest of 1970 marked a stage in a process, part of a long-term evolution of network practices, rhetoric and ideologies surrounding the definition and value of the television audience. We cannot fully understand that transition and its significance without considering the two decades of network philosophies and practices that led up to it.

All of which suggests several points by way of conclusion. Charting the quest for "quality demographics" as an evolutionary process rather than an explosion reminds us of the risks inherent in "Great Man" accounts of history—in this case the attribution of the sea change circa 1970 to the personal vision of Klein at NBC and Wood at CBS. Taking these "single-handed" accounts at face value obscures the complexities and ambiguities of the process, ignores the development of these practices (and the rhetoric) over time, and overlooks the *continuities* of practice and strategy that were in fact being maintained at both networks. Gitlin, for example, quotes Wood extensively on his apparently single-handed hauling of CBS into the demographic age, with Dann (whom Gitlin did not interview) painted unilaterally as the foot-dragging, ratings-hungry voice of the old guard. This young turk versus old guard version of events is complicated most obviously by Dann's own 1967 cancellations, but also by his programming of the upmarket *He and She,* his scheduling of the controversial *Smothers Brothers Comedy Hour* and his advocacy for *All in the Family,* not to mention, a few years earlier, his reported defence of prestige drama during the Aubrey regime.[57] It is also worth noting that Wood, for whom "relevant" was the watchword of the new CBS in 1970, had the previous year canceled the high-rated, topical, young-skewed—and controversial—*Smothers Brothers Comedy Hour* on the pretext of a missed production deadline.[58]

Likewise, to understand Klein's actions at NBC, one must recognize that the quality/upscale audience agenda had begun well before he arrived at the network in 1961. Demographic information data was part of the ratings currency by the late 1950s, and the NBC research department under Hugh Beville, Jr (Klein's predecessor as vice president) increasingly exploited it. As noted earlier, NBC was trumpeting the demographic superiority of its daytime lineup as early as 1953, scrutinizing prime-time audience composition by 1960, and making audacious claims of "young adult" leadership by 1963. The point here is not to defend Dann's forward-thinking nature, or to replace Klein with Beville as the rightful author of the NBC "young adult" propaganda campaign, but to caution against such simplistic accounts of individual authority, to highlight the complexity of the historical terrain, and to argue, quite simply, for a broader, longer, and deeper perspective. As in any industry, television executives do have real power and they exert it, setting policies and making decisions that have measurable impact on the cultural landscape of programming and schedules. But they do so within organizational constraints, and upon a foundation of established systems. Wood and Klein did not revolutionize network practices, they maintained and adapted existing ones.

The real impact of those practices is also worth considering in a much more careful fashion. Beyond the concrete if tenuous effect on programming (vis-à-vis retention and development), we need to cast a more critical eye on the notion of "quality" itself, both as it was used by the industry in the 1960s and 1970s to refer to audiences and programming, and as it has been invoked in academic history. In reviewing the rhetoric of quality demographics, it is difficult to ignore the tone of condescension, bordering on contempt, for less desirable audience segments, especially older and rural viewers. To say that such viewers were undervalued in the new demographic thinking is an understatement—they were explicitly unwanted. And if the older, rural viewers were at the fringes of the radar, racial minorities might as well have been in another solar system. The unstated but implicit word in every network construction of "young adult" or "urban, educated" was of course, "white," While this is not the place for an extended discussion of the implications of the network discourse on "quality," the relevant tensions at play in the industry as the demographic mindset took hold are intriguing. On the one hand the networks—especially NBC—increasingly trumpeted their ability to deliver younger more affluent audiences to their advertisers. Meanwhile, advocates for older viewers and some industry insiders were arguing that the networks were missing a large and lucrative market by overlooking the fifty-plus age group in their quest for younger viewers, while still other observers proposed that the importance ascribed to the young adult audience by advertisers was in fact "far in excess of their numbers or their definable buying power."[59] (This could help explain why in practice the networks' demographic talk tended to outstrip their concrete programming action.)

Similarly, while networks executives solemnly called on producers to incorporate broader and more accurate portrayals of black people in their shows,[60] both the networks' rhetoric and their programming strategies made it clear that their ideal target audience was predominantly the white middle and upper-middle class. The plea for more integrated casting could itself be seen as much as a reflection of, and/or appeal to, the liberal sensibilities of the upscale audience as it was an attempt to do the right thing—but perhaps this is too cynical. In any case, while some critics have argued that US television was doing its audience a disservice by programming innocuous, escapist fare during a time of wrenching social change, it is just as reasonable to argue that the pursuit of a young, urban, educated, affluent (white) audience segment was a betrayal of the medium's democratic promise, as well as a breach of broadcasters' responsibility to serve the public interest. In the final analysis, of course, the arrogance, ageism and implicit racism of the rhetoric is ultimately more disturbing than the practice, for as we have seen, the networks continued to programme by and large for the masses, trying to garner the upscale audience as part of the bargain, all the while hoping for the breakout hit. Nevertheless, the explicit proclamations that the eighteen-to-thirty-five, urban, college-educated, upper-income viewer constituted the "quality" audience means, of course, that the other 60%–80% were considered inferior on all fronts; the ostensible quest for a certain demographic profile at the exclusion of others raises fundamental questions about the broadcasters' moral and social responsibility during this period.

That said, if the industry language of demographic quality often seems smug and elitist, we should recognize that the same core assumptions that ground the network rhetoric of the 1960s and 1970s have often tended to form the basis for our own accounts and evaluations as historians and critics, with the pursuit of upscale demographics applauded for raising the sophistication level of prime time and clearing away the vulgar, raucous escapism of the wasteland years. It was "again worth our while" to watch television; it was "something that could be lived with." In other words, with the advent of the Norman Lear and MTM shows, cinema scholars and English professors discovered television. "Television for us," as it were. And in embracing a certain type of programme, there was clear demarcation between acceptable texts and unacceptable ones, and, by extension, a subtle (or sometimes not so subtle) derision of the tens of millions of viewers who might actually have found meaning and pleasure in the likes of *Gunsmoke* or *The Beverly Hillbillies.*

The corollary to the first signs of television studies' acceptance within academia in the mid 1970s was that, moving forward, the medium's scholars focused almost without exception on contemporary texts, and the programming landscape of the 1960s was left largely unexplored. This was not just a question of timeliness (or trendiness), but returned to that issue of value. *Hill Street Blues, Twin Peaks* and *Six Feet Under* are obviously art, but what can be made of *The Beverly Hillbillies*? In short, 1960s television was presumed to be understood well enough (and not all that worthy of serious attention anyway). Lynn Spigel and Michael Curtin, in the introduction to their recent anthology on 1960s television (a first—and more than two decades overdue), write that even at that late date (1997) "1960s popular television is still largely conceptualized as 'Wasteland,' (or in some circles, 'Camp'), fare."[61] US television has not been accorded anything like the sustained, systematic historical exploration that cinema has, but the decade between the quiz show scandals of 1958–59 and the "renaissance" of 1970 has been especially overlooked. It is an open question whether, say, the tragicomic moralizing of *M*A*S*H* was ultimately more uplifting and artistic than the surreal populism of *Green Acres,* but thus far the notion of a "renaissance" and the sophistication ostensibly bred by the demographic revolution has been largely accepted as self-evident—mythicized rather than analyzed.

The 1970 and 1971 seasons undeniably mark a significant period for US television, but considered in context it was clearly more a denouement than a dawn. We need to acknowledge that the foundation for the demographic strategies of the early 1970s was put in place over time, and also recognize the role, thus far overlooked, that demographics played in shaping *1960s* television—not, perhaps, a profoundly dramatic role, but no less influential than the one that played out in the 1970s. Indeed, the *continuities* of "demographic thinking" across the 1950s, 1960s and early 1970s are striking, with every supposedly radical, abrupt or audacious ploy of Klein or Wood circa 1970 echoing actions carried out years under earlier network regimes.

And the continuities extend to this day. In recent years CBS has increasingly, albeit tentatively, indicated a willingness to embrace the older audience that has long been its traditional strength, and that its competitors have sought to avoid. While CBS has not gone so far as to trumpet itself as the number one network among aging suburbanites, it has taken another look at the data, not simply equating "quality" audience with "young urban," but acknowledging and reacting to the buying power of older adults, and trying to convince advertisers of their value.[62] This could be interpreted as much as acceptance of an established niche as an active strategy to cultivate an audience, but such "spin" should hardly be surprising—it is the mirror image of NBC's own rhetorical tactics for going on thirty years. And those tactics remain essentially unchanged from the template set in 1963, as NBC continues to crown itself the number one network among young adults—in those years when it does not lead in overall ratings, that is.[63] The sense of déjà vu that accompanies such pronouncements underscores the truly seminal nature of the practices and propaganda of "quality demographics" in the 1960s, which set the stage for the manoeuvres and machinations of the early 1970s and beyond.

Notes

1. Les Brown, *Televi$ion: The Business Behind the Box* (New York, NY: Harcourt Brace Jovanovich, 1971).
2. Ibid, pp. 29, 55–6, 182, 241.
3. Jane Feuer, Paul Kerr, and Tise Vahimagi, *MTM: "Quality Television"* (London: British Film Institute, 1984), p. 3.
4. Muriel Cantor, *Prime-Time Television Content and Control* (Beverly Hills: Sage, 1980), p. 77.
5. Sally Bedell, *Up the Tube* (New York, NY: Viking, 1981), pp. 31–6.
6. Todd Gitlin, *Inside Prime-Time* (New York, NY: Pantheon, 1983), pp. 210–18.
7. Bedell, *Up the Tube,* p. 34.
8. For similar accounts, all of which cite Brown, see James L. Baughman, *The Republic of Mass Culture* (Baltimore, MD: Johns Hopkins University Press, 1992); Laurence Bergreen, *Look Now, Pay Later* (New York, NY: Mentor, 1980); David Marc, *Demographic Vistas* (Philadelphia, PA: University of Pennsylvania Press, 1984); Robert Metz, *CBS: Reflections in a Bloodshot Eye* (New York, NY: Signet, 1975); Lisa A. Lewis, *Gender Politics and MTV: Voicing the Difference* (Philadelphia, PA: Temple University Press, 1992); Robert J. Thompson, *Television's Second Golden Age: From* Hill Street Blues *to* ER (New York, NY: Continuum, 1996).
9. Richard Corliss, "Happy days are here again," in Horace Newcomb (ed.), *Television: the Critical View* (Oxford: Oxford University Press, 1982), pp. 64–76.
10. Horace Newcomb, "American television criticism, 1970–1985," *Critical Studies in Mass Communication,* vol. 3, no. 2 (1986), p. 220.
11. Based on the British series *Till Death Us Do Part* (BBC, 1966–75).
12. For an informative account of the "relevance" wave, see Harry Castleman and Walter J. Podrazik, *Watching Television* (New York, NY: McGraw Hill, 1982), pp. 221–3.
13. Brown, *Televi$ion,* p. 241.
14. The NBC Research and Planning Bulletins and Research Highlights consulted for this paper are housed at the Wisconsin Center for Film and Theatre Research at the State Historical Society in Madison. For brevity in the text and footnotes, I cite the Research and Planning Reports, Research and Planning Bulletins, and Research Highlights as Reports, Bulletins, and Highlights, respectively. Note that numbering systems associated with these documents were not consistent throughout the years. When an issue number exists, it is cited. Documents that are not designated as part of any particular series (Reports, Bulletins, Highlights) are cited by their discrete title.
15. For example: Highlights, December 1952, no. 2; Highlights, January 1953, no. 2; Highlights, "Nielsen TV pocket piece—2nd October report," 30 November

1953; "Advance Trendex ratings show NBC new shows closing the gap on CBS," 11 October 1957; "November 1957 Trendex report—NBC improves competitive position against CBS," 14 November 1957.

16. Report, "TV network audience leadership—facts vs. fantasies," 4 June 1953; Hugh M. Beville, Jr., NBC interdepartmental correspondence, 26 October 1954; Highlights, "Latest competitive network standings show NBC no. 1 position," 21 October 1958.

17. Bulletin, "'Ding Dong School' analysis," no. 50, 13 May 1953.

18. Bulletin, "The characteristics and buying habits of the daytime TV audience," no. 1, 3 February 1956. Eight other bulletins in the series, based on a Home Testing Institute study, followed, ending 1 March 1956.

19. Hugh Malcolm Beville, Jr., *Audience Ratings: Radio, Television, and Cable* (Hillsdale, NJ: Lawrence Earlbaum Associates, 1988), pp. 37, 112–114; Douglas Gomery, "How Nielsen and Arbitron became the ratings kings," *The Library of American Broadcasting Transmitter,* vol. 3, no. 1 (2001), pp. 3, 7. URL: www.lib.umd.edu/umcp/lab.

20. Bulletin, "ARB audience composition," no. 202, 21 April 1960.

21. Albert R. Kroeger, "They're dealing new hands in Detroit," *Television,* March 1961, pp. 49–50 ff.

22. Murray Horowitz, "Plot sickens for half hours," *Variety,* 17 October 1962, p. 21. See also "Why the rush to hour-long shows?," *Broadcasting,* 17 April 1961, pp. 108–9, which likens participating sponsorship to the way "the prudent investor spreads his investment capital over a number of stocks rather than plunging it all on a single company."

23. Highlights, "The number one evening network: NBC-TV," 14 November 1961; Highlights, "NBC—the #1 television network," 6 November 1961.

24. Highlights, "What's in a home," 9 January 1963, p. 1; Highlights, "For your analysis—*Eleventh Hour,*" 8 April 1963; Highlights, "NBC emerges as the leading network for upper income, upper educated young adults (which network is really first, a look behind the average ratings," 19 November 1963.

25. Highlights, "NBC emerges"; Bulletin, "The size and quality audience of NBC's anthology programs," no. 262, 25 November 1963; Bulletin, "The young adult audience—NBC leadership confirmed by 26 ARB local market reports," no. 263, 3 November 1963; Bulletin, "NBC has 5 of the top 10 young adult programs," 3 December, 1963; Highlights, "Half hour wins among young adults by network," 6 November 1963.

26. Bulletin, "Another look behind the ratings," 11 December 1963.

27. NBC Research Highlights Bulletin, 6 January 1964.

28. Highlights, "*TW3*—the urban 'Beverly Hillbillies,'" 13 January 1964.

29. Among numerous examples, circa 1965–66: Highlights, "NBC—the number one network among young adults," 1 November 1965; Bulletin, "Summary of network audience 1963–64 season," no. 266, 5 May 1964; Highlights, "TV-Q indicates that NBC is the preferred network among the college-educated adults," April 1965; Highlights, "The golden dozen," 6 November 1966; Highlights, "NBC attracts record number of young (18–49) adults," 27 November 1966.

30. Highlights, "The latest data on *Run for Your Life*'s audience," 9 May 1966; Bulletin, "NBC has higher ratings in the top US markets," 17 August 1966.

31. Highlights, "NBC increases its lead as number one adult network," 22 July 1965.

32. Bulletin, "ABC's home built on crumbling (not building) blocks," 8 February 1965; Highlights, "Batman's TvQ profile," 28 February 1966; Highlights, "Monkees are 'top banana,'" 12 November 1966.

33. Highlights, "NBC continues to have TV's most-viewed programs," 11 November 1964; Highlights, "NBC dominates top ten charts," 29 November 1964; Highlights, "The top five programs in reach are NBC's," 8 February 1965; Highlights, "NBC's number one position (with honor) is reaffirmed," 15 March 1965; Highlights, "NBC wins first Nielsen nationals of the season," 12 October 1966.

34. NBC Research Bulletin, no. 264, 26 March 1964; NBC Research Bulletin, "Summary of ARB national color TV survey," no. 272, 24 March 1965; Bulletin, "A profile of color TV set owners and prospective buyers," no. 278, 21 May 1965; Bulletin, "A product usage profile of color TV set owners," 3 December 1965.

35. George Rosen, "'64–'65: Nielsen in full color," *Variety*, 8 July 1965 p. 19; NBC Research Bulletin no. 272, "Summary of ARB national color TV survey," 24 March 1965.

36. Bulletin, "How NBC color programs compare with selective magazines in reaching a 'class' audience," 27 November 1965.

37. Rosen, "For those who think young," *Variety*, 20 January 1965, p. 47.

38. Walter Spencer, "TV's vast grey belt," *Television*, August 1967, p. 74; Richard K. Doan, "Why shows are cancelled," *TV Guide*, 15 June 1968, reprinted in Barry G. Cole (ed.), *Television* (New York, NY: The Free Press, 1970), p. 124. Klein cites *The Rogues* in the Spencer article, and comments on *Tarzan* in the Doan interview. See also Highlights, "Tarzan—an all-family program," 22 March 1967.

39. Spencer, "TV's vast grey belt," p. 55.

40. Richard Donnelly, "They're off! (as often as not)," *Television*, March 1967, p. 24.

41. Highlights, "*Bonanza* lead over *Smothers Brothers* biggest ever," 16 February 1969. On the demographic makeup of these and other programmes, see Dick Hobson, "Who watches what," *TV Guide*, 27 July 1968, reprinted in Jay S. Harris (ed.), *TV Guide: The First 25 Years* (New York, NY: Simon and Schuster, 1978), pp. 147–50; Richard Donnelly, "Television's big target: young marrieds," *Television*, January 1967, pp. 52–3.

42. Highlights, "Sock it to em!," 3 April 1968.

43. Herm Schoenfeld, "Quo vadis TV: class or corn?," *Variety*, 26 June 1963, p. 27.

44. CBS promotional booklet for *The Defenders*, 1962. Reginald Rose papers, Wisconsin Center for Film and Theatre Research at the State Historical Society.

45. For a superb critical analysis of 1960s TV documentary, see Michael Curtin, *Redeeming the Wasteland: Television Documentary and Cold War Politics* (New Brunswick, NJ: Rutgers, 1995).

46. Richard Oulahan and William Lambert, "The tyrant's fall that rocked the TV world," *Life*, 10 September 1965, p. 94.

47. George Rosen, "Paley's pouch-money, that is," *Variety*, 27 January 1965, p. 33.

48. CBS advertisement, *Variety*, 27 January 1965, p. 82; NBC advertisement, *Variety*, 24 February 1965, p. 37.

49. "CBS reshuffle: emphasis on youth," *Broadcasting*, 27 February 1967, p. 25; Richard K. Doan, "End of the line," *TV Guide*, 17 June 1967, reprinted in Harris (ed.), *TV Guide*, pp. 132–4.

50. On the demographics of *Gunsmoke* (and other shows), see Donnelly, "Television's big target," pp. 52–3.

51. Single-sponsor shows accounted for between 3% and 7% of prime-time shows by 1970, depending on the source consulted. Leo Bogart (ed.), *The Age of Television* (New York, NY: Frederick Ungar, 1972), pp. 425–6, proposes 7% and Sydney W. Head, *Broadcasting in America* (Boston, MA: Houghton Mifflin, 1972), p. 267, offers 3%.

52. Dann is quoted in Jack Stanley, *A History of Radio and Television Western Dramatic Series* Gunsmoke, *1952–1973*, Ph.D. Dissertation, University of Michigan, 1973 (Ann Arbor, MI: University Microfilms), pp. 177–81.

53. Spencer, "TV's vast grey belt," p. 81.

54. Ralph Tyler, "The 1967–68 season," *Television*, June 1967, p. 37. The shows were both thematic and institutional forebears of the MTM stable of comedies. Not only did *He and She* and *Good Morning World* depict young urban professionals trying to "make it" career-wise, both had reflexive, entertainment-industry premises. The former was created by Bill Persky and Sam Denoff, regular *Dick Van Dyke Show* writers, the latter directed by *Van Dyke* veteran Jay Sandrich. All three worked on the young/urban-slanted *That Girl* in 1966; Sandrich would go on to become a key director on *Mary Tyler Moore,* and Persky and Denoff later wrote for MTM's *The Betty White Show* (1977).

55. Dwight Whitney, "Irreverent is the word for the Smothers Brothers," *TV Guide,* 10 February 1968, reprinted in Harris (ed.), *TV Guide* p. 143.

56. Brown, *Televi$ion*, p. 29.

57. Metz, *CBS: Reflections in a Bloodshot Eye*, pp. 44, 293–305, 320.

58. Bert Spector, "A clash of cultures: The Smothers Brothers vs. CBS television," in John E. O'Connor (ed.), *American History/American Television* (New York, NY: Frederick Ungar, 1983), pp. 159–83; Steven Alan Carr, "On the edge of tastelessness: CBS, the Smothers Brothers, and the struggle for control," *Cinema Journal,* vol. 31, no. 4 (1992), pp. 3–24.

59. Eugene Feehan, "The over-50 age group," *Television,* June 1967, pp. 20–21, 44–7; Donnelly, "Television's big target," p. 23.

60. Murray Horowitz, "CBS, NBC reiterate pro-Negro stand on casting but meaningful drama on integration still lacking," *Variety,* 31 July 1963, p. 22.

61. Lynn Spigel and Michael Curtin, *The Revolution Wasn't Televised: Sixties Television and Social Conflict* (New York, NY: Routledge, 1997), p. 12.

62. CBS's public stance on the older audience over the past decade has ranged from "comfortable" to "eagerly pursuing." See "Producers miffed as CBS shuns youth-oriented shows to woo an older crowd," *TV Guide,* 30 September 1989, South Texas edition, pp. 49–50; Rick Kogan, "A show of neglect," *Chicago Tribune,* 6 August 1992, section 5, pp. 1, 11; Jane Glenn Haas, "Networks warned of perils in ignoring viewers over 50," *Chicago Tribune,* 1 October 1993, section 5, p. 3; Marl Hart, "Mature viewers gain stature in ratings war," *Chicago Tribune,* TV Week, 31 November 1996, p. 1; Steve Johnson, "Out with old, in with 18–49," *Chicago Tribune,* 21 October 1999, section 5, pp. 1, 8.

63. In spring 1999, with all the numbers in, CBS regained its spot as the most-watched network for the first time in five years—and NBC discounted the victory because CBS trailed in attracting the eighteen-to-forty-nine demographic; the same scenario played out again in May 2001. Yet in 2002, when NBC had bragging rights to first place in the ratings, the network trumpeted its mass Nielsen status, remaining curiously quiet about its demographic superiority. See Allan Johnson, "CBS wins network title, rivals are unimpressed," *Chicago Tribune,* 27 May 1999, section 3, p. 1; Sharon Waxman, "Zucker targets NBC's aging nightly lineup," *USA Today,* 24 June 2001, p. G01.

Negotiating Civil Rights in Prime Time
A Production and Reception History of CBS's
East Side/West Side

Aniko Bodroghkozy

"The Vast Wasteland" was FCC Chairman Newton Minow's characterization of American television in the early 1960s. The prime-time schedule ran amok with "broads, bosoms, and fun," to use CBS-TV president James Aubrey's alleged description. A perceived golden age of quality live drama had given way to a mass cultural dreck of talking horses, friendly Martians, and Hollywood hillbillies. By the late 1950s, television critics and commentators, who had held such high hopes for the new medium, now despaired at the nosedive in quality (Boddy 1990, 233–41). Yet, despite the formulaic drivel, ownership of sets skyrocketed to saturation levels in the early 1960s.[1]

Onto this seemingly debased stage of popular entertainment came a group of programs that historian Mary Ann Watson has dubbed "New Frontier character dramas" (Watson 1990, 43). Lawyer shows like *The Defenders,* doctor shows like *Ben Casey* and *Dr. Kildare,* classroom dramas like *Mr. Novak,* and the social work series *East Side/West Side* all attempted to deal with social problem topics of the day. They provided networks a way to deflect at least some of the criticism leveled at them from commentators and FCC commissioners for the mindlessness of their programming fare. The New Frontier programs also functioned as significant popular culture sites for mediating Kennedy-era liberalism and social change. Watson has noted how these series echoed the "service to society" ideals of the Kennedy years, especially the optimism that concerned professionals and institutions could ameliorate, if not solve, problems like poverty, racism, and juvenile delinquency.

East Side/West Side which joined the CBS lineup in the fall of 1963, was not one of the era's most successful social problem dramas, but it was certainly the most audacious, controversial, and daring. One of the first prime-time entertainment shows to introduce an African American in a continuing role,

Aniko Bodroghkozy, "Negotiating Civil Rights in Prime Time: A Production and Reception History of CBS's *East Side/West Side*." From *Television & New Media,* August 2003, Vol. 4, No. 3, pp. 257–282, copyright © 2003 by Sage Publications, Inc. Reprinted by permission of Sage Publications, Inc.

the show featured newcomer Cicely Tyson as an assistant to the show's main character, social worker Neil Brock (George C. Scott). Like other dramas of its type, episodes of *East Side/West Side* focused on issues like juvenile crime, urban renewal, prostitution, and the death penalty. However, the show's greatest significance—and its greatest controversy—rested on its handling of a number of episodes that dealt directly with race relations. *East Side/West Side* brought issues of racism, black rage, white guilt, and liberal responses to them all into prime-time entertainment with unprecedented urgency and directness.

In this article, I explore how this show, both at the level of production and at the level of reception among viewers and critics, manifested many tensions associated with white liberalism of the period—especially the challenges to race relations from the civil rights movement. As a mass-media cultural text, *East Side/West Side* provides a revealing case study of how educated middle-class whites were using a piece of popular culture to begin an often painful process of working through the meanings of fundamental social change.

This article joins a dialogue with other scholars working within cultural studies paradigms about the ways prime-time television has participated in the social circulation of meanings about American race relations. Most of this scholarship has tended to focus on contemporary programs and their production/reception contexts. Jhally and Lewis (1992), Fiske (1996), and Gray (1995) have all provided important studies of how blackness and racial meanings have been negotiated in American television in the 1980s and early 90s. In their ethnographic analysis of audience responses to *The Cosby Show*, Jhally and Lewis (1992) found that many white viewers used the series with its affluent black family as a justification for their opposition to the continued need for affirmative action and other policies and programs associated with the agenda of the civil rights movement. Whereas Jhally and Lewis's work looks at television in the post–civil rights era, my study examines how both producers and audiences negotiated racial issues in the very midst of that movement's profound challenge to racial norms. As historical analysis, this study has to find other ways in which to reconstruct audience meaning-making strategies. Jhally and Lewis's use of focus groups and interviews are impossible in this kind of analysis. Instead, I analyze audience letters written to the network (and collected in the papers of the show's producer David Susskind at the State Historical Society of Wisconsin), along with articles in the popular press, to suggest how (mostly white) Americans were responding to the challenges of the civil rights movement.[2]

The assumption underlying this study is that television programming, both in the production stage ("encoding") and in the reception stage ("decoding") participates in and serves as a terrain for the cultural negotiation over changing social and political experiences (Hall 1980; Fiske 1987). Gray (1995) shows how fictional and nonfiction television were crucial sites for both the entrenchment and challenge to Reagan-era ideologies of blackness. Similarly, Fiske (1996) shows how a number of racially-obsessed early 90s media spectacles—from the Rodney King beating video, to the Anita Hill–Clarence Thomas hearings, to the O.J. Simpson case—all served as points of maximum visibility over racial matters, inviting discursive engagement and struggle. Gray (1995) argues that it is possible—indeed, very often necessary—to approach commercial culture as a place for theorizing about black cultural politics and the struggles over meaning that are played out there. Hence, I want to suggest that commercial culture serves as both a *resource* and a *site* in which blackness as a cultural sign is produced, circulated, and enacted. (P. 2)

As this study will show, I see *East Side / West Side* as both a "resource" and a "site" for the circulation and enactment of the sign of blackness but also, more generally, the signs of race relations and Kennedy-era liberalism.[3] But as we will see, it was the series' two high-profile episodes on race issues that brought to maximum discursive visibility a cultural preoccupation with questions of the place of African Americans in American society and the appropriate response of white liberals.

"Entertainment" Versus "Urgent Issues": CBS and the Creation of *East Side/West Side*

East Side/West Side was not a easy show to get onto network television. Produced for CBS by David Susskind's Talent Associates–Paramount, Ltd., the project was notably out of step with the programming strategy of the network. CBS had found itself with a winning prime-time schedule filled with unsophisticated, rural-oriented, "hayseed" shows. *The Beverly Hillbillies* and *The Andy Griffith Show,* both comedies extolling the virtues of country living and lore, exemplified the pattern of entertainment programming more and more associated with the network. The Susskind project, on the other hand, took place on the mean streets of New York City, and—unlike most television shows in that era of burgeoning telefilms—the series was entirely shot on location in the metropolis.[4] The series focused on the cases taken on by an angry crusader for social justice, social worker Neil Brock who worked for an independent welfare agency, the Community Welfare Service (CWS). The problems Brock dealt with were the problems of urban America—a world away from the warm-hearted dilemmas faced by the gentle folk of Mayberry RFD. The CWS was located in a slum neighborhood, and many of Brock's clients suffered from the vicissitudes of poverty and social neglect.

Network head James Aubrey was unimpressed. According to Robert Metz in his chatty history of the network, Aubrey loathed the show and tried to have the CWS relocated to Park Avenue. David Susskind reported Aubrey declaring, "They've got just as big social problems on Park Avenue and that's where I want the goddam show to be" (Metz 1975, 228). Despite Aubrey, the show's locale remained gritty, poor, and needful of social assistance.

Philosophically, the show seemed to owe more to the era of live anthology dramas with their frequently urban locations and social problem themes. Susskind himself had begun his career in television as a producer of respected anthology series. However, in the new world of "escapist" television fare so successful with Nielsen families and with sponsors wanting "happy people with happy problems" sandwiched between their advertisements, *East Side / West Side* not only wasn't escapist, but as far as the network was concerned, it wasn't even entertainment.

Memos from CBS executives reveal a semiotic struggle over the definition of *entertainment* when the material concerned the "urgent issues" of the times. As far as the network was concerned, explorations of such issues were best left to news and documentary programming where "an objective and dispassionate approach is possible." CBS's director of program development, Lawrence White, in a memo dated 10 July 1963 (Susskind Papers, box 66, file 18), during the show's development, argued that examinations of proposed story ideas about

> fall out shelters, the Birch Society, sympathy picketing, negro [*sic*] ghettos, etc., etc., is certainly out of the show's domain. The dramatized treatment of important current social and political questions must, for impact, take either an editorial point of view or endorse solutions, which automatically seems to eliminate the objective view.

Uncritically buying into the myth of reportorial objectivity, White set up a binary between news and drama. Fictional narratives dealing with topical issues somehow lacked the requisite mechanisms whereby reportage could maintain a (politically safe) proper distance. White's concerns about objectivity were likely grounded in a fear of alienating potential viewers who might disagree with the social change agenda implicit in a series about social work and the amelioration of urban problems. The network stance also suggests the philosophy behind the "escapist" programming CBS was perfecting. If the news, public affairs, and documentary sections of the network were handling treatments of such issues, then the entertainment section should eschew those topics entirely—as shows like *Mr. Ed* appeared to do—to properly separate the two areas of network operation.

CBS also had problems with *East Side/West Side* because, by focusing on *social* issues, narratives, did not concentrate with appropriate emphasis on the problems of individual characters with whom audiences could identify. White argued,

> You must understand that the problem of the individual based on an emotional need which finds some relief, some understanding and some compassion from the character of Neil Brock is the true subject matter of our series. . . . His commitment must always be to the human—to the individual—to hope.

By committing to the individual, however, the narrative would be unable to commit to a program of social change and social movement. Individual problems needing Brock's assistance would thus not have a fundamental social or economic basis.

The network seemed particularly concerned about the tone of the program. It had an "over-grim documentary feel." And whereas unhappy endings may have been acceptable for such reality-based material, the network was concerned that this fictional project lacked humor. In an internal memo from White to CBS Programming Head Michael Dann, dated 7 May 1963 (Susskind Papers, box 66, file 18), White argued,

> We all know that what makes life bearable for the inhabitants of the jungle that many parts of our world have become; what makes people live with poverty

and lack of hope is the God-given ability to laugh at oneself, to hear the laughter of children in the worst tenement.

White's Pollyanna view suggests a strategy the network wanted the show's producers to use to defuse whatever incendiary material they were encountering. Presumably, tenement problems of poverty and economic distress could somehow be mitigated if viewers could be convinced that poor people still had a wealth of laughter at their disposal.

East Side/West Side producers attempted to negotiate with CBS over this issue. While not backing away from the "urgent issues," they assured Lawrence White in, for instance, a letter from Talent Associates' Larry Arrick dated 2 July 1963 (Susskind Papers, box 66, file 18) that scripts with a lighter, more comic tone had been commissioned, including a love story involving Neil Brock. However, writers and producers for the show engaged in a certain amount of self-censorship over the types of urgent issues they would endeavor to examine. One project involved police brutality in Harlem. CBS countered by suggesting a story about an individual "sick cop" whose singular sadistic tendencies ruined an otherwise perfect neighborhood. The project's scriptwriter, along with George C. Scott, refused to entertain CBS's proposal. In a letter to David Susskind dated 29 May 1963 (Susskind Papers, box 66, file 18), the writer argued, "I felt that approach was a whitewash of police brutality after weeks of research in Harlem and the Lower East Side with social workers." He recommended dropping the story ideas as just too "hot" a topic.

Despite the network's reservations about the entertainment values of *East Side/West Side*, and despite poor responses from test audiences who reportedly found the pilot too "harsh" and "severe," the series went ahead more or less as Susskind, Scott, and Talent Associates wanted it.[5] However, in publicity materials, the production company tried to negotiate a preferred reading of the series that emphasized CBS's definition of entertainment. Talent Associates issued a press release to television editors at 1,800 newspapers on 31 August 1963 (Susskind Papers, box 67, file 1) with copy reading:

> . . . television should reflect reality and "East Side/West Side" does just that but within a framework of showmanship and entertainment. We want the viewer to be absorbed, involved, entertained and informed—all by the same program! . . . The subject matter in "East Side/West Side" is unusually varied. Some of the programs are actually comedies because life even at its most corrosive level is sometimes that or it could not be lived at all.

George C. Scott took a similar message to journalists who interviewed him about his role. In one newspaper article (Susskind Papers, Clippings, box 66, file 16), he argued,

> We have a drama on urban renewal. It presents all sides of the problem—the landlord's, the tenant's, the city planner's, the bureaucrat's, etc. You think this might be dull? Well, it isn't. We do it as entertainment. Here's a point I wish to emphasize. Any show must, first of all, be entertaining, told with action, drama, humor and conflict. There's nothing deadlier than pure propaganda. That's the reason so many plays with messages fail.

The debates over the entertainment value of this television project indicate anxiety about prime time as a venue for narratives with a social conscience. How should mass-distributed fictional texts interact with a newly activist political and social climate? The early 1960s witnessed an interventionist liberalism in Washington, bolstered by optimism that both government and private social welfare organizations could eradicate systemic social ills. Grassroots movements agitating for fundamental social change, like the civil rights campaigns, were further transforming the political culture of the nation. Yet, American network television, which came of age in the more politically quiescent 1950s, when McCarthyist Red scares discouraged questioning of the status quo, may have been having a tough time understanding the new sentiment blowin' in the wind. Despite protestations of journalistic objectivity, television coverage of the civil rights movement, most notably the clashes between desegregation activists and Bull Connor's dogs and fire hoses in Birmingham, ended up functioning as movement propaganda. Martin Luther King actively sought out television cameras to film the suppression suffered by his movement's nonviolent participants. The networks complied. They also complied with the Kennedy Administration, providing often-fawning coverage of the telegenic chief executive (Watson 1990). However, in fictional programming, the networks seemed mired in a 1950s fear of the consequences of representing any kind of critique of the dominant social or economic order—even when the White House was sanctioning those critiques, to some extent at least.

Fans of the show also participated in the debate over the issue of what entertainment meant. *East Side/West Side*'s travails with the ratings system encouraged a notable number of obviously educated viewers to construct mass/elite arguments about the television industry and its mass audience. One viewer, a Ph.D. from Roosevelt, New Jersey, condemned the show's cancellation and CBS as a broadcast network

> for a complete disregard of responsibility towards a good many of its viewers and towards the use of TV as a medium for cultural enhancement and intellectual enlightenment. I simply do not think that it is fair to lower TV standards to the lowest common denominator who may be some poor, ignorant, bigoted person in some section of the country.

Letters like this one constructed television as a battlefield where the debased political and intellectual capabilities of the mass were destroying the promise of the medium. Escapist entertainment television was something the "stupid masses" enjoyed—and inflicted on the more discriminating minority. A viewer in Dallas noted, "Since you have no hillbillies, no glamor [*sic*], no pies in the face, and no stupid fathers, your show is almost foredoomed to be way down in the ratings." A married couple from Utica, New York, sent the network a telegram warning, "If our television viewing is to be dictated by either economic groups or bigots, you may be assured that this family in addition to many others will de-plug the black box and terminate our interest in television broadcasting" (Susskind Papers, Viewer mail, box 67, file 4).

Over and over again, these viewers, who constructed themselves as a discriminating minority able to appreciate the value of a series like *East Side/West Side,* took pains to geographically locate the dumb, bigoted masses whose tastes they felt were adversely influencing programming: entertainment was being defined by dumb Southerners. The vast majority of viewer letters relating to the series in the David Susskind papers displayed Northeast, Midwest, or Southern California addresses. Most letter writers came from urban areas. These viewers either implicitly or explicitly constructed the dumb masses and their reactionary politics as nonurban and from the South. A viewer from New York City fumed, "Frankly, I am just fed up with TV catering to the southern group that is against humanity & humans" (Susskind Papers, Viewer mail, box 67, file 4). Such views neatly located bigotry and ignorance away from the letter writer's locale.

The first phases of the civil rights movement and its coverage on television may have encouraged viewers to think about racism and reactionary politics as a Southern problem. The early 1960s saw little attention paid to miseries of ghetto life and poverty in Northern and West Coast cities. That poverty was better hidden until the explosion of urban black riots that began with the 1965 Watts Uprising in Los Angeles. Poverty and discrimination that did exist in the North were, presumably, being dealt with by the interventionist liberalism that *East Side/West Side* mirrored. But the South, at least from the perspective of some Northerners, was something else. A Northern liberal construction of a Southern Other shouldered the responsibility for debased popular culture and debased politics.[6]

Just as some Northern fans of the show felt that conservative Southern sensibilities and prejudices were infecting what they could see on their TV screens, some Southerners seemed to have felt equally inundated with Northern liberal propaganda. A columnist for a newspaper in Jackson, Mississippi (Susskind Papers, Clippings, box 66, file 16), railed against an episode that criticized traditional morality around youthful sexual activity.

> I wonder if certain propagandists are misusing entertainment . . . to catch the sympathies of Americans for philosophies that can sicken this country. . . . What [the story] all adds up to is that we need a more advanced society planned by far-sighted and understanding experts (just, by coincidence, like the social worker in the play).

This reviewer was clearly alarmed by the managerial, social engineering qualities of activist liberalism that the show, despite CBS's admonitions, attempted to express. And because its political morality was at such odds with the reviewer's worldview, the show could not possibly be entertainment.

However, charges that the show was propagandistic were not limited to the South. A reviewer in Camden, New Jersey (Susskind Papers, Clippings, box 66, file 16), condemned the show as "a vicious propaganda vehicle for tearing down morals and social order." Anxieties about mass media and its role in a perceived degradation of the country's moral fiber were certainly not new. However, the Mississippi and New Jersey critics clearly considered *East Side/West Side* as a kind of cheering section for the policies of the Kennedy Administration.

The Impotent Hero

The social conscience and political change attitudes of *East Side/West Side* were not the only areas of controversy surrounding the show's production. Equally problematic for the network and for some critics was the figure of Neil Brock. In a number of significant ways, the character did not satisfy traditional expectations of the narrative male hero. As feminist film theorists in particular have pointed out, the leading male character is narratively active, making things happen, commanding the diegetic space of the fictional world, merging his gaze with that of the camera, thus encouraging spectators of the drama to identify themselves with him and his desires (Kaplan 1983; Mulvey 1975).

A number of critics zeroed in on the ways Brock did not measure up to these expectations. *Saturday Review* critic Robert Lewis Shayon titled an article on the show "The Powerless Hero," and observed that Brock was "socially impotent; his clients are victims of society. Neither he nor they transcend their limitations with any high quality of word or action." A critic for a paper in Lynn, Massachusetts, argued that Brock did not have much to do. He "mostly stands around looking grim or sits in his office looking concerned." Characters typically worked out their problems on their own. A reviewer at the *Los Angeles Times* indicated that a weakness of the series was that Brock as social worker was essentially a passive force, ranting at social conditions but unable to improve them (Susskind Papers, Clippings, box 66, file 16).

Brock's "impotence" may have been an inadvertent statement about the limits of interventionist liberalism to ameliorate social problems. The early 1960s evidenced a great deal of optimism that rationally planned and suitably funded projects, such as the soon-to-be-inaugurated Great Society programs put forth by Kennedy's successor to the presidency, Lyndon Johnson, would finally wipe out the remaining "pockets" of poverty in America. The "can-do" vigor inspired by President Kennedy's rhetoric about the opportunities and challenges faced by a new generation of Americans were inspiring to resurgent liberals who, like John Kenneth Galbraith, saw poverty not as a structural aspect characteristic of capitalism but rather as a faulty distribution of wealth correctable by an affluent society. Properly focused public spending, according to Galbraith, would take care of the final vestiges of poverty (Galbraith 1958; Matusow 1984). Neil Brock's inability to right the social wrongs may have been a harbinger warning that liberal tinkering with the social order would not be effective in promoting truly emancipatory change.

Although *East Side/West Side* was noteworthy for its handling of various contemporary social welfare problems, it has been recognized most widely for the unprecedented way in which it dealt with Northern, urban race relations. On 4 November 1963 and on 2 December 1963, the series aired two highly publicized, discussed, and debated episodes that have come to exemplify the show's historical importance.[7] "Who Do You Kill?" starred newcomers James Earl Jones and Diana Sands as an impoverished Harlem couple whose baby was killed after being bitten by a rat; "No Hiding Place" featured Ruby Dee as part of a black couple who had just moved into a previously all-white Long

Island neighborhood in the throes of unscrupulous real estate agents' tactics of "blockbusting." The episodes were broadcast at a particularly key moment as far as the relationship between television and the civil rights campaigns were concerned. The two shows also bookended another landmark television moment: the assassination of President Kennedy and the resulting four days of continuous coverage of its aftermath.

On 20 June 1963, Martin Luther King brought more than 250,000 people to the nation's capital for the March on Washington, in an attempt to ensure passage of the Civil Rights Bill. The event received massive and supportive coverage from all three networks. A few months before, the networks had carried shocking images of black children and old men being attacked by dogs and high-pressure water hoses organized by Birmingham's police chief, Bull Connor. Both of these events functioned as media spectacles, especially for Northern whites. Suddenly, television was transformed into a primary site whereby Americans were having their previously naturalized notions about race questioned. Televised representations of black struggle shocked many into rethinking what America stood for, especially when it came to the rights of black people. The shocking quality of the images impelled numerous Northern whites—mostly idealistic college students—into actively joining civil rights campaigns. However, most viewers did not end up going down south to participate in voter registration campaigns or other such activism. Nevertheless, the searing quality of the images challenged spectators to react in some way to what they were seeing night after night. What made this particular moment in broadcast history so significant was not only the fact that viewers were inundated with journalistic representations of the struggle for social change but that they were also being confronted with fictional representations of the same struggle. The *East Side/West Side* episodes may not have been seen by as many viewers as the news coverage of civil rights activity, but they functioned in a similar way: they forced viewers (in often painful ways) to confront racism and their own implications within that system.

The following section of this paper examines how viewers negotiated meanings around racism, liberal responses, and white guilt within a context of heightened intensity about those issues—heightened largely by television coverage. The reading strategies viewers adopted in relation to these two shows provide useful clues about how many Northern white Americans were coming to grips with the shocks of racial social transformations that so many Americans experienced via mediation by their television sets. Press commentary and the response of *East Side/West Side* viewers suggest a complex set of negotiations as white viewers found themselves having to grapple with the no-longer-invisible struggles of African Americans within a white social order.

"Who Do You Kill?"

According to memos in the David Susskind papers, the philosophical debates between the show's producers and CBS, evident during the series' initial stages, continued during the preproduction of this episode. Written by Talent Associates producer Arnold Perl, the script was supposed to be both a love story amidst the tenements and an exposé of appalling Harlem living conditions. James Earl Jones played Joe, the frustrated and angry young husband who could not seem to get a decent job despite taking night courses. He minded the baby while his more optimistic wife, Ruth, worked as a waitress. Crisis struck when a rat bit their sleeping baby. In a nightmarish scene, Joe ran out into the dark Harlem streets clutching his child, unable to get any taxi to stop and take them to a hospital. When the child died, the normally vibrant Ruth, the functional head of the family, collapsed emotionally, losing all sense of hope. Brock and Jane, the Cicely Tyson character, attempted to offer assistance to Joe and Ruth at the hospital. In a much-quoted piece of dialogue, Joe exclaimed, "If a white man stick a knife in my back and another white man pull it out and stick on a bandage, you think I'm going to kiss his hand?"

CBS objected to the first draft script's "editorializing" and "tract"-like qualities. The network wanted a more universal love story of a young couple dealing with difficult circumstances. Larry White, speaking for the network, particularly objected to the "sermonizing" about slumlords, quotas, and over-crowded hospitals that he argued "vitiated" the drama. In a 2 September 1963 memo from Arnold Perl describing his meeting with White (Susskind Papers, box 67, file 1), Perl noted that White disliked the background given to explain why Ruth withdrew after her baby's death. White argued that it wasn't needed: "It is universal." Perl responded that neither his nor White's child would ever be bitten by a rat in a slum.

> When I added that this was the whole point of the show—that these were not people even as you and I, but an average Negro couple living and trying to make out in an average Harlem existence, he moved to another point.

The network wanted an uplifting story only coincidentally about impover-ished black ghetto dwellers. Harkening back to the distinction White made between drama and journalism, any narrative that incorporated material about documented social conditions somehow would no longer be effective drama. However, universalizing the story would, of course, make it politically safer. The universal human condition would be less likely to generate interventionist polit-ical movements or respond to historically specific mechanisms of social change.

The *Los Angeles Times,* praising the show, argued, "It was not a story of color but of the eternal struggle of man in an imperfect world" (Susskind Papers, Clippings, box 66, file 16). Such a reading was unconsciously racist, because the specificity of African-American struggles with poverty and racism were being so aggressively denied. The more hegemonically palatable "man" displaced the ideologically loaded and uncomfortable signifier "color." If this was a universally human story, then it could be a white story, too.

One reviewer who disliked the episode castigated the show for *not* doing precisely what the *Los Angeles Times* critic thought the show did so well. This reviewer argued that the difficulties faced by the young black couple "are indigenous to poverty. They're problems that know no color barrier. . . ." She went on to explain that black performers had fared much better when they were "integrated" into story lines, such as on *The Nurses, The Defenders, The*

Fugitive, Ben Casey, and *Mr. Novak* in "unostentatious" ways. "What's objectionable [in *East Side / West Side*] is the automatic raising of the racial question every time a Negro appears in a dramatic scene" (Susskind Papers, Clippings, box 66, file 16). The reviewer seemed uncomfortable with any representations of black people that pointed to difference. As long as black images refrained from discomfiting whites by pointing to unresolved and contentious issues of race relations—as long as they integrated themselves into familiar narratives and representations, then all was fine.

While reviewers appeared to be confused about whether the episode was unique to the African-American experience of poverty or whether it was a universal story of struggle, the episode's director, Tom Gries, appeared incoherent on the issue. In an interview on the filming of the program, he argued that while the narrative was a "Negro story, native to Harlem," it could just as easily have been a story about white people, because it was so universal. Then, apparently thinking the matter over, he said,

> No . . . I guess the story belongs to Harlem. Do you know Harlem? I didn't. Those people will all go to heaven because they live in hell now. We shot for three days at 118th St. and Lennox Ave. and I didn't believe it—I didn't believe people lived that way. (Susskind Papers, Clippings, box 66, file 16)

The broadcasting of this episode generated a great deal of discussion and was preceded by an exceptional amount of publicity. Producer Susskind persuaded his good friend New York Senator Jacob Javits to view an advance copy of the episode and to praise it on the floor of the Senate.[8] Talent Associates also launched a word-of-mouth letter-writing campaign to a hundred "outstanding American leaders," including Martin Luther King. The leaders were sent a copy of the script and asked to inform friends and members of their organizations about the upcoming broadcast. Enough interest had been generated by the story that almost all television critics were expected to write on the episode. Ratings were generally quite good: its initial broadcast garnered a 38-percent share of the television viewing audience.[9]

Two of CBS's Southern affiliates, however, decided against broadcasting the episode. KSLA-TV in Shreveport, Louisiana, claimed the show had to be pre-empted for a televised debate between candidates for a local political race. The general manager of WAGA-TV in Atlanta, according to a 5 November 1963 New York *Newsday* article (Susskind Papers, Clippings, box 66, file 16), opined that the show was "too rough for prime-time television" and that "it would be detrimental to the cause of good race relations in Atlanta and surrounding areas." Even though the drama had nothing to do with Southern race relations, these affiliates still felt their white racial sensibilities under attack.

The episode generated a relatively heavy amount of viewer mail, if the number of letters in the David Susskind papers is any guide (Susskind Papers, Viewer mail, "Who Do You Kill?" box 69, file 10). There are 204 letters and postcards; all but five praise the episode. It is important to note that this selection of letters cannot stand in for the larger audience who did not write about their responses, nor can their reading strategies be considered unproblematically representative of the millions who watched the program. At best, viewer letters provide us with qualitative clues suggesting tendencies in historically specific moments of mass-audience meaning-making strategies.

Considering that viewers watching the episode would also have been exposed to imagery and news stories about civil rights activity, it is no surprise that many linked the program's impact to that of the movement. A Massachusetts letter writer wrote that "the impact of the story was worth a million sit-downs or protest marches." A Pomona, California, viewer argued that "programs of this sort will do more to help our country solve this problem than all the pleading, marching[,] praying or legislation." Although well-meaning, these responses suggest white viewers who were not entirely comfortable with black people protesting, marching, and agitating for civil rights. Fictional representations may have felt less threatening, less confrontational, and less immediate in their effects. Other viewers read the episode as part of a continuum of civil rights activity: the program continued and extended the political goals of the movement. A New Jersey fan wrote, "The program dramatically and graphically made believable and immediate the protests we have heard before only in speeches." Another viewer hoped the show "will lend impetus to the 'Freedom Now' movement to free all oppressed all over this land." Thus, rather than being a substitute for the direct action practices of the movement, the *East Side / West Side* episode was itself a political intervention. Unsympathetic viewers opposed to civil rights also read the show as connected to civil rights politics. Another New Jersey viewer condemned the episode as "nauseous propaganda. . . . Even the 'reverend' was made up to look like that rabble rouser, Martin Luther King."

Although this viewer's oppositional reading indicated an unwillingness to see herself implicated in Northern mechanisms of racism, many others found themselves compelled to examine their own whiteness and its accompanying privilege in relation to an oppressed black Other. A Weymouth, Massachusetts mother wrote, "I am ashamed to be one of the so-called white Christians who have let such a situation exist. I feel guilty as I look around my clean suburban home and my small ones sleeping in clean beds." A priest in Fargo, North Dakota, wrote, "I was both angry and guilty. Angry because of the awful agony of the young couple. Guilty because as a white man I am partially responsible for anguish so rife and unnecessary and damaging." Many viewers were self-conscious about identifying themselves as white, and many engaged in similar bouts of liberal guilt. Whiteness for these viewers had become something that needed attention—whiteness had social and political consequences. Skin color was connected to power and to distinctions. The progressive potential of this fictional drama lay in the ways it forced many of its viewers to recognize, perhaps for the first time, that as middle-class whites, they were caught up in power relations of race and privilege. The denaturalizing of that set of relations was clearly painful but potentially emancipatory.

Other viewers caught up in white liberal guilt expressed a degree of helplessness in changing the system of race relations with which they were suddenly grappling. One woman pleaded,

> Please someone let us know what we as citizens, better yet, as human beings who *care* about other human beings—what can we do to help. . . . Do we

write the Mayor, our Congressman, our Senator? I feel helpless but I must help in some way.

A woman in Scarborough, Ontario, asked, "is there something a white Canadian can do to begin to help change things? Not patronizingly but sincerely. I can't think of anything specific and feel sick about the whole thing." A woman in Brooklyn wrote, "We were moved to write to you because in our sense of helplessness over the dramatic situation presented, this was the only positive step we, as viewers, could take."

The palpable agonizing these viewers expressed raises some perplexing questions. Clearly, these white viewers were moved enough by the representations of black poverty, discrimination, and despair that they wanted to engage in some form of intervention to effect social change. Yet, at that very moment in time, a coordinated, organized movement expressly committed to racial social justice was mobilized and active. Although viewers made the connections between the civil rights movement and this program, they did not seem to make the further connection that if they wanted to engage in ameliorating race relations, they needed to become politically active. As predominantly white Northerners (plus one non-American), it is possible that these viewers constructed civil rights activism as strictly a black, as well as Southern, phenomenon—something that just did not interpellate them from their subject positionings. These viewers may have been unable to conceive of themselves participating in a social change movement. Their desire to do something was channeled into writing letters to the show's producers. Supporting *East Side / West Side,* which was already threatened with cancellation, became a substitute for involvement with civil rights activity. Fandom for the series functioned as an alternative way to express a nascent political position.

Although the program may not have created new white foot soldiers for the era's civil rights campaigns, it did appear to encourage some profound soul searching among viewers about their own internalized racism. One viewer who had grown up on Chicago's South Side admitted,

> Even as a loving Christian, [I] have very little love and understanding for my negro [*sic*] brother. But the picture last night has opened my mind and heart to the negro and I can honestly say that I now have a deeper insight to the terrific plight of the negro.

Another Chicago family used the show to engage in some painful self-exploration of the limits of their own racial tolerance. The letter writer described family members being reduced to tears. Their sixteen-year-old daughter asked why Negroes had to live like that.

> Finally, after going through the whole bit about the unfairness of our treatment of the negroes [*sic*], she remarked, "Yes, but you wouldn't want them living next to you, would you?"
>
> Now, I had always thought that we—as a family, were unusually tolerant and understanding, but I realize now that our sterilized life in the suburbs has *and is* producing another generation of segregationists. No maybe I wouldn't like to live next door to negroes, but how do I know? I never have

tried. But, whether I like it or not, it is morally wrong that I even feel this antipathy towards them when I have had absolutely no socializing with them.

In the end, perhaps the show's most noteworthy achievement, based on clues in these letters, was a contribution to consciousness raising among whites. This piece of fictional entertainment programming did much the same in forcing white Americans to face the truth of racial injustice and inequality endemic in their society. Prime-time series like *East Side/West Side,* along with news specials and evening newscasts, worked to set a foundation of sympathy among many white television viewers for the goals of a movement they engaged with only via their television sets.

Although none of these viewers seemed to have been ready to engage in any form of direct action in response to what they had seen in the program, such was not the case for a group of intrepid executives from Kinney Service Corporation. According to an article dated 11 December 1963 in *Daily Variety* (Susskind Papers, Clippings, box 66, file 16), the group decided to take a tour of Harlem to ascertain whether housing conditions were as bad as the episode suggested. Shocked to discover they were, the businessmen decided to choose a block and clean it up—exterminate the vermin, paint, cart away garbage, and so forth. Using their business clout, they were able to prevail over slumlords who wanted no outside interference with their property. After cleaning up the block, a passing policeman, watching the cleanup, alerted the group to an even filthier block up the street. The businessmen resolved to clean it up, without even bothering to contact the landlord. The story is a perfect illustration of the can-do spirit animating the early days of the War on Poverty. The urban blight that Harlem represented could be fixed with enough good old determination and resolve.

"No Hiding Place"

East Side/West Side's other famous episode on race relations was aired the week network television resumed its regular schedule after the four days of continuous coverage of the Kennedy assassination and funeral. Written by formerly blacklisted screenwriter Millard Lampell, the show was a complex look at how a middle-class, white suburban community, and one liberal family in particular, reacted when unscrupulous real estate agents attempted to blockbust their neighborhood. The community of Maple Corners already had one black family—the couple was impeccably educated, with all the markers of (white) middle-class respectability. Nevertheless, shady real estate agents attempted to panic white homeowners with visions of a black invasion, encouraging them to quickly sell their houses at a loss. The agents in turn would sell the houses at a large profit to unwitting black families eager to move to a nice suburban neighborhood. At the end of the process, a previously all-white neighborhood would be mostly black.

Neil Brock's friend Chuck Severson and his Southern wife Anne found themselves in the difficult position of wanting to do the right thing and resist racist appeals to panic selling but fearing the economic consequences of their good intentions. The couple, on Brock's advice, hosted an awkward party to introduce their anxious white neighbors to their eminently respectable new black neighbors. Racial rapprochement appeared possible until one of the for-sale homes sold to a successful but uneducated and unrefined black man. The narrative reached its crisis. Anne, portrayed perhaps too broadly and superficially as the exact opposite of a Southern racist, wanted to stay and put up the good fight for integration and color-blind civility. As a woman, however, the narrative dilemma did not hinge around her desires or decisions. Husband Chuck, referred to in the show as "Larry Liberal," was the center of attention. Brock exposed Chuck's implicit racism by commenting, "You were expecting a white Negro, and you got a black one." Brock went on to observe, "If he went to Harvard, if he plays golf, and talks like a Boston gentleman, and looks like a Philadelphia lawyer, then fine, let him have brown skin. Only not too brown. Sure, Chuck believes in equality: *but . . .*" The episode ended without any resolution.

Like "Who Do You Kill?" "No Hiding Place" garnered a significant amount of attention from both the press and viewers.[10] Although the seventy-three letters and postcards in the Susskind papers written in response to the show were mostly favorable, a significant number (eleven) indicated that some viewers were deeply uncomfortable about the prospects of black people living in their midst (Susskind Papers, Viewer mail, "No Hiding Place," box 69, file 12). White viewers may have responded with less conflict to the Harlem story because the issues explored in that drama were spatially removed from their own lives. They could feel badly for Joe and Ruth and wish to help in some vague way, but they would never have to worry that the couple would move in next door. The December 4 show hit many of the series' white, middle-class, suburban viewers literally where they lived—and any fearful or racist responses that the subject matter might elicit from them would find "no hiding place." The drama interpellated white viewers in such a way that many would have little choice but to accept the positioning of themselves as "Larry Liberals" and face their own embedded anxieties and prejudices about the black Other. Like the Chicago family whose daughter forced the issue about integrated neighborhoods, "No Hiding Place" may have forced many viewers to grapple with the question of whether or not they were a new generation of segregationists.

One viewer, like the fictional family in the show, lived in a Long Island neighborhood that included one lone black family. Her response indicates how profound the impact of this episode could be:

> Because of your programs, I find myself re-examining my own position toward integration. I am very indignant towards bigots when I watch a show like the "Rat Bite," but when I hear the fears and doubts expressed by "Chuck" in "No Hiding Place" I understand and sympathize with them. I haven't resolved any of my conflicts on this subject because of your series. I have become more aware of my own bigoted attitudes, which surprised me.

This liberal and well-intentioned viewer appeared to understand that racism was not only the activities and discourses of grossly and hatefully intolerant rednecks. Racism had a more insidious and subtle form as well. And she saw herself implicated in this gentler version. However, by forcing this viewer to realize her own previously unexamined bigotry, the episode helped to create a potentially emancipatory experience. The viewer's nonracist racism was suddenly apparent to her. The discomfort it caused could encourage her to reexamine her assumptions and begin a process of personal change.

A number of other viewers who praised the show and mentioned their own support for integrated housing felt the need to mention, usually parenthetically ("by the way" or "incidentally" or "perhaps I should add") that they were white. Such self-consciousness may indicate that these viewers saw the struggle for racial integration as essentially a black issue. They suddenly found themselves having to negotiate their own racialized subject positions within this terrain. Such self-consciousness could be potentially emancipatory because their own whiteness, previously naturalized as a nonposition (because invisible), was suddenly visible to them. A number of these viewers indicated that they were actively working for integration in their own neighborhoods, suggesting that recognition of "the wages of whiteness" might be a first step to active engagement with civil rights activism (Dyer 1997).

Whereas the program may have had this potentially emancipatory impact on some viewers, others negotiated different readings. The drama's lack of closure and refusal to mandate a solution left viewers free to construct readings determined by their own social positioning and experiences. A white musician and published writer from Brooklyn wrote a long, narrative letter to David Susskind to praise him for the episode and to recount her own experience of being blockbusted. She described a formerly clean, safe, beautifully appointed street where she could walk late at night after coming home from the Academy of Music. All of a sudden, her neighbor's house was sold and a "car load of Negroes" moved in:

> Then the horror began. There is no other word for it. One by one the fine houses sold for two or three thousand dollars. Negroes moved in. Noise replaced peace and quiet. Prostitutes yelled from windows at night and were carted off by police kicking and screaming. No one was safe. Cockroaches became a torment. Relief tenants ruined the houses, leaving their front doors open night and day for the drinks. I had Negroes on both sides of me.

Fearful of going out at night, and with the captain of police urging her to move, the letter writer made her decision:

> So, I sold my lovely home with its black walnut woodwork, its high ceilings, spacious rooms, hundreds of paintings specially lighted, thousands of books. I had a splendid library, many books out of print. I went about the house lovingly touching the walls and apologizing for deserting them. I knew it would be turned into a rooming house for Negroes and it was right away.

The writer's class position as well as her whiteness put her at odds with her new neighbors. What is particularly noteworthy here, however, is the fact that this letter writer felt the episode justified her opinions and attitudes. She praised the show, asserting that the people in the play should leave, as she was forced to do. Susskind and scriptwriter Millard Lampell may not have welcomed such a reading of their show, but the open-ended quality of the narrative and the fact that Lampell allowed no closure may have made such readings easily negotiable. At the end of the episode, we are left with Anne's closing dialogue to Chuck: "You've got to decide, love. . . . You're gonna have to decide. . . ." This letter writer made her decision and managed to find support for her racism in that ambiguous ending.

Few viewers constructed such idiosyncratic readings. Numerous letter writers connected the show to their own efforts in promoting integration. A number of clergymen and laypeople involved in attempts to fight for integrated housing praised the episode as helpful in assisting the movement. Yet, rather than emphasize the need for collective action and broad-based organizing to achieve these goals, many letters emphasized individual solutions. One White Plains, New York, letter asserted, "While [the episode] left no questions answered, this is consistent with the realities because the questions can only be answered by each individual himself." A pastor in Xenia, Ohio, echoed this sentiment: "You left the decision there in the hands of the individual, and this is, of course, where the race crisis must ultimately be solved." As was the case with some of the viewers of "Who Do You Kill?" here again we find a certain amount of reluctance on the part of some white viewers to admit that integration and racial amelioration would require political and activist intervention. If solutions were ultimately in the hands of individuals, then a political movement (such as the civil rights movement) was not really necessary. Lampell's script, interpellating viewers as rational, liberal individuals who could make appropriate individual decisions, may have privileged these readings. Connected to this perspective was the presumption that if antiracist solutions were up to individuals, then racial bigotry was likewise a problem of individuals rather than a systemic condition related to whiteness.

Other viewers had a much more antagonistic reaction to the episode's portrayal of white bigotry. They appeared resentful and alarmed at having their whiteness and its attendant powers held up to them as problematic. An anonymous letter from "a disgusted viewer" stated, "Instead of helping, you are just making it worse. You rile up the colored people against the whites everytime they see a show of this sort." Unwilling to confront their own bigotry, these viewers felt under siege. Integration and civil rights had nothing to do with ameliorating injustice to blacks but rather with punishing whites. These viewers rejected the interpellation to see themselves as "Larry Liberals" who needed to make decisions about how they were implicated in racism. What they saw instead was a form of reverse discrimination. A viewer from East St. Louis fumed, "It is amazing how all the negroes [*sic*] inadequacies can conveniently be blamed on the white race." These oppositional readings suggest the kinds of struggles that manifest themselves when a previously naturalized worldview suddenly gets exposed and questioned. Although these viewers indicated they weren't buying the message, they tended to worry very much that others would be brain-washed by the media into believing that racism had something to do with white power.

The African-American press welcomed this kind of unmasking of hegemonic racism and the discomforts it caused. The *Pittsburgh Courier,* a black newspaper that circulated fairly widely in the black community, praised the episode for emphasizing that Northern whites could no longer assume that racism was just a Southern problem (Garland 1963). The columnist observed,

> During the racial violence in Mississippi, Alabama, and other Southern states, Northern whites shook their heads sadly and pointed an accusing finger at the South. . . . Now the scene shifts to the North, and while we don't have segregationists like Barnett and Wallace defying the Federal government, the sentiments coming from many Northerners on the question of integrating are just as bitter.

The *Courier* was correct in predicting that Northern whites would have a difficult time coming to terms with their own racism, as the letters about "No Hiding Place" make clear; however, some Northern viewers were still insisting on believing that the problem was most acute in the South. A Chicago viewer asked, "Will this show be seen in the South—you must educate the *whole* country not just the north." A Great Neck, New York, viewer lamented, "I'm sure the program did not reach the areas where it would do the most good." She did add, however, "We in the North are very much in need of programs of this type."

These viewers, like the ones who protested "dumb Southerners" dictating the kinds of debased entertainment fare available on television, indicated how geographically divided the nation remained over questions of race, questions of taste, questions of entertainment, and questions of what it meant to be an upstanding white American. A discursive form of civil war continued to wage. However, white Southerners as well as Northern and Southern blacks, for the most part, did not join the site for discursive struggle offered by "No Hiding Place." Southerners may have had a difficult time finding the show on the airways because, according to an interview with Susskind in the *Philadelphia Daily News* on 5 February 1964 (Susskind Papers, Clippings, box 66, file 16), twenty-six CBS Southern affiliates dropped the series.[11]

The show—and the series itself—also did not appear to generate a great deal of attention from blacks either. Little, if any, of the viewer mail in David Susskind's file of audience letters appears to have come from black viewers. The African-American press, likewise, paid only perfunctory attention to the series. A few articles in the *Pittsburgh Courier* and the *Chicago Defender* praised the series but focused mostly on the banning of *East Side/West Side* and other "integrated" series from some Southern television markets. One might assume that one of the first television series to feature both an integrated cast, along with highly publicized episodes about race relations, would have generated heavy interest from African-American critics and television viewers. Whereas the lack of letters from blacks in the Susskind papers cannot serve as empirical evidence that blacks did not watch the series in significant numbers, the lack of significant coverage in the black press is more suggestive. The relative absence of interest indicates that *East Side/West Side* and the other New Frontier character dramas were addressing white audiences—especially liberal whites in Northern urban areas. "Who Do You Kill?" may have depicted an urban black reality, but the episode was constructed as a white problem to be solved by white liberals. "No Hiding Place" positioned white liberals at the center of the drama and asked them to choose how they wished to respond to the black presence. To some extent, the black characters in both of these episodes functioned as objects of narrative action (or inaction, as the case may be) rather than as subjects. The black press may have had relatively little interest in the series, also, because the arenas of struggle for African Americans in 1963 were not focused, as they had been in the past and would be again in the future, on black representations in entertainment media. In 1951, before the advent of the civil rights movement, the appearance of *Amos 'n' Andy* on network television did function as a key terrain of cultural and political struggle, especially for middle-class African Americans and the NAACP (Ely 1991). In the early 1960s, with civil rights activism receiving large amounts of mostly sympathetic media coverage from network news television and other mainstream media outlets, questions of black representation on entertainment television may have seemed less pressing in the struggle over positive images.

Sponsorship, Ratings, Cancellation

Although *East Side/West Side* consistently won its time slot in the Nielsen ratings, the series was never fully sponsored. Adding to this problem was the fear, and actual fact, of CBS Southern affiliates refusing to carry the show. Despite respectable ratings, critical praise for the series and numerous awards, including Emmys and a citation from B'nai Brith, the show's one-year run always operated under the cloud of imminent cancellation.

The situation led numerous viewers to engage in a form of rhetorical bargaining with the network. Recognizing the commercial basis of the medium whereby the function of programming is to deliver up audiences to advertisers, letter writing viewers promised to be extra good consumers if the network would continue serving up *East Side/West Side*: "If the show SHOULD remain on the air, I promise faithfully to buy and promote every single product that sponsors the show—whether I can use such products or not." "Perhaps other viewers feel as I do and are so pleased with the show they will promote sponsors' products to others to show their approval" (Susskind Papers, Viewer mail, box 69, file 10). "I was only aware of one sponsor, *White Rain* but next Monday when I watch this show I will take notice of the other sponsors and gladly buy their products if they continue to show me programs like this one." "I'm running to stock up on '*White Rain*'" (Susskind Papers, Viewer mail, box 69, file 12). On the other side, of course, a few viewers declared that they would refuse to buy the sponsors' products because the show so offended their racial sensibilities.

Many viewers railed against the fundamental attributes of commercial network television with its reliance on ratings and sponsors, but by bargaining with this system and by asserting that they would buy the products sponsored, these viewers also implicitly accepted the capitalist/consumerist foundations of that system. They negotiated with the system and attempted to make it work for them but could do so only by accepting as given a commodity structure in which their only power was in being "extra good consumers" in exchange for their favored programs. Although these promises may have been only rhetorical, they nevertheless pointed out the extent to which commercial television had been naturalized to viewers. Rather than call for a noncommercial form of television that would potentially provide a more congenial environment for serious, critical programming like *East Side/West Side,* viewers allied themselves with sponsors and a network system that could never comfortably allow these kinds of shows to flourish.

Inevitably perhaps, CBS cancelled the series. Whether it did so because of Southern affiliate grumbling or ratings or sponsor problems, the network found itself with a politically unappealing series that seemed to serve up nothing but unwanted controversy. Rather than blame the network, many Northern white viewers blamed Southern racists for the show's demise. Susskind, perhaps attempting to defuse the geographical tension, admitted that the network could not sell two minutes of the show's airtime to advertisers, thus losing $84,000 a week on the series. The producer praised CBS for keeping the show on the air as long as it did, even as it lost a reported $2 million in the process (Susskind Papers, Clippings, box 66, file 16).

Conclusion

Americans in the 1960s found themselves in a tumultuous period of social change as activist movements challenged previously naturalized racial, generational, gender, and foreign policy regimes. By 1963, nightly news broadcasts at two of the three networks had expanded to thirty minutes. Television, at least in its news and documentary arenas, found itself devoting more and more of its newly developed news-gathering abilities to documenting the social and political movements with all the attendant drama and exciting visuals they tended to provide. The crucial role played by television coverage of key civil rights battles in Birmingham and Selma and in the coverage of the 1963 March on Washington has been much commented on (Garrow 1978; McWhorter 2001). Less attention has been paid to the role played by entertainment television programming during this period. And whereas assumptions have been made that viewers must have had their preconceptions challenged about race (and later about the war in Vietnam) by television coverage, little qualitative work on this issue has yet appeared. Obviously, it is difficult to reconstruct almost forty years later how television viewers may have used the medium to think about changing race relations in the wake of that uprising for racial equality and empowerment. This article has attempted to reconstruct how some viewers used a couple of key episodes of one entertainment series to think about race within that context. *East Side/West Side* was clearly a terrain of struggle for mostly Northern, mostly white Americans trying to negotiate positions around race and around Kennedy-era liberalism. That Southern whites were mostly silent and that Northern whites so castigated them indicates how important the divide between the two halves of the country remained a century after the civil war. That black Americans appeared not to have found the series of particular salience suggests that during this moment at least, the politics of representation in popular culture was not at the top of many African Americans' lists of important issues. That the network broadcasting this series appeared profoundly uncomfortable with it suggests that television executives, after perfunctorily appeasing broadcast reformers like FCC head Newton Minow, wanted to go back to business as usual in the entertainment branch of their operations. Later in the decade, network television would find more politically palatable ways to bring questions of race to the small screen by constructing postintegration worlds, where blacks fit into white worlds without problems (*I Spy, Star Trek, Julia*).[12] *East Side/West Side* presented a more troubling representation for viewers and for broadcasters. In the relatively optimistic climate of America in the early 1960s, a liberal-inflected program that did not provide answers and solutions may have been prescient but was doomed to failure.

Notes

1. By 1962, 90 percent of American households had at least one television set (Steinberg 1980).

2. Historical studies of African Americans and American television are surprisingly scant in the literature. Some recent articles include Classen (1997, 305–24), Harper, (1997, 62–81), Haralovich (1999, 98–119), and Bodroghkozy (1992, 143–67).

3. For an analysis of *East Side/West Side* from a political economy perspective, see Brook (1998).

4. By the late 1950s, the mode of television production began changing over from New York–based live programming to Hollywood-based filmed series, usually in episodic formats (Vianello, 1984, 204–18; Boddy, 1990).

5. This information is contained in a CBS interoffice memo titled "Preliminary Report on East Side, West Side (Program Analysis,)" dated 9 April 1963 (Susskind Papers, box 66, folder 18).

6. Such fears were not without some merit. MacDonald (1983) has noted in his history of African Americans in television that when Southern stations finally were able to hook up to the broadcast networks, programmers became notably more conservative in their programming choices, not wanting to offend what they considered to be Southern sensibilities, especially around race issues.

7. Watson (1990) discusses both of these episodes at some length in her book, as does MacDonald (1983). Marlon Riggs's important documentary on the history of African Americans in television, *Color Adjustment,* also features excerpts from the programs (Riggs 1991; see also Brook 1998).

8. In a letter to Senator Javits, dated 29 October 1963, David Susskind wrote, "Jack, this show needs all the help it can get from people with important pulpits. . . . [T]hose people who finally allowed ["Who Do You Kill?"] to be scheduled should be praised to the skies on the floor of the Senate" (Susskind Papers, box 67, folder 1).

9. Nielsen and Arbitron ratings information on every episode of the series is available in the Susskind papers, box 68, file 1. In general, *East Side/West Side* "won" the

ratings race against the NBC and ABC offerings broadcast during the same time slot. In general, the show's "share" hovered around the 30-percent range—a respectable, if not superior, performance. Other programs from this era with similar ratings did not necessarily get cancelled after one season.

10. The episode's ratings were similar to the other program, as well. According to the Nielsen numbers, "No Hiding Place" captured 37 percent of the viewing audience (Susskind Papers, box 68, file 1).

11. Another unidentified newspaper clipping in the Susskind papers indicates that CBS disputed this contention, arguing that only one station dropped the show but that the network experienced difficulty selling airtime to sponsors for the series.

12. Although *Julia*, which ran from 1968 to 1971, presented viewers with a most unthreatening black character—a widowed nurse raising a precocious six-year-old son—viewers still managed to construct an array of differing responses, some surprisingly racist (see Bodroghkozy 1992).

References

Boddy, W. 1990. *Fifties Television*. Urbana and Chicago: University of Illinois Press.

Bodroghkozy, A. 1992. "Is This What You Mean by Color TV?": Race, Gender, and Contested Meanings in NBC's *Julia*. In *Private Screenings: Television and the Female Consumer*, edited by L. Spigel and D. Mann. Minneapolis: University of Minnesota Press.

Brook, V. 1998. Checks and Imbalances: Political Economy and the Rise and Fall of *East Side/West Side*. *Journal of Film and Video* 50(3): 24–39.

Classen, S. 1997. Southern Discomforts: The Racial Struggle Over Popular TV. In *The Revolution Wasn't Televised: Sixties Television and Social Conflict*, edited by L. Spigel and M. Curtin. New York: Routledge.

Dyer, R. 1997. *White*. London. Routledge.

Ely, M. P. 1991. *The Adventures of Amos 'n' Andy: A Social History of an American Phenomenon*. New York: Free Press.

Fiske, J. 1987. British Cultural Studies and Television. In *Channels of Discourse*. Chapel Hill: University of North Carolina.

———. 1996. *Media Matters: Race and Gender in U.S. politics*. Minneapolis: University of Minnesota Press.

Galbraith, J. K. 1958. *The Affluent Society*. Boston: Houghton Mifflin.

Garland, H. 1963. Video Vignettes. *Pittsburgh Courier* 14 December, Final edition.

Garrow, D. J. 1978. *Protest at Selma*. New Haven, CT: Yale University Press.

Gray, H. 1995. *Watching Race: Television and the Struggle for "Blackness."* Minneapolis: University of Minnesota Press.

Hall, S. 1980. Encoding/Decoding. In *Culture, Media, Language*, edited by S. Hall et al. London: Hutchinson.

Haralovich, M. B. 1999. *I Spy's* "living Postcards": The Geo-Politics of Civil Rights. In *Television, History, and American Culture*, edited by M. B. Haralovich and L. Rabinovitz. Durham, NC: Duke University Press.

Harper, P. B. 1997. Extra-special Effects: Televisual Representations and the Claims of "the Black Experience." In *The Revolution Wasn't Televised: Sixties Television and Social Conflict*, edited by L. Spigel and M. Curtin. New York: Routledge.

Jhally, S., and J. Lewis. 1992. *Enlightened Racism: The Cosby Show, Audiences, and the Myth of the American Dream*. Boulder, CO: Westview.

Kaplan, E. A. 1983. Is the Gaze Male? In *Women and Film: Both Sides of the Camera*. New York: Methuen.

MacDonald, J. F. 1983. *Blacks and White TV: Afro-Americans in Television since 1948*. Chicago: Nelson-Hall.

Matusow, A. 1984. *The Unraveling of America: A History of Liberalism in the 1960s*. New York: Harper and Row.

McWhorter, D. 2001. *Carry Me Home: Birmingham, Alabama*. New York: Simon and Schuster.

Metz, R. 1975. *CBS: Reflections in a Bloodshot Eye*. Chicago: Playboy Press.

Mulvey, L. 1975. Visual Pleasure and Narrative Cinema. *Screen*, 16 (3): 6–18.

Riggs, M. T. 1991. *Color Adjustment*. San Francisco: California Newsreel.

Steinberg, C. S. 1980. *TV Facts*. New York: Facts on File.

Susskind, D. Papers. Wisconsin State Historical Society. Manuscript division.

Vianello, R. 1984. The Rise of the Telefilm and the Network's Hegemony over the Motion Picture Industry. *Quarterly Review of Film Studies*, 9 (Summer):3–21.

Watson, M. A. 1990. *The Expanding Vista: American Television in the Kennedy Years*. New York: Oxford University Press.

Innovating Women's Television in Local and National Networks
Ruth Lyons and Arlene Francis

Marsha Cassidy and Mimi White

Newsweek's cover story on 19 July 1954 called Arlene Francis "the quick queen of television."[1] In the same year, *Look* magazine reported that Ruth Lyons was known as "Miss Ohio" because her "chitchat" had "the force of law."[2] These tropes of feminine power acknowledged an ascendant force in early American television—the "femcee," a charming, witty, middle-aged hostess who presided over daytime broadcasts aimed at women viewers. The star personalities of these two women, shaped by regional variance and contrasting taste cultures, were integrally linked to local-versus-network power struggles over programming dominance. Comparing the work of Lyons and Francis—in particular, their professional biographies, the formats of their signature programs, and the reach of their audience/advertising support—reveals the interplay between early television's regional/network dynamics and the search for a taste culture that would attract the widest possible audience.[3] During the years when local and national companies vied for the control of daytime profits, Lyons and Francis came to represent distinct versions of the feminine cultural sphere in postwar America. In the industry's struggle for national hegemony, early renderings of femininity on TV implicated issues of class, taste, and region. These issues prominently emerge in the personae of Lyons and Francis and serve to inform their ultimate place on American television. Like other women who were influential in early television, Lyons and Francis often fail to appear in official television histories, yet their signifying and economic power in the industry suggests their irrefutable agency in the formative stages of broadcast history.

Born within two years of one another (Lyons in 1905, Francis in 1907), Lyons and Francis led strikingly parallel lives, albeit in different domains—Lyons in Cincinnati, Ohio, and Francis in New York City. Both women successfully established radio careers during the 1930s and moved into television early. Ruth Lyons transported her Cincinnati-based daytime radio show, *The Fifty Club*, from WLW Radio to the Crosley television network in 1949, and she hosted the program until her retirement in 1967. Arlene Francis, a radio, stage, and screen actress based in New York City, starred in a number of television shows in the industry's earliest days, gaining national recognition as a regular panelist on CBS's popular primetime quiz show *What's My Line?* in 1950. In 1954, she was selected to anchor NBC's ambitious daytime show *Home*. Both women acquired prestige and clout within these separate daytime spheres—Lyons in the lucrative TV cities of Cincinnati, Dayton, Columbus, and later Indianapolis, and Francis in NBC's rapidly expanding national market, which encompassed sixty-one cities by 1956. These two "television girls" commanded astronomical yearly salaries— over $100,000 in the mid-1950s—and exerted considerable power in a man's world. Lyons, called a "dictator" by some (but "Mother" by those who worked closely with her), wielded iron control over her own program and its sponsors, and she was the only woman on the Crosley board of directors. Francis did not control production decisions on *Home*, but her ability to satisfy sponsors—and please audiences—secured her influence at the network.[4]

Lyons and Francis are also centrally identified with innovations in daytime genres that relied on the charm of a femcee, as each star established a sense of "personality" through the magazine format of consumer television. (Indeed, both of their programs functioned, among other things, as ongoing and endless commercials.) In their public personae, they share an improvisational, conversational, and witty mode of performance, and neither of them was beautiful in the classical or traditional sense. Despite their prominence within their respective media domains—and both were profiled in national magazines— they were intertextually promoted as mothers and wives, devoted to family and home, even though their professional trajectories were clearly at odds with this image of conventional domesticity. They even both attended the coronation of Queen Elizabeth II in June of 1953. One wonders if they ever met, though no evidence of this has yet emerged in our research.

While both Lyons and Francis played key roles in the development of daytime broadcasting, contrasts between their public images and programs illuminate divergent trends in 1950s television. In dress, voice, performance style, and studio design, Lyons reproduced a frankly Midwestern and middlebrow culture at the center of her empire, from her trademark "flower bouquet" microphone to a bright plaid three-seat rocking chair that served as the centerpiece of her set. In contrast, Francis's style was rooted in the New York City scene, where she appeared weekly on *What's My Line?* dressed in an elegant gown, exchanging quips with the country's wittiest celebrities. With her glamour and sophistication, Francis fit comfortably into *Home*'s broadcast studio, an opulent circular set that mimicked modernist theatrical space. Ironically, Lyons hosted a show called *Fifty-Fifty* (referring to the size of her live studio audience) while Francis hosted the domestically referenced *Home*.

Biographical Sketches

Ruth Reeves was born in Cincinnati, Ohio, in 1905, where she was raised in a conservative, religious, middle-class home. Her formal education ended after one year of college at the University of Cincinnati. Working as a piano player in a sheet music store, Lyons met professional singer Howard Hafford, who hired her as the assistant musical director at WKRC Radio in 1929. Later that year, she went on the air with a fifteen-minute program of piano music and became the hostess of *The Woman's Hour,* which offered music, recipes, interviews, and spontaneous conversation before a live studio audience.

In 1932, Ruth married her longtime boyfriend, Johnny Lyons, but continued to work arduously at the radio station, appearing on air and developing new programs. When Johnny accepted a promotion and transfer to Cleveland, Ruth chose to remain in Cincinnati—in part to remain close to her ailing parents—as her career in local radio blossomed. Ruth maintained an active long-distance marriage for a while, but Johnny's frequent job transfers strained their relationship. They were formally divorced in 1939, though Ruth kept the Lyons name throughout her professional career.

Ruth's reputation advanced in 1937 when a major flood in Cincinnati created emergency conditions. Ruth stayed on the air around the clock, keeping listeners abreast of developments and raising more than $50,000 in donations for the Red Cross. As a result of this activity, she was promoted to program director at WKRC. By the late 1930s, she produced and hosted a number of programs, including *The Woman's Hour, Open House,* and a half-hour commentary program called *A Woman Views the News.* Most important, she was developing a stellar reputation among sponsors for selling products. Her influence with listeners was verified during the 1939 Christmas season when Lyons and her coworkers visited the local children's hospital to entertain its young patients. Donations for toys came pouring into the station after Lyons detailed the children's plight to her audience. (This was the origin of the "Ruth Lyons Children's Christmas Fund," which still survives today, administered by WLW-TV.) In 1942, Lyons was offered and accepted a position with the prestigious Crosley Broadcasting Corporation's WLW and WSAI radio stations, a move that would enhance her career significantly. Years later, her WKRC boss Hulbert Taft lamented his decision not to retain Lyons, noting that for a difference in salary of ten dollars a week he had lost a million-dollar personality. Crosley announced its hiring coup in the Cincinnati newspaper and sponsored a contest to name Lyons's new daytime show, finally selecting the doubly feminized *Petticoat Partyline.* In this same watershed year for Lyons, she remarried, wedding Herman Newman, a Unitarian minister and social worker who later became a professor of English and semantics at the University of Cincinnati.

As her career advanced, Lyons hosted a number of popular programs for Crosley, including *WLW Consumers' Foundation,* where two hundred women tested products to be advertised on radio; *Morning Matinee,* an audience-participation show with music, talk, and games; and the game show *Collect Calls from Lowenthal's.* By now Ruth was considered a favorite with sponsors.

When she recommended a product, sales markedly increased in her listening area. Her growing popularity and salesmanship yielded her new industry clout. For example, when Herman contracted scarlet fever in 1943 and Ruth was quarantined with him, Crosley installed special lines so Ruth could broadcast her programs from home.[5] More important, Lyons was able to exert increasing control over her own programs. This included the right to abandon a tightly scripted format—a privilege granted only to Lyons—and the freedom to ad-lib program content, including commercials. Lyons also insisted that she personally approve all sponsors for her shows. In this way, Lyons established two of the practices key to sustaining her success and power in broadcasting: her chatty personal style and the right of acceptance and refusal of products for promotion on her programs.

On the personal side, Lyons became a mother in 1944. Although she delivered a stillborn child, she came home with an orphan born a few days earlier at the same hospital. Candace "Candy" Newman made her first appearance on her mother's radio show at the age of six weeks and, as she grew older, became a frequent guest on the television show. Lyons's relationship with her daughter, on whom she doted both publicly and privately, reinforced Lyons's popular reputation as an "ordinary housewife" who just happened to do radio shows, an image widely promoted by Lyons herself and the Crosley network.

In 1946, Lyons launched *The 50 Club* on WLW Radio. The program, scheduled at midday, featured a live studio audience of fifty guests who were served lunch in conjunction with the program. The show combined interviews, games, music, and stunts.[6] In 1949, the program moved to WLW-TV and was quickly added to the schedules of the other television stations in the Crosley network (WLW-D and WLW-C, and when it joined the network in 1957, WLW-I).[7] Originally one hour long, the program was extended to ninety minutes as its popularity grew. When the size of the studio audience doubled, the program was renamed *The Fifty-Fifty Club*. In August of 1957, *The Fifty-Fifty Club* became the first locally produced show in the area telecast in color, and in September of 1957, the program began airing on WLW Radio as a simulcast. As a result, the program reached an extensive audience beyond television. Ruth Lyons was promoted as the most-watched and most-listened-to personality in Ohio and Indiana, also reaching legions of radio fans in Kentucky, West Virginia, western Virginia, and southern Michigan—the scope of WLW Radio, with its 500,000-watt clear channel signal.[8]

As *The Fifty-Fifty Club* secured ratings supremacy, Ruth Lyons's reputation as a premier saleswoman soared to new heights. WLW publicity material consistently emphasized the appeal of her program for sponsors, bragging, "Ruth Lyons is both a byword and a 'buy' word in tens of thousands of homes" ("Backgrounds"). The station's promotional literature documents her astonishing market impact: a gelatin zooms from seventy-six gross to five hundred gross sales in one Cincinnati distribution area after just one month on Lyons's show; in ten weeks, a line of canned vegetables jumps from seventh to first place among Lyons's viewers in all three of her metropolitan markets. These and other stories tout her singular skill in selling products, an ability closely tied to her personal charisma. According to WLW selling brochures, on Lyons's show, a commercial, "always live and always ad-lib," becomes "a warm, meaningful personal recommendation from one woman to another."[9] Because her endorsement of products had immediate and visible impact in her markets, sponsors lined up to be included on her program.

With its substantial Midwestern audience, popularity with sponsors, and unwavering admiration of local fans, *The Fifty-Fifty Club* was able to attract preeminent guest celebrities. Over the course of her show, visitors included Guy Lombardo, Vic Damone, Rudy Vallee, Cab Calloway, Liberace, Arthur Lee Simpkins, Van Cliburn, Joe Garagiola, Hedda Hopper, Helen Hayes, Eva Gabor, Troy Donahue, Dick Powell, Rita Moreno, Andy Williams, Efrem Zimbalist, Michael Landon, Jack Webb, Henry Cabot Lodge, Sargent Shriver, Carol Channing, Milton Berle, Bob Hope, Jimmy Durante, Dr. Albert Sabin, Wally Post, and Jesse Owens, among many others.[10]

Despite several failed experiments with broadcasting her show nationally (a topic we will discuss in detail later), Lyons maintained an unmatched eminence in the context of the Crosley stations, where her impact and power on *The Fifty-Fifty Club* persisted unabated for many years, earning her frequent mention in national publications. *Cosmopolitan* magazine called her "A Million Dollar Dynamo,"[11] while *Ladies' Home Journal* featured her as "the Midwest's most influential housewife."[12] By the early 1960s, Lyons had achieved extraordinary success as a programmer, producer, hostess, and musician. She even released albums featuring songs she had composed and launched a signature line of high-fashion dresses, the "Ruth Lyons Autograph Collection."[13]

The likely avenue to television stardom for women during the 1950s is corroborated by the career of Arlene Francis, whose professional trajectory paralleled Lyons's in many respects. However, important distinctions between them—and between their public personae—are firmly rooted in their regional origins and the taste cultures of their social worlds. While Lyons's achievements were centered in the Midwest, Francis's career was inextricably linked to her lifelong devotion to acting and to New York City's social and theatrical milieu.

In her 1978 memoir, Arline (later changed to "Arlene") Francis Kazanjian remembers the events of her childhood as a perpetual clash between competing forces—her personal ambitions for a life in the theater versus a more traditional future imagined by her adoring but old-fashioned parents. While her maternal grandfather, Alfred Davis, a minor English actor, was moved to tears by Francis's childhood recitations, her Armenian-born father, a successful portrait photographer, sternly discouraged her pursuit of acting.[14] When Francis was seven, the Kazanjians moved from Boston to New York. There she was enrolled in a convent boarding school, where all thoughts of the theater were to be expunged. Yet after graduation, Francis was as determined as ever to succeed as an actress. She and her mother traveled to Hollywood, and Mrs. Kazanjian, without her husband's knowledge, helped Arlene land a part as a prostitute in David O. Selznick's production of *Murders in the Rue Morgue,* working opposite Bela Lugosi as the archfiend.[15] When Mr. Kazanjian saw his daughter nailed to a cross in a nightgown on a movie poster promoting the film, he insisted that Arlene return to New York at once; she was subsequently enrolled in Finch Finishing School, where she says she "got partially finished," and became the respectable proprietress of "D'Arlene Studios" on Madison Avenue, a "gifte shoppe" financed by her father. The store was an immediate money-loser, and it devolved into a hangout for Francis's friends and out-of-work actors. One of the shop regulars suggested Francis try out for a job playing bit parts on the radio show *King Arthur's Round Table* for Young and Rubicam. She was thrilled to land the role for $100 per week, variously imitating dogs, cats, goats, princesses, and beggars.[16]

Working in the nation's radio industry offered Francis a way to appease her father and still fulfill her irrepressible desire to act. Because Mr. Kazanjian admired broadcasting's commitment to commercial values and family entertainment, Francis was free to pursue an active career in radio performance. During the 1930s, her deep-timbered voice was heard on more than twenty soap operas, as well as on *The March of Time, Cavalcade, Betty and Bob,* and *Forty-Five Minutes from Hollywood* (in which she simulated the performances of famous movie stars, such as Katharine Hepburn and Bette Davis). "I'd run from one studio to another in the same day, changing my accent en route," she remembers (26, 21–27).

Francis's career ascended rapidly, and she soon became known as radio's "Oomph Girl" because of her vitality and charm.[17] By 1938, she was selected as the first woman to cohost a quiz show. On *What's My Name?,* Francis applied her talent at mimicry to impersonate the voices of public figures for contestants to guess. More important, she honed her ability to improvise before a live audience.[18] By 1943, she was picked to host a second successful game show, *Blind Date,* a program with patriotic overtones that featured contestants from the military competing for a date with a beautiful model or actress. It was this program that would move to television in 1949 and make Francis instantly recognizable wherever she went (86).

Overlapping her broadcasting endeavors were intermittent stage roles both on and off Broadway (her father finally relented). During the 1930s and 1940s, she appeared in some twenty plays, beginning with Mercury Theater's production of *Horse Eats Hat* in 1936, directed by Orson Welles. Happily "over-employed," Francis balanced a demanding radio career with a string of theater credits (48). Another Welles play, *Danton's Death,* not only continued her theatrical involvement, but also hastened the end of her marriage to Neil Agnew, a wealthy Paramount executive fifteen years her senior (35). Francis's long-standing partnership with radio star and theatrical producer Martin Gabel began during *Danton's Death,* when Francis and Gabel spent ten minutes waiting alone together each night in a movable set below stage. Francis divorced Agnew in 1946 and was married to Gabel the same year.

After the war and her marriage to Gabel, Francis reluctantly moved to Hollywood to follow her husband's work in film production. Their son Peter was born in 1947. In Hollywood, Francis managed to land a part in Arthur Miller's film *All My Sons* (dir. Irving Reis, US, 1948), but her career stymied in California as she found herself viewed as a producer's "wife."[19] Although the Gabels partied with Hollywood's elite—including Ira Gershwin, Rex Harrison, Lilli Palmer, Bob Benchley, Tallulah Bankhead, Preston Sturges, Ronald Colman, Greer Garson, Lauren Bacall, and Humphrey Bogart—Francis considered herself a "New Yorker-in-exile."[20] When Peter was eight months old, Francis defied postwar mores and resumed her professional life on the East Coast, leaving husband and baby in California to accept a leading role in *Cup of Trembling* on Broadway (83). Although the play failed miserably, the move east served to reestablish the family in New York City, as husband and son eventually followed Francis and her unstoppable career in broadcasting.

With Francis back on board, the TV version of *Blind Date* became a national hit on ABC in 1949. Almost overnight, she became "Arlene" to millions of television viewers. A year later, she was selected to appear as a regular Sunday evening panelist on CBS's *What My Line?* Dressed in elegant evening clothes, Francis and three other high-profile humorists—Dorothy Kilgallen, Fred Allen, and Bennett Cerf—guessed the unusual occupations of everyday contestants. Moderated by John Daly, *What's My Line?* quickly became a national institution and anchored Francis's career for almost twenty-five years. From 1952 to 1954, soon after the completion of the transcontinental cable, Francis, one of television's brightest stars and "busiest women,"[21] was seen coast-to-coast on all three networks: she appeared on *Who's There?* and *By Popular Demand* on CBS; *Talent Patrol, The Comeback Story,* and *Soldier Parade* on ABC; and, of course, *Home* on NBC. Within a three-month period during 1954, Francis's face appeared on the cover of *Newsweek, Look,* and *TV Guide.*[22] *Newsweek* raved that she was "the best . . . and the nicest of American femcees,"[23] and *American Magazine* called her "one of the most successful performers in the whole entertainment world."[24] When *Home* premiered on 1 March 1954, Francis's television career reached its apex.

During the height of her television fame, Francis mingled with the country's most cosmopolitan citizens, socializing with show people, trendsetters, intellectuals, politicians, and society doyennes. Walter Winchell helped arrange the details of her marriage to Gabel; Judy Garland sang "Somewhere over the Rainbow" at a party in her home in the East Seventies; Frank Sinatra took the Gabels yachting; the Gabels dined routinely at the Stork Club, the Oak Room, and Billy Reed's Little Club with John Daly and other show people; and the Gabels were invited to (or hosted) the most chic parties in town, performing a comedy skit at Swifty Lazar's fiftieth birthday celebration, for example. The public persona Francis brought to the *Home* show inevitably connected her to this trendy social circle. Yet by all accounts, Francis excelled on television precisely because she did not come across as a snob. To audience and friends alike, she exuded "charm"; in fact, in 1960, she was commissioned to write a book about "charm at work." *That Certain Something: The Magic of Charm* recorded definitions of charm gathered from distinguished figures.[25]

In good part because of her charisma, Francis, like Lyons, was also recognized as a preeminent television saleswoman. *Newsweek* reported that she spent more time rehearsing commercials than practicing the script for *Home* itself,[26] and Francis's workday was often interrupted by unexpected meetings with sponsors or by preset luncheons.[27] In her autobiography, Francis recalls being presented with an award in the grand ballroom of the Waldorf-Astoria Hotel for her skill as a saleswoman, joking that her earlier ambition to be "Actress of the Year" had evolved into being "Sales-woman of the Year."[28] Since both Lyons and Francis anchored programs designed to function as highly effective sales tools, each star was called on to perfect an approach that would integrate programming content, personal charm, and selling.

Signature Daytime Programming for Women

The Fifty-Fifty Club and *Home* were typical of daytime programs for women in early television in terms of the consumer format they adopted and their persistent commercial appeals. The two programs shared a common genre that allowed for flexibility, profitability, and innovation: the magazine show. The magazine format was characterized both by a fragmented design, modeled after the sections of a women's magazine, and by multiple sponsorships.[29] *The Fifty-Fifty Club* and *Home* offered a hybrid of the magazine program, one that incorporated entertainment, celebrity guests, "expert" service talk, and musical numbers alongside home economics material. *The Fifty-Fifty Club* also included the participation of a live audience, often invited in conjunction with product promotion.

Indeed, both programs were suffused with sponsorship and product promotion. Even in the initial responses to *Home,* which praised its quality, reviewers feared that empty materialism might overshadow substance. After watching the show for a week, *New York Times* critic Jack Gould noted that *Home* "might become a 'television department store' just as easily as the women's magazine of video."[30] A month later, Robert Lewis Shayon criticized *Home* in *Saturday Review* for its preoccupation with things, rather than thoughts. "The Thing," he wrote, "is 'Home's' hearthgod. . . . 'Home' appeared a heavenly department store, a valhalla of gadgets and gimmicks, a cloud of electronic dust returning to dust."[31] In 1956, *Coronet* magazine, referring to the way in which program content readily slid into product promotion, wrote that if *Home* was like a magazine, then most of the time viewers were "flipping through pages of advertisements."[32] A segment on fashions you could make at home was readily apparent as an advertisement for Simplicity Patterns, as sewing expert Lucille Rivers demonstrated how to build a slip right into the chiffon skirt of a party dress. It's "simplicity to make," Rivers promised.[33] Another segment found Hugh Downs explaining the nuances of pepper, "an ancient and honorable spice," while small turntables on the counter displayed a number of "quite attractive" shaker sets, all for sale.

The promotional aspects of *The Fifty-Fifty Club* could be considered even more blatant. Ruth Lyons wielded extraordinary control over her program and its advertising. Because she was not rigidly tied to a script or to carefully timed ad breaks, she could arbitrarily vary the time spent on specific product promotions, occasionally even dashing through her list of featured products non-stop, as she did when Bob Hope was the guest. (She quite explicitly admitted this, saying she was going to just run through all the products she had to promote as fast as she could in order to have more time to talk with Hope.)

Lyons was afforded this flexibility because she spent considerable time discussing sponsored products in the usual course of things. Whole segments of the program came down to nothing but extended ads, as Lyons chatted with the audience about one product after another. She might sit down at the piano to extemporize a song that turned out to be a jingle for pretzels and end up with the whole studio audience singing along. ("T-e-m-t-e-e, How good can a pretzel be?" was sung in harmony, for example, on 1 March 1951.)[34] On many days, the bulk of Lyons's use of audience interaction was closely tied to product promotion. Lyons would raffle off "prizes"—specifically the products advertised on her show—and audience members would readily parrot the promotional scripts that they regularly heard on the program. During a broadcast in 1963, Lyons asked if anyone in the studio had never tried Knorr soup. When one woman raised her hand, Lyons stepped into the studio space to interrogate her: "There sits a woman, in the prime of life, who hasn't enjoyed Knorr soups. . . . What's your trouble? Are you just stubborn or what?"[35] Another common sight on *The Fifty-Fifty Club* was children selling products: a thirteen-year-old boy named Robert was asked to identify a brand of mattress, for example, and readily supplied the appropriate response.[36] Similarly, many of her celebrity guests were performing in the Cincinnati area and used their interviews with Lyons for self-promotion. Segment after segment, it was difficult to draw clear distinctions between program content and advertising.

In this hyperconsumerist context, typical of early television, both *The Fifty-Fifty Club* and *Home* emphasized the discernment and imprimatur of their femcees in relation to the panoply of products they sold. Lyons and Francis were widely known as women who only sold products they personally used, tested, or approved in advance. In the case of Lyons, this relationship included exercising personal control over her sponsor base. Indeed an emphasis on Lyons's selective endorsement was explicitly incorporated into her extemporaneous chatter about products on her show. Francis, too, portrayed herself as a woman who "dug gadgets" and who was committed to being honest with viewers about the products she sold.[37] Regarding her forty sponsors on *Home*, Francis reports, "I tried everything, did everything, ate everything and usually bought everything they offered. . . . If I sold it, I was sold on it."[38] Francis was not the producer of her own program and, under the aegis of the network, had nothing resembling the very direct control Ruth Lyons exerted on her own program. But the network relied on Francis's personality and popularity to appeal to viewers with the insistent claim that she only promoted products she personally supported (and even used). This was the case even though it was unlikely that she made her own clothes with Simplicity patterns or scoured her sink spotless with Old Dutch Cleanser.[39] Even in the case of Lyons, with her "ordinary housewife" persona, it is hard to imagine that she waxed her own kitchen floors with Simoniz waxes, ironed her own clothes with Easy-On Spray Starch, or gave herself home permanents with Toni products.

Two Taste Cultures

In their analogous career paths, their ability to infuse the magazine format with charisma, and their feminized selling power, Ruth Lyons and Arlene Francis helped define the feminine cultural sphere of early daytime television. Yet Lyons and Francis represented divergent taste cultures. While Lyons positioned herself at the summit of Midwestern values, fashions, and conventions, Francis was aligned with New York City elitism, situated at the pinnacle of urbane coastal sophistication.

The distinctive set design of each program telegraphed significant regional and class distinctions. Lyons surrounded herself with the accoutrements of middlebrow taste. Like the decor in her own home, featured in a cover story for *The American Home* in April of 1958, Lyons's stage decorations were constantly updated. In the 1950s, her stage, a cozy arena embellished daily with flower arrangements, included a faux early American coffee table and skirted sofa and chairs. The 1960s brought an even closer imitation of the middle-class furnishings Lyons had adopted in her own home, including a double-seated print rocker at center stage; a wrought-iron chandelier; a brick walk backdrop, louvered doors, wood paneling, and bookcases; and later in the decade, an imitation Mondrian adorning the wall at stage right. All of the set's embellishments referenced Lyons's middlebrow taste for what *American Home* called "provincial informality."[40] In less flattering terms, *The Ladies' Home Journal* characterized Lyons's decoration style as "Rampant Early American."[41]

In contrast, *Home*'s sprawling set was the program's most talked about novelty, an experimental floor plan that rejected domestic verisimilitude. Costing over $200,000 to build, the circular studio was packed with electronic gadgets, stage turntables, platforms that moved up and down, and even a moving electric signboard called a "flashcast." The round arena was divided into various wedges that represented the program's multiple departments, with cameras and crew stationed at the center.[42] A revolving monkey-arm camera, mounted on the ceiling, provided an overhead perspective that routinely disrupted the illusion of televisual realism. In the manner of modernist theater so revered during the 1950s, *Home*'s minimalist set revealed its theatrics, calling attention to the show's artifice. *Home*'s repeated use of the extreme long shot from overhead, the moving camera that trucked behind Francis as she crossed the set, or the familiar view of the crew clustered in the central circle maneuvering their cameras, reminded viewers that homemaking on *Home* was a staged contrivance.

Home's "alienation effect" exposed the program's representations of domestic life as performance. For example, during a commercial skit promoting DuPont products, Francis and a young girl are dressed in matching DuPont nylon bathrobes in what appears to be the child's bedroom.[43] It's bedtime, and the girl takes off her robe as Francis tucks her into bed. The camera zooms in slowly to the girl and then holds on a close-up of the DuPont nylon sheets (just long enough to allow Francis off-camera time to remove the robe she is wearing over her shirtwaist). Then, in a sequence typical on *Home,* the camerawork proceeds to nullify the bedroom mirage, cutting to a tracking shot that follows Francis straight across the diameter of *Home*'s arena, the bedroom set behind her revealed as a staged fiction. As stagehands pull up her microphone cable, Francis keeps walking, past the center core of the set, past the cameras gliding into new positions, past Hugh Downs, who speaks a brief greeting, past "Dick" (probably producer, Dick Linkroum), past two crew members adjusting a monitor at the right, until she finally steps onto the almost barren wedge where she will conduct her next interview. Francis's modernist passage across the set dispels the illusion of a tranquil suburban bedtime.

While *Home*'s set fostered distanciation and showcased a cultivated Broadway actress as hostess, the mise-en-scène of *The Fifty-Fifty Club* reflected a star whose performance style and inter-textual persona were comfortably Midwestern—but with a twist. As Ruth Lyons sat center stage on her rocking loveseat, the camera seemed to peer through a fourth wall into a suburban Cincinnati living room. Yet Lyons performed a version of femininity that transgressed middle-class strictures. One national journalist described her as "a completely uninhibited, supercharged, somewhat brassy virago" who "alternately browbeats, tickles, and charms her audiences."[44] Powerful and self-assured, Lyons presided daily over a subordinate cast of characters who both indulged and celebrated her bossiness and performative whims. In 1957, the *Saturday Evening Post* explained that the format of *The Fifty-Fifty Club* "is exactly what comes to Ruth's mind when she is before the cameras."[45] Lyons's reputation for controlling every aspect of her ninety-minute program was widely acknowledged. Enemies called her "a dictator at work," while fans said they admired a woman who was obviously "the boss over a lot of men" and was free to say exactly what was on her mind (113). Supporting the loquacious narcissism of this high priestess of Midwestern daytime television in 1957 were Willie Thall, Lyons's number one affable male "foil"; Cliff Lash, conductor of Lyons's seven-piece band and number two straight man; and three female blonde vocalists that looked like younger versions of Ruth herself—Ruby Wright, Marian Spelman, and Bonnie Lou.[46]

The universe of *The Fifty-Fifty Club* also embraced audience participation. During an episode that aired in September of 1960, Lyons turns to her studio audience and says in mock exasperation, "I just hope sometime . . . I can do my own show without you running it!"[47] Lyons nurtured a teasing but respectful rapport with her daily studio visitors. Lyons's goal was to keep the audience "responsive at all times" during a broadcast, immediately changing the subject or involving the audience if the show lagged.[48] She might reprimand her studio participants—"Are you going to be one of those dull groups?"[49]—or heckle them, asking a man in the audience, "What's the matter? Can't you keep a job?"[50] At her remote broadcasts in sister cities, Lyons cordially shook hands with hundreds of women because she knew many of them had been waiting since dawn to meet her.[51] Lyons's interplay with the audience also extended to viewers at home, who were called by telephone to participate in quizzes and contests. And, of course, women in the audience routinely helped out with commercials.

If the *Home* show was self-revelatory in its camerawork, *The Fifty-Fifty Club* strove to make the television cameras as unobtrusive as possible. When Lyons made the shift from radio to television broadcasting, she rebelled against the station's dictates for standard television practices. Accustomed to moving freely about the studio during her radio broadcasts, she complained about being instructed "where I must stand, sit, where I should be when talking with the women in the audience, and that I must always face the camera" (71). Lyons insisted that the cameras be placed as inconspicuously in the studio as possible, so that the cameras would never come between her and her audience—one centered in the back of the studio, another tucked into a studio corner, and a third at stage left, near the commercial product area.[52] Lyons's improvisational style frustrated directorial planning, however. Occasionally, Lyons yanked one of her cameramen into the antics on stage and sent the control booth scrambling.[53] Lyons's former director Ron Wilson remembers, "As a director, I never knew what she was gonna do or where she was gonna go next. It was totally unpredictable."[54]

Using brash improvisation, Lyons perfected a stage personality that mediated between a Midwestern disdain for the pretensions of high culture and access to that culture. Lyons's mantra was, "You can't talk down to your viewers,"[55] and she promoted herself as an unaffected Midwestern housewife, "completely unsophisticated."[56] In 1958, *American Home* attributed her broadcasting success to "being first a homemaker and then a showman,"[57] and in an autobiographical piece for *Ladies' Home Journal,* Lyons asserted in 1960, "I am primarily a homemaker [and] mother of a fifteen-year-old daughter, Candace" (despite her employment of two full-time housekeepers).[58]

Yet Lyons mastered the art of cautious cultural mobility, allowing her viewers to sample vicariously the pleasures of elite culture. On her program, she chatted with the most famous celebrities in America, but she never gushed or fawned. Lyons repeatedly interrupted Bob Hope with stories about her own travels to Russia, improvised at the piano with Steve Allen and Victor Borge (who ended up clowning *under* the piano), insisted Carol Channing reveal what was under her turban (hair rollers), and insulted Gloria Swanson about her age.[59] Lyons consistently affiliated herself with the material culture of her middle-class viewers, but she also publicly tested out the pleasures of elite consumerism, sharing her excitement on air over a new fur coat, an expensive ring, or a vacation to Europe.[60] As Lyons explained it, "I get a big kick out of buying and doing things I couldn't afford at one time, and I share that kick with my audience."[61] When Lyons departed for England to attend the coronation of Queen Elizabeth II, five hundred fans gathered to see their cultural emissary off—yet her fans were equally delighted to learn that Lyons had tucked two chocolate bars into the top of her Christian Dior original in case she got hungry during the four-hour ceremony in Westminster Abbey.[62]

With *Home,* as with many other programs, NBC president Pat Weaver was trying to negotiate between taste cultures as he plotted the network's entry into the heartland of America. By the early 1950s, Weaver had adopted a philosophy of broadcasting that came to be known as "Operation Frontal Lobes," promising to bring culture and education to the masses in a palatable form.[63] Michele Hilmes and Lynn Spigel demonstrate convincingly that Weaver did not invent either the magazine format or the homemaking show.[64] However, what Weaver did bring to *Home* was a novel interpretation of the low-budget homemaking format, a "quality" show for housewives, unabashedly aspiring to introduce New York City to the country at large.[65] From its inception, *Home*'s roster of department "editors" serving under Arlene Francis linked the show directly to New York City's leading cultural communities. *New York Post* writer Dr. Rose Franzblau provided advice on family relations and child psychology; Dr. Leona Baumgartner, *Home*'s health expert, doubled as New York City's health commissioner; Vassar graduate Poppy Cannon, whose husband, Walter White, served as president of the NAACP, headed *Home*'s food department. Former actress Eve Hunter offered fashion and beauty advice, while Sydney Smith, daughter of Broadway star Loring Smith, handled home decorating.[66] The "quality" of the guests Francis interviewed further confirms *Home*'s mission for edification. As chief writer Fred Freed put it, "Whenever we get a chance to stop treating the housewife like a dull dame with a dust mop . . . we give her something worthwhile."[67] Francis interviewed Pearl S. Buck, Helen Keller, Joseph Welch, Margaret Truman, John and Jacqueline Kennedy, Justice William O. Douglas, cabinet secretary Maxwell Rabb, attorney general Herbert Brownell, former president of the United Nations Carlos Romulo, Norman Vincent Peale, Billy Graham, senator Margaret Chase Smith, and the duchess of Windsor, to a name but a few.

Francis herself embodied a New York City chic that never quite meshed with the middle-class suburban lifestyle of *Home*'s target audience. In keeping with *Home*'s attempt to mix "upper-class fantasy with tropes of averageness,"[68] Francis's television persona perpetuated an unresolvable split between NBC's commitment to the diffusion of "enlightenment" and the imperatives of mass appeal. Although Francis proclaimed herself to be "the world's prize consumer" in her private life, installing a new kitchen every time *Home* changed sponsors,[69] her star persona set her apart from the middle-class suburban ideals of the decade. "When they were first putting *Home* together," she said in an interview in 1956 with Alfred Bester, "they want[ed] the girl-next-door. . . . I talked them out of it and persuaded them to let me do it my way." In Bester's view, typical of the received wisdom about Francis circulating in the popular press at the time, Francis and *Home* did not quite fit together: "I couldn't figure what a hip chick like Arlene was doing on such a [square] show."[70] In the public eye, she was a seasoned New York actress, a determined career woman who earned an astronomical salary, and someone whose erudition, verbal style, and wit transgressed middle-class norms. As the "quick queen" of television, Arlene Francis was the ambiguous ruler of both "pots and puns."[71] To counter her sophisticated aura, Francis's publicity emphasized her pursuit of two careers—"television and her home"—and she succeeded in coming across on television as personable and accessible.[72] "I'm a home-body," Francis told Bester later in the *Holiday* interview. "Our show comes right into people's houses. They know me. They like me. And I like them."[73] Francis's devotion to motherhood was also a recurrent theme, and magazine photographs often featured shots of her at home with Peter. If charm, warmth, and motherhood were a palliative to snobbishness, they could not finally eradicate the sophistication of Francis's image. Francis suffused *Home* with a sense of imbalance; she was nonjudgmental and warm, but also at ease in an elite world. In the few surviving kinescopes of *Home,* Francis's grace in highbrow culture becomes evident. In one episode, Francis reports viewing a French film called *Le diable au corps* [Devil and the flesh] (dir. Claude Autant-Lara, 1947) three times, judging it "a brilliant picture."[74] During a remote broadcast on Memorial Day in 1956, Francis sails in a lagoon beside Belvedere Island in California, then tours a nearby artists' community as part of *Home*'s focus on elegant "West Coast living."[75] During an ambitious broadcast from Independence Hall in Philadelphia, Francis orchestrates an arty sound montage that celebrates America's path to independence.[76]

Most memorably, in 1957, Francis interviewed the duchess of Windsor, who was promoting a "gay and glittering April in Paris Ball" to be held that evening at the Waldorf-Astoria Hotel, a benefit intended to encourage the exchange of artists between France and the United States.[77] This episode, more than any other that survives, reveals Francis as unruffled even in royal society, reviewing ball gowns with the duchess, observing historical French tableaux, admiring the gilded dishware on which chef Philippe was to reproduce the wedding meal of Lafayette that night, and listening in awestruck silence to a costumed actor recite the "Declaration of the Rights of Man." Francis even supplies the duchess with a wit's ideal straight line: "What do you think makes a man well dressed?" The duchess's instant reply, "His wife generally, I think," affirms Francis's easy repartee with the smart set. Finally Francis tells her viewers that she plans to attend the ball herself.

Particularly in this episode—but evident in others too—Francis assumes an effortless sophistication, embodying elite taste culture rather than the middle-class folksy rapport Ruth Lyons so successfully establishes with her audience. Where Lyons solidifies a sense of community as she promotes everyday household products, Francis often seems out of character carrying out the mundane selling duties of *Home:* a lover of French film praising the virtues of vinyl flooring; an admirer of luxurious West Coast living promoting "sanforized" cotton play clothes that "never shrink";[78] a celebrated Broadway actress modeling a party cap constructed out of aluminum foil. These discords in Francis's star persona echoed the contradictory imperatives that lay at *Home*'s foundation; caught in the class versus mass conflict, Francis strove to temper coastal stylishness with middlebrow attitudes.[79] Hugh Downs, Francis's male sidekick, regularly served to deactivate snobbery. With his quiet manner and boyish looks, he enacted Midwestern pragmatism. During the April in Paris preball fashion show, for example, Downs looks on as the women speak of "Cinderella dresses" and "magnificence in royal blue." The ladies murmur "Magnifique!" as a model displays a dress studded with jewels, but Downs calls her "a walking jewelry store. . . . She sleeps in a safe."

Despite her ad-lib wordplay, her reputation for down-to-earth charm, and her easy sense of humor, Arlene Francis retained a cultivated high polish, like *Home* itself. In Ruth Lyons's judgment, "the trouble with television" in the years of her success was exactly this elitist stance. Lyons criticized the coastal insularity of network television creators, especially those who spent "their days lunching in the East Fifties of New York."[80] Although she never referred to the *Home* show, Lyons questioned the class appeal of East Coast broadcasting in an interview with the *Ladies' Home Journal:* "My show appeals to salt-of-the-earth people, real people. Such people exist in Boston and Atlanta as well as Cincinnati and Indianapolis. I know that because when I was on national network these women wrote to me. They told me that most women performers on TV give them a pain, with their minks and affected voices and private show-biz jokes. . . . What does this kind of woman know about a housewife?" (162). Ruth Lyons prided herself on her place in the Ohio community as just another housewife, but she also offered her viewers a sampling of elite culture—either by bringing the world to Cincinnati or by traveling as an ambassador to unfamiliar spheres. In contrast, the Manhattanite Arlene Francis, higher up in the cultural hierarchy than Lyons to begin with, remained a friendly outsider, moderating Fifth Avenue values to the Main Streets of America. Francis's voice was well modulated, carefully trained for theater and radio. For her, *dark* was *dahk,* the hard *t* in *thirty-three* well enunciated, the *rs* rolled slightly. Her signature props were high-fashion glasses, which she wore for reading, and gaudy but expensive necklaces. Like the cliché of the bespectacled woman in Hollywood cinema, Francis signified the "intellectual woman" who "looks and analyses."[81] Her signature diamond-studded heart necklace, a love token from her husband, along with other showy jewelry, prominently signaled her class status.

By contrast, Ruth Lyons's voice, though low-pitched like Francis's, was described as "somewhat sharp," "a sandpaper voice," one "as unmistakably Midwestern as the *Chicago Tribune*."[82] Lyons's signature prop was the flower-bouquet microphone, an affectation of middlebrow femininity, matched by the purse she carried and the white gloves she often wore on stage. It became a tradition for studio guests to wear white gloves to the program too. In a regular feature that highlighted these dainty accessories, the women in the audience waved to the camera as they sang the notorious "Waving Song," a segment taped and then replayed for their amusement after the show:

> Let's wave to the folks who are watching
> Say hello to the folks listening in
> We want you to see
> And hope you'll agree
> We really look lovely on color TV.[83]

The difficulty of imagining Arlene Francis carrying a purse on *Home*'s set or waving to the audience in white gloves, or Ruth Lyons redecorating her stage in a minimalist design, underlines the distinctive versions of feminine taste culture each woman came to represent.

Local/National Presence

The public personae of Ruth Lyons and Arlene Francis outlined above are inextricably linked to competing industry forces during the 1950s, as regional and national interests battled for control of the daytime dollar. Ruth Lyons, by celebrating her Midwestern origins and tastes, built a regional empire that profited the locally owned Crosley enterprise (later purchased by Avco); Arlene Francis propagated a more sophisticated taste culture from Manhattan for national consumption, helping NBC to successfully colonize local markets. Ruth Lyons and *The Fifty-Fifty Club* were able to retain a distinctive place in local television against the incursions of network programming, establishing a stronghold that enabled the rise of Phil Donahue and daytime syndication (first through Avco and later with Multimedia). Arlene Francis and *Home* offer a significant early example of an opposite pressure: NBC's preemptive move into daytime television devised to displace locally controlled programs, concentrating economic and programming power with national networks. *Home* became the model for a legacy of network-controlled magazine programs that still survives today.

Lyons's endurance against the pressures of the national networks exemplifies her exceptional success within local daytime television. To a considerable degree, this success is closely tied to her strong local connection to the Ohio community, a connection she actively nurtured. For example, Ruth Lyons established a strong presence through her well-publicized Christmas Fund, which benefited hospitalized children. In 1995, the Cincinnati Historical Society mounted an exhibit honoring Ruth Lyons. When visitors were asked to fill out questionnaires sharing their memories of Ruth, many recalled receiving toys when they were hospitalized as children; many other respondents remember Lyons because they were members of her studio audience. In the course of her career, Ruth Lyons remained strongly connected to her audience through sustained efforts at local visibility. Although based in Cincinnati, every spring and fall the program traveled to other cities in the Crosley network for live broadcasts. As described in station promotional material, "Because of the tight ticket situation [in Cincinnati] (tight?—they're unobtainable!), it is felt that listeners and viewers in and around the areas of WLW-T's sister stations should have the opportunity of seeing 'The Fifty-Fifty Club' 'In Person' at least once a year."[84] In Cincinnati, tickets were indeed almost unobtainable. It was typical for three years' worth of tickets for *The Fifty-Fifty Club* to sell out after only a single announcement of availability, even after audience capacity had been increased to 130 places.[85]

Lyons's community presence fortified her power as a regional star, and her ratings were astronomical. In 1965, her total TV viewership in the four WLW markets numbered approximately 400,000 per average quarter-hour, with another 70,000 radio fans listening to the simulcast.[86] In the face of network forays into local markets, the enduring success of *The Fifty-Fifty Club* is all the more notable. Ruth Lyons was unbeatable in her time slot.

It is likely that her reign would have endured for many more years, but family misfortune cut her career short. In December 1964, Lyons suffered a minor stroke and was briefly hospitalized. A year later, Lyons's twenty-year-old daughter Candy was diagnosed with breast cancer and died in 1966 on a family trip. In a human response that transcended publicity or persona, Lyons never fully recovered from this loss. She returned to host *The Fifty-Fifty Club*, but missed many of the broadcasts. On 27 January 1967, Lyons's retirement from the show was announced, and she never again appeared before cameras. Secluded at home, Ruth Lyons spent the next few years writing her autobiography, *Remember with Me*. She died a Cincinnati legend in November 1988. Lyons's influence on television history did not end with her retirement in 1967, however. In the same year, Phil Donahue adapted Lyons's extemporaneous style and premiered a revamped form of the audience participation show in Dayton, Ohio, on Crosley's TV station WLW-D.[87] Honoring Lyons after her death in November of 1988, Donahue acknowledged her impact on his history-making career: "If there had not been a Crosley Broadcasting with a commitment to local programming, and if there had not been a Ruth Lyons, I probably wouldn't be here."[88]

Although *Home* only lasted a few years, it, too, altered the course of television, representing a major network initiative to capture the daytime market. With a format perfectly suited to multiple sponsors, it also tapped into an immense new range of small-ticket advertisers that expanded NBC's revenue base.[89] While *Home* was cancelled after only three years, it had succeeded in providing access to new viewers and new accounts for the network. In her memoirs, Arlene Francis recognizes that *Home* was a "victim of the rating game."[90] Despite steady profits, from the very beginning *Home* lagged behind the variety and audience participation shows CBS programmed in competition.[91] Even in its final season (1956–57), when NBC moved *Home* to an earlier time slot (10–11 AM) in which the competition was not as keen, the show still failed to win its hour.[92] The NBC network, which had used *Home* to begin the march into daytime programming for women, quickly realized that other, cheaper formats, like the quiz show, garnered greater profits during the day. While *Home* retained a loyal and vociferous following, it was not lucrative enough to survive within the daytime economic environment it had helped to create.[93] "The rest of NBC's daytime schedule kept hitting new rating and sponsor highs," explained *Variety*, while *Home* merely held steady. In NBC's search for daytime dollars, "*Home* became an embarrassment in the overall daytime picture. It had to go."[94]

While the professional life of Arlene Francis faltered briefly after *Home*'s demise, her career as an actress continued to prosper for many years, including screen roles and stage appearances. In broadcasting, Francis went on to host a shorter midmorning program on NBC called *The Arlene Francis Show* during the 1957–58 season; continued to appear as a regular panelist on *What's My Line?* in both its CBS and syndicated versions until 1975; made numerous guest appearances over the next thirty years, from *The Jack Paar Show* in the late 1950s to *Scarecrow and Mrs. King* in the mid-1980s;[95] and was heard daily on New York City's prestigious WOR Radio until 1990, the year she turned eighty-three. Having received the Broadcasters Award for Lifetime Achievement in 1987, Francis spent a long retirement in San Francisco, where she died on 31 May 2001.[96]

In the history of daytime television, *Home,* under the engaging leadership of Arlene Francis, emerged as something of a triumphant failure. In industry terms, *Home* succeeded in achieving Weaver's agenda by advancing the network's presence in morning television. At the same time, refashioning the homemaking genre on a grand scale helped naturalize daytime broadcasting as a feminine sphere, a radio legacy that was probable but not inevitable for American television. Weaver's ostensible failure thus paved the way for network ascendancy in the years to follow and initiated a long line of *Home*-style imitators, including such programs as ABC's *The Home Show* (1988–94), *Martha Stewart Living* (syndicated in partnership with CBS, 1993), and NBC's *Later Today* (1999). Yet *Home*'s contradictions, responsible in part for the show's cancellation, expressed television's ongoing uncertainty about how to construct American femininity. Francis herself offered the lingering possibility that women of substance and wit could exist in the feminine cultural sphere, a possibility sustained by her ongoing presence in broadcasting after *Home*'s demise, when she was no longer expected to be an exemplar of all-American womanhood. *Home*'s failure does not diminish the fact that its specific means of inscribing feminine public culture were central to refiguring network institutions and infrastructures in the effort to dominate daytime television programming aimed at a female audience.

Going National

During an era in which competing forces in daytime television strove to seduce the nation's housewives, neither Arlene Francis and *Home* nor Ruth Lyons and *The Fifty-Fifty Club* ever attained a national hegemony. *Home*'s early cancellation—along with Lyons's tenacious but region-bound success—indicates that while the national networks never fully dominated local markets during the day, even the most successful local programming met obstacles to achieving a national reach. Unresolved contentions over region versus nation, middlebrow versus highbrow, and local power versus national power were fully operative in the histories of *Home* and *The Fifty-Fifty Club*.

In the case of *Home,* the show's cancellation in 1957 served as a cautionary tale about the country's tolerance for Weaver's version of highbrow taste. In unabashedly promoting the urban taste culture of New York City, Weaver had miscalculated how to reach the new national television audience that was shifting rapidly from a predominantly urban-centered demographic to a broader viewership.[97] Yet Ruth Lyons, who had perfected a public persona and mode of address that successfully attracted a Midwestern audience, also failed to find the formula for national appeal. In both 1951–52 and 1958, the NBC network courted Lyons, but the merger never worked. These two unsuccessful forays into NBC's national lineup brought into sharp focus conflicts over region, taste, and power central to daytime television's evolution. Like Francis, Lyons failed to embody a national mode of femininity.

In October 1951, the first half-hour of *The Fifty Club* began a fifty-two-week run on the NBC network, the first season of what was to be a three-year contract. It appears that neither party was unhappy when the agreement terminated after only one year. In April of 1958, Ruth Lyons briefly cohosted *The Today Show* on NBC with Dave Garroway, one of several women guest hosts brought in during Helen O'Connell's maternity leave. This was apparently supposed to test Lyons as a network personality, but she quickly returned to her home base. In both cases, the contemporary claim is that Lyons eschewed the national broadcasting context, feeling too constrained by the strictures of the network, the rigid scheduling of commercials, and the need to work from a script. Given the nature of her own program, and the degree of control she was able to exercise, it is likely that she was unwilling to relinquish her power. After all, Lyons's control at Crosley extended to the conditions of her own broadcast, including almost no recording of her shows. Certainly the network would not have secured this kind of luxury. Lyons was keenly aware that kinescopes or tapes of her program would enable others to access and control her image and performance.[98] Lyons further claimed that she was a "Midwest personality" and "content to remain one," a position reiterated by a WLW staffer, who explained,"Her roots lie deep in Ohio, and most of the appeal of her show is local."[99]

It is also the case that Lyons's local version of middle-class femininity and taste did not measure up to national standards. When *The Fifty Club* debuted on the NBC network in 1951, John Crosby of the *New York Herald Tribune* clearly expressed this perspective. Sounding the voice of New York elitism, he disparaged Lyons's performance in a scathing review. Crosby mocks events on the show that he considers laughably second rate but which were, in fact, at the core of Lyons's community-based success:

> [Lyons] and one of her assistants by the name of Willie fell to discussing her cough, which is getting deeper. The symptoms were very interesting if you like other people's symptoms, and I'm sure that you do. . . . That brought us handily to lucky number time. The lady in the audience who held the lucky number . . . turned out to be some one who knew Ruth's sister "a real long time." She and Ruth talked about her little boy, who is now in Edgewater School or some such place. If this is entertainment, my mother ought to be in Joan Davis's shoes. She's wonderful at this sort of thing. . . . The high point of this divertissement—to me at least—was Miss Lyons and her sidekick singing the commercial for A-1 sauce. I've heard love songs before but never such passion as this. . . . I don't see how A-1 could move elsewhere. That's her song. "My Man" belongs to Fanny Brice, A-1 belongs to Ruth Lyons.[100]

Seven years later, when Lyons appeared as cohost for a week on the *Today* show, these taste clashes and their link to locality were ignited again. This time, the Cincinnati press and Lyons's faithful fans perceived a network snub. The local *Cincinnati Enquirer* reported that after twenty minutes on the air, Lyons "was permitted only two brief appearances," her final contribution a mere one-minute reading of news headlines.[101] Later in the week, Lyons found herself literally concealed between two potted palms while delivering a commercial. In her autobiography, Lyons remembers the intense local furor evoked by her *Today* show appearance: "My viewers had expected that I would chat with Dave Garroway in the same way in which they were accustomed to seeing and hearing me on my own show. Obviously they were disappointed. . . . For days, and even weeks, the newspapers and hundreds of letters from viewers . . . protested that I had been treated very shabbily by the entire network." Lyons reports that she made every attempt to dissipate the controversy but concludes, "In vain I tried to explain to my audience that Dave and the entire cast, as well as representatives of NBC, were wonderful to me, but it was all to no avail!"[102]

Lyons, affirming her own values, tacitly accepted her audience's rejection of New York elitism and its exclusionary impulse. In the battle over taste cultures and, concomitantly, in the battle for broadcasting power, Lyons refused network subjugation and continued to cultivate her perfect fit in the Midwest. Even though Bob Hope told Lyons that the NBC network was still "kinda Ruth-minded" as late as 1963,[103] Lyons rejected modifying her persona for the national scene. The same can be said for Arlene Francis. While her brand of intelligence, wit, and sophistication fell short in daytime's mass national market, the career of her later life in New York City succeeded on its own terms.

Ruth Lyons and Arlene Francis marked off separate regimes of industry power during the 1950s. As the histories of *The Fifty-Fifty Club* and *Home* demonstrate, Lyons and Francis were potent figures in the intense competition over local-versus-network control of daytime programming, embodying television's contentions over middlebrow/highbrow and region/nation. While achieving personal success as public career women, they were also complicit in helping establish daytime television as a feminine site within television, aimed to capitalize on the demographics of the female marketplace. They accomplished this by participating in influential programs that offered different approaches to the feminine cultural sphere. Their shows clearly addressed viewers as domestic consumers, preoccupied with cooking, sewing, decorating, and cleaning. But they also routinely promoted a broader purview, embracing eminent figures from the worlds of popular entertainment, high culture, and politics. With their unique, discrepant styles, both Lyons and Francis demonstrated a distinct knack for successfully bringing these elements together for the benefit of the daytime television audience. Their different approaches retrospectively provide us with a way of testing the modes of femininity that would come to signify the new postwar woman in the context of American daytime television. Ultimately, neither Lyons nor Francis was able to offer an enduring model for a national audience. Francis was too urban, too knowing, too remote; Lyons was too folksy, too brash, too local. Yet each forced an assessment of women's representations on television—in local and national contexts.

Both women were highly visible in helping create and define the nature of daytime television, despite the demise of Francis's signature program on national television and Lyons's failure to capture a national audience. Moreover, these women are exemplary rather than singular. Their stories parallel the careers of other women who routinely populated the earliest daytime formats and who participated in defining daytime television's models of femininity, through varying success and failure.[104] Ruth Lyons and Arlene Francis thus emerge as significant figures of feminine power during daytime television's formative years—women, shaped by history, who helped shape history.

Notes

1. "Arlene Francis: The Quick Queen of Television," *Newsweek*, 19 July 1954, 50+.

2. "They Love Ruth Lyons," *Look*, 20 April 1954, 68.

3. Victoria Johnson addresses related issues regarding primetime. See *"Jubilee, U.S.A.! Populist Address and Local Values in 1950s Network TV"* (paper presented at the Society for Cinema Studies annual conference, San Diego, CA, 4 April 1998).

4. Biographical details were compiled from Arlene Francis, *Arlene Francis: A Memoir* (New York: Simon and Schuster, 1978); "Arlene Francis: TV's Busiest Woman," *Look*, 4 May 1954, 52–56; James A. Maxwell, "The Lady Lays Down the Law," *Saturday Evening Post*, 6 April 1957, 24–25; Cynthia Keller, *Remembering Ruth Lyons: 1905–1988* (Cincinnati, OH: Cincinnati Historical Society, 1995); Mary Wood, "Ruth Lyons: A Living Legend," *Cincinnati Enquirer Magazine*, 27 September 1981, 3; and Ruth Lyons, *Remember with Me* (Garden City, NY: Doubleday, 1969).

5. Keller, *Remembering Ruth Lyons*, 72–73.

6. "Backgrounds and Beginnings," Publicity Archives, Ruth Lyons Collection at WLWT-TV, Cincinnati, OH, ca. 1958.

7. Mary Wood, "Remembering Ruth," *The Cincinnati Enquirer*, 8 November 1988.

8. "Backgrounds."

9. "She SELLS, too—and How!" Publicity Archives, Ruth Lyons Collection at WLWT-TV, Cincinnati, OH, ca. 1958.

10. "Company Comes," Publicity Archives, 1961, Ruth Lyons Collection at WLWT-TV, Cincinnati, OH, 18–19.

11. Martin Abramson, "Million-Dollar Dynamo," *Cosmopolitan*, April 1953, 140–43.

12. Betty Hannah Hoffman, "She Speaks to Seven Million Women," *Ladies' Home Journal*, April 1960, 149.

13. "She Shall Have Music," Publicity Archives, 1961, The Ruth Lyons Collection at WLWT-TV, Cincinnati, OH, 4.

14. Francis, *Arlene Francis*, 10.

15. Ibid, 19; see also "A Tribute to Arlene Francis," available at www.arlenefrancis.com, accessed January 2001.

16. Francis, *Arlene Francis*, 20–21.

17. "Tribute," www.arlenefrancis.com.

18. Francis, *Arlene Francis*, 44.

19. "Tribute," www.arlenefrancis.com.

20. Francis, *Arlene Francis*, 72–78.

21. "Arlene Francis: TV's Busiest Woman," 52.

22. Katherine Pedell, "What's Her Line?" *TV Guide,* 9 July 1954, 4–6.

23. "Arlene Francis: Quick Queen," 54.

24. Roul Tunley, "You Don't Have to Be Beautiful," *American Magazine,* October 1954, 114.

25. Arlene Francis, *That Certain Something: The Magic of Charm* (New York: Messner, 1960).

26. "Arlene Francis: Quick Queen," 54.

27. Alfred Bester, "Antic Arts: At Home with Arlene Francis," *Holiday,* October 1956, 79–80.

28. Francis, *Arlene Francis,* 136.

29. See Lynn Spigel, *Make Room for TV: Television and the Family Ideal in Postwar America* (Chicago: University of Chicago Press, 1992), 75–80; Inger L. Stole, "There Is No Place Like Home: NBC's Search for a Daytime Audience, 1954–1957," *Communication Review* 2.2 (1997): 135–61; Michele Hilmes, *Radio Voices: American Broadcasting, 1922–1952* (Minneapolis: University of Minnesota Press, 1997), 271–81.

30. Jack Gould, " 'Home,' Daytime Show for Women on NBC, Starts Ambitiously," *New York Times,* 5 March 1954, 26.

31. Robert Lewis Shayon, "The Hurry of 'Home,' " *Saturday Review,* 10 April 1954, 38.

32. James C. G. Conniff, "Arlene Francis: The Lady Is a Wit," *Coronet,* February 1956, 53–57.

33. Kinescope, videotape #4010.3, 12 November 1956, Museum of Broadcast Communications, Chicago.

34. Kinescope, videotape #MI 95–19, 1 March 1951, Cincinnati Historical Society, Cincinnati, OH.

35. Kinescope, videotape #MI 94–6, 1963, Cincinnati Historical Society, Cincinnati, OH. Lyons's friend Carol Channing said of Lyons, perhaps only half joking, "I was afraid not to buy what she said to buy" ("Ruth Lyons: First Lady of Broadcasting," videotape, WXIX-TV, #MI-94–4, undated, Cincinnati Historical Society, Cincinnati, OH).

36. Kinescope, videotape #MI 95–19, September 1960, Cincinnati Historical Society, Cincinnati, OH.

37. Bester, "Antic Arts," 80.

38. Francis, *Arlene Francis,* 136.

39. Kinescope, 20 May 1954, Collection of J. Fred MacDonald and Associates, Chicago.

40. Jean Austin, "Why Ruth Lyons' Homemaking Program Is Midwest's Tops," *American Home,* April 1958, 17.

41. Hoffman, "She Speaks," 162.

42. "Be It Never So Humble," *Life,* 29 March 1954, 50–51.

43. Kinescope, videotape #13376, 21 September 1954, Museum of Television and Radio, Beverly Hills, CA.

44. Abramson, "Million-Dollar Dynamo."

45. Maxwell, "The Lady," 114.

46. Ibid, 25; other notable regulars during the show's run were singers Doris Day and Rosemary Clooney and sidekicks Peter Grant, Bob Braun, Nick Clooney, and Frasier Thomas. See also Keller, *Remembering Ruth Lyons,* 105.

47. Kinescope, videotape #MI 95–19, September 1960, Cincinnati Historical Society, Cincinnati, OH.

48. Lyons, *Remember with Me,* 87.

49. Hoffman, "She Speaks," 150.

50. Abramson, "Million-Dollar Dynamo," 140–43. In a questionnaire distributed by the Cincinnati Historical Society in 1995, Jim Welch, one of Lyons's last stage managers, remembered the "distinct and thoughtful philosophy about how you treat the audience" that he learned from Lyons. He said that on Lyons's show, "the audience came before any of us or any other work-a-day concerns" (Welch questionnaire, 20 December 1995 "Ruth Lyons Project Box," Broadcast Archives, Cincinnati Historical Society, Cincinnati, OH).

51. Lyons, *Remember with Me,* 134.

52. See Maxwell, "The Lady," 25. File photographs in the Ruth Lyons Collection at WLWT-TV, Cincinnati, OH, confirm these placements.

53. Abramson, "Million-Dollar Dynamo."

54. "Ruth Lyons: Portrait of a Legend," videotape, WLWT, 3 October 1986, Collection of WLWT-TV, Cincinnati, OH.

55. Maxwell, "The Lady," 110.

56. Abramson, "Million-Dollar Dynamo," 140–43.

57. Austin, "Why Ruth Lyons," 14.

58. Lyons, *Remember with Me,* 152.

59. "Ruth Lyons: First Lady of Broadcasting"; Maxwell, "The Lady," 114, 117.

60. Maxwell, "The Lady," 113; Hoffman, "She Speaks," 150.

61. Maxwell, "The Lady," 113.

62. Lyons, *Remember with Me,* 99–100.

63. Pam Wilson, "NBC TV's 'Operation Frontal Lobes': Cultural Hegemony and 50s Program Planning," *Historical Journal of Film, Radio, and Television* 15 (1995): 83–105.

64. Spigel, *Make Room for TV,* 80–81; Hilmes, *Radio Voices,* 277–87.

65. *Home's* family affairs editor, Phyllis Jenkins, said the show prided itself on segments that "raised people's spirits and standards" (Interview with Marsha Cassidy, Santa Monica, CA, 12 August 1996).

66. "For the Girls at Home," *Newsweek,* 15 March 1954, 92.

67. Bester, "Antic Arts," 82.

68. Spigel, *Make Room for TV,* 83.

69. Francis, *Arlene Francis,* 136, 145.

70. Bester, "Antic Arts," 80.

71. "Arlene Francis: Quick Queen," 50; *Newsweek* cover.

72. Tunley, "You Don't Have to Be Beautiful," 117.

73. Bester, "Antic Arts," 80.

74. "April in Paris Ball," Kinescope, videotape #B:03679, 11 April 1957, Museum of Television and Radio, Beverly Hills, CA. *Le diable au corps* is a mildly scandalous film about an affair between an adolescent boy and a woman whose husband is away at war. They fall in love, are separated, and she dies giving birth to his child. The story is told in flashback from his point of view as he follows her funeral from a distance.

75. "Memorial Day on Belvedere Island," videotape, 30 May 1956, Collection of J. Fred MacDonald and Associates, Chicago.

76. "*Home* in Philadelphia," kinescope, videotape #B:02626, 22 October 1956, Museum of Television and Radio, Beverly Hills, CA.

77. "April in Paris Ball."

78. Kinescope, 20 May 1954.

79. See Stole, "There Is No Place Like Home," 135–61.

80. Hoffman, "She Speaks," 162.

81. Mary Ann Doane, "Film and the Masquerade: Theorising the Female Spectator," *Screen* 23.3–4 (1982): 74–88. Reprint in *Feminist Film Theory: A Reader,* ed. Sue Thornham (New York: New York University Press, 1999), 140.

82. Maxwell, "The Lady," 114; Hoffman, "She Speaks," 149.

83. Lyrics, Ruth Lyons Collection at WLWT-TV, Cincinnati, OH.

84. "The Fifty-Fifty Club Today," Ruth Lyons Project Box 2–6–N-2, and "Sponsors," 1961, 26, Cincinnati Historical Society, Cincinnati, OH.

85. "Backgrounds."

86. " '50–50 Club' Analysis," Publicity Archives, Collection at WLWT-TV, Cincinnati, OH.

87. Alex McNeil, *Total Television: The Comprehensive Guide to Programming from 1948 to the Preset,* 4th ed. (New York: Penguin, 1996), 657.

88. Quoted in Bob Greene, "Early TV-Show Hostess Succeeded with Class," unidentified newspaper clipping marked November 1988, in Ruth Lyons Collection at WLWT-TV, Cincinnati, OH. Other television notables were devotees of *The Fifty-Fifty Club.* David Letterman, Jane Pauley, and Erma Bombeck acknowledged Lyons's influence on their performance styles and careers. See "Ruth Lyons: First Lady of Broadcasting."

89. See Spigel, *Make Room for TV,* 82; Stole, "There Is No Place Like Home," 10; and Pat Weaver with Thomas M. Coffey, *The Best Seat in the House: The Golden Years of Radio and Television* (New York: Knopf, 1994), 250.

90. Francis, *Arlene Francis,* 160.

91. In *Home*'s first and second season, for example, *Strike It Rich,* scheduled against *Home*'s second half-hour (11:30 AM to noon), pulled an average 9.75 rating, while *Home* delivered only a 3.0. In raw numbers, this meant that in the fall of 1954, *Home* reached into 746,000 households every day, with an approximate viewership of 1 million. Thanks to Lawrence Lichty, professor of radio/TV/film at Northwestern University, Evanston, Illinois, for these numbers.

92. On CBS, *The Garry Moore Show* averaged a 6.5 rating from 10–10:30 AM and *Arthur Godfrey Time* a 7.5 between 10:30–11:00 AM, while *Home* slipped to a new low of 2.5 (Lichty).

93. Arlene Francis attributes *Home*'s demise to Weaver's philosophy of uplift. She views *Home* as an intelligent, ambitious, and educational program that struggled to compete in a ratings-dominated business where mass appeal ruled. In her memoirs, she writes, "Sad to say, the networks have always demonstrated that it is not their job to educate the public" (*Arlene Francis,* 159–60).

94. Bob Chandler, "Decline and Fall of 'T-H-T,' " *Variety,* 14 August 1957, 42.

95. David Inman, *The TV Encyclopedia* (New York: Perigee, 1991), 327.

96. "Tribute," www.arlenefrancis.com; e-mail with Peter Gabel, 21 February 2001.

97. Wilson, "NBC TV's 'Operation Frontal Lobes,' " 101.

98. Because she refused to allow most of her programs to be recorded in any form, very few of them still exist. Instead, her legend looms large, grounded in a standard repertoire of oft-repeated stories and anecdotes that circulate in magazine and news stories, Crosley publicity materials, and interviews with scant verification. This absence of a visual record, dictated by Lyons from the start, may also be linked to her performance style: she was free to improvise, make slips, and be brash because there would be no record of either her triumphs or her failures.

99. Hoffman, "She Speaks," 159.

100. Clipping of *New York Herald Tribune* review, undated, Publicity Archives,

Ruth Lyons Collection at WLWT-TV, Cincinnati, OH. Joan Davis was a highly regarded comedienne who had begun in radio and was popular in early television.

101. Charlton Wallace, *Cincinnati Enquirer,* 21 April 1958, Ruth Lyons Collection at WLWT-TV, Cincinnati, OH.

102. Lyons, *Remember with Me,* 94.

103. Kinescope, videotape #MI 94–6.

104. See David Weinstein, "Women's Shows and the Selling of Television to Washington, D.C.," *Washington History* 11.1 (1999): 4–23; Mark Williams, "Considering Monty Margetts's *Cooks Corner:* Oral History and Television History," in *Television, History, and American Culture: Feminist Critical Essays,* ed. Mary Beth Haralovich and Lauren Rabinovitz (Durham, NC: Duke University Press, 1999), 36–55; Inger L. Stole, "'The Kate Smith Hour' and the Struggle for Control of Television Programming in the Early 1950s," *Historical Journal of Film, Radio, and Television* 20 (2000): 549–64; Mary E. Beadle and Michael D. Murray, eds., *Indelible Images: Women of Local Television* (Ames: Iowa State University Press, 2001); Donna L. Halper, *Invisible Stars: A Social History of Women in American Broadcasting* (Armonk, NY: Sharpe, 2001); Robert Alley and Irby Brown, *Women Television Producers, 1948–2000* (Rochester, NY: University of Rochester Press, 2001); and Cary O'Dell, *Women Pioneers in Television: Biographies of Fifteen Industry Leaders* (Jefferson, NC: McFarland, 1997).

Ethnic Masculinity and Early Television's Vaudeo Star

Susan Murray

Many of the obituaries and tributes to Milton Berle published in the days following his death on March 27, 2002, emphasized the ways in which the comic's Jewishness either informed his comedy or was central to his stardom. In the *Wall Street Journal,* Joseph Epstein wrote that "everyone had to know that Berle was Jewish," while the *Baltimore Sun*'s television critic detailed the ways Berle's Jewishness was central to the rise and decline of his program *The Texaco Star Theater* and, more generally, to the future representation of Jews on television.[1] Franklin Foer put it bluntly (and rather lovingly) in his Salon.com article by calling the comedian a "very Jewy Jew."[2]

While it may be easy for contemporary critics to speak frankly about Berle's ethnicity and its impact on his popularity, there was no such commentary in the mainstream coverage of the star when he was first dubbed Mr. Television and America's Uncle Miltie. Rather, the signs of his Jewishness were read through his historical connections to such things as vaudeville, New York, and a particular type of ethnic masculinity.

After the proven commercial success of early variety programs, such as *The Texaco Star Theater* (1948–1953, NBC), vaudeville-trained performers became the most-sought-after personalities in television. Jack Benny signed an unprecedented ten-year contract with CBS worth almost $1 million in 1950. And, during the following year, Berle penned a deal with NBC that would cost the network up to $200,000 a year for thirty years. Clearly, networks and advertisers were confident about the long-term earning potential of such stars—in fact, it would seem that they assumed television's "vaudeo" trend would continue in perpetuity ("vaudeo" is an industry term that conjoins vaudeville with video).

What actually occurred is that vaudeo would be absorbed into the sitcom format by the end of the decade and many of the genre's top stars would watch their careers fizzle out by the early sixties. But during this early period, the variety performer's brash, stagy, New York vaudeville style became one of the most significant prototypes of the television star. The broadcast industry was

Susan Murray, "Ethnic Masculinity and Early Television's Vaudeo Star." From *Cinema Journal,* Vol. 42, No. 1 (Fall 2002), pp. 97–119. Copyright © 2002, University of Texas Press.

initially interested in exploiting ex-vaudeville stars for the way in which their performance style emphasized the visuality, spontaneity, immediacy, and intimacy of the television medium. Also, on a very practical level, ex-vaudevillians were a convenient pool of talent from which to draw, as many of them were New York regional performers and the television networks were all broadcasting from flagship stations in Manhattan.

Yet, as a consequence of poaching vaudeville performance styles, the television industry was forced to confront the more indelicate aspects of variety-format humor that threatened to erupt unexpectedly on live television. Ex-vaudevillians had a tendency to ad-lib sly sight gags, asides, and subtle gestures to connote sexual references or situations. So, in this perilous terrain of a live, visual, domestic-entertainment medium, not only did the bawdy antics of stage comedy have to be eliminated from the script in preproduction but their spontaneous appearance in the program also had to be anticipated. One way to ease the reception of such content was to contain or construct rhetorically a personality for the comedian that would befit the values of the television audience.

In relying on the proven variety format and using older vaudevillians and radio performers, the television industry was referencing a traditional form of entertainment (hoping in this way to secure its audience) while simultaneously promoting the novelty, the "newness," of the medium itself. It is in this context that the analysis of the appeal and cultural resonance of the early television comics becomes so significant. Considering the somewhat morally tenuous state of the variety format and the aging, ethnic, and somewhat flexible masculinity of the top comedy stars, alongside the industry's desire to be perceived as a natural extension of the American family, the television industry might appear to have been working at cross-purposes. However, these apparent contradictions in the construction of early comedy stars bespeak rather coherent symbolic constructions of ethnicity, masculinity, and anxieties over the changing demographics of the American cultural landscape.

This article argues that, although a variety performer's particular ethnic identity was rarely addressed outright in television, traces of his "Jewishness" were embedded in the star's persona and performance style. Specifically, the cultural and religious heritages of such individuals as Milton Berle, George Burns, Sid Caesar, and Jack Benny were obliquely referenced through their connection to the traditions of vaudeville, their affiliations with particular geographic areas/neighborhoods, their relationships with their extended families, and their representations of a historically and culturally located feminized masculinity. The subtle nature of these ethnic cues helped these comedians address the cultural experiences of the largely northern and urban television audience of the late forties without completely alienating viewers from other regions.

Comedy, Nostalgia, and Urban Ethnic Masculinity

The industry's presumptions about the connection between live television and stage work and the presold celebrity of ex-vaudevillian headliners led to the hiring of a large number of male vaudevillians. Many of these performers, including Berle (formerly Milton Berlinger), Caesar, Ed Wynn, Burns (Nathan Birnbaum), and Benny (Benjamin Kubelsky), had embarked (with varying degrees of success) on radio and film careers before their entry into television. For example, Benny was one of the most popular radio stars of the thirties and forties. Although he was initially reluctant to enter into television production (largely because of the work involved in reconceiving and performing his program for the new visual medium), both NBC and CBS considered him to be a guaranteed ratings winner. After accepting a capital-gains deal from CBS in 1948, Benny was eventually lured into television work by the promise of a larger audience and salary. Berle, though, was a risky investment for NBC as his radio program, *The Philip Morris Playhouse*, and the radio version of *Texaco Star Theater* were largely considered disappointments. Yet the physical comedy and sight gags Berle acquired during his years on the vaudeville circuit forecast a nice fit with the still-developing aesthetic economy of television.

Given the collection of performers who were the early stars of television, it is a bit curious that an industry so concerned with emphasizing the visual aspects of the new technology chose individuals so significantly older and less glamorous than their counterparts in film. As postwar Hollywood promoted the virile hero and the psychologically tormented detective, television offered a less traditional vision of maleness. In 1948, the year Berle became a household name with *Texaco Star Theater*, films were released starring Montgomery Clift (*The Search, Red River*), John Wayne (*Red River*), Humphrey Bogart (*Key Largo, The Treasure of the Sierra Madre*), and Clark Gable (*Command Decision*) in roles as war heroes, prospectors, tough guys, and cowboys. Although film noir presented psychologically troubled and morally conflicted protagonists during these years, the presentation of masculinity through Hollywood product was still within the traditional white Anglo-Saxon masculine paradigm. Even Hollywood screen comedy had moved away from the anarchistic, vaudeville-inflected format and toward the narratively integrated romantic comedy that highlighted stars such as Gable and Cary Grant. The vestiges of the vaudeville aesthetic in film were found in the teams of Dean Martin and Jerry Lewis and Bob Hope and Bing Crosby (with each pair containing a romantic and an "adolescent" lead—all four of whom were already popular broadcast stars).

Compared to the more hardened male types found in film, the goofy, gangly, mugging Berle hardly appeared to be anyone's ideal man, or man to be. Nevertheless, his awkward physicality and psychological vulnerability expressed through self-deprecating humor were integral to the currency of his urban-based character. In his study of Berle's career, Arthur Frank Wertheim found that Berle "personified a flippant city slicker—a character most viewers could understand."[3] Berle's character mobilized nostalgia for turn-of-the-century city culture, and more specifically for working-class theater (which depended on a revisionist history of its original "amoral" discursive construction). While Berle certainly was not the last word in postwar virility, he possessed a homey familiarity and nostalgic resonance that was paramount to his popularity. And, surprisingly, his gender play and brash sensibilities actually worked for an audience whom the industry assumed was seeking moral reassurance and reinforcement of middle-class values from the new domestic medium.

Masculinity, in a strategic cultural performance of signifiers, is mobilized in relation to other social constructions and positions. In reading the personas of television stars of the late forties and early fifties, the functions of ethnicity and class are often difficult to disentangle from gender codes since they work to inform one another. In discussing the process of identification, Judith Butler points out that individuals may wish to see coherence and authenticity in gender identity, but "[words, acts, gestures, and desire] are fabrications manufactured and sustained through corporeal signs and other discursive means."[4]

A consequence of understanding masculinity as performance is that its mobilization as a congruency of signs within the system of media representation produces a mirroring effect that is overwhelming in its obfuscation. In television, as in film, performers represented and reconstituted signs present in contemporary culture that were meant to signal a specific form of gender identity. Thus, the performance of gender witnessed in everyday "reality" is replayed for viewers through these individuals' screen acts, words, and gestures and contributes to a further distancing of the signs of identity from its human object. Nevertheless, by discussing the various reference points each type of performance is aiming to incorporate, we can perceive an underlying structure informing individual characterizations of specific identity types. In the case of many early television stars, the "fabrications" of gender, class, and ethnicity are vital not only to their extratextual performance of functionally idealized public identities but also to their on-screen allusions to historically and generically defined characterizations. Their on- and off-screen personas, which are most often codetermined, are constituted via the text of the television shows in which they perform as well as through the historical and rhetorical devices and intentions of the culture at large.

Vaudeo stars were peculiarly adept at playing with signs of gender and ethnicity, as they were required by the variety format to inhabit numerous character types simultaneously. Sid Caesar, for example, was known for his portrayals of a regular cast of characters. While in his role as host of *Your Show of Shows,* he would perform a rather straight version of himself—or at least a consistent representation of who he was purported to be in the press. In his sketches, however, he created characters such as storyteller Somerset Winterset, the German professor, jazz musicians Progress Hornsby and Cool Cees, and, along with his partner, Imogene Coca, Doris and Charlie Hickenlooper, an "average" middle-class Staten Island couple. It would seem that with Caesar's ability to take on so many characterizations, locating one stable identity for him would be difficult for the audience. Yet, as prolific as his representations of different identities were, his construction through the cultural legacies that arose out of the variety format, along with the publicity materials that accompanied his rise to television stardom, assembled a context for Caesar's reception as an individual and hinted at his own "authentic" gender and ethnic identity.

Most important to the creation of such a context was the origin of the vaudeo performance style. The variety format was understood as a modern extension of turn-of-the-century vaudeville, an industry populated largely by working-class performers of particular ethnic backgrounds, the most predominant being Irish and Jewish. Many vaudeo stars, including Caesar, had begun their careers in the vaudeville circuit and had later performed in the "Borscht Belt," a collection of Jewish hotels in the Catskill Mountains, emphasizing the performers' ethnic and religious affiliations further.

The publicity generated for Caesar, Berle, and Burns consistently referred to their early careers in Borscht Belt venues, as well as to their childhood and familial connections in such New York ethnic neighborhoods as Harlem, Yonkers, and the Lower East Side. In some instances, articles would reveal not only the neighborhood of a performer's birth but also the exact street address.[5] These elements formed the basis for these performers' reception as men who maintained affiliations with specific regional and cultural conceptions of what it meant to be a man. They were clearly not raised to become traditional Anglo-Saxon heroes in the form of cowboys, drifters, or tough guys. Instead, their roles as comedic performers were constructed and received through historically and culturally specific signifiers of ethnic masculinity. In addition, the variety format in which they worked (with its emphasis on multiple characters, ethnic humor, and drag) granted them the room in which to play with these signifiers and to further complicate assumptions about stable, traditional American masculinity.

Many of the stock characters comedians such as Berle and Benny created for their variety programs were amalgams of American assumptions about masculinity and ethnicity. The implementation of easily recognizable class, ethnic, gender, and regional traits into vaudeville characters allowed for the lean economy of the form's truncated narratives and "olio" structure. Jewish characters, which did not become popular in vaudeville until the early 1900s, were often created through the donning of a long, pointed beard, large spectacles, a long black coat, and a dark plug hat.[6]

Michele Hilmes notes that this vaudevillian practice continued in golden-age radio, but since it was required to reside in the purely aural, the skills of the ethnic dialectician were emphasized.[7] Race, ethnicity, and class were fashioned through vocal cues and underscored by stereotyped behaviors. This practice of turning performance into an identity shorthand was picked up in vaudeo, allowing a similar economy to inform variety-show production. Although dialect continued to play a role in broadcast variety programs, there was also a reemphasis on visual display, as performers could again rely on mannerisms and dress to connote identity.

Although the vaudeo star's own ethnicity did not always dovetail with the ethnicity of the characters he or she created, the audience may have assumed a certain amount of cross-fertilization between performers' on-stage characters and their authentic identities. As Richard Dyer has pointed out, the question of the performer's "real" identity in relation to his or her character is theorized as pivotal to audience relationships with the star/performer.[8] Moreover, the vaudeville aesthetic overtly courted the conflation of on-stage/off-stage personas by breaking the boundaries of theatrical realism, making possible a higher degree of intimacy between performer and audience.

Variety television programs borrowed much of the style of vaudeville and continued to emphasize the relationship between performer and audience through such devices as direct address and studio-audience interaction. Television also courted audience assumptions about the authenticity of television performers through its persistent claims to intimacy. Because television was watched within the domestic sphere and was initially live, the industry sold itself to audiences as being more intimate and real.

Furthermore, because television performers were required to act sincere and trustworthy in order to sell their sponsors' wares, they often worked to come across as more genuine. For vaudeo stars, the representation of what could be construed as their authentic on- and off-stage personas occurred while they were acting as their show's host—during monologues and in their (relatively) straight interactions with their guest stars. They would then go on to perform in sketches as a number of different characters, but, in self-referential asides to their audience, they would often return to what might be understood to be their core personality.

The identities of early-television comedians interacted with and was influenced by both the operations of television stardom and those of comedy performance. Moreover, the ethnicity and sexuality of these stars were at stake both in their on-screen performance of specific character types and in the construction of their off-screen personas. As such, the disruptive nature of what Steven Seidman calls "comedian-centered comedy" has ramifications for the audience's subsequent perceptions of the comedian's "authentic" identity in relation to his or her characterizations.[9] Recent work on the comedy genre by Seidman, Henry Jenkins, and Frank Krutnik, among others, reveals the ways in which comedian-centered gag or slapstick comedy often disrupts classical narrative continuity by enabling the audience to linger on the spectacle of the performance. In discussions of film comedy, examples such as Hope's cross-dressing in *Road to Rio* (Norman Z. McLeod, 1947) are used to elucidate the way in which the comedian's over-the-top performance can intrude into an otherwise coherent, stable narrative.

Scholars also suggest that such narrative ruptures may destabilize a comedy star's characterization/identity. Speaking specifically about classical Hollywood comedy, Krutnik argues that "the comedian figure deforms familiar conventions of film heroism, unified identity, and mature sexuality." He concludes that, in the play of narrative disruption and containment, these films "circulate around questions of gendered identity."[10] The variety format is not as coherent in its structure as the classical Hollywood film. However, the vaudeo star's ability to cross over from one sketch to another, to embody numerous characters, to provide a base or stable personality in his role as host, and spontaneously to interrupt guest performances reveals similar moments of disjuncture caused by the seemingly uncontrolled nature of the lead performer.[11] Vaudeo's presentational, comedian-centered, gag and slapstick style figures the vaudeo comic's persona as one that is fluid in its relation both to narrative and to constructions of authenticity and performance. Specifically, vaudeo appears to be fascinated with the reticulations of gender and ethnicity. The vaudeo star plays with the signs of both these categories of identity and complicates them through his decentered position within the narrative and his intimate relationship with his audience.[12]

Berle's performance style provides a good example of this process, as he was known for constantly interrupting his show's sketches and guest stars' performances. While a sketch was in progress, Berle would make asides to his audiences out of the sketch's character, often references or inside jokes to what the audience knew of his on-stage persona. While performing his drag bits, Berle's extreme physical plays on femininity (such as batting his false eyelashes or pursing his overly made-up lips in a faux-seductive manner) were often disrupted by moments when he would lower his voice and speak to the audience in his normal baritone. For example, in one 1951 episode of *Texaco Star Theater,* Berle opened the show as a bride escorted by a portly groom. The audience howled as he swished his hips and batted his eyes as he sang a ditty about how he married an elephant. As the groom left the stage, Berle continued his monologue in his own voice and as Berle, but with the occasional feminine gesture. Still dressed as a woman, Berle discussed the confinements and conflicts of marriage from a male point of view, commiserating with the married men in the audience. He ended by taking off his wig and introducing the evening's guest star. Moments like this served to disrupt the continuity of Berle's characterizations, highlighting their artificiality and confusing the distinctions of gender codes. Berle also "spontaneously" broke into the acts performed by his musical guests. The mini-narratives of even these smaller moments within the variety format were made discontinuous by Berle's intrusive persona.

Although Berle is an extreme example of the decenteredness of the vaudeo star, Burns and Caesar also went in and out of character. In fact, Burns's oft-discussed movement across genres as the simultaneous host and sitcom star of *The Burns and Allen Show* (1950–1958, CBS) is an excellent example of the way such a performer could enter and exit a self-contained narrative. This process resulted in a destabilization of all characterization, emphasizing the constructed nature of identity, but at the same time it reasserted the relatively consistent personality that existed beneath the performances of these stars.

Jewish Identity and the Vaudeo Star

The strong conflation of "real life" and "reel life" that occurred in the reception of the television comedian was contained within the destabilized identity that is part of the narrative play in comedian-centered comedy. Thus, the comedian's persona may have been rendered as contradictory or even incoherent. In attempting to forge a unified identity for these performers that satisfied the perceived desires of the domestic broadcast audience, the network publicity offices and talent agencies had to assemble a narrative for the lives of the stars that assimilated the various, and often disjunctive, aspects of the comedians' sexuality and ethnicity. This was most often achieved through discourses on the "real-life" ethnic and familial pasts of vaudeo performers. Many of the men who were heralded as the first comedians to consolidate a regular viewing audience were fashioned as ethically (and ethnically) justified recipients of television fame. This meant that discourses on domesticity were constructed around these men that spoke to pertinent social concerns and memories that were circulating in the postwar culture.

Discourses that served to remind viewers of the ethnic and immigrant makeup of the urban areas from which performers came were particularly important elements in positioning the domestic histories of the typical vaudeo star. However, the very ethnic identities and working-class origins of these vaudeo stars that were comforting reminders of America's immigrant past could also be deleterious elements of their personas in the years immediately following World War II. Therefore, few openly acknowledged their ethnicity—especially those who were Jewish—except for occasionally noting their birth name (i.e., that Eddie Cantor was born Edward Israel Iskowitz), the use of Yiddish words such as *tuchus* or *kishkas*, or, in the case of George Burns and Gracie Allen, acknowledging a "mixed" marriage. Instead, covert signs of ethnic identity were embedded in the representations of the performers' work and familial histories, their constructions of feminized masculinities, and their imbrication in urban values.

Barry Rubin asserts that in the immediate postwar era relatively few Jews living in the public eye would play openly on their backgrounds since "for most, the market's dictate did more than any prejudice to make it preferable not to seem too Jewish lest this cut one off from the best opportunities and widest audience."[13] Rubin remarks that, although comedy was dominated by Jews and Jewish humor, "the Jewish comedians, all products of Orthodox, Yiddish-speaking homes, retained none of these characteristics themselves." Instead, audiences could infer a performer's ethnic background through the stories told about his past as well as subtle inflections, gestures, and regional references.

Rubin notes that Americans in the fifties developed a fascination with Jewish culture since it represented difference in an era of extreme homogeneity. He quotes Robert Alter, who wrote frequently on Jewish identity, as saying that it was significant during this period that "the Jew has a special language, a unique system of gestures, a different kind of history which goes much further back than that of other Americans, a different cuisine, a kind of humor and irony that other Americans don't have, the colorfulness and pathos which other Americans aren't supposed to possess anymore."[14] These differences acted as nostalgic reminders of the diverse nationalities and cultures that had been assimilated into the country's urban culture during the waves of immigration in the nineteenth century.

Although the label of immigrant was not synonymous with a particular ethnicity, the influx of immigrant groups into poor and working-class neighborhoods of New York at the turn of the century led to the confluence of an individual's ethnic background with the urban space in which he or she was raised. For example, much of Burns's extratextual material mentioned his years growing up as the child of immigrants on New York's Lower East Side. Although not every resident of this area was of Jewish extraction, it was historically known by East Coast Americans as a largely Jewish enclave: a first stop for Eastern European Jews in their initiation into U.S. culture. Thus, the performance and speaking style George Burns acquired from the Lower East Side were clues to his ethnic and religious background.

Sid Caesar gave similar clues to his background. Karen Adair suggests that "though Caesar never made a point of his Jewishness while performing, nevertheless it did emerge in some of his inflections and phrasings, such as 'Darts, they're playing.' The almost Talmudic lament of 'It'll be a miracle!' is the sort of thing Jewish mothers wail when their kids are growing up."[15]

Henry Jenkins's study of Cantor's film persona reveals the ways in which the comedian's Jewishness was assimilated into general connotations of urbanity in the late twenties and early thirties as a way to appeal to film audiences in regions outside East Coast urban centers.[16] As a result, Cantor (who had made much of his Jewishness in publicity materials early in his career) was forced to avoid direct references to his ethnicity and instead allowed his persona to retain only "subtle textual traces of his Jewishness, all but invisible to regional viewers, yet potentially meaningful to minority audiences."[17] What happened to Cantor during the late twenties and early thirties is similar to the management of the vaudeo persona that occurred twenty years later. Although early vaudeo stars were playing to largely urban audiences who would recognize ethnic tropes and allusions, performers such as Burns, Berle, Benny, and Caesar allowed tales of their origins and urban sensibilities to speak softly for their Jewish heritage, so as not to offend rural and suburban viewers,[18] even though, as Jewish historian Arthur Hertzberg reminds us, Jews themselves were becoming a part of suburban postwar life and entering into a period of rather intense assimilation.[19]

The portrayal of stars' domestic lives was an essential extratextual element of the production of star personas during this period. It was particularly important for television stars, as the industry was trying to construct television as a family-friendly entity that rightfully belonged in the center of American home life. Although the popular press often initially portrayed the married vaudeo male as the head of his own happy family, this narrative often had to be rewritten in light of domestic discontent. Benny and Burns, both well known in the broadcasting industry from their success on radio, were easy to portray as family men since both worked closely with their wives and adopted children during their broadcasting careers. Berle also adopted a daughter during his tenure as "Uncle Miltie," but his role as fifties patriarch was tainted by marital problems. In early 1950, *Redbook* reported that "the domestication of Milton Berle has proved a challenge even to the persuasive resources of his wife, a former showgirl billed as 'Joyce Matthews, the prettiest girl in America.' There have been troubled moments in the union, including a divorce."[20] After divorcing Berle for the second time, in 1952 Matthews attempted suicide in the apartment of her married lover, theatrical producer Billy Rose.

In light of the threat such scandals posed to the stars' credibility as "happy family men," it was far more advantageous for publicity agents to emphasize the performers' extended families over their nuclear ones. Vaudeville was a handy tool in this process because it provided the appropriate backdrop for the typical American success story. Moreover, cultural memories of the massive influx of immigrants arriving in the U.S. in the early 1900s were potentially stimulated by the move of more than one million Americans from cities to suburbs during the postwar era. Douglas Gomery elucidates the connection between these two significant demographic shifts:

> To appreciate the scope of this internal migration compare it to the more famous transatlantic movement from Europe to the United States around the turn of the century. In 1907, when migration was at its peak, more than one million Europeans landed in the United States. This was precisely the magnitude of the suburban migration of the late 1940s and early 1950s.[21]

The press often described vaudeo performers as having successfully renegotiated their working-class positions through hard work, humor, and a kind of ethnic pluck. They were providers who enabled their often large families to escape the poverty of urban immigrant neighborhoods. Berle, Burns, and Caesar, all child vaudeville stars raised in poor Jewish neighborhoods, were quick to describe how their families had been integral to their success in the theater. They variously worked with their siblings, were pushed by their strong-willed mothers, or were inspired by the wish to provide for their large working-class clans. Many told stories of how they resisted the Old World traditions of their immigrant parents in order to better succeed in American society. Burns related his ambivalence toward the religious voracity of his cantor father, and Benny repeatedly told how his father hit him in the head with a prayer book as punishment for arriving late to Yom Kippur services.[22] Rubin argues that

> the contrast between unpleasant Jewish childhoods and high American aspirations characterized the life of most Jews growing up between the 1890s and 1930s . . . powerful emotional force pushed them toward success in American society and away from Jewish identity. But equally ashamed of abandoning it, they often retained a strong sentimental attachment for that background.[23]

Berle, whose mother, Sandra, regularly appeared in his television act, had been discovered at the age of five when he won five dollars in a Bronx talent contest for mimicking Charlie Chaplin. His early years as a child actor in vaudeville and in silent film were often portrayed in the popular press as a struggle to keep his Harlem-based family together. Describing his father as ineffectual in supporting his family, Berle often told stories of his mother's undying support for his career and of how he helped his financially strapped family. Sandra was a constant presence in Berle's life and performances and acted as a continuing reminder to the public of his troubled beginnings and of his unending mother-love.

On television, Uncle Miltie was also cleverly crafted as a family entertainer, not only through his relationship with his mother (who was often in the studio audience) but also through his implied relationship with viewing families. He always had special goodnight greetings for the children in the audience and did television specials and benefits for children. In one such special, *Uncle Miltie's Christmas Party* (1950, NBC), water, powder, and pies were thrown in Berle's face. Although this was a rather common vaudeville joke, it also allowed Berle's masculinity to be subjugated, helping to make him everybody's favorite uncle: a nonsexual, nonthreatening member of the family.

Vaudeo stars also emphasized their personal relationships with one another, which were often described as close-knit kinships. Countless articles in the popular press told of dinner parties, card games, and golf rounds attended by vaudeo stars and their nuclear families. These events were not understood as business-related but as gatherings of close friends. Furthermore, they were described with the reverence and fervor usually reserved for blood ties.

Jack Benny was portrayed as the center of this off-hours social group, acting as host and introducing many of its key players. Danny Kaye, Fred Allen, and Cantor were all regular visitors to the Benny household, but it was Burns and Allen who were Benny and his wife's closest friends. After Benny's wife, Mary Livingston, introduced Allen to Burns, the foursome became virtually inseparable. Many of the articles that were supposed to be about one of the comic couples mentioned the other, describing Livingston and Allen's shopping trips or Burns and Benny's constant attempts to make each other laugh. Although it was said that Burns made Benny laugh the hardest of any of his comedian friends, Burns told *Cosmopolitan* that "because Benny is such a great audience, in fact that greatest audience, he has everybody in the business working for him. I know lots of comics would rather do an hour's entertainment for Jack, in Jack's living room, than play a week in a big theater in New York."[24] Even Benny's marriage connected him to another comic family, since Livingston (née Sadie Marks) was related to film comedian Zeppo Marx. Close bonds among vaudeo stars were privileged in these stars' promotional campaigns and served to reassert the stars' affiliations with extended familial networks.[25]

References to vaudeo performers' extended families and their ethnic working-class upbringings resonated with the pasts of many urban television viewers. But such allusions may also have stimulated sentimental memories of extended familial structures (which were now threatened by encroaching suburbanization) as well as earlier ethnic politics and processes of assimilation occurring during the twenties and thirties. In the years immediately following World War II, the vaudeville aesthetic reminded white Americans of a time when ethnic politics appeared, in retrospect, to be comparatively uncomplicated. Revelations of the Holocaust and fears associated with the Cold War came to weigh heavily on the minds of many Americans in the years following the war. (In retrospect, the turn-of-the-century waves of immigrants, which brought significant numbers of European Jews to the U.S., experienced a relatively smooth assimilation.) In addition, the State of Israel was proclaimed in May 1948 as a safe haven for Jews. In light of the discourses on the Holocaust, the television vaudevillian, largely understood as "ethnic" and most often Jewish, was a comforting sight to many Americans who had only recently learned of Nazi Germany's attempt to exterminate the Jewish people. Henry Popkin, who complained bit-

terly about the lack of Jewish characters or performers in film during the immediate postwar period, wrote in a 1952 edition of the conservative magazine
Commentary:

> Whatever may happen in the future, one fact is encouraging; in television, as
> in radio during its heyday, there prevails what might be called the New York
> idea, that Jewishness is not freakish or embarrassing and there might as well
> be Jewish comedians as any other kind. Hence one finds the sort of Jewish
> reference, whether comic or not, that stands in refreshing contrast to the rest
> of our antiseptically "Aryanized" popular culture: a Yiddish phrase spoken, a
> Jewish dialect or intonation, an identifiably Jewish ironic quality. All of this
> expresses no attitude, breaks no lances against anti-Semitism; it only recog-
> nizes one fact of experience: that Jews do exist.[26]

Despite the fact that subtle references to ethnicity may have been comforting to urban and Jewish viewers of early television, Jewish performers were
in many ways suspicious figures in American culture during the late forties and
early fifties. The implementation of the broadcasting blacklist after the publication in 1948 of *Red Channels: A Report on Communism in Broadcasting*
revealed that many Jewish performers were unfairly targeted as Communists
because of their ethnic heritage. For some, the Rosenberg trial in 1952 was
the pinnacle of the rhetorical confluence of anti-Semitism and anti-commu-
nism. Some Jewish organizations and leaders tried to distance themselves from
the stain of communism by engaging in a bit of red-baiting themselves:

> For American Jews, the Rosenberg case became a major test of loyalty. For
> anti-Communists, who had grown more strident since 1948, it meant disso-
> ciation with Jewish Communists and denial that the Rosenberg case had any-
> thing to do with anti-Semitism. Most Jews ran for cover during the Rosen-
> bergs' trial, feeling not only that it was a major test of their loyalty but also
> that it might be turned into an orgy of anti-Semitism. At the deepest levels,
> I suspect, it triggered all sorts of reactions associated with the Holocaust fears
> that had never been acknowledged or dealt with.[27]

A rather direct coupling of the Rosenberg case with the commercial image
of Benny was even united through the infamous Jell-O box that Julius Rosenberg supposedly used as a password in his covert transactions. In some accounts,
upon exchange of the Jell-O box, either the phrase "Benny sent me" or "Benny
from New York sent me" was passed verbally between the two men.[28] Even
without this direct reference to Benny, most Americans would have automatically connected the gelatin product with the comedian. As Marjorie Garber
points out, "So closely did American audiences link Benny and Jell-O that in
a poll taken in 1973 of middle-aged listeners asked to name his radio sponsor,
most answered 'Jell-O,' although in fact Benny was subsequently sponsored
by Lucky Strike cigarettes for almost twice as long as he had been by Jell-O."[29]
Garber goes on to note that Benny's Jewishness was significant in the cultural
resonance of the Jell-O aspect of the Rosenberg trial, as was the product's
complicated relationship to Jewish law (i.e., the non-Kosher origins of gelatin
but its eventual kosher certification after manufacture).

Events such as the publication of *Red Channels* and the Rosenberg trial belie the complicated, and frequently treacherous, signifiers that often piggybacked on the codes of Jewishness. So, while Jewish ethnicity may have been essential in the revitalization of the vaudeville aesthetic and, subsequently, in the naturalization of the television medium as a legitimate form of cultural production, it was difficult to acknowledge a performer's Jewish ethnicity routinely or overtly. Instead, ethnicity was commonly moderated through the codes of urbanity and immigrant childhoods and family.

Yet another significant way to reference Jewishness obliquely was through the performance of masculinity. The male vaudeo star's multivalent sexuality had the potential to activate long-standing assumptions about the nature of his ethnic background.

Mobilizing Ethnicity by Troubling Masculinity

Although his on-screen comedy was based largely on wordplay, insulting jokes, and topical gags, Berle's costume acts were the most popular segments of *Texaco Star Theater*. The comedian was known for his female impersonations of, for example, Cleopatra, Carmen Miranda, and the opera star Dorothy Kristen (who was so insulted by his portrayal of her that she took him to court). As the *New York Times* wrote in a 1990 retrospective article, Berle "was a man who wasn't afraid of a dress and for four years he owned Saturday night."[30] Although crossdressing was a long-standing practice in vaudeville and was not often directly described in the press as being sexually transgressive, a 1951 article in *Sponsor* implied that sponsors and broadcasters were aware of such tensions:

> Some eyebrows in the trade are up more or less all the time at TV's tolerance of "swish" routines and impersonations. They think that's going too far, projecting a special brand of big city tenderloin into the family circle. Other observers are more relaxed about the "swish" stuff, think it will be interpreted as nothing more than a spoofing of sex characteristics.[31]

Berle's propensity for donning a dress would have been especially potent when considered in relation to his ethnicity since many theorists have argued that femininity has long been considered a concomitant feature of male Jewishness. Citing examples from the early church to Nazi propaganda films, Garber notes that "not only sartorially, but also scientifically and theoretically, the idea of the Jewish man as 'effeminate' as well as 'degenerate' has a long and unlovely history in European culture."[32] The characteristics that seemed to set Jewish men (particularly those of the Hasidic sect) apart—the way they spoke, dressed, gestured—were regarded by many gentiles as not only foreign but "woman-like."

Daniel Boyarin, in his detailed analysis of Jewish masculinity, suggests that the European conception of the Jewish man as half man, half woman was asserted by the Jewish culture itself. It is a reaction to the marginalization of the culture, since "Jewish society needed an image against which to define itself and produced the 'goy'—the hypermale—as its countertype, as a reverse of its social norm."[33] Boyarin goes on to suggest that this alternative gender typing is a historical strategy for cultural survival: instead of imitating their oppressors, Jewish men embraced the antithesis of Anglo "hyper-masculinity."[34] Although Boyarin never specifically mentions any of the vaudevillians who worked on television, Garber ultimately finds Berle's form of cross-dressing a strategy that reasserted feminization of the Jewish man. She claims his drag impersonations were a "prerogative" of power because he chose to cross-dress and, in doing so, he directly confronted the stigmatization of the Jewish man as feminine. Garber writes that "for a Borscht Belt comedian like Milton Berle, whose routines so often included a drag act, to cross-dress for success, recuperating, however unconsciously, this 'feminization' of the Jewish man, and deploying gender parody is an empowering strategy."[35]

Beyond referencing the feminization of Jewish masculinity, another determinant of Berle's "feminization" was his relationship with his mother. His publicity material, which focused primarily on his childhood performances as a working-class Harlem native, repeatedly emphasized his overbearing yet loving Jewish mother. In an article entitled "My Son, Uncle Miltie," published in the *L.A. Examiner* on Mother's Day 1952, Sandra Berle writes: "As for a good many years, wherever he went I did go, getting the bookings, fighting the would-be managers and agents and talent developers, cooking over a can of Sterno in hotel rooms for the both of us, living out of a trunk. Those were the hard days, and then came the good ones, all these good ones."[36]

Berle's attachment to his mother managed to domesticate him, to connect him with family life, yet, at the same time, it demasculinized him further, even if his attachment was couched in the comforting discourse of immigrant culture. The brashness and sexual innuendoes of Berle's live performances were tamed, and the long-standing stereotype about Jewish mothers and their sons was clearly reinforced for the television audience. Berle told Gladys Hall, a writer for *Radio/TV Mirror,* that he always included Sandra in his life and performances because of all she did for him during his childhood: "Some forget, when they grow up what their mothers did for them and gave to them. I don't forget. I remember . . . all the sacrifices she made for me and the things she went without so that I could succeed. I don't think there is ever enough that you can do for your mother. Ever."[37] In a 1989 interview, Berle expressed concern over his feminized image. When asked why he had so many extramarital affairs, Berle responded by saying, "Maybe I had to prove my manhood to the outside world that always saw me with my mother and wearing dresses in my act. Is she his 'beard'? Is he gay? Maybe that's why I played around so much."[38]

Jack Benny, whose vanity, posture, and gestures could have been construed as feminine, was a tamer version of the Jewish male comic and much slower to appear on television. Unlike Berle, Benny often avoided the use of the puns and slapstick moves of traditional vaudeville routines, choosing instead to place his radio and television narratives within a situational context. However, Benny's use of the cheapskate stereotype, his violin playing, and his reliance on self-disparaging humor were definite components of both his vaudeville performances and his ethnic background. According to Hilmes and Margaret

McFadden, Benny's feminization originated in his radio program. Hilmes writes:

> Jack comically violated all the norms of American masculinity. Obviously wealthy but unable to spend money, thinking himself the pinnacle of masculine attractiveness but unable to interest women, suave and debonair but unable to handle simple situations, the authoritative host of a major radio program but unable to command the respect of his employees (and, later, a white man totally dependent on his black servant, a relationship with strangely homoerotic implications).[39]

McFadden argues that the construction of Jack and Rochester as an interracial couple is undermined by both characters' pursuance of women within the text of the TV program. She argues, therefore, that the subversive potential of their relation is contained, as "their aggressive heterosexuality, like that of the other men in the cast, obscures their all-male family and thus makes it acceptable. Further, this ambiguity allows the construction of a family where certain non-threatening women and some feminine qualities in men are permitted, but where no culturally idealized wives and mothers intrude."[40] Denise Mann contends, however, that Benny's "aggressive heterosexuality" in relation to the female film stars that appeared on his show actually feminized him further, at least momentarily, by placing him in the role of ogling fan.[41]

Still, Benny had little trouble fitting within mainstream America's conception of a domestic entertainer. This was, in part, the result of a consistent publicity campaign that depicted him as a benevolent family man. Benny's stage persona as a curmudgeonly, vain penny pincher was disavowed in numerous press releases and publications about his real life during the late forties and early fifties. Unlike the publicity surrounding other vaudeo stars of the period that worked to conflate a performer's on-screen personality with that of his off-screen identity, articles and press releases about Benny often denied any direct connection between his two identities. This may be because the situational narrative of *The Jack Benny Program,* unlike the shows featuring Berle and Caesar, required Benny to remain in one character during the entire broadcast. And, although the Benny character could be endearing at times, he could also be quite despicable. To prevent broadcast audiences from believing that Benny was really as vain and cheap as his on-screen character, Benny and his publicists carefully managed to retain the most positive aspects of Benny's broadcast persona while denying the "reality" of the most offensive aspects of that image. Stories about his rise to fame as a child violinist, as well as about his generosity and his role as a dedicated family man and loyal friend, were circulated as means to this end. In a 1944 article in *American Magazine,* Benny's radio personality was suggested to be a great psychic burden to the "real" Benny. Jerome Beatty writes: "If you or I made $10,000 every Sunday we wouldn't care if the world thought we were Jo-Jo, the dog-faced boy. But Jack Benny, at 50, takes life and public opinion as seriously as a candidate for the U.S. Senate and spends most of his spare time chasing his shadow, trying to stamp it out."[42]

In a 1949 CBS press release, Mary Livingston claimed, "Jack has his own hair and teeth, is not anemic, is in perfect physical condition, can play a pretty good violin and in my opinion, and in the opinion of almost everyone who really knows him, is the greatest guy in the world."[43] In addition, Benny often played with the constructed nature of his broadcast character and public image. For example, a 1951 layout of Benny and his family in *Look* parodied the supposed "real-life" publicity photos that Hollywood stars typically had taken of them in staged domestic settings. Stanley Gordon writes facetiously in the introduction that "from now on, Benny intends to be photographed like the Hollywood stars in movie magazines—in cozy family scenes to warm the hearts of his many fans, pictures to show that the Bennys are, after all, 'just plain folks.' "[44] Jack, daughter Joan, and Mary are in the accompanying photos of them doing the dishes, working on Joan's homework, cleaning the car, singing at the piano. A caption for a shot of Jack hanging laundry on the line reads, "The domestic type: Jack hangs out a few things in the laundry yard (A full-time laundress is really the one who does the family wash daily.)" Another caption, accompanying an image of Jack, Mary, and Joan sitting around the piano singing and playing the violin, reads "After dinner, the Bennys always gather round the piano for a musicale. (In fact, Jack keeps violin in bathroom, plays only on his CBS program.)"

By pointing out the media fabrication of stars and their home lives through these joking asides, Benny destabilized the authenticity of his fictional persona. In so doing, he was able to pick and choose which characteristics he wished to emphasize and which he would deemphasize. He could remain the vain fall guy on screen or in radio, but he was also able to claim that he was still "authentic" in the way that the public would value (i.e., he was trustworthy, caring, and generous), thereby making him an acceptable role model and product pitchman.

Although the assumptions of Jewishness and a peculiarly feminized masculinity mobilized around Benny continued to make him popular throughout his career, they were also denied, perhaps in an effort to bolster his fiscal and social standing in the 1950s. By recreating an image of the hard-working, generous, and often guilt-ridden Benny, the home viewing audience could be more comfortable with his extraordinarily glamorous lifestyle—and, specifically, with his much-publicized post–talent raid salary. But even the revised Benny, although now in recoil from some of the more long-standing Jewish stereotypes of his earlier persona, was still entrenched in the mythic struggle of a working-class boy made good. This struggle, as I have shown, was firmly imbricated with nostalgia for the immigrant and extended family and for domestication of the vaudeville aesthetic.

Conclusion

The form of ethnic (read Jewish) masculinity that helped shape the careers and personas of early-television comedians had a limited utility in the subsequent development of the medium's industrial and cultural operations. For a brief period, coinciding with the years of the Federal Communication Commission's freeze on licenses, performances by men who cultivated a flexible yet historically defined and culturally determined gender identity dominated television. The industry was able both to exploit and to counter the signs of an alternative form of masculinity during its campaign to enter the American home by mobilizing the cultural memory of an audience unsettled by recent social upheavals and the breakup of the extended family.

By the mid-1950s, the variety show was clearly in decline. As many television historians have noted, this was due, at least in part, to the lifting of the FCC's freeze on licenses and the changing demographics of the television audience. No longer primarily urban and as ethnically mixed, the audience was now increasingly middle class and lived in rural as well as suburban areas. The cultural references made by Jewish vaudeville comedians ceased to be familiar to a large part of the audience.

Furthermore, as Lynn Spigel argues, during the early 1950s when government officials were focusing much of their attention on television content, vaudeo bore the brunt of the censorship debates.[45] Concerned about the bawdy antics, ethnic jokes, and sexual asides of vaudeo comedians, these politicians pointed to the format's New York sensibility as the root source of its offensiveness.[46] In *Television Program Production,* Carroll O'Meara contends that

> What many entertainers fail to realize, actually, is that the areas containing the bistros, night spots, and bright lights are only a segment of America. And yet, somehow, they insist on broadcasting to the entire nation comic and other material which is definitely not acceptable in the average American home. . . . Our nation consists of 160 million citizens, most of whom live in small towns, go to church on Sunday, attempt to bring up their children decently, and do not regard burlesque as the ultimate in theater.[47]

The public calls for censorship by public officials and cultural critics made sponsors nervous. Out of fear of losing their consumer base, they were forced to reconsider many of the basic tenets of vaudeo humor. A 1951 article in *Sponsor* claimed that television carried with it a greater risk of offending viewers than radio or film and recommended that sponsors censor problematic program content:

> Advertisers are by now pretty well briefed, or they ought to be, as to the everyday hazards lurking in racial jokes, dialects, characterizations, and superiority-inferiority situations. The pictorial factor in TV increases the danger. . . . So long as the sponsor's goal is universal good will for his products and services he cannot indulge in heavy-handed kidding and race-trait burlesque and then is surprised if Italians or Mexicans, or Irish, or Jews pass him by at the retail firing line.[48]

The ethnic and brash urban personalities that made vaudeo such a success in the late 1940s were now considered inappropriate for the increasingly national, middle-class audience. As a result, critics and politicians singled out the vaudeo star as an example of the tastelessness of network broadcasting. Many vaudeo producers responded by altering the structure and sensibility of their programs by introducing sitcoms, erasing ethnic references, and making their programs more family-friendly overall. However, these changes would not ultimately save the vaudeo comedians who built early television. By 1953, Dick Powell, president of the Television Writers of America, was claiming that the "death of video comedy stars is being caused by censorship. . . . If Will Rogers were alive today, he would probably go back to rope-twirling."[49]

During the early 1950s, the television industry was also forced to appease audiences and critics who were becoming bored with vaudeo performers and sponsors who had tired of paying their exorbitant salaries. Consequently, the frequent and forceful cries of sponsors and trade critics for new faces and formats had a significant impact on the industry's eventual embrace of the sitcom. More concerned with the repetitious nature of vaudeo than with its inability to resonate culturally outside the East Coast, some sponsors and critics expressed concern as early as 1950 about the long-term viability of the vaudeville performance style and the age of its television headliners. Sponsors were also deeply worried about the financial implications of what *Variety* dubbed the "New Talent Crisis," a period in the early 1950s when the industry, feeling the strain of its prior disregard for talent development, allowed vaudeo star salaries to skyrocket and dramatically increase the overall production costs of the variety format. As a result, the sitcom, with its emphasis on narrative and its reliance on a regular cast (rather than expensive, high-profile guest stars), looked like an economically viable venture for sponsors and independent producers alike, especially since successful examples were already on the air.

Although traces of the vaudeville tradition were still present in television comedy, plot-driven, "realistic," suburban sitcoms dominated network program schedules by the late 1950s and early 1960s. This format offered viewers a new vision of domesticity, identity, and consumer culture that differed dramatically from that of early variety shows and ethnic sitcoms. George Lipsitz suggests that "for Americans to accept the new world of fifties consumerism, they had to make a break with the past."[50] In the case of television, the industry and its audience were ready to break with vaudeo, as the format's references to prior traditions of ethnic masculinity and immigrant life were no longer culturally relevant to viewers now eager to embrace the "good life" promised in suburbia.

Notes

I am indebted to Janet Staiger for her suggestions and support for this article from its very inception and to Janet Thumim, who was instrumental in refining the most recent versions of this article.

1. Joseph Epstein, "Have You Heard the One about the Jewish Comic," *Wall Street Journal*, April 1, 2002, A12, and David Zurawik, "Mr. Television," *Baltimore Sun*, March 29, 2002, 1E.

2. Franklin Foer, "Kaddish for Uncle Miltie, Television's No. 1 Jew," Salon.com, posted March 28, 2002.

3. Frank Wertheim, "The Rise of Milton Berle," in John O'Connor, ed., *American History/American Television*, (New York: Fredrick Ungar, 1983), 56.

4. Judith Butler, *Gender Trouble: Feminism and the Subversion of Identity* (New York: Routledge, 1992), 136.

5. It was reported in 1949 that Berle was born on W. 118th Street. Robert Sylvester, "The Strange Career of Milton Berle," *Saturday Evening Post*, March 19, 1949, 38.

6. Douglas Gilbert, *American Vaudeville: Its Life and Times* (New York: Dover, 1940), 287.

7. Michele Hilmes, *Radio Voices: American Broadcasting, 1922–1952* (Minneapolis: University of Minnesota Press, 1997), 89.

8. Richard Dyer, "*A Star Is Born* and the Construction of Authenticity," in Christine Gledhill, ed., *Stardom: Industry of Desire* (New York: Routledge, 1991), 132–40.

9. Steven Seidman, *Comedian Comedy: A Tradition in Hollywood Film* (Ann Arbor: UMI Research Press), 1981.

10. Frank Krutnik, "A Spanner in the Works? Genre, Narrative, and the Hollywood Comedian," in Kristine Brunovska Karnick and Henry Jenkins, eds., *Classical Hollywood Comedy* (New York: Routledge, 1995), 29, 36.

11. Berle was quoted as saying, "Some people say I'm in the show too much and some people say I'm not in it enough. They accuse me of interrupting the acts but there's a difference between interruption and integration. . . . To come from left field and interrupt an act without any thought given to how it will look would be dangerous. If there isn't any actual reason to come into the act, I assure you I will never do it. "How Milton Berle Got into Television," *L.A. Examiner*, April 29, 1951, 21.

12. Although borrowing from film theory to elucidate television can be a questionable endeavor, the interpenetration of performance styles and narrative strategies in and among television, radio, film, and vaudeville during this period warrants close comparisons. Part of the difficulty in studying early-television comedy is the lack of research on the genre with regard to the specific characteristics of the medium. In future work, I plan to explore this area further.

13. Barry Rubin, *Assimilation and Its Discontents* (New York: Times Books, 1995), 98.

14. Ibid.

15. Karen Adair, *The Great Clowns of American Television* (Jefferson, N.C.: McFarland, 1988), 77.

16. Henry Jenkins, "Shall We Make It for New York or for Distribution?: Eddie Cantor, Whoopee, and Regional Resistance to the Talkies," *Cinema Journal 29*, no. 3 (spring 1990): 43.

17. Jenkins notes that "while the question of ethnic identity was a key concern within urban areas where the immigrant masses struggled to define their place in American society, and therefore a prime field for the construction of jokes, it did not prove as amusing in the hinterlands, which either found the question irrelevant or too threatening to provide much humor." Ibid., 46.

18. Even the relatively innocuous signs of urbanity caused problems for the entertainers as critics complained that their "big-city values" were offensive to small-town, middle-class viewers. References to performers' urban sensibilities were used in this context to connect their geographic origins negatively with the use of blue and ethnic humor and sexual innuendoes. Consequently, the same signs used to place a performer in a particular cultural milieu were also seemingly suspect to and potentially offensive to many television critics during this period. An argument could be made that there were anti-Semitic undertones to this conflation. Leslie Fiedler argues that "the discovery in the Jews of a people essentially urban, essentially Europe-oriented, a ready-made image for what the American longs to or fears he is being forced to become." Fiedler, "Saul Bellows," in Irving Maline, ed., *Saul Bellow and the Critics* (New York: New York University Press, 1967), 2–3.

19. Arthur Hertzberg, *The Jews in America—Four Centuries of an Uneasy Encounter: A History* (New York: Columbia University Press, 1986), 304–20.

20. Edwin H. James, "Anything for a Laugh!" *Redbook*, January 1950, 94–96, 100.

21. Douglas Gomery, *Shared Pleasures: A History of Movie Presentation in the United States* (Madison: University of Wisconsin Press, 1992), 85.

22. Rubin, *Assimilation and Its Discontents*, 68–69.

23. Ibid.

24. Maurice Zolotow, "The Fiddler from Waukegan," *Cosmopolitan*, October 1947, 138.

25. The Friar's Club can be seen as an extension of this narrative, albeit a more private one. Most of the preeminent vaudeo performers of the period were members and socialized regularly at its New York facilities.

26. Henry Popkin, "The Vanishing Jew of Our Popular Culture: The Little Man Who Is No Longer There," *Commentary*, October 1952, 50.

27. Morton Horowitz, "Jews and McCarthyism: A View from the Bronx," in Marjorie Garber and Rebecca L. Walkowitz, eds., *Secret Agents: The Rosenberg Case, McCarthyism, and Fifties America* (New York: Routledge, 1995), 262.

28. See Marjorie Garber, "Jell-O," in Garber and Walkowitz, *Secret Agents*, 11–21.

29. Ibid., 15.

30. Jeremy Gerard, "Milton Berle Browses at Home and the TV Audience Gets a Treat," *New York Times*, December 11, 1990, C15.

31. "Be Careful on the Air: On TV, the Risk of Offending Is Even Greater than on Radio or in the Movies," *Sponsor*, September 24, 1951, 36–37, 76–80.

32. Marjorie Garber, *Vested Interests: Cross-Dressing and Cultural Anxiety* (New York: Routledge, 1992), 224.

33. Daniel Boyarin, *Unheroic Conduct: The Rise of Heterosexuality and the Invention of the Jewish Man* (Berkeley: University of California Press, 1997), 4–5.

34. Robert Meeropol (the son of Ethel and Julius Rosenberg) contends that the government and the press feminized his father during the years of his incarceration, trial, and execution. He writes,

> The fonts of conventional wisdom also helped popularize the characterization of my mother as dominant and my father as submissive. Such a relationship was widely viewed as "unnatural" in the 1950s. Morris Ernst, co-counsel for the ACLU, first offered to represent my parents if they would confess, and then offered the FBI his analysis of the dynamic of my parents' relationship. Ernst, the amateur psychologist who had never met my parents, concluded that "Julius is the slave and his wife Ethel is the master."

Meeropol, "Rosenberg Realities," in Garber and Walkowitz, *Secret Agents*, 241–42.

35. Garber, *Vested Interests*, 233.

36. Sandra Berle, "My Son, Uncle Miltie," *L.A. Examiner*, May 19, 1952, 21.

37. Gladys Hall, "Everybody's Uncle Miltie," *Radio/TV Mirror*, June 1951, 80.

38. Dorothy Rader, "The Hard Life, the Strong Loves of a Very Funny Man," *Parade*, March 19, 1989, 6. Besides gossip about his extramarital affairs, there were many rumors about the very large size of Berle's penis. Perhaps this discourse can be interpreted as an attempt to assert a more conventional masculinity for Berle to thwart questions about his sexual preference.

39. Hilmes, *Radio Voices*, 194.

40. Margaret T. McFadden, "America's Boyfriend Who Can't Get a Date: Gender, Race, and the Cultural Work of *The Jack Benny Program*, 1932–1946," *Journal of American History* (June 1993): 126.

41. Denise Mann, "The Spectacularization of Everyday Life: Recycling Hollywood Stars and Fans in Early Television Variety Shows," in Lynn Spigel and Denise Mann, eds., *Private Screenings: Television and the Female Consumer* (Minneapolis: University of Minnesota Press, 1992), 41–70.

42. Jerome Beatty, "Unhappy Fiddler," *American Magazine,* December 1944, 28–29, 142–43.

43. Mary Livingston, "By His Own Doing, He's the 'Most Maligned Man in the World,' Says Mary Livingston of Husband Jack Benny," CBS press release, February 7, 1949, Publicity File, Jack Benny collection, UCLA Television Archive, Los Angeles.

44. Stanley Gordon, "The Rebellion of Jack Benny," *Look,* May 8, 1951.

45. In 1952, indecent content on television was just one concern of government officials: "At the moment five main areas offer continuing problems: (1) plugs that fail; (2) beer and wine commercials; (3) indecency; (4) racial stereotypes; (5) violence." Bert Briller, "TV Code Has Upped Necklines, but Long Plugs, Beer Blurbs, Violence, Race Carbons Still Pose Problems," *Variety,* December 31, 1952, 20, 27. Also see Lynn Spigel, *Make Room for TV: Television and the Family Ideal in Postwar America* (Chicago: University of Chicago Press, 1992), 147–49.

46. New York–produced live anthology dramas were also thought to appeal to only "urban tastes." For more on this, see William Boddy, *Fifties Television: The Industry and Its Critics* (Chicago: University of Illinois Press, 1993), 93–107.

47. Carroll O'Meara, *Television Program Production* (New York: Ronald Press, 1955), 14–16.

48. "Be Careful on the Air," 36–37, 76–80.

49. "Low State of Comedy Blamed on Censorship, Pressure Groups," *Variety,* February 25, 1953, 1.

50. George Lipsitz, "The Meaning of Memory: Family, Class, and Ethnicity in Early Network Television Programs," in Spigel and Mann, *Private Screenings,* 75.

Identity, Power, and Local Television
African Americans, Organized Labor, and UHF-TV in Chicago, 1962–1968

Nathan Godfried

"The Negro as a normal human being doesn't exist in the programming eye of the local Chicago television stations." So noted John H. Sengstacke, editor and publisher of the African-American newspaper the *Chicago Daily Defender*, at public hearings held by the Federal Communications Commission (FCC) in March 1962.[1] Testifying before a meeting of the House Committee on Education and Labor in New York City 7 months later, Diahann Carroll, Godfrey Cambridge, and other African-American actors and entertainers described a continuing, pervasive, and calculated discrimination against blacks in television and radio. Singer and actress Abbey Lincoln commented that "it is as if the Negro performer were invisible; more than that, as if the black man as part of the society in this country, does not exist."[2] Television comedy and dramatic series, like Hollywood movies before them, placed African Americans in only limited and highly stereotyped roles and situations. Television thus "continued to reinforce white racist ideas, while further destroying a meaningful self-image" for African Americans.[3]

Studies of television programming conducted during the 1950s and 1960s revealed a similar neglect and distorted representation of working-class Americans and their labor unions. Although working-class characters appeared in only a small percentage of television programs, concluded a 1956 investigation, "the gross tendency of these portrayals is mainly to convey negative images, of working-class individuals."[4] Subsequent studies found that television generally "avoided any realistic presentation of work, workers, and workers' organizations."[5] While recognizing these image problems, organized labor leaders also feared the political and economic repercussions of corporate control over television. In 1963, for example, officials of the American Federation of Labor-Congress of Industrial Organizations (AFL-CIO) complained that television and other mass media remained "for the most part in the hands of

Nathan Godfried, "Identity, Power, and Local Television: African Americans, Organized Labor, and UHF-TV in Chicago, 1962–1968." From *Historical Journal of Film, Radio, and Television*, Vol. 22, No. 2 (2002), pp. 117–134. Reprinted by permission of Routledge/Taylor & Francis Ltd. (http://www.tandf.co.uk/journals).

people who are antagonistic to organized labor and create an atmosphere in which it is difficult to conduct responsible collective bargaining."[6]

Faced with the established television industry's power to define and thereby obfuscate or pervert their social, political, and economic goals and even their own identities, African-American community and organized labor leaders sought greater access to and participation in the mass medium. Engaged in an intensified quest for economic, political, and social justice during the late 1950s and 1960s, African Americans in particular challenged the mass media's stereotyped and sometimes malignant image of themselves. They demanded that the world of white television fully utilize the available talented black actors, writers, directors, and technicians. As they pursued integration into the national television system, many African-American activists also urged the establishment of black-oriented television programming, especially at the local level. Such programming might enlighten whites and blacks about the battle for social change; increase employment opportunities for minority artists; and, in general, enhance the black community's own political, psychological, and cultural consciousness, unity, and power.

Efforts to create such programming, however, raised political and social questions within the African-American community and the larger society. The National Association for the Advancement of Colored People (NAACP), for example, demanded an end to racial discrimination in the television industry, but feared that black-oriented television would exacerbate divisions among Americans. Although leaders of the AFL-CIO understood the desire of subordinated groups to maintain access to the means of ideological and cultural production, they nonetheless worried that creating black-oriented programming would weaken the ideal of an integrated, harmonious social system that increasingly rested on a bourgeois consumer culture. This ideal also led them to favor television programming that cultivated organized labor's image as a good citizen.

This article explores these tensions over television's role in enhancing or undermining a group's power and sense of self by describing and analyzing the competition over an ultra-high frequency (UHF) television outlet in Chicago during the 1960s. UHF-TV Channel 38 became the prize in a contest between the Chicagoland TV Company and the Chicago Federation of Labor (CFL). The owners of Chicagoland, as well as its supporters among local civil rights activists, wanted a station that would program primarily for the city's African-American community. Leaders of the CFL sought a television outlet that would, among other things, highlight the organized labor movement's contributions to the general welfare and public interest. Although the end result was that neither organization made use of Channel 38, the debate between the two reveals much about how African-American community activists and conservative trade union officials perceived a role for television in modern society.

Examining television's formation and growth within a local context fits Douglas Gomery's call to attend to "TV's historical development from the bottom up"—a modification of the classic mandate from social historians. Moving from the national to local scene fits radio and television history in part because the FCC, throughout most of the latter half of the 20th century, directed broadcasting stations to assess and serve the needs and interests of their local communities. As Michael Curtin and other historians have explained, however, ascertaining the local public interest remained highly problematic because the majority of the nation's television stations were located in urban centers with large populations that frequently divided along some combination of ethnic, racial, class, or religious allegiances. In Chicago, the respective groups that coalesced behind the Chicagoland and CFL television applications represented different constituencies and held conflicting definitions of the local community needs. Reviewing the CFL-Chicagoland battle thus helps us to examine, as Curtin has argued in a related context, "the complex historical interactions among different groups and forces." in American society as well as the perceived role of television in such interactions.[7]

African-American communities throughout the United States recognized and criticized the political and racial biases of television networks and stations during the 1950s and 1960s. Although black entertainers played a significant role in the medium's first years, especially in variety-show formats, national television of the 1950s presented the same racist stereotypes of African Americans that had dominated radio and film. Even as civil rights protests commanded the attention of the national press in the early 1960s, "blacks had not really 'arrived' in TV."[8] Sampling the programming of the New York City affiliates of the National Broadcasting Company (NBC), the Columbia Broadcasting System (CBS), and the American Broadcasting Company (ABC) for 2 weeks in April 1962, researchers from the City College of New York found that "if one viewed television for 5 hours on any channel at any time on any day, he would see two Negroes, one for less than 3 minutes and one for more than 3 minutes." Investigators discovered that in the vast majority of their television appearances, blacks either performed as musicians, singers, or dancers, or played the role of domestics in dramatic or comedy series, or participated in sporting events. African Americans rarely acted in daytime serials or appeared in children's shows.[9] Media scholar Marilyn Fife has explained that the television industry's "inexcusably poor record for minority hiring" and its ignoring or under-reporting of "issues of pertinence to black communities" reinforced "the 'invisible man' tendency of American culture." Television neither valued nor recognized nonwhite communities.[10]

In Chicago leaders of black community groups and institutions faulted local television stations and their news and entertainment shows for neglecting the complex problems of segregation and discrimination and for excluding African-American workers from program development and production. Television editorials dealing with race relations became a particularly heated site of controversy by the early 1960s. In 1961 WBBM-TV, the CBS-owned and operated affiliate, supported the reappointment of the controversial superintendent of the Chicago public school system. Echoing the city's political hierarchy, WBBM dismissed the substance of civil rights protests against the schools and labeled the protestors as disciplinary problems. The Reverend Carl A.

Fuqua, executive director of the Chicago branch of the NAACP, criticized the station's failure to address the crisis of racial segregation in the schools.[11] The next year the *Chicago Defender* declared John Madigan, WBBM's editorial writer and spokesman, intellectually bankrupt for siding with "die-hard segregationists" and denying that the city's public schools were dangerously segregated.[12] Chicago's black community increasingly saw local television as part of the city's discriminatory infrastructure and as defender of the racial status quo.

A handful of people addressed race issues during FCC-sponsored hearings on local television in the spring of 1962. Fuqua deplored the myopia of local stations as they excluded "any substantial programming that deals with . . . the problems of interracial adjustment and understanding." While commending some local programs for their efforts at integration, *Chicago Defender* publisher Sengstacke regretted that these shows aired after midnight. He complained that local stations elided any comprehensive examination of segregation. Aside from news shows, African Americans were "almost nonexistent in local TV. But even on the newscasts, the reporting of Negro activities is almost always confined to the sensational or criminal story." Sengstacke emphasized that television needed to portray blacks realistically as clerks, bricklayers, teachers, doctors, and athletes and to incorporate them as both secondary and major participants in the programming.[13]

By 1963 the NAACP and other national organizations had condemned broadcasters and advertisers for their "pitiful" effort at "even token hiring." They demanded that Hollywood producers and unions address employment discrimination in television and films. But attentive observers still would have been hard-pressed to "find a Negro face" at the 1963 meeting of the National Association of Broadcasters in Chicago. The television industry as a whole continued to perpetuate "a picture of a lily-white America."[14] With national networks reluctant to integrate black workers and themes into television shows, some community activists and entrepreneurs turned to independent, specialized stations that would cater to the black audience.

Commercial interest in developing specialized broadcasting for African Americans had first manifested itself in the rapid spread of "black appeal" radio stations during the 1950s. As the development of television preoccupied broadcasting networks in the late 1940s and early 1950s, "the radio industry's control over national programming, advertising, and listenership collapsed." Local radio stations sought more profitable uses for their wavelengths—that is, new audiences and sponsors—and considered programming for large demographic groups defined by age, ethnicity, race, or gender. In urban markets where African Americans constituted a significant percentage of the population, economics led some local radio stations to commit "their entire broadcast schedules to programming by and for African Americans."[15] This was particularly true in Chicago where the percentage of blacks living in the city increased from 9.3 to 23.6% of the total population between 1944 and 1960 and where the total number of black-oriented radio programs in the metropolitan area correspondingly exploded from 56 hours weekly in 1944 to more than 600 hours weekly in 1960. Black populations, incomes, products, and radio all grew simultaneously.[16]

The lure of profits motived radio entrepreneurs in selected areas to program for black audiences, but African Americans and the FCC embraced this development for other reasons. Black-appeal radio offered new job opportunities to unemployed or underemployed black radio workers and those aspiring to become broadcast technicians, disc jockeys, or journalists. African-American audiences welcomed these radio stations' efforts to address black economic, social, and political needs. In addition, as local disc jockey Norman Spaulding explained, Chicago's black-appeal radio became widely popular because it utilized "the cultural forms of music and language indigenous to its audience."[17]

For its part, the FCC recognized that minority groups might possess legitimate unique needs and interests that could be serviced best by broadcasting outlets with focused programming. In 1962, for example, the commission weighed the concerns of New York City's black population in deciding between two applicants for a new FM-radio license. Station WLIB-AM, which already concentrated its programming on the city's African Americans, proposed to develop a similar focus on the FM dial. Community leaders testified that cultural, social, and economic divisions within the city's black population notwithstanding, African Americans confronted common problems in housing, education, and employment. In addition, they needed educational and "cultural enrichment, information concerning nonwhite nations and cultures, and improved employment opportunities for Negro talent." Acknowledging that the competing applicants appeared "to be essentially equal" on such criteria as capital requirements and technical experience, the FCC granted the FM license to WLIB because it had "demonstrated substantial needs for Negro-oriented programming." This decision, in the words of the commission, served "the public interest, convenience, and necessity."[18]

The commercial forces and public policies that opened black access to a competitive local radio market offered some hope for the concentrated national television industry. By the end of the 1950s a handful of very high frequency (VHF) channels operated in major metropolitan areas. Those outlets, in general, fell under the control of the three national networks and powerful local businesses. In Chicago, for example, affiliates owned and operated by NBC, CBS, and ABC dominated the VHF market, with only two independent stations, WGN, a component of the *Chicago Tribune* media conglomerate, and WTTW, an educational broadcaster. Concentrated and centralized control of television programming alarmed some FCC officials who increasingly believed that local service was "the cornerstone of American broadcast regulation." Drawing on Section 307(b) of the 1934 Communications Act, the commission proclaimed in 1952 that "as many communities as possible should have the opportunity of enjoying the advantages from having local outlets that will be responsive to local needs."[19] In the aftermath of his "vast wasteland" speech in May 1961, FCC chairman Newton Minow urged viewers to voice their ideas and concerns about television at public hearings that he planned to hold at the community level.[20]

The first of these hearings, held in Chicago in March and April of 1962, aimed to assess the efforts of the VHF-TV stations to determine the local programming needs and interests of Chicago's residents and to produce local programming that effectively met those needs and interests. The hearings also promised to gauge the extent of public demand for additional or different types of local television programs.[21] As Christopher Anderson and Michael Curtin have argued, the hearings demonstrated the difficulty of defining local interests when the community encompassed a large population divided by class, race, ethnicity, gender, and religion. Chicago's white middle class—the presumed demographic, economic, and psychological core of the city—debated the merits of a national mass consumer culture versus those of an indigenous local culture. At the same time, "special interest" groups, including African Americans and broadcasting unions, attacked the established television industry for failing to develop diverse local programming that addressed Chicago's particular political, economic, and social problems. Local television's critics and the FCC, however, appeared unable to resolve "the question of how television stations might best account for the city's social diversity." The federal regulatory agency "settled for the stations' rationale, which was to identify the community interest with an essentially market-driven image of consensus, a knowable community of white, middle-class consumers."[22]

Nevertheless, a few government officials as well as observers of the Chicago television scene imagined another solution to the problem of homogenized network programming. *Chicago Sun-Times* reporter William Braden, for example, suggested that securing more independent, non-network stations, through the use of the ultra-high frequency spectrum, would expand and vary Chicago programming. Newton Minow could not agree more. As part of his effort to diversify television programming and to provide greater choice for American viewers, Minow sought to create a viable UHF broadcasting system. Responding to pressure from the FCC chairman, Congress ordered that television sets manufactured after January 1963 be equipped with UHF (channels 14–84) as well as VHF (channels 2–13) receivers. Interest in ultra-high frequency broadcasting subsequently increased as more sets could receive UHF signals and as the available UHF channels far outnumbered VHF ones. From 1964 to 1973, the FCC approved the addition of 111 UHF stations compared to only 47 VHF stations.[23]

Chicago's WCIU-TV, among other UHF-TV licensees, developed "special interest programming" as an alternative to the network fare of most VHF stations. Channel 26, the city's first UHF station, debuted on 6 February 1964 and quickly distinguished itself by airing entertainment and informational shows for Chicago's ethnic and racial minorities. A weekly variety show, *Grecian Panorama*, included, among other novelties, "the gyrating pelvises of veiled belly dancers," for the city's approximately 150,000 Greek Americans. The local Hispanic population could watch unedited Mexican bullfights "complete with bleeding bulls and trampled matadors" as well as a 50-episode adaptation of Charles Dickens's *Great Expectations* in Spanish. A regular showing of foreign-language films, newscasts in Polish and Spanish, polka shows, and programming for the city's Irish, Italian, German, and Swedish enclaves also filled WCIU's schedule. The station arranged for Fred Wall, general manager of the

African-American weekly newspaper the *Chicago Courier*, to produce a weekly discussion program for, by, and about Chicago's black community. WCIU president John Weigel also lined up reruns of *Amos 'n' Andy*, which the CBS network had produced for television in 1951–1953. While Weigel considered the series an "American Classic," many African Americans proclaimed the show "an affront to the Negro people" and organized a campaign to have the series removed from the air.[24] Such controversy did not diminish the possibility that programming for ethnic and racial minorities might prove profitable.

Market surveys suggested that African Americans purchased higher priced brands of food, clothing, and incidentals than white people and engaged in above average television viewing. "The social and moral problems involved in integration are intricate and solemn," concluded the trade journal *Broadcasting* in 1963, "by comparison the study of the Negro as a market is simple and encouraging."[25] That same year white-owned companies in Los Angeles and Washington, DC, each with experience in black-appeal radio, inaugurated UHF stations aimed at black audiences. Operated by news, engineering, and advertising staffs that were 75% African American, Washington, DC's WOOK-TV scheduled jazz with Oscar Brown, gospel music with Mahalia Jackson, *Teenarama Dance Party, Aunt Mary's Birthday Party* for young children, professional wrestling, movies, black night club acts, and a weekly charm school and other programming that catered to "the Negro drive for self improvement." WOOK's news and public affairs programs tended to "lean hard on civil rights developments."[26]

The new station had its detractors within the local African-American community. Some local leaders denounced the FCC for its willingness to license broadcasters who sought "to further segregate the air waves." Chuck Stone, editor of an area black newspaper, worried that the station's commercial impulses would lead to relatively escapist programming: "WOOK-TV will sell hair straightener to the Negro without facing up to the racial problem which makes the Negro want to buy hair straightener." Stone and others believed that the station "skirted the real problems" confronting African Americans, thus missing "an opportunity to contribute to the educational and cultural life of the Negro community." Richard Eaton, the owner of WOOK, admitted that the station avoided controversy, but insisted that it would provide opportunities for young African-American entertainers to develop their talents, discuss the problems of the black community, and "show interracial activities which are harmonious."[27] The debate that raged around WOOK-TV also came to characterize the battle over Channel 38 in Chicago.

Chicagoland TV Company formed in 1962 under the direction of Frederick B. Livingston and Thomas L. Davis. Both men, neither of whom was African American, had lived in the Chicago area for several decades, worked in radio and/or television, and actively participated in ethnic, racial, and civic organizations. Livingston, a public relations expert, had experience in advertising, the promotion of broadcasting stations, and television production. As organizer for the Back of the Yards Neighborhood Council's annual fair, Livingston became familiar with the city's numerous ethnic and racial minorities.

In addition to his responsibility to secure capital for the venture, Livingston's primary role in Chicagoland was to supervise overall public relations and advertising.[28] Tom Davis served as manager of Chicago radio station WAAF, although he had some financial and administrative interests in radio stations in Indiana and Iowa. From 1952, when he became station manager, Davis pursued the "high road" of putting WAAF into the African-American market by presenting programs that both black and white listeners would enjoy, that publicized African-American social and civic organizations, and that generally served "the Negro as . . . an integral part of the community." Norman Spaulding characterized WAAF's programming as "a marketing format for middle-class Blacks," while the station sales manager observed that it "featured more white-accepted Black artists" than other black-appeal stations. Davis, who was to serve as Chicagoland's general manager and sales manager, would administer and supervise the station's daily operations.[29]

Livingston and Davis discussed their broadcasting plans with African-American and ethnic community leaders in 1961 and 1962. Their original scheme included programming that utilized local talent to entertain and inform foreign nationality groups about the customs and history of their homelands. The bulk of the proposed station's schedule, however, aimed at meeting African Americans' desire for programs that presented "Negroes and white participants together," offered "a more favorable image of the Negro," afforded blacks greater opportunities to appear on television, and featured subjects of interest to the black community.[30] Chicagoland TV Company applied for Channel 38 in late October 1962. Other groups also filed for the UHF channel, but by 1965 only the CFL remained to challenge Chicagoland.

Officials of the CFL and its radio station WCFL-AM had a long-standing interest in television, declaring in the late 1940s that the new medium would prove "as essential for the protection of Labor's interests as Radio has been." WCFL applied for Chicago's VHF-TV Channel 11 in 1953, offering to turn over daytime hours to educational organizations while retaining the evenings for commercial broadcasting and whatever other purposes it wished to pursue. Although the FCC awarded Channel 11 to local educational groups in 1954, the CFL supported WTTW with free publicity and financial donations. CFL president William Lee served on WTTW's Board of Directors and considered the station "a vital institution in our community."[31] But the CFL maintained that it wanted a television station of its own. In the fall of 1964 as the deadline approached for filing an application for the last of the city's available UHF channels, Lee ordered employees of the CFL newspaper and WCFL to put together a program proposal, financial data, and a rationale for owning a television station. Despite promising to spare no effort or expense in preparing the CFL's case for a license, Lee and his close associates remained blissfully ignorant of their television proposition.[32]

The authors of the television application conceptualized a role for the station that reflected the conservative ideology of the CFL leadership. They proposed "to run a diversified program service" that would remain independent of the network system. Rejecting the approach of some nascent UHF stations to program for specified demographic markets, the CFL promised to "present programming attuned to the needs and interests of all the socio-economic–ethnic–religious groups residing within the proposed service area." The labor federation acknowledged the social diversity of both the city and the labor movement, but it nevertheless maintained that they both remained one unified whole. "Men and women, white and colored, Catholics, Protestants and Jews, and many national origins" were all represented among the CFL's trade union members, delegates, and officials, yet they all came together as Chicagoans to participate in a plethora of civic organizations and public activities. The CFL application noted that the Chicago area needed "television programming directed toward the labor community," but neither the documents accompanying the application nor subsequent public testimony by CFL representatives produced any evidence to support this assertion.[33]

WCFL-TV instead promised a broadcasting schedule that would adhere to standards of integrity, honesty, and fair dealing, that would promote community improvement, and that would help to create an active, informed citizenry. It proposed to offer enlightening and interesting women's programs, to encourage local educational and cultural bodies to make use of the station, and to find, develop, and present the best local talent regardless of race or ethnicity. The CFL even insisted that it would make the station into a valuable and trusted advertising vehicle by avoiding shoddy and dishonest commercials. References to workers and their unions included ambiguous commitments to offer accurate and fair news coverage, to discuss important public issues, and to have public affairs shows reflect community needs and problems.[34]

The tentative schedule for WCFL-TV's first year of operation indicated approximately 13.5 broadcast hours per day, 7 days a week. Almost 75% of all the programming would be sponsored, with just over 25% sustained by the station. Of the approximately 58 hours of entertainment programming per week, WCFL-TV would show 9 hours of syndicated drama, action, or children's series and 29 hours of feature motion pictures. The CFL hoped that public and private organs which produced their own films for educational, informational, or advertising and propaganda purposes would supply labor television with the bulk of its entertainment shows. The Department of Defense, for example, might furnish films for *Armed Forces Journal*, a half-hour program on Saturday mornings. CFL officials touted this show as providing "insight into one of the most significant undertakings of government"—that is, preparation for national defense. An entertainment and educational show dealing with science and industry would rely on film from the archives of the National Association of Manufacturers and local industrial and research companies. For a weekly travelogue program, labor television proposed using promotional films produced by major airlines. Talk shows on health would draw materials from the Red Cross' films on infant care, first aid, and swimming instruction. The station planned to produce its own documentaries on community institutions such as the Salvation Army, the Mental Health Society of Greater Chicago, the YMCA and YWCA, the Illinois Children's Home and Aid Society, the Chicago Board of Trade, the NAACP, and the Urban League.[35]

Only two programs in the tentative schedule dealt directly with labor issues. *Federation News,* a 15-minute live news show, would air weekdays at 5:35 PM Anchored by Irwin E. Klass, editor of the central body's newspaper, the show would report on labor-related news, interview guests, and show film clips and short documentaries relating to topics such as union health services and pension funds, union-management-government cooperation, consumer advice, and apprenticeship programs.[36] The other program with labor content was *Pros and Cons,* a 30-minute panel discussion show slated for Saturdays at 9:00 PM Here, depending upon the subject matter, representatives of management, labor, civic organizations, the public, or legislative bodies would participate on the panel. Topics of direct interest to workers included the minimum wage, employment discrimination, the effects of labor negotiations on the community, union support for political candidates, and arbitration and labor-management relations. Among the broad labor-related issues that the show promised to address were fair housing, fair employment practices, poverty and unemployment, education, de facto segregation and neighborhood schools, and urban renewal.[37] These latter subjects constituted some of the burning issues confronting Chicago's African-American and white working-class communities during the 1960s. The application emphasized them because no broadcast outlet purporting to serve the public interest could ignore race relations and because it illustrated that a station owned by organized labor could satisfy a broad public mandate, thereby negating any need for specialized programming for racial minorities. Several black community leaders and activists refuted this last point while testifying on behalf of the Chicagoland TV Company.

Joining Chicago Urban League director Edwin C. Berry at FCC hearings held in April 1965 were attorney and activist Anna R. Langford, public school administrator Virginia F. Lewis, and radio station WAAF news director Louis E. House, Jr., among others. Chicagoland's lead attorney, Robert L. Heald, asked these witnesses to identify what they believed were the principal needs of Chicago's black community; comment on television's potential role in dealing with these problems; explain how well and to what extent the local VHF-TV stations fulfilled that role; and, finally, opine whether Chicagoland's proposed schedule would serve the interests of Chicago's African-American population.

Berry began by explaining that Chicago's black citizens required "equality of opportunity in all areas of human endeavor, but particularly in the bread and butter issues of jobs, education, and housing." Langford, the "feisty attorney" who represented civil rights protestors in their ongoing battle with the city's public school system, discussed how racial discrimination had produced "very highly specialized" needs in the black community. In particular, she noted the need to rectify the inferior education students received in heavily segregated black schools. Virginia Lewis, an assistant superintendent of the Chicago public school system's educational extension, and Morris Harrison Tynes, a Baptist minister, pointed to how widespread racial prejudice produced "perceptual distortion" among African Americans. According to Lewis, Chicago's black population needed "opportunities for presenting the Negro as he sees himself . . . and as he would be seen by his fellow Americans. Opportunities to know more . . . about his own heritage and to have others know more about his contributions to the society of which he is a part." Tynes called for "a massive effort to enable the Negro to rediscover who he is." Expanding upon this theme, Berry remarked that the black community required a way to interpret its bread and butter issues "to the broader community" and, equally important, to explain "what important things would happen to our total community if the needs were fulfilled on a basis of human equality."[38]

Chicagoland's witnesses agreed that television could address African-American needs, but that the medium had done very little thus far. Berry called television "a very powerful instrument of public interpretation" that had not yet sufficiently confronted the problem of racism. Television had to transcend racial stereotypes, employ more blacks as actors, writers, and technicians, produce specific programs dealing with race issues, and integrate African Americans into programming. Langford believed that television could become an "effective means of education," citing the role that the medium already had played in enlightening audiences about the civil rights movement.[39] Tynes implied that television might become the agent for helping Americans to overcome racial stereotypes and rediscover their real identities.[40]

Echoing a familiar complaint, Tynes called the African American "the silent spectator and almost invisible man" in Chicago television. Louis House, news director for black-appeal radio station WAAF, concurred that "we don't see enough of ourselves from baby up on to death on television." Chicago's dominant "white television" industry kept racial minorities "uninformed, misinformed, and propagandized."[41] Tynes complained that Chicago television had failed to create "a positive and constructive image and self-image" for African Americans. "There is very little in Chicago television to give the Negro a sense of self-appreciation, of self-identification, of self-understanding or a consciousness of being a member of a more inclusive aspiring community, a more integrated community."[42] Berry knew of no "single sustained program on any local television station that was designed to treat the problem of discrimination and segregation in race relations." He particularly lamented the lack of integrated programming for children. If television was all that children knew, "they would think that the society of the United States was all of these bleached complexions with the blue eyes." Berry also criticized the "almost lily white" staffs of Chicago television stations for making "very slow" progress toward training and employing black technicians and performers.[43]

Chicagoland proposed to meet African-American community needs by presenting integrated live shows; affording opportunities for individual black citizens and groups to appear on television; and treating topics of particular interest to African Americans.[44] The witnesses judged that Chicagoland's tentative schedule could potentially benefit the city's black population and its white communities as well. Concerned with education and self-image, Langford, Lewis, and Tynes applauded shows focusing on young children and adolescents. The *Children's Hour, Teenarama, Chicago High School News,* and *Teenage Problem Clinic* would bring together African American and white children to entertain, to discuss common problems, and to explore differences. Lewis stressed that "Negro children need to see and to feel a part" of the city and Chicagoland's youth shows seemed to contribute to this end.[45]

A 2-hour, 5-night-a-week live entertainment show, *Chicago Scene,* constituted the heart of Chicagoland's prime time entertainment. Similar in format to the NBC network's successful *The Tonight Show,* this program would originate "from Chicagoland's studio in an informal setting, featuring a Negro master of ceremonies, with guests from all parts of Chicago society." Community activists assumed that *Chicago Scene* would utilize under-employed black talent and inevitably would examine matters of concern to all African Americans. Berry expected that people like Sidney Poitier or Lena Horne, who might appear on the show, would discuss the problems of segregation and discrimination and the fight for equal rights in America because such things "are important in their lives." The show's description "very much impressed" Tynes, who argued that Chicago's black population wanted an African American "featured in the category of a Johnnie Carson type show." The Baptist minister averred that "this will give an added dimension of self-respect to the Negro citizenry."[46]

Other positively reviewed programs included *Americana, Open Lens,* and *This Is My Heritage.* These shows promised to promote greater racial understanding and cooperation by delving into the contemporary problems as well as "the history and background of various ethnic and racial groups." While appreciating the import of blacks learning about the ethnic roots and concerns of their white neighbors and vice versa, African-American community leaders emphasized how these programs might educate black audiences about the meaning of the black experience in Chicago and the United States. They anticipated that such knowledge would enhance the pride of and generally strengthen the black community.[47] All in all, Langford found it "very unrealistic" that the existing stations could either comprehend the depth of racial discrimination experienced by African Americans or do anything about it. Thus the Chicagoland proposal "to me is realism. This has a possibility" of working.[48]

Attorneys for the CFL disagreed, alleging that black-oriented programming would segregate the air waves. James E. Greeley, a CFL lawyer, repeatedly asserted that "a program schedule which is of particular interest and tailored to the desires of the Negro community" tends "to separate the Negro, rather than integrate him into society." He also dismissed the argument that the black community's unique demands required specialized programming from a broadcasting outlet and he wondered what would happen once the peculiar needs disappeared. In general, the CFL attacked the idea of using the public air waves to serve the claimed special needs of a minority audience, rather than using the public resource for a broadly-defined public interest.[49]

Chicagoland and its attorneys denied that the station intended to program solely for African Americans. "To the contrary," explained Heald, the programming "is designed for all people but deals with the subject of Negroes." Witnesses such as Langford concurred, observing that Chicagoland's shows had the potential to "educate the white person as well as the Negro to the cultural backgrounds of the Negro." Such programs would improve the African

American's self-image and correct white people's distorted perceptions of blacks.[50] But Urban League director Berry, while not desiring "a segregated air wave," nevertheless saw the need for a "specialized effort to deal with the problem" of racism. Given the systemic segregation that already divided Chicago, "it is no violation of my code to recommend specialized treatment of a special problem that society has caused. And under these circumstances as we have separated people, it is necessary that we communicate with those people and help them to use their own strength and ingenuity to break out of the shackles of separation." Berry's position, although rooted in a commitment to integration, also demonstrated a belief in enhancing the black community's own power vis-à-vis white society.[51] The CFL rejected both this black power approach and the entire concept of black-oriented television as dangerous to the public good.

Relying upon a city-wide network of contacts, including those in the political machine of Mayor Richard J. Daley, the CFL gathered together its own black community representatives to argue against the Chicagoland application. Contesting the arguments of Berry, Langford, Lewis, Tynes, and House were, in particular, Theodore Robinson and Ralph Metcalfe. Robinson, a technical advisor in the Illinois State Labor Department, served on the Executive Board of WCFL and participated in several municipal bodies including the Housing Committee of the city's Commission on Human Relations. Daley had selected Metcalfe, a former Olympic sprinter with high stature in the black community, but no political experience, to serve as a committeeman for the city's predominantly black Third Ward in 1952. Metcalfe subsequently became a City Council alderman and "dutifully supported the Machine" until the early 1970s.[52]

In general, the CFL's witnesses embraced the official position of the city's white power structure. They contended that African Americans already possessed basic rights and opportunities in Chicago and that they were following the path of earlier ethnic immigrants in becoming assimilated into the dominant society. This perspective dismissed accusations that Chicago was "the most segregated city above the Mason and Dixon Line." Mayor Daley insisted that the city possessed no ghettoes and that it had never deprived anyone of the right to vote. He refused to consider inadequate housing, jobs, and schools as "race problems," preferring instead to call them "problems of people in a community." The city's white political and economic structure found nothing wrong with the status quo and denounced demands for changes in the city's racial policies as the ranting of trouble-makers.[53]

When asked about the city's most pressing problems, Metcalfe told the FCC that the city had to develop more civic pride. While blacks wanted integration, they did not seek "to be set aside separate and distinct from other particular groups." Chicago did not need a local television station to focus on black themes and use black talent because an increasing number of black entertainers already had secured access to television programming and because most blacks did not want "anything specifically directed towards" them. Indeed, according to Metcalfe, specialized programming could alienate Chicago's white citizens, the very "people that we would most want to reach and to tell our story." Metcalfe praised television for its "terrific impact" upon the community and, in particular, for improving "the intelligence of our youngsters today."[54]

Theodore Robinson acknowledged the need to reduce segregation and discrimination, but he refused to categorize housing, employment, and education problems as solely black worries. Housing, for example, was not a racial problem per se, but rather a matter of inadequate residences for the city's poor population. Robinson believed that television could help improve communications among different urban groups as well as aid people "to adjust to the conditions of the entire city." But just as he "objected to concentrating public housing in the Negro area because it isolates and separates people," Robinson vigorously opposed "separate but equal facilities in communication . . . or anything else." Black-appeal television would perpetuate the "feeling of separateness on the part of the Negro people" when what "we really need is to get into the main-stream of life in a community and force the main-stream of life in this community to receive us and do business with us." Robinson also found it "very socially undesirable" to establish a television station solely to create employment opportunities for African Americans.[55]

Unlike many community leaders who attacked the city's racial policies, Carl Fuqua did not testify on behalf of Chicagoland. The director of the local NAACP chapter concluded that the African-American community did not require specialized television shows. Fuqua agreed that local television stations had engaged in mere "tokenism" when it came to employment and programming. Nevertheless, he questioned whether the proposed black-oriented television station would dramatically improve upon the rather "shallow and stereotyped" programming already aired over the city's black-appeal radio stations. Programming designed "for any minority group, specifically Negroes in Chicago, is probably programming that ought to involve the total population because there is a need to have education as well as a need to be fulfilled in terms of the total city." As for the question of employment, Fuqua called for the elimination of all discriminatory barriers in the Chicago television industry and the application of equal opportunity for all qualified personnel.[56]

WCFL attorneys insisted that their witnesses had identified fatal flaws in Chicagoland's application. Black-oriented television programming, for example, would intensify rather than diminish racial divisions in the city. Moreover, Chicagoland had failed to establish a need for such programming because it had not conducted a comprehensive poll or survey of the city's black population to determine its needs and interests. Lawyers for the CFL also maintained that their witnesses held greater stature in the African-American community than did Chicagoland's witnesses. The words of a NAACP director or elected city official had to "be given greater weight than" those of a grass-roots activist or broadcast journalist. In the end, contended WCFL, Chicagoland had failed "to establish that in the total frame of reference, there is either a public need or public interest for the type of Negro oriented operation it proposes in Chicago."[57]

The testimony and affidavits of the VHF-TV stations in Chicago generally reinforced WCFL's position. WBBM-TV argued that its "program schedule is designed to interest and inform all of the television audience within the station's service area, and the station generally does not present programs aimed at any single audience component such as an ethnic group." WBBM officials nevertheless insisted that in presenting "a balanced program which meets . . . the diverse needs and interests of its audience," the station often aired "programs that have . . . been of particular interest 'for Negroes and ethnic groups.' " Echoing the CFL, the local television industry implied that surrendering to the demands of special interest groups and emphasizing the political, economic, social, or cultural differences among Chicago's citizenry only would serve to divide the community and weaken its overall welfare.[58]

WCFL's own definition of broadcasting in the public interest, however, remained flawed and self-serving. Leaders of the CFL, especially William Lee, had little desire to develop programming that might build labor solidarity, offer a labor perspective on crucial contemporary issues, or challenge the status quo of white bourgeois society. Lee and his colleagues were quintessential business unionists who favored "negotiations to strikes and conciliation to confrontation" and rarely questioned Chicago's economic or political status quo.[59] Working with local business and government to support the prevailing distribution of economic and political rewards, the CFL maintained labor peace and the image of an interracial cross-class harmony of interests. Its future television station aimed to entertain a wide audience, create good will for labor among the general public, and demonstrate to corporate officials and the public at large that the labor perspective was identical to that of liberal government and big business.[60] Equally important, Lee wanted a television station to generate significant revenues for the CFL. Despite the considerable rhetoric of meeting community needs and interests, the CFL remained primarily interested in the bottom line. This became apparent when the designated general manager of the new station told the press that "we're hoping to come up with another Ken Draper to direct our programming department." Draper, as general manager of WCFL radio, had guided that station's shift to a Top-40 rock music format and its rise to among the three highest rated radio stations in the city. Like WCFL radio, WCFL-TV aimed "to make a strong play for the younger audience" and the lucrative advertising dollars that accompanied it.[61]

Labor leaders may have genuinely believed that Chicagoland's proposed black-oriented programming was "socially regressive" and that it was not "in the public interest to authorize a Negro oriented station which would tend to alienate or segregate Negroes or in any way inhibit Negroes from entering the mainstream of American life."[62] But such arguments should be juxtaposed with the Chicago labor movement's highly problematic actions regarding the black working class. Despite giving lip service to the goals of integration and social equality during the 1960s, CFL officials looked the other way as their constituent unions, especially in the building trades, flagrantly stymied efforts to integrate area workplaces and vocational schools. The CFL remained a staunch supporter of, and apologist for the contentious racial policies of the Daley administration in the crucial areas of education and housing.[63] In the end, the labor federation wanted a television station to maximize its revenues, its political reputation, and its social-political ideology. The latter's guiding tenet was that labor, business, and government had entered into an alliance to enhance the public welfare by, among other things, expanding a mass consumption-centered society.

Chicagoland TV Company also sought to make a profit and certainly did not challenge mass consumption. But its definition of broadcasting in the public interest, at least as interpreted by the neighborhood activists who testified on its behalf, addressed real and perceived needs in the black community. African-American leaders urged the creation of a television station that would enlighten its audience as to the causes and possible solutions to segregation and discrimination in housing, education, and employment and that would, at the same time, enhance racial consciousness and pride. The testimony of Berry, Langford, Tynes, et al., revealed an intuitive understanding that the broadcast media in the United States were public property and not exclusively the domain of the private interests that owned them. These activists thus perceived that television could serve as a means of communicating among community-based organizations and between those groups and the larger society.[64]

The debate between the CFL and Chicagoland over black-oriented television reflected in part the complicated struggle between advocates of *integration* and those of *black power*. As historians have recently demonstrated, this was no simple dichotomy: civil rights activists "strategically used integrationist and nationalist tactics in their struggles" against racism.[65] Nevertheless real differences existed between the two. Proponents of integration sought to end discriminatory behavior and systems through institutionalizing "broadly inclusive rules of participation in all areas of social life . . . in schools, housing, jobs, politics, commerce, culture." Hence the opponents of black-appeal television, both within and outside the African-American community, embraced, at least in theory, equal opportunity for racial minorities within the existing broadcasting system. The black power approach emphasized redistributing "power and initiative to the black community" as a precursor to the destruction of black subordination in all areas of political, social, and economic life.[66] In demanding black-oriented television, proponents of Chicagoland pushed for cultural and informational power that the African-American community itself could utilize in struggling for social and economic justice.

FCC officials had little comprehension of the larger issues at stake as they considered the conflicting arguments advanced by the CFL and Chicagoland. In the end, the commission's Broadcast Bureau interpreted the position of Chicagoland's supporters to mean that:

> what is desired is not programming directed exclusively or primarily to the Negro community but rather greater opportunity for participation by Negroes on a regular basis in programming directed to the community as a whole. The record is overwhelmingly clear that Negroes strongly desire to have Negro participation in television to a much greater extent than at present.[67]

Although FCC bureaucrats and commissioners found merit in this goal and in Chicagoland's proposed programming, they assigned Channel 38 to the CFL. Financial considerations and not programming concerns ultimately resolved the competition: Chicagoland did not possess the requisite finances to establish and operate a station while the CFL did.[68]

With final FCC approval in June 1968, WCFL-TV arranged for the construction and installation of a transmitter and antenna at the John Hancock Center. The proposed station never materialized. CFL leaders soon realized that the nascent station would be a financial drain rather than a revenue generator. Few stations, even VHF ones, made profits during their first years of operation. The question of UHF-TV economic viability had plagued the FCC as early as 1965 when the commission considered requiring applicants for UHF channels in major cities "to demonstrate an ability to survive three years of competition from the three network-affiliated VHF stations" in those markets. In 1968, only two out 37 independent UHF-TV outlets reported a profit. Unsure as to the economic potential of its UHF station, the CFL began searching for a buyer of the license in the fall of 1970. Labor officials eventually sold the station to the Atlanta-based religious organ, Christian Communications of Chicagoland, Inc., for $1 million. The FCC approved the license transfer in early 1976 and WCFL-TV left the television world without broadcasting a program.[69]

A decade after the Chicagoland–CFL debate, the city of Chicago found itself without a television station that might have offered an alternative to the dominant corporate and white broadcasting structure, from either a class or racial perspective. Like their counterparts in the city's business (including television) and government sectors, CFL officials posited that television served only a single unified public interest. At its best, the function of a television station owned by organized labor was to allow for trade union elites to communicate information with rank-and-file workers and the general public; it was not to facilitate communication within the working classes or to offer class-based cultural products. On the other hand, activists within the African-American community questioned the existence of a unified public interest. In advocating black-oriented television, these community leaders recognized the possibility that a multitude of publics with differing concerns co-existed in Chicago. At best, they wished to maximize public access to television and democratize the medium. At the very least, they sought a television outlet that would allow for a freer exchange of ideas and opinions than available on existing stations and that would enhance their own cultural identity and power.[70]

Notes

1. *Chicago Sun-Times*, 22 March 1962, p. 1.
2. US House of Representatives, *Hearings before the Committee on Education and Labor: investigation of discrimination practices in the performing arts*, 87th Congress, 2nd session (Washington, DC, 1963), pp. 13, 56, 87 (quote).
3. Marilyn Diane Fife, Black image in American TV: the first two decades, *The Black Scholar*, 6 (1974), p. 8 (quote); Sharon Albert-Honoré, Empowered voices: freedom of expression and African-American community radio, PhD dissertation, University of Iowa, 1995, pp. 27–35.
4. Frank Gentile and S. M. Miller, Television and social class, *Sociology and Social Research*, 45 (1961), p. 263. One of the few television shows in the 1950s to offer a sophisticated portrayal of working-class culture was the local Chicago program *Studs'*

Place. See Chad Raphael, Utopia out of place: *Studs' Place*, popular front culture and the blacklist in Chicago television, *Quarterly Review of Film and Video*, 16 (1999), pp. 253–270.

5. Ralph Arthur Johnson, World without workers: prime time's presentation of labor, *Labor Studies Journal*, 5 (1981), p. 206. See also Jerry Rollings, Mass communications and the American worker, in Vincent Mosco and Janet Wasko (eds), *The Critical Communications Review, Volume I: labor, the working class, and the media* (Norwood, NJ, 1985), pp. 131–152.

6. Sara U. Douglas, *Labor's New Voice: unions and the mass media* (Norwood, NJ, 1986), p. 32; *Federation News*, 12 January 1963, p. 8; *AFL-CIO News*, 2 February 1963, p. 4 (quote); Elizabeth A. Fones-Wolf, *Selling Free Enterprise: the business assault on labor and liberalism, 1945–1960* (Urbana, IL, 1994).

7. Douglas Gomery, Rethinking television historiography, *Film and History*, 30 (2000), pp. 17–27, 19 (first quote); Christopher Anderson and Michael Curtin, Mapping the ethereal city: Chicago television, the FCC, and the politics of place, *Quarterly Review of Film and Video*, 16 (1999), pp. 289–305; Michael Curtin, Connections and differences: spatial dimensions of television history, *Film and History*, 30 (2000), p. 59 (second quote).

8. J. Fred MacDonald, *Blacks and White TV: African Americans in television since 1948*, 2nd edn (Chicago, 1992), pp. 3–57 passim; Fife, Black image in American TV, pp. 7–11, 11 (second quote); Jannette L. Davis and William Barlow (eds), *Split Image: African Americans in the mass media*, 2nd edn (Washington, DC, 1993), pp. 267–327.

9. *Investigation of Discrimination Practices*, pp. 22–28, 24 (quote).

10. Marilyn Fife, Promoting racial diversity in US broadcasting: federal policies versus social realities, *Media, Culture, and Society*, 9 (1987), p. 484.

11. *Chicago Daily Defender*, 5 July 1961, p. 3.

12. *Chicago's American*, 13 April 1962, p. 18; *Chicago Daily Defender*, 16 August 1962, p. 13 (quote); Arvarh E. Strickland, *History of the Chicago Urban League* (Urbana, IL, 1966), pp. 234–235. John Madigan became WBBM-TV's news director in 1963 and quickly clashed with the station's news anchor and star reporter, Frank Reynolds. Madigan, who believed that "Reynolds concentrated too heavily on racial news," changed the format of WBBM's premier news show by dropping in-depth coverage of selected stories and adopting "a broader approach." Marjorie Fox, News in the heartland: WBBM-TV, Chicago, in Michael D. Murray and Donald G. Godfrey (eds), *Television in America: local station history from across the nation* (Ames, IA, 1997), p. 232.

13. *Chicago Sun-Times*, 22 March 1962, p. 1 (first quote); *Chicago's American*, 21 March 1962, p. 6 (second quote); *Chicago Daily News*, 21 March 1962, p. 3. For details on the FCC hearings see, Anderson and Curtain, Mapping the ethereal city.

14. *Broadcasting*, 65 (29 July 1963), p. 91, (19 August 1963), p. 59 (first and second quotes); *Chicago Daily Defender*, 2 April 1963, p. 15 (third quote), 11 June 1963, p. 12 (fourth quote).

15. William Barlow, *Voice Over: the making of black radio* (Philadelphia, PA, 1999), p. 108 (quotes); Nathan Godfried, *WCFL: Chicago's voice of labor, 1926–1978* (Urbana, IL, 1997), pp. 256–258; Kathy M. Newman, The forgotten fifteen million: black radio, the "Negro market" and the Civil Rights Movement, *Radical History Review*, 76 (2000), pp. 115–135.

16. Norman W. Spaulding, History of black oriented radio in Chicago, 1929–1963, PhD dissertation, University of Illinois, Urbana-Champaign, Illinois, 1981, pp. 40–51, 179.

17. Ibid., p. iv.

18. Federal Communications Commission, *Federal Communications Commission Reports*, Vol. 33, *July 13, 1962 to December 29, 1962* (Washington, DC, 1964), pp. 37–46, 44 (first quote), 45 (second and third quotes), 46 (fourth quote); Barlow, *Voice Over*, pp. 217, 223, 230, 233–234, 268.

19. Eric D. Berkowitz, Low power television and the doctrine of localism: the need to reconcile a medium with its message, *University of San Francisco Law Review*, 18 (1984), pp. 520 (first quote), 521 (second quote); Anderson and Curtin, Mapping the ethereal city, pp. 292–295.

20. *New York Times*, 10 May 1961, p. 1; Mary Ann Watson, *The Expanding Vista: American television in the Kennedy years* (New York, 1990), pp. 18–26; James L. Baughman, *Television's Guardians: the FCC and the politics of programming, 1958–1967* (Knoxville, TN, 1985), pp. 60–69.

21. *Broadcasting*, 62 (26 February 1962), pp. 35–36. For details on the hearings, see Anderson and Curtin, Mapping the ethereal city, pp. 295–301.

22. Anderson and Curtin, Mapping the ethereal city, p. 301.

23. *Chicago Sun-Times*, 25 March 1962, p. 10; Berkowitz, Low power television and the doctrine of localism, pp. 520–522; Christopher H. Sterling and John M. Kittross, *Stay Tuned: a concise history of American broadcasting* (Belmont, CA, 1978), pp. 356–359, 381, 417.

24. *Chicago Sun-Times*, 10 January 1964, p. 32, 27 January 1964, p. 36, 9 March 1964, p. 36, 19 March 1964, p. 62; *Chicago Daily News*, 7 February 1964, p. 37; *Jet*, 23 April 1964, p. 61, 18 June 1964, p. 60; *Chicago Daily Defender*, 30 May–5 June 1964, pp. 1 (fourth quote), 2 (fifth quote); *The Wall Street Journal*, 19 February 1965, p. 1 (first, second, and third quotes); MacDonald, *Blacks and White TV*, pp. 28–35; Melvin Patrick Ely, *The Adventures of Amos 'n' Andy: a social history of an American phenomenon* (New York, 1991).

25. *Broadcasting*, 64 (17 June 1963), p. 96. See Robert E. Weems, *Desegregating the Dollar: African American consumerism in the twentieth century* (New York, 1998).

26. *Broadcasting*, 64 (4 February 1963), p. 56; *Jet*, 7 February 1963, p. 62; *Chicago Daily Defender*, 11 February 1963, p. 16; *Sponsor*, 22 October 1962, pp. 14–15, 50, 17 August 1964, pp. 53, 57; *The Wall Street Journal*, 19 February 1965, p. 1 (quotes).

27. *Chicago Daily Defender*, 18 February 1963, p. 13 (first quote), 11 February 1963, p. 16 (second, third, and fifth quotes); *Broadcasting*, 71 (5 September 1966), p. 59 (fourth quote).

28. Proposed Findings of Fact and Conclusions of Law on behalf of Chicagoland TV Company, 27 September 1966, pp. 3–5, Docket No. 15668, Box 113, Folder: Vol. 7, General Records of the FCC 1946–1979, Record Group 173, National Archives, College Park, MD (hereafter cited as Findings of Fact . . . Chicagoland, followed by pages, RG 173).

29. Findings of Fact . . . Chicagoland, pp. 3, 5, 6 (first and second quotes), RG 173; Spaulding, History of black-oriented radio, p. 164 (third and fourth quotes).

30. Findings of Fact . . . Chicagoland, pp. 6–8, 8 (quotes), RG 173.

31. *Federation News*, 13 May 1950, p. 5 (first quote), 7 March 1953, p. 7, 11 December 1954, p. 7, 17 March 1956, p. 5 (second quote), 1 April 1961, p. 8, 18 March 1961, p. 7.

32. *Federation News*, 31 October 1964, p. 5, 6 February 1965, pp. 5–6, October 1966, p. 12; Irwin E. Klass, interview with author, 12 July 1991, Chicago; Official Report of Proceedings before the FCC at Washington, DC, 10 and 11 May 1966, Vol.

30, pp. 1658–1711, 1713–1724, 1778–1805, 1810–1819, Box 112, Folder: Vol. 5, Docket No. 15668, RG 173; Report of Proceedings at Washington, DC, 22 June 1966, Vol. 37, pp. 2492–2510, Box 113, Folder: Vol. 6, Docket No. 15668.

33. Direct Written Testimony of Chicago Federation of Labor and Industrial Union Council, Vol. 2, CFL-UIC Exhibit No. 30, Proposed television programming, p. 1 (first and third quotes), and CFL-UIC Exhibit No. 31, General program standards and policies, p. 1 (second quote), Folder: Vol. 9, Box 114, Docket No. 15668; Findings of Fact . . . Chicagoland, p. 39 (fourth quote), RG 173.

34. CFL-UIC Exhibit No. 31, pp. 1–3, Folder: Vol. 9, Box 114, Docket No. 15668, RG 173.

35. CFL-UIC Exhibit No. 30, Proposed television programming, pp. 5–56, 7 (quote), Folder: Vol. 9, Box 114, Docket No. 15668, RG 173.

36. CFL-UIC Exhibit No. 31, pp. 31–32, Folder: Vol. 9, Box 114, Docket No. 15668, RG 173.

37. Ibid., pp. 43–44.

38. Report of Proceedings before the Federal Communications Commission at Chicago, 6 April 1965, Vol. 10, pp. 296 (first, seventh, and eighth quotes), 369 (third quote), 7 April 1965, Vol. 11, p. 553 (fifth quote); 9 April 1965, Vol. 13, 882 (fourth quote), p. 883 (sixth quote), Box 111, Folder: Vol. 2, Docket 15668 (hereafter cited as FCC Proceedings at Chicago, followed by the date and volume, pages, box and folder, RG 173); William J. Grimshaw, *Bitter Fruit: black politics and the Chicago machine, 1931–1991* (Chicago, 1992), p. 123 (second quote).

39. FCC Proceedings at Chicago, 6 April 1965, Vol. 10, pp. 297 (first quote), 298, 370, 371 (second quote), Box 111, Folder: Vol. 2, RG 173.

40. FCC Proceedings at Chicago, 9 April 1965, Vol. 13, pp. 883, 884 (quote), Box 111, Folder: Vol. 2, RG 173.

41. FCC Proceedings at Chicago, 9 April 1965, Vol. 13, p. 897 (first quote), 8 April 1965, Vol. 12, pp. 777 (fourth quote), 783 (second quote), 789 (third quote), Box 111, Folder: Vol. 2, RG 173.

42. FCC Proceedings at Chicago, 9 April 1965, Vol. 13, p. 897, Box 111, Folder: Vol. 2, RG 173.

43. FCC Proceedings at Chicago, 6 April 1965, Vol. 10, pp. 334 (first quote), 342 (second quote), 349 (remaining quotes), Box 111, Folder: Vol. 2, RG 173.

44. Findings of Fact . . . Chicagoland, p. 9, RG 173.

45. Ibid., pp. 10–12; FCC Proceedings at Chicago, 6 April 1965, Vol. 10, p. 382; 7 April 1965, Vol. 11, pp. 556–559, 558 (quote); 9 April 1965, Vol. 13, pp. 888, 891, Box 111, Folder: Vol. 2, RG 173.

46. Findings of Fact . . . Chicagoland, p. 10 (first quote), RG 173; FCC Proceedings at Chicago, 6 April 1965, Vol. 10, pp. 335–341, 337 (second quote); 8 April 1965, Vol. 12, pp. 780–781; 9 April 1965, Vol. 13, pp. 887 (third quote), 888 (fourth and fifth quotes), Box 111, Folder: Vol. 2, RG 173.

47. Findings of Fact . . . Chicagoland, pp. 11–12, 13 (quote), RG 173; FCC Proceedings at Chicago, 6 April 1965, Vol. 10, pp. 376–377; 7 April 1965, Vol. 11, p. 559; 8 April 1965, Vol. 12, pp. 774–775, Box 111, Folder: Vol. 2, RG 173.

48. FCC Proceedings at Chicago, 6 April 1965, Vol. 10, pp. 404 (quotes), 341, Box 111, Folder: Vol. 2, RG 173.

49. FCC Proceedings at Chicago, 6 April 1965, Vol. 10, p. 330, Box 111, Folder: Vol. 2, RG 173.

50. Ibid., pp. 362 (first quote), 372 (second quote).

51. Ibid., pp. 331 (quotes), 353–354.

52. FCC Proceedings at Chicago, 13 April 1965, Vol. 14, p. 922, Box 112, Folder: Vol. 3, RG 173; James R. Ralph, Jr., *Northern Protest: Martin Luther King, Jr., Chicago, and the Civil Rights Movement* (Cambridge, MA, 1993), pp. 81–82; Paul Kleppner, *Chicago Divided: the making of a black mayor* (DeKalb, IL, 1985), p. 86 (quote); Grimshaw, *Bitter Fruit*, pp. 134–135, 108–112.

53. *Chicago Daily Defender*, 29 June 1961, p. 11, 3 July 1961, p. 1 (first quote); Alan B. Anderson and George W. Pickering, *Confronting the Color Line: the broken promise of the Civil Rights Movement in Chicago* (Athens, GA, 1986), pp. 347, 405–406; Strickland, *History of the Chicago Urban League*, p. 260; *Chicago Daily News*, 17 February 1964, p. 45 (second and third quotes).

54. FCC Proceedings at Chicago, 13 April 1965, Vol. 14, pp. 987–998, 993 (first quote), 998 (second quote), 991 (third quote), Box 112, Folder: Vol. 3, RG 173.

55. Ibid., pp. 924–935, 928 (first and third quotes), 927 (second quote), 933 (fourth and fifth quotes), 934 (sixth quote).

56. FCC Proceedings at Chicago, 14 April 1965, Vol. 15, pp. 1110–1121, 1113 (first and second quotes), 1112 (third quote), Box 112, Folder: Vol. 3, RG 173.

57. Chicago Federation of Labor and Industrial Union Council, Brief in support of exceptions, 23 March 1967, pp. 4 (first quote), 6 (second quote), Box 114, Folder: Vol. 10, Docket No. 15668, RG 173.

58. Stipulations, Exhibit 1, WBBM-TV (quotes) and Stipulations, Exhibit 2, WGN-TV, Box 113, Folder: Vol. 7, Docket No. 15668, RG 173; testimony by John Wilkinson Taylor, executive director of the Chicago Education Television Association, WTTW-TV, in FCC Proceedings at Chicago, 14 April 1965, Vol. 15, pp. 1077–1088, Box 112, Folder: Vol. 3, RG 173; Anderson and Curtin, Mapping the ethereal city, pp. 299–300.

59. *Chicago Tribune*, 17 June 1984, sec. 3, p. 8 (quote).

60. Godfried, *WCFL: Chicago's voice of labor*, pp. 240–243.

61. *Chicago Sun-Times*, 6 January 1968, p. 22 (quotes); Godfried, *WCFL: Chicago's voice of labor*, p. 281.

62. Brief in support of exceptions, 23 March 1967, pp. 5–6 (quotes), Box 114, Folder: Vol. 10, Docket No. 15668, RG 173.

63. Ralph, *Northern Protest*, pp. 70–71; Milton Derber, *Labor in Illinois: the affluent years, 1945–1980* (Urbana, IL, 1989), pp. 58–60, 73–79; *Chicago Daily Defender*, 21 August 1961, p. 1; *Federation News*, 2 September 1963, p. 29, 5 October 1963, p. 4.

64. Ralph L. Stavins (ed.), *Television Today: the end of communication and the death of community* (Washington, DC, 1969), pp. 24, 199–239.

65. Jeanne F. Theoharis, "We saved the city": black struggles of educational equality in Boston, 1960–1976, *Radical History Review*, 81 (2001), p. 62.

66. Anderson and Pickering, *Confronting the Color Line*, pp. 44, 412 (quotes).

67. Broadcast Bureau's Proposed Findings of Fact and Conclusions of Law, 23 December 1966, p. 32, Box 114, Folder: Vol. 10, Docket No. 15668, RG 173.

68. FCC, *Federal Communications Commission Reports, January 5, 1968 to March 22, 1968*, Vol. 11, 2nd series (Washington, DC, 1969), pp. 101–108, 137–138.

69. *Federation News*, January 1968, p. 1, June 1968, p. 1, October 1968, p. 8, August 1969, p. 4, November 1970, p. 7, October 1973, pp. 4–5; Ward L. Quaal, interview with author, 10 August 1990, Chicago; Rolla Edward Park, Cable television, UHF broadcasting, and FCC regulatory policy, *The Journal of Law and Economics*, 15 (April 1972), pp. 207–208; Klass interview; *Broadcasting*, 68 (22 March 1965), p. 118 (quote), (23 August 1971), p. 37, (1 August 1975), p. 30 (2 February 1976), p. 52;

FCC, *Federal Communications Commission Reports, July 25, 1975 to September 5, 1975,* Vol. 54, 2nd series (Washington, DC, 1976), pp. 471–476. Chicagoland apparently made an unsuccessful last ditch effort to secure Channel 38 when the CFL put it on the market in the early 1970s. Jerrold Oppenheim, Channel 44 license illegal?, *Chicago Journalism Review,* 5 (May 1972), p. 8.

70. Albert-Honoré, Empowered voices, pp. 4, 94–95, 152; Stavins, *Television Today,* pp. 61–69, 199–239.

PART 2

The Production Context

Studies of television production processes, like studies of problems in the history of television, have increased in recent years. This is due in part to a recognition that production practices have never been quite so routine as some would suggest. It also results from the realization that some of these practices are in processes of change, altered by developments in technologies, economic factors, and the expansion of distribution outlets. But the driving questions still focus on problems of making meaning within culture industries, problems that encompass issues of constraint and creativity in industrial settings. Essays in this section address these matters from a number of perspectives, some of them rather unusual, in order to offer a range of models for further work.

Elana Levine pursues what is by this point a "traditional" approach by applying Richard Johnson's "circuit of culture" model to soap opera production. The value of such a model is that it examines interactions across a range of influential sites, from those most material aspects such as the economic factors underlying commercial media to the more "cultural" factors such as language, race, and gender. Levine outlines five categories involved in production. Much of this work is based on her observations of the actual production of *General Hospital,* a program she also followed as a viewer. As she notes, access to such "on the ground" resources was gained rather easily by request. In my own experience and that of numerous students, this is not unusual. Levine's model, her categories, and the intersections that cross them could be applied to other genres as well, and useful comparisons would emerge from an expanded body of production research.

A very different type of research and analysis informs Caroline-Isabelle Caron's study of the translation processes involved in preparing *Star Trek* for a francophone audience. Issues of language and language transfer are central to understanding the global influence of American and British television, yet relatively little work has been done on translation, dubbing, or other forms of linguistic transformation. Clearly, the export of television programs has been a fundamental aspect of the economic model for the U.S. television industry and a fundamental issue for importing television systems. When Caron concludes that the translation of *Star Trek* changes the original text "into a different yet related cultural product," she raises the sort of precisely focused analytical problem that should inform studies of other production topics. Such efforts not only result in altered understanding of the television materials themselves but also expand our knowledge of cultural distinction.

Another "atypical" approach to questions involving production is found in Greg Siegel's essay on large-screen video displays. Siegel calls prompt attention to the expansion of what we might mean by "television" in current social contexts. The presence of video screens in commercial and other public settings suggests the need for equally expanded modes of analysis. Especially in the context of stadiums and arenas, large-screen television "competes" with "real" events taking place before crowds of fans and spectators. In other settings as well, such as political conventions, trade shows, or religious gatherings, the use of magnified images has become part of everyday experience. While Siegel concludes that LSVD (large-screen video display) is "not television," his notion of remediation actually calls attention to the fragile notion of television that has dominated our general understanding of the term, and also our critical and analytical approaches to it. Students using this collection should seek other forms of the medium that are "not television" but which teach us more about what "television" is.

From the very large to the very precise—Yeidy M. Rivero's essay on *Mi Familia*, Puerto Rico's first locally produced situation comedy to cast black actors in principal roles, turns to the media professionals who worked on the show for source material. Their perspectives are key to understanding the production of the series not only because of its specific content but also because that content was developed in the context of generalized Puerto Rican assumptions and claims about race. Professing a kind of democratic racial hybridity, Puerto Rico remains, in Rivero's analysis, a society beset with its own forms of "racism." Her interviews with actors, producers, and executives demonstrate how deeply held assumptions shape media content. Here again is a model for analysis of other examples of television content. Those involved in television production work with stated and unstated perspectives that shape details ranging from set design to plot structure. Articulation of these points of view, by those involved or by the analyst who engages them in conversation, often provides new ways of understanding televised material.

This is also the case with Amanda D. Lotz's study of *Any Day Now,* another television program focused in part on issues of race and identity. The special significance of the program, however, is that it was developed and programmed on the Lifetime television network, a network billed as television for women. Unlike Rivero's essay, however, which addressed a large problem for national cultural identity and self-definition, Lotz focuses on how changes in the U.S. television industry indicate changes in what might be understood as "television culture." Like other authors in this collection, she raises issues related to the proliferation of cable television channels and applies the term "post-network television" to describe this still-developing context. The analysis, then, has a doubled perspective, each narrowing the focus of narrative strategies in the serialized melodrama she examines—not just female friendships on a network for women but also a biracial friendship covering a "lifetime" connection. As with previous essays, Lotz has drawn material from on-set observations and interviews with production personnel, and I note again that such arrangements are not difficult to establish. Others should be encouraged by these examples.

Toward a Paradigm
for Media Production Research
Behind the Scenes at *General Hospital*

Elana Levine

Cultural studies of media have made significant contributions to our under-standing of the social and political implications of mediated representation and the contextually-dependent meanings made of media by their audience mem-bers. The study of media production, however, has received much less atten-tion from cultural studies scholars. This gap in research is *not* intrinsic to the field's models of cultural circulation. In fact, models such as those provided by Stuart Hall (1980) and Richard Johnson (1986/87) explicitly call for atten-tion to cultural production and for the integration of production analyses and studies of texts, audiences, and contextual influences. In this essay, I argue that cultural studies scholarship can be usefully expanded and nuanced both by tak-ing on more production-centered research and by drawing upon the media production scholarship of those working under other theoretical and method-ological perspectives (Gans, 1979; Tuchman, 1979; Cantor, 1971; Cantor & Cantor, 1992). The development of theoretically and methodologically rigor-ous and sophisticated approaches to production studies can offer cultural stud-ies researchers, as well as communications scholars working within other par-adigms, new insights and heretofore unrecognized connections between media production, media texts, media audiences, and the social contexts within which they circulate. To demonstrate the benefits of such a broadened strategy, I here analyze the production process of *General Hospital,* a U.S. broadcast tele-vision network daytime soap opera, and suggest ways in which production fac-tors relate to questions about texts, audiences, and social contexts.

The cultural studies bias toward analyses of texts and audiences over pro-duction has existed to varying degrees throughout the field's studies of media. Inspired by Stuart Hall's (1980) encoding/decoding model, various cultural

Elana Levine, "Toward a Paradigm for Media Production Research: Behind the Scenes at *General Hospital.*" From *Critical Studies in Media Communication,* Vol. 18, No. 1 (March 2001), pp. 66–82. Reprinted by permission of Taylor & Francis Ltd. (http://www.tandf.co.uk/journals).

studies projects of the early and mid-1980s did include industrial analyses along with their presentations of audience readings. But because the most revelatory aspect of Hall's model was its recognition of contextually-influenced variability in audience decoding, much of the scholarship in its wake focused disproportionately on audiences over industries. Studies of soap operas, including those by Hobson (1982), Ang (1982), and Brown (1994), have exemplified this trend, examining such issues as the gendered address of the soap opera text, the rewards and costs of soap viewing, and the negotiations audiences make with the raced, classed, and gendered norms of both the soap world and the social world within which soap viewing occurs.

This text-and audience-centered bias has understandable origins in cultural studies history. Founded, at least in part, as a reaction against economically determinist interpretations of commercial culture, cultural studies has logically emphasized the resistive power of audience readings over the constraining forces of production. At the same time, an ongoing debate between political economy and cultural studies has kept production-centered scholarship largely in the hands of political economists, where it serves as a reliable marker of difference from their less classically marxist cousins.[1] With production-oriented scholarship practiced for so long by those more interested in the circulation of money than the circulation of meaning, it has been difficult for cultural studies scholars to connect production practices to the questions of discourse and power (aside from economic power) that the field most frequently addresses. While cultural scholars readily admit that capital plays a chief role in commercial media production, they tend to stop their thinking there, failing to look for the roles of discourse, knowledge, and daily practice in cultural production.

In attempting to broaden the cultural studies approach to media along such lines, this essay offers a case study of soap opera production and thereby puts Richard Johnson's (1986/87) circuit of culture model into practice. Johnson's model poses a mutually influential relationship between production, texts, audiences, and contexts. To get at this relationship, he urges a two-pronged analysis of production. The examination of material means and the capitalist organization of labor are one prong, but Johnson suggests that production scholarship should also engage in exploring a range of *cultural* elements, such as rules of language and discourse and classed, raced, and gendered struggles over these rules as they occur within the production sphere (p. 55). Having advocated this two-pronged analysis of the production process itself, Johnson also suggests two means of relating production to the other spheres of cultural circulation. First, he argues for the examination of production moments as distinct and particular, as specific acts, not just general conditions. Secondly, and at first glance contradictorily, he argues for a *lack* of distinction between production, texts, and audiences. He urges, for example, careful analysis of the "productive" elements in cultural *consumption,* thereby retaining the cultural studies insistence upon active audiencehood (p. 57–58). Instead of negating his call for the distinctiveness of production, this second suggestion avoids economic determinism while remaining materially grounded in audience experience and production practice.

How the various aspects of the production process contribute to texts and shape possibilities for audience readings are the focus of the rest of this essay. I here categorize, describe, and analyze five major factors that shape a particular kind of cultural production, U.S. broadcast network television production. Even more narrowly, I examine the production of one particular television soap opera. The five categories I outline—production constraints, the production environment, production routines and practices, the production of characters and stories, and the role of the audience in production—have grown out of interviews and observations I conducted on-site at the *General Hospital* studio. I spent two weeks of August 1997 on the set, in the control booth, and around the offices of the show. I chose this particular program largely because I had spent the last sixteen years as a devoted viewer and thus had an immense backlog of information about its storylines, style, and personnel. I gained access by writing a letter to the executive producer, explaining my academic project and my interest in *General Hospital*. The coordinating producer called me months later and invited me to visit. The ease with which these arrangements were made illustrates the potential accessibility of commercial production to interested scholars. The ease with which a long-time fan was able to become a critical researcher and a critical researcher was able to turn back into a long-time (albeit somewhat more jaded) fan has helped me to analyze the similarities and differences between audience experience and the production world in ways unavailable to the more traditionally "objective" researcher. While the resulting analysis should offer useful insights to those interested in television soap opera, my aim here is also to provide a model for further research of television production practices, and possibly even for other forms of commercial culture.

Production Constraints

This first area of cultural production focuses on the production history and constraints of *General Hospital* in order to better understand the way the production process is shaped by its own background. While production as a whole is seen as a limiting or constraining factor in theories of media culture, I here illustrate some of the large-scale constraints that shape not only the resultant text, but the rest of the production process, as well. While mainly economic in origin, these large-scale constraints also have cultural impact. They influence the environment within which employees work and the routines and practices they follow, as subsequent categories will demonstrate. This section focuses on the large-scale constraints of ownership structure, the program's own production history, and the status of soaps in the contemporary television industry. While constraints can be imposed by the histories and specificities of the medium, the genre, the show, and the people who create it, as well, the three constraints I touch on here were particularly salient during my research trip and seem particularly formative to *General Hospital*.

While most U.S. broadcast network television programming is produced by independent production companies that license their products to networks for a fee, *General Hospital* is wholly owned and produced by ABC/Disney itself.

While all of ABC's soap operas are network-owned, they are the only one of the three major networks with that arrangement. As Joe Montrone (personal communication, August 20, 1997), ABC executive in charge of daytime production for the west coast explained, "Technically, everybody on the show is an employee of ours, whether they're contracted, daily hire, or full staff with benefits. They all get an ABC paycheck." Because of this, there is intense network involvement at every level, with ABC's west coast executive in charge of daytime programming attending weekly story meetings between the executive producer and head writers, ABC Daytime publicity handling media relations, and ABC network offices in New York holding the budgetary purse strings. As a result, when network policies forbid guns to be held directly to characters's heads or restrict the explicitness of sex scenes, the show's staff sometimes feels creatively constrained. Yet the backing of ABC and its parent company, Disney, has benefitted the show by providing a degree of financial security less likely for a soap owned by an independent production company. According to one *GH* staff member who had previously worked at a soap not owned by its network, *General Hospital* has larger budgets for sets, wardrobe, and other such necessities than does this other soap because the production company owning the other show is unwilling (or unable) to spend as much, given its smaller size.

The show's own history also affects its production, setting it apart from even the other ABC-owned soaps. The enormous success of *General Hospital* in the early 1980s not only changed the soap opera industry, but earned *GH* a certain status with its network from which it still benefits today. According to coordinating producer Marty Vagts (personal communication, August 12, 1997):

> What we heard in those days was that ABC Daytime . . . was dropping 67% of the network profits. Right to the bottom line. We were clearing 67%. . . . And the pack was led by *General Hospital*. It was a giant cash cow. . . . And *General Hospital* had the ability to go to the well, the network well, and say that we needed a prop budget of X number of dollars or we needed a scenery [budget] of X number of dollars and we would get it. The other shows did not have that ability.

The material benefits the show received during the 1980s continue to pay off in substantial back-stocks of wardrobe, sets, and props; in the contractually secured earnings of star performers; and in the current studio space itself, which was constructed specifically for the show in the late 1980s and is substantially larger than the studios for ABC's New York–based soaps. Such historically earned perks set *GH* apart from other soaps, allowing it an opulence that is increasingly rare in the financially strained soap industry of the 1990s and 2000s.

Soaps are no longer the "cash cows" they once were for the broadcast networks. The soap opera audience, at least as it is measured by Nielsen, has shrunk drastically since the 1980s, a change attributable to the increasingly fractured television marketplace and the growing numbers of women in the workforce. Both of these trends have eroded the industry's formerly solid base of housewife viewers and have kept the genre from attracting newer, young audiences, who, 20 years ago, might have begun watching with their mothers or grandmothers (Parney and Mason, 2000, p. 13). Since the early 1990s, soaps have lost more than 20 million daily viewers, or about 25% of their total audience (Johnson, 1999, p. 1E; McFadden, 1999, p. D1). As a result, today's highest-rated soap hovers around a 7.2 rating while the lowest-rated ones survive on ratings in the 2.0 range. In August 1997, at the time of this study, *General Hospital* floated in the middle of this range, rating a 4.6, at least 6 to 8 million viewers less than in the early and mid-1980s. As a consequence, ABC and the other networks are making less and less money on these productions, resulting in decreased budgets for the shows. One specific result has been the virtual elimination of remote location shooting, a practice *GH* once engaged in up to seven times a year. Another has been a reduction in the show's clothing budget. According to costume designer Bob Miller (personal communication, August 20, 1997), "Our budget next year will probably be the same budget that we had in 1986. And clothing has probably tripled [in cost]."

As with any kind of constraints, the show's staff works to maintain a certain level of quality within these budgetary limits. For example, the wardrobe department sells used clothing to a specialized television and film resale shop, returning $70,000 to their budget from one year of these proceeds. Miller and co-designer Steve Howard make 3 or 4 wholesale shopping trips to New York design houses each year, purchasing high-fashion clothing a season in advance at much-reduced prices. Part of the reason they are able to do this is Miller's 10 year employment history with the show, a background that has provided him with a strong sense of the clothing many characters will need. But the wardrobe department's ability to reduce costs in this way is also assisted by the fact that, "Our gals are in a size range from 0–2 to 6 mainly" (B. Miller, personal communication, August 20, 1997). The clothing they purchase will fit, or else can be slightly altered to fit, a number of different actresses. Even the body types of performers shape the production process, their similar, extremely small, sizes allowing advance, wholesale wardrobe shopping that saves money and establishes a high-fashion, designer look.

This variety of physical and fiscal production constraints illustrates just a few of the distinctive shaping factors that media scholars might consider in analyses of television production. Though production is frequently understood as limiting or constraining texts and readings, these examples point to the constraints within such constraints. The limits of commercial culture are more complicated than simple profit motivation or the exploitation of workers. They can affect studio size and body size, the scope of the on-screen world and the scope of femininity. An understanding of such factors not only informs the interpretation of texts, but helps us to comprehend the priorities of capitalism, the imperatives of the television medium, and the reasons behind the products the medium offers. De-naturalizing the television world in these ways is the first step to not only knowing that world, but understanding the particular ways its power is shaped and its money and meanings are circulated.

Production Environment

Large-scale industrial factors, and the specific production details through which they have an impact, necessarily constrain the rest of the production process, even the environment in which ABC's employees work. Exploring this environment can uncover relevant economic determinants, such as the role of labor unions in the production process. But it can also provide insight to the cultural issues at stake within production situations. Hierarchies of gender and institutional positioning, for example, operate in *General Hospital* production and affect production routines and practices, as well as the television narrative constructed through the work process. Two aspects of the production environment that best bring to light these economically and culturally shaped processes are the overall work-place milieu and the organizational hierarchy.

Though the *General Hospital* work environment functions like any other television production in many ways, it is significantly different, as is any soap, because of the continuous, unending nature of the work. With preemptions no more than one or two times a year and production running only 2 to 3 weeks in advance of airing, the staff must produce an entire episode each day of the week. Thus, every task must be executed as efficiently as possible. The *General Hospital* studio must constantly negotiate high-level efficiency, technological intricacy, and creative selectivity. The tenuous blend of a tight production schedule and the emotionally-charged material endemic to soap operas escalates the tensions already present in any dramatic production.

These contradictory working conditions play out in the weekly production meetings, held one week in advance of the actual production. Here, issues up for discussion range from the kind of undergarments needed for a scene where a character disrobes to the maneuverability of the cameras in a new set. The meetings are a carefully balanced combination of practical or technical details and creative speculation on character motivation and story progression. While the director, who coordinates discussion of his or her particular episode, tends to work on the side of the practical and technical, questions of character motivation inevitably intervene, such as how vitally important it is for the abandoned-at-the-altar Brenda, now in a precarious emotional state, to rid herself of all remnants of her wedding, even her dress. This character motivation then requires practical back-up, as in the decision to slightly re-design Brenda's wedding gown to cover the undergarments she will wear as she sheds the dress in her hurt and angry post-wedding scene.

These tensions and their practical repercussions continue in daily production. While the director must be concerned with technical details of camera placement, lighting, and sound, he or she is also responsible for imparting performance notes to the actors. While these duties are no different than those of any television director, the pace at which the soap opera director must work, shooting 25–30 "items," or scene segments, per day, makes concerted attention to all these factors impossible. As such, the line producer (a duty rotated among 3 of the show's producers) gives the director notes on all these aspects throughout the shoot, though she tends to comment most often on aesthetic and creative issues over technical ones. While performance notes often originate with the producer, they are usually relayed by the director or through the floor manager at the director's request. The director is also freed from attending too closely to performance because the show has an acting coach on staff who works with the actors off-set or confers with the line producer and director in the control booth.

The distinctions in duty between the director and the line producer operate as gendered distinctions as well as efficiency-motivated time-savers. While all of the *GH* line producers are women and most of the directors are men, the gendering of their duties is not determined by the workers who fill the roles. In the *GH* production world, bodily aesthetics, questions of emotion, and delicate personnel issues are distinguished from technical matters and time constraints. The socially feminized aspects of production remain the exclusive domain of the producers and other "artistic" departments, while the more masculinized aspects are less selectively assigned. While the show certainly employs technical specialists in areas such as lighting and editing, the producers can and do dictate decisions in these areas. But technical personnel, often including the directors, remain far removed from the producers' reign over the more feminized concerns. For example, when an actress known for wanting excessive rehearsal time slowed down a scene with questions about character motivation, the technical director discounted her concerns, commenting, "That's not our business; that's not what we're here for," to his cohorts in the control booth. The production staff surrounding him agreed, emphasizing their prioritization of efficiency above all else. The line producer handled the actress.

The divisions in duty and agenda are also matters of positioning within the organizational hierarchy. Because the socially feminized areas are handled by those highest in the institutional ranks, the feminine is distinguished, but not necessarily disempowered, in this production environment. The producers have authority over so many areas, and particularly more delicate ones like talent relations, because of their prominent institutional status. Gendered distinctions meet organizational ones and result in the validation of socially feminized concerns. As the exasperation with the actress' demands suggests, resistance to such concerns is also a factor, be it in the name of efficiency, technology, or masculinized disinterest (such as when crew members watched broadcast feeds of golf matches on their camera viewfinders during particularly time-consuming scenes). Certainly, such differences in duty and agenda result from the soap opera's dual imperatives of cost- and time-efficient production and emotionally intense, time-consuming drama. But the fact that these economically motivated constraints become distinguishable elements with gendered overtones suggests that the production environment is as culturally shaped as it is economically determined.

The production environment is also shaped by those personnel less visible in the daily work process. The writing staff is one of those nearly invisible influences. During my visit, it was clear that the current head writing team was temporary, as the show worked through complicated contractual negotiations to re-hire a former, well-regarded head writer. Because the current head writers, as well as their most recent predecessors, lived in New York, and the rest of the writing team worked out of their homes, the writers held a mysterious, and somewhat revered, place within the organizational hierarchy.[2] The writers, at least according to assistant David Goldschmid (personal communication, August 11, 1997), often feel isolated from the rest of the show and are hungry for information on how their work is received in-house. The only people in-house who have contact with them are the writers' assistants, the executive producer, and the network programming executive, illustrating the physical and conceptual isolation of soap writers from the activities on the set and in the control booth.

The executive producer and the network programming executive, who hold the highest positions within the organizational hierarchy, were also physically removed from daily production. Their remove was only partial, however, as they would watch the onset action from monitors in their offices and frequently call the line producer in the control booth with comments and suggestions. While many employees, particularly actors, claimed that executive producer Wendy Riche has an "open door" policy and that they are always welcome to speak with her about storylines and their characters, her physical door was rarely open, her physical presence rarely visible, and any physical contact with her filtered through her two protective assistants. Yet the fact that I would often be referred to her to answer my questions illustrated her controlling involvement in nearly all aspects of the work process. The isolation of Riche and the writers from the rest of production (and from me as researcher, for that matter) was telling of the institutional hierarchy and of the physical and experiential distance between high-level decision-making and daily production. Those highest in the institutional hierarchy were most removed from daily production, though they controlled it in ways unobservable to most employees.

The production environment and its complicated tensions of efficiency and creativity, hands-on labor and removed, hierarchical control, demonstrate that struggles in soap opera production occur along cultural as well as economic lines, between duties and agendas distinguished and hierarchized by gender and institutional positioning, as well as by the larger-scale constraints of ownership structure, production history, and industrial trends. All of these constraints can affect the program they're meant to produce by determining the time and attention paid to performances, the allocation of budget to salaries or equipment or production elements like sets and wardrobe, and the shifts in meaning or emphasis as the production passes through the hands of network executives, executive producer, writers, line producers, actors, and production staff and crew. The environment within which these players are positioned is crucial to an understanding of their impact upon the resulting program.

Production Routines and Practices

While the weekly production meeting and the role of the director in daily tapings are some of the most significant routines and practices at *General Hospital,* a host of other routines and practices inform the production process. Such practices continue to speak to the cost- and time-efficiency demanded of soap operas. But they affect the program in other ways, as well, influencing the kinds of stories that get told and the paths by which those stories proceed. I discuss the practices of writing and production scheduling here to illustrate the way daily work routines negotiate textual meaning, at times fracturing it and at times fixing it. The continuity practices running throughout this daily work are the main method employed to stabilize such meaning before the program is offered up to audiences.

The vast quantity of stories and scripts required of a daily, hour-long dramatic production makes even the creative practice of writing a routinized one. Head writers plan stories that outline writers break down into daily segments and scriptwriters translate into dialogue and action. Despite this fractured system, continuity checks are built in to encourage consistency. Scriptwriters are given detailed, scene-by-scene summaries of each episode's happenings in the script outlines. Writers' meetings and producer notes help to hammer out questions about character motivation and plot convolutions. And continuity questions are asked and answered throughout each production day. Script continuity thus serves as the first line of defense against unstable meaning, against holes in the fictional world.

In addition to battling the writing system itself, continuity must fight against the idiosyncracies of the daily scriptwriters, each of whom has his or her own character biases. As scriptwriter Elizabeth Korte (personal communication, August 18, 1997) admitted:

> I have a real affinity for dark, driven, really scarred, very screwed up characters . . . However, you can't give good characters short shrift. You have to make them interesting, too . . . you have to try hard to guard against having every single scene be about the characters that you like.

Yet character consistency and balance does not happen just by writers trying very hard to be fair. Writers sometimes find alternative ways to write for "their" characters. As writer's assistant David Goldschmid (personal communication, August 11, 1997) explained:

> I've seen examples where certain writers of ours, they would love characters so much that they would trade scenes with other writers. [Say] you have writer A and writer B. Writer A will say, "Oh, I'd KILL for the Jason/Robin stuff in your day." And writer B will go, "Well, that was kind of giving me some problems. If you do those scenes for my script, can I pick up your Kevin/Lucy scenes?"

Such internal negotiation of scenes is part of the process by which *General Hospital* writing practices work to stabilize textual meaning. Jason and Robin are identifiable characters with consistent voices because of such trades and because the layering of writers builds character and story continuity checks into the writing process.

Despite such checks, however, continuity slips inevitably occur. The writing staff must sometimes make leaps of logic to keep the plots coherent. Elizabeth Korte (personal communication, August 18, 1997), who handles script continuity as well as writing scripts, explains a slip that occurred when the character of Robin said she was leaving for Paris the next day and actually left that evening:

> There's this thing called justifying where it's like, maybe we can believe that it was so traumatic that she broke up with Jason that she left earlier. Or we do this; this is our favorite thing that we do. It's the yellow sticky. This is a willing suspension of disbelief ticket and sometimes when I'm just asking people to believe, I'm like, take a yellow sticky. It's like, that's what you get, we're doing it, it's gotta be that way.

The willing suspension of disbelief operates as a substitute for continuity when production efficiency disallows re-writes or re-takes of problematic scenes. The writing team, along with the audience, agrees to suspend their doubts about situational particularities and even the fictional status of the world itself in favor of the character and relationship motivations that drive the narratives in the first place. In both the successes and failures of continuity within the writing process, textual meaning is fractured and fixed, disputed and conceded, all before the script is even produced.

The production schedule also opens up multiple opportunities for fractured meanings and confused plots. While the ideal situation is the full production of an entire episode in one day, this is rarely the case at *General Hospital*. Because only a limited number and configuration of sets can fit on the stage on any given day, and because the cast of approximately 35 contract players has a myriad of personal and professional scheduling conflicts, each day's production schedule is organized by grouping together related scenes, not by proceeding in a linear fashion through an episode. Coordinating producer Marty Vagts and his assistants try to schedule as much of one day's episode per shooting day as possible, but inevitably plan pre-and post-tapings of other episodes because of cast or set conflicts. The implications of this production schedule are numerous. Pre- and post-taped shows mean higher fees for the director, per Director's Guild rules. The long production days (rarely less than 10 hours) mean overtime pay for the unionized crew. Actors are rarely present en masse, instead working on set for only portions of the day. The makeup and hair room oscillates between periods of intense activity and no activity. Meanwhile, actors (and the producers who guide them) must conceptually shift their focus between scenes that are not necessarily taped in chronological order, adjusting their responses and emotional expression according to the character's place in the story, a place they have not yet worked through in their performance.

Like the writing process, the production schedule requires continuity checks to secure the potentially errant meanings it might produce. Wardrobe, hair, and makeup constantly take Polaroid photos of the actors, along with extensive notes on their appearance, so that they can replicate their looks on other shooting days which are supposed to be the same story day in the on-screen world. The production office provides an item-by-item breakdown for every shooting day, noting special props, wardrobe and makeup, or special effects and unusual technological requirements. The production continuity person then carefully tracks such details throughout the day and across days, making sure, for example, that performers carry their purses in and out of rooms and that the degree of rainfall is consistent across concurrent scenes on different sets. While such details seem trivial, they occupy an immense amount of time for many different workers on the *General Hospital* set and ultimately create coherent textual meaning out of a fractured work process.

While even the most effective of continuity practices can never close down the meanings that audiences might make of a given program, they do shape those potential meanings in foundational ways. The negotiations between writing practices, production scheduling, and continuity work to make the fictional world seamless and congruous. Routinized production practices allow for the routinized reliability of the soap opera's daily textual installments, where consistent character emotions, homes, and hairstyles provide justification for the on-screen world's believability, despite its extreme plots or the extraordinary attractiveness of its inhabitants. The preoccupation with details and the persistence of assembly-line routines are in some ways necessitated by the textual form, in some ways by audience expectations, and in some ways by economic imperatives. Their effect on the text and on potential readings of it is to offer a provisional baseline of meaning upon which characters and stories are built.

Production of Characters and Stories

The meanings audiences make of *General Hospital* proceed beyond a baseline of plot coherence and character consistency. They operate on more complex levels of story and character, as well, in both the world of production and that of audience consumption. The ways that characters and stories, in all their ideological intricacy, are produced involves nearly all *GH* employees to some extent. Most salient, however, are the writers, actors, and production departments that bring the characters to life and the stories to fruition. Each contributes to the characters and stories, bringing together layers of narrative significance that can be decoded in a range of ways, depending on which layers are deemed significant in any given moment of reception.

Since soap opera characters are first created through writing, the way that writers conceive of characters is an influential aspect of their generation. Scriptwriter Elizabeth Korte (personal communication, August 18, 1997) described her characters as living beings, "[Sonny] loved Brenda, but she was horrible for him. And he honored Lily but did not love her . . . She was in every way the perfect wife for him. He wasn't unstable around her. . . . She was like human lithium. She calmed him down." But Korte also conceived of her characters as archetypes, explaining how this particular love triangle was a retelling of such classic stories as *The Godfather* and *Gone with the Wind*:

> Scarlett O'Hara, that's Brenda, is sure she's in love with Ashley Wilkes. Which,
> I know Sonny doesn't seem like Ashley, but if you really take a step back from
> it, he is, he's a person who lives according to this archaic code. . . . He's gonna

be a gentleman, he's gonna be a mobster, even if the world he was raised to
be in is no longer there.

Characters like Sonny and Brenda are constructed, then, not just in the minds
of their creators, but through cultural constructions of tragic sagas and tortured romance. While the textual analyst or the lay audience member might
make such connections by watching the program, the fact that the program's
writers also view their characters in these ways suggests that similar meaning-
making processes occur during stages of production, reception, and perhaps
even critical analysis. The originary location of the intertextual connection
between Sonny and Brenda, Ashley and Scarlett, is insignificant. What does
matter is that cultural archetypes consciously operate within production decisions about characters, that production processes are invested in and influenced
by the surrounding culture.

Industry practice also involves itself with the surrounding culture in actors'
conceptions of their characters. The fact that actors tend to discuss their characters as living beings, often as beings with experiences parallel to their own,
is a telling reminder of the fluidity between lived experience and cultural production. Twenty year cast member Jackie Zeman (personal communication,
August 14, 1997) collapsed her own life, her conception of her audience's
lives, and her character's life when commenting on audience reaction to her
character, Bobbie:

> The first half of your life is one way and you finally hit 40 and now what
> becomes normal to you was never normal; it's a big deal. And so just having
> a husband and a child and a house and a home and a job and a family and a
> husband that's not fooling around or lying or drinking or taking drugs or
> doing any bad things, this is like, oh my God, I made it.

Zeman expressed pride in her own family life elsewhere in this discussion,
assumed a similar interest in family experience for her audience, and applied
both to her understanding of Bobbie's life and the audience's response to it.
Such belief in the authenticity of the character's tribulations helps many of the
show's actors to sustain their characters for years on end. According to *GH*
acting coach John Homa, (personal communication, August 20, 1997) one of
the primary difficulties of acting is that, "You as an actor must suspend your
disbelief. You've got to quit bitchin' and moanin' about this being real or not
real and just make it work." Much like the suspension of disbelief that the writers employ to make sometimes far-fetched events cohere, so too do soap actors
suspend their disbelief, justify actions through reference to character motivation, and call upon their own knowledge of human relationships to make sense
of narrative events.

But neither writers nor actors solely determine the construction of characters and stories. The various production departments—Set design & decoration,
Makeup & Hair, Wardrobe, and Lighting, for instance—also produce characters and stories. For example, Sonny and Brenda's last romantic dinner before
their wedding (a wedding the production staff knew would never take place) was
a long and drawn out series of "items" because of the intense attention to detail

during them. Not only were the actors dressed in formal-wear and elaborately coiffed, but senior supervising producer Julie Carruthers halted taping while Makeup matched Sonny's facial bruise to its previous incarnation and Props arranged the candles and table settings to look opulent, but not cluttered. Pink gels and screens were placed on the lights and the studio air conditioning was turned off because it kept putting out the candles around the set. When discussing the following day why the previous one had run so late, Carruthers (remarks made on set, August 21, 1997) explained how important it was to take the extra time to relight and perfect the romantic scene because, "It was their dance . . ." Her justification for the extra work demonstrates how production details not only support, but help to construct, narrative significance. Because this scene was lit a certain way, because special care was taken with makeup and wardrobe, because the staff used valuable production time to perfect one scene of many scheduled for that day, this scene became more important to everyone in the studio. It also became more distinctive within the flow of its episode, since it would look different than most other scenes. Because it featured the couple's final romantic moments before Sonny's last minute decision to run away by himself to save Brenda's life, it merited this extra time and attention. The meaning of the scene was constructed through writing and performance, but also through production details. This major story and character moment was constructed as a moment about romance and poignancy (as opposed to, say, sex and excitement) because of these details.

While the production of characters and stories seems more obviously meaning-laden than other aspects of production, exploring the ways in which character and story construction *generate* meaning and significance can help to demystify the creative process. This demystification can then help to expose cultural products and their messages as constructed as opposed to real or natural. Studying the production of Sonny and Brenda's final moments in this way can allow media scholars to point out how culturally constructed ideals of love and romance are perpetuated, in this case through intertextual associations, careful attention to visual details, and extended preparation time. To understand the way characters and stories are specifically created is to understand how cultural images and narratives hold and, more significantly, execute their power.

The Audience in Production

Lurking throughout all aspects of production is the audience, the industry's conception of the audience, the processes of audience decoding that both precede and follow any given *General Hospital* production day, and the actual audience around whom so much scholarship has centered. Though the audience figures implicitly into many aspects of production, such as in continuity efforts to stabilize textual meaning, the audience can also play an explicit role at certain moments. One such moment is the handling of audience response by the production team. Another way in which audiencehood figures into production evokes Richard Johnson's (1986/87) perspective on the lack of distinction between production, text, and audience. Processes of audience meaning-making, such as speculating about future storylines and tracking character knowledge of potentially explosive information, also occur during the production process, and suggest new ways of thinking about production itself. Finally, the meeting of production, audience, and critical research, as discussed here in my relationship to *General Hospital,* can offer new insights to the role of the audience—and the media scholar—in cultural production.

The way *General Hospital* handles its audience response is telling of the limited presence of actual audience members in the production process. The show's production team fits audience responses into an established system that allows for efficient categorization and acknowledgment. When fan mail arrives at the show, those letters addressed to actors are tallied and sent unopened to the actors themselves. Those letters addressed to the writers go to one of the writer's assistants, who reads them and summarizes their responses in a monthly report that includes selected quotes from letters encapsulating what many people are saying. A large chunk of the mail is addressed to the producers or to the show itself. This mail is opened and tallied by the student interns, who register whether the response is negative (if the writer says he or she will stop watching the show), positive (even if they have specific criticisms, as long as they don't threaten to stop watching), or requires a response (to which the interns send one of a series of form letters). The writers' mail report and all the numerical tallies go to the assistant to the executive producer, who compiles them into a monthly report for the producers, head writers, and network executives. The interns are additionally responsible for summarizing the phone messages left daily on a viewer response voice-mail box. The assistant to the executive producer types and distributes these summaries to the producers and head writers. Lastly, the network sends regular summaries and choice selections from postings in the ABC Daytime Online bulletin boards about the shows. The network also conducts viewer focus groups a few times a year to get additional audience feedback.

While the system in place to handle audience response is thorough and efficient, it does not really account for most viewers' perspectives, as the letters must be neatly classified into positive or negative categories and the actual words of audience members are only rarely seen by anyone higher in the chain of command than a writer's assistant. Additionally, the writing and production schedule requires storylines to be mapped out several months in advance, so viewer responses to just-aired episodes can have little direct or immediate impact. Still, the network and the producers are interested enough in audience response that they have, on rare occasion, adjusted storylines accordingly. Predictably, the more established actors were less invested in audience response than were the newer performers and the producers were more interested in viewer feedback than were other employees. Overall, the specific opinions and perspectives of audience members were valued less than their general responsiveness. For example, the production staff appreciated the fan war being waged between those viewers wanting Brenda to be paired with Sonny versus those wanting her paired with Jax more for its vociferousness than for the specific opinions offered on the dysfunction or strength of the relationships.

But audiencehood played another, less expected, role in production, when meaning-making processes usually associated with reception were enacted by production personnel. Crew members would discuss storylines, expressing disgust with devious characters or adoration for blossoming romances as would any other viewer, despite the fact that actors were playing out those storylines in front of their very eyes. The writing staff spoke as passionately about characters and their motivations as do soap fans chatting with their peers on the Internet. As Elizabeth Korte (personal communication, August 18, 1997) in script continuity explained, her job requires her to keep track of the different characters' points of view, to know what they've done, seen, or said previously. It has been well-documented in studies such as Brown's (1994) and Allen's (1985) that audience members engage in the same kind of tracking, eagerly awaiting the revelation of some vital piece of information a character does not yet know.

The fact that show employees frequently have as little information about future storylines as do audiences assists in this sort of audience-like speculation. In one between-takes conversation between actresses, for example, the two women debated who would turn out to be the father of Carly's baby. Like any audience members uninformed about future storyline, they weighed the ramifications of A. J. being the father instead of Tony. (Their consensus: It would most likely be A. J. because of all the future storylines with his family it would open up.) While a plethora of storylines serves production interests, it also serves audience interests, and rumination about storyline possibilities is a common feature of audience discourse on soaps (Hobson, 1982; Ang, 1982). The actresses's lack of power to control the parentage of Carly's baby, given their position within the *General Hospital* institutional hierarchy, makes their speculation and prediction more like audience activity than like producer machination. While such audience activity can be understood as "producerly" for its actions upon the text, such production activity can be understood as "audience-like" for its refusal to accept textual meaning as pre-determined.

The third role of the audience in production is more accurately that of the audience in the *study* of production. If media scholars hope to research Johnson's circuit of culture (1986/87), we need to make room for ourselves within that circuit. Particularly if we choose to engage in on-site production research, media scholars should consider the role of the researcher in relation to production (much as cultural scholars have done in considering the role of the researcher in relation to audiences under study). When the media researcher is also an audience member (as most are likely to be, whether as fan or as critic), audiencehood enters into production through an otherwise non-existent channel. During my trip to *GH*, I functioned as researcher by interviewing people, sitting in on meetings, observing my surroundings, and taking notes. But I was also an audience member, coming close to tears while watching the taping of a goodbye scene between Sonny and his father and momentarily thrilling at sitting at the bar of Luke's blues club. I'm less certain about how my presence affected the production process itself, though having a stranger sitting in the corner of the control booth or jotting on a notepad on set each day may have subtly shifted the work process.

My interpretations of the processes I observed have also undoubtedly been shaped by my long-time viewership. For example, I easily chatted with cast members in their dressing rooms due, at least in part, to my intense familiarity with their on-screen selves. Though I knew I was a stranger to them, they felt like old friends to me. Instead of challenging my researcher's professionalism or blocking my objectivity, my audiencehood provided me with a perspective on the production process potentially more valuable than that of a disinterested observer. My view of the production process was the audience view as well as the researcher's view. Since audiencehood has been historically privileged within cultural studies of media, exploring the role of the audience in production, even literally *within* the production environment as a researcher/audience member, helps to keep production scholarship from losing sight of the other spheres of cultural circulation. Analyzing the distinctiveness of production, both economically and culturally, while continuing to explore the continuities among production, texts, audiences, and social contexts, can keep cultural studies true to its theoretical models while moving the field beyond its text- and audience-centered focus.

Conclusion

These five categories for analyzing the television production process suggest one of many potential templates for organizing industry-centered scholarship. Certainly other forms of television programming, other television systems, other media, and other temporal and spatial contexts could lead to other categorizations. Neither the categories nor their implications can serve as universal truths about all cultural production or all U.S. broadcast network television production or even all soap opera production. Hopefully, however, they demonstrate the significance of production-centered scholarship to a broad understanding of the entire cultural circulation process.

Putting Johnson's model of cultural circulation into practice involves recognizing that production contains both economic and cultural elements, that it is both a distinctive process and a process intertwined with other spheres of cultural circulation. Conducting analyses of cultural production along these lines, as well as drawing upon the production scholarship executed by political economists, mass communications analysts, and sociologists, can help cultural studies scholarship gain a fuller picture of the intricacies of cultural circulation. In addition, those scholars working in paradigms other than cultural studies might find new insights to the production processes they are already investigating. As a range of media communication scholars have realized and continue to realize, production-centered research can demonstrate the links between commercial media's capitalist base and their ideological messages. In addition, delineating specific production practices can alert media activists to vulnerable points at which to intervene and can assist scholars in unmasking the constructed naturalness of media images. If media researchers seek to understand the paths through which media products come to exist, if they seek to understand the constraints that shape the products available to us, then this sort of rigorous, layered attention to production processes is vital.

Notes

1. The 1995 *Critical Studies in Mass Communication* colloquy on the debate between political economy and cultural studies exemplifies this trend.

2. The scattering of soap opera writers outside the confines of the studio and even the city of production challenges traditional notions of authorship, even of television authorship, which is acknowledged to be less univocal than most. The work processes of writers, so vital to soap opera production and yet so removed from the production space, are significant elements of the production process that deserve further exploration and analysis.

References

Allen, R. (1985). *Speaking of soap operas*. Chapel Hill and London: The University of North California Press.

Ang, I. (1982). *Watching Dallas: Soap opera and the melodramatic imagination*. (D. Couling, Trans.). London and New York: Methuen.

Brown, M. E. (1994). *Soap opera and women's talk: The pleasures of resistance*. Thousand Oaks, California: Sage Publications.

Cantor, M. (1971). *The Hollywood TV producer: His work and his audience*. New Brunswick: Transaction Books.

Cantor, M. and Cantor, J. (1992). *Prime Time Television: Content and Control*, 2nd Edition. Newbury Park, CA: Sage.

Colloquy. (1995). *Critical studies in mass communication*, 12, 60–100.

Gans, H. (1979). *Deciding What's News*. New York: Random House.

Hall, S. (1980). Encoding/decoding. In S. Hall, D. Hobson, A. Lowe, P. Willis (Eds.), *Culture, media, language: Working papers in cultural studies 1972–1979* (pp. 128–138). London: Hutchinson.

Hobson, D. (1982). *Crossroads: The drama of a soap opera*. London: Methuen.

Johnson, K. V. (1999). Soaps in a lather. *USA Today*, 2 July, 1E.

Johnson, R. (1986/87). What is cultural studies anyway? *Social text*, 16, 33–80.

McFadden, K. (1999). Another era leaves *Another World* kaput. *The Seattle Times*, 24 June, DI.

Parney, L. and Mason, M. S. (2000). Selling soaps. *The Christian Science Monitor*, 7 July, 13.

Tuchman, G. (1979). *Making News*. New York: Free Press.

Translating Trek
Rewriting an American Icon in a Francophone Context

Caroline-Isabelle Caron

Italian translators use a now well-known cliché: "Traduttore, traditore." Translating is betraying. It refers to the tension between the necessity of rendering meaning (or interpretation) and that of rendering style, metaphors, and images within the original source text. This tension is a profound one in literature. In translating television dialogues and in dubbing episodes, many more exigencies come into play. Television translators have to take into account questions of synchrony, linguistic limitations, the various dubbing traditions of different countries, and their own poetic license. The main challenge of television translation is to find a balance between being true to the source text and the sometimes necessary falsification of the original dialogue in order to accurately render the story being told. Those factors come into play when translating *Star Trek*, created by Gene Roddenberry. The largely visual Trek universe, with its own vocabularies and traditions, is a special challenge for translators.

This is especially true when translating *Star Trek: The Original Series* into French. In 1971–1972, all seventy-nine episodes were dubbed in Montreal, and the series was renamed *Patrouille du Cosmos (Cosmos Patrol)*. It has aired nearly every year since. Sonolab (now a subsidiary of Covitec) was responsible for the dubbing; the texts were written by Michel Collet and the dubbing actors worked principally under the stage direction of Michel Georges.[1] The translation available to all French audiences is *Patrouille du Cosmos*, though in France it was re-entitled *Star Trek: Classique*.[2]

Dubbers often translate for audiences that may or may not be familiar with the universe of the story being told (Dutter; Luyken 155). When dealing with *TOS*, these difficulties are more than obvious. *Patrouille du Cosmos* was one of the very first television series ever dubbed in Quebec.[3] The Quebec dubbing tradition was still being invented when this translation was produced. The dubbers had to adapt and interpret dialogues taking place on other planets, pronounced by aliens in silly make-up and starship officers wearing goofy clothes.

Caroline-Isabelle Caron, "Translating Trek: Rewriting an American Icon in a Francophone Context." From *The Journal of American Culture*, Vol. 26, No. 3 (Sept. 2003), pp. 329–355. Copyright © 2003, Blackwell Publishing/American Culture Association.

Furthermore, these shows were metaphors for profoundly American stories of frontier exploration and for societal debates that meant very little to the average Québécois in the early 1970s. The dubbers needed to make all of this intelligible to French-speaking audiences while remaining true to the original concepts, storylines, and ultimate moral messages of each episode. As I will show here, they had varying levels of success.

Today, *Patrouille du Cosmos* is as widely known in Quebec and France as *Star Trek* is in the United States.[4] But *Patrouille* is not quite the same show as *TOS*. The "filter" of translation has created a similar yet distinct cultural product from its original English version. In this study, I will explore how the transformations resulting from the dubbing process have changed *Star Trek* into *Patrouille du Cosmos,* and how, as a result, Francophone audiences have been watching a different show than Anglophones. This study is based on a review of all seventy-nine episodes, and I will refer to fourteen selected episodes representing all three seasons. When quoting dialogue, parentheses ( ) indicate off-screen dialogue, E indicates the original English text, Q the Quebec translation, and LT the literal English translation of the Quebec text. The literal translations are my own. For E and Q, the dialogue is in quotation marks, since it was actually spoken, as opposed to LT. Character name codes and the names of the dubbing actors are in Appendix 1. I will give examples of the various types of transformations and of some of the most striking translation challenges faced by the dubbers. The purpose of these examples is to offset how the *TOS* stories and characters were modified—in short, how they were "betrayed." I will also posit hypotheses as to how *Patrouille du Cosmos* was incorporated into the French-language collective imagination and culture.

The Challenges of Dubbing Trek

The process of dubbing a television show poses special challenges for the translators. Television shows, like all audiovisual productions, "have generally as much to do with music, images and acting as with words" (Luyken 149). Translators, therefore, have to take into account that the texts must be spoken (their "actability") and that the sounds of the translated texts must more or less fit what is being seen, especially the lip movements (Whitman-Linsen 14; Ladouceur 20–21). In short, the translated text must be in synchrony with the visual portion of the production. In her book *Through the Dubbing Glass,* Candace Whitman-Linsen breaks down the different types of synchronies into categories that are both intertwined and mutually dependent. As she explains, "All of the types are highly woven in with semantic, phonetic, psychological, aesthetic and semiotic considerations" (19).

Whitman-Linsen divides between visual/optical and audio/acoustic synchronies (19). Of the former, she identifies lip synchrony, syllable articulation synchrony, length of utterance synchrony (gap synchrony or isochrony), and gesture and facial expression synchrony (kinetic synchrony). Of the latter, she categorizes idiosyncratic vocal type, paralinguistic elements (tone, timber, pitch of voice), prosody (intonation, melody, tempo), cultural variations, and accents and dialects. In order to produce high-quality versions into other languages, most (ideally all) of these synchronies must be realized; failing that, the viewers may not believe the televised performance they see and hear.

Television translators and dubbers also face practical constraints. The dubbing of audiovisual media is almost always done with a minimal budget and under strict time constraints. It is therefore difficult to produce quality dialogue (Pommier 104–45). The casting of actors is not always easy and is always expensive.[5] In a few *patrouille du Cosmos* episodes, the same actor dubbed two characters, changing his voice and accent in the process. Most of the time, only a very attentive ear will detect it. But this can also lead to problems. In "Balance of Terror"/ "Zone de terreur," for example, the actor dubbing Scotty also dubbed another character, Lieutenant Stiles. In most episodes, this would not be a problem, since the second character would usually have so few lines that the actor's double duty would go unnoticed. But in a scene where both characters have to speak in close proximity, this difficulty had to be resolved somehow. This is what happens in Act 4:

> K:　E "Weapons' status."
> 　　 Q "L'état des armes?"
> 　　 LT The state of the weapons?
> (Sc):　E "We've only the forward phaser-room, Captain."
> 　　 Q [line omitted]
> K:　E "Fully operable, Scotty?"
> 　　 Q "En état de marche, Scotty?"
> 　　 LT In working order, Scotty?
> (Sc):　E "Yes, sir. But specialist Tomlinson is manning it alone. No stand-by crew available."
> 　　 Q [line omitted]
> St:　E "Sir, my first assignment was weapon's control."
> 　　 Q "Monsieur, ma première affectation était le maniement des faisseaux."
> 　　 LT Sir, my first affectation was beam handling.

The narrative was clearly modified here. It was decided to omit Scotty's lines altogether. Contrary to the original, when Kirk calls Scotty, he only hears silence and his questions serve to emphasize Scotty's lack of response. What the Quebec version implies is that the engineer has been hurt in the previous battle and cannot answer the bridge. The original indicated that Scotty had his hands full in engineering and needed help. But in French, when Stiles offers to man the forward phaser room, he is acting as a proficient officer replacing an injured comrade. The result is a dramatic scene in which the actor did not have to speak the lines of two different characters in succession and give himself away.

Such acting constraints are compounded by the techniques used for voice-overs in various countries. In French-speaking countries, dubbing is done with the *bande rythmo* method in which the source text is divided into one-minute segments and shown to the dubbing actors on a screen at the top or bottom of which is a timing indicator and a scrolling band (see Appendix 2). On the band is the dubbed text, as well as indications for rhythm, tone, accentuation, and emphasis. As the text scrolls past the timing indicator, the actors know exactly when to pronounce which syllable and make which sound.

The result is usually very tight synchrony and isochrony. Often, however, the outcome is a flattening of the general tone of the acting performance, as the actors are never acting more than a minute of dialogue at a time. It can also lead to overacting. The *bande rythmo* technique prevents the dubbing actors from fully interpreting any given scene. Most French dubbing technical manuals explain that the actors must keep an eye on the dubbed scene at all times, keep the other on the scrolling band, and pronounce every word, every syllable at the precise moment when they scroll past the timing indicator, a veritable ocular gymnastic (Pommier 39; Whitman-Linsen 75). As a result, the dubbers' acting performance is not always believable, or simply not very inspired, no matter how good the translated text (Pommier 105–06). Most *Patrouille du Cosmos* episodes suffer from this kind of flattening. As a result, the grand eloquence of William Shatner is more tame, and Spock's original neutral, logical tone is sometimes nothing short of somber in the Quebec version.

Inevitably, dubbing is a difficult process. The linguistic elements (vowels, syllables, lip movements, and so on), paralinguistic elements, facial expressions, body movements, and breathing are inherent to all performed texts (Ladouceur 20–21). The translation of dialogues must therefore provide for coherence in all of those categories. This is not always possible. In every case of visual media translation, the translators and dubbers are forced to accept some level of compromise.

In some cases, compromising means sacrificing meaning for better lip synchrony. For example, in the episode "Assignment: Earth"/"Mission: Terre," the principal character "Gary Seven" becomes "Gary Savant" in French. The number seven translates as "sept" in French, and clearly couldn't be used. Since Seven's main characteristic is his advanced knowledge, the choice of "Savant" fits both synchrony and the overall storyline. Even if the use of a number would have underscored the fact he is not of planet Earth, his French last name serves a similar purpose. In the episode "Miri," the crew lands on a planet inhabited by children who turn out to be over three hundred years old. "Grups" (the name the children gave to adults, short for grown-ups) was translated as "Grands Pieds," literally "Big Feet." Translation erased the original meaning and its obvious reference to kiddy-talk, while introducing a quirky reminder that adults have bigger feet than children. However, it assured lip synchrony, as the bilabial sounds found in "Grups" are also found in "Grands Pieds." The same happens with the name the children gave themselves, "Onlies" (because they are the only ones left), which is translated as "Élus," or "Chosen," as if the children had concluded that the adults killed by the "Life Prolongation Project" had died in divine punishment.

At other times, the translators compromise synchrony to ensure stronger dramatic effects or grammatically correct sentences. The episode "A Journey to Babel"/"Un tour à Babel" contains several examples of this, the most evident of which is heard during the party scene in Act 1.[6] After a heated dis-

cussion between Spock's father Sarek, Andorian ambassador Shras, and Ter-
ralite ambassador Gav, the conversation comes to a close with a retort by
Spock's mother Amanda:

> Sh: E "Have you met Gav before, Ambassador?"
>   Q "Avez-vous rencontré Gav auparavant, ambassadeur?"
>   LT Have you met Gav before, Ambassador?
> Sa: E "We debated during my last council session."
>   Q "On s'est affronté lors de la dernière session du conseil."
>   LT We confronted each other during the last council session.
> A: E "Ambassador Gav lost."
>   Q "Ça s'est soldé par la défaite de Gav."
>   LT It ended with Gav's defeat.

Amanda's line means essentially the same in both versions, but the length
and number of syllables are quite different. The Quebec version has eleven syllables instead of the six quick syllables in English. A literal translation like
"Ambassadeur Gav a perdu" would not have had the same kind of punch as
the original, and would have provided for even worse synchrony. To resolve
this problem, the dubbers chose to end Amanda's line while her face was partially hidden by her hand bringing a drinking glass to her mouth. The result
is that the viewers would notice the lack of synchrony, but the dubbing would
not look as bad as it could have under other circumstances.

In reverse, shortcuts are sometimes taken in the dialogue because the
French version would simply require too many words to render exactly. This
is the case in the episode "Balance of Terror"/ "Zone de terreur." In a complicated scene in Act 1 where Spock briefs the crew on the situation at the
border of the Neutral Zone, the visuals show close-ups of Spock interspersed
with shots of various crew members listening to him. The translator had to
write a text that would explain the situation as precisely as in the source text,
but that would still be isochronic. In short, every time Spock comes into view,
the French text must say the same thing as the original, and the explanation
must not run longer that it does in English.

> Sp: E "Referring to the map on your screens, (you will note beyond the mov-
>   ing position of our vessel, a line of Earth outpost stations. Constructed on
>   asteroids, they monitor the Neutral Zone, established by treaty after the
>   Earth-Romulan conflict of over a century ago. As you may recall from your
>   histories, this conflict was fought, by our standards today, with primitive
>   atomic weapons and in primitive space vessels) *which allowed no quarter,*
>   *no captives, nor was there even ship-to-ship communication. (Therefore, no*
>   *Human, Romulan or ally has ever seen the other.) Earth believes the Romu-*
>   *lans to be warlike, cruel, traitorous. And only the Romulans know what they*
>   *think of Earth.* (The treaty set by subspace radio, established this Neutral
>   Zone, entry in which, by either side, would constitute an act of war.) The
>   treaty has been unbroken since that time. Captain."
>   Q "Vous référant à la carte qui est sur votre écran, (vous noterez au-delà de
>   les chemins suivie par notre vaisseau une ligne de stations interspatiales. Con-
>   struites sur des astéroïdes, elles surveillent la Zone Neutre, qui fut déter-
>   minée après le conflit qui survint entre la Terre et Romulus il y a un siècle.

Si vous voulez bien vous souvenir, les combattants utilisèrent de primitifs vaisseaux spatiaux et de non moins primitives armes atomiques. Ce fut une véritable hécatombe.) *Il n'y eu ni blessés, ni captifs. Il n'y eu aucun corps-à-corps visuel pendant les combats. (Par conséquent, il n'y a même pas eu de contact humain entre les combattants.) Les Terriens croyaient que les Romulans étaient sauvages, cruels, traitres. Il n'y avait que les Romulans qui connaissaient les Terriens.* (Le traité de paix établi par radio déterminait une Zone Neutre, qui ne devait être violée par aucun des partis sous peine d'une nouvelle guerre.) Le traité n'a jamais été rompu depuis ce temps. Capitaine."

LT Referring to the map on your screen, you will note beyond the route followed by our vessel a line of interspace stations. Constructed on asteroids, they monitor the Neutral Zone, which was determined after the conflict which occurred between Earth and Romulus a century ago. If you would recall, the combatants used primitive space vessels and no less primitive atomic weapons. It was a veritable slaughter. *There were no casualties, no captives. There was no visual hand-to-hand during the battles. Consequently, there was not even human contact between the combatants. Terrans believed that the Romulans were savage, cruel, traitorous. Only the Romulans knew the Terrans.* The peace treaty established by radio determined a Neutral Zone, which was not to be violated by either party, lest the beginning of a new war. The treaty was never broken since that time. Captain.

The italicized sentences posed the most difficulty for the translator and are ultimately inaccurate. Clearly, this passage also shows that the translator was forced to cut out less important details in favor of isochrony. The depth of the episode was lost to the necessity of making it all fit visually (Fodor 77–79).

In other cases, translators compromise by modifying the actual text of the dialogue to better render the overall storyline. The result is a better understanding of the story, but a different rendition of what the text originally said. In Act 3 of the same episode, the Romulan Commander and his officer Decius do not agree on the proper course of action. The former would rather go home, but the latter is eager to go back into battle against the *Enterprise*.

D: E "We are in the Neutral Zone. They will not enter. If you refuse, permit me the glory of the kill, commander."

Q "Ils n'entreront jamais en Zone Neutre. Si vous refusez, accordez-moi la gloire de me tuer, commandant."

LT They will never enter the Neutral Zone. If you refuse, allow me the glory of killing myself, commander.

Here, the French-language version better emphasizes Decius's eagerness than does the original, and implies that he would not go home alive without having destroyed their enemies. As such, he compounds later lines by the Romulan Commander, played by Mark Leonard. In Act 4, he explains to Kirk that Romulans are "creatures of duty" ("créatures de devoir"), after which he honorably activates his ship's self-destruct mechanism.

As in the previous example, sometimes a translator will choose to add meaning, lines, jokes, or details that do not appear in the source text in order to beef up the story being told. In *Patrouille du Cosmos,* the most common form of these transformations is the addition of jokes. In the episode "Bread and Circuses"/ "Sur les chemins de Rome," there are several instances of striking changes, including additional gags.[7] Many of the added jokes build upon dialogue already in the source text. At the beginning of Act 1, for example, Spock detects noticeable levels of air pollution similar to twentieth-century Earth's. The Francophone gag is stronger here than the Anglophone.

Mc: E "The word is 'smog.'"
Q "Ça s'appelait le 'smog.'"
LT It was called 'smog.'

Sp: E "Yes, I believe that was the term. I had no idea you were that much of a historian, doctor."
Q "Je crois bien que c'était le terme. Oh! Je ne vous connaissais pas ce talent d'historien, docteur."
LT I well believe that it was the term. Oh! I did not know you had the talent of a historian, doctor.

Mc: E "I am not, Mister Spock! I was simply trying to stop you from giving us a lecture on the subject! Jim, is there anything at all we know about this planet?"
Q "Je n'en suis pas un, Monsieur Spock! Je voulais seulement éviter l'énumération complète de ce qui compose le smog, Spock. Jim, à part le smog, y a-t-il autre chose que l'on connaisse sur cette planète?"
LT I am not one, Mister Spock! I only wanted to avoid the complete enumeration of what comprises smog, Spock. Jim, besides smog, is there anything else we know about this planet?

In the French-language passage, the smog gag in set up more strongly by McCoy, by insinuating clearly that this is superfluous knowledge about an otherwise unknown planet. In that episode, however, the best added gag is found in the very last lines of the episode in Act 4. After having escaped with their lives and finally understanding that they had been among Romans and Christians, Kirk tells Chekov that it is time to leave:

K: E "Wouldn't it be something to watch, to be a part of it, to see it happen all over again. Mister Chekov, bring us out of orbit. Warp factor one."
Q "J'aimerais bien y assister, en faire partie, voir ce qui arrivera, seulement une fois. Monsieur Chekov, sortons de l'orbite chrétienne. Mach facteur un."
LT I would like to see it, to be part of it, to see what will happen, only once. Mister Chekov, let us leave the Christian orbit. Mach factor one.

C: E "Yes, sir."
Q "Ave, César!"
LT Hail, Caesar!

The added gag underscores the plot of the entire episode by inserting a play on words. "Sortir de l'orbite chrétienne" can mean "To leave the Christian orbit," but also "To leave the Christian zone of influence" in much the same way the Romans were trying to do in the episode. Chekov's witty retort only adds to this, by mockingly placing Kirk in the position of imperial leader of the *Enterprise*.

Other changes completely transform the original text in order to add a passage that would be much funnier and more intelligible to Franco-phones. At the very end of "Miri," Act 4, Yeoman Rand, Kirk, and McCoy reflect on the events that just took place. Rand is worried about the children:

R: E "Just children. Simply to leave them there with a medical team . . ."
        Q "Ce n'était que des enfants. Ils ont besoin d'être sous contrôle médical, Jim."
        LT They were only children. They need to be under medical control, Jim.

K: E "Just children. Three hundred years old and more. I've already contacted Space Central. They'll send teachers, advisors . . ."
        Q "Des enfants? Le plus jeune avait trois cents ans. J'ai contacté les autorités compétentes. Ils vont leur envoyer des éducateurs."
        LT Children? The youngest was three hundred years old. I contacted the proper authorities. They will send them educators.

Mc: E "And truant officers, I presume."
        Q "Des fonctionnaires, comme d'habitude."
        LT Civil servants, as usual.

K: E "They'll be all right."
        Q "Probablement."
        LT Probably.

The theme of the incompetent civil servant is an extremely familiar one to Francophones of Quebec and France. It comprises the very old cliché of civil servants who do not know what they are doing and sleep at their desks all day. Clearly this is what the translator refers to here. The implied image is that the civil servants sent to the planet will be completely overrun by those three-hundred-year-old children, and will in no way be able to control them. Doctors, on the other hand, might have better luck, as Rand implies.

As the previous example shows, it is sometimes necessary for translators to change the cultural references in the source text in order to make it funnier, or simply more intelligible to the target (other-language) audience. For example, in "Bread and Circuses"/ "Sur les chemins de Rome," when commenting on the extent of the similarities with Earth, Spock explains,

Sp: E "Complete Earth parallel. The language here is English."
        Q "Vraiment, on se croirait sur Terre. Jusqu'à la langue qui est française."
        LT Truly, one could believe to be on Earth. Even the language is French.

Since the language spoken in the Quebec version is French, a literal translation of this passage would have made little sense. Spock could not have commented in French that the language heard by him and the audience was English. A change of cultural allusion was necessary.

Most of the time, referential substitution provides meaningful information to replace cultural allusions that the target audience would not normally possess (Leppihalme 37–77). With the new cultural allusions in place, the target audience can now make sense of the dialogue or the storyline being depicted. In the case of *Star Trek*, most of the allusions to beasts, literary authors, or other cultures are invented and integrated into the overall Trek universe. There is little need to cut out a reference to a Denebian Slime Devil in order to replace it with another reference; it is self-explanatory. The only reason to do so would be to solve difficulties in synchrony.

This is what happened in "A Journey to Babel"/ "Un tour à Babel." During the aforementioned party scene, immediately after the passage discussed earlier, Amanda reveals to McCoy that her son Spock had a pet as a child. In English, she describes the *sehlat* as "Sort of like a . . . a fat teddy bear." Teddy bears are part of the Quebec cultural universe, and comparing a *sehlat* to an "ourson" or an "ours en peluche" would have made perfect sense. However, it would have allowed for terrible synchrony. The translator therefore chose to change the comparison to "Une sorte de gros cheval de bois" (a kind of a big wooden horse). The number of syllables is the same, the lip movements are synchronized, and the passage keeps its original reference to a child's toy. However, the mental image created by the dialogue is quite different. This image is further changed by Spock's additional description:

> Sp: E "Not precisely, doctor. On Vulcan the teddy bears are alive, and they have six inch fangs."
>
> Q "Non, pas tout à fait, docteur. Sur Vulcain, un cheval de bois, ce n'est pas en bois. Ça vit et ça a des canines d'éléphant."
>
> LT No, not precisely, doctor. On Vulcan, a wooden horse, it's not made of wood. It lives and it has elephant canines.

The spirit of the dialogue and the impression of the alien quality and the possible threat posed by the beast are kept intact, though the actual image has changed.

On the other hand, some changes made by the translator were not necessary. Meanings and words were changed significantly, even if a literal translation would not have been problematic. There is a certain amount of poetic license in the choices made by the writer of the Quebec text. Often, the balance between necessity and preference is not always detectable. In most scenes, questions of synchrony complicate matters. However, in a scene where most of the text is in voice-over (no lip movement), one could expect a literal translation to take place. But this is not always the case. "The Cloud Minders"/ "Nuages" has a good example of this. In Act 1, while Kirk and Spock are resting in the cloud city of Stratos of the planet Ardana, the latter reflects on the situation at hand and announces to the audience the main plot twists of the episode. The entire speech is in voice-over, with shots of the sights and characters of the episode. It is necessary to give it in full here:

> (Sp): E "This troubled planet is a place of the most violent contrasts. Those who receive the rewards are totally separated from those who shoulder the burdens. It is not a wise leadership. *Here on Stratos, everything is incomparably beautiful and pleasant.* The High Advisor's charming daughter Droxine particularly so. The name Droxine seems appropriate to her. I wonder: can she retain such purity and sweetness of mind and be aware of the life of the people on the surface of the planet? There, the harsh life in the mines is instilling the people with a bitter hatred. The young girl who lead the

attack against us when we beamed down was filled with the violence of desperation. If the lovely Droxine knew of the young miner's misery, I wonder how the knowledge would affect her."

Q "Cette planète est le siège des plus violents contrastes. Ceux qui font les profits se désolidarisent complétement de ceux qui accomplissent les tâches. Ce qui ne pourrait être une façon peu orthodoxe de mener les choses. *Ici, sur Stratos, tout n'est que luxe, calme et volupté, comme l'a si bien dit un poète terrien.* La fille du Grand Officier ne dépare en rien cette cité idyllique. Comme le disait Plassius son père, c'est le plus beau des chefs d'œuvres. Une chose m'étonne. Elle semble être confinée dans un univers calfeutré et ethéré. Loin, très loin des contingences de sa planète. Cependant, des conditions de travail rigoureuses ont insufflé une haine implacaple dans l'esprit des mineurs. La jeune fille qui conduisait l'attaque dirigée contre nous lors de notre arrivée semblait animée par la violence du désespoir. Si la charmante Droxine arrivait à sentir la misère de ces jeunes mineurs, je me demande quelle serait sa réaction."

LT This planet is the stage of the most violent contrasts. Those who make the profits completely dissociate themselves from those who accomplish all the tasks. That which would not be an orthodox way of doing things. Here, on Stratos, all is luxury, calm, and opulence, like it was so well said by a Terran poet. The daughter of the High Officer does not mar in any way this idyllic city. As Plassius her father said, she is the most beautiful of masterpieces. One thing surprises me. She seems to be confined to a closed and ethereal universe. Far, far away from the exigencies of her planet. In the meantime, the rigorous work conditions have insufflated an implacable hatred into the minds of the miners. The young girl who was leading the attack directed at us at the time of our arrival seemed to be animated by the violence of desperation. If the charming Droxine found a way to feel the misery of these young miners, I wonder what would be her reaction.

None of these changes was necessary, since there was no synchrony to take into account. In the Quebec version, there is no mention of Spock's opinion of Droxine's name, but there is an insistence on her exceptional beauty. There is also a paraphrase of *Invitation au voyage* by the Terran poet mentioned in the underlined sentence, Charles Baudelaire: "Là, tout n'est qu'ordre et beauté/Luxe, calme, et volupté" ("There, all is order and beauty/Luxury, calm, and opulence") (67). There is a stronger emphasis on her ignorance of the conditions below than in the source text. It better underscores the contrasts spoken of at the beginning of the passage. This also furthers the comparison with Baudelaire's poem by enhancing the impression that Stratos is like the luxurious and comfortable room he described. Notable is the use of the words "calfeutré et ethéré" ("closed and ethereal"), which aptly describe both the city and a Baudelairean atmosphere.

Another subtle change is the use of the verb "se désolidariser" ("to dissociate oneself") in the first sentence. The verb in French clearly implies a socialist/marxist outlook. In the original episode, there was an evident anti-slavery message, referring back to America's controversial institution. The translator chose to turn the Troglyte miners' strife for emancipation into a class struggle by using a word that would inevitably remind the audience of the his-

tory of unionized labor. Since the vocabulary used to describe Stratos is eminently bourgeois, the effect is inflated further. Thus, the dubbed speech alters
the viewers' outlook on the entire story in just a few words. The insertions of
new cultural allusions served to add meaning and to emphasize a particular
interpretation of the events taking place. "By altering dialogue and performance," Jeff Davidson explained, "plots can by re-routed, characters re-mod-
eled, bad jokes re-funnied" (Whitman-Linsen 166).

Translating the Untranslatable

Profound alterations, like those shown so far, sometimes come into play because
of greater translation difficulties. Translators often have to deal with sentences,
names and designations, even entire storylines that cannot be translated easily,
if at all. Imaginative solutions are often the only way to resolve such tough problems. In *TOS,* this is especially true in high-concept episodes where intricate
vocabularies and colloquial speech types were invented. In "The Way to Eden"/
"Le chemin d'Éden," the space hippies looking for a mythical planet called those
who disagreed with them "Herbert." That word caused particular difficulties for
the translator because it is not easily pronounceable by Francophones. It was
translated as "Sceptique," ("Skeptic," or unbeliever). That choice served to better explain the hippies' opposition to those who would doubt them. But the
choice had significant consequences in the translation of the rest of the episode.
In Act 1, when Kirk asks Spock to define "Herbert," the Vulcan is embarrassed:

> Sp: E "It is, em, a somewhat, em, uncomplimentary, Captain. Herbert was a
> minor official, notorious for his rigid and limited patterns of thoughts."
> Q "C'est ainsi, euh, qu'ils surnomment, euh, je vous demande pardon,
> qu'ils surnomment les irrécupérables, les conservateurs, les tenants de
> l'aphorie, méthodiques, ceux qui se mettent la tête dans le sable. Les
> autruches, quoi."
> LT This is how, em, they call, em, forgive me, how they call unsalvage-
> ables, conservatives, proponents of rigid thought, methodicals, those who
> bury their heads in the sand. In short, ostriches.

Because of the choice of "Sceptique" for "Herbert," the translator was forced
to change the definition Spock states. In doing so, he had to do away with the
familiar incompetent civil servant theme, but found an imaginative way of inflat-
ing the joke. Since Kirk was constantly being called "Herbert" in the episode,
his being compared to an ostrich makes Spock's comments (and William Shatner's subsequent facial expressions) hugely funny.

The opening of Act 1 in the same episode was difficult because of the hip-
pie-like slang the Eden seekers were using. Ideally, the translator would have
had to look for a way to stay true to the spirit of the dialogue, while ensuring
that the lines sounded "hip." Instead, he chose another path:

> Sp: E "one."
> Q "Logos."
> LT Logos.

Se: E "We are one."
     Q "On a le Logos."
     LT We have the Logos.
Sp: E "One is the beginning."
     Q "Logos est la Raison Suprême."
     LT Logos is the Supreme Reason.

By using the Greek word "Logos" to name the ideal the space hippies were striving for, the translator went around the near impossibility to solve this translation. Logos was the name of the supreme deity in Stoicist doctrine. Clearly, the translator tried to turn the space hippies into Neo-Stoicists who follow "the Supreme Reason," thus giving them a little more credibility in the eyes of the Quebec audience. By changing them into a philosophical movement with Greek origins, the translator changed the message of the episode. The Eden seekers were no longer a reference to a contemporary phenomenon, and the story no longer served as social commentary. By displacing the cultural allusion, the translator made the cultural background of this episode even more foreign, as well as more respectable. This choice also made the translation of the next lines easier. Had Spock said "un" in lieu of "one," the whole dialogue would have sounded a little off. To render the meaning implied in the English dialogue, "unité" would have been a proper term, but synchrony would have been gravely compromised. Although "Logos" is not much better, it does allow for a better flow in the subsequent lines.

As the last example shows, some passages are extremely difficult to render in French. In such cases, the translator has had to use feats of imagination in order to circumvent those problems. Technobabble is more often that not a major pitfall. For example, *Star Trek* has customarily used naval terminology in its dialogues. This has served the franchise well. However, the equivalent French terminology is rarely synchronic. Trek translators have the unenviable choice of either sacrificing synchrony for exactitude, or the reverse. In the case of *Patrouille du Cosmos,* the choice has often been the former. "Bridge" and "deck" are always replaced by their exact French naval equivalent "passerelle" and "pont." In the same vein, "shuttle" and "shuttlecraft" are almost always translated as "navette." However, the latter word also was given sometimes as "maraudeur," meaning "marauder" or "prowler." This is an ingenious choice in that it emphasizes the maneuverability of the craft.

Invented technology posed the greatest difficulties. How does one translate "warp," "phaser," "transporter," and "sensors"? Each was dealt with differently. "Warp"—meaning the warping of the space-time continuum in order to achieve faster-than-light speeds using the principals of continuum distortion propulsion (Sterbach and Okuda 54–74)—would translate as "distorsion" or "déformation." "Warp factor three" would then become "facteur de distorsion trois." This would not do very well visually.[8] In light of the necessity of making it sound technical, the dubbers chose to translate "warp" as "mach," despite the fact that it refers to the speed of sound, not light. In some instances, the translator avoided using the term altogether, like in the last scene of "Bread and Circuses"/ "Sur les chemins de Rome" mentioned earlier. At other times, phrases such as "poussée facteur un" ("thrust factor one") were used, like in Act 4 of "Arena"/ "Arène."

"Phasers" were also a problem. The translator could have kept the acronym exactly as it was, the same way the acronym "laser" was accepted as is in the French language.[9] For some reason, the translator chose several other words, including "laser," that were used indiscriminately during the three seasons. The most common were quite imaginative. When referring to the ship's phasers, the term "faisseaux" was generally spoken. It translates as "beams," and as such is more generic than the original. Yet it defines exactly what the viewer is seeing on the screen: beams shooting out of the *Enterprise*'s hull. Therefore, in Act 3 of "Balance of Terror"/ "Zone de terreur," Lieutenant Stiles can call out:

St: E "Paris pattern. All phasers fire."
       Q "Ordre du capitaine. Tous les faisseaux, feu."
       LT By order of the captain. All beams, fire.

In this quote, the translator also had to deal with the "Paris pattern" of the phaser shots, which is not translatable literally in French. His solution erased a cryptic passage in the original, and emphasized the vessel's chain of command—an elegant solution. From the beginning of the second season, phasers (especially the hand-held models) were also called "fuseurs," meaning "fusers." This solution had the advantage of sounding technical, even though the implied function of the device is different. Instead of producing beams of phased directed energy, fusers shoot beams that evidently fuse the matter they hit. A secondary meaning can be implied, since the French verb "fuser" means "to spurt," hinting to the great strength of the jets of energy the devices emit.

The "transporter" received two translations. In the first half of the series, "transbordeur" was generally used. In naval terms, this is a literal translation of "transporter-platform." The word is a derivative of the verb "transborder," or "to transship." In the second half of the series, the inventive "salle de téléportation," in lieu of "transporter room" became the norm. "Téléporteur"—from the Greek prefix *tèle* meaning "at a distance" and the Latin *portare*, "to carry"—became the habitual translation for the "transporter." It renders more exactly the function of the device—so much so that, even in English, "teleportation" had become the generic term designating the principle of matter–energy conversion transport. (See Sterbach and Okuda 102–09.)

"Sensors" might not have been a problem, were it not for the fact that, in both English and French, the word is a homonym of "censors." The potential confusion had to be avoided. As with the previous examples, the translators used different terms at different times in the series. "Radars" was a frequent choice, but the most ingenious solution was the invention of the term "scruteurs" (literally, "scrutinizers"). While maintaining lip and syllable articulation synchrony, the word better explains the actual function of the sensors as devices that intensely examine the ship's surroundings and identify minute details.[10]

Dealing with such difficulties forced the translators to modify greatly the dialogues in order to make them intelligible in French. A short exchange between Kirk and Scotty in Act 1 of "Bread and Circuses"/ "Sur les chemins de Rome" is a perfect example:

K: E "Wait. I can prove we're telling the truth. A small device. I'll take it out slowly. Kirk to *Enterprise*. Come in."
  Q "Un instant. J'ai la preuve de nos bonnes intentions. Ce n'est qu'une petite boîte. Je vais la sortir doucement. Kirk à l'*Entreprise*. [Words omitted. Lips move with no sound.]"
  LT A moment. I have proof of our good intentions. It is only a small box. I will take it out slowly. Kirk to *Entreprise*.

(Sc): E "Scott here, captain."
  Q "Scott à l'inter, capitaine."
  LT Scott at the intercom, captain.

K: E "Scotty, lock in on my transmission beam. Scan us."
  Q "Scotty, branchez les scruteurs sur ma fréquence. Vous nous voyez?"
  LT Scotty, connect the scrutinizers on my frequency. You see us?

(Sc): E "Scanning, sir."
  Q "Je vous ai dans l'écran."
  LT I have you on the screen.

The technobabble was rendered in such a way here that, even if the terms used are different, Kirk's orders and the devices used are perfectly understood. However, this passage also has its own problems: Kirk's first line, "Come in," was not translated as "Répondez" ("Respond"), as it usually was in the series. In French it was cut out, which left Shatner's lips moving without a sound.

The more unusual devices also posed problems. In "Mirror, Mirror"/ "Miroir," the "agony booth" of the mirror universe's *ISS Enterprise* was referred to as "salle de torture" ("torture room"). It was also quickly called "cabanon," a very awkward translation that means both "hut" and "cell." In Quebec, a "cabanon" also commonly refers to a backyard storage shed. Since it is spoken very fast in the French-language dialogue, most viewers would probably miss it. In the same episode, the hand-held punishment device called an "agonizer" could have been translated as "agoniseur." Rather, it became the "auto-destructeur" ("self-destructer"), which implies that the device kills, contrary to the original intention of the authors (Okuda, Okuda, and Mirek 3). In short, the dubbers have invented their own technobabble—though not as standardized as in the original—and in so doing altered the stories being told.

What the previous examples show is that the translator could not always translate the source text literally. Michel Collet sometimes had to rewrite the dialogue completely. This works well in most instances, but some scenes and even entire episodes can prove themselves utterly untranslatable. This is the case in "Bread and Circuses"/ "Sur les chemins de Rome." Several examples taken from that episode have already been analyzed in this article. The reason for so many instances of text modification is that the episode is based on an untranslatable premise. At the heart of the story, the *Enterprise*'s crew members face a situation started by their inability to understand a simple play on words. The away team meets escaped slaves who call themselves "Children of the *Son*," as in the Son of God, since they are Christians. Kirk and the others understand the phrase as "Children of the *Sun*." Thinking they are dealing with Sun worshippers, they go about the episode wondering how they can advocate peace. It is not until the end of the story that Uhura figures it out:

> U: E "I'm afraid you have it all wrong, Mister Spock, all of you. I've been monitoring some of their old-style radio waves. The Empire spokesman trying to ridicule their religion. But he couldn't. Don't you understand? It's not the Sun up in the sky? It's the Son of God."

The problem facing the French-language translator was that the episode is based on a homonym untranslatable into French: "sun" is "soleil," and "son" is "fils." In literature, there are typically four translating strategies used to solve such a problem (see Henry). Whenever possible, a translator should strive for an isomorphic translation, where a play on words is rewritten into another play on words that is as close to a literal translation as possible. Usually this is impossible with puns (see Lendvai; Politzer; Hetzron; Marino). A homomorphic translation would, for example, replace a pun with another different pun. Here, however, it was simply impossible to rewrite the slaves' religion into an entirely different set of beliefs where a homonym would be possible. A heteromorphic translation would replace it with a different type of play on words. Although not inconceivable, the confusion of the away team would have quite a different foundation than in the original dialogue. In the end, purely written strategies would not work. The translator chose to do a free translation, where plays on words are translated into regular prose and sometimes prose is turned into gags. As mentioned earlier, this episode is rich with such cases.

The translator was forced to accept the fact that the basic premise of the episode would not make any sense to French-language viewers. "Soleil" and "fils" are not homonyms, and there is no escaping it. And so, when they meet the escaped slaves, the latter do not ask "Êtes-vous des Enfants du Fils?," but "Êtestes-vous des Enfants du Soleil?," even if it makes no sense whatsoever that Christians would refer to themselves as "Children of the Sun." Uhura's explanation of the away team's error makes little sense either:

> U: Q "J'ai bien peur que vous soyez dans l'erreur, Monsieur Spock et vous tous. J'ai passé mon temps à étudier les messages qu'ils envoyaient par radio-phonie et l'emetteur de l'Empire essayait de ridiculiser cette religion. Mais sans résultat. Mais ne réalisez-vous pas qu'il ne s'agit pas du Soleil. C'est le Fils du Dieu."
> LT I'm afraid you are in the wrong, Mister Spock and all of you. I spent my time studying the messages they sent by radio broadcasts and the Empire's transmitter trying to ridicule this religion. But with no results. But don't you realize that it's not the Sun [Soleil]. It's the Son [Fils] of God.

It seems evident that the translator was rather frustrated by the challenge of this episode. Overall, it was very well translated, with imaginative solutions to problems that might have been left dangling in other episodes. For example, the Roman television announcer's lines in Act 3 are nearly perfect:

An: E "And first tonight, ladies and gentlemen, a special surprise extra. In the far corner, a pair of highly aggressive Barbarians. Strong, intelligent, with strange ways and I'm sure full of surprises. And facing them, two favorites here from previous encounters, Achilles and Flavius. [pause, applause and cheers] Victory or Death? And for which of them? Well, ladies and gentlemen, you know just as much about that as I do because this is your program. *You Name the Winner!"*

Q "Le premier combat que nous vous offrons est une surprise extraordinaire. Dans le coin le plus éloigné, une paire de terrifiants barbares, forts, intelligents, qui se battent de façon étrange. Ils nous réservent bien des surprises. Ils feront face à deux de nos combattant favoris, Achille et Flavius. [pause, applause and cheers] Combat à mort. Qui sera le vainqueur? Eh bien, je n'en sais pas plus que vous et je vous laisse à votre programme. *Cherchez le vainqueur!"*

LT The first fight that we give you is an extraordinary surprise. In the farthest corner, a pair of terrifying Barbarians, strong, intelligent, who fight in a strange manner. They have surprises in store for us. They will face two of our favorite fighters, Achilles and Flavius. [pause, applause and cheers] Fight to the death. Who will be the victor? Well, I do not know any more than you and I leave you to your program. *Find the Victor!*

However, the episode also contains several instances where the translator has added gags and inserted plays on words in the French text. For instance, in the last scene of Act 4, McCoy refers to the now-late Flavius as a "fils du soleil," literally "son of the sun." As such, it seems the translator has simply taken his revenge by creating lines that could never be translated back into English! The Roman television announcer's last lines are a wonderful example of this. The italicized pun in the channel's French slogan is untranslatable into English:

An: E "Good evening, ladies and gentlemen. Before tonight's first heat, a simple (execution. The *State Unitas Channel* has a lot of excitement coming your way)."

Q "Bonsoir, mesdames et messieurs. En intermède avant nos émissions, nous vous présentons (une simple exécution. Mais restez branchés sur le *Canal des Arènes* pour vos jeux favoris. *Canal des Arènes, la Reine des canaux!)"*

LT Good evening, ladies and gentlemen. As an interlude before our broadcasts, we present to you a simple execution. But stay tuned to the *Arena Channel* for your favorite games. *Arena Channel, the Queen of channels.*

The examples presented so far show transformations of the source text, at times spectacular ones. Individually, each underscores the different types of changes that translation has caused, the results of difficulties inherent in any translation process. Put together, they create a significantly different cultural product than the original. Different allusions have been added to shift the cultural background of the show, such as references to specific poets and philosophers. Many changes are quite profound. If the stories are different, so are the characters.

Transfigurations

In *Patrouille du Cosmos,* characterization is the result of several factors, only some of which are inherent in the original Anglophone version. The dubbing actors' performance, their stage direction, French-language dubbing traditions, and the allusions made in the translated dialogues all alter the viewers' ultimate perceptions of the characters. Kirk in French is not the same as in English; neither are the other members of the *Enterprise*'s crew.

One striking change is a consequence of the way the characters are played by the dubbing actors. The fact that dubbed performances are often flatter and more aloof has already been mentioned. If that often means that their acting is somewhat uninspired, it also results in an impression that the characters are stoic and unemotional. In French, Starfleet officers are not easily moved or exited by the situations around them. Kirk's grandiloquent speeches are spoken in a poised and reflective tone. Scotty's excited commentaries are transformed into determined analyses and cynical retorts.

The way in which the other characters address each other is also different.[11] During season one, the "Sir" used by the crew to address Kirk was almost always translated as "Monsieur." But given the obvious visual difference of the words, the translator found an inventive solution. In seasons two and three, "Sir" is often rendered as "Chef" ("chief")! In the Francophone version of "Miri," Janice Rand calls Kirk "Jim," which she never does in English. What these changes imply is a looser, friendlier chain of command than what would be deduced from the action on the screen. Kirk's original nickname for McCoy served a similar purpose in *TOS* by underlying the friendship between the two men. However, "Bones" presented quite a challenge to the translator. The literal translation "Os" would have been nothing short of silly. It could not be "Doctor" either; the difference would have been too obvious to the viewer. Perhaps the translator allowed himself to be inspired by the French version of Walt Disney's *Snow White.* In *Patrouille*, Kirk's nickname for McCoy is "Prof," the same as the French name of the dwarf Doc. However, what the French nickname implies is the reverse of the crew's use of "Chef." "Prof" underscores the extent of McCoy's knowledge and education, and his position of authority both on the ship and in his friendship with Kirk. It places him on a higher level and produces the opposite effect of its source word. Even in the most casual of contexts, "Prof" has a deferential aspect. The chief medical officer is then presented as the older, wiser friend of the brash captain of the *Enterprise.* The various scenes where McCoy counsels Kirk take on a much deeper meaning in that light.

These changes in tone and implied narrative are compounded by an aspect of French dubbing tradition that always significantly alters spoken dialogues. French-speaking audiences as a whole insist on linguistically and stylistically correct dialogue (Luyken 138). This has significant consequences. In a large proportion of French-language dubbed audiovisual media, the level of the spoken language is quite high. The language used is what is known as *Français International,* a version of the language devoid of regional indicators. Accents and phrases are neutral and standardized so that the geographical origins of the speaker cannot be identified. Until the end of 1970s, this was the language commonly used in Francophone-dubbed shows and films, and was considered the only proper way to speak in audio and visual media. The German language has a similar form, *Hochdeutsch,* which is the preferred language for dubbing in Germany even today (Herbst 295–303). Both *Hochdeutsch* and *Français International* are more comprehensive forms of language standardization than "Received Pronunciation" is for the English language, as they also affect language structure and ideally eliminate all region-specific colloquialisms. However, there is a social (class) component to both Received Pronunciation and International French, of which *Hochdeutsch* is largely exempt.[12]

In *Patrouille*, characters speak International French. The result is that most audible regional indicators in the original dialogue are erased. There is no difference to be heard between characters who originally spoke with various British or American accents. This is true for Scotty's heavy Aberdeen accent, Lieutenant Kyle's Irish inflections,[13] and McCoy's Southern drawl. Their "quaint ethnic" phrases have been eliminated as well. Scotty's wearing of a kilt in a few episodes and the occasional reference to Scotland are the only reminders of his origins. Audibly, he is ethnically indistinguishable from Kirk. McCoy's Southern US origins have completely disappeared, since there are no visual signs of his provenance. He is no longer the "good-ol' family doctor" he was in the original version. Spock and Kirk's origins were established mostly in dialogue (and in the Vulcan's pointed ears), and so are still present, but only within those limits.

The end result of all of this is that the *Enterprise*'s crew speaks in a manner that implies an extensive education, some degree of refinement, great psychological strength in the face of danger, and an underlying uniformity of social provenance. The wide spectrum of regional accents in French certainly would have allowed for an approximation of the ethnic differences within the *Enterprise*'s crew. But if Scotty were to have spoken with a Marseille accent, he would not have been a Scot but a French Southerner; McCoy speaking like a Montrealer would not have made him an American Southerner but a Québécois. As Whitman-Linsen points out, "Target language 'correspondences' have a disconcertingly incongruous effect and tend to sound completely misplaced" (51). Standardization was unavoidable.

However, even with a uniformization of the language, some accents can still be heard in *Patrouille*. Chekov is still played with a very heavy, caricatural Russian pronunciation, like in *TOS*. The reason is that a Russian accent is feasible in French, unlike a Southern drawl. Other accents were added. This is especially true of Sulu. In the original American version, Sulu is the quintessence of excellent elocution, and George Takei played him in the best of the King's English. On the other hand, Daniel Roussel's Sulu speaks grammatically correct French but in a very strong mock-Asian nasal accent. Sulu is a "truer" and more believable Asian because of it.[14] It is a sad fact that in early 1970s Quebec, an accentless Asian would not have been believable, in the same way that an accentless Black would not be believable to an audience in France even today (Plourde i–ii). Thankfully, Uhura has only a very slight (and ethnically indistinguishable) accent in *Patrouille du Cosmos,* due to the dubbing actress's own inflections.[15] The greatest change in her character has much to do with pronunciation, however, though not with accent. In *Patrouille,* she is named "Uhara." This modification is meant to facilitate French elocution, since the *h* sound in the middle of Uhura would not be pronounced in French; [u-u-ʀɑ] is difficult to say, but [u-ɑ-ʀɑ] flows quite well.

The change in accents serves the same purpose as most modifications in cultural allusions in translated texts (Whitman-Linsen 125). Accents and stereotypes reflect internalized moral values, shared political and historical identity, and collective aesthetic tastes that infiltrate the plot and are widely taken for granted by the audience. A certain accent, a certain "ethnic" reference can ensure that viewers believe in the characters being played and understand the relative positions of the characters within a given story. Consequently, as the previous examples show, these changes sometimes imply having to cater to prejudices and stereotypes common to the target audience in order to make the narrative come alive for them.[16] A most stunning example is found in "Bread and Circuses"/ "Sur les chemins de Rome." Spock is fascinated by the similarities between planet Eight Ninety-Two-IV and Earth. He voices his thoughts on the people they meet at the beginning of Act 1. The Roman slave Flavius makes a remark about Spock's ears:

> F: E "Where are you from? What do you call those?"
>   Q "Et vous, d'où venez-vous? C'est quoi ces choses?"
>   LT And you, where are you from? What are those things?
> Sp: E "I call them ears."
>   Q "Ces choses sont mes oreilles."
>   LT These things are my ears.
> F: E "Are you trying to be funny?"
>   Q "Est-ce une plaisanterie?"
>   LT Is it a joke?
> Sp: E "Never. Colloquial twentieth-century English. An amazing parallel."
>   Q "Non, des oreilles. C'est le type parfait de l'Italo-Américain du vingtième siècle, de la mafia."
>   LT No, ears. He's the perfect type of twentieth-century Italian-American, from the mafia.

In the Quebec version, when responding to Flavius's insult, Spock makes an ethnic slur, obviously meant as a joke by the translator. The likable Roman brute in the source text becomes an archetypal mafioso. Besides simply pursuing the succession of jokes written into earlier parts of the scene, the slur also creates a mental image and allowed the 1970s Quebec viewers to better believe in the Earth parallel. By playing with the prejudices of his target audience, the translator underscored what the original authors were trying to convey.

The unfortunate result is a much different philosophy in the show than in Gene Roddenberry's original vision. Characters in *Patrouille du Cosmos* are sometimes frankly xenophobic or intolerant, where *TOS* was not. In the original, McCoy often would throw slurs at Spock to provoke an emotional response in the Vulcan. In the translation, his comments don't seem to be said so half-jokingly as before, like in Act 4 of "A Journey to Babel"/ "Un tour à Babel":

Mc: E "That thick-headed Vulcan stamina. I couldn't have pulled them through without it."
Q "Ces bourriques de Vulcains sont obstinées mais sans leur ténacité, j'aurais échoué."
LT These Vulcan asses [*donkeys*] are obstinate but without their tenacity, I would have failed.

Scotty was also one to pass judgment on a person's appearance or behavior, but here too his reactions are stronger than in the original. In the trailer of "The Way to Eden"/ "Le chemin d'Éden," he is quite stunned by the appearance of the space hippies. In the original, he refers to the group he has just beamed aboard as "a nice lot too!" In French, he proclaims he has never seen "une si jolie brochette de clowns!" ("such a pretty string of clowns!"). From simple surprise, Scotty's lines now pass judgment.

Gender relations also are affected. There is a definite slant toward a more sexist dialogue in the Quebec version of *TOS*. The original is far from exempt of sexism—the entire plot of "Turnabout Intruder"/ "L'Important" is proof enough.[17] However, Roddenberry was famous for trying to be as egalitarian with female characters as the network would allow.[18] In *Patrouille du Cosmos*, dialogue alterations move away from these attempts.

Over the course of the seventy-nine *TOS* episodes, the original stories whose plots or characters (good or bad) denigrated women—such as "Turnabout Intruder"/ "L'Important" or Nomad's attack on Uhura in "The Changeling"/ "Le Korrigan" because she was an illogical female[19]—only serve to inflate the added sexist comments of the Quebec version. The result, in today's eyes, can be disconcerting. In the final scene of "Balance of Terror"/ "Zone de terreur," Kirk goes to the ship's chapel to give his condolences to Ensign Angela Martine, whose fiancé was killed in the last Romulan attack:

K: E "Never makes any sense. We both have to know that there was a reason."
Q "Les mots ne veulent rien dire. Je voulais vous dire que je suis avec vous."
LT Words mean nothing. I wanted to tell you that I am with you.
Ma: E "I'm all right."
Q "Je vous remercie."
LT I thank you.

The dialogue has been completely transformed. Still, Kirk easily could have said something like "C'est insensé, enseigne. Nous devons nous demander s'il y avait une raison" ("It does not make any sense, ensign. We have to ask ourselves if there was a reason."); Martine could have answered: "Ça ira" ("It'll be all right"), with few synchrony problems. The spirit of the original dialogue would have been kept. Why the translator chose to change both characters' lines is debatable, especially considering that the dubbed dialogue poses serious synchrony problems (both actors are shot in close-up). It makes more sense when contextualized over the three seasons of *Patrouille du Cosmos*. Quebec dialogues regularly appear to emphasize female inferiority and emotionalism. In the previous passage, it is logical to posit that Michel Collet did not think the audience would believe that a grief-stricken woman would say she was "all right." Perhaps he did not believe it himself.

A character like Kirk, known for his success with women, would likely be affected by such a downward slant—and he was, though often subtly. However, the shift in "Miri" is nothing less than blatant. In the previously mentioned last scene, when McCoy, Kirk, and Rand recapitulate the events of the episode, Rand concludes on the title character, a three-hundred-year-old adolescent girl:

> R: E "Miri. She really loved you, you know."
> Q "Miri. Elle était tombée amoureuse de vous."
> LT Miri. She had fallen in love with you.
> K: E "Yes. I never get involved with older women, Yeoman."
> Q "Oui. Personnellement, je dois dire que j'aime assez les fruits verts."
> LT Yes. Personally, I must say that I rather like green fruits.

In the original, Kirk's comment was partly ironic. The audience understands he would not have gotten involved with an adolescent, no matter how old and no matter how tempting. He feels compassion toward her. In French, on the contrary, the comments are rather offensive for today's ears. Kirk is proving himself a veritable macho who likes younger women, whom he can pluck at a time when they still do not have the experience to resist. The sentence structure of Kirk's French retort also indicates a much more categorical rejection of Miri, and a measure of spite toward older women. This fact is compounded by Yvon Thiboutot's tone in the dubbed passage. In the original (in light of Kirk's reaction to the girl in the previous scenes), his rejection of Miri is a question of propriety, not necessarily a lack of attraction. In the Quebec dialogue, only her great age justifies the rejection. His obvious attraction to the girl in the previous scenes then seems to prove his preference for very young, inexperienced women.

Kirk's character was changed in other aspects as well. The same way that McCoy and Scotty's spoken improprieties were exaggerated in *Patrouille du Cosmos,* so was Kirk's sometimes brusque irreverence. In many *TOS* episodes, Kirk's impatience with officials and ambassadors only underlined what would later be defined as "cowboy diplomacy" by *Star Trek: The Next Generation*'s Captain Jean-Luc Picard.[20] In *Patrouille*, it is a more complicated matter. At times, Kirk is simply impolite. In Act 3 of "A Journey to Babel"/ "Un tour à Babel," in the heat of a battle against an unknown assailant, the diplomats on board are worried:

> U: E "Captain, the intercoms are jammed. All the ambassadors are asking what's going on."
> Q "Capitaine, les communications intérieures sont rompues. Les ambassadeurs demandent ce qui se passe."
> LT Captain, internal communications have been severed. The ambassadors are asking what's going on.
> K: E "Tell them to take a good guess, but clear that board, lieutenant."

Q "Dites à ces messieurs de prendre un verre! Ce n'est pas le moment de
nous embêter, lieutenant."
LT Tell these gentlemen to have a drink! It's not the time to bother us,
lieutenant.

Kirk's response is significantly different in the French version. Whereas in the
original Kirk made Uhura keep order on the ship and ensure reliable communications, the French-speaking Kirk dismisses the ambassadors as bothersome.
In the first, Shatner said his line in such a way that the viewers would understand that Kirk wished to say something impolite but refrained. In the second,
Thiboutot's line as Kirk is simply rude, and he played it with audible spite in
his voice.

In light of the innumerable modifications made in the dialogues and the
adjustments in the stories that followed, there is little doubt that translation
into French has significantly metamorphosized *TOS* into a related yet distinct
cultural product. In many ways, the French-language show is much more of a
comedy than the original, since so many of its episodes were "re-funnied."
Patrouille du Cosmos is not the "Wagon Train to the Stars" that *TOS* was:
McCoy is no country doctor and Kirk is no cowboy. Furthermore, the latter
is sexist and rude in measures the original was not. Similar comments could
be made for most characters of the series. Despite what the original opening
narration states, the *Enterprise* is not exploring the frontier.[21] It is on Cosmos
Patrol; it is there to maintain order in space. One need only ask how this cultural icon has been incorporated into French-language culture.

Bring the Spock!

The question of audience perception of a cultural product can be addressed in
two ways. The first is directly, by asking questions to a chosen sample. The
second is indirectly, by looking at the reappropriation of a cultural product.
For the purpose of this article, the latter approach is more interesting. It allows
for the understanding of how a product has been integrated into the common
vocabulary of a culture, whereas the first approach opens a door only on an
audience's impressions of the viewed product.[22] With *TOS,* the question of
appropriation becomes interesting because one must take into account the
mediation resulting from its translation into *Patrouille du Cosmos.* Because
Patrouille is not quite the same as *TOS,* the result of its acculturation should
affect its place in common culture.

Fan fiction in French, from France or Quebec, would be a particularly good
window into this phenomenon. However, there is very little French-language
Trek fan fiction to be found, with virtually none inspired by *TOS,* and none from
France.[23] This reveals that *Patrouille du Cosmos* has not inflamed the imagination of its audience like *TOS* has in the United States. Rather, Japanese *anime*
serials, *Buffy contre les vampires,* and other popular dubbed television shows have
the favor of Quebec and French fan fiction writers.[24] What little *TOS* fan fiction
in French there is comes exclusively from Quebec and is in text. Yet the two
audiovisual exceptions I have found offer an interesting explanation.

In 1990–1992, a group of audiovisual media and communications students at the Cégep de Jonquière (Qc)[25] chose for their two-year project to write, produce, and shoot an original twenty-eight-minute episode of *TOS*. Entitled "Le Juge" ("The Judge"), the episode was written by Daniel Lavoie (who plays Spock) and produced by Éric Bédard (who plays McCoy). It features all of the main characters, as well as Klingons, a mysterious and beautiful female alien, and an omnipotent being standing in judgment of humanity. The episode is a mix of several familiar storylines and decors, mostly taken from "Arena"/ "Arène" and "The Empath"/ "L'Impasse." At first glance, "Le Juge" could be interpreted as paying homage to *TOS*, as a filmed role-playing game that offered a group of dedicated fans the opportunity to act out their favorite characters. Sets, costumes, and camera movements and angles have been very carefully and successfully reproduced. Original music and sound effects also were used. Visually, it is extremely close to *TOS*. But this is misleading. In reality, "Le Juge" is an episode of *Patrouille du Cosmos*.

The dialogues are very well written in impeccable International French. They include all of the aforementioned features of *Patrouille,* including the opening monologue and a racial slur by McCoy, who again compares Spock to a donkey. The actors, though all amateurs and not all talented, try their best to reproduce the characteristics of their respective characters—and there lies the paradox. They must emulate the physical acting styles and typical body movements of William Shatner, Leonard Nimoy, and DeForest Kelley, but imitate the vocal performances of Yvon Thiboutot, Régis Dubost, and Michel Georges. The best actor in the group is Carl Poulin, who plays Kirk. An examination of his performance is very revealing. When sitting in the command chair on the bridge, Poulin's physical movements (his hitting of the comm button on the chair's right arm, his swinging of the chair to look at Uhura or Spock, and so on) are all typical of Shatner's Kirk. However, his poised vocal tone, his intonations, and his careful enunciation are strikingly reminiscent of Thiboutot. The result is similar to watching *TOS* in French. The performances are all a little off the mark, not only because of their amateurism, but mainly because fluctuating kenetic synchrony is an inherent feature of *Patrouille du Cosmos*. The actors' movements and facial expressions do not always fit what is being said. Clearly, *Patrouille du Cosmos*'s main characteristic is the result of the dubbing process, otherwise Bédard, Lavoie, and the others would not have attempted to reproduce it so closely. They have assimilated these elements and presented them on the screen, both as fans and as members of the Quebec audience. The second example emphasizes this to its fullest. *Star Trek: The Sitcom* is a 2001, three-minute short produced for Montreal's Kino project (a forum for the creation and presentation of film shorts by budding and underground directors) by Éric Dupuis and Richard Lacombe. In it, an array of visibly handheld *TOS* action figures tell inane jokes. We discover that Captain Kirk is really Batman (played by Gumby) in search of the Joker, who has snuck on board the Enterprise. The entire short is voiced by the two men speaking in equally flat and false tones, clearly evoking dubbing. The dialogues are also written in perfect International French. Dupuis and Lacombe intentionally

reproduced and exaggerated the linguistic characteristics and uninspired acting inherent to most dubbing performances. In doing so, not only is the dialogue ridiculous because of its content, its very form focuses on and makes fun
of *Patrouille du Cosmos*' nature as a translated cultural product. Though, Bédard
and Lacombe's works are generally inspired by American popular culture and
genre movies, they normally use these references to criticize today's society.
Their other science fiction short, *Odyssée 2001,* plays on the Kubrick classic's
visuals as a moving exploration of mental illness. *Star Trek: The Sitcom* is their
only short with no redeeming social qualities whatsoever.

Star Trek: The Sitcom's deliberate use of bad dubbing voices and *Le Juge's*
familiar storyline and paradoxical acting prove that the effect *Patrouille* has had
on its audience is more about form than about content. *Patrouille* is a common vocabulary that can be spoken and acted. It is a cultural allusion in and
of itself. When reproduced in the visual and audible spirit of the original, the
result is undeniably a hybrid of two cultural worlds. However, in the face of
the virtual nonexistence of French-language *TOS* fan fiction, the obvious conclusion would be that *Patrouille du Cosmos* serves a different function in the
Francophone collective imagination than among Anglophones.

This can be seen in science fiction shows written and shot in Quebec. One
must first notice just how few there have been. Of all science fiction television
shows to have played on Quebec television from the 1960s to the end of the
1980s, fewer than ten were produced in Quebec and all were child-oriented
programs.[26] The rarity of Quebec science fiction shows cannot only be
explained by budget constraints. The fact they are all youth programs hints at
a particular perception of the genre that will become evident in the next para-
graphs. Since 1990, their rarity has not changed and the shows still have the
same target audience.

From 1999 to 2001, the space adventure/slapstick comedy/satire *Dans
une galaxie près de chez vous* ("In a galaxy near you") was the only Quebec-
made science fiction program on Quebec television. It targeted the early adolescent viewers of the youth cable network *Vrak.tv* (who now enjoy twice daily
reruns). During its three seasons and sixty-five episodes, *Dans une galaxie* presented the adventures of Capitaine Charles Patenaude and his crew aboard the
Planetary Federation spaceship *Romano Fafard* in the early 2030s. The opening narration states their mission: to find a suitable planet to which the human
population can escape Earth, now deprived of its ozone layer, and to go "where
the hand of Man has never set foot."[27]

The series has all of the expected characteristics of a spaceship show. In
addition to the opening narration and stereotypical storylines, the vessel
Romano Fafard looks like it was made out of tin cans. But it also has all of
the features of a Starfleet starship, with primary and secondary hulls and a warp
nacelle. It has a multicultural and mixed crew, but of various intellectual capacity and dexterity, all of them prone to pie-in-the-face physical comedy. Yet this
is not simply another *Red Dwarf; Dans une galaxie* is clearly spoofing *Patrouille*
on several levels.

Capitaine Charles Patenaude (played by Guy Jodoin) is a dashing officer, ready to run into danger to accomplish his mission. Here too, language plays a key role in the captain's character definition. Patenaude expresses himself in poised yet pathos-filled, long-winded speeches. His accent and vocabulary are perfect International French. He only breaks from this when he speaks in aside, where he uses Quebec dialect in order to emphasize a scene's gags. Patenaude mentions poets and philosophers, though in ridiculous combinations. Physically, his movements are grand and theatrical. In short, he speaks and moves like a captain should—that is, he moves and speaks like Kirk does in *Patrouille du Cosmos*. The major difference is that here, the comedic effect is intentional and exaggerated.

The audiovisual vocabulary of *Patrouille* appears in *Dans une galaxie* for the same reason (but for the opposite effect) than in *Le Juge*. In order to be a recognizable science fiction spoof, *Dans une galaxie* must first be recognizable as a science fiction show. It therefore contains recognizable elements of the best-known science fiction show to have played on Quebec television. Because the audio and visual elements of *Patrouille* are not perfectly coherent, and because the costumes and make-up (especially when seen today) are somewhat silly, the effect may be comedic. Using this, the writers and producers of *Dans une galaxie près de chez vous* built a comedy and a satire of the entire science fiction genre.

This aspect of *Patrouille du Cosmos* (and older science fiction television in general) is constantly used in Quebec television in order to produce comedic effect. *TOS* references in Quebec television are not many, but they are always used to produce a laugh. As a cultural allusion, *Star Trek* equals ridicule.

This fact is nowhere better illustrated than in the works of comedic playwright and author Claude Meunier. His television and film works contain several references and allusions to the *TOS* universe. In 1991, Meunier alluded to *TOS* in *Ding et Dong—Le Film*. This feature film presented the comic duo Ding and Dong (Serge Thériault and Claude Meunier), whose dismal attempts at success lead them on one ridiculous adventure after another. At one point, they trap a movie producer in his office in an effort to pitch him a project. Ding and Dong play an out-of-control action scene, during which they proceed to destroy his office. It is a hodgepodge of allusions to a dozen popular American movies of the 1980s, from *Raiders of the Lost Ark* to *Rocky*. One particularly surreal moment in that scene has Claude Meunier (Dong) throw himself on the intercom, press the speak-button and scream in broken English, "Capitaine Kirk! Capitaine Kirk! Brrrrrrrrrring de Spock!" *TOS* is one of many allusions to American cultural icons that serve two purposes in the scene.

At first glance, the Trek reference adds to the sheer madness of the scene and gets a laugh. On a second level however, the allusions to American popular culture collectively serve to underscore how desperate for success Ding and Dong have become. At that point in the film, they have sunk to their lowest level ever. In the following scenes, they will be forced to sell their schtick door to door. This "action scene" actually caters to a common belief in Quebec that, no matter how exciting and hugely popular, American culture is a subquality culture, and American television and movies are generally intellectually inferior and banal (see Atkinson). When Ding and Dong invade the offices of Roger Ben Hur Productions, the audience understands that they are willing to stoop to the level of American popular culture to attain success. On both levels, their passing reference to *TOS* emphasizes it as funny and camp.

In 1992, Ding and Dong made another reference to *TOS* in Meunier's television special *Le merveilleux monde de Ding et Dong* ("The Wonderful World of Ding and Dong"). The show featured a skit where the two title characters insert themselves into the *TOS* universe, with hysterical consequences. The *Entreprise*'s crew, having been sexually abstinent in space for years, find themselves on a planet inhabited by women, and laughter ensues. However, this spoof of the *TOS* episode "Spock's Brain" / "Le cerveau de Spock" is very different from a similar reenactment in *The Wonder Years*. The latter, entitled "Just Between You and Me . . . and Kirk and Paul and Carla and Becky," underscores the main characters' realization of the power of women over their growing bodies: an essentially nostalgic allusion. Meunier's Ding and Dong simply played on the ridiculousness of the women's planet premise and its potential for slapstick.

This function of *TOS* in Meunier's work culminates in 1996. *La Petite Vie* ("The Little Life," as in ordinary life) is Quebec television's most successful series of all time. At its highest peak, virtually all of the province's French-speaking adults would be watching, almost four million viewers.[28] The sole writer of the series, Meunier used its quirky characters to satirize and criticize the most common cultural traits of those of Quebec, with dialogues emphasizing their absurdity. Therefore, the main characters are Quebec archetypes: Popa, the distant father with a garbage bag fetish (played by Meunier), Moman, the overbearing mother with a turkey fetish (played by a man, Thériault), and their adult children, among whom are Rod (the mama's boy) and Caro (the hysterical daddy's girl). In the series's four seasons and sixty episodes, Meunier explored and ridiculed everything from Quebec's inferiority complex with France, to game shows and stardom, to old-age homes and homosexual marriage. Inevitably, *Star Trek* would eventually come into play.

The third season episode "Le rêve de Moman" ("Moman's Dream") features Moman dealing with her monopolizing family and Popa's toothache by escaping into a Trek dream. In it she is Capitaine Skirt and her husband is Monsieur Spot on the bridge of their vessel, a mix of the *Enterprise*'s command center and their pink harborite kitchen. They are attacked by Klingons and surly aliens who turn out to be family members wanting an invitation to Sunday dinner. This episode is typical of the series, as it contains one absurd gag after another, and Moman's dream is marginally more surrealist than her "real" little life.

Meunier has used Trek typology to underscore the ridiculousness of his characters as much as the comedic potential of the *TOS* universe. Moman's turkey fetish, for example, appears in her dream in the form of turkey drumsticks in lieu of her ship's warp nacelles.[29] Monsieur Spot's bridge console is a brightly colored work bench. The transporter is a functioning shower head. The relationship between Popa and Moman also hints back to Kirk and Spock. Sexually frustrated for years, Moman in her dream echoes Kirk's active libido. Of course, Skirt is attracted to Spot, but he refuses her advances, stating that such actions are illogical.

It is because of the fact that Trek, as known in Quebec, is perceived as silly that Meunier could replay its themes in his works. Meunier's use of *TOS* allusions shows how well integrated *Patrouille du Cosmos* is in the Quebec collective imagination. Because it was so popular and was rerun year after year, Spock's ears and Kirk's sexual attractiveness are immediately recognizable.

Concluding Thoughts

The translation of *Star Trek: The Original Series* into *Patrouille du Cosmos* has changed the former into a different yet related cultural product. Through the filter of translation, the Trek universe was not simply transposed; rather, it was altered so that original stories, dialogues, and even character definitions were not the same in the version viewed by French speakers. This both allowed and affected Trek's integration into Quebec's common culture. Trek is a vocabulary, a set of commonly known archetypes that can be reused in order to transmit a message. Trek is a cultural allusion all its own, but because of its dubbing, the nature of this allusion—the set of expected meanings understood in its Quebec version—differs in part from that which is implied in the original English.

Like everywhere, Kirk is remembered for his active libido, Spock for his ears. The costumes and sets are immediately recognizable. Episode structures and storylines, space vessel shapes, and alien make-ups are familiar to viewers of both languages. The differences in the referential nature of *TOS* are mostly the result of the approximate synchronies of *Patrouille*. Kirk's sexist remarks and other characters' racist comments are not a part of the English common knowledge of Trek. McCoy's depiction of Vulcans as donkeys is a catch phrase in French, whereas the ever-famous "Beam me up" is without an equivalent. In short, visual allusions are similar, language-based allusions are not.

The most striking differences, however, can be inferred from the reuse of Trek vocabulary and imagery in Quebec television. *TOS* references are typically used to emphasize and ridicule, for kitsch and silliness. It is as such that Quebec popular culture knows *Star Trek*. It is the campiness of 1960s Trek and its status as an archetypal American television series that take precedence. Many French-language episodes were intentionally written to be funnier than the original, thus turning this science fiction icon into something of a space comedy. Furthermore, Trek is used because it is visually and audibly silly, because it is recognized as an antiquated American—thus foreign—icon of the 1960s and 1970s.

Of course, American television and film have no shortage of Trek spoofs, from numerous episodes of *The Simpsons*[30] to the recent movie *Galaxy Quest*. But where such references, designed to make the audience laugh, have equivalents in Quebec television and movies, there is a high number of American Trek references that denote a certain amount of nostalgia, even behind the laughter. Like in the episode of *The Wonder Years* mentioned earlier, nostalgia for the 1960s is a common theme in many American television shows. The *X-Files*'s Fox Mulder was depicted in childhood flashbacks wearing full Spock regalia in "Dreamland II." These images date from a time before Mulder's sister was abducted by aliens, at a time when extraterrestrials were still make-believe to him. Even William Shatner's famous 1986 "Get a Life!" skit on *Saturday Night Live* has a certain nostalgic aspect to it, as it shows him regretting the better days before Trekkies, when people still knew this was "only a TV show!" Both cases refer to simpler, more innocent times.

Nothing of the sort appears in Quebec television's references to Trek. The inadvertent ridiculousness of *Patrouille du Cosmos,* from the dated looks to the gaps in synchrony, have done for *TOS* what its incorporation into American culture could not. Like monster movies and dubbed Chinese kung-fu features, *Patrouille* is psychotronic. It is with this in mind that Daniel Lavoie and his colleagues at the Cégep de Jonquière filmed *Le Juge.* Otherwise, they would not have been so careful to replicate the synchronic gaps found in *Patrouille* and would have endeavored to create a purely *TOS* episode, or even to do a *TNG* or *DS9* story.[31] This better than any other argument proves the independence of Quebec popular culture before such a watershed cultural phenomenon as *Star Trek*.

Appendix 1:
Character Name Codes and Dubbing Actors

French-language texts: Michel Collet
Principal dubbing stage direction: Michel Georges

Character codes: Characters—dubbing actors
Narrator: Daniel Roussel, Yvon Thiboutot
K: Captain James T. Kirk—Yvon Thiboutot
Sp: Commander Spock—Régis Dubost
Mc: Doctor Leonard McCoy—Michel Georges
Sc: Engineer Montgomery Scott (Scotty)—Julien Bessette, François Cartier
Su: Lieutenant Hikaru Sulu—Daniel Roussel
U: Lieutenant Nyota Uhura (Q = Uhara)—Arlette Sanders
C: Ensign Pavel Chekov—André Montmorency
R: Yeoman Janice Rand—Elizabeth Lesieur
D: Romulan Officer Decius—Edgar Fruitier
Sh: Andorian Ambassador Shras—Benoit Marleau

Character codes: Other characters—unknown dubbers
A: Amanda (Mrs. Sarek)
An: Roman television announcer
F: Flavius
G: Tellarite Ambassador Gav
Ma: Ensign Angela Martine
Sa: Vulcan Ambassador Sarek
Se: Doctor Sevrin
St: Lieutenant Stiles

Source: "Patrouille."

Appendix 2:
Dubbing Studio Using *Bande Rythmo* Method

Key: (1) Mixing engineer (2) In-line computer (3) Mixing console (4) Projection room (5) Sound speaker (6) Monitor (7) Soundproof glass (8) Stage manager or director (9) Dubbing actors (10) Timing indicator (11) Bande rythmo (© Dave Leclerc, 2003, d@studiobionic.com) Source: Plourde lxis.

Notes

1. The history of Quebec's dubbing industry is yet to be written.

2. This is very unusual, considering French laws concerning the broadcast of visual media dubbed outside of France. Since 1978, only forty-two hours of Quebec-dubbed shows were allowed per broadcaster per year. Since 1996, all Quebec-dubbed American television shows have been forbidden on France's major networks (Lagueux and Charron; Saint-Germain 35–38) In Francophone countries, *Patrouille du Cosmos* is distributed by various Paramount-affiliated companies, such as Viacom Enterprises Canada for Quebec. Until the end of 2001, *Patrouille du Cosmos* played on Canal D in Quebec, and is currently playing on Canal Jimmy in France. Canal Jimmy shows episodes in English with French subtitles and in repeat in French (*Canal Jimmy; GEOS*).

3. Sonolab purchased dubbing equipment from France in 1968 (information given by Hélène Rozon).

4. The only contender for *Patrouille du Cosmos*'s success is *Cosmos 1999*, the Quebec-dubbed version of *Space 1999*, which also has had considerable airtime both in Quebec and France, though much less than *Patrouille*. In any case, both in the Francophonie and in the United States, the later series has enjoyed considerably less influence on collective cultures and imaginations. Yet *Cosmos 1999* is one of the few "clas-

sic" American sci-fi series to be the subject of fan fiction in French, a status that *Patrouille du Cosmos* does not enjoy. See *Franco FanFic* Web site.

5. For average cost statistics for Europe, see Luyken 89–109; for Quebec, see "L'industrie du doublage au Québec."

6. Note the play on words in the Q title, taken from the phrase "La tour de Babel/The Tower of Babel."

7. Note the word play in the Q title, referring to the known proverb, "Tous les chemins mènent à Rome/All roads lead to Rome."

8. Nevertheless, the French translators of *TNG* have chosen to sacrifice synchrony and use this exact phrase. In fact, synchrony is generally sacrificed in preference of meaning in this particular version, because these dubbers lean toward a nucleus-synch approach rather than simple lip-synch. Nucleus-synch favors matching the nuclei (stressed syllables) of the target-language dialogue with "the movements of the [actors'] body, slight nods, raising of the eyebrows," and all other gestures that "always coincide with the stressed syllables" in speech (Luyken 160–61). Because a one hundred percent accurate lip synchrony is impossible, an accentuation of the visual performance of the actors often provides a greater impression of naturalness in the dubbed version (see also Herbst 292–95).

9. This is what the translators of *TNG* chose to do. In the real world, "laser" stands for "light amplification by stimulated emission of radiation." In the Trek universe, "phaser" stands for "phased energy rectification," which refers to the method by which "stored or supplied energy entering the phaser system was converted to another form for release toward a target" (Sterbach and Okuda 123).

10. Again, the translators of *TNG* have moved away from synchrony in favor of precision and generally translated "sensors" as "détecteurs" ("detectors").

11. Such changes are inevitable when translating from a Germanic to a Romance language. For similar examples from Italian to English, see Ulrych.

12. Since the 1970s, two philosophies for French-language dubbing have come into existence and have been the subject of considerable debate. The first is that of using International French in all revoicings, even in films set in regions and social classes that have distinctive accents in the source language. The result is similar to the case examined in this article. However, an increasing number of dubbed films in Quebec and France are done in these regions' respective dialects and reflect the differential accents of each country's social classes. Lower classes speak *Parisian Argot* or *Verlan* for France, and *Joual* for Quebec. Higher classes speak grammatically perfect French in varying accents. Translations that present social and geographical dialects in the target language have become more acceptable in the last two decades. The result is that Parisian translations are not necessarily understandable to Montrealers, though they tend to be more so than the reverse. Therefore, one country's translations are not readily acceptable to the other country's viewers, and are often considered inferior, both to the original and to their own country's version. French laws against foreign French-language dubbed material only inflate the mutual acrimony (see Paquin).

13. Recurring character in all three seasons, relief helmsman and transporter technician, played by John Winston (Okuda, Okuda, and Mirek 255).

14. See what Plourde has to say about the social meaning of such an accent, especially in his conclusion. See also Whitman-Linsen 48–53; Danan; Robyns.

15. It is therefore very surprising (and a relief) to note that *TNG*'s Geordie LaForge has no accent whatsoever in the French version of the show.

16. This is especially important when cultural mores and what is considered acceptable in the source culture's film and television differ from those of the target culture. For examples from Russian to Italian, see Salmon Kovarski.

17. This shameful episode depicts a Dr. Janice Lester driven stark raving mad by the fact that she was not allowed to become a starship captain due to her sex. The depiction of women is caricatural and the dialogue is overacted. Ultimately, women are proven psychologically unstable and Starfleet's discrimination is justified. The true irony is that this episode was originally meant to denounce the sexism of 1960s American society and of the television networks that would not allow female authority figures on their shows.

18. The female executive officer Number One, played by Majel Barrett in *TOS*'s first pilot, "The Cage," was just one of those instances when Gene Roddenberry attempted to include female authority figures in the show (Okuda, Okuda, and Mirek 328–29). In this case, his attempt failed and she was cut from the regular cast. Nevertheless, footage from the pilot was used, with the Number One character intact in the two-parter "The Menagerie, Parts I and II"/ "La ménagerie, première et deuxième parties."

19. More precisely, Nomad attacks Uhura because he finds her illogical and paradoxical. Spock justifies Uhura's internal conflicted nature by the fact that she is a woman. He asserts this matter-of-factly, as a nondebatable reality.

20. In an argument with Spock in "Unification, Part II."

21. There were two different translations of the "Space. The final frontier" narration. The first monologue was a close approximation of the original and was voiced by Daniel Roussel, who usually played Sulu. In the second half of the series, the narration departed from its source text and is voiced by Yvon Thiboutot, the voice of Kirk:

Q   "Espace. Frontière de l'infini vers laquelle voyage notre vaisseau spatial. Sa mission, explorer de nouveaux mondes étranges, découvrir de nouvelles vies, d'autres civilisations et, au mépris du danger, reculer l'impossible."

LT   Space. Border of infinity toward which travels our space vessel. Its mission, to explore strange new worlds, discover new lives, other civilizations and, in defiance of danger, push back the impossible.

22. On methodologies for identifying television audiences and publics, see Proulx. For an example of a comparative reception study (in the case of *Dallas*), see Katz and Liebes.

23. Most fan fiction stories to be found in French are set in the *TNG* and *DS9* timeline, like the several fan fiction novels published online on the Web site of *Star Trek Québec,* an email role-playing game club. France has several similar sites. They depict original ships and crews, and are novelizations of the club's scenarios. Rare *TOS* exceptions are the works of a few members of *Star Trek Québec,* such as Sylvie Manseau who wrote "L'Ultime mission," a *TOS/TNG* crossover story. In France, *Virtual Star Trek Season Project* was launched in 2000 but has yet to produce a single story. The only *TOS* fan "fiction" found to date on the French Internet or in print are "doctored" erotic pictures of the women of Trek, both of dubious quality and very bad taste on Thierry Le Trekker's Web site.

24. A quick internet search on *Yahoo! France* or *La Toile du Québec* with keywords like "anime," "Sailor Moon," "Buffy contre les vampires," or "Dawson" will reveal hundreds of fan fiction sites. See also *Franco FanFic* Web site.

25. Cégep = Collège d'enseignement général et professionnel. Cégeps are Québec educational institutions providing two- and three-year programs, and are an obligatory level of education between the fifth year of secondary schooling and the first year of university.

26. The most important were *Les Chiboukis, Les 100 tours de Centours, Les Oraliens, Kosmos 2001, Opération-mystère,* and *Les Égrégores.* There also have been a few sci-fi inspired kids' game shows, most notably *Les Satellipopettes.* See the *Les émissions de notre enfance* Web site.

27. The narration changed slightly every season to follow the timeline and, in Season 3, to criticize Canada's federal television funding policies. In Season 1, the narration was as follows:

Q   "Nous sommes en 2034, la situation sur la Terre est catastrophique; la couche d'ozone est complètement détruite par la gaz carbonique des voitures, l'industrie chimique et le "pouche-pouche" en cacane. Résultat: la Terre cuit sous les rayons du Soleil, les récoltes sont complètement brulées, il n'y a presque plus d'eau potable et les companies de crème solaire s'enrichissent. La situation devient urgente. Il faut trouver une nouvelle planète pour y déménager 6 milliards de tatas. C'est ainsi, que le 28 octobre 2034, le vaisseau spatial *Romano Fafard* quitte la Terre en route vers les confins de l'Univers. Là où la main de l'Homme n'a jamais mis le pied."

LT We are in 2034, the situation on Earth is catastrophic; the ozone layer is completely destroyed by carbon dioxide from cars, the chemical industry, and "push-push" in a can. The result: Earth bakes under the rays of the Sun, harvests are completely burnt, there is almost no drinking water left, and sunscreen companies are getting richer. The situation is becoming urgent. One must find a new planet to which move 6 billion bozos. This is why on 28 October 2034 the space vessel *Romano Fafard* left Earth toward the ends of the Universe. There where the hand of Man has never set foot.

28. In 1995–1996, at the time of the example studied here, *La Petite Vie* had fallen to fifth place, with an average of 1,422,000 viewers, which nevertheless amounted to nearly a third of Quebec's adult population (*Info Presse Communication* 52).
29. Meunier had used a similar gag in *Le merveilleux monde de Ding et Dong*.
30. Among many, *Deep Space Homer* contains numerous Trek references, like the usual "Beam me up Scotty" joke and an Itchy and Scratchy skit entitled "Scar Trek: The Next Laceration." In *Itchy and Scratchy: The Movie*, the family watches a promotional trailer of "Star Trek XII: So Very Tired," featuring a very old Kirk and a very fat Scotty.
31. Like, among numerous others, the amateur series *Star Trek: Hidden Frontier,* executively produced by Rob Caves of the USS-Angeles club in Los Agneles, California.

Works Cited

Atkinson, Dave. "L'américanisation de la télévision: qu'est-ce à dire?" *Variations sur l'influence culturelle américaine.* Ed. Florian Sauvageau. Sainte-Foy: PUL, 1999: 59–72.
Baudelaire, Charles. *Les fleurs du mal.* Paris: Booking International, 1993.
Canal Jimmy. 5 May 2002 <http://www.canaljimmy.fr>.
Danan, Martine. "Dubbing as an Expression of Nationalism." *Meta* 36.3 (1991):605–14.
Dutter, Anne, and Georges Dutter. "Le plaisir des mots." *Notes* 149 (Sept.–Oct. 1996). Accessed on 5 May 2002. <http://www.sacem.fr/kisoque/notes/doublage/dutter.html>.
Fodor, Istvan. *Film Dubbing. Phonetic, Semiotic, Esthetic, and Psychological Aspects.* 3rd ed. Hamburg, Germany: H. Buske, 1976.
Franco FanFic. 5 May 2002 <http://www.francofanfic.com>.
GEOS: The Global Episode Opinion Survey. 5 May 2002 <http://www.swd.net.au/geos/>.

Henry, Jacqueline. "Communiquer l'intraduisible, ou traduire les jeux de mots." *Translation—The Vital Link/La traduction au cœur de la communication.* Ed. Catriona Picken. London/Brighton: Institute of Translation and Interpreting 1993: 92–99.

Herbst, Thomas. "Dubbing and Dubbed Text-Style and Cohesion: Textual Characteristics of a Special Form of Translation." *Text Typology and Translation.* Ed. Anna Trosborg. Materdam/Philadelphia: J. Benjamins, 1997: 291–308.

Hetzron, R. "On the Structure of Punchlines." *Humor* 1.1 (1988): 39–48.

Info Presse Communication 12.1 (1996): 52.

Katz, Elihu, and Tamar Liebes. "Moyens de défense et vulnérabilités: typologie de la réaction des téléspectateurs face aux émission de télévision importées." *Souveraineté et protectionisme en matière culturelle. La circulation internationale des émissions de télévision à la lumière de l'expérience canado-américaine.* Ed. Dave Atkinson, Ivan Bernier, and Sauvageau Florian. Sainte-Foy/Sillery: PUQ, 1991: 147–59.

La Toile du Québec. 5 May 2002 <http://www.toile.qc.ca>.

Ladouceur, Louise. "Les paramètres de l'adaptation théâtrale au Québec: de 1980 à 1990." Thesis. U de Montréal, 1991.

Lagueux, Michèle, and Danielle Charron. *Le doublage. Étude réalisée dans le cadre du rapport sur l'avenir de la télévision francophone.* Québec: Direction des communications du Ministère des communications du Québec, 1985.

Lendvai, Endre. "Translating 'Untranslatable' Russian Jokes." *Translation—The Vital Link/La Traduction au cœur de la communication.* Ed. Catriona Picken. London/Brighton: Institute of Translation and Interpretting, 1993: 105–09.

Leppihalme, Ritva. *Cultural Bumps: An Empirical Approach to the Translation of Allusions.* Clevedon: Multilingual Matters, 1997.

Les émissions de notre enfance. 5 May 2002 <http://www.emissions.ca>.

Luyken, Georg-Michael. *Overcoming Language Barriers in Television: Dubbing and Subtitling for the European Audience.* London: European Institute for the Media, 1991.

Manseau, Sylvie. *Chroniques Star Trek.* 5 May 2002 <http://www.9bit.qc.ca/~smanseau/startrek.htm>.

Marino, M. "Puns: the Good, the Bad, and the Beautiful." *Humor* 4.1 (1991): 61–108.

Meunier, Claude. Interview with Bernard Derome. *La Grande Aventure de la télévision.* Productions SociétéRadio-Canada. 8 Dec. 2002.

Ministère de la Culture et Communications du Québec. *L'industrie du doublage au Québec. Consolidation et nouveaux marchés.* Aug. 1997. Acessed on 5 May 2002 <http://www.mcc.gouv.qc.ca/publications/doublage.pdf>.

Okuda, Michael, Denise Okuda, and Debbie Mirek. *The Star Trek Encyclopedia: A Reference Guide to the Future.* 2nd ed. New York: Pocket Books, 1997.

Paquin, Robert. "Le doublage au Canada: politiques des langues et langues des politiques." *Meta* 45.1 (2000): 127–33.

Plourde, Éric. "Le doublage de *The Simpsons:* divergences, appropriation culturelle et manipulation du discours." Thesis. U de Montréal, 1999.

Politzer, R. "A Brief Classification of the Limits of Translatability." *Modern Language Journal* 40 (1956): 319–22.

Pommier, Christophe. *Doublage et postsynchronisation.* Paris: Dujarric, 1988.

Proulx, Serge, ed. *Accusé de réception. Le téléspectateur construit par les sciences sociales.* Québec: PUL, 1998.

Robyns, Clem. "Translation and Discursive Identity." *The Translator* 3.1 (1997): 57–78.

Saint-Germain, Maud. "Doublage-traduction ou doublage-trahison? Les enjeux identitaires et socio-économiques du doublage des films et de l'audiovisuel au Québec." Thesis. U de Montréal, 1998.

Salmon Kovarski, Laura. "Problemi di intraducibilità culturale nel film russo-sovietico: l'ambiguità di *Taxi Blues*." *Traduzione multimediale per il cinema, la televisione e la scena*. Ed. Christine Heiss and Rosa Maria Bollettieri Bosinelli. Bologna, Italy: Clueb, 1996: 251–77.

Star Trek Québec. 5 May 2002 <www.trekquebec.com>.

Star Trek: Hidden Frontier. 5 May 2002 <http://www.hiddenfrontier.com/>.

Sterbach, Rick, and Michael Okuda. *Star Trek: The Next Generation Technical Manual*. New York: Pocket Books, 1991.

Thierry Le Trekker. 5 May 2002 <http://thierry-the-trekker.chez.tiscali.fr/>.

Ulrych, Margherita. "Film Dubbing and the Translatability of Modes of Address: Power Relations and Social Distance in *The French Lieutenant's Wife*." *Traduzione multimediale per il cinema, la televisione e la scena*. Ed. Christine Heiss and Rosa Maria Bollettieri Bosinelli. Bologna, Italy: Clueb, 1996: 139–60.

Virtual Star Trek Season Project (France). 5 May 2002 <http://www.multimania.com/fvsp/startrek.html>.

Vrak.tv. 5 May 2002 <http://www.vrak.tv>.

Whitman-Linsen, Candace. *Through the Dubbing Glass: The Synchronization of American Motion Pictures into German, French, and Spanish*. New York: P. Lang, 1992.

Yahoo! France. 5 May 2002 <http://fr.yahoo.com>.

Audiovisual Works

"A Journey to Babel"/ "Un tour à Babel." *Star Trek*. Epi. #44. Writ. D. C. Fontana. Trans. Michel Collet. Paramount. 17 Nov. 1967.

"Arena"/ "Arène." *Star Trek*. Epi. #19. Teleplay Gene L. Coon. Story Fredric Brown. Trans. Michel Collet. Paramount. 19 Jan. 1967.

"Assignment: Earth"/ "Mission: Terre." *Star Trek*. Epi. #55. Teleplay Art Wallace. Story Gene Roddenberry and Art Wallace. Trans. Michel Collet. Paramount. 29 Mar. 1968.

"Balance of Terror"/ "Zone de terreur." *Star Trek*. Epi. #9. Writ. Paul Schneider. Trans. Michel Collet. Paramount. 15 Dec. 1966.

"Bread and Circuses"/ "Sur les chemins de Rome." *Star Trek*. Epi. #43. Writ. Gene Roddenberry and Gene L. Coon. Trans. Michel Collet. Paramount. 15 Mar. 1968.

"The Changeling"/ "Le Korrigan." *Star Trek*. Epi. #37. Writ. John Meredyth Lucas. Trans. Michel Collet. Paramount. 29 Sept. 1967.

Dans une galaxie près de chez vous. Television series. Motion International Montréal (Qc), 1999–2001.

"The Cloud Minders"/ "Nuages." *Star Trek*. Epi. #74. Teleplay Margaret Armen. Story David Gerrold and Oliver Crawford. Trans. Michel Collet. Paramount. 28 Feb. 1969.

"Deep Space Homer." *The Simpsons*. Epi. #1F13. Writ. David Mirkin. Fox. 24 Feb. 1994.

Ding et Dong—Le Film. Writ. Claude Meunier. Dir. Alain Chartrand. Max Films Productions, 1991.

"Dreamland II." *The X-Files*. Epi. #6X05. Writ. Vince Gilligan, Frank Sponitz, and John Shiban. Fox. 6 Dec. 1998.

"The Empath"/ "L'Impasse." *Star Trek*. Epi. #63. Writ. Joyce Muskatt. Trans. Michel Collet. Paramount. 6 Dec. 1968.

Galaxy Quest. St. David Howard. Scr. David Howard and Robert Gordon. Dir. Dean Parisot. Dream Works, 1999.

"Itchy and Scratchy: The Movie." *The Simpsons.* Epi. #9F03. Writ. John Swartzwelder. Fox. 3 Nov. 1992.

"Just Between You and Me . . . and Kirk and Paul and Carla and Becky." *The Wonder Years.* Epi. #2X11. Writ. Matthew Carlson. ABC. 18 Jan. 1989.

La Petite Vie. Television series. Writ. Claude Meunier. Avanti Ciné-Vidéo, 1993–1999.

Le Juge. St. Daniel Lavoie. Dir. Éric Bernard and Marie-Éve Cloutier. C de Joliette (Qc), 1992.

Le Merveilleux Monde de Ding et Dong. Television special. Writ. Claude Meunier with Louis Saïa and Serge Thériault. Avanti Ciné-Vidéo Inc./La Société des Ha! Ha! Enr., 1992.

"Le rêve de Moman." *Le Petite Vie.* Epi. #45. Writ. Claude Meunier. SRC. 1996.

"The Menagerie, Parts I and II"/ "La ménagerie, première et deuxième parties." *Star Trek.* Epi. #16. Writ. Gene Roddenberry. Trans. Michel Collet. Paramount. 17 Nov. 1966.

"Miri"/ "Miri." *Star Trek.* Epi. #12. Writ. Adrian Spies. Trans. Michel Collet. Paramount. 27 Oct. 1966.

"Mirror, Mirror"/ "Miroir." *Star Trek.* Epi. #39. Writ. Jerome Bixby. Trans. Michel Collet. Paramount. 6 Oct. 1967.

Odyssée 2001. Writ. and prod. Éric Dupuis and Richard Lacombe. Kino'02, 2001.

"Patrouille du Cosmos." *Film àvenir au cinéma.* 5 May 2002 <http://www.films.qc.ca/doublage/patrouillecosmos.html>.

Saturday Night Live. Epi. #225. Host William Shatner. NBC. 20 Dec. 1986.

"Spock's Brain"/ "Le cerveau de Spock." *Star Trek.* Epi. #61. Writ. Lee Cronin. Trans. Michel Collet. Paramount. 20 Sept. 1968.

Star Trek: The Sitcom. Writ. and prod. Éric Dupuis and Richard Lacombe. Day 3/Cabaret Kino'02, 2001 <http://www.kino00.com/film/startrek.ram>.

"Turnabout Intruder"/ "L'Important." *Star Trek.* Epi. #79. Teleplay Arthur H. Singer. Story Gene Roddenberry. Trans. Michel Collet. Paramount. 3 June 1969.

"Unification, Part II." *Star Trek: The Next Generation.* Epi. #207. Teleplay Michael Piller. Story Rick Berman and Michael Piller. Paramount. 11 Nov. 1991.

"The Way to Eden"/ "Le chemin d'Éden." *Star Trek.* Epi. #75. Teleplay Arthur Heinemann. Story Michael Richard and Arthur Heinemann. Trans. Michel Collet. Paramount. 21 Feb. 1969.

Double Vision
Large-Screen Video Display and Live Sports Spectacle

Greg Siegel

In the summer of 1980, the first-ever large-screen color video display system was installed in Dodger Stadium in Los Angeles (Mitsubishi Electronic Corporation 1996). Debuted during that year's Major League Baseball All-Star Game, the Diamond Vision large-screen video display (LSVD), designed and manufactured by the Mitsubishi Electronic Corporation,[1] offered sports spectators something unprecedented: a sharp, full-color, electronic image—moving image—of the action on the field. Despite its novelty, Dodgers fans, many of whom had been watching sports on television for decades, could not have been confused as to the "purpose" of the colossal contraption rearing up behind the left-field bleachers. This was TV—live sports television to be precise—and it had migrated from the cozy comfort of the living room to the "friendly confines"[2] of the ballpark, even if, along the way, it had mutated into a larger-than-life simulacrum of itself.[3]

Since 1980, throughout the United States and Canada, the sports-stadium LSVD[4] has been transformed from a technological marvel and cultural curiosity to an economic necessity and architectural obligation. While this is particularly true for the scores of stadiums aligned with professional sports leagues in North America, such as Major League Baseball (MLB), the National Football League (NFL), the National Hockey League (NHL), and the National Basketball Association (NBA), it is increasingly the case that college and minor-league sports facilities are being equipped with LSVDs (Carroll 1999; Mitchell 1999).[5]

This article analyzes LSVD in terms of, and often against, theories of the televisual apparatus, paying particular attention to the ways in which LSVD inflects and/or problematizes notions of presence, liveness, immediacy, and postmodern simulation. I argue that LSVD is properly understood as a hybrid apparatus,[6] one distinct from but dependent on the varied and variable forms, functions, and meanings of television, as well as cinema, the telescope and the public-address system. Furthermore, I contend that the LSVD apparatus alters the nature of the live event, as well as the spectator's relationship to and experience of it, by inducing and sustaining a mode of spectating practice characterized by the dynamic oscillation between immediate and mediated views of the game.

Presence

We are used to thinking about media screens as portals to be passed through en route to somewhere else. The movie screen provides a means of easy escapism, whisking us away, if only for a couple of hours, from the harsh realities and tiresome mundanities of our everyday lives, absorbing us into the fantastical mise-en-scène of the elsewhere, the "elsewhen." In a darkened theater we sit and stare, immobile and immersed, captivated by the immense luminosity of the silver screen in front of us, mistaking *representations* of reality for *perceptions* of reality (Baudry 1999a),[7] hallucinating our own transportation.

The television screen brings this visual vehicularity back home. Not only are our peregrinations privatized, but TV's claim to liveness ensures that, unlike cinema, we and the event we are watching share the same temporality, as though we were witnessing, firsthand, the unfolding, in and through time, of an authentic happening.[8] Television, moreover, explodes the singularity and boundedness of the film format, turning a one-stop, one-time voyage into a ceaseless "flow" (Williams 1990) of multiple embarkations and arrivals, available, at least for those with cable, each and every second, 24 hours a day. Today, the digital screen, from high-definition television (HDTV) to CD-ROM to the World Wide Web to virtual reality (VR), refashions and extends, or "remediates" (Bolter and Grusin 1999),[9] this promise of psychical transport in ways that are myriad and complex.

The LSVD screen, by contrast, is *not* a portal to be passed through en route to somewhere else. This is because it is already *there*, always already present at the event it is presenting/presence-ing.[10] Cinema, television, the World Wide Web—all of them, we have been told, take us from where we are and deliver us, mechanically, electronically, or digitally, to where we want to be. With LSVD, on the other hand, we are delivered *before* viewing not *because* of it, where the term "before" means both "prior to" and "in front of." Which is to say that LSVD is encountered not at the point of one's imaginary departure but at the site of one's actual destination (i.e., the sports stadium). With regard to what Samuel Weber (1996) calls a medium's "differential specificity," this is the difference that makes all the difference.

LSVD's sphere of reception equals its sphere of production equals its sphere of transmission, forming a kind of self-reflexive closed circuit, or what Douglas R. Hofstadter (1979/1999) refers to as a "strange loop."[11] LSVD's onscreen images are (often) visible offscreen, where they appear not as electronically generated representations but "in the flesh." The images' referents, in other words, are immediately incarnate, proximately available. Similarly,

LSVD's offscreen space overlaps, or is coterminous with, the actual space of exhibition. The viewing machinery inhabits the "pro-filmic" space; the viewing takes place in the place of the viewed.

The upshot of this strange spheric overlap is not the *replacement* of the immediate view by the mediated view, as with television, but rather the *double displacement* of each onto/into each other. *The mediated view subsumes the immediate view, even as the immediate consumes the mediated, resulting in an entirely new view characterized by neither the one nor the other but by the dynamism of their mutual interrelation.* Governed by an impossible logic that splits visual subjectivity in the process of reframing it, the two views alternately reflect,[12] refract, and reduplicate each other; they complement, comment on, and complicate each other. But they do not substitute, supplant, or stand in for each other, as so many representations for the real or realities for their representations. LSVD does not represent the game and does not generate representations of the game. It *co-presents* the game, doubling its discourse— augmenting it, supplementing it, enhancing it, accompanying it, envisioning it. In this sense, then, LSVD is spectacularly redundant.

Television overcomes distance, closing the spatial gap separating subject and object. LSVD does not (have to) overcome distance. Or rather the distance LSVD overcomes—between, say, spectators in the back rows of the upper balcony and the playing surface below—differs from the distance television overcomes in both degree (quantitative) and kind (qualitative). It differs in degree because television's overcoming is reckoned in miles, whereas LSVD's overcoming is reckoned in feet. It differs in kind because television transmits images of persons, places, and things that are not in one's immediate line of sight or field of vision. No amount of squinting will bring TV's referents into direct view; no amount of "fine-tuning" will incarnate its succession of iconographics. Nor will any other optical technology—a telescope, for instance— help close the gap between viewer and viewed, for the simple reason that television does not provide an enlarged *version of the visible,* as does LSVD, but rather a particular *visualization of the out-of-sight.*

> In contrast to the telescope, television does not merely allow the viewer to "see at a distance" things that otherwise would be invisible. It *transports vision as such* and *sets* it immediately *before* the viewer. It entails not merely a heightening of the naturally limited powers of sight with respect to certain distant *objects;* it involves a transmission or transposition of vision itself. (Weber 1996, 115–16)

LSVD's mode of mediating distance, together with the impulse behind and effects of that mediation, has as much in common with the magnifying functionality of the telescope (or opera glasses or binoculars) as it does with the "space-annihilating" function of television.[13]

Hypermediation and Narrativization

LSVD functions both as an opaque object, *screening out* the stadium spectator's immediate view of the game, and as a narrativized objectivity, *screening in* the game in/as a serial flow of conventionalized images. I will address each of these in turn.

For Jay David Bolter and Richard Grusin (1999), the diachronic process of remediation, which concerns the formal and functional correspondences and disjunctures between and across media technologies, is structured according to, and propelled by, the "twin logics of immediacy and hypermediacy" (p. 5). Immediate media aspire to pure transparency, absolute invisibility. The user is encouraged to forget or disavow the enabling interposition of the medium at hand (i.e., the fact of mediation), thereby achieving a state of unadulterated transcendence. "Immediacy is transparency: the absence of mediation or representation. It is the notion that a medium could erase itself and leave the viewer in the presence of the objects represented, so that he could know the objects directly" (Bolter and Grusin 1999, 70). The concept of transparent immediacy recalls the claim made earlier that media technologies such as cinema, television, the Internet and virtual reality often function—or at least have been widely and loudly trumpeted—as portals to be passed through en route to somewhere else.

Whereas we look *through* a transparent medium, we look *at* a hypermedium (Bolter and Grusin 1999, 41). One is a crystal-clear window, the other a graffiti-emblazoned brick wall. From medieval illuminated manuscripts, with their painstakingly intricate adornment, to windowed multimedia applications, with their splashy graphic layerings, hypermedia are supremely spectacular and patently nonillusionistic, beseeching "us to take pleasure in the act of mediation" (Bolter and Grusin 1999, 14). Just as hypermedia are opaque where immediate media are transparent, so the former ask us to remember or recognize the medium where the latter persuade us to forget or disavow it. "Hypermediacy is opacity—the fact that knowledge of the world comes to us through media. The viewer acknowledges that she is in the presence of a medium and learns through acts of mediation or indeed learns about mediation itself" (Bolter and Grusin 1999, 71).

LSVD is a hypermedium, a dazzling opacity. Stadium spectators, as temporary inhabitants of a decidedly nonillusionistic environment, are not disposed to forget either the resistant materiality of the LSVD screen or the hulking steel gondola (or massive concrete scaffolding) supporting it. This is because LSVD is less a *medium-that-channels* that which is out of reach than an *intermediary-that-obstructs* (and *constructs,* as we will see shortly) that which is already at hand. In the parlance of spectator sports, the term "obstructed view" is usually reserved for those vantage points marred by a partially occluded or otherwise restricted view of the playing surface. However, the view of the playing surface mediated by LSVD can also be understood as a kind of obstructed view, insofar as it momentarily blocks off—or, more precisely, *screens out*—the direct view of the action on the field/rink/court. By repeatedly threatening to seize the spectator's sightline and redirect the intensities of his/her gaze, LSVD *interferes with* the spectator's immediate apprehension of the game. Yet this intermittent interference, this saccadic "noise," is precisely the desired effect. For Henning Eichberg (1995), LSVD actualizes an entirely new way of seeing, what he calls "hypervisuality":

Increasingly, we see large screens inside the arenas used to present the events in visual detail. They are able to enlarge on selected scenes; they reproduce processes in slow motion and split the visual impression up into a multiplicity of pictures. This is no longer the visuality of the traditional modern stadium—it is hypervisuality. (P. 340)

The stadium spectator's willful, if intermittent, withdrawal from the immediacy of the real (i.e., the direct view of the action taking place on the field/rink/court) in favor of the hypermediation of LSVD contrasts with the television viewer, whose only access to the real is via its mediation. To avert one's eyes from the TV screen (and close one's ears or mute the audio track) is to sever one's connection to the medium, even if only momentarily, and thus to that which is being depicted. There can be no apprehension of the event, or any part of the event, without the conveyance of sights and sounds by/through the televisual medium. Averting one's eyes from LSVD, however, does not effect the severing of such a connection, for the spectator is enveloped by the event on all sides and at every moment. One can refrain from watching the game on LSVD, but not without another aspect of the event coming in to view (assuming, of course, one's eyes remain open).

No doubt, part of LSVD's allure has to do with its ability, as a hypermedium, to produce in/for the spectator "a feeling of fullness, a satiety of experience, which can be taken as reality" (Bolter and Grusin 1999, 54).[14] But this explanation only goes so far, for it tells us nothing about the singularity of LSVD's appeal as compared to other possible and actual manifestations of today's in-stadium hypermedia, such as interactive informational kiosks, "smart seats," video games, cable-access televisions, and internet-wired computers.

A more revealing answer lies in the way LSVD iconographics appropriate and adapt the formal "objectivity" and rhetorical conventions of televised sports. Television, of course, does not simply *transmit* a sporting event; it carefully *constructs* it, and does so "in the form of a coherent narrative or story" (Goldlust 1987, 87). John Goldlust (1987) argues that

> the essential narrative and dramatic structure of all sporting contests [is] very much the same. Any sporting event is a contest between protagonists (or teams of protagonists) who compete according to a set of rules administered by authoritative adjudicator(s), so that ultimately a result emerges. From such a simple and seemingly limited structure, television[,] using its technical and creative resources, proceeds to construct a style of sporting drama best suited to one of the primary dictates of the medium—the accumulation of audiences. (P. 88)

For Goldlust (1987), the ability to accumulate audiences for sports telecasts hinges on the medium's widely touted capacity for instantaneous transmission, along with the aura of immediacy that is its inevitable by-product.

> The most inclusive narrative form is the complete live telecast of the sporting event. Until the introduction of videotape into television production in the 1950s, this was, of necessity, the most widely employed form of sports television and despite the subsequent development of others, remains the type

that attracts consistently large viewing audiences. The strength of its appeal lies in providing the television audience with an ostensibly complete and *immediate* [emphasis added] experience of the sporting event. (P. 88)

Goldlust (1987, 89–91) identifies six "visual components" of the typical sports telecast: (1) pre-prepared material on tape or film, including opening title and ending credit sequences, taped interviews, background material, archival footage, and viewer competitions; (2) graphics, including titles, credits, names of participants, statistics, scores, symbols, explanatory diagrams, analysis of particular plays, and promotional material for future telecasts; (3) game action, including temporary "breaks built into the structure of the sport" (p. 89); (4) slow-motion replays; (5) "spontaneous or prearranged live coverage of nonaction elements of the game or stadium event" (Goldlust 1987, 90), including crowd shots, reaction shots of coaches and other off-field personnel, shots of celebrities attending the game, and brief interviews with participants, coaches, former players, and celebrities; and (6) commercial interruptions and sponsored logos superimposed over action sequences. These same visual components, along with the logic underlying their organization, make up a substantial portion of LSVD iconographics, provided we substitute "in-house promotions" or "sponsored features" for "commercial interruptions."[15] Indeed, whether it uses images taken directly from the broadcast television feed, or those coming from the team's/stadium's own dedicated cameras, or some combination of the two, the basic visual style, structure, and flow of LSVD programming frequently hews to the line of sports television—a fact that goes a long way in explaining LSVD's attraction for the stadium spectator.

There can be little doubt that television's narrativized construction of the sporting event provides "a privileged cognitive and aesthetic experience" (Goldlust 1987, 90), insofar as the medium's formal elements (mise-en-scéne, videography, editing, sound) are manipulated and mobilized to accentuate, even hyperbolize, the game's supposedly intrinsic capacity for drama and spectacle. The facial close-up, for example, is repeatedly used to signify what are believed to be the intense psychological states of the participants (concentration, elation, anguish, frustration, etc.) (Goldlust 1987, 93), while the slow-motion replay, at once oneiric and scientific, "allows the analysis and appreciation of body movements which are normally inaccessible to view" (Morse 1983, 49).[16] The fact that much of LSVD programming copies or closely approximates the "language" of sports television can be seen as a solution to a particular problem, namely the problem of how to recreate, within the confines of the stadium itself, the experience of televised sports for the generation(s) of fans accustomed to its sensorially aggrandized and affectively intensified construction of the game.

While in the past, watching televised sport was generally considered a secondary and therefore a relatively impoverished version of direct spectatorship, the defining power of television as the authoritative interpreter of the sporting experience has successfully inverted the social validity of this assumption. The view of the sporting contest mediated by television has established itself as the primary experience. The giant video screen is there to attract people to the stadium event and to ensure that by attending they will not be deprived of the "television experience." (Goldlust 1987, 174)[17]

Whatever its alleged advantages, LSVD's cooptation of sports television's visual codes can also precipitate bouts of perceptual disorientation for the stadium spectator. To see why this is the case, a brief detour is necessary.

Sports television follows the conventions of Hollywood- style continuity editing, which is designed "to create a smooth flow from shot to shot" (Bordwell and Thompson 1997, 285). This "smooth flow" is achieved through the systematic employment of an ensemble of techniques, including the establishment of an imaginary "180-degree line" or "axis of action" or "center line,"[18] which works to ensure the immediate legibility of spatial relations across edits, or in the case of live television, across camera-to-camera "switches." In televised football, the axis of action runs from one end zone (or goal post) to the other. The same is true for basketball and hockey, where the 180-degree line cuts through the middle of the court/rink latitudinally, from goal net to goal net. (The situation is somewhat more complicated in baseball, but in general, the principle holds.) Most of the 20-plus cameras used to shoot a typical televised sporting event are arrayed on the *same side* of the axis of action or on the line itself. As long as the director does not switch to a camera on the other side of the 180-degree line, the constancy of screen direction will be ensured.[19] That is, Team A will always appear on the left side of the screen, moving right during offensive moments (and left when on the defensive), and Team B will always appear on the right side of the screen, moving left during offensive moments (and right when on the defensive).

For the television viewer, this technique, and the conventions of continuity editing in general, create the sense of a coherent, contiguous space, one in which the action unfolds in a clear, continuous manner. But for some stadium spectators this is not the case. Say that Team A appears on the left side of the LSVD screen and advances right, while Team B appears on the right side of the LSVD screen and advances left. Now imagine, as a stadium spectator, that one's orientation vis-à-vis the field/rink/court is such that Team A is positioned to one's right and advances left, while Team B is positioned to one's left and advances right. The result is that the LSVD image *reverses,* as though in a mirror, the spatial relationships obtaining in one's immediate view of the game. Every time one glances at the LSVD screen and then back at the playing surface (or vice versa), one has, in effect, crossed the center line and violated the 180-degree rule, flip-flopping the directionality of vectorial motion, breaching the coherent contiguity of perceptual space and disrupting the clear continuity of the unfolding action.

To be sure, over the course of a game, *every* spectator who uses LSVD must perform countless mental reorientations, as he/she switches back and forth from a fixed and immediate vantage point to a mobilized and mediated one. At any given moment, LSVD offers the spectator an alternate (i.e., mediated) perspective of the game at hand, conferring on him/her an ocular option unavailable to the pre-LSVD stadiumgoer.[20] But for those spectators for whom the LSVD image is effectively inverted, these mental reorientations are even more involved, in that they entail a constant succession of specular reversals. And they can be more complicated still, as it is customary in many sports for the opposing teams to change sides during designated breaks in the action (i.e., at half-time or the end of a period/quarter). All of this means that over the course of a game the spatial relations established by LSVD are in constant flux vis-à-vis one's direct view of the action.

Sound

According to Goldlust (1987, 91), there are four "audio components" of the typical sports telecast: (1) audio soundtracks accompanying pre-prepared material; (2) music; (3) "international sound," that is, the "natural" sound emanating from the stadium event; and (4) commentary from broadcast professionals. For all intents and purposes, LSVD's "voice" is the stadium public-address (PA) system, and that system routinely mediates both prerecorded music and voices (e.g., pop songs, the synched sound of prepackaged video montages) and "live" music and voices (e.g., organ/keyboard instrumentals, PA announcements).[21] Although LSVD does not tap into the broadcast television feed for its audio, as it often does for its video, it is certainly not without its analogues to numbers 1 and 2. As for number 3, the stadium PA system does not record or amplify ambient sound.[22] Nevertheless, because television *does* record ambient sound, the phenomenon figures into the experiences of both stadium spectator and television viewer, albeit, of course, to different degrees. What about number 4?

Doubtless, the most glaring sonic discrepancy between LSVD and TV is that the former's presentation of the game is often "mute," whereas aural "dead air" is anathema to the latter. In accordance with MLB, NFL, NHL, and NBA rules and regulations (Bob Becker, personal communication, 24 August 1999), the stadium PA system falls silent during those moments when the game is underway to avoid distracting the players on the field/rink/court. The only noises the stadium spectator detects at such times are ambient, not amplified, emanating "naturally" from the surrounding persons and objects, not mediated by the enormous woofers and tweeters encased in the stadium speakers. The television viewer, however, hears something more, something *on top of* the stadium's accidental acoustics: the seemingly incessant chatter of the commentators. This point is hardly negligible, as the verbal exposition and explication delivered by trained broadcasters plays a central role in the narrative construction of televised sports.

> There is perhaps nothing that better illustrates the mediational role of television than the curious phenomenon of the television sports commentary. Instead of providing the viewer with a "direct" access to the event through visual images of the contest mixed with the international sound, the commentary team attempt[s] to present a coherent exposition, analysis, evaluation and assessment of the on-going game and stadium events, as well as locating a particular game in the broader context of a historically developed subcul-

ture that draws upon previous performances of present day participants, as well as the noteworthy champions and "legendary" contests of previous eras. Thus, in the manner that the television newsreader or the narrator of a documentary presents a comprehensive and consistent story that coherently binds together the somewhat disparate and unanchored visual images being presented, similarly, the role of the sports commentator is to act as an authoritative guide to the "reading" of the sports contest for the benefit of the television audience. (Goldlust 1987, 91–2)

While sound helps anchor, organize, and interpret the mediated visuals for the television audience, LSVD helps anchor, organize, and interpret the immediate "visuals" (i.e., direct perceptions) for the stadium audience. By means of the systematic deployment of a wide variety of readily intelligible, affectively charged audiovisual cues—televisual iconographics, electronic alphanumeric messages (appearing on the stadium's "matrix boards")[23] and theatrical lighting techniques in conjunction with PA-boosted music, monologue, and sound effects—the LSVD apparatus shapes spectators' awareness and understanding of the sporting event taking place in front of them and the "stadium event"[24] taking place around them.

The Distracted Glance

With respect to the question of motivation, the LSVD spectator's relationship to the medium is fundamentally different than that of the film, television, or cyber/virtual spectator. For the latter group, the screen figures (as) the primary projection of desire. One attends the cinema because one wishes to see a particular film or because, more generally, one wants to experience the peculiar pleasures associated with cinema spectatorship. Much the same can be said for the television viewer and cyber/virtual spectator, however "distracted" he/she might be. The reasons for going to the movies, watching television, or exploring cyberspace may differ, but the expectation of, and desire for, a communion with the medium, or with the content of the medium, obtains in every case. Significantly, this communion is not achieved as a byproduct of some other activity or commitment, related or not, but rather is the principal incentive driving the viewing process. It does not matter, for our purposes, what underpins or constitutes the desire of the film spectator or television viewer or internet surfer; nor does it matter what one hopes to gain or obtain as a result of the viewing act (escape, titillation, relaxation, education, amusement, enlightenment, etc.). It does not even matter if one's expectations are fulfilled. What matters is that a *prior intentionality* is almost always built into the structure of film, television, and cyber/virtual spectatorship. That is, the anticipatory desire to engage the medium is the condition of possibility for spectatorship. One's investment in the medium precedes one's encounter of it. The medium is actively sought out for its own sake, or for its content, in any case, for the gratifications it and only it can afford. The viewing experience (again, whether distracted or not) is held to be an end in itself, not the product of happenstance. The film, TV, or cyber/virtual spectator is a spectator because spectatorship—this spectatorship and not that—is deliberately chosen.

By contrast, one does not attend a sporting event for the express purpose of viewing LSVD, but rather goes to see the game and/or to experience the broader event of which the game is a part. It is arguable that today's sports spectator, living in a media-saturated society—one in which the economic imbrication of the sports and media industries is widely known and highly visible—expects the stadium to be equipped with one or more LSVD screens. He/she might even look forward to the privileges and pleasures such mediation promises. But in regard to his/her decision as to whether to attend the event, the fact of LSVD's presence in the stadium is unlikely to be the make-or-break criterion. LSVD is not the chief motivation, not the ultimate reason for going to a sporting event, but rather an accident of circumstance, something to be enjoyed (or not, as the case may be) as "value-added." As noted earlier, LSVD is an augmentation, a supplement, an enhancement, an accompaniment, a spectacular redundancy. LSVD is sensational *and* superfluous—not to one's spectating experience, it must be stressed, but with respect to one's spectatorial raison d'être.

We are compelled, in light of the above, to reconsider that old bugbear of television theory: the distracted glance. For John Ellis (1992), television's poor image quality, diminutive screen, and domestic sphere of reception conspire to elicit a distracted glance as opposed to cinema's sustained gaze. In this view, the magnetic pull of the televisual medium is relatively weak; one's attention—or, more precisely, one's *concentration*—is in perpetual danger of being torn asunder by a thousand peripheral forces. What I want to highlight is the fact that, embattled though it is, the activity of television viewing still assumes center stage in Ellis' account. Distractions, whether endemic to the medium (e.g., screen size) or intruding from without (e.g., domestic obligations), figure in a scenario in which watching television is both the viewer's principal goal and the theorist's manifest object of study.

Enter the LSVD spectator. We cannot—must not—assume that watching LSVD is the spectator's principal goal, even though this activity constitutes our present object of study. The stadium spectator is first and foremost a consumer of live sports and only secondarily—consequentially, circumstantially, accidentally—a consumer of mediated images. While I agree with John Thornton Caldwell (1995) that Ellis' concept of the distracted glance ("the surrendered gaze") is highly problematic vis-à-vis television,[25] it nevertheless gains new resonance, perhaps even new respectability, when applied to LSVD. For as Bolter and Grusin (1999) point out, "the viewer experiences such hypermedia not through an extended and unified gaze, but through directing her attention here and there in brief moments" (p. 54). There is simply no getting around it: the stadium spectator *does* glance at the LSVD screen. I do not mean to suggest, of course, that all spectators use LSVD to the same extent or in the same way. But it is highly unlikely that *any* spectator should be inclined to gaze at LSVD for hours at a time, as though it were a cinema screen or television set or computer monitor. To the extent that today's stadium spectator can be said to possess/project any gaze at all, it is doubtless a compromised gaze, a gaze riddled with glances, perforated by wayward looks, not the inviolable, laser-like stare of the traditionally construed filmgoer. To be precise, the contemporary stadium spectator glances at both—switches between—the LSVD screen and the action on the field/rink/court. At bottom, any comprehensive theory of the LSVD spectator must come to grips with the following radical reversal: one is not distracted *from* LSVD; one is distracted *by* LSVD.

Framing the Game

Writing in reference to televised football, Brien R. Williams (1977) distinguishes between three embedded layers of "events" taking place simultaneously.

> They are (1) the *game event,* defined as the action on the field plus directly related activities taking place on the sidelines, (2) the *stadium event,* defined as the total sequence of activities occurring in the stadium, both perceived and participated in by the fans and including the game event, and (3) the *medium event,* defined as the total telecast of which coverage of the game event is part. (P. 135)

According to this schema, the game event is embedded in the stadium event, which is embedded in the medium event.[26] "The medium event incorporates the game and stadium events but supplements these with the commentary, interviews, graphics and other visual inserts, advertising material from sponsors and station promotions" (Goldlust 1987, 85–6) (see Figure 1).

LSVD complexifies this picture by multiplying Williams's embedded layers to the point that they resemble nothing so much as a set of Chinese boxes. Like television, LSVD frames both the stadium event and the game event, making it a medium event in its own right. (To distinguish between the television medium event and the LSVD medium event, I will henceforth call them "TV event" and "LSVD event," respectively.) But it is more complicated than this because LSVD does not simply frame the stadium event and game event directly; it also frames part of the TV event, to the extent that it appropriates

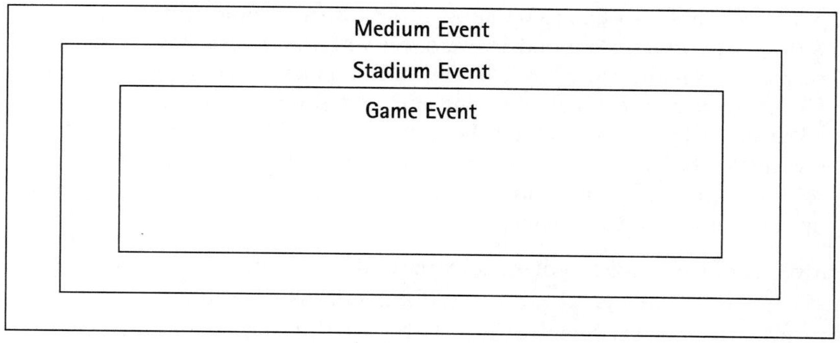

Figure 1

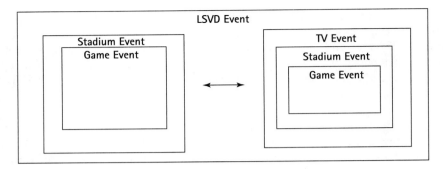

Figure 2

the broadcast television signal to supplement its programming. The LSVD event, then, is comprised of the coordinated exchange and interplay of the TV event (which includes the stadium and game events) and its own framing of the stadium event (which includes the game event) (see Figure 2).

Complicating matters further is the fact that the LSVD event is itself part of the stadium event (i.e., part of "the total sequence of activities occurring in the stadium, both perceived and participated in by the fans and including the game event"). This raises a key question: Does the LSVD event, which is subsumed under the stadium event, belong *inside* or *alongside* the game event (i.e., "the action on the field plus directly related activities taking place on the sidelines")? Within Williams's narrow definition, it would not seem as though LSVD could be framed by the game event. However, players and coaches *do* use LSVD for informational and strategic purposes. Consider the following anecdotes offered by Kyle Ritchie (personal communication, 8 October 1999), Scoreboard Operations Manager for the Carolina Panthers football team and current 1st Vice President of the Information Display and Entertainment Association:

> [NFL players] Cris Carter and Desmond Howard have admitted they use the video screens to their advantage. I think it was Cris who said that, while he was running a pattern one day, he looked up at the screen and could tell the pass was coming to him. Sure enough, he turned around and, boom, there was the ball. When Desmond Howard was with the [Green Bay] Packers, the year they won the Superbowl, he ran back a punt return for a touchdown. He let up at about the 30-yard line and started getting all fancy. The press asked him why he did that and he said something like, "I let up because I saw on the board that no one was behind me. Why run harder than I have to?" The cover of *Sports Illustrated* told the same story: his eyes are straight up, looking at the video screen.

Clearly, LSVD is implicated in, and part of, the game event (see Figure 3). Strictly speaking, this is where the embeddedness ends for the stadium spectator; only the television viewer knows the final frame (see Figure 4). Yet in a more liberal sense, both the stadium spectator and the television viewer experience the overall event as framed by television.

Television must produce a form of entertainment that ensures a maximisation of the sale of commercial time and therefore the staging of the sports event is increasingly susceptible to changes in structure and form that television professionals assess will be most favourable to this end. This has led to the most visible and widely commented on influences on sport attributed to television—changes to the internal structure of sporting contests through manipulation of rules, scoring, conditions of play and control over decisions affecting time, place and duration of the event. (Goldlust 1937, 145)

In any case, it should be clear from the above that LSVD demands that we acknowledge the altered nature of the game and stadium events, as well as the stadium spectator's altered relationship to and experience of them.

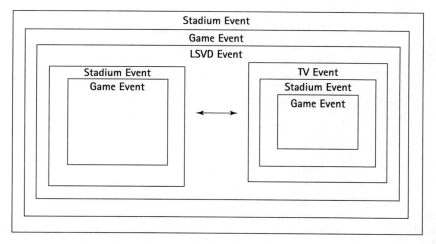

Figure 3

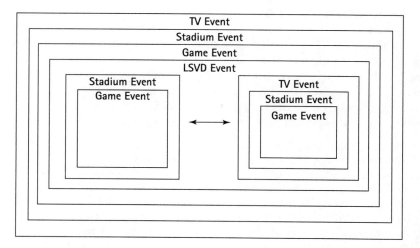

Figure 4

The Specter of Simulation

Up to this point, I have been drawing primarily on television and film theory as a means of analyzing LSVD's differential specificity. But the nature, function, and effects of the LSVD apparatus could also be interrogated through the prism of postmodernist theory.[27] For instance, with regard to the issues of presence and programming, we might inquire as to whether the spectatorial effects of LSVD's manipulations of onscreen time (e.g., slow-motion replay) and space (e.g., the 180-degree rule) could be elucidated with reference to the postmodern experience of time and space, as theorized by, say, David Harvey (1990) or Fredric Jameson (1997) or Manuel Castells (1997). Although he does not use the term "postmodern," Brian J. Neilson (1995), writing about baseball, broaches this idea:

> [LSVD] has altered our experience of the stadium, by eroding the unity of time and space by which we locate ourselves and determine "reality." If the effect of previous technological interventions upon the game of baseball has been to dislocate the game on the field from the rhythm of the days and the seasons, and from the crossed lines of our collective history, the effect of [LSVD] is to dislocate us from the moment itself. I have often seen a crowd withhold its applause after an exceptional play until it has consulted the televised replay; this sequence surely describes a unique epistemological reversal in the history of human consciousness. (Pp. 66–7)

A more obvious application of postmodernist theory to LSVD, however, would hinge on Jean Baudrillard's (1995) notion of simulation.

A Baudrillardian analysis of LSVD might argue that the game's electronic simulation is necessary to underwrite the "reality" of the experience for postmodern spectators because in our cultural economy the media screen hypostasizes the real.[28] It might argue that in the contemporary sports stadium the live event and its mediation, once ontological opposites, converge and merge into a single seamless spectacle. Or it might argue, simply, that today the difference between simulated liveness (TV) and live simulations (LSVD) makes no difference.

Although this (hypothetical) line of reasoning is provocative in its abstraction, I do not think it is particularly useful in assessing the LSVD apparatus. The problem is that it assumes the categorical antonymy between, and subsequent "implosion" of, the live and the mediated, rather than seeing them as two shifting points on a discursively constructed continuum. Philip Auslander (1999) makes this point in reference to live performance:

> Thinking about the relationship between live and mediatized forms in terms of ontological oppositions is not especially productive because there are few grounds on which to make significant ontological distinctions. Like live performance, electronic and photographic media can be described meaningfully as partaking of the ontology of disappearance ascribed to live performance, and they can also be used to provide an experience of evanescence. Like film and television, theatre can be used as a mass medium. . . . I am not proposing, however, that live performance and mediatization partake of a

shared ontology. . . . I am suggesting, rather, that how live and mediatized forms are used is determined not by their ostensibly intrinsic characteristics but by their positions within a cultural economy. To understand the relationship between live and mediatized forms, it is necessary to investigate that relationship as historical and contingent, not as ontologically given or technologically determined. (P.51)[29]

LSVD's insertion into the stadium does not instigate or symbolize an ontological implosion of the live and the mediated. What it *does* signal, though, is that the latter is now an integral element in the meaning and experience of the former. Today, significantly, this is true not only of spectator sports, but increasingly, of live "performance" in general, including dramatic theater, musical concerts, religious services,[30] political speeches, performance art, stand-up comedy, fashion shows, consumer demonstrations, business conventions, and educational seminars.

This goes back to something I have argued at various points and in various ways throughout this article: LSVD reconfigures the stadium event as the energized interchange between direct presentation and mediated copresentation. Baudrillard's theory, however, cannot account for this structuring oscillation, this restless movement negotiating the immediate view of the playing surface and the mediated view of the LSVD screen. Indeed, only synthetic inertia, not dialectical alternation, exists where the poles of the real and the simulated have collapsed into one another. Where the difference makes no difference, there can only be self-identical stasis. Implosion, in other words, is tantamount to death.

Yet not even LSVD's shrillest detractors—those purists for whom the apparatus' incursion into the stadium represents the "contamination"[31] of liveness—make the charge that it deadens the distinction between the live and the mediated, much less that it deadens the intensity of the overall event. On the contrary, their critique alleges something altogether different, namely that LSVD interjects an overbearing spectacularity and disjointed hyperactivity into the proceedings, suffusing the stadium with the sensationalist values of show business.[32] Thus, despite what some postmodernists would have us believe, the LSVD phenomenon is not about death by means of simulation but about liveness by means of simulation's appropriation.

Conclusion

LSVD is not television, but it remediates the comparatively low resolution of its pixelated image and the generic codes and formal conventions of live sports telecasts. LSVD is not cinema or theater TV circa 1948–1953 (Hilmes 1990), but it remediates the immense scale of their screens and the commercial communality of their spheres of reception. LSVD is not a telescope, but it remediates its ability to magnify the already-in-sight. LSVD is not a "spectacular" electric sign in the mold of those adorning New York City's Times Square (Starr and Hayman 1998), but it remediates its optoelectronic technology and eye-catching effulgence. LSVD is not a scoreboard, but it remediates its alphanu-

meric display and statistical functionality. LSVD is not a PA system, but it remediates its informational, promotional, and participatory modes of address.

For sporting-event attendees, the hybridized technocultural assemblage
that is LSVD facilitates and encourages, perhaps even demands, a new mode
of spectating practice, a new type of experiential enthrallment. Today's stadium spectator possesses a degree and kind of perceptual agency denied to
spectators of previous generations, insofar as he/she is able to alternate at will
between points of view that are, on the one hand, direct and (relatively) fixed,
and on the other, mediated and mobilized. The former viewpoint registers the
familiar unidirectional temporality and embodied spatiality of everyday (waking) experience; the latter registers the elliptical, expanded, and iterative temporality and conventionalized spatial relations of narrativized visual media, particularly television and cinema.

In the end, what makes the LSVD apparatus so remarkable, what makes
it more than simply "TV in a public place" (à la theater television) or the latest example of simulation's colonization of the real (a Baudrillardian phan-
tasm), is that it does not position the spectator at any *single* or *stationary* point
on the spectrum of engagement, but rather shuttles him/her back and forth
along the length of its axis. He/she is neither the fully present "live" spectator, nor the telepresent television viewer, nor the postmodern subject for whom
such a distinction has ceased to matter. Instead, like LSVD itself, the contemporary stadium-goer is something of a hybridized entity—by turns near
and far, now and then, sedentary and mobilized, centered and decentered,
emplaced and displaced.

Notes

I am grateful to Lawrence Grossberg, Ken Hillis, and Victoria E. Johnson for their
helpful comments on earlier drafts of this article.

1. Other LSVD manufacturers include Sony (JumboTron), Daktronics (ProStar),
SACO (SmartVision) and Panasonic (AstroVision).

2. This a colloquialism for Chicago's Wrigley Field.

3. The notion that LSVD is simply a larger-than-life television will be problematized in what follows. My point here is that television was, and still is, the obvious cultural and technological touchstone for sports fans who use LSVD.

4. Unless otherwise indicated, all subsequent references to LSVD concern its use
in contemporary sports stadiums in the United States and Canada. In other words,
"LSVD" should be taken to mean "sports-stadium LSVD." Neither the multiple worldwide applications of LSVD technology, nor its increasing utilization as part of nonsporting events (e.g., rock concerts, corporate seminars, mass gatherings) and exhibitions (e.g., billboard-style advertising), will be considered here. That said, I believe that
many of the observations and arguments I make in this article could be used, with some
modification, to shed light on LSVD's utilization in nonsporting events.

5. According to Kyle Ritchie (personal communication, 8 October 1999), Scoreboard Operations Manager for the Carolina Panthers football team and current 1st Vice
President of the Information Display and Entertainment Association.

[LSVD have] been catching on like wildfire at the college ranks. It's an important recruitment tool. These high-school recruits come in and see the college players getting introduced on the video board—that's a big deal to them. It's becoming a necessity for colleges to keep up with the Joneses, because if you don't have it, another school will.

6. Following Jean-Louis Baudry (1999b), I use the term "apparatus" to denote the complex convergence of media technology, iconographic content, viewing conditions, and psychophenomenological disposition of the viewer.

7. It's actually more complicated than Baudry (1999a, 1999b) lets on, because the film screen's present representations are the filmmaker's—or, more precisely, the film camera's—past "perceptions."

8. Perhaps the most celebrated—and, in the eyes of critics such as Jane Feuer (1983), most mystifying and ideological—of television's inherent properties is its capacity to broadcast "live," to depict (distant) events at the very instant of their occurrence, that is, as they occur, as they are occurring. More than any other feature, so the argument goes, this claim to liveness, together with its correlatives, "immediacy" and "presence," constitutes the medium's stock-in-trade, its mark of distinction.

9. Jay David Bolter and Richard Grusin (1999) define "remediation" as "the formal logic by which new media refashion prior media forms" (p. 273).

10. It will be objected that this is not always the case. On special occasions, for instance, as during the championship playoffs, many franchises invite fans to watch the team's "away" game on the LSVD screen(s). In this scenario, the spectator is not in the physical presence of the event being depicted. True enough. I would argue, however, that we are no longer talking about the LSVD apparatus, insofar as the viewing conditions, if not the material medium, have been radically modified. In fact, the viewing conditions have been modified to those of late-1940s/early-1950s theater television (Hilmes 1990).

11. "The 'Strange Loop' phenomenon occurs whenever, by moving upwards (or downwards) through the levels of some hierarchical system, we unexpectedly find ourselves right back where we started" (Hofstadter 1979/1999, 10). Although the analogy is not perfect—for one thing, the notion of a hierarchy of levels does not apply—I nevertheless wish to suggest something of the specular circularity that obtains when the sites of production, transmission, and reception collapse into (the space) each other, as they do in the case of the LSVD apparatus.

12. For some stadium spectators, LSVD registers a mirror-like inversion, a strange phenomenon that is bound up with televised sports' conventionalized editing practices (i.e., the "180-degree rule"). I will elaborate on this point shortly.

13. In truth, LSVD does not magnify everyone's view of the game. On the contrary, for spectators sitting or standing close to the field/rink/court, LSVD often provides a broader, more inclusive perspective on the action.

14. Bolter and Grusin (1999) hasten to point out that the kind of "reality" hypermedia evoke is not the metaphysical kind, but rather is "defined in terms of the viewer's experience: it is that which would evoke an immediate (and therefore authentic) emotional response" (p. 54). Unfortunately, they never adequately explain what constitutes an "authentic" emotional response.

15. At one time it was not uncommon for television commercials to be shown on LSVD. Today, however, the practice is speeding toward extinction. Not that advertising does not play a part in LSVD programming—far from it. But the overwhelming majority of today's LSVD producers insist on "airing" promotions created exclusively

for LSVD, particularly those that elicit audience participation. Bob Becker (personal communication, 24 August 1999), Director of In-Game Entertainment and Production for the Carolina Hurricanes hockey team, explains,

> If Toyota came to us and said they wanted to do a 30-second spot per game, we'd steer them away from doing a commercial and try to develop a promotion for them. We'd say something like, "No, we don't want to run a commercial, but how about sponsoring a trivia question?" So it would be the Toyota Trivia Question, and then afterwards the PA announcer would say, "Hey fans, don't forget to check out your local Toyota dealer!" When I was with the Florida Marlins, instead of doing a commercial we did this Toyota "drive-around." A Toyota truck came through the center-field fence and cruised around the ballpark with Billy the Marlin [mascot] shooting off Marlins cushions or T-shirts or balloons or water guns, whatever. We tried to turn it into something entertaining for the fans. No one wants to sit there and watch a commercial.

Likewise, Kyle Ritchie (personal communication, 8 October 1999) considers TV commercials anathema to a "fan-friendly" stadium environment:

> Some stadiums still just say, "Send us your ad and we'll run it." It's an ad-fest and it's awful. Thankfully, the number of teams doing that is way down. No one wants to be bombarded with commercials; there are more creative ways of doing things, for instance, sponsored features. When a company asks us to run their commercial, we say to them, "Here's what we know the fans will embrace better." Then we show them examples and, all of a sudden, they're sponsoring a Jeep race or a "Guess the Movie" clip or one of our player features—"Hit of the Week," "Play of the Week," "Touchdown of the Week," "Player of the Week." They can also do giveaways in the stands, sponsor tailgate parties—the sky's the limit.

16. In the same article, Morse (1983) writes, "The most memorable shots . . . are the ones shown in slow motion, where violent force and speed are electronically invested with grace and beauty" (p. 51).

17. Several other commentators put forth essentially the same argument. Margaret Morse (1983):

> The electronic reshaping of the game appears to have maintained the delicate balance necessary to the game while increasing spectacle. The television event may indeed be a better vehicle to give form to the fantasies which animate the cultural model of sport. The process of transformation has begun to affect the stadium event as well. Not merely the requisites of television but television techniques have invaded the arena itself: an up-to-date stadium now possesses an instant replay screen and many spectators bring television sets with them as well, doubling the pleasures of the crowd with the novelistic pleasures of the screen. (P. 54)

Philip Auslander (1999):

> Spectators at many sporting events now watch significant portions of the games they are attending on giant video screens. The rhetoric of mediatization embedded in such devices as the instant replay, the "simulcast," and the close-up, at one time understood to be secondary elaborations of what was originally a live event, are now constitutive of the live event itself. (P. 25)

Geraint John and Rod Sheard (1997):

> [LSVDs] are not just gimmicks but an essential element in managements' array of techniques to win back spectators from the comfortable alternative of watching sports events free of charge, with close-up shots, action replays and the like in the comfort of t:wrote,

As the sophistication of the television operators increased, and the demographic profile of the fans changed toward younger people raised on televised sports, the use of the screens was expanded in order to make the experience in the stadium more like that of watching a game on television. (P. 66)

John Bale (1994):

Television has become the defining reality of sport to the extent that a form of technology intended originally for sports viewers in the comfort of their own homes is today installed in the very stadiums where the games are held. Large TV screens are now virtually obligatory elements of the big stadium landscape. (P. 177)

18. Bordwell and Thompson (1997):

In the continuity editing system, [the 180-degree line or axis of action is] the imaginary line that passes from side to side through the main actors, defining the spatial relations of all the elements of the scene as being to the right or left. The camera is not supposed to cross the axis at a cut and thus reverse those spatial relations. (P. 477)

19. As Morse (1983) points out, there is one occasion when the violation of the 180-degree rule is officially sanctioned:

The rules of continuity editing are followed, in that all the cameras tape from one side of the field (except in those few instances when a "reverse-angle replay" on screen signals that the 180 degree rule has been broken and the opponents will have appeared to "change sides" on screen). (P. 49)

20. For Eichberg (1995), the stadium spectator's newly acquired power to switch between views ("zapping") brims with sociological import:

The view is zapping from the grass to the screen, from picture to picture. And the zapping spectatorship opens up a new world of simulation in sports—virtual sports. . . . The zapping pattern may destroy some important traditional habits of sport spectatorship. . . . By actualizing a dimension of visuality which, to be sure, had always been present, it gives change, variation and multiplicity a new societal significance. This may be the view of a new type of society. (P. 340)

21. My conception of the LSVD apparatus includes the stadium's PA system and "matrix boards" (see note 23). The in-house entertainment "script" I received during a visit to the production facilities at Raleigh's Entertainment and Sports Arena (January 11, 2000) makes explicit the programming connection between LSVD, matrix boards, and PA system. Each page is organized into seven columns, the last three of which are "J- Tron" (JumboTron), "Audio," and "Matrix." The script, whose designation is telling but which is actually more like a cross-indexed timetable or schedule, indicates what images and sounds are planned for every second of the Carolina Hurricanes hockey game.

22. This raises the issue of presence again: the amplification of ambient sound is unnecessary since one is already there, that is, within earshot.

23. The matrix board can be understood as a kind of technological linchpin uniting, on one hand, the preelectronic scoreboard, whose informational function it both subsumed and greatly expanded, and on the other hand, the black-and-white video board of the 1970s, which paved the way for present-day LSVD. Moreover, unlike the old black-and-white video boards, which, beginning in 1980, were gradually phased out in favor of full-color LSVDs, matrix boards are still widely—and heavily—utilized in most sports stadiums.

24. I address the notion of a "stadium event" later in this article.

25. "Caldwell (1995) takes Ellis to task for his 'surrendered gaze theory,' which could not be a less accurate or useful description of emergent televisuality. . . . This distracted surrender gaze theory seems so far from an accurate portrayal of contemporary television consumption that one wonders whether glance theorists base their explanations of TV only on primitive shows produced in the early, formative years of the medium" (p. 25).

26. Although Williams's three-layered framework is useful, it is also somewhat misleading because it implies that the medium event is all-encompassing. In truth, the medium event never encompasses every aspect of the game event (i.e., television's construction of the game is always incomplete) and it encompasses even less of the stadium event.

27. Until now, I have been careful to avoid invoking the word "postmodern." There are a couple of reasons for this. First, there is the notorious difficulty of ascribing to the term anything approaching a coherent, inclusive, and unanimously agreed-on definition. Second, postmodernist analyses of contemporary phenomena, from architecture to identity to virtuality, often come off as pro forma exercises, in which it is all too obvious that the object under investigation is not of interest for its own sake, but rather only insofar as it can be marshaled in support of an omniscient theoretical doctrine (i.e., postmodernism) whose usefulness has been determined in advance. There is the danger, in other words, that a rote postmodernist reading of the LSVD apparatus would dismiss it as merely another symptom of postmodernity, the latest instantiation (and proof of the existence) of a postmodern society characterized by, among other things, rampant mediatization and, correlatively, the ascendancy of "hyperreality."

28. Philip Auslander (1999) suggests as much:

> Whereas mediatized performance derives its authority from its reference to the live or the real, the live now derives its authority from its reference to the mediatized, which derives its authority from its reference to the live, etc. The paradigm that best describes the current relationship between the live and the mediatized is the Baudrillardian paradigm of simulation: "nothing separates one pole from the other, the initial from the terminal: there is just a sort of contraction into each other, a fantastic telescoping, a collapsing of the two traditional poles into one another: an IMPLOSION." (P. 39)

29. Auslander does not seem to realize this claim implicitly contradicts his earlier pro-Baudrillard assertion (note 28).

30. It is interesting to note that the very first JumboTron system was installed, in 1985, in Southern California's Crystal Cathedral, a televangelist church (Sony Corporation 1997).

31. Auslander (1999) observes that several theater critics/scholars, such as Patrice Pavis, routinely bemoan "the inevitable 'technological and aesthetic contamination' of live performance in the economy of repetition" (pp. 40–41).

> All too often, such analyses take on the air of a melodrama in which virtuous live performance is threatened, encroached upon, dominated, and contaminated by its insidious Other, with which it is locked in a life-and-death struggle. From this point of view, once live performance succumbs to mediatization, it loses its ontological integrity. (Pp. 41–2)

32. In the eyes of Brian J. Neilson (1995),

> the temporal rhythm of baseball is looping, elliptical, nominally linear but nonuniform, always expanding and contracting. It doesn't follow secular time but is a kind of pat-

terned meandering, impelled forward only by the internal logic of events on the field. But television brings into the ballpark the implacable urgency of its own logic, which is that of "entertainment," continuously discontinuous, all meaning fragmented, a relentlessly compressed linear juxtaposition of images. Television now pays the bills and underwrites the current opulence of the sport. Once introduced into the ballpark, however, it obeys a McLuhanesque imperative, subsuming all that it encompasses into itself, making it television. The ballpark, instead of being an autonomous, extraterritorial free zone, with its own temporal laws—that is, the remembered ballpark of our youth—becomes, increasingly, a colonial outpost of the expanding, imperial tele-realm. (P. 67)

References

Auslander, Philip. 1999. *Liveness: Performance in a Mediatized Culture*. London: Routledge.

Bale, John. 1994. *Landscapes of Modern Sport*. London: Leicester University Press.

Baudrillard, Jean. 1995. *Symbolic Exchange and Death*. Iain Hamilton Grant, trans. London: Sage.

Baudry, Jean-Louis. 1999a. The Apparatus: Metapsychological Approaches to the Impression of Reality in Cinema. In *Film Theory and Criticism: Introductory Readings,* edited by Leo Braudy and Marshall Cohen, 760–77. New York: Oxford University Press.

———. 1999b. Ideological Effects of the Basic Cinematographic Apparatus. In *Film Theory and Criticism: Introductory Readings,* edited by Leo Braudy and Marshall Cohen, 345–55. New York: Oxford University Press.

Bolter, Jay David, and Richard Grusin. 1999. *Remediation: Understanding New Media*. Cambridge: MIT Press.

Bordwell, David, and Kristin Thompson. 1997. *Film Art: An Introduction*. 5th ed. New York: McGraw-Hill.

Caldwell, John Thornton. 1995. *Televisuality: Style, Crisis, and Authority in American Television*. New Brunswick, NJ: Rutgers University Press.

Carroll, Rick. 1999. Gameday Looks to Plano Office for Big Screen Sales. In *Dallas Business Journal,* 29 November [Online]. Available from MasterFILE Premier.

Castells, Manuel. 1997. *The Rise of Network Society*. Oxford, UK: Blackwell.

Eichberg, Henning. 1995. Stadium, Pyramid, Labyrinth: Eye and Body on the Move. In *The Stadium and the City,* edited by John Bale and Olof Moen, 323–47. Keele, UK: Keele University Press.

Ellis, John. 1992. *Visible Fictions: Cinema, Television, Video*. Rev. ed. London: Routledge.

Feuer, Jane. 1983. The Concept of Live Television: Ontology as Ideology. In *Regarding Television: Critical Approaches—An Anthology,* edited by E. Ann Kaplan, 12–21. Los Angeles: American Film Institute.

Goldlust, John. 1987. *Playing for Keeps: Sport, the Media and Society*. Melbourne: Longman Chesire.

Harvey, David. 1990. *The Condition of Postmodernity: An Enquiry into the Origins of Cultural Change*. Cambridge, UK: Blackwell.

Hilmes, Michele. 1990. *Hollywood and Broadcasting: From Radio to Cable*. Urbana: University of Illinois Press.

Hofstadter, Douglas R. [1979] 1999. *Gödel, Escher, Bach: An Eternal Golden Braid*. Reprint. New York: Basic Books.

Jameson, Fredric. 1997. *Postmodernism, or, the Cultural Logic of Late Capitalism.* Durham, NC: Duke University Press.

John, Geraint, and Rod Sheard. 1997. *Stadia: A Design and Development Guide.* 2d ed. Oxford, UK: Architectural Press.

Mitchell, Eric. 1999. Stadium Construction Boom Could End in U.S. In *Washington Business Journal,* 2 August [Online]. Available from MasterFILE Premier.

Mitsubishi Electric Corporation. 1996. *Diamond Vision: Large Scale Video Displays.* Brochure. Tokyo: Mitsubishi Electric Corporation.

Morse, Margaret. 1983. Sport on Television: Replay and Display. In *Regarding Television: Critical Approaches—An Anthology,* edited by E. Ann Kaplan, 44–66. Los Angeles: American Film Institute.

Neilson, Brian J. 1995. Baseball. In *The Theater of Sport,* edited by Karl B. Raitz, 30–69. Baltimore, MD: Johns Hopkins University Press.

Sony Corporation. 1997. *JumboTron: Large-Screen Color Video Display System.* Brochure. Tokyo: Sony Corporation.

Starr, Tama, and Edward Hayman. 1998. *Signs and Wonders: The Spectacular Marketing of America.* New York: Currency-Doubleday.

Weber, Samuel. 1996. *Mass Mediauras: Form, Technics, Media.* Stanford, CA: Stanford University Press.

Williams, Brien R. 1977. The Structure of Televised Football. *Journal of Communication* 27 (3): 133–39.

Williams, Raymond. 1990. *Television: Technology and Cultural Form.* London: Routledge.

Erasing Blackness
The Media Construction of "Race" in *Mi Familia*, the First Puerto Rican Situation Comedy with a Black Family

Yeidy M. Rivero

> People sit down to watch *Mi Familia* as if it were a white, yellow or blue [family]. There is no color, there is nothing established. And since we do not touch that subject.... And it was not that we did not want to talk about it.... At the beginning we realized that we did not have to talk about it. It is a Puerto Rican family, period.[1]
>
> *Mi Familia*'s production personnel, July 1997, personal communication

On 14 September 1994, after 40 years of local programming, Telemundo's network affiliate in Puerto Rico (Telemundo, WKAQ-Channel 2) began to broadcast *Mi Familia*, the first and only locally produced situation comedy to cast black actors in principal roles.[2] Produced by locally renowned Puerto Rican producer Paquito Cordero and influenced by US black-oriented situation comedies such as *The Jeffersons* and *The Cosby Show*, *Mi Familia* recreates the life of a black lower-middle class Puerto Rican family, the Meléndez and their neighbors. Currently, *Mi Familia* has been on the air for more than five years, and in September 1999, it began airing on Telemundo's network affiliates in New York and Miami.

This article analyzes some of the ways in which media professionals involved in *Mi Familia*'s production re-appropriated Puerto Rico's *mestizaje* (very approximately, cultural and racial hybridity) and racial democracy discourse—both are discussed below—and the possible implications for the show's conceptualization. As a member of *Mi Familia*'s production personnel indicated, "there is no color, there is nothing established [. . .] it is a Puerto Rican family, period." The construction of the Meléndez family as "non-racial" foregrounds Puerto Rico's racial and cultural *mestizaje* and creates a televisual

Yeidy M. Rivero, "Erasing Blackness: The Media Construction of 'Race' in *Mi Familia*, the First Puerto Rican Situation Comedy with a Black Family." From *Media, Culture & Society*, Vol. 4, No. 4 (July 2002), pp. 459–480, copyright © 2002 by Sage Publications, Inc. Reprinted by permission of Sage Publications, Inc.

'imagined community' that re-articulates the flattening out of ethnicity as the center of the island's culture and identity (i.e. *Ia gran familia puertorriqueña* hegemonic discourse).[3] To conceive of *Mi Familia* as a local cultural artifact we need to understand Puerto Rico's political, legal, economic, and cultural relationship with the US.

First, as a result of the Spanish-American War in 1898, Puerto Rico was annexed as a US territory that year. Today Puerto Rico is defined as a "commonwealth" territory, a highly contradictory and ambiguous political status that nationally situates the island as autonomous within the US, even while it is completely beholden to it in practice. However, although Puerto Rico is not sovereign, it has a distinct culture based on a common heritage and history, a culture that makes it both Latin American and Caribbean in ways visible in no other part of the US. As Morris (1995:14) notes, "national identity may refer to a sense of belonging to a nation that does or does not have its own territory, that does or does not have political autonomy." Despite constant and multidimensional efforts by the US and Puerto Rican governments to "Americanize" the country and the existence of three political parties largely differentiated by their stance on the island's status (pro-statehood, pro-commonwealth, and pro-independence), many Puerto Ricans do not feel culturally attached to the US (Morris, 1995: 169). Rather, the need to constantly reaffirm the island's cultural uniqueness overshadows the web of racial domination embedded in the internal construction of Puerto Rican culture, identity, and racial discourses.

Second, and obviously interrelated to US–Puerto Rican political relations, the island's media are regulated by the Federal Communication Commission (FCC). Thus the Commonwealth government has no sovereignty over its communication systems. Third, although local commercial stations were originally owned by Puerto Ricans, US and multinational conglomerates currently own every single commercial television station and sponsor most programming.[4] Finally, and central to this research, since 1954 when television began in Puerto Rico, many locally produced programs have been influenced by successful US programming concepts.[5] Nonetheless, the shows that have "borrowed" ideas from the US have always been adapted to Puerto Rican culture by recreating the island's distinctive social, political, cultural, and economic discourses in particular historical periods. Consequently, to examine *Mi Familia*'s constructions of "race" I will focus on the ways in which the island's culture and identity were re-constituted in the show's conceptualization and the implications for scripting the first situation comedy to represent a black Puerto Rican televisual family.

The essay's arguments are drawn from data that include personal interviews conducted during Summer 1997 and Winter 1999 with *Mi Familia*'s producer, assistant producers, writer, director, actors, and sales director, sales representatives, programmer, and technical staff at Telemundo de Puerto Rico. I investigated in detail *Mi Familia*'s situation comedy genre, production processes, and the professional, social, and economic backgrounds of the people involved in *Mi Familia*'s production. Because of the potential for controversy over the participants' answers, their names and professional affiliations have been omitted. To facilitate the analysis, data are divided into two main categories: *Mi Familia*'s production personnel (MFPP) and Telemundo de Puerto Rico's media professionals (TMP). Furthermore, space constraints dictate that this essay exclude a detailed textual analysis of *Mi Familia*'s constructions of "race," blackness and whiteness. As part of a larger body of my research, the present analysis establishes an initial discussion regarding Puerto Rican commercial television's articulation of the island's racialized discourses, culture and identity.

To contextualize media professionals' characterization of "race," this article begins with a discussion of the various racial categories that comprise Puerto Rico's national identity and their interconnections to historical, social, cultural and political discourses. Drawing from theories of racial and cultural *mestizaje* and Puerto Rico's racial discourses, the argument moves to an analysis of *Mi Familia* and Telemundo media professionals' descriptions of the situation comedy genre in general and the show's black family in particular. The article ends by problematizing the media professionals' characterization of "race" and *negritud* [blackness] and the implications for this and other locally produced programs.

Black, White, and Other Categories: Puerto Rico's Racial Spectrum

Guillaumin (1995: 35) maintains that the ideology of "race" is informed by specific social, political and economic practices in Western societies. If we understand ideology as shared ideas, beliefs and traditions in a particular society that promote the interest of a specific group, and if we consider that the elites in Latin America imitated the Western model of modernity by situating blacks and indigenous people as the "antithesis of the modern nation" (Hanchard, 1994: 173), then "race" in Puerto Rico and Latin America may be viewed as a social construction influenced by Western (colonial and racial) ideologies, but which manifests itself in particular cultural practices. In other words, even though there might be similarities regarding "race" and racial constructions around the (Western) world in general and Latin America in particular, "race" responds to specific "racial formations," a distinct social structure, and historical and cultural contexts (Omi and Winant, 1994). Thus, to understand Puerto Rico's racial ideologies and racism, we must also consider the construction of the national culture and identity, the racial and cultural *mestizaje* which inform this construction, and the ongoing tension between the island and the US.

This US–PR cultural political and social tension on the island creates cultural discourses based on the "differences" between these two nations. Within these discourses of "difference," "race" and "race" relations in Puerto Rico are generally located as a distinctly superior antithesis to US racial ideological discourses and practices.[6] Thus, by establishing a polarity between Puerto Rican and US cultures and racial ideologies, a dominant misconception emerges that prejudice is effectively non-existent in Puerto Rico.

Significantly, people on the island see themselves as part of an ethnic collective—Puerto Ricans. Rodríguez (1989: 52) theorizes that in Puerto Rico, "racial identification [is] subordinated to cultural identification." Although Rodríguez's theory has been criticized as an over-generalisation of Puerto Rican racial identities, specifically in the context of US Puerto Rican communities (James, 1998: 223; Rodríguez-Morazzani, 1996: 161–162), her work provides a basis for examining issues of cultural and racial identification. The "cultural identification" espoused by Rodríguez does not mean, however, that the island is a racially homogeneous society.[7] This is clearly seen in the ongoing racial prejudice against Puerto Rican blacks in general, and, more recently, against Dominican immigrants in Puerto Rico. These immigrants, who are primarily mulattos and blacks, have been cast as scapegoats for the island's economic and social problems (Duany, 1990, 1992, 1998).

On the one hand, one can argue that similarities exist in the ways whiteness and blackness operate in Puerto Rico and the US, particularly in terms of the marginalization of black cultures and communities and the construction of whiteness as the ideological force behind hierarchical racial categorizations. Nonetheless, by contrast with the US, Puerto Rico's racial ideologies respond to the *mestizaje* discourse and the creation of a unified national space.

Mestizaje, or racial mixing, is a key factor in the construction of a racially integrated nation, since everyone, regardless of skin color, is racially mixed and thus, an equal member in society (Wade, 1997; Winant, 1994). However, behind the comforting screen of racial *mestizaje* lies the racist ideology and process of *blanqueamiento* [whitening] where racial mixing with white (European) people make populations "white," thus erasing supposedly inferior black and Indian racial traits (Wade, 1997). Culturally, *mestizaje* highlights the egalitarian fusion of European, African and indigenous cultures and traits constructing a nationally mixed culture and identity. Yet even though Puerto Rico's *mestizaje* hegemonic discourse creates and promotes a "color blind" and culturally mixed socio-cultural space, a series of racial categorizations and cultural practices that comprise the vernacular defy the myth of *mestizaje* and operate in ways equivalent to racial equality.

Unlike the US where "a black is any person with any known African black ancestry" (Davis, 1991 cited in Stokes, 1996–7: 56), racial categories in Puerto Rico are most clearly associated with physical appearance and social status, not the specifics of biological descent (Duany, 1998). A range of racial classifications includes "negro, blanco, trigueño, trigueñito, indio, moreno, prieto, jabao" (Crespo, 1996: 32). It is extremely difficult to translate these terms since they are rooted in the island's vernacular language. However, in general, *negro, moreno,* and *prieto* mean black; *trigueño* and *trigueñito* are shades of brown and can be categorized as *mulatto; indio* means Taino-looking; *jabao* refers to a person whose skin color is white but who has features commonly associated with black people, and *blanco* means white. In addition, like some of the previous categorizations (*trigueño, trigeuñito* and *prieto*), *gente de color* [colored people] and *negrito* have been used in Puerto Rico and in some Latin American societies to avoid using the term *negro* [black] (Zenón-Cruz, 1975:

250). This tendency responds to racial discourses which construct this racial term as derogatory.[8]

Negrito/a [diminutive for black] is currently used in Cuba and Puerto Rico and is sometimes employed as a derogatory reference to black people. Although *negrito/a* and *negro/a* may be used in reference to blacks, in Puerto Rico it has also been adopted as a term of affection regardless of "race." A person may be called *negrito/a* or *negro/a* despite the fact that this individual could be of white skin. Likewise, a series of phrases rooted in racial stereotyping inform the vernacular and espouse a problematic construction of blackness. For example, *el que no tiene dinga, tiene mandinga* [the one who does not have dinga has mandinga], is used to describe the mixing of other blood with black blood.[9] On the other hand, *mejorar la raza* [improve the "race"] denotes that black and mulatto people marry white individuals to improve or *blanquear* [whiten] their "race."

Certainly, the issue of racial consciousness is a key factor in the recurrent use of the socially and culturally normalized proverbs which inform Puerto Rico's vernacular culture. Hanchard (1994: 15) defines racial consciousness as:

> the dialectical result of antagonism between two or more groups defined as races in a given society. It represents the thought and practice of those individuals and groups, who respond to their subordination with individual or collective action designed to counterbalance, transpose or transform situations of racial asymmetry.

In Puerto Rico there has never been any large-scale political and social mobilization against racism. Jiménez-Román (1996: 11) contends that those who have protested against racism on the island "have been labeled overly sensitive, as suffering from an inferiority complex, or as unwitting victims of an imported, i.e. alien, racial ideology." In other words, protests against racism generally reactivate the US–Puerto Rico cultural contentions and the historical differences between the two nations' racial relations and discourses.

In terms of media representations (and misrepresentations) of *negritud* [blackness] a particular example demonstrates the ongoing debate between Puerto Rican and US racial ideologies and cultures. In 1973, Telemundo de Puerto Rico produced the *telenovela El hijo de Angela María* which presented two "black" characters played by white actresses in "blackface" (*Panchita* and *Chianita*). When both characters appeared in Puerto Rico's televisual space, a group of black actors created a coalition to protest against the misrepresentation of blackness. This group of artists protested against the use of "blackface" and the fact that Puerto Rican television's construction of *negritud* was synonymous with a lack of education, a lack of social skills, and backwardness (Rey, 1973: 74–6; Ríos, 1973: 70–2). Nonetheless, these protests did not eliminate the use of "blackface" in Puerto Rican television. Actually, one of the characters, *Chianita*, became an icon in the island's popular culture and appeared on Puerto Rican television until 1985.

Several factors should be considered in the black actors' opposition to "blackface." First, the main strategy of the black actors' coalition compared their situation to the "progress" of black actors in the US during the 1970s, which of course responded to 1960s Civil Rights movement. By establishing comparisons between Puerto Rico and the US, this discussion might have activated the different histories of these two nations' race relations while concomitantly articulating the issue of Puerto Rico's hegemonic constructions of nationality and *mestizaje*. Second, no major mobilization in Puerto Rico's public sphere supported the black actors' coalition. In other words, the 'people' (audience) and other media professionals apparently did not acknowledge the presence of racism and prejudice. Finally, and possibly a key element in the televisual construction of *negritud,* how could transformations occur within Puerto Rican television given the national culture's construction around and promotion of the ideology of racial equality (democracy) and *mestizaje?*

Puerto Rico's public debate has focused (among other issues) on the island's political status quo and economy, the English–Spanish language debate, and the US historic colonial exploitation of local resources (land and people). These issues are important aspects in the public sphere since they provide a foundation for debates over US imperialism and local sites of resistance. Nonetheless, a need to discuss the internal colonialism that informs the national culture persists. This internal colonialism, although influenced by US domination, transcends the year of 1898 and has its origins in the construction of the island's national identity and culture. Given these perennial roots, how can one overturn racial and racist ideologies that have been part of the national imaginary for centuries, that remain a fundamental recurring cultural and political strategy for ensuring a unified ethnic and cultural space, and that also inform the island's media institutions? Certainly, as Díaz-Quiñones (1993) observes, without a "decolonization of the imaginary" and without a revision of the internal colonialism that permeates the culture, changes will be difficult to accomplish.

Taking these racial, social, cultural, and historical elements into consideration, this essay argues that *mestizaje* and racial democracy ideologies were the center of *Mi Familia*'s conceptualization and thus created a cultural artifact that normalized Puerto Rico's hegemonic construction of a racially integrated-non-racist national culture, identity and society. Some of *Mi Familia*'s and Telemundo media professionals' characterizations of *negritud* function in contrast to US black-oriented shows (specifically *The Jeffersons* and *The Cosby Show*) and the cultures represented in them. Through comparisons between *Mi Familia* and US black-oriented programming, television became the location for articulating the differences between US and Puerto Rico's racial discourses, blackness and cultures.

Media Professionals' Understanding of "Race" in *Mi Familia*

Although *Mi Familia* was the first and remains the only locally produced program that recreates the life of a lower-middle-class black Puerto Rican family, it should be noted that during 1994, three independent producers expressed interest in producing a sitcom with black actors for other "local" stations. When informants were queried about this sudden interest, they concluded that since a show with a black cast would be something new in Puerto Rico's local television market it could potentially become as successful as black-oriented shows in the US (MPP and TMP, July 1997, personal communication). Nonetheless, despite the possibility that three shows with a black cast could have been produced on different "local" stations, Paquito Cordero, *Mi Familia*'s producer, was the only producer who achieved his goal.[10]

According to some sources, Cordero's power and prestige in Puerto Rico's media industry helped him become the first producer to be awarded a contract with Telemundo, the island's most successful television station.[11] Moreover, they observed that the other producers decided to abandon the project since it was no longer something unique. Other informants declared that the other two independent producers discarded their projects because Cordero had hired the most renowned black comedians on the island, thereby diminishing the likelihood that their programs would have *ganchos* [actors with market appeal]. Therefore, in a general sense, the producer's impulse to develop a sitcom with a black family in 1994 seems to be related to the success of black-oriented situation comedies in the US and the market possibilities attached to this "new" type of cultural product in Puerto Rico.

When *Mi Familia* began production on 14 September 1994, a newspaper advertised the show as "the first colored family in Puerto Rican television" (Cordero, 1994: 55) while another avoided the family's "race" by describing the show as a "new Cordero production" (Torresgrosa, 1994: 116). The description of a "colored family" infuriated some production members who argued that the family's "race" was black and that the term "colored" was a racist remark. As one participant observed, "a colored family? Which color? Yellow, blue, orange?" (MPP, July 1997, personal communication). However, not a single one of my respondents commented upon the article that focused on *Mi Familia*'s authorship, and avoided the family's "race." The fact that none of the articles described the show as a sitcom with a black family can be viewed as a response to normalized cultural practices which situate the racial term *negro* as derogatory.[12]

Besides criticizing the use of "colored peopled," some informants expressed disappointment over the fact that although *Mi Familia* had originally planned to address racism, none of the show's scripts had ever dealt with the issue. As one participant stated:

> When they talked to me about the idea, they told me that this was going to serve as a channel to break with this country's molds, that it was going to be something different, that it was going to deal with themes of racism, social topics such as drugs, everything, everything. Almost nothing has been done, but it is not Paquito's (the producer) fault; it is Telemundo's fault. (MPP, July 1997, personal communication)

Another source attributed the absence of racial themes to a combination of factors which included the Catholic Church, politicians, Telemundo and Puerto

Rican society in general. During the interview process, this individual continually used the phrases *la mentalidad isleña* [the island's mentality], "colonialism" and "internal colonialism" to explain the absence of racial themes in *Mi Familia* and the racism that permeates Puerto Rican society in general and local television in particular. As the source observed:

> There is a need to create more work for black people. I have met many talented individuals who are black who do not want to be part of this environment (television) because they think it is for whites. Yes, there is prejudice, but if you have talent, prejudice cannot stop you. It is necessary to untie the internal chains. (MPP, July 1997, personal communication)

Even though one cannot claim that these views are representative, the remarks depict an illuminating analysis of the various and interconnected levels that are used to construct "race" and racism in Puerto Rico and in other nations with black and "other" minority communities (Brah, 1996; Essed, 1991; Twine, 1998; Winant, 1994).[13]

Despite the fact that some of the production members were displeased by the lack of racial and social themes in *Mi Familia*'s narrative, they believed that the show was a "positive space" for the representation of blackness, especially since some white comedians on Puerto Rican television still dress in "blackface."[14] In several newspaper articles and television magazines, actors identify *negritud* as a pivotal element in *Mi Familia*. Otilio Warrington ("Bizcocho"), *Mi Familia*'s principal actor notes:

> I consider that the show has been successful first, because it satisfies a need, it fills an empty space. [. . .] Second, because it is the first program with blacks that has been produced in Puerto Rico, something that Paquito Cordero wanted to do for a long time. I think that being the only program in its genre, *Mi Familia* causes a sensation and also attracts black people who completely identify with us (*Mi Familia*'s black family). (Brugueras, 1998: 4–6)

Furthermore, Judith Pizarro, the show's principal actress, also emphasizes the importance of producing a show with black actors. "When Paquito Cordero called me with this in mind, I accepted immediately. In addition, it was the first time that someone created a space for blacks in Puerto Rico (i.e., on television)" (Rivera-Esquilín, 1997: 18).

Even though some of the interviewees identified *negritud* as an important element in *Mi Familia,* others evaded the topic and categorized the show as a sitcom with a Puerto Rican family. It should be clear that during the interviews, most made references to *Mi Familia* as a show with "colored people" thus avoiding the term black. In responding to questions about the process of selecting black actors, some of *Mi Familia*'s production personnel and Telemundo's media professionals expressed ideas about "race" that were completely different from those presented by the previous interviewees. One source observed that:

> Here, regardless of the success of *Cosby* and *The Jeffersons* and multiple shows with *colored families,* this topic was never explored. We talked about how we

were going to develop the show, what we were going to do. For me, the interesting thing is that from the beginning we never dealt with that issue ("race"). In Puerto Rico, people see them (the black family) as any other family. In the US it is not like that. Those are programs about *colored people*. They have a way of talking, dressing, and we do not have to use that. Here, there is no color (in the program); it does not frame anything. (MPP, July 1997, personal communication; emphasis added)

This interviewee assumes that since the sitcom never addresses racial themes, *negritud* is erased from its narratives; thus, audiences see the Meléndez as "any other family." This reference to "any other family" can be associated both with Puerto Rico's hegemonic "imagined community" and with previous family sitcoms featuring white performers/families. According to this participant, "race" is neutralized in *Mi Familia* by creating a "colorless" space whose racial and cultural frames of commonality between audiences and the program is ethnicity. By positioning the narrative as colorless, the participant normalizes the *mestizaje* discourse as the parameter for the family's "race."

Furthermore, to sustain the point, the informant foregrounds differences between *Mi Familia* and US black-oriented shows while concomitantly establishing the ways in which racial identities and "race" operate in both nations. According to this view, black shows in the US present cultural elements associated with the African American community ("colored people") which create differences not only in relation to Puerto Rican blacks but also regarding racial, cultural, and ethnic relations in both nations. Certainly, there are differences between African Americans' and Puerto Rican blacks' vernacular cultures and identities. However, the above account underplays cultural aspects associated with Puerto Rico's black and mulatto populations that have been part of *Mi Familia*'s narratives.[15] In the case of Puerto Rico, the interviewee maintains that there is no need to establish distinct cultural traits since presumably, no racial, ethnic, or power differences exist within the island's culture.

A curious aspect of the comments just cited relates to the ways in which US black shows such as *The Jeffersons* and *The Cosby Show* are read. Even though these sitcoms did not explicitly address racial struggles and power inequalities (Downing, 1988; Fuller, 1992; Gray, 1995), for this source, the presence of black bodies and cultural elements constructed the show as "colored" (black). In other words, US television's representation of blackness is perceived as a unified racial and cultural space. Gray (1995) maintains that despite the fact that these shows present black culture in a pluralist environment (*The Jeffersons*) or in multiculturally diverse settings (*The Cosby Show*), they operate within dominant US discourses of whiteness, middle classness and social mobility. In a similar way, *Mi Familia* functions within Puerto Rico's racial, social, historical and cultural discourses and normalizes *mestizaje* and racial equality as the center of the island's culture. Nonetheless, what is peculiar about such views is that in the case of US television, the predominant inclusion of black bodies and culture encodes the shows as "colored" even though such programs do not explicitly address racism and power inequalities that inform the US racial struggle. On the other hand, in the case of *Mi Familia,* the absence of racial themes positions the show as "colorless" despite the fact that the family is black and that the show incorporates cultural elements associated with black and mulatto Puerto Rican communities. Thus, from this standpoint "colored people" and "blackness" are equivalent only to US African American communities, bodies, cultures and their televisual representations.

Another interviewee noted that:

> . . . the only difference that exists is that by chance they are *negritos,* but it could be a white family because racial themes are never addressed, or any type of *crime.* Actually, you see it [the program] and you would not notice that they are *negritos* because they are *normal* (my emphases). (MPP, July 1997, personal communication)

The second source's remarks clearly operate within a racist framework even though he/she might not be aware of the racism embedded in his/her comments.[16] As previously mentioned, *negrito* is sometimes used pejoratively to construct black as an inferior category in relation to white. By using *negritos* instead of *negros* and by juxtaposing *negritud* with "crime" and abnormality, black-bodied citizens become symbols of the "Other" undesirable sociocultural element in Puerto Rican society. According to this last source, within a dignified representative of a Puerto Rican family in the sitcom's fictional space *negritud* had to be neutralized by constructing a "non-racial" and "normal" (white) family. Also, like the previous participant, the present participant contends that the absence of racial themes erases the family's *negritud*.

This last view creates a binary construction of whiteness and blackness by directly assigning specific social, cultural and ethical values to members of these racial groups. In light of Dyer's (1994: 70) contention that the ideology of whiteness carries and symbolizes apparent neutrality but also a claim to moral and aesthetic superiority, in this case, whiteness becomes the symbol of respectable cultural morality and standards of decency within Puerto Rican society.

Finally, when addressing the use of black actors and its possible impact on *Mi Familia*'s sponsors, one of Telemundo's media professionals explained that:

> . . . the fact that the program was about *colored people* (my emphasis) was never an issue. Besides, you have to understand that "Bizcocho" (*Mi Familia*'s principal actor) is a very commercial actor, the audience likes him. No, the sponsors never had a problem. Besides, here (in Puerto Rico) there are white, black, and *trigueño/a* people. (July 1997, personal communication)

The last participant presents an openly commercial position regarding *Mi Familia* as a cultural product. The sponsors had no problems with the actors' "race," especially since Puerto Rico is a racially mixed society. As was noted, Puerto Ricans are comprised of many "shades." More important was the fact that the main actor is highly marketable, an aspect that erases any possible problems since, as the participant observed, "Bizcocho" is popular with audiences and has been a successful and profitable actor for local stations, producers and for himself.[17] Furthermore, even though "Bizcocho" is publicly outspoken in favor of Puerto Rico's independence from the US and has openly discussed racial topics, his television characters have never explored these issues. As an actor, "Bizcocho" has limited power in television's hierarchical structure and this may explain his characters' silence about them.

In sum, the sponsors, the station and some of the *Mi Familia* media professionals did not perceive a show with "colored people" as an obstacle; rather, *negritud* was commodified as something new and different when compared to other locally produced television shows. Yet, this commodification of "Otherness" does not represent a threat to Puerto Rico's racial-cultural status quo (whiteness). On the contrary, it becomes a location within which *mestizaje* and racial democracy discourses are normalized.

The De-colonization of the Televisual Imaginary

The analysis of the participants' descriptions presented here delineated the interconnections between their characterizations of "race" and Puerto Rico's historically racialized discourses. The inclusion of the participants' remarks should not be construed as an attempt to identify individuals as racist, to quantify how many people made racist or non-racist remarks, or to establish how many participants were more or less alert to Puerto Rico's racial ideologies. Reducing racism to individual psychology radically diminishes the issues involved, for as Lipsitz (1998: 2) observes, "race" is a construction "with sinister structural causes and consequences." "Race" is a social and historical construct that responds to economic, political and cultural conditions in specific temporal and geographical locations. In examining *Mi Familia,* it was important to locate the ways in which media professionals conceived of ideologies of "race"/*negritud* and the possible implications for the production of a show featuring a black Puerto Rican family.

As was evident in some of the participants' remarks, the *mestizaje* discourse and the articulation of Puerto Rican ethnicity as the main signifier of racial and cultural unity (expressed by the construction of a "non-racial" family), definitively stamped the first and only locally-produced sitcom with a black Puerto Rican televisual family.

Three primary and interconnected reasons for the *Mi Familia* production staff's "erasure" of blackness emerge from their descriptions. First, as was previously observed, Puerto Rico's culture relies on a hegemonic discourse that racial prejudice is effectively non-existent on the island. This construction is traceable to the island's nation-building era and has been a recurring element in Puerto Rico's public, cultural, social, and political arenas. Second, some of the people directly involved in *Mi Familia*'s production firmly believe that racism is not part of the culture, even though some of their comments implied their acceptance of racist categories. The categorization of *Mi Familia*'s black family as "colorless" and therefore "normal" clearly articulates a racial bias informed by the hegemonic discourse of a racially mixed nation.

Finally, there is the issue of television censorship, an omnipresent unwritten code that affects Puerto Rican television production in general and *Mi Familia* in particular. Censorship comes from three types of intertwined sources: social, industrial and personal. As a family sitcom, the show maintains a middle ground, keeping a safety net for both audiences and sponsors (Marc, 1997). Through Telemundo's and the sponsors' constant, yet tactful, vigilance, *Mi Familia* is constrained to performing within the parameters of Puerto Rico's dominant and conservative ideological discourses. Therefore, even though some of *Mi Familia*'s media professionals expressed an interest in exploring racism, drugs, politics and social themes, they tried to avoid conflicts with the station and the sponsors.

Notwithstanding this, one should consider that, as some interviewees observed, the mere presence of black bodies in the Puerto Rican family sitcom genre constructs a different representation of the Puerto Rican nation by re-inscribing this marginalized community into televisual, societal and cultural discourses. Television representations of black Puerto Ricans as members of a television family might transform racially and culturally stereotypical constructions of this community in the Puerto Rican social imaginary while counterbalancing previous television depictions.[18] Since former representations of *negritud* connoted low social class, illiteracy, poor language, "black dialect," and lack of self-esteem (Zenón-Cruz, 1975) and since white actors continue to use "blackface" to represent blackness, perhaps *Mi Familia* should be considered as a potentially open terrain for re-interpretations of televisual *negritud*.

I do not want to suggest that since *Mi Familia* uses black bodies, and that since they are almost absent in other locally produced programs, the producer and Telemundo are the only ones who carry the "burden of [black] representation" (Mercer, 1994). This would expect too much from the first and only show to date that has presented a black family in Puerto Rico's 48-year commercial television history. Rather, producers of all locally produced programs need to revise radically the ways in which "race," as well as ethnicity, gender and sexuality, are re-articulated in their programs' narratives.

Finally, and pertinent to this study, there is a need for research about media representations of "race" across different geographical and cultural regions. In addition, scholars should pay particular attention to the encoding processes and the individuals involved in the production of media's cultural products. This type of research opens the possibility for establishing dialogues with media professionals by creating a space for transformations, both in the media and in academia.

Notes

I would like to thank Stephen Berrey, Gilberto Blasini, and specially John Downing for their comments and suggestions.

1. Due to space constraints, this essay only includes English translations of interviews conducted in Spanish. All of the translations presented herein were done by the author.

2. Unless indicated, Telemundo refers to Telemundo's affiliate in Puerto Rico.

3. *La gran familia puertorriqueña* [the big Puerto Rican family] is an ideological discourse created during the 19th century by the Puerto Rican elite to forge class and racial solidarity against the Spanish colonialist government (Díaz-Quiñones, 1985; Guerra, 1998; Quintero-Rivera, 1976). According to Díaz Quiñones (1985) the concept of *la gran familia pueriorriqueña* has been central to debates over Puerto Rican identity. Hegemonic racial democracy and *mestizaje* discourses were prominent in Puerto Rican politics and culture after 1898 and again during the 1950s when the US and the island's government implemented a new series of economic, social and cultural reforms targeting the country's development (Díaz Quiñones, 1985).

4. Currently there are four major "local" commercial stations in Puerto Rico (WKAQ-Telemundo, WAPA-TV Channel 4, WSTE-TV Channel 7, and WLII-TV Channel 11). Although all these stations are owned by US and multinational conglomerates, they function as semi-independent entities. The stations establish commercial autonomy through local productions, business arrangements with independent producers, programming, audience viewing measurements and sponsors.

5. Some of these examples are the situation comedy *Mapy y Papi* and the variety show *Show de Shows,* produced in 1954 and which were adaptations of *I Love Lucy* and *Your Show of Shows,* respectively, and *Tres muchachas de hoy* and *Soltero y sin compromiso* produced during the 1970s. These 1970s Puerto Rican situation comedies were influenced by US family situation comedies which represented "families" made up of friends or individuals outside of strict "blood ties" (Hamamoto, 1989; Marc, 1997; Taylor, 1989).

6. See Blanco's (1937/1985) *El prejuicio racial en Puerto Rico* and an analysis of the "racial" debate in Puerto Rico in Betances (1972), Guerra (1998), and Quintero-Rivera (1976).

7. At least until 2000, Puerto Rico's census did not include "race" as one of the categories; therefore, there is no data regarding the island citizens' racial composition.

8. The origin of *negro* as a negative connotation is related to the institution of racial slavery. The term "colored people" was originally used during the Spanish colonial period to show courtesy and warmth to black and mulatto individuals (Alvárez-Nazario, 1974).

9. This phrase originated in South America and connoted that a person who does not have "inga-Inca" (Indian blood) has *mandinga* (African blood) (Alvárez-Nazario, 1974, cited in Zenón-Cruz, 1975: 256).

10. Paquito Cordero has worked in Puerto Rican television since its origins in 1954 when he began as an actor and a scriptwriter. In 1960 he founded his own company (Paquito Cordero Productions). For 40 years, Cordero has produced movies, television situation comedies, variety shows and musical shows. In addition, during the 1970s, through his Hit Parade record company, Cordero served as a singers' promoter and produced variety shows in Puerto Rican nightclubs and in New York City.

11. In Puerto Rico's television market, Telemundo maintains the highest ratings and shares. According to an April 1999 prime-time audience report issued by Mediafax, the company that offers television audience measurements in Puerto Rico, Telemundo obtained a 41 percent of share followed by WLII with 28 percent, and WAPA with 22 percent. Cable television obtained a 7 percent share followed by Puerto Rico's government television station with 5 percent.

12. See previous section on Puerto Rico's racial categories.

13. The oppression and racism against South Asians and black communities in the UK (Brah, 1996), the "everyday racism" experienced by black women in the Netherlands and "non-racial racism" in the US (Essed, 1991), and the ongoing prejudice in Brazil against blacks masquerading as racial democracy and *mestizagem* (Twine, 1998;

Winant, 1994), recreate the ways in which racial ideologies and oppression operate in the global context.

14. "Blackface" has been part of Puerto Rico's cultural space since the end of the 19th century. The first representations of "blackness" in Puerto Rico's cultural melange can be traced to the Cuban bufo comedic tradition. This theatrical genre, whose origins are traceable to France and Spain, flowered in Cuba by the 19th century (Muguerica, 1984) and prescribed the ways in which "black" characters were first portrayed on Puerto Rico's stage, radio, and later, television. Some of Puerto Rican television's stereotypical representations of blackness in "blackface" are: Diplo and Reguerete (main characters in the 1954 variety show *La taberna India*), Panchita and Chianita (in the 1973 adaptation of the Venezuelan *telenovela El hijo de Angela María*), and Pirulo el Colorao (in the 1990s comedy *Al aire libre*).

15. *Mi Familia*'s scripts have incorporated cultural elements that are generally associated with Puerto Rico's black, mulatto, and working class populations. For example, some scripts include *salsa* and *merengue* performers as secondary characters. Also, *Mi Familia*'s characters mainly listen to *salsa*, rap, and *merengue* musical styles which have been socially constructed as working class cultural artifacts.

16. During our conversation, this source was worried about comments made regarding gay people and US shows with gay characters. This person expressed views about gays because of complete trust in my confidentiality. Nonetheless, when this person made the aforementioned comments about blacks, no worries were expressed about disclosing his/her name or possible repercussions related to these comments.

17. Otilio Warrington ('Bizcocho') is one of the most famous comedians in Puerto Rican television. He began his television career during the 1970s and has participated in numerous locally produced sitcoms, variety shows and comedies.

18. See previous description of "blackface" in Puerto Rican commercial television.

References

Alvárez-Nazario, M. (1974) *El elemento afronegroïde en el español de Puerto Rico*. San Juan, Puerto Rico: Instituto de Cultura Puertorriqueño.

Betances, S. (1972) "The Prejudice of Having No Prejudice in Puerto Rico," *The Rican* (2): 41–54.

Blanco, T. (1985). *Tomás Blanco: El prejuicio racial en Puerto Rico*. Río Piedras: Huracán.

Brah, A. (1996) *Cartographies of Diaspora, Contesting Identities*. London: Routledge.

Brugueras, M. (1998) "TV día," *El nuevo día*, November 15: 4–6.

Cordero, S. (1994) "Television," *El vocero*, September 1: 55.

Crespo, E. (1996) "Domestic Work and Racial Division in Women's Employment in Puerto Rico, 1899–1930," *Centro* VIII (1 & 2): 30–41.

Davis, J.F. (1991) *Who is Black? Our Nation's Definition*. Philadelphia: Pennsylvania State University Press.

Díaz-Quiñones, A. (1985) "Tomás Blanco: Racismo, historia, esclavitud," in T. Blanco (ed.) *El prejuicio racial en Puerto Rico*. Río Pedras, Puerto Rico: Huracán.

Díaz-Quiñones, A. (1993) *La memoria rota*. Río Piedras, Puerto Rico: Huracán.

Downing, J.D. (1988) "*The Cosby Show* and American Racial Discourse," pp. 46–73 in G. Smitherman-Donaldson and T. van Dijk (eds) *Discourse and Discrimination*. Detroit: Wayne State University Press.

Duany, J. (1990) *Los dominicanos en Puerto Rico: migración en la semi-periferia*. Río Piedras, Puerto Rico: Huracán.

Duany, J. (1992) "Caribbean Migration to Puerto Rico: A Comparison of Cubans and Dominicans," *International Migration Review*, 26(1): 46–66.

Duany, J. (1998) "Reconstructing Racial Identity: Ethnicity, Color, and Class among Dominicans in the United States and Puerto Rico," *Latin American Perspectives* 25(100): 147–72.

Dyer, R. (1994) *White*. London: Routledge.

Essed, P. (1991) *Understanding Everyday Racism*. London: Sage.

Fuller, L.K. (1992) *The Cosby Show: Audiences, Impact, and Implications*. Westport, CT: Greenwood Press.

Gray, H. (1995) *Watching Race: Television and the Struggle for "Blackness."* Minneapolis, MN: University of Minnesota Press.

Guerra, L. (1998) *Popular Expression and National Identity in Puerto Rico: The Struggle for Self, Community, and Nation*. Gainesville, FL: University of Florida Press.

Guillaumin, C. (1995) *Racism, Sexism, Power and Ideology*. London: Routledge

Hamamoto, D.Y. (1989) *Nervous Laughter: Television Situation Comedy and Liberal and Democratic Ideology*. New York: Praeger.

Hanchard, M. (1994) "Black Cinderalla?: Race and the Public Sphere in Brazil," *Public Culture* (7): 165–85.

James, W. (1998) *Holding Aloft the Banner of Ethiopia: Caribbean Radicalism in Early Twentieth-century America*. London: Verso.

Jiménez-Román, M. (1996) "Un hombre (negro) del pueblo: José Celso Barbosa and the Puerto Rican 'Race' Towards Whiteness," *Centro* VII (1/2): 8–29.

Lipsitz, G. (1998) *The Possessive Investment in Whiteness*. Philadelphia, PA: Temple University Press.

Marc, D. (1997) *Comic Visions: Television Comedy and American Culture*. Oxford: Blackwell Publishers.

Mediafax (1999) *TV Audience Measurements, Puerto Rico* (Press Release). San Juan, Puerto Rico: Mediafax Inc.

Mercer, K. (1994) *Welcome to the Jungle: New Positions in Black Cultural Studies*. New York: Routledge.

Morris, N. (1995) *Puerto Rico: Culture, Politics, and Identity*. Westport, CT: Praeger.

Muguercia, M. (1984) "El 'teatro de arte' en Cuba entre 1936 y 1950," *Revista Tablas* 4: 2–15.

Omi, M. and H. Winant (1994) *Racial Formations in the United States*. London: Routledge.

Quintero-Rivera, A. (1976) *Conflictos de clase y política en Puerto Rico*. Río Piedras, Puerto Rico: Huracán.

Rey, R. (1973) "Silvia del Villard ataca a los 'negros' pintados," *Teve guía* 4: 74–6.

Ríos, B. (1973) " 'Chianita' nació por casualidad," *Teve Guía* 4: 70–2.

Rivera-Esquilín, E. (1997) "Judith Pizarro . . . entre el drama y la comedia," *El vocero* 17 December: 18.

Rodríguez, C. (1989) *Puerto Ricans Born in the USA*. Boston, MA: Unwin Hyman.

Rodríguez-Morazzani, R. (1996) "Beyond the Rainbow: Mapping the Discourse on Puerto Ricans and 'Race,'" *Centro* VIII (1/2): 149–70.

Stokes, C. (1996–7) "Race and Revolution in Cuba," *Race & Reason* 3: 55–61.

Taylor, E. (1989) *Prime-time Families: Television Culture in Postwar America*. Berkeley, CA: University of California Press.

Torresgrosa, A.L. (1994) "Teve cuñas" *El nuevo día* 11 September: 115–16.
Twine, F.W. (1998) *Racism in a Racial Democracy: The Maintenance of White Supremacy in Brazil.* New Brunswick, NJ: Rutgers University Press.
Wade, P. (1997) *Race and Ethnicity in Latin America.* London: Pluto Press.
Winant, H. (1994) *Racial Conditions.* Minneapolis, MN: University of Minnesota Press.
Zenón-Cruz, I. (1975) *Narciso descubre su trasero.* Humacao, Puerto Rico: Furidi.

Textual (Im)Possibilities
in the U.S. Post-Network Era
Negotiating Production and Promotion Processes on Lifetime's *Any Day Now*

Amanda D. Lotz

By the late 1990s, the economy of the U.S. television industry had been significantly reconfigured from the fairly static relations that had characterized it from its 1950s origin to the mid 1980s. A variety of factors—including the success of cable and satellite transmission, the appearance of new broadcast networks, increased ownership conglomeration, decreased regulation, and the emergence of new technologies—combined to usher in a new era of industry competition, forcing adjustments by traditional broadcast networks. During the decade from approximately 1985 to 1995 these factors substantially altered the institutional environment of the U.S. television industry, a rupture commonly identified as the transition to a post-network or neo-network era.

This study examines the negotiations that producers Nancy Miller and Gary Randall engaged in during the production and promotion of their Lifetime Television series *Any Day Now* (1998–2002), one of the first successful original narrative series produced for a cable network. I explore how the producers' creative goals of expanding social discussion about ethnic difference and racism challenged ideological norms mandated by a commercial media system, and how the changed competitive structure of the post-network era helped make possible textual content that would probably have been too controversial for the network era. The information supporting this article was gathered during observation of the series' production and writing process and through interviews with series' staff held in August of 1999 (also see Newcomb & Lotz, 2002). During the visit, I observed writers' meetings in which many of the second season episodes were planned, attended a "tone" meeting with the director for the episode they were preparing to shoot, and sat in on a promotional strategy meeting as well as daily episode shooting and events such as a

Amanda Lotz, "Textual (Im)Possibilities in the U.S. Post-Network Era: Negotiating Production and Promotion Processes on Lifetime's *Any Day Now*." From *Critical Studies in Media Communication,* Vol. 21, No. 1 (March 2004), pp. 22–43. Reprinted by permission of Taylor & Francis Ltd. (http://www.tandf.co.uk/journals).

photo shoot for *Entertainment Weekly*. I argue that changes in determinations of the audience size and attributes deemed necessary for commercial success have significant consequences on textual possibilities. This case also illuminates the complicated nature of periods of industrial transition in which industry workers face new possibilities while some residual practices, perceptions, and norms continue to constrain their pursuits.

The Post-Network Era and Institutional Analysis

The post-network era refers primarily to changed institutional structure and industrial practice; however, these adjustments cannot be isolated from the industry's creative output: television texts. John Caldwell (1995) documents how these changes in industrial dynamics redefined production and promotion processes and resulted in programming shifts toward "excessive style" and "visual exhibitionism," using the term "televisuality" to describe series' and networks' increased attention to style (pp. 2–5). Caldwell also notes the importance of audience fragmentation in explaining changing stylistic norms, as smaller audiences throughout the television universe increased the value of niche audience groups, potentially enabling more experimentation with visual form and ideological content.

A more traditional concern about the effect of the post-network competitive environment on television texts emerged from political economists who were particularly concerned about increased ownership conglomeration and expanding deregulation. Much of this scholarship argues that concentrated ownership structures lead to the homogenization of culture and decrease the independence of those who produce television content, particularly in the case of journalism (Bagdikian, 1997; Garnham, 1990; McChesney, 1999; Schiller, 1992). In supporting his argument about the massive scope of conglomeration's restrictions on media content, Bagdikian (1997) cites many examples in which disseminating public information took second place to maintaining business and political relationships among media empires and their commercial backers.

Case study analysis of the post-network era performed by Michael Curtin (1999) maintained, however, that synergies of media conglomeration might increase the diversity and multiplicity of cultural forms because profitability in this environment requires a search for diverse audiences who desire different media products. Curtin (1999) uses three case studies to illustrate that "popular culture remains an active site of social and political contest" despite the conglomerated ownership of the post-network era; he even believes "the media industries may be more open to alternative forms of cultural expression today, simply because executives are not certain from where the next hit will come" (p. 64). Although this era is characterized by few owners with multiple media holdings, great internal competition "toward niche operations that cater to particular tastes" still exists (Curtin, 1996, p. 191).

This case-based work of Caldwell, Bagdikian, and Curtin helps explain how post-network structural changes affect the types of programming created in the

US television industry and how the reconfigured competitive environment has altered conventional programming, production, and promotion processes. The discrepancies in their findings suggest a lack of uniformity characteristic of a time of uncertainty and transfiguration. Examinations of individual series' production processes illustrate the differentiation of post-network industrial practices and indicate the benefits and limitations this competitive environment might offer representations and discourses absent or marginalized during the network era, particularly those that challenge white supremacist, capitalist, or patriarchal norms. This article consequently proceeds from the assumption that focused examinations of individual series, networks, and audience markets provide information and analyses that enable a more precise understanding of new competitive configurations and their consequences for critical media research. Case studies such as the one provided here can be seen as distinct examples, while indicating the possibilities explored by individuals and groups in search of strategies viable in a new economic, regulatory, and sociocultural context.

With some notable exceptions, critical studies of the institutional process of television series production remain relatively rare in comparison with textual analyses, despite the fact that examining the process of production and promotion provides useful information about conventions and practices that create industrial norms (Cantor, 1971; d'Acci, 1994; Gitlin, 1985; Levine, 2001; Newcomb & Alley, 1983; Turow, 1982). Such studies often seek to illustrate the complicated process of ideological production by describing and analyzing the obstacles producers encounter during production and their struggles to negotiate specific goals within the expectations and desires of distribution networks.

The critical frameworks through which researchers develop these studies vary considerably. Todd Gitlin (1985) researched *Inside Prime Time* during the waning years of the network era and examined how the business practices and internal politics of commercial media enterprises constrained textual content. Gitlin's (1979) theoretical framework for understanding television remains more traditionally Marxist than the neo-Marxist frameworks emerging from the theories of British cultural studies scholars such as Stuart Hall and David Morley. The British cultural studies approach, which supports the research of those such as d'Acci (1994), du Gay (1997), Gray (1995), and Levine (2001), addresses the intertwined nature of economic and discursive power by seeking to incorporate analyses of economic and material factors while affording the audience some power in negotiating ideology present in mediated texts.

I use the critical trajectory supported by the British cultural studies approach to production study because of its understanding of cultural production as complicated and varied and its utility in considering the anti-racist and feminist discourses that distinguish my case study. This foundation does not presuppose economic determinism; it views the creation and dissemination of cultural texts as complex and contradictory and as resulting from factors that cannot be reduced to a simple economic base, while still acknowledging the role of economic and business forces (Grossberg, 1995). Additionally, it recognizes the integrated nature of questions about texts, audiences, and social contexts that are informed by analysis of the production process (Johnson, 1986/87; Kellner, 1997). This framework aids this article's dual focus of analyzing the production process as a tool for understanding discursive and ideological features related to telling stories about gender and ethnicity, as well as exploring how the competitive dynamics of the post-network era might enable variation in discursive possibilities.

The series this articles examines, *Any Day Now,* aired from August 1998 to March 2002, completing four full seasons and a total of 88 episodes. The series differentiated itself through unconventional feminist and anti-racist discourses and aired on the cable network Lifetime Television, best known for its promotional slogan "Television for Women." A series such as *Any Day Now,* with its focus on the friendship of two female characters who are ethnically different, may illustrate new possibilities for telling stories directed to female audiences; however, the series' efforts to incorporate discourses about ethnicity, class, and other identity-based differences led to conflict with a network that defined its niche more broadly. Although some have suggested that the multiplicity of programming outlets characteristic of the post-network era indicates that a more expansive range of ideological perspectives may now circulate, close examination suggests that multiplicity might yield only slightly more ideological diversity, and then only when the audience niche is considered valuable by advertisers. The case study illustrates how the co-existence of traditional network era practices and new practices that constitute the post-network era lead to a work environment that is difficult for industry workers to negotiate. As industry workers struggle to identify new norms, academic critics must adapt theories and assumptions about the production of culture that acknowledge shifting industry practices. This essay aids in expanding critical understandings of the post-network era by specifying the various kinds of institutional forces operating throughout the pre-production, production, and promotion process of a particular text.

Situating Lifetime's "Television for Women" and *Any Day Now*

Lifetime Television Network emerged as a powerful cable competitor at the close of the 20th century, building on its nearly 20-year history to become the most watched cable network in prime time in 2001 with an average of 1.58 million households (Top 25, 2001). Lifetime began its reign as the most-watched cable network in prime time during the first quarter of 2001, a title it held until faltering in the first quarter of 2003 when it slipped to second amidst a surge by cable news networks covering the path to war in Iraq. Caldwell (1995) and Curtin (1999) substantially explain Lifetime's ascendancy and dominance through their arguments about the importance of niche audiences in post-network era competition. The specific female-focus of Lifetime's programming hails a particular niche interest group—but a comparatively sizable one. Feminist media analyses of Lifetime and its programming strategy have explored the feminine and feminist discourses of the network's programming and promotion and generally found the network to feature themes associated with a traditional femininity (d'Acci, ed., 1994; Meehan & Byars, 2000). Lifetime competes with other basic cable networks (those networks generally available on the cheapest tier of cable service that consequently reach the most homes) such as Turner Network Television (TNT), Turner Broadcasting System (TBS), and USA Network. It reaches 86 million cable and satellite homes, which makes the network nearly universally available to the 84 percent of US homes receiving cable or satellite service (Cable Advertising Bureau, 2003; Top 25, 2002). Lifetime earned the 17th highest revenue among all U.S. television networks in 2002, with $790 million (Top 25, 2002).

Due to this established institutional position, Lifetime was able to create and sustain original narrative series beginning with the drama *Any Day Now* and sitcoms *Maggie* and *Oh Baby* in 1998. The development of these series mark the network's second attempt at developing original series, with a first attempt as early as 1989 with its continuation of the NBC series *The Days and Nights of Molly Dodd,* then series such as *Confessions of Crime, The Hidden Room,* and *Veronica Clare* in 1991. Those series Lifetime originated performed dismally in comparison with the network's original films and were cancelled after airing less than a full season of episodes (Johnson, 1994; Wilson, 1994).

The steady audience gains throughout the cable industry during the 1990s led several of the financially stronger basic cable networks to compete more directly with broadcast networks by creating narrative series similar to, and with budgets approaching the level of, those on broadcast television. Original cable series are able to take content risks because of cable's less stringent regulations and the smaller audience size required to succeed. Producing original series is usually substantially more costly for cable networks than airing the off-air syndicated series that provide plentiful filler for many networks (Petrozzello, 1998). Original narrative series production remains a crucial step in establishing a network brand and expanding the audience base and reputation of a network, but only cable networks in a solid financial position appear able to replicate this competitive strategy. Other basic cable original narrative series include A&E's *100 Centre Street,* TNT's *Witchblade,* USA's *La Femme Nikita* and *Monk,* and FX's *The Shield. Any Day Now* provided a good match for Lifetime because of its emphasis on two female characters, but the series also brought content about racism that had not been as central to the Lifetime brand.

Any Day Now explores the friendship of two women, one white, one black, who were childhood companions in the civil rights hotbed of 1960s Birmingham, Alabama. The narrative of each episode is split between events occurring in the 1990s and those of their 1960s childhood. The series begins as Rene Jackson returns to Birmingham for the funeral of her father James, a man who was instrumental in desegregating Birmingham and spent his life seeking civil rights justice. After growing up in Birmingham, Rene attended the historically black Spelman College and became a corporate lawyer in Washington, D.C. When Rene returns, she and her childhood best friend, Mary Elizabeth O'Brien, have not spoken for over 25 years. Their estrangement results from harsh words exchanged after 18-year-old Mary Elizabeth became pregnant and was angered by Rene's suggestion of abortion as a solution. After Rene returns to Birmingham, the women rekindle their friendship.

Rene takes over her father's law firm and moves back into her childhood home with her mother, Sara. During Rene's absence and immediately after high school, Mary Elizabeth married Colliar Sims, her childhood sweetheart; they now have two teenaged children. Colliar works as a contractor, but initially has trouble maintaining work after a disabling back injury, which makes money tight for the Sims. Despite lifelong dreams of being a writer, Mary Elizabeth's family has occupied nearly all her time. Once her children reach their teens, however, she takes college courses and gradually writes a novel based on her childhood experiences with Rene.

Any Day Now adheres to a conventional U.S. dramatic television format. Stories grounded in the ongoing relationship between the two principle characters and their relationships with friends and family exhibit the seriality common in soap operas (and increasingly common in most television melodrama). These relationship-based problems are never-ending and irresolvable. In contrast to the ongoing nature of relationship stories, the series also usually contains explorations of specific social and political issues within individual episodes. (For example, gay rights are explored in an episode in which Rene represents a lesbian couple wishing to rent a public facility for a commitment ceremony, but this story is introduced and resolved within a single episode). This formal organization often makes the series seem like an issue-oriented program, as the episodic plots tackle distinct topics, such as rape or gay rights. Stories about racism and ethnic difference transcend episodes to become a recurrent and defining theme, but in a trans-episodic structure (rather than the more conventional use of multi-episode plot arcs).

The most unconventional aspect of the series' form is the incorporation of two time periods within each episode. Each 1960s plot with Mary Elizabeth and Rene as girls amplifies the 1990s crisis the characters face. When adult Mary Elizabeth and Colliar experience a lack of intimacy, for example, the 1960s plot shows the events leading to their first kiss. Most importantly, however, the 1960s plots often recall the overt racism of the era and depict the civil rights struggle. The dual time periods provide an additional layer to the cumulative narrative, so that regular viewers bring knowledge of the extensive role ethnic difference has played in the lives of the characters as they confront obstacles to their friendship in both the 1960s and 1990s.

If *Any Day Now* had debuted 10 years earlier, its content, such as its discourse on issues of ethnicity and racism, quite probably would have been identified as unconventional for a dramatic series. By 1998, however, what was once novel and exceptional content was increasingly common within the competitive dynamics of the post-network era. Series appeared on network schedules that presented stories about two women in a dramatic series (*Cagney & Lacey*, CBS, 1982–1988) or explored stories about racism set in both the present (*In the Heat of the Night*, NBC/CBS, 1988–1994) and the past (*I'll Fly Away*, NBC, 1991–1993; *Homefront*, ABC, 1991–1993). Consequently, *Any Day Now*'s attention to past and present racism and its emphasis on dramatic stories about two female characters were neither wholly innovative nor unique. The narrative exploration of these areas, however, remained uncommon on U.S. television. There is not space to address the critical scholarship exploring black representations on U.S. television or the institutional factors important in their development, but this article is informed by this work (Gray, 1995; Hall, 1986, 1992; Jhally & Lewis, 1992; Means Coleman, 1998; Zook, 1999).

Any Day Now provides a useful case study for clarifying the industrial and cultural significance of post-network era programming strategies because it offers uncommon depictions and discourses related to gender and ethnicity and because of its status as an early cable foray into original series production. Executive producers Miller and Randall sought to make a deliberate creative intervention with this series, which they expressed as a desire for *Any Day Now* to instigate "water-cooler conversation" about racial politics in America (N. Miller, personal communication, August 19, 1999). This explicit desire to achieve a goal broader than economic gain and the producers' efforts toward intervening in cultural debates reveal a great deal about the challenges producers face in telling stories with non-dominant ideological emphases. I acknowledge that this may overstate the nobility of Miller and Randall's goals for the series, but my visit with them and their actions in regard to the series support their assertion. For example, they lobbied Lifetime to conduct a televised "Town Hall Meeting on Race in America" following a particularly political episode, and they also participated in fora held at universities that used the narrative content to spur discussion of racism in America. In my interview, Miller expressed that she had earned enough money writing stories about rape victims and other unempowered women to be in a personal financial position to remain committed to her narrative vision regardless of the economic consequences.

Unlike the series *Cagney & Lacey,* which set precedent with its dramatic narrative emphasis on two female characters and their relationship (d'Acci, 1994), Miller and Randall had little difficulty compelling Lifetime to permit a focus on the personal struggles of Rene and Mary Elizabeth and their relationship. As the following analysis explores, topics and themes related to racism were much more problematic to Lifetime's programming department. Content struggles related to the series' emphasis on exploring ethnic difference may be expected; nevertheless, considering the sites at which they emerge is valuable for understanding the complexity of textual production and ideological transmission.

Creating, Producing, and Promoting Television for Women: The Struggle of a Lifetime

Simply bringing *Any Day Now* to television was an unusually formidable challenge, and the difficulties faced by its creators indicate the potential innovations and limitations of post-network programming. Miller and co-creator Deborah Joy Levine sold their original concept for the show to CBS in 1990 (Nancy Miller & Gary Randall, 1999). This version was a comedy/drama blend about the interracial friendship of two girls growing up in 1960s Birmingham. Orion, headed by Gary Randall, was to produce the series. Randall pulled the show days before it was to begin production because he believed the time was not right for a series about children. Miller then spent eight years trying to find an outlet for the series and became partners with Randall shortly before Lifetime contacted her. Two of the executives who were at CBS when the network ordered *Any Day Now* had moved to Lifetime and remembered Miller's script. Lifetime was preparing to launch its first drama and wanted Miller's project if she could add a contemporary dimension to the show by also depicting the girls as adults. Miller and Randall reconfigured the series to meet Lifetime's request.

Although there may be few "conventional" stories of series creation, Miller's persistence and the conditions under which Lifetime ultimately purchased the series extend beyond the usual circumstances. The seven-year memory of the CBS/Lifetime programming executives illustrates the insularity of the executive community, as well as the potential value of such insularity for ideas presented "before their time." The jump from the generally-oriented CBS network of the early 1990s and a dramedy about two girls to the niche-focused Lifetime and its desire for a more dramatic emphasis and adult focus exemplifies how particular network brands with specific programming emphases emerge as a result of the differentiation mandated by the post-network competitive environment.

Despite Lifetime's offer, Miller and Randall had difficulty finding a studio that would produce the series. In the typical arrangement, Miller and Randall would partner with a production studio that would finance the series beyond the per-episode license fee paid by Lifetime and then retain ownership of the series for later syndication sales to recoup the investment. Concerns about the rate of return on a series that was produced for a first-run on a cable network, probably in concert with the series' unconventional content, made finding a studio uncommonly difficult for a series already granted a pilot commitment.

The struggle Miller and Randall experienced at this stage in the production process is illustrative of larger issues relating to post-network programming strategies. To set the broadest institutional context, a variety of factors created concern about the series' viability for syndication. First, a standout original series success had not yet been produced by any of the basic cable networks. Lifetime's endeavor with *Any Day Now* (the creation of a quality original drama series with a budget approaching that of a broadcast network series) was uncharted territory for the U.S. television industry in 1998. (USA had just begun *La Femme Nikita* at this point, but this was a shared venture with Canadian, British, and Italian companies that ensured multinational distribution.) The second-run viability of a series originally viewed by only three million households on a cable network was largely unknown. *Any Day Now*'s broadcast-like budget and production values comprised part of its innovation, while also contributing to its risk. It was possible that viewers in second-run markets would not recognize the series as exceptional from other syndicated dramas, increasing its second-run value, but the lack of a prior case made investors uncertain.

Second, in 1998, the rankings of basic cable networks had not yet shifted to validate the strategy of networks with clear and distinctive network brands (sometimes called "boutiques"), as opposed to general interest networks such as TNT, USA, TBS, FX, and TNN (Higgins, 2001). Because the conventional thinking of the cable industry validated the general interest cable networks, Lifetime's attempt to create original programming seemed an exceptional gamble. Lifetime's success with *Any Day Now* and its other original series is arguably a crucial factor in the network's rise to basic cable prominence by 2001.

Finally, Miller was also looking for a studio at a time during which the effects of eliminating the financial interest and syndication rules were beginning to emerge throughout the industry. Networks increasingly purchased series produced by their own studios during the late 1990s, and Lifetime's lack of a narrative production studio provided challenges for Miller which would have been less likely had a network with a co-owned production studio purchased the series.

Unquestionably, *Any Day Now*'s distribution on a cable network provides the key defining institutional aspect of this series and contributes to the problem of risk outlined here. Lifetime's network history, brand identification, and audience penetration each contribute to the construction of *Any Day Now*'s form and audience. Airing on a cable network dramatically alters the audience size required for success. At the time, a top-rated cable series often drew only five to eight million households and could rank in the top 25 shows viewed on cable per week with as few as two million households. In comparison, top broadcast shows in 1998–1999 drew about 17 million households, with the top 25 reaching at least nine million. In its first season, *Any Day Now* averaged 1.6 million households, increasing to just over two million in season two and peaking at 3.1 million for its two-hour movie in October 1999. The smaller audiences required on cable allow for the success of unconventional programming, while the degree to which cable networks struggle to get audiences to sample their programming still provides substantial risk for investors. Consequently, demographic and economic factors must also be understood as the cultural factors that underlie fundamental aspects of television texts. The business of television cannot be separated from the artistic content in a commercial system, which allows considerations that would normally seem purely economic to play a considerable role in the creation and dissemination of cultural texts. These intersections are at the center of any attempt to understand the textual variance enabled by post-network industrial configurations.

Any Day Now's planned emphasis on the ethnic differences of its lead characters also contributed to the assessment of risk. Randall acknowledged that there was a perception that stories about U.S. racism would not sell well internationally (G. Randall, personal communication, August 19, 1999). Perception, founded in empirical research or not, is a crucial and arbitrary aspect of cultural production that affirms convention and encourages the reworking of known forms and themes. Obvious parallels to the history of U.S. racism—conflict among Israelis and Palestinians, Pakistanis and Indians, conflict structured by religion, class, caste—suggest the broad applicability of the series' stories, despite industry beliefs of their U.S. specificity. The perception that *Any Day Now* would not sell well internationally is similar to perceptions networks often acknowledge about the limits of content that audiences will find acceptable: perceptions that tend to err on the side of caution and convention. Havens (2000, 2002) has not found ethnicity to be a problem in the international syndication of situation comedies featuring black casts such as *The Cosby Show, The Fresh Prince of Bel Air,* and *Family Matters,* but did find some international buyers to be hesitant of purchasing comedies with more of an emphasis on the black American experience, particularly those featuring slang and African American speech patterns, such as *Martin* and *The Jamie Foxx Show.* Importantly, and as Havens (2002) emphasizes, the reality of whether international audiences would embrace stories about U.S. racial politics is unimportant because distributor perceptions often lead to a self-fulfilling prophecy. Those shows perceived to have little appeal do not receive the promotion required to succeed, or even may not be purchased or produced, as was nearly the case for *Any Day Now.*

Lifetime acted as both production studio and network for the pilot episode in order to advance production while Miller and Randall sought a studio. A network and an external production company would usually split these roles, and assuming both functions created a tense relationship between Miller and Randall and the Lifetime executives. The network needed to take full responsibility for both the quality of the content (production studio emphasis) and the budget (network emphasis), a difficult balance in the pilot phase since quality is often improved by increasing expenditures. A production company might put more financial resources into a concept (pilot) they suspect will be profitable in the long run in order to get past the barrier of an initial purchase of episodes, while the network is more interested in limiting its financial expenditures on a product to which it is not yet committed. The initial tension in the relationship between Miller and Randall and the network may have contributed to struggles over content and promotion that developed later.

Miller and Randall eventually reached an agreement with Spelling Entertainment to produce the series. Randall attributes the eventual success of the deal to the fact that Spelling, Miller, and he all employed agents from the same firm, and that the agents' perseverance in constructing the deal resulted from their common stake (G. Randall, personal communication, August 19, 1999). The challenges the series faced in this typically uncontested stage of production indicate the complexity of negotiating conventions during a time of industrial change. Further, the fact that a resolution came through the chance of mutual representation illustrates the complicated distribution of power among various roles in the creation of cultural productions (Turow, 1997).

Production Struggles: Negotiating Content

Even after finding a distribution outlet at Lifetime and a studio willing to take a risk on a product attempting an unconventional endeavor, the producers of *Any Day Now* were still only at the beginning of a complicated process. Examining the negotiations surrounding what producers Miller and Randall intended for the series and what Lifetime executives desired for their schedule reveals how the complex process of program creation continues in the post-network era. The sites of contention between the network and producers expose some of the limitations in representing non-dominant themes and identity groups, limitations that remain intact despite expansion in niche audience possibilities. Two sites emerge as points of contention: first, the amount of creative autonomy Lifetime afforded the producers, and second, the network's positioning of the series through scheduling, marketing, and in relation to the Lifetime brand. Content that narrowed the potential audience (too focused on ethnicity issues, addressing women of certain age groups) and the series' tone ("nice" women's stories versus "exploitation" themes) proved particularly contentious in the struggle over creative autonomy.

Miller followed conventional practice and received approval for plot ideas from Lifetime both when the ideas existed as "broad stroke" episode outlines and through their development into scripts, which allowed the network some influence in the content and form of the series. Despite the requirements of this constant approval, *Any Day Now*'s writers were generally happy with the relationship with Lifetime and the content it allowed. Lifetime permitted the series to use the racist epithet "nigger" in order to express accurately the speech of southern whites in the 1960s and approved other references generally unacceptable in public speech in an effort to maintain the verisimilitude of often awkward discussions of ethnicity and racism. This laxity in content restriction is particularly important to the series' explicit exploration of the often unspoken significance of ethnicity in contemporary U.S. society and in retelling painful stories of racism in America's past.

Miller and Randall, however, were frustrated that their stories were shared with such a small audience because of their broader creative goal for the series to provoke cultural discussion of racial politics. They acknowledged that smaller audiences were a consequence of the increased creative freedom made available on a cable network, and Miller affirmed Lifetime as her preferred outlet if given the choice of airing on Lifetime or having the broader audience exposure that would come only with more stringent creative limitations common on broadcast networks. The post-network era may make niche audiences commercially viable, but creators seeking to tell stories with unconventional content are also faced with a Hobson's choice of small audiences or none at all. This is an improvement from the network era in which there were no options available for stories such as Miller's, but it must be understood as a measured gain.

Conflicts about content developed despite the series' positioning on Lifetime, and primarily resulted from Lifetime's determination of which audiences are most demographically valuable and the network's sense that Miller's stories did not appeal enough to this group. For example, one of the writers proposed a plot about aging, which Miller quickly rejected based on her awareness of the audience age group Lifetime desired. "Keep it young and contemporary" appears as one of four sets of "words of wisdom" hanging on the wall in Miller's office as a reminder to the writers. At this time the lead characters would have been 46 in a realistic account of the narrative, but Lifetime did not want to emphasize that the characters were approaching 50 or even offer plots that would acknowledge they were in their forties. Lifetime sells its time to advertisers based on its number of female audience members between the ages of 18 and 49, although audiences in the 18-to-34-year-old age range attract even more advertising dollars. Lifetime consequently seeks stories perceived to resonate with women in their mid thirties or below, rather than those approaching 50. By the end of *Any Day Now*'s second season, it drew equivalent ratings in the categories women 18-to-49 and women 50-plus (1.7 each). The series earned a 1.9 rating in women 25-to-54 and a 1.3 rating in women 18-to-34.

Again, perception plays an important role in the suggestions and mandates the network provided to the creators. To increase numbers of younger viewers, *Any Day Now* focused more on Mary Elizabeth's teenage daughter Kelly in the final seasons of the series, as she became pregnant and married before graduating from high school. The show maintained its emphasis on racial politics by having Kelly marry a black man, but the increased narrative time afforded to Kelly decreased the time spent on stories about Mary Elizabeth, Rene, and their relationship. Despite opening space for dramatic stories about two female characters and their ethnic difference, Lifetime remained bound by advertisers' preference for younger audiences. This is not to say that younger women are unconcerned with stories about issues such as aging, but that the network placed particular value on signifiers such as a central teen character that they perceived would lead more young viewers to the series.

A more contentious area of content negotiation between Miller and Lifetime evolved from the series' emphasis on racial politics. Throughout the series' four-year run, Miller and her staff wrote stories about racism that were aggressively confrontational and challenged audiences with contemporary topics including interracial dating and marriage, the color caste system, affirmative action, stereotypes, racial epithets, "passing," and racial profiling, in addition to giving dramatic depth to historical stories such as the march on Washington, the 16th St. Baptist church bombing, Martin Luther King Jr.'s assassination, KKK terrorism, civil rights activism and organizing in the Jackson home, as well as everyday racism and segregation. A note from Lifetime midway through the writing of the second season suggested that the series' past plots focused too heavily on civil rights stories, which led Miller to de-emphasize these stories. The network was not wholly averse to civil rights stories; rather, they sought more diversity in the events represented from the 1960s (the series instead placed more emphasis on aspects of 1960s popular culture). The shift away from regularly including stories about America's racist history was noticeable and prevented the series from continuing what had been a distinguishing narrative feature from its first season. "Past" plots commenting on racism or race-related topics dropped from 56 percent of shows before the Lifetime note to 17 percent of shows following (through the end of the second season).

Lifetime probably believed that Miller's anti-racist discourse could diminish the size of the audience by alienating those for whom Miller's agenda was too aggressive. Thus Miller had to negotiate her desire to tell provocative stories about racism with Lifetime's desire to not alienate potential audience members who might be estranged by the show's uncompromising anti-racist position. My point here is to acknowledge that even though Lifetime allowed a more expansive presentation of stories with explicit anti-racist themes, Miller and her staff were not given carte blanche. The request for fewer civil rights-focused past plots was announced during my visit. I do not have direct knowledge of other similar requests, but it is certainly reasonable that receiving this note from the network shaped the stories the staff proposed and their perception of what the network would accept, as illustrated by self-censorship regarding the aging example.

Another suggestion from Lifetime addressed the tone of the series. One writer noted that comments from Lifetime often included suggestions to heighten the amount of drama, perhaps best understood as melodramatic conflict (M. Israel, personal communication, August 18, 1999). This request is especially significant when considered in relation to the made-for-Lifetime films earning the network some infamy for constructing stories that characterize women as victims (A Dangerous Affair, 1995; A Kiss So Deadly, 1996; A Loss of Innocence, 1996). These films provide the strongest ratings performance for the network, but they have also garnered criticism for their emphasis on women who are victims or in peril, who are confronted with agonizing decisions in their personal lives, but who succeed and defeat their victimizer in the end (Byars & Meehan, 1994; Hundley, 1999; McAdams, 1999; Meehan & Byars, 2000).

The perception that excessive melodrama and exploitation themes attract female audiences has often led female-focused series to heighten these elements. D'Acci (1994) chronicles the struggles the writers of Cagney & Lacey experienced when the network realized exploitation plots—sensational content often incorporating sex and violence—performed well. The success of exploitation plots in increasing audience size led CBS to push for more of these plots, while these were not always the stories the writers primarily wished to tell. In their discussion of story ideas, the Any Day Now writers expressed recognition of the difference between exploitation plots and what one writer termed the series' status as a "nice chick show"; a distinction acknowledging the series' emphasis on interpersonal and familial crises rather than more extreme cases of violence and threats to the family's continued existence. Balancing elements of exploitation and being a nice women's show was a constant negotiation.

An example of a script change that may have resulted from efforts to heighten drama occurred in the rewriting process of an episode originally about an atheist teacher who is suspended when parents fear she is sharing her beliefs with students. The writers composed the broad strokes for this script and pitched the idea to Miller during my visit. Over the next few days Miller and the writers discussed where they personally, as parents, would want to draw the line in terms of other aspects of a teacher's identity they would find unacceptable. The writers asked Miller, who does not have children, if she would have any trouble with an atheist as a teacher. She responded, "Probably not if it [atheism] didn't come into anything." When asked if she would have trouble with a Wiccan—someone participating in the Wicca religion, which is often connected to witchcraft—she answered, "Yes, I'd get my kid out of school if a witch was teaching them" (N. Miller, personal communication, August 19, 1999). Miller later asked Randall the two questions, receiving two "no" answers. She then asked him, "What if the teacher were a Nazi?"—to which he said he would take them out of school. When the episode aired, the teacher was a Wiccan rather than an atheist, and was fired, although the series presented the grounds for her appeal as promising.

Based on conversations in which the creative team expressed a sense that a Wiccan was more dangerous or controversial than an atheist, this transition from original plot to the episode that aired (a process I was not present for) might be understood as a decision to increase the sensational aspects of the story. The series also included more typically exploitative plots, including a stalker's harassing of Rene (season one) and Mary Elizabeth's encounter with a burglar at work and consequent post-traumatic stress (season two). Lifetime's request for the series to heighten its drama resulted from its perception of which stories are valued by female audiences and illustrates another way Miller's vision was subordinated to network mandates, despite the other opportunities resulting from airing on a niche network.

Promotion Struggles: "We Are So Much More than Bubble Baths and Tea Cups"

In addition to struggles over storylines, the conflict between Lifetime's aims for the show, the producers' creative vision, and the precarious position of niche targeted series can be seen in the strategies Lifetime used to promote *Any Day Now*. The series' promotion can be viewed as conventional in many ways, but a range of factors contributed to a struggle between the series' producers and Lifetime's promotion department over promotional definition and strategy. Miller and Randall's concern resulted from how promotion contributed to the size and type of the audience, but also to what viewers expected from the series. Miller and Randall's intentions for the series as the basis of water-cooler conversations led them to criticize Lifetime's promotional campaign. In Miller's words: "We wasted our first year, as far as getting the show out there because we trusted them [Lifetime] to do it" (N. Miller, personal communication, August 19, 1999). Their sense of a wasted effort resulted both from Lifetime's limited promotion of the series outside the network and the type of promotional strategy used.

Miller argued that Lifetime's promotions depicted the series as all "tea cups and bubble baths"; a comment on Lifetime's heavy use of promotional teases depicting the women's conversations and of images connected with the "soft" content of a series about friendship. These promotions constructed the series as about the life-long friendship of two women instead of bringing to the fore the often controversial issues that threatened their friendship in each episode. A print advertisement in *Entertainment Weekly* from the first season exhibits this strategy. On a full-page split graphically in half—black on the top, pink on the bottom—the following promotion appears:

> It's hot, it's cold, it's funny, it's tragic, it's forever, it's whatever. Must be a friendship between two women.

The advertisement does not mention the stars, the genre, or the defining aspect of a story set in two time periods that examines not only a friendship, but also an interracial friendship between two women in the U.S. south. Randall argued that "every [cable] network that has succeeded in promoting their program-ming and getting ratings numbers has succeeded in promoting either the provocative or the salacious aspects of that show," citing *South Park* and *The Sopranos* as examples.

As second season episodes began airing, Miller mandated that her writing staff "give Lifetime no choice," meaning that her staff should offer them noth-ing soft to promote. Throughout the second season, some promotion reflected Miller's pleading with the network. Specifically, Lifetime promoted the two-part episode "It's Not About the Butter" with emphasis on the political con-tent of the episode. Lifetime aired this episode as a special event, presenting it as a two-hour movie in the time slot usually featuring made-for-Lifetime films and followed it with a "Town Hall Discussion of Race in America." The advertisement for the episode superimposes written sentences—"You will be shocked. You will be angry. You will think twice."—over some of the most emotionally charged scenes of the episode. After clips from the episode's dia-logue, the narrator announces, "Lifetime presents an explosive two-hour *Any Day Now*. Two hours you'll never forget." The promotion closes with a line of Rene's dialogue, "Sometimes what's at stake is more important than being safe," which is followed by Mary Elizabeth gasping, "My god," when she sees a cross burning in her front yard.

This style of promotion is more in line with what Miller and Randall sought and was replicated to a lesser extent in subsequent promotions. Instead of images of Rene and Mary Elizabeth talking to each other on the phone or over a cup of coffee, a common first season image, these later promotions focused more on the issue of the episode. For example, one promotion depicts Mary Elizabeth finding a condom falling out of her daughter's boyfriend's jacket and then shows Bill arriving at Rene's house—months after calling off their wed-ding—where she is entertaining her new, white boyfriend. Such promotions reveal the week's controversy to viewers without exposing its resolution. Notably, emphasizing controversy is in accord with Life-time's strategy for pro-moting its films; these promotions feature the exploitative elements of the sit-uation, the "woman in danger" motif of the films. In many ways, this is the type of promotion Miller desired.

Particular frustration with Lifetime's efforts in promoting the anti-racist discourse of the series led Miller and Randall to pursue what they termed a grassroots campaign to help audiences seeking casts with ethnic diversity to find the series. (They went so far as to hire a public relations consultant, in addition to the one hired by Lifetime.) This struggle over how to promote the show occurred during the summer of 1999, at the same time the NAACP and other organizations representing non-dominant ethnic groups received exten-sive press coverage of their protests over the lack of diversity in ethnic repre-sentations in the programs the broadcast networks were preparing to launch. In many ways it was a veritable promotional bonanza waiting to happen, but Miller could not draw attention to the series because the advocacy groups focused only on broadcast networks. Consequently, *Any Day Now,* a show exemplifying the advocacy groups' calls for diversity in front of and behind the camera went unmentioned in their highly publicized assault on the "television industry" as defined by network era standards.

When the publicists pushed Miller and Randall to describe the "call to action" they sought, the curious circumstances of the campaign emerged. Miller and Randall sought for the publicists to mobilize members of groups such as the National Council of Negro Women to write letters both to Lifetime in praise of the show (so that they might continue their emphasis on racism and ethnic difference) and to major press outlets to draw attention to the show. This was an unusual request of audience members, who typically only mobilize in letter writing campaigns when a network threatens cancellation of a show. There was, however, no apparent threat; according to Miller, Lifetime was very happy with the ratings the series received and she did not believe the show would face danger of cancellation unless its audience dropped below half a million households (once established, the series consistently drew two million) (N. Miller, personal communication, August 19, 1999). The publicists were uncertain of how to proceed without a cancellation threat, based on their perception of how viewers practice and understand their role. Extending *Any Day Now*'s viewership in an effort to advance cultural discussions about racism was certainly a worthwhile enterprise, but viewers and public relations executives have an understanding of the transaction involved in being audiences and creating audiences. How to circumvent traditional practices for an uncommon series with a goal beyond commercial success, however, remains unclear.

Promotion is particularly crucial in the post-network era because so many networks now compete for the attention of audiences. Lifetime's lack of promotion of the series outside the network was particularly limiting, as non-Lifetime viewers had little awareness of the series. Additionally, the series' deviation from conventional "Television for Women" themes could have attracted a broader audience or at least other specific audience segments. Even once the network moved to issue-oriented promotion, the racial politics were not nearly as central in promotion as they were in the episodes, and the network continued to offer no indication of the past plots in promotion. These promotion practices also suggest a concern about how the series' anti-racist politics and attention to issues of ethnic difference might be received. By not emphasizing Miller's anti-racist agenda in promotion, Lifetime forfeited audiences for whom these themes would have particular appeal.

Ron Becker (1998) uses the term "slumpies" (socially liberal, urban-minded professionals) to describe the audience psychographic that many advertisers sought in the 1990s (psychographic measures incorporate lifestyle components and values as another way to categorize audiences). Becker focuses on the slumpies' importance to the expansion of gay friendly programming, but slumpies could also be reached with anti-racist and feminist programming such as *Any Day Now*. In constructing its promotion of *Any Day Now*, Lifetime apparently calculated that downplaying the series' unconventional anti-racist discourse to appeal to those accustomed to the less politically progressive Lifetime brand would provide a larger audience than emphasizing the slumpie-friendly themes (anti-racist and feminist discourse) that may have drawn new or infrequent viewers to the network. This is contrary to the way a network such as Showtime promotes their series *Queer as Folk,* perhaps a quintessential example of post-network programming. This show clearly defines its "edge" and effectively disinvites those intolerant of gay identities. *Any Day Now*'s status as a preliminary original cable series may explain Lifetime's use of a more conventional—arguably network era—strategy, further illustrating the complexity of industrial practices during a period of transition.

Conclusion

Examining the creative process involved in the creation, production, and promotion of *Any Day Now* contributes a range of information valuable for critical media inquiry. The adjustments of the post-network era have altered the boundaries of textual possibility within which the industry functioned for many years. Some practices have changed radically (channel expansion and competition, audience sizes needed for viability), while other practices remain intact (program funding by studios who seek sizable profits in secondary markets, ways of promoting programming to women, networks exerting creative control over series' creative staff). Not all of these practices are in flux, and the process of transition varies by network, series, and over time. Still, to truly understand the textual ramifications of institutional adjustments, one needs to attend to the shifting institutional and economic practices throughout the pre-production, production and promotion process. Bagdikian (1997), Curtin (1996, 1999), and Caldwell (1995) arrive at their assessments of the post-network era by focusing on only a handful of institutional rearrangements, rather than the entire process. Although this study only considers a singular case, it is more holistic in understanding the myriad forces that impinge upon the final textual strategies of the series, including issues of channel identity, audience size, competitive environment, program funding practices, and promotional efforts in relation to texts, producers, and networks.

Within the context of a holistic approach to a singular case, this study illuminates two sets of information. First, the specifics of this case support the truism of commercial cultural production that an audience niche must achieve a size deemed "substantial" and possess attributes valued by advertisers in order to be served. On its face, this statement provides little innovation; however, as a case occurring during the post-network era, the struggles and success of *Any Day Now* illustrate adjustments in which audiences are now perceived as "substantial." Secondly, periods of industrial change can enable unconventional products; yet the uncertainty of new rules can also make variance from convention difficult during the process of transition. Media industry pundits have often noted that no one in Hollywood wants to be first, but that everyone is lining up to be second. It is this fear of failing when trying something new, paired with the desire to be among the first when a new trend emerges, that accounts for the industry's reliance on tested concepts and formats, which are reinvigorated through endless recombination and subtle variation.

The Commercial Viability of Smaller Audience Niches Enables
Unconventional Programming

Many established norms and processes shifted from the time of Miller's first pitch of the series in 1990 to the time she ultimately secured the Lifetime contract. The emergence of Lifetime as a niche network able to support original narrative programming is an important development for those who study how changing industrial relations constrain and enable shifts in programming. Lifetime selected Miller's series because of the congruence of its story with the network's focus, and Miller consequently experienced little of the network interference endured by the creative team of *Cagney & Lacey*. The case of *Any Day Now* on Lifetime, however, also makes clear that producers still face many limitations in telling stories and reaching audiences. The anti-racist message of the series became a primary point of contention between the creators and the network precisely because *Any Day Now* aired on Lifetime. The central role of Mary Elizabeth and Rene's relationship might have developed as an issue of contention if a network that did not primarily define itself as "Television for Women" distributed the series. Ironically, many of the series' struggles in both negotiating content with Lifetime and finding an appropriate promotion strategy illustrate how a series that defines itself (or is defined) differently from an audience niche perceived to be profitable faces challenges similar to those of more broadly defined series in the network era. If *Any Day Now* had aired on "The Network for Anti-Racist Women of All Ages," its content might have been considered conventional enough to avoid some of the conflicts it experienced on Lifetime, but the market has yet to indicate that such a precise niche might be profitable.

Lifetime had not explicitly connected its brand identity to anti-racist ideologies and the exploration of ethnic diversity until *Any Day Now,* although its self-promotion often emphasizes multicultural depictions of women in a manner that could be described as providing "window-dressing." Admittedly, Lifetime has a better record of including ethnically diverse casts than dramatic series about women airing on broadcast networks that overwhelmingly feature white, straight, upper-middle class, single, career women. Still, Lifetime's contribution should be considered as only a measured gain. The dramas Lifetime has developed since *Any Day Now* (*Strong Medicine,* 2000–; *The Division,* 2001–; *For the People,* 2002–2003) illustrate the network's apparently preferred strategy of including characters with diverse ethnicities without regularly emphasizing the discrepant privilege afforded as a result—an emphasis *Any Day Now* maintained.

The success of the Lifetime venture in providing series for women should be noted, but not overstated, as little evidence of similar success for other under-represented and non-dominant identity groups exists. Despite some recognition of the slumpie preference for narratives with themes about social justice, no network has built a brand identity around this psychographic sensibility. The recent multiplication of cable networks targeting women and the expansion of dramatic series centering female characters across all networks results from conventional perceptions about household buying patterns and women's status as a sizable demographic group (Byars & Meehan, 1994). At half the population, women are hardly a niche, although programming targeted toward them continues to be perceived in that way. Successive cable original narrative series have emerged from generally targeted networks such as A&E, TNT, FX, and USA and have not contested the white patriarchal norms of broadcast schedules. Only pay cable network Showtime has attempted and succeeded with original dramas challenging the white norms of U.S. television (*Soul Food, Resurrection Blvd.*), but these shows are only available to those willing and able to pay a monthly premium.

Periods of Industrial Change Enable Textual Innovation, but Residual Norms Deter and Simultaneously Counteract New Possibilities

This case provides particularly valuable information about how the emergence of *Any Day Now* during a period of institutional transition affected the negotiation of dominant ideological and industrial practices. Moreover, it indicates which possibilities the new institutional environment might enable for deviation from ideological norms. As noted in multiple locations, perceptions, regardless of their validity, provide some of the most substantial barriers to unconventional types of shows (original narrative cable series) and unconventional content (stories about racism). For *Any Day Now,* perceptions that only US audiences—and certain segments at that—would be interested in stories about the history and present reality of US racism nearly prevented production, while the perception that the series must expand the role of its teen characters to increase the number of younger viewers led to adjustments in narrative emphases.

Although many of the conditions that challenged *Any Day Now*'s production team resulted from factors that seem economic in nature, such as syndication, demographics, budgets, audience size, and audience markets, it is important to recognize these factors as inseparable from the cultural contribution of narratives. Neither the texts nor the industrial context explain the situation in full, but a comprehensive picture emerges from examining their intersections. A study of another series would vary in specific details, but studies of what occurs in writers' rooms, director's meetings, promotional strategy sessions, and conversations with networks reveal the interconnections within the process of the creation and dissemination of cultural texts. Some scholars might use the compromises Miller made in her narrative as evidence of the impossibility for texts to challenge ideological norms. Instead, I see the case of *Any Day Now* as an indication of the complex struggle and process of negotiation in which a dominant ideological structure clearly exerts itself, but also proves to be permeable. Miller may have compromised the idealized version of her story in a variety of ways, but she was still able to produce and disseminate a series that challenged racist institutions in a consistent and repeated manner. It may be that the success of programs that defy conventions will alter perceptions about viable content and forms (as *The Cosby Show* once did) but, as this case shows, this is a long and slow process of negotiation.

Many features of industrial practice have changed in response to the post-network competitive environment, while much also remains the same. Many of the most difficult struggles Miller and Randall faced resulted from others (Lifetime, production studios, NAACP) adhering to the conventional logic of the network era, despite its obsolescence. The emerging nature of the post-network era makes it an invaluable site of study for determining larger patterns, perhaps before they become historical rather than contemporary practices. The post-network era is still very much defined by uncertainty for both its practitioners and academic researchers. As producers such as Miller and Randall struggle to determine the new rules and possibilities available to them, so must we engage the emerging debates, dilemmas, and practices that lend insight into the processes of cultural creation that are both enabled and constrained by this developing competitive environment.

Notes

An early version of this research was presented at the Console-ing Passions Conference, Notre Dame, IN (May 2000).

The author would like to thank the two anonymous reviewers, the journal's editors, Timothy Havens, and her dissertation co-advisors, Horace Newcomb and Janet Staiger, for their close readings of various drafts and extremely helpful suggestions.

References

Bagdikian, B. (1997). *The media monopoly* (5th ed.). Boston: Beacon Press.

Becker, R. (1998). Prime-time television in the gay '90s: Network television, quality audiences, and gay politics. *The Velvet Light Trap, 42,* 36–47.

Byars, J., & Meehan, E. R. (1994). Once in a Lifetime: Constructing "the working woman" through cable narrowcasting. *Camera Obscura (special volume on Lifetime: A Cable Network "For Women," edited by J. d'Acci), 33–34,* 12–41.

Cable Advertising Bureau. (2003). *Cable TV facts: 2003.* New York: Cable Advertising Bureau.

Caldwell, J. T. (1995). *Televisuality: Style, crisis, and authority in American television.* New Brunswick, NJ: Rutgers University Press.

Cantor, M. (1971). *The Hollywood TV producer, his work and his audience.* New York: Basic Books.

Curtin, M. (1996). On edge: Culture industries in the neo-network era. In R. Ohmann, G. Averill, M. Curtin, D. Shumway, & E. Traube (Eds.), *Making and selling culture* (pp. 181–202). Hanover, NH: Wesleyan University Press.

Curtin, M. (1999). Feminine desire in the age of satellite television. *Journal of Communication, 49,* 55–70.

d'Acci, J. (1994). *Defining women: Television and the case of* Cagney & Lacey. Chapel Hill: University of North Carolina Press.

d'Acci, J. (Ed.). (1994). *Camera Obscura (special volume on Lifetime: A Cable Network "For Women"), 33–34.*

du Gay, P. (Ed.). (1997). *Production of culture/Cultures of production.* London: Sage.

Garnham, N. (1990). *Capitalism and communication: Global culture and the economics of information.* Newbury Park, CA: Sage.

Gitlin, T. (1979). Prime time ideology: The hegemonic process in television entertainment. *Social Problems, 26,* 251–266.

Gitlin, T. (1985). *Inside prime time.* New York: Pantheon Books.

Gray, H. (1995). *Watching race: Television and the struggle for Blackness.* Minneapolis: University of Minnesota Press.

Grossberg, L. (1995). Cultural studies vs. political economy: Is anybody else bored with this debate? *Critical Studies in Mass Communication, 12,* 72–81.

Hall, S. (1986). Gramsci's relevance for the study of race and ethnicity. *Journal of Communication Inquiry, 10,* 5–27.

Hall, S. (1992). What is the "black" in black popular culture? In G. Dent (Ed.), *Black popular culture* (pp. 21–33). Seattle: Bay Press.

Havens, T. (2000). "The biggest show in the world": Race and the global popularity of *The Cosby Show. Media, Culture & Society, 22,* 371–391.

Havens, T. (2002). "It's still a white world out there": The interplay of culture and economics in international television trade. *Critical Studies in Media Communication, 19,* 371–392.

Higgins, J. M. (2001, June 11). Five blind mice: How the big cable nets lost their way. *Broadcasting & Cable, 131,* 20–27.

Hundley, H. L. (1999). Defining feminine programming and co-opting liberal feminism: A discursive analysis of Lifetime's original movies. Doctoral dissertation, University of Utah.

Jhally, S., & Lewis, J. (1992). *Enlightened racism:* The Cosby Show, *audiences, and the myth of the American dream.* Boulder, CO: Westview Press.

Johnson, E. (1994). Lifetime's feminine psychographic space and the Mystery Loves Company series. *Camera Obscura (special volume on Lifetime: A Cable Network "For Women," edited by J. d'Acci), 33–34,* 42–74.

Johnson, R. (1986/1987). What is cultural studies anyway? *Social Text, 16,* 38–80.

Kellner, D. (1997). Overcoming the divide: Cultural studies and political economy. In M. Ferguson & P. Golding (Eds.), *Cultural studies in question* (pp. 102–120). London: Sage Publications.

Levine, E. (2001). Toward a paradigm for media production research: Behind the scenes at *General Hospital. Critical Studies in Media Communication, 18,* 66–82.

McAdams, D. (1999, October 18). Opportunity of a Lifetime: Carole Black girds Lifetime for its first direct challenge. *Broadcasting & Cable, 129,* 21–29.

McChesney, R. (1999). *Rich media, poor democracy: Communication politics in dubious times.* Urbana: University of Illinois Press.

Means Coleman, R. (1998). *African American viewers and the Black situation comedy: Situating racial humor.* New York: Garland.

Meehan, E. R., & Byars, J. (2000). Telefeminism: How Lifetime got its groove, 1984–1997. *Television & New Media, 1,* 33–51.

Nancy Miller and Gary Randall executive producers. (n.d.). Retrieved December 20, 1999, from http://www.lifetimetv.com/onair/anyday/cast/frameset.shtml/miller_interview.html.

Newcomb, H., & Alley, R. S. (1983). *The producer's medium.* New York: Oxford University Press.

Newcomb, H., & Lotz, A. D. (2002). The production of media fiction. In K. B. Jensen (Ed.), *A handbook of media and communication research* (pp. 62–77). New York: Routledge.

Petrozzello, D. (1998, October 26). Only on cable. *Broadcasting & Cable, 128,* 42.

Schiller, H. I. (1992). *Mass communication and American empire* (2nd ed.). Boulder, CO: Westview Press.

Top 25 networks. (2001, November 26). *Broadcasting & Cable, 131,* 46–56.

Top 25 networks. (2002, December 2). *Broadcasting & Cable, 132,* 24–28.

Turow, J. (1982). Unconventional programs on commercial television: An organizational perspective. In D. C. Whitney & J. Ettema (Eds.), *Mass communicators in context* (pp. 107–129). Beverly Hills, CA: Sage Publications.

Turow, J. (1997). *Media systems in society: Understanding industries, strategies, and power*. White Plains, NY: Longman.

Wilson, P. (1994). Upscale feminine angst: *Molly Dodd*, the Lifetime cable network and gender marketing. *Camera Obscura (special volume on Lifetime: A Cable Network "For Women," edited by J. d'Acci), 33–34*, 102–131.

Zook, K. B. (1999). *Color by FOX: The FOX network and the revolution in Black television*. New York: Oxford University Press.

PART 3

The Programming Context

The majority of essays in this section focus, as in previous editions, on tele-vision's programs. While many of these are entertainment programs—primarily drama and comedy—there are also explorations of political comedy-talk shows, of documentary, and of the larger questions of television "formats" and net-work programming strategies. As the range of television offerings expands in terms of both genre and specific instance (episode, movie, etc.), the vocabu-laries of analysis expand as well. New questions emerge and different examples are cited. But the range of topical content has expanded as well.

Like many other "newer" television programs on both network and cable channels, *Will and Grace* is indicative of content more precisely targeted to specific audiences and interests. Its success, however, may also indicate that "narrowcast" or targeted programs may often spill over assumed boundaries of interest, taste, even ideology to attract attention and delight in the larger potential audience. But even if this is the case, the show is also an example of television's attempt to deal with "identity" in ways perhaps thought uncom-mon in the heyday of the big three networks, and in that sense is yet another indication that the "network era" has passed. Some boundaries or assumed propriety regarding sexual orientation, preference, and expression has blurred or disappeared, and even though "backlash" may at times emerge, shows such as this one, though dealing with a range of cultural categories, can be found throughout the television schedule. Christopher Castiglia and Christopher Reed explore *Will and Grace* as a complex and complicated fictional world, pointing to what could be considered shortcomings when compared with the real culture and politics of gay experience, but also acknowledging the range of possibilities included in the narrative. Their analysis should be a model for dealing with other television materials so specifically constructed, always remembering that though an example may not be fully "adequate" to lived experience, it is also the case that "no television show could be."

Jason Mittell's examination of *The Simpsons* appeared before publication of his superb book *Genre and Television: From Cop Shows to Cartoons in American Culture* (2004), but its close analysis of the role of genre provides an excellent exploration of the cartoon series, an important show to be discussed in this collection. Central to Mittell's approach is a fully developed perspective on the role of genre in television, a much used analytical category, not always systematically applied. A major part of his argument demonstrates that genre is not merely an industrial or formal designation but a flexible, evaluative, active means of cultural meaning construction. Mittell argues that his "account of genre and *The Simpsons*" has "demonstrated how generic terms, definitions, and meanings serve as a discursive framework for the program's cultural comprehension." This more complicated notion of genre is also more useful and should be applied widely in understanding other examples.

Trevor Parry-Giles and Shawn J. Parry-Giles offer another way of understanding the cultural significance of television fiction in their analysis of *The West Wing*. There they argue that it is possible to "read" television programs in sociocultural contexts, in this case reading the show "against the cultural anxieties and ambivalences about the contemporary presidency." They suggest that the television series models a romanticized vision of the institution of the presidency. Such symptomatic readings of television fiction are provocative and useful precisely because they invite consideration of alternative understandings and approaches, but also because they invite analysis of other television programs that might deal with similar content (consider *Jack and Bobby* or *24*), or because they might invite examination of other television programs that might take other approaches toward "cultural anxieties and ambivalences" related to other institutions. How, for example, might this close analysis become a model for understanding medical or legal programs, or programs treating "the family"? This is an excellent model for analysis of other programs and genres.

Jane Arthurs's essay on *Sex and the City* yet again calls attention to "forces shaping programmes in the digital, multichannel era of television." It also frames the results of the changes (opportunities?) afforded by this new industrial and economic context in terms of gender(ed) politics, that is, how this "sexualised mode of address . . . might be understood in the light of debates about the politics of postfeminist culture." As in the studies of *Will and Grace* and *The West Wing*, this linkage of television fiction and sociopolitical issues is common in television studies. What has become more remarkable, however, are the problems related to understanding the links in the "post-network" era in which the general cultural roles and functions of "television" seem to have shifted. Debates over *Sex and the City* mirror the kinds of generic distinctions and hierarchies of value discussed by Mittell in his study of *The Simpsons*, more heavily freighted, perhaps, by the codes of "realism" and "comedy" surrounding *Sex and the City*. Arthurs concludes then, as so many analyses of television must, by pointing to the achievements of the program while also indicating its limitations.

A similar perspective informs "Girls Rule! Gender, Feminism, and Nickelodeon," by Sarah Banet-Weiser. Her conclusion, stated in several ways, has a familiar ring: "Nickelodeon's efforts to include girls as lead characters may be understood as a lucrative market strategy to capitalize on the cultural fad of girl power, but programs such as *Clarissa Explains It All, As Told by Ginger,* and *Nick News* nonetheless provide a different cultural script for both girl and boy audience members, a script that challenges conventional narratives and images about what girls are and who they should be." Or again, "In this sense, the easy dismissal of girl power as a media-created new commercial avenue that has no connection with any kind of real politics is both inaccurate and misleading about the nature of reality in the 21st century." Supporting these claims is an important analysis of programming strategies of a network. Thus, Banet-Weiser's essay should be linked to Lotz's production analysis of *Any Day Now* on the Lifetime network, and in other ways to Deborah L. Jaramillo's examination of *The Sopranos* as part of the AOL Time Warner/HBO corporate strategy. By placing "programs" in the context of a "specialty" network, Banet-Weiser again contributes to our repertoire of approaches.

Topics related to gender and sexuality are also the subject of Sheldon H. Lu's "Soap Opera in China: The Transnational Politics of Visuality, Sexuality, and Masculinity." As this title indicates, Lu's focus extends over a substantial range of topics. In providing this overview he demonstrates once again the tangled features considered in the best analyses of television—questions of specific production practices, of specific practices of representation, and of the ways in which these factors interact on the national level with features of cultural identity. Moreover, he calls attention to the fact that "national" or "cultural" identities now interact with, even when not subordinated to, the "transnational." Television's cross-border realities must be studied in specific contexts, as this essay indicates.

This concern also comes to the fore in Silvio Waisbord's "McTV: Understanding the Global Popularity of Television Formats." As Waisbord makes clear, with trade and adaptation of television formats the patterns of programs such as *Big Brother* or *Survivor* "travel" to countries around the world. Waisbord argues that these formats can be adapted to local or regional purpose and culture, but that the larger structural feature of format licensing and use tends to prevent creation and distribution of other forms of television. In the case of these examples, economic principles tend to override social and cultural concerns, but that, too, is a matter of degree. As with so much of television, the questions tend to focus on the oscillation between positive and negative aspects of specific practices.

John Corner's analysis of the roles and functions of music in documentaries turns to a more formal aspect of television all too often ignored, the significance of the audio track. But Corner goes beyond merely noticing music as background. He demonstrates the ways in which music affects specific content and calls attention to the problems that can emerge from the process.

Does music provide specific cues? If so, is this form of manipulation contradictory to the stated purposes of "documentation"? And finally, he considers new possibilities for extending the roles of music. The essay should suggest numerous opportunities for further studies of this type.

Jeffrey P. Jones also turns to a different kind of television that has taken on increasing importance. Whether this, too, is the result of changes in the economic and technological contexts of the medium, or represents "logical" developments in certain types of programming, there is little question that what he refers to as the "new political television" is taken seriously not only by viewers but also by advertisers, owners, and those who practice "real" politics. Jones's primary subjects are Bill Maher, whose program *Politically Incorrect* began on the cable network Comedy Central, then migrated to ABC, then returned in different form to HBO; Dennis Miller, who has also had several different program venues; and Jon Stewart, who also appears on Comedy Central in *The Daily Show with Jon Stewart*. He contrasts these comedians with the "pundits" of the "network era" who appeared and still appear on programs such as *Meet the Press, Nightline,* or *Face the Nation.* Jones concludes that "new political television offers viewing audiences the ability to watch nonexperts discussing politics with comedian hosts who roast political distortions and fakery when they see it, yet who offer opinionated and thoughtful ruminations that aren't always designed to be taken *too* seriously."

This section concludes with David Thorburn's classic essay, "Television Melodrama." Though few of the examples cited there will be familiar to users of this collection, the concepts remain central to television. Indeed, they may be more central today than when the essay first appeared. Thorburn's focus on structures of melodrama and on the centrality of the actor/character in television should today be applied to the full range of "reality television" as well as to fictions—perhaps more appropriately one should say, as well as to other *types* of fictions, for the reality of reality television must be constantly called into question. Certainly, however, it is the case that programs such as *Survivor* or *Big Brother, Jerry Springer* or *Dr. Phil,* rely on melodramatic sensibilities, processing key sociocultural issues in the restricted boxes, the staged performances, or the intense "counseling" of these programs. And they are perhaps far more personality focused and driven than even the most detailed performance of actors. This essay reminds us that there are certain aspects of television that have, so far, remained fundamental to our best understanding.

It still remains to try to understand how all these features of the medium, all these types of representation, narrative, and media practice, are made part of the lived experience of viewers. That is the subject of essays in the next section.

"Ah, Yes, I Remember It Well"
Memory and Queer Culture in *Will and Grace*

Christopher Castiglia and Christopher Reed

Memory, Gay Identity, and the Television Sitcom

Cultural identities depend crucially on memory, collective as well as personal. The cultural critic Stuart Hall goes so far as to define "identities" as "the names we give to the different ways we are positioned by, and position ourselves in, the narratives of the past."[1] Hall's formulation stresses the mutable, reciprocal nature of identity as a constant negotiation of memory closer to what some theorists call "identifications" than to notions of identity as essentialized and static.[2] Assaults on memory—on particular memories and on the value of memory itself—therefore threaten not only our knowledge of the past, but our ability to imagine, reshape, and make claims for identifications in the present and future as well.

Assaults on gay memory in particular have been virulent in recent years, abetting the forces that would render us sexually anxious, isolated in dynamics of shame and guilt. Such assaults are often overtly homophobic: initiatives to prevent affirmative acknowledgment of homosexuality in history classes, campaigns to obscure the same-sex attractions of historical figures in museum exhibitions, objections to the designation of gay neighborhoods, and so forth.[3] But antipathy to gay memory runs deeper than these examples. The mainstream press plays up arguments over the locutions of "gay" versus "queer," emphasizing generational differences in conceptions of sexual self-definition in ways that frustrate efforts to strengthen bonds among people—old and young, male and female, straight and gay—outside conventional sex/gender norms.[4] Even the not-overtly-homophobic media rehearse versions of gay history as victims' tales, in which sexual and political self-assertion leads to violent assault. While the murders of Harvey Milk and Matthew Shepard are important to gay history, we lose something when these become the primary paradigms of the gay past, of cultural memory. The mainstream's focus on gay martyrs, moreover, follows two decades of stories featuring the doomed homosexual vic-

Christopher Castiglia and Christopher Reed, "'Ah, Yes, I Remember It Well': Memory and Queer Culture in *Will and Grace*." From *Cultural Critique*, No. 56 (Winter 2004). Copyright © 2004, University of Minnesota Press.

timized by an immature culture that in the 1970s promoted the "promiscuity" that led to AIDS. In this view, the solution to the "problem" of memory is a willed amnesia, in which gay men forget our past in order to assimilate to purportedly healthier mainstream norms.

This campaign for amnesia has been abetted by both nominal allies and media-appointed spokesmen for the gay community who urge us to renounce forms of gay culture generated by sexual dissidents in earlier decades. *New York Newsday* columnist Gabriel Rotello, for instance, played a central role in a National Public Radio feature, calling on gay men to make "a complete break with the past" in order to "totally rethink the way they conceive their sexual behavior." This is typical of calls on gay men to reject the legacy of the immediate post-Stonewall generation and to reinvent ourselves along supposedly cleaner, healthier lines that end up looking just like the borders of "normalcy" defined by a coupledom conceived as monogamous and (at least in Vermont) state-sanctioned, and by property rights, including the production of progeny.[5]

Please pause a beat here for comic timing. Then repeat with Jack McFarland's sarcastic hesitancy: "I'm not really getting the theme of this party." Jack's reaction when he finds his "man-tan reunion" has become a play-date for gay couples with children encapsulates his blissful obliviousness to what we've just described as a range of sex-negative, club-negative, camp-negative impulses at work in and on gay culture. In contrast, Jack's happily wholehearted identification, through his memory of past parties, with the clichés of gay culture—disco, musicals, fashion trends—constitutes a principle pleasure of *Will and Grace,* helping to make it, according to one study, the most-watched television show for gay audiences.[6] If the chat rooms devoted to the show are any indication, not "Just Jack" individually, but the way *Will and Grace* as a whole revels in the rich resources of gay memory arouses strong identification with the forms of subculture it models from a wide range of viewers manifesting the various forms of antagonism to heteronormativity yoked by the term "queer."[7]

It might seem unlikely that a sitcom should recoup such powerful assaults on subcultural memory. Our claims, it should be clear, are not assertions of fact, but the outcome of a strategy of interpretation that, like Jack, finds pleasure and subcultural identification in areas overlooked or dismissed by a more authoritative gaze.[8] *Will and Grace* has been criticized by mainstream media critics for characters they perceive as superficial and self-involved, while a major study of "gay visibility" in mass culture gave up all pretense of analysis of the show it said was

> a puzzle. Dabbling in double standards yet indubitably gay. Apolitical yet surreptitiously aware. Familial yet hedonistic. Gay male centered yet with two of the strongest female characters on TV. Devoid of larger community yet assuredly not tokenized. . . . And, through it all, very funny.[9]

But television entertainment—and sitcoms in particular—have often gone where news and drama feared to tread. In the 1970s, Norman Lear's hit series, including *All in the Family, Maude,* and *The Jeffersons,* famously troubled dominant attitudes toward race, gender, class, and the political ruptures of the Vietnam era.[10] Even before these overtly political sitcoms, the alibi of humor allowed shows like *My Three Sons* and *Green Acres* to visualize certain queer potentials. The three sons of Fred MacMurray demonstrated more about male intimacy, with the help of gruff Uncle Charlie, than almost any show on television, while Hooterville was inhabited by a fashion-crazy drag-wannabe, a female carpenter who always wore her tool belt loaded, several elderly gentlemen who lived alone, and a man in love with a pig.

More broadly, sitcoms, by presenting sympathetic, recurring characters whose eccentric misreadings of their environments constitute the primary pleasure of the genre (Eva Gabor's Lisa Douglas in *Green Acres,* Uncle Martin on *My Favorite Martian,* and all the characters except—tellingly—the Professor on *Gilligan's Island*), validated strategies of non-normative interpretation that are a hallmark of subculture. A T-shirt seen in gay-identified neighborhoods lists three names—Buffy, Jody, Sissy—with a red check next to the last name, a joke that presumes not only common memories of *Family Affair* but also shared strategies of pleasureful misreading.

In addition to the plots and characters of television sitcoms, phenomenologies of the medium and genre have unique importance in the construction of minority sexual identity. Television, George Lipsitz argues, powerfully "addresses the inner life," not only because its "dramatic and social locus is the home," but because the formal logic of productions for the small screen—zoom shots, tight framing, quick cuts, and so on—"focus attention inward." In "maximizing the private and personal aspects of existence," as Lipsitz puts it, television permits an especially intense bond between individual experience (the affective pleasures of viewing) and collective formations (the shareable set of references, or memory-narratives, made available by the diegesis) that transcend kin.[11] At the same time, the seriality of the sitcom format, flexible and prone to revision, subordinates presumptions of identity as unchanging historical fact to more playfully malleable and self-willed models of identification. For Lipsitz, the way "television colonizes intimate areas of human sexuality and personality" is part of its invidious undermining of political identities organized around race, ethnicity, class, and family.[12] But what about sexual identity, which is almost invariably formed outside—and in opposition to—racial, ethnic, and class bonds nurtured in families, and requires an ability to revise the personal memory narratives (revaluing that same-sex crush in the first grade, for instance, while downplaying heteronormative participation in a high school prom)? Accommodating such nonfamilial identifications, television sitcoms' fascination with non-normative or chosen families from *I Dream of Jeannie* and *The Courtship of Eddie's Father* through *The Brady Bunch* to *Cheers* and *Friends* suture the privatized affect of domestic viewership to increasingly self-motivated, collectively maintained forms of affiliation.

This analysis suggests links between the histories of television entertainment and of sexual identity overlooked by studies focused on plotline and character (though encapsulated in the playwright Neil Bartlett's claim, "The history of mainstream entertainment is the history of gay culture").[13] The sitcom's roots lie in the nineteenth-century forms of "commercialized leisure" that, Lipsitz argues, replaced traditional rituals of communal memory with theaters where "role playing . . . suggested identities could be changed," where "theatrical 'time' presented an alternative to work time," encouraging "audiences to pursue personal desires and passions," and where "theatergoers . . . shared these intimate and personal cultural moments with strangers." The same historical forces that replaced community rituals with commercial theater—increasing social and geographic mobility, rapid urbanization, and higher levels of disposable incomes—helped generate modern gay culture.[14] Although Lipsitz ignores sexual community, his descriptions of the characteristics of mediated memory suggest its ties with emergent gay culture, which often took shape in the commercial spaces of popular entertainment and shared its constitutive features. Particularly relevant is mass media's yoking of collective memory and anonymity, in marked contrast with more conventional forms of remembering that assume unmediated memory (of family, of village) as the basis of identity. Mass media allow audiences to share intimacy without familiarity and to create new memories—and hence identities—from seemingly impersonal and specularized encounters. Lipsitz's description of the dynamics of popular theater—"The unfamiliarity of the crowd with each other provided a kind of protective cover—a 'privacy in public' whereby personal feelings and emotions could be aired without explanation or apology"—echoes recent historical analysis of the sexual counterpublics that allowed simultaneous anonymity and community formation, secrecy and collective code-making, defying stereotypes of both the exclusively heterosexual "public" and the isolated gloom of the "closet."[15] These parallels between the viewing logic of televised entertainment and gay identity suggest that sitcoms in general—and, with its unprecedented gay focus, *Will and Grace* in particular—should be a rich site for explorations of the dynamics of gay memory as they play out in constructions of subcultural sexual identity today.

The Players

Like other classic sitcoms (*All in the Family* is an obvious model), *Will and Grace*'s weekly episodes focus on the interaction of characters who are less coherent, believable people than embodiments of competing attitudes or social positions.[16] Two pairs of characters—Will and Grace on one hand, Jack and Karen on the other—represent (among other things) different attitudes toward memory and, because of that, toward sexuality, self-worth, and community.

Jack is the "gayest" character. That is, he most exemplifies gay cultural codes, many of which he enacts through rehearsals of gay memory to create sexual and social bonds with other gay men. In one paradigmatic scene, when Jack and another man, after eying each other in a store, start to speak, they perform an updated version of the lyrics from the 1958 movie musical *Gigi*, adapted to express a series of sexual memories ("We met in Soho. / It was the Village. / Gay Pride? / Wigstock. / Ah, yes, I remember it well. / In a cage. / On a box. / Vodka neat? / On the rocks. / Ah, yes, I remember it well").[17] Here memory (both of gay cruising habits and of midcentury movie musicals) allows Jack to connect with another gay man and to affirm his sexuality in a way that merges gay eroticism with camp knowledge of movies like *Gigi*, cultural geography, and community events (Gay Pride, Wigstock). This scene is paradigmatic in the way it presents memory neither as just individual nor particular to these two men, but as the basis of gay identity. With Jack on-screen, *Will and Grace* offers television audiences the unprecedented spectacle of gay subcultural interaction depicted as a practice of shared pleasure for those involved and deployed to include viewers who take their own pleasure in recognizing (which is to say remembering) the sexual scenario and camp allusions.[18] In contrast to the long history of films and television shows that deployed gay codes in ways that isolated or pathologized particular characters, expanding that effect to viewers who wondered, "Do others see what I see? Does that make me sick?" *Will and Grace* affirms gay memory as a viable basis for identity.

In contrast to Jack, Will has a more ambivalent relationship to memory and consequently to gay cultural codes. Except when under Jack's influence, he lacks Jack's enthusiasm for the memories attached to camp or cruising, and his own memory-narratives regularly rehearse experiences of humiliation and shame: breakups, missed opportunities, childhood embarrassments. Will's is typically the conservative voice, criticizing Jack for his campy deployments of gay codes and for his unembarrassed enjoyment of his sexuality. As a result, unlike Jack, who often mentions friends in what seems an extended gay network, Will seems oddly and unhappily isolated, locked into a heterosexual-seeming relationship with Grace (in the show's first episode, they pretend to be newlyweds).

When Will does use memory to make a "love connection," the results don't pay off for him as they do for Jack. This is clear in the episode titled "Love plus One," in which Jack, working as a Banana Republic salesman, is smitten with a handsome shopper.[19] Sensing that Matthew is a "smarty," Jack convinces Will to hide in a dressing room, feeding him dialogue through a headset. Will proffers references that are both straight (John Updike's *Rabbit Run,* for example, which Jack turns, John Waters–like, into *Rabid Nun*) and "high cultural" (shopping for art at the Spielman Gallery). The elite and non-gay quality of their memories grounds Will and Matthew's relationship in the dominant cultural values that quickly become its undoing: a few episodes later they break up when Matthew refuses to challenge his boss's homophobia and acknowledge Will as his lover (by comparison, Jack's carefree display of affection with his latest boyfriend unwittingly "outs" the boss's son to his dad).[20]

Not only within the plot of these episodes, but also in relation to the show's audience, Will's rejection of Jack's uninhibited homoeroticism and campy range of reference frustrates ambitions toward community. As numerous chat room commentators complained, we never see Will and Matthew share an intimate moment.[21] The self-contained nature of their coupledom seems to echo the self-contained quality of the memory references on which their relationship is founded. Will and Matthew's initial connection comically exaggerates the mainstream's fixation on individualism: the same individual salesperson at one private gallery tried to sell the same unique work of art to each of them—a memory none of us can share. Where the audience is distanced by Will's range of reference, however, Jack's allusions include us in a community that, although it falls short of the individualistic ideals of "high" culture, succeeds in reproducing collective pleasure. Throughout the scene in which Will and Matthew meet through Jack's headset, Jack continually intrudes collective queer memory into their conversation (finding that Matthew works on television, Jack, thinking immediately of the gay cult show *Buffy, the Vampire Slayer*, exclaims, "Oh my god. I love *Buffy*. *Buffy* is my life. . . . I'm so into Willow being a lez. Did you have anything to do with that?"). Because he counters their more "serious" pretensions, Jack, as always, is reproved by Will (and now Matthew) as childish and uncontrolled. Jack seems to speak for the viewing audience, however, when, tired of being excluded by Will and Matthew, he interrupts their conversation with a petulant, "Hey, can we talk about something I'm interested in?"

But although Jack is the gayest character, Will is not not-gay: one of the greatest attractions of *Will and Grace* is its recognition of a range of positions within gay identity. Will often stands up for "gay pride" against straight and potentially homophobic audiences: he organizes a sensitivity training for police officers, insists that his closeted lover acknowledge his sexuality, and is himself vocally "out" in the workplace. Significantly, Will's memory-narrative of his sexual identity, staged in the flashback-heavy Thanksgiving 2000 special, credits Jack with pulling him out of the closet. Camp and cruising, represented by Jack, are thus acknowledged as a deep history that enables and remains allied with the more mainstream gay politics represented by Will.

In the original conception of *Will and Grace*, Will's friendship with Jack was balanced by Grace's relationship with her socialite secretary, Karen. Will and Grace, the more normative title characters, share, among other things, a difficult relationship to memory, marked by embarrassment and shame (an episode in which guilt motivates Grace's return to Schenectady to apologize to a grade school classmate whose malicious nickname she initiated, only to be called a "bitch" in front of a funeral parlor full of strangers, is typical).[22] Even the bond between Will and Grace is founded on a shared memory of humiliation occasioned by their failure to achieve heterosexual fulfillment. This is the theme of the hour-long 2000 Thanksgiving special, which rehearses their dysfunction in twinned plots—"the story I like to call 'When Mary Met Sally,'" quips Jack—set simultaneously in the past and present (this structural assertion of the formative relevance of memory is reinforced by the plot, in which these memories are recalled in order to explain to a woman they meet in a bar why her relationship with her boyfriend is failing). Not coincidentally, Grace is, like Will, socially awkward and sexually anxious (Karen calls her "Prudence McPrude, Mayoress of Prudie Town").[23] Nevertheless, Grace, like Will, is capable of fierce loyalty to her gay friends and of an imaginative relation to her own sexuality. If Will's pride relies on his memory of Jack's campy influence, so Grace's relies on her memory of Will's steadfast friendship: memory thus fosters bonds, not only across differences within the gay community, but across supposed divides of gay and straight, male and female, as well.

This passing of memory across boundaries of gender and sexuality is clearest in the character of Karen, nominally a straight woman, who matches Jack's pleasure in eroticism and his repertoire of camp references. Karen's cheerful failure to sustain any conventional social role associated with subordinate femininity—caring wife, nurturing mother, helpful secretary—is linked to Jack's status as the happy homosexual in her response when he asks why she never makes coffee in the office: "For the same reason you don't have a wife and three kids: that's the way god wants it."[24] While Grace is getting called a bitch in Schenectady, Karen tells Jack fondly, "You're simple, you're shallow, and you're a common whore: that's why we're soul-mates." And when they argue, Karen is equally equipped from the arsenal of camp knowledge, suddenly quoting *Gypsy,* for instance, as she spits at Jack: "You ain't gettin' 88 cents from me, Rose!"[25] (In a riposte several episodes later into their quarrel, Jack invokes *The Wizard of Oz* to instruct Karen, "Now be gone before someone drops a house on you!")[26] Despite her always offstage husband and children, Karen's participation in gay cultural memory "queers" her in ways that become occasionally explicit: when Jack first hears about the man-tan reunion, he tells Grace she can't come because it's "gay guys only," then murmurs to Will, "Remind me to invite Karen."[27] This remark recognizes Karen's character as a hilariously exaggerated projection onto an urban matron of stereotypes of gayness as a self-centered combination of ruthless materialism and devastating wit.

In a television genre that claimed documentary veracity, this attribution of gay stereotypes to middle-aged femininity might seem just one more tediously offensive reminder of the links between homophobia and misogyny; the humiliation of actress Sharon Gless as the pro-gay mom in Showtime's *Queer as Folk* comes to mind as an example.[28] In the stylized structure of the sitcom, however, the over-the-top projection of Karen as a best friend for Jack can be enjoyed as a campy inversion of a genre of mainstream films (the 1997 blockbuster *My Best Friend's Wedding* and the derivative *The Next Best Thing*), which projected gay characters (played in both cases by Rupert Everett) solely as handsome and attentive best friends for straight women, but with no lives—certainly no gay plots—of their own. This tried-and-true dynamic was the original premise of *Will and Grace* and remains, presumably, some part of its audience appeal. In the early episodes, Karen and Jack appeared separately and only as sidekicks for Grace and Will.[29] With *Will and Grace*'s success, however, came its confidence to engage directly the common, but little discussed, phenomenon of heterosexual women who share enthusiastically in queer cultural codes, as—in a related development—the Jack/Karen relationship grew at least as important as the Will/Grace duo.[30] These shifts coincided, in *Will and Grace*'s second season, with several jabs at the movie precedent: jokes on Grace's insistence that she looks like Julia Roberts, the star of *My Best Friend's Wedding* (Karen responds, "The only thing you two have in common is horse teeth and bad taste in men"),[31] an episode titled "My Best Friend's Tush," and, most noticeably, the ongoing plot in which Karen arranges Jack's marriage of convenience to her maid, mocking the heterosexual romantic conventions of the films from which the show derived.

For our purposes, what is significant in these characters is that their abilities to revise stereotypes and to make community across identities often conceived as antagonistic are enabled by memory: personal memories of the characters' shared histories, and, more important, cultural memories shared by a community of viewers. Insisting that gay cultural memory can create community across differences of sexual politics, gender identity, or class position, *Will and Grace* embodies the ways memory can not only cohere, but also transform ("queer") contemporary notions of identity.

"Jack Has Originality": Memory and Collective Reference

The pleasure we take in *Will and Grace* derives in part from the scarcity of popular representations of subcultural memory. The hunger for such representations is often belittled in mainstream television commentary, but one sign of the dominant culture's privilege is its failure to recognize its own rehearsals of collective memory for what they are. People invested in normative identities (whiteness, maleness, heterosexuality) that are continually reinforced by mainstream media as the makings of unique individuality can afford to ignore the collective aspect of those memories. To be a privileged citizen is to imagine oneself an autonomous individual, though that "individuality" looks much like everyone else's.

For those outside mainstream culture, however, memories on which to ground alternative social identities must be more self-consciously recognized, cultivated, and shared. This self-consciousness, performed in relation to mass culture, is the basic component of "camp," the colloquial term for the pleasurable misreading that transforms mass-cultural phenomena into subcultural memories that help to cohere and strengthen gay identity in ways that challenge dominant cultural beliefs, including the belief in autonomous individuality. As a disruptive mode of interpretation that inverts authoritative claims to meaning and hierarchies of value, "camp" is notoriously hard to define, except by example.[32] We'll take our example of camp's power from the *Will and Grace* episode "I Never Promised You an Olive Garden" (itself a campy memory reference to Lynn Anderson's 1970 hit, "I Never Promised You a Rose Garden"). In this episode, Karen goads Jack into overcoming his traumatic memories of grade school bullies so that he will accompany her to a principal's conference at her stepchildren's posh academy. Once there, Jack encounters John, who is being bullied into heteronormativity just as Jack was. Identifying with John, Jack thwarts the bullies first by camping it up (he grabs Karen's purse and condemns physical aggression from a fashion standpoint: "This macho bully schoolyard crap is *so* 1983 I could vomit. Now scram!"), then by sharing gay cultural codes with John (showing him how to perform "Just John" with Jack's signature "jazz hands"). Here the camp frivolity of fashion, femininity, and song-and-dance trumps the thudding viciousness of the normative hands down—or, rather, up. In the most explicit demonstration of the power of memory to form collective identity, Jack teaches John how to be himself, a self that is both Jack and John. Here queer memories are rescued from the trauma of isolated individualism (being alone, being beaten up) and transformed into a shared identity that empowers and delights both participants. "Thanks for your help," John says. "Same here," Jack replies.[33]

The difference between mainstream and camp deployments of memory and the different kinds of subjectivity they produce are explicitly at issue in "My Best Friend's Tush." In this episode, Jack invents a cushion for mass-transit riders called the "Subway Tush" (already his focus is on a collective experience of public pleasure outside the mainstream American identification with the individualism of the automobile and the privacy of bodily sensation). When Will's refusal to fund Jack's scheme is overcome by Grace (typically, using a heterosexualizing plot that infantalizes Jack, she pleads to Will, "I work all day. You work all day. He comes home at 3:00 to an empty house. I worry about him"), Will arranges a meeting with potential investors. Although Jack makes Will promise to talk to the investors, once they assemble Jack can't resist bursting into song ("Hey *mon frère* / If your *derrière* / Needs a little cush . . ."). The investors are sold by Jack's campy performance, but want the straight-laced Will out of the venture, because he thinks "too small." To spare Will's feelings, Jack lies about the investors' motives, but when Will asserts they are backing out because "you turned a meeting with my colleagues into Circus-O-Gay," Jack tells the truth, profoundly upsetting Will's sense of himself as the acceptable face of homosexuality for these capitalists. Will's funk lasts until Grace reveals that Jack is quitting the venture out of loyalty to Will. When Will interrupts the meeting where Jack plans to dismiss his investors, he bursts in with a speech promoting Jack ("Jack has . . . passion, he has vision, and most of all, Jack has originality. There is not an idea in this man's head that is not fresh, unique. . . ."), only to learn that the deal has foundered because Jack stole the idea for the Subway Tush from "an ex-lover of Swedish extraction."

In this plot, Jack and Will express very different notions of "originality" and what they imply for individuality and community. For Will, originality—individual uniqueness—is the basis of vision and passion. Jack, however, has knowingly both taken the idea for the Subway Tush from Bjorn and derived his campy promotional shtick from commercial jingles. Jack's undeniable passion and vision do not, as Will claims, derive from his originality. In episode after episode, Jack's erotic and social repertoire recycles mass-media memories—montage and medley are his fortes—to succeed. If Jack's performances are who he is (his cabaret act is called "Just Jack!"), then it is notably untrue that "Jack has originality." Jack's identity—and his passions—are clearly constructed through his sharing of gay subcultural bonds (including his sexual relationship with Bjorn). Will, in his rush for mainstream acceptance, mislabels these acts as "originality," failing to value them—at least for this audience of suits—as moments of queer memory.[34]

For some critics, Will's pandering to potential investors might be paradigmatic of what is wrong with *Will and Grace*. Critiques of mass media for selling out gay culture through a combination of niche marketing for gay audiences and assimilationist depictions of gay men are not wrong, just incomplete.[35] The evolution of gay identity in tandem with emerging forms of commercial entertainment suggests a more symbiotic relationship between the two, in which mass-media niche marketing helps to create what it presumes: a community that shares a set of references and attitudes.[36] Primary among those attitudes is gay identity as camp, a practice of pleasure first nurtured and taught in niche commercial spaces (primarily bars and theaters) and, later, in niche commercial publications—including some academic venues—where critics lovingly explicated the camp subtexts of mass-marketed entertainments (primarily films and novels).[37] As a strategy for the useful misreading of popular culture, camp, at least in some measure, reciprocates the mass media's corrosive effects on gay subculture, cultivating an actively ironic viewership in place of the gullible passivity presumed of audiences by the mass media's harsher critics.

Will and Grace's depiction of camp strategies circulating within an explicitly gay context opens a new commercialized venue for the cultivation of gay memory, and the Subway Tush investors' fascination with Jack's campy advertising jingle seems self-consciously to parallel the campy Old Navy ads (featuring Megan Mullally, the actress who plays Karen) that punctuate holiday airings of the show. Though this is a shift more in scope than in kind from earlier commercial circulations of camp, the new scope does, significantly, widen the interpretive community for gay memory that is synergistically presumed and created by any performance of camp. Undoubtedly, some of the intensity and subversiveness of gay subcultural identification is traded for wider relevance—a move that echoes the broader cultural shift from relatively separatist and small "gay" and "lesbian" communities to the broader but vaguer "queer" identity. Jack's performances of camp deploy a repertoire of codes available to anyone—male or female, gay or straight—with access to the same forms of mass media. *Will and Grace* allows the straight women characters to pick up on Jack's strategy of using media references to disrupt conventional logics of conversation and plot. Karen's cultural references are perfectly in sync with Jack's, but even the more normative Grace has her moments: in a scene where Will tries to distance Grace by hissing bitterly, "You might as well be my wife," Grace deflects the insult by pretending to mishear him, responding incredulously, "Marcus Welby is my wife?" To camp on mass culture may make one less "original," less possessed of the unique individualism signaled by one's embodiment of a stable, autonomous "identity." But to dismiss mass entertainment for "selling out" gay culture misses the complex interactions between commercial co-optation and resistant interpretation, autonomous identity and cross-cultural identifications, individualism and the imagined community of viewers. The practices of camp viewing that *Will and Grace* depicts, however, show that queers co-opt mass culture—not only the other way around—allowing through such acts of reappropriative interpretation the possibilities for *collective originality* to emerge.

"I Guess Weddings Just Bring Out the Worst in Me"

The challenge that the recycling of queer cultural memory poses to the oxymoron of conventional individuality extends to that corollary of individualism:

the perfect couple. What most distinguishes Will and Grace from Jack and Karen may be their differing relationship to the ideal of the all-consuming self-sufficiency of the couple. Will and Grace seem happiest, as evidenced in the failed experiment with Grace moving across the hall, when they are in the same apartment, uninterrupted by visits—usually presented as "intrusions"—by Jack and Karen. What the title characters reinforce, then, is an overdetermined image of the conventional nuclear family: Mom and Dad happily ensconced in a privately owned home, with two unruly interlopers (boy and girl child) who must be affectionately indulged, though not treated as equals. This depiction has troubling consequences: it desexualizes Grace and Will (especially Will, whose homosexuality is repeatedly blamed for their failure to find complete fulfillment in each other); it presents queers as developmentally immature (emotional "children" who will grow into a "mature" recognition of the values represented by Will and Grace); and, above all, it validates a way of life cut off from the pleasures brought by more communal social formations.

Jack and Karen, in contrast, circulate promiscuously. While we typically see Will and Grace only at home or at work unless brought to another space by Jack and Karen, the latter are often in stores, restaurants, gyms, hotels, schools: all spaces that enable interaction with people—often queer people—who float in and out of the plot, often without names or fully developed characters.[38] These spaces and interactions allow Jack and Karen more fluid and expansive definitions of relationships, community, and identity. Despite—or maybe because of—their outrageous narcissism, which grandly assumes that everyone they encounter shares their sensibility, there is an element of generosity in Jack and Karen's relationship to the broader social world that is lacking in Will and Grace's tightly controlled, hermetic environment. Jack and Karen's disruption of the couple-centric dynamic is a crucial part of the appeal of *Will and Grace,* allowing the show to take its place with *Friends* (another hit sitcom that—to judge from chat room discussions and network marketing strategies—shares a significant component of its audience of young adults with *Will and Grace*) as a forum in which the contradictory dynamics of couple and community are negotiated for viewers at the stage in life when mainstream norms demand the prioritization of coupledom and marriage over friendship networks created in school.

These issues may be most explicitly at play in the episode titled "Coffee and Commitment," which involves the four regulars in the commitment ceremony of Joe and Larry (the former fast-life gay couple turned suburban dads already mentioned in connection with the failed man-tan reunion). "I love weddings" is Grace's immediate couple-centric response. "Well, it's not strictly a wedding; it's a same-sex civil union, which affords many of the same rights as a marriage," responds Will, articulating his legalistic grasp on the limitations of the dominant culture's acceptance of gay coupledom. Will and Grace's reflections of the usual range of liberal debate on this issue is interrupted by Jack, who bursts in, in a caffeine-induced delirium, announcing, "Did you see that? I almost did the half nelson. I almost bruised my delicates, my delicates, my domo arigato Mr. Tomatoes. Huge news! I have met—Are you ready for this?

Mr. Right. Well, Mr. Right-Now, anyway. Ba-da-bum. Good night, folks, I'm here all week. Jack 2000!" Conventional coupledom doesn't stand a chance in the face of this promiscuous collapse of boundaries, not only between couples, but between languages, between denotation and euphemism, between authentic expressions of individual emotions and cultural clichés, between personal conversation and public performance.

The episode goes on to contrast the mock-hetero gay couple to the addictions of Jack (to caffeine) and Karen (to booze and pills), with Will and Grace angrily debating their own emotional and financial commitment to one another. This pairing of plots functions as a metaphor for the situation of sexual minorities today, caught between stereotyped ideals of coupledom indistinguishable from heterosexuality and equally stereotyped diagnoses of gay culture as a morass of disease and addiction. The sly yoking of "commitment" and "addiction" suggests that one can end up addicted to the conventional rituals of the exclusive couple (in the final scene, Grace says of the wedding cake she is addictively gobbling, "It's got nine layers of chocolate and a Snickers bar in the middle. I may move into it"). This addiction, the episode suggests, has particularly bad effects on gay men, who end up "picking up the bill" (Will is angry throughout the episode because of Grace's assumption that he will pay for all their joint ventures). More figuratively, gay men pick up the bill for conventional coupledom by submitting themselves to conventional gender roles (Larry and Bob wonder which one of them is the bride), social isolation (no more man-tan parties in the Hamptons for this happy couple; in a later episode, Larry and Bob cancel a trip to Morocco with Will, unwilling to leave their daughter Hannah behind), and a sense of shame about alternative erotic or romantic arrangements. As Will tells Grace, "I guess weddings just bring out the worst in me."

Representing an alternative—and today often vilified—gay legacy, Jack and Karen, the more explicitly "addicted" characters, end up supplying each other with a form of companionship and support that is both harder to ritualize and hence to name (they decide to get over the D.T.'s by "touching each other inappropriately"), but no less trustworthy for that. And *their* addictions—to pleasure in its myriad forms—lead again, not to exclusion and shame, but to inclusion (Jack flirts with a man who offers him a cigarette, while Karen finds booze by seeking out the inevitable "sad sister," shamed by her single status at the marriage of her gay brother). If addiction to coupledom brings out the worst in Will and Grace, addictions to pleasure—reinforced through the expansive communities built through shared memory and circulated cultural codes—bring out the best in Jack and Karen. This episode suggests that the collective identities built through gay memory model at least one alternative to gay (or even, in the case of Will and Grace, queer) marriage and the exclusive couple at its center.

The History of the Queer Future

Out of our memories comes our future. Not only what we remember, but *how* we remember—with pleasure or pain, generosity or anxiety—shapes the futures we will enjoy (or endure) as communities or as individuals. This is the theme of the episode "There but for the Grace of Grace," in which Will and Grace make a pilgrimage to visit a beloved college professor, Joseph Dudley. They find him disillusioned and embittered, locked in a battle of resentments with his longtime companion, Sharon. Watching the two snipe at one another, Will and Grace recognize aspects of their own relationship. Grace exclaims to Will, "Them. They're us," adding, "when he put down the bottle of Correctol by her lamb chop, she said 'Ew.' I say 'Ew.' Will, she is exactly who I'm going to be." Ironically, this return to the past gives Grace a vision of her future, a vision she uses to change the course of her history. When Grace tells Sharon that she terminated an engagement after Will disapproved of the man, Sharon confronts Grace with "Because god forbid there should be any other man in your life besides Will." Sharon recognizes that coupledom has prevented her and Joseph from exploring the potential range of their pleasures, locking them into a life of frustrated resentment. Will and Grace seem to learn their lesson from this trip down memory lane: several episodes later, Will encourages Grace to pursue a relationship with her new romantic interest, Nathan, and in the process meets a man he has admired bashfully from afar. Will and Grace use the past, strategically, to avoid the exclusive interdependence of the conventional couple that has doomed Joseph and Sharon.

Of course, Grace's immediate history always held a potentially "queer" future. Her own mother, Bobbi (played by Debbie Reynolds), is never depicted with her husband; instead, we see her with her effeminate accompanist, with whom she performs a camp repertoire of show tunes and disco hits. Although Grace asserts her difference from her mother, they both share a love of gay men and the culture they produce (Bobbi asks Grace, "What do the boys make out to these days? Is it still Judy?").[39] Unlike Grace's often fraught relation with gay men, Bobbi takes self-affirming pleasure in that relation, seeing it as compatible with more conventional connections (Bobbi has a husband and children). Grace's past, rightly remembered, thus offers her another means of escape from Sharon's frustrations into the pleasures and possibilities of a queer future.

Grace, in a later episode, offers Will a similar view into his queer future, giving him a visit to a clairvoyant, Psychic Sue, as a birthday gift. Sue predicts that Will will be contacted by a "strawberry blonde" with whom he once had a relationship and to whom he never got a chance to say goodbye. When she identifies this blonde as a "she," Will dismisses Sue's predictions as heterosexist smoke and mirrors, only to return home to find a package from his mother containing the collar of his beloved childhood pet, a strawberry blonde dog who died while Will was away at college. Sue has plunged Will back into his past, and his memory, like virtually all his memories, is at best bittersweet, associating affection with loss and disappointment. It is Grace who queers Will's memory: when he takes out the dog collar and announces it belonged to "Ginger," Grace asks, "That drag queen you and Jack hung out with last summer?" Will's memory takes him to his nuclear family, always for him a site of pain. Grace's comment, however, suggests a competing history: not of pain but of pleasure, not of heterosexuality but of queer gender-bending, not of childhood innocence but of adult sexual play. Above all, the memory Grace evokes is collective, involving not just Jack but also someone with at best a contingent relation to Will's life (someone he "hung out with" for a summer) who has nevertheless functioned as a source of queer pleasure, and the pleasure of this memory—for the laughing audience if not for Will—defuses the heavy sentimentality of Will's maudlin family memory.

As textual critics like to say, this scene is foreshadowing, for when, convinced now of Sue's psychic acumen, Will returns for a second visit, he wants to know what, sexually, awaits him in his future. Slowly, Sue reveals to him that he will spend the rest of his life with someone named . . . Jack. Will is traumatized by this revelation, and much of the episode's humor centers on his hysterical distaste for the idea of sexual union with Jack. Two narratives run side by side here. In one, Will seeks pleasure in a memory rooted in a past dominated by the heterosexual nuclear family (a memory that, we can see even if he doesn't, brings him pain). This familial memory, projected into the future, conjures a kind of mirror image: another man exactly like Will to play the missing half of his ideal couple. In contrast, the *queer* memory—of the drag queen who might have worn a dog collar—takes Will to another future, shared with Jack. That future will be very different from Will's normative ideal: when Jack learns of Sue's prediction, he insists that, in his "marriage" to Will, each must have his own apartment and his own boyfriends. The future with Jack—a future predicated by a "memory" of a summer spent "hanging out" (as opposed to Will's usual mode, "staying in")—busts the conventional couple wide open, suggesting a future founded in pleasure, gender-nonconformity, sexual play, and, above all, expansive community, not in the sentimental innocence of the exclusive couple.[40]

In all these episodes, *Will and Grace* suggests that memories can function not as signposts toward a future for which we are inevitably fated (or doomed), but as the materials from which we can construct new relationships with ourselves and our communities. Using memory to create new futures takes several steps, as these episodes demonstrate. First, queers must learn to identify not according to biological "sameness" (sons must follow their fathers), but across cultural differences of sexuality, gender, and lifestyle. While these queered identifications may disrupt the nuclear family (Will's relationship to his own childhood) and the conventional couple (Will and Grace's sense of themselves as almost-married), they open up possibilities for new and expansive communities, which may include biological relations (like Bobbi) or conventional couples (like Larry and Bob) but are not restricted to them. Our memories take us, then, to places and people who, in our past, gave us pleasure (sexual pleasure, perhaps, but also the pleasure of good conversation, new experiences, fresh perspectives). These people and places are often erased by conventional sources of memory (albums featuring photos only of weddings, babies, or family gatherings), but their memories are carried by the traces of mass culture that allowed us to meet them in the first place and that gave us a shared vocabulary of remembrance. These cultural sources carry the memories of collective pleasure, whether in Bobbi's rendition of the disco hit "Gloria," in Karen's citations of *Gypsy,* or Grace's reference to drag, any one—or all—of which recall a history of gender nonconformity and campy defiance. Out of these memories, *Will and Grace* forms a new community and invites us, if we're willing to let the memories be ours as well, to share its pleasures.

Conclusions: Thanks for the Memories

Debates over gay history and identity can make us feel that we must choose sides. What'll it be: memory or amnesia, community or coupledom, subculture or assimilation? One of the pleasures of *Will and Grace* is its use of humor to stage an optimistic hope for a resolution of debilitating debates within the gay community between the positions Michael Warner describes as "the dignified homosexual" and the "queer who flaunts his sex and his faggotry, making the dignified homosexual's stigma all the more justifiable in the eyes of straights."[41] In place of this antagonistic scenario, *Will and Grace* repeatedly shows Jack pulling Will from his isolation, encouraging him into rehearsals of gay memory. Together they recall sexual exploits and perform apparently spontaneous yet carefully choreographed campy duets that suggest Will's unacknowledged store of gay memory. In return, Will protects Jack, providing him the emotional and financial support that allow him to pursue his more transgressive behaviors. This rapprochement between forms of gay identity that are often presented as antagonistic is crucial to the show's appeal, defusing a disabling sense of incoherence not only among different kinds of gay men, but within individuals defining their own sexual identity. "I am totally like Will, but I have a flouncing Jack inside of me waiting to come out and meet people," reads one posting in the show's chat room.[42]

Another aspect of *Will and Grace*'s appeal is its delight in exploring the bonds between certain forms of gay male and straight female identity and, by extension, the validation it offers for relationships between gay men and straight women, reversing the pejorative view of both parties implied in the common epithet "faghag."[43] The affirmation *Will and Grace* offers a queer community of gay men and their straight women friends does not depend primarily on plot, however. Other television shows have presented supposedly gay characters in friendship plots without gaining the powerful allegiance of gay viewers (the short-lived *Normal, Ohio,* which ran during *Will and Grace*'s third season, for example). What *Will and Grace* offers beyond demographic representation is a range of relationships to gay memory and identity, and, most important, the continual, delighted, and delightful engagement of the audience in the dynamics of queer identity formation through memory. As references to the gay past and contemporary queer mores whiz past, we recognize, we recall, we repeat these remarks in ways that value not only the specific allusions to elements of gay history, but the related strategies of campy interpretation and performance that lie at the heart of gay identity.

Will and Grace's role in identity formation is reflected in many remarks posted in chat rooms dedicated to the show, where the recognition-recall-repeat dynamic is described again and again. The question, "Are any guys/girls in a 'Will and Grace' friendship?" elicited such responses as:

My best friend and I are SOOOOOOOO Will and Grace.

It's scary sometimes because a lot of the things that happen on the show resemble things that have happened to us. . . . Sometimes we all get together and have Will and Grace night at someone's house.

My best friends ARE most definitely Will and Grace, no doubt about it. We love the show and although we can't always be together to watch it, we always analyze it soon after. And we are always quoting the show.

My best friend and I watch the show together every week and more and more I see W&G jokes popping into our every day conversations! We continue to frighten people wherever we go.[44]

This dynamic is especially clear in a posting from "Eddie T." who writes: "I'm really tuning in to Jack & Karen each week. Sean & Megan make the world seem a little safer for those of us who are still inventing ourselves, but in spite of the reception we get, are not unpleased with where we've gotten so far—any day now we're gonna find that pony."[45] Eddie recognizes that the viewer's identification is not with a simple demographic category (I'm a gay man so I identify with a gay character), but with the process of "inventing" identity as part of a social relationship and using the stuff of cultural memory—he concludes his posting with a reference to one of Karen's lines from the show.

The importance of such references is also registered in queries motivated by viewers' desires to expand their abilities to understand and deploy camp references and attitudes. "I really wanna know the name of the song Will and Jack sang to the baby," opened one thread. About Karen, female posters confess, "at times I wish that I had the nerve to say what she says to people who tick me off! My fav line: 'Love ya like a cold sore!' " and "Karen is the woman I want to be! . . . To be able to completely overlook all my MANY flaws and just roast everyone I see. That takes guts and quite a bit of confidence."[46] We are not claiming that the world will change because one more person can identify Patti LaBelle's 1974 "Lady Marmalade" or somebody somewhere learns to stand up for herself with a quick and campy put-down. But the accumulated instances of recognition and repetition of such moments—using *Will and Grace* itself as a new mass media source of queer memory—just might ground future identities in pleasure, which seems a far more sustainable foundation than assimilationist ideals to have our differences "tolerated" by the mainstream.

Not that the world of *Will and Grace* is adequate to the needs of queer representation. No television show could be, of course, and the limitations of class, race, geographical setting, and other particulars begs for other shows—and other cultural phenomena—to address a wider demographic range of queerness. Even within the demography *Will and Grace* claims as its own, two failures are glaringly evident: the absence of lesbians and of explicit gay eroticism. For a show that otherwise is so good on the dynamics of queer inclusion, the missing lesbians reflect long-outdated notions that gay men and lesbians exist in entirely separate cultural spaces (when lesbians *are* referred to, it's almost always in a put-down by Jack, reinforcing old stereotypes of misogynistic gay men). Several lesbians who are central figures in queer cultural memory—Martina Navratilova, Sandra Bernhard, Ellen DeGeneres—have made cameo appearances on the show, but the lesbian presence in mass media that these figures represent has yet to be mined as part of the queer memory *Will and Grace* builds on. By the same token, the enormous contribution of lesbians to queer social and political organizations goes oddly and unhappily unreflected in the community modeled by *Will and Grace,* an absence registered in the lack of self-identified lesbian participants in the show's chat rooms.

The other major shortcoming, which viewers who do log onto the chat rooms regularly lament, is the absence of gay physicality on the show, this in contrast to the way heterosexuals kiss, cuddle, and appear in bed together with some regularity.[47] In the episode "The Young and the Tactless," for instance, Grace is seduced by a neighbor, Nathan, whom she professes to find repulsive until he overcomes her torrent of words with a kiss.[48] By contrast, in the following episode Will is allowed only a quick peck on the lips with the young video store clerk he is dating. In a dynamic where gay eroticism can be discussed, but never pictured, this trumping of words by visualized deed allows heterosexuality to trump homosexuality in the show's hierarchy of pleasures. Significantly this is the same episode where certain verbal taboos are broken, with an overt display of homophobia directed at Will and Jack by Karen's mother-in-law. The show's apparent willingness to stage visual heteroeroticism and verbal homophobia but not visual homoeroticism remains a disappointing reflection of mainstream squeamishness.

Despite these shortcomings, however, the theme of the final episode of *Will and Grace*'s 2001 season returned to the power and promise of queer memory. In this episode, Jack is set up to believe that he is finally going to meet his father, Joe Black, only to discover that his father died some years ago.[49] When Will tries to comfort Jack, they express their different understandings of memory.

Jack: He'll never teach me to ride a bike or throw a ball or kiss a man. I'm totally alone.

Will: Jack, what have you really lost here? I mean, it would have been great if you'd gotten to know him, but he wasn't part of your life before, he's not part of your life now. What's really changed?

Jack: But I loved him.

Will: But you didn't *know* him.

Jack: But I loved him.

Will: Maybe you loved the *idea* of him.

In contrast to Will's belief that memories must be based on "actual" relations (particularly biological ones), Jack understands that memories are concepts ("ideas") that ground who we are in the present. Telling Will "he was the source of all my talents," Jack affirms what viewers of *Will and Grace* have already seen: Jack's "talents" arise from an affectionate attachment to self-generated memories, the products of mass media and camp (Jack's notion of filial affection is derived, typically, from a movie, rather than from biological kinship; throughout the episode he sings Barbra Streisand's *Yentl* hit, "Papa Can You Hear Me?"). Out of these memories, Jack develops self-affirmation (noting that his talents are his father's, Jack, in claiming that he "loves" his father, is really saying he loves himself) and collective attachment (without his memories, Jack is alone).

More important, having detached his memories from his particular history, Jack allows them to circulate in unpredictable ways. Strikingly, it is Grace's new boyfriend, Nathan, who proves best able to understand Jack's affectionate relationship to memory. Proposing a memorial service where he, Jack, and Will share memories that are necessarily self-generated (none of them knew Joe Black), Nathan makes the following toast:

> We're born, we grow, we live, we die. If we're lucky, we have family and friends who know us and love us. I never knew my dad. But it doesn't matter, because wherever we go and whatever we do, we know that the spirit of the mother and the spirit of the father are alive in each of us, that everything good already exists within ourselves. So, here's to Joe, the father in all of us.

Like Jack, Nathan understands that each of us has a "Joe," a memory we use to bolster our talents and everything else that is best in us. That memory is less a register of an actual event or person than a projection of a desire for connection, for kinship, for community. If making such memories into a "father" that gives rise to a present-day "family" seems heterosexualizing and patriarchal, the circulation of this memory between Nathan and Jack ensures that fathers can be gay (indeed, in a subplot of the episode, Jack discovers he is the father of a boy, conceived from a sperm donation), and that families are what we make, not just what we are born into. In short, "family" functions here as shorthand for community, and the community the show imagines, built from the stuff of queer memory (here conventional notions of family are queered), extends across identities, sexualities, and genders.

Of course, one can never fully enter into a community made with the dead—or, for that matter, with characters on television sitcoms—but there is even something queer about the friction between individual affect and fictive collectivity, echoing what Christopher Nealon describes as an ongoing tension within gay representation between "the unspeakability of desire . . . and group life," as manifest in collective cultural forms.[50] While we are not urging an uncritical relation to either mass media or to the queer cultures it enabled and shaped, we are asserting the value of taking pleasure in a continually changing and multifaceted gay memory and in the mass media that are its repository. The memories generated by television run the risk, as Lipsitz warns, of making "culture . . . seem like a substitute for politics, a way of posing only imaginary solutions to real problems" or, at worst, "internalizing the dominant culture's norms and values as necessary and inevitable." Yet, as Lipsitz recognizes, "culture can become a rehearsal for politics" and most often "a form of politics." At its best, the television sitcom extends the legacy of the popular theater as "a kind of free space of the imagination," "a place where desire does not have to be justified or explained."[51] But the best of the medium demands the best of its viewers: our willingness to use the pleasureful identifications it arouses to transcend passive consumption and become the embodied practice of community. In so doing, we might see the pleasures produced by mass culture, even the most anonymous of its media, television, as the means to code-making systems of memory- and affect-production that allow the shared discourse of queer community in the present and the future.

Notes

Funding for the research and writing of this paper was provided by the Gay and Lesbian Alliance Against Defamation Center for the Study of Media and Society. Additional research funding was provided by the Richter Scholar Program of Lake Forest College. For their support and contributions to this essay, we would like to thank Ron Gregg and our research assistants, Ryan Inton and Becca Shrier.

1. Stuart Hall, quoted in Andreas Huyssen, *Twilight Memories: Making Time in a Culture of Amnesia* (New York: Routledge, 1995), 1.

2. Diana Fuss, *Essentially Speaking: Feminism, Nature, and Difference* (New York: Routledge, 1989), 1–21, 97–112; *Identification Papers* (New York: Routledge, 1995), 1–19.

3. Specific recent examples include a referendum in Oregon to preclude affirmative mention of homosexuality in public schools, which was only narrowly defeated; the opposition whipped up by the *Washington Post* to the curatorial acknowledgment of Romaine Brooks's lesbianism in the exhibition on display at the National Museum of Women in the Arts over the summer of 2000 (see July 9 review, and on August 9 a letter, and an article about the letter, under the headline "Lesbianism may be all the rage, but what does it have to do with an artist's work?"), and the subsequent whitewashing of same-sex eroticism in major exhibitions on Thomas Eakins and Andy Warhol (Holland Carter, "Everything about Warhol but the Sex," *New York Times,* July 14, 2002, at www.nytimes.com). On controversies over the designation of a gay neighborhood in Chicago, see Christopher Reed, "We're from Oz: Marking Ethnic and Sexual Identity in Chicago," *Environment and Planning D: Society and Space* 21, no. 4 (August 2003): 425–40.

4. This paper, therefore, uses "gay" and "queer" as overlapping terms, with the latter intended to stress continuities among those at odds with conventional heteropatriarchy.

5. This argument is made in more detail in Christopher Castiglia, "Sex Panics, Sex Publics, Sex Memories," *boundary 2* 27, no. 2 (summer 2000): 149–75.

6. Better World Advertising reported *Will and Grace's* lead among television audiences of gay and bisexual men in the San Francisco Bay area, among whom it earned a 36 percent share as opposed to its 6.3 percent rating in this area's population as a whole ("Surprise, Surprise," *Chicago Free Press,* November 29, 2000, 2).

7. Unless otherwise specified, chat room references are to the *Will and Grace* discussion group on the NBC site at http://nbc-tvclubs.nbci.com/willandgrace/forums.

8. Neither of us is trained in—though both teach courses in—media studies. Our interest in our students' and our own pleasures in (some) television motivates our purposeful divergence from academic approaches to mass media that seem to equate negativity with critical rigor. This tendency in film studies is demonstrated by the overwhelming influence of Laura Mulvey's "Visual Pleasure and Narrative Cinema," with its stated aim of destroying pleasure by analyzing it, over the same author's other writings analyzing her own viewing pleasures (most notably "Afterthoughts on 'Visual Pleasure and Narrative Cinema' Inspired by King Vidor's *Duel in the Sun*," both in her

Visual and Other Pleasures [Bloomington: Indiana University Press, 1989], 14–38).
The roots of this bias against pleasure are too numerous and complex to go into here,
though they have been analyzed by some of the most provocative and lively writers in
the humanities and social sciences. See, for instance, Pierre Bourdieu on intellectuals'
need to claim an "ethical superiority" associated with "cultural capital"—an impulse
intensified by the confluence of popular taste and intimidating economic capital in mass
entertainment (*Distinction: A social Critique of the Judgment of Taste,* trans. Richard
Nice [Cambridge: Harvard University Press, 1984]), or Jane Gallop's analysis of the
psychic drama of criticism as an act of aggression in which the critic triumphs by debas-
ing his or her objects of study ("Psychoanalytic Criticism: Some Intimate Questions,"
Art in America 72 [November 1984]: 9–15).

9. Suzanna Danuta Walters, *All the Rage: The Story of Gay Visibility in America*
(Chicago: University of Chicago Press, 2001), 111.

10. On *All in the Family*'s gay plots, and the ire they aroused in the Nixon White
House, see Larry Gross, *Up from Visibility: Lesbians, Gay Men, and the Media in America* (New York: Columbia University Press, 2001), 81.

11. George Lipsitz, *Time Passages: Collective Memory and American Popular Culture* (Minneapolis: University of Minnesota Press, 1990), 19.

12. Ibid., 18.

13. Quoted in Paul Burston, "Just a Gigolo?" in *A Queer Romance: Lesbians, Gay
Men, and Popular Culture,* ed. Paul Burston and Colin Richardson (London: Routledge, 1995), 120.

14. For an influential articulation of this argument, see John D'Emilio, "Capitalism and Gay Identity," in *Powers of Desire: The Politics of Sexuality,* ed. Ann Snitow,
Christine Stansell, and Sharon Thompson (New York: Monthly Review Press, 1983),
100–113.

15. Lipsitz, *Time Passages,* 7–8, 16. For comparison, see, for example, George
Chauncey, *Gay New York: Gender, Urban Culture, and the Making of the Gay Male
World, 1890–1940* (New York: Basic, 1994).

16. The origins of this tradition—long before early sitcom characters or their prece-
dents in the stock characters of nineteenth-century vaudeville and light opera—
in Molière's plays and the "masks," as the characters were called, of the commedia
dell'arte of the Renaissance, suggests a longer history of the social effects of popular
entertainment than that sketched by Lipsitz.

17. "Whose Mom Is It, Anyway?" (season 2, episode 5). All scripts quoted from
www.durfee.net/will/scripts.

18. One possible—but brief—precedent for such deployment of gay memory was
the "coming out" season in the sitcom *Ellen,* but Ellen's obliviousness to—and outright denial of—subcultural allusions during the protracted buildup to the coming out
(as described by Gross, *Up from Visibility,* 157–58, and Walters, *All the Rage,* 83) left
little time for their development before the show's cancellation. What Walters describes
as the "snatches of gay life" in the last shows of the season (88–90) did manifest many
of the dynamics we find in *Will and Grace,* however.

19. Season 3, episode 6.

20. "Brothers, a Love Story" (season 3, episode 13).

21. In response to the thread, "Do you think the reason everyone loves Jack so
much is because he is stereotypically gay and Will acts like he's straight? Do you think
it will help when Will gets a boyfriend?" came replies such as "I would definitely love
to see him with a partner or significant other and would not mind at all if they called
on me!" and "I would love to see Will play a more gay role, more real to life. Yes,

actually dating and relationship issues with other gay men would be a plus." Although viewers can imagine Will with a "boyfriend or significant other" or celibate, they reject the idea that Will should have serial partners. As one viewer put it: "he does deserve someone in his life. But I do not think they should put him around with all kinds of guys. Will is usually the one with emotional attachments and I think to have this with all the guys would go against his character." Not surprisingly, those who identify more strongly with Jack see a connection between his serial attachments and his more fluid notion of identity.

22. "Alice Doesn't Live Here Anymore" (season 3, episode 20).

23. "Love plus One" (season 3, episode 6).

24. "Coffee and Commitment" (season 3, episode 10).

25. "Ben? Her?" (season 2, episode 23). That straight women characters prove as adept at camp as gay men is not surprising, given the history of camp, which often arose from figures—Bette Davis or Mae West, for example—who appealed to female and gay male viewers because of similar traits of endurance, self-assertion, and erotic inventiveness.

26. "Fear and Clothing" (season 3, episode 2).

27. Season 3, episode 6. Gay novelist Andrew Holleran, characterizing Karen as a "cross between Leona Helmsley, Lorena Bobbitt, Jacqueline Susann, Mother Goddam, and Margo Channing," claims her as "let's face it—the only really gay character on the whole sitcom: the straight woman." For Holleran, gay identification with Karen is a function of a nostalgic and collective yearning arising from strong cultural memory: "We miss Paul Lynde. We miss Wayland Flowers and Madame. We miss Bette Davis. We even miss the Golden Girls" ("The Alpha Queen," *Gay and Lesbian Review 7*, no. 3 [summer 2000]: 65–66). The perceived gayness of Karen's character seems also reflected in the Los Angeles Gay and Lesbian Center's selection of actress Megan Mullally (who declines to discuss her own sexuality) for its 2001 Creative Integrity Award, and in her starring role in Old Navy commercials, spoofing old-fashioned showgirl musical numbers.

28. Howard Buford, president of the advertising agency behind the campaign to market *Queer as Folk*, described his premise: "It's relevant to a broader audience if you convince them the show is an authentic slice of gay and lesbian life" (in Stuart Elliot, "Advertising," *New York Times*, November 28, 2000). Mainstream TV critics bought this claim, rehearsing clichés of the "hard-hitting" *Queer as Folk* as praiseworthy for the realistic "fullness of the characters" in contrast to the "role-model material" of shows like *Will and Grace*, and quoting *Queer as Folk*'s executive producer on the need "to be honest" (Steve Johnson, "On Television: On the Gaydar," *Chicago Tribune*, November 30, 2000).

29. In yet another rehearsal of memory, NBC reran the premier of *Will and Grace* during prime time on April 12, 2001.

30. The NBC chat room devoted to the show reveals that Jack and Karen's relationship at least equals—and threatens to overwhelm—the draw of the show's original couple. Discussion threads "Will & Grace or Jack & Karen?" and "Who's funnier Will and Grace or Jack and Karen" elicited only responses favoring Jack and Karen (typical among them, "I have been calling it [the show] Jack & Karen for a long time now"), with the exception of two participants who tactfully urged that the two pairs were equally funny. See also the discussion thread "Who loved that episode?"

31. "To Serve and Disinfect" (season 2, episode 7).

32. The pioneering attempt at definition, Susan Sontag's 1964 "Notes on Camp" (reprinted in *A Susan Sontag Reader* [New York: Vintage, 1983], 105–19) is largely a

list of examples. Sontag's pre-Stonewall assumption that camp was apolitical has been supplanted by numerous scholars; see especially Andrew Ross, "Uses of Camp," in *No Respect: Intellectuals and Popular Culture* (New York: Routledge, 1989), 135–70; and three anthologies: Fabio Cleto, ed., *Camp: Queer Aesthetics and the Performing Self— A Reader* (Edinburgh: Edinburgh University Press, 1999); Moe Meyer, ed., *The Politics and Poetics of Camp* (New York: Routledge, 1994); and David Bergman, ed., *Camp Grounds: Style and Homosexuality* (Amherst: University of Massachusetts Press, 1993).

33. "I Never Promised You an Olive Garden" (season 2, episode 3). The power of this image of camp mentorship is registered in such chat room postings as "My favorite episode was when Jack came to the rescue of the young boy in the school hallway. We all could have used a Jack when we were that age!" (http://htmlgear.lycos .com).

34. Jack's attitude toward his "theft"—acknowledging but unconcerned—implies a queer critique of the dominant culture's valorization of individuality in several ways. First, mainstream culture grants married heterosexuals a notion of collective property that it denies gay couples; if Jack and Bjorn were straight and married, the fact that this product was Bjorn's idea would be less troubling. Second, Jack reveals the fallacy behind presumptions that capitalism or the law represents the triumph of "originality": the jingles he recycles in his performance are attractive because they are repeated in commercials, and the legal case the investors threaten Jack with would be built on a derivative notion of precedent.

35. For a strong critique of niche marketing, see Alexandra Chassin, *Selling Out: The Gay and Lesbian Movement Goes to Market* (New York: St. Martin's, 2000), 101–43. Chassin acknowledges "leaving aside" issues of gay and lesbian "cultural expression, taste, subjectivity, and lifestyle" (xx). For the argument that *Will and Grace,* along with other American television and film, presents assimilationist queer characters that leave mainstream viewers' prejudices unchallenged, see James Keller, *Queer (Un)Friendly Film and Television* (Jefferson, N.C.: McFarland, 2002).

36. This case has been made particularly strongly for the niche-marketed physique magazines of the 1950s and 1960s. These offered men "membership" (as subscriptions were called) in a community that valued homoeroticism along with other pleasures of the body and challenged authoritative legal and medical definitions of normality and probity, creating a far closer precedent to the activist forms of gay community that emerged in the late 1960s than the earnestly assimilationist political magazines. Though the circulation of the physique magazines were hundreds of times greater than that of the political periodicals, political histories of the gay movement have been blinded to their influence by assumptions of the apolitical nature of mass culture (to the extent of ignoring and denying the political commentary that accompanied the beefcake pictures). See Christopher Nealon, *Foundlings: Lesbian and Gay Historical Emotion before Stonewall* (Durham, N.C.: Duke University Press, 2001), 99–139.

37. Until recently, the most enabling queer scholarship on film and television explicated depictions of homosexuality not named as such in mainstream film and television. The chapter "The Way We Weren't" in Vito Russo's pioneering *The Celluloid Closet: Homosexuality in the Movies* (New York: Harper & Row, 1981) set a standard for this kind of work; another valuable example is Richard Dyer, *The Matter of Images: Essays on Representations* (London: Routledge, 1993).

38. A partial catalog might include the African-American girl Jack competes with on e-Bay, a trick named Mipanko and his unnamed father, a delivery boy, a temperance-oriented soccer mom, an INS officer, a crowd of "recovering" gays and lesbians, Martina Navratilova, a crew of ballet-dancing cater-waiters, a gay-acting heterosexual named Scott, a weeping woman in a bar, and a porn director.

39. "Whose Mom Is It, Anyway" (season 2, episode 5).

40. "Gypsies, Tramps, and Weed" (season 3, episode 7).

41. Michael Warner, *The Trouble with Normal: Sex, Politics, and the Ethics of Queer Life* (Cambridge: Harvard University Press, 1999), 32.

42. Thread: "Which character do you relate to the best? Why?"

43. This validation has been a long time coming, as television lags behind social trends registered in well-known sociological studies since the 1970s; see Rebecca Nahas and Myra Turley, *The New Couple: Women and Gay Men* (New York: Seaview, 1979); and Catherine Whitney, *Uncommon Lives: Gay Men and Straight Women* (New York: Plume, 1990).

44. In addition to these responses to the thread "Are any guys/girls in a 'Will and Grace' relationship?" other posters identify with the Karen/Jack duo. One woman posted, "My friend Joel is my 'Just Jack.' He's every girl's best friend" (thread: "Will & Grace or Jack & Karen"). Another female viewer acknowledged, "While watching Will & Grace, I never wanted to be a gay man so badly." Not surprisingly, she identifies especially with Jack: "I love Jack (sounds corny but true)!!!!!!" (http://htmlgear .lycos.com). Another female viewer writes, "I'd have to say I'm a lot like Jack. Which is kinda sad because I'm a 13 year old female and he's a 30 year old gay guy. Ah, it doesn't bother me, but he acts like I do in so many ways (which may be why I love him so much) he could maybe even pass for my brother or something"—the "or something" here reveals the glimmer in this young viewer's mind of a possibility for a relationship outside the norms of the nuclear family (thread: "Which character do you relate to the best? Why?"). The fluidity of identifications fostered by *Will and Grace* is truly queer and clearly contradicts assumptions that all gay people identify with "positive images" like the one presented by the character of Will, or that only gay men benefit from the forms of identification and self-esteem arising from gay-identified cultural forms like camp and cruising.

45. http://htmlgear.lycos.com.

46. Threads: "Is it the gay thing or do we really like the show?" and "Which character do you relate to the best? Why?"

47. This point is made repeatedly in the chat rooms: one participant characterizes *Will and Grace* as "show[ing] two gay men who only kiss and have sex with women. . . . I appreciate *Will and Grace*. I'd just appreciate it more if they didn't shy away from being gay" (thread: "Gay Representation on TV"); see also thread "Kiss Tally."

48. Season 3, episode 20.

49. "Sons and Lovers" (season 3, episode 22).

50. Nealon, *Foundlings*, 13.

51. Lipsitz, *Time Passages*, 16, 9.

Cartoon Realism
Genre Mixing and the Cultural Life of *The Simpsons*

Jason Mittell

It's an odd thing when a cartoon series is praised as one of the most trenchant and "realistic" programs on TV, but there you are.
—Josh Ozersky, media critic (quoted in Ozersky 11).

It's just a cartoon. People shouldn't pay that much attention to a cartoon.
—Andy Schulze, fifteen year old (quoted in Shahid, "Hey, Dude")

Few television programs exemplify 1990s media like *The Simpsons*—popular culture sensation, marketing phenomenon, generic mixture, (alleged) embodiment of postmodernism, and representative of the post-Fordist network era. Yet before celebrating (or critiquing) the show as the program of the decade, I believe we must stop and examine some of the assumptions that have been made about 1990s media and postmodern culture. Specifically, *The Simpsons* provides a valuable case study to examine issues of niche marketing, genre mixing, and postmodernism that mark our understanding of contemporary media. In order to discuss these issues, I will focus on how *The Simpsons's* generic status affected its larger cultural circulation. I contend that the show's genre mixing is crucial to understanding the program and that genre has had deeper and more significant ramifications than one might presume by following the typical approaches to genre study, namely, identifying generic definitions and meanings. Instead, by conceptualizing genre as a discursive process of categorization and hierarchization, rather than as a core textual component (a theoretical move I discuss below), we might be able to view the cultural workings of genre as it relates to television programming such as *The Simpsons*. Specifically, I want to focus on how genre impacts *The Simpsons* regarding issues of cultural hierarchies, assumptions about target audiences, codes of realism, and the impli-

Jason Mittell, "Cartoon Realism: Genre Mixing and the Cultural Life of *The Simpsons*." From *The Velvet Light Trap*, No. 47 (Spring 2001), pp. 15–28. Copyright © 2001, University of Texas Press.

cations of genre parody, all of which can add to our understanding of contemporary media landscapes.

Before offering a generic analysis of *The Simpsons*, we must reconcile how
to approach a program that is often labeled "postmodernist," a term that has
implied generic transcendence for many critics (see Perloff for examples of this
argument). Postmodernism, as might befit its theoretical pedigree, is a slippery
signifier, producing new meanings and implications practically every time the
word is spoken or cited. Instead of weighing in as to whether *The Simpsons*
should be viewed as postmodernist or not, I wish to question the term's value
in studying *The Simpsons* and 1990s media culture. How will labeling the show
"postmodern" better our understanding of either the text or its cultural context and circulation? Most critics who have lauded *The Simpsons* as an example of postmodern media call attention to its hyper-reflexivity and self-
awareness. Jim Collins labels an instance of Bart watching his own Macy's
Thanksgiving Parade float on television "emblematic of a postmodern textuality" (335–36). Likewise, Matthew Henry points to the show's "shattering of
the fictional illusion" as fulfilling one of postmodernism's "prerequisites"; he
exemplifies this point with an episode's opening sequence in which the family
runs into the living room, over-shoots, and ends up off the frame of the "film"
and into the realm of sprocket holes (95). Yet to celebrate these aspects of the
program as indicative of postmodernism ignores some substantial continuities
within media history. As John Caldwell suggests, *Simpsons*-style reflexivity and
intertextuality have been features of television comedy since its first decade.
Caldwell cites numerous examples such as the oft-mentioned *Ernie Kovacs Show*
and *Burns and Allen Show* but also less notably reflexive shows like *Texaco Star
Theater, Your Show of Shows,* and *I Love Lucy* (23). For Caldwell, if the textual
practices that typify postmodernism have run throughout television history,
there is little benefit to such a label that cannot effectively demarcate the
medium's historical eras or aesthetic movements.

However, the textual ancestry of *The Simpsons* predates even television, as it
is certainly part of a longer tradition of animated film. Reflexivity has always been
a defining component of animated shorts, dating back as early as 1914's *Gertie
the Dinosaur*—definitely prepostmodern. Donald Crafton has argued that the
early years of animation were marked by the central tendency of "self-figuration,
the tendency of the filmmaker to interject himself into his film," an aesthetic
technique that has recently been hailed as typically postmodern but clearly predates any claims for a postmodern era (*Before Mickey*, 11). Later animation in
the 1930s and 1940s was well known for its reflexivity and self-awareness, regularly breaking down the artifice and illusion of the medium; these techniques
are most often tied to Tex Avery's work but were also employed by nearly every
animation studio in Hollywood. Even the specific example Henry uses from *The
Simpsons* to typify the show's postmodern tendencies is in itself a specific allusion to 1953's *Duck Amuck*, Chuck Jones's celebrated deconstruction of Daffy
Duck's animated universe. I thus regard these claims to *The Simpsons's* postmodern textual aesthetic with skepticism, as the very same techniques that are
hailed as typically postmodern have clear roots in the show's generic precursors.

Another aspect of postmodernism that bears direct relevance upon our understanding of *The Simpsons,* especially regarding the show's generic status, is the role of parody in textual practice.[1] There is little question that parody is an operative mode within *The Simpsons,* but the scholarly implications of this parody are less clear. Does the show's use of parody make the program emblematically postmodern or an anachronistically modernist relic? One way of resolving the debate is to consult the vast scholarship concerning parody and postmodernism. We might look to Fredric Jameson's oft-cited nomination of pastiche as postmodern "blank parody"—parody without the critical edge of satire typical to modernist works (16–19). Alternatively, we could consider Linda Hutcheon's discussion of postmodernist "ambivalent parody" that both follows and ridicules a genre's conventions (*A Poetics*). Holding up these definitions of postmodern parody to *The Simpsons,* we might be able to itemize the elements of the show's parodic tendencies and label it postmodern or not according to these (or other) schemas. But so what? How does this really further our understanding of the text or its cultural life?

This is not to say that parody is not a vital aspect of *The Simpsons;* I will return to this topic as I investigate the show's mode of genre mixing. However, I see little point in locating the program's use of parody within larger trends of postmodernism—this usage does not correlate with the categories that either producers or audiences use to make sense of the text. It is more productive to analyze media in actual cultural circulation than theoretical abstraction. After all, what does it matter to our goal of understanding the cultural life of *The Simpsons* that it is (or is not) "postmodern" according to one definition? If "postmodern" were an active term that many critics, audiences, and producers used to make sense of the program, then it might be worth further inquiry. However, the only audience that uses this label to understand *The Simpsons* is academics (and just a small group at that). Unless we are interested in charting the discursive reception of the show within academic circles (which is not my project here), the postmodern label seems unnecessary to this analysis. In fact, I view it as a hindrance, as there is a common assumption that postmodern texts transcend genre definitions through radical eclecticism and boundary blurring.[2] I contend that *The Simpsons* as well as other generically mixed and parodic texts often labeled postmodern activate genre categories *more* than so-called pure genre texts, a position I explore below through the intersection of the program and television genres.

If we want to study genre and *The Simpsons,* what is it exactly that we should examine? I would like to propose a number of questions concerning television genre that we must consider if we are to understand the circulation of *The Simpsons* more fully. How does the show work in relation to the family sitcom genre? How does it work as an animated cartoon? How do audiences and critics make sense of the show's generic mixing? How are the conventions of each genre tied to assumptions of "proper" subject matter and audience? How are the multiple genres of *The Simpsons* configured within cultural hierarchies and norms? How does *The Simpsons*'s use of genre parody complicate its generic position? How might scholars approach these questions of genre regarding a generically complex and mixed program such as *The Simpsons?* Finally, what are the ultimate implications of genre for *The Simpsons* as well as the implications of *The Simpsons* for television genre study? To answer questions such as these, we need to revise our notions of genre and how we might study generic practices.

While I explore these theoretical issues of television genres in more depth elsewhere, I wish to briefly lay out a model of examining genres as cultural categories (see Mittell, "A Cultural Approach"). Rather than just looking at genres as collections of textual conventions or core meanings, I believe we should examine genres as culturally circulating sets of practices that work to categorize television texts and link together various cultural assumptions. Following the work of Rick Altman, Robert Allen, Steve Neale, and Ralph Cohen ("History and Genre"). I consider genres as cultural categories in process. Instead of looking at genre as a static category that may be precisely defined, I examine the processes of definition that are constantly undertaken by audiences and industries regarding genres. Instead of interpreting the meaning of genres as expressed within the deep structure of narrative texts, I look at the discursive meanings that are culturally articulated to both narrative and non-narrative genres and that are under negotiation within specific historic moments. Instead of assessing the cultural values expressed by genres, I look at how generic categories are culturally evaluated and tied to important hierarchies that situate genres within power relations. In short, I look at genres as dynamic cultural categories, comprised of discursive practices of definition, interpretation, and evaluation and constituted through the interactions between texts, industries, audiences, and contexts.[3]

Rather than offering a more detailed theorization of this approach to genre here, I will explain my method through an applied case study. To examine the generic processes of definition, interpretation, and evaluation that are intertwined with the numerous genre categories running through *The Simpsons,* I have examined a variety of discursive sites, including popular press reviews, editorial commentaries, trade journal accounts, interviews with creative personnel, and academic critiques. I focus on the program's early years, as the show's initial novelty and controversial reception led to intense discussions and debates on how to make sense of this program. Through an analysis of these discursive sites, I will explore the competing uses of generic terms such as sitcom, cartoon, animation, and parody. I am not trying to arrive at the "proper" categorization of the show through this analysis; instead, I want to examine the discursive operation of genre surrounding the cultural life of *The Simpsons* to see how notions of genre helped constitute a framework of understanding for this unusual and controversial program and how this show is exemplary of 1990s media practices.

Generic Discourses and *The Simpsons*

It is obvious to even the most casual or inexperienced television viewer that *The Simpsons* is on some level a mixture of domestic sitcom and animated cartoon. It is hardly worth the effort to attempt to prove this categorical combination via either textual analysis or discursive examination. However, while it may be clear *what* genres the show draws upon, it is not always clear what the ramifications of this generic mixing are. How does this generic cross-fertilization affect the viewer? How do audiences make sense of these two genres in tandem? What meanings of the genres do they see at play within the show? What historical predecessors are linked to the program within both genres? How do these genres establish a framework of understanding for *The Simpsons* that impacts how the show has been figured as a cultural object? By looking at the critical discourse and press coverage of the show's emergence, we can address these questions and point to the larger consequences of the program's generic mixing in action. Specifically, I will focus on the ramifications of the show's generic processes as they concern issues of cultural hierarchies, implications of target audience, codes of realism, and notions of parody. In exploring the discourses circulating around the emergence of *The Simpsons*, I am not offering a detailed reception study per se but instead engage in a contextual analysis of the program's circulation and larger cultural life beyond the text itself. Thus my use of critics and press commentaries is not meant to stand in for the audience at large but rather to point out how the program became activated within broader cultural circulation. Audience members might have drawn upon these contextual frameworks, but I am not arguing that they necessarily are typical of broader reading strategies.[4]

Critics regularly label *The Simpsons* a sitcom first and foremost. As advertising executive Betsy Frank suggests. "[T]hat's absolutely all that it is—a situation comedy that happens to be animated" (quoted in Williams). But what specific visions of this wide-ranging genre are put forward? The press discourse surrounding the program regularly evokes the domestic family sitcom tradition: television critic Tom Shales calls the Simpson family "the flip, dark side of the Nelsons, the Andersons, the Bradys and all other sitcom families from the dawn of television" ("The Primest Time").[5] A celebration of the program in *Time* magazine suggests that the family "seem[s] to be a typical sitcom family—the Honeymooners with kids, the Flintstones in suburbia—with typically outlandish dilemmas to face and resolve each week" ("Simpsons Forever!"). Another critic specifically notes the antecedent of *The Simpsons*'s hometown: "When *The Simpsons* first went on the air, viewers and critics alike were surprised that the show had exhumed one of television's hoariest formulas: a sitcom, albeit animated, about a blue-collar family living in a standard-brand American suburb, and not just any old suburb but a town called Springfield, just like the locale of *Father Knows Best,* the blithely Utopian sitcom of the 1950s" (Morgenstern). Some contemporary sitcom examples also stand in opposition to *The Simpsons:* "The slightly skewed perspective of *The Simpsons* makes them a far more human and believable family than such carefully conceived, endlessly responsible TV facsimiles as the Huxtables, the Keatons, et al." (Lewis).[6]

This family sitcom ancestry is echoed in quotations from production personnel: creator Matt Groening noted, "[A]t an early age I was most strongly affected by *Leave It to Beaver* and *Ozzie and Harriet. [The Simpsons]* is my

skewed reaction to those shows." Even as he asserts the importance of these previous sources, Groening asserts the show's violations of the genre's conventions:
"[T]he show has all the elements of its live-action family-oriented prototypes,
with a twist" (quoted in Mason).[7] Specifically, Groening notes that, unlike the
sitcom tradition of limited numbers of characters and settings, the show's animated form gives the writers and animators freedom to open the genre outward
from the typical domestic setting. Thus he suggests that the show is "a halluci-
nation of a sitcom" or "a sitcom, but there's no 'sit' " (quoted in O'Connor; see
also Clark). As I will discuss below, the specifics of the show's blending complicate easy definitions of a single generic tradition.

Other critics specifically link *The Simpsons* to a more recent trend within
the domestic sitcom genre. While wholesome programs like *The Cosby Show*
and *Family Ties* were among the genre's most popular incarnations in the
1980s, the most successful new sitcoms of the late eighties and early nineties
constituted a backlash against this vision of the successful and happy American family. Typically, critics pointed to the highly popular (and controversial)
triumvirate of *Married . . . with Children, Roseanne,* and *The Simpsons* as representing "a new development of the situation comedy. Each program . . .
focuses on a family marked by visual styles and characterization as bleak and
miserable as those of former TV families had been handsome or cheerful"
(Ozersky 11; see also Berkman). One *TV Guide* reader characterized this phenomenon more aptly than any critic by suggesting that such "antifamily" backlash is typical whenever "there's an abundance of family sitcoms"—whether it
is *Roseanne* as a response to *Growing Pains* in the 1980s or *The Addams Family* and *The Munsters* turning the 1960s family into literal monsters (see Pierce).

Critics also focus on *The Simpsons*'s place within the genre of television
animation or cartoons. The discursive difference between "animation" and
"cartoon" is significant. "Animation" works as a fairly neutral term, connot-
ing a technological process and visual technique. "Cartoon," on the other hand,
is more loaded, implying predominantly a children's (or childish) audience,
whimsical content, and questionable social value, having been linked to notions
of Saturday morning cartoons since the 1960s. Thus even though critics regularly use the term *cartoon* to describe *The Simpsons,* they often have to qualify it with additional markers of legitimacy or clarification. Hence critics label
the show a "cartoon family show," a "half-hour adult cartoon series," "the
most multilayered cartoon since *Rocky & Bullwinkle*," and "more than a cartoon, it's TV's most intelligent comedy" (Zoglin, "The Fox Trots Faster";
David; "From Toddlers to Teens"; Siegel). Clearly, critics are working against
dominant meanings of cartoons as just "kid's stuff" and unsophisticated entertainment by citing the show's intelligence and quality in the face of the low
expectations of the cartoon genre.

Critics point to how the show successfully aspires to levels generally
reserved for live-action programming to counter the traditional hierarchy that
places all things live over all things animated. One critic labels the show "a
prime-time cartoon series that's livelier and more vividly human than most live-
action shows" (Morgenstern). Another dismisses the question "too much fuss

over a cartoon show?" by citing the show's openness to "interpretive calisthenics," its high level of "topical satire," and numerous "cultural references," all attributes that legitimate the program in the face of cultural stigmas against animation (Shales, "*The Simpsons:* They're Scrapping Again"). Even an adolescent audience member asserts this hierarchy by denying the show's cartoonishness: "It's not really like a cartoon . . . but that makes it better" (Shakia Jackson quoted in Anderson). However, the cartoon's pejorative qualities and low cultural status are never far from the surface, as one critic describes the show's wild success and ensuing controversy and notes, "[T]he whole thing's totally improbable: we're talking about a half-hour cartoon" (Waters, "Family Feuds").

We do see an indication of these hierarchies' origins within press discourse as well. One *USA Today* article interviews animation historian Charles Solomon regarding the success of *The Simpsons* with all age groups:

> We tend to forget that what we think of as the great cartoons—the Warner Brothers cartoons of the '40s and '50s, the Disney cartoons of the '30s—were made for general audiences and could appeal to the most sophisticated member of the audience as well as the least. During the '60s and '70s, animation became stereotyped as a children's medium because of Saturday morning, which was a distortion. There's always been a big audience for animation, and this is one of the first projects that's been sophisticated enough in its approach to once again appeal to adults as well as to children. (Quoted in Shahid, "*The Simpsons*")

Solomon's argument has been borne out, as numerous other animated programs followed *The Simpsons* to succeed with an adult audience (*Beavis & Butthead, Dr. Katz, King of the Hill,* and *South Park*). The rise of the Cartoon network as a highly successful twenty-four-hour exhibition site of animated programming, airing the very same animated shows that were once stigmatized as "just" children's programming on Saturday morning, further suggests the constitutive role of industrial practices in defining a genre's audience.[8]

The Simpsons is often explicitly contrasted with Saturday morning programming. One critic praises *The Simpsons* compared to a characterization of the genre in 1990; "cartoons are either toy-oriented syndicated strips or huggable Saturday morning specials where a real crisis occurs when a bear loses his sweater" (Horn). Groening echoes these sentiments: "[I]f there's anything this show has to overcome, it's adults considering it just another one of those crummy cartoons on TV" (quoted in Schefelman). Just as he cites *Ozzie & Harriet* as a formative text for *The Simpsons,* he names *Rocky & Bullwinkle* and other Jay Ward programs (like *George of the Jungle*) as the only previous examples of successful television cartoons to combine animated form and sophisticated humor (Anderson). *The Flintstones* and *The Jetsons,* prime-time animated sitcoms, are often mentioned as key predecessors, but *The Simpsons* is generally held up as more sophisticated and critical of both its sitcom and animated form, "an anti-*Flintstones* cartoon" (Reese).[9] Thus while the show draws on a wide range of sitcom ancestors as satirical fodder, it has a more distant relationship with most previous cartoons.

The show's creators offer a number of textual instances of *The Simpsons* working against cartoon traditions. Executive producer James L. Brooks notes some of the benefits of the animated form, such as the ease of changing "locations" and including many characters, but adds, "[D]ucks won't talk . . . But little girls will play great blues on the saxophone! And women will have their money hidden in their hair" (quoted in Shales, "The Primest Time"). Thus while the world portrayed on *The Simpsons* refuses to violate certain codes of realism, it does take advantage of its animated form in ways that a live-action show simply could not manage or afford. Groening further suggests, "[T]here's a rule in drawing *The Simpsons* that they can never go cross-eyed, like all those cartoon characters on Saturday morning" (quoted in Morgenstern). Elsewhere, he remarks that "we're the only cartoon show where, when people hit the ground, they actually get bruised and bloody" (quoted in Brioux).[10] Finally, he points to other typical genre conventions that *The Simpsons* violates: "[T]he characters' heads do not get crushed by anvils. Their eyeballs do not pop out of their heads, and their jaws do not drop to the ground. Also, we have no laugh track" (quoted in Schefelman).[11] Thus Groening suggests how the show ignores particular conventions of both animation and sitcom genres.[12]

The key exception to the rules Groening and Brooks offer is, of course, the show's cartoon within the cartoon, *The Itchy & Scratchy Show*. A direct parody of *Tom & Jerry* as well as other classic chase cartoons, *Itchy & Scratchy* works to bring the cartoon's generic conventions to the forefront, highlighting how *The Simpsons* as a whole abandons them. Paul Cantor offers a compelling explanation:

> If you are going to distinguish a cartoon within a cartoon, you must raise its cartoonicity to a higher power. In *Itchy & Scratchy*, anything that is not pure cartoon has been ruthlessly stripped away to leave us facing the meaningless and gratuitous violence that is the quintessence of cartoon. . . . The total flatness of the cat-and-mouse world gives a rounded quality to the world of the Simpson family, and the humans no longer seem quite so cartoonish.

Cantor's analysis points to the strategic use of certain generic conventions within *Itchy & Scratchy* that not only allow it to parody typical cartoons but further separate *The Simpsons* as a whole from the connotative links to mindless children's entertainment that the cartoon genre has accrued over the years on television.

The case of *Itchy & Scratchy* points us toward important issues of parody and genre mixing. Before getting into the specificities of parody and *The Simpsons,* we should consider the ways in which critics frame the program as a generic mixture. As already suggested, critics often point to the show's dual generic identity, but we should consider how they see the dual genres in relation to one another. Not surprisingly, the sitcom is noted more as the *object* of the show's satire, while the animated form becomes the *vehicle* for undermining the more typical sitcom genre. One critic called *The Simpsons* "the Antichrist of television sit-coms, with no surrender to tedious convention. The animated form unshackled the producers and opened the series to wild flights of irreverent fantasy" (Carman). Critics also note the simultaneous rebellion against typical animation techniques as well: "[T]he script is wickedly anti-sitcom; the animation is viciously unDisneylike" (Lichfield). Another critic notes its violation of both genres: "[S]ophisticated and satirical dialogue ensures that the humour is not typical of a cartoon series and unlike other cartoons, the characters are not cute and lovable. The producers deliberately avoided a 'sitcom' feel and the script has been described as, 'like Woody Allen writing for the Road Runner'" (Hetherington).

The two major effects of the show's generic mixture concern the breadth of the show's target audience and the paradox of realism. The issues of target audience and genre are explicitly and inextricably linked—genres are often defined (especially industrially) by whom their audiences are surmised to be, such as soap operas as dramas for house-wives or sports as magnets that deliver men to advertisers. The sitcom traditionally has been a mass format that appeals to all demographic groupings; the domestic sitcom has been specifically framed as entertainment "for the whole family." The genre has often been more targeted than this—think of the early 1970s rise of urban "quality" sitcoms (like *All in the Family* and *Mary Tyler Moore*) as part of the turn toward a younger, more urban, and more affluent audience than the rural fans of *The Beverly Hillbillies* and *Green Acres*. But there is no traditional linkage of the sitcom as a whole with any narrow group beyond general notions of "family entertainment."

The cartoon has been far more bound to specific audiences in its history on television, with the genre clearly marked as children's programming. As the earlier quotation from Solomon suggests, however, this has not always been the case. The same animated short films that entertained mass audiences in 1930s, 1940s, and 1950s cinemas became redefined as "kid's stuff" following the industrial shifts that took shorts out of theaters in the 1950s and onto Saturday morning television in the 1960s. There is nothing inherently "childish" about the animation genre in terms of textual form—most cartoons from this era were created for adult senses of humor and contain many references that sail above children's heads. But the genre and the Warner Bros. (among other studios) animated texts that found themselves in both of these two contrasting eras of animation took on new meanings through these industrial practices.[13] Hence we must look to the genre's assumed appropriate audiences in the discourses of industrial practices that place shows on the television schedule and commentators and critics who work to situate programming within frameworks of comprehension for their readership.

The Simpsons, as noted in nearly every mention of the program in 1990, was the first network prime-time cartoon since *The Flintstones* shifted to Saturday mornings in 1966.[14] Groening often relates the troubles of getting a prime-time cartoon on the air, as network executives were reluctant to target only kids but also assumed that adults would not watch a cartoon. He was given his chance primarily because Brooks had a successful track record, and Fox's fringe position in the late 1980s allowed it to take significant risks in hopes of unexpected payoffs. Additionally, in the late 1980s Groening had introduced the characters in short segments on *The Tracey Ullman Show* (Fox), a program with a narrow but dedicated following among a sophisticated adult audience. *The Simpsons* debuted on Sunday nights at 8:30 eastern standard time, a time slot that Shales suggests is typically conducive to "family fare" more than any other night of the week ("The Primest Time"). *The Simpsons* succeeded beyond all expectations, providing Fox with its first top ten ratings hit and crossing demographic boundaries to reach "a huge and still-expanding audience of little kids, trend-wise teens and hip adults" (Morgenstern). The program had a huge initial college following and successfully merchandised to children and adults alike (Cary; Ozersky 11).

As is now clear, the program transcended the expectations of the cartoon genre, reaching the broad-based audience more typical of the sitcom.[15] But how did critics make sense of the show in terms of its target audience? Most reviewers insisted that *The Simpsons* was intelligent, clever, and sophisticated, moving the program away from typical preconceptions about animation. As the show progressed, ratings and widespread merchandising demonstrated that the program was drawing a significant audience among young children as well, prompting a quick backlash. People who opposed the show's cynicism, satiric edge, or representations of Bart's mischief critiqued the reasons that kids were watching. One editorial argued, "*The Simpsons* is really an adult program whose cynical message appeals to people bored with conventional programs on other channels. Because the program is a cartoon and is broadcast early in the evening, it attracts many children" ("Bad Bart"). This editorial draws upon generic assumptions tied to animation to critique the show's "adult" content and representations of disruptive children and troubled families, implying that cartoons should stick to their place—fringe programming times and unchallenging, non-confrontational content.

More enthusiastic critics offered differing views for the show's popularity with kids: "*The Simpsons* is an unusual-for-TV, kid's-eye-view of the world, managing to tap genuine emotions and experiences, from violent video games to the euphoria of learning that school's been canceled by the season's first heavy snow. Yes, this is that rare series about kids that is written by people you can envision actually having been kids" (Rosenberg). *Newsweek*'s Harry Waters offered, "[T]here's little mystery to why the saga of the Simpsons enthralls the young. The series shamelessly panders to a kid's-eye view of the world: parents dispense dopey advice, school is a drag and happiness can be attained only by subverting the system." He goes on to suggest that children view the program as "real," a position that he juxtaposes with more adult views of the program as hip and sophisticated. Another critic summed it up by arguing that the show "appeals to kids who like cartoons, to intellectuals who like satire . . . and to thugs who like a troublemaking hero" (Hughes).

Even as critics looked for ways to explain the show's appeal to diverse audiences, Groening insisted that they were writing for adults, not kids. He went on to assert the particular brand of family entertainment that *The Simpsons* offered: "I like to think it's something that's going to be family entertainment in a new sense. It's going to offer something for every member of the family, depending upon whatever level they're going to meet the show. Adults are going to enjoy the witty dialogue and the funny story turns and kids are going to enjoy some of the wild sight gags" (quoted in Clark). Brooks similarly noted that "we finally found out what 'family entertainment' is, or should be. I've sat there watching the show with my folks and my young children and we all laughed at different things. I like that" (quoted in Shales, "*The Simpsons: They're Scrapping Again*"). Clearly, the show's producers conceived of a broad audience, even if they were (at least initially) aiming for the adults and were happy to pick up the kids without effort.

But while Fox was certainly ecstatic to be able to reach such a broad audience, enabling the fledgling network to establish itself as a legitimate contender, *The Simpsons*'s broad reach spurred a number of controversies. The program debuted to critical praise and high ratings but soon became the target of critics and commentators who decried the show's "antifamily" content and questioned this prime-time cartoon's suitability for children. The show's success generated a wave of marketing and merchandising, but just as Bart Simpson T-shirts became ubiquitous in elementary schools across the United States, new debates emerged as to whether "Underachiever and Proud of It" was an appropriate slogan for American youth, leading to school bans and public outcry.[16] Given these critical discussions surrounding the show's audience base, what are the linkages between these controversies, the program's assumed target audiences, and the role of genre in the cultural life of *The Simpsons*?

Notions of the "proper" audience for a given program, as often tied to the show's genre, are cited and mobilized in a variety of ways to further specific positions surrounding such cultural controversies. Thus the above-quoted anti-*Simpsons* editorial cites the "cartoon-for-kids" assumption to criticize the show's rebellious characterizations and cynical attitude as inappropriate. Another writer suggests that the program is primarily a satirical critique of family politics and that his kids "misinterpret" the show as a celebration of Bart's actions; thus their cartooncentric appeals are "misplaced," even though the show's adult appeals are held up as admirable (Tommy Dentine quoted in Glynn 66–67). Finally, a mother of a child whose school banned Bart T-shirts directly criticizes the controversy in generic terms: "They're blowing it way out of proportion. It's only a cartoon . . . To me, it's comical" ("Principal Expels Bart Simpson"). For this viewer, the show's genre serves to locate the program both as appropriate for children and as not worthy of "serious" cultural consideration.

As these three examples demonstrate, there is nothing inherent in the genre to suggest that cartoons have particular meanings, appeals to audiences, or even proper viewers. They each use the same claim to "cartoonishness" to further quite different arguments. Since *The Simpsons* is often labeled a cartoon and thus appropriate viewing for kids, viewers can alternately use these assumptions to support both adult anxiety over the show's rebellious attitude and the perceived ridiculousness of this anxiety over what is culturally positioned as an "insignificant" form of entertainment. Viewers and critics use the generic history of animation and its ensuing linkages with children's programming to situate the program within hierarchies of taste and cultural value. Just as some voices label *The Simpsons* a cartoon to call for greater industrial responsibility in targeting its assumed childish audience, others use the low cultural value of animation to dismiss moral concerns over such an inherently unrealistic and fantastic (and therefore culturally harmless) genre.[17] But this latter notion of "only a cartoon" needs to be expanded on more fully, as numerous critics and audience members highlight the show's realism—a trait that seems to directly contradict dismissive remarks about the irrelevance of a cartoon—as one of the defining and pleasurable features of *The Simpsons* as a generic mixture.

As suggested in this essay's epigraphs, there is a certain ironic paradox in *The Simpsons*'s "realistic" vision of the American family as achieved through the traditionally antirealist mode of animation. In discussing the notion of realism concerning *The Simpsons,* I use the term not as an uncritical and uncontested concept but as a marker of struggle that audiences, industries, and critics mobilize to further their points. Realism has long been a topic of debate within media studies, as the term is marked by both a variety of definitions and assumed ideological impacts. Rather than arguing whether the show is realistic or not, I examine the ways discourses of realism became articulated to the cartoon genre surrounding *The Simpsons,* as critics point to this paradox as key to the show's success. In discussing Barbara Bush's negative reaction to the program, one critic calls the show an "all-too-real TV cartoon series" (Radcliffe). Shales notes that "they are funny-mirror reflections of what's weird and askew in American society, characters who have achieved a level of affection beyond that of most sitcoms performed by mere mortals" ("*The Simpsons:* They're Scrapping Again"). Another critic suggests that "the animation disguises the fact that it consists of what we laughingly call in TV 'adult humor.' It is the most serious program we have about family relationships, the decline of education, the failure of parents, and the fact that kids today are no damn good" (Kitman). Perhaps most interestingly of all, a survey of schoolchildren in Australia voted *The Simpsons* "the most realistic program on TV after the news" (Flew 19).

This paradox of animated realism becomes more explicit when *The Simpsons* is compared to other live-action programs. One common comparison is to *The Cosby Show,* specifically motivated by Fox's decision to program *The Simpsons* directly opposite *The Cosby Show* in the 1990 fall schedule. This clear juxtaposition—between a live-action family that embodies nearly impossible to realize economic achievements (especially exceptional for an African-American family) and few real-life counterparts and an animated family whose socioeconomic situation and emotional tenor looked more real to viewers—provoked numerous commentaries. "Johnny Carson observed in a monologue that even though the idealized Huxtables on *The Cosby Show* are played by flesh-and-blood humans and the Simpsons are mere cartoon characters, *The Simpsons* seems more realistic. Family life at the Simpson home probably reminds more families of their own households than do the relatively homogenized antics of the Huxtable clan" (Shales, "*The Simpsons:* They're Scrapping Again"). Similarly, an article quotes a street vendor selling bootlegged Bart T-shirts: "*Cosby* is the way it is supposed to be. *The Simpsons* is the way it really is—that's life" (Walters). Thus even though some of the cartoonish goings-on in Springfield might be somewhat unpredictable and unusual, many found the perfect family life of a black doctor and lawyer more inexplicable in contemporary American culture.

The Simpsons is also described as more real than its cohort of "antifamily" sitcoms in the early-1990s. "Gross and funny in roughly equal measure, *Married . . . With Children* turns the TV family into a vicious cartoon. *The Simpsons,* a real cartoon, is actually much closer to recognizable human life" (Zoglin, "Home" 86). Another critic similarly suggests that *Married's* Bundys, "like all sitcom characters, aspire to the televisual purity of cartoon characters, but are stuck in rubbery bags of protoplasm with nothing but one-liners and a laugh track to hide behind. The Simpsons, oddly, are freer than other TV families to act human" (Ozersky 14). Groening himself points to *Married's* more outrageous "cartoonish" take on the family while claiming that *The Simpsons* moves away from outrageousness in exchange for "a family that is desperately trying to be normal" (quoted in Sullivan). Other critics compare *The Simpsons* to *Roseanne* as well and conclude that the animated family is more revealing and realistic than the Conners (Elm; Berkman 68–69). But how might we explain this seeming paradox of a cartoon being hailed as highly realistic, in spite of the genre's strong tradition of violating codes of realism?

Groening points to certain strategies that the producers employ in creating *The Simpsons:* "I think the show delivers on our goal, which is to tell stories that people can connect to, that are funny and actually have some sort of emotional resonance you don't expect in a cartoon. We don't go for laughs for laughs' sake; we really are trying to tell stories that make you forget from time to time you're watching a cartoon" (quoted in Rense 106). Executive producer Sam Simon credits James Brooks for his "marching orders to do a show based on the emotional inner lives of its cartoon characters, and that's really never been done before" (Schembri). Thus despite their animated form, the characters are as (if not more) three-dimensional as those on most sitcoms. But since they are "only cartoons," the writers can heap indignities and trauma upon them without making audiences feel bad for the characters. As Solomon suggests, "[I]f they were too real, you'd become too sympathetic and too sensitive about their feelings. But because they're obviously not real people, you can exaggerate and make things funnier without feeling any pain" (quoted in Shahid, "*The Simpsons*").

Dave Berkman furthers this argument, suggesting that unlike *Roseanne's* visual realism of working-class struggles, "there is an even more devastating reality to *The Simpsons,* one which succeeds only because, as a stylized cartoon, it is visually unreal" (69). He goes on to itemize the ways in which *The Simpsons* breaks the taboos of American television, portraying the threats of nuclear power, the negative effects of excessive television viewing, and the "deceits perpetuated by American education"—aspects of reality that can only be seen on television when rendered by a team of cartoonists. Whereas the standard sitcom traditionally reaffirms the family through its weekly restoration of equilibrium, *The Simpsons* works within its cartoon form to pose problems, more akin to those of real life, that simply cannot be solved within a half-hour. The show then regularly solves these very problems in spite of itself, demonstrating both the artificiality of the sitcom tradition and the power of animation to represent "realities" that cannot be captured in a three-camera studio or before a live audience.

One of the many examples of this dual use and abuse of the sitcom formula is the episode "King-Size Homer."[18] The far-fetched premise of this episode is that in order to qualify for disability benefits, thus allowing him to stay home instead of going to work at the nuclear power plant, Homer gains sixty-one pounds to become medically obese. Once this goal is achieved, Homer both revels in his governmentally enabled flexibility and experiences discrimination as an overweight person. Throughout the course of the episode, Homer's weight gains and subsequent treatment of his "disability" both violate the decorum of the normal sitcom and express the flexibility of the animated format to represent that which would be unfeasible for a live-action program, drawing upon the convention of cartoon size changing paradigmatically expressed in Tex Avery's *King-Size Canary*.

The show's resolution highlights (and undercuts) the sitcom's need to restore equilibrium, relocating the show firmly in the realm of the sitcom while simultaneously parodying the genre's conventions. Homer's negligence in performing his job duties from home—he goes to a movie matinee, leaving his computer terminal, which monitors the nuclear power plant's safety, unattended—causes a potential meltdown, a typical dig that questions the nuclear power industry in a way that most live-action shows could not politically sustain. He ends up saving the day by falling to his seeming death into the exploding nuclear tank, though his enlarged size gets him stuck in the tank's vent, thus sealing the rupture and averting the crisis. As Lisa notes, "I think it's ironic that Dad saved the day while a slimmer man would have fallen to his death," highlighting the typical machinations of the sitcom's pat narrative resolution. Finally, in order to restore the show's situation to its beginning equilibrium, Mr. Burns agrees to pay for a liposuction to restore Homer to his normal 239-pound size in time for next week's episode. Thus *The Simpsons* works to strategically assert the conventions of its sitcom genre while simultaneously parodying the assumptions the genre typically requires. This type of explicit generic parody and reference is typical of other episodes as well, with common allusions to the lack of continuity between episodes and the characters' loss of memory of past events.

This combination of both denial and exaggeration of the norms of the sitcom form suggests the ways in which *The Simpsons* uses parody to define itself generically. Linda Hutcheon has argued that we should look to parody not just as a textual element or formal attribute but as a "pragmatic" component of texts in their cultural encoding and decoding (*A Theory*). Thus the parodic realism of *The Simpsons* emerges not only in the text but also in the interpretative insights of critics attempting to make sense of the show. One critic notes, "[T]hey are caricatures, not just of *us*, but of us in our national delusion that the life of the sitcom family is the way things are 'supposed' to be" (McConnell 390). Similarly, another argues, "*The Simpsons* is satire. Rather than engage in the pretentious misrepresentation of family life that one finds in the 'model family' shows (from *The Donna Reed Show* to *The Cosby Show*), this program admits that most parents aren't perfect" (Rebeck). The program's realism emerges not in its adherence to norms of live-action programming but from its parodic dismantling of unreal live-action sitcom conventions.

Parody surfaces in the debate surrounding the show's legitimacy for children as well. Peggy Charren, president of Action for Children's Television, defends the show on satirical grounds; she suggests that principals who banned Bart's image from school would probably interpret Jonathan Swift's classic satire "A Modest Proposal" as a legitimate cause to worry about child abuse (Arnold). At the other extreme, a writer described how his children watched the show, unaware that it was parody. He claims that after he intervened by teaching them to understand the show's "proper" parodic framework, they stopped watching the show because they disliked thinking of the show as satire, ultimately supporting his claim that it was not well suited to children (quoted in Glynn 67). *The Simpsons*'s parody, and an audience's "failure" to interpret it as such, can serve both to argue for the show's inappropriateness for kids and to refute such age-based condemnations of the program.

Through parodic conventions such as caricature and hyperexaggeration that are typical of animation, *The Simpsons* forces us to question the codes of realism associated with live-action systems of representation. Likewise, critics point out that satire is often missed, leading to "mistaken" interpretations that may cause viewers to either enjoy or condemn the program. But in all cases, parody is held up as a legitimating trait, a sign of *The Simpsons*'s legitimacy as more than just an average cartoon. Critics note the show's satirical edge in order to legitimate the adult pleasures of the text, even if kids (or other adults) miss them. Just as the program's animated form is often tied to its lack of cultural value, its parodic take on the sitcom (and nearly every other American cultural norm) works to elevate the position of *The Simpsons* within cultural hierarchies.

This brief account of parody within the text and contexts of *The Simpsons* differs significantly from a postmodernist account of either blank parody or generic dilution. Through the show's use of parody, I contend that the discourses of genre are reiterated and foregrounded explicitly, not "flattened out" or disrupted. Of course, these enunciations of genre are often framed critically, calling the assumptions of genre into question. Whether this happens through undermining sitcom realism by highlighting the genre's artificial narrative structure or by exploding the assumptions of the cartoon through the hyperbolic violence of *Itchy & Scratchy*, *The Simpsons* does not work to *destroy* generic codes but to *highlight* their cultural circulation and common currency among the show's media-saturated audience. By calling attention to these generic assumptions and mocking cultural conventions, the show can certainly serve as a site of opposition, treating traditionally marginalized topics (from problems of nuclear power to a "realistic" nuclear family) and questioning the very media system that circulates the show (as demonstrated most pervasively in the unusual episode "The Simpsons Spin-off Showcase").[19] Thus the animated form of *The Simpsons* enables a critical take on the sitcom genre, probably the most conventional and mainstream television genre.

But just as our approach to genre necessitates examinations of the specificities of individual instances and contextual circulation, we need to avoid sweeping generalizations about parody "always" leading to opposition, co-optation, or postmodernism. Parody must be regarded as a historical and contextual mode of production and reception, in addition to its more common textual conceptions. We must also recognize how parody can work to support more dominant and traditional notions of television culture. Jonathan Culler aptly points out how genre parody can further dominant meanings even in the face of seeming "oppositional" content. He argues that "pseudo-parody" can create the illusion of resistive critique of the ideological conventions of a genre, providing readers an oppositional position in relation to the conventions of the form. But often this mode of parody serves only to "forestall a possible objection" for the reader, establishing a level of goodwill with an audience to create the sense of opposition, even as the text works to reassert the norms of the parodied genre (Culler 148–52). Thus many viewers have commented that while *The Simpsons* mocks the norms of the sitcom genre, ultimately the show contains the same level of sentimentality and "family values" of the shows it allegedly satires. I do not wish to resolve this debate between "real" or illusionary oppositional content and *The Simpsons* here—such arguments need to be supported by research and analysis aimed more at this particular question than my generic inquiry. Rather, I want to point to the problems with sweeping claims of a genre's (or genre parody's) inherently oppositional content or attitude. Such generalizations are one of the central reasons why genre analysis has fostered such a bad reputation within contemporary media studies.

I have not resolved the paradox of this essay's epigraphs: if *The Simpsons* is figured as quite "realistic," can it be "just a cartoon"? I would argue that *The Simpsons* does work as both realistic animation and just a cartoon. By looking at the ways in which *The Simpsons* has been linked to generic codes of realism, notions of cultural validity, and assumptions of target audience, we can see how the discourses surrounding a program work to locate new cultural phenomena within already extant hierarchies of cultural norms and values. *The Simpsons* was figured as "just a cartoon" by those wishing to dismiss its cultural value or positioned as inappropriate to the cartoon genre in order to question its legitimacy for children. Other critics hailed the show's parodic take on the sitcom as "realistic" and therefore "quality" television, working against the normally held cultural conception of animation as children's programming. For these critics, animation was the generic addition that, ironically, enabled *The Simpsons* to be the era's most effective and realistic critique of the live-action sitcom. Thus even though traditionally cartoons have figured low on cultural hierarchies, in the case of *The Simpsons* the animation genre worked to raise the program above the ordinary sitcom and critique that conventional genre's vaunted place within American culture.

In my account of genre and *The Simpsons,* I have demonstrated how generic terms, definitions, and meanings serve as a discursive framework for the program's cultural comprehension. Assumptions about animation and family sitcoms situate the program within hierarchies and systems of power relations that impact the show's reception and the ensuing controversies that emerged. But it would be a mistake to regard this generic framework as fixed or static. Just as the show is positioned within already extant generic codes and discourses, *The Simpsons* and its circulation have worked to reconstitute and change the very generic notions that were partially formative of its initial cultural understanding. The success of the show with adults, partially overcoming the stigmas of animation's "childish" audience, have somewhat eroded these notions. We can see the effects of this generic shift most dramatically in industrial practices, as numerous successful adult animated sitcoms have followed *The Simpsons,* from Fox's similar family sitcom *King of the Hill* to the even more adult targeted cable programming of *Beavis & Butthead* and *South Park.*

But the generic assumptions of animation have not simply disappeared in the wake of *The Simpsons,* as both *Beavis & Butthead* and *South Park* have been embroiled in similar controversies surrounding the programs' appropriateness for a children's audience that is assumed to be the "natural" target of animation. What these instances indicate most clearly is that an account of genre is necessary to understand how audiences and industries make sense of these mixed and parodic programs, and thus we cannot simply apply the rubric of the "postmodern" and deny the show's generic markers. While "postmodernist" may be a compelling categorization of this program textually, we must look beyond the text to see how cultural discourses in a variety of realms work to articulate and constitute generic assumptions and conventions that may work against tenets of postmodern criticism. The discursive hierarchies that are linked to both the sitcom and animation are accrued over time and constantly undergoing reformation. Additionally and most importantly, the site of genre definition and meaning is not intrinsic to the media text. Genres are formed within the dynamic interactions between texts, industries, audiences, and historical contexts, not statically embedded within programs. Thus if our goal is to understand the cultural life of a program like *The Simpsons* and contemporary media culture, we must critically explore the shifts and implications of its genres as discursive processes found in the interactions between these spheres of media practice. If we are to better understand the complex operations of television programs like *The Simpsons* within contemporary society, we must look beyond the media text and explore the contextual relationships and issues like genre that constitute a show's "cultural life."

Notes

1. Note that parody is another hallmark of animated cartoons. For further discussion on parody in animation, see Crafton, "The View from Termite Terrace."

2. Collins implicitly suggests this in his discussion of *Twin Peaks;* see Cohen, "Do Postmodern Genres Exist?" for a compelling discussion and refutation of this argument.

3. This approach to media studies—examining the interrelations between industry, audience, text, and context—is drawn from D'Acci; see also Hall; Johnson.

4. For discussions of critical discourses and reception studies, see Staiger; Klinger.

5. Shales's quote refers to *Ozzie & Harriet's* Nelson family, *Father Knows Best's* Anderson family, and *The Brady Bunch* as *The Simpsons's* sitcom forefamilies from the 1950s and 1960s.

6. The Huxtables inhabited *The Cosby Show* and the Keatons were on *Family Ties,* two highly successful 1980s family sitcoms.

7. Similarly, Groening has been widely quoted as calling *The Simpsons* a "mutant Ozzie and Harriet" (see Ozersky 11).

8. I explore this case study in further depth in Mittell, "Telegenres."

9. This is not to say that *The Flintstones* was thought of as safe children's entertainment in the 1960s; I am merely using critical references to the show in the 1990s to provide a contrast with *The Simpsons.*

10. Note that exceptions to this certainly do emerge, such as Homer's noted trait of being nearly impervious to physical harm, especially head injuries.

11. The lack of laugh track is notable, as previous prime-time cartoons such as *The Flintstones* and *The Jetsons* had adopted the sitcom convention of the laugh track, even though they were clearly not "filmed before a live studio audience."

12. For a compelling argument as to how various conventions of typical cartoons such as "stretch & squash" came to be the dominant mode of animation, see Thompson.

13. I deal with this shift in industrial practice concerning the cartoon genre more fully in Mittell, "Telegenres."

14. *The Flintstones* remained on the air in Saturday morning and syndicated reruns; new variations occasionally appeared on Saturday morning.

15. Note that many articles suggest that the show did have an unusually high following among children as compared to other family sitcoms.

16. For accounts of these controversies, see Glynn; Fiske.

17. See Snead (84–85) for an account of animation's "rhetoric of harmlessness."

18. *The Simpsons,* "King-Size Homer," originally aired November 5, 1995. While I have focused on the discursive circulation that surrounded *The Simpsons* in the early 1990s, this midseries episode is representative of typical generic practices used throughout the series' run.

19. *The Simpsons,* "The Simpsons Spin-off Showcase," originally aired May 11, 1997.

Works Cited

Allen, Robert C. "Bursting Bubbles: 'Soap Opera,' Audiences, and the Limits of Genre." *Remote Control: Television, Audiences, and Cultural Power.* Ed. Ellen Seiter, Hans Borchers, Gabriele Kreutzner, and Eva-Maria Warth. New York: Routledge, 1989, 44–55.

Altman, Rick *Film/Genre.* London: BFI, 1999.

Anderson, John. "Cool Cartoon Causes Kooky Craze." *Newsday* 5 March 1990: B4.

Arnold, David. "Bart a Class Act?" *Boston Globe* 13 October 1990: 1.

"Bad Bart." *Boston Globe* 17 October 1990: 18.

Berkman, Dave. "Sitcom Reality." *Television Quarterly* 26.4 (1993): 63–69.

Brioux, Bill. "Keeping up with *The Simpsons.*" *TV Guide* 29 March 1997.

Caldwell, John Thornton. *Televisuality: Style, Crisis, and Authority in American Television.* New Brunswick, NJ: Rutgers UP, 1995.

Cantor, Paul A. "In Praise of Television: The Greatest TV Show Ever." *American Enterprise* September 1997: 34–37.

Carman, John. "Don't Have a Cow! TV Hit Few Highs." *San Francisco Chronicle* 30 December 1990: 46.

Cary, Alice. "Big Fans on Campus." *TV Guide* 18 April 1992: 26–31.

Clark, Kenneth R. "*The Simpsons* Proves Cartoons Not Just for Kids." *Chicago Tribune TV Week* 14 January 1990: 3.

Cohen, Ralph. "Do Postmodern Genres Exist?" *Postmodern Genres.* Ed. Marjorie Perloff. Norman: U of Oklahoma P, 1988. 11–27.

———. "History and Genre." *New Literary History* 17.2 (1986): 203–18.

Collins, Jim. "Postmodernism and Television." *Channels of Discourse, Reassembled.* Ed. Robert C. Allen. Chapel Hill: U of North Carolina P, 1992. 327–53.

Crafton, Donald. *Before Mickey: The Animated Film, 1898–1928.* Rev. ed. Chicago: U of Chicago P, 1993.

———. "The View from Termite Terrace: Caricature and Parody in Warner Bros. Animation." *Film History* 5.2 (1993): 204–30.

Culler, Jonathan. *Structuralist Poetics: Structuralism, Linguistics, and the Study of Literature.* Ithaca, NY: Cornell UP, 1975.

D'Acci, Julie. *Defining Women: Television and the Case of Cagney & Lacey.* Chapel Hill: U of North Carolina P, 1994.

David, Hugh. "Cartoon Kickback on the Sidewalk." *Independent* 29 July 1990: 17.

Elm, Joanna. "Are the Simpsons America's TV Family of the '90s?" *TV Guide* 17 March 1990: 7–8.

Fiske, John. *Media Matters: Everyday Culture and Political Change.* Minneapolis: U of Minnesota P, 1994.

Flew, Terry. "*The Simpsons:* Culture, Class and Popular TV." *Metro Magazine* 97 (1994): 14–19.

"From Toddlers to Teens." *TV Guide* 2 March 1991: 6–15.

Glynn, Kevin. "Bartmania: The Social Reception of an Unruly Image." *Camera Obscura* 38 (1996): 60–91.

Hall, Stuart. "Encoding, Decoding." *The Cultural Studies Reader.* Ed. Simon During. New York: Routledge, 1993. 90–103.

Henry, Matthew. "The Triumph of Popular Culture: Situation Comedy, Postmodernism and *The Simpsons.*" *Studies in Popular Culture* 17 (1994): 85–99.

Hetherington, Lesley. "Here Comes *The Simpsons.*" *Green Guide* February 1991.

Horn, John. "*The Simpsons,* from the Maker of *Life in Hell,* Offers a Twist on Cartoons." *Associated Press* 10 January 1990.

Hughes, Mike. "Groening: Life in the Big Leagues." *Gannett News Service,* 29 July 1990.

Hutcheon, Linda. *A Poetics of Postmodernism.* New York: Routledge, 1988.

———. *A Theory of Parody: The Teachings of 20th- Century Art Forms.* New York: Methuen, 1985.

Jameson, Fredric. *Postmodernism or, the Cultural Logic of Late Capitalism.* Durham, NC: Duke UP, 1991.

Johnson, Richard. "What Is Cultural Studies Anyway?" *Social Text* 6.16 (1987): 38–80.

Kitman, Marvin. "That Quirky Simpsons Spark *The Simpsons.*" *Newsday* 6 December 1990: 85.

Klinger, Barbara. *Melodrama and Meaning: History, Culture, and the Films of Douglas Sirk.* Bloomington: Indiana UP, 1994.

Lewis, Randy. "Let's Give the Kids a Break on the Bart Simpson T-Shirts, OK?" *Los Angeles Times* 13 May 1990: 55D.

Lichfield, John. "Giving New Meaning to Family Viewing." *Independent* 8 July 1990: 11.

Mason, M. S. "*Simpsons* Creator on Poking Fun." *Christian Science Monitor* 17 April 1998: B7.

McConnell, Frank. "'Real' Cartoon Characters." *Commomecal* 15 June 1990: 389– 90.

Mittell, Jason. "A Cultural Approach to Television Genre Theory." *Cinema Journal* forthcoming 2001.

———. "Telegenres: Television Genres as Cultural Categories." Ph.D. diss., U of Wisconsin, 2000.

Morgenstern, Joe. "Bart Simpson's Real Father." *Los Angeles Times* 29 April 1990: 12.

Neale, Steve. "Questions of Genre." *Film Genre Reader II.* Ed. Barry Keith Grant. Austin: U of Texas P, 1995. 159–83.

O'Connor, John J. "Prime-Time Cartoon of Unbeautiful People." *New York Times* 21 February 1990: C18.

Ozersky, Josh. "TV's Anti-Families: Married . . . with Malaise." *Tikkun* 6.1 (1991): 11–14, 92–93.

Perloff, Marjorie, ed. *Postmodern Genres.* Norman: U of Oklahoma P, 1989.

Pierce, W. "Letter: Leave It to Bart." *TV Guide* 14 April 1990: 41.

"Principal Expels Bart Simpson." *Associated Press* 28 April 1990.

Radcliffe, Donnie. "Marge to Barb; Don't Have a Cow, Ma'am." *Washington Post* 12 October 1990: B1.

Rebeck, Victoria A. "Recognizing Ourselves in the Simpsons." *Christian Century* 27 June 1990: 622.

Reese, Michael. "A Mutant *Ozzie and Harriet.*" *Newsweek* 25 December 1989: 70.

Reuse, Rip. "The Mainstreaming of Matt Groening." *Emmy* August 1990: 104–08.

Rosenberg, Howard. "Bart & Family Try to Make the Grade." *Los Angeles Times* 11 October 1990: F1.

Schefelman, Dan. "Mutants Make His Nuclear Family Funny." *Newsday* 1 February 1990: 69.

Schembri, Jim. "Bart's Blues." *Age* November 1991.

Shahid, Sharon. "Hey, Dude. What Do You Think about *Simpsons?*" *USA Today* 14 June 1990: 11A.

———. "*The Simpsons:* Kids Like to Be Gross, Shock Their Parents." *USA Today* 14 June 1990: 11A.

Shales, Tom. "The Primest Time: Sunday Night Television, from *The Ed Sullivan Show* to *The Simpsons.*" *Washington Post* 11 March 1990: G1.

———. "*The Simpsons:* They're Scrapping Again—But This Time It's a Ratings Fight." *Washington Post* 11 October 1990: C1.

Siegel, Ed. "Hey, Dudes! They're Back!" *Boston Globe* 11 October 1990: 57.

"Simpsons Forever!" *Time* 2 May 1994: 77.

Snead, James. *White Screens/Black Images: Hollywood from the Dark Side.* New York: Routledge, 1994.

Staiger, Janet. *Interpreting Films: Studies in the Historical Reception of American Cinema.* Princeton, NJ: Princeton UP, 1992.

Sullivan, Jim. "Animation's Answer to the Bundys." *Boston Globe* 14 January 1990: A1.

Thompson, Kristin. "Implications of the Cel Animation Technique." *The Cinematic Apparatus.* Ed. Teresa de Lauretis and Stephen Heath. New York: St. Martin's P, 1980. 106–19.

Walters, Laurel Shaper. " 'In' T-Shirts of Bart Simpson Are out at Some Schools." *Christian Science Monitor* 27 September 1990: 14.

Waters, Harry F. "Family Feuds." *Newsweek* 23 April 1990: 58–63.

Williams, Scott. "Move over, Flintstones. *The Simpsons* Have Arrived." *Associated Press* 7 February 1990.

Zoglin, Richard. "The Fox Trots Faster." *Time* 27 August 1990: 64–67.

———. "Home Is Where the Venom Is." *Time* 16 April 1990: 85–96.

The West Wing's
Prime-Time Presidentiality
Mimesis and Catharsis in a Postmodern Romance

Trevor Parry-Giles and Shawn J. Parry-Giles

On December 13, 2000, millions of Americans turned to their television sets at 9:00 P.M. EST to view a program about politics. NBC had promised its viewers a gripping and insightful exploration of the impact of a presidential assassination attempt on senior White House staff members. Not only were these eager viewers to learn about the psychological toll of presidential assassinations, but they were also to experience, as they did every week, a behind-the-scenes glimpse of life in *The West Wing*.

Those viewers may have been disappointed when the presidential politics of *The West Wing* were replaced by the "real" politics of Campaign 2000. Instead of the soothing, surrogate presidency of Josiah Bartlet, these viewers heard the compelling oratory of Vice President Al Gore and Texas Governor George W. Bush as they responded to the Supreme Court's decree ending the Florida recount. The strange coincidence of December 13, 2000, when the quest for the presidency preempted the dramatic exercise of power in *The West Wing*, points to the powerful collusion of "reality" and "fiction" in contemporary U.S. political culture. Indeed, Americans are increasingly finding fictionalized representations of presidents and the presidency in literature, film, and on television.[1] These fictionalized presidents regularly engage serious issues and define presidential leadership in powerful and meaningful ways, reflecting the cultural preoccupation with this institution and its place in our national culture.[2]

The presidency is an institution created by Article II of the Constitution, which has evolved over more than two centuries, but neither its institutionality nor its history fully defines what the presidency means. The nature of presidential leadership and the relationship between presidents and their publics

Trevor Parry-Giles and Shawn J. Parry-Giles, "*The West Wing*'s Prime-Time Presidentiality: Mimesis and Catharsis in Postmodern Romance." From *Quarterly Journal of Speech,* No. 88 (May 2002), pp. 209–227. Reprinted by permission of Taylor & Francis Ltd. (http://www.tandf.co.uk/journals).

demand attention to the discourses about the executive branch that circulate outside political campaigns, the news, and the academy.

We articulate and define a construct that we title "presidentiality,"[3] which speaks to the larger political and cultural understanding of the presidency. *By presidentiality, we refer to an ideological rhetoric that helps shape and order the cultural meaning of the institution of the presidency.* Presidentiality is an amalgam of different voices and divergent texts that use as a referent the office of President of the United States and the individuals who hold that office. Presidentiality, thus, is responsive to context and collective memory and it defines, in part, the national community by offering a vision of this central office in the U.S. political system.

Because popular culture is a significant voice in U.S. political culture, we examine how *The West Wing* (*TWW*), a one-hour NBC television drama about the fictional presidency of Josiah Bartlet, manifests a specific presidentiality.[4] *TWW* occurs at a historical moment when the presidency and its meaning are in flux. Richard W. Waterman et al. contend that "There are indeed serious problems with the state of the presidency as we come to the end of the twentieth century."[5] Arguably, the presidency has been transformed as an institution, initiated in part by the postmodern turn[6] and also by scrutiny resulting from the Vietnam War, Watergate, the Iran-Contra situation, the Clinton impeachment, and the 2000 election.[7] The postmodern turn coincided with the presidential scandals and a growing commitment to adversarial journalism to produce a cynical U.S. public that is suspicious of the officeholder's character and critical of past presidential heroes (e.g., slave-owning Washington and Jefferson, philandering FDR and JFK).[8] Thus, the presidency's role in public life and in political affairs is constantly reassessed even as it represents the locus of political attention and reflects larger cultural anxieties about U.S. political life and leadership.

Coming at the end of the twentieth century, *TWW* puts forth a provocative and compelling version of presidentiality for the national polity, addressing the cultural trepidation about the precise nature of the presidency during a conflicted moment in U.S. history. The program has become, in the words of *George* magazine, "a zeitgeist show, a reflection of the tenor of our times."[9] Broadly speaking, *TWW* reflects larger political-cultural conflicts. James Chesebro argues that although "the media shape and influence the economic, political, and social institutions . . . they also depend upon these external institutions for their existence and are therefore constrained and ultimately defined by these external institutions."[10] In its mimetic portrayal of presidential politics, *TWW* offers a romantic narrative reflective of the postmodern condition in U.S. culture. To a certain degree, this political drama disrupts images of traditional political power, depicting a chaotic, inclusive, and communal presidentiality dominated by a collectivity of appealing heroes. Although polyvalent,[11] we argue that the ideological disruption of *TWW*'s postmodern take on the presidency is ultimately contained and controlled by its simultaneously conventional discourse of presidential politics; such a political vision offers a hopeful and cathartic vision of presidentiality yet one reliant on the ideologies of intellectualism, militarism, masculinity, and whiteness. In support of this reading, we first consider existing definitions of the presidency, moving to an assessment of the mimetic nature of popular culture in portraying this institution and the role that romantic narratives assume in conceptions of presidentiality. We also offer background information about *TWW* and discuss its portrayal of a chaotic, postmodern vision of presidentiality. Finally, we detail the more conservative and cathartic characterizations of presidentiality offered by *TWW*, ending with an assessment of contemporary presidentiality in U.S. political culture.

Cultural Visions of Presidentiality in U.S. Politics

Despite the turbulence that surrounds the office, the presidency arguably is the most important and symbolically meaningful institution of the U.S. system of government. No other branch of the federal government—not Congress, not the Supreme Court—is the focal point of public discussion, cultural angst, or political hope in the same way as the presidency. Moreover, the individuals who occupy the office stand in for the national polity. "The president became the most visible landmark of the political landscape, virtually standing for the federal government in the minds of many Americans," notes presidential historian Fred Greenstein.[12] These leaders represent the U.S. community internationally and become the expression and receptacle of communal identity and ideology.

Most presidential commentators who assess the nature of the institution and individual presidents tend to ignore the symbolic importance of the presidency as a cultural force in U.S. political life.[13] Their focus is on presidential leadership, greatness, and strength as barometers of institutional/political power. Political scientist Stephen Skowronek, for instance, rereads presidential history to discern the politics that presidents make. His telling of this history is, as might be expected, a search for the "*institutional* logic of political disruption," as he challenges sacrosanct notions of institutional order to reinscribe a vision of our nation's chief executives.[14]

Nowhere is the tendency to ignore the cultural power of the presidency more apparent than in the analyses of the "rhetorical presidency." The rhetorical power of the office, according to Jeffrey Tulis, is "a way of constituting the people to whom it [presidential rhetoric] is addressed by furnishing them with the very equipment they need to assess its use—the metaphors, categories, and concepts of political discourse."[15] Of course, the president is the definitive and constitutive agent in this framework, offering the vocabulary and discourses necessary for the larger public to form their national identity and essence.

There is nothing wrong with highlighting definitive rhetorical characteristics of presidential leadership,[16] but presidential oratory is not alone in constituting the presidency. There is a significant difference, as Martin J. Medhurst points out, between the rhetorical presidency and presidential rhetoric.[17] To fully appreciate the ideological and rhetorical demarcation of the presidency requires an engagement with the vast collection of discourses that also figure in the cultural and political meaning of the office and the people who occupy it.

Popular Culture and Mimetic Portrayals of the Presidency

Foretelling the increased attention to its aesthetic dimensions, Thomas Farrell argues that "rhetoric is the only art responsible for the imitation and expression of public thought."[18] Fictionalized representations of politics are powerful and accessible rhetorical forms, increasingly influential as they improve in technological sophistication and mimetic capacity. Such discourses play a central role in the definition and expression of political culture and political leaders.[19]

The ancient concept of mimesis begins to explain the role and meaning of fictionalized presidencies for contemporary political culture. Mimesis refers to the ability of a discourse to imitate or copy lived experience. Rooted in the *Poetics* of Aristotle, the mimetic experience generates "a world of appearances, of semblance, and the aesthetic." Although it might be tempting to dismiss mimetic renditions as replicated fakery because they belong "to a nonempirical order of knowledge," such dismissal would be a mistake.[20] The mimetic process creates a material reality and, ultimately, "designates not a passive process of reproduction but the process of creation, representation, or enactment."[21]

Mimetic representations of the presidency frequently offer audiences new visions of this political institution or revised biographies of the nation's chief executives. Such representations work precisely because they approximate a reality of the presidency that is persuasive and credible. Popular culture, as it represents political activity and the presidency in U.S. politics, must strive for a high degree of perceived verisimilitude to secure audience acceptance. As Lee Sigelman notes, the "mimetic aspect is the key to the popularity and the political significance of the Washington novel."[22] The same is true of portrayals of politics in film or on television.[23]

When offering mimetic portrayals of the presidency, political dramas and films often rely on romance as a central emplotment strategy, a narrative that resonates in presidential discourse as well. In the aftermath of the Vietnam War and Watergate, Chesebro maintains that "Americans apparently found romantic conceptions increasingly satisfying and reliable" in their favorite television shows.[24] As President Jimmy Carter worked unsuccessfully to overcome problems with the economy, the Iranian hostage crisis, and the Cold War, Walter R. Fisher argues that the "stage was set for the entrance of a heroic [i.e., romantic] figure as president"—Ronald Reagan.[25] The conflation of romantic narrative in both popular television and presidential discourse is not surprising. "Art cannot in essence be different from other cooperative social processes," Christopher Caudwell reveals.[26] Or, put differently by Northrop Frye, romance "is essentially a verbal imitation of ritual or symbolic human action."[27]

For many romance narratives, the juxtaposition of the hero and the villain is an instrumental strategy, representing a glimpse into the hierarchy of the larger culture and its discourses. Frye argues that "In every age the ruling social or intellectual class tends to project its ideals in some form of romance, where the virtuous heroes and beautiful heroines represent the ideals and the villains the threats to their ascendancy."[28] Within legal discourse, William Lewis suggests that romantic texts "reinforce the authority and legitimacy of current legal structures and their related conceptions of order."[29] The popularity of romance, according to Frye, is grounded in the assumption that such a quest narrative "avoids the ambiguities of ordinary life, where everything is a mixture of good and bad, and where it is difficult to take sides or believe that people are consistent patterns of virtue or vice."[30]

In contrast, we contend that contemporary romance discourse, like the political culture that produces it, can reflect deep-seated ideological dissonance. "The stark good-versus-evil of romances often proves problematical for politics,"[31] notes Lewis; John M. Murphy likewise reveals that in some contemporary campaign histories, many of which were written during the turn to postmodernism, "the villain is not purely evil nor [is] the hero purely good."[32] These ideological complexities mirror cultural conflict and authenticate the mimetic features of romance texts. A postmodern presidential romance, which provides "for a freedom from tradition" and an "activation of difference," offers a complex depiction of presidentiality.[33] This polyvalent image is trapped between a more progressive, community-based notion of inclusivity and an individualistic image that perpetuates the traditional, conservative vision of a white/male hero embodying infinite power for righteous ends.

The Chaotic Presidency of *The West Wing*

NBC debuted *The West Wing* on September 22, 1999. Written by Aaron Sorkin, the program features the activities of the senior staff in President Josiah Bartlet's White House. The central characters in the show include the Chief of Staff (Leo McGarry), the Communications Director (Toby Ziegler), the Deputy Chief of Staff (Josh Lyman), the Deputy Communications Director/Speechwriter (Sam Seaborn), and the Press Secretary (C.J. Cregg). Other characters include the First Lady (Abigail Bartlet), the President's daughter (Zoe Bartlet), the President's Personal Assistant (Charlie Young), and the assistant to the Deputy Chief of Staff (Donna Moss). Much of the action occurs in the "west wing" of the White House. Critically acclaimed, *TWW* has won numerous awards including the 2000 and 2001 Emmy Awards for Best Drama and the 2001 Golden Globe Award for Best Television Drama.[34]

Much of the praise for *TWW* results from its alleged "realism," with many commentators noting that the show portrays for its viewers what the presidency is really like. Former White House Press Secretary Marlin Fitzwater, a *TWW* consultant, concludes that the program "very accurately portrays so many elements of presidential life—the frantic urgency about issues and decisions."[35] To achieve such mimetic sensibilities, the show's producers hired consultants with political experience, including former White House Press Secretary Dee Dee Myers, Jimmy Carter's pollster Patrick Cadell, and journalist and former U.S. Senate staffer Lawrence O'Donnell. As *US* magazine notes, such experts "help ensure accuracy on the set."[36] As if to reinforce the realism of the program, a *TV Guide* cover story in July 2000 profiled all of the cast members of *TWW* and their "real-life" White House counterparts.[37] *TWW* consultants

Patrick Cadell and Laurence O'Donnell were regular commentators on MSNBC and CNBC during the 2000 campaign and election, conflating further the distinctions between reality and image. *Brill's Content* even concludes that *TWW* "presents a truer, more human picture of the people behind the issues than most of today's White House journalists."[38]

Central to the "realism" of *TWW* is its depiction of presidentiality as the management of chaos and uncertainty, reflecting the conflict inherent in the romance narrative.[39] With *TWW,* though, chaos represents an integral theme rather than a plot device to be resolved quickly at the end of each hour's episode. Such chaos reigns throughout the first 18 of 22 episodes of the premiere season. Indeed, much of the first season of *TWW* highlights the incapacity of the Bartlet administration to manage its chaotic problems. Because the program concerns what Joshua Meyrowitz calls the "backstage" dimensions of the presidency,[40] the personal anxieties of the president (and his staff) magnify and intensify the turmoil characteristic of the first season. The result is a series that reveals the contingent nature of presidential action and the anxiety of those who confront national problems.[41]

TWW offers other elements that depart from a traditional romance narrative, evidencing its postmodern characteristics. The program presents more complex relationships between heroes and villains;[42] even the show's dark sets with low lighting reflect images associated with the "enemy" (e.g., "darkness," "confusion," "winter") rather than the archetypal hero (e.g., "dawn," "light," "spring"). Although the regular characters are more heroic than not, *TWW,* in part, communicates a sense of *collective heroism* embodied in a communal presidentiality rather than the construct of the archetypal individual hero (personifying "communal values and traditions").[43]

TWW's pilot establishes the parameters of the Bartlet administration's chaotic presidency. It features a largely absent President Bartlet who crashed his bicycle into a tree earlier in the day; it also reveals how little the staffers know about the problems they confront. One plot line, for instance, concerns a Cuban boatlift headed toward Florida. Attempting to solicit information about its scope, Chief of Staff Leo McGarry realizes he has no information and asks his deputy, "True or false: If I were to stand on high ground in Key West with a good pair of binoculars, I'd be as informed as I am right now?"[44] Speechwriter Sam Seaborn summarizes the chaos of the episode:

> I just found out the *Times* is publishing a poll that says a considerable portion of Americans feel the White House has lost energy and focus. A perception that's not likely to be altered by the video footage of the President riding his bicycle into a tree. As we speak, the Coast Guard is fishing Cubans out of the Atlantic Ocean while the Governor of Florida wants to blockade the Port of Miami. A good friend of mine's about to get fired for going on television and making sense, and it turns out I accidentally slept with a prostitute last night.

Succeeding episodes exacerbate the uncertainty and self-doubt that resonates throughout the first season of the Bartlet presidency. Romance often develops through "a conflict between the hero and his enemy,"[45] but with *TWW,* this dialectic is often internalized in Bartlet. In *TWW's* fifth episode, "The Crackpots and These Women," the staff confronts numerous citizens with often fringe concerns that demand their attention. As the episode closes, President Bartlet confides to Toby Ziegler his own internal insecurities, offering the ultimate in "backstage" understanding of presidential motives and anxieties:

> Bartlet: I know I disappoint you sometimes. I mean, I can sense your disappointment. And I only get mad because I know you're right a lot of the times. . . . The other night when we were playing basketball, did you mean what you said? My demons were shouting down the better angels in my brain?
>
> Toby: Yes sir. I did. . . .
>
> Bartlet: I suppose you're right.
>
> Toby: Tell you what though, sir. In a battle between a president's demons and his better angels, for the first time in a long while, I think we might just have ourselves a fair fight.

Such a postmodernist rendition of romance is enhanced further by the revelation in episode 12 ("He Shall from Time to Time") that President Bartlet is suffering from a form of multiple sclerosis that has been hidden from the public. The President is even portrayed as weak by a Supreme Court justice who charges that he lacks the "guts" that the American people require of their President (episode 9—"The Short List"). Bartlet's character, thus, is humanized and flawed by inner conflict. Although the stature of his character is lessened by a more "common man" image, such humanization potentially strengthens the identification with viewers' insecurities and foibles. Indeed, as Caren Deming concludes, characters constructed in this way are "heroic" because they "keep trying" in the face of adversity.[46]

 TWW's construction of presidentiality also posits, at times, a more reluctant commitment to military force, which further alters the traditional vision of the drama's romantic hero. This ambivalence is established during the second episode ("Post Hoc, Ergo Propter Hoc") when President Bartlet confides his insecurity to an aide: "I'm an accomplished man, Morris. I can sit comfortably with prime ministers and presidents, even the pope. Why is it every time I sit with the Joint Chiefs, I feel like I'm back at my father's dinner table?" President Bartlet even acknowledges that his lack of "violent" feelings toward the nation's "enemies" may make him appear weak. Robert W. Connell notes that the United States often preserves male power through such institutions as the military.[47] *TWW's* presidentiality, like the political culture at large,[48] questions the commitment to militaristic power. This ideological interrogation is evident in *TWW's* fallible hero battling external and internal exigencies while questioning a commitment to violence as a means to combat external foes.

 These psychological and political struggles also involve his staff; *TWW's* presidentiality thus expresses a collectivist notion of the institution, deviating from the stereotypical romantic hero-president. Military decisions are portrayed, for example, as collective decision-making efforts involving the Joint

Chiefs of Staff, the President, and the President's Chief of Staff. In episode 3, "A Proportional Response," this collectivity expands to include the backing of the "Western coalition" (e.g., Britain and Japan) in retaliation for the downing of a U.S. jet in the Middle East. As the President anxiously prepares to speak publicly about the retaliatory bombing, all of the President's staffers busily assist him during the chaotic scene. The episode ends on another note of collectivism when the President invites Charlie to "come help us out" in getting the cop killer bullets that killed Charlie's mom outlawed by Congress. Later in the season, we are given a behind-the-scenes look into how the gun bill actually passed in Congress when Bill 802 comes to fruition through the collective efforts of Josh, Leo, and the Vice President. Not only is the President uninvolved in securing the remaining five votes, he is sleeping during the bill's passage because of a backache that required medication (episode 4—"Five Votes Down"). Such depictions disrupt the romantic notion of a heroic president as "the self-determining, autonomous individual."[49]

Heroism likewise is problematized in these scenes. In "Five Votes Down," the President's disengagement is accented by his pain killer induced interactions with his staff, leading him to expound nonsensically on Toby's "nice name," for example. Josh is portrayed as the one responsible for delivering four of the five swing votes, yet he wins over one recalcitrant congressional leader by using political threats: "Vote yes or you're not even going to be on the ballot two years from now." Leo's "heroism" is notable because he convinces the Vice President to deliver the remaining congressional leader's vote. Leo's valor, however, is contextualized within the revelation of his past drug and alcohol dependency and his wife's quest for a divorce because he paid more attention to his job than to his marriage. The Vice President also is presented as self-interested when he obtains the final vote for Bill 802, declaring that he's "going to be President of the United States one day." Thus, *TWW*'s presidentiality is predicated, in part, on a collective vision of leadership that destabilizes the heroes of the collective as well as the President's claims to valor.

TWW's collective, though humanized, also demonstrates the producers' commitment to issues of inclusiveness and multiculturalism, as the drama seeks to mimic the larger cultural campaign to have a presidential administration that looks like the nation.[50] During the first season, two white women are part of the President's inner circle, C.J. Cregg (Press Secretary) and Mandy Hampton (political consultant); both are strong women who often competently compete with their peers. In response to not being informed about Sam's relationship with a prostitute, C.J., for example, confronts Josh and Sam, establishing her power while confronting negative stereotypes about women:

Josh: You're overreacting.
C.J.:   Am I? . . . as women are prone to do?
Josh: That's not what I meant . . .
C.J.:   That's always what you mean.
Josh: You know what C.J.? I think I'm the best judge of what I mean . . . you paranoid, Berkeley, shiksa, feminista. Wow, that was way too far.

> C.J.:   No, no. Well, I've got a staff meeting to go to and so do you, you elit-
> ist, Harvard, fascist, missed the dean's list two semesters in a row, Yan-
> kee jackass.

C.J. also demonstrates her power to Sam by asserting: "I'm your first phone call . . . before, now, in the future. . . . Anytime you're into something and you don't know what, you don't keep it from me. I'm your first phone call, I'm your first line of defense. You have to let me protect you, and you have to let me protect the President." At the conclusion of the heated exchange, C.J. ends the conversation: "We're done talking now, you can go" ("A Proportional Response"). Assuming such an assertive and protective role with her colleagues disrupts more traditional lines of authority in which men are usually portrayed as the "protectors" of women.[51]

Mandy's character is similarly constructed as a powerful figure who rejects the hierarchy established by her colleagues. In a turf battle with Josh, Mandy's former boyfriend, Josh pronounces, "You answer to me and you answer to Toby." Mandy retorts: "[I]n your dreams, in your little dreams" ("Post Hoc, Ergo Propter Hoc"). Mandy also challenges the President not to speak like an "economics professor with a stick up his butt" (episode 5—"The Crackpots and These Women"). In addition, Mandy describes herself as "accomplished and brilliant" because of her political consulting experience and her Ph.D. in political science, her M.A. in communication, and her B.A. in art history. Such depictions of C.J. and Mandy are partial disruptions of traditional feminine characterizations, which typically represent a "romantic sentiment" of "dependence and goodwill that gives the masculine principle its romantic validity and its admiring applause," contends Susan Brownmiller.[52]

In some ways, *TWW* also expresses a commitment to diversify its characters along racial lines. Interestingly, *TWW* appeared on the NBC schedule at the same time that the major broadcast networks faced criticism for their predominantly white casts; when the networks announced the 1999–2000 fall schedule, some groups held hearings and threatened boycotts to protest the lack of diversity in network programming.[53] Charlie emerged at the beginning of the season as the one person of color among the President's inner circle, constituting *TWW*'s most significant response to the call for greater diversity on television.

Diversity on *TWW* usually involves characters that are not part of the core group of advisors in the Bartlet White House. The Attorney General, although never featured in the first season, is identified as an African American ("A Proportional Response"), as is the Housing and Urban Development Secretary, played by CCH Pounder (episode 15—"Celestial Navigation"). The Bartlet administration also diversifies the Supreme Court by placing the first Latino American on the bench in a storyline that spans multiple episodes (episode 9—"The Short List" to episode 18—"Six Meetings Before Lunch").

The Chairman of the Joint Chiefs of Staff, Admiral Fitzwallace, is an African American who is granted considerable power and authority during *TWW*'s first season. He not only is an expert on foreign policy, but also has greater knowledge and wisdom than the President on military matters. In "A Proportional

Response," Fitzwallace tells Leo: "You're going to have to set him [the President] down." When Leo asks for counsel, Fitzwallace offers sage, parental advice: "Tell him it's always like this the first time. Tell him he's doing fine." Leo retorts: "He's not doing fine." Fitzwallace counters: "Yeah, he is." This particular example illustrates the *postmodern* romance, as people other than the President are granted the authority and wisdom usually reserved for the drama's white hero. Although Herman Gray is troubled by the tendency of television programs like *TWW* to incorporate notions of "blackness" into its scripts "without necessarily challenging or disturbing that order," Gray also acknowledges that "cultural struggles" over the "representation of blackness in our *present*, help to prepare the groundwork, to create spaces for how we think about our highly charged racial *past* and possibilities for our different and yet-contested future."[54] Postmodern struggles over representation commingle in popular culture and in presidential discourse, with *TWW*'s presidentiality mimicking ongoing cultural contestation over whiteness.

Chaos predominates during the first 18 episodes of the *TWW*'s inaugural season. The dominant narrative features a conflict-ridden President who experiences problems controlling, managing, and meaningfully affecting the uncertainties and contingencies of presidential politics and governance. The season finale exacerbates this depiction with the dramatic portrayal of the ultimate in presidential chaos—an assassination attempt. The disruption of *TWW*'s heroic presidentiality is increased by a more inclusive vision, featuring strong women, people of color in positions of power, and a critique of violence. As Murray Edelman contends, "works of art may bring new ways of seeing and understanding."[55] The presidentiality of *TWW* challenges traditional romantic images of the powerful and valiant, solitary white male just as the larger culture wrestles with complicated visions of presidential heroism among its "real life" chief executives.

At the same time, however, a more postmodern conception of presidentiality does not exist apart from its symbiotic "other." John Fiske writes, "we don't live in a completely postmodern world." Rather, "we live in a world where the modern and the postmodern . . . coexist uneasily."[56] *TWW* links postmodern and modern images, containing much of the ideological angst of the first season in a discourse of traditionalism.

The West Wing's Ideologically Modern Presidentiality

TWW's reliance on more traditional images is not surprising given the conservative nature of romance narratives.[57] Although art may offer new understandings, Edelman writes that "[a]t any historical period the most widely promulgated and accepted perceptions reflect and reinforce the dominant social relationships."[58] The postmodern urge to disrupt the modern is constrained by a reliance on conservative constructs, and *TWW* reflects this ideological tension. Although chaos dominates the first 18 episodes of *TWW*, the ideological angst lessened in episodes 19–21, beginning with episode 19, "Let Bartlet Be Bartlet." In this instance, *TWW*'s narrative resembles the *discovery* process of romance narratives, in which the protagonist "prove[s] himself to be a hero even if he does not survive the conflict."[59] The individuals who people the show continue to face complex problems and difficult psychological conflicts, but these emerge within reassuring ideological frameworks that order *TWW's* presidentiality as a cathartic and conservative response to cultural anxieties about presidential leadership.

Like the larger culture that produced it, *TWW* reflects contradictions in its portrayal of issues of inclusion and multiculturalism, often resorting to militarized, masculine, and white images that arguably overpower the more progressive ones. *TWW's* presidentiality, thus, mimics the dissonance embedded in the phrase, "the world we want and the world we don't want," reflecting the sentiment that we are "enthralled" by the same "networks of power" that we "abhor."[60] Although the culture embraces, at times, the disruption of status quo power that is *perceived* to accompany a celebration of multiculturalism, it often finds solace in more nostalgic images of heroism personified by the white, male, presidential hero.

In addressing the chaos that swirls around him, Bartlet's hesitant, tentative presidentiality comes to its apotheosis in "Let Bartlet be Bartlet." Facing conflicts over gays and lesbians in the military, low approval ratings in polls, an internal memo questioning the capacity of the administration to exert leadership, and a general malaise among the staff, President Bartlet and his Chief of Staff redirect the administration's focus. In the process, this episode articulates a presidentiality that is ideologically meaningful, characterized by a commitment to honesty, candor, and an unbridled pursuit of policy and ideals. Such a vision of presidentiality emerges powerfully in the oddly therapeutic conversation between Bartlet and Leo:

> Bartlet: I don't want to feel like this anymore.
> Leo: You don't have to.
> Bartlet: I don't want to go to sleep like this.
> Leo: You don't have to.
> Bartlet: I want to speak.
> Leo: Say it out loud. Say it to me.
> Bartlet: This is more important than reelection. I want to speak now.
> Leo: Say it again.
> Bartlet: This is more important than reelection. I want to speak now.
> Leo: Now we're in business!

The episode ends with Leo mobilizing the senior staff with each declaring, "I serve at the pleasure of the president."

In the next episodes, a more decisively heroic President emerges. As the President sits in bed at the end of episode 20, "Mandatory Minimums," the entire senior staff, anxious over the events of the day, comes to his bedroom, one by one, seeking sage advice, solace, or forgiveness. The President calmly listens yet commands:

> There'll be more meetings tomorrow. In the meantime, everybody calm down.
> Leo's got your engines fired like you're running Daytona. That's fine, keep

them there. Guess what. Mistakes are going to be made. Minimize them, fix them, move on. . . . Listen to me. I have never lost an election in my life. If we do this right, people are going to respond.

At the end of the episode, the President confides to Leo, "I'm sleeping better. And when I sleep, I dream about a great discussion with experts and ideas and diction [sic] and energy and honesty. And when I wake up, I think, I can sell that." Although the notion of the collective is still present in *TWW*'s romantic presidentiality, individualism is more prominent; the President ends the day alone in his bedroom, preparing to dream of greatness as the lone romantic leader of the nation.

Images of the president as an intellectual reinforce the notion of individual heroism. In romance narratives, Chesebro writes that "romantic agents must be intellectually superior to others" and be capable of "exercising superior control" over "their environment."[61] Such an image is often juxtaposed in the collective memory of presidents with that of the "common man." *TWW* rejects "common man" depictions, presenting an "intellectual" president instead. During the first season, President Bartlet is rarely seen in situations that emphasize his links to the people (e.g., shaking hands, seeking input from the public, giving speeches). His intellectualism is firmly established in the second episode, "Post Hoc, Ergo Propter Hoc," when Bartlet quizzes his staff over the meaning of *post hoc, ergo propter hoc,* Josh consequently dubs him, "Jed Bartlet, Nobel Laureate in Economics, three-term congressman, two-term Governor." In the same episode, a military officer tells Bartlet, "You have a once in a generation mind, sir." Bartlet frequently performs his intellectualism. In "A Proportional Response," he laments the inability of the United States to protect its citizens around the world:

> Did you know that two thousand years ago a Roman citizen could walk across the face of the known world free of the fear of molestation. He could walk across the earth unharmed, cloaked only in the words *Civis Romanis,* I am a Roman citizen. So real was the retribution of Rome, universally understood as certain, should any harm befall even one of its citizens. . . . Where is the retribution for the families and where is the warning to the rest of the world that Americans shall walk this earth unharmed, lest the clenched fist of the mightiest military force in the history of mankind comes crashing down on your house?

Both the historical allusion and his vocabulary reflect Bartlet's knowledge and his ability to apply it to his official duties, projecting the image of an intellectually heroic president. *TWW* constructs its president as the antithesis of the "common man"—as a romantic individual who possesses the "once in a generation" mind necessary to navigate the challenges of the contemporary presidency.

The modern romantic hero of *TWW* comes to rely on military action to resolve foreign policy disputes, mimicking the practice of many hero presidents. Historically, U.S. political culture has valued presidents who successfully led the nation in war; virtually every list of great presidents features Washington, Lincoln, Wilson, and FDR.[62] Furthermore, U.S. political campaigns have become "ritual substitutes for war, battles between the forces of good and the forces of evil."[63] At bottom, U.S. conceptions of presidentiality are infused with a rhetoric of war and power.

Although expressing ambivalence toward violence, *TWW* also portrays Bartlet in situations demanding a military response and displaying his ability to carry out such responsibilities. After President Bartlet confides to a military aide (Morris) that he is insecure about his standing with the military in "Post Hoc, Ergo Propter Hoc," he reacts almost viscerally after that military aide's plane is shot down in Syria. Bartlet is so upset that he threatens to "blow them off the face of the earth with the fury of God's own thunder." In the next episode, "A Proportional Response," a similarly emotional Bartlet challenges military leaders on the validity of proportional responses to terrorism. After acceding to the proportional response, Bartlet proclaims: "Let the word ring forth from this time and this place, you kill an American, any American, we don't come back with a proportional response, we come back [bangs fist on table] with total disaster!"

TWW's presidentiality, thus, ultimately cloaks the presidency in a discourse of militarism, furthering the symbiotic relationship between the presidency, militarism, and heroism. Military leaders never are shown in a negative light, and peacemaking or peacekeeping are not activities undertaken by the Bartlet administration. Perhaps nothing demonstrates the militarism of *TWW* more clearly than the absence of a Secretary of State or any diplomatic arm of the U.S. Government. Indeed, a national security team is not established in *TWW* until the second season, and even then, the official presented is the National Security Advisor, not a Secretary of State. The Chairman of the Joint Chiefs of Staff is a recurring character, and military personnel are everywhere, but the diplomats, the peacemakers, are entirely absent.

The militarism of *TWW* accentuates the masculine nature of its presidentiality. Although Bartlet's character is obviously polyvalent, the militaristic moments of *TWW* coincide with a vision of a more masculine and thus ideologically conventional President Bartlet. Bartlet, for example, is often engaged in masculine activities and expressions, playing basketball with the male staffers ("The Crackpots and These Women") or telling Charlie and C.J. that he "could take George Washington" (episode 18—"Six Meetings Before Lunch") or claiming, "I still got it [machismo]" when he has a 101.9 degree temperature ("He Shall From Time to Time"). The President is stereotypically masculine in certain interpersonal interactions, advising Leo over his failed marriage, "You're the man, [so] fix it" ("Mr. Willis of Ohio") or teasing Toby about his ex-wife wearing "the pants in the family" ("Mandatory Minimums") or warning Leo about a fair weather friend: "It's not hard to like a guy when he's doing well; the measure of the man is how does he behave when things are otherwise" ("Take Out the Trash Day").

Another notable example of *TWW*'s masculine presidentiality emerges in a conflict between the President's staff and the First Lady's assistants. Generally, the First Lady is not a prominent character in *TWW*'s first season and does not appear until the seventh episode; even then she is featured infrequently. Significantly, she is a medical doctor who is outspoken privately and publicly, yet her medical expertise is performed only in reference to the President and his health. She is marginalized and diminished in a culminating dispute with the President during "The White House Pro-Am" (episode 17). In an Oval Office confrontation, Bartlet reveals his frustration about the perception that he is being handled by his wife in relation to a controversial child labor bill. In the end, the First Lady admits her errors, stating, "I concede I was wrong about the thing." President Bartlet retorts, "Good." When the First Lady attempts to rebut, the President declares, "Just be wrong. Just stand there in your wrongness and be wrong. And get used to it." Even though the two share a humorous, warm, and touching moment at the conclusion of the confrontation, hierarchy is preserved as the First Lady concedes her errors ("The White House Pro-Am"). Such constructions are not surprising. "Heroic leaders," notes Bruce Miroff, "are drawn to, and sometimes obsessed by, proofs of masculinity."[64]

Several additional dimensions of *TWW*'s masculine presidentiality relate to the drama's construction of women. Although C.J. and Mandy are portrayed as strong and of equal status to their peers, they also are shown making frequent mistakes. In the pilot, the first image of C.J. is of her falling down on a treadmill; Mandy is shown driving recklessly and chasing political colleagues down the lawn of a federal building. Other mishaps are more significant, as when C.J. makes a public statement that inaccurately describes how the President is required to nominate a Democrat and a Republican to the Federal Election Commission. Leo, in response, calls C.J.'s error "a dumb mistake" (episode 20—"Mandatory Minimums"). Mandy's mishap involves her leak of a memo over Bartlet's vulnerabilities that represents a significant public relations problem for the President and his staff ("Let Bartlet Be Bartlet"). Mandy's character disappears from the show not long thereafter.

Although the men also make errors, C.J. and other women are the characters who occasionally lack a clear understanding of certain governmental activities. In episode 6—"Mr. Willis of Ohio," for instance, C.J. seeks out instruction from Sam about the conflict over census sampling; despite her status as a high-ranking White House functionary, she does not grasp the basics of the U.S. census. In another episode, she announces her lack of economic aptitude, proclaiming, "I really don't understand anything" ("The White House Pro-Am"). In these instances, she functions as a stand-in for those in the audience who may lack understanding of important governmental and political functions. Donna, Josh's secretary, often plays the role of quizzical citizen asking her boss about the reasons that the Democrats do not wish to give back the budget surplus to taxpayers ("Mr. Willis of Ohio") or what the FEC does ("Let Bartlet Be Bartlet").

Finally, a scene from "The Crackpots and These Women," positions the women of *TWW* at the margins. At the end of the episode, President Bartlet offers an encomium to the women gathered in the White House for a celebration. Leo, Josh, and the President are positioned in the scene oddly, giving them the ability to gaze and comment on the women around them surreptitiously. Their comments, while praise-worthy, are highly gendered and illustrative of *TWW*'s masculine presidentiality:

Bartlet: We were talking about these women.
Josh: Yeah?
Leo: We can't get over these women.
Bartlet: Look at C.J. She's like a fifties movie star, so capable, so loving and energetic.
Leo: Look at Mandy over there. Going punch for punch with Toby in a world that tells women to sit down and shut up. Mandy's already won her battle with the president. The game's over, but she's not done. She wants Toby.
Bartlet: Mrs. Landingham. Did you guys know she lost two sons in Vietnam? What would make her want to serve her country is beyond me, but in 14 years, she's not missed a day's work, not one.

All of the women are valued and praised, but in gendered ways. C.J. is noticed for her energy and appearance, and Mrs. Landingham for her motherhood and her faithful dedication. Even when Mandy is admired for her perseverance and commitment, this trait is contextualized as a gender role reversal. The episode separates male from female by positioning the females as an object of gaze and comment.[65] Although there are positive depictions of women, the drama is often dismissive of the feminine, further coupling masculinity and presidentiality.

Similarly, *TWW* marginalizes persons of color. Conceived in a Constitution that wrote slavery into the founding of the republic, and dominated for 213 years by white men, the presidency is defined by its whiteness—a "social location" that is "perceived as if it had a normative essence."[66] With *TWW*, the President's whiteness is reified through the drama's valorization of its past white presidents and through Bartlet's repeated epideictic to Western knowledge. In response, African American characters almost always are called on to perform blackness (and Latinos their Hispanicity) in some capacity even as *TWW* evidences a commitment to multiculturalism.

Obviously, President Bartlet embodies whiteness through his performance of the presidency. Subtly, though, *TWW*'s pervasive visual encomium to white presidential heroes is mimetic and legitimates the whiteness of this *fictional* president. The backdrop of all episodes is replete with pictorial representations of such romantic heroes as George Washington, Abraham Lincoln, Theodore Roosevelt, and FDR; these historical markers promote the individualism of *TWW*'s presidentiality and embody the country's normalization of whiteness.

TWW's whiteness is perpetuated by Bartlet's love of Western knowledge. The President, for example, excitedly picks out a book entitled, "*The Nature of Things: A Didascalic Poem* translated from the Latin of Titus Lucretius Carus" for his daughter's Christmas present (episode 10—"In Excelsis Deo"). President Bartlet is given a copy of the U.S. Constitution translated into Latin as he prepares for his State of the Union address, which he proceeds to read and translate aloud. Finally, the President cites St. Augustine in a debate over the death penalty, all of which accentuates his intellectualism and his epistemological commitment to the West and Western knowledge (episode 12—"He Shall From Time to Time"). As Homi K. Bhabha notes, the historical and contemporary "culture of the west," assumes a level of "authority," which for many scholars, reifies whiteness.[67]

Most African Americans who appear during the first season give testimony to the state of racial politics in the United States. Before Charlie is hired, for example, Leo consults Admiral Fitzwallace (the Chairman of the Joint Chiefs of Staff) about the racial implications of this decision. The Chairman's response is instructive and reveals the series' ideological orientation toward racial matters. Reacting to Leo's concern over having "a young black man waiting on the president," Fitzwallace asks, "You gonna pay him a decent wage?" "You gonna treat him with respect in the workplace?" When Leo responds affirmatively, the Chairman prophesizes, "Then why the hell should I care. . . . I've got some real honest to God battles to fight, Leo. I don't have time for the cosmetic ones."

This scene and others communicate that African Americans exist to comment on issues of race regardless of their position. In this way, African Americans always perform race and are subject to the white gaze. Fitzwallace's comments accomplish the ideological dismissal of racial concerns in White House hiring practices. Coming from an African American character of some authority stresses that important questions about wages and respect should overwhelm concerns about race and ethnicity. Read in the context of protests against the networks' casting prejudices, *TWW* denigrates racial politics, suggesting that just as Leo's questions about Charlie's race are "cosmetic," so, too, are the concerns raised about the networks' casting decisions.

Stereotyping people of color also is abundant in *TWW*, particularly as people of color are associated with violence. Throughout the first season, Charlie's relationship with the First Daughter is repeatedly discussed in relation to the violent white supremacists who threaten them repeatedly and who motivate an entire Secret Service investigation. The assassination attempt that ends the first season is attributed to racial hatred against Charlie. In addition, Leo plays the race card with an African American Congressman who is opposing a gun control bill. To him, Leo pleads, "God, Mark. The bodies being wheeled into the emergency room are black. These guns aren't going to Scottsdale, Mark, they're going to Detroit, they're going to Philadelphia. An entire generation of African American men are being eaten alive by drugs and poverty" ("Five Votes Down"). In "The State Dinner," Indonesians are characterized as "gangs of roving people beheading those they suspect of being sorcerers." In each case, people of color are defined in relation to violent or aberrant behavior. These examples reduce race to clichés and stereotypes while reifying the unempowered lives of people of color who spend time combating violence.

At base, *TWW* is a predominantly white show that features mostly white characters that perpetuate an ideology of whiteness. The power of whiteness is most visible when the HUD Secretary, a woman of color, is forced to apologize publicly for calling Republicans "racist." Leo commands, "We need their votes on any number of issues. . . . Your role first and foremost is to serve the

President, a task today at which you failed spectacularly" (episode 15—"Celestial Navigation). This is the same episode in which the white staffers from the White House compel the Latino Supreme Court nominee to ignore the indignity of racial profiling in order to secure appointment to the High Court. Within these instructive scenes, whiteness is empowered and privileged and so, too, is the authority of the presidency.

The West Wing's Constructed Presidentiality

In the opening scenes of *TWW*'s pilot, the camera moves us from the well-lit, secured entryway of the White House past the guards, down the hallway, and through the doors to the darkened, chaotic, fast-paced west wing. As the camera moves backstage, to a place where most have never been, we enter a scene that promises to offer a "real" glimpse of the U.S. presidency. We soon learn that *TWW*'s presidentiality expresses and confronts the same ideological tensions as the United States at the turn of the twenty-first century.

TWW's postmodern depictions emphasize a humanized vision of our heroic president, a presidentiality complete with the same insecurities and weaknesses that plague people every day. This postmodern romantic hero, Jed Bartlet, does not have all the answers and cannot control the chaos of his world. To allay his doubts and to order that world, he relies on a collective, albeit ideologically dissonant, heroism that includes women and people of color and in which insecurities are expressed, anxieties are acknowledged, and heroic actions are questioned.

TWW's modern presidentiality, however, also presents a more traditional president as the lone individual fighting against the country's enemies. President Josiah Bartlet is smart, white, male, and militaristic because that is what all U.S. presidents are in the romantic narratives that define them. This modern presidential hero can manage the chaos, fight for what is right and oppose what is wrong, all the while supported by a competent but ultimately inferior staff.

TWW's presidentiality is thus complex and multi-layered. *TWW*'s presidentiality evidences its postmodernity by disrupting traditional images of power, but it also reifies the same romantic images that are predicated on the power of the white, male hero. As such, the postmodern critique that *TWW* offers the audience is limited because it emerges from within a modernist narrative framework.

Various consequences result. First, *TWW*'s modern, romantic rendition of presidentiality may restore a sense of idealism to politics. A 2001 study completed by the Council for Excellence in Government recognizes *TWW* for "giving elected officials the second most improved image" recorded among all occupations, moving these workers ahead of business leaders and teachers in public esteem. This study reveals the power of presidential images emanating from popular culture; the Council notes, for example, that such a rise in esteem is due to the "depth of its [*TWW*'s] characters" and to its focus on "real issues and sincere commitments" that reject the "cynical" vision of politics.[68]

The modernist and romantic depictions in *TWW* are ideologically troubling, however, because they also instantiate traditional images of the U.S.

presidency that are decidedly masculine, white, individualized, intellectualized, and militarized. The mimesis of popular culture's presidentiality is critical to the ideological impact of such discourses. "That [art] *seems* to be such a mirror strengthens its potency as ideology," contends Murray Edelman.[69] If the United States ever hopes to achieve a representative politics that looks like its citizenry, popular culture renditions must disturb the all too common and comfortable narrative emplotments that have demarcated the presidency within traditional, modern, romantic parameters.

To some extent, the postmodern, oppositional tendencies of *TWW,* while limited, are still productive. As women and people of color are placed in positions of power, the drama works gradually to naturalize the diversification of power. Given the mimetic features of popular culture, viewers become accustomed to an altered presidentiality that articulates a more collective, nonviolent, and inclusive vision of leadership. If the Council for Excellence in Government's study is valid, the mimetic features of *TWW* affect perceptions of government employees, which must inspirit, at least unconsciously, a more progressive attitude toward a more multicultural executive. Over time, popular culture's mimesis can continue the erosion of the presidency's traditional and exclusionary characteristics.

In this postmodern age of presidential politics, citizens are schooled, at least partially, in the postmodern critique of power, as they are taught to discern the fallibility and foibles of presidential "heroes" (e.g., Kennedy, Johnson, Nixon, Ford, Carter, Reagan, Bush, and Clinton). Such guardedness is productive and necessary. A more adversarial public and a more questioning citizenry may prove to be a more political public. The postmodern presidentiality of popular culture, as expressed in *TWW,* reminds us of that fallibility and perhaps lessens the unproductive expectation that presidents should be seen in mythic and heroic ways. Those popular culture texts give a glimpse of the "backstage" and a sense of the tortured individual leader, working in contradistinction to the highly managed, frontstage imaging of contemporary presidents. They add a depth and a richness to our understanding of the U.S. presidency and the men who have occupied that office.

Measured against a modern romantic vision, all future presidents will without question fail, and historians will continue to remind us of the failures of our past presidential heroes. *TWW* is a reminder that it is time to stop longing for the mythic hero's return. It invites us, instead, to seek a postmodern leader who may be flawed and conflicted but who will succeed in bettering the lives of *all* who live in this increasingly diverse and complicated nation.

Notes

An earlier version of this essay was presented at the annual convention of the National Communication Association, Atlanta, 2001.

The authors wish to thank Sharon Downey and the QJS reviewers for their helpful comments and Karlyn Kohrs Campbell for her meticulous editing of this manuscript.

1. According to the Internet Movie Database (http://www.imdb.com/), 31 feature

films were released in the 1990s and in 2000 that feature the president or members of the president's family or staff, including: *Absolute Power* (1997), *Air Force One* (1997), *The American President* (1995), *Angel of Pennsylvania Avenue* (1996), *Bad Trout* (2000), *Chain of Command* (2000), *Clear and Present Danger* (1994), *The Contender* (2000), *Dave* (1993), *Deep Impact* (1998), *Deterrence* (1999), *Dick* (1999), *Executive Power* (1997), *Executive Target* (1997), *Feed* (1992), *First Daughter* (2000), *First Kid* (1996), *Hot Shots, Part Deux* (1993), *Guarding Tess* (1994), *In the Line of Fire* (1993), *Independence Day* (1996), *Jefferson in Paris* (1995), *JFK* (1991), *Mars Attacks!* (1996), *My Fellow Americans* (1996), *Nixon* (1995), *The Peacekeeper* (1997), *Primary Colors* (1998), *Shadow Conspiracy* (1997), *The War Room* (1993), and *Wild, Wild West* (1999)

2. John M. Murphy reveals the power of popular culture and its depictions of the presidency when he suggests the possibility of a return to a heroic tradition for presidential rhetoric in his admiration for such mediated presidents as Morgan Freeman in *Deep Impact*, Harrison Ford in *Air Force One*, Bill Pullman in *Independence Day*, Michael Douglas in *The American President*, Kevin Kline in *Dave*, and Martin Sheen in *The West Wing*. See John M. Murphy, "The Heroic Tradition in Presidential Rhetoric," *Rhetoric & Public Affairs* 3 (2000): 466–70.

3. For a more extended discussion of presidentiality, see Shawn J. Parry-Giles and Trevor Parry-Giles, *Constructing Clinton: Hyperreality and Presidential Image-Making in Postmodern Politics* (New York: Peter Lang, forthcoming). The term "presidentiality" rarely appears. It occurs once in memos written to President Gerald Ford by aide Foster Channock about the 1976 elections and the need to communicate Ford's "presidentiality." See "Thoughts on Presidentiality," Foster Channock Files, Gerald R. Ford Library, Grand Rapids, Michigan. Mark Crispin Miller uses "presidentiality" to designate the "presidential" adjectives that George W. Bush lacks. See Mark Crispin Miller, *The Bush Dyslexicon: Observations on a National Disorder* (New York: W. W. Norton, 2001), 32.

4. Our analysis concerns the first season of *TWW* (1999–2000), with some references to the first episode of the second season.

5. See Richard W. Waterman, Robert Wright, and Gilbert K. St. Clair, *The Image-Is-Everything Presidency: Dilemmas in American Leadership* (Boulder: Westview Press, 1999), 161. Addressing the impact of the Clinton impeachment, Richard A. Posner contends that "The mystique of the Presidency became a casualty of the narration in the Starr Report and of the public interrogation of the President by a grand jury before a global audience." See *An Affair of State: The Investigation, Impeachment, and Trial of President Clinton* (Cambridge, MA: Harvard University Press, 1999), 265. Others studies include Colin Campbell and Bert A. Rockman, eds., *The Clinton Legacy* (New York: Chatham House, 2000); and Mark J. Rozell and Clyde Wilcox, eds., *The Clinton Scandal and the Future of American Government* (Washington, DC: Georgetown University Press, 2000).

6. John Fiske contends that the postmodernist "refutes any hierarchicalization of the different truths produced by the different modes of representation." Accordingly, concentrations of power are criticized and distinctions between truth and falsehood are problematized, politicized, and associated with "specific historical time and geographical region." See *Media Matters: Race and Gender in U.S. Politics* (Minneapolis: University of Minnesota Press, 1996), 62. See also Linda J. Nicholson, ed., "Introduction," in *Feminism/Postmodernism* (New York: Routledge, 1990), 4.

7. Several commentators note the decline of the contemporary presidency. See Stephen Paul Miller, *The Seventies Now: Culture as Surveillance* (Durham: Duke University Press, 1999); and Bruce J. Schulman, *The Seventies: The Great Shift in American Culture, Society, and Politics* (New York: Free Press, 2001).

8. Many observers discuss a rise of cynicism occasioned by adversarial journalism.

See W. Lance Bennett, *News: The Politics of Illusion,* 2nd ed. (New York: Longman, 1988); Joseph N. Cappella and Kathleen Hall Jamieson, *Spiral of Cynicism: The Press and the Public Good* (New York: Oxford University Press, 1997); William Chaloupka, *Everybody Knows: Cynicism in America* (Minneapolis: University of Minnesota Press, 1999); Roderick P. Hart, *Seducing America: How Television Charms the Modern Voter* (New York: Oxford University Press, 1994); and Thomas E. Patterson, *Out of Order* (New York: A. Knopf, 1993).

9. Sharon Waxman, "Inside *The West Wing's* New World," *George* (November 2000): 54–9; 94–6.

10. James W. Chesebro, "Communication, Values, and Popular Television Series— A Seventeen-Year Assessment," *Communication Quarterly* 39 (1991): 220. We do not rely on Chesebro's conclusion that in mimetic communication characters mirror the audience.

11. Audiences evaluate messages differently, resulting in polyvalent texts reflecting their ideological positioning. See Jodi R. Cohen, "The 'Relevance' of Cultural Identity in Audiences' Interpretations of Mass Media," *Critical Studies in Mass Communication* 8 (1994): 442–54; Celeste Michelle Condit, "The Rhetorical Limits of Polysemy," *Critical Studies in Mass Communication* 6 (1989): 103–22; Brenda Cooper, "The Relevancy and Gender Identity in Spectators' Interpretations of *Thelma & Louise,*" *Critical Studies in Mass Communication* 16 (1999): 20–41; and Bonnie J. Dow, *Prime-Time Feminism: Television, Media Culture, and the Women's Movement Since 1970* (Philadelphia: University of Pennsylvania Press, 1996).

12. Fred I. Greenstein, *The Presidential Difference: Leadership Style from FDR to Clinton* (New York: Martin Kessler Books/Free Press, 2000), 3.

13. See Barbara Hinckley, *The Symbolic Presidency: How Presidents Portray Themselves* (New York: Routledge, 1990).

14. Stephen Skowronek, *The Politics that Presidents Make: Leadership from John Adams to Bill Clinton* (Cambridge, MA: The Belknap Press of Harvard University Press, 1997), 15, emphasis added.

15. Jeffrey Tulis, *The Rhetorical Presidency* (Princeton, NJ: Princeton University Press, 1987), 203.

16. Analyses of presidential rhetoric include Karlyn Kohrs Campbell and Kathleen Hall Jamieson, *Deeds Done in Words: Presidential Rhetoric and the Genres of Governance* (Chicago: University of Chicago Press, 1990); Richard J. Ellis, ed., *Speaking to the People: The Rhetorical Presidency in Historical Perspective* (Amherst: University of Massachusetts Press, 1998); Wayne Fields, *Union of Words: A History of Presidential Eloquence* (New York: Free Press, 1996); Carol Gelderman, *All the Presidents' Words: The Bully Pulpit and the Creation of the Virtual Presidency* (New York: Walker and Company, 1997); Samuel Kernall, *Going Public: New Strategies of Presidential Leadership,* 3rd ed. (Washington, DC: CQ Press, 1997); and Martin J. Medhurst, ed., *Beyond the Rhetorical Presidency* (College Station: Texas A & M University Press, 1996). A review of the literature on the rhetorical presidency is offered by Mary Stuckey and Frederick J. Antczak, "The Rhetorical Presidency: Deepening Vision, Widening Exchange," *Communication Yearbook* 21 (1998): 405–41.

17. Martin J. Medhurst, "Introduction," in *Beyond the Rhetorical Presidency* (College Station: Texas A & M University Press, 1996), xi.

18. Thomas B. Farrell, "Rhetorical Resemblance: Paradoxes of a Practical Art," *Quarterly Journal of Speech* 72 (1986): 17.

19. The most famous example is Bill Clinton's 1992 appearance on the *Arsenio Hall Show.* During the 2000 election campaign, Al Gore and George W. Bush appeared on *Oprah, Late Night with David Letterman, The Tonight Show,* and *Live with Regis,*

among others. For discussions of this phenomenon, see Richard Davis and Diana Owen, *New Media and American Politics* (New York: Oxford University Press, 1998); and Edwin Diamond and Robert A. Silverman, *White House to Your House: Media and Politics in Virtual America* (Cambridge, MA: MIT Press, 1997).

20. Gunter Gebauer and Christoph Wulf, *Mimesis: Culture, Art, Society,* translated by Don Reneau (Berkeley: University of California Press, 1992), 317. See also Thomas Twining, "On Poetry Considered as an Imitative Art," in *Aristotle's 'Poetics' and English Literature: A Collection of Critical Essays,* edited by Elder Olson (Chicago: University of Chicago Press, 1965), 45–6.

21. Gebauer and Wulf, *Mimesis,* 119.

22. Lee Sigelman, "Taking Popular Fiction Seriously," in *Reading Political Stories: Representations of Politics in Novels and Pictures,* edited by Maureen Whitebook (Lanham, MD: Rowman & Littlefield, 1992), 151.

23. James Combs argues, "Movies are part of the communication process wherein a political-culture-in-time is defining what's happening politically in the context of temporal immediacy." See *American Political Movies: An Annotated Filmography of Feature Films* (New York: Garland, 1990), xii.

24. Chesebro, "Communication, Values, and Popular Television Series," 213.

25. Walter R. Fisher, "Romantic Democracy, Ronald Reagan, and Presidential Heroes," *Western Journal of Speech Communication* 46 (1982): 302.

26. Christopher Caudwell, *Romance and Realism: A Study in English Bourgeois Literature,* edited by Samuel Hynes (Princeton, NJ: Princeton University Press, 1970), 37.

27. Northrop Frye, *The Secular Scripture: A Study of the Structure of Romance* (Cambridge, MA: Harvard University Press, 1976), 55.

28. Northrop Frye, *Anatomy of Criticism: Four Essays* (New York: Atheneum, 1967), 186.

29. William Lewis, "Of Innocence, Exclusion, and the Burning of Flags: The Romantic Realism of the Law," *Southern Communication Journal* 60 (1994): 12.

30. Frye, *The Secular Scripture,* 50.

31. Lewis, "Of Innocence, Exclusion, and the Burning of Flags," 12.

32. John M. Murphy, "Knowing the President: The Dialogic Evolution of the Campaign History," *Quarterly Journal of Speech* 84 (1998): 30.

33. See Jeff D. Bass, "The Romance as Rhetorical Dissociation: The Purification of Imperialism in *King Solomon's Mines,*" *Quarterly Journal of Speech* 67 (1981): 259, 268; Diane Elam, "Feminism and the Postmodern: Theory's Romance," in *The Feminist Reader: Essays in Gender and the Politics of Literary Criticism,* 2nd ed., edited by Catherine Belsey and Jane Moore (Malden, MA: Blackwell, 1997), 196; and Wendy B. Faris, "Scheherazade's Children: Magical Realism and Postmodern Fiction," in *Magical Realism: Theory, History, Community,* edited by Lois Parkinson Zamora and Wendy B. Faris (Durham: Duke University Press, 1995), 185.

34. A complete list of the awards and honors received by *TWW* and its cast can be found at http://www.geocities.com/westwing01/.

35. Waxman, "Inside *The West Wing's* New World," 94.

36. Julian Rubinstein, "Politically Correct," *US,* October 1999, 74.

37. Mary Murphy, "House Call," *TV Guide,* July 22–28, 2000, 15–24.

38. Matthew Miller, "The Real White House," *Brill's Content,* March 2000, 88. A *New York Times* article assesses the realism of *TWW,* noting areas in which "the show is much glossier than the reality." See "'West Wing' Fact and Fiction," *New York Times,* July 2001, 14.

39. Frye, *Anatomy of Criticism,* 187.

40. Joshua Meyrowitz, *No Sense of Place: The Impact of Electronic Media on Social Behavior* (New York: Oxford University Press, 1985), 268–304.

41. Other television exigencies explain why the characters on *TWW* are routinely shown multitasking as they circulate through the offices and corridors of the White House. Lewis Grossberger noted that "the producers realized the show would be big on talk." Conversation is not visually exciting "so the actors have to shout their lines while rushing past each other and racing in and out of each other's offices. Everyone is constantly in motion, spouting political gibberish." Such activity reinforces a sense of turmoil and uncertainty, which becomes central to *TWW*'s vision of presidentiality. See Lewis Grossberger, "Now and Before," *MediaWeek,* October 18, 1999, 82.

42. Caren J. Deming notes that unlike most melodramas, which are "essentially a modernist form," the police drama *Hill Street Blues* did not offer "moral absolutes" or heroes with "certainty of virtue." See Caren J. Deming, "*Hill Street Blues* as Narrative," *Critical Studies in Mass Communication* 2 (1985): 7.

43. See Lois Parkinson Zamora, "Magical Romance/Magical Realism: Ghosts in U.S. and Latin American Fiction," in *Magical Realism: Theory, History, Community,* edited by Lois Parkinson Zamora and Wendy B. Faris (Durham: Duke University Press, 1995), 511; Chesebro, "Communication, Values, and Popular Television Series," 215; and Murphy, "The Heroic Tradition in Presidential Rhetoric."

44. Most citations from *TWW* derive from videotapes of the episodes, but some citations are from transcripts of the program previously found at http://www.testytoads .com/TWW/. This site has ceased operation, and all transcripts from this site were matched to the videotaped version of the episode.

45. Frye. *Anatomy of Criticism,* 187.

46. Deming, "*Hill Street Blues* as Narrative," 15.

47. Robert W. Connell, *Gender and Power: Society, the Person, and Sexual Politics* (Stanford, CA: Stanford University Press, 1987). See also Shawn J. Parry-Giles and Trevor Parry-Giles, "Gendered Politics and Presidential Image Construction: A Reassessment of the 'Feminine Style,'" *Communication Monographs* 63 (1996): 337–53.

48. The Clinton administration worked with Hollywood to lessen the amount of violence in television and film, and the president called on the entertainment industry to work with the administration to create more positive television programming for children in his 1996 "State of the Union" address. See William Jefferson Clinton, "1996 State of the Union Address," January 23, 1996, http://clinton4.nara.gov/textonly/ WH/New/other/sotu.html.

49. Lesley Johnson, "'As Housewives we are Worms': Women, Modernity, and the Home Question," in *Feminism & Cultural Studies,* edited by Morag Shiach (Oxford: Oxford University Press, 1999), 478.

50. In 1992, Bill Clinton promised to create a White House that looked like the nation. When *TWW* first aired, DeWayne Wickham, of *USA Today* maintains that Ben Johnson of President Clinton's Initiative for One America visited with *TWW*'s producers to encourage greater diversity on the program so as to help "this nation escape the bog of our racial division." See DeWayne Wickham, "TV's White House is Just Too White," *USA Today,* March 21, 2000, available at www.usatoday.com/news/ comment/columnists/wickham/wick073.htm.

51. See Nick Trujillo, "Hegemonic Masculinity on the Mound: Media Representations of Nolan Ryan and American Sports Culture," *Critical Studies in Mass Communication* 8 (1991): 291.

52. Susan Brownmiller, *Femininity* (New York: Linden Press/Simon & Schuster, 1984), 16.

53. See "Media Advisory: NAACP to Take New Actions to Increase Television Diversity," May 24, 2001, available at http://www.naacp.org/news/releases/TV div52401.shtml.

54. Herman Gray, *Watching Race: Television and the Struggle for "Blackness"* (Minneapolis: University of Minnesota Press, 1995), 171–2. Thomas K. Nakayama discusses the tendency to "(re)construct white heterosexual masculinity [i.e., power] in the wake of an emasculating Vietnam experience, and with a white society facing a multicultural future." See "Show/Down Time: 'Race,' Gender, Sexuality, and Popular Culture," *Critical Studies in Mass Communication* 11 (1994): 162–79.

55. Murray Edelman, *From Art to Politics: How Artistic Creations Shape Political Conceptions* (Chicago: University of Chicago Press, 1995), 63.

56. See Fiske, *Media Matters*, 62. See also Stephen H. Browne, "Remembering Crispus Attucks: Race, Rhetoric, and the Politics of Commemoration," *Quarterly Journal of Speech* 85 (1999): 186; and Eva Illouz, "The Lost Innocence of Love: Romance as a Postmodern Condition," *Theory, Culture & Society* 15 (1998): 161–86.

57. Images of "realism" typically are "conservative" because of the "acceptance of society in its present structure." See Frye, *The Secular Scripture*, 164.

58. Edelman, *From Art to Politics*, 63.

59. Frye, *Anatomy of Criticism*, 187.

60. See Frye, *The Secular Scripture*, 58; and John A. McClure, "Postmodern Romance: Don DeLillo and the Age of Conspiracy," *South Atlantic Quarterly* 89 (1990): 353.

61. Chesebro, "Communication, Values, and Popular Television Series," 206.

62. Robert K. Murray and Tim H. Blessing, *Greatness in the White House: Rating the Presidents*, 2nd ed. (University Park: The Pennsylvania State University Press, 1994).

63. Forrest McDonald, *The American Presidency: An Intellectual History* (Lawrence: University Press of Kansas, 1994), 433. See also Shawn J. Parry-Giles and Trevor Parry-Giles, "Meta-Imaging, *The War Room*, and the Hyperreality of American Politics," *Journal of Communication* 49 (1999): 28–45; Samuel L. Popkin, *The Reasoning Voter: Communication and Persuasion in Presidential Campaigns* (Chicago: University of Chicago Press, 1991); and Theodore O. Windt, Jr., "Presidential Rhetoric: Definition of a Field of Study," *Central States Speech Journal* 35 (1984): 24–34.

64. Bruce Miroff, *Icons of Democracy: American Leaders as Heroes, Aristocrats, Dissenters, and Democrats* (New York: Basic Books, 1993), 354–5.

65. Laura Mulvey, *Visual and Other Pleasures* (Bloomington: Indiana University Press, 1989).

66. Thomas K. Nakayama and Robert L. Krizek, "Whiteness: A Strategic Rhetoric," *Quarterly Journal of Speech* 81 (1995): 293.

67. Homi K. Bhabha, "The Other Question: Difference, Discrimination and the Discourse of Colonialism," in *Out There: Marginalization and Contemporary Cultures*, edited by Russell Ferguson, et al. (New York: The New Museum of Contemporary Art, 1990), 71–2. See also Edward W. Said, *Orientalism* (New York: Vintage Books, 1979); and Nakayama, "Show/Down Time," 162–79. John A. McClure implicitly connects western ways of knowing with modernist expressions. See McClure, "Postmodern Romance," 347.

68. "Changing Images of Government in TV Entertainment," Council for Excellence in Government, June 5, 2001, available at http://www.excelgov.org/index.htm.

69. Edelman, *From Art to Politics*, 62 (emphasis in original).

Sex and the City and Consumer Culture
Remediating Postfeminist Drama

Jane Arthurs

Introduction

A new approach to the representation of women's sexuality in television drama has emerged in the form of Home Box Office's (HBO) hit comedy series *Sex and the City* (1998–). The aim of this article is to show how the success of *Sex and the City* is symptomatic of the forces shaping programmes in the digital, multichannel era of television that allow for innovation in its sexualised mode of address. I also want to suggest how this development might be understood in the light of debates about the politics of postfeminist culture. I will explore how the creation of a successful brand in this crowded market depends on the ability to innovate within a pattern of predictable pleasures to create a recognisable identity for a product that appeals to a commercially attractive audience (John Ellis 2000: 165–9). The novelty of *Sex and the City*, I argue, lies in the migration of a woman-centred and explicit sexual discourse into television drama. Its distinctive appeal arises from its ability to "re-mediate" the familiar forms of the television sitcom and the glossy women's magazine. Remediation is used by Jay David Bolter and Richard Grusin as a term to describe the forms in which new media arise, as each medium "responds to, re-deploys, competes with and reforms other media" (1999: 35).

Sex and the City can be compared to previous examples of postfeminist, woman-centred drama produced for prime-time network television in the US. These are dramas that in the wake of second-wave feminism selectively deploy feminist discourses as a response to cultural changes in the lives of their potential audience, an audience that is addressed as white, heterosexual, and relatively youthful and affluent. They emerged out of a hybridisation of genres driven by a desire to maximise audiences by creating drama that appealed to both men and women. The feminisation of crime genres such as cop shows (*Cagney and Lacey*) and legal dramas (*LA Law, Ally McBeal*) allowed for an exploitation of the generic pleasures associated with the masculine, public world of work and

Jane Arthurs, "*Sex and the City* and Consumer Culture: Remediating Postfeminist Drama." From *Feminist Media Studies*, Vol. 3, No. 1 (2003), pp. 81–96. Reprinted by permission of Taylor & Francis Ltd. (http::/www.tandf.co.uk/journals).

the feminised, private world of personal relationships (Julie D'Acci 1987; Bonnie J. Dow 1996; Amanda D. Lotz 2001; Judith Mayne [1988] 1997; Rachel Moseley and Jacinda Read 2002). Their responsiveness to changes in the sociopolitical context had also allowed for an engagement with liberal feminist issues arising from women's relation to the law and to work. A focus on women as protagonists, whose actions drive the narrative, replaced the marginal and narrow range of roles available previously to women characters in these genres. Although it shares their incorporation of feminist themes and their focus on the liberal, heterosexual, white, metropolitan, career woman, *Sex and the City* is very different from these networked dramas. These differences arise, I would argue, from the institutional conditions of its production and distribution. It was made not as prime-time network TV but as subscription cable television. This has a number of consequences for the form that it takes.

One of the consequences of the multiplication of channels has been a diversification in television's address to audiences. Specialist channels catering to particular social groups or taste cultures have proliferated. It moves the television industry much closer to the magazine industry, which addresses niche markets and where there is very little overlap between men's and women's titles. This has a number of consequences. One is that it draws the audience into a different economic relation to the product, where the tastes of the audience-as-market, as direct purchasers of the channel, are not as obscured by the normalising processes of the mass market. This segmentation allows for a pluralism that recognises previously marginalised cultures, albeit limited by their ability to pay. It also encourages polarisation, especially between male and female audiences (Benjamin Compaine and Douglas Gomery 2000: 524). *Sex and the City* is addressed to affluent, white women as a segment of the market, in which it re-mediates the address developed in the established women's media, namely glossy women's magazines. This reverses the trend towards the hybridisation of masculine and feminine genres that has characterised prime-time drama on network television.

The argument introduced here is developed in the following sections where I look at how the programme remediates the content and address of women's magazines for television and the Internet; how its brand identity is established across the interlocking circuits of the media, celebrity, and fashion to construct an address to the "bourgeois bohemians"; the resultant instability in its aestheticised mode of address as it oscillates between complicity and critique of a consumer lifestyle; and, finally, the consequences this has for its construction of women's sexuality.

Having It All

In the hybrid, women-centred, work-based drama characteristic of postfeminist television in the 1980s and 1990s, one of the main issues has been the division between the world of work and the private world of the domestic sphere that prevents women "having it all." In *Sex and the City,* the world of work largely disappears from view as a distinct space and set of hierarchical relations, although the women's autonomy from men is underwritten by their economic independence. For three of the four women who make up the main characters in the series, work is collapsed into the private sphere and becomes another form of self-expression, alongside consumption, thereby side-stepping the postfeminist problematic. Carrie's sex life and those of her friends act as research for her weekly newspaper column, which she writes from home. Samantha works in public relations, a job where her physical attractions and personal charm are intrinsic to her success. Charlotte manages an art gallery in a manner that suggests it is more of a hobby. This might be regarded either as a magical resolution of a continuing contradiction in women's lives or a realistic reflection of the opportunities for educated urban women in the contemporary labour market. Only Miranda feels the contradiction between her private life and her career success as a lawyer.[1] Even so, when Miranda accidentally becomes pregnant (in Season 4) and has the baby without getting married, she gets by with the help of her friends, including the child's father.

There is a generic expectation that postfeminist drama will be about single women wanting to get married. *Sex and the City* was initially marketed as such to feed into those expectations. The video blurb for the first season states "Sexy, hip, smart and sassy, *Sex and the City* charts the lives and loves of four women and their quest to find the one thing that eludes them all—a real, satisfying and lasting relationship. Is such a thing possible in New York?" (*Sex and the City* 1999–2001). But unlike other postfeminist narratives, in *Sex and the City* the responsibility for single women's unhappiness isn't laid at the door of feminist women choosing a career over a man. Of the four women only Charlotte is unequivocal in her desire to get married but is quickly disillusioned when she does. The traditional romance narrative is still there but as a residual sensibility, a slightly old-fashioned version of femininity that doesn't work in practice. Charlotte's belief in romance and saving yourself for your husband is undercut by his impotence on their wedding night and her discovery that he can be aroused only by a porn magazine in the bathroom, thereby completely puncturing the romantic myth (Episode 45 "Hot Child in the City").[2] When Carrie and friends visit a former New Yorker for her baby shower (Episode 10 "The Baby Shower") they aren't shown envying the woman her home in the country, her husband, and her coming baby—rather it accentuates the gulf which separates them from her—and they return to their single lives in New York with a huge sigh of relief.

The women's single state is rather a necessary precondition for their central preoccupation—sexual relationships and how to achieve sexual satisfaction—not previously considered a suitable topic for television drama. The series publicly repudiates the shame of being single and sexually active in defiance of the bourgeois codes that used to be demanded of respectable women. It self-reflexively interrogates media representations of the single woman although the emotional power of these residual stereotypes is acknowledged. For example, when Carrie appears looking haggard and smoking a cigarette on the front of a magazine under the strapline "Single and Fabulous?" it sparks a discussion amongst the four women about why the media want to persuade women to get married (Episode 16 "They Shoot Single People Don't They?"). Despite their intellectual critique, the rest of the episode explores the emotional vulnerabilities of their situation before concluding that it's better to be alone than faking happiness with a man. There is no shame attached to being alone. It ends with Carrie eating by herself in a restaurant, with no book to read as armour, to assert her belief that she really is "Single and Fabulous"! (with no question mark).

This exploration of women's sexuality is enabled by changes in the regulatory regime of television as a consequence of digital convergence. It has moved closer to the freedoms enjoyed by the print media and the Internet as compared to the sensitivity to religious Puritanism historically shown by the television networks.[3] In a context freed from the moral constraints of network television, *Sex and the City* is able to exploit fully the glossy women's magazines' consumerist approach to sexuality, in which women's sexual pleasure and agency is frankly encouraged as part of a consumer lifestyle and attitude. In this respect, *Sex and the City* has moved a long way from the kind of family-centred or wholesome peer-group sitcoms that have previously dominated the network schedules, in which embodied desire provided the repressed subtext rather the primary focus of the dialogue and action. Hybridisation of the discourse of women's magazines with the codes of the television sitcom has provided the "licensed space" for an exploration of sexual taboos and decorum (Jane Arthurs 1999; Steve Neale and Frank Krutnick 1990).

This hybridisation has also allowed for the consumer attitude to be lightly satirised, a response that is argued to be characteristic of an aestheticised relation to the self. It is this sensibility that allows for the adoption of ironic ways of consuming and a self-reflexive attitude to one's own identity, appearance, and self-presentation. Michael Featherstone (1991) characterises the aestheticised relation to the self as one in which consumers enjoy the swings between the extremes of aesthetic involvement and distanciation, a sensibility he argues is characteristic of the new middle classes of postmodern culture. It is a form of controlled hedonism that oscillates between complicity with the values of consumer culture, and critique. This allows a certain section of the "baby-boomer" generation the simultaneous satisfaction of the sensual pleasures allowed by material success along with the placating of their guilty, liberal conscience. It emerged in the "Yuppie TV" of the work-obsessed 1980s, where both envy and guilt were deliberately evoked in response to the affluent lifestyles of its protagonists. In *LA Law* for example, the guilt was differentiated by gender. For men it was guilt at their material success whereas for women it was guilt at their lost opportunity for marriage and children (Jane Feuer 1995).

The almost exclusive focus on sexual relationships and consumption in *Sex and the City* speaks instead to the wider cultural influence in the 1990s of the "bourgeois bohemians." This class fraction has, David Brooks (2000) argues, replaced the Yuppies as the new dominant class in the US (and other Western economies). The key feature of this new class fraction is their ability to reconcile the contradictions between bourgeois and bohemian values and lifestyles. Sexual permissiveness, that in the bohemian movements of the 1960s was articulated with radical anti-capitalist political values, has been re-articulated to con-form, not only with the materialist priorities of consumer culture, but also with the emancipatory politics of the 1970s and 1980s. One effect has been to free white, middle-class women from the sexual constraints required by bourgeois respectability.[4]

A scene from the first season of *Sex and the City* (Episode 6 "Secret Sex") encapsulates this brand identity, that is to say the emotions, attitudes, and lifestyle with which it is associated and the specificity of its address. In an episode that explores the shame that some sexual experiences can provoke, Carrie, the series central character, gathers a group of her friends together for the launch of a new publicity campaign promoting her weekly column called "Sex and the City." They wait on the sidewalk for a bus to pass by carrying the poster for her brand on its side. They are in a mood of excited anticipation, marred only by the regret that Mr. Big, the new man in her life, has failed to show up to share this proud moment. The revealing dress she is wearing in the poster is the dress that she had worn on their first date, when, despite her best judgement, they had sex. As the bus approaches, the excitement turns to dismay, and Carrie hides her face in shame. There is the poster with Carrie's body stretched in languorous pose along the full length of the bus, under the strapline "Carrie Bradshaw knows good sex." But as we pan across her body, next to her seductively made-up lips a crudely drawn outline of a large penis is revealed.

This short scene exemplifies the series' dramatic terrain, namely the explo-ration of women's sexuality in a postmodern consumer culture. It is a culture produced by capital's restless search for new and expanded markets, and char-acterised by the commodification of the individual's relation to the body, self, and identity, just as we see here in the relation of Carrie to her billboard image. The scene also exemplifies the programme's tone and style which mixes the display of celebrity lifestyles for our emulation, as in women's magazines, with a comic puncturing of these aestheticised images. The idealised image of bour-geois perfection in the image of Carrie on her billboard is momentarily satirised by the obscene graffiti. It is an eruption of the repressed "other" to bourgeois femininity in a deliberate disruption of its codes of sexual decorum. This, plus Big's absence, are both reminders of women's vulnerability to loss of self-esteem when it relies too exclusively on body image and its sexual appeal to men. The presence of Carrie's friends is important though in providing the support and reassurance she needs to regain her composure. Their shared cul-ture of femininity offers an alternative to heterosexual dependence.

Feminist evaluations of *Sex and the City* have conflated it with other exam-ples of postfeminist culture in which comedy and satire has replaced any serious, ethical commitment to challenging the power relations of patriarchy, a challenge that they argue is undermined by complicit critique. The postfeminist irony in texts such as *Bridget Jones* or *Ally McBeal* allows for a constant emphasis on women's appearance and sexual desirability as a source of worth whilst simulta-neously subjecting this attitude to ridicule (Germaine Greer 1999; Imelda Whelehan 2000). In this view, the ironic oscillations in our relation to the bour-geois women who people the fictional world of *Sex and the City* are complicit with the aestheticised values of consumer culture and its unequal structuring of the "look." It assumes women in the audience are invited to share this male gaze to the extent that it is internalised in women's narcissistic relation to their own bodies. This objectifies women's bodies and renders them powerless. In a counter-argument, feminine cultures of consumerism and fashion have been considered as a source of pleasure and power that is potentially resistant to male control. Indeed they can offer women an alternative route to self-esteem and autonomy that overcomes the damaging division that second-wave feminism constructs between feminism and femininity (see Joanne Hollows 2000; Celia Lury 1996; Angela McRobbie 1997 for an overview of these debates).

These contradictory evaluations need not be presented as alternatives. Part of the problem for academic feminism is to develop arguments that capture the complex contradictions of postfeminism in popular culture. In her discussion of the emphasis on the spectacle of women's bodies in women's magazines, Hilary Radner (1995) draws attention to the way this is counteracted by a textual commentary that variously endorses or asks us to question the extent to which women's worth resides in her looks. In arguing the limitations to metacritical feminist discourse in capturing women's reading practices in everyday life, Radner highlights the potential of feminine culture to "displace the political onto the minute decisions of a contingent day to day practice in which absolute categories cannot be maintained from moment to moment" (1995: 178). Consumption is thereby redefined as an active process that has unpredictable ideological consequences. In Scott Lash's (1990) view, the ubiquity of images in postmodern consumer culture in itself produces contradictory juxtapositions that undermine any secure position from which to interpret the world. This, he argues, has the potential to produce self-reflexive, nomadic identities in which gender, for instance, is open to re-definition (Lash 1990: 185–98). *Sex and the City* self-consciously explores the instability of feminine identity in a postfeminist, postmodern consumer culture.

Its commodity form precludes a straightforward celebration of the feminist potential of consumer culture, however. This promotes, according to Susan Willis (1991), an alienated and fetishised relationship between people defined by the exchange of commodities. Moreover, the codification of class, race, and gender differences in the stylistic details of commodities normalises and perpetuates notions of inequality and subordination (Willis 1991: 162–3). The professional middle classes have, in her view, been duped by the signs of privilege into confusing the individualised freedom to consume with real political power. Argues Willis, "The production of resistant meanings by individuals will always be assimilated by capitalism for the production of fresh commodities" (1991: 175).

Sex and the City exemplifies these features of the commodity. Its stylistic features contribute to the cultural hegemony of the incorporated resistance of the bourgeois bohemians. Its culture of femininity provides an alternative to heterosexual dependence but its recurring promise of a shameless utopia of fulfilled desire always ends in disappointment for the cycle of consumption to begin again next week.

Remediation

New technologies of representation proceed by reforming or remediating earlier ones, while earlier technologies are struggling to
maintain their legitimacy by remediating newer ones.

(Bolter and Grusin 1999:61)

Sex and the City is the product of an emerging form of globally dominant
television. It is a quality comedy drama series with high production values produced for the subscription cable channel, Home Box Office (HBO). America
Online/Time Warner, who merged in 2000, owns HBO. They also bought
IPC (International Publishing Corporation), the magazine publisher, in 2001.
This economic convergence has produced an international media conglomerate covering the Internet and print media, as well as television. HBO has to
sell itself first to its subscribers in the US, on the basis of its appeal to a sufficiently affluent segment of the potential market, before syndicating to other
distributors in a global market. Arguably, its relative freedom from government regulation and from the restraints imposed by advertisers in comparison
to the networks makes it more responsive to the tastes and values of new social
groups (Lury 1993: 40–51).

The high production costs of "quality" drama have provoked fears of its
demise when the amounts for production are more thinly spread across a multiplicity of channels. Instead, as the case of HBO demonstrates, it may well
migrate to subscription-based services (Ellis 2000: 174). For HBO "quality"
drama has been used successfully to enhance both its visibility and its reputation in a context where cable television has had to struggle to gain any cultural status at all. In 2001 *Sex and the City* won the Emmy for Outstanding
Comedy series, the first time a cable television show has ever taken top hon-
ours for best series in any category (http://www.hbo.com/city/insiders?
guide/news). News items and features relating to *Sex and the City* appear regularly in the print media and work to maintain its visibility and status as "must
see TV." Its success has been achieved by generic innovation to address a niche
market. Rather than offering a mixed schedule or hybridised genres for family
viewing, as the networks do, HBO's brand name acts as an umbrella for multiple channels that separate out programmes designed for specific audiences. A
whole channel is addressed to women: HBO Signature, "Smart, sophisticated
entertainment for women." In a week during July 2001 it was offering a Friday night with "back to back" *Sex and the City*, plus movies themed as
"Romance Feature" or "Leading Ladies Feature—a different leading lady every
Friday night" (http://hbo.com/schedule).

Print media influence the form of *Sex and the City*. Adapted from a book
written by Candace Bushnell ([1996] 1997), a New York journalist, it is structured around the fictionalised writing of a weekly newspaper column. It retains
the first-person mode of direct address, using Carrie's voice-over to comment
on the action in which a question is posed, journalistic research is undertaken
and some conclusions proposed in a personalised, witty and aphoristic style.

The questions range from the frivolous to the taboo. They can be serious but not too serious. They don't deal with rape or sexual harassment as in *LA Law* or *Ally McBeal*.

> Can women have sex like a man? . . . Are men commitment phobes? . . . In New York has monogamy become too much to expect? . . . Is motherhood a cult? . . . Can sex toys enhance your sex life? . . . Does size matter?

Each of the ensemble cast provides a different perspective on the week's question. Their stories are told as alternatives for viewers to weigh up, just as articles in women's magazines offer a variety of personal anecdotes to their readers to exemplify a particular issue and how different people have responded in practice. These are loosely tied together by Carrie's final voice over in a provisional conclusion that is often tentative in tone. "Maybe . . ." The bulletin board on the *Sex and the City* website then invites viewers' comments on the episode, asking questions like "What do you think of the new men in Carrie's life? . . . Talk about it with other fans on the Bulletin Board . . . Do you identify with Carrie? . . . Talk about it with fellow fans" (http://www.hbo.com/city/community). Thus multiple perspectives are actively encouraged within a tightly structured, repetitive format in which the characters are bound into a relatively unchanging situation in order to guarantee continuation of the pleasures offered by the brand (Lury 1993: 86–7).

Sex and the City's treatment of sexuality can be understood as a re-mediation of the content and address of women's magazines for television. These women are updated versions of the "Cosmo" woman who is dedicated to self-improvement and economic independence (Ros Ballaster, Margaret Beetham, Elizabeth Frazer, and Sandra Hebron 1991).[5] The function of sexual imagery and talk in *Sex and the City* is quite different from pornographic magazines and cable channels where sexual arousal is assumed as the purpose for consumption. *Sex and the City* dramatises the kind of consumer and sexual advice offered by women's magazines. This is a sphere of feminine expertise in which it has been argued that women are empowered to look—not only at consumer goods but also at their own bodies as sexual subjects (Radner 1995). Sexuality is presented in this context as a source of potential pleasure for which women should make themselves ready, whether through internalising the beauty and fashion advice that will attract the right men, or through following advice on sexual technique. Carrie's billboard slogan draws attention to this pedagogic function; "Carrie Bradshaw *knows* good sex" (emphasis mine). It is an expertise rooted in everyday life and experience. When called upon to give a lecture to a roomful of women on how to get a date, Carrie fails miserably. But she succeeds brilliantly the following week when she takes the women to a bar, where she guides them in how to work the room by reading the sexual signals, giving them the confidence and expertise to act on their desires (Episode 46 "Frenemies").

The series is able to go beyond the catalogue function of magazine fashion spreads, or the list of ten tips on how to improve foreplay. A consumer lifestyle is presented not as a series of commodities to be bought but as an integrated lifestyle to be emulated. The clothes and shoes become expressions of the different moods and personalities of embodied, empathetic characters in an authentic setting. This function is in fact most explicit on the programme's website, which differs in tone and emphasis from the television series and more closely matches the look and address of a woman's magazine. It relies on the relationship fans already have with the programme, guiding viewers in how to convert their knowledge about the series into knowledge they can use in their own lives, as discerning consumers of fashion, as creators of "a look" and a lifestyle. This is represented as a set of active choices that are an expression of individual character and mood. We are invited to conceive of emotional states as a trigger for particular types of consumption and clothing choices, such as the photograph of Carrie that is captioned "The dress that shows she is finally going to split from Mr. Big" (http://www.hbo.com/city_style). The site anticipates, encourages, and attempts to shape fan behaviour that will convert into consumerism (Miriam Rivett 2000).

Bourgeois Bohemians

As a successful brand *Sex and the City* influences the continuing transformations in fashion that characterise consumer culture. News stories about fashion regard it as an important influence. Sarah Jessica Parker (who plays Carrie) is a fashion icon in women's magazines and in newspaper columns; celebrity exposure is being touted as a replacement for the era of catwalk shows and supermodels.[6] The British fashion journalist who tracked down and bought Parker's horse head handbag and then wrote about it in a British national newspaper provided publicity for the TV show, the makers of the bag, and Parker as a celebrity (Victoria Lambert 2001). It also contributed to New York's reputation as city "brand" in the global system of capitalism as a source of new fashion ideas. A report on the New York fashion shows in the *Guardian* was headed "Fashion in the city; cult show underpins style" (Charlie Porter 2001). It comments on the "power of the cult drama" to create a fashion trend, whether for Jimmy Choo stiletto heels, corsages, or purses in the shape of a horse's head. The report is focused on the House of Field who act as stylists for *Sex and the City*. Theirs is a bohemian look, made newly respectable as mainstream fashion, but retaining in the thrift-store elements reference to the anti-materialist values that characterised the hippie bohemianism of the 1960s. It incorporates the psychedelic patterns of that era and an individual eclecticism achieved by mixing retro and new clothing, the avant-garde and the mass-produced.

The horse's head handbag works within this kitsch aesthetic, in which objects are redefined as "cool" through a process of irony. It reminds the *Daily Telegraph* journalist of My Little Pony and her 9-year-old self, and it is cheap to buy in comparison to most designer handbags ($165). The HBO website offers *Sex and the City* merchandise for sale, but they have no pretensions to be designer goods. They are cheap items: T-shirts, mugs, and glasses printed with the *Sex and the City* logo and New York skyline (doubly ironic now). The trash aesthetic of *Sex and the City* anticipates the ironic response that, in the

1980s for example, was developed as a sub-cultural, camp response to *Dynasty* (Feuer 1995: 142). In the decade or so that separates *Dynasty* from the incorporated irony of *Sex and the City*'s trash aesthetics, camp irony has moved from the margins to the centre. It exemplifies the way in which an attitude to mass culture originating in a gay response to their cultural marginalisation, has been appropriated by the mainstream media in order to address niche markets in the affluent middle classes. It is the culmination of a trend that accelerated in the 1960s, and is associated with the rise of the consumer society and the generation that grew up with it (Andrew Ross 1989). *Sex and the City* is simply part of a wider cultural trend, one that at its most broad can be described as postmodernism, a commodified aesthetic in which irony is a central component (Naomi Klein 2000).

The style also expresses a bohemian attitude to women's sexuality. But the clothes do not simply replicate the rather demure look for women of the hippie era, when sexual liberation, enabled by the separation between sex and reproduction that the pill made possible, still meant women responding to men's sexual initiatives. The *Sex and the City* version of bohemian fashion is post punk, post Madonna; it incorporates an assertive sexualised imagery for women that consciously plays with the transgressive sexual connotations of leather, bondage, and underwear as outerwear. One garment, "open to below the navel before swooping under the crotch, had an immaculate cut, even if the look was purposefully wanton . . . [Y]ou could easily see Carrie giving the look a try, maybe out at the Hamptons" (Porter 2001). "Wantonness" combined with "a perfect cut" epitomises the reconciliation of bourgeois with bohemian values in the aesthetics and lifestyle that *Sex and the City* expresses and promotes.

The specificity of this taste culture is made clear in the series itself through the way the four main characters' style and codes of sexual behaviour are defined against other social groupings. There are the restrained (and boring) bourgeois women, untainted by bohemian values, in whom sexual expression is kept under strict control. These are exemplified by the women who look increasingly scandalised as Charlotte, the most "preppy" one of the four, at a reunion dinner with her university Fraternity friends, reveals the fact of her husband's impotence and her own frustration. "Don't you ever feel like you want to be fucked really hard"? she enquires as they recoil in disgust (Episode 46 "Frenemies"). Or by Natasha, Big's wife. His boredom with her is defined by her taste in interior design, "Everything's beige." Then there are the people who live outside the city, and whose adherence to traditional gender roles is an indicator of their being either low class or simply old-fashioned. On a trip to Staten Island (the ferry marking the boundary) "real men" offer a tantalising sexual fantasy for Samantha, but when faced with the reality in the cold light of a working day, her liaison with a fireman doesn't seem such a good idea (Episode 31 "Where There's Smoke . . .").

In traditional bourgeois cultures unbridled sexual appetites or loose speech are a mark not only of the lower classes but of the unruly woman, who inverts the power relations of gender and has sex like a man (Arthurs 1999; Mary Russo 1995). Samantha's guilt-free promiscuity is exemplary here, although even she has her limits. She is shocked by a new acquaintance who dives under the restaurant table to "give head" to a man they have just met (Episode 36 "Are We Sluts"). Indecorum is a sign of lack of respectability, which for women has been a sexual as well as class category associated with prostitution. *Sex and the City* works through the problem of establishing the boundaries of respectability in a postfeminist culture where women share many of the same freedoms as men, but in which the residual effects of the double standard are still being felt. It strives to be sexually frank without being "vulgar."

These women are of a generation old enough to have been influenced by feminism (in their thirties and forties) but too old to participate in a newly fashionable queer culture, despite their appropriation of camp as a style. They are resolutely heterosexual, despite occasional short-lived encounters with gays, lesbians, and bisexuals that simply reconfirm it. "I'm a tri-sexual," says Samantha jokingly. "I'll try anything once," and indeed she does, briefly, have one lesbian lover. Carrie's relationship with a 26-year-old bisexual founders when she can't handle the thought that he's been with a man, nor does she feel comfortable with his gender-bending friends. "I was too old to play this game," she tells us in the voice-over (Episode 34 "Boy, Girl, Boy, Girl . . ."). These episodes, like the one where Samantha dates an African American, simply mark where their sexual boundaries are drawn. Thus the women's particular mix of bourgeois bohemianism is normalised.

Their transgression of bourgeois sexual decorum marks the foursome as "unruly," a challenge to patriarchal structures of power, but their adherence to the sleek control of the commodified body makes this compatible with capitalism. Unlike Edina or Patsy, the unruly women in *Absolutely Fabulous* (BBC2 1992–4, BBC1 1995–6), a British comedy that is located in a similar cultural milieu, if the women are made to *look* ridiculous it is a momentary aberration that causes embarrassment (as in the billboard scene). In contrast, the British comedy persistently satirises consumer culture and the feminine world of fashion, PR, and women's magazines, through a farcical exaggeration of fashion styles and a slapstick mode of comedy that undermines the bodily control and discipline that underpins glamour (often as a result of drug-taking or excessive drinking, a bohemian legacy of the 1960s in contemporary consumer society that plays a very minor role in *Sex and the City* in comparison) (see Arthurs 1999; Pat Kirkham and Beverley Skeggs 1998 for further discussion of *Absolutely Fabulous*). The comedy in *Sex and the City* depends instead on verbal wit and ironic distancing, a more intellectual, and, in class terms, a more bourgeois form than slapstick. It also enables the complicit critique that is considered to be characteristic of postmodernism (Feuer 1995; Klein 2000; Lash 1990).

The Aestheticised Self and Sexual Relations

The advert for Bailey's Cream, the corporate sponsors of *Sex and the City*, exemplifies how in consumer culture the body as the bearer of sensation replaces the ethical self as an ideal. It presents a sensuous image of swirling, creamy liquid with the slogan "Let your senses guide you." Rachel Bowlby refers to the ideal modern consumer as, "a receptacle and bearer of sensations, poser and posed, with no consistent identity, no moral self" (1993: 23). In this aestheticised culture the question has become, does it look good or feel good rather than, is this a good thing to do? Although *Sex and the City* rejects the traditional patriarchal dichotomy of virgin and whore, insisting in its explorations of the women's multiple sexual experiences their rights to seek sexual satisfaction without shame, this doesn't mean that there are no limits. Aesthetic boundaries replace moral boundaries so that men who can't kiss very well, who smell, who are too short, or whose semen tastes peculiar are rejected on those grounds.

Despite the radical roots of this bohemian attitude, developed in opposition to the rationalist, puritan ethos of nineteenth-century industrial capitalism (in Romanticism and Surrealism as well as Dandyism), it is now fully integrated into consumer marketing and its appeal to our hedonistic impulses and imaginings. Lury explains that:

> [A]n important part of this calculating hedonism is an emotional and cognitive distancing on the part of the individual since it is this distance which introduces the possibility of reflection on consumption and facilitates the adoption of playful and ironic ways of consuming. (1996: 76)

Yet for women, Lury argues, this relation to an aestheticised, self-reflexive identity in which commodities are used creatively to re-fashion the self is more problematic than for men (1996: 118–55). This is because they occupy an unstable position in relation to the aestheticised self, an instability that is enacted in the oscillations in tone that characterise *Sex and the City* and its exploration of women's sexuality in a consumer culture.

For the women in *Sex and the City,* it often appears as though hedonism and narcissism have displaced the masochist position they occupy in patriarchal structures of desire. The grotesque "other" of sadistic masculinity has been repressed (and displaced into *The Sopranos,* another successful HBO "quality" drama). In this economy of desire the city streets have lost the danger of a sadistic or reproving masculine gaze. Instead of intimating the dark dangers that kept respectable women off the streets, New York is shown to be a place of freedom and safety—the worst that can happen is that their clothes might be splashed by a passing car (as happens to Carrie in the title sequence). These women move freely around the cafes and boutiques, with a confident sense of possession, enjoying the multiple pleasures of consumption in the company of other women and gay men. In this way their dependence on male lovers for emotional and sensual satisfaction is displaced; they always disappoint or disempower, as Mr. Big does in the billboard scene by not showing up. A designer stiletto shoe, Carrie's trademark obsession, is different. It's always there to be possessed, offering a fetish substitute for the satisfactions denied by men. The autoeroticism legitimated by the narcissistic structure of the look in consumer culture offers the possibility of doing without men at all. The show's promotion of vibrators as a route to sexual satisfaction has resulted in a huge increase in sales of the "rabbit" model that was featured (Episode 9 "The Turtle and the Hare") (Clarissa Smith 2002).

The programme's representation of the women's dissatisfaction with their male lovers could be regarded as encouraging a rejection of men as a source of emotional and sexual satisfaction in favour of a feminine culture of gossip and shopping. It is the tight-knit relationship of the four women that is the only constant in the series. But they don't live together as in the cosy but adolescent comedy series *Friends*. The recurring message that for grown ups living in Manhattan means living alone constructs the single household as the norm, a trend that has been cited as one of the major stimuli to consumption in modern cities (Lury 1996).

Sex in this context becomes like shopping—a marker of identity, a source of pleasure—knowing how to choose the right goods is crucial. But men in *Sex and the City* are the only objects of desire that create consumer dissatisfaction. The women treat men as branded goods—the packaging has to be right but the difficulty is to find one whose use value lives up to the image. The quest becomes one in which they are looking for the phallus that would bring an end to a seemingly endless chain of desire. "In a city of infinite options there can be no better feeling than that you only have one," is the aphorism Carrie offers at the end of one episode (Episode 7 "The Monogamists"). And yet there is a recognition that the phallus will never live up to its promise of satisfaction and fulfilment. "In a city of great expectations is it time to settle for what you can get?" wonders Carrie (Episode 9 "The Turtle and the Hare"). The women try men out to see if they "fit for size," as Carrie tells a potential husband, but they never do. This is literally the case when promiscuous Samantha unexpectedly falls in love (Episode 12 "Oh Come All Ye Faithful"). When she has sex with her new lover after two weeks of uncharacteristic abstention, she is devastated. His dick is only three inches long! In *Sex and the City* size *does* matter.

Sex and the City incorporates the ambivalence in feminist evaluations of the aestheticised self—showing it to be both a source of confident autonomy and of disempowerment in its unstable oscillations. For instance, Carrie's performance is constructed around her role as a successful and famous journalist researching her newspaper column that bears the same name as the TV show. She is shown as a detached observer of her own and her friends' sexual desires and experiences. She self-reflexively and playfully deliberates on their consequences, not in terms of some overarching ethical position but from an aesthetic point of view of someone who has to write a witty, readable column that will enhance her professional status. Sexual ethics are converted into a controlled display of witty aphorisms and the comedy of embarrassment. The same is true of the show's address to its viewers. As an audience we are positioned as detached observers of this sexual play, not as we would be in pornography for physical arousal and the satisfactions of masturbation, nor as lessons in morality, but to be amused.

When the oscillation swings back to close involvement, the mood is one of unsatisfied yearning not playfulness. Carrie's emotional involvement with the main man in her life produces the feeling that she is out of control—her desire for him can never be fully satisfied. Again this is considered characteristic of a consumer lifestyle in which consumers "experience moderate swings from being in control to being out of control and back again . . . Their lives are balanced between feelings of completeness and incompleteness" (Elizabeth

Hirschmann cited in Lury 1996: 77). In this scene the consequences of an aestheticised relation to sexual relations are shown to be debilitating—for women.
Carrie craves authenticity, and constantly wants to establish whether her relationship with Big is real or not. In one episode, where she is particularly dis-
tressed by her powerlessness in relation to Big, Carrie offers a poignant critique of the masquerade as a strategy of female empowerment.

> I think I'm in love with him, and I'm terrified in case he thinks I'm not per-
> fect . . . you should see what I'm like round him—its like—I wear little out-
> fits. I'm not like me. Sexy Carrie. Casual Carrie. Sometimes I catch myself
> actually posing—its exhausting!' (Episode 11 "The Drought")

Later that evening Big visits her flat for the first time. She is nervous about this
as another test of her self-presentation, but is reassured, "I like it just the way it
is," he says. On seeing a couple having sex in the flat opposite, offering a distanced but explicit spectacle, Big turns to her and says, "Hell—we can do better than that!" The voice-over from Carrie, "And then he kissed me," places the
scene in the realm of a Mills and Boon erotic novel for women—the unobtainable object of the heroine's desire succumbs when he recognises her true worth.
Yet it also marks a return to the distancing that characterises the dominant, comic
mode of the series. Carrie's worries about her unstable and inauthentic identity
are resolved through the aestheticised pleasures of erotic spectacle and generic
parody. And there is no end to these oscillations; its serial form doesn't provide
the plenitude of narrative closure; instead its repetitions offer the consumer satisfactions of "diversity within sameness that is comfortable and comforting to
most people" (Hirschman cited in Lury 1996: 77).

Conclusion

The fragmentation of the television market has allowed a sexually explicit and
critical feminist discourse into television comedy, albeit within the parameters
of a consumer culture and the limitations this imposes. This is a welcome innovation in women's representation on television in that it assumes and promotes
women's right to sexual pleasure and validates women's friendship and culture. At the same time the contradictions of its comedic and serial form exposes
this culture to interrogation and critique, thereby encouraging intellectual
analysis. The analytic approaches used in this article are not confined to an academic elite but are available to a broad segment of educated women, the bourgeois bohemians, who read the quality press alongside women's magazines. An
ability to see ourselves in these characters works not simply to confirm our
sense of self but to question the costs as well as the benefits of living in a postfeminist consumer culture. It is in the messy contingencies of the everyday that
feminism is produced or inhibited in practice, and it is this quality that *Sex and
the City* is able to capture.

This establishes a space in popular culture for interrogation of our own
complicity in the processes of commodification—women's narcissistic relation
to the self, the production of fetishistic and alienated sexual relations—that

continue to undermine our self-esteem and contentment. The programme offers evidence of the deleterious effects of economic liberalism in a society where moral and religious values are in decline, with no alternatives to the hedonistic and selfish values of capitalism. Whether this has the power to translate into feminist political action is beyond the scope of this article (but see Klein 2000; Whelahan 2000; Willis 1991 for scepticism in this respect). What remains more hidden from view is the gap between the lifestyle depicted and the experience of the majority of the women in the world, who are often the most disadvantaged by the economic inequalities on which the freedom to pleasurable consumption rests (Klein 2000; McRobbie 1997; Willis 1991). Yet in a post September 11 context, the connotations of *Sex and the City*'s logo of the Manhattan skyline has changed. The guiltless triumph of consumer values no longer seems so secure.

Notes

I would like to thank Gillian Swanson, Sherryl Wilson, and Helen Kennedy, as well as the anonymous reviewers for this journal, for their helpful comments on earlier versions of this article.

1. In a series of interviews with writers of the series that appeared on the website in July 2001 they were asked which characters they identified with most strongly. They all chose Miranda (http://www.hbo.com/cityinsiders_guide; accessed July 26, 2001).

2. The identification of the episodes follows the continuous numbering of the website episode summaries rather than the video compilations, which start again at number one for each season.

3. As technological and economic convergence gathers pace, regulatory frameworks are also converging. The Internet has been an important driver in this respect, resetting the boundaries for the public circulation of sexual material (Bernt Stubbe Ostergaard 1998).

4. The kind of attention given to women's sexual freedom and pleasure in second-wave feminism arises from the very specific social and political history of the white middle-class women who dominated the movement. It is quite different from the political agenda around sexuality that arises from the historical positioning of black or working-class women as the embodied "other" of the white bourgeoisie (Donna Haraway 1990).

5. The four main characters' signature cocktail is called a "cosmopolitan," signalling this sorority. The show's title echoes that of a book, *Sex and the Single Girl* written by Helen Gurley Brown in 1962 who went on to be the founding editor of *Cosmopolitan* magazine in 1965 (Radner 1995).

6. Radner's (1995: 51–5) discussion of Cybill Shepherd's role in the television comedy *Moonlighting* (1986–7) also highlights the way intertextuality allows for differing inflexions of the same celebrity persona.

References

Arthurs, Jane. 1999. "Revolting Women: The Body in Comic Performance," in Jane Arthurs and Jean Grimshaw (eds.) *Women's Bodies: Discipline and Transgression*, pp. 137–64. London and New York: Cassell.

Ballaster, Ros, Margaret Beetham, Elizabeth Frazer, and Sandra Hebron. 1991. *Women's*

Worlds: Ideology, Femininity and the Woman's Magazine. Basingstoke: Macmillan Education.

Bolter, Jay David and Richard Grusin. 1999. *Remediation: Understanding New Media*. Cambridge, MA and London: MIT Press.

Bowlby, Rachel. 1993. *Shopping with Freud*. London and New York: Routledge.

Brooks, David. 2000. *Bobos in Paradise: The New Upper Class and How they Got There*. New York: Simon and Schuster.

Bushnell, Candace. [1996] 1997. *Sex and the City*. London: Abacus.

Compaine, Benjamin and Douglas Gomery. 2000. *Who Owns the Media?: Competition and Concentration in the Mass Media Industry*. Mahwah, NJ and London: Lawrence Erlbaum Associates.

D'Acci, Julie. 1987. "The Case of *Cagney and Lacey*," in Helen Baehr and Gillian Dyer (eds.) *Boxed In: Women and Television*, pp. 203–26. London: Pandora.

Dow, Bonnie J. 1996. *Prime-time Feminism: Television, Media Culture and the Women's Movement Since 1970*. Philadelphia: University of Pennsylvania Press.

Ellis, John. 2000. *Seeing Things: Television in the Age of Uncertainty*. London and New York: I. B. Tauris.

Featherstone, Michael. 1991. *Consumer Culture and Postmodernism*. London: Sage.

Feuer, Jane. 1995. *Seeing Through the Eighties: Television and Reaganism*. Durham, NC: Duke University Press.

Greer, Germaine. 1999. *The Whole Woman*. London: Doubleday.

Haraway, Donna. 1990. "Investment Strategies for the Evolving Portfolio of Primate Females," in Mary Jacobus, Evelyn Fox Keller, and Sally Shuttleworth (eds.) *Body/Politics; Women and the Discourse of Science*, pp. 139–62. London and New York: Routledge.

Hirschmann, Elizabeth. 1992. "The Consciousness of Addiction: Towards a General Theory of Compulsive Consumption." *Journal of Consumer Research* 19 (September): 155–79.

Hollows, Joanne. 2000. *Feminism, Femininity and Popular Culture*. Manchester and New York: Manchester University Press.

Kirkham, Pat and Beverley Skeggs. 1998. "*Absolutely Fabulous*: Absolutely Feminist?," in Christine Geraghty and David Lusted (eds.) *The Television Studies Book*, pp. 287–300. London, New York, Sydney, and Auckland: Arnold.

Klein, Naomi. 2000. *No Logo*. London: Flamingo.

Lambert, Victoria. 2001. "Horseplay with a Handbag." *Daily Telegraph*, July 4: 15.

Lash, Scott. 1990. *Sociology of Postmodernism*. London and New York: Routledge.

Lotz, Amanda D. 2001. "Postfeminist Television Criticism: Rehabilitating Critical Terms and Identifying Postfeminist Attributes." *Feminist Media Studies* 1 (1): 105–21.

Lury, Celia. 1993. *Cultural Rights: Technology, Legality and Personality*. London and New York: Routledge.

Lury, Celia. 1996. *Consumer Culture*. Cambridge: Polity Press.

Mayne, Judith. [1988] 1997. "LA Law and Prime Time Feminism," in Charlotte Brunsdon, Julie D'Acci, and Lynn Spigel (eds.) *Feminist Television Criticism: A Reader*. Oxford and New York: Oxford University Press, pp. 84–97. First published in *Discourse* 10 (2): 30–47.

McRobbie, Angela. 1997. "Bridging the Gap: Feminism, Fashion and Consumption," *Feminist Review* 55 (Spring): 73–89.

Moseley, Rachel and Jacinda Read. 2002. "'Having It Ally': Popular Television (Post)Feminism." *Feminist Media Studies* 2 (2): 231–49.

Neale, Steve and Frank Krutnick. 1990. *Popular Film and Television Comedy*. London: Routledge.

Ostergaard, Bernt Stubbe. 1998. "Convergence: Legislative Dilemmas," in Dennis McQuail and Karen Suine (eds.) *Media Policy: Convergence, Concentration and Commerce*, pp. 95–106. Euromedia Research Group. London, Thousand Oaks, CA, and New Delhi: Sage.

Porter, Charlie. 2001. "Fashion in the City: Cult Show Underpins Style." *Guardian*, September 10: 5.

Radner, Hilary. 1995. *Shopping Around: Feminine Culture and the Pursuit of Pleasure*. New York: Routledge.

Rivett, Miriam. 2000. "Approaches to Analysing the Web Text: A Consideration of the Web Site as an Emergent Cultural Form," *Convergence* 6 (3): 34–60.

Ross, Andrew. 1989. "The Uses of Camp," in *No Respect: Intellectuals and Popular Culture*, pp. 135–70. New York and London: Routledge.

Russo, Mary. [1994] 1995. *The Female Grotesque: Risk, Excess and Modernity*. New York and London: Routledge.

Sex and the City. 1999–2001 (video recording). Home Box Office. Seasons 1–3.

Sex and the City (website). Home Box Office. On-line. Available: http://www .hbo.com/city (July 2001).

Smith, Clarissa. 2002. "From Oppression to the Jelly Rabbit," paper presented at the Third Wave Feminism Conference, Exeter University, UK, July 23–25.

Whelahan, Imelda. 2000. *Overloaded: Popular Culture and the Future of Feminism*. London: The Women's Press.

Willis, Susan. 1991. *A Primer for Daily Life: Is there More to Life than Shopping?* London and New York: Routledge.

Girls Rule!
Gender, Feminism, and Nickelodeon

Sarah Banet-Weiser

In June 2000, the Museums of Television and Radio in both New York and Los Angeles presented a three-month retrospective that honored the children's cable network Nickelodeon. The retrospective, "A Kid's Got to Do What a Kid's Got to Do: Celebrating 20 Years of Nickelodeon," featured screenings of past and current programming, hands-on workshops, an interactive gallery exhibit, and seminars for families. One of the seminars, titled "Girl Power! Creating Positive Role Models for Girls," lauded Nickelodeon's efforts over the past 20 years to challenge traditional gender stereotypes on children's television by featuring girls as primary lead characters. A "girl power" seminar had a particular cultural resonance in 2000: the connection between these two concepts—"girl" and "power"—once thought to be completely absent from the world of children's popular culture, had become normalized within the discourses of consumer culture. In the contemporary cultural climate, in other words, the empowerment of girls is now something that is more or less taken for granted by both children and parents, and has certainly been incorporated into commodity culture.

Indeed, the rhetoric of girl power has found currency in almost every realm of contemporary children's popular culture. In the mid-1990s, The Spice Girls, a manufactured, pop-music girl-group, adopted "Girl Power!" as their motto. And, at the same time, the alternative internet community the Riot Grrrls incorporated girl power ideology in their efforts to construct a new kind of feminist politics (see, for example, Baumgardner & Richards, 1999; Currie, 1999; Douglas, 1999; Driscoll, 2002; Kearney, 1998; Shugart, Waggoner, & Hallstein, 2001). T-shirts emblazoned with "Girls Kick Ass!" and "Girls Rule!" became hot new items for both high-school and elementary school girls, and Nike's "Play Like a Girl" advertising campaign skillfully used the concept of "commodity feminism" to sell athletic gear (Goldman, 1992; Sturken & Cartwright, 2001). In the sporting world, the success of the 1999 Women's Soccer World Cup tournament, the public focus on tennis superstars Venus

Sarah Banet-Weiser, "Girls Rule! Gender, Feminism, and Nickelodeon." From *Critical Studies in Media Communication,* Vol. 21, No. 2 (June 2004), pp. 119–139. Reprinted by permission of Taylor & Francis Ltd. (http://www.tandf.co.uk/journals).

and Serena Williams, and the creation of the Women's National Basketball Association brought new attention and prestige to powerful female athletes. In the world of popular psychology and everyday culture, books such as Mary Pipher's (1995) *Reviving Ophelia: Saving the Selves of Adolescent Girls* and Rosalind Wiseman's (2002) *Queen Bees and Wanna-Bes: Helping Your Daughter Survive Cliques, Gossip, Boyfriends, and Other Realities of Adolescence*, recognized problems unique to young girls growing up in the 1990s and immediately became bestsellers.

In the world of children's television, programs about self-confident, assertive, and intelligent girls such as Nickelodeon's 1991 hit, *Clarissa Explains It All*, and more recent animated programs such as *As Told by Ginger*, *Rocket Power*, and *The Wild Thornberries* initiated a new trend in programming that actively rejected the conventional industry wisdom that children's shows with girl leads could not be successful (see, for example, Seiter, 1995). Aside from these types of entertainment programs, Nickelodeon also addresses gender issues on its non-fiction news program, *Nick News*, with episodes devoted to body image, bullying, and girls' sports, among others. This essay focuses on the cultural context that produces girl power practices and commodities, and specifically situates the cable television network Nickelodeon as a key producer of girl power culture. Is contemporary media—and Nickelodeon in particular—simply capitalizing on a current trend, or does girl power ideology signify a new direction for feminist politics? I argue here that girl power is not just a fad, although it is that; it is not just about empowerment, although it is that as well. Girl power powerfully demonstrates the contradictions or tensions that structure Third Wave feminist politics, especially for young girls. It is not my aim to "resolve" these tensions or to expose Third Wave feminism or girl power as a commercial hoax. It is my goal, rather, to theorize how the often contradictory media representations of girl power function as a kind of feminist politics. Because of the importance of media representation to all kinds of politics, it is also important to situate media powerhouses within this kind of context. Nickelodeon, for example, does not simply exploit the commercial market of girl power; the network is also a significant *producer* of girl power culture—especially since Nickelodeon is one of the most influential producers of children's programming and media in the U.S., and it attracts a large audience of pre-adolescent and adolescent girls.

It is this tension between Nickelodeon's embrace of the girl power consumer market and its role as a producer of girl power ideology that I will explore here. But what does it mean to say that a huge corporate entity such as Nickelodeon enables girls to be *producers* of their own culture? Certainly, it can be argued, as Mary Celeste Kearney does, that alternative cultural productions along the margins of mainstream popular culture—'zines, for example, or Riot Grrrl websites—illustrate how girls can produce girl power culture (Kearney, 1998). But Nickelodeon programs are hardly "alternative," and are squarely a part of mainstream, commercial culture. To get at how Nickelodeon demonstrates the tensions within girl power culture, I analyze three of the network's programs: *Clarissa Explains It All*, which first aired in 1991; *As Told by Ginger (ATBG)*, a contemporary popular animated series, and *Nick News*, the weekly news program for children that is hosted and produced by Linda Ellerbee. I chose to examine *Clarissa* because the program is widely noted as a "break-through" show in girl power programming—it was among the first children's series to feature a strong, independent girl lead character, and through this program Nickelodeon became well-known in the industry as a champion for girls. I then look at ATBG as a way to account for the trajectory of girl power ideology in the decade since Clarissa first aired, taking specific note at the program's use of irony and self-reflexivity as a more current rhetorical strategy of girl power. Finally, I examine *Nick News* for its representation of girl power themes, as well as its role as a producer of girl power culture through both the themes of the episodes and the figure of the host, Ellerbee, herself. Although *Nick News* differs from the other programs in that it is non-fiction, the themes on the news program—body image, popularity, parental authority—are similar to the themes in the entertainment programs, and thus it makes sense to look at all three as rich examples of mass-mediated girl power. The content of these particular Nickelodeon programs illustrates some of the contradictions within the relationship between media visibility, commercialism, and the production of girl culture—the same kinds of contradictions that also structure Third Wave feminism.

Girl Power and Generational Differences: Feminism for Whom?

Girl power programming on Nickelodeon is part of a general trajectory in the contemporary mass media that can, in part, be attributed to Third Wave feminism.[1] Third Wave feminism (or sometimes "Girlie feminism") embraces commercial media visibility and enthusiastically celebrates the power that comes with it. In this way, Third Wave feminism situates issues of gender within commercial and popular culture, and insistently positions Third Wave feminist politics as not only fundamentally different from Second Wave feminist politics,[2] but because of the embrace of media visibility and the commercial world, as also more representative for a new generation of women. Indeed, one of the most impassioned discourses involving feminism lately has not been generated by differing particular political platforms, or a specific egregious act of discrimination against women, but from the arguments, contradictions, and general disavowals between Second and Third Wave feminism. The lack of generational cohesion here between the two movements makes it difficult to figure out one's position within feminism; as Susan Douglas (1994) has argued, the different stances on the consumer world between generations leads to a broader ambivalence about feminism: "Once this sense of generational collectivity *as a market* evaporates, so does the sense of political collectivity" (p. 292, my emphasis). That is, differences between Third Wave and Second Wave feminists are often represented as a generational rather than political problem. And yet, as Lisa Hogeland (2001) points out, generation is not a significant explanation for differences. The alternative, recognizing problems within feminism, means confronting the "unevenness" of the movement itself and "fundamental differences in our visions of feminism's tasks and accomplishments" (p. 107). One of these differences concerns media visibility. Whereas many Third Wave feminists seem to regard consumer culture as a place of empowerment and as a means of differentiating themselves from Second Wave feminists, Second Wave feminism has tended, on the whole, to be critical of the misogyny of popular consumer culture.

The embrace of consumer culture is the site for tension within girl power programming on Nickelodeon as well. Once feminism (as represented through girl power), becomes part of the mainstream it has traditionally challenged, can we still talk about it as political? Can feminism be represented and enacted within popular culture, or is popular culture by design hostile to feminism? Are we simply living in, as Naomi Klein (2000) claims in her book *No Logo*, a "Representation Nation," where visibility in the media takes precedence over "real" politics? Jennifer Baum-gardner and Amy Richards (2000), authors of the Third Wave feminist tract *Manifesta: Young Women, Feminism, and the Future*, argue to the contrary, and claim that this kind of media visibility is absolutely crucial to politics. On Nickelodeon, not only are there strong female characters on the programs, there is a general tone of empowerment and activism that shapes the network's self-image.

In fact, we have arrived at a point where much of (liberal) feminism is part of mainstream media culture; that this is not a problem could be taken as a measure of what Second Wave feminism has accomplished (Dow, 1996). Baumgardner and Richards (2000) argue that young women who make up the Third Wave are "born with feminism simply in the water," a kind of "political fluoride" that protects against the "decay" of earlier sexism and gender discrimination (p. 83). The struggle for positive representations in the media is certainly not over, but we also do not experience the same media that we did even ten years ago, when, as Douglas (1999) contends, the most pervasive media story remained "structured around boys taking action, girls waiting for the boys, and girls rescued by the boys" (p. 293). There has been a clear historical trajectory of incorporating feminist ideologies into mainstream popular culture, ranging, as Bonnie Dow (1996) points out, from the 1970s television show *One Day at a Time* to shows in the 1980s and 1990s such as *Murphy Brown* and *Designing Women*. And yet, as Dow argues, while the liberal feminist politics of equal opportunity and equal pay for equal work have been somewhat normalized (although the material reality of these politics is not always or even often achieved), it is also the case that the process of mainstreaming an oppositional politics often functions as a hegemonic strategy to dilute those very politics. In other words, the normalization of feminism has prevented it from existing as a discrete politics; it rather emerges as a kind of slogan or a generalized "brand."

As a contemporary social and political movement, then, feminism itself has been rescripted (but not disavowed) so as to allow its smooth incorporation into the world of commerce and corporate culture—what Robert Goldman (1992) calls "commodity feminism." Current feminist politics involve a complex dynamic that is not only directly concerned with general gender issues, but also with issues of cultural territory: as part of a general self-identification, Second Wave feminism is at times overly romanticized in terms of its commitment to social protest politics, and there seems to be a kind of reluctance on the part of Second Wave feminists to rethink and redefine politics according to the stated needs and desires of Third Wave feminism (Susan Brownmiller, in a now infamous *Time* magazine interview about Third Wave feminists claimed, "they're just not movement people"; Bellafante, 1998, p. 60). This territorialism that surrounds some of the current politics of feminism seems to be about salvaging the name of feminism (and, presumably, the politics that ground and historicize the name). Baumgardner and Richards (2000), Barbara Findlen (1995), and Naomi Wolf (1994), for example, participate in this kind of salvation project, the project of not necessarily appropriating a historical concept of feminism, but widening its borders to include more contemporary manifestations of the politics. While in theory this makes sense, and certainly these authors at times do justice to the legacies of feminisms, Baumgardner and Richards (2000) also insist that "underneath all of these names and agendas is the same old feminism" (p. 80). However, it is precisely *not* the same old feminism that structures the politics of Third Wave feminism. The insistence that it is stems from a range of sentiments, from nostalgic yearnings for real social protest movements to respectful acknowledgements of political practices that open up economic and social opportunities to a sheer base desire to belong to something. Without discounting these sentiments, it is also the case that lingering in this generational territory battle between Second Wave and Third Wave feminism has paralyzed the debate, and prevented the further development and refinement of a feminist praxis and material feminist politics. As Hogeland (2001) points out, "Generational thinking is always unspeakably generalizing: one reason we react so vehemently to accounts of 'our' generation is that changes in feminist ideas, and the social, political, and institutional impact of feminism itself have been so uneven" (p. 110).

In fact, the idea that we all share a feminist politics, that we all want the same thing, is highly problematic. Not only does this make the same mistake as many Second Wave feminists who insisted on a universal feminist standpoint, but it also functions as a kind of refusal to identify what the "thing" is that we all apparently want (see particularly Hartsock, 1998). The politics of feminism are quite obviously different for different generations, and Third Wave feminists are produced in a very different cultural and political context to Second Wave feminists. This, then, is what situates the specific politics of girl power as a politics of contradiction and tension: the dynamics between the ideological claims of this cultural phenomenon—girls are powerful, strong, independent—and the commercial merchandising of these claims demonstrate a profound ambivalence about these feminist politics in general.

Nickelodeon produces its own kind of commodity feminism through its original programming. The television shows on Nickelodeon engage the audience member as an important consumer group, but the other components of girl power—media visibility and cultural production—are also part of the programming. The girl power programming on Nickelodeon, as well as the net-work's outspoken commitment to girls as lead characters, forces us to inter-rogate the connections and contradictions between children's television and empowerment. In fact, "empowerment" became the buzzword of the 1990s—not in marginalized political communities, but squarely within mainstream commercial culture. While this kind of empowerment obviously references eco-nomic power and the recognition of adolescent (and pre-adolescent) girls as an important market segment, it also seems to address a politico-social power represented in terms of feminist subjectivity. Indeed, Nickelodeon has built its entire self image around this concept of empowerment. Addressing children as empowered beings, as kids with rights, is a very different message from earlier television programming, which tended to address children as either unsophis-ticated or in need of protection (Hendershot, 1999; Jenkins, 1998; Kinder, 1999; Seiter, 1995; Spigel, 1992). And, within the context of girl power, the relationship between empowerment and children's television is especially charged because of television's history as a medium that favors boy characters and boy-based programs. Thus, while part of an emphasis on the empower-ment of youth signals a larger cultural shift in definitions of childhood itself, it is also reflective of shifting feminist politics, where access to female empow-erment is increasingly found within commercial culture, rather than outside the hegemonic mainstream.

Obviously, to invoke the term "power" in direct connection with girls is an ideologically complex move, and has several different facets. The most eco-nomically significant way in which power connects to girls is the increasing recognition of young girls and adolescents as an important consumer group—a group that has more and more money to spend each year on girl power prod-ucts (McNeal, 1992; Quart, 2003).[3] Another important way in which power is connected with girls in the media context of Nickelodeon is through the particular gender representations on the network's original programming. As Ellen Seiter (1995) points out, it was not really until the 1980s that children's television began creating shows that featured girls as lead characters. Although the heroines of such 1980s programs as *My Little Pony* and *Strawberry Short-cake* were not necessarily powerful, intelligent characters, they were at least female, which challenged the earlier invisibility of girls on children's television. Historically, a "cross-over" audience has seemed to work only in favor of boys (in other words, according to conventional wisdom, boys *and* girls would watch boys on television, but boys would not watch girls on television). In the past decade, however, the representation of girls on television has been influenced by the more general mainstreaming of feminist rhetoric, and Nickelodeon has led the way in terms of children's television.

In 1991, Nickelodeon launched its hit "tween" program, *Clarissa Explains It All,* featuring a young girl as its lead character. The network's commitment to strong girl characters (a commitment that has demonstrated itself in more and more programming that features girls as lead characters) is an important part of its public persona: the aforementioned Museum of Television and

Radio's retrospective on Nickelodeon featured the network's commitment to girls as a main focus. Curator David Bushman commented:

> I think Nickelodeon has empowered kids in a lot of ways . . . but I think they've specifically empowered young girls, and that's a really important thing that Nickelodeon deserves a lot of credit for. This whole idea that you could not make girl-centric shows because boys wouldn't watch them, they disproved that theory. (Heffley, 1999, p. 45)

Indeed, some industry professionals mark the debut of *Clarissa Explains it All* as a crucial turning point for Nickelodeon, the moment in which the network established itself as an organization dedicated to taking risks to more accurately represent and appeal to a child audience. In this sense, Nickelodeon is an important *producer* of girl power politics, as it explicitly connects commercial representation and the sheer visibility of girls on television with a larger recognition of girls as important empowered subjects in the social world.

Of course, the claim that representation and greater visibility of girls in the media results in a particular kind of empowerment assumes several things. First, to assume that media visibility leads to empowerment is to consider adolescent television audiences as active agents who position themselves in a variety of relationships with the ideological structures and messages of the media. While this may be true, it is also certainly true that these very same ideological structures and messages of the media privilege a commercial context that connects social power with consumption activity. Second, the acknowledgement that adolescent girls comprise an active, empowered audience does not necessarily free them from the commercial power of the mass media. To the contrary, as we witness with the increasing visibility of gay and lesbian representations on television, this kind of recognition insists on the ever-more important connection with the commercial power of the mass media (see, for example, Canclini, 2001; Dow, 2001; Gross, 2001; Miller, 1998). The cultural dynamics that produced girl power within the constant flux of media representations of gender in the 1990s not only produced a hip new slogan, but were also part of a more general shift toward mainstreaming feminism into popular and dominant culture (Dow, 1996). Undoubtedly, this kind of media visibility carries with it a kind of power, in a cultural context where visibility is so often conflated with power and influence.

Another aspect of empowerment behind the girl power movement is a more institutional one and involves the accounting of girls as producers of their own culture (rather than simply consumers). It also entails the transformation of the media industry itself, where more and more executives and producers are female. While, as Joy Van Fuqua (2003) argues, the relationship between women in positions of power at networks and the proliferation of strong female characters is certainly not guaranteed, it is also worth noting that, for example, the former president of Nickelodeon, Geraldine Laybourne, led the way in the children's television market in terms of creating programming with powerful girl lead characters. *Nick News* is not only hosted but also produced by Linda Ellerbee, a known feminist and children's activist. This institutional side of girl power production coexists with a proliferation of less mainstream forms of girl power culture, such as 'zines including *Bust* and *Hues* and "do it yourself" (DIY) forms of cultural production (Kearney, 1998).

These elements of empowerment—as a consumer group, as media visibility, and as cultural producers—are all part of girl power. The dynamics between these variations within the theme of empowerment are complicated, and represent significant tensions and even ambivalence within feminisms. Media visibility is an important component of empowerment, but it is far from unproblematic, as scholars such as Stuart Hall (1997), Herman Gray (1997), Larry Gross (2001), and Bonnie Dow (2001) have pointed out. As Gross (2001), writing about the increasing media visibility of gays and lesbians, succinctly put it: "as we're learning, visibility, like truth, is rarely pure and never simple" (p. 253). The power behind girl power is also complex, and is often contradictory. One of the key tensions regarding girl power exists not between the mainstream media and feminism, but rather within feminism itself, and the assumed generational differences between Second and Third Wave feminists.

Nickelodeon and Girl Power Programming

Catherine Driscoll (2002), in her recent study of adolescent girl culture, points out that

> the opposition between pleasure in consumption figured as conformity and pleasure against the grain of such conformity does not provide a useful model for considering girl culture, where resistance is often just another form of conformity and conformity may be compatible with other resistances. (p. 12)

In other words, concepts such as conformity and resistance are assumed to be oppositional, but in fact are mutually constituitive categories. The ideological themes of girl power that are represented in Nickelodeon programs such as *Clarissa Explains It All* and *As Told by Ginger,* where the girls are strong, independent, and often unruly are situated in relation to normative definitions of girls as obedient and docile—even as these "resistant" themes are marketed as a particular kind of product. So, for example, during the commercial break for an episode of *As Told by Ginger,* an animated program that features a group of intelligent and often ironic middle-school girls, one could often see an ad for a girl power doll: girls playing with Barbie, or something similar, dressed up in sporty clothes carrying a skateboard (or one for the new Mattel Flavas dolls, hip-hop dolls of various ethnicities positioned on a cardboard wall covered in grafitti). Indeed, this kind of juxtaposition so often shown on the media, between a kind of political agency and a commitment to consumerism, is one of the reasons that it is so difficult to theorize what exactly girl power is, as well as whether or not it is a feminist discourse and practice. That is to say, the typical categories that are used to talk about agency do not really apply to this contemporary context, since girl culture is ambiguous from the ground up (see, for example, Driscoll, 2002).

Discussing the exaggerated negative reaction to the Spice Girls and the subsequent dismissal of the group by critics as inauthentic and manufactured,

Driscoll (2002) asks: "Can feminism be a mass-produced, globally distributed product, and can merchandised relations to girls be authentic?" (p. 272). Driscoll understands girl culture to be primarily characterized by "unresolvable tensions" between agency and conformity. She argues, "To actually embrace the community alternative girl culture imagines requires a degree of complicity with systems with which they claim to be incompatible, and they produce legitimated models of agency within the systems they say exclude them" (p. 278). This complicity with the system is precisely where Nickelodeon steps in; the discourse of girl power created a new niche in television programming and led to the creation of girl-centered and girl-powered shows. Nickelodeon programs can be seen as potentially innovative efforts to address gender representation in children's television. However, the presentation and rescripting of gender identity for girls on Nickelodeon is not as seamless as the network's subtext of girl power would lead one to believe. Nickelodeon demonstrates Driscoll's point about the unresolvable tensions between agency and conformity: the network overtly situates gender identity (or positive gender portrayal) as an important element of programming, and was the first children's network to air a program that featured a girl character in a leading role, with their 1991 live-action show, *Clarissa Explains It All*. At the same time, the network's definition of empowerment is part of a larger system of consumer citizenship, where the recognition of an audience as a potentially lucrative one confers power on that same audience.

Clarissa Explains It All

With the debut of *Clarissa,* Nickelodeon became known for risk-taking in programming, and was specifically recognized as a champion for girls in television. The success of *Clarissa* has undoubtedly been a motivation for not only Nickelodeon to continue to produce shows about girls—it has followed *Clarissa* with other successful programs: *The Secret World of Alex Mack* (1994), *The Mystery Files of Shelby Woo* (1996), *The Wild Thornberries* (1998), *The Amanda Show* (1991), and *As Told by Ginger* (2000), among others—but also for other networks to create programming that challenges "the boys-won't-watch-girls" myth. According to the Nickelodeon press release about the show, the main character, Clarissa Darling (played by Melissa Joan Hart) "is an imaginative and very contemporary teenager who makes no bones about detailing her likes, dislikes, and fantasies. Breaking many conventions of the sitcom and using special video effects to highlight Clarissa's thoughts and plans, the series examines life through her eyes" (Nickelodeon press release, 2000). The idea of portraying life through the eyes of a young girl is innovative in and of itself, especially given the historical context of 1991. Nickelodeon very purposefully marketed *Clarissa* as a break-out kind of show, and the success of the program illustrated the effective marketing: boys seemed to watch the program along with girls, and the show clearly seemed to tap into the burgeoning cultural climate of girl power. The early 1990s were already emerging as a new era for pre-adolescent and adolescent boys and girls in terms of their spending power and consumption habits, and the character of Clarissa seemed to fit perfectly in this context. Indeed, Clarissa is not the stereotypical feminine heroine who relies on a man (or a boy, in this case) to save her from the various scrapes of contemporary teenage life. Although boys are featured regularly on the show— Clarissa has a younger brother, Ferguson, who often provides the annoying foil for Clarissa's thought processes, and her best friend, Sam, is a boy her own age with whom she has a platonic relationship—the program truly does revolve around the antics of Clarissa.

As the lead character, Clarissa is portrayed as an unusually mature teenager who narrates her life to the audience as one that is full of surprises, haphazard coincidences, and typical teen dilemmas. Her parents, Janet and Marshall Darling, are caricatured as ex-hippies, and their (media-defined) sense of social responsibility shapes each episode (for example, Clarissa's mother, Janet, is a health nut, and her father, Marshall, is an environmentally aware architect). Each episode opens with a monologue by Clarissa, where she voices some clever remark about the theme of that day's show. Often these opening remarks are sarcastic and self-reflexive; for example, in the episode "The Misguidance Counselor" (June 14 1992), Clarissa begins the show with a sardonic statement: "Okay, time for another normal start of another normal day in the ever-normal Darling household." This episode goes on to spoof normal families, with the central narrative organized around an obviously ridiculous plan of the school's guidance counselor for Clarissa to "fit in." The program in general is very intertextual in that other television shows and films are often referenced and used as part of the plot: for example, at one point in this specific episode, the show parodies early family television shows such as *Ozzie and Harriet* by depicting a black and white television set featuring the show *Oh! Those Darlings,* complete with a head shot of Clarissa in nostalgic 1950s garb, and a credit line "Clarissa Darling as Big Sis" underneath. Another episode also demonstrates this kind of ironic self-construction, where the opening line of "A Little Romance" (August 14, 1993) has Clarissa saying: "I think that it was either William Shakespeare or Sting who said, 'love is blind; love is madness; love is reason without reason.' Personally, I agree. Love is nuts!"

John Hartley (1999) identifies *Clarissa* as an interesting example of a particular kind of potential civic behavior. Locating the politics of citizenship within a variety of cultural artifacts and technologies within the "mediasphere," he argues that within media and commercial culture, we have moved through a series of different levels of citizenship, ranging from civic to cultural citizenship. The present moment is characterized by yet another form of citizenship, called DIY or "Do It Yourself" citizenship (p. 179). DIY has its roots in British punk rock and has been recognized as a particular kind of alternative cultural production (especially in terms of girl power ideology) such as 'zines and riot grrl websites (Kearney 1998; McRobbie, 1991). Interestingly, Hartley identifies the very mainstream *Clarissa Explains It All* as illustrative of DIY citizenship because the character of Clarissa is smart, in control of her environment, and she disrupts conventional modes of representation by talking directly to the camera. As Hartley argues, the character of Clarissa marks an important departure from conventional representations of young girls on television because she is the "undis-

puted centre of her show . . . a mainstream, fully-formed, 'adult' character, articulate, interesting, full of initiative, clever and congenial" (p. 184).

Hartley continues by arguing that Clarissa is a particular kind of citizen
(albeit a problematic kind of citizen), in a world of children's media that often
excludes children as citizens, both ideologically and in practice. He identifies
Clarissa Explains It All as a program that specifically attends to issues of citizenship for girls and, in that way, the show disrupts cultural mythologies of
gender for young girls: the victim, the unintelligent, the dependent. Clarissa
is quite plainly the opposite of all of these personality characteristics, but not
only that, the show itself is often organized as a kind of *critique* of the constructed nature of cultural mythologies—of girls, of boys, of romance, of popularity. In this way, the character of Clarissa represents the kind of contradictions present in the broader politics of girl power: she is the typical powerless
adolescent girl in the sense of her position in a larger culture that privileges
both adults and males, but she is nonetheless a powerful figure within commercial culture. Hartley describes DIY citizenship as bringing about a kind of
"semiotic self-determination" where representation of agency *becomes* agency
in a particular televisual society; in this way, Clarissa represents a kind of girl
power feminism that makes sense in this particular historical moment, and
under these particular conditions.

Through its intertextuality, its unconventional methods such as narrating
directly to the camera, and its casting as lead a kind of wacky teenage girl, the
show represents some of the important themes of girl power ideology. For
example, in the episode "Can't Buy Me Love" (September 8, 1992), Clarissa
opens the show with these remarks: "What's in and what's out: two harmless
little questions that make otherwise rational people break out in hives." The
recognition here of both the importance of fitting in socially, and the superfi-
ciality of that desire to fit in, mirrors the larger tensions of girl power ideology. The episode continues when Clarissa's brother Ferguson is befriended by
the local rich kid, predictably named J. Elliot Fundsworth III, and is asked to
pledge to join an exclusive yacht club, the Young Americans' Junior Yacht
Club. Within this relationship, Ferguson is transformed from the solidly middle-
class boy that he is to a pretentious snob, interested only in elite membership
at the club. J. Elliot Fundsworth III, not surprisingly, is a fraud who befriends
Ferguson only to gain access to Clarissa, on whom he has a crush. Although
Ferguson is constantly at odds with Clarissa in the show, it is Clarissa who
saves him from the clutches of the elitist, arrogant boy.

The episode is peppered with subtle (and some not so subtle) messages
about class politics; although they are certainly not radical in that the episode
focuses only on the very wealthy, there is nonetheless a pro-social message
intended. More interesting, however, is the role that Clarissa herself plays as
the savior of her brother, and the one who rejects the love interest of the selfish rich boy. She is the lead character in the program, and each episode centrally revolves around not only her experiences as a young adolescent girl, but
also around the contradictions between political action and individual subjectivity that are inherent in current definitions of girl power culture. The last

episode of the program, "The Last Episode," which aired October 1, 1994, depicted these contradictions on several different levels. The episode revolved around Clarissa's decision to go to college in Cincinnati to study journalism. Although her decision about college had ostensibly been made, when Clarissa wrote an article for a local newspaper about teen angst and malls (could there be a more illustrative girl power topic?), she was offered an internship at the *New York Daily Post*. She then was faced with choosing between college and career, a plot theme that carried on the show's explicit connection of gender identity with a kind of agency or citizenship.

Clarissa can be seen as an important Third Wave feminist icon. Her empowerment as a particular kind of citizen is assumed to be more generally connected to an increase in empowerment in the media and in the larger social world (in fact, "The Last Episode" is reminiscent of another media power player when Clarissa plays Murphy, of *Murphy Brown* fame, in a spoof called "Murphy Darling"). And, like Third Wave feminism itself, the agency of the character of Clarissa is reflective of a contradictory version of citizenship; the empowerment that it articulates for young girls does not include a model for how to *access* that citizenship except through representation. Indeed, girl power is defined by the tensions between representing girl power citizenship through the media and accessing that citizenship in a way that has larger implications for gender ideologies and practice.

As Told by Ginger

As Told by Ginger (ATBG) is a Nickelodeon original animated production, currently airing twice a week. The show features a main cast of five 12–13-year-old girls, and generally revolves around the issues that surround this group in their school, Lucky Middle School. Although the program does feature three younger boys (all of whom are siblings of the main characters), the episodes are primarily concerned with issues that pertain to the girl characters. The program has enjoyed some critical acclaim: it has been nominated twice for an Emmy award (Animated Series in Less Than an Hour category), but lost to *The Simpsons* and *Futurama*. Like those other animated programs, *ATBG* also presents social commentary within each episode; the girl power issues that garner a kind of social power, such as popularity, cliques, the culture of "cool," are presented in this program within a context of critique. *ATBG* is at times self-reflexive, using parody and irony to critique social norms and standards about gender and class. The main theme of the show revolves around some of the very same issues that *Nick News* covers in real life; Ginger Foutley, the lead character, is accepted into both the popular, cool clique at school, as well as by her long-time friends who are also represented as intelligent nerds.

In fact, one fan describes Ginger is described in the following manner:

> Ginger Foutley is a regular kid—although maybe a bit more reflective than most—who's still trying to figure out who she is. The social structure of Lucky Junior High grosses her out, but she's also kind of obsessed with it. If she were part of the cool clique, she swears she would do things differently. Yet her bluff is called when Courtney, a princess of cool, decides Ginger can hang.

> With one foot in each crowd, Ginger constantly flip-flops between her loyalty
> to her old friends and her desire to be cool with a capital C . . . Welcome to
> junior high! (As Told By Ginger, 2003a)

The profound tensions that define Ginger's character are mirrored by the contradictions that surround girl power culture specifically and Third Wave feminism more generally. In particular, the tensions between wanting to "be cool
with a capital C" in a commercially driven culture and the dedication to genuine female friendship are a marker of girl power. While this is certainly not a
new theme in children's programming (the subject of the cool crowd seems
to be a staple of programming targeted to the tween segment of the market),
the refusal to resolve the issue makes *ATBG* unique.

In other words, most other children's programs that deal with issues of
popularity seem to claim the moral high ground and come out for "genuine"
friendship at the expense of the obviously more superficial popular social group.
Yet *ATBG* plays with the tension more, even with characters other than Ginger. For example, Courtney Gripling, "the princess of cool," is cast in a Professor Higgins sort of role, a popular girl who wants to re-make Ginger:

> Totally self-absorbed and opportunistic, Courtney takes her position as Most
> Popular Girl very seriously. She prides herself on the diplomatic control and
> manipulation of her classmates. She's intrigued and baffled, however, by Gin-
> ger's backbone and real friendships. So she sets out to pluck the "unknown"
> from the dregs of everyday life and make her a "Popular Girl." (As Told By
> Ginger, 2003a)

In this role, Courtney is at times more successful than others, but there is a
general refusal to cast the characters universally as either superficial or genuine.
Again, this kind of ambiguity, formulated within the dynamics of consumerism
(the foundation upon which the concept of cool hangs) and a discourse of the
genuine, is symptomatic of Third Wave feminism and girl power culture, a politics which at times rather defensively insists that these two discourses and practices are not mutually exclusive.

This tension is not simply a side theme of *ATBG;* rather, it forms the substance of almost every episode. The tension is often represented through a
strategy of parody and self-reflexivity: there is a general subtext that mocks the
distinctions between social groups and characterizes the groups as trivial, even
while the show constantly focuses on social groups, thus legitimating them for
the tween audience. For example, in one episode, "Family Therapy" (May 25
2002), the contradictions between the superficial cool group and the genuine
real group are brought into bold relief through the figure of Ginger's friend
Macie Lightfoot. Macie, definitely not a member of the cool group, is riddled
with neuroses and is an incredibly insecure, self-conscious character. In this
particular episode, the program's theme revolves around the fact that Macie
and one of the cool girls, Mipsy, both have birthdays on the same day. While
Mipsy's birthday is announced at a school assembly and the cool girls immediately begin to plan a party (complete with a sushi chef flown in from Japan),
Macie waits for what she anticipates will be a surprise party given by her par-

ents. Unfortunately, her parents, both child psychologists, forget her birthday, and need to be reminded about the date by Ginger. In an effort to compensate for their forgetfulness, they shower Macie with attention. However, they are so unconnected to their daughter that they don't realize that she is turning 13, and treat her instead as if she was a five-year-old—they throw her a party with a petting zoo, they give her a swing-set for a present and, for her party, she dresses in a dress more appropriate for a very young child.

The social commentary of the program—the child psychologists forgetting their own child's birthday, the hyperbolic character of Mipsy's birthday party, the embrace of the juvenile attention by Macie—characterizes this program within the same popular cultural realm as *The Simpsons* or other programs like it that offer ironic critique as part of the entertainment. *ATBG* is different from *Clarissa*—for one thing, it is produced at a very different historical moment to *Clarissa Explains It All,* and the increased normalization of feminist rhetoric since 1991 (when *Clarissa* was first aired) has an obvious presence on the program. The issue of cliques, although always part of the landscape in adolescent culture, occupies a new position of salience in the early 21st century, where attention to girls has not only led to an increase in commercial products for this audience, but also increased public attention to the issues that characterize girl culture.

Nick News

Cliques, popularity, intelligence and empowerment are some of the girl power themes in Nickelodeon's original entertainment programming. These themes, however, not only provide interesting entertainment content, but are also represented in the non-fiction programming on the network's award winning children's news program, *Nick News. Nick News* is a half-hour weekly news program, shown every Sunday evening. Each regular edition *Nick News* covers three or four topics, and there is also a special edition *Nick News,* which devotes an entire show to one theme or special topic. *Nick News* is clearly different from *Clarissa* or *ATBG* because it is non-fiction; as a news program, it arguably provides a kind of "public sphere" for its youth audience. As David Buckingham (2000a) has argued, "for all its short-comings, news journalism remains the primary means of access to the public sphere of political debate and activity" (p. 186). The show is hosted by Linda Ellerbee, a public figure who is not only well known as a feminist, but also as an important children's advocate.

According to Buckingham, the key to *Nick News*'s success is the willingness of the program to be more adventurous with information and to "rethink politics" for children and thus address the youth audience as a slightly different kind of citizen. *Nick News* at times achieves the goal of establishing the relevance of traditional politics, but it is also an example of the kind of tension present in girl power programming, a tension between a more official political rhetoric and the rhetoric of consumer politics. At times, *Nick News* does address children as "political actors," as Buckingham asserts. That is to say, children's voices, desires, and opinions are treated with respect and without condescension, and the program offers specific instruction on how to act politically—by writing to one's congressperson, by refusing the social rules of an elitist clique, or simply by educating the child audience in what free speech means. So, for example, in one episode of *Nick News* (October 6, 2002), the first story involved cross-burning, after a recent case in the southern U.S. This was a significant program in that it articulated the complexities surrounding issues of free speech, and Ellerbee asked the children in the studio whether, for example, the KKK has a right to free speech, pushing the children to answer why and why not.

After this story, the show cut to a commercial break. At the return of *Nick News*, Ellerbee immediately began the program by discussing how one's dreams can come true—but as a rock star. The program then went on to detail the story of "O-Town," a manufactured boy-band that came into existence as a result of the reality television show, *The Making of the Band*. The odd juxtaposition of these two stories exemplifies the specific tension found in girl power programming between a more typically political form of address and a more commercial address that emphasizes consumer choice. In fact, in a special episode of *Nick News*, "The Fight to Fit In" (December 2, 2002), Ellerbee specifically references the contradictions I am identifying more generally in girl power ideology: "Grown ups will tell you how easy it is to be a kid. Kids know better. There is, at your age—at any age really—a natural struggle between the desire to be part of a group and the desire to be an individual."

Nick News more expressly addresses girl power in several different ways: there are some special editions, such as "The Fight to Fit In," or "The Body Trap" (November 25, 2002), that focus on issues thought to be relevant to girl culture such as body image, girls' personal identity, as well as on issues of inclusion in a male-dominated world. (Indeed, many of the girl power issues covered on *Nick News* explicitly reference the social world as largely male dominated, surely a recognition of the mainstreaming of feminist thought into children's consumer culture.) In "The Body Trap," *Nick News* devoted an entire issue to problems related to body image and contained a scathing critique of the popular culture industry's privileging of thin girls as ideals. Featuring not only celebrity Rosie O'Donnell as an "expert," but also graphic visual footage of a young girl suffering from anorexia, "The Body Trap" is an important counter-argument to the hundreds of images of impossibly thin models within popular culture that so powerfully become the norm for young girls. The episode featured a group of children and adolescents, both boys and girls, telling their personal stories about wanting to be thin, feeling stigmatized, and so on. Although this kind of personalized, individual story-telling is important in terms of recognizing the problem, it also functions to distract audiences from larger social issues that are a result of "The Body Trap," such as gender discrimination, racism in the media, and so on.

Even in the regular *Nick News* schedule, girls are often featured as important story subjects (there are, of course, many stories that appeal to a crossover audience of both boys and girls). For example, issues such as the fledgling National Women's Football League was covered in one episode, where the story made an explicit argument about the unequal playing field for girls and boys sports, and argued that girls "are as tough as boys" (October 20, 2002). Other episodes of *Nick News* dealt with the issue of cruelty and gossip among girl cliques. For example, in an episode of *Nick News* aired on November 3, 2002, Ellerbee begins by saying: "Sugar and Spice and everything Nice, that's what little girls are made of . . . NOT!" In fact, Ellerbee continues, girls can be just as mean as boys, and even meaner. The episode then depicts several young girls recounting their stories of cruelty at school, featuring author Rosalind Wiseman (of the aforementioned *Queen Bees and WannaBes*) on the voice-over stating that the "girl who has the most social power gets to do what she wants to the girl who doesn't." The episode also discusses the contradictions between societal expectations of girls—primarily that they be silent and passive rather than aggressive and active—and that this expectation has led to a unique kind of cruelty that relies not on overt aggression but rather a more subtle, and arguably more insidious, type of malice such as gossip and secrets. Directly connecting girl cruelty to popular culture, *Nick News* argues that girls learn "that to move up they have to pull somebody else down" through glossy magazines, music videos and other forms of popular culture that privilege a kind of brutal competition among girls. The segment ends with a discussion of Wiseman's "empower program," *Owning Up*, where she encourages girls to stand up for themselves if another girl is being cruel. As *As Told by Ginger* suggests in an entertainment format, some of the more pressing issues of the early 21st century, at least when it comes to children, have to do with the dominant practices of femininity, self-esteem, and popularity in the social and cultural world. These topics have provided a broader cultural context for *Nick News* to address similar sorts of issues.

Finally, another way in which *Nick News* is an example of girl power programming comes not in the form of representation, but in a more extratextual way, through the host Linda Ellerbee herself. Ellerbee is a well-known journalist who has been outspoken on the problems of sexism and ageism in the field of journalism. Her production company, Lucky Duck Productions, not only produces *Nick News,* but also programs for Lifetime Television and WE (Women's Entertainment Network). Her work in journalism has garnered numerous awards, including several Emmys and the duPont Columbia award (*Nick News* itself has won three Peabody awards). Ellerbee is also a public speaker; she is a breast cancer survivor and speaks nationally about her experience. She is well known for her respect for both women and children, and is the author of an adolescent reading series, "Get Real," about a young girl reporter.

Henry Jenkins (1998) positions Ellerbee as an important figure in the world of children's media regarding the treatment of children as political and social agents, rather than impressionable beings that need protection from the media. He argues that Ellerbee

> creates television programs that encourage children's awareness of real-world problems, such as the Los Angeles riots, and enable children to find their own critical voice to speak back against the adult world. She trusts children to confront realities from which other adults might shield them, offering them the facts needed to form their own opinions and the air time to discuss issues. (p. 32)

As the producer of *Nick News,* Ellerbee is also a producer of children's culture—and in this specific case, a producer of girl power culture. Although *Nick News* is clearly not a DIY form of cultural production, or an alternative girl power 'zine, it nonetheless manages to function as an important producer of girl power ideology (Kearney, 1998).

Nick News is shaped in part by these different dimensions of girl power. The program's focus on girl power issues, in a children's news program that targets a youth audience, is an important form of media activism. *Nick News* claims to specifically empower children through the distribution of information. As Nickelodeon describes the show, "Every week *Nick News* keeps you in the know about the issues that are important to you, from personality profiles to interviews to polls and special guests . . . It's the news the way YOU want it, with help from kids everywhere!" (Nickelodeon website, 2003). However, not only is it difficult to determine precisely what issues are important to all kids, but *Nick News* has the same problem as most news programs: how to connect the issues on the program with the politics of a child's material life. As Buckingham (2000b) argues, "young people need to be provided with opportunities to engage in political activity, rather than simply observing it from a distance—in other words, that they are entitled to be political actors in their own right" (p. 187). *Nick News* is a program that, like citizenship itself, is fraught with tension about the various meanings of empowerment, and what it means to be a political actor. The girl power episodes on *Nick News* create even more of a contradiction: on the one hand, the programs do encourage an awareness of the various issues surrounding contemporary gender politics. On the other hand, these very same gender politics are the products not necessarily of political action, but of media visibility and the commercial realm. The issue of body image, for example, is an important feminist concern, and *Nick News* acknowledges this, but also approaches it from within the commercial realm of the media—a site that helps to produce dominant norms of femininity in the first place.

Girl Power: Citizenship or Consumerism?

Nickelodeon's efforts to include girls as lead characters may be understood as a lucrative market strategy to capitalize on the cultural fad of girl power, but programs such as *Clarissa Explains It All, As Told by Ginger,* and *Nick News* nonetheless provide a different cultural script for both girl and boy audience members, a script that challenges conventional narratives and images about what girls are and who they should be. Susan Douglas (1999), writing about the Spice Girls, argues that

> when adolescent girls flock to a group, they are telling us plenty about how they experience the transition to womanhood in a society in which boys are still very much on top. Girls today are being urged, simultaneously, to be independent, assertive, and achievement oriented, yet also demure, attractive, soft-spoken, fifteen pounds underweight, and deferential to men. (pp. 47–48)

Nickelodeon programming, including the shows discussed in this essay, incorporates these kinds of tensions as part of their narrative logic, and in so doing provides a context in which both girls and boys can question dominant narratives of gender.

Bonnie Dow (1996), when discussing prime time television shows of the 1980s and 1990s that were assumed to contain a feminist message, argues that while the gender ideology on shows such as *Murphy Brown* and *Designing Women* may not create policy change or affect material politics, they nonetheless represent a kind of feminism. In other words, that these shows are being aired in the mainstream media (a place that historically has demonized feminism) does not mean they are anti-feminist:

> To use the word "feminist" to describe them is not a mistake: within the limits of commercial television, they offer a version of feminist ideology. However, that ideology is one suited to television's needs, not to the needs of a feminist politics committed to the future of all women regardless of race, class, sexuality, or life situation. (p. 214)

Indeed, I see girl power shows on Nickelodeon as also representing a kind of feminism, one that is fundamentally about tension and contradiction. Girl power television is more closely aligned with Third Wave feminism than any kind of post-feminist ideology that disavows feminism. On the contrary, girl power programs such as *Clarissa* and *As Told by Ginger* are visibly situated within a Third Wave ethos, where empowerment and agency define girls more than helplessness and dependency. However, this empowerment is represented as an individual choice, and at times resembles other commercial choices we all make. In other words, Nickelodeon is an important producer of a kind of feminism, but commercial and media visibility is an important part of what *legitimates* that feminism. This does not mean that girl power television is *not* feminism; but it does mean that a significant component of Third Wave and girl power feminism is about media visibility. The mixing of political addresses within the programming and advertising on Nickelodeon—both feminine and feminist, both social and individual—reflects the kind of dynamic Third Wave feminists adopt as part of their subjectivity. Thus, the network itself speaks to its child audience in a mix of conflicting feminist voices.

The images young girls and adolescents watch on Nickelodeon—images of Clarissa Darling, or Ginger Foutley, or the real girls on *Nick News*—are empowering, at least within a specific context. They are diverse, and they represent a range of options and models, and in many ways these images are a refreshing and politically authorizing change from traditional images of femininity. While obviously the commercial shaping of girl power cannot be denied, girl power, like other forms of feminism, is about a particular kind of recognition. This is not simply a recognition that so-called "women's issues" such as sexual harassment, equal work for equal pay, and legal policies on rape and abuse are important issues that need to be addressed in the public sphere. It is also a recognition of women as contributing members of society now meriting a kind of visibility. And increasingly, the kind of visibility that carries with it an important dimension of power is media or cultural visibility.

In this sense, the easy dismissal of girl power as a media-created new commercial avenue that has no connection with any kind of real politics is both inaccurate and misleading about the nature of reality in the 21st century. The charge by Second Wave feminists regarding the apparent lack of real politics in Third Wave feminism may very well indicate, in part, the latter's preoccupation with personal issues and individualism. But this sentiment not only romanticizes the feminist movements of the 1960s and 1970s as concerned only with the social and material spheres; it also caricatures feminist politics of the 1990s as narcissistic and vacuous. As Susan Douglas (1994) has pointed out, the representation of women and girls in the media has historically encouraged a kind of love/hate relationship, where seemingly contradictory messages about being strong and weak, beautiful and business-like, assertive yet demure, have been offered to female (and male) audiences as a model for subjectivity. The media address of Third Wave feminism and girl power ideology is no different: it is also about tension and contradiction, about the individual pleasures of consumption and the social responsibilities of solidarity. Although obviously the political landscape has changed since the 1960s, and it seems evident in many contemporary examples that individual concerns have taken precedence over larger community or social issues, it is too easy to dismiss girl power as only or simply media fluff. The collectivist drive that defined the feminist movement during the Second Wave emerged not only because the feminists of that era were particularly politically minded, but also because the civil rights movement, the gay rights movement and the anti-war movements (as well as other political upheavals during this time) provided a rich context for collective protest. For contemporary women, the focus on individualism and the increasing significance of commercial culture provides a context for a very different kind of feminism to materialize. One project for feminists, then, is to attempt to understand the discourse of Third Wave feminism on its own terms, and not always through comparison to an imagined and nostalgic golden age of feminism of the 1970s.

Notes

1. Third Wave feminism is generally characterized as a movement centering on female self-empowerment that emerged in the 1990s. Third Wave feminism often uses both mainstream and marginalized popular and commercial cultures as mechanisms to celebrate female sexuality and access empowerment. The cultural expression of Third Wave feminism is often playful and ironic, exemplified in television such as *Buffy the Vampire Slayer,* activist groups like Riot Grrrl and 'zines such as *Hue* and *Bitch*. Third Wave activists, most often in their 20s and 30s, are focused on a broad range of feminist issues, ranging from abortion rights to individual self-esteem.

2. Second Wave feminism generally refers to the women's movements of the 1960s and 1970s. Second Wave activists were focused on fighting for gender equality in the workplace, abortion rights, economic parity, violence against women, and other issues. The Second Wave of feminism was defined by the collectivist drive that motivated the movement, and focused not only on the equality of women with men, but also on the liberation of women from patriarchy. Some of the important legislative measures that occurred as a result of the efforts of Second Wave feminists are, to name a few, the Equal Pay Act 1963, Title VII, the Civil Rights Act 1964, and the Equal Rights Amendment.

3. Boys also influence the purchasing power of their parents. Children in general have been increasingly recognized as a very important market because of not only their

own power as a group, but also the extended power that comes from their influence on their parent's commercial decisions.

References

As Told by Ginger website. Retrieved March 1, 2003, from Character section, http://www.cooltoons.com/ginger

Aucoin, D. (1999, March 21). At 20, Nickelodeon is top-rated—and it's the channel that changed kids TV. *The Boston Globe* p. N4.

Baumgardner, J., & Richards, A. (1999). *Manifesta: Young women, feminism, and the future*. New York: Farrar, Straus and Giroux.

Bellafante, G. (1998, June 29). It's all about me! *Time*, p. 57.

Buckingham, D. (2000a). *The making of citizens: Young people, news and politics*. London: Routledge.

Buckingham, D. (2000b). *After the death of childhood: Growing up in the age of electronic media*. London: Polity Press.

Canclini, N. G. (2001). *Consumers and citizens: Globalization and multicultural conflicts*. Translated and with an Introduction by George Yudice. Minneapolis: University of Minnesota Press.

Currie, D. (1999). *Girl talk: Adolescent magazines and their readers*. Toronto: University of Toronto Press.

Douglas, S. (1994). *Where the girls are: Growing up female with the mass media*. New York: Times Books/Random House.

Douglas, S. (1999). Girls 'n spice: All things nice? In Daniel M. Shea (Ed.), *Mass politics: The politics of popular culture* (45–49). New York: St. Martin's Press.

Dow, B. (1996). *Prime-time feminism: Television, media culture, and the women's movement since 1970*. Philadelphia: University of Pennsylvania Press.

Dow, B. (2001). Ellen, television, and the politics of gay and lesbian visibility. In *Critical Studies in Media Communication, 18* 123–140.

Driscoll, C. (2002). *Girls: Feminine adolescence in popular culture and cultural history*. New York: Columbia University Press.

Findlen, B. (Ed). (1995). *Listen up: Voices from the next feminist generation*. New York: Seal Press.

Goldman, R. (1992). *Reading ads socially*. New York: Routledge.

Gray, H. (1997). *Watching race: Television and the struggle for the sign of blackness*. Minneapolis: University of Minnesota Press.

Gross, L. (2001). *Up from invisibility: Lesbians, gay men, and the media in America*. New York: Columbia University Press.

Hall, S. (1997). *Representation: Cultural representations and signifying practices*. London: Sage Books.

Hartley, J. (1999). *Uses of television*. London: Routledge.

Hartsock, N. (1998). *The feminist standpoint revisited and other essays*. Colorado: Westview Press.

Heffley, L. (1999, June 3). Family arts zone: Then along came lively shows for kids, in the nick of time. *Los Angeles Times*, p. 45.

Hendershot, H. (1999). *Saturday morning censors: Television regulation before the V-chip*. Durham: Duke University Press.

Hogeland, L. M. (2001). Against generational thinking, or, some things that "Third Wave" feminism isn't. *Women's Studies in Communication, 24* 107–121.

Jenkins, H. (1998). *The children's culture reader*. New York: New York University Press.

Kearney, M. C. (1998). Producing girls: Rethinking the study of female youth culture. In S. A. Inness (Ed.), *Delinquents and debutantes: Twentieth century American girls' cultures* (pp. 285–310). New York: New York University Press.

Kinder, M. (Ed.). (1999). *Kids' media culture*. Durham, NC: Duke University Press.

Klein, N. (2000) *No logo*. New York: Picador.

McNeal, J. U. (1992). *Kids as customers: A handbook of marketing to children*. New York: Lexington Books.

McRobbie, A. (1991). *Feminism and youth culture: From Jackie to Just Seventeen*. Boston: Unwin, Hyman.

Miller, T. (1998). *Technologies of truth: Cultural citizenship and the popular media*. Minneapolis: University of Minnesota Press.

Nickelodeon press release (2000, September). In press packet for "A Kid's Got to Do What a Kid's Got to Do: Celebrating 20 years of Nickelodeon." New York: Museums of Television and Radio, June 1, 2000.

Nickelodeon website. Retrieved May 31, 2000, from http://nick.com/all_nick/tv_supersites/display_show.jhtml/?show_id = new

Pipher, M. (1995). *Reviving Ophelia: Saving the selves of adolescent girls*. New York: Ballantine Books.

Quart, A. (2003). *Branded: The buying and selling of teenagers*. Cambridge: Perseus Publishing.

Seiter, E. (1995). *Sold separately: Parents and children in consumer culture*. New Jersey: Rutgers University Press.

Shugart, H. A., Waggoner, C. E., & O'Brien Hallstein, D. L. (2001). Mediating Third Wave feminism: Appropriation as postmodern media practice. *Critical Studies in Media Communication, (18)* 194–209.

Spigel, L. (1992). *Make room for TV: Television and the family ideal in postwar America*. Chicago and London: The University of Chicago Press.

Sturken, M., & Cartwright, L. (2001). *Practices of looking: An introduction to visual culture*. London: Oxford University Press.

Van Fuqua, J. (2003). "What are those little girls made of?": The *Powerpuff Girls* and consumer culture. In C. A. Stabile & M. Harrison (Eds.), *Prime time animation: Television animation and American culture* (pp. 205–219). New York: Routledge.

Wiseman, R. (2002). *Queen bees and wannaBes: Helping your daughter survive cliques, gossip, boyfriends and other realities of adolescence*. New York: Crown Publications.

Wolf, N. (1994). *Fire with fire: The new female power and how to use it*. New York: Fawcett Books.

Soap Opera in China
The Transnational Politics of Visuality, Sexuality, and Masculinity

Sheldon H. Lu

This article is a study of Chinese soap opera, a form of television drama that emerged and flourished in the 1990s. Television drama is the most widely watched form of entertainment in contemporary China by virtue of the high rate of television penetration in Chinese households. Although television drama dates back to 1958, when television was first seen in China, there was an explosion in the 1990s in the nation's production, broadcasting, and consumption. In 1994, more than six thousand episodes of television dramas were produced in China; in 1995, more than seven thousand episodes; and in 1996, more than ten thousand episodes. In 1978, there were only 1.5 million TV sets, but by 1996, there were 280 million, and the estimated TV audience was 800 million.[1] This exponential growth in TV sets and the spread of TV programming is a direct reason for the decline in film audiences in the People's Republic of China (PRC).

Television Drama in China: A Historical Overview

Television broadcasting in China began at seven o'clock in the evening, Beijing time, on May 1, 1958, during the era of the "Great Leap Forward." The first Chinese television drama, a thirty-minute play, *Yikou cai bingzi* (*A Veggie Cake*), was produced and aired live on the Beijing Television Station on June 15, 1958. Hu Xu, the director of this drama, coined the term *dianshi ju* (literally "television drama") for this new form. This term harked back to the *guangbo ju* (literally "radio drama" or "radio play") in China. It was only fitting that television dramas had a parallel name.

For Hu Xu and many critics, the birth of Chinese TV drama was an indigenous phenomenon, not an act of imitating the foreign. In addition to Beijing TV and China Central TV (CCTV), television stations in Shanghai, Harbin, Guangzhou, Changchun, and Tianjing produced and broadcast their own dra-

---

Sheldon H. Lu, "Soap Opera in China: The Transnational Politics of Visuality, Sexuality, and Masculinity." From *Cinema Journal*, Vol. 40, No. 1 (Fall 2000), pp. 25–47. Copyright © 2000, University of Texas Press.

mas beginning in 1958. From 1958 to 1966, called the "direct telecast period" (*zhibo qi*) by Chinese TV historians, China produced nearly two hundred single-episode TV dramas; all were simultaneously produced, performed, and telecast live. Television drama production came to a halt during the Cultural Revolution and was not resumed until 1978.[2]

From the late 1970s through the 1980s, Chinese TV stations produced indigenous dramas and showed foreign television shows. American TV serials aired in China included *Man from Atlantis, Hunter, Falcon Crest, Remington Steele, Matt Houston,* and *Dynasty.* It is even reported that *Dynasty* was Chinese leader Deng Xiaoping's favorite program.[3] The Japanese soap opera *Oshin* was also tremendously popular when it aired on CCTV in the summer of 1986.

Beginning in 1981, the PRC began producing its own serials as opposed to single-episode dramas. *Xin xing* (*New Star*), for example, was a twelve-episode drama produced by Taiyuan TV but telecast on the national network in 1986. One of the most widely watched of these programs, it took on the topical issues of the time: economic and social reform.[4]

Since the 1990s, television drama has experienced unprecedented growth and popularity, so that it now occupies the preeminent place in contemporary cultural entertainment. Given the vast output, Chinese critics attempt to distinguish among subgenres and terminological differences within the television drama format. They speak of *lianxu ju* (television serial), *tongsu ju* (popular drama), *qingjie ju* or *yanqing ju* (melodrama), *shinei ju* (indoor drama), *feizao ju* (soap opera), *xiju* (comedy), *qingjing xiju* (sitcom), *lishi ju* (historical drama), *wuxia ju* (martial arts drama), and *jingfei ju* (detective and crime drama). The longest-running Chinese drama to date, *Da Qin diguo* (*The Great Qin Empire*), had 136 episodes. Such top-rated and widely watched dramas as *Kewang* (*Yearnings*, 50 episodes, 1990) and *Beijingren zai Niuyue* (*Beijingers in New York*, 21 episodes, 1993) marked the maturity of "soap opera" as a full-blown Chinese genre. Similarly, *Bianjibu de gushi* (*Stories of the Editorial Office*, 25 episodes, 1991) was regarded as the birth of "situation comedy," Chinese style.[5]

Chinese television serials are funded and produced by a variety of sources, involving both private and public funds. Yet they are all aired on public and state TV stations at the national, provincial, and municipal levels. Advertisements constitute a regular part of the programs and provide their main source of income. In China, as in the West, the televisual text is a "supertext" that consists of the particular program and the introductory and interstitial materials, such as announcements and advertisements.[6] Of course, the term "soap opera" in America derives from the fact that detergents and cleaning products were often advertised during such programs. The genesis of soap operas in China can also be examined in this light.

As mentioned earlier, *Yearnings* (dir. Zheng Xiaolong, CCTV and Beijing TV, 1990), the most successful Chinese TV drama, has been taken to be the first Chinese soap opera. The serial's narrative intertwines the stories of two families. Most of the episodes take place in a home and are shot in a studio. Therefore, the drama is also credited with being the first "indoor drama" (*shinei ju*) in China. Critics have pointed out an indissoluble link between the commercials and the story itself:

> There was always a commercial before the drama was telecast every time. The commercial was for a detergent, "Dailaoli" (literally "Save your labor"), to be used in the water tank of a toilet at home. The commercial was like a byproduct of this enchanting television drama. It traveled to almost every home in mainland China along with the drama. The commercial was like part of *Yearnings*. We seemed to be used to the commercial when we watched the drama. If we did not see Dailaoli first, *Yearnings* would not begin. The commercial seemed to exist at the margins of the story. Only when the two were connected would things become a whole.[7]

In an uncanny way, this Chinese TV drama was "soap opera" in the classic sense in that commercials for soap products were built into the very fabric of the television supertext. American in origin, soap opera has become a global form of television programming in many parts of the world, including (post)socialist China.[8]

Imaging National Identity in the Age of Transnationalism and Globalization.

Since full-fledged soap opera developed in China relatively late in comparison to the situation in many other parts of the world—North America, Latin America, and Europe—the subject has received very little critical attention in the West. Even in the U.S., "it was not until the 1980s that soap operas began to be taken seriously as texts."[9] Since then, however, television studies, media studies, and cultural studies have adopted a variety of approaches and orientations to TV drama: for instance, textual analysis, ideological analysis, ethnographic research, genre study, and gender analysis. To analyze the political economy of TV programs, scholars have attempted to determine the correlations and antagonisms among the televisual text, audience response, commodification, capitalist hegemony, and the status quo. Critical positions often fall somewhere between two extremes: populist celebration of potentially emancipatory moments in some TV programs and wholesale condemnation of the TV industry for its role in perpetuating capitalist ideology.[10]

In an effort to move beyond purely textual and ideological studies, much emphasis has been placed recently on ethnographic research that focuses on the audience's reception of given programs.[11] Critics thus dwell on the changing configurations of resistance, struggle, and negotiation on the part of the viewer in relation to the television text and the industry.[12] The leftist critical legacy has desired to avoid reductive oversimplifications and binary oppositions and to build on and revise two earlier traditions: the denunciation of mass culture as ideological deception in the fashion of the Frankfurt School or the total embrace of youth culture by British cultural studies enthusiasts. Thus, Jane Feuer points out the importance of "deconstructing three sets of opposing terms that have structured leftist discourses around Reaganism and around television: pop-ulist/elitist, complicity/critique, and commodity/art."[13] One should take a bal-anced critical stance that relies on neither John Fiske nor Jean Baudrillard, nei-ther "the ahistoricism of Jean Baudrillard's concept of resistance" nor "the totalizing endorsement of the subordinate resisting reader in John Fiske."[14]

The scholarly advances in the West may offer some heuristic guides for the examination of the contemporary Chinese scene, but they cannot be trans-ferred wholesale to such a different cultural and social setting. As a postso-cialist, developing country, China poses a unique set of problems for cultural studies. If one continues to speak of "resistance," "opposition," "negotiation," and "pleasure," one might ask, What is there to resist and oppose in China? Capitalist hegemony? Socialist politics? What kind of audience pleasure is avail-able? Officially, the PRC is a socialist/communist state; yet increasingly it has steered toward a capitalist market economy. Such a basic contradiction between politics and economics is captured in the official slogans of the state itself: build a "socialist market economy," build "socialism with Chinese characteristics."

In analyzing the social condition of contemporary Chinese television drama in this time of depoliticization, globalization, and consumerism, some critics have identified three major forces in public culture: (1) official discourse and state ideology, (2) elite culture (*jingying wenhua*), and (3) emergent "plebeian culture" (*shimin wenhua*), the culture of the masses and the populace.[15] In the PRC, official discourse and state ideology refer to the cultural policies and reg-ulations of the socialist regime, state-sponsored artworks, and cultural activi-ties. Elite culture consists of the discourse of intellectuals and humanists who purport to be the guardians of knowledge and high culture and who are com-mitted to the reconstruction of humanism and subjectivity. Though more allied with the forces of mass culture, popular soap opera has to negotiate with all three constituencies. The televisual text necessarily embodies a mixture of oppo-sition, co-optation, negotiation, and confluence all at once. In analyzing a Chi-nese TV serial, then, the critic must be attentive to a number of concerns: state ideology and censorship, capitalist commodification, humanist discourse, and the sentiments of the masses.

In this study, I specifically address the issue of national identity. What is "China" in the global cultural imaginary at the beginning of the twenty-first cen-tury? As an abstract social totality, or "a-thing-in-itself," China remains inac-cessible to the cognitive cartographer. China is visible to the human eye insofar as it projects itself as an image or a self-image or, more precisely, as an endless *series* of images and simulacra. The task at hand is to investigate the production and consumption of the self-image of the PRC in contemporary Chinese visual and narrative texts, specifically as represented in prime-time TV soap operas.

Day and night, the Chinese consumer is swamped in a vast, inescapable sea of visual images: TV, video, film, billboards, and magazines. Out of this fragmented collective of simulacra, an illusory image of China is constructed in both the public sphere and the private fantasy world. Whether it is the pic-ture of a Western fashion model on the front cover of a magazine sold by a peddler on the street or the representation of "foreign babes" in a prime-time

TV program, the PRC fashions images of itself and the other on a map of global cultural geography. In such a manner, visuality in contemporary China partakes of a transnational, cross-cultural politics of representation.[16]

In the post–Cold War era, which is characterized by both globalization and fragmentation, it may no longer be feasible to speak of a divide between Third World "national allegory" and American postmodern culture.[17] No country, certainly not China, can be treated as a homogeneous entity. It is all the more important, therefore, to analyze China's need to fashion coherent images of its national and cultural identity, to create a semblance of an "imagined community," precisely because of the present state of fragmentation and transnationalization in its culture and economy. To borrow a term from Fredric Jameson, it is necessary to inquire into the *geopolitical unconscious* of contemporary China—that is, the vision of the social, the public, and the national-within-the-global—through the tales and images of the private, the sexual, and the psychic in media representations. We need not treat these texts as national allegories but, rather, as images of *imagined national identity* in the paradoxically *transnational* postmodern hyperreality.[18] Transnational flows of capital, images, and people between China and the world have opened up new avenues for inventing nationhood and creating self-understanding.

In the domestic and global arena of image production and consumption, we may distinguish two opposite yet complementary strategies in the politics of the self-representation of China. In the global cultural market, Chinese artists offer localized narratives and images. They employ self-exoticization and self-eroticization for the gaze of the Western spectator. China appears as an ethnic other. Such a "(self-)ethnographic" approach is most evident in the New Chinese Cinema, especially the films of Chen Kaige, Zhang Yimou, Zhou Xiaowen, and Xie Fei that circulate in the international market.[19] Othering the self is what sells in global consumption; art *cum* commodity must be stamped with some intrinsic "Chineseness" to be purchased and consumed around the world.

In the Chinese domestic cultural market, however, the strategy is the opposite. To fulfill the expectations, fantasies, desires, and self-knowledge of indigenous, local Chinese, the media must project a sense of globalism, not "tribalism." The other, the foreign, must be exoticized, eroticized, and, at times, subalternized. Moreover, the initial exoticization of the foreign must ultimately be accompanied by domestication, taming, and a literal marriage of foreigners and Chinese—often within the traditional courtyard (*sihe yuan*). (An example is a TV serial about American girls in Beijing, discussed below.). As both a late-comer nation-state and an ancient empire, China vindicates itself in the narrative of the universal history of capitalism and modernity. In such a politics of visual representation, the public, national agenda of modernization and globalization must be narrated through the private fantasy world of a transnational libidinal economy.

In the course of my analysis of the interrelations of the media, popular culture, and the public sphere, the focus will be on the formation of what I call a new "transnational male imaginary." Specifically, I examine the mass media's attempt to reconstruct a male subjectivity in the context of 1990s transnational public culture. This recuperation of masculinity is a crucial component of popular culture in contemporary China.

The Emergence of Transnational Libidinal Economy

Broadly speaking, the popular discourse of masculinity in the New Era (late 1970s late 1980s) played a subversive, critical, and antihegemonic role in the public sphere.[20] In the 1990s, new popular genres—which were initially introduced from Hong Kong, Taiwan, and the West—largely supplanted older forms of literary, artistic, and cultural production. Ironically, the triumph of this new popular culture also implied its gradual acceptance and co-optation by the state. The PRC's integration into global capitalism in the 1990s brought new possibilities, desires, and anxieties for the male gender in discursive and social space. The construction of a male imaginary or the establishment of a male subjectivity has thus been an urgent task for the mass media and public culture at large. The goal would be to recuperate a functional masculinity.

During the mid-1980s, in the post-Mao era, the liberation and reassertion of individuality *cum* masculinity became a major concern in public culture. The "search for men" was a predominant theme in both intellectual discourse and popular culture. The term "men" (*nanzi han*) is here understood as "tough," "rough," "masculine," "manly." A redundant expression, it is indicative of the problematic nature of the Chinese discourse on masculinity under construction. Such a critique is part and parcel of the larger critique of Chinese society. For instance, one of the most celebrated writers of the 1980s, Zhang Xianliang, lived in prisons and labor camps for two decades. His stories, such as *Nanren de yiban shi nüren* (*Half of Man Is Woman*), depict the emasculation and sexual impotence of Chinese men caused by political oppression. The theme of dysfunctional masculine sexuality is thus turned into an allegory of the fate of the nation as a whole.

The critique of injured masculinity is necessarily accompanied by its positive reconstruction, as in Zhang Yimou's *Hong gaoliang* (*Red Sorghum*, 1988), which was a box-office hit in China. A reenactment of the resurrection of Chinese masculinity, the film depicts the psychical and libidinal liberation of Chinese men in a legendary past. The theme songs, such as *Meimei ni dadan di wanqian zou* (*Little Sister, Go Forward Bravely*), were later taken up by popular singers. Cassettes of popular songs about northwestern China, the Shaanxi area, the cradle of Chinese civilization, entitled *Xibei feng* (*Northwestern Wind*) and *Shaanbei 1988,* galvanized the minds and hearts of tens of millions of young Chinese. These popular songs, sung in a hoarse male voice, are myths of regained virility and of the revival of the ancient land. In these popular refashionings of the male image, masculinity is no longer the refined, reserved, effeminate scholar-intellectual type prevalent in Chinese culture but a projection of primitive vitality.

The 1990s marked a continued "search for men" in Chinese culture. In Xie Fei's *Xiang hun nü* (*Women from the Lake of Scented Souls*), co-winner of the Golden Bear Award at the 1993 Berlin Film Festival, the critique of masculinity is still strong. Set in a village in contemporary China, the film tells the story of a Chinese woman, who, typical of the Chinese "socialist market economy," starts a joint venture with a Japanese investor to export high-quality sesame oil to Japan. Despite her business success, she has to struggle with a dysfunctional family: a crippled husband and a mentally retarded son. Male impotence has led to lack of libidinal and emotional fulfillment for her and her daughter-in-law. Women in some of Zhang Yimou's later films confront similar situations: for instance, the title characters in *Ju Dou* (1990) and *The Story of Qui Ju* (1993).

The contemporary Chinese discourse on masculinity in the era of transnational capitalism necessarily has its "Chinese characteristics." The new agenda shared by both the state and popular culture is the creation of a strong "socialist market economy," an economy that will ultimately catch up with those of the advanced countries in the West. The competition between the PRC and the West is a rivalry for the accumulation of capital and economic development. As portrayed in popular culture, however, this competition sometimes turns into a libidinal one. The reassertion of Chinese masculinity takes the form of a transnational fantasy, the wish-fulfillment of competing successfully with foreigners for the possession of capital and women. Romantic triumph, therefore, is directly linked to the struggle in the global financial arena. This transnational male imaginary is thus a manifestation of a collective geopolitical unconscious that amounts to the psychic counterpart of the economic. In the case of gender discourse, the potential danger is that a new masculinity projected in the mass media will be easily appropriated for nationalistic and patriarchal causes.

In the 1990s, a cluster of narrative and visual texts—stories, novels, films, and nighttime soap operas—described the trafficking between Chinese and foreigners in China. They usually involved titillating, sensational transnational and/or transcultural love between Chinese and foreigners in China or between ethnic Chinese and non-Chinese in diasporic conditions. Products of this fledgling minigenre include autobiographical novels such as *Beijingers in New York* (*Beijingren zai Niuyue,* by Cao Guilin), *A Chinese Woman in Manhattan* (*Manhadun de Zhongguo nüren,* by Zhou Li), *He Married a Foreign Woman* (*Quge waiguo nüren zuo taitai,* by Wu Li), and *My Experience as a Lawyer in the U.S.* (*Wo zai Meiguo dang lüshi,* by Zhang Xiaowu and Li Zhongxiao); nighttime soap operas, such as *Beijingers in New York,* based on the novel of the same title, *Chinese Ladies in Foreign Companies* (*Yanghang li de Zhongguo xiaojie*), *Shanghainese in Tokyo* (*Shanghairen zai Dongjing*), *Russian Girls in Harbin* (*Eluosi gunian zai Harbin*), and *Foreign Babes in Beijing* (*Yangniu zai Beijing*); and films such as *A Wild Kiss to Russia* (*Kuangwen Eluosi*). Below, I will focus on soap operas in order to detect certain shared strategies in the Chinese media for imaging the self and the other.

In 1993, *Beijingers in New York* (dir. Zheng Xiaolong and Feng Xiaogang, CCTV and Beijing TV, 1993), a 21-episode serial drama, captivated the attention of the entire nation.[21] This was the first Chinese television drama shot entirely outside China. Director Zheng Xiaolong from Beijing TV was already a famous figure for his role in producing such top-rated dramas as *Yearnings* and *Stories of the Editorial Office.* Nonetheless, it was an ordeal for him to finance this new drama. The production budget was 1.5 million U.S. dollars, or the equivalent of ten million yuan at the time. Beijing Television Art Center and CCTV signed a contract to be co-partners in the production. CCTV agreed to allow three minutes of advertising time in each episode during the first run of the series, up to a total of sixty minutes for the entire show.

The production team at Beijing TV Art Center borrowed the 1.5 million dollars from the Beijing branch of Bank of China. At first, Bank of China was reluctant to approve the loan, afraid that Beijing TV might not be able to pay it back if the drama, to be shot entirely in New York, turned out to be a failure. At the point of desperation, Zheng and his associates took the daring step of asking the Central Committee of the Chinese Communist Party (CCP) to intervene on their behalf. Li Ruihuan, a reform-minded leader, was then in charge of artistic and ideological matters in the Party hierarchy. At the urging of the Central Committee, Bank of China approved the loan, and the production team went to New York to shoot the serial.[22] After a first run on CCTV in the fall of 1993, the series was popular enough to be aired on Chinese-language channels in the U.S. in spring 1994.

The drama follows the life of Wang Qiming (Jiang Wen), a Chinese artist and new immigrant in New York City; his wife, Guo Yan; daughter, Ning Ning; mistress, Ah Chun; and business competitor, David McCarthy. He comes to the United States as a viola player but cannot find a suitable job. He and his wife then start working as cheap laborers in a sweater factory. His wife later leaves him for the owner of the factory, David, a white male. Wang subsequently establishes his own business and becomes an entrepreneur himself. At the end of the series, he defeats David in a financial competition and takes over his factory.

This plot illustrates the ambitions and frustrations of Chinese males in the 1990s, and, in fact, it is the tale of transnational capitalism itself. It recounts the transformation of an artist-intellectual into a capitalist who will do anything to survive and win. Further, the man is competing with a white male for the possession of both capital and women. Finally victorious, the Chinese man wins on the financial, economic, and libidinal battleground vis-à-vis his American competitor.

In one scene, Wang Qiming pays a local symphony orchestra to perform with him. He is able to resume his artistic career for a moment and, because of his new-found financial power, to command a large orchestra. Another telling sequence involves Wang being entertained by a white prostitute. He holds a large number of bills in his hand and asks the half-naked, buxom prostitute to say "I love you." Compromising scenes such as these invite the spectator to speculate on some possible deep political unconscious of Chinese nationals in the global arena. They project a quite different self-image of the Third World subject. Rather than being portrayed as a deprived and impoverished citizen, in the realms of sex and business the Chinese male is transformed into an aggressive and confident player, even on the home turf of advanced Western nations.

The TV series ends with a scene at a street intersection. After gambling away his entire savings in Atlantic City, Wang Qiming sticks out his middle finger and says "fuck you" to a white woman driver who is yelling at him for blocking traffic. This open ending leaves to the imagination what Wang will do next, though he may have just revealed his desire subconsciously in his obscene gesture. The insertion in this program of Chinese males in the global circulation of capital, people, and desire provided potent images of both wish-fulfillment and self-caricature for the Chinese male audience. Although audience responses to and assessments of the show diverged drastically in regard to the main character, viewers were fascinated with the show because of its attempt to define Chinese identity in the global cultural imaginary of the 1990s.[23]

The show offered Chinese viewers a close look at the sights, sounds, scenery, and landscape of New York. Yet, as critics have pointed out, these postcard images had less to do with America and more to do with Chinese sentiments toward it. A Chinese woman journalist, now residing in the United States, describes the drama as one that shows "Western scenes through tinted glasses." For her, the drama was concocted from the formula of "xenophobia + patriotism + patriarchy + anti-imperialism and the criticism of capitalism." As a propaganda set-piece, it won the applause of officials, ordinary people, and intellectuals alike in China.[24]

Critics have also noted that Wang's mindset resembles that of Ah Q in Lu Xun's masterpiece story *Ah Q zhengzhuan* (*The True Story of Ah Q*), written in the early twentieth century.[25] Ah Q is the archetypal Chinese national character who projects an exaggerated sense of greatness but in reality is a pathetic weakling and loser in the modern world. Similarly, Wang grew up in the era of the Cultural Revolution and has come to America in search of opportunities. At times he detests capitalism and exploitation and makes fun of his own transformation into a capitalist; at other times, he wants to be rich and on top of the world. He often curses America: "What is America? When we [Chinese] were human beings, they were still apes!" Nonetheless, he brings his family to America to fulfill his dream. He is ashamed of the backwardness of China yet proud of its civilization. As an artist-intellectual-capitalist-hooligan, he embodies a split Ah-Qesque character. Through Wang, the drama reveals the contradictory nature of Chinese national identity and nationalism in a trans-Pacific setting.

An equally popular novel about successful overseas Chinese, Zhou Li's autobiographical *A Chinese Woman in Manhattan* (1992), also relates the rags-to-riches tale of a Chinese in the financial capital of the world. The difference is that the protagonist is a Chinese woman who marries an American man. Despite the tremendous popularity of the novel, it was never transformed into a TV program. Given the libidinal dynamics of Chinese transnational public culture, the story of a Chinese woman being "taken" by an American man, however successful she may have been in New York, would probably not have fared well with a large share of the domestic male TV audience.

Romancing the Other:
Russian Girls in Harbin and Chinese Men in Russia

Because of the success of *Beijingers*, a number of soap operas on the theme of Chinese abroad or foreigners in China followed suit. In fact, the very names of these soap operas indicate the influence of *Beijingers: Shanghainese in Tokyo, Russian Girls in Harbin,* and *Foreign Babes in Beijing.* However, none of these latter dramas had the impact or shocking effects on the audience as the original program.[26] Often regarded as pale imitations of *Beijingers,* they have not received the critical attention they are due.[27]

Most Chinese TV serials are mini-serials, not as long as those in many other countries where they may last many years. Nevertheless, seriality is a fundamental feature of Chinese TV dramas, and they are relatively open-ended narratives. The appearance of various characters who stand for different beliefs and personalities, commercial interruptions, narration in serial installments, and an almost perpetual delay in reaching closure make these dramas more or less multivoiced dialogic discourses and polysemic texts. Although it is difficult or impossible to offer a definitive decoding of the meanings in these dramas, issues of national and cultural identity in the age of transnationalism and globalization loom large.

It has been reported in the Chinese tabloid press and in other mass media that, because of the dire economic situation in the former socialist bloc countries, large numbers of citizens have fled to other countries, including China, in search of better jobs. It is said that Russian women have appeared in numerous Chinese cities, not only along the coastline but in places in the hinterland where foreigners have never come in the past. These women, described as having "blonde hair and blue eyes" (*jinfa biyan*), work in restaurants, bars, dance halls, hotels, and fashion shows. Business thrives wherever they work, as Chinese men patronize these places in order to be served by these "exotic" Westerners.

To be sure, the Western woman is not a new figure in Chinese gender discourse. While the Chinese peasant woman often serves as a signifier of feudal oppression, the white woman has been a trope of Western lifestyle and the incarnation of modernity throughout the twentieth century.[28] In contemporary China, popular magazines frequently feature pictures of white fashion models to attract the male gaze. The white woman functions as an object of both male desire and female mimicry. A good example is Zhou Xiaowen's film *Ermo* (1994). The comedy juxtaposes scenes of the imaginary world of romance and love-making as seen in American soap operas such as *Dynasty,* which has been run and rerun on Chinese TV since the 1980s, with the drab and difficult world of daily life in rural China.[29] Ermo, the title character, has an illicit love affair with her neighbor and thereby reenacts a subconscious behavior derived from televisual images of the U.S. lifestyle. This is not to suggest that Chinese women did not have sexual desire prior to viewing *Dynasty* but to point to the catalytic effect of such foreign media images.

The twenty-episode TV series *Russian Girls in Harbin* (*Eluosi gunian zai Harbin,* dir. Sun Sha, CCTV and Heilongjiang Studio/Tian'e Film, 1994) is a good example of the transnational trafficking of Chinese men and foreign women in contemporary Chinese mass media. The series focuses on a group of Russian girls who come to Harbin looking for work and wealth. Harbin is a large city in northeast China, near the Sino-Russian border, which has a long history of Russian influence; today it is a major center for trade between the countries. Consistently foregrounded in the drama is the (imaginary) central position of Chinese men in relation to women, whether Chinese, Russian, or otherwise. The centrality of Chinese men is established, confirmed, and reconfirmed as they are positioned as the owners of power and capital. Foreign women are the "subalterns," subject to the men's gaze and desire.

Russian Girls has multiple narrative strands, plots, and characters, however, one of the overarching narrative threads is a triangular love story involving Fang Tiancheng (Jiang Wu), a young Chinese entrepreneur; his former Chinese girlfriend, Liu Ying; and a newcomer—a Russian girl named Olia. The serial begins with the story of Olia, whose family suffered during the economic decline of Russia. Although a caring parent, her father is a helpless alcoholic who cannot lift the family out of poverty. Olia leaves her family and boyfriend for China in hopes of finding a good job. At Suifen River, she is in danger of being attacked by Chinese mobsters, but at the critical moment, Fang Tiancheng appears, beats back the bad guys, saves Olia, and then leaves the scene. Eventually, they run into each other in Harbin, where, overjoyed by their reunion, Tiancheng helps Olia find a job and an apartment.

In a particularly provocative scene, over a dinner between Tiancheng and Olia, Tiancheng bitterly recalls past events in Sino-Soviet history and tells Olia that China has always been a generous country. However, in the difficult years following the Sino-Soviet split in the late 1950s and early 1960s, he says, the Soviet Union unfairly demanded that China pay back its debt and thus caused tens of millions of Chinese people to endure hardship and hunger. The ungrateful way of the Soviets contrasts sharply with the generosity of Tiancheng toward Olia. While Tiancheng goes on with his tirade, Olia silently listens. At one point, she tells him he is cruel to animals since he shot down a pigeon to prepare a special dish for her. Although there is a degree of self-mockery and irony in conversations such as these, it is significant that, as a result of the "cunning of history," China has finally earned the right to teach its long-time rival Russia a lesson or two through the mouth of Tiancheng. That similarities exist between the personae of Fang Tiancheng in *Russian Girls* and Wang Qiming in *Beijingers* is no coincidence, for Fang Tiancheng is portrayed by none other than Jiang Wu, the younger brother of Qiang Wen, who plays Wang Qiming in *Beijingers*. The resemblance between the two actor-brothers is all too obvious.

In the last episode of the series, most of the Russian girls leave Harbin for Russia by train. The moment of parting is agonizing for both Tiancheng and Olia, who have had an on-and-off love affair. The final sequence unleashes the lovers' pent-up feelings and anxieties. Olia runs toward Tiancheng from a long distance in slow motion, while Tiancheng waits for her by his motorcycle. In the final scene, the two ride off on a motorcycle into the horizon. The two lovers are united, and, metaphorically, so are their two countries.

Throughout the series, the Russian girls are exoticized and eroticized.[30] Most work as waitresses and entertainers in a Harbin hotel. They all have beautiful singing voices and appear sensuous and vivacious. The manager of the hotel, a Chinese woman, has to teach them Chinese demeanor. She tells them that rather than being flirtatious with the guests, they should be modest.

Although Olia stands out as virtuous and intelligent, her body is often eroti-cized. For instance, in a scene in which Tiancheng brings her breakfast in bed, his gaze fixes on her voluptuous, revealing body of Olia, his "sleeping beauty." In a shower scene, the camera slowly caresses the woman's upper body, back, hair, and neck as she washes herself. In her "being-looked-at-ness," the Rus-sian woman, as the ethnic other, bares and surrenders herself to the eyes of the local Chinese spectator.

Another noteworthy visual text is the film *A Wild Kiss to Russia* (*Kuang-wen Eluosi*, dir. Xu Qingdong, Beijing Film Studio, 1995). Ranked as the tenth-highest-grossing Chinese-made film of 1995,[31] this comedy recounts the romantic adventures of two Chinese businessmen in Russia. The protagonist is a poor intellectual named Da Jiang (Feng Gong). At the beginning of the film, Da Jiang's seven-year marriage has just ended after his wife left him for a rich man, so he decides to go to Russia to pursue his dream: selling Chinese goods. Once in Russia, his friend and business partner, Shuang Cheng, has an affair with Natasha, while Da Jiang falls in love with Natasha's younger sister, Katya. Katya is an aspiring ballet student who wishes to go to Moscow to pur-sue her studies but has no money to fulfill her wish. For some time, Da Jiang is determined to make enough money to send Katya to Moscow, but the two are unable to be united. After completing their business deal in Russia, both Shuang Cheng and Da Jiang return to China. Shuang Cheng becomes the owner of a bar where Russian dancers regularly entertain the guests. When Da Jiang's buddy invites him to the bar, Katya suddenly appears and performs a segment of *Swan Lake* for the guests. The film ends with Da Jiang and Katya being reunited and embraced in a "wild kiss."

Throughout this comedy, the economic ascendancy of Chinese men vis-à-vis their former Russian "big brothers" is portrayed. Moreover, the Chinese men's wealth is exchanged for Russian love just as the men's ownership of cap-ital soon leads to an overflow of libidinal energy. Throughout the film, Rus-sian men and women are depicted as poor people who work for (invariably male) Chinese bosses. The Russians are all too eager to receive *renminbi* (Chi-nese currency).

In one scene, Katya is about to sell her piano to get some cash. Da Jiang comforts her and holds her in his arms while saying, "There will be bread, there will be milk, and there will be everything." Many Chinese viewers would immediately recognize that this line is a verbatim quotation from the film *Lenin in 1918* (Mikhail Romm, 1939), one of the most popular Soviet films of the Mao era. Lenin says these words to comfort an old Russian woman during a very difficult time in Soviet history. In this new context, Da Jiang's words become a parody of Lenin's original phrase. Numerous instances like this not only mock the former relationship between China and Russia but also reverse their relationship. The Russian revolution is no longer a model and an inspi-ration for the Chinese; it is now the Chinese who provide the "bread," "milk," "piano," and "everything." Although self-parody and self-deflation are part of the humor of the comic star Feng Gong, his reiteration of a familiar line from a sacred revolutionary text highlights that circumstances have changed between the neighboring countries.

It is not difficult to discern the underlying nationalist, sexist undertones in such media representations. In the nineteenth century, China was bullied, humiliated, and defeated by czarist Russia many times. In the twentieth century, Stalin's Soviet Union was the model society to be emulated by the Chinese during their communist revolution. The Chinese Communist Party was a little brother under the shadow of its big brother. In the 1960s and 1970s, the Soviet Union was regarded as China's ideological rival and number-one enemy. Yet, by the end of the century, China remained intact and capitalist economy was flourishing, whereas the former Soviet Union was socially and economically disintegrating. The victory that Chinese men are able to score with foreign women symbolizes not only the resurrection of Chinese masculinity but also a triumph of the Chinese nation itself.

Domesticating the Foreign: American Babes in Beijing

The twenty-episode soap opera *Foreign Babes in Beijing* (*Yangniu zai Beijing*, dir. Wang Binglin and Li Jianxin, Beijing Film Studio) aired on prime-time Chinese TV in 1996. As a top-rated program in a country where "TV penetration . . . is at over 95 percent or so," "*Foreign Babes* had a first-run audience of about 600 million viewers" and has been rerun several times since.[32] The melodrama focuses on several ordinary Chinese families living in a traditional Chinese courtyard (*sihe yuan*) and on a group of foreign students in Beijing. The main narrative strand revolves around the love affairs of the two Li brothers, Tianming and Tianliang, and two American students, Louisa and Jessie.

The first episode begins with a scene on a crowded Beijing bus. Among the passengers are two American students, Robert and Louisa. As the passengers push their way around, Robert comments that people in China lack civility (*wenming*). His remark enrages Li Tianliang, and after they all exit the bus, Tianliang and Robert get into an argument about civility and civilization. Tianliang tells Robert that he is the one being rude. When Robert refuses to apologize and asks Tianliang if he has the courage to beat him up, Tianliang throws a heavy punch at Robert, knocking him down. While all this transpires, Robert's friend Louisa feels no less than "love at first sight" for Tianliang, whom she persistently pursues. Eventually, she marries Tianliang and moves to the traditional Beijing family compound, where, as a virtuous, lovely, dutiful wife, Louisa lives harmoniously with her Chinese in-laws.

Meanwhile, Louisa's friend Jessie (Rachel DeWoskin) relentlessly pursues Tianliang's elder brother, Li Tianming, with whom she eventually has an affair. The trouble is that Tianming is married and has a young son. Their crosscultural relationship proves stronger than infatuation and obsession; in fact, the two seem to be genuinely in love. At the end of the series, Tianming divorces his wife and leaves for America with Jessie.

The two brothers and the two "American babes" are at opposite poles and thus present a varied and complex picture of the Chinese and the foreigners. The younger brother, Tianliang, is portrayed as patriotic, righteous, and straightforward. Although he remains a faithful and loving husband after marrying Louisa, the interests of his country and his state-owned company always come first.

In one episode, Louisa's father, Jack, the head of an American company doing business in Beijing, is on the verge of bankruptcy and desperately needs to sell his technology and equipment to a Chinese buyer. Tianliang's family urges Tianliang to help his in-law by buying his equipment. However, to save money for his company and China, Tianliang decides to buy from a Japanese company at a cheaper price. Apparently, the episode shows that Tianliang places national interest above personal interest. Although his course of action seems cruel and incomprehensible to the "Chinese" feelings of his family members, Louisa loves him all the more for his incorruptibility and professionalism. Later on, Tianliang manages to take care of both sets of concerns by introducing Jack to another Chinese buyer. In one scene, after the crisis is settled, Tianliang and Louisa go out to the suburbs to relax. With the silhouette of the Great Wall in the background, Tianliang has a few things to teach his attentive American wife about the "Chinese way," that Chinese people really "respect human rights."

The older brother, Tianming, contrasts with Tianling dramatically. Tianming is opportunistic and self-promoting and seizes any chance to move up the social ladder. His American lover, Jessie, is also very different from Louisa. She appears at first to be only impetuous and irresponsible, but their affair certainly puts her and Tianming's moral character in question. As the story develops, however, their love and self-determination become the saving grace for Tianming and Jessie.

Although the series dwells on the commonality of human feelings across racial and national boundaries, it also explores the comic elements of cultural differences. For instance, the Li family is heartbroken to find out that their eldest son had an illicit affair with a Western woman. Not only is this cruel to their beloved daughter-in-law, but it is also a disgrace to the family, their ancestors, and their neighbors. In one episode, Mr. Li, a rather traditional father as well as a comic figure, tries to get Jack, Tianming's boss, to dissuade Tianming from divorcing his wife for the sake of Jessie. In his traditional Chinese reckoning, Jack could certainly stop Tianming's action since he is not only Louisa's father but, more important, the "leader" of Tianming's "work unit" (*danwei lingdao*). To his surprise, Jack responds that he has no right to interfere with Tianming's personal life and must respect the separation of the private and public spheres even though he is his boss. As a matter of fact, he was married four times. For Jack, divorce is the "beginning of a new life" (*xin shenghuo de kaishi*)! The mindsets of the two parents, though now related by marriage, could not be further apart.

In the libidinal arena, the American boy, Robert, is necessarily positioned as the loser. Although he has known Louisa since childhood, he loses her to Tianliang. At the end of the series, Robert has contracted a kind of cancer that is incurable in America. The only hope is traditional Chinese medicine and exercise. One of the final shots of the series shows Robert exercising amid a group of Chinese.

Also noteworthy is the marginalization of Chinese women represented by the character of Qin Fen. As Tianming's wife and Huzi's mother, she is a traditional Chinese woman. Even after her divorce from Tianming, she does not rebel against the Li family but remains on good terms with them and committed to raising her son. Qin Fen does not remarry. The finale of the soap opera shows the characteristic Chinese New Year family dinner, a time of reunion. As her ex-husband, Tianming, leaves for America with Jessie, Qin Fen, still a member of the Li family, shows up at the Lis' home to join the happy gathering. Thus, the image of Qin Fen is of a woman who silently swallows sorrow, bears suffering, and accepts what fate has in store for her. This representation, designed to win the sympathy and affection of broad segments of the Chinese TV audience across age and gender lines, can be traced not only to both traditional Chinese literature and modern film but more specifically to the archetype fashioned by the character Liu Huifang in *Yearnings* (*Kewang*). According to Rachel DeWoskin, who plays Jessie:

> All of my writhing, naked love scenes with Tianming are juxtaposed to scenes of his wife doing virtuous things—walking down rows and rows of the factory, working overtime, and patiently teaching their baby how to read. She breaks her back in a factory and then runs home to cook beautiful dinners for the family. She watches the clock, waiting for Tianming, refusing to believe what she suspects might be true. I actually cried watching the show when his wife leaves the family home.[33]

The "American babes" are clear winners as opposed to the Chinese women in the soap opera. Furthermore, in contrast to *Russian Girls in Harbin,* Louisa's and especially Jessie's families are represented as wealthy in relation to their Chinese counterparts. In *Russian Girls,* Russian families are told to be poor. What is even worse, Olia's father is an irresponsible alcoholic. The comparative financial situations of the Chinese, Russian, and American families is an allegory of the uneven economic strength of the three countries in the post–Cold War period.

The Transnational Politics of Sexuality and Masculinity in the Chinese Media

In both *Russian Girls* and *Foreign Babes,* there is undeniably a marginalization of the local Chinese woman in favor of the white woman in the racial, transnational politics of Chinese men, whose desire and gaze motivate the flow of the respective narrative.[34] The foregrounding of white female sexuality is a symptom of an insecure male subjectivity. The imaginary conquest of the white woman is a male defense mechanism, an attempt to do away once and for all with the stereotype and self-perception of inadequate Asian/Chinese masculinity and sexuality.

The psychosexual dynamics in these Chinese soap operas may also be understood in the light of the writings of Frantz Fanon, a foundational figure in the genealogy of postcolonial studies. In his seminal book *Black Skin, White Masks,* Fanon theorized the subject-positions of black men and women and their sexual and marital relationship with white men and women. Psychoanalysis provides him with a vantage point to investigate colonialism and racism. On the one hand, he criticizes black women in the Antilles for their desire to marry white men. He accuses these women of being complicit in the emasculation of the native black male. Their wish for gaining white acceptance through marrying white men is contemptuously described by Fanon as "whitening," "lactification." On the other hand, he is more sympathetic to the desire of black men to marry white women. In Chapter Three "The Man of Color and the White Woman," Fanon writes, "I wish to be acknowledged not as black but as white. Now—and this is a form of recognition that Hegel had not envisaged—who but a white woman can do this for me? By loving me she proves that I am worthy of white love. I am loved like a white man."[35]

It is through such a dialectical reversal that the Third World subject, be he an "oversexed black male" or an "undersized Asian male," as popular stereotypes go, is able to reassert his manhood in terms of sexual, political, and economic power. It is obvious that this type of anticolonial, counterhegemonic thought is embedded in masculinist, patriarchal, nationalist discourse. Mary Ann Doane points out that "For Fanon, a psychoanalytical understanding of racism hinges on a close analysis of the realm of sexuality. This is particularly true of black-white relations since blacks are persistently attributed with a hypersexuality."[36] Similarly, the relationship between race and sexuality becomes equally important in the Chinese context, since the Chinese or Asian male has been dismissed as lacking in masculinity in racist discourse and some popular perception. Historically, in Hollywood fiction, the "Chinaman" has always been a creature of problematic masculinity.[37] When interracial romance does happen in a positive light, it is usually the situation of a "white knight" taking a submissive Chinese lady (Suzie Wong, etc.) In the international film market, the heroics and antics of Asian masculinity are given expression in Hong Kong action and martial arts films. Yet, even in such genres, libidinal economy is kept at a minimum, and the male heroes appear to be single-minded, desexualized fighting machines.[38] Hence, the resexualization of Chinese masculinity through the white woman on prime-time national TV in mainland China is a significant development in the self-imaging of China. Although these TV programs are not intended for international primary audiences, they serve the function of reversing existing images of interracial relations on the home front.

If the white woman has represented a figure of "modernity," "beauty," and most of all a trope of "alterity" in the Chinese public culture,[39] her latest transformation and domestication within China betokens a new moment in the self-other binarism in the male imaginary. She is no longer an "other," an object of the gaze, a figure distant from the self. She is now within reach, and turns into a vehicle for the self-aggrandizement of the male ego. If Western soap operas such as *Dynasty* offer titillating televisual images of the romantic other for mass cultural consumption and yet hold that "fantasy world" at arm's length away from the local Chinese consumer during the 1980s, as vividly reenacted in a fictional film such as *Ermo*,[40] Chinese media have created their own tales of wish-fulfillment. Meanwhile, the Chinese male, purportedly bearing the burden of the entire collective, displaces his erstwhile subalternity and replaces it on the foreign female.

The circulation of these stories and images of regained masculinity in the mass media reveals something about the nature of contemporary Chinese public culture. Although there is no official pronouncement on these matters, the state acquiesces to such portrayals in national TV programs, newspapers, and magazines. In contrast, the censors have been rather strict on other types of representation of Chinese masculinity in international film culture. Here I refer to, for example, films by Zhang Yimou and Chen Kaige. Zhang's depiction of Chinese men has radically changed since his first film *Red Sorghum* (1988). In his later works—*Ju Dou* (1990), *Raise the Red Lantern* (1991), *The Story of Qiu Ju* (1993), and *To Live* (1994)—Zhang depicts Chinese masculinity in dysfunction and crisis. The spectator sees impotence, incest, concubinage, polygamy, injured male organs, and the inability of men to save their spouses and children. There are also Chinese critics who point out that the films seek to cater to the taste of the Western audience by selling out spectacles of the exotic Orient. Although the images of dysfunctional, impotent Chinese masculinity may fare well with the Western audience, for whatever reasons, they run contrary to the public discourse and the mass media in China. If there is still any use for the notion of "national allegory" as formulated by Fredric Jameson in his discussion of Third World literature in the era of multinational capitalism, one may tentatively conclude that the libidinal economy of the public culture of a "post–Third World" country (a former Third World country in the Cold War era) such as China in the era of transnational capitalism is a fable of the embattled situation of the post–Third World in relation to the dominant Euro-American political and libidinal economy. Soap operas such as the ones I mentioned offer an opportunity for us to map the Chinese geopolitical unconscious, namely, the correlation between the psychic, the sexual, the private and the social, the political, the public. As the Chinese economy is the process of being integrated in a competitive global economy, it is foreseeable that such tales of libidinal adventures will continue to figure prominently in Chinese popular media.

The cultural, political, and libidinal economy in contemporary China is necessarily related to developments in the global arena. The events in China are in part a function of a world situation that has been described by critics as "global capitalism" or "transnational capitalism."[41] The alliance between popular culture, patriarchal discourse, and transnational capital should raise concerns for media critics. At this juncture, my critical project shares the same goal with what has been termed "transnational feminist practices"—that is, "an attention to the linkages and travels of forms of representation as they intersect with movements of labor and capital in a multinational world." In other words, "we are interested in how patriarchies are recast in diasporic conditions of postmodernity—how we ourselves are complicit in these relations, as well as how we negotiate with them and develop strategies of resistance."[42] We should be more aware of the intersections and imbrications among libidinal economy, global capital, social labor, private fantasy, nationalism, and patriarchy.

It is evident that the extended serial form of Chinese soap operas, which involve complicated plot lines and different personalities, may not offer a hardened, single message and that the meaning of a soap may vary among the audience, especially if we deal with a heterogeneous audience as large as several hundred millions in the Chinese case, as some claim. Moreover, these visual texts are replete with ironies, parodies, and self-deflations that an insider would easily spot. Yet critical reception of these texts in the West sometimes interprets them as expressions of a wave of neonationalism in China.[43] Such a reading sees only one side of the political dynamics of visual and narrative representation. In that case, the transnational male imaginary in the 1990s would be an unabashed self-assertion of the male ego. Public culture would then reinforce and perpetuate the dominance of the position of the patriarch-state-capital. It is therefore necessary for us to rethink the condition, possibility, and necessity of maintaining a critical public space both inside and outside China. However, I would also argue that these television dramas, as products of mass media and popular culture, are varied and complex enough to be more than packaged nationalism. The description of the private passions of Chinese masculinity in these texts, often at the expense of indigenous women, explore the possibilities, limits, fallacies, and fluid boundaries of national identity, not necessarily nationalism, in the circumstances of an increasingly *trans*national, deterritorialized global economy in the post–Cold War era.

Notes

Parts of this article were presented at the Convention of the American Association for Chinese Studies at the University of Maryland in 1996; the "Critical Theories: China and the West" conference in Changsha, China, in 1997; the "Gender, Visuality, Modernity in Twentieth-Century China" symposium at the University of Pittsburgh in 1997; the Convention of the Association for Asian Studies in Chicago in 1998; the "Globalization and the Future of the Humanities" conference at Beijing Language and Culture University in 1998; and the "Asian Cultures at the Crossroads: An East-West Dialogue in the New World Order" conference at Hong Kong Baptist University in 1998. I thank those audiences for their challenging comments. I especially want to thank several people who provided assistance and useful critique at various stages of the writing: Lucy Fischer, Perry Link, Anne T. Ciecko, Rachel DeWoskin, Yingjin Zhang, David Desser, Stanley Abe, *Cinema Journal* Editor Frank P. Tomasulo, and the anonymous readers of *Cinema Journal*.

1. For statistical figures and estimates, see Zhu Kuoliang, "Yijiu jiuliu nian dianshi ju chuangzuo shitai" (The state of television drama production in 1996), *Dianying yishu* (Film Art) 5 (September 1996): 67–74, and Xie Xizhang, "1995: Zhongguo dianshi ju huigu" (1995: Chinese television drama in retrospect), *Dangdai dianying* (Contemporary Film) 4 (July 1996):80–89.

2. See Hong Shi, "Zhiboqi Zhongguo dianshi ju de shijian he guannian" (The practice and concepts of Chinese television drama in the period of direct telecast), *Dangdai dianying* (Contemporary Film) 1 (January 1994): 87–92; Guo Zhenzhi, *Zhongguo dianshi shi* (History of Chinese Television) (Beijing: Zhongguo renmin daxue chubanshe, 1991).

3. Judith Marlene, "The World of Chinese Television," in Donald Altschiller, ed., *China at the Crossroads* (New York: H. W. Wilson, 1994), 207.

4. For a discussion of this drama and Chinese television in general, see James Lull, *China Turned On: Television, Reform, and Resistance* (London and New York: Routledge, 1991).

5. Xie Mian and Zhang Yiwu, *Da zhuanxing: hou xinshiqi wenhua yanjiu* (The great transformation: A study of the culture of the post-New Period) (Harbin: Heilongjiang jiaoyu chubanshe, 1995), 345–92.

6. For a clarification of this concept, see Nick Browne, "The Political Economy of the Television (Super) Text," in Horace Newcomb, ed., *Television: The Critical View*, 4th ed. (New York: Oxford University Press, 1987), 585–99. Given the latest developments in digital television and computerized image-making, the television "supertext" is perhaps evolving into an electronic "hypertext," which may further expand the experience and definition of television viewing.

7. Xie and Zhang, *The Great Transformation*, 362–63. For discussions in English, see Lisa Rofel, "The Melodrama of National Identity in Post-Tiananmen China," in Robert C. Allen, ed., *To Be Continued . . . Soap Operas around the World*, (London: Routledge, 1995), 301–20, and Jianying Zha, *China Pop: How Soap Operas, Tabloids, and Bestsellers Are Transforming a Culture* (New York: The New Press, 1995), Chap. 2, *Yearnings*, 25–53. My translation.

8. For a new study of global television and global soap opera, see Chris Barker, *Global Television: An Introduction* (Oxford, U.K.: Blackwell, 1997).

9. Allen, *To Be Continued*, 6.

10. See, for example, Douglas Kellner, "TV, Ideology, and Emancipatory Popular Culture," in Newcomb, *Television: The Critical View*, 471–503, and Todd Gitlin, "Prime Time Ideology: The Hegemonic Process in Television Entertainment," in Newcomb, *Television: The Critical View*, 507–32.

11. For assertions about the importance of ethnographic research, see Ien Ang, "Culture and Communication: Toward an Ethnographic Critique of Media Communication in the Transnational Media System," in John Storey, ed., *What Is Cultural Studies? A Reader* (London: Arnold, 1996), 237–54, and James Lull, *Inside Family Viewing: Ethnographic Research on Television Audiences* (London: Routledge, 1990).

12. Douglas Kellner cautions us that any overhasty ethnographic research may result in various fetishisms—the "fetishism of struggle," the "fetishism of audience pleasure," and the danger of "celebrat[ing] resistance *per se* without distinguishing between types and forms of resistance." Kellner, *Media Culture: Cultural Studies, Identity and Politics between the Modern and the Postmodern* (London: Routledge, 1995), 38–39.

13. Jane Feuer, *Seeing through the Eighties: Television and Reaganism* (Durham, N.C.: Duke University Press, 1995), 151.

14. Ibid., 4. For John Fiske's views, see his *Television Culture* (London: Routledge: 1987) and *Understanding Popular Culture* (London: Unwin Hyman, 1989). Fiske highlights the ability of the viewer to "make do" with the popular cultural texts that he/she confronts in everyday life (by way of the theory of Michel de Certeau).

15. Xie Xizhang and Wu Di, "Wenhua toushi: tongsu ju de xingsheng yuanyin ji jiazhi quxiang" (A cultural perspective: The reasons for the flourish of popular dramas and their axiological choices), *Dangdai dianying* (Contemporary Film) 6 (November 1994): 79–84.

16. Needless to say, transnational and crosscultural interactions have occurred throughout the history of world cinema. Witness Hollywood's appropriation of foreign directors from the silent era (German, Swedish, etc.), all the way to its current flirtation with Hong Kong directors. Hollywood has also featured the "exotic" Western woman

in a Chinese setting from early on, for example, Marlene Dietrich in Josef von Sternberg's *Shanghai Express* (1932). I describe "transnational politics" in a rather specific historical and social context. I emphasize the strategy of China's TV industry to target China's *domestic* audience by using the resources and opportunities afforded by the transnational flow of images, commodities, and capital in the 1990s. For a historical overview of aspects of transnationalism in Chinese filmic discourse, see Sheldon H. Lu, ed., *Transnational Chinese Cinemas: Identity, Nationhood, Gender* (Honolulu: University of Hawaii Press, 1997), "Introduction," 1–31. For a study of transnationalism in modern China, see Aihwa Ong and Donald M. Nonini, eds., *Ungrounded Empires: The Cultural Politics of Modern Chinese Transnationalism* (New York: Routledge, 1997).

17. See Fredric Jameson, *The Geopolitical Aesthetic: Cinema and Space in the World System* (Bloomington: Indiana University Press, 1992), 1–6. Here Jameson outlines his concepts of the geopolitical unconscious, allegory, space, and representability and offers them as solutions to the form-problems of the postmodern era.

18. Heuristic as it may be, Jameson's theory of national allegory has been the subject of reconsideration and debate. See Ahmad Aijaz, "Jameson's Rhetoric of Otherness and the 'National Allegory,'" *Social Text* 17 (fall 1987):3–25, and Madhava Prasad, "On the Question of a Theory of (Third) World Literature," *Social Text* 31/32 (spring 1992):57–83.

19. See Rey Chow, *Primitive Passions: Visuality, Sexuality, Ethnography, and Contemporary Chinese Cinema* (New York: Columbia University Press, 1995).

20. For a periodization of stages of cultural history in the Deng era from the late 1970s to the 1990s, as well as discussions of Chinese postmodernism and popular culture, see Sheldon H. Lu, "Postmodernity, Popular Culture, and the Intellectual: A Report on Post-Tiananmen China," *Boundary 2* 23, no. 2 (summer 1996): 139–69; Lu, "Art, Culture, and Cultural Criticism in Post-New China," *New Literary History* 28, no. 1 (winter 1997): 111–33; Lu, "Global POSTmodernIZATION: The Intellectual, the Artist, and China's Condition," *Boundary 2* 24, no. 3 (fall 1997): 65–97; and Lu, "Universality/Difference: The Discourses of Chinese Modernity, Postmodernity, and Postcoloniality," *Journal of Asian Pacific Communication* 9, nos. 1–2 (1999): 97–111.

21. The drama aroused heated debates in China. For pertinent discussions in English, see Geremie R. Barmé, "To Screw Foreigners Is Patriotic: China's Avant-Garde Nationalists," *China Journal* 34 (July 1995): 209–34; Pamela Yatsko, "Inside Looking Out: Books and TV Dramas about Life Overseas Reflect Existing Chinese Biases," *Far Eastern Economic Review*, April 11, 1996, 58–59; Mayfair Mei-hui Yang, "Mass Media and Transnational Subjectivity in Shanghai: Notes on (Re)Cosmopolitanism in a Chinese Metropolis," in Ong and Nonini, *Ungrounded Empires*, 287–319; and Lydia H. Liu, "What's Happened to Ideology: Transnationalism, Postsocialism, and the Study of Global Media Culture," *Working Papers in Asian/Pacific Studies* (Durham, N.C.: Asian/Pacific Studies Institute, Duke University Press, 1998).

22. For an insider's account of the financing of the TV drama, see Peng Xin'er, "Da dao Niuyue qu—neimu jiemi" (Fighting Their Way to New York—Exposing a Secret), *Dazhong dianying* (Popular Cinema) 6 (1993): 10–15. For a story on Robert Denbo, who played David McCarthy in the drama, see Fang Jin, "Yige zai Beijing de Niuyue ren—yanggemen'er 'Dawei'" (A New Yorker in Beijing—foreign brother "David"), *Dazhong dianying* (Popular Cinema) 12 (1993):14. For a report on Wang Ji, who played the role of Ah Chun in the drama, see Zhao Wentao, "Wang Ji yiran liunian Beijing" (Wang Ji still loves Beijing), *Dazhong dianying* (Popular Cinema) 12 (1993):16.

23. Xie and Zhang, *The Great Transformation*, 380–86.

24. Zha Xiduo (Jianying Zha), "Youce yanjing li de xiyang jing—Beijing ren de Niuyue meng" (Western scenes through tinted glasses—the New York dream of Beijingers), *Jiushi niandai* (The Nineties) (February 1994): 16–17.

25. Wu Di, "Beijing tongsu lianxu ju chuangzuo jianxi: cong Kewang dao Beijing ren zai Niuyue" (A brief analysis of the creation of Beijing popular serials: From *Yearnings* to *Beijingers in New York*), *Beijing dianying xueyuan xuebao* (Journal of Beijing Film Academy) 1 (1994): 146–63.

26. *Shanghainese in Tokyo* tells the story of Chinese students in Tokyo. To some critics, this drama is more truthful and realistic than *Beijingers*, but not as shocking and powerful as the latter. See Yu Haiyi, "Guanyu dianshi lianxu ju *Shanghairen zai Dongjing* de taolun zungshu" (An overview of the discussions regarding the television serial *Shanghainese in Tokyo*), *Shehui kexue* (Social Sciences) (Shanghai) 4 (April 1996): 76–77.

27. See He Ma, "Chuangche mofang he shi xiu" (Is there an end to repetition and imitation?), *Zhongguo yinmu* (China Screen) (August 1997): 40.

28. For an informative study of the symbolism and politics of the white woman in contemporary China, see Louisa Schein, "The Consumption of Color and the Politics of White Skin in Post-Mao China," *Social Text* 41 (winter 1994): 141–64.

29. See Anne T. Ciecko and Sheldon H. Lu, "*Ermo*: Televisuality, Capital, and the Global Village," *Jump Cut* 42 (1998): 77–83.

30. Exoticizing and eroticizing the ethnic other is also a recurrent feature in China's representation of its ethnic minorities, whose women are supposed to be good dancers and singers just as foreign women (Russian girls) are assumed to be. For a parallel study, see Dru C. Gladney, "Representing Nationality in China: Refiguring Majority/Minority Identities," *Journal of Asian Studies* 53, no. 1 (February 1994):92–123.

31. The list of the ten highest-grossing Chinese-made films of 1995 is found in *Dianying yishu* (Film Art) 3 (May 1996): 4. For an inside look at the shooting of the film in Russia, See Long Luowan, "Zouchu guomen de dianying ren" (The filmmakers who stepped out of the Chinese border), *Dazhong dianying* (Popular Cinema) 12 (1994): 12–13.

32. Bob Young and Rachel DeWoskin, "Foreign Babe in Beijing," *Transpacific* 67 (1996): 14. For a look at the international cast of the drama, see Ru Dai, "*Yangniu'er zai Beijing* zhong de waiguo yanyuanmen" (The foreign actresses and actors in *Foreign Babes in Beijing*), *Dazhong dianying* (Popular Cinema) 7 (1995): 20–21.

33. Young and DeWoskin, "Foreign Babe in Beijing," 16.

34. A white female graduate student from America was spat on in Harbin by a Chinese woman, who apparently mistook her for another "Russian girl" in the area. The event is a telling example of cultural stereotypes and misunderstandings effected by the media in contemporary China.

35. Frantz Fanon, *Black Skin, White Masks*, trans. Charles Lam Markmann (New York: Grove Press, 1967), 63.

36. Mary Ann Doane, *Femmes Fatales: Feminism, Film Theory, Psychoanalysis* (New York: Routledge, 1991), 217.

37. See Gina Marchetti, *Romance and the "Yellow Peril": Race, Sex, and Discursive Strategies in Hollywood Fiction* (Berkeley: University of California Press, 1993).

38. For studies of images of Chinese masculinity, see Steve Fore, "Jackie Chan and the Cultural Dynamics of Global Entertainment," in Lu, *Transnational Chinese Cinemas,* 239–62; Anne T. Ciecko, "Transnational Action: John Woo, Hong Kong, Hollywood," in Lu, *Transnational Chinese Cinemas,* 221–37; Mark Gallagher, "Masculinity in Translation: Jackie Chan's Transcultural Star Text," *Velvet Light Trap* 39 (spring

1997): 23–41; and Tony Williams, "Space, Place, and Spectacle: The Crisis Cinema of John Woo," *Cinema Journal* 36, no. 2 (winter 1997): 67–84.

39. This issue has been closely analyzed in Schein, "The Consumption of Color," 141–64.

40. See Ciecko, "Transnational Action," 221–37, and Ciecko and Lu, "*Ermo:* Televisuality, Capital, and the Global Village," 77–83.

41. See Arif Dirlik, *After the Revolution: Waking to Global Capitalism* (Hanover and London: Wesleyan University Press, 1994), and Dirlik, "The Postcolonial Aura: Third-World Criticism in the Age of Global Capitalism," *Critical Inquiry* 20, no. 2 (winter 1994): 328–56.

42. Caren Kaplan and Inderpal Grewal, "Transnational Feminist Cultural Studies: Beyond the Marxism/Poststructuralism/Feminism Divides," *Positions: East Asia Cultures Critique* 2, no. 2 (fall 1994), 439. See also Kaplan and Grewal, eds., *Scattered Hegemonies: Postmodernity and Transnational Feminist Practices* (Minneapolis: University of Minnesota Press, 1994).

43. These soap operas about Chinese men dating Western women are interpreted by some as expressions of neonationalist sentiments. For example, see Barmé, "To Screw Foreigners Is Patriotic"; Keith B. Richburg, "Embracing 'Foreign Babes': China Wary of Cross-Cultural Dating, but Delights in TV Show," *Washington Post,* July 21, 1996, A1 and A27; and Wendell Yee, "Foreign Babes and *Post* Chauvinism," *Transpacific* 67 (1996):8. For a different response and a defense of the drama, see Rachel DeWoskin, "Foreign Babes," at Website—http:www.iht.com/iht/edlet/let0821.html (August 21, 1996).

McTV
Understanding the Global Popularity of Television Formats

Silvio Waisbord

Back in the 1980s, global television seemed headed toward becoming a "wall-to-wall Dallas," as Hollywood's domination of television screens was dubbed in Europe. In the context of profound changes in the structure of European television, such a prospect raised concerns about the future of national television and cultural imperialism amid the onslaught of U.S. media. Lately, it seems that global television is likely poised to be a "wall-to-wall format." Around the world, television is filled with national variations of programs designed by companies from numerous countries. Formats are programming ideas that are adapted and produced domestically. The commerce of formats is not new. For decades, formats of "reality" and "fiction" programming have been produced and sold in international markets (Moran 1998). But, as the trade press has recently described it, "format television" has taken the industry by storm. In recent trade fairs, studio executives have pontificated about the virtues of formats and industry panelists have discussed the differences between formats of "reality" and "scripted" programs.

The popularity of formats is more than just another trend in an industry perennially hungry for hit shows and eager to follow them. It reveals two developments in contemporary television: the globalization of the business model of television and the efforts of international and domestic companies to deal with the resilience of national cultures. The analysis of these developments allows us to reexamine how economics and culture are related in the process of media globalization. In the first section of this article, I argue that when understood as a set of media policies and technological developments, globalization has intensified interconnectivity among television industries worldwide. Interconnectivity happens through structural and institutional linkages among television systems and industries worldwide. The result is the emergence of an increasingly integrated business governed by similar practices and goals. In the second section, I delve into what the popularity of television formats reflects about national cultures in a globalized world. On the surface, the global dissemination of formats may suggest not only the global integration of the economy of the indus-

Silvio Waisbord, "McTV: Global Trade in Television Formats." From *Television & New Media*, November 2004, Vol. 5, No. 4, pp. 359–383, copyright © 2004 by Sage Publications, Inc. Reprinted by permission of Sage Publications, Inc.

try but also the standardization of content. What better evidence of cultural homogenization than format television? A dozen media companies are able to do business worldwide by selling the same idea, and audiences seem to be watching national variations of the same show. At a deeper level, however, formats attest to the fact that television still remains tied to local and national cultures. Bringing up examples of Latin American cases, I argue that television is simultaneously both global and national, shaped by the globalization of media economics and the pull of local and national cultures.

Privatization and Demand for Format Programming

The massive changes in the structure of television systems in the 1980s and 1990s have connected television systems that, until then, functioned in relative isolation. When television was conceived as a national, protected industry, the global trade of programming ran into regulatory stonewalls. In the past decades, privatization, liberalization, and deregulation of the airwaves removed such limitations and opened television systems to flows of capital and programming. The result has been the increasing homogenization of systems on the principles of private ownership and profit goals.

Together with structural changes, technological developments increased the demand for programming. Before the last wave of globalization, most television industries had a limited number of hours that they needed to fill. The emergence of a multichannel, liberalized environment raised the possibility that large producers would benefit from increased demand generated by the explosion in the number of television hours. With extensive libraries, well-established distribution networks, and an unparalleled marketing machine, Hollywood companies were poised to profit enormously from those changes. The globalization of television industries seemed unequivocally designed to benefit Hollywood. The fact that most systems shifted toward an "American" model of television gave a substantial advantage to the industry that had invented it.

However, as the principles of commercial television became standardized and industries matured, other domestic industries could also produce and export programming, particularly if they catered to audience niches. What was good for Hollywood could, under the appropriate conditions, also be good for other production companies based in other countries as long as they could master the game of commercial television. Consequently, dozens of television companies based in Western Europe, Australia, and New Zealand gained more than a foothold in the global television market. This is put in evidence by the trade of program formats. Many Western European companies are the copyright holders of recent hit formats. The trade press has dubbed Europe "the leader of reality programming" (Fry 2000). The success of Britain's Celador and Pearson, Holland's Endemol, or Sweden's Strix television is evidence that the pool of producers is no longer limited to traditional Hollywood companies. Pearson Television boasts to be "Britain's only truly global television producer, with over 160 programs currently in production in almost 35 countries around the world." Its hit *Who Wants to Be a Millionaire* has been sold to 79 countries (Schneider

2000). The BBC has sold *The Weakest Link* to 38 countries. Telefónica-owned Endemol has blanketed the world with *Big Brother* and other reality programming. Strix created the widely popular *Expedition: Robinson* (known as *Survivor* around the world) and *The Bar*. Moreover, the success of these companies has been mentioned lately as evidence of important changes in the European media and tougher competition for Hollywood (Andrews 2000; Carter 2000). They have accomplished what seemed reserved only to a handful of British productions until not so long ago—that is, to sell formats in the almost impenetrable U.S. television market (see O'Regan 2000). These developments have led some observers to talk of a "two-way transatlantic" flow (Guider 2000), while others, stretching the point, conclude that "U.S. influence is slipping" (Jensen 2000) and that "TV imperialism goes into reverse" (Moyes 2000).

Although it is true that some European production companies are able to capitalize on the changes that globalization promoted in the last decades, such statements rush to conclusion, failing to recognize the enormous inequalities that still exist in the global trade of audiovisual products. To speak of Hollywood's influence as "slipping" or facing "competition" based on the strength of a handful of non-U.S. companies is absurd considering that Hollywood has expanded its worldwide presence through the promotion of globalization policies. No question, in addition to European firms, a number of non-Western companies also became important producers and exporters of television programming. The number of booths at international trade fairs, such as National Association of Television Program Executives (NATPE) and Marche International des Films et des Programmes pour la TV, la Video le Cable et les Satellites (MIPCOM), grew steadily, featuring new sellers of diverse television programs. Japanese firms, whose traditional exports consisted mainly of cartoons and documentaries, now sell dramas and game-show formats. Hong Kong, Egyptian, and Indian producers consolidated their presence in their respective linguistic regions as well as in diasporic markets (Sinclair, Jacka, and Cunningham 1996). Mexican and Brazilian media powerhouses found new opportunities in global television, mostly through the sale of telenovelas (Sinclair 1999; Straubhaar 1991). In recent years, some Latin American producers have also exported formats to the United States and many European countries.

However, the rise and consolidation of television exports from several regions can hardly be considered evidence that Hollywood's dominant position in global television is challenged or, more generally, that inequality in the flows of television and information has been eliminated (Biltereyst and Meers 2000; Golding 1998). Notwithstanding the success of some third world producers, Western domination of the global television market remains undisputed in terms of program sales (and, more broadly, the structure of the industry). Although the pool of global exporters has expanded beyond traditional Hollywood studios as industries matured, companies based in big and wealthy countries have better chances to become global exporters. The largest ten exhibitors at recent MIPCOM meetings were companies based in the United States, Western Europe, or Japan. In the late 1980s, the "U.S. accounted for 71 percent of the total world traffic in television material." As television industries matured and domestic programming topped ratings, it was estimated that the percentage of U.S. shows dropped to 60 percent in 1995 (Segrave 1998). Local preference for domestic or regional shows does not necessarily mean that Hollywood's fortunes have decreased. Recent calculations are that the six major Hollywood studios raked in $4.5 billion to $5 billion in 2001, more than the rest of the world combined (Pursell 2001). Although it has become more diversified in terms of the number of producers and more complex in terms of patterns of programming flows, the field of television exports hardly seems leveled.

Explaining the Popularity of Television Formats

The popularity of formats has been the result of many developments. First, it has been the unintended by product of the existence of protectionist laws in some television systems. In some countries, such as Indonesia, the use of subtitles is banned, and programs are broadcast in English or local languages. Such protectionist restrictions prompted broadcasters to purchase foreign scripts (instead of canned shows) and produce them domestically without subtitles. Also, quota policies favor formats over canned shows. Informed by concerns about national culture and the promotion of "national" television, many European countries, for example, have quotas that primarily aim to curb the import of Hollywood programs (Grantham 2000; Tunstall and Machin 1999). Programming quotas have loopholes that allow foreign ideas (rather than foreign shows) to enter as long as they are produced domestically. Format programming, then, is part of business strategies to bypass local programming quotas. If stations broadcast domestic versions of foreign shows, those versions help to satisfy quota requirements; if they buy canned foreign shows, they do not. So peddling formats allows Hollywood studios and Latin American producers, for example, to enter protected markets in Europe by selling scripts, packaged formats, or partnering with domestic companies in coproduction arrangements.

Besides protectionist laws, television formats have recently caught on like wildfire partially because of the huge success of "reality shows" such as *Survivor* and *Big Brother,* particularly in the United States. Like other cultural industries, the television industry is ruled by the "nobody knows" principle (Craves 2000; Gitlin 1983), with constant ebbs and flows in programming trends. Because there is no certainty about the prospects of specific programs and genres, hit shows inevitably engender trends that are followed until exhaustion. Coping, imitation, and jumping on the band-wagon of whatever seems to work at the moment have been typical in the television industry since its origins and, arguably, have become even more common lately as conglomerization has increased pressures for higher profits in shorter periods of time.

Before the latest phase of globalization, trends tended to be limited to national boundaries. Back in the days when television systems were organized around different principles, station executives could not easily adopt successful trends from U.S or European commercial television. What worked in private television could not necessarily be applied in public broadcasting systems or in government-controlled television and vice versa. Structural regulations and institutional expectations limited programming choices. For programming trends to become truly globalized, television systems needed to be patterned along the same principles. Once such limitations were eliminated and commercial principles became dominant, then, what works in one television system could be adopted elsewhere. In standardizing the structure of television, globalization encouraged the tendency toward imitation and reluctance to promote innovation that underlies commercial broadcasting.

Globalization also accelerated the integration of television systems through business and professional networks. The global presence of media corporations has laid the ground for standardization of television output. International corporate networks are conduits for information about what works and what doesn't. Corporate executives may not be completely familiar with programming trends and audience preferences in every country, but they carry around the world their own experiences that in most cases have been nurtured in television industries in the West and are likely to be updated about current trends in the United States. Although they may be sensitive to local tastes and may give autonomy to domestic personnel familiar with local audiences, their commercial and aesthetic judgments are likely to be informed by trends and production values that are common in the West. Such experiences inform decisions to green-light programming ideas. So domestic programming chiefs are more likely to get approval if they acquire a format that is known to their bosses in Miami, London, or Los Angeles or if they pick a show with aesthetic and production values that are familiar to corporate executives. The growing homogenization of the professional sensibilities among television executives worldwide, embedded in Hollywood's worldview, is an important aspect of "the new international division of cultural labor" (Miller et al. 2001) that needs to be studied. Globalization has nurtured the formation of a cosmopolitan class of industry professionals who, from New York to New Delhi, increasingly share similar concepts and attitudes about "what works" and "what doesn't" in commercial television. Moreover, the globalization of the television business has introduced and improved the formation of informal networks for the dissemination of information about the industry. Television executives are more likely to be familiar with programming hits and duds, trends and preferences, particularly in the United States. Hollywood, arguably, may not be the undisputed seller of television programming worldwide as it was in the early decades of television. U.S. television, however, remains the fishbowl of the global television industry. Executives from around the world immediately take note of whatever seems to work (or fail) in U.S. television.

Attendance at annual trade meetings, exposure to the same trade publications, and regular electronic communications have helped maintain frequent interpersonal contacts that facilitate familiarity with global trends. The number of participants in trade fairs and conferences substantially grew in the last decade. These meetings are places for cultivating a similar business mindset among industry executives. MIPCOM's motto frankly states it: "MIPCOM speaks the unifying dialogue of the industry: Business." Also, the number of trade publications with international distribution and readership grew. Some weeklies and monthlies regularly feature special sections devoted to international television and to the state of the industry in regions and countries from around the world. Finally, the availability of communication technologies such as cable, satellite, and the internet provide easy access to a wealth of information about programs worldwide. With these interpersonal and technological networks in place, it has become easier, and also professionally imperative, for television executives to know about global trends.

In this sense, the popularity of television formats reflects the globalization of television trends; the adoption of programming that circumstantially offers some predictability in terms of its potential commercial success. In times when such dynamics are almost universal, then, formats satisfy the double demand of finding low-cost programming with a track record. Private television, no matter where it is situated, constantly demands new and cheap programming that can deliver audiences to be sold to advertisers. Buying formats, then, is a cost-saving strategy that eliminates some of the highest fixed costs that fiction programming demands. Some of the most popular formats such as game shows and "reality" shows usually require smaller investments than fiction as they don't need to hire actors and well-known writers. The average cost of ABC's *Who Wants to Be a Millionaire* is $750,000 compared to $1.2 million for ABC's *The Practice;* NBC's *Twenty-one* costs not more than $700,000 versus $1.4 million for an episode of *Law and Order;* and an installment of *Survivor* costs $200,000, three times less than $600,000 for each episode of *King of Queens* (Weinraub 2000). In Britain, it was estimated that an hour of a high-rating quiz show costs £200,000 compared to £1 million for a drama (Hughes 2001). Not surprisingly, then, from Argentina to the United States, labor unions representing actors, writers, and technical staff have resisted the rush to format television on the grounds that it threatens their jobs.

Besides lower costs, imported formats offer some measure of predictability based on their past performances in numerous countries. The constant and increasing pressures for turning profits means that there is little, if any, time for innovating or trying new ideas. All incentives are to reach out for proven ideas that can help diminish uncertainty. Formats, then, are the ultimate risk-minimizing programming strategy. Format owners provide extensive experience that includes the record of shows in different countries, what worked and what didn't, and details on national variations. Game-show producers, for example, bring a plethora of statistics about the records of different games and detailed information about production that draws from hundreds of hours of programming in several continents.

Some format shows (particularly "reality" shows) are also attractive to television companies because they give the opportunity to draw large audiences to their websites that feature interactive games, polls, and details about the contestants. Format copyright owners have been pitching their wares worldwide, stressing that their productions are able to integrate television and the internet, thereby increasing revenues and much-needed net traffic. Also, companies can make additional revenues through the publishing of fanzines and magazines about the shows and newfound celebrities.

Formats and the Globalization
of Intellectual Property Rights

Whereas successful programs and trends, especially in the United States and a new other Western countries, used to be blatantly imitated, the illegal copying of programs has become problematic. Using someone else's ideas in the production of television shows is certainly not new. Since the beginning of the industry, television executives have freely appropriated program ideas without acknowledging their origin or paying royalties. In an industry that has long been characterized by sameness and repetition, borrowing ideas across geographical borders has been common. This practice has not disappeared. Producers continue to find inspiration in other shows. More interconnectivity among television industries and easy access to what is playing around the world means that executives have better and faster information about an expanding pool of potential ideas. Moreover, controversies over the legal rights of program ideas and shows continue. Because intellectual property laws across countries do not grant similar rights, television companies have intensified lobbying efforts to pass legislation that protects their programs. Although violations are more closely monitored than in the past, companies have battled in each other in court over "original" authorship of highly profitable program formats. In the past years, there have been various copyright lawsuits and accusations. U.K.-based companies Planet 24 and Castaway Television Productions have unsuccessfully sued Endemol for "theft of format," arguing that the latter's *Big Brother* resembled *Survivor*. CBS initiated legal actions against Fox claiming that *Boot Camp* stole ideas from *Survivor*. Celador sued Denmark Radio for copyright infringement of *Who Wants to Be a Millionaire*.

These legal battles illustrate the rising importance of intellectual property issues in the agenda of global cultural producers and Western governments. The reasons for why these debates have become prominent recently are many (e.g., the coming of digital technologies, the separation of form and content) and are common to all cultural industries. Issues specific to the television industry need to be mentioned, however. Globalization has facilitated the "stealing" of programs by fostering increasing interconnection among industries. The expansion of cable and satellite signals and the gradual articulation of integrated global business networks provide a constant source of programming ideas that can be appropriated. Simultaneously, globalization has improved the chances for companies to monitor and litigate copyright violations. Like large content producers in other industries, television companies have become increasingly interested in detecting and persecuting violators. Having extensive operations in the most important television markets, large producers have better chances to find transgressors. As a result of these concerns, format producers gathered at the 2000 Cannes Marche International des Programmes de Television (MIPTV) launched the Format Recognition and Protection Association (FRAPA). Members of the Monaco-based organization include major television companies interested in investigating and preventing piracy. FRAPA created an International Television Paper Format Registry.

In terms of intellectual property rights, the effects of globalization on television companies have been similar to the ones on the "copyright industries" at large. For all content producers, globalization has posed a challenge—namely, how to harmonize copyright laws and improve enforcement at a global level, particularly in markets where piracy is rampant and governments are "uncooperative" in meeting corporate objectives.

In summary, the popularity of formats is largely the result of fundamental institutional changes in the global television industry—namely, the domination of the private model of television, the standardization of commercial practices, and rising concerns about copyright infringements.

Television Formats and National Cultures

It would be limiting to try to understand the popularity of formats by only addressing changes in the structure of television systems. It also reflects where economics and culture meet in global markets. International flows of standardized, delocalized formats prove that audiences cling to local and national consciousness. This may seem ironic only if we assume that globalization inevitably eliminates cultural diversity and breeds homogenization. The dichotomy between globalization as the agent of cookie-cutter commercial cultures or the force for cultural hybridity and resistance is false, however. Global media and the national are not antithetical but, actually, are integrated in complex ways.

The popularity of television formats is at the crossroads of global and local dynamics of the cultural economy of television. Contemporary television is a Janus-faced industry that in the name of profitability needs to commodify real and imagined nations while being open to global flows of ideas and money. The global circulation of formats responds to programming strategies to bridge transnational economic interests and national sentiments of belonging. Such strategies neither follow patriotic concerns nor suggest that television dutifully respects the diversity of national cultures. Rather, they result from the intention to maximize profits while "the national" continues to articulate cultural identities. In turn, television programming recreates and perpetuates national sentiments. Formats reflect the globalization of the economics of the television industry and the persistence of national cultures in a networked world. They make it possible to adapt successful programs to national cultures. In comparison to canned shows, they provide television executives with a reliable and malleable solution to produce potential hit shows. Most foreign shows often run into cultural barriers and, thus, are less likely to become ratings boosters. They can be cheaper than domestic productions and a low-cost strategy to fill more television hours, but they are unlikely audience magnets.

Compared to canned programming, the question of culture is thematized differently in formats. Formats carry meanings that are not necessarily attached to national cultures. Formats are culturally specific but nationally neutral. The DNA of formats is rooted in cultural values that transcend the national. Textual readings of popular formats such as game shows suggest that they champion the culture of consumption (Fiske 1990; Otnes 1996). "Reality shows" like *Sur-*

vivor can be read as the global projection of capitalism, naked individualism, and competition. However, format shows are less prone to have specific references to the local and national, precisely because they are designed to "travel well" across national boundaries. Formats purposefully eviscerate the national. Could we say that *Survivor/Expedition: Robinson* is unequivocally a Dutch show? What makes *The Bar* Swedish and *Taxi Orange* Austrian? How does *Waku Waku* represent Japanese national identity? What is British about *Who Wants to Be a Millionaire*? Because formats explicitly empty out signs of the national, they can become nationalized—that is, customized to domestic cultures. For commercial television, this is the advantage of television formats over ready-made shows. Because formats are conceived as flexible formula, traces of national belonging are downplayed and even eradicated. The result is a pasteurized, transnational product detached from national cultures. Formats, then, reveal the dynamics of "glocalization" (Robertson 1992) in the pursuit of profit: the adaptation of programming formula to the tastes of domestic audiences.

Hollywood-filled television schedules around the world might suggest that domestic audiences prefer U.S. programs or that the latter enjoy the "competitive advantage of narrative transparency" (Olson 1999). Neither audience preference nor the presumed textual universality of programs account for the wide presence of Hollywood fare, however. Such arguments downplay or simply ignore the structure of the global cultural economy and the institutional workings of the television industry that make certain choices available. Audiences' choices follow industrial dynamics and decisions. To suggest that schedules accurately reflect audience tastes falls into "consumer sovereignty" arguments that ignore the variety of forces and decisions that shape programming schedules. When television is organized on the basis of commercial principles, explanations for why schedules feature foreign or national programming depend on profit calculations and the business savvy of producers in selling their wares in different markets.

More than audience tastes, trade practices and costs better explain the content of schedules. Programming decisions are often contingent on whether owners believe that substantial investments are required to turn a profit. Those calculations depend on the fact that not all television industries offer similar conditions for national production. When the economic conditions are propitious (e.g., substantial economy of scale, advertising investments, sizable domestic market), companies are more likely to produce programming even though the costs are higher than buying foreign shows. Even under these conditions, television companies might opt to produce cheap (talk shows, news, variety shows, game shows) over expensive genres (fiction, documentaries), particularly in countries with small economies of scale and infant television industries. However, even when domestic conditions could allow some production, filling schedules with foreign canned programming is preferred because it's significantly cheaper.

In the last decade, ratings have confirmed that when given a choice, audiences prefer domestic and regional content to foreign programs (Hoskins, McFayden, and Finn 1997; Langdale 1997; Waisbord 2000a; Waterman and

Rogers 1994). This is hardly an indication of the leveling of opportunities for television industries to produce content that, at least in principle, reflects better local realities. Audiences might prefer local content, but domestic industries might not produce it. Only under specific economic and industrial circumstances is local programming able to knock Hollywood shows off prime-time schedules, and Hollywood productions are used as fillers in off-peak hours when audiences and advertising revenues are smaller. Not all television industries have the capacity to produce a significant number of hours to satisfy demand, however.

Against the backdrop of different possibilities for domestic production, audiences' localism is an important factor, particularly when markets are sizable and wealthy. This is the reason why many cable and satellite networks decided to split their signals along cultural lines by offering regional services. MTV, ESPN, and other cable networks have realized that programming in local languages that taps into local talent and preferences is more profitable than monolingual, "American"-only broadcasts (Hils 1998; Koranteng 1999). These services increasingly feature a higher percentage of locally and regionally produced content. It is not easy to pin down exactly what it is that audiences prefer about domestic content. The industry comes up with mostly ad hoc, post facto explanations about why certain programs were hits. Explanations do not necessarily guarantee that programs with similar characteristics would perform similarly. It is generally believed that audiences choose programming that resonates with their own cultures. To examine this issue, I analyze the relation among formats, narratives, and language by looking at the experience of Latin American television.

Formats and Narratives

The conventional wisdom in the industry seems to be that audiences like to recognize familiar themes, places, and characters on television. Humor and drama are favorites because they are commonly rooted in local and national cultures. Likewise, the appeal of news and mediated sports lies in the fact that they continue to cultivate linkages to the local and the national. Newscasts anchor a sense of community by relaying information about current events. Televised sports provide opportunities for representing and reenacting local and national sentiments. It continues to operate as an arena in which national identities retain important commercial and ideological functions (Whannel 1993).

Although universal stories and foreign places may be appealing, television audiences consistently prefer narratives that incorporate familiar elements. This is why audiences prefer productions coming from countries that share "cultural proximity" (Straubhaar 1991). However, audiences may find remote even coproductions among companies based in countries that share cultural elements such as language. A case in point is the commercial failure of Latin American telenovelas that featured multinational casts and stories that evolved in many countries in the region. According to television executives I interviewed, these programs flopped because they were a hodgepodge, a "Latino-pudding" that unsuccessfully tried to articulate a common regional identity.

The result was that they featured a collection of scattered references to national cultures that ultimately lacked cultural specificity. Even the presence of popular, national stars did not help to deliver bigger ratings in their own countries.

Audience preferences for domestic content presents television executives with a dilemma: content that is strongly embedded in local and national cultures has a better chance to be successful domestically, but it is less likely to find interested buyers and enthusiastic audiences abroad. Because foreign sales are, for most Latin American companies, secondary business strategies, the success of telenovelas hinges mainly on the domestic market. Moreover, because metropolitan markets capture the lion's share of audience ratings and advertising revenues, it is not unusual that telenovelas unmistakably reflect the local culture of big cities (where production companies usually are based). In Argentina, for example, the greater Buenos Aires area has 78 percent of media advertising and 60 percent of television homes. No wonder, then, that audiences in the interior find that most productions are too "*porteñas*" (as Buenos Aires culture/people are called).

Because domestic and, particularly, metropolitan markets continue to be central to television economics, producers are inclined to incorporate local stories, humor, and characters in their programs, even though it potentially deters marketability abroad. This is why productions that in the industry lingo are "too local," such as "period" telenovelas or those heavily immersed in local politics, have a harder time finding international markets than programs that are detached from the local. In Latin America, there is a long tradition of telenovelas that place classic love stories and family conflicts amid historical and political struggles. It has been argued that many have been profitable domestically precisely because they offer audiences opportunities to recognize themselves as members of a cultural community (Allen 1995; Martin-Barbero 1993). Their exportability is limited, however. If they are sold, it is usually because of their low costs. The relative higher costs of Hollywood productions in small and impoverished television markets in Eastern Europe and Asia benefited Latin American productions in the 1980s and 1990s.

In contrast to "national" productions, telenovelas that tell universal love stories (e.g., rags-to-riches, Cinderella-themed plots), without specific local references and featuring known stars have fewer problems in crossing cultural boundaries. The best example has been Mexico's Televisa-produced telenovelas. Their remarkable success in countries as diverse as Russia and the Philippines has been explained by the fact that besides the charisma of lead stars, national references are almost absent from the stories. Particularly compared with Brazilian "period" and contemporary telenovelas (Trinta 1998) or TV Azteca's telenovelas that address political "headlines" issues, Televisa's productions typically feature universal stories.

Unlike canned shows that are steeped in specific national cultures, formats are open texts that can be adapted. Within the constraints dictated by their owners, domestic productions can fit local narratives, histories, humor, events, and characters into the basic formulas that they purchase. Because formats are essentially open, they cannot be seen simply as transmission belts for Western values. In his thoughtful study of formats, Albert Moran (1998) argues that formats are places for negotiation between domestic and foreign cultures rather than Trojan horses of Western culture. Formats neither crystallize a static notion of national culture nor are pure impositions of external values. They are texts in which different understandings of national identity are projected and redefined against the backdrop of imported formulas. To conclude that national cultures are the casualties of television formats, Moran suggests, is to ignore the flexibility of formats and the active role of audiences in consuming television (also see Skovmand 1992).

Format television shows, then, organize experiences of the national. Even "reality" shows, which unlike "period" or "contemporary" fiction are not ostensibly designed to articulate national narratives, provide spaces for the representation of national cultures. Particularly in times when private television has little incentives to produce fiction and prefers to churn out low-cost shows, one should not ignore the fact that game shows, variety shows, or "reality" shows also offer opportunities for audiences to recognize themselves as members of national communities. The question of how the national is expressed and recreated in those genres, however, has not received sufficient attention. Studies have generally prioritized the textual analysis of "highbrow" programs (dramas, documentaries) that purposefully delineate cultural boundaries through historical narratives and appealing to collective memories. Aside from the textual characteristics of specific genres, television is intertwined with the national in multifaceted ways. More than in specific moments when programming appeals to nationalistic discourses, television has the power of naturalizing cultural connections in everyday viewing.

Language and Formats of Television Fiction

One way in which television turns "the national" into a pregiven, constitutive reality is through broadcast languages. Arguments about globalization qua cultural homogenization pay inadequate attention to the fact that language remains a pillar of cultural distinctiveness and national identities in a globalized world. Notwithstanding the consolidation of English as the world's lingua franca, the linkages between language and nation are still important and, in some cases, fundamental to an understanding of processes of cultural unification and difference. The formation of national identities continues to be inseparable from language (De Swaan 1991; Edwards 1985). Language is the basis for the politics of inclusion and exclusion that are at the center of processes of identity formation (Anderson 1983; Hall and du Gay 1996).

From this perspective, it is important to consider the relation between media and language. Languages delineate cultural boundaries that articulate flows of television programming. This is the main finding of the argument that global patterns of television flows are articulated around "geolinguistic markets" (Sinclair, Jacka, and Cunningham 1996). So, even at a time when global television audiences arguably seem to be watching the same or similar shows, television programs in vernacular languages continue to anchor a sense of cultural belonging and function as a privileged site for the reproduction of nations. In a world saturated by Hollywood content, mediated vernaculars are both cultural binders and reminders of belonging to distinctive cultural communities.

The force of broadcast language (or mediated language, in general) lies in its invisibility, on the fact that we rarely notice it. Language constitutes an example of "banal nationalism" (Billig 1995). Billig (1995) argues that the ideological habits that enable nations to be reproduced "are not removed from everyday life. . . . Daily, the nation is indicated, or 'flagged,' in the lives of its citizenry" (p. 6). For him, the image of "the flag hanging unnoticed on the public building" (p. 8) is one of the best illustrations of banal nationalism. Language can be understood along similar lines. The common belief that languages and nations are "naturally" inseparable hides, for Billig, the artificiality of such relation (also see Anderson 1983).

Following Billig's argument, we can understand broadcast language as a way in which nations are daily reproduced. Television normalizes the ties between language and nations. The force of televised language lies in its ordinariness, in continuously weaving a seamless linkage between nation and language. Television "flags" nationhood often through regular programming in specific languages. This is different from "media events" (Dayan and Katz 1992) that purposefully appeal to the nation through communal media experiences. "Media events" such as official funerals, the signing of international treaties, or global sports are moments of collective mobilization in the name of the nation; television is put in the service of nationalism as a political movement. Every day, however, television perpetuates national bonds in the mold of "banal nationalism." It is the active reminder more than the active mobilizer of national consciousness. While the broadcast of momentous occasions that congregate extraordinarily large audiences is sporadic, television regularly keeps nationhood alive by "flagging" spoken languages and drawing and sustaining linguistic boundaries such as "diasporic" media that maintain national identities through perpetuating linguistic bonds among immigrant communities (Sinclair and Cunningham 2000).

Perhaps because of the invisibility of broadcast language, this point has not been sufficiently emphasized. Whereas literary studies have focused on how media narratives and storytelling articulate nations, historical-sociological studies have addressed the role of public broadcasting and media industries in "imagining" nations (Scannell and Cardiff 1991; van der Bulck 2001). It is also necessary to consider that the media propagates and reinforces national sentiments through perpetuating linguistic bonds. Contemporary television, like newspapers in the nineteenth century (Anderson 1983), contributes to the perpetuation of national cultures by spreading a vernacular and reinforcing linguistic bonds among populations. Thus, programs in vernacular languages that are not explicitly interested in articulating national cultures also provide a place for the representation of the national. In legitimizing some and excluding other languages, television allows for the recognition of language-based cultural communities. The need for dubbing and subtitling imported programs and films implicitly acknowledges that any attempt to produce cultural uniformity clashes with the resilience of vernacular languages.

The global popularity of formats attests to the resilience of language as a constitutive element of national identities. Compared with "reality" programs, fiction is more difficult to be formatted and adapted. Scripted programming, including fiction, tends to be more culturally specific and is more expensive to produce. Despite these difficulties, fictional programming has also been formatted for two main reasons: linguistic barriers and the cultural nature of drama and comedy. Even when countries have a similar linguistic and cultural base such as Britain and the United States, original programs are steeped in different webs of meaning that are lost when they cross borders (Miller 2000). Formats, then, offer a way to adapt not only the content but also the language of original productions.

Latin America offers an interesting case to examine this issue because amid the intensification of regional trade of programming in the last decades (Sinclair 1999), the Spanish/Portuguese divide continues to be one of the most visible fault lines in the region's cultural geography. The division is certainly not as pronounced as in Europe, where media projects intended to create a regional culture have run up against linguistic fragmentation and the strength of vernacular languages (Kilborn 1993). Still, the issue of language divisions remains an important one, particularly in relation to regional trade of television. Serialized fiction, namely telenovelas, continues to be the backbone of television programming in Latin America. Although schedules feature a heavy diet of "reality" programming, television executives view telenovelas as the fundamental pillars of daily schedules. Language has been a sticking point in the regional trade of telenovelas. Since the 1970s, many Spanish-dubbed Brazilian telenovelas have been shown in Spanish-speaking Latin America (as well as in Spain), and some continue to be very popular. But as television industries matured and state-owned television stations were privatized (Waisbord 2000b), more Spanish-language productions from different countries became available in the international market. This made programming executives from Spanish-speaking countries less enthusiastic about importing Brazilian telenovelas. Although the latter generally have superior production values, gripping stories, and often feature breathtaking outdoor scenery that is appealing to audiences, they hit a cultural wall. One obstacle is arguably the fact that some of the most popular Brazilian telenovelas are embedded in national histories, politics, and myths that do not resonate with global audiences. Simultaneously, however, these characteristics work in favor of Brazilian productions, branding them as "the exotic other" in international markets. In many Latin American countries, however, the main obstacle has been linguistic. Even the best dubbing cannot make up for the fact that they are not originally spoken in Spanish. This cultural distance has been more acute in countries with substantial domestic production (such as Mexico), where audiences are accustomed to programming in their own language both domestic productions and dubbed Hollywood shows.

Something similar happens on the other side of the linguistic divide. In Brazil, a country that produces a significant amount of programming, only a small amount of foreign programs is aired on terrestrial television. As one of the largest global media corporations and the country's long-standing dominant television company, Globo has produced thousands of hours of programming for decades. Its annual production was estimated at 2,239 hours in 2000 (Fernandez 2001). It produces 80 percent of its schedule (Cajueiro 2000). SBT and Bandeirantes also produce a considerable number of hours, particularly variety and talk shows. Hoping to chip away at Globo's audience share, both networks occasionally decided to import programs from Spanish-speaking countries to keep costs down, particularly when a downturn in the economy slowed down advertising revenues. Because of language differences that Portuguese dubbing cannot completely bridge, they purchased formats of successful telenovelas. SBT has purchased formats of Televisa telenovelas that are produced in Brazil with local actors. Bandeirantes acquired from Argentina's Telefe the hit children-oriented novela *Chiquititas*. Under Telefe's supervision, the Portuguese version with Brazilian actors was filmed in Buenos Aires. Globo, which did not buy programs from Spanish-speaking Latin American countries for decades, bought the script of the Colombian hit "Betty la Fea" for $100,000, a paltry sum considering that the cost of an hour of its lavish telenovelas is several times higher. Whereas Globo justified the purchase by stating that it would produce a version adapted to Brazilian culture and television, observers speculated that Globo's decision was motivated by a different interest—namely, to prevent SBT and Bandeirantes, who traditionally rely on successful telenovelas from Spanish-speaking countries, from acquiring the Brazilian rights of a potential hit.

But linguistic screens are not limited to the presence of different languages; the multiplicity of Spanish accents is another cultural barrier in the trade of television shows in the region. One could argue that accents, not simply Spanish, became visible markers of national identity in Spanish-speaking Latin America. As Nancy Morris (1999, 55) writes, "accent . . . is perhaps one of the strongest ways of establishing a local identity."

The old quip is that Latin America is a region divided by the same language. In a region where the Spanish empire imposed cultural homogeneity through language over a variety of indigenous languages, language did not become the distinctive marker of national identity in the postindependence period, as it did in other postcolonial societies (see Mar-Molinero 2000). Because most states (excluding Brazil and the English-, Dutch- and French-speaking Caribbean islands) shared the same language, they could not be defined as nations in terms of language. Only in a few countries did indigenous languages (e.g., Guarani in Paraguay) gain official acceptance as part of the national imaginary, but they had limited, if any, presence in the national media. With little sensitivity to linguistic diversity within Latin American nation-states, radio, film, and television have greatly contributed to making specific accents distinctive signifiers of the nation. Not only did they nationalize Spanish, particularly among illiterate populations scattered through vast and hard-to-reach territories, but they also nationalized the accents of the capital cities, where the largest media industries historically have been based (Martin-Barbero 1993).

At the regional level, television was responsible for the expansion of Mexican accents. This was the consequence of two developments. First, for decades, Latin American audiences have watched Hollywood film and television productions dubbed mainly into Mexican-accented Spanish. Second, Televisa has exported telenovelas and children's shows throughout the region, some of which were massively popular, since the early 1970s. The result was that Mexican accents became the lingua franca of Latin American television and are widely believed to be more "neutral" than any other accent. This gave Televisa a huge competitive advantage over television producers from other countries. Televisa's success was based on the fact that audiences were familiar with Mexican accents, a familiarity that its productions reinforced. This advantage was not limited to South America, but it also extended to the United States given Televisa's long-standing presence as the leading program provider in the Spanish-language television market. Besides culture, Televisa certainly enjoyed other economic advantages; it expanded regionally earlier than other television industries and produced a substantial number of television hours.

Because Spanish-speaking audiences are generally used to Mexican accents, productions in any other accents sound "foreign." This fact certainly has not escaped Brazilian producers, who prefer Mexican dubbing of their productions for Latin American distribution. It has also been a main difficulty for other Latin American producers to enter regional markets. Besides business obstacles, they have also faced accents as a cultural wall. For Argentine programs, for example, accents are a major cultural hurdle to export their productions north of Ecuador. The situation is different in the Southern Cone as well as in Bolivia and Peru where audiences are more familiar with Argentine accents, particularly after the satellite signal of Telefe and other Buenos Aires–based regional cable networks started operations in the 1990s. But elsewhere, audiences reject the Argentine accent, particularly in countries where, given the absence of indigenous fiction and the reluctance of media moguls to support production (such as in Central America), audiences have watched Mexican programming for decades.

Having been exposed mostly to national accents, Mexican audiences find other accents foreign. Equipped with an enormous production capacity and vast libraries, Televisa has accustomed domestic audiences to Mexican accents. Its limited foreign programming is overwhelmingly Hollywood productions, particularly films (Sanchez-Ruiz 2000). Aiming to reduce Televisa's audience share, newcomer TV Azteca resorted to in-house and independent productions and, in some opportunities, to regional shows. But recognizing the difficulty of jumping over the accent barrier, it opted to produce versions of popular shows from the region, such as the Argentine hit *Chiquititas*.

Accent barriers are also evident in the trade of programming between Spain and Latin America. Television audiences are not used to each other's accents.

Only a small amount of Spanish productions has been aired on Latin American television. Spanish audiences have been accustomed to national accents in both domestic and foreign programming. If interested in shows from across the Atlantic, Spanish networks are more likely to buy the libretto and formats instead of canned shows. In recent years, for example, they bought formats of Argentine programming (variety shows, novelas, game shows, and dramas) and produced domestic versions that incorporated news headlines, local references, and characters.

To Globalize, McDonaldize

The traffic of television formats in Spanish- and Portuguese-speaking countries suggests that formats allow companies to jump over linguistic barriers. This is what Hollywood companies recently learned: because of domestic preference for "national languages" (and national programming), they cannot rely solely on the old practice of dumping programs to conquer international markets. The time when television systems went on a buying binge and loaded up on Hollywood productions to fill increasing demand for terrestrial television has changed, particularly in large and wealthy markets. In a world of linguistic diversity and more developed television industries, Hollywood television studios had to find new and creative ways to do business. Coproducing local-language programs with domestic companies and other forms of partnership illustrate the "think globally, program locally" mantra that currently dominates the global television industry. Format television shows "glocalization" at work—that is, the merits of a business "multicultural" strategy that is "sensitive" to cultural diversity. Such sensitivity is not informed by respect for or interest in preserving "multiculturalism" but rather to maximize opportunities for commercial gain. For global television companies, cultural difference is not an obstacle, but, if incorporated properly, it could be a boon. Programming hybridity makes sense because it makes money. In the international division of cultural labor, domestic companies are more attuned to local sensibilities than global corporations and, consequently, are better at manufacturing programs that incorporate the local and the national. In the traffic of global television brands, the partnership of global and domestic companies aims to address cultural diversity as a component of global markets. Cultural difference is a business matter rather than a political project.

Grappling with the reality of globalized economics and localized cultures, the global television industry has found formats as convenient instruments to leap over cultural boundaries while taking economic advantage of the substantial transformations that domestic television industries experienced in the past decades. Formats are a form of McTelevision. Shorthand for the McDonald's fast-food chain, the prefix *Mc* stands for a business model characterized by efficiency, calculability, predictability, and control that caters products to specific local requirements, usually informed by cultural factors (Ritzer 1998). Applied to the television industry, formats represent the global commercialization of an efficient and predictable program that can be tweaked according to local tastes. McTelevision is the selling of programming ideas with a track record that are sufficiently flexible to accommodate local cultures to maximize profitability. The national origin of the format is less important than its effectiveness. Formats are de-territorialized (see Tomlinson 1999); they have no national home; they represent the disconnection between culture, geography, and social spaces that characterizes globalization. Signs of cultural territories are removed so domestic producers can incorporate local color and global audiences can paradoxically feel at home when watching them. Locality needs to be evicted so it can be reintroduced as long as it does not alter the basic concept. Although any television company can come up with such formula and market it globally, Hollywood and some European television companies maintain substantial advantage in the selling of formats. The popularity of formats suggests that global television industry is becoming a giant cultural vacuum cleaner that constantly sucks in ideas from around the world and turns them into commodities. In a global world, capital flows encounter fewer obstacles in crossing borders than in the past, but canned programming continues to run into cultural and linguistic barriers. Economic and cultural boundaries do not seem to be eroding similarly.

Where the Global Meets the Local

The evolution of the global television industry has largely shaped arguments about the circulation of television programming. Since the 1960s, analyses have reflected not only political and theoretical debates but also the state of international television flows. Theories of media imperialism and "one-way street" flows expressed the first phase in the 1960s and 1970s, which can be characterized by the domination of Hollywood productions and infant industries worldwide. In the 1980s and 1990s, arguments about multiple flows responded to a new phase that featured the rise and consolidation of new producers and exporters, particularly in the third world. At the cusp of a new century, a new phase seems to be emerging, one characterized by the increasing complexity of flows of capital and programming and novel developments in the economics, production, and export of television.

One of the new developments is the appeal of television formats both for exporters and buyers. The contemporary trade of formats puts in evidence that the globalization of media economics and culture are intertwined but are not identical. Globalization has been responsible for major transformations in the structure of television systems. Privatization and deregulation have opened the doors to cross-border flows of capital and technology. Those changes opened new ways for media business to expand into international markets through output deals, joint ventures, programming sales, and production arrangements. Globalization has unsettled past linkages between state and capital, geography and business, the local and the global. No longer do conflicts neatly fit in the "national versus foreign" mold. Multiple alliances and conflicts have emerged. Governments and domestic companies tried to fend off foreign powerhouses through requirements of national citizenship for media owners and limitations on the percentage of foreign ownership of domestic business (Morris and Wais-bord 2001). Such attempts to harness the global traffic of capital are bypassed by international and domestic corporations, who, having realized that they mutually need each other, decide to partner in different ways.

Amid these dynamics, the industry became more integrated as a whole. The structure of television systems became streamlined along the lines of the private model. Business is the name of the game, regardless of where company headquarters are located. As some domestic industries matured, a new slew of producers began peddling programs worldwide. Consequently, flows of capital and television programming are more complex than in the past. The globalization of television economics has not made national cultures irrelevant. Even when screens have been inundated with Hollywood fare, television remains a central place for articulating the national. Media narratives and spoken language continue to organize a sense of cultural belonging.

Formats are not the catalysts for cultural sameness or the loss of cultural diversity; adaptations provide opportunities for reimagining nations in various ways (Moran 1998). Global audiences are watching the same formats, but they engage culturally in ways that are not predetermined. Formats are ultimately contained in local and national meanings. It would be a mistake, however, to celebrate formats as harbingers of cultural diversity. Just because formats are "glocalized," they do not necessarily usher in multiculturalism or stimulate cultural democracy. First, formats are not entirely malleable. Copyright holders ultimately determine what changes can be incorporated; they remain "the author" of the text despite a variety of national adaptations and audiences' interpretations. Second, adaptations run a whole gamut of possibilities, partially related to the fact that some genres (drama) are more open-ended than others (game shows) (Moran 1998). We can't simply assume that because formats are adapted, they express national cultures in similar ways. How is the national expressed in formats? Unlike versions in Northern Europe, the Spanish producers of *Big Brother* decided to include outdoor swimming pools because of better weather. The Russian producers of *Who Wants to Be a Millionaire* eliminated the "ask the audience" lifeline because people intentionally give the wrong answer to contestants. The Argentine edition of *The Price Is Right* had to make room for winners to celebrate effusively with the friendly host and to include more games with low-price prizes (people there prefer more opportunities to win cheaper items than fewer chances to win big-ticket consumer goods). The Brazilian version of a Mexican tele-novela brings home settings and references familiar to domestic audiences. These adaptations evoke and materialize different meanings of local/national cultures. Can we say that format adaptations equally reflect national culture or nurture a sense of local/national community? What kind of opportunities do different television genres and format adaptations offer for organizing a sense of cultural belonging?

These questions need to be examined by expanding our thinking about the consequences of globalization in the television industry. The issue of the "effects" of international television flows needs to be asked not only in terms of "effect/audience activity" but also in terms of "missing opportunities" for cultural diversity to be expressed. The contemporary popularity of "reality show" formats as a cheap programming alternative arguably elbows out genres such as drama and comedy that, when compared with "reality" programming and game shows, offer different possibilities for the expression of national experiences. When profit is the bottom line and "reality" formats are available at a fraction of the cost of fictional programming, commercial television does not have to bother to produce fiction, to paraphrase Manuel Alvarado (2000). Format television does not eradicate national cultures, but as a reflection of a global industry solely concerned with quick commercial success and no patience for innovation, it decreases opportunities for diverse and complex representations of "the ties that still bind" (Waisbord 1998) local and national communities.

References

Allen, Robert. 1995. *To be continued: Soap operas around the world.* London: Routledge.

Alvarado, Manuel. 2000. The "value" of TV drama: Why bother to produce it? *Television & New Media* 1 (3):307–19.

Anderson, Benedict. 1983. *Imagined communities: Reflections on the origins of nationalism.* London: Verso.

Andrews, Edward L. 2000. Europe's "reality" TV: Chains and Big Brother. *The New York Times,* April 11.

Billig, Michael. 1995. *Banal nationalism.* London: Sage.

Biltereyst, Daniel, and Philippe Meers. 2000. The international telenovela debate and the contra-flow argument: A reappraisal. *Media, Culture and Society* 22 (4):393–413.

Cajueiro, Marcelo. 2000. "If it ain't broke." *Variety,* April 3.

Carter, Bill. 2000. At TV Bazaar, US companies look to buy, not just sell. *The New York Times,* October 9.

Craves, Richard. 2000. *Creative industries: Contracts between art and commerce.* Cambridge, MA: Harvard University Press.

Dayan, Daniel, and Elihu Katz. 1992. *Media events: The live broadcasting of history.* Cambridge, MA: Harvard University Press.

De Swaan, Abram. 1991. Notes on the merging global language system: Regional, national, and supranational. *Media, Culture and Society* 13: 309–23.

Edwards, John. 1985. *Language, society and identity.* Oxford: Blackwell.

Fernandez, Angel. 2001. El boom de la telenovela. *El Mundo* (Spain). http://www.elmundo.es/2001/02/22/television/957968.html.

Fiske, John. 1990. Women and quiz shows: Consumerism, patriarchy, and resisting pleasures. In *Television and women's culture: The politics of the popular,* edited by Mary Ellen Brown. London: Sage.

Fry, Andy. 2000. Europe secure as leader of reality programming. *Variety,* September 25, M4–M8.

Gitlin, Todd. 1983. *Inside prime time.* New York: Pantheon.

Golding, Peter. 1998. Global village or cultural pillage? The Unequal inheritance of the communications revolution. In *Capitalism and the information age,* edited by Robert W. McChesney, Ellen Meiksins Wood, and John Bellamy Foster. New York: Monthly Review Press.

Grantham, Bill. 2000. *"Some big bourgeois brothel": Contexts for France's cultural wars with Hollywood.* Bedfordshire, UK: University of Luton Press.

Guider, Elizabeth. 2000. Two-way transatlantic. *Variety,* September 25, M1–M2.

Hall, Stuart, and Paul du Gay. 1996. *Questions of cultural identity.* London: Sage.

Hils, Miriam. 1998. MTV sings in local lingos. *Variety,* August 10, p. 24.

Hoskins, Colin, Stuart McFayden, and Adam Finn. 1997. *Global television and film.* Oxford: Oxford University Press.

Hughes, Janice. 2001. Rewriting the traditional broadcast revenue model. *Financial Times* (London), June 19, p. 2.

Jensen, Elizabeth. 2000. The changing face of international TV. *Los Angeles Times,* October 27, F1.

Kilborn, Richard. 1993. "Speak my language": Current attitudes to television subtitling and dubbing. *Media, Culture & Society* 15:641–60.

Koranteng, Juliana. 1999. TV goes local: Pan-regional networks launching local channels. *Advertising Age* 70 (2):32–3.

Langdale, John V. 1997. East Asian broadcasting industries: Global, regional, and national perspectives. *Economic Geography* 73:305–21.

Mar-Molinero, Clare. 2000. *The politics of language in the Spanish-speaking world.* London: Routledge.

Martin-Barbero, Jesus. 1993. *Communication, culture and hegemony: From the media to mediations.* London: Sage.

Miller, Jeffrey S. 2000. *Something completely different: British television and American culture.* Minneapolis: University of Minnesota Press.

Miller, Toby, Nitlin Govil, John McMurria, and Richard Maxwell. 2001. *Global Hollywood.* London: BFI.

Moran, Albert. 1998. *Copycat TV: Globalization, program formats, and cultural identity.* Luton, UK: University of Luton Press.

Morris, Nancy. 1999. US voices in UK radio. *European Journal of Communication* 14 (1):37–59.

Morris, Nancy, and Silvio Waisbord, eds. 2001. *Media and globalization: Why the state matters.* Lanham, MD: Rowan & Littlefield.

Moyes, Jojo. 2000. TV imperialism goes into reverse as British shows invade the US. *The Independent* (London), August 4.

Olson, S. R. 1999. *Hollywood planet.* Mahwah, NJ: LEA.

O'Regan, Tom. 2000. The international circulation of British television. In *British television: A reader,* edited by Edward Buscombe, 303–22. Oxford: Oxford University Press.

Otnes, Cele. 1996. A critique of daytime television game shows and the celebration of merchandise: *The Price is Right. Journal of American Culture* 19 (3):51.

Pursell, Chris. 2001. To import or to format? That is the question. *Electronic Media,* January 15, 64.

Ritzer, George. 1998. *The McDonaldization thesis: Explorations and extensions.* London: Sage.

Robertson, Roland. 1992. *Globalization: Social theory and global culture.* London: Sage.

Sanchez-Ruiz, Enrique. 2000. Globalization y convergencia: Retos para las industrias culturales Latinoamericanas. Typescript.

Scannell, Paddy, and David Cardiff. 1991. *A social history of British broadcasting: Serving the nation, 1923–1939.* Oxford: Blackwell.

Schneider, Michael. 2000. Whiz quiz hits global jackpot. *Variety,* July 17.

Segrave, Kerry. 1998. *American television abroad: Hollywood's attempt to dominate world television.* Jefferson, NC: McFarland.

Sinclair, John. 1999. *Latin American television: A global view.* Oxford: Oxford University Press.

Sinclair, John, and Stuart Cunningham. 2000. Go with the flow: Diasporas and the media. *Television & New Media* 1 (1):11–31.

Sinclair, John, Elizabeth Jacka, and Stuart Cunningham, eds. 1996. *New patterns in global television: Peripheral visions.* Oxford: Oxford University Press.

Skovmand, Michael. 1992. Barbarous TV international. In *Media cultures: Reappraising transnational media,* edited by Michael Skovmand and Kim Christian Schroeder, 84–103. London: Routledge.

Straubhaar, Joseph. 1991. Beyond media imperialism: Asymmetrical interdependence and cultural proximity. *Critical Studies in Mass Communication* 8:39–59.

Tomlinson, John. 1999. *Globalization and culture.* Chicago: University of Chicago Press.

Trinta, Aluizio R. 1998. News from home: A study of realism and melodrama in Brazilian *telenovelas.* In *The television studies book,* edited by Christine Gerghty and David Lusted, 275–86. London: Arnold.

Tunstall, Jeremy, and David Machin. 1999. *The Anglo-American media connection.* Oxford: Oxford University Press.

van der Bulck, Hilde. 2001. Public service television and national identity as a project of modernity: The example of Flemish television. *Media, Culture and Society* 23:53–69.

Waisbord, Silvio. 1998. The ties that still bind: Media and national cultures in Latin America. *Canadian Journal of Communication* 23:381–411.

Waisbord, Silvio. 2000a. Industria global, cultural y política locales: La internacionalización de la televisión Latinoamericana. *America Latina Hoy* (Salamanca) 20 (August): 77–85.

Waisbord, Silvio. 2000b. Media in Latin America: Between the rock of the state and the hard place of the market. In *De-Westernizing media studies,* edited by James Curran and Myung-Jin Park. London: Routledge.

Waterman, David, and Everett M. Rogers. 1994. The economics of television program production and trade in Far East Asia. *Journal of Communication* 44 (3) 89–111.

Weinraub, Bernard. 2000. Sudden explosion of game shows threatens the old TV staples. *The New York Times,* February 9, E1, E3.

Whannel, Gary. 1993. *Fields in vision. Television sport and cultural transformation.* London: Routledge.

Sounds Real
Music and Documentary

John Corner

Within the aural profile of television, music plays varying roles and functions, quite apart from its vital job in signalling programme identity through signature title tunes. These functions include generating *thematic* support for what is on the screen—indications of historical time, of geographical place and of appropriate mood being prominent—and providing *formal* support for programme organisation, pacing and the shifting intensities of portrayal. In all these modes of application, the way in which rhythm, tempo, harmony, melody, etc., feed into contextual, associative patterns of cultural meaning will be a matter for careful production judgement, however "intuitively" exercised. Clearly, a challenge is posed for analysis in tracing the specific dynamics of this process across its diverse formal and contextual factors (Tagg 1987 poses the terms of this challenge most suggestively from within a semiotic perspective).

In this article, I want to concern myself largely with the varied function of music within factual programming. In particular I want to look at that range of factual programmes still identified loosely and sometimes nervously as "documentary," despite the further strain placed on this leaky category by recent developments in "reality television" (Dovey 2000 provides a good critical review). How does music figure within television's documentary aesthetic and, as the whole area of factual programming undergoes shifts of form and function, in what ways might the mode of its employment change? Given the lack of writing on this topic to date, an exploratory and provisional approach seems appropriate.

Music and the Documentary Aesthetic

In assessing the use made of music in documentary production we have to recognise from the outset documentary's widely varying profile and emphases. It is a genre of inquiry and argument, of observation and illustration and, particularly in the last few years, of diversion and amusement. Within British television, a strong journalistic dimension to documentary emerged quite rapidly

John Corner, "Sounds Real: Music and Documentary." From *Popular Music*, Vol. 21, No. 3 (2002), pp. 357–366. Reprinted with the permission of Cambridge University Press.

in the early 1950s, as the medium became a primary source of national news and public knowledge. This contrasted sharply with the promotional and propagandistic uses to which cinematic documentary was often put during the 1930s and 1940s. It is perhaps not surprising that the more the representational scheme of a documentary is framed by rationalistic imperatives and concern about "balance," the more likely it is that music will seem extraneous if not wholly suspect, an importer of unwelcome emotion and feeling. But the history of documentary's musical relations is not simply a matter of its proximity to the journalistic. For perhaps the biggest broad movement in international documentary since the 1950s has been that influenced by the "vérité" and "direct cinema" traditions of sustained observational film-making. These have often embraced a degree of depictive purism that places question marks alongside anything likely to adulterate a direct relaying of the primary events, circumstances and interactions before the camera.

Taken together, then, what we might call *journalistic rationalism* and *observational minimalism* have acted to keep many producers (and quite possibly sizeable sections of the audience) concerned about the risk of a musical ingredient somehow subverting programme integrity. There has been work outside of these protocols of course, including various kinds of expansive, more freely expressive reportage and dramatised productions. In these, music has continued to be important.

It might be worth noting here the basic differences between musical accompaniment to fictional narratives, on the one hand, and to documentary-style programmes on the other. These have to be treated as indicative rather than definitive, and they collapse altogether in the case of drama-documentary productions, but recognition of them is analytically useful. Musical soundtrack in scenes of acted narrative and dramatised setting, perhaps underneath dialogue, guides us in our imaginative response to a fictional world, a world that it is the rhetorical project of the film or programme to encourage us to be drawn within. The music works to position us in terms of this diegetic containment. However, documentary's images, interviews and commentaries work largely within the terms of display and exposition. Our involvement here is different from the way in which we are spectators to a "visible fiction." We may be the addressees of direct, spoken address, images may be offered to us as an illustration of explicit propositions, we may be cued to watch sequences as witnesses to the implicit revelation of more general truths. In this context, musical relations are likely to become more self-conscious, and less intimate, than when watching fiction.

Some indication of how the use of music is viewed from within the perspectives of documentary production can be gleaned from the latest edition of what is undoubtedly the most widely used production manual. This is Michael Rabiger's *Directing the Documentary* (Rabiger 1998). In his bullet point notes on post-production, Rabiger comments as follows:

- Music should not inject false emotion.
- Choice of music should give access to the inner life of a character or the subject.

- Music can signal the emotional level at which the audience should investigate what is being shown (Rabiger 1998, p. 310).

What we see here, I think, is clearly both a sense of risk and of possibility. Music is regarded as primarily emotional in its effects, either by way of signalling appropriate levels of emotion or, more indirectly, by providing support for an interiority which cannot itself be visualised or perhaps even spoken ("inner life"). There are some awkward questions raised by this, certainly. How are we to judge the "falseness" of an emotion and by what independent means will the conditions of "inner life" be available to producers so that they may be secure in indicating it musically? But questions of documentary integrity are notoriously difficult to resolve cleanly by sole resort to evidence lying outside of individual creative judgement. In the light of what I shall say below, it seems to me particularly appropriate that the third rubric uses "investigate" rather than simply "respond to." An invitation to some kind of participatory dynamic, not a conditioned reflex, appears to be part of the plan, at least in this account.

In pursuing my brief exploration into music and the documentary aesthetic I shall draw on a number of examples, some of them recent. However, I want to start with a consideration of how music figures in one of the classics of the British documentary tradition—Humphrey Jennings' 1941 film *Listen to Britain* (Crown Films). Although it is an example drawn from documentary cinema, it seems to me that some aspects of the way this film works have a very useful bearing both on practice and on potential in television.

Listen to Britain and the Arts of Looking

The film that finally became *Listen to Britain* started out on the drawing-board as a film about music and the military, potentially organised around the idea of marching tunes. The final version, a film offering different sights and sounds of wartime work and life in Britain over a twenty-four hour cycle, departs radically from this initial plan but preserves the emphasis on music (see Vaughan 1983). Throughout its length, the film "finds" its music from marching bands, dance bands, canteen concerts, orchestral concerts, small groups of singers (fireman, soldiers and children) and different radio programmes. Since these are almost all sourced within the film's visual presentation, they form part of its invitation to "listen to Britain." They are offered as Britain's own sounds, not an added soundtrack, but they are expanded across scenes other than their source scene. Between the music, a range of other sounds is heard too. These are the overheard sounds of work and play, of aeroplanes, of trains, of factories and of fragments of casual conversation in a variety of settings. Perhaps the most radical element of the film is that it completely eschews commentary. It proceeds entirely through its succession of linked images, music and sounds, organised within a subtle and always implicit sense of relationship and development.

What does this emphasis on the hearing of music and sounds but not words mean for the way in which we watch the film, for our experience as viewers? I think the answer here is that it greatly intensifies our engagement with the images. It helps provide the resources for a viewing disposition allowing us to respond fully to the charge of meanings in each composition and actively to read the screen not only in the detail of the shot but in its relationship within an associative sequence. Music saturates the images, informing them by fusing its meanings with their own, and at the same times it bonds the shots together through its own aesthetic continuity. It frees them from the literalism of commentary and underwrites the possibility of delivering surprise and juxtaposition as well as of expected connections. Through listening to Britain, we are enabled properly to *look* at it. For this to work, what we are offered visually must have sufficient resonance and depth to hold active attention without accompanying speech. This is partly a matter of generating a formal interest (through such factors as framing, composition, lighting and movement within the shot). But it is also, in close combination, very much a matter of *what* is shown and the wartime viewer's social and personal relation to the depicted sights and the connoted themes. In Jennings' film, the contemporary audience's ability to connect directly and powerfully with what they saw, as elements of a common present and of shared hopes and anxieties, could be assumed. Clearly, these conditions cannot be met so easily if at all with other kinds of topic, intended audience or viewing situation.

We can also ask some closer questions about the form. What would be the effect were Jennings' images to be shown with actuality sound but either with no music at all or with music only within those shots depicting its source? First of all, I think screening the images unaccompanied would have critically depleted the contemporary audience's experience, reducing its emotional fullness and pushing it too far towards a communicative uncertainty. The codes for watching silent depictions are relatively undeveloped in Western culture. Watching a real event in silence is one thing, the existential fact of *being there* closing the potential distance between self and circumstance. Moreover, the silence is a motivated part of the watching itself. Watching a silent representation involves a very different relationship. Even watching on television a minute's silence being observed at the start of a football match carries an awkwardness for the viewer which is distinctive to the secondary status of the experience and to the fact that it is the representation, not us, which initiates the silence. There are other, cognate, experiences we might want to consider, for instance a visit to an art gallery or a photo exhibition. Here, however, the silent contemplation of the exhibits is accompanied by purposive movement through the physical space of the gallery; though it may be silent, the experience is partly one of motivated behaviour. Once again, the silence essentially belongs to us, not the depiction, from which no sound can be expected. The post-sound technology screen offering its *deliberately* silent images to a static audience poses a challenge to comfortable viewing relationships. It raises questions about the informational yield, aesthetic satisfaction and directed thoughtfulness that the image track can successfully generate within the viewer on its own. Even the silent cinema used inter-titles and, often, live accompaniment as a partial 'solution' to this. Silence presents the possibility of an embarrassing insufficiency of meaningfulness and a more embarrassing uncertainty about whether this insufficiency is essentially in the work or in the viewer. One very basic function of music, then, is to reduce the risk of the attention frame slipping towards *too much* self-consciousness and loss of focus in this way.

In *Listen to Britain,* restricting the music to source-scenes only would clearly be better than the complete loss of musical accompaniment. However, it would occasion a radical loss of continuity and of cumulative force across the film's design, marking a separation of scenes and settings instead of using form to strengthen thematic interconnection. The duration of many scenes, wonderfully constructed though they are, would be seen to out-run their perceived interest even by an audience for whom they were thick with wartime significance.

Of course, *Listen to Britain* is not the only film of the British Documentary Movement to use music imaginatively. Other classic works such as *Coalface* (GPO Films, 1935) were in many ways more inventive in this respect, using special compositions to work, often dialectically, with the images (see the discussion in Corner 1996). However, they also used a commentary too, thus stabilising their audio-visual aesthetic around the words of an information flow directly addressed to the viewer. In *Coalface,* Benjamin Britten's score is used to suggest machine noises related to the visual portrayal and to fit in with, and further emphasise, the speech rhythms of the commentary. This, in addition to performing the more conventional functions of enhancing the viewing experience, signalling shifts of mood and giving a strengthened continuity and development. Its percussive and dissonant modernism would provide a challenging aural input on its own, but in combination with the mechanistic energy of the film's images it forms an integrated experience.

Listen to Britain is unusual in the trust it shows in supporting images through music alone and also, in some scenes, in supporting the music through the images. That is why its visual experience is so distinctive. Key scenes here include shots of a canteen full of workers singing along to Flanagan and Allen on stage, of female lathe operators joining in with the rendition of "Yes, My Darling Daughter" coming over the Tannoy and of a National Portrait Gallery performance of a Mozart piano concerto performed by an RAF orchestra (with, pointedly, Dame Myra Hess as soloist). The latter is played across shots of the Queen and various members of the concert audience (predominantly armed service personnel) as well as across street scenes and panoramas of wartime London. The example of this film, though distinctive to a period both of cinematic and social history, is one that can help us in thinking more creatively as well as more critically about television practice and its continuing possibilities.

"To Document": Subgeneric Variety and Audio-Visual Codes

The imperative "to document" is a broad one, admitting a wide range of approaches and making the generic idea of "documentary" resistant to clear codification. What counts as "documentary" has been, since the 1930s, very much a pragmatic matter of particular purposes and opportunities, informed by contemporary developments in audiovisual technology and culture. In Britain, a decisive shift in the general profile of documentary occurred with the development of national television services in the late 1940s and early 1950s. Documentary in effect "migrated" from cinema to television, taking some key personnel with it. It was now predominantly conceived in terms of programmes addressed to homes rather than films addressed to the darkened auditorium. Its defining, although by no means exclusive, function also shifted. From being a project of national publicity and celebration it became increasingly characterised as one of reportage, drawing selectively on the established traditions of radio journalism and concurrent developments in television news. Both the shift from public to domestic address and the shift away from the publicity mode carried implications for the auditory profile by which the genre as a whole was characterised. One factor here was the move towards a quieter, less declamatory mode of address, with a reduced commitment to affective impact. This clearly had consequences for the future use of musical soundtrack.

In looking at how music has been employed across television's documentary output, two axes of documentary type can be useful guides, however approximate they may be and however much the one needs often to be mapped on to the other. First of all, there is the axis running from "serious" to "light," an axis regularly subject to changing criteria and one which has been made newly prominent in the schedules by the last decade's developments in "reality television." Secondly, there is the axis from "Art" to "Record," to use the terms that I have found more generally helpful in thinking about documentary practice. Along this axis can be plotted a number of issues to do with authorship, self-consciousness, stylistic range and what we can call the particular "reality claim" of the programme (see Winston 1995).

In relation to the first axis, a strong tendency has been for music to be employed more frequently the "lighter" the topic and/or treatment. Right from the 1950s, this can be seen in documentaries seeking to place a comic, sentimental or lightly ironic framing on their subjects. So for instance, a programme on the job of street cleaning in London (in the series *Look in on London,* ATV 1956) has an occasional soundtrack of jaunty, banjo music accompanying its images of refuse barges and the industrial riverside. The music is used formally, to punctuate the development of the account, but also thematically. It offers a cue both for reading location (the East End, working-class settings) and for reading tone (informative but relaxed and slightly amused). Placed across sections where the commentary is minimal or temporarily absent, it provides a pleasing context of sound within which to attend to the images in the spirit of informative diversion (for a full analysis of this programme, see Corner 1996, chapter 4). Unlike in *Listen to Britain,* there is little symbolic density or resonance sought in the crafting of the shots, so they are even less able than in the earlier film to support an unaccompanied viewing.

As a documentary topic and approach becomes more serious, a matter of issues and problems, of controversy and argument, then there is likely to be a more strategic kind of attention paid to the "mood cueing" that music brings. There is also likely to be more uncertainty about the *kind* of music that should be used, should it be considered at all. The possibilities offered by classical works are likely to be found in some cases more appropriate than popular forms. Brief passages, perhaps just a phrase, can reinforce a more sombre and contemplative viewing experience but they still need to be used with care and sparingly. Jazz is interestingly placed here. Within British television, scores in the John Dankworth orchestral idiom are used in the late 1950s and 1960s to connote "the city" and sometimes "youth." A typical scene might have bluesy saxophone-led phrases over a shot of a London night scene, borrowing the American connotations for a wider resonance. Yet problems of class are raised by the use of Jazz, since it has never been a popular working class form in Britain. For a period, Jazz was a preferred music for mapping the indigenous documentary subject within an essentially cosmopolitan, "noir-ish" view of urbanism and its new restlessness.

In relation to the second axis, that between art and record, the tendency here has been for music to be used more extensively in those programmes which operate confidently within a sense of themselves as artefacts, as authored "works." This need not mean a claim to high aesthetic status, it simply indicates a level of self-consciousness about the crafting and styling of the account, the degree of creative and imaginative freedom exercised in its construction. Clearly, *Listen to Britain* worked strongly within a version of this mode of documentation, as did many films from the British Documentary Movement.

One relevant example from the television of the 1950s is Denis Mitchell's *Morning in the Streets,* made for the BBC in 1959. Essentially an impressionistic portrait of aspects of life in northern working-class communities, the film varies in tone between a relaxed whimsicality and a serious sense of constraint and of hope. Its extensive use of different musical material is doubly licensed by the frequent lightness of tone, as positioned on my earlier axis above, and its clear status as an *auteur* piece (a status confirmed in its winning of the Prix Italia in the following year).

As well as the line of "audio-visual essays" in this broad vein, continuing through to current schedules, there are other stands of documentary that have exercised a creative licence as "art" more freely than mainstream output. Here, biographical documentaries, with their directly personal focus, have drawn extensively on music to establish both tone and circumstance. Dramatisations of all kinds (including reconstruction "emergency" series like the BBC's *999*) have often been keen to use it in order to support their attempt at offering some of the narrative development and emotional intensities associated with fiction. Archive series, committed to a grounding in "record" but also often involved in kinds of imaginative projection, have needed it not only to sustain and to shift mood but also to help fill out a basic communicative profile otherwise depending extensively on silent footage and commentary. For a rather similar reason, wildlife series and the increasing range of popular science and history series, both using lengthy sequences without significant actuality sound, have resorted to it more frequently over the last decade. Against such exercises in directorial styling and affective address, we can place the modes of reportage and observation noted earlier.

Within the formats of documentary reportage, the news-based protocols of journalism have tended to place the use of musical soundtracks as an intrusion in programmes offered essentially as professional reporting and analysis.[1] This is so both at the level of form (a well organised report does not need any extra dynamics) and of theme (what to feel should be a matter of individual viewer reaction to what is shown and said). In the latter case, a risk of manipulation, and perhaps a breach of impartiality requirements, has also been perceived. This is particularly so in those sequences of a programme where interview testimony and/or visual evidence is being placed within a framework for assessment on a matter of established controversy. At points like these, the journalistic function is at its most accountable, not simply documenting but organising the terms of a conflict of opinion. Both the established professional broadcaster codes as well as institutional protocols and (in some cases) national legislation are at issue here.

An example can be taken from a study I carried out with colleagues on British television and video accounts of the debate about nuclear energy in the late 1980s (Corner et al. 1990). One of the programmes we looked at, the last episode in a series of three BBC programmes entitled *Taming the Dragon* (BBC2 1987) examined the safety record of the British nuclear industry in the wake of the Chernobyl disaster. In exploring this record through voiced-over film and interview, it made extensive use of an eerie, slow, electronic soundtrack, connecting the account to recent fictional portrayals of nuclear mishap, including the BBC thriller series *Edge of Darkness,* screened to popular success in the previous year. There is little doubt from the viewing analysis we undertook that this music made a significant contribution to the sense of threat carried in parts of the programme. However, the programme's ostensible journalistic purpose, carried in the commentary and interview structure, was precisely to explore the existence and level of this threat. The addition of such a soundtrack can be seen as working to reinforce a conclusion about nuclear risk that the journalistic discourse was still only entertaining as one interpretation among others. Not surprisingly, in the nuclear industry (and amongst a few of our researched respondents) there was some dissatisfaction expressed with this kind of premature closure of judgement, especially when achieved in such an indirect, affective manner. No discussion of audio-visual practices in public information could fail to recognise the real problems posed by cases like this. Whatever the degree of musical inhibition introduced into television documentary practice by journalism across its very wide range of descriptive work, in its core "forum" functions, as a means of reporting and assessing public dispute, the issue of covert judgement will require continued care.

Within the very different framework of observational filming, there has been a commitment, not to informational impartiality, but to the delivery of a raw viewing experience—the witnessing of ongoing action and overheard speech in the most direct of modes. Here, the apparent spontaneity and naturalism of the approach, the very artlessness of its rhetoric, has worked against the employment of musical soundtrack. The inhibitions here have not been grounded in ideas of propriety or legal requirement, like those of journalism.

They have been seen as an essential part of successful recipes for generating and sustaining the effect of "directness." It is significant, for instance, that even *Big Brother* (Endemol Entertainment for Channel 4, 2000 and 2001), the most innovative and successful factual entertainment format of the last few years, preserves its naturalistic address by using music only for title sequences and break points.

Re-imagining Documentary: New Spaces for Music?

I have set out a situation in which the use of music in documentary television has been characterised both by its conventional employment as a supplementary, affective stimulant and, often, by a degree of restraint. The twin television emphases on journalistic integrity and on observational directness (the latter reinforced by the raw effect sought by many recipes for "reality" programming) have, in different ways, positioned music as a potential intrusion. More imaginative forms of reportage (for instance, those based on travel) have introduced it as a device to point up a theme or underscore an irony but they, too, have often been wary of a bolder use. Most frequently, it has been seen as useful in getting the viewer through "bridging" sequences, including journeys. Again, the advice in Rabiger (1998) is instructive:

> Transitional sequences of any kind can benefit from music, especially if it lifts the film out of a prevailing mood. Music can highlight an emotional change when, for instance, an aspiring football player learns he can join the team, or when someone newly homeless lies down for the first night in a doorway. (Rabiger 1998, p. 286)

As the varieties of audio-visual documentation are further dispersed and hybridised, it would be a pity to see music as *merely* offering a more widely used set of clichés for injecting punctuation, pace and intensity into the viewing experience. With game shows, gardening, holiday and cookery programmes and a whole range of lifestyle output increasingly trading on varieties of the documentary image, this will undoubtedly be one mode of use. Here, the energies of the music sometimes appear to be compensating for the paucity of visual interest and perhaps even the perceived limitations of the speech. Not surprisingly, a number of low-budget and rapidly shot location programmes, especially holiday and sports series, contrive to keep things bright and strong in this way. Philip Tagg (1987) comments illuminatingly on the diverse categories of "catalogue" music designed expressly to be used in such kinds of professional application.

Other possibilities, however, still remain under-explored—possibilities that would allow a more considered connection with visual portrayal. As in *Listen to Britain,* this is music providing us with the time to *look* properly, giving us a framework in which to gaze and to *think*. To refer back to my quotation from Rabiger, it is music as part of "investigation." Such an approach goes along with the use of more generous shot lengths and with restraint in voiced-over speech, at least for given segments. It encourages a more adventurous approach to the television image at a point where the technology can do full justice to audiovisual creativity. This is after decades of development that have tended towards visualisations cut back to the demands of speech and of narrative pace. As I suggested earlier, this bolder musico-visual approach is not just another mode of musical subservience, since there is a clear sense in which our experience of the music itself (whether "borrowed" or specially written) benefits from the combination. And although the music's generated meanings will tend to fuse with those of the image sequence, the very directness of the approach means that we are conscious of listening to music as well as of attending to the screen. Moreover, the aesthetic options extend well past their cliché instances (e.g. rural lyricism, the bustle of the city) and await further, committed innovation.

One notable, recent example is *Wisconsin Death Trip,* a film made for the BBC2 *Arena* series (and transmitted in 2000) but also distributed to independent cinemas (see the website at www.wisconsindeathtrip.com). Working imaginatively from local newspaper records and photo archives that document one year in the nineteenth-century history of the township of Black River Falls in northern Wisconsin, this programme offers a potent combination of data and mood. A key element in its portrayal of past events, an exploration using archive stills and reconstructed action, is the specially written orchestral score (including work by John Cale). Mixing the rhythms and textures of different American musics, including traditional forms, this provides the essential medium in which the evocative power of the images and commentary works. It opens up the space to look properly and thoughtfully at the visual record in its localised times and places and is central to the film's resonance and success.

Another example comes from the winner of the 2001 Grierson award for the best documentary series, Icon Film's *Indian Journeys* (screened on BBC in April 2000). Throughout this series, music was used effectively in the conventional thematic way to deliver a stronger sense of Indian culture alongside the visuals and the commentary. However, at points, there was also a more prominent role given to it. In the episode following a journey to the source of the Ganges ("Shiva's Matted Locks"), the arrival of the presenter at the source glacier in the Himalayas is initially the occasion both for voice-over and to-camera presentation. But then music (a song) works with the camera to provide a more provocative, wordless, encounter with the scene. The programme slows down, as it were—its busy rhythms of interview, exposition and travel sequence relax to offer a more focused sense of place, space and significance. This is much more than simply a chance to admire the scenery, a touristic moment. It is a chance to take in something of how the setting works as an experience for the visitor, including the pilgrims whose route the programme has followed. It thereby encourages an active perception that allows us, at least partly, to discover and to ponder our own terms of relation to the represented inside the terms of the representation. Despite the spectacular landscape, this is the aesthetics of engagement rather than of display. It brings a cognitive enhancement, not just an increased viewing delight.

Such an attempted extension of the visual language of documentary in combination with music, pushes well beyond the experience of the documentary image provided by journalism, by the varieties of *tele-vérité* or even by those transitional moments of music-image combination indicated in Rabiger's account. For many years, the mixing of the creative and the factual on television was viewed with suspicion by those who, unlike the pioneers of documentary cinema, drew on too rigid a sense of demarcation between imagination and knowledge. After this false separation, there has come a kind of false conflation suggested by such terms as "infotainment." This is false because it too easily suggests, both for advocates and for critics, that it is only within a limited range of novelty formats that certain aesthetic "boundaries" can be crossed.

Documentary reportage around controversial issues will clearly continue to want to keep some of its core discourses free of the kinds of prematurely evaluative closure that I discussed earlier. But documentary exposition includes much more than journalism, and even within documentary journalism I believe there is more room for expressive depiction and for the musico-visual exploration of topic than is currently being used.

The real potential that television offers for connecting knowing to feeling, and hearing to viewing, remains larger than we might guess from what is now in the schedules. A more varied, inventive and risk-taking employment of music within television documentary would be a welcome part of the wider and continuing exploration of the role of art in the quest for understanding.

Note

1. The way in which news practices influence work in other factual genres is worthy of further research. Of historical interest here is the first of two *Times* articles written about the state of television journalism by the broadcasters John Birt and Peter Jay (Birt and Jay 1975). In it, a tension is noted between the "newsroom model" and the "movie model" of current-affairs programming. The authors see the latter as leading to an undesirable emphasis on filmic criteria, such as narrative incident, animated talk and exciting locations, rather than exposition and analysis. It seems clear that music would be seen as a further, diversionary element of the "movie model."

References

Birt, J., and Jay, P. 1975. "Television journalism: child of an unhappy marriage between newspapers and film," *The Times,* 30 September
Corner, J. 1996. *The Art of Record* (Manchester)
Corner, J., Richardson, K., and Fenton, N. 1990. *Nuclear Reactions: Form and Response in Public Issue Television* (London)
Dovey, Jon. 2000. *Freakshow: First Person Media and Factual Television* (London)
Rabiger, M. 1998. *Directing the Documentary* (London)
Tagg, P. 1987. "Musicology and the semiotics of popular music," *Semiotica* 66, 1/3, pp. 279–98.
Vaughan, D. 1983. *Portrait of an Invisible Man* (London)
Winston, B. 1995. *Claiming the Real* (London)

From Insiders to Outsiders
The Advent of New Political Television

Jeffrey P. Jones

The airing of political talk on television has always assumed one crucial point: that those doing the talking should have direct "insider" knowledge of what they are talking about. The assumption by television producers has been that "expertise" should be the defining characteristic of who gets to speak—either by politicians who are directly involved, their handlers or strategists, or the journalists and opinion columnists whose job it is to study and report on their activities. The assumption is built on the belief that such speech is designed primarily to inform or educate, not fulfill other functions of political communication. By maintaining such a standard, however, a whole series of logical outcomes follow: that the subjects, issues, and players that properly constitute politics are the self-evident product of this expertise; that audiences are only interested in hearing expert opinions on politics; and that other forms of political discourse do not merit airing in the public sphere that television provides.

Such assumptions of speakers and audiences are, most certainly, the product of a political culture with expectations of an informed citizenry, a culture that has held the conduct of rational political thought as the discursive ideal.[1] They are also the product of a time in which social scientists, journalists, and even philosophers had a more prominent place in the national political dialogue conducted in the press and through mass-circulated magazines and journals prior to the arrival of television. And as various histories of political talk on television remind us, this thinking is the product of the history of network news bureaus that developed the shows, as well as the role and place that journalists felt they occupied as arbiters of political discussion and opinion.[2]

Over three decades later, these assumptions have changed. Although talk by political experts continues to dominate both network and cable political programming,[3] the decade of the 1990s ushered onto the stage a series of new programming types and specific cable channels that explicitly offered new forms and approaches to political talk on television. In particular, that change has

Jeffrey P. Jones, "From Insiders to Outsiders: The Advent of New Political Television." Reprinted from Jeffrey P. Jones, *Entertaining Politics: New Political Television and Civic Culture,* Rowman & Littlefield (2005), pp. 35–62. Reprinted with permission of the publisher.

been associated with the addition of talk not by political insiders, but inclusive now of those who position themselves outside the conventional wisdom and sense making of political elites. These new voices and programming types challenge the assumptions of what constitutes knowledge, who gets to speak, what issues can be addressed, as well as what types of political talk audiences will find both informative *and* pleasurable.

I chart the evolution by first examining political talk on television from the network era through the first generation of cable programming (to the late 1980s), and then exploring how a series of developments and changes in the economic, political, cultural, and technological realms of American society in the 1980s and early 1990s provided the fertile soil from which new political programming would grow. Included here is a discussion of these changes in television that resulted from increased competition that was brought on by cable, leading to new risk taking, new programming stylistics, and attempts at new relationships with audiences. The discussion then turns to the rise of new forms of political talk television, beginning with the populist talk radio-style imitators that arose on cable and leading eventually to a transformation of cable news channels into ideologically driven talk programming. The analysis then turns to humorous political talk shows, including a comparison with their competition during that time slot—that is, late-night comedy talk shows. I examine how these new programs position themselves as both alternatives to and critiques of the fakery in news programming, pundit shows, and other late-night talk shows. I conclude with a discussion of the new role these programs play as alternative political voices, including the guests and topics they host and the political stances they assume.

Pundit Talk in the Network Era

For much of television's history, political talk programming[4] has grown from the roots of journalism, in particular the practices of interviewing and op-ed writing. The earliest manifestations of this on network television were the shows *Meet the Press* on NBC (1947) and *Face the Nation* on CBS (1954), where newspaper and broadcast journalists interviewed government officials and newsmakers of the day.[5] The names of these shows, of course, signal the press's understanding of their role as representatives of the public and public interest through their journalistic interrogational style. That tradition lives on today through these shows, but also through descendants such as *Nightline* and *The NewsHour with Jim Lehrer*. Another type of early political talk program is the journalist roundtable discussion, first developed in 1969 through *Agronsky and Company*, hosted by television and radio journalist Martin Agronsky, and broadcast on public television. The show derives from the op-ed journalistic tradition and featured four journalists and Agronsky offering their opinions of the week's news events. The show was based in the belief that, because journalists are the closest independent observers of actions occurring in the political arena, they would offer the most informed yet impartial opinion of what was *really* going on. *Agronsky* (later renamed *Inside Washington*) became the model upon which programs such as *Washington Week in Review* (1967 on PBS), *The McLaughlin Group* (1982 on PBS), and *Capital Gang* (1988 on CNN) were formulated.

It is from this type of programming that critics have derisively given the participants the name "pundits," derived from the ancient Sanskrit word meaning "learned man." But as the word made its way into the English language, it became not only a reference for someone who gives authoritative opinions, but is also used in "mocking the pretensions of those who nag politicians through public and widely circulated observations."[6] Rather than simply an annoying gadfly role, critics contend that pundit programs are, in essence, somewhat dangerous because these journalists tend to spout opinions on all sorts of issues and events that they generally have little knowledge of as reporters (hence, they aren't really expert thinkers, just expert talkers). As Dan Nimmo and James E. Combs contend, "They now constitute a source of opinion-formation and opinion-articulation, agenda-setting and agenda-evaluation, so vast as to make the United States a punditocracy: a nation where the mediation of opinion by important and highly visible media figures is paramount."[7]

The last type of political talk show is somewhat an amalgam of the first two, whereby one or two commentators hold a discussion (rather than an interview) with a guest, thus creating a context in which opinions are freely forthcoming, albeit connected to political actors of the day. The pioneer and, in many ways, defining show in this sub-genre is *Firing Line*, a syndicated program first offered by RKO in 1966, featuring the firebrand conservative and founder of the *National Review*, William F. Buckley Jr.[8] Programs of similar structure that have developed over the years include *Crossfire* (1982 on CNN) and, to some extent, *This Week with David Brinkley* (1981 on ABC). On *Firing Line*, Buckley took the concept of televised political debate seriously and would resort to all manner of rhetorical techniques (both fair and out-of-bounds) to win his encounters. Buckley's producer even conceived the show as "an intellectual version of Friday night at the fights."[9] Buckley's take-no-prisoners approach to political discourse, complete with name-calling, physical threats, interruptions, and put-downs, was the presentational model of televised political discourse from which many subsequent programs have drawn.

Indeed, although the typology of shows offered above is based on the structural features of the programming and the arrangement of the cast that conducts those discussions, a more fruitful approach might be to chart the lineage of political talk based on the ideological leanings and discursive style that these shows offer. In such a formulation, the logical progression moves from the pedantic style and postwar libertarian brand of conservatism offered by Buckley to the belligerent style and Reagan school of neo-conservatism in John McLaughlin, to the inanely blowhard style and rabid right-wing reactionary Bill O'Reilly, the current king of agonistic political talk on cable television. This reformulated lineage also recognizes that the *quality* of political talk has seen a marked devolution from the days of *Firing Line,* not to mention the ideological triumph of conservativism.[10] Buckley, whom most people (including his archenemies) concede possessed a high level of intelligence, has spawned

O'Reilly, who almost singlehandedly has shown that a talk show host need know nothing about anything to hold forth on every issue in stunning ignorance and yet draw the largest audience in cable political talk (and be a best-selling author to boot!). And, of course, O'Reilly is simply one of many manifestations of political talk in the rotisserie league of programming now found on the cable channels Fox News, MSNBC, CNN, and CNBC.[11]

Although this review of the genre of pundit-based political talk is cursory, the detailed histories provided by Alan Hirsch, Eric Alterman, and Nimmo and Combs lead to three primary conclusions about the nature of these shows, their participants, and the talk that is offered there.[12] First, and perhaps most importantly, the independent and impartial observer of politics that the journalistic form assumes is, in fact, neither of those things. That is to say, although most pundits retain jobs as columnists for major newspapers and news magazine weeklies, their participation in televised political talk has clearly shown how closely connected to power they are. Indeed, several prominent pundits (or their wives) have been employed in various presidential administrations.[13] Yet they all are active participants in the political sphere, employ an epistemology often called "inside-the-beltway" thinking, and contribute to the conventional wisdom and general circulation of meanings of politics that emanate from the nation's capital. Perhaps more damning, these pundits are full-scale participants in the spreading of rumors, the settling of scores, and intrabureaucratic power struggles typical of Washington politics.[14] *Media Week* reporter Alicia Mundy notes the important role that Sunday morning talk shows play in Washington political maneuverings: "These shows aren't mere entertainment, nor are they simply commentary," she writes. "Today, politicians use these shows to make news and to make waves. They use them to send signals to their allies and to the opposition. And they use them to evaluate their own packaging and marketing efforts."[15] In short, these pundits are not commentators on the system—they and their shows *are* the system.

The second, and related, conclusion about television's pundits is that they are not just journalists, but celebrity elites in their own right. As pundit Robert Novak notes, "When I'm recognized now it is as a television celebrity. Not even as a television commentator!"[16] As such, they are guests in the Georgetown social circles and maintain personal friendships with politicians, including many a president. They not only command larger salaries than their non-televised peers but also parlay their celebrity status into enormous speaking fees on the lecture circuit.[17] In short, they are the visible face of political opinion, and as a result have a vested interest—as all celebrities do—in maintaining that image by staying within the bounds of the celebrity system that created them.[18]

The final and overriding conclusion that can be drawn from pundit television is that its reality belies the argument that those with high levels of political knowledge will offer the highest forms of rational political discourse. What pundit television has clearly shown is that more often than not, their public presentations are pure spectacle. As noted above, the rhetorical flourishes of Buckley have only grown into full-blown circuses on programs like *The*

McLaughlin Group, perhaps the flagship show in this regard. Most pundits, regardless of the program on which they appear, have learned the lessons of what makes for good television. Calm, thoughtful, introspective, and compromising demeanors are not among them. Audiences also recognize the spectacle nature of these talk "shows," but the incestuousness of the participants and their banter ultimately limits its audience appeal beyond those who can both keep up with the demands of insider knowledge yet also stomach the bellicose displays of showmanship.[19]

In sum, then, what has become the dominant form of political talk on television does not adhere to the journalistic ideals of objectivity, dispassion, or rational thought from which it was supposedly born. What has developed in its stead are programs that feature celebrity commentators who are intimately connected to power, who participate in a circumscribed system of political thinking, and who construct a discursive spectacle with limited appeal beyond the political cognoscenti or political junkies. Although it has been argued that these programs probably do more in greasing the wheels of the establishment than in informing and educating an electorate, as far as television political talk is concerned, these programs have generally been the only game in town. In turn, the viewing and voting public has received the media's message: "*This* is politics—love it or leave it." Of course, what was shown through the tremendously low levels of voter turnout in the 1988 presidential and 1990 congressional elections was that people were, in fact, leaving it in droves.

Hence, as a series of changes in the political and economic climate began to take hold in the 1980s and early 1990s, television producers recognized the weaknesses in the system and began to offer new forms of political talk programming they believed audiences were interested in seeing. Any objections that these new forms of political talk programming would be illegitimate because of their using celebrity hosts, or allowing people who were not experts to talk, or producing an entertainment spectacle all seemed moot because of what pundit television itself had become. Before discussing that programming, however, we must understand the changes in politics, technology, culture, and the economics within the media industries that laid the groundwork for these new types of programs.

Contextual Changes

The most significant factor in shaping politics and political culture in the 1980s was the election and popularity of Ronald Reagan.[20] As a Hollywood celebrity, he maintained the credentials to effectively communicate his outsider status and his conservative populist mantra that government is not part of the problem—rather, it *is* the problem. To a great extent, Reagan's popularity was not built on actual policies or programs that benefited the vast majority of Americans who supported him, but rather on his posturing against government as a negative force in American life.[21] By the 1988 presidential election, both Republican and Democratic candidates Pat Robertson and Jesse Jackson attempted to assume Reagan's populist mantle by running "outsider" campaigns.[22] Although unsuccessful in their electoral bids, the populist rhetoric they offered from both the far right and far left would appear again two years later when populist angst became a driving force in several "Throw the Rascals Out" campaigns in the midterm congressional elections.[23] Two years hence, such angst again found its embodiment in Ross Perot's outsider presidential campaign with his "common sense" approach to government and town hall meetings to find out what "the people" really wanted from government.[24] Perot also led the way in using popular, nonpolitical television talk shows as a primary means of communicating with the public. Indeed, his candidacy was a product of his appearance on *Larry King Live* in which he informed the audience that if the American people wanted to draft him to run, he was willing to finance that effort himself.[25] As the campaign progressed, all of the presidential candidates appeared on similar types of "populist" entertainment talk shows to communicate directly with "the people" as well as to avoid the more confrontational questioning that typically occurred in forums with the press.[26] Yet again, two years later many citizens signed up with Republicans who now joined the populist bandwagon by promising fail-safe legislative guarantees through written "contracts" with the public.[27]

A component of this populist upsurge was the language of "common sense." Citizens and politicians embraced common sense as the Holy Grail of the legitimacy crisis, a cure-all remedy that would supposedly bring sanity, clarity, and efficiency to out-of-control politicians and bureaucrats.[28] Vice President Al Gore sought to sell his efficiency-in-government report by dressing it up as a voting man's beer commercial—*Common Sense Government: Works Better and Costs Less.* Around the same time, lawyer Philip K. Howard produced a best seller called *The Death of Common Sense: How Law Is Suffocating America,* which, in turn, attracted fawning Democratic and Republican suitors at both the national and state levels who wished to align themselves with this popular manifesto.[29] The rhetoric of common sense also sought codification by becoming one of the ten commandments of the Republican Party's "Contract with America," including a piece of legislation advanced in Congress known as "The Common Sense Legal Reform Act of 1995."[30]

This same period also witnessed the fluidity between the fields of politics and media. The traditional revolving door between government and industry became much more high profile. Politicians who once garnered media attention while serving in some capacity as government officials or political candidates became media celebrities after departing government service by working for media corporations that attempted to exploit their celebrity name-value. Oliver North, Mario Cuomo, Ross Perot, Jesse Jackson, Jerry Brown, Susan Molinari, George Stephanopoulos, David Gergen, and Pat Buchanan, among others, all found work in some capacity as on-air personalities. This movement toward "politician as celebrity," however, was simply a continuation of the dwindling loss of public identification with political parties and widespread public emphasis on choosing among politicians as *individuals* whom they "get to know" through media exposure.[31] As public frustration with government increased, politicians distanced themselves from traditional political structures, posturing as political "outsiders" not beholden to any interest except the mandate of "the people."

In summarizing the changes in the political climate, then, the decade of the 1980s and early 1990s witnessed an intermixing of celebrity and politics, the appeal to commonsensical ways of talking and thinking about politics, and a concurrent upsurge in populist anti-politics by a public that was increasingly finding the political arena repugnant. Audiences therefore tuned in to politicians on entertainment talk shows precisely because these shows did *not* produce the traditional staid political talk they had grown accustomed to. Instead, audiences now found that they too were allowed to ask questions of the candidates, and that responses came in a language that was more accessible and commonsensical than the highly cloaked and guarded language of spin offered in other venues.[32]

In the technological realm, political anxiety mixed with social expectations and technological opportunities to produce a degree of populist hope. The 1990s saw the flowering of potentialities developed in the 1980s through the microcomputer and cable television revolutions. The Internet became a commercial, social, and political reality, especially for middle- and upper-class citizens at that time. Expectations of media-driven political change rose amid a rhetoric of technological progress, exemplified by claims of five hundred cable channels, electronic town hall meetings, worldwide communication in the global village, easy access to political information in the form of citizen-centered presidential debates, candidate appearances on phone-in talk shows, congressional e-mail addresses, and the ability to organize and identify with like-minded people in cyberspace.[33] The frontiers of space and time had seemingly been conquered, and the divisions between elite and mass discourse seemingly overcome. Problems associated with recalcitrant politicians and bureaucracies would disappear as people became empowered by new communication technologies to participate in the decisions that govern their lives (or at least to make better and easier choices from the menus provided).[34]

In the cultural realm, citizens waged ideological battles in what is often called the "culture wars."[35] Roughly speaking, the term refers to the prolonged disagreements between liberals and conservatives over issues such as sexual orientation, racial identity, physical access equality, media representations, religion, public morality, and gender relations. These battles have been conducted as much through social institutions or cultural patterns and behaviors (such as media, language, "lifestyle," academia, religion) as through formal politics. The battlegrounds are quite fluid, though, to the point where cultural battles can be waged in political forums (judicial rulings, impeachment hearings, etc.),[36] and political battles may be waged in cultural forums such as talk television. "Political correctness" became the term used by conservatives and moderates alike to derisively chide efforts by liberals and progressives to alter what were seen as harmful, stereotypical, or ideologically loaded practices in society. Political correctness mandated certain behaviors, critics claimed, and resistance to such efforts in a strongly individualistic American society appeared with great frequency in public life, including on television talk shows.

Also in the realm of popular culture came a general displacement of afternoon soap operas with syndicated, issue-oriented talk shows. Although these types of shows had their initial success through male-hosted programs such as *Donahue* and *Geraldo* in the 1980s, it was the success of Oprah Winfrey and a bevy of imitators such as Jenny Jones, Sally Jessy Raphael, and Ricki Lake that led to the enormous expansion of the genre in the early to mid-1990s.[37] As has been examined in numerous scholarly works, these shows typically discuss personal issues such as anorexia, teenage pregnancy, incest, homosexuality, and so on, and involve both experts and laity on stage with the host moderating. Eventually in each program, the audience participates in the discussion, and it is here that scholars have argued that laity has successfully offered challenges to institutionally based expertise.[38] These programs have since grown into what has been called "trash television," featuring guests who appear on the program to reveal bizarre sexual and personal peccadilloes, or who appear so they can "confront" other people in their lives, all for the camera to record and witness as exotic spectacle. The king and queen of trash television, many people widely acknowledge, are hosts Jerry Springer and Ricki Lake.[39]

In the economic realm of media industries, the wisdom of "the people" also became a value that producers realized could be commodified. Talk radio formats became the godsend of AM stations nationwide as listeners and participants revived a flailing industry with populist political talk. Talk radio host Rush Limbaugh led the way, but a bevy of conservative copycats were also spawned nationwide by Limbaugh's success, such as Ken Hamblin ("The Black Avenger"), G. Gordon Liddy, and Sean Hannity.[40] Trying to model the success of talk radio, as well as tap into the interactive capabilities brought on by the Internet craze, cable television entrepreneurs developed talk television channels and programming strategies that sought to mobilize populist angst by showcasing commonsense commentary of the average person and exploiting interactive technologies to intensify the connection with the viewing audience. CNN developed an hour-long daily program, *TalkBack Live* (1994); MSNBC's precursor was America's Talking (1994); Multi-Media/Gannett produced the Talk Channel (1994) (renamed NewsTalk Television in 1995); C-SPAN introduced its morning call-in show, *Washington Journal;* Republican party activists produced National Empowerment Television (1993; renamed America's Voice in 1998), a channel that actually billed itself as explicitly "populist." Around the same time, two comedians stepped forward with shows that featured entertaining political talk in new and unusual formats for both the political and entertainment genre: *Dennis Miller Live* appeared on HBO in 1994, and Comedy Central introduced *Politically Incorrect* in 1993, only to lose it to network television four years later.

In sum, then, by the early 1990s, an environment existed in which populist rhetoric and thinking had become a popular vehicle for addressing political anxiety, where "common sense" became a catchall solution to complex problems, and where political celebrity became the point of public identification with new types of politics that might provide a more appealing solution. This is a social environment where communication technologies offered hope and optimism for overcoming one-way flows of communication from distant forces of bureaucracy and control, thereby giving people greater voice, access, and choice. It is a cultural environment in which political struggles are increasingly played out in cultural forums such as talk shows, and it is an economic environment where media industries competitively struggle to create programs and channels that are cheap to produce, yet innovative and popular with audience tastes. Also important to note here is how interrelated these processes are: disillusionment in politics leads to hopeful answers in technology and new media; frustration with government finds an outlet in culture, including the primary currency in popular culture of "celebrity"; cultural wars become political wars (and vice versa), and hence, attractive content for conflict-driven media programming; technological convergence produces opportunities for political and economic exploitation; economic competition results in new forms of programming related to politics featuring technology.

In understanding the type of political programming that would develop from this context, it is important that we examine in some detail the television industry's specific response to the increased competition brought on by the rapidly expanded offerings made available by cable. That is, it bears asking: What specific measures did programmers take (in particular, for both new and existing cable channels) not only to mark themselves as appealing to audiences, but also to establish different *relationships* with audiences based on that appeal?

Televisual Style, Audiences, and "Outsider" Talk

Two major things occurred in the postnetwork period of the late 1980s and early 1990s that speak to the issues at hand: the television industry's change in programming style to appeal to audiences in new and different ways, and the concomitant popularity of syndicated audience participation shows in afternoon programming and their effect in altering assumptions about such issues as authority, voice, knowledge, and participation in television's presentation of public issues. It is from these two major developments that new political television was formed, leading to a style of political programming inclusive of "outsider" political voices provided by both comedians and the nonexpert public itself.

The first of these developmental changes was produced as a result of the rise of competition to the network oligopoly from cable programmers. For the networks, consumers were now able to choose from a broad array of more narrowly defined options on cable for their viewing pleasures (sports, music, news, etc.). For new and existing cable channels, the challenge was to provide some level of interesting and attractive content that would draw viewers away from their former habits of attending to network programming, but also away from *other* cable competition. In the process, it was necessary to give the network a specific "brand image" in viewers' minds. The increased competition led one network executive in 1993 to state, "It's not business as usual anymore. We have got to find ways to recreate this business so that it will survive into the next decade."[41] In addition to this increased competition, the industry was also experiencing changing production factors such as advances in audio-visual technologies and changing costs of production, both allowing for newer presentational aesthetics and altered appeals to audiences.

John Thornton Caldwell offers perhaps the most thorough and illuminating analysis of the ways in which the industry responded. The means the networks used to fight for survival, he argues, involved an intensive program of innovation and stylistic development. The new look offered is what he calls "televisuality," an aesthetic tendency toward excessive style. "Television moved from a framework that approached broadcasting primarily as a form of word-based rhetoric and transmission," he notes, "to a visually based mythology, framework, and aesthetic based on extreme self-consciousness of style."[42] Style became the subject, the defining practice of television as a means of attaining a distinctive look in the battle for audience share. Excessive style, however, is more than simply a visual phenomenon. Instead, it becomes a means of developing a "look" by individualizing programs in viewers' minds via their distinctive appeal.

A driving force behind the need for this new exhibitionism was the changing relationship between audiences and the televisual product. "The individuation and semiotic heterogeneity evident in televisual excess," he argues, "means that such shows are from the start defined by, and pitched at, niche audiences who are flattered by claims of difference and distinction."[43] These new rules affect both viewers and industry, and the texts that exist between them. Viewers are positioned as savvy and self-conscious televisual consumers by the industry, while the texts "demand a more conscious form of viewer negotiation."[44]

Simultaneous with this reconfiguration of industry perspective was the increasing popularity and multiplicity of syndicated issue-oriented afternoon talk shows, often called audience participation programs. As noted above, an enormous body of scholarly work has been devoted to exploring these programs and their place in society. What merits our attention here are the conclusions these scholars make in two regards: first, how (through the inclusion of studio audience participation in creating these programs) these shows led the way for audiences to question what constituted "authority" and "expertise" in televised talk about issues of public concern, including questioning who has the right to speak and be heard about such issues; and second, how such programming has eroded the boundaries between the differing programming genres of talk (e.g., the "entertaining" and the "serious"). Paulo Carpignano, Robin Andersen, Stanley Aronowitz, and William DiFazio argue that audience participation programs "problematize the distinction between expert and audience, professional authority and layperson." For them, these shows "constitute a 'contested space' in which new discursive practices are developed in contrast to the traditional modes of political and ideological representation."[45] Through talk that often pits "experts" against "laity," these authors highlight the importance of the studio audiences' (and perhaps the viewing audiences' as well) rejection of the claims offered by authority figures:

> What is expressed is a refusal not of knowledge but of expertise. The talk show rejects the arrogance of a discourse that defines itself on the basis of its difference from common sense. In debate, the authority of the expert is replaced by the authority of a narrative informed by lived experience.[46]

Similarly, in their study of British and American talk shows, Sonia Livingstone and Peter Lunt make an analogous argument by expanding upon Jürgen Habermas's conception of a separation between the life-world and system-world, that is, the differences between the organic knowledge derived from lived lives and that of the specialized knowledge produced within the professionalized and institutionalized logic of "the system." They contend that these shows "adopt an anti-elitist position which implicitly draws . . . alternative epistemological traditions, offering a revaluation of the life-world, repudiating criticisms of the ordinary person as incompetent or ignorant, questioning the deference traditionally due to experts through their separations from the life-world and their incorporation into the system, and asserting instead the worth of the 'common man.' "[47] Livingstone and Lunt find these altered patterns to be so substantive that they read into the British media at large a tendency for movement "away from critical exposition and commentary. Letting ordinary people speak for themselves is replacing critically conscious social realism."[48]

The second conclusion from this literature is that contemporary talk shows are a distinctive field of discourse composed of intergeneric and crossgeneric features where the boundaries between the "serious" and the "popular" or "entertaining" are increasingly blurred.[49] The reason this is possible, argues Wayne Munson, is that the talk show is a contingent and malleable form of programming—a hybrid, by definition. The talk show, he contends, "combines two communicative paradigms, and like the term itself, the 'talkshow' fuses and seems to reconcile two different, even contradictory, rhetorics. It links conversation, the interpersonal—the premodern oral tradition—with the mass-mediated spectacle born of modernity."[50] Within it, there is space for the creation of multiple points of audience identification, as well as the opportunity for programmers to "refresh" the televisual landscape. He argues,

> the talkshow mingles the "professional" or "expert" with the "amateur," the guest or participant who appears by virtue of particular personal experience or simple audience membership. It shrewdly combines the folk and the popular with the mass, the immediate and interpersonal with the mediated, in a productive dialectic that both reflects and constructs an image economy's "voracious need for change and innovation" and for "continually changing the rules, and replacing the scenery," as Andrew Ross puts it.[51]

The result of these changing and recombinatory forms is the fact that the audiences for such programming are increasingly "fragmented." Echoing Caldwell's claim that television producers sought to create new relationships with niche audiences who are flattered by claims of distinction, Andrew Tolson argues that there "is no longer the general 'popular' audience (targeted by mass advertising), but rather it is diversified into cults and cliques, characterized by different kinds of 'knowingness.' "[52]

In short, this literature illuminates features that would also become distinguishing characteristics of new political television. These features include the cross-generic construction of programming, the inclusion of "ordinary voices," the range of diverse positions presented, the challenge to "expert" authority, the informal conversational style, and the usage of a common vernacular and "common sense" thinking about issues and solutions that were traditionally approached through professional languages and knowledge. These features are

important in that they offer a qualitatively different approach to the more paternalistic political discourse offered through pundit television. Combined with
Caldwell's observations about stylistic excess in postnetwork television, programmers of the new populist brand of political television (discussed below) utilized angry political talk as a stylistic marker, a distinctive presentation of excess
wrapped in the gadgetry and buzz of new communication technologies. Furthermore, viewers were flattered by a rhetoric that their voices mattered, and
that America was waiting to hear what they had to say. A new relationship was
built on viewer activity around the televisual text, rewarding the viewer as an
"engaged" citizen as he or she helped construct the programming. Television's
search for style, then, its search for a new and different look, actually opened up
new modes of discourse and new forms of participation and presentation for
political talk on television that had previously been ignored or disregarded.

Vox Pop Programming
and the Transformation of Cable News

Cable television in the mid-1990s gave birth to a handful of programs and
channels offering an eclectic array of programming featuring audience-centered
political talk. NBC, Multi-Media/Gannett, CNN, C-SPAN, and the Free Congress Foundation all constructed programs or entire cable channels dedicated
to offering an "outsider" political voice in the mode of talk radio.[53] As a cheap
form of programming, these groups attempted to ride the waves of success not
only of talk radio, but also of the populist rhetoric of the anti-politics/anti-
government groundswell and the buzz over new communication technologies.
Indeed, cable programmers attempted to access these citizen/viewer dissatis-
factions with politics via the promise of communication technologies, thereby
allowing programmers to establish both stylistic and content changes relatively
inexpensively while providing enormous potential for including its audience
within the programming beyond talk radio's disembodied voices. Political commentary and opinions from viewing audiences could become part of the
programming via e-mail, faxes, voice mail, phone calls, chat rooms, videoconferencing, and bulletin board systems. The stylish new programming also
offered high-tech sets and gadgetry featuring fax machines, screen "crawls,"
computer screens, video kiosks in malls and shopping-centers, and other visual
displays of "the people's voice" in action.

As Caldwell argues, competition in the cable marketplace required these
distinctive stylistic markers but also required an appeal for new and more significant relationships with viewers. The move to "the people's voice" in cable
programming created different temporal and spatial relationships with viewing
audiences as networks encouraged viewers to extend their participation in the
program prior to, during, and after a particular show's airing by joining in discussions via chat rooms, bulletin boards, e-mail, and voice mail. In short, audiences were tired of elite-centered political and social discourse, cable network
executives argued, and therefore were perceived as interested in consuming
new forms of talk programming that included their own voices and concerns.

Efforts in this regard include NBC's attempt to exploit synergies between their broadcast and cable properties by creating America's Talking on July 4, 1994, a new channel dedicated to all-talk programming (which became MSNBC two years later). America's Talking (A-T) was NBC's effort to expand the limited talk television concept that it was featuring on CNBC during prime-time hours into an all-talk format. With talk radio's enormous popularity in mind, the network hired Roger Ailes, former Republican Party strategist and the executive producer of Rush Limbaugh's syndicated television program, to head both America's Talking and CNBC. As a result, Ailes brought the impulses he developed with Limbaugh to the new network, offering initial program lineups and an overall channel concept that mirrored the success Limbaugh was having with his "common man" persona and rage-against-the-liberal-system populism.

With programs like *Pork* (about government waste and corruption), *Bugged!* (billed as "primal scream therapy brought to you courtesy of the information superhighway"), and *AM I Nuts?* (about the stresses of everyday life), Ailes sought to construct the network as an outlet for the perceived frustrations viewers were supposedly experiencing with modern life.[54] He also emphasized that the network was "trying to represent real people."[55] A-T sought to position itself on the cutting edge of televisual difference by acting on the assumption that audiences don't passively watch television anymore but instead actively participate in constructing programming. Twelve of A-T's programs incorporated on-line bulletin boards, polling, electronic mail, and chat room services.[56] The linking of technology and populist politics was intended to flatter and involve a certain niche audience, thereby not waiting for an audience to appear, but in many ways attempting to create it.

The same populist impulse was seen in the programming of National Empowerment Television (NET), a small cable channel officially associated with the Free Congress Foundation—a conservative political organization founded by Republican party activist Paul Weyrich. NET launched on December 6, 1993, and was run as a tax-exempt, nonprofit entity. The primary purpose of the channel was not to make a profit, but to impact politics. Its mission was simple: empower people to hold (liberal) political elites accountable. That task would be achieved, they argued, first, by providing programming that would bypass the media elite, presenting their viewers "unbiased" and "truthful" information necessary to see the lies they were being told by mainstream media and elite politicians; and second, by providing the means—interactive call-in programming—through which Americans could "talk back to Washington" and thereby "put government on the defensive."[57] "Our bent is populist," proclaimed Burton Pines, vice chairman of the network. "America has a grievance against Washington. We will be on America's side, not Washington's side."[58] The network sought to empower its viewers (and achieve their loyalty) primarily through its programming, 80 percent of which incorporated viewer call-ins. But as a network that arose alongside the conservative populism of Newt Gingrich et al. and the "Republican Revolution" of 1994, the network found that it could not sustain itself as those forces subsided, and ultimately it declared bankruptcy in January 2000.

One final example of the move toward featuring "outsider" audience voices in cable programming came from CNN. In an effort to bolster its afternoon ratings when no news stories merited extensive coverage, the network introduced *TalkBack Live* on August 22, 1994. *TalkBack* was a one-hour public affairs talk show that aired in the heart of CNN's afternoon schedule (3:00 PM EST), and sought the traditional town hall meeting as its romantic corollary. Upon its launch, CNN argued that the program would create a national forum for dialogue, a place to build bridges and seek commonality, a place where publics could interact with policy makers who had power to "change things." Whereas America's Talking incorporated interactive technologies for both stylistic and populist purposes, *TalkBack* embraced a rhetoric of democratic utopianism— technology as a means of reviving democracy, providing access to power, and bringing the nation closer together. "The point is to re-create an old-time town meeting using the most advanced technology to create a connection that I think we lack," said Teya Ryan, the show's executive producer.[59] "People are interested not simply in what the experts have to say, but what their fellow Americans have to say," she noted elsewhere.[60]

Like America's Talking, *TalkBack* would employ numerous technological vehicles to incorporate the lay voice into the program, including phone calls, electronic mail, faxes, videoconferencing, and chat groups. The show's original host, Susan Rook, argued, "This is 'Crossfire' for real people."[61] The studio set was built to visually represent the interactive nature of the program (as well as effectively merge the spheres of business, consumption, and politics into one seamless whole). Constructed in the atrium lobby of CNN Center in downtown Atlanta, the set would seat up to 150 people, including tourists, shoppers, workers, and local residents. In addition to a live audience, the program integrated the voices and messages of viewers at home by including a table in the middle of the set with a ten-line telephone, a fax machine, and computer terminal. Producers off-screen would also integrate viewer opinions and questions via video remotes and on-line comments while allowing faxes to pop out of the machine on stage.[62]

As both the populist and techno-euphoric mood of the country receded substantially by the turn of the century, the overt rhetoric of angry voters, town hall meetings, alienation from Washington, and electronic democracy largely left with it. With *TalkBack Live*'s cancellation on March 7, 2003, only C-SPAN's morning call-in show, *Washington Journal*, has survived as a program solely dedicated to interactive viewer participation centered on politics.[63] What this discussion offers, however, is insight into how cable television programmers attempted to exploit the mood and context of the moment, and in turn challenged the normative conceptions of who gets to speak about politics on television and what will be spoken about. America's Talking, National Empowerment Television, and *TalkBack Live* altered the landscape by insisting that the audience was not simply to be spoken *to*, but also to be spoken *with*. The audience was welcomed into the conversation and flattered—not only for what they know, but also for their technological savvy and abilities to connect to information and share it with others. Television had finally asserted that politics isn't just what occurs inside the beltway but rather is also what people make of it in their daily experiences and activities of living. These programs and channels were venues, according to the producers, where citizens could express themselves, connect to power and to each other, and create political change. Each of these three encouraged, to various degrees, an "us versus them" approach in attracting disaffected audiences to political talk—a marked change from the pundits' assumption of a public as a singular "us."[64]

The legacy of this programming for new political television is twofold. First are the formal components of the programming that are active today in other talk shows. The outsider public voice is still present in political programming in various ways. For instance, *Crossfire* changed its format to include viewer e-mail, as well as beginning performing before (and fielding questions from) a studio audience that formerly did not exist. Many of the other talk programs on cable news networks (such as the popular *The O'Reilly Factor*) also feature viewer e-mail.

Perhaps the most substantial and lasting legacy of Vox Pop programming, however, has been the stunning success of Roger Ailes and his almost single-handed transformation of the genre of cable news programming. When America's Talking became MSNBC in 1996 (Microsoft and NBC's effort to up the technological ante by further enhancing the linkages between television news and on-line viewer activity), Roger Ailes left the network to become programming chief at Fox News. Whereas Ailes had generally failed to capitalize on his efforts to feature conservative, populist, and bombastic rhetoric with *The Rush Limbaugh Show* and America's Talking, here he found success by cloaking it in the mantle of journalistic "objectivity." Featuring overtly conservative talk show hosts and programming and outright ideologically biased news reporting, the network nevertheless brands itself "Fair and Balanced." The network has also retained its alignment with "the people" from Ailes's Vox Pop days by using slogans such as "we report, you decide" in its promotional materials. In some ways, the network doesn't shy from the conservative label placed on it by critics because it argues that "the American people" believe the news media is liberal, and hence the network is therefore offering a corrective choice.[65]

Since 1996, Fox News, CNN, and MSNBC have been the leading networks featuring political talk programming on cable. In general, these "news" channels have experienced a weakening in the audiences for the hard news format of CNN, an enormous rise in the audiences for the opinionated talk programming of Fox News, and a complete about-face for the programming strategies employed at MSNBC in the wake of its dwindling viewership.[66] In short, what has occurred is that these "news" channels actually program more hours of talk shows than news.[67]

Waving American flag banners in the corner of the screen, Fox News became the cable news leader after the terrorist attacks of September 11, 2001. The political mood had changed from one of know-it-all viewers in a robust America to a public desperate for answers after one of the most puzzling and disturbing events in American history.[68] Fox News embraced the flag and its own patriotic hubris in establishing a connection with its viewers in America's "War on Terrorism," employing the same "us versus them" rhetoric of the Vox Pop days, only now with a different "enemy." The "people's voice," it seems, would be that of Bill O'Reilly, with his common-sense rhetoric and his use-and-abuse style with guests who just don't get it. Or perhaps that voice is Geraldo Rivera, the surrogate American qua Fox News reporter rummaging through the caves of Tora Bora, Afghanistan, with a pistol on his hip in search of Osama bin Laden! In sum, it may be talk television under the label of "news," but the excessive style of discursive spectacles (whether through lay or expert voices, screaming hosts, or roving reporters) and the alignment with and flattering of the viewing public (through e-mails and studio audiences, ideological sensibility, or patriotic zeal) is still a fixture in political talk programming on cable.

The arbitrary boundaries between experts and nonexperts are now much more fluid, and the variety of ways in which programs intentionally recognize and flatter their audiences have greatly increased from the earlier model of political talk programming. Whether the exaggerated claims of political "empowerment" for viewers by "talking back" to power made by Vox Pop producers in the mid-1990s were ever achieved is questionable. What did occur in the process, however, is a reformulation by television producers and audiences of what counts as desirable and attractive political talk on television. What also occurred concurrent with Vox Pop programming was the appearance of two comedy-driven talk shows with politics at the center of the discussions.[69]

Humorous Political Talk Shows and Late-Night Television

Late-night network television is generally dominated by two types of programming: the local newscast of network affiliates, followed by the late-night talk shows featuring David Letterman and Jay Leno, among others.[70] The problem with this programming for three comedians—Bill Maher, Dennis Miller, and Jon Stewart—is that these forms of programming have lost all relevance as either meaningful forums for public discourse and/or entertainment. Indeed, these comedians argue that the talk and comedy on the late-night shows offer the public nothing but boring banter with celebrities pitching their latest project and politically irrelevant comedy from uninspired hosts. The local and national broadcast and cable news is also deficient, offering "news" that is manipulative, trivial, and fatuous, so much so that reporters have turned reporting into entertainment. Each of these comedians, over the course of the 1990s and early 2000s, set out to address these deficiencies by offering their own brand of politically humorous talk show as antidote. Indeed, from what the record shows, their intention in crafting these shows seems to have been as much an effort to address deficiencies in programming as it was to redress the lack of meaningful *political* talk available to citizen-viewers. What has resulted, however, is the emergence of three politically engaged, aggressively iconoclastic, sharp-tongued, and sharp-witted comedian-hosts who have offered truly original political programming that addresses the fakery in public life as manifest in news and late-night television talk.

The three programs that led the way in the development of the humorous political talk show are *Politically Incorrect with Bill Maher, Dennis Miller*

Live, and *The Daily Show with Jon Stewart.*[71] . . . [H]ere they are examined for what they share in common: their critique of the fakery in news, late-night television, and political rhetoric in general; and their crafting of a subgenre of late-night talk that shares certain distinctive characteristics that mark them as both political and entertaining.

A Response to Fakery

These three comedians, with their producers and writers, have defined themselves in opposition to their competition. That is to say, each of their shows was created (somewhat) as a response to the deficiencies of both the talk and humor offered in late-night television, as well as the fakery of television news reporting and the politics reported there. Indeed, fakery is the defining trait that all of these programs critique—from the frivolous and scripted chitchat that Letterman conducts with guests, to the toothless political jokes in Leno's monologues, to the feigned objectivity and rampant sensationalism of news programs, to the empty and misleading rhetoric of politicians that appear there. These comedians express a desire for honesty in public life, resulting most often in a take-it-or-leave-it criticism of the political and social landscape that they encounter and respond to in the course of each day or week. Hence, the contribution of Maher, Miller, and Stewart to new political television is this: They have intentionally set out to say what can't or isn't being said elsewhere on television.

Bill Maher has made it perfectly clear, from the beginning of his show's run until its cancellation by ABC, that the program was designed in response to the type of television that irritated him. "The genesis for this show," Maher noted in 1993, "comes in some ways from my frustration with doing talk shows over the past 10 years and always being shoved away from controversial material."[72] Therefore, when Maher pitched his program idea to producers, he says he "sold the idea that there wasn't anything that lived up to being a talk show. Talk shows had become boring, publicity-driven promotional shows with one guest at a time. They were missing the two biggest areas of humor: the connection of guests and controversial subjects."[73] Maher wanted a show in which guests would actually interact with each other, and that interaction would be based on things in life that actually matter—two features he felt were not present anywhere in the late-night talk show conversation.[74] "The original point of the show," he notes, "was to get out of people what they're like at a cocktail party. We want to have people talk about real things, but in an amusing way that's not forced."[75] And after being cancelled nine years later, Maher again offered a defense for why his program should be seen as an important contribution to public awareness of current affairs, as opposed simply to blurring the line between entertainment and politics. "Anyone who would make the choice to watch 'Politically Incorrect' was at least interested in something of substance. . . . I was doing a show pitted against two other purely entertainment shows that would not even attempt to tackle the subjects we were tackling."[76]

Maher is also critical of the type of humor offered by Leno and Letterman. Although Maher maintains that he has made his own share of "Bush is dumb" jokes, he nevertheless prides himself on also holding President George

W. Bush's "feet to the fire on every single thing he's ever done. That's what Leno hasn't done." Maher contends that comedians need to plumb the depths of Bush's public deceits and propaganda ploys, but they don't. "That's what I want Jay Leno and the others to make fun of. But they won't. They make fun of him for mispronouncing a word."[77] Dennis Miller has been less overtly critical of his comedic peers, but he has made it clear that he considers the type of humor they offer monotonous. When his show debuted, he noted that he wanted to "put the spine of vitriol in that staggering rag doll known as comedy."[78] Although each program begins with a traditional comedic monologue (similar to his competition), it is his signature five-minute breathless exposition known as the "rant" that has won him acclaim as a political commentator. When asked if his comedy might get lost on some of his viewers as they struggle to make sense of what he calls his "arcane simile" approach to comedy, he says, "I think a high percentage of the people want to have to figure it out a little. . . . I'll just bet you that most lay people out there are upset that they're treated like such morons."[79] His head writer also notes that Miller's first syndicated talk show, the one that was cancelled in 1992, was "a little ahead of its time. . . . They hired him to be another Johnny Carson . . . and Dennis is a different type of comedian. He's a much edgier type of comic."[80] Miller's conception of political talk is aggressive and demanding for audiences, yet he recognized that this type of comedy is what was missing at the time.

Finally, Jon Stewart has also expressed his dismay over the artifice of public life—whether it is news reporting, political rhetoric, or entertainment talk. Indeed, *The Daily Show* directly parodies the news program by pretending to be one, complete with the fake anchor role played by Stewart, a team of faux correspondents and commentators, and the tongue-in-cheek moniker, "The Most Important Television Show—Ever!" As a parody of television news shows, it skewers the absurdity and contradictions that pass for "news." "We find a lot of material in . . . how the news has been entertainment-ized," he says. "You'd think news has a higher mandate than entertainment, but, apparently, it doesn't."[81] Head writer for *The Daily Show*, Ben Karlin, offers his opinion of how the show positions itself in the void of late-night programming: "[Our show is] not a straightforward talk show, so we don't have to be this thing that people turn to for comfort and direction. And it's not a news show, so it doesn't have too much of what is essentially this artifice of objectivity."[82] Because the program ridicules both politicians and journalists for being fakes, critics have charged it as being liberal. Stewart offers a telling response, though "fakery" is not his word of choice: "The point of view of this show is we're passionately opposed to bullshit. Is that liberal or conservative?"[83]

This is the standard these programs define themselves against. They also share a level of similarity that helps define this type of humorous political talk as a subgenre of political talk programming.

Characteristics of New Political Television

The first defining feature shared by *Politically Incorrect with Bill Maher, Dennis Miller Live,* and *The Daily Show with Jon Stewart* is that they are entertainment shows that are unafraid to deal with politics directly or aggressively. Political subjects dominate the content of the shows, and through parody, conversation, or ranting, each places politics squarely in its comedic crosshairs. Johnny Carson believes that comedians can't be social commentators because seriousness and humor, in his view, are incompatible.[84] David Letterman intentionally chooses to remain apolitical in his comedy, noting that "I'd hate to think there were people in America saying, 'Well, hell, Letterman likes him; let's vote for the son of a bitch.' "[85] Maher, Stewart, and Miller, on the other hand, have taken advantage of the cable forums they operate in (or originated from) and have built shows around politics in all of its manifestations. Maher and Stewart frame their shows around issues and events that appear daily in the news, and hence provide running commentary on everything from the O. J. trial, Whitewater, the presidential sex scandal and impeachment, to the 9/11 terrorist attacks, homeland security, and the war in Iraq. Miller's discussion topics are more broad-based, allowing for a more wide-reaching rant, but nevertheless they are centered on issues such as race, Republicans, homosexuality, political correctness, freedom of speech, activism, funding for the arts, liberals, and the electoral system. None of the hosts claims an expertise in politics, and indeed, some even proclaim a level of nonsophistication on the subject. Miller, for example, says, "I am the definitive layman. If I see something that (ticks) me off, I have a childlike urge to just say it (ticks) me off, instead of trying to figure it out."[86] Moreover, when they speak, it is not with a voice that assumes insider knowledge. Instead, it derives from a commonsensical layman's version of understanding that comes from reading newspapers and watching television—just like many of their viewers.

A second feature for the programs by Miller and Stewart is the way the show is divided between political commentary and guest interview (although for Maher, these are somewhat combined by having his guests talk on the topic of his choosing, that is, politics). Both *Dennis Miller Live* and *The Daily Show* begin with their own brands of political commentary, and then segue halfway through the show into an interview with a guest that may or may not have anything to do with the preceding political critique. Sometimes the guest is related to the topic—for instance, Miller had Surgeon General Joycelyn Elders on the same show as his rant on teenage pregnancy, and Stewart has had Madeleine Albright on the show to discuss Middle East diplomacy. But again, this need not always be the case, for Stewart is just as likely to discuss the war in Iraq in the first part of the show, then bring on (as he says) "the girl from *Felicity*" for a fawning celebrity chat.[87] The point here is that these shows have no problem balancing politics and entertainment in the same half-hour of programming.

The third related feature of these programs regards the types of guests they host. At least for Maher and Stewart, their shows include celebrities as well as guests who are not household names (indeed, guests who can be outright obscure for some in the viewing and studio audience). Maher's show was perhaps the most pronounced in this regard for several reasons. The central premise of the show was to assemble a mélange of people from various walks of life (film and television, politics, sports, music, literature and journalism, and political/social activism) as well as of differing ideological stripes. In producing a show with four guests, five nights a week, over the course of nine years, *P.I.* almost always included obscure guests. The show even hosted a "citizen panelist" for part of its run, selecting a "Joe or Jane American" from various cities across the nation to participate in the discussions. Most of the guests, however, were public persons, but again, not necessarily someone who was simply a celebrity. Miller and Stewart have also hosted the occasionally obscure guest, such as *Harper's Magazine* editor Lewis Lapham (a person who is not known for his entertaining demeanor, nor a magazine that is typical table reading for the eighteen- to thirty-four-year-old demographic), a former UN weapons inspector, or a former official with the Federal Aviation Administration to discuss airport security. To be sure, the fact that these shows are about politics—not simply celebrity pop culture—leads to these guests' inclusion. The point here is that the show's hosts are unafraid to bring on guests who they think will provide an interesting take on public affairs, irrespective of the fact that the channel-surfing audience could vote with their changer not to stay with an unfamiliar face. . . . [M]any in the audience actually enjoy the guest variety as well as hearing people with whom they are unfamiliar. They also like hearing the political opinions of celebrities whom they have never heard hold forth on political issues—sometimes to their shock and dismay and other times to their pleasant surprise.[88]

Fourth, these shows are distinctive in that the political discussions are conducted in front of a *live* studio audience (unlike almost all other political talk shows). Indeed, holding political discussions in the presence of audiences—who naturally laugh, jeer, cheer, applaud, and occasionally heckle both the hosts and guests—adds a powerful dynamic to the televised sense making of politics. Political oratory is participatory, and just because it is being televised does not negate the audience's natural impulse to respond to that which they feel strongly about. As such, no longer can political commentators and guests (especially those who are particularly partisan or ideologically driven) trot out inanities without also having to hear how these formulations play with the public. When Jon Stewart offers various video clips of government officials spouting ridiculous statements, or clips of manipulative news broadcasts, the audience doesn't even wait for Stewart to make a joke or to reference the clip; they are quite capable of knowing when and where to laugh, and generally do so with great exuberance.

The dynamics of how a live audience can affect televised political discourse can be seen very clearly on an episode of *Real Time with Bill Maher*. Maher held a conversation via satellite with Sandy Rios, president of the Concerned Women for America, to discuss President Bush's proposed constitutional amendment to ban gay marriages. Rios boldly proclaimed, "Bill, we have a crisis in our country. Even if you were in favor of gay marriage, we've got anarchy going on, especially in San Francisco," at which point the audience erupted in laughter at her fevered assertions. But she continued, "This is a breaking of law. This is lawlessness," only to be greeted again with a loud burst of laughter. Her only recourse at that point was to respond by saying, "I don't know why your audience is laughing [followed by more audience laughter]. If it were an issue they were against, they would be very upset about this."[89] Surely Rios followed the letter of her particular script despite the audience's wholesale rejection of her thinking. Nevertheless, the tenor and tone of the conversation (and that which viewing audiences at home were presented with) was altered as a product of simply allowing citizens to witness and participate in (even if only through laughter) such televised political discourse.

The ways in which these shows mix their serious and humorous components comprise the fifth feature of similarity. Indeed, there really is no segregation of these features (such as serious rant, then humorous talk with a celebrity). The humor, anger, amusement, dismay, and disagreement are all mixed in the narrative flow each show creates. On *P.I.*, the guests may find themselves yelling at each other at the tops of their lungs, only to have Maher or a fellow comedian remind everyone that perhaps they are taking themselves too seriously by offering a pithy rejoinder. *P.I.*, in particular, tries to include different guests who can provide both seriousness and humor to the discussion. Miller's rants are not just diatribes or polemics. He makes his political points *through* his humor, pointing out the contradictions and absurdities of a situation, while offering a smirking smile and outraged tone simultaneously. The rant allows him to thumb his nose at the rigid boundaries of stand-up humor that have traditionally required the comedian to offer a line and wait for the laugh. Instead, by being humorous and serious at the same time, the comedian becomes an essayist, opening up the opportunity to make points without the obligation to simultaneously score laughs within a line or thought. And for Stewart's program, the parody is, by definition, a combination of serious humor. The humor is delivered with a straight face (or at least a repressed grin) until the audience catches on.

Yet by freely mixing humor with political talk, critics have tended to assume that the former trivializes the latter. For instance, one critic has argued, "By providing a hideous burlesque of political debate, in which semi-literate rock stars, stand-up comics and think-tank ideologues flogged one another's so called opinions, *Politically Incorrect* did more to encourage stupidity than an army of Tom Greens."[90] Wayne Munson, however, argues that talk shows that employ such playfulness with "discursive boundaries and identities" are threatening to "critics (who) are desperate for clear labels and stable structures—in other words, for a representational 'purity' the talkshow will not allow."[91] The executive producer of *P.I.*, Scott Carter, asserts that the show's "format acknowledges the blurring of the line between news and entertainment," but he suggests that such lines are essentially meaningless to most audiences.[92]

What this mixture has allowed for (the sixth common feature of these shows) is the development by each comedian of a political persona built on his particular type of humor. Yet having a politically opinionated persona (something avoided by hosts such as Leno and Letterman) automatically reduces their audience appeal at the mass level (though not for the small and paying audiences associated with cable viewing).[93] Critics have commented on Miller's supposed "smugness factor," contending that "most of the time, he seems mighty pleased with himself and his brand of high-IQ comedy."[94] Maher too has been charged with a know-it-all quality, or for being shrill and condescending to his guests, especially by nonfans (as demonstrated in online discussion forums . . .). Some critics have also noticed how such posturing has played itself out with audiences to a level of positive outcomes. In regard to Miller, one journalist wrote, "Once, his comedy was tinged with a hipper-than-thou attitude; to some, Miller seemed to be smirking, setting himself above his audience. Now, he and the fans are on closer terms; he invites them into his exclusive little circle, and they respond eagerly."[95] If this journalist is correct, the crafted political persona as savvy but humorous commentator plays well with audiences who appreciate the cultish and cliquish distinction that such a relationship seemingly bestows.

Which leads to the seventh point: how these shows demand a level of sophistication or knowledge about both politics *and* popular culture. Critics often contend that these shows are the equivalent of a "Politics for Dummies" manual. Even Jay Leno contends that in political humor, "the audience has to know what you're talking about or else you'll be sunk. . . . You can't know more than anybody watching. And we've found that once you get past secretary of state—and even that is a stretch—no one knows what you're talking about."[96] These political comedians, through their performances to date, obviously disagree. Maher and Stewart quite often employ in their jokes less-than-common-name political figures that many viewers may not recognize, such as Russian Prime Minister Yevgeny Primakov, UN leader Kofi Annan, Treasury Secretary Paul O'Neill, and Deputy Secretary of Defense Paul Wolfowitz. Miller is perhaps the most aggressive comic in drawing from a catalog of obscure news, literary, and pop culture figures to make a point. In one of his rants inveighing against the "death of common sense," for instance, he cries:

> Christ, we're so bogged down in procedure, we make Radar O'Reilly look like Henry David Thoreau. You couple that with a Blanche DuBois–like denial of personal responsibility for the crap in our lives, and it's no wonder we're in a malaise that makes a bout of Epstein-Barr seem like a Laker Girl doing the Watusi after four triple lattes with a Dexatrim chaser.[97]

Although some critics contend that these shows contribute to ignorance about current events in young people, Jon Stewart argues that to even understand his show, one has to retain some level of knowledge about what is going on in the world. "I honestly don't think that young people can avoid getting news," he says. "I mean, news and information surround you almost on a molecular level these days. . . . And if you don't inform yourself, or have some sense of what's going on, our show won't even make sense to you."[98] The point to be made here is that far from trafficking in idiocy, these shows actually demand a high level of viewer savvy about the world and a more conscious viewer negotiation of the text for sense to be made from it. Furthermore, these shows are less inclined to care if the viewer doesn't get the reference, for they provide the type of cliquish knowledge that cable generally trades in. If the audience is too slow, dumb, or ill informed to get it, then that is their loss and the joke is on them. The networks, of course, provide programming tailor-made for such audiences. For the audiences who do "get it," they are rewarded for their savvy and distinctiveness as such.

The last two points of commonality refer to these shows' brevity and their mildly populist appeal. All three of the shows are only thirty minutes in length (as opposed to Leno and Letterman, who often fill their time with meaningless banter between the host and band leader), therefore offering a taste of interesting and digestible conversation about politics while refusing to beat the audience over the head with redundant arguments. The result, as audience data show, is that this generally leaves them wanting more.[99] Also, all three comedians recognize their place as representative of other outsider voices, and hence maintain some populist feature in their program or in their thinking. Miller takes phone calls from viewers during the interview segment of his show; Maher allows "citizen panelists" to join the conversation from time-to-time; and Stewart says he speaks for the "politically disappointed" and "represents the distracted center."[100] In short, each of the three shows offers some level of respect for their audience, its opinions, and its time.

Alternative Political Talk

Over the last decade, the presentation of political talk on television has changed. Although pundit talk still dominates both cable and network political programming, we have witnessed new forms of political talk that have taken advantage of their cable origins, home, or sensibilities to transform the genre and develop alternative approaches. For critics of humorous political talk, these shows have blurred the lines between serious and entertaining programming, and hence have made politics a frivolous matter. For these new talk hosts, however, the shows they produce offer a measure of honesty that combats the fakery that dominates both politics and entertainment in public life. Their programs allow for seriousness and humor to mix through the flow of conversation—the way that it does, they contend, everywhere in life *except* on television.

Yet that response to fakery is also a desire to call a spade a spade when it comes to government lies. That is, these new political television programs not only cover politics in humorous ways, but they also seek to illuminate the artifice of public discourse (by other talk shows, news, politicians) and those who refuse to hold those in power accountable (e.g., government officials, corporations, journalists). [T]hese comedian-hosts discuss certain topics, make certain connections, and point out "realities" that they contend are plainly obvious but that the news media and pundit shows—as the consummate political insiders—either refuse to cover or tend to handle in very similar ways. For instance, here is a small sample of topics covered by *The Daily Show* in 2003: Iraq and Halliburton; the FCC's media ownership vote; Bush dodging questions about weapons of mass destruction; gay marriage; the new head of the Environmental Protection Agency; tax cuts for the rich; why white collar crime does pay; faith-based government aid; the California governor recall election; Texas congressional redistricting; and the role of media during wartime.

Through subjects such as these, the comedian-hosts are not held simply to repeating the government's position on these matters. Instead, they doggedly attack those things that they find disturbing, puzzling, or outright lies and fabrications.

In sum, we can conclude several points about this move from political insiders to outsiders and the advent of new political television. Politics and culture are not separate spheres but are intimately interconnected. People are now allowed to talk about politics on television without being *in* politics. That is, people outside the political clubhouse are allowed to hold publicly televised conversations with and about those who *are* in politics. The language used in those conversations tends to be both politically basic and culturally obscure, which in essence turns the pundit/journalist formula on its head (i.e., politically obscure and culturally basic). The issues and events are not covered from the standard pundit/journalist approach, and the things said offer alternative perspectives from an outsider position. The shows are intended to uncover the fakery that dominates public life and politics. Finally, audiences have shown (by tuning in over the course of twelve years) that they want these new connections to politics and culture because such connections mirror their own political habits and cultural behaviors. To state it quite succinctly: new political television offers viewing audiences the ability to watch nonexperts discussing politics with comedian hosts who roast political distortions and fakery when they see it, yet who offer opinionated and thoughtful ruminations that aren't always designed to be taken *too* seriously. All of this is mixed with other cultural artifacts that the audience cares about and is invested in. As one reporter has noted, "These are not your father's late night talk shows."[101] Indeed. But on the other hand, neither are they your father's pundit talk shows.

Notes

1. See Schudson's argument about periods of civic culture in American history, including the Informed Citizen model that grew out of the Progressive Era reforms of the early twentieth century and that, in many ways, we still operate under today. Michael Schudson, *The Good Citizen: A History of American Civic Life* (New York: The Free Press, 1998).

2. Eric Alterman, *Sound and Fury: The Making of the Punditocracy* (Ithaca, N.Y.: Cornell University Press, 1999); Alan Hirsch, *Talking Heads: Political Talk Shows and Their Star Pundits* (New York: St. Martin's Press, 1991). Alterman provides an interesting discussion of the history of punditry on television dating back to Walter Lippmann's writings in newspapers. See also Bernard Timberg, *Television Talk: A History of the TV Talk Show* (Austin: University of Texas Press, 2002).

3. Indeed, Nielsen ratings for the Sunday morning talk shows suggest that over ten million audience members still tune in to these programs. For instance, average audience ratings for the Sunday morning pundit talk shows for the 2001–2002 television season are: *Meet the Press* (4.5 million); *Face the Nation* (2.9 million); *This Week* (3.0 million) (A. C. Nielsen Company).

4. Included in this discussion is political talk programming that appeared with the first generation of cable programming; that is, on CNN during the 1980s. Although

appearing on cable, this approach to political talk was very similar to that found on public television and the networks, with only slight modifications that led to an increase in spectacle performances. It was not until the 1990s when numerous new cable channels began appearing (what I call the second generation of cable programming) that pundit political talk would be both challenged by other forms of talk and expanded upon using similar generic features.

5. See Rick Ball, *Meet the Press: Fifty Years of History in the Making* (New York: McGraw-Hill, 1998).

6. Dan Nimmo and James E. Combs, *The Political Pundits* (New York: Praeger, 1992), 6.

7. Nimmo and Combs, *Political Pundits*, 8.

8. William F. Buckley Jr., *On The Firing Line* (New York: Random House, 1989).

9. Hirsch, *Talking Heads*, 13.

10. For reasons that have been hard to identify, liberals have never been successful as hosts of pundit programming. MSNBC tried to counterprogram against Fox's conservatism by making Phil Donahue their lead prime time host in 2002, but his show was cancelled just as America was preparing to invade Iraq (a war that Donahue opposed) in 2003. Allison Romano, "Liberal, and Proud of It," *Broadcasting & Cable* (15 July 2002): 12.

11. The ever-changing lineup has included shows such as *Hardball with Chris Matthews, Hannity and Colmes, The Drudge Report, Equal Time, Politics Today, The Beltway Boys, Special Report with Brit Hume, Imus in the Morning, Scarborough Country,* and the old talk show stalwarts, *Geraldo* and *Donahue*, which were reformatted for cable. See Alterman, *Sound and Fury,* for a more thorough accounting of these shows.

12. Hirsch, *Talking Heads;* Alterman, *Sound and Fury.*

13. Pat Buchanan was Richard Nixon's speechwriter and also worked in the Reagan administration; John McLaughlin was personal friends with Reagan, and his wife was appointed secretary of labor by Reagan; Chris Matthews worked for Jimmy Carter; George Will was close personal friends with Ronald and Nancy Reagan, and his wife worked in the Reagan White House and was also a manager in Bob Dole's 1996 presidential bid.

14. The case of television pundit and columnist Robert Novak's "outing" of an undercover CIA agent at the behest of "unnamed" Bush administration officials in 2003 is perhaps the most glaring recent example of this.

15. Alicia Mundy, "Showtime in the Capitol," *Media Week* 6 (15 January 1996): 20–22.

16. Hirsch, *Talking Heads,* 181.

17. Nimmo and Combs, *Political Pundits,* 43–44.

18. As Alan Hirsch warns, since success breeds imitation, most commentators "now travel the celebrity path" and probably will not heed the warning of celebrity pundit Jack Germond: "Celebrity impinging on your ability to do your job well is a genuinely serious concern and it requires people to be damned careful." Hirsch, *Talking Heads,* 182–83.

19. As Wayne Munson asks, "Is it 'talk' or 'show'? Conversation or spectacle? Both? Neither?" Wayne Munson, *All Talk: The Talkshow in Media Culture* (Philadelphia: Temple University Press, 1993), 15.

20. Although one might argue that Jimmy Carter, with his outsider positioning and homespun persona, began the current trend, it was Reagan who essentially ran against the job he wanted to occupy. He took anti-politics to a new level, one we are still living through today.

21. Or as Robert Dallek puts it, Reagan's "pronouncements on everything from abortion to welfare proved to be more symbolic than substantive" proving his "extraordinary mastery of public symbols that resonated so effectively with millions of Americans." His "public goals satisf(ied) psychological needs as much as material ends." Robert Dallek, *Ronald Reagan: The Politics of Symbolism* (Cambridge, Mass.: Harvard University Press, 1999), viii, xiv, xxiv.

22. See Allen D. Hertzke, *Echoes of Discontent: Jesse Jackson, Pat Robertson, and the Resurgence of Populism* (Washington, D.C.: Congressional Quarterly Press, 1993).

23. Michael Oreskes, "As Problems Fester, Voters Send Pink Slips," *New York Times,* 23 September 1990, 4:5; John Dillin, "American Voters Disgusted, Angry with Politicians," *The Christian Science Monitor,* 17 October 1990, 1.

24. For analyses of Perot as a "populist," see Dennis Westlind, *The Politics of Popular Identity* (Lund, Sweden: Lund University Press, 1996): Linda Schulte-Sasse, "Meet Ross Perot: The Lasting Legacy of Capraesque Populism," *Cultural Critique* (Fall 1993): 91–119.

25. See Larry King, with Mark Stencel, *On the Line: The New Road to the White House* (New York: Harcourt Brace and Company).

26. Maureen Dowd, "Populist Media Forums and the Campaign of 92," *New York Times,* 3 November 1992, A14.

27. Harvey Mansfield, "Newt, Take Note: Populism Poses Its Own Dangers," *Wall Street Journal,* 1 November 1994, A1. For a more general assessment of the 1990s as a "populist" political era, see Sean Wilentz, "Populism Redux," *Dissent* 42 (Spring 1995): 149–53: Paul Piccone and Gary Ulmen, "Populism and the New Politics," *Telos* 103 (Spring 1995): 3–8. For commentary on how the populist overtones of the decade don't live up to the "true" definition of "populism," see Molly Ivins, "Just What Is a Populist, Anyway?" *Austin-American Statesman,* 6 February 1996, A9; Michael Kazin, *The Populist Persuasion: An American History* (New York: Basic Books, 1995).

28. See E. J. Dionne Jr., *Why Americans Hate Politics* (New York: Simon and Schuster, 1991); Seymour Lipset and William Schneider, *The Confidence Gap,* 2d ed. (Baltimore: Johns Hopkins University Press, 1987); Susan Pharr and Robert Putnam, eds., *Disaffected Democracies: What's Troubling the Trilateral Countries?* (Princeton: Princeton University Press, 2000); Christopher Lasch, *The Revolt of the Elites and the Betrayal of Democracy* (New York: W. W. Norton and Company, 1995).

29. Albert Gore, *Common Sense Government: Works Better and Costs Less* (New York: Random House, 1995); Philip Howard, *The Death of Common Sense: How Law Is Suffocating America* (New York: Random House, 1994).

30. See "Bad Justice," editorial, *New York Times,* 21 February 1995, A18; Joe Klein, "The Birth of Common Sense: Bill Clinton Outflanks the Republicans on Regulatory Reform," *Newsweek* 125, 27 March 1995, 31.

31. David Marshall, *Celebrity and Power: Fame in Contemporary Culture* (Minneapolis: University of Minnesota Press, 1997).

32. In the 1992 presidential election, Thomas Patterson compared ten questions asked of candidates by citizens with ten questions asked by journalists in campaign debates and press conferences. One of the conclusions he arrives at is that the press conducts its business in a language that is foreign to the concerns of the citizenry. Thomas Patterson, *Out of Order* (New York: Random House, 1993), 55–56.

33. For instance, John Thornton Caldwell quotes a former adviser to the FCC and the White House and board member of the National Association of Broadcasters as saying, "'There will be a plethora of niche [cable] networks responsive to the needs of specific cultural groups within our multicultural society.' In addition to providing 'own-

ership opportunities' for minorities, 'these culturally specific niche networks will require management teams that are sensitive and responsive to the needs of their target audience.'" John Thornton Caldwell, *Televisuality: Style, Crisis, and Authority in American Television* (New Brunswick, N.J.: Rutgers University Press, 1995), 257.

34. A representative work of this utopianism is Howard Rheingold, *Virtual Community: Homesteading on the Electronic Frontier* (New York: Simon and Schuster, 1991). For a critical assessment of the false illusions presented by communication technologies, see Theodore Roszak, *The Cult of Information* (Berkeley: University of California Press, 1994). The polarizations of utopianism and distopianism became so pronounced by the end of the decade that a group of "middle-of-the-roaders" went so far as to advance what they call a "technorealism" movement, a manifesto grounded in "reality" that should ground us all. See Andrew Shapiro, "Technorealism: Get Real!" *The Nation* 266, 6 April 1998, 19–20.

35. Todd Gitlin, *The Twilight of Common Dreams: Why America Is Wracked by Culture Wars* (New York: Metropolitan Books, 1995).

36. The impeachment and trial of President Clinton were examples of the culture wars for *New York Times* columnist Frank Rich. He argues, "The cultural fault lines of the moment are those of 30 years ago, and potentially just as explosive. The right-wing rage once aimed at long-haired, draft-dodging, sexually wanton hippies (a caricature of the left even then) is now aimed at Bill Clinton, whose opportunistic, split-the-difference politics is actually closer to the old mainstream G.O.P. than to the 60's left but who nonetheless has become the right's piñata for all it hates about the Vietnam era's social and sexual revolutions." Frank Rich, "Let It Bleed," *New York Times*, 19 December 1998, A15.

37. For a representative example of scholarly works focusing on these types of talk shows, see Munson, *All Talk*; Jane M. Shattuc, *The Talking Cure: TV Talk Shows and Women* (New York: Routledge, 1997); Timberg, *Television Talk*; Andrew Tolson, "Televised Chat and the Synthetic Personality," in *Broadcast Talk*, ed. Paddy Scannell (London: Sage, 1991), among others.

38. See Sonia Livingstone and Peter Lunt, *Talk on Television: Audience Participation and Public Debate* (London: Routledge, 1994); Paolo Carpignano, Robin Anderson, Stanley Aronowitz, and William DiFazio, "Chatter in the Age of Electronic Reproduction: Talk Television and the 'Public Mind,'" in *The Phantom Public Sphere*, ed. Bruce Robbins (Minneapolis: University of Minnesota Press, 1993).

39. Doug McIntyre, a writer and guest on *Politically Incorrect*, once called these shows "human cockfighting." See Joshua Gamson, *Freaks Talk Back: Tabloid Talk Shows and Sexual Nonconformity* (Chicago: University of Chicago Press, 1998); Laura Grindstaff, *The Money Shot: Trash, Class, and the Making of TV Talk Shows* (Chicago: University of Chicago Press, 2002); Kevin Glynn, *Tabloid Culture: Trash Taste, Popular Power, and the Transformation of American Television* (Durham, N.C.: Duke University Press, 2000).

40. See Peter Laufer, *Inside Talk Radio: America's Voice or Just Hot Air* (New York: Carol Publishing Group, 1995), and Howard Kurtz, *Hot Air: All Talk, All the Time* (New York: Times Books, 1996), for accounts of talk radio's success and the personalities that drove it. For an analysis of talk radio's supposed influence on political behavior, see David C. Barker, *Rushed to Judgment: Talk Radio, Persuasion, and American Political Behavior* (New York: Columbia University Press, 2002).

41. Caldwell, *Televisuality*, 292.

42. Caldwell, *Televisuality*, 4.

43. Caldwell, *Televisuality*, 251.

44. Caldwell, *Televisuality*, 256.

45. Carpignano et al., "Chatter."

46. Carpignano et al., "Chatter," 116–17.

47. Livingstone and Lunt, *Talk on Television,* 102.

48. Livingstone and Lunt, *Talk on Television,* 178. They argue that this is occurring in British televised drama, documentary, and current affairs programming.

49. Tolson, "Televised Chat," 198.

50. Munson, *All Talk,* 6.

51. Munson, *All Talk,* 15.

52. Tolson, "Televised Chat," 198.

53. This section is based upon a more complete discussion found in Jeffrey P. Jones, "Vox Populi as Cable Programming Strategy," *Journal of Popular Film & Television* 31 (Spring 2003): 18–28.

54. John Dempsey, "Newest Cable Act Child: America's Talking," *Daily Variety,* 27 June 1994, 32.

55. Rich Brown, "America's Talking Cable Channel Takes Off," *Broadcasting & Cable* 124 (4 July 1994): 16.

56. Scott Williams, "America's Talking—The All-Talk Cable Network—Bows on July 4th," *Associated Press,* 1 July 1994.

57. Dennis Wharton, "Debuting Cable/Sat Net Tuned to the Right," *Daily Variety,* 29 November 1993, 4.

58. Linda Moss, "'C-SPAN with Attitude' Will Launch December 6," *Multichannel News* 14, 15 November 1993, 14.

59. Phil Kloer, "CNN Interactive Program Will Raise Back Talk to a New Level," *Atlanta Journal and Constitution,* 11 July 1994, A1.

60. Marc Rice, "People, Faxes, Computers Debate the Issues on New CNN Program," *The Associated Press.* 22 August 1994.

61. Bob Sokolsky, "'TalkBack Live' Touts Town Meeting Format," *The Press-Enterprise* (Riverside, Calif.), 5 August 1994, B5.

62. Rice, "People, Faxes."

63. CNN cancelled *TalkBack* as America geared up for war on Iraq in 2003. CNN noted the decision for change was based on a "heightened news environment." Yet as America debated the need to go to war when most of its allies did not support such a decision, CNN obviously was uninterested in hearing what viewers and audience members had to say about such a decision. The show averaged between 600,000–700,000 viewers (many over 55 years old). Caroline Wilbert, "CNN Pulls Plug on Afternoon 'TalkBack,' " *Atlanta Journal-Constitution,* 8 March 2003, 1E.

64. As discussed in [a later chapter of *Entertaining Politics* (Lanham, M.D.: Rowman & Littlefield, 2005)].

65. Dan Trigoboff, "3 Nets: News, Views, Confused," *Broadcasting & Cable,* 11 March 2002, 10.

66. That is to say, MSNBC moved from news to almost all talk programming in the summer of 2002. It eventually fired liberal talk host Phil Donahue and tried to imitate Fox News by hiring ultra-conservative hosts such as former Republican Congressman Joe Scarborough. Douglas Quenqua, "MSBNC Shifts Focus from Reporting to Commentary," *PR Week* (10 June 2002): 3.

67. For the typical weekday programming schedule in September 2002, for instance, CNN aired talk shows from 2:00 PM to 5:00 AM (EST), Fox aired talk from 4:00 PM to 6:00 AM and MSNBC aired news only from 9:00 AM–12:00 PM Tim Rutten, "Talk Is Cheap, or at Least Cheaper Than Newscasts," *Los Angeles Times* (7 June 2002): D2.

68. Nimmo and Combs conclude that talk show punditry is persistent in American television because it offers the nation a form of "symbolic healing," providing viewers a therapeutic medicine of symbols and myths in confusing and complex times. Nimmo and Combs, *Political Pundits,* 167–69. The continued prominence of "expert" voices in cable talk programming perhaps reflects this theoretical observation.

69. *Politically Incorrect* began on Comedy Central in 1993, followed by *Dennis Miller Live* on HBO in 1994. *The Daily Show* did not appear until 1996, and Jon Stewart did not fill the "anchor" chair until 1999.

70. *Nightline* on ABC also airs at this time, but with it consistently running third in the ratings, I don't consider it a "dominant" type.

71. Although the first two were cancelled after nine years, both Maher and Miller have reappeared in 2003–2004 with new shows on cable in a similar vein–*Real Time with Bill Maher* (HBO) and *Dennis Miller* (CNBC).

72. Lawrence Christon, "Not For the Humor-Disabled: A Talk Show with No Holds Barred," *The Record,* 7 September 1993, D08.

73. Wayne Walley, "NCTA Surfer: Clashing Opinions Fuel 'Incorrect,'" *Electronic Media,* 8 May 1995, 39.

74. An exception to that claim might be *The Late Late Show* featuring Tom Snyder or *Later with Bob Costas,* but in both instances, those shows were interview programs simply conducted in an informal manner (not to mention the very late time slot in which they appeared).

75. Terry Kelleher, "Comedy Central's Cocktail Party," *Newsday,* 25 July 1993, 3.

76. Jack Tapper, "The Salon Interview: Bill Maher," *Salon.com,* 11 December 2002, http://archive.salon.com/people/interview/2002/12/11/maher/print.html.

77. Tapper, "The Salon Interview."

78. Mary Voelz Chandler, "Dennis Miller Gets the Last Laugh," *Rocky Mountain News,* 16 September 1994, 3D.

79. Ray Richmond, "Saturday Night Live: Dennis Miller Gears Up for HBO," *Los Angeles Times Weekend Magazine,* 26 March 1993, 20.

80. John McKay, "Miller Rants Come to Canadian TV," *The Ottawa Citizen,* 18 January 1999, C11.

81. Terry Morrow, "'The Daily Show' Mocks Presentation of TV News," *Pittsburgh Post-Gazette,* 12 June 2000, D5.

82. David Folkenflik, "Humorists Enter the War Zone," *Baltimore Sun,* 20 April 2003, 2F.

83. Bruce Fretts, "In Jon We Trust," *Entertainment Weekly,* 31 October 2003, 30–35.

84. Rodney Buxton, "The Late-Night Talk Show: Humor in Fringe Television," *The Southern Speech Communication Journal* 52 (Summer 1987): 377–89.

85. Buxton, "The Late-Night Talk Show."

86. Phil Rosenthal, "Worker Bee Dennis Miller Has Jokes, Not Answers," *Tampa Tribune, Florida Television.* 12 May 1996, 7.

87. Stewart explains that the inclusion of celebrities, as opposed to more high-powered political guests, is a product of the show's understaffing; that is, it's easier to do celebrity interviews. "Honestly, one of the reasons that it's there is we just can't write that much. We've tried to make the interview segment somewhat different from what you might see on other [late night shows]. But the truth is, it is what it is and we do the best we can with it. It's not part of the show that any of us necessarily go,

'I can't wait to get hold of that interview segment and make it happen,' " Aaron Wherry, "News and Laughs at 11." *National Post*, 5 October 2002.

88. See audience data in chapter 8 [of *Entertaining Politics* (Lanham, Md.: Rowman & Littlefield, 2005)].

89. *Real Time with Bill Maher*, HBO broadcast, 27 February 2004.

90. Josh Ozersky, "The 'Correct' Thing to Do: Kill the Show," *Newsday*, 27 March 2002.

91. Munson, *All Talk*, 111.

92. Scott Carter, interview by Jeffrey P. Jones, 5 February and 29 March 1999.

93. Indeed, perhaps political television is unique in that it invites certain viewers to watch the show because they explicitly dislike or disagree with certain persons or opinions found there but enjoy the political engagement or rhetorical challenge nonetheless.

94. Don Aucoin, "In the Midnight Hours: A New Generation of Hosts Livens Up the Late Shows," *Boston Globe*, 23 May 1999, N1.

95. Robert Laurence, "Room for Rant: From Stand-up to Sports, Dennis Miller's Trademark Diatribes Belie a Man Riding the Raves of Success," *San Diego Union-Tribune*, 12 August 2001, F1.

96. Bernard Weinraub, "The 2000 Campaign: The Comedians: Election's Barometer: Barbs of Late-Night TV," *New York Times*, 19 January 2000, A16.

97. Dennis Miller, *Ranting Again* (New York: Doubleday, 1998), 143.

98. Judy Woodruff, "Jon Stewart," *Inside Politics*, CNN, 3 May 2002; see also Jane Ganahl, "'Daily Show' Host Jon Stewart is TV's King of Irony," *San Francisco Chronicle*, 23 April 2002, D1, for another response.

99. According to Maher and *Politically Incorrect*'s producers, as well as my own observations of fan comments in viewer mail and on-line, one of the most frequent questions from the audience was why the show lasted only thirty minutes.

100. Stephen Armstrong, "I Can Scratch the Itch," *The Guardian* (London), 17 March 2003, 8.

101. Aucoin, *Midnight Hours*, N1.

Television Melodrama

David Thorburn

> I remember with what a smile of saying something daring and inacceptable John Erskine told an undergraduate class that some day we would understand that plot and melodrama were good things for a novel to have and that *Bleak House* was a very good novel indeed.
>
> Lionel Trilling, *A Gathering of Fugitives*

Although much of what I say will touch significantly on the medium as a whole, I want to focus here on a single broad category of television programming—what *TV Guide* and the newspaper listings, with greater insight than they realize, designate as "melodrama." I believe that at its increasingly frequent best, this fundamental television genre so richly exploits the conventions of its medium as to be clearly distinguishable from its ancestors in the theater, in the novel, and in films. And I also believe, though this more extravagant corollary judgment can only be implied in my present argument, that television melodrama has been our culture's most characteristic aesthetic form, and one of its most complex and serious forms as well, for at least the past decade and probably longer.

Melo is the Greek and word for music. The term *melodrama* is said to have originated as a neutral designation for a spoken dramatic text with a musical accompaniment or background, an offshoot or spin-off of opera. The term came into widespread use in England during the nineteenth century, when it was appropriated by theatrical entrepreneurs as a legal device to circumvent statutes that restricted the performances of legitimate drama to certain theaters. In current popular and (much) learned usage, *melodrama* is a resolutely pejorative term, also originating early in the last century, denoting a sentimental, artificially plotted drama that sacrifices characterization to extravagant

David Thorburn, "Television Melodrama." Reprinted from *Television as a Cultural Force,* ed. Douglass Cater and Richard Adler, by permission of Praeger Publishers, Aspen Institute Program on Communications and Society, and the author. Copyright © 1976 by David Thorburn.

incident, makes sensational appeals to the emotions of its audience, and ends on a happy or at least a morally reassuring note.

Neither the older, neutral nor the current, disparaging definitions are remotely adequate, however. The best recent writings on melodrama, drawing sustenance from a larger body of work concerned with popular culture in general, have begun to articulate a far more complex definition, one that plausibly refuses to restrict melodrama to the theater, and vigorously challenges long-cherished distinctions between high and low culture—even going so far as to question some of our primary assumptions about the nature and possibilities of art itself. In this emerging conception, melodrama must be understood to include not only popular trash composed by hack novelists and filmmakers—Conrad's forgotten rival Stanley Weyman, for example; Jacqueline Susann; the director Richard Fleischer—but also such complex, though still widely accessible, artworks as the novels of Samuel Richardson and Dickens, or the films of Hitchcock and Kurosawa. What is crucial to this new definition, though, is not the actual attributes of melodrama itself, which remain essentially unchanged; nor the extension of melodrama's claims to prose fiction and film, which many readers and viewers have long accepted in any case. What is crucial is the way in which the old dispraised attributes of melodrama are understood, the contexts to which they are returned, the respectful scrutiny they are assumed to deserve.[1]

What does it signify, for example, to acknowledge that the structure of melodrama enacts of fantasy of reassurance, and that the happy or moralistic endings so characteristic of the form are reductive and arbitrary—a denial of our "real" world where events refuse to be coherent and where (as Nabokov austerely says) harm is the norm? The desperate or cunning or spirited stratagems by which this escape from reality is accomplished must still retain a fundamental interest. They must still instruct us, with whatever obliqueness, concerning the nature of that reality from which escape or respite has been sought. Consider the episode of the Cave of Montesinos in *Don Quixote,* in which the hero, no mean melodramatist himself, descends into a cavern to dream or conjure a pure vision of love and chivalry and returns with a tale in which a knight's heart is cut from his breast and salted to keep it fresh for his lady. This is an emblem, a crystallizing enactment, of the process whereby our freest, most necessary fantasies are anchored in the harsh, prosaic actualities of life. And Sancho's suspicious but also respectful and deeply attentive interrogation of Quixote's dream instructs us as to how we might profitably interrogate melodrama.

Again, consider the reassurance-structure of melodrama in relation to two other defining features of the form: its persistent and much-contemned habit of moral simplification and its lust for topicality, its hunger to engage or represent behavior and moral attitudes that belong to its particular day and time, especially behavior shocking or threatening to prevailing moral codes. When critics or viewers describe how television panders to its audience, these qualities of simplification and topicality are frequently cited in evidence. The audience wants to be titillated but also wants to be confirmed in its moral sloth, the argument goes, and so the melodramatist sells stories in which crime and criminals are absorbed into paradigms of moral conflict, into allegories of good and evil, in which the good almost always win. The trouble with such a view is not in what it describes, which is often accurate enough, but in its rush to judgment. Perhaps, as Roland Barthes proposes in his stunning essay on wrestling, we ought to learn to see such texts from the standpoint of the audience, whose pleasures in witnessing these spectacles of excess and grandiloquence may be deeper than we know, and whose intimate familiarity with such texts may lead them to perceive as complex aesthetic conventions what the traditional high culture sees only as simple stereotypes.[2]

Suppose that the reassuring conclusions and the moral allegorizing of melodrama are regarded in this way, as *conventions,* as "rules" of the genre in the same way that the iambic pentameter and the rimed couplet at the end of a sonnet are "rules" for that form. From this angle, these recurring features of melodrama can be perceived as the *enabling conditions* for an encounter with forbidden or deeply disturbing materials: not an escape into blindness or easy reassurance, but an instrument for seeing. And from this angle, melodrama becomes a peculiarly significant public forum, complicated and immensely enriched because its discourse is aesthetic and broadly popular: a forum or arena in which traditional ways of feeling and thinking are brought into continuous, strained relation with powerful intuitions of change and contingency.

This is the spirit in which I turn to television melodrama. In this category I include most made-for-television movies, the soap operas, and all the lawyers, cowboys, cops and docs, the fugitives and adventurers, the fraternal and filial comrades who have filled the prime hours of so many American nights for the last thirty years.[3] I have no wish to deny that these entertainments are market commodities first and last, imprisoned by rigid timetables and stereotyped formulas, compelled endlessly to imagine and reimagine as story and as performance the conventional wisdom, the lies and fantasies, and the muddled ambivalent values of our bourgeois industrial culture. These qualities are, in fact, the primary source of their interest for me, and of the complicated pleasures they uniquely offer.

Confined (but also nourished) by its own foreshortened history and by formal and thematic conventions whose origins are not so much aesthetic as economic, television melodrama is a derivative art, just now emerging from its infancy. It is effective more often in parts of stories than in their wholes, and in thrall to censoring pressures that limit its range. But like all true art, television melodrama is cunning, having discovered (or, more often, stumbled upon) strategies for using the constraints within which it must live.

Its essential artistic resource is the actor's performance, and one explanation—there are many others—for the disesteem in which television melodrama is held is that we have yet to articulate an adequate aesthetics for the art of performance. Far more decisively than the movie-actor, the television-actor creates and controls the meaning of what we see on the screen. In order to understand television drama, and in order to find authentic standards for judging it as art, we must learn to recognize and to value the discipline, energy, and intelligence that must be expended by the actor who succeeds in creating what we too casually call a *truthful* or *believable* performance. What happens when an actor's performance arouses our latent faculties of imaginative sympathy and moral judgment, when he causes us to acknowledge that what he is doing is true to the tangled potency of real experience, not simply impressive or clever, but *true*—what happens then is art.

It is important to be clear about what acting, especially television-acting, is or can be: nothing less than a reverent attentiveness to the pain and beauty in the lives of others, an attentiveness made accessible to us in a wonderfully instructive process wherein the performer's own impulses to self-assertion realize themselves only by surrendering or yielding to the claims of the character he wishes to portray. Richard Poirier, our best theorist of performance, puts the case as follows: "performance . . . is an action which must go through passages that both impede the action and give it form, much as a sculptor not only is impelled to shape his material but is in turn shaped by it, his impulse to mastery always chastened, sometimes made tender and possibly witty by the recalcitrance of what he is working on."[4]

Television has always challenged the actor. The medium's reduced visual scale grants him a primacy unavailable in the theater or in the movies, where an amplitude of things and spaces offers competition for the eye's attention. Its elaborate, enforced obedience to various formulas for plot and characterization virtually require him to recover from within himself and from his broadly stereotyped assignment nuances of gesture, inflection, and movement that will at least hint at individual or idiosyncratic qualities. And despite our failure clearly to acknowledge this, the history of television as a dramatic medium is, at the very least, a history of exceptional artistic accomplishment by actors. The performances in television melodrama today are much richer than in the past, though there were many remarkable performances even in the early days. The greater freedom afforded to writers and actors is part of the reason for this, but (as I will try to indicate shortly) the far more decisive reason is the extraordinary sophistication the genre has achieved.

Lacking access to even the most elementary scholarly resources—bibliographies, systematic collections of films or tapes, even moderately reliable histories of the art—I can only appeal to our (hopefully) common memory of the highly professional and serious acting regularly displayed in series such as *Naked City, Twilight Zone, Route 66, Gunsmoke, The Defenders, Cade's County, Stoney Burke, East Side, West Side, The Name of the Game,* and others whose titles could be supplied by anyone who has watched American television over the past twenty or twenty-five years. Often the least promising dramatic formulas were transformed by vivid and highly intelligent performances. I remember with particular pleasure and respect, for example, Steve McQueen's arresting portrayal of the callow bounty hunter Josh Randall in the western series, *Wanted: Dead or Alive*—the jittery lean grace of his physical movements, the balked, dangerous tenderness registered by his voice and eyes in his encounters with women; the mingling of deference and menace that always enlivened his dealings with older men, outlaws and sheriffs mainly, between whom this memorable boy-hero seemed fixed or caught, but willingly so. McQueen's subsequent apotheosis in the movies was obviously deserved, but I have often felt his performances on the large screen were less tensely intelligent, more self-indulgent than his brilliant early work in television.

If we could free ourselves from our ingrained expectations concerning dramatic form and from our reluctance to acknowledge that art is always a commodity of some kind, constrained by the technology necessary to its production and by the needs of the audience for which it is intended, then we might begin to see how ingeniously television melodrama contrives to nourish its basic resource—the actor—even as it surrenders to those economic pressures that seem most imprisoning.

Consider, for example, the ubiquitous commercials. They are so widely deplored that even those who think themselves friendly to the medium cannot restrain their outrage over such unambiguous evidence of the huckster's contempt for art's claim to continuity. Thus, a writer in the official journal of the National Academy of Television Arts and Sciences, meditating sadly on "the total absence" of serious television drama, refers in passing to "the horrors of continuous, brutal interruption."[5]

That commercials have shaped television melodrama decisively is obvious, of course. But, as with most of the limitations to which the genre is subjected, these enforced pauses are merely formal conventions. They are no more intrinsically hostile to art than the unities observed by the French neoclassical theater or the serial installments in which so many Victorian novels had to be written. Their essential effect has been the refinement of a segmented dramatic structure peculiarly suited to a formula-story whose ending is predictable—the doctor will save the patient, the cop will catch the criminal—and whose capacity to surprise or otherwise engage its audience must therefore depend largely on the localized vividness and potency of the smaller units or episodes that comprise the whole.

Television melodrama achieves this episodic or segmented vividness in several ways, but its most dependable and recurring strategy is to require its actors to display themselves intensely and energetically from the very beginning. In its most characteristic and most interesting form, television melodrama will contrive its separate units such that they will have substantial independent weight and interest, usually enacting in miniature the larger patterns and emotional rhythms of the whole drama. Thus, each segment will show us a character, or several characters, confronting some difficulty or other; the character's behavior and (especially) his emotional responses will intensify, then achieve some sort of climactic or resolving pitch at the commercial break; and this pattern will be repeated incrementally in subsequent segments.

To describe this characteristic structure is to clarify what those who complain of the genre's improbability never acknowledge: that television melodrama is in some respects an *operatic* rather than a conventionally dramatic form—a fact openly indicated by the term *soap opera*. No one goes to Italian opera expecting a realistic plot, and since applause for the important arias is

an inflexible convention, no one expects such works to proceed without interruption. The pleasures of this kind of opera are largely (though not exclusively)
the pleasures of the brilliant individual performance, and good operas in this
tradition are those in which the composer has contrived roles which test as
fully as possible the vocal capacities of the performers.

Similarly, good television melodramas are those in which an intricately formulaic plot conspires perfectly with the commercial interruptions to encourage a rich articulation of the separate parts of the work, and thus to call forth
from the realistic actor the full energies of his performer's gifts. What is implausible in such works is the continual necessity for emotional display by the characters. In real life we are rarely called upon to feel so intensely, and never in
such neatly escalating sequences. But the emotions dramatized by these
improbable plots are not in themselves unreal, or at least they need not be—
and television melodrama often becomes more truthful as it becomes more
implausible.

As an example of this recurring paradox—it will be entirely familiar to any
serious reader of Dickens—consider the following generically typical episode
from the weekly series, *Medical Center*. An active middle-aged man falls victim to an aneurysm judged certain to kill him within a few years. This afflic-
tion being strategically located for dramatic use, the operation that could save
his life may also leave him impotent—a fate nasty enough for anyone, but psychologically debilitating for this unlucky fellow who has divorced his first wife
and married a much younger woman. The early scenes establish his fear of
aging and his intensely physical relationship with his young wife with fine lucid
economy. Now the plot elaborates further complications and develops new,
related central centers of interest. His doctor—the series regular who is (sometimes) an arresting derivation of his television ancestors, Doctors Kildare and
Ben Casey—is discovered to be a close, longtime friend whose involvement in
the case is deeply personal. Confident of his surgeon's skills and much younger
than his patient, the doctor is angrily unsympathetic to the older man's reluctance to save his life at the expense of his sexuality. Next, the rejected wife,
brilliantly played by Barbara Rush, is introduced. She works—by a marvelous
arbitrary coincidence—in the very hospital in which her ex-husband is being
treated. There follows a complex scene in the hospital room in which the former wife acts out her tangled, deep feelings toward the man who has rejected
her and toward the woman who has replaced her. In their tensely guarded
repartee, the husband and ex-wife are shown to be bound to one another in
a vulnerable knowingness made in decades of uneasy intimacy that no divorce
can erase and that the new girl-wife must observe as an outsider. Later scenes
require emotional confrontations—some of them equally subtle—between the
doctor and each wife, between doctor and patient, between old wife and new.

These nearly mathematic symmetries conspire with still further plot complications to create a story that is implausible in the extreme. Though aneurysms
are dangerous, they rarely threaten impotence. Though impotence is a real
problem, few men are free to choose a short happy life of potency, and fewer
still are surrounded in such crises by characters whose relations to them so fully

articulate such a wide spectrum of human needs and attitudes. The test of such an arbitrary contrivance is not plausibility of the whole but the accuracy and truthfulness of its parts, the extent to which its various strategies of artificial heightening permit an open enactment of feelings and desires that are only latent or diffused in the muddled incoherence of the real world. And although my argument does not depend on the success or failure of one or of one dozen specific melodramas—the genre's manifest complexity and its enormous popularity being sufficient to justify intensive and respectful study—I should say that the program just described was for me a serious aesthetic experience. I was caught by the persuasiveness of the actors' performances, and my sympathies were tested by the meanings those fine performances released. The credibility of the young wife's reluctant, pained acknowledgment that a life without sex *would* be a crippled life; the authenticity of the husband's partly childish, partly admirable reverence for his carnal aliveness; and, especially, the complex genuineness of his ambivalent continuing bonds with his first wife—all this was there on the screen. Far from falsifying life, it quickened one's awareness of the burdens and costs of human relationships.

That the plots of nearly all current television melodramas tend, as in this episode of *Medical Center,* to be more artificially contrived than those of earlier years seems to me a measure not of the genre's unoriginality but of its maturity, its increasingly bold and self-conscious capacity to *use* formal requirements which it cannot in any case evade, and to exploit (rather than be exploited by) various formulas for characterization. Nearly all the better series melodramas of recent years, in fact, have resorted quite openly to what might be called a *multiplicity principle:* a principle of plotting or organization whereby a particular drama will draw not once or twice but many times upon the immense store of stories and situations created by the genre's brief but crowded history. The multiplicity principle allows not less but more reality to enter the genre. Where the old formulas had been developed exhaustively and singly through the whole of a story—that is how they became stereotypes—they are now treated elliptically in a plot that deploys many of them simultaneously. The familiar character-types and situations thus become more suggestive and less imprisoning. There is no pretense that a given character has been wholly "explained" by the plot, and the formula has the liberating effect of creating a premise or base on which the actor is free to build. By minimizing the need for long establishing or expository sequences, the multiplicity principle allows the story to leave aside the question of *how* these emotional entanglements were arrived at and to concentrate its energies on their credible and powerful present enactment.

These and other stratagems—which result in richer, more plausible characterizations and also permit elegant variations of tone—are possible because television melodrama can rely confidently on one resource that is always essential to the vitality of any artform: an audience impressive not simply in its numbers but also in its genuine sophistication, its deep familiarity with the history and conventions of the genre. For so literate an audience, the smallest departure from conventional expectations can become meaningful, and this creatures endless chances for surprise and nuanced variation, even for thematic subtlety.

In his instructive book on American films of the forties and fifties, Michael Wood speaks nostalgically of his membership in "the universal movie audience" of that time. This audience of tens of millions was able to see the movies as a coherent world, "a country of familiar faces, . . . a system of assumptions and beliefs and preoccupations, a fund of often interchangeable plots, characters, patches of dialog, and sets." By relying on the audience's familiarity with other movies, Wood says, the films of that era constituted "a living tradition of the kind that literary critics always used to be mourning for."[6]

This description fits contemporary television even more closely than it does those earlier movies, since most members of the TV audience have lived through the whole history of the medium. They know its habits, its formulas, its stars, and its recurring character actors with a confident, easy intimacy that may well be unique in the history of popular art. Moreover, television's capacity to make its history and evolution continuously available (even to younger members in its universal audience) is surely without precedent, for the system of reruns has now reached the point of transforming television into a continuous, living museum which displays for daily or weekly consumption texts from every stage of the medium's past.

Outsiders from the high culture who visit TV melodrama occasionally in order to issue their tedious reports about our cultural malaise are simply not seeing what the TV audience sees. They are especially blind to the complex allusiveness with which television melodrama uses its actors. For example, in a recent episode of the elegant *Columbo* series, Peter Falk's adventures occurred onboard a luxury liner and brought him into partnership with the captain of the ship, played by Patrick Macnee, the smooth British actor who starred in the popular spy series, *The Avengers*. The scenes between Falk and Macnee were continuously enlivened not simply by the different acting styles of the two performers but also by the attitudes toward heroism, moral authority, and aesthetic taste represented in the kinds of programs with which each star has been associated. The uneasy, comic partnership between these characters— Falk's grungy, American-ethnic slyness contrasting with, and finally mocking, Macnee's British public school elegance and fastidiousness—was further complicated by the presence in the show of the guest villain, played by yet another star of a successful TV series of a few years ago—Robert Vaughn of *The Man from U.N.C.L.E.* Vaughn's character had something of the sartorial, upperclass *elan* of Macnee's ship's master but, drawing on qualities established in his earlier TV role, was tougher, wholly American, more calculating, and ruthless. Macnee, of course, proved no match for Vaughn's unmannerly cunning, but Falk-Columbo succeeded in exposing him in a climax that expressed not only the show's usual fantasy of working-class intelligence overcoming aristocratic guile, but also the victory of American versions of popular entertainment over their British counterparts.

The aesthetic and human claims of most television melodrama would surely be much weakened, if not completely obliterated, on any other medium, and I have come to believe that the species of melodrama to be found on television today is a unique dramatic form, offering an especially persuasive resolution of the contradiction or tension that has been inherent in melodrama since the time of Euripides. As Peter Brooks reminds us in his provocative essay on the centrality of the melodramatic mode in romantic and modern culture, stage melodrama represents "a popular form of the tragic, exploiting similar emotions within the context of the ordinary." Melodrama is a "popular" form, we may say, both because it is favored by audiences and because it insists (or tries to insist) on the dignity and importance of the ordinary, usually bourgeois world of the theatergoer himself. The difficulty with this enterprise, of course, is the same for Arthur Miller in our own day as it was for Thomas Middleton in Jacobean London: displacing the action and characters from a mythic or heroically stylized world to an ordinary world—from Thebes to Brooklyn—involves a commitment to a kind of realism that is innately resistant to exactly those intense passionate enactments that the melodramatist wishes to invoke. Melodrama is thus always in conflict with itself, gesturing simultaneously toward ordinary reality *and* toward a moral and emotional heightening that is rarely encountered in the "real" world.

Although it can never be made to disappear, this conflict is minimized, or is capable of being minimized, by television—and in a way that is simply impossible in the live theater and that is nearly always less effective on the enlarged movie-screen. The melodramatic mode is peculiarly congenial to television, its inherent contradictions are less glaring and damaging there, because the medium is uniquely hospitable to the spatial confinements of the theater and to the profound realistic intimacy of the film.

Few would dispute the cinema's advantages over the theater as realistic medium. As every serious film begins of reminding us, the camera's ability to record the dense multiplicity of the external world and to reveal character in all its outer nuance and idiosyncrasy grants a visually authenticating power to the medium that has no equivalent in the theater. Though the stage owns advantages peculiar to its character as a live medium, it is clearly an artform more stylized, less visually realistic than the film, and it tests its performers in a somewhat different way. Perhaps the crucial difference is also the most obvious one: the distance between the audience and the actor in even the most intimate theatrical environment requires facial and vocal gestures as well as bodily movements "broader" and more excessive than those demanded by the camera, which can achieve a lover's closeness to the performer.

The cinema's photographic realism is not, of course, an unfixed blessing. But it is incalculably valuable to melodrama because, by encouraging understatement from its actors, it can help to ratify extravagant or intense emotions that would seem far less credible in the theater. And although television is the dwarf child of the film, constrained and scaled down in a great many ways, its very smallness can become an advantage to the melodramatic imagination. This is so because if the cinema's particularizing immediacy is friendly to melodrama, certain other characteristics of the medium are hostile to it. The extended duration of most film, the camera's freedom of movement, the more-than-life-sized dimensions of the cinematic image—all these create what has been called the film's mythopoeic tendency, its inevitable effect of magnification. Since the natural domain of melodrama is indoors, in those ordinary and enclosed spaces wherein most of us act out our deepest needs and feelings—bedrooms, offices, courtrooms, hospitals—the reduced visual field of television is, or can be, far more nourishing than the larger, naturally expansive movie-screen. And for the kind of psychologically nuanced performance elicited by good melodrama, the smaller television screen would seem even more appropriate: perfectly adapted, in fact, to record those intimately minute physical and vocal gestures on which the art of the realistic actor depends, yet happily free of the cinema's malicious (if often innocent) power to transform merely robust nostrils into Brobdingnagian caverns, minor facial irregularities into craterous deformities.

Television's matchless respect for the idiosyncratic expressiveness of the ordinary human face and its unique hospitality to the confining spaces of our ordinary world are virtues exploited repeatedly in all the better melodramas. But perhaps they are given special decisiveness in *Kojak,* a classy police series whose gifted leading player has been previously consigned almost entirely to gangster parts, primarily (one supposes) because of the cinema's blindness to the uncosmetic beauty of his large bald head and generously irregular face. In its first two years particularly, before Savalas's character stiffened into the macho stereotype currently staring out upon us from magazine advertisements for razor blades and men's toiletries, *Kojak* was a genuine work of art, intricately designed to exploit its star's distinctively urban flamboyance, his gift for registering a long, modulated range of sarcastic vocal inflections and facial maneuvers, his talent for persuasive ranting. The show earned its general excellence not only because of Savalas's energetic performance, but also because its writers contrived supporting roles that complemented the central character with rare, individuating clarity, because the boldly artificial plotting in most episodes pressed toward the revelation of character rather than shoot-em-up action, and because, finally, the whole enterprise was forced into artfulness by the economic and technological environment that determined its life.

This last is at once the most decisive and most instructive fact about *Kojak,* as it is about television melodrama generally. Because *Kojak* is filmed in Hollywood on a restricted budget, the show must invoke New York elliptically, in ingenious process shots and in stock footage taken from the full-length (and much less impressive) television-movie that served as a pilot for the series. The writers for the program are thus driven to devise stories that will allow the principle characters to appear in confined locations that can be created on or near studio sound-stages—offices, interrogation rooms, dingy bars, city apartments, nondescript alleys, highway underpasses, all the neutral and enclosed spaces common to urban life generally. As a result, *Kojak* often succeeds in projecting a sense of the city that is more compelling and intelligent than that which is offered in many films and television movies filmed on location: its menacing closeness, its capacity to harbor and even to generate certain kinds of crime, its watchful, unsettling accuracy as a custodian of the lists and records and documents that open a track to the very center of our lives. *Kojak's* clear superiority to another, ostensibly more original and exotic police series, *Hawaii Five-O,* is good partial evidence for the liberating virtues of such confinement. This latter series is filmed on location at enormous expense and is often much concerned to give a flavor of Honolulu particularly. Yet it yields too easily to an obsession with scenic vistas and furious action sequences which threaten to transform the program into a mere travelogue and which always seem unnaturally confined by the reduced scale of the television screen.

That the characters in *Kojak* frequently press beyond the usual stereotypes is also partly a result of the show's inability to indulge in all the outdoor muscle-flexing, chasing, and shooting made possible by location filming. Savalas's Kojak especially is a richly individuated creation, his policeman's cunning a natural expression of his lifelong, intimate involvement in the very ecology of the city. A flamboyant, aggressive man, Kojak is continually engaged in a kind of joyful contest for recognition and even for mastery with the environment that surrounds him. The studio sets on which most of the action occurs, and the many close-up shots in each episode, reinforce and nurture these traits perfectly, for they help Savalas to work with real subtlety—to project not simply his character's impulse to define himself against the city's enclosures but also a wary, half-loving respect for such imprisonments, a sense indeed that they are the very instrument of his self-realization.

Kojak's expensive silk-lined suits and hats and the prancing vitality of his physical movements are merely the outer expressions of what is shown repeatedly to be an enterprise of personal fulfillment that depends mostly on force of intellect. His intelligence is not bookish—the son of a Greek immigrant, he never attended college—but it is genuine and powerfully self-defining because he must depend on his knowledge of the city in order to prevent a crime or catch a criminal. Proud of his superior mental quickness and urban knowingness, Kojak frequently behaves with the egotistical flair of a bold, demanding scholar, reveling in his ability to instruct subordinates in how many clues they have overlooked and even (in one episode) performing with histrionic brilliance as a teacher before a class of students at the police academy. Objecting to this series because it ratifies the stereotype of the super-cop is as silly as objecting to Sherlock Holmes on similar grounds. Like Holmes in many ways, Kojak is a man who realizes deeply private needs and inclinations in the doing of his work. Not law-and-order simplicities, but intelligence and self-realization are what *Kojak* celebrates. The genius of the series is to have conceived a character whose portrayal calls forth from Savalas exactly what his appearance and talents most suit him to do.

The distinction of *Kojak* in its first two seasons seems to me reasonably representative of the achievements of television melodrama in recent years. During the past season, I have seen dozens of programs—episodes of *Harry-O, Police Story, Baretta, Medical Center*, the now-defunct *Medical Story*, several made-for-TV movies, and portions at least of the new mini-series melodramas being developed by ABC—whose claims to attention were fully as strong as *Kojak's*. Their partial but genuine excellence constitutes an especially salutary reminder of the fact that art always thrives on restraints and prohibitions, indeed that it requires them if it is to survive at all. Like the Renaissance sonnet or Racine's theater, television melodrama is always most successful when it most fully embraces that which confines it, when *all* the limitations imposed upon it—including such requirements as the sixty- or ninety-minute time slot, the commercial interruptions, the small dimensions of the screen, even the consequences of low-budget filming—become instruments of use, conventions whose combined workings create unpretentious and spirited dramatic entertainments, works of popular art that are engrossing, serious, and imaginative.

That such honorific adjectives are rarely applied to television melodrama, that we have effectively refused even to consider the genre in aesthetic terms is a cultural fact and, ultimately, a political fact almost as interesting as the artworks we have been ignoring. Perhaps because television melodrama is an authentically popular art—unlike rubber hamburgers, encounter group theater or electric-kool-aid journalism—our understanding of it has been conditioned (if not thwarted entirely) by the enormous authority American high culture grants to avant-garde conceptions of the artist as an adversary figure in mortal conflict with his society. Our attitude toward the medium has been conditioned also by even more deeply ingrained assumptions about the separate high dignity of aesthetic experience—an activity we are schooled to imagine as uncontaminated by the marketplace, usually at enmity with the everyday world, and dignified by the very rituals of payment and dress and travel and isolation variously required for its enjoyment. It is hard, in an atmosphere which accords art a special if not an openly subversive status, to think of television as an aesthetic medium, for scarcely another institution in American life is at once so familiarly *un*special and so profoundly a creature of the economic and technological genius of advanced industrial capitalism.

Almost everything that is said or written about television, and especially about television drama, is tainted by such prejudices; more often it is in utter servitude to them. And although television itself would no doubt benefit significantly if its nature were perceived and described more objectively, it is the larger culture—whose signature is daily and hourly to be found there—that would benefit far more.

In the introduction to *The Idea of a Theater,* Francis Fergusson reminds us that genuinely popular dramatic art is always powerfully conservative in certain ways, offering stories that insist on "their continuity with the common sense of the community." Hamlet could enjoin the players to hold a mirror up to nature, "to show . . . the very age and body of the time his form and pressure" because, Fergusson tells us, "the Elizabethan theater was itself a mirror which had been formed at the center of the culture of its time, and at the center of the life and awareness of the community." That we have no television Shakespeare is obvious enough, I guess. But we do already have our Thomas Kyds and our Chapmans. A Marlowe, even a Ben Jonson, is not inconceivable. It is time we noticed them.[7]

Notes

1. The bibliography of serious recent work on melodrama is not overly intimidating, but some exciting and important work has been done. I list here only pieces that have directly influenced my present argument, and I refer the reader to their notes and bibliographies for a fuller survey of the scholarship. Earl F. Bargainnier summarizes

recent definitions of melodrama and offers a short history of the genre as practiced by dramatists of the eighteenth and nineteenth centuries in "Melodrama as Formula," *Journal of Popular Culture* 9 (Winter, 1975). John G. Cawelti's indispensable *Adventure, Mystery, and Romance* (Chicago, 1976) focuses closely and originally on melodrama at several points. Peter Brooks's "The Melodramatic Imagination," in *Romanticism: Vistas, Instances, Continuities,* ed. David Thorburn and Geoffrey Hartman (Cornell, 1973), boldly argues that melodrama is a primary literary and visionary mode in romantic and modern culture. Much recent Dickens criticism is helpful on melodrama, but see especially Robert Garis, *The Dickens Theatre* (Oxford, 1965), and essays by Barbara Hardy, George H. Ford, and W. J. Harvey in the Dickens volume of the Twentieth-Century Views series, ed. Martin Price (Prentice-Hall, 1967). Melodrama's complex, even symbiotic linkages with the economic and social institutions of capitalist democracy are a continuing (if implicit) theme of Ian Watt's classic *The Rise of the Novel* (University of California Press, 1957), and of Leo Braudy's remarkable essay on Richardson, "Penetration and Impenetrability in Clarissa," in *New Approaches to Eighteenth-Century Literature,* ed. Phillip Harth (Columbia University Press, 1974).

2. Roland Barthes, "The World of Wrestling," in *Mythologies,* trans. Annette Lavers (Hill and Wang, 1972). I am grateful to Jo Anne Lee of the University of California, Santa Barbara, for making me see the connection between Barthes's notions and television drama.

3. I will not discuss soap opera directly, partly because its serial nature differentiates it in certain respects from the prime-time shows, and also because this interesting subgenre of TV melodrama has received some preliminary attention from others. See, for instance, Frederick L. Kaplan, "Intimacy and Conformity in American Soap Opera," *Journal of Popular Culture* 9 (Winter, 1975); Renata Adler, "Afternoon Television: Unhappiness Enough and Time," *The New Yorker 47* (February 12, 1972); Marjorie Perloff, "Soap Bubbles." *The New Republic* (May 10, 1975); and the useful chapter on the soaps in Horace Newcomb's pioneering (if tentative) *TV, The Most Popular Art* (Anchor, 1974). Newcomb's book also contains sections on the prime-time shows I am calling melodramas. For an intelligent fan's impressions of soap opera, see Dan Wakefield's *All Her Children* (Doubleday, 1976).

4. Richard Poirier, *The Performing Self* (Oxford, 1971), p. xiv. I am deeply indebted to this crucial book, and to Poirier's later elaborations on this theory of performance in two pieces on ballet and another on Bette Midler (*The New Republic,* January 5, 1974; March 15, 1975; August 2 and 9, 1975).

5. John Houseman, "TV Drama in the U.S.A.," *Television Quarterly* 10 (Summer, 1973), p. 12.

6. Michael Wood, *America in the Movies* (Basic Books, 1975), pp. 10–11.

7. Though they are not to be held accountable for the uses to which I have put their advice, the following friends have read earlier versions of this essay and have saved me from many errors: Sheridan Blau, Leo Braudy, John Cawelti, Peter Clecak, Howard Felperin, Richard Slotkin, Alan Stephens, and Eugene Waith.

PART 4

Audiences, Viewers, Users

The search for meaningful ways to understand how people view, understand, and perhaps "use" television has been a major aspect of television studies for more than three decades. Variously approached as questions of "reception" or "interpretation," or "active viewership," as well as in some instances, as a matter of "effects," a range of approaches has filled gaps in our knowledge in this area. Debates have circulated around whether or not it is even important to know how individuals deal with television, given more expansive issues of ideology, corporate control, or conventional content.

The essays in this section refuse to ignore the role of audiences/viewers/users. Equally important, however, they study these processes with full awareness of the large issues involved. They represent a continuing commitment to probing a complex intellectual problem and represent a range of possible approaches to that problem.

Ron Lembo comes to the issues of television use from a fully developed sociological perspective. Wary of large generalizations on the one hand and of small-scale individualistic accounts on the other, he establishes modes of viewing that are linked to other daily activities. The richness of this strategy is that it both demystifies the act(s) of viewing television, yet notes with precision how viewing is its own form of behavior. He adopts the term "sociality" to describe and partially define television use. The sociality of the viewing culture describes the "complexity of meaning that is involved in people's day-to-day television use." While this may seem an obvious conclusion, Lembo turns it to powerful advantage in placing his own analysis alongside other approaches to viewer activity.

Annette Hill examines audiences with a different sociological strategy, relying on survey data as well as interviews. She also places her primary object of study, *Big Brother*, in relation to other forms of "factual entertainment," other "gamedocs" such as *Survivor*, as well as programming built around crime, medical, or makeover content. Her conclusions are not meant to establish large-scale explanations of what television viewing "means." Rather, her analysis is particularly valuable for explaining particular viewing strategies developed for understanding and enjoying particular program types. If we assume that many, if not most, television viewers master multiple viewing strategies, Hill's approach can be adapted to analysis of other viewing contexts. In the end, this type of analysis is not so far removed from Lembo's attempts to generalize viewing behaviors. His own work indicates a similar strategic "use" on the part of television viewers. The more we know of such specific contexts, the better our map of the problem of television viewing.

That figurative map is expanded geographically and culturally by the next two essays, Antonio C. La Pastina's "Telenovela Reception in Rural Brazil: Gendered Readings and Sexual Mores," and "Sex Appeal and Cultural Liberty: A Feminist Inquiry into MTV India," by Jocelyn Cullity and Prakash Younger. Both studies use detailed interview techniques. In La Pastina's case these interviews might best be understood as part of an "ethnographic" project in which he lived in the same context he was studying. His study focuses on a specific text, a popular *telenovela*, and suggests that "geographical isolation and the local patriarchal culture mediated the process of reception, interpretation, and appropriation of telenovelas." Significantly, Cullity and Younger examine the "global" spread of television of a particular sort. Their interviews were supplemented with participant observation in the MTV India studios and surveys administered to a number of groups. In their words, "the main body of the essay illustrates how MTV India programming is understood to affirm the primacy of the local and is perceived to provide an empowering 'space' for young, middle-class women." Each of these essays is significant for the precision of its analysis. Like other approaches to both texts and viewers, these acknowledge opportunities while never diminishing problematic aspects of television production, distribution, and use. While it may be the case that few readers of this collection will engage in audience studies in such specific international settings, the models provided here can be applied in any "local" context.

Kim Bjarkman takes audience studies into a new direction. The focus on "fans" is hardly surprising, of course. What is innovative here is the linkage between "fandom" and the ability of fans to "collect," to "archive," to become expert in special areas. Given that for a substantial portion of its history television was considered an "ephemeral" medium, a medium that offered up "content" or "programs," "series," or "shows" that could only be recalled, remembered, discussed, the advent of recording devices such as the videotape recorder opened new possibilities. Bjarkman conducted extended interviews with three collectors. Each is in some way a specialist. Each has developed a rationale, almost a philosophy of collecting and archiving, rationales and philosophies that extend to modes of documentation and categorization. And while the information presented here is significant as a mode of audience behavior and as indication once again of the difficulties involved in generalizing too widely about "viewing" or about "audiences," it is also important for demonstrating the difficulties involved in capturing television's "past."

That the past is taken as valuable is in itself a form of audience practice, one that engages broader cultural assumptions about the value of the medium and its offerings. Those are, of course, the issues underlying this entire collection of essays. Analysis and criticism, the development of "television studies" are all evidence of viewership, use, reception. Essays in the next section address some of these issues more directly.

Components of a Viewing Culture

Ron Lembo

The social experience of people who watch television has not been conceptualized or documented adequately by social theorists, social scientists, or, more recently, by cultural studies analysts. In contrast to earlier sociological views, cultural studies does, in fact, accord television watching a legitimate place in its account of power, but it fails to adequately theorize the context of television watching as a new and distinctive cultural form. While cultural studies tends to examine texts as exemplars of ideology or discursive power, understanding them in terms of the social and historical conditions under which they are produced, I argue that, unless critical analysts generate categories of reception, of use, that can document the social function of television, the emphasis on textual reading among audience members remains incomplete and perhaps misses what is arguably most important about television use.

I use the construct of *sociality* to incorporate and move beyond ideas about discourse and textuality, and to systematically explore how television is used in ways that allow me to focus on more than just the dynamics of power and resistance, at least as they have typically been formulated in cultural studies' accounts. My strategy is to work through ideas about power by grounding them empirically in reconstructions of the practical uses that people make of television on a day-to-day basis.

The social world of television use is no doubt a complicated one. Its complexities—the differences in mindfulness that emerge there, the variety of ways that people construct social relations with others, as well as the ways that television fits with everything else that people do in their everyday lives—are certainly understandable as power effects, but not *only* as power effects. The language that we use to analyze and account for the complexities of this world must be able to say, with clarity and precision, what *else,* besides power and resistance, they are about.

Generally speaking, conceptualizing television use involves reconstructing the practical ways that people who watch television situate themselves with the medium on a day-in, day-out basis. Contrary to appearances, television use is a multifaceted activity, one that is much more complicated than meets the eye.

Ron Lembo, "Components of a Viewing Culture." Reprinted from Ron Lembo, *Thinking Through Television,* Cambridge University Press (2000), pp. 99–113. Reprinted with the permission of Cambridge University Press.

Assessing its meaning for people and the significance it carries in their lives involves nothing short of the analytical reconstruction of it as a distinctive kind of culture. I have referred to this elsewhere as "the viewing culture" (1994).

The sociality of the viewing culture can best be understood by proceeding in the following way. First, analysts must recognize that television is a powerful medium, that its power works simultaneously through multiple symbolic forms, and that the objective structuring of those forms can be documented empirically. There is a long line of work, both inside and outside of cultural studies, that understands power as a constituent feature of television, and this work must be incorporated into any analysis of the viewing culture. But, because people typically approach television practically rather than analytically, the medium's power is not their primary concern, even though they recognize at times the influence that it has in their lives. For this reason, it is best that the reconstruction of their television use *not* begin by focusing directly on issues of power (or resistance). The second strategy follows from this idea. Analysts of the viewing culture must be cognizant of television's power, but they must then set aside power constructs in order to examine how particular kinds of viewers, whose lives are situated in particular ways, concretely construct their own meaningful relations with television. Once this reconstruction of the various kinds of routine practices that are involved in television use is underway, power constructs can then be brought back into the picture by looking at how television and its symbolism works to construct the sociality of those viewing practices.

The Turn to Television

Typically, individuals must come to television from some other aspect of their lives, and, similarly, they must turn off the set and fit television back into their lives. This progression, from turning to television, to interacting with it, to leaving it and fitting it back in one's life is the basic cultural pattern in which viewers make their experience with television meaningful. When a person thinks about watching television, it is usually in a specific situation and often has something to do with what that person is thinking and feeling. Different things may go through different people's minds and they may feel a variety of things as they go about the business of situating themselves with television or in choosing to do other things. For various reasons, some of these situations, along with the thoughts and feelings that people have in them, recur regularly. Over time, particular situations, with their accompanying thoughts and feelings, serve as typical points of departure for watching television or engaging in any number of other activities. Turning to television, like turning to other activities, becomes a ritual part of people's everyday life. Because it takes shape amidst a multitude of factors that constitute the contingencies of daily living, the turn to television carries meaning on its own terms, quite apart from viewing itself. Furthermore, because turning to television becomes a habit, a ritual, it in turn shapes the contours of the broader context of people's lives. And, finally, it is this broader context of a person's life, including the place that television use has within it, that shapes in important ways the meaning of viewing itself.

To understand the meaning that turning to television has for people, analysts must consider more concretely just what is involved, socially speaking, in the situational contexts that give rise to television use. Since people do not ordinarily organize their lives exclusively around television: analysts must proceed by first stepping back from any inquiry into the turn to television per se, and instead gain some understanding of what it is that people do with the rest of their lives. Do they work? If so, what shift do they work? Does the shift vary or stay the same over time? If they are not compelled to do shift work, do they keep regular hours none the less? If so, what are they? What do they actually do at work? What are the pros and cons of the job? If people do not work for employers outside the home, how is it that they support themselves?—or, if this is not an issue for them, then analysts must inquire as to how they typically structure their day. Are they self-employed? Is their day structured around child care and household responsibilities? Do they attend school regularly? My research focused on working people, and as you might expect, work outside the home was certainly central to the way that they organized their everyday lives. But I also found that household work, child-care responsibilities, and the comings and goings of school-age children were independent factors that worked in conjunction with employment schedules to constitute people's everyday routines within the home. The interrelationship of work, family, and household routines is what structures the availability of free time for people, and in this way it constitutes an important, initial component of the structural contexts that can serve as a point of departure for their turn to television.

Once this more basic structuring of situational contexts is understood, the meaningful complexity of the contexts themselves must be accounted for. Even at this broad level of analysis, analysts do not want to focus exclusively on the turn to television because, in any given situation, people can just as easily turn to a variety of other activities, including hobbies, crafts, the use of other media, as well as visits with neighbors, family, or friends in order to relax and enjoy themselves. Once something of people's work, family, and household routines are known, analysts can then inquire as to which situations typically provide people with the opportunity to watch television or do any number of other things, too. What do people do before work, after work, before school, after school, before dinner, after dinner, late at night, on Saturday or Sunday afternoons? These are the more objective determinants of the situations that need to be accounted for. For any typical situation, determining the significance that turning to television holds for people is best accomplished by first accounting for where viewing fits amidst these other activities. In any given situation, it matters if people turn exclusively to television, if it is one activity chosen among other non-media activities on a regular basis, or, if it is turned to relatively infrequently.

As I said earlier, the power of television to shape people's experience must become a part of this analysis. Television is first and foremost an object of consumption. It is purchased in the market-place and, depending on the model, the make, and its specific features, the television set by itself can serve as a marker of status and consumer well-being. In comparison to friendships, family relations, hobbies, crafts, and even household chores and responsibilities, the turn to television, like the turn to radio, exposes people to discourses of consumption and orients them to the market-place, whether or not they are persuaded to buy products or identify with the imagery being sold. The simple questions of how often and for how long television is turned to, are important indicators of the ways in which discourses of consumption are extended into the private and personal space of the home. By situating the turn to television amidst the routine choices that people make in carrying out their daily activities, the analyst is able to document how television works differently in different people's lives to extend these discourses of consumption into their meaningful experience.

Beyond this recognition that television use exists as one among many activities, analysts face the far more difficult task of documenting the mindful and emotional qualities exhibited by viewers at different stages of their turn both to television and to other activities; and, beyond that, they must also be able to assess where it is that people end up, mindfully speaking, after they have become involved in watching television or doing other things. Are people typically feeling tired, bored, anxious, alert, relaxed, or some other way when they turn to television in any given situation? Do they typically feel the same, similar, or different when they turn to any of a variety of other activities in these same situations? Furthermore, we need to know more about how people decide to watch television and do other things. How mindful are they in turning to television or to other activities at different times? Television viewers that I have interviewed often display or express knowledge of having engaged in decision-making processes that range from sheer habit to highly reflective ones as they orient themselves to television and to other activities. Is the turn to television or to other activities done out of habit, for escapist pleasure, with an eye toward a playful kind of interactive engagement, or perhaps to engage oneself more seriously in whatever it is that one chooses to do? By documenting the mindfulness involved in turning to television and comparing it with the mindfulness exhibited in turning to other activities, the more concrete conditions in which people bring television into their lives can be analytically reconstructed. We gain insight into the meaning of television use that simply would not be possible if we were to focus directly on viewing or if we were to examine only the turn to television, without examining how it is situated amidst other activities. Examining the specific, mindful ways that people typically turn to television and other activities can tell us something about how their capabilities to act as a self are realized differently in their everyday lives.

Since turning to television is not all that people do in their time away from work, school, child care, and household responsibilities, analysts also need to assess where it is that people typically end up in these different situations by comparing the mindfulness of their involvement in television viewing and other activities. Different activities may have differing potentials when it comes to how mindful people can be while they take part in them, and some charting and profiling of this is in order if we wish to comparatively analyze the meaning of television use. When it comes to activities, I have found it to be especially important to determine whether or not the participation is active or passive, if the person can control the pace, if he or she is able to integrate their participation from one occasion to the next—that is, if the activity has a developmental course—and the degree to which the person is able to be reflective and gain insight about themselves, their society, or their environment. Taken together, participation, pace, developmental course, and possibility for insight are important dimensions of any activities, and their documentation will enable a comparative analysis of the actual activities, including television viewing, that people routinely become involved in.

Television Interaction

Once television is turned to as an activity, the real-life context that may have shaped the turn does not recede completely into the background. Yet, the attention of viewers tends to be focused on television imagery. Despite the apparent simplicity of much television programming and the taken-for-granted nature of the set's presence in people's homes, the viewing culture is, in fact, a quite complex social world. In attempting to determine the meaning of viewing per se, there are numerous factors to consider, including the ways in which the different symbolic forms of programming work in constituting the mindful and emotional quality of viewing relations, and how the meaning of these viewing relations, may be constituted differently depending upon whether or not people watch alone or with others.

In discussing the turn to television, I pointed out that it was necessary for the analyst to recognize the structuring role that television often plays in exposing people to discourses of selling and consumption on a scale and with a repetitiveness that is unmatched by their involvement in other activities, save perhaps for radio listening and shopping itself. This is true, too, with what I am calling viewing relations: the analyst must be able to determine something of the power that these particular discourses have in ordering and organizing people's mindful and emotional experience. But analysts must do more than that, too. In order to consider how television works once people have turned to it, they obviously need to focus more directly on their viewing relations. And it is important that they do so by first accounting for the complexity of the symbolic forms that comprise programming, since the meaning of viewing is constituted in large part by the mindful involvement that people have with these symbolic forms.

The Symbolic Forms of Programming

Discursive Symbolism

In the first place, there are numerous levels of what we might term a "persuasive logic" that typify the marketing strategies of various individuals, groups, and corporate entities. For example, there are the advertisers, politicians, televangelists, and direct marketers whose symbolism ranges from hard-sell pitches to the more comforting imagery of national brand advertising manufactured by Madison Avenue firms; there is the image-making and rhetoric of politicians; the personalities that bring infomercials to life; the promotional pitches for upcoming films and television shows; and, most recently, the seemingly never-ending stream of goods and testimonials that comprise the home-shopping networks. The strategies may be more rational, relying primarily on words to convey the correctness of purchasing decisions, or more emotional, relying instead on the feel of visual imagery to suggest in subtle and sometimes unrecognizable ways the pleasure and satisfaction to be had through association with the product. Symbolically speaking, the net effect of all of this strategizing is to make it possible for viewers to experience varied encounters with the goods and imagery of selling on a continuous basis.

Then there are the conventions of story-telling to consider. Typically, it is realism along with genre, plot, and characterization that serve as the most important focal points of people's attention, since these are the features that are most salient in the representation of social action as if it were real. They provide the symbolic basis for a wide range of people's interpretations of programming, including what in the scenes, stories, and characterizations they find to be plausible as well as what they deem worthy of criticism. In a typical home, television programming provides people with a wide range and increasingly eclectic mix of story-telling conventions that are now available on upwards of forty channels simultaneously. At all levels—scenes, characterizations, plots—story-telling conventions can be more or less formulaic, depending upon the degree to which marketing considerations predominate over craft concerns in shaping programming. Story-telling conventions are intertextual as well, frequently making reference to depictions of plot and characterization found in films, previous television programs, and in the production of celebrity more generally. This layering of possible meanings in the symbolism of story-telling conventions adds up to rather complex depictions of social life in which the reference points for meaning-making on the part of people can shift quite easily from the real to the intertextual to the real over the course of any particular viewing session. Both persuasive messages and story-telling conventions refer to ideas about social life that unfold temporally as action develops in programming.

Presentational Symbolism

In using the term presentational symbolism, I have adopted Suzanne Langer's (1957) term to focus attention on how images may evoke or signify meaning without relying on the linear or temporal development that we typically associate with the workings of story-telling conventions or persuasive messages.

One kind of presentational symbolism is the esthetics of visual imagery. The work of creative people, including the writing of dialogue, the appearance and performance of actors, the impression made by visual images, including the effects of lighting, composition, camera angles, and color contrasts, as well as editing techniques that result in various kinds of juxtapositions and movements of visual images—all of this presents itself to the people who watch as a distinctive kind of symbolism. It provides an objective basis in people forming a range of mindful and emotional relationships with programming. But these mindful and emotional relationships do not necessarily exhibit the unfolding of meaning that we typically find in people's encounters with either persuasive symbolism or the symbolism of story-telling conventions. From the standpoint of the people who watch, the esthetics work by way of a spatial rather than a temporal logic. The unfolding of social action is not needed for programming to become meaningful. Visual imagery works along the lines of what Walter Benjamin (1968) described as the "shock effect" of the film: emotionally powerful encounters that stimulate people's imaginative powers, perhaps leading to brief moments in which many different meanings are superimposed, one upon the other, as they call to mind multiple associations they may have with imagery.

Another kind of presentational symbolism consists of depictions of cultural life in which meaning may be more visual than ideational. This includes visual imagery that may serve as a premise for scenes of social action within a show; as a more visually oriented starting-point for the plausibility that is necessary if viewers are to involve themselves in a story; or simply as looks or actions that are repeated across different genres of programming and across different programs within genres and are recognizable as such by people. For example, the combination of furniture, decor, layout, and architecture of home interiors lends a decidedly upper-middle-class quality to the settings of shows. Similarly, the combination of mannerisms, modes of dress, hair styles, and facial features, among other things, conveyed in the image projected by a good many characters on television, signifies the middle and upper-middle classness, the conventional gender distinctions, and the heterosexual orientation of the characters that populate these shows.

By referring to these kinds of depictions of cultural life as "presentational," I am attempting to clarify how the symbolism of programming works in ways that do not seem to demand the same kind of attentiveness that we typically associate with the interpretations of persuasive messages or story-telling conventions. While each depiction of cultural life or impression made by visual imagery may be traceable to the intentions of creative people, including a show's producers, or to programmers, the broader patterning of these depictions and impressions need not be intentional, and yet the patterns do exist, objectively, and can be documented empirically as a form of symbolism available for meaning-making by the people who watch. These patterns of presentational symbolism are closer to what Deleuze (Deleuze and Parnet, 1987) and others have called "assemblages": the patterns of cultural life that are produced unconsciously and thereby emerge from a place beneath or beyond intentionality. For Deleuze and others, these patterns take their place in the realm of what is cultural.

Commodity Forms of Symbolism

Finally, there are what I term the commodity forms of symbolism that serve as the most direct extensions of a marketing logic in programming. In the business of television, network executives and programmers are most concerned with maintaining and expanding market shares for their product. By doing so, they generate increases in advertising revenue. It is, after all, this interest in profitability that drives the delivery of programming into the home. But, in order for profits to accrue, this economic interest must be translated into the cultural currency that we encounter as programming. In the process, distinctive symbolic forms emerge that become part and parcel of the meaning making process for people who watch. First, there is the flow of programming that generates a continual circulation of imagery. Second, there is the segmented programming structure, composed of 15-, 30-, and 60-second commercial spots as well as half-hour, hour, and two-hour program blocks, that works by breaking up this flow of programming. Taken together, flow and segmentation generate disjunctures in the symbolic field of programming, where, unlike the discursive symbolism of persuasion and story-telling conventions, the movements and combinations of imagery do not develop normative continuity; and, unlike even presentational symbolism, the logic of these movements and combinations work to destabilize whatever cultural coherence may be depicted in the symbolism of visual images themselves. Third, conventions of story-telling are repeated again and again in different programs and then circulated on a daily (syndicated shows), weekly (network series), and season-long basis across numerous channels. This results in a distinctive, manufactured quality to the symbolism of programming that viewers can certainly distinguish from the rendering of real-life in the story-telling conventions themselves. Like flow and segmentation, this symbolism of repetition also derives from a marketing logic, which means that it does not necessarily work to order social experience in normative ways. When they become mindfully engaged with these commodity forms of symbolism, people make meaning by disengaging themselves from the real world that television purports to represent and instead rely on their practical knowledge, gained through repeated exposure to television and other media, that programming is a world of manufactured, manipulated, and manipulable images.

Television programming, then, is symbolically complex, and it can mean different things at different times to different people. Yes, it is composed, as we would expect, of persuasive messages of different kinds as well as the various conventions by which the stories of television are told. These discourses, as they have come to be called, serve as points of departure for a variety of viewing relations. In ranging across different channels it is commonplace for people to encounter different scenes, characterizations, and story-lines and to interpret them differently, depending on both the depictions themselves and what people bring to them in terms of social knowledge. In short, despite the mainstreaming tendency of these discourses, viewing is a symbolically rich and highly ambivalent activity. But these discourses, even in all their complexity, are not all there is to the symbolism of television programming. There is the presentational symbolism of programming, which is itself multi-layered and serves as a point of departure for the construction of a rich and complicated imaginative world on the part of people. And then there are the commodity forms that impart a manufactured quality to programming and generate discontinuities and disjunctures in the symbolic field, all of which exist quite apart from discourse and even the workings of presentational symbolism. Each of these symbolic forms can be documented as distinctive patternings of programming, and each works differently and simultaneously to constitute a multiplicity of viewing relations. Analysts of television must account for this symbolic complexity in their attempts to document the meaning of television viewing.

Viewing Relations

Once the symbolic complexity of programming is understood, analysts face the difficulty of documenting how viewers actually situate themselves with television and make use of this symbolism. I have found that a wide range of mindful and emotional relationships with imagery are possible and, in fact, probable. Viewing can occur in solitary situations and in group situations. In solitary situations, people can or cannot become mindfully engaged with any and all of the symbolic forms of programming. At one extreme, they can relate to television as an object, using it simply for background noise or to have some company in the house while they do other things or otherwise occupy themselves. Or they may intermittently attend to what is on the screen, using the flow of programming to follow only the most exciting scenes of a program, and then quickly turning their attention to other things unrelated to television. People may watch what is on the screen, but they are not really thinking too deeply or getting too involved in anything they see. With the flow enabling them to just watch things go by, they may focus attention on the presentational symbolism and create meaning with visual images in a variety of ways—some related and others unrelated to the depictions at hand. They may watch a good portion of a single program in this way, alternatively spacing out and returning to the visual imagery or even the action as it develops on the screen. None of this, mind you, could be considered attentive viewing. People can become more mindfully engaged with the specifics of the story-telling conventions, they can get interested in the plot, the action of scenes, or with the characters themselves. They can be attentive enough to recognize how things are put together, or they can follow the scenes or what the characters do and concern themselves with why things come out as they do. In instances such as this, people are more consistently focused on the discourse of programming. At the other extreme, they can become so involved in the story, the action, or with the characters, that the depictions seem real to them, leading them to feel as if they are there, in the situations and a part of what is happening. In some cases, people may be attentive enough to make connections between what they are watching and things they have watched on TV in the past, or things they have seen in films, or even things they have had happen in their own life. Sometimes, this leads them to think reflexively about their own lives and, as a result, they feel enriched or more knowledgeable about themselves or their world. It is important to bear in mind, though, that people do not simply accept everything that they see, even when they watch in what appears to be attentive ways. They may be mindful of what is on in different ways. Sometimes they may merely recognize the implausible and make a mental note of it. At other times, if something that they feel strongly about does not make sense, they react to it verbally or with gestures to make their distance from the depiction that much more explicit.

Viewing also occurs in group situations where the same range of viewing relations that we can find in solitary viewing can occur; only now, their occurrence is complicated by the fact that interaction among people is an ongoing feature of television use. At one extreme, there are situations in which the relationship of each person to the television set is of primary importance. In these instances, the meaning of viewing is to be found by analyzing the separate, mindful relations of each person with the symbolic forms of the programming they encounter. And here we can assume it is the story-telling conventions that are most pertinent to their mindful involvement; although it is possible that they might find the presentational symbolism or even the repetition of programming more interesting to watch. At the other extreme, interaction among people can be so thoroughly integrated with their attention to programming that viewing becomes a highly organized social world in which people can play what one viewer aptly called "the game of television." This begins with viewers settling in to watch a favorite show or one that they like to see regularly. With the program serving as a focal point for their attention, different viewers can voice their opinions about what they are watching in order to elicit comments from the others and initiate some discussion. Then, the give and take of conversation (some of it highly critical) around specific scenes or characters' actions—and, usually, it is the story-telling conventions and the "real world" they depict which interests people most—enables shared meanings to emerge. Most of the time, however, the meaningful quality of group viewing lies somewhere between these two extremes. In some instances, people may all be gathered in the same room to watch, but each in their own way may be sufficiently distracted by other thoughts or by continued involvement in other activities of various sorts so that they pay less than full attention to what is on. Or, people may be gathered with the intent to watch a particular program closely, but it may turn out that the program does not hold their attention. In situations such as these, numerous scenarios are possible, depending upon how well the people know one another, their respective moods, and whatever else they may decide to do, to name just a few of the more important factors to be considered. Sometimes, sporadic commentary about television or other matters may emerge and take on a life of its own as people use the flow of programming or the presentational symbolism as something to fall back on during lulls in the conversation, or when they want to disengage themselves from social interaction. At other times, one or another person may leave the room to attend to other things then return to focus once again on what is on the screen, hoping that things had changed enough for the program to now hold their attention.

It should be clear from this discussion that the task of understanding the meaning that television viewing has for people can become quite complicated. So, too, can the task of specifying how the power of television works in constituting their mindful and emotional relationships with programming. People's presence of mind is constantly shifting while they watch. Still, the analyst must be able to determine if it is television or people themselves who are responsible for maintaining this presence of mind. Generally speaking, significant changes in people's presence of mind must be understood in relation to the workings of the different symbolic forms that I have mentioned. Discursive symbolism is not the sole determinant of the meaning of their viewing experience.

Leaving Television and Fitting It Back Within Daily Life

Beyond people's turn to television and their interaction with programming lie the issues of what they think, feel, and do as a result of using the medium. First, there are behavioral effects of viewing to consider. Analysts need to account for the seemingly small and insignificant ways that our behavior may be transformed as a consequence of what we encounter on television. How do depictions of characters and celebrities become incorporated into people's daily routines? How do such depictions alter the meaning of people's actions? This world of behavior and behavioral change does not lend itself easily to documentation because it is sometimes too personal, too close, too much about who people are becoming for them to reveal it to the analyst. Furthermore, the television-driven world of behavior can easily shade into fantasy, where the lived reality of things becomes more imaginary and sometimes that which separates the two realms is not so easily identified. But what is more easily identified is the conversation that people have with others, when they are no longer watching, about what they have seen on television. Conversation may sometimes lead people to reinterpret what they have seen or heard. Over time this talk may change the very way that they watch television—not only what they watch, but, more importantly, what they find believable or worthy of criticism. So, the analyst must be able to determine whether or not people talk regularly, with the same people, about what they watch. Do they talk about the same shows? Is it important for them to discuss their favorite shows or favorite characters on a regular basis? What sorts of story-lines or characters' actions typically elicit their commentary and provoke the most enthusiastic kinds of talk? What does "critical talk" consist of? If talk about television does not take place regularly, it may still occur, only it may be more random and infrequent. If so, what does that talk consist of? Is it focused on favorite shows, is it limited to comments about special shows such as sporting events, award shows, political debates, mini-series, and the like, or is it some combination of the two? Questions such as these mark only a beginning of an inquiry into the meaning of people's conversations regarding television.

Television can figure importantly in the ways that people think about and deal with problems or issues in their own lives. Do the ways in which particular characters deal with fictional situations, such as marital or family problems, job stress, relations with supervisors, alcoholism, drug use, and so on become incorporated into the ways in which people who watch handle similar situations in their own lives? If so, what is it, specifically, about televised depictions that resonate with their own lives? Similarly, do they witness depictions of "real life" on television that serve as clear indicators of what *not* to do if they are confronted with the same or similar circumstances in their own lives?

Leaving television and fitting it back within daily life also encompasses the formation of attitudes and opinions that emerge from television use and that people may carry around inside their heads and draw upon in making sense of themselves and their world, especially the world beyond their own day-to-day experiences. People certainly think about their world, the social relations they are a part of, the people and places they come into contact with, including what they see on television and in other media. They develop attitudes and formulate opinions on a wide variety of things. When it comes to television, analysts have to document how viewers think differently, and how what they already think is supported as a result of what they watch. When viewers accept particular television presentations of, say, inner-city police or criminal lawyers as plausible, does this have a direct bearing on how they understand inner-city police or criminal lawyers in the real world? It seems problematic to focus only on specific interpretations people make while watching television and then to extrapolate these interpretations to stand for some more diffuse knowledge that they have of the world—say, of inner-city police or criminal lawyers. To depart from such a strategy of documentation would mean to deal more directly with how it is that specific interpretations or even more stable and consistent patterns of interpretation based on viewing favorite shows or recurrent themes in programming are actually fit by people into their everyday lives. Some of what people interpret may become meaningful in actual behavior and some in fantasy. But if attitude and opinion research offers us any indication, there may be yet another realm in which some of what people watch takes on meaning as more diffuse and free-floating ideas about the world that are simply stored in their preconscious or unconscious mind. These ideas may surface when real world occurrences or encounters with the media or both provoke people to recall the "televisual knowledge" they have stored away and use it to elaborate the meanings associated with such occurrences and encounters in their own minds. Armed with a prior understanding of the symbolic forms of programming, and knowledgeable regarding the viewing habits of people, including their favorite shows and characters, the analyst can then identify the kinds of depictions that resonate most with particular people and, on that basis, attempt to reconstruct how these more diffuse, free-floating ideas about the world take shape in their everyday lives.

Conclusion

Television use involves a complex process of meaning-making, one that is mindfully and emotionally constituted in a variety of ways, ranging across the three components that I have mentioned—the turn to television, interaction with programming imagery per se, and leaving television and fitting it back within daily life. Understanding how television is situated in people's everyday lives necessitates that we analytically reconstruct their use of the medium in all its complexity. In considering the turn to television, analysts need to know how a person's responsibilities structure everyday life and create the opportunities for turning to television in the first place. Typically, these responsibilities include work, school, child care, and housework. Analysts need to know the situational contexts that typically serve as a point of departure for television use. This includes documenting the feelings people have in these situations, their mindfulness in turning to television and to other activities, the activities themselves, as well as their mindful potential. In analyzing the second component, television interaction, analysts should proceed knowing that there is more to programming than discourse. The presentational and commodity forms of symbolism work along with discursive symbolism in providing an objective basis for people's continual movements in and out of a variety of viewing relations. Analysts need to know what these viewing relations are, what typifies the movements between them for different people, and when and how the television constitutes the meaning of these viewing relations, and to distinguish this power from the directive role that people's identities and sense of self play in giving meaningful form to their viewing. And, finally, with regard to the third component, leaving television and fitting it back into daily life, analysts need to know how television imagery becomes situated in people's everyday lives. They need to reconstruct the act of turning off the television so as to better understand the emotional complexities that attend to it. They need to know both what people do differently as a result of their viewing as well as how what they do, if not noticeably different from what they have done in the past, is nevertheless solidified as a result of watching television. Furthermore, analysts need to understand people's talk about television, whether or not they find what they watch helpful in dealing with personal problems and issues, the ideas they formulate about the "real world" as a consequence of watching television, and the daydreams and fantasies that might be stimulated by television use.

I refer to this complexity of meaning that is involved in people's day-to-day television use as the sociality of the viewing culture. In talking about this sociality, it is crucial that analysts account for television's power by identifying the different ways that it can work: as an object of consumption, discourses of persuasion, story-telling conventions, visual symbolism, flow, a segmented structure of programming, and as a repetition of manufactured images. It is in all of these ways that television can shape the sociality of the viewing culture. Certainly, discourse is powerful. But understanding the sociality of the viewing culture involves much more than accounting for power and resistance.

References

Adorno, Theodor. 1974. "The Stars Down to Earth." *Telos* 19. 1957. "How to Look at Television." In *Mass Culture: The Popular Arts in America,* edited by B. Rosenberg and D. White. New York: The Free Press. 1945. "A Social Critique of Radio Music." *Kenyon Review* 7:2.

Adorno, Theodor, and Max Horkheimer. 1972. *Dialectic of Enlightenment.* New York: Seabury.

Allen, Robert., ed. 1987. *Channels of Discourse.* Chapel-Hill: University of North Carolina.

Ang, Ien. 1985. *Watching Dallas: Soap Opera and the Melodramadic Imagination.* London: Methuen.

Anzaldua, Gloria. 1987. *Borderlands.* San Francisco: Spinsters/Aunt Lute.

Bandura, Albert. 1965. "Influence of Models' Reinforcement Contingencies on the Acquisition of Imitative Responses." *Journal of Personality and Social Psychology.* 2, 1–55.

Barthes, Roland. 1972. *Mythologies.* New York: Hill and Wang.

Benjamin, Walter. 1968. *Illuminations.* New York: Harcourt.

Berelson, Bernard. 1971. *Content Analysis in Communication Research.* New York: Hafner. *Psychology.* Vol. 2, 359–69.

Blumer, Herbert. 1969. *Symbolic Interactionism.* New York: University of California. 1933. *Movies and Conduct.* New York: MacMillan and Co.

Bourdieu, Pierre. 1977. *Outline of a Theory of Practice.* Cambridge University Press.

Brunsdon, Charlotte. 1991 "Text and Audience." In *Remote Control: Television, Audiences, and Cultural Power,* edited by Ellen Seiter, Hans Borchers, Gabriele Kreutzner, and Eva-Maria Warth. New York: Routledge.

Butler, Judith. 1995. *Bodies That Matter.* New York: Routledge. 1990. *Gender Trouble: Feminism and the Subversion of Identity.* New York: Routledge.

Cantril, Hadley. 1935. *The Psychology of Radio.* New York: Harper.

Clark. T. J. 1984. *The Painting of Modern Life.* Princeton University Press.

DeFleur, Melvin and Sandra Ball-Rockeach. 1982. *Theories of Mass Communication.* New York: Longman.

Deleuze, Gilles. 1983. *Nietzsche and Philosophy.* New York: Columbia.

Deleuze, Gilles and Claire Parnet. 1987. *Dialogues.* New York: Columbia.

Deleuze, Gilles, and Felix Guattari. 1983. *Anti-Oedipus: Capitalism and Schizophrenia.* Minneapolis: University of Minnesota.

Dunn, Robert. 1991. "Postmodernism: Populism, Mass Culture and the Avant-Garde." *Theory Culture and Society* 8, 111–135.

Durkheim, Emile. 1967. *The Elementary Forms of the Religious Life.* London: G. Allen and Unwin. 1938. *The Rules of Sociological Method.* New York: The Free Press.

Ellis, John. 1982. *Visible Fictions: Cinema, Television, Video.* Boston: Routledge and Kegan Paul.

Fiske, John. 1987. *Television Culture.* London: Methuen.

Foucault, Michel. 1986. *The Care of the Self: History of Sexuality, Volume III.* New York: Vintage. 1985. *The Use of Pleasure: The History of Sexuality, Volume II.* New York: Vintage. 1980. *The History of Sexuality, Volume I.* New York: Vintage. 1970. *The Order of Things.* New York: Pantheon.

Gerbner, George, Larry Gross, Michael Morgan, and Nancy Signorielli. 1986. "Living With Television: The Dynamics of the Cultivation Process," in Bryant, Jennings., and Zillman, Dolf., eds. *Perspectives on Media Effects.* Hillsdale, N.J: Lawrence Erlbaum. 1982. "Charting the Mainstream: Television's Contribution to Political Orientations." *Journal of Communication,* 30:2. 1980. "The Demonstration of Power: Violence Profile No. 11." *Journal of Communication* Summer. 1980.

Gerbner, George, Larry Gross, Nancy Signorielli, Michael Morgan, and Marilyn Jackson-Beets. 1977. "The Demonstration of Power: Violence Profile No. 10." *Journal of Communications* 29:3, 177–196.

Gitlin, Todd. 1983. *Inside Prime Time.* New York: Pantheon. 1980. *The Whole World is Watching: The Media in the Making and the Unmaking of the New Left.* Berkeley, CA: University of California Press. 1979. "Prime-Time Ideology: The Hegemonic Process in Television Entertainment." *Social Problems* 26:3, 251–266. 1978. "Media Sociology." *Theory and Society* 6:2, 205–254.

Goffman, Erving. 1979. *Gender Advertisements.* New York: Harper. 1959. *The Presentation of Self in Everyday Life.* Garden City, NJ: Doubleday.

Goodwin, Andrew. 1992. *Dancing in the Distraction Factory: Music Television and Popular Culture.* Minneapolis: University of Minnesota Press.

Grossberg, Lawrence. 1988. "'It's a Sin': Postmodernity–Popular Empowerment and Hegemonic Popular." Paper presented at Rice University Conference on the Sociology of Television, Houston, TX. 1987. "The In-Difference of Television." *Screen* 28, 28–45.

Grossberg, Lawrence, Cary Nelson, and Paula Treichler (eds.). 1992. *Cultural Studies.* New York: Routledge.

Hall, Stuart. 1980. "Cultural Studies: Two Paradigms." *Media, Culture, and Society* 2, 57–72. 1975. "Television as a Medium and Its Relation to Culture." Stencilled

Occasional Paper, Centre for Contemporary Cultural Studies. Birmingham, England.

Hall, Stuart, Dorothy Hobson, Andrew Lowe, and Paul Willis, (eds.). 1980. *Culture, Media, Language*. London: Hutchinson.

Hewitt, John. 1989. *Dilemmas of the American Self*. Philadelphia: Temple University Press.

Hoggart, Richard. 1966. *The Uses of Literacy*. Boston: Beacon.

Iyengar, Shanto. 1991. *Is Anyone Responsible?* University of Chicago Press.

Iyengar, Shanto and Donald Kinder. 1987. *News That Matters*. University of Chicago Press.

Jameson, Fredric. 1991. *Postmodernism Or, The Cultural Logic of Late Capitalism*. Durham: Duke University. 1983. "Postmodernism and Consumer Society." In *The Anti-Aesthetic: Essays on Postmodern Culture*, edited by Hal Foster. Port Townsend, WA: Bay Press.

Katz, Elihu and P. Lazarsfeld. 1955. *Personal Influence*. New York: The Free Press.

Kellner, Douglas. 1990. *Television and the Crisis of Democracy*. Westview Press: Boulder, CO.

Klapper, Joseph. 1960. *The Effects of Mass Communication*. Glencoe, IL: The Free Press.

Kubey, Robert William, and Mihaly Csikszentmihalyi. 1990. *Television and the Quality of Life*. Hillsdale, NJ: L. Erlbaum.

Lacan, Jacques. 1977. *Ecrits: A Selection*. New York: Norton. 1968. *The Language of the Self: The Function of Language in Psychoanalysis*. New York: Dell.

Langer, Suzanne. 1957. *Philosophy in a New Key*. Cambridge: Harvard University Press.

Lasswell, Harold. 1938. *Propaganda Techniques in the World War*. New York: P. Smith.

Lazarsfeld, Paul, Bernard Berelson, and Hazel Gaudet. 1948. *The People's Choice*. New York: Columbia University Press.

Lazarsfeld, P. and R. Merton. 1977. "Mass Communication, Popular Taste, and Organized Social Action." In *The Process and Effects of Mass Communication*, edited by W. Schramm and D. Roberts. Chicago: University of Illinois Press.

Lembo, Ron. 1994. "Situating Television in Everyday Life: Reformulating a Cultural Studies Approach to the Study of Television Use." In *From Sociology to Cultural Studies*, edited by Elizabeth Long. Boston: Blackwell Publishers, pp. 203–233.

Lembo, Ron, and Ken Tucker. 1990. "Culture, Television, and Opposition: Rethinking Cultural Studies." *Critical Studies in Mass Communication* 7, 97–116.

Macdonald, Dwight. 1983. *Against the American Grain*. New York: Da Capo Press.

Mahler, Margaret. 1975. *The Psychological Birth of the Human Infant: Symbiosis and Individuation*. New York: Basic Books.

Malamuth, Neil, and Victoria Billings. 1986. "The Functions and Effects of Pornography: Sexual Communication versus Feminist Models in Light of Research Findings." In *Perspectives on Media Effects*, edited by Dolf Zillmann and Jennings Bryant, Hillsdale, NJ: Ablex.

Marcuse, Herbert. 1964. *One Dimensional Man: Studies in the Ideology of Advanced Industrial Society*. Boston: Beacon Press.

McRobbie, Angela. 1991. *Feminism and Youth Culture*. Boston: Unwin Hyman.

Mead, G. H. 1934. *Mind Self and Society*. University of Chicago Press. 1932. *The Philosophy of the Present*. University of Chicago Press.

Merton, Robert. 1968. *Social Theory and Social Structure*. New York: The Free Press. 1946. *Mass Persuasion: The Social Psychology of a War Bond Drive*. New York: Harper & Bros.

Meyrowitz, Joshua. 1985. *No Sense of Place: The Impact of Electronic Media on Social Behaviour*. Oxford University Press: New York.

Miller, Mark Crispin. 1988. *Boxed In: The Culture of TV*. Evanston, III: Northwestern University Press.

Morley, David. 1994. *Television, Audiences, and Cultural Studies*. New York: Routledge. 1986. *Family Television and Domestic Leisure*. London: Comedia. 1980. *The Nationwide Audience*. London: British Film Institute.

Nietzsche, Friedrich. 1968. *The Will To Power*. New York: Random House.

Postman, Neil. 1985. *Amusing Ourselves to Death*. New York: Viking.

Press, Andrea. 1992. *Women Watching Television*. Philadelphia: University of Pennsylvania.

Rabinow, Paul and Hubert Dreyfuss. 1983. *Michel Foucault: Beyond Structuralism and Hermeneutics*. University of Chicago Press.

Radway, Janice. 1984. *Reading the Romance*. Chapel Hill: University of North Carolina.

Rosaldo, Renato. 1989. *Culture and Truth*. Boston: Beacon Press.

Seldes, Gilbert. 1957. *The 7 Lively Arts*. New York: Sagamore Press.

Shils, Edward. 1969. *Literary Taste, Culture, and Mass Communication*. Englewood Cliffs, NJ: Prentice-Hall.

Silverstone, Roger. 1995. *Television and Everyday Life*. New York: Routledge.

Spigel, Lynn. 1992. *Make Room for TV: Television and the Family Ideal in Postwar America*. University of Chicago Press.

Thompson, E. P. 1966. *The Making of the English Working Class*. New York: Vintage.

Tichi, Cecilia. 1991. *Electronic Hearth: Creating an American Television Culture*. New York: Oxford University Press.

Wellman, David. 1993. "Honorary Homeys, Class Brothers, and White Negroes: Mixing Cultural Codes and Constructing Multicultural Identities on America's Social Borderlands," Paper Presented at the American Sociological Association Annual Meetings, Miami Beach, Florida.

Williams, Raymond. 1983. *Culture and Society*. New York: Columbia University. 1982. *The Sociology of Culture*. New York: Schocken. 1974. *Television, Technology, and Cultural Form*. London: Fontana.

Willis, Paul. 1978. *Profane Culture*. London: Routledge, Kegan, Paul. 1977a. *Learning to Labor*. London: Saxon House.

Winnicott, D. W. 1971. *Playing and Reality*. New York: Tavistock. 1965. *The Maturation Processes and the Facilitating Environment*. Madison, Wisconsin: International Universities Press.

Wright, Charles. 1975. *Mass Communication: A Sociological Perspective*. New York: Random House.

Zillmann, Dolf and Jennings Bryant. 1982. "Pornography, Sexual Callousness and the Trivialization of Rape." *Journal of Communication* 32:9.

Big Brother
The Real Audience

Annette Hill

Big Brother is a new format in factual entertainment that has been subject to much speculation in the press, on TV, the internet, and by the public. As the *Big Brother* (BB) format was quickly adopted by different countries, this speculation focused primarily on the negative: was *Big Brother* voyeuristic? Why were viewers addicted to watching a reality show about nothing? I want to focus on BB in relation to audience attraction. In doing so, I draw on John Corner's theory of "postdocumentary culture.". . . . Corner's argument concerning documentary as diversion is helpful when considering audience attraction to a hybrid genre such as BB. This gamedoc's focus on the microsocial, display and confession, performance and actuality, ordinary and celebrity, works toward a viewing experience that is far removed from traditional documentary.

Some commentators have argued that BB is popular because it is voyeuristic (McLean 2000). Others have argued that BB is popular because it is interactive—we decide the winners and the losers (Jones 2001). Neither argument seems to me to capture the viewing experience that is BB. If some viewers did achieve sexual pleasure from watching contestants engage in nude mud painting or intimate moments under the duvet, it still does not explain why BB is so popular with the viewing public as a whole. There may be a "nosey sociability" (Corner 2000) to watching BB, but this does not make it "voyeur-TV." It is certainly the case that some audiences enjoy interacting with the BB experience. However, evidence suggests that interactivity is one of the least favorite aspects of the BB experience for general TV viewers.

I want to outline the context of factual entertainment and its audience, and the specific experience of watching BB. Seen in relation to factual entertainment as a whole, BB is one of the least popular examples of "documentary as diversion." Seen in relation to gamedocs, BB is one of the most popular examples of new factual entertainment. My reflections on BB therefore serve two purposes. The first is to examine the viewing experience for factual

Annette Hill, *"Big Brother:* The Real Audience." From *Television & New Media,* Vol. 3, No. 3 (August 2002), pp. 323–340, copyright © 2002 by Sage Publications, Inc. Reprinted by permission of Sage Publications, Inc.

entertainment as a whole. Viewers prefer informative, behind the scenes factual entertainment, preferably concerning law and order, or homes and gardens, and are skeptical of the more "performative" entertainment programs about real people. Thus, in the factual programming market, BB is not an all-round entertainer, but rather an extraordinary "media event" whose life span may be short lived. The second is to examine the BB viewing experience. Research indicates that attraction to BB is based on the social and performative aspects of this new type of factual entertainment.[1] Viewers watch BB for many reasons—it's something new, you can vote people you don't like off the show—but perhaps the most striking reasons for watching BB are that everybody else is watching and talking about it, and everybody else is forming judgments on the contestants and how they act up for the cameras. The focus on the degree of actuality, on real people's improvised performances in the program, leads to a particular viewing practice: audiences look for the moment of authenticity when real people are "really" themselves in an unreal environment. This, I argue, is the popularity of the gamedoc, evident in its early incarnation, BB, and writ large in BB spin-offs, such as *Survivor* (ITV, U.K.; CBS, U.S.), *Temptation Island* (Sky, U.K.; CBS, U.S.), or *The Mole* (Channel 5, U.K.; ABC, U.S.), which capitalize on the tension between performance and authenticity, asking contestants and viewers to look for the "moment of truth" in a highly constructed and controlled television environment.

Watching *Big Brother* Around the World

The rise in international formatted reality programs, such as BB, *Survivor*, or *Popstars* (ITV, U.K.), indicates the economic success of selling a global format that is locally produced. Although traditionally the domain of game shows, *gamedocs* offer competitive and new hybrid formats in the international TV marketplace. Buying an established format such as BB reduces the costs of production and attenuates the risks associated with new programming. BB's global performance points to a strong, at times remarkable, market share. Although my focus in this article is to consider the "use value" of BB, its exchange value is equally important.

During the first series of BB in Holland (John de Mol Productions, Veronica), up to 6 million viewers tuned in to watch an intimate moment between two contestants. In Germany, the first series of BB (Endemol Entertainment, RTL2 and RTL) was so successful that a second was commissioned immediately for the autumn 2000 schedule. RTL2, a small TV station, with an average 3.9 percent market share, managed a 15 percent market share with the second series. Based on this, a third series ran directly after Christmas until May 2001, although the ratings were disappointing for the third series.[2]

Other European countries followed suit. In Portugal, TVI, a small TV station, had much success broadcasting BB between September and December 2000 (Endemol Entertainment). TVI's average share is 9 percent, and with BB its market share rose to over 50 percent, with its highest rated episode at 74 percent in the final week.[3] This ratings success has been repeated with the second series. Spain broadcast BB from April to July 2000 on Tele 5 (Zeppelin Television). Tele 5's average market share is 21 percent. BB started slowly with only a 13.7 percent share but quickly reached a more respectable 30 percent, peaking at 70 percent for the final show—more people tuned in to watch BB than the Champions League semifinal match between Real Madrid and Bayern Munich. Belgium's television channel, Kanaal 2, has an average 9 percent market share; after it had broadcast BB from September to December 2000 (Endemol Entertainment), the audience share increased to nearly 50 percent. In Switzerland, BB also ran in autumn 2000 (B&B Endemol, TV3); TV3's average market share is 2.5 percent, but with BB this increased to 30 percent.

Only in Sweden and the United States did BB fail to achieve a similar increase in market share. In Sweden, BB broadcast during autumn 2000 (Metronome Film and Television, Kanal 5); it managed an average 10 percent market share, which is no different from Kanal 5's normal market share.[4] In the United States, BB was shown from July to December 2000 (Evolution Film and Tape, CBS). Although the premiere attracted a 23 percent market share, BB's average share was only 12 percent, and it failed to achieve the runaway success of *Survivor* (CBS), which in some ways stole the thunder from the BB U.S. experience. However, the average ratings for BB in Sweden and America did not stop Kanal 5 or CBS from commissioning a second, modified, series.

Outside Europe and America, BB has performed well in Australia (Southern Star Endemol, Channel 10), appealing to 50 percent of nineteen- to thirty-nine-year-olds, the target audience for Channel 10.[5] In Argentina, the first series of BB, which was transmitted from March to July 2001 on Telefe, a private terrestrial channel, the ratings for the eviction show averaged 20 percent of the market share. Telefe were so pleased with the success of BB that they commissioned a second series, which aired August 2001, only a month after the finale of the first series.[6] The BB format has yet to be acquired in other Latin American countries, or in Asia or the Middle East.

A more detailed breakdown for BB U.K. (GMG Endemol Entertainment, Channel 4) reveals the extent of the success of BB across converging media. Channel 4 had the best Friday night ratings in its history. BB began with 3 million viewers and gradually increased to a 46 percent market share during the week the contestants uncovered Nasty Nick, and peaked at 10 million viewers (56.5 percent share) on the final night. Overall, BB averaged a 26 percent market share. Sixty-seven percent of the population watched BB at least once. More than 7 million viewers telephoned Channel 4's hotline to vote for the winner, which broke the record for viewer participation in a U.K. TV program. As for the web site, it received 3 million page impressions each day, which made it Europe's top web site during the summer of 2000. On the day when Nasty Nick was uncovered by contestants, the web site received a record-breaking 7.5 million page impressions.

The second series of BB was also successful, averaging 4.5 million viewers, and giving Channel 4 more than a 70 percent increase on their average broadcast share. Channel 4 digital youth channel E4 screened BB2 continuously and at peak moments in the BB house (e.g., Paul and Helen's candlelit tryst), attracted record figures, propelling the digital channel ahead of terrestrial minority channels.[7] By using interactive TV handsets or phone lines, 15.6

million viewers voted to evict contestants. The web site received a total of 159 million page impressions, and 16.4 million video streams were requested.[8]

Based on this economic evidence, it is no wonder the BB format sold so well in the international TV marketplace. In an uncertain factual programming market, this new breed of factual entertainment promises to deliver audiences. As the figures above show, BB also promises to enhance channel identity, as small TV companies become perceived as risk takers, stripping the schedules for newcomers like BB. For most TV companies, the risk paid off. The consequences of this for factual programming as a whole remain to be seen as audience interest in gamedocs has yet to be tested in the long term. Certainly, the poor performance of *Survivor* (ITV1) in the United Kingdom, compared to its success in the United States, suggests that not all gamedoc formats are guaranteed winners, especially for mainstream channels.[9] As many TV companies revise the BB format for its second and subsequent series, there is concern that the popularity of BB has peaked. According to a study conducted by E-Poll in July 2001, only 39 percent of regular viewers of reality TV feel there is room for more programs, with 35 percent claiming they are only interested in watching a couple of new reality shows. BB is now a familiar formula and must work hard to maintain its ratings success in a competitive environment.

Who's Watching Factual Entertainment?

What types of factual entertainment do the general public like to watch on TV? My research (funded by the Economic and Social Research Council, Independent Television Commission [ITC], and Channel 4) aims to present a broad picture of British audiences and factual entertainment.[10] I used a multimethod approach, combining quantitative and qualitative techniques. The survey included a representative sample of more than 9,000 TV viewers taken from the Brodcasters' Audience Research Bureau (BARB), aged four to sixty-five plus, who were contacted during August 2000.[11] This was also the month that BB made headlines in the United Kingdom.

The answer to the question "who's watching factual entertainment?" is everyone. Factual entertainment programs were watched by 72 percent of children aged four to fifteen (80 percent of the over 10s), and the more popular types of factual entertainment (see below) were watched at least occasionally by 70 percent of adults. Although there are minor variations in age, gender, social class, education, household makeup, and ethnicity, what is so surprising is the homogeneous audience for factual entertainment: it appeals to everyone.[12]

The answer to the question "what *types* of factual entertainment do the general public like to watch on TV?" is more complicated. The types of factual entertainment watched most often by the British public were police/crime programs (e.g., *Police, Camera, Action!* [ITV]), which were watched either regularly or occasionally by 72 percent of adults and 71 percent of children; "places" programs (e.g., *Airport* [BBC]), which were watched by 71 percent of adults and 75 percent of children; home/garden shows (e.g., *Changing Rooms* [BBC])—67 percent of adults and 84 percent of children. Among the under 16s (in particular, the under 13s), pet shows (e.g., *Animal Hospital* [BBC]) were as popular as the categories cited above. These were watched by 83 percent of children and 63 percent of adults.

It is also necessary to break down factual entertainment into subgenres. There are three main subgenres, although programs can overlap within these categories. In the survey I conducted with the ITC, the subgenres were identified as follows:

> *Observation* programmes are often about watching people in everyday places (e.g. *Airport*). *Information* programmes use true stories to tell us about something, like driving, first aid, or pets (e.g. *999*). *Created for TV* programmes are about putting real people in a manufactured situation, like a house or an island, and filming what happens (e.g. *Big Brother*).

The subgenres of factual entertainment liked most by the general public were observation (67 percent), information (64 percent), and created for TV (28 percent). Across all social groups, the created for TV category was much less popular. If we break it down by age, the outcome improves for the created for TV category. Only 28 percent of adults and 44 percent of children liked this type of factual entertainment, but 48 percent of sixteen- to twenty-four-year-olds, and 69 percent of thirteen- to fifteen-year-olds, liked the created for TV category. However, it is still the case that the general viewing public prefer more "traditional" (i.e., familiar) and "informative" factual entertainment.

When considering factual entertainment as a whole, we might expect BB to score poorly. BB fits into the created for TV category, it does not contain clearly informative elements within the program, and its raison d'être is to maximize the use of intrusive cameras. The characteristic of factual entertainment most liked by the general public was information (75 percent); least liked was intrusive cameras (68 percent). BB also fits into the category of "real people" programs, which, compared to police, places, or pets programs, scored poorly in the survey. Table 1 details the occasional and regular viewers of real people programs: occasional viewers (22 percent) were more likely to watch factual entertainment about real people if the viewers were female, sixteen to thirty-four years old, ABC1 social grade, college or university students, with children in the household, and with access to the internet.[13] Thus, although we could not expect BB to appeal to a cross section of the public, unlike other factual entertainment shows, it should appeal to the target audience for Channel 4, a minority channel that aims to attract the younger, upwardly mobile viewer.

Two more reflections on general viewers of factual entertainment need to be made before turning to the BB audience. These relate to public attitudes to actuality and performance. Table 2 shows how much the British public distrust the "reality" of stories in factual entertainment. More than 70 percent of the sample questioned the authenticity of the content of factual entertainment. Expectations were so low that half the population claimed stories about real people were sometimes made up in TV programs. Out of this 50 percent, there was little difference in terms of demographic variables such as gender, age, or social class.[14]

Table 1. Factual Entertainment ("Real People" Programs)

Watching Real People Programs (e.g., Big Brother)	Adults Occasional (22 percent of sample) (Percentage)	Adults Regular (12 percent of sample) (Percentage)
Males	21	9
Females	23	15
16–24	29	32
25–34	32	22
35–44	25	11
45–54	22	7
55–64	15	3
65+	12	2
AB	25	11
C1	23	13
C2	21	14
DE	20	11
15+ education	19	4
16+ education	23	13
17–18 education	29	13
19+ education	27	12
Students	37	24
With children	30	16
Without children	21	7
With internet access	29	14
Without internet access	22	8

NOTE: unweighted base = 8,216.

Table 2. Audience Attitudes to Actuality in Factual Entertainment

Actuality	All Adults (Percentage)
I think the stories in entertainment programs about real people really do happen like this	12
I think the stories in entertainment programs about real people happen like this, but parts of them are exaggerated for TV	23
I think the stories in entertainment programs about real people sometimes happen like this and are sometimes made up	50
I think the stories in entertainment programs about real people are all made up	2

NOTE: Base = 8,216.

Table 3. Audience Attitudes to Performance in Factual Entertainment

Performance	Agree All Adults (Percentage)	Disagree All Adults (Percentage)	Not Sure All Adults (Percentage)
Members of the public usually act the same on TV as in real life	8	60	21
Members of the public usually overact for the cameras	70	4	16
I can always tell the difference between someone's actual story being caught on camera, or being re-created for TV	36	8	45

NOTE: Base = 8,216.

Table 3 consolidates this portrait of the viewing public as cynical of the reality of real TV and alert to the performative nature of factual entertainment. Almost half of the sample (45 percent) were uncertain as to whether they could tell the difference between someone's actual story being caught on camera or being re-created for TV. As many as 70 percent of the sample agreed members of the public usually overacted for the cameras. Again, as with the question of actuality, there was little demographic difference in opinion.[15]

What sort of picture is painted by these statistics? On one hand, factual entertainment is popular with all groups of TV viewers, especially as the sort of TV program to be watched occasionally. There are particular types of factual entertainment people prefer: programs about institutions or places are popular, particularly if they contain informative, "behind the scenes" content that captures real stories on camera. As factual entertainment has established itself as a strong, all-round TV product for primetime audiences, there has arisen a deep distrust and ambiguity concerning the reality of real people's stories. In particular, the popularity of observation programs, for example, docu-soaps, which primarily focus on members of the public "performing the real" for the camera (Roscoe forthcoming), has perhaps led to high expectation that real people overact in front of cameras. This adds weight to the argument that "documentary as diversion" is little more than "performative TV" (Corner 2000; Bruzzi 2000; Dovey 2000). On the other hand, programs such as BB, which can be classified as created for TV factual entertainment, or real people programs, and which are a natural development from docu-soaps, are one of the least popular types of factual entertainment. Although much of this article highlights the success of BB, we should remember that in the factual programming market, BB is not an all-round entertainer. It is a successful format for minority channels who aim to attract young, upwardly mobile viewers. However, at this moment in time, even young viewers (16–24) prefer observational (75 percent) and informative (67 percent) factual entertainment to the created for TV category (52 percent). This suggests a cautious approach to new developments in factual entertainment (Hill 2005).

Who's Watching *Big Brother*?

In keeping with this caution over the success of BB for the British public, only 30 percent of the sample watched BB during the month of August, at its height of success. Although Channel 4 claimed that 67 percent of the population watched BB at least once, this was a testament to the "media event" that was the summer of BB, rather than its general popularity. If only 30 percent of the population watched BB during August, then many more tuned in toward the end of the series, when the media event reached its climax in September 2000, to find out what all the fuss was about and to see who won the show.

Table 4 compares viewers of BB and viewers of created for TV factual entertainment. There is little difference between groups, and this confirms the picture from the previous section that people are more likely to watch BB as an example of created for TV factual entertainment if they are young and educated. Twenty-eight percent of men and 34 percent of women watched *Big Brother*. Sixteen- to thirty-four-year-olds were two times more likely to have watched it than older viewers. Fifty-one percent of viewers with college education saw the series, compared with an average of 33 percent of those without. There was not much differentiation by social grade. In addition to this, adults were twice as likely to have seen *Big Brother* if they lived in households with children. The reason for this may be related to the fact that BB U.K. was shown during the summer school holidays, and parents tuned in to see what their children were watching and talking about.

A greater percentage of adults with access to the internet than those without watched *Big Brother* (41 percent and 22 percent, respectively). This raises an important distinction. Out of our sample, the majority of adults (83 percent of men and 85 percent of women) and children (74 percent of ten- to fifteen-year-olds) had not accessed web sites related to factual entertainment. The principal reason cited (by 57 percent of adults and 40 percent of children) was not having access to the internet. A further 36 percent of adults and 25 percent of children said that they had not visited the sites because they are not interested in them. Despite the fact that 50 percent of sixteen- to twenty-four-year-olds have access to the internet, 82 percent did not access these web sites.

When we explored this during the qualitative fieldwork, many fans of BB explained they hadn't visited the site because it was too difficult to download to their home computers, and, more significantly, they wanted to watch the TV show in order to join in conversations about BB. Thus, although more adults with access to the internet watched BB, it does not necessarily mean these viewers accessed the BB site. In fact, so few people accessed the site in this sample, it would suggest viewers of the BB TV series may be different from visitors of the BB web site. Table 5 shows the least popular BB experiences are visiting the internet site and talking in chat rooms (each liked by only 15 percent). Similar evidence from Germany also suggests a distinction between

Table 4. "Created for TV" Factual Entertainment and *Big Brother*

Viewer Profile	Watching Big Brother (30% of adults) (Percentage)	Like Created for TV Factual Entertainment (28% of adults) (Percentage)
Males	28	22
Females	34	32
16–24	58	52
25–34	50	43
35–44	36	26
45–54	25	20
55–64	15	16
65+	9	14
AB	35	27
C1	34	29
C2	30	29
DE	27	25
15+ education	15	22
16+ education	33	29
17–18 education	38	31
19+ education	33	33
Students	51	46
With children	41	37
Without children	22	24
With internet access	40	32
Without internet access	33	27

BB TV viewers and internet users (Mikos and Prommer 2001). Forthcoming research on BB internet users should hopefully clarify this issue. Channel 4's decision to stream live footage of the BB house, during the second series of BB, via their digital youth channel E4, indicates forward thinking as viewers can utilize the interactive elements of the web site (watching contestants twenty-four/seven, voting) while watching TV and experiencing few of the technical difficulties associated with web sites.

In relation to the TV series itself, Table 5 outlines the favorite BB features and experiences. Respondents were presented with a list of program features (e.g., group conflict) and a list of BB experiences (e.g., visiting the web site). The BB experience enjoyed by the greatest percentage of all respondents was watching the live "eviction" show (59 percent), followed by seeing ex-contestants talk about their experiences (58 percent), watching the nightly TV program (55 percent), and talking about the program with friends/family (51 percent). These experiences involve watching the TV show and talking about it before, during, and afterward. As Scannell and Couldry point out . . . , talk about TV is not a minor part of TV experience, but arguably one of the most important features of television and everyday life (see also Gauntlett and Hill

Table 5. *Big Brother* Characteristics (Likes)

Big Brother *Characteristics*	*Like—Adults* *(30% of sample)* *(Percentage)*
Seeing people live without modern comforts, e.g., TV	72
Watching group conflict	68
Seeing contestants visit the confession room	65
Seeing people do tasks set by the TV makers and viewers	61
Watching people do everyday things	60
Watching the live eviction program	59
Seeing ex-contestants talk about their experience	58
Watching individual people under stress	57
Watching the nightly TV program	55
Choosing the winner	52
Talking about the program with friends/family	51
Choosing the losers	48
Suggesting tasks	46
Watching people do private things	35
Media coverage of the program	31
Visiting the 24-hour internet site	15
Talking about the program in chat rooms	14

1999). Those aspects of the BB experience that were most "interactive," choosing winners and losers, were not so popular with viewers (52 percent and 48 percent), although this changed with BB2 in 2001, which utilized interactive voting via the Channel 4 digital youth channel E4. Media coverage of BB also rated poorly with viewers (31 percent). Clearly, media coverage helped to make BB a "media event" but also saturated the market with BB gossip. Viewers preferred to be part of the media event through firsthand experience (watching and talking about BB) rather than reading about it secondhand.

The aspect of BB content that was liked by the greatest percentage of all respondents (72 percent) was seeing people live without modern comforts. Perhaps, part of the attraction to watching people live without modern comforts is related to how real people cope in a manufactured situation, whether this be the BB house, or an island, or a jungle environment. Lacking contact with the outside world, contestants were forced to interact with each other, and this often led to conflict, the second most popular content (68 percent) in BB. Tensions within the group would also drive contestants to the confession room, the third most popular content (65 percent). The format for BB encouraged tension, and this was particularly popular with Channel 4's target audience: younger viewers, especially with college education, were more likely to enjoy seeing group conflict (83 percent of sixteen- to twenty-five-year-olds) than older viewers.

The aspect of BB content least liked was watching people doing private things (35 percent). This is puzzling. Statistics show the British public do not like intrusive cameras in factual entertainment, and perhaps watching people doing private things in the BB house was equated with "intrusiveness." However, one cannot watch BB without cameras positioned to be "intrusive" and trained to follow people engaged in private activities.

We explored the statistical results in the qualitative fieldwork, and the findings point to another explanation for viewer attraction to BB. On one hand, when choosing from a list of features in the survey, the majority of respondents opted for "people living without modern comforts" and shied away from the more private aspects of the BB house, although, arguably, if there had been a category for "performance," the results may have been different. The findings in the qualitative data back up the statistics in the survey, which showed a high level of expectation that real people act up for the cameras in factual entertainment. The findings also relate to research of German viewers of BB, which argues that talk about contestants is influenced by questions of authenticity (Mikos and Prommer 2001).

Although there isn't space to do justice to the qualitative data on factual entertainment (see Hill 2005), nevertheless, some extracts will illustrate the type of dialogue that accompanies watching BB. This dialogue does focus on the personal; however, watching people doing private things is interpreted in relation to self-display. Viewers watched BB, in particular scenes that involved group conflict (e.g., Nasty Nick scene) and looked for moments of truth that could be glimpsed through the improvised performance of BB contestants. The contestants were, after all, taking part in a game show, and viewers expected contestants to play to cameras:

> Maybe you put yourself in that situation and see . . . it's like I watch it and see if I was on BB, I'd want everyone to like me or I think of myself as an alright person. And if I was on there, I'd be acting different, I got to do this because people gotta like me, so, maybe that's why I think they're acting up. They must have thought about everything they've done and said before they actually said and done it. (29-year-old male salesman)

Not only did viewers expect contestants to act up for the cameras, they also expected this improvisation to break down:

> I think at the beginning they definitely weren't acting themselves, they were strange people in that programme, but as it unraveled, I don't know, I think they did become themselves more. . . . I don't know how much they could react to the camera because there is only a certain amount that you can control your emotions. (22-year-old unemployed female)

However, caution is needed in referring to authenticity and artifice in factual programming. In documentary theory, much discussion has taken place as to the "authenticity" of tele-representation, especially in observational filmmaking (see Corner 1996; Winston 1995, 2000; among others). This discussion is relevant to my argument about viewers' perception of authenticity in BB primarily because general viewers of BB are unfamiliar with academic and industry debate about the reality of depicted behavior in documentary TV. Indeed, the general viewer of all types of factual entertainment, including BB, is unfamiliar with most documentary, and they choose to watch popular factual because they perceive it as more accessible than traditional documentary.

Although many viewers are aware of press reports questioning the truthfulness of popular factual, and my research illustrates their cynicism about the reality in factual entertainment, this does not mean audiences have rejected the *idea* of authenticity in factual TV. In fact, audiences have developed viewing strategies that foreground authenticity in a highly constructed TV environment. For the average TV viewer, judging authenticity in popular factual programs such as BB is related to judging the integrity of the self. When contestants in BB are faced with emotionally difficult situations, they often reveal their "true" nature. Audience attraction to judging levels of authenticity in BB is primarily based on whether contestants stay true to themselves, rather than whether the program is truthful in its depiction of contestants.

If we consider factual entertainment as a whole, viewing strategies for BB are linked to a general attraction to the management and/or transformation of the self in popular factual. Although there is not space to explore this fully, a constructive way to consider BB is from the point of view of self-management. Although we are watching contestants in a gamedoc, we are also watching non-professional actors negotiate difficult situations. These real people experience a transformation from ordinary person to celebrity, and also a transformation of the self. Many contestants leave the BB house and tell us how much they learned about themselves, how being in the BB house was not primarily related to money but to personal development. In this sense, they are all winners. Much factual entertainment focuses on transformation, whether this be transformation of the self or of the home, and this is often achieved through self-display, where the viewers are asked to judge for themselves how much a person, object, or space has been altered for the better. Viewing strategies for BB, which foreground authenticity in relation to the self, are connected to a general development in formatted factual TV to highlight self-display and personal improvement, a highly attractive characteristic of factual entertainment.

Conclusion

Clearly, BB is part of a new development in factual entertainment, one that foregrounds performance. Other examples of factual entertainment, such as docu-soaps, have capitalized on real people "performing the real" in front of cameras, and BB, and its cousins, take this a stage further. Thus, in *Celebrity Big Brother* (GMG Endemol, Channel 4), we see professional actors in private, performing for a public charity. Such developments in audiovisual documentation have led to a marked uneasiness on behalf of audiences of factual entertainment. The general public does not believe in the reality of real-TV, which is thought to be exaggerated or even made up, and, in relation to this, the public expects real people to perform for the cameras. In this ambiguous, playful environment, BB performed strongly. The format proved to be successful across different cultures, tapping into a desire for new factual programming, and was successful with segments of viewers, in particular the much coveted sixteen- to thirty-four-year-old, educated, upwardly mobile viewer.

What impact will BB have on factual entertainment, and on viewers' interpretive frameworks for audiovisual documentation? It is too early to say how BB, and other gamedocs will survive in the long term. Certainly, in relation to audience attraction to all types of factual entertainment, BB scores poorly. A general TV audience wants to see informative programs, which go behind the scenes and capture someone's real story on camera. In fact, there is much evidence to suggest that audiences are tired of the performative documentary and want to see more hidden camera programs, where real people are "really" themselves in a natural, more often unnatural, environment (see Hill 2005). While this may ring alarm bells in terms of "surveillance" . . . it points to a desire for less artifice and more actuality in factual entertainment.

Viewers' strategies for watching factual TV are, in my opinion, several moves ahead of the game. If part of the attraction in watching BB is to look for a moment of authenticity in relation to selfhood, then audiences are responding to the hybrid of performance and reality that has come to characterize much factual entertainment. The "game" is to find the "truth" in the spectacle/performance environment. There is an evolution in viewing strategies, and despite the trend for more performative gamedocs at present, it would be surprising if viewers asked for more artifice in factual TV. In John Corner's postdocumentary culture, the audience is looking for evidence of the real, especially in relation to the presentation of the self in television.

Notes

1. My audience research is funded by the Economic and Social Research Council, the Independent Television Commission, and Channel 4. The research involves quantitative and qualitative methods. A survey was conducted during August 2000 involving a representative sample of 8,216 adults (ages sixteen to sixty-five plus) and 937 children (ages four to fifteen) TV viewers; focus groups were conducted during November 2000 (twelve groups, plus three pilot groups); in-depth interviews with families in their homes are currently under way for a six-month period.

2. All figures in this section are taken from press packs for *Big Brother* (Channel 4 press pack), published ratings data (Broadcasters' Audience Research Bureau [BARB] and Nielson), and the industry magazine Channel 21 International Nov/Dec 2000 (p. 42).

3. Thanks to Cosette Castro for information regarding *Big Brother* in Portugal. According to TVI, the average share was 61 percent for the first series of *Big Brother*.

4. The ratings only paint one picture of *Big Brother* in Sweden; despite average ratings, the show was popular and much discussed in the public domain.

5. Jane Roscoe refers to the production context and ratings for BB in Australia in her article "Big Brother Australia: Performing the Real Twenty-Four Seven" (forthcoming).

6. Thanks to Edgardo Garcia for information regarding *Big Brother* in Argentina.

7. The Broadcasters' Audience Research Bureau (BARB) ratings for Wednesday 11 July 2001 show that 626,000 viewers tuned in to watch E4, compared to 300,000 viewers for Channel 5 and 400,000 viewers for Channel 4 at the same time, 11 PM.

8. See Broadcast 31 July 2001.

9. The ratings for *Survivor* in the United Kingdom in no way mirrored the huge success of *Survivor* in the United States: BARB ratings for June 2001 confirm that *Survivor* began with more than 6 million viewers, but this dropped to an average of 4 million for the rest of its run, a poor performance for ITV1.

10. Caroline Dover is assisting me in this research project, and her analysis of the survey has been used extensively in this article.

11. The sample has been weighted in the analysis to ensure that variables such as sex, age, and social class are fully representative of national and regional populations. The population targets were those estimated by BARB.

12. There is not space in this article to report on the full findings of the survey—a report is available from the Independent Television Commission. Ethnicity was one variable we were unable to explore in our research, owing to the makeup of the BARB sample: this is a pity as data are needed on ethnic audiences and factual entertainment.

13. Thirteen- to fifteen-year-olds and, especially, sixteen- to twenty-four-year-olds are more likely than other age groups to like intrusive cameras, seeing the reactions of the public to presenters/real people, arguments and disagreements, up-to-the-minute stories, and looking into other people's lives. For example, 53 percent of thirteen- to fifteen-year-olds and 60 percent of sixteen- to twenty-four-year-olds like seeing arguments, compared with 30 percent of under-13s and 38 percent of older adults.

14. The only difference occurred in relation to age and education (56 percent of sixteen- to twenty-four-year-olds compared to 40 percent of sixty-five and older; 44 percent fifteen and older terminal education compared to 56 percent nineteen and older terminal education).

15. The only differences occurred in relation to age, education, and internet access (74 percent sixteen- to twenty-four-year-olds, compared with 63 percent sixty-five and older; 67 percent fifteen and older terminal education compared with 79 percent students; 78 percent with internet access, compared with 68 percent without internet access).

16. See Ien Ang (1985) and Dorothy Hobson (1982) among others for research in TV viewers and soap operas.

References

Abercrombie, Nicholas, and Brian Longhurst. 1998. *Audiences: A Sociological Theory of Performance and Imagination*. London: Sage.

Ang, Ien. 1985. *Watching Dallas: Soap Opera and the Melodramatic Imagination*. Translated by Della Couling. London: Methuen.

Bruzzi, Stella. 2000. *New Documentary: A Critical Introduction*. London: Routledge.

Corner, John. 1996. *The Art of Record*. Manchester, UK: Manchester University Press.

———. 2000. What Do We Know about Documentary? *Media, Culture and Society* 22:5.

Dovey, John. 2000. *Freakshows: First Person Media and Factual* TV. London: Pluto.

Gauntlett, David, and Annette Hill. 1999. *TV Living: Television, Culture and Everyday Life*. London: Routledge.

Hill, Annette. 2005. *Reality TV: Audiences and Popular Factual Television*. London: Routledge.

Hobson, Dorothy. 1982. *Crossroads: The Drama of a Soap Opera*. London: Methuen.

Jones, Janet. 2001. *Pore-Close TV: Big Brother and the Internet*. Unpublished paper.

McLean, Gareth. 2000. You Are Watching *Big Brother*. *Guardian*, 3 August, p. 6.

Mikos, Lothar, and Elizabeth Prommer. 2001. Watching *Big Brother* in Germany. Unpublished paper.

Moores, Shaun. 2000. *Media and Everyday Life in Modern Society*. Edinburgh, Scotland: Edinburgh University Press.

Roscoe, Jane. Forthcoming. *Popstars:* The Ultimate Docu-Soap. *Continuum: Journal of Critical Studies*.

Winston, Brian. 1995. *Claiming the Real: The Documentary Film Revisited*. London: British Film Institute.

———. 2000. *Lies, Damn Lies, and Documentary*. London: British Film Institute.

Telenovela Reception in Rural Brazil
Gendered Readings and Sexual Mores

Antonio C. La Pastina

During my fieldwork in Macambira,[1] the small rural community at the center of this ethnographic account, a song from the previous carnival season was still popular among local residents who playfully danced the new steps learned from television shows. *Na boquinha da garrafa* (roughly translated as "on the mouth of the bottle") alluded to a bottle, typically beer, placed upright on the floor with a woman rhythmically dancing around it, slowly lowering herself over the bottle until she nearly touched the phallically positioned stem with her crotch. This became a disturbing image for me after seeing young girls, none more than 12 years of age, dancing to this tune during a celebration in school and again during a political rally honoring one of the mayoral candidates. My perception that these children were being sexualized could be the result of my "foreign gaze," which might have lost its "Brazilian sensibilities" after many years of socialization in the U.S., or it could be the result of observing young boys in the audience whistling and making sexual remarks. This precocious sexualization, which also concerned many in the community, indicates a connection between popular media, especially television, and sexual mores that originate in the southern urban centers of Brazil where most television shows are produced. Television, at least in this context, seems to be located at the center of a process through which viewers learn, question, and sometimes incorporate new norms, values, and behaviors.

Since its creation in the early 1950s, the Brazilian television system has spread to 99% of Brazil's municipalities (Faria & Potter, 1994), connecting a large territory and providing rural and isolated viewers with a glimpse into the life of the urban south, mainly Rio de Janeiro and São Paulo. Television, and the highly popular primetime serials called telenovelas, expose local viewers to attitudes and behaviors that many residents in Macambira deem foreign to the local culture. Several studies have investigated the reception of telenovelas among rural audiences in Brazil (Almeida, 2001, 2003; Costa, 1997; Kottak,

Antonio C. La Pastina, "Telenovela Reception in Rural Brazil: Gendered Readings and Sexual Mores." From *Critical Studies in Media Communication*, Vol. 21, No. 2 (June 2004), pp. 162–181. Reprinted by permission of Taylor & Francis Ltd. (http://www.tandf.co.uk/journals).

1990, 1991, 1992; La Pastina, 1995, 1999, 2001, 2003a, 2004; Pace, 1993; Pennacchioni, 1984; Prado, 1987, 1995; Sluyter-Beltrão, 1993; Triguero, 1987). These studies have found that in many cases local viewers, especially youth, emulate fashion and slang as a way to participate vicariously in the national urban culture. But few studies have investigated how traditional gender norms and rural isolation mediate the reception of telenovelas (Martin-Barbero, 1987/1993).

The present study discusses how rural viewers appropriated telenovelas in their daily lives and how the meanings assigned to the texts are mediated by the local patriarchal culture and by Macambira's peripheral location in relation to the urban context presented on screen. The isolated location of Macambira intensified the perceived gap between the local lifestyle and the urban reality constructed by the telenovelas. The conflicts between traditional gender roles, the economic necessity of relying on women's labor, and the penetration of foreign southern values created a fissure in the life of the community, challenging values, norms, and sexual behaviors, and perhaps promoting change. This work is located in this transitional time for residents of Macambira, a time in which telenovelas became entwined in viewers' lives as an alternative to their own reality, as a guide to urban forms of leisure and entertainment, and as a tool to challenge the traditional patriarchal order.

The ethnographic data discussed in this study were collected over a year-long period from March 1996 to February 1997 in Macambira, a community of roughly 2,000 inhabitants in the dry *Sertão do Seridó*, an area where unpredictable rainfall and soil exhaustion have created a culture of migration and economic dependence on government subsidies and female artisanal labor. For two generations, women have embroidered fine linen for wealthy patrons in the state capital 200 miles away.

Within the context of poverty that dominated the interior of northeastern Brazil, Macambira seemed to defy the images normally associated with the dry backlands. The paved main roads and white cinder block houses gave first-time visitors the impression that Macambira was a wealthy community. But a walk on the outskirts changed that perception. Of the 400 homes in the community, about 10% had no electricity, all used septic tanks, and several had no running water. The majority of the population lived with limited resources, while a few, normally white and male, dominated the economy through land ownership, political patronage, or commerce.[2]

While local commerce was limited and offered only the staples, many residents periodically traveled to Caicó, a city of 50,000 and the largest urban center in the region, to purchase other consumer items. Most residents regularly wore shorts and T-shirts, normally from political campaigns or from a carnival block, dressing up only for parties or special occasions. Some, mostly women, had their clothes sewn by one of several local seamstresses who purchased fashion magazines so their customers could pick a style. But most already had a clear idea of the clothes they wanted: usually the dress of an actress on a telenovela. The community's geographical isolation means that it has limited access primarily to one television network as well as limited physical and economic access to urban consumer culture, hindering the potential to reproduce lifestyles presented on television.[3]

Of the 203 households sampled in a survey conducted in Macambira (Rios-Neto, Miranda-Ribeiro, & Potter, 1998), 24% of the respondents said that television was their preferred form of entertainment, followed by chatting (22%), strolling (15%), and listening to music (9%). Other self-reported leisure activities mentioned were religion (5%), partying (6%), and household tasks (3%). From these data, it is clear that for most residents television and music dominated leisure opportunities, along with chatting and strolling—activities rooted in a pre-technological era. Nevertheless, radio and television were more than forms of entertainment; they also represented symbolic class ascension through the acquisition of knowledge. Beyond a passive form of entertainment, they represented access to the outside world. In the remainder of this essay, I will discuss established approaches to the study of telenovela reception, introduce the community where the ethnographic fieldwork was conducted and propose how a specific telenovela interpretation was mediated by the local patriarchal culture and the community's geographical isolation.

Interpreting Telenovelas

In the last three decades, the role of telenovelas in Brazilian society has attracted growing attention among scholars who have looked at their popularity and the sophistication of their production values (Mattelart & Mattelart, 1987/1990) to raise questions regarding ideological domination, imperialism, and their potential to promote social change. Some scholars have argued that Brazilian telenovelas reproduce Hollywood's imperialistic discourse (Herold, 1988; Oliveira, 1990), while others have examined the export of Brazilian programs to challenge the argument of cultural imperialism and defend the growth of regional production centers (Sinclair, 1996). Still others have argued that telenovelas have the potential to promote beneficial social change (Faria & Potter, 1994; McAnany, 1993; Vink, 1988). Reviewing the Latin America literature on telenovela reception, McAnany and La Pastina (1994) found that most studies did not attempt to understand the interconnectedness of societal (economic, political, cultural) and textual factors that influence viewers' meaning creation and appropriation of these texts. In order to comprehend the reception process, there is a need to understand how different contextual factors influence viewers' interpretations and how the contextual factors, in concert with the telenovelas, might reproduce patriarchal power structures that traditionally privilege men over women.

Most audience studies, particularly telenovela reception projects in Latin America, ignore men in their data collection. There is an assumption, erroneous in the case of Brazil, that men are not part of the telenovela audience. Most media researchers in Brazil seem to have bought into the Globo network's[4] constructed notion of telenovelas as female texts that are predominantly consumed by female viewers (Hamburger, 1999), even though Ortiz,

Borelli and Ramos (1988) demonstrated through ratings data that close to 40% of the audience of Brazilian telenovelas was male.[5]

Telenovela reception studies also have been limited to one particular telenovela (or two in the case of Prado, 1987), but all seem to make references to other telenovelas mentioned by viewers (McAnany & La Pastina, 1994). Tufte (1994, 2000) expanded the focus from one telenovela by analyzing the case of an actress, Regina Duarte, and her insertion in telenovela texts. However, what becomes clear from the selection of media texts used in these research endeavors is that the issues perceived and debated by viewers are directly related to the narratives within the text. Sluyter-Beltra$tio's (1993) viewers talked about political issues not only because her interviewees were more politicized, but also because the text she was using represented a clear parody of the Brazilian political system. Leal's (1986, 1988) women discussed their personal relationships in relation to the women in the telenovela who also were discussing their own relationships. Tufte's (1994, 2000) respondents articulated their experiences of class and racial discrimination relating to a leading character in a telenovela who was going through similar situations. Tufte also cites the example of a *mulatta* woman who recalled from her repertoire of telenovela memories the discrimination suffered by the character of a black architect in the telenovela *Corpo a Corpo* ("Body to body") aired in 1984–1985 to explain her views on the problem of discrimination in the telenovela they were discussing. These examples seem to indicate that telenovelas can provide interpretive frames that allow viewers to construct meaning in the interface between the available textual material, viewers' cultural capital (Bourdieu, 1984), and the contextual elements in the viewing environment (La Pastina, 1999, 2001, 2004).

Martin-Barbero (1987/1993) proposes that instead of studying the relation between viewers and texts from "the logic of production and reception . . . we [should] start with the mediations where the social materialization and the cultural expression of television are delimited and configured" (p. 215). The mediations are the

> place from where one can understand the interaction between the space of production and reception: that which is produced on television does not necessarily relate uniquely to the requirements of the industrial system . . . but also to the demands of the cultural web and from the ways of seeing. (Martin-Barbero & Munõz, 1992, p. 20, my translation)

With the mediations project, Martin-Barbero is attempting to decenter media, arguing that media is losing "its specificity and becoming an integral part of the economic, cultural and political system" (Richeri's study as cited in Martin-Barbero, 1987/1993, p. 215). This "abdication of mediacentrism" is the result of social movements that push media to be integral to the economic system. Mediations are then the "structures encrusted in the social practices and the everyday" (Lopes, Borelli, & Resende, 2002, p. 39, my translation). Therefore the mediations become a central sphere where media functions and interpretations can be understood in relation to everyday life because they "produce and reproduce the social signification, thereby creating a *sphere* which makes the understanding of the interactions between production and reception possible" (Tufte, 2000, p. 21). Orozco (1991) argues it is important to consider multiple sites of mediation. Telenovela appropriation in a small rural community, such as Macambira, is mediated by social talk (gossip), knowledge of genre rules, viewers' cultural capital (particularly regarding urban lifestyles), the local patriarchal culture, and geographical isolation. This study will focus on the role of these last two spheres of mediation.

Approaching reception through mediations can represent an important alternative to the understanding of the relationship between viewers and text. In focusing on particular spheres of mediation, we can understand how different contextual factors interact with viewing practices, viewers' values and beliefs, and the text, providing a more dynamic framework to analyze different layers of interpretation.

Audience Ethnography: Theory and Practice

Tufte (2000), supporting the relevance of audience ethnography, presented a valuable analysis of the distinctions between reception and ethnographic approaches to studying audiences. He argues that reception studies have traditionally been short-term, focused on one place of reception, normally the house, and relied mostly on interviews using a deductive approach to the data. Audience ethnography, on the other hand, relies on long-term immersion, locating the process of engagement between viewers and media texts in the everyday life through an inductive, multi-method approach of collecting and analyzing data.

The ethnographic process that Tufte (2000) refers to allows the researcher to gain exposure to a wide range of community members, to observe the insertion of cultural and media products in the local reality, and to locate the reception practices within a broader context more suited to understanding the dynamics shaping this engagement process. In attempting to understand those dynamics, most of the information presented here was collected through extensive informal conversations; structured, unstructured, and ethnographic interviews (Lindlof & Taylor, 2002); and participant observation. Repeated in-depth interviews with a select group of residents, 30 in total, were conducted in an attempt to engage with telenovela viewers across class, gender, age, race, and educational boundaries. Many of the accounts collected in these interviews reinforced information gathered from other residents with whom I maintained extensive informal contact. Data from two surveys conducted in the community, as well as archival data, focus groups, and participant observation, were used in the weaving of this account of the engagement between the telenovela and its interpretation by local residents. The data collected through these different methodologies over the period of the fieldwork were, in traditional ethnographic practice (Sanjek, 1990), analyzed and reanalyzed through several readings and siftings of the data that allowed me to develop categories and refine them in ways that reflected my experience in the field.

Mankekar (1999) uses ethnography "to evoke the contexts in which texts are interpreted and to demonstrate the inextricability of the text from the context" (p. 20). For her, "television cannot be reduced to the text on the screen, but instead must extend to the spaces occupied by television in the daily lives and practices of viewers" (p. 21). I agree with Mankekar that when investigating the interrelation between television and viewers' everyday lives, ethnographic practices allow researchers to position themselves within the process of consumption and observe the patterns of interaction, incorporation, or rejection, the ways in which the texts are embodied, and the "articulation of experience with structures of power and inequality" (Mankekar, 1999, p. 21).

The process of operationalizing audience ethnography has been problematized by several scholars (La Pastina, 2003b; Murphy, 1999; Murphy & Krady, 2003; Tufte, 2000). And great emphasis has been placed on the community "entry." Mine was facilitated by distant interpersonal connections, but my actual entry into community life happened only three weeks into my stay as the result of torrential storms that flooded my room in the elementary school lockers. Suddenly there were three empty houses I could rent. At that point I had started to teach English at the local high school as a substitute, which established my role in the community's social fabric. Even after my duties were finished I was still referred to as the *professor*.

My native status as a Brazilian, fluent in Portuguese, did not transfer to a local or native status. Instead I remained an outsider, even if one with strong ties with some residents and the national and local culture. My de facto or perceived cultural, economic, social, and symbolic capital enabled me to have access to certain groups in the community but hindered access to others, particularly marginalized members of the community. To overcome those barriers I took advantage of extended networks through friendship and socialization. But without the help of Mira, a local nurse who conducted bi-weekly house visits, access to more peripheral sectors of the community would have been almost impossible.

The Cattle King in Macambira

Context

In her book on soap operas and women's talk, Brown (1994) argues that women "can enjoy soap operas [and telenovelas] even though [these soaps] may be ideologically consistent with dominant values. But, at the same time, they may take up these pleasures and use them to critique these same values" (p. 5). For Brown, much of the pleasure in soap opera fanship lies in women's ability to talk about programs that are produced with them in mind. Brown is attempting to demonstrate how women appropriate soap opera narratives to subvert dominant hegemonic structures. This patriarchal hegemonic discourse that she argues women can subvert in their interaction with telenovelas is central to understanding the engagement between viewers in Macambira and telenovelas.

Faria and Potter (1994) suggest that telenovelas might have a role in promoting changes in established patriarchal relationships in Brazil. They believe that gender relations might have been one area in which telenovelas helped create a point of conflict and allowed women's agency to push for change. They also argue that telenovelas may erode male authority while promoting female autonomy. Kottak (1990, 1992), in an extensive ethnographic study of five communities in Brazil, also argues that TV viewing has the potential for liberating attitudes toward gender roles. In many cases, it seems that television becomes a bridge that links traditional local gender roles and urban, outside views. Pace (1993), researching in Gurupá, and Kottak (1990, 1991, 1992), working in Arempebe, both villages in rural Brazil, argues:

> Television has extended Brazilians' horizons beyond home and community, forming a bridge between family and nation. Operating on a daily basis, the TV set has become the main mechanism by which images, and people who are not relatives, friends or neighbors enter the home. It introduces otherwise unfamiliar settings and types of people. Country people glimpse urban life, city dwellers meet rural folk. (Kottak, 1992, p. 271)

In Macambira, television was a source of pleasure and information, as well as the main leisure activity available to most residents. Men and women had distinct preferences regarding what they watched and explained these gender preferences in terms of men's and women's tastes. Males and females perceived that men's preferences were news, sports, and action films, while women's were romance and variety programs. The division between the tastes of men and women seemed to follow a traditional patriarchal view of gendered television usage, but the living room politics described by Morley (1986) did not apply to this community, due primarily to limited access to other channels and to women's empowerment within many households.

The lack of available job opportunities for males and the increasing demand for embroidered textiles by the growing tourist industry in the region's coastal cities has resulted in women having, on average, a greater income than their male partners. This reliance on embroidery has slowly shifted the perception of women's roles in the community and tilted the gender balance, leading to different household arrangements. In some homes, the man was the primary provider, but those were few and normally the man held a political position or owned a small business in which the woman assisted. In a few cases, the men were liberal professionals, but less than 10% of the population fit that profile. Those homes normally owned a satellite dish and the man controlled the remote.

The second category included those men who boasted they supported their families, but their wives helped substantially, even when the husbands did not acknowledge it. There was a perception among many residents that men whose wives were the breadwinners had their self-esteem damaged, leading to emotional distress and alcoholism. For some, there was an impression that women were reveling in their economic power, demanding more freedom as men became more submissive.

There was a third category in which the breadwinner was clearly the wife who worked as an embroiderer and provided for the household. This group was divided into men who did not help with household chores and those who were the main caretakers. In those households, some of the men had temporary jobs, depending on their qualifications, the availability of jobs and the network to which they belonged, and their commitment to helping within the household.

There were few monoparental households that were not multigenerational. Normally when the woman was left or left her partner, she returned to her parents' home or moved in with a brother or sister. The few exceptions had a difficult time supporting the household and taking care of domestic chores. Multigenerational households were the norm. Many younger couples lived with the family of one of the spouses until they could get their own homes, which normally involved the patronage of the mayor who would build a house for the new family with federal funds. Multigenerational households were also advantageous in terms of reduced expenses and distribution of duties. Different activities were assigned to different members of the households, increasing the time for women to embroider. In some families, this arrangement reduced even further the males' roles in the household.

Nevertheless, patriarchal relationships with clear gender role definitions were still present in the local imagination. *Machista* households were based on certain expectations regarding gender roles. There was a clear definition of what pertained to male and female domains. The wife was supposed to care for the house and children, while the husband worked outside the house and supported the family. When the wife worked, she was helping support the household, even if hers was the main source of income, while the husband who did any household chores was only helping. The man's sexuality was not contained by the marriage. His escapades (or adultery) were perceived as wrong but not socially punished, while the wife was to remain loyal to her husband.

The realization that a woman could bring more money into the household if she devoted more hours to embroidery led many couples to rethink the traditional male and female duties within the household. A growing number of men openly told me about cooking, cleaning, and caring for children. Many, however, were still reluctant to acknowledge caring for the household, because of concerns about their image, their authority, and, ultimately, their masculinity. One local man set the limits of a man's household share at washing clothes. It took me a while to realize that washing clothes for most people in Macambira was still a public activity, involving carrying the clothes to the water hole and washing them bent over the water.[6] There was still reluctance among males to publicly engage in activities perceived to be feminine. Nevertheless, the economic context of shrinking opportunities for men and the growing reliance on women's labor forced many to question the traditional patriarchal ideals and adapt their lifestyles to fit their economic needs. In the households described above, women exerted a growing role as breadwinners and consequently had a greater influence over family decisions and leisure opportunities, including the choice of channels to watch. It is in this conflictive terrain, where men and women experienced the challenges of adapting to new gender roles, that media, perceived as foreign to the local values and traditions, became an important source of information and point of contention.

These media images led many in Macambira to question their sense of belonging in the national and global culture. Among the majority of the population a gap existed between desire and access, promoting the local population to deal continuously with a sense of alienation from the televised nation. Television seemed continuously to reinforce this position of isolation and difference, while allowing viewers to be connected to a broader world and know about what was going on in other places. As Pace (1993) found in Gurupá, following the arrival of television, people knew more than before about the outside world and events in Brasilia, the national capital, and other nations. But they also knew more about the nation and the world than they knew about regional and state politics. For people in the remote Gurupá in the Amazon region, the state capital of Belém became more remote and less interesting than the geographically remote urban centers of the south. This was a sentiment shared by many in Macambira. A constant complaint was that they knew less about what was going on in Natal, the state capital, than they knew about the south, especially São Paulo and Rio de Janeiro. In part, this was because local newscasts were underdeveloped and viewers with a satellite dish could not access them anyway. This displacement from the regional level reduced political and economic knowledge about the state capital as well as access to consumption opportunities. While the novelty of television in Gurupá created an intense desire for news and knowledge about the outside world, the long-term relationship with television in Macambira (where there had been some exposure to the medium since the early 1980s) increased residents' desire to know more about their own region.

Text

The narrative of *The Cattle King* begins in the World War II years on coffee farming land in rural Brazil where the children of two enemy Italian families fell in love. The narrative then moves to the present, where the son of the renegade couple, Bruno, is a wealthy cattle rancher. His family life is falling apart; his wife has betrayed him, and his spoiled children, Lia and Marcos, are involved in drugs and relationships of which he disapproves. In the midst of this crisis he meets a poor woman, Luana, a member of a group of landless peasants who invaded his farm. He falls in love with her, only to discover that she is his cousin through her mother's side, a family he still hates for mistreating his parents. The narrative weaves three locations, both urban and rural, and two main themes: romantic conflicts and land reform.

The romantic couples in this narrative represented adultery (Leia betrayed Bruno, Zé do Araguaia betrayed Donana, and the senator "almost" betrayed his wife), battering of women (Leia was battered by her lover/new husband Ralf), and class and age differences (Leia and Ralf, Bruno and Luana, and Lia and Pirilampo). Leia was freed from an abusive relationship only after another jealous husband killed her abusive lover. The class differences between Luana and Bruno and Lia and Pirilampo play out through most of the narrative, lead-ing to conflict and periodic separation.

Bruno is the central axis in the narrative. As in his two previous telenovelas, the author Benedito Rui Barbosa wrote a man's saga and the story of the land he conquered and tamed. In *The Cattle King*, however, he expanded the set-ting from a local to a national one, incorporating the debate over land reform into one man's tale. But ultimately, the narrative is not about that setting or the riches and power that were part of it. That is the background; the story is about Bruno's own voyage of rediscovery, a process of humanization of mas-culinity. In this telenovela the author presented a new masculinity, an *anti-macho* hero. He was still rugged and brave, successful and manly, but at the same time he was loving and forgiving, not afraid to show his emotions and share his feelings. He gave part of his fortune to the ex-wife who betrayed him, left his empire to his children, moved back to his roots to rebuild his life with his new wife, accepted his daughter's pre-marital sex, and understood his son's insecurities in his relationship with Liliana, the senator's daughter he impreg-nated and left standing in the altar. Asked about his representation of mas-culinity through this *anti-macho* male, Barbosa said he had no intention of presenting such an image or raising a debate (Nascimento, 1997). There may have been no intentionality in the hero's portrayal, but the shattering of some *machista* convictions, such as pardoning the adulterous wife, was perceived by some in Macambira as excessive.

With its subplots on agrarian reform politics, cattle ranching, and coffee farming, many local viewers perceived *The Cattle King* as a realistic text. While the rural subtext was enjoyed by women, telenovelas—and *The Cattle King* was no exception—were seen as being mostly about romance. Men often looked to find a reason to follow telenovelas, arguing that only telenovelas with his-torical, realistic, or rural themes attracted them. In contrast, women expected telenovelas to provide a romantic text in which couples slowly built a rela-tionship through conflict, external opposition, and overcoming adversities to fulfill their love. This gender ordering of television taste also was found by Morley (1986) among urban working class viewers in England. Women view-ers in Macambira understood the melodramatic roots of the genre and expected these conventions to be followed by the writers. The modernization of the genre in Brazil, which incorporated contemporary social and political elements (Hamburger, 1999), seemed to some viewers to be distancing it from its melo-dramatic roots, raising complaints among female viewers that Globo's tele-novelas were no longer romantic. The local culture and context, with its patri-archal values and sense of isolation, impacted both men's and women's readings, and in some instances gender distinctions emerged based on view-ers' appropriation of these texts to either question the local norms or the mod-ern urban nation represented in the narratives.

Patriarchy and Telenovela Interpretation

While viewers in Macambira were quick to blame television for community problems such as drugs and teen sex, it was their perception of telenovelas as a threat to the established order that underscored the gender differences in their readings. Men saw telenovelas as a threat to their roles and rights within the local culture, while women saw them as representing an alternative to the gender norms that ordered local life.

Both men and women complained about violence and drugs and said that children misbehaved and no longer respected parents and elders. But the most common accusation was that television, and telenovelas in particular, were showing too much sex, making children excited and prone to engage in it. Many in Macambira perceived *The Cattle King* as a source of values and ideas foreign to those considered the norm in the community. A third person effect model (Davidson, 1983) seemed to be espoused by many viewers who saw television affecting only other people and never the person speaking. In many instances, especially in cases such as *The Cattle King* where a woman had committed adultery, women were seen as potential victims of these television images and messages. It seems that only adult males were perceived to be immune to the impact of television.

Embodying the local patriarchal values expressed in Macambira, Requião, an important local politician and father of three daughters, felt television was threatening traditional morals and values. He did not watch telenovelas, although he had when he was young. He had decided to stop watching because he felt he was "hooked" on them. Early in my stay we were talking about the sexual life of the community and he told me about the increasing number of young women who would have sex with their boyfriends, who, in many cases, they did not marry. He never considered mentioning the boyfriends were also having sex prior to marriage. For him, as for most in the community, it was taken for granted that men would have pre-marital sexual experiences. According to Requião, few couples married; most just moved into cohabitation. For him, television was the main reason there was such a change in values: "TV is always teaching that to have sex is good and fun. People see [it on TV] and they just want to do it."

Requião had a reputation for being a womanizer. By the end of my stay I had heard of many affairs, including a scandal around election time when he supposedly had sex with a 15-year-old girl. Several people criticized the young girl for always being after him, "not giving him a break." This relationship was constructed as the result of her pursuing him and ultimately breaking his self-control. The general view seemed to be that women, unlike men, could exert self-control over their sexuality.

This patriarchal culture, challenged by the changing roles of women in the local economy, mediated viewers' readings of issues such as pre-marital sex and adultery. In both situations, women were constructed as more responsible for their sexual acts, while men's behavior was perceived to be the result of natural urges. Television and telenovelas were seen as responsible for breaking this patriarchal order, influencing children and teenagers, and especially girls and young women, to engage in precocious sex, undermining the gender norms that held women responsible for saving themselves for the right men.

In seeing television as responsible for the spread of new ideas about sexuality and pleasure, parents acknowledged the media's role in disseminating views that conflicted with the accepted set of moral codes in the community. Some women saw the potential for their children to learn about safe sex, but generally the view was that telenovelas and other shows were undermining the structure of society by promoting the idea that young women could have sex prior to their marriage and be independent of their families and/or protective male figures, such as fathers, boyfriends, or husbands. When discussing the adulterous wife in the telenovela, many viewers saw her behavior as pernicious for bringing ideas not to teens but to women. These representations, coupled with the growing independence of many local women, increased the perception of telenovelas as a threat to the fragile local patriarchal structure.

It was the interpretation of the adulterous wife in the telenovela that clearly presented a schism between men's and women's reliance on local patriarchal values. Eusébio, the town barber, verbalized most male views about *The Cattle King*. He liked the telenovela a lot until Bruno, who had already been betrayed, pardoned his adulterous wife. "After he brought his wife back home I got sick of it and stopped watching it . . . Men here don't like that." The view of a man befriending his adulterous wife, proposed by the telenovela, produced an image of a "new man," an image of a more sensitive, respecting and understanding male, shedding patriarchal attitudes of privilege. This new male, however, had little resonance with male viewers in Macambira.

August held a transitional view. Comfortable with his wife working out of town at night as a nurse, he acknowledged that a woman's reputation was still much more vulnerable than a man's. His view was that women in the telenovelas, and consequently in larger centers, were already liberated and engaging in practices that were still perceived to be wrong in a small town such as Macambira. He believed that women, even in rural communities, had gained more freedom and that society was more accepting. He saw Leia as a bad example but felt that her husband forgiving her was a positive lesson for traditional communities such as Macambira.

The most traditional split between men's and women's views of her adultery was seen in their explanations of why she did it. For most men she was a *safada*, a "no-good." For most women she was bored, lonely, and frustrated by her husband's extensive absence to care for his farmers. The fact that he was a provider seemed to justify for most men his frequent absence and lack of attention to his wife. However, most women did not seem to feel that providing for the family was the most important element in a relationship.

During an interview with Everton and Maria Antonia, married for more than 12 years with two children, a distinction between their views about Leia and her adultery became noticeable, symbolizing a gap between men's and women's readings. In contrast to his wife, Everton could see no possible explanation for Leia's behavior and had no understanding of her motivations. This underlined the awareness among local women of an unjust balance between men's and women's rights and roles within relationships. While men seemed more prone to judge Leia as responsible for the downfall of her family and son (who at a certain point in the narrative was accused of killing her lover), women seemed more understanding and aware of Leia's motivations for committing adultery, even if they recriminated her actions. Several women, and no men, mentioned Bruno's acknowledgment of his faults as a husband and father as partly responsible for the demise of their relationship.

There was a clear sense from the interviews I conducted and the time I spent talking with these viewers that most believed those programs had a role in promoting behaviors that many deemed inappropriate. Ultimately, telenovelas seemed to be showing a society in which gender relations were different from what was accepted locally, and in doing so they presented the danger of subverting established norms. Perhaps telenovelas were not responsible for any behavior change, as many viewers claimed, but it was undeniable that telenovelas were perceived to be responsible for the promotion of these new urban lifestyles. Telenovelas represented a reality on the screen that, even if remote, seemed to indicate the way their lives might be in the future.

On the Nation's Periphery

While viewers in Macambira saw *The Cattle King* as a realistic narrative, they felt it was remote and uncharacteristic of their own lived experiences. This perceived gap was stressed by the conflict between morals and values presented in the telenovelas and those experienced in their own lives. For many, the core distinction between urban and rural lifestyles was located in the lack of privacy in small towns such as Macambira.

This difference between these two worlds, one urban and modern, the other rural and traditional, also created a sense of being in a peripheral state. Many saw Macambira at the edge of modernity as seen on TV. They could only catch a glimpse at the center of the nation through the screen. At the same time, these viewers were anxious to view this alternative reality; they wanted to see telenovela characters engaging in activities perceived to be urban in nature and location. They were curious to see where these characters dined and were entertained, and how they dressed, spoke, and worked. This desire informed their views of lifestyles as well as the perceived gap between their own choices and those in urban centers. Nevertheless, it seemed that this gap between urban and rural attitudes and values underscored another split between viewers. Men and women did not necessarily share the same opinion on this perceived distance between their own lived experiences and those presented in the telenovelas. Many female viewers were more reluctant than male viewers to read those differences solely in terms of their geographical location.

Dinalva, a 27-year-old mother of two children, thought that women in larger cities could act more freely, like the women in the telenovelas. "In the larger cities the rights [between men and women] are more equal; there is not as much gossip. Here men and women have the same rights but men have more freedom; the woman is marked if she does anything; there is a lot of gossip." In Dinalva's case, gossip exerted a damaging form of social control on women's lives in Macambira, while she believed women in larger cities were immune to those social pressures. For her, equal rights between men and women were assumed but qualified: "Men have more freedom." Zefa Nega echoed Dinalva: "In the big cities it is different, like the old saying: No one sees anything, no one knows about your life or sees the time you get in . . .".

The telenovela seemed to reinforce this perception of a gap between norms and behaviors in urban and rural settings as well as a gap in gender relations. The patriarchal culture of Macambira reinforced men's perceived inherited rights to freedom, while women were limited by the risk of shattering their reputations. While telenovelas might challenge those ingrained beliefs, many viewers maintained that a gap separated their lifestyles from those in urban cities presented in the telenovelas. Viewers of both genders perceived these gaps. Men related the representation of urban norms and values as something distant and, in many ways, unacceptable. Alternatively, women perceived their constraints in comparison to those presented in the telenovelas. For men, this gap was about northeastern rural culture versus urban southern culture; for women it was about freedom and equal rights.

Gedião, a 32-year-old, college-educated, small-business owner, married young when his wife got pregnant. Even though he went through a forced marriage, he had very traditional views on gender issues. He thought that if a woman were not a virgin, a man might not marry her. He saw virginity as good, with symbolic capital ingrained in the local and regional patriarchal culture. Gedião saw strong distinctions between his world and the one represented in the media from the south. These views pervaded his interpretation of telenovelas and the world around him. For him, the telenovela senator's acceptance, understanding, and support of his daughter's pregnancy were characteristic of urban centers in the south. He believed that a major gap existed between parental styles in the two regions. In the case of Macambira, he thought fathers would not be as supportive.

For Gedião, the adulterous Leia provided another example of the distinction between local and urban cultures: "If a woman 'puts horns on his head,' for the rest of his life he will be marked. There are things no one can accept here, you see. And in the south is not like that. I hear that there (in the south) it is common; the woman betrays him and the guy accepts her back." It seems that television was the source for this reading of different levels of acceptance of betrayal between the urbanized south and Macambira. Certainly the stories told by people from the community who moved to the south as temporary workers served to fuel imaginations about licentious behavior and loose sexual mores in the south.

Thirty-year-old Anizio was married to Iná, who was younger and better educated than he. For several years they dated without her parents' approval. When we talked about Leia's adultery, he focused on what he perceived to be the gap between what happened in Macambira and what happened in the telenovelas. He thought that it would be impossible for a man betrayed by his wife to befriend her after they separated. His wife, who had been listening up to that point, started talking about a couple in Macambira who separated and remained friends. He quickly pointed out that they were an exception, and "besides she had not betrayed him." For him, the gap between telenovela and reality was also a gap between urban and rural, anonymity and community intimacy, private and public.

Like Iná, several other women challenged males' readings of characters based solely on the peripheral condition of the community. Benedita named several young women who were single mothers and lived at home with their families, questioning the view that this practice would be acceptable only in the south. The perception of distance between Macambira and the locus of modernity presented in the telenovelas was manifest in the desire of some viewers to have the telenovelas present more of the lifestyles of the characters. At the same time these images served as a reminder of their peripheral status, allowing for the circulation of new trends that could be absorbed and digested by the viewers. This distance also served to reinforce their identity as northeasterners, *Sertanejos,* and small town folk. A typical comment was: "I could never live in São Paulo; it is too dangerous, too big, too crazy." At the same time people were talking about the amenities available for those living in urban centers: more leisure activities, greater shopping opportunities at cheaper costs, and anonymity. In this peripheral state, in which urbanity was perceived as central, viewers in Macambira were constructed as others. As others, these viewers consumed modernity through the media at the same time they isolated what were perceived to be undesirable consequences of this modern reality. This dichotomy forced viewers to seek a position between the two realities; one that was peripheral, but lived, and the other that was central, but only accessible through the screen.

Conclusions

In the opening of this article, I expressed my discomfort with the young girls dancing to a popular carnival song. This feeling about the local sexual mores and norms was also experienced by many residents who consumed telenovelas and other media products and saw a gap between their culture, values, and traditions and those represented on the screen. It is in this sphere—between the local and the televised—that the mediations that structured viewers' interpretations of *The Cattle King* are located. Mediations are the sphere where production and reception interact, creating a space where interpretations can be understood in relation to the broad social, cultural, political, economical, and historical context. In raising issues of sexuality, trust, and moral norms, this telenovela fed viewers with material that, to some, resembled their own experiences. For others, it questioned the local patriarchal culture and exposed the gaps between representations of life in urban centers and their own lives in Macambira. And some had their concerns over the telenovela's content reinforced.

I have discussed how viewers' reception of *The Cattle King* in Macambira, a small rural community in the interior of northeast Brazil, was mediated, among several factors, by the local patriarchal culture and its peripheral location in relation to the urban centers represented in the text. This telenovela's popularity was unquestioned in Macambira, even when elections were attracting most of the town's attention. Viewers followed the telenovela, asking friends and neighbors about what happened when they missed episodes, and watching segments between meetings and rallies. Young and old talked about characters, used language from the telenovela, and knew about the main characters. Few residents had no information about the telenovela.

Established gender norms, attitudes, and the changing political economy of Macambira structured in many ways the levels of interaction between viewers and text. Women's increasing economic power, due to their work as embroiderers, and the increasing dependence of men on women's income, have created a fracture in the traditional male-female domination patterns. This has allowed women to question their roles and men's roles in the household and community. The telenovela seemed to be one way through which women observed alternatives, which were then appropriated to assess their own lives and the life of the community in relation to that of the characters in the south. This finding supports earlier reception study findings by Leal (1986) and Vink (1988) that demonstrated how telenovelas were used by women to explain their lived experiences. Nevertheless, women wanted these contemporary contexts presented within the framework of traditional melodramatic narratives. The telenovela women could be independent and hard working and the men could be sensitive and understanding, but in the end the romantic couples had to finish the narrative happily together. Several women perceived the contemporizing, which pushed telenovelas to become a venue for social and political discourse, as a distraction from the central objective of these narratives—the characters' relationships.

Men, on the other hand, saw this process of contemporizing as a bridge to what they perceived to be a realistic narrative, which justified their viewing and enjoyment of the telenovela. However, the established norms and attitudes regarding gender roles in the community still limited the possibilities for males to acknowledge the melodramatic as enjoyable. Telenovelas, for these males, were valued according to their perceived informational/realistic content. There was a perception that their masculinity, questioned by their inability to provide for their households, could be damaged even more by their association with a feminized text such as a telenovela. Men watching the telenovela preferred to talk about issues that interested them; in the case of *The Cattle King* it was land reform and the rural lifestyle (La Pastina, 1999). Even if the text were perceived as feminine, males used the rural lifestyle and the political narrative to think about their lives in relation to the urban, modern south (La Pastina, 2001). Their interest in these elements of the narrative seemed to indicate that perceived gender norms and patriarchal values did in fact hinder male viewers' engagement with the more traditional melodramatic elements of class ascension, love, and betrayal. This, however, does not mean that males did not pay attention to those elements or were oblivious to them. It means they took a greater interest in elements associated locally with the male sphere, such as politics and farm techniques, rather than engaging with elements normally associated with the female sphere, such as child rearing and romance.

Telenovelas, as I was told many times, have a central role in community life. The television set functions as an electronic storyteller, a bard (Fiske & Hartley, 1978), bringing into the community tales of "distant" lands and "foreign" practices. In this process, television exposes viewers to "practical inadequacies in the culture's sense of itself" (p. 88). People incorporate and challenge values, norms, and beliefs presented in the telenovelas, which often destabilizes the culture from within. It is hard, if not impossible, to attribute causality between telenovelas and social change in Macambira. In this environment, television has created a bridge to another reality that slowly, even if some try to keep it at bay, is permeating community life through fashion, language, behavior, ideals, and aspirations.

Audience ethnographies allow for the possibility of assessing the different elements involved in the reception process and how these elements interact within the context of the locality in which the observation takes place, as well as with the culture and identity of the community members. Television audiences are fluid; they present different characteristics in different situations and toward different programs. Thus, "watching television should be seen as a complex and dynamic cultural process, fully integrated in the messiness of everyday life, and always specific in its meanings and impacts" (Ang, 1991, p. 161). Ethnography provides a domestic context of television and telenovela reception among different groups in the community. It also facilitates an understanding of how the reception context can affect the interpretation of the message by viewers, individually and in groups. The ethnographic approach employed in this study permits the examination of the phenomena in their immediate social, political, and economic contexts, allowing for the mediations proposed by Martin-Barbero (1987/1993) to become apparent and the resulting interpretations to be grounded in the specific context.

Notes

Data reported in this paper were collected over a year of ethnographic work conducted as part of a larger research endeavor entitled "The Social Impact of Television on Reproductive Behavior in Brazil" undertaken by the following institutions in Brazil and the U.S.: Centro Brasileiro de Análise e Planejamento (CEBRAP), Federal University of Minas Gerais, School of Communications at the University of São Paulo, Núcleo the Estudos Populacionais at the University of Campinas, and the Population Research Center at the University of Texas at Austin. Grants from the Mellon and Hewlett Foundations funded the ethnographic work reported here.

The author would like to thank Emile G. McAnany, Karin G. Wilkins, Joseph D. Straubhaar, Joseph Potter, Esther I. Hamburger, Heloisa Buarque de Almeida, Katherine I. Miller, Michael T. Stephenson, Dale A. Rice and the anonymous reviewers and co-editors of CSMC who provided enlightening suggestions for revisions.

1. Macambira, a plant found in the interior of northeastern Brazil that is not only beautiful but resourceful, is the name I assigned to the community in which I conducted this ethnographic work. I also assigned pseudonyms to all informants mentioned in this study.

2. Race was a topic of discussion in Macambira and a constant reminder of the unequal distribution of capital in postcolonial societies that based their development on forced slave labor. Phenotypically, people in Macambira were hard to define; there were some people who identified themselves as whites and some who saw themselves as blacks, but the racial continuum and the indigenous presence in the ethnic make-up made the region quite complex to describe, especially if we were to adopt U.S. racial categories (Bourdieu & Wacquant, 1999). In Macambira most of the wealth was in the hands of the white inheritors of the white settlers who owned the land. In the last three decades increasing interracial marriage has drastically changed the local racial make-up, pushing most of the narratives about racial discrimination to the past tense, even if the present is still tied to inequalities resulting from past racism in Macambira and Brazil. Due to its complexity, race and ethnic perceptions of otherness within the community and by community members of televised representations of otherness deserves an independent treatment far more complex than space permits in this article.

3. Globo, the leading network in Brazil was the only one received by all the households in Macambira. Its reception was only possible because the town had acquired, in the early 1990s, a satellite dish and retransmission tower that allowed the signal of one network to be received and rebroadcast to the surrounding area. In the mid-1990s, with a growing economic instability, many households in Macambira acquired a satellite dish, which increased their access to 14 or 16 channels, depending on the size of the dish.

4. The Globo network is the largest in Brazil and the main producer of telenovelas. It has kept a hold on audience ratings since the early 1970s.

5. Since the early 1990s, many audience scholars have called for more studies that include male viewers (Allen, 1989; Livingstone, 1992). Seiter (1999), nevertheless, raises some of the problems of conducting joint interviews with male and female respondents because these practices might silence female participants. I share Seiter's concern and acknowledge that in the patriarchal context in which this study was conducted, group interviews with male and female participants would have hindered data collection. However, in some situations when I interviewed couples, that process revealed a tension in their readings that I was then able to pursue in individual conversations.

6. Many families washed their clothes in the *açude* (water hole) to save water. It is important to remember that washing clothes in the *açude* was part of most women's lives until recent years. It also had a role in women's socialization in a space off-limits to men.

References

Allen, R. (1989). Bursting bubbles: Soap operas, audiences and the limits of the genre. In E. Seiter, H. Borchers, G. Kreutzner, & E. Warth (Eds.), *Remote control* (pp. 16–43). London: Routledge.

Almeida, H. B. (2001). *"Muitas mais coisas" Telenovela, consumo e gênero ["Many more things:" Telenovela, consumption and gender].* Unpublished doctoral dissertation, Universidade de Campinas, Campinas, São Paulo, Brazil.

Almeida, H. B. (2003). Telenovela and gender in Brazil. *Global Media Journal.* Retrieved on August 5, 2003 from http://lass.calumet.purdue.edu/cca/gmj/contents.htm.

Ang, I. (1991). *Desperately seeking the audience.* New York Routledge.

Bourdieu, P. (1984). *Distinction: A social critique of the judgment of taste.* Cambridge: Harvard University Press.

Bourdieu P., & Wacquant, L. (1999). On the cunning of imperialist reason. *Theory, culture & Society, 16,* 41–58.

Brown, M. E. (1994). *Soap opera and women's talk: The pleasure of resistance.* Thousand Oaks, CA: Sage.

Costa, S. R. (1997). *Recepção de telenovela: Um estudo de caso em Serra da Saudade-MG* [Telenovela reception: A case study in Serra da Saudade-MG]. Unpublished master's thesis. Universidade Federal de Viçosa, Viçosa, Minas Gerais, Brazil.

Davidson, P. (1983). The third-person effect in communication. *Public Opinion Quarterly, 47,* 115.

Faria, V., & Potter, J. (1994, February). *Television, telenovelas and fertility change in Northeast Brazil.* Paper presented at the seminar on Values and Fertility Change, Geneva, Switzerland.

Fiske, J., & Hartley, J. (1978). *Reading television.* London: Methuen.

Hamburger, E. I. (1999). *Politics and intimacy in Brazilian telenovelas.* Unpublished doctoral dissertation, Department of Anthopology, University of Chicago, Chicago.

Herold, C. M. (1988). The "Brazilianization" of Brazilian television: A critical review. *Studies in Latin American Popular Culture, 7,* 41–57.

Kottak, C. P. (1990). *Prime time society: An anthropological analysis of television and culture.* Belmont, CA: Wadsworth.

Kottak, C. P. (1991). Television's impact on values and local life in Brazil. *Journal of Communication, 41,* 70–87.

Kottak, C. P. (1992). *Assault on paradise: Social change in a Brazilian village* (2nd ed.). New York: McGraw-Hill, Inc.

La Pastina, A. (1995). *Television and telenovelas in a rural community in Northeast Brazil: A pilot study for an ethnography of telenovela reception.* Unpublished manuscript.

La Pastina, A. (1999). *The telenovela way of knowledge: An ethnographic reception study among rural viewers in Brazil.* Unpublished doctoral dissertation. University of Texas, Austin.

La Pastina, A. (2001). Product placement in Brazilian primetime television: The case of a telenovela reception. *Journal of Broadcasting & Electronic Media, 45,* 541–557.

La Pastina, A. (2003a). *Does national programming promote national identity? A case study of rural Brazil.* Paper presented at Media in Transition Conference, May, Massachusetts Institute of Technology, Cambridge, MA.

La Pastina, A. (2003b). "Now that you going home are you going to write about the natives you studied?" Telenovela reception, adultery and the dilemmas of ethnographic practice. In P. Murphy & M. Krady (Eds.), *Global media studies: An ethnographic approach* (pp. 125–146). London: Routledge.

La Pastina, A. (2004). Selling political integrity: Telenovelas, intertextuality and local elections in Brazil. *Journal of Broadcasting & Electronic Media.*

Leal, O. F. (1986). *A leitura social da novela das oito.* [The social reading of the eight o'clock telenovela]. Petrópolis, Brazil: Editora Vozes.

Leal, O. F. (1988). Class interpretations of a soap opera narrative: The case of the Brazilian novela "Summer Sun." *Theory, Culture and Society, 5,* 81–88.

Lindlof, T. R., & Taylor, B. C. (2002). *Qualitative communication research methods* (2nd ed.). Thousand Oaks, CA: Sage.

Livingstone, S. M. (1992). The meaning of domestic technologies: A personal construct analysis of familial gender relations. In R. Silverstone & E. Hirsh (Eds.), *Consuming technologies: Media and information in domestic spaces* (pp. 113–130). London: Routledge.

Lopes, M. I., Borelli, S. H., & Resende, V. R. (2002). *Vivendo com a telenovela: Mediações, recepção, teleficcionalidade* [Living with the telenovela: mediations, reception and tele-fiction]. São Paulo: Summus Editora.

Mankekar, P. (1999). *Screening culture, viewing politics: An ethnography of television, womanhood, and nation in postcolonial India.* Durham, NC: Duke University Press.

Martin-Barbero, J. (1993). *Communication, culture and hegemony: From the media to the mediations* (E. Fox & R. White, Trans.). Newbury Park, CA: Sage. (Original work published 1987)

Martin-Barbero, J., & Munñz, S. (Eds.). (1992). *Televisión y melodrama.* Bogotá: Tercer Mundo.

Mattelart, M., & Mattelart, A. (1990). *The carnival of images: Brazilian television fiction* (D. Buxton, Trans.). New York: Bergin & Garvey. (Original work published 1987)

McAnany, E. G. (1993). The telenovela and social change. In A. Fadul (Ed.), *Serial fiction in TV: The Latin American telenovelas* (pp. 135–147). São Paulo, Brazil: Robert M. Videira.

McAnany, E. G., & La Pastina, A. (1994). Telenovela audiences: A review and methodological critique of Latin American research. *Communication Research, 21,* 828–849.

Morley, D. (1986). *Family television: Cultural power and domestic leisure.* London: Comedia.

Murphy, P. D. (1999). Media cultural studies' uncomfortable embrace of ethnography. *Journal of Communication Inquiry, 23,* 205–221.

Murphy, P., & Krady, M. (Eds.). (2003). *Global media studies: An ethnographic approach.* London: Routledge.

Nascimento, M. (Executive Producer). (1997, February 24). *Roda Viva* [Television Broadcast]. São Paulo: TV Cultura.

Oliveira, O. S. (1990, May). *Brazilian soaps outshine Hollywood: Is cultural imperialism fading out?* Paper presented at the International Communication Association, Intercultural and Development Division, Dublin.

Orozco, G. (1991). Mapa para abordar las mediaciones en el processo de recepción televisiva: Una aproximación metodólogica. [Map to investigate the mediations in the television reception process: A methodological discussion]. *Cuadernos de comunicación y practices sociales, 2,* 53–64. México: Universidade Iberoamericana.

Ortiz, R., Borelli, S., & Ramos, R. (1988). *Telenovela: História e producão.* [Telenovela: History and production], São Paulo: Brasiliense.

Pace, R. (1993). First-time televiewing in Amazonia: Television acculturation in Gurupá, Amazonia. *Ethnology, 32,* 187–206.

Penacchioni, I. (1984). The reception of popular television in Northeast Brazil. *Media, Culture and Society, 6,* 337–341.

Prado, R. M. (1987). *Mulher de novela e mulher de verdade: Estudo sobre cidade pequena, mulher e telenovela.* [Telenovela women and real women: A study about small town women and telenovela], Unpublished master's thesis, Museu Nacional, Universidade Federal do Rio de Janeiro, Rio de Janeiro, Brazil.

Prado, R. M. (1995). Small town, Brazil: Heaven and hell of personalism. In D. Hess & R. Damatta (Eds.), *The Brazilian puzzle* (pp. 59–84). New York: Columbia University Press.

Rios-Neto, E. L. G., Miranda-Ribeiro, P., & Potter, J. (1998, January). *I saw it on TV: Television and demographic change in Brazil.* Paper presented at the Workshop on the Social Dynamics of Fertility Change in Developing Countries, National Academy of Sciences, Washington, DC.

Sanjek, R. (1990). On ethnographic validity. In R. Sanjek (Ed.), *Filednotes: The makings of anthropology* (pp. 385–418). Ithaca: Cornell University Press.

Seiter, E. (1999). *Television and new media audiences.* Oxford: Oxford University Press.

Sinclair, J. (1996). Mexico, Brazil, and the Latin World. In J. Sinclair, E. Jacka, & S. Cunningham (Eds.), *New patterns in global television: peripheral vision* (pp. 33–66). New York: Oxford University Press.

Sluyter-Beltrão, M. (1993). Interpreting Brazilian telenovelas. In A. Fadul (Ed.), *Serial fiction in TV: the Latin American telenovelas* (pp. 63–76). São Paulo, Brazil: Robert M. Videira.

Triguero, O. M. (1987). *A TV Globo em duas comunidades rurais da Paraiba: Estudo sobre a audiência da televisão em determinados grupos sociais* [Globo network in two rural communities in Paraiba: Audience study among specific social groups]. Unpublished master's thesis, Universidade Federal Rural da Paraiba, Paraiba, Brazil.

Tufte, T. (1994). *Living with the Rubbish Queen: A media ethnography about telenovelas in everyday life of Brazilian women.* Unpublished doctoral dissertation, University of Copenhagen, Denmark.

Tufte, T. (2000). *Living with the Rubbish Queen: Telenovelas, culture and modernity in Brazil.* Luton: University of Luton Press.

Vink, N. (1988). *The telenovela and emancipation: A study on TV and social change in Brazil.* Amsterdam: Royal Tropical Institute.

Sex Appeal and Cultural Liberty
A Feminist Inquiry into MTV India

Jocelyn Cullity and Prakash Younger

This essay discusses findings from an ethnographic study of MTV India. After a brief feminist analysis of MTV India's content, the main body of the essay illustrates how MTV India programming is understood to affirm the primacy of the local and is perceived to provide an empowering "space" for young, middle-class women. To understand this perspective requires a consideration of the historical role women played in traditional versions of Indian nationalism and the ideological constraints they face today. A coda situates the findings of the study in terms of the broader effects of globalization.

Our study is based on interviews with feminist media professionals, feminist scholars and activists, members of the All India Democratic Women's Association (AIDWA), and television producers in Delhi and Mumbai. Please see the full list of interviews that follows the essay. Also included in this study is a female student discussion group at Saint Xavier's College in Mumbai, led by lecturer Shilpa Phadke.

The study also incorporates textual analysis of selected programming, as well as results from two qualitative surveys with women students at Jawaharlal Nehru University (JNU) in Delhi and Saint Xavier's College in Mumbai. An initial survey, distributed and collected by college teachers at JNU and St. Xavier's, ascertained that the thirty-five women were from Indian middle-class families. We aimed our questions at the students' lifestyles. Questions ranged from queries about favorite music and clothes, role models, and whether students worried about their weight to questions that elicited responses about future careers and marriage. A section on television asked the students questions about their favorite shows, television role models, and their perceptions of images on television, including questions specifically concerning their sentiments about images on MTV India. Additional questions sought their ideas about influences on women by a variety of media (for example, magazines, film, newspapers, television). Participant observation took place in the MTV-

Jocelyn Cullity and Prakash Younger, "Sex Appeal and Cultural Liberty: A Feminist Inquiry into MTV India," *Frontiers,* Vol. 25, No. 2 (2004), pp. 96–122. Copyright © 2004, University of Nebraska Press.

India studio and in public spaces frequented by "the MTV generation." This latter method produced conversations with young women throughout our fieldwork, which we recorded in daily field notes and which, of course, informed our thinking. Unless otherwise specified, the word "informants" used throughout this essay refers to all of the groups described above. Our findings reflect those situations where there were overwhelming majorities of opinion with regard to specific questions. The aim of our research is to provide a transnational, feminist perspective on how young, middle-class Indian women might negotiate global television programming.

The original intention behind our case study of MTV India was to look at television images that might register to the viewer as "Western" and examine how they function in an Indian context. Our research, however, revealed that MTV India programming had been largely indigenized or "Indianized" so that MTV could stay afloat in the robust Indian television market. Furthermore, findings pointed to the emergence of a new form of cultural nationalism, seen in the "indigenization" of global media. This essay explores some of the implications of this new nationalism from a gender perspective.

Owned by Viacom in New York, MTV was launched in the United States in 1981 as a twenty-four-hour cable program service presenting a continuous flow of music videos that featured pop and rock songs.[1] MTV tried to distinguish itself from other channels by being unconventional. With hosts making on-air mistakes on messy sets and under poor lighting, programming came across as spontaneous and casual.[2] Vee-jays, or VJs, MTV's on-air announcers, are pivotal to providing the desired image of hip irreverence and relaxed informality.[3] MTV invented the self-contained music clip, something that has become entrenched in Western popular culture.[4] AT the same time, the content of MTV videos clips stimulates consumer purchase, particularly in the fashion industry.[5] In the late eighties and nineties, MTV extended its reach, broadcasting in Latin America, Japan, Australia, Russia, and Asia.

MTV started in India as MTV Asia, carried by Star TV; in 1994, it broke from Star, launching out alone as MTV India. When MTV first entered India, it simply tried to relocate Western MTV products, like Western pop music.[6] According to informant Natasha Malhotra, a vice-president and executive producer at MTV India, this programming was "not convincing."[7] Moreover, viewers saw it as a cultural invasion.[8]

A severely declining share of the market forced MTV India to go off the air in 1995 to reconsider its strategies or face closing down altogether. In the MTV India studios in Mumbai, the new, entirely Indian creative staff (Malhotra came on board at this time) realized they had to dramatically "Indianize" to stay alive. Research on record sales in India showed that the most popular genre in the country—at 70 to 80 percent of record sales—was Hindi film music.[9] MTV therefore replaced its Western music videos with Hindi film clips, popular song and dance numbers taken from hit films that make for autonomous, self-standing videos. Seventy percent of MTV's music was now Hindi music, with Western music videos continuing to air in non-prime-time slots.

Indian VJs with Indian accents replaced foreign VJs. In most cases, producers localized the programming "environment," featuring Indian street scenes with Indian people. MTV India kept its Western format and its focus on youth culture but indigenized it to suit Indian middle-class tastes. This decision effectively turned things around to make the channel the third or fourth most popular MTV in the world.[10]

During the 1990s, globalization gave birth to a new form of cultural nationalism in India, seen most clearly in this active and self-conscious indigenization of global media, distinct from the traditional forms of nationalism found in the ideologies of India's Congress party and the Hindu right. The markers of the "Western" and the "Indian" were no longer stable or easy to identify.

Processes of globalization are generally associated with the remaking or reworking of existing gender divisions.[11] If the spread of satellite television in India has in some sense democratized media, in what capacity have Indian women participated in this process? To what extent have patriarchal structures been dismantled? In what new forms have they been reconstituted? Does the cultural hybridity of the new images provide the idiom for a new hybrid form of patriarchy? While a thorough examination of such questions is beyond the scope of this essay, we will examine the possibility, persistently affirmed by our informants, that the images in question create a valuable imaginative space for middle-class women that did not exist in earlier versions of the national public sphere.

To appreciate the most basic context within which this assertion registers, it is necessary to recall the place of women within those earlier narratives. As Partha Chatterjee has argued, the ideological work of nation-building depended on the distinction between the "Home," a spiritual realm in which the irreducible core of Indian culture would be reproduced, and the "World," the realm in which Indians would appropriate the potentials of modernity.[12] To maintain this delicate balance, the nationalist project required a "new woman" who would keep up the spiritual purity necessary to "Indianness" while passively supporting the progressive projects of modernity. With this distinction in place,

> the new norm for organizing family life and determining the right conduct for women in the conditions of the modern world could now be deduced with ease. Adjustments would have to be made in the external world of material activity, and men would bear the brunt of this task. To the extent that the family was itself entangled in wider social relations, it too could not be insulated from the influence of changes in the outside world. Consequently, the organization and ways of life at home would also have to be changed. But the crucial requirement was to retain the inner spirituality of indigenous social life. The home was the principal site for expressing the spiritual quality of the national culture, and women must take the main responsibility for protecting and nurturing this quality. No matter what the changes in the external conditions of life for women, they must not lose their essentially spiritual (that is feminine) virtues; they must not, in other words, become essentially Westernized. It followed, as a simple criterion for judging the desirability of reform, that the essential distinction between the social roles of men and women in terms of material and spiritual virtues must at all times be maintained. There

would have to be a marked *difference* in the degree and manner of Western-ization of women, as distinct from men, in the modern world of the nation.[13]

In our reading of Chatterjee's model, the constraints of maintaining this balance function to keep women bound to the ideological construct of the "Home" even as they actually move into the sphere of the "World" through work, education, and other activities. Without denying the important historical differences that distinguish competing versions of this model (that is, those associated with the Congress party, the Hindu right, the Marxist left, etc.) and the stages in its evolution from the nineteenth century to the present, one can nonetheless recognize a generally pervasive ideological identification of "Woman" and "Home" to which middle-class Indian women are still subject today.

In contrast to the restrictions implicit in this model, the new pop-cultural nationalism manifest in the production and reception of MTV India images seems to provide a strategic rhetorical means for middle-class women to assert their independence by participating in the patriotically inflected project of globalizing the local and localizing the global. Strongly evident as we pursued our inquiry was that informants perceived the images of women on channels like MTV India as a challenge to the discourses of purity, patrilineality, and authenticity that characterize older nationalist constructions of the "Home." By providing images of "worldly" women who are at the same time understood to be fully "Indian," MTV India is understood to help legitimate women's claims to equal participation in realms beyond the domestic.[14]

In what follows, we will first examine the images themselves, assessing how their formal and semiotic designs might function to reproduce or challenge existing gender relations. We will then proceed to consider how middle-class young women engage with these images.

Feminist Analysis of MTV Images in the U.S.A.

To create a point of departure, it is useful to look at studies already done on MTV content in the West, to see if Indian MTV content differs at all. Although MTV in the United States does have a department that views videos for objectionable content, targeting drug use, excessive alcohol consumption, and sex,[15] female images depicted on the channel in the United States show that MTV is far from achieving a "gender-balanced communication," where representations of the female are not vastly diminished beings. Though male rap artists have helped to lessen the domination by white men, historically MTV in the United States has foregrounded white male characters at the expense of women and minorities.[16]

In music video narratives, women are consistently "put down" and "kept in place," and caricatures of traditional personality attributes for gender are employed—for example, men are more aggressive and violent; women are more affectionate and fearful.[17] Stereotypes of gender occupations distort reality, with women portrayed as cheerleaders, secretaries, fashion models, and telephone operators. In most cases women are not portrayed as involved in the production of music but are frequently positioned as dancers, sometimes as back-up singers, or as simply present, surrounding the male artist.[18] The constant repetition of these roles means that women accept that success or stardom comes from being models or dancers,[19] or more generally, objects for male entertainment.

In the continuous stream of similarly formatted videos and ads, sexual images make a product stand out from the clutter. Sex sells the videos, which in turn are there to sell the viewer CDs and tapes.[20] Most of the video story-lines are male sexual dream worlds or fantasies about being desired and accepted by women, including older men's fantasies about younger women. Parties with lots of women, at times resembling orgies, are common. The not-so-implicit message is that women's bodies are fair game.[21] Studies show that half of the women portrayed, as opposed to one tenth of the men, wear provocative cloth-ing.[22] In U.S. videos, women get in and out of clothes a lot, frequently strut-ting across the screen in undergarments. Camera angles reduce women to shapes and outlines, or to objects. Some devices for achieving this effect are panning over the body, looking down onto a woman's breasts, and fragment-ing body parts, swooping over a leg, or, often with female artists, shooting between her legs.[23] Sexual violence is made to appear normal: women are some-times caged; and female flight, a woman running away from a man, always ends by turning into actual desire for the male pursuer. *No* really means *yes.* The way women are touched and handled is manipulative but made to look natural. Guns enhance the masculinity of their users.

All these dangerous qualities are not necessarily explicit but are subtle enough to fit in "normally."[24] The question is what effect do all these images have on the real world, on how men and women think about each other and sex?[25] Linking these images to crimes such as date rape, studies have concluded that MTV's portrayal of heterosexual sexual interaction constitutes a serious danger for young women and girls.[26] On the basis of the images themselves, this danger is now being inadvertently welcomed into Indian middle-class culture.

Western Patriarchy Goes Local?
A Feminist Analysis of Images from MTV India

For the purposes of this study, we selected and analyzed a sample of MTV India programming using, as a foundation, a list of dangerous types of images of women in the media produced by the organization Media Watch. A textual analysis of women's images, from the stream of Hindi film clips to the VJs and other on-air personnel, showed the following major themes or commonalities in programming content on MTV India.

The Female Body Focus

The female as a body is predominant in all facets of MTV India programming, often through an intense focus on clothes. In Hindi film clips, women frequently switch between, in particular, halter tops and short skirts and the *salwar kamiz* or *sari.* Although women do appear in clothes that cover more of the body than in Western videos, the emphasis in all videos is definitely on appearances in bikinis, or in minis and plastic bras. In both Indian and Western videos on MTV India, the male artist's "mate" frequently appears throughout his song in a man's shirt and nothing else. In almost all of the videos analyzed, men were fully dressed, wearing trousers, even if portrayed in a hot climate surrounded by women in bikinis. In one Hindi film clip, the female artist is in a dress so short that the viewer is allowed to glimpse her underwear throughout the song. On a promo for the MTV show *Style Check,* a woman holds a square of cardboard in front of her body with a bra and underwear painted on it. "You are what you wear," she says, while changing into a gold dress that stops at the top of her thighs. In the very popular video "Habibi," three women in three separate rooms fixate on what they themselves are wearing, eventually emerging to find they have all chosen the same outfit. This focus on attire makes for a very common storyline in videos featuring Indian female artists.

In the early nineties, the controversial hit film song "What's Beneath the Blouse" was one of the first to use camera shots that lingered on the female artist's breasts.[27] In just a few years, the camera has grown used to lingering quite a bit more. In the last decade, Hindi films have become much more sexually explicit, exposing more of the body.[28] While the links have yet to be explicitly established, there is a general sense that the traditionally sublimated eroticism of Bollywood films has given way, especially in musical sequences, to a frankness derived in part from their dual status as music videos.

On MTV India, camera shots include frequent close-ups of female body parts. In "Habibi," editing techniques fragment the woman's body, the screen splitting into frames showing the three women in parts. In this video, the camera also rests on the female artist's breasts before moving up to her face. One of the most common camera angles on MTV India is the shot of a woman's flat stomach with a male artist singing right next to it, his head and her stomach filling the frame. Here, the MTV aesthetic takes a traditional pose of sublimated Bollywood romanticism and by reframing it desublimates it. Perhaps the most explicit shot in the programming analyzed—a quick one at about two seconds long, but there nonetheless—is the shot of an Indian woman's jean buttons undone.

On *The Grind,* an MTV show produced in the United States and still aired on MTV India, editors mix shots of dancers in a studio with video clips from one particular song that plays continuously throughout all visuals. The studio camera shots here are low, looking up at bouncing breasts, and cameras are also situated above the dancers, focusing downward into cleavage. Straight on, close-ups of dancers' breasts in tight T-shirts are a constant. Informants referred to *The Grind* as the only Western show on MTV India. But what is striking is that the clothes, the dance moves, and the body focus on what used to be perceived as a relatively shocking show now appear the same, visually, as those on other (Indian) shows on MTV India.

The Female VJ as Cultural Icon

Letter after letter read aloud by female VJs on-air goes like this: "We have something in common. We are both women! I want to be a VJ like you." On one show almost every letter mentioned the fact that the writer loved the VJ's hairstyle. The female VJs on the programming selected for analysis all wore low-cut tops. The preferred body shape is slim; if curvy, this is emphasized. It's clear that the female VJ's value depends on her attire (a major fashion indicator) and general appearance—which is significant when viewed alongside MTV producers' and other informants' comments that herald the woman VJ as an important cultural icon and new role model.

But it is necessary to remember that MTV India's overall programming focus privileges male artists—both Indian and Western—in the videos and in interviews with artists. In the programming analyzed, there was only one instance where two Indian female artists played back-to-back in the music lineup and one instance of two Western female artists playing back to back.

Most commonly, MTV India portrays women as dancers. Like props on the steps of a *ghat* or on a beach, women dancers often surround the male artist while he sings or plays an instrument. An ad calling for television developers illustrates a general sense of the male as intellectually dominant. The camera pans across a group of male clones and then focuses on one man who is forcing open an animated box around him. A graphic with "find your space" dances above his head. The ad is for jobs at MTV India.

Male Fantasy

The implicit male spectator of music video fantasies is evident in the many images of women "waiting" in bedrooms, or laid out on beds, while, in contrast, we view the active male artist, who is the object of identification, singing on his motorbike. A classic example of such fantasies is the Indian male artist surrounded by cooing women in a pool. One video storyline follows two older Indian men who get up in the middle of the night, leaving their fat, middle-aged wives asleep while they take turns peeping through a telescope at girls splashing about in a pool. The fat wives wake up and catch their husbands, chastising the two now forlorn-looking men. This portrayal of older, fat women as a negative—a familiar-enough image in Western popular culture—is a decidedly new female image in India.

Even with images that make for the strongest cases of empowerment, visual stylistics and storylines do not stray outside a patriarchal framework. Women may be represented as "free," but only to a certain extent. Between-the-legs shots reduce and make vulnerable the strong female artist, while men ultimately win "the battle of the sexes" narratives featured in music videos. For instance, the female artist may be depicted as an independent woman driving a car by herself, but by the end of the song she will have found her mate, and he will be driving a motorcycle, she happily behind him, her arms wrapped around his waist. While the editing of Indian videos and Hindi film clips is perhaps not as aggressively exploitative as it can be in both Western videos and films, the diminishment of the female as a full person, as subject rather than object, is nonetheless similar.

In contrast to this image-ghetto within which the Indian woman is generally contained, the Indian male is often empowered on a global scale through his acquisition of an international array of women. In one instance, an exotic crowd of women of all nationalities dressed in short-shorts surround a male singer on a palm-fringed beach. In another example, a male Indian jumps out a bedroom window to get away from a white father with a gun who has found out his whereabouts. And in an ad for CDs, a male voice-over sings: "I gotta girl in Rome, I gotta girl at home."

The Primacy of the Local Reception:
MTV India as a Strategic Cultural Opportunity

The above interpretation of MTV India images stem from conventional Western feminist textual analysis. However, there is a vast difference between this account and that of our Indian informants. Feminist activists, scholars, television producers, and women students alike firmly resisted such a reading. They instead saw the images as presenting new and vital spaces for women, noting that in the past images of women were generally limited to portrayals of wives, mothers, and father's wives. They emphasized the need to add voices and imaginative options and not to begin subtracting them. "It's a broadcast media," Ranjan Bakshi at Zee Network said, "not a narrowcast band."[29]

Through programming such as that found on MTV India, new spaces for women are perceived to enable a range of activity in both the local and global realms. How exactly does programming on MTV India create these new spaces? Our informants stressed that it is possible to recognize that MTV images served a *strategic* function. The female VJ is not necessarily seen as someone who empowers politically or is felt to be incredibly lucid about women's rights. In fact, women students often described MTV India's VJs as "hyper" and "chirpy."[30] However, VJs were among those that our informants cited as emerging images of strong women taking control of the work-sphere.[31] Rahul Roy, whose independent documentary films focus on gender relations, stressed this, saying VJs are one of the new female images on TV focusing on "aspiration and dreams" and that such images are "psychologically supporting the [women's] movement."[32]

Students surveyed described MTV India as having a "carefree attitude" and a " freshness," stating that MTV India's shows "represent the youth of today."[33] There was a general sense of agreement among informants with the words of Cyrus Oshidar, creative director at MTV India, who said the VJs "are comfortable in what they wear, confident in what they wear, and they are well spoken enough. They do project an image of confident young women in a male society. I think you need more of that."[34]

Informants like Professor Chaudhuri at Jawaharlal Nehru University and well-known writer and women's activist Anita Anand promoted the new image of the single, independent woman who lives alone, one who is "not being cheated out of leisure and pleasure," and who has the choice to get married or not.[35] Vijaya Nidadavolu, a media consultant at Delhi's International Center for Research on Women, emphasized that "individualism has arrived. Having an opinion, an attitude, is seen as a positive attribute."[36] In our surveys and in the discussion group, students commonly used the adjectives "assertive,"

"individual," and "liberated" to illustrate their choice of preferred role models on television.[37]

In our interviews and surveys, women and men saw the support of female
television employment, both on and off the screen, as essential. During this
study, the entertainment sections of newspapers often quoted Natasha Malhotra, a vice president and executive producer at MTV India. Informants
referred to her as a role model for the working woman, someone particularly
significant to the up-and-coming, career-conscious younger generations. (All
female students surveyed saw themselves in careers in five years' time; only half
saw themselves married as well.)

Generally, our informants saw a potential empowerment and liberation
within images of women in music videos. Documentary filmmaker Rahul Roy
and Madhu Kishwar, Indian activist and publisher of *Manushi* magazine,
insisted that while it may be commodifying, "flaunting your assets" is "a power
trip, too."[38] Getting away from the "vamp," the fact that heroines and not
just villainesses now smoke and drink (albeit rarely), was another positive aspect
noted about new images. As Anita Anand said, "Now there are more diverse
roles than Bollywood's Vamp or Miss Goody Two-shoes."[39] This good girl–bad
girl binary, essential to Hindi films and other aspects of Indian popular culture in the post-Independence period, was a principal means of reproducing
the Home-World distinction. By erasing this distinction, perhaps inadvertently,
MTV images thus work to dismantle a key element of earlier versions of nationalist patriarchy. Our informants were keenly aware of this effect.

It is essential to remember that though cultural hybridity is not something
new to Indian culture (it has in fact been a conspicuous feature of popular film
since Independence), it has traditionally been a quality that belonged almost
exclusively to men. The best-known reference point for this quality is the refrain
from Raj Kapoor's famous song "Mera juta hai japani" ("My Shoes Are Japanese") in *Shri 420* (Raj Kapoor, 1955):

> My shoes are Japanese,
> My trousers are English,
> On my head is a red Russian hat,
> But my heart remains Indian.

As both Rachel Dwyer and Sumita Chakravarty have shown, this cultural
hybridity has been a constant for male stars up to the present.[40] In Chakravarty's
model of "imperso-nation," the complex cultural hybridity of the male star's
image performs an essential function in reconciling the heterogeneous elements
that make up India's pop-cultural, as opposed to official, identity as a nation.[41]
But though ease in moving back and forth between traditional and Western
culture has always been a defining characteristic of the Bollywood hero, until
recently the same freedom has generally been denied to the heroine. Instead,
roles for women were strictly divided between Westernized bad girls or vamps
and "pure" Indian good girls. For instance, in *Shri 420* the character Maya
("Delusion") wears fish-tail gowns, smokes cigarettes in a holder, lives in her
own apartment, speaks English as well as Hindi, and hangs out in nightclubs.

A traditional good girl, the schoolteacher Vidya ("Knowledge") in the same film lives with her crippled father, wears *saris,* speaks Hindi, and is rewarded with the hero's love. Over the course of the 1990s, this rigid figurative binary broke down somewhat, and female romantic leads or heroines are allowed a limited engagement with Western culture through fashion, dancing in night-clubs, and other forms of spectacular consumption.[42] While the variety of engagements with the "World" female characters are permitted is still drasti-cally limited when compared to the range available to male characters, and while, in the final analysis, narratives still tend to reward a female allegiance to tradition and the "Home," the emerging cultural hybridity of Bollywood hero-ines represents a clear opening up of possibilities, something that is strongly presented on MTV India.

A common theme among informants was that a sexual revolution, one referred to as being similar to that which took place in the West in the 1960s, is now taking place in India—and that new images on a station like MTV India give this revolution space, celebrating affirmative sexuality. Shilpa Phadke, writer and lecturer at St. Xavier's College in Mumbai, stressed, "Sexuality is both liberating and problematic—in the same ways as it was found to be dur-ing the Western sexual revolution."[43] Informants felt strongly about taking care not to shut this revolution down by negating MTV India images. In our discussion group, students affirmed this revolution for the basic reason that, again, this was another opportunity to present women who were "strong," with "minds of their own."[44]

Informants linked a perceived increase in dating and premarital sex for both young adult men and women to images of sexual relationships. Sandeep Bindra, owner of Moet's Restaurant, one of the first "pub ventures" in Delhi that now attracts middle-class youth, said the most significant change between his generation and the younger generation is that young women today are "more free. They don't mind they're with one boy today; tomorrow with another boy. They don't mind being seen."[45] Over 90 percent of women stu-dents surveyed, as well as the young women we spoke to informally, felt that new television shows had increased dating.[46] MTV India's Cyrus Oshidar expressed a similar view as other informants on this topic:

> Dating is good—to help break down the barriers you get in arranged mar-riages. It's a positive, independent, young person's thing. You defy a lot of tradition to do it. If this country's going to go anywhere, the young people have to be involved. They have to have a point of view. Even if it starts with getting laid, dating, mating. At least it's empowerment. At least it's a fucking point of view."[47]

Twenty-eight-year-old Vijaya Nidadavolu equated MTV images with a need to start giving space to women in their late teens and twenties in "pubs and clubs where a lot of young women smoke and drink, wear sleeveless shirts in the street, and don't give a damn if people are looking at them."[48] While informants did not necessarily glorify these activities in themselves, they clearly valued them as a legitimate means of asserting the freedom of the female indi-vidual in the teeth of constricting moral ideologies.

The images in question also provide a means for women to affirm participation in a new social development in local-global intermingling. Young, middle-class women feel a part of the vitalized middle-class community nurtured and reflected in MTV programming, a community dotted with new Indian musicians and other artists. The placement of women in foreign locales as they sing or dance represents a claim to international mobility and the freedom to choose one's destination. The global claim is inherent in these portrayals of women as cosmopolitan and fluid, switching back and forth between values of a bigger world and those of the *desi,* or Indian world. As well, fashion decisions, that more often now include jeans and spaghetti-strap tops, generally seem to symbolize a new freedom to hypothetically choose whatever she wants. Strikingly, over two-thirds of women surveyed saw jeans as an "Indian" style, as opposed to a "Western" style. But Vijaya Nidadavolu put it this way:

> The twenty-one-year-old is not seeing the image of the independent type as Western—or Western clothes as Western. They're something for herself, as her life, her reality. She can choose who to be. She doesn't think she's Indian, American, European by her dress or attitudes. Young, Indian women fit in anywhere in the Diaspora. They fit into India, England, America. . . . TV is a huge influence on this. Essentially I'm Indian but somewhere my values are identifiable across the world. When I wear these clothes I'm still Indian. But I wear them because I choose to. It's me. If a girl takes on an attitude or way to be it's what she's comfortable with, rather than rooting it to a particular culture. . . . It's about choice. It's about deciding for yourself."[49]

A worrisome twist on this global and local fluidity is the recent popularity of the skinny look in India. Of the students surveyed, twice as many worried about their weight over those that said they did not.[50] Schoolgirl diets are a new phenomenon, one that two-thirds of all our informants felt was related to MTV and Star TV "right in your homes, blaring all the time."[51] Writer and magazine editor Madhu Kishwar, whose feminism is inflected with her own unique brand of nationalism, sees the indigenization of such ideals as a hazardous development: "The film stars have become all anorexic types—the flat bellies are as recent as last year. They used to be buxom and healthy; now they aren't successful if they are happy and plump film actresses. We used to say this was Western, but the moment your own film stars start displaying this look, it's going to be a real problem. It becomes dangerous."[52]

In this context, we should briefly note the existence and significance of pop-cultural phenomena relating to new images of Indian women. Perhaps the most important element of this larger cultural matrix is the much-discussed success of Indian women at international beauty contests. In one sense the "new Indian woman" that MTV India has a hand in creating is a cultural artifact of the beauty contests, which are felt to be international triumphs. Informants referred to related impacts, to the facts that grooming schools have opened all over India,[53] that the beauty industry is booming, and that parents aspire for children to become beauty queens. Birthday parties for seven-year-old girls in Delhi neighborhoods feature the games "walk the ramp" and "act like the model."[54] Needless perhaps to say, the ideal body shape has been altered by the heavy social focus on these contests. The sudden appearance of weight-loss clinics in cities like Delhi and Mumbai, providing a new outlet for an intense concentration on skinniness, is a principal marker of identification with this new ideal.

Shilpa Phadke at St. Xavier's College emphasized the need for balance:

> On MTV—wearing those clothes, displaying that attitude—is equal to liberation, modernization. But MTV is selling those images and icons. As long as we are able to see this, that's okay. Don't ban the beauty contest. You can make money. Beauty contests are a career for some women, with huge sums of money. You have the right to become famous. Just as long as people know it's not what it appears to be. MTV is selling a product. All of us don't have to look like that.[55]

In the college surveys, students *were* strikingly unified about relating anorexic images to MTV India. Yet the skinny, skin-exposed woman is perceived as one that belongs to India now, not something that belongs to the West—as perceived in earlier days. The social impact of the skinny woman image is something that remains to be judged in the years to come.

The Primacy of the Local: Empowering Images, Ambivalent Reality

Although new television images were generally affirmed, one-third of our informants questioned whether images had really changed on a deeper level, even though they had superficially gone through a total revolution, seen, for example, in changes to the dress code from the sari to the mini.[56] Vijaya Nidadavolu thought core values had not really changed, saying that a woman may wear jeans but would still have an arranged marriage.[57] Informants also referred to the fact that males remain heads of households, regardless of empowering new roles for women reflected in new television images. Ananya Bannerjee, chief producer at India's government-run national station, Doordarshan, said that Bollywood film images remain the most influential, and she felt that the images of women in these films had not undergone a change, pointing out that the story still centers around the male lead.[58]

One-third of our informants did feel that new images of women on television caused some tension. Akhila Sivadas, coordinator of the Media Advocacy Group headquartered in Delhi, said that those born after 1979 were fine with the new media but that women over forty suffered from anxiety, often attributed to the storylines of popular soaps on channels other than MTV India. Parents, she said, frequently had more problems with television than their kids did. Sivadas's studies focus on older women, because of the Media Advocacy Group's impression that young people are taking the new programming in stride.

But other informants alluded to issues for the "MTV generation," stating that messages for young people in India today are very confusing. A common example was that dating and the intrinsic value of the family represent very different needs. Sharika Sharma, a woman in her mid-twenties who works for

Trisoft Design, felt the younger generation maintains beliefs in traditional values, seeing the family as extremely important, and yet at the same time they do want to have sex with their boyfriends.[59] Another informant commented on women being less mobile and still very much in the home, and that dating means lying to one's family,[60] which creates tension for the individual.

We should mention here that generally speaking the assumption among all our informants and in the viewed images themselves was an implied compulsory heterosexuality. For lesbians in India, things are changing but very slowly. This is according to Cath Sluggett, a British woman who, along with several Delhi women, started Sangini, a phone helpline for gay women open two days a week. Sangini also offers counseling and support group meetings. Sluggett thought there was a slow awareness growing, citing the fact that she knew of one gay club in Mumbai and a Dehli bar that catered to gay women and men one night a week. Sangini receives calls from all over the country, where gay women, she said, are still very much hidden in their homes. "In the West, perhaps you can access any space you want," she said, "but here it's just starting." Sluggett said women and men still had very traditional values, that the beliefs and stereotypes surrounding sexuality had not changed. She felt that new senses of independence and choice for women were superficial, stating that it would be "a long time before women especially get autonomy for themselves."[61]

The maintenance of both a career and a domestic life seems to be another difficult issue for young, middle-class women. When asked what kind of women they would like to see on television, students surveyed, as well as those in the discussion group led by Shilpa Phadke at St. Xavier's College overwhelmingly responded that they wanted more of the "independent" and "strong" characters, "self confident women who can manage both home and office" or "a blend of a perfect career woman and a housewife."[62] To illustrate the discrepancy between a mediated image-world and reality, Sivadas contrasted the successful balance between the realms on television and the imbalance or pressure that would immediately be applied to a young working woman if she refused to stay home after her mother-in-law had taken sick.[63] Other informants cited tension or pressure in the image of the perfect woman who has a perfect job, perfect children, and keeps a perfect house.[64] Phadke said, "For a lot, the role models who are out there are working, have achieved, are earning good salaries, and have homes. They are balanced. They are somewhere between the radical and the traditional. Young women are trying to have it all."[65] Scholars and activists, as well as students who in fact simultaneously called for more of these images, felt images that represent having it all, being perfect both inside and outside the house, are particularly difficult to live up to.

There appeared to be some confusion over reading the new images. For instance, MTV's creative director, Cyrus Oshidar, firmly stated that VJs were not chosen because they were slim but because they were well spoken. He said that Miss India's articulation and independence were key in MTV's choice in the mid-nineties to take her on as a VJ. Within five minutes of this discussion, however, in a reference to fads in Mumbai, Oshidar said, "They are so desperate to have icons from these stupid fucking beauty contests. In the papers, they are saying 'Lara [a current beauty queen], we are proud of you. We love you. God bless you, you have done your country proud.' And I'm like, she's in a bikini and says she wants to help the poor and, sorry, I don't get it." He then immediately backed up his earlier statement by saying, "In a strange way, maybe it's good."[66]

Informant Responses to MTV India and the Struggle for Women's Rights

Overall, informants perceived that new images of working women and those exhibiting independence indicate a sense of expanding choice for middle-class women, in graphic contrast to the "long-suffering" images of the past, with images generally changing for the better over the last ten to twelve years.[67] They emphasized the need for more diversity and plurality of viewpoints in representations of women, particularly pointing to a need to keep fighting for the portrayal of women as strong and independent, the latter, as already stated, a common wish in the college surveys of women students.

Overwhelmingly, our informants asserted that this is happening through images on MTV India and on other channels, agreeing with Professor Chaudhuri at JNU who emphasized choice as a key concept.[68] They called for extensions to those images newly in place.[69] Informants said they sensed that new images represented something deeply positive happening for women, even if what this is has yet to be properly defined or understood. They felt there was more than commodification of women's bodies and lifestyle choices occurring and that this still unknown entity was something not to be disturbed.[70]

India's winning of several beauty contests, including Miss World, in the 1990s created heated debate over sexual politics (about the contests themselves and about Indian women's participation in them), a debate in which the government got involved and one that ultimately forced feminists into defensive positions, stifling any protest against female commodification in the contests.[71] In response to the Hindu right's attack on Western culture and its patriarchal version of "authentic" Indian culture, those sensitive to women's rights have shown a strong aversion to defining Indian culture at all. Left-minded citizens have reacted intensely to conservative elements in society that, for instance, criticize women wearing jeans in college. Cultural producers like Oshidar and Malhotra are busy reacting to political decisions to arrest television producers and their studio audience participants for risqué behavior on-air. During research for this study, a competing music channel's game-show contestants stripped down to their underwear on-air and were consequently arrested. This sort of action on the part of authorities has caused a terrific protest from the television industry.

The urge to defend MTV India images becomes fully comprehensible when one considers the discursive regime that those who criticize them would put in their place. If the original nationalist formula allowed for a qualified engagement with modernity, the new nationalism of the Hindu right reinscribes women only in terms of traditional values. Hence the debate over these images overdetermines and infuses them with values that seem far in excess of what the images themselves represent. In this regard, one might consider the public controversy surrounding the film *Fire* as roughly analogous to any debates around channels like MTV India. Depicting the emergence of a lesbian relationship amidst the claustrophobic atmosphere and constraints of a patriarchal joint-family, the film produced an inflamed response from the right, which used it as a springboard to extend its ideological campaign against "Western" values and for the return of "Indian" ideals of feminine virtue. Despite some reservations about the film within the Indian left, the strategic imperatives imposed by the attacks on it served to mobilize support in defense of freedom of expression, secularism, and the rights and existence of Indian gays and lesbians.[72] Despite their basic differences as cultural objects, both MTV India and *Fire* give rise to a largely similar discourse on the right, one which opposes an alien notion of "the West" to the comfort and virtue of indigenous culture; in denying such a binary opposition those who defend such objects posit, recognize, and assume another model of what it is to be Indian.

In countering such debates about what is Indian and what is not Indian, producers, scholars, and activists rejected any blame for negative cultural traits on external forces (like an imposed Western culture). Almost always, they instead stated that Indian culture must take responsibility for its own negative elements. "Indian culture at one level has always been about beauty and color consciousness, about making girls aware of their physical attributes early on," said Akhila Sivadas. "All popular culture is economic. You could repackage the entire cosmetic industry around the Indian bride. You don't have to do it by MTV."[73]

Shohini Ghosh, documentary film instructor at Jamia Millia Islamia University, whose work includes writing on gender, media, and representation and on the emergence of queer spaces in postsatellite television, and who vehemently opposed seeing new media images as dangerous or negative agreed. Ghosh found it dangerous to blame negative images on the media, saying one needed to "decenter MTV," that "a huge cultural churning" was happening. The "manipulation argument—that TNCs or MNCs lure women to do things they are actually opposed to, that they have no agency—is not going to get us far," she said. She stressed instead the family and "lived experience" as those that needed attending to: "Media manipulation may be one part of the story. But the family is complicit, and overlooked. . . . It's much easier to attack TV than my lover or best friend."[74]

Like the "West," the "media" can be used to describe the relations between culture and the individual as a form of alienating contamination by an external source. Comments such as those above suggest that the paternalistic protective assumptions in such description also entailed debilitating implications about those whose "authenticity" requires protection. As Leela Rao notes, the question of "Westernness" and "inauthenticity" consistently gets raised whenever women articulate the inequalities of gender in the media.[75]

The construction of the Indian, including the role of the Indian woman, causes intense Indian press debate. Fierce leftist public reaction against these constructions has meant resistance to criticizing television images out of a valid fear of possibly replicating arguments by the Hindu right. This caution not to make any political statements, to ensure no inadvertent link-up with fundamentalist politics, has effectively muffled the voices of the women's movement. Feminists in India today are confronted with the difficult task of finding a new language that avoids political co-option.[76] The political environment seems to have put women in the unfortunate position of battling unsuccessfully against being reduced to two polarized sets of images, as evident in the words of Geetanjali Misra, program officer of Sexuality and Reproductive Health at the Ford Foundation in New Delhi: "We want the jeans, but we don't want the exploitation because of the jeans. If you forget the MTV woman, then a whole new set of problems appears: family, tradition, and the pure woman."[77]

In addition, India's women's movement seems to be experiencing another, different kind of setback. New programming and new images have come into India at a time when the women's movement is very sensitive to accusations of not being diverse enough.[78] It has suffered from a general accusation about negotiating on behalf of others, instead of "bringing in the voices of the so many that are left out,"[79] resulting in a cry for more pluralism in the movement itself, with active outreach to include other points of view. Many feminists therefore hesitate to criticize images they see as associated with younger and possibly differently classed women. The images on MTV define new places for women that they will not condemn.

There are thus complex reasons for resisting criticism of television images like those on MTV India. While the disempowering potentials inherent in the imagery remain a serious cause for concern, the larger picture we have reconstructed from informants' responses indicates that this imagery is only one term in a tricky political-cultural situation. As former MTV India VJ and former Miss India-Canada Rishma Malik said, "In the current environment, there's no room for discernment yet."[80]

Coda: Beyond the Middle Class—
MTV India and the National Divide

In certain respects, the contrast between our reading of the MTV India images and that of our informants might be taken to affirm the priority of their reception over any sexist quality inherent to them. The context-specific strategic reading of the images also allows them to be understood in terms of well-known theories of globalization. To take one instance, we can treat the cultural hybridity of MTV India images as, in Homi Bhabha's words, a "third space," "a fluctuating movement of occult instability" that destabilizes the debilitating binaries of postcolonial oppression (that is, the West/Modernity/the Future vs. India/Tradition/the Past) and thus allows the local to define its own relation to the global.[81] The work of Ien Ang is also relevant and can lead to a similarly positive assessment. In her model of globalization, the local and global are not seen to be separate realms; instead, the local reproduces itself precisely through the ways in which it appropriates and refunctions the global flows of mass media forms like MTV.[82] While those with allegiance to older, specifically modern forms of cultural nationalism might see such images as dissolving the ties of tradition that ground communities and politics, Ang emphasizes the creative potential of such postmodern forms of nationalism. While noting the dangers of romanticizing an agency that is only "imaginative," her model identifies readings such as that of our informants as "deeply politicized" nodes where ideological tensions find expression or resolution.[83]

The work of these two theorists and others puts an affirmative spin on the processes of globalization because they generally consider only one set of power relations, focusing on a "global" and a "local," each of which is taken to stand for a larger whole (that is, Western multinational capitalism vs. the Indian nation-state). Thus MTV India can come to represent an instance in which, in Bhabha's terms, the former colony of India vaults into the post-modern future by subverting the conceptual binary that kept it mired in the traditional or modernist past. But to assess the political substance of such subversion requires that we have a fuller understanding of the empirical relationships between the instance of the local treated in a given analysis (in this case, young middle-class women) and the larger whole for which it has come to stand (in this case, India as a whole). While our subjects' refunctioning of MTV India's images may seem to be a positive development when viewed from within the middle-class enclave, it is also important to consider its place in the larger context from which we extracted it in delimiting the scope of this study—that is, in terms of the realities of Indian society beyond the middle class. What relationships do MTV India's brand of hybrid cultural nationalism presuppose or engender among India's population as a whole? While it will not be possible for us to treat this question in full detail, we would like to conclude this study with a few observations concerning this broader context.

The first and most basic point to emphasize is that the "nation" affirmed by this new form of nationalism excludes all those outside the middle class. MTV India, according to Sangeeta Gupta, director of Strategy and Research at MTV India, targets three hundred million people, putting aside, "first and foremost . . . seven hundred million in rural India."[84] The confident, upwardly mobile dynamism of MTV India's version of the Indian nation is thus predicated on a disavowal of the peasants and working-class people who make up 70 percent of the country's population. This detail of market research reveals the contours of a fundamental inversion of values. The Indian peasant rooted in the land, who had been the primary icon of the older nationalism, has now been replaced by the figure of the mobile nonresident Indian. If the middle class had been forced to sublimate its consumer desires during the decades in which India's identity was built around socialist ideals, India's peasantry now must inhabit a regime of media images in which their reality can only be recognized in the fetishized form of "ethnic chic."[85]

Lacking the buying power of those in the middle class, the rural majority of India's population lives within a national imaginary that must appear inaccessible and alien. Because they are subject to a complex matrix of class, caste, and gender-based oppression, the perspective of women peasants on new

images of women is especially different from that of their middle-class counterparts. Village women face a complex array of gender-based problems—for
example, most women are in *purdah,* their faces covered with veils, and are
liable to severe punishment for any infringement of this and other codes of
feminine modesty. In most cases, they bear the responsibility of fetching the
daily water supply for their families, a role that has been well documented to
leave women and girls prey to sexual harassment and rape. There are no toi-
lets in the villages, and landlords forbid their tenants, who are in many cases
their bonded labor, to use a portion of their land—the land the peasants live
on—for such a purpose. Village women thus have the daily task of finding safe
places to relieve themselves. Such problems sketch out the context for protests
and resistance against images that are seen to exacerbate them. To illustrate
one instance of protest, in the small town of Rohtak, seventy kilometers north-
west of Delhi, members of AIDWA, the All India Democratic Women's Association, have won the right to monitor film posters with explicit shots of women
pasted on walls around the town to advertise upcoming films. They perceive
these images as responsible for creating an environment that is alienating,
oppressive, and dangerous. In a courtroom discussion there, cinema-hall owners questioned the women's right to monitor the posters, stating that such
images were in any case already available on television courtesy of channels like
MTV India. Women responded to this statement by saying that the television
could be turned off. Rather than the liberation such images represent for
middle-class Indian women, rural women perceive these images as encouraging harassment, conditioning the fantasy lives of men who would nonetheless
punish them severely if they ever actually departed from traditional codes of
dress and behavior.

Because of their very different strategic concerns, the particular cultural
effects of globalization we have been considering can be said to divide Indian
women in terms of class and location. While for one group the new images
might promise to effect a growing parity with their male counterparts, for
another they radicalize and inflame longstanding patterns of oppression and
isolation. Any full assessment of globalization must project and consider the
long-term social and political consequences of such radical divergences.

Imperialism of language and culture thus also occurs, of course, within a
country[86] and relates to any questions of hegemony or power. The cultural
dynamics this study has considered need to be viewed in relation to their function within Indian society as a whole. Are new middle-class rules and values economically and culturally colonizing the lower classes of society in India? In 1976,
communications scholar Herbert Schiller wrote, "Freedoms that are formally
impressive may be substantively oppressive when they reinforce prevailing
inequalities while claiming to be providing generalized opportunity for all."[87]
While this statement should certainly also be regarded from a gender perspective, it relates well to this deeper stratification between middle and lower classes
that seems to have embedded itself in India throughout the nineties. Based on
the frequent number of times media personnel and young women we spoke to
in public spaces casually repeated the phrase, "There are too many Indias in one,"

there seems to be a growing sense within the middle class that they could do without the rest of India. These broader power relations are crucial to evaluating the deeper dimensions of the findings outlined in the essay presented here.

Notes

With sincere thanks to Judy Polumbaum, Jael Silliman, and Bonnie Sunstein at the University of Iowa. We are very grateful for their insights, for Dr. Polumbaum's help with final revisions, and also for the guidance provided by *Frontier*'s reviewers. This article is for our daughter, Leela.

1. Jack Banks, *Monopoly Television: MTV's Quest to Control the Music* (Colorado: Westview Press, 1996), 1.

2. Ibid., 34.

3. Ibid.

4. Throughout this study, we use the adjective "Western" to designate those forms of culture that are perceived to be Eurocentric or nonindigenous; we do not mean to suggest that an East-West binary is in any sense natural or absolute.

5. Banks, *Monopoly Television*, 2.

6. David Page and William Crawley, *Satellites over South Asia: Broadcasting, Culture, and the Public Interest* (New Delhi: Sage Publications, 2001), 149.

7. Natasha Malhotra, interview by author, tape recording, Mumbai, Maharashtra, July 28, 2000.

8. Page and Crawley, *Satellites over South Asia*, 149.

9. Cyrus Oshidar, interview by author, tape recording, Mumbai, Maharashtra, July 28, 2000; Malhotra, interview.

10. Ibid.

11. Nina Laurie, Claire Dwyer, Sarah L. Holloway, and Fiona M. Smith, *Geographies of New Femininities* (New York: Pearson Education, 1999), 3.

12. Partha Chatterjee, *The Nation and Its Fragments: Colonial and Postcolonial Histories* (Princeton: Princeton University Press, 1993), 116–34.

13. Ibid., 126.

14. Purnima Mankekar's valuable study of women's reception of television programming during the 1980s and early 1990s provides us with a relatively immediate context that helps explain the valorization of the new images that began to emerge in the mid-1990s. As her ethnography of women's responses to Doordarshan demonstrates, programming during the period typically situated the historical dilemmas of Indian women (that is, being placed in a double bind regarding tradition and modernity) within a nationalist framework; though there were many other ways in which the representation of women on television engaged the experience of female viewers, the basic tendency of "women-oriented" narratives during this period was to legitimate the reconfiguration of traditional and modern values with reference to the nationalist Home/World formula outlined earlier in this essay. In the epilogue to this study, Mankekar discusses the extent to which the transnational quality of images such as those of MTV India have displaced and posed a challenge to the ideology that has been hegemonic for most of India's history as an independent nation, shifting the focus from the politics of nation and community to the politics of family, sexuality, and intimacy. While the new images and narratives generally register for her informants as having less of an immediate relation to their own lives, she suggests (following the work of anthropologist Anne Allison) that the images articulate a *fantasy* of liberation that has important

effects on the lives of Indian women, establishing a basis for frustration in some cases, creating forms of pleasure and possibility in others. (*Screening Culture, Viewing Politics: An Ethnography of Television, Womanhood, and Nation in Postcolonial India* (Durham, NC: Duke University Press, 1999.)

15. Banks, *Monopoly Television*, 175.

16. Ibid., 2–3.

17. Ibid., 3.

18. *Dreamworlds 2: Desire/Sex/Power in Music Video,* VHS, written, edited, narrated by Sut Jhally (Northampton, MA: Media Education Foundation, 1995).

19. Ibid.

20. Ibid.

21. Ibid.

22. Banks, *Monopoly Television,* 3.

23. *Dreamworlds 2.*

24. Ibid.

25. Ibid.

26. Ibid.

27. Monika Mehta, "What Is Behind Film Censorship?" (paper presented at "Gender, Globalization, and Representation in South Asia" conference, Syracuse University, Syracuse, New York, March 31, 2001).

28. Cath Sluggett, interview by author, tape recording, New Delhi, Delhi, June 29, 2000.

29. Ranjan Bakshi, interview by author, tape recording, New Delhi, Delhi, July 20, 2000.

30. Women students at Jawaharlal Nehru University, New Delhi and Saint Xavier's College, Mumbai, surveys by author, July to October, 2000.

31. Rahul Roy, interview by author, tape recording, New Delhi, Delhi, June 29, 2000.

32. Ibid.

33. Women students at Jawaharlal Nehru University, New Delhi and Saint Xavier's College, Mumbai, surveys.

34. Oshidar, interview.

35. Maitrayee Chaudhuri, interview by author, tape recording, New Delhi, Delhi, July 6, 2000.

36. Vijaya Nidadavolu, interview by author, tape recording, New Delhi, Delhi, July 6, 2000.

37. Women students at Jawaharlal Nehru University, New Delhi and Saint Xavier's College, Mumbai, surveys; Shilpa Phadke, St. Xavier's College, Mumbai, July 2000.

38. Roy, interview, and Madhu Kishwar, interview by author, tape recording, New Delhi, Delhi, June 30, 2000.

39. Anita Anand, interview by author, tape recording, New Delhi, Delhi, June 28 and July 4, 2000.

40. Rachel Dwyer, "Bombay Ishtyle," in *Fashion Cultures: Theories, Explorations and Analysis,* ed. Stella Bruzzi and Pamela Church Gibson (New York: Routledge, 2000); Sumita Chakravarty, *National Identity in Indian Popular Cinema, 1947–1987* (Austin: University of Texas Press, 1993).

41. Chakravarty, *National Identity,* 7–9.

42. Dwyer, "Bombay Ishtyle," 182–86.

43. Shilpa Phadke, interview by author, tape recording, Mumbai, Maharashtra, July 28, 2000. Geetanjali Misra also commented on the fact that a sexual revolution like

that in the West in the 1960s was taking place in India today, except that now of course it carries the threat of AIDS (interview by author, July 3, 2000).

44. Discussion group led by Shilpa Phadke.

45. Sandeep Bindra, interview by author, tape recording, New Delhi, Delhi, July 20, 2000.

46. Women students at Jawaharlal Nehru University, New Delhi and Saint Xavier's College, Mumbai, surveys.

47. Oshidar, interview.

48. Nidadavolu, interview.

49. Ibid.

50. Women students at Jawaharlal Nehru University, New Delhi and Saint Xavier's College, Mumbai, surveys.

51. Kishwar, interview.

52. Ibid.

53. Misra, interview.

54. Chaudhuri, interview.

55. Phadke, interview.

56. Gargi Sen, interview by author, tape recording, New Delhi, Delhi, July 1, 2000.

57. Nidadavolu, interview.

58. Ananya Bannerjee, interview by author, tape recording, New Delhi, Delhi, July 4, 2000.

59. Sharika Sharma, interview by author, tape recording, New Delhi, Delhi, June 20, 2000.

60. Sluggett, interview.

61. Ibid.

62. Shilpa Phadke, discussion group; women students at Jawaharlal Nehru University, New Delhi and Saint Xavier's College, Mumbai, surveys.

63. Akhila Sivadas, interview by author, tape recording, New Delhi, Delhi, July 3, 2000. Perhaps we can see a reaction to this sort of traditional role in a comparison of matrimonial sections in the *Hindustan Times* (May 1990 and July 2000). The most striking difference in descriptions was the number of grooms in 2000 who advertised stating they had their *own* houses.

64. Nidadavolu, interview.

65. Phadke, interview.

66. Oshidar, interview.

67. Bannerjee, interview.

68. Chaudhuri, interview.

69. Some informants complained that female image content was the same as it always had been, but was now dressed up in a new form: "Same content, different form." Women said that, in images of women, the woman had the license to be independent and to wear what she wanted until she got married. Then the clothes would change, and the husband automatically became the head of the household. However, emphasis still remained on extending these images, not on spending time attacking them.

70. Sen, interview.

71. Phadke, interview; Brinda Karat, interview by author, tape recording, New Delhi, Delhi, June and July 2000.

72. An excellent overview of the controversy can be found in Sujata Moorti, "Inflamed Passions: *Fire,* the Woman Question, and the Policing of Cultural Borders," *Genders* 32 (2000), http://www.genders.org/g32/g32_moorti.html.

73. Sivadas, interview.

74. Shohini Ghosh, interview by author, tape recording, New Delhi, Delhi, July 7, 2000.

75. Leela Rao, "Facets of Media and Gender Studies in India," *Feminist Media Studies* 1, no. 1 (2001): 46.

76. Karat, interview.

77. Misra, interview.

78. Karat, interview.

79. Phadke, interview.

80. Rishma Malik, phone interview by author, Toronto, Ontario, April 5, 2001.

81. Homi Bhabha, "Cultural Diversity and Cultural Differences" in *The Post-Colonial Studies Reader,* ed. Bill Ashcroft, Gareth Griffiths, and Helen Tiffin (New York: Routeledge, 1995), 208.

82. Ien Ang, *Living Room Wars: Rethinking Media Audiences for a Postmodern World* (New York: Routeledge, 1996), 153.

83. Ibid., 9, 137.

84. Sangeeta Gupta, interview by author, tape recording, Mumbai, Maharashtra, July 28, 2000.

85. Dwyer, "Bombay Ishtyle," 185.

86. Amos Owen Thomas, "Global-diasporic and Subnational-ethnic Audiences for Satellite Television in South Asia," *Journal of International Communication* 3, no. 2 (1996): 73.

87. Herbert Schiller, *Communication and Cultural Domination* (New York: International Arts and Sciences Press, 1976), 45.

Bibliography: Interviews

All India Democratic Women's Association. Haryana and Rohtak District members, including Vidya, Manjeet, Sabita, Kamlesh, Rajo, and Jagmati. Interviews: July 2000.

Anand, Anita. Women's Feature Service. Interviews: June and July 2000.

Bakshi, Ranjan. Vice President, Corporate Communications, Zee Network. Interview: July 2000.

Bannerjee, Ananya. Chief Producer, Doordarshan. Interview: July 2000.

Bindra, Sandeep. Owner, Moet's Restaurant. Interview: July 2000.

Chaudhuri, Maitrayee. Writer, Associate Professor, School of Social Systems, Jawaharlal Nehru University, New Delhi. Interview: July 2000.

Ghosh, Shohini. Reader, Video and TV Production, AJK Mass Communication Research Center, Jamia Millia Islamia University. Interview: July 2000.

Gupta, Sangeeta. Director, Strategy and Research, MTV India. Interview: July 2000.

Karat, Brinda. All India Democratic Women's Association. Interviews: June and July 2000.

Karkara, Ravi. Training and Gender Consultant. Interview: June 2000.

Kishwar, Madhu. Publisher and Editor, *Manushi*. Interview: June 2000.

Malhotra, Natasha. Vice President and Executive Producer, MTV India. Interview: July 2000.

Malik, Rishma. Former VJ, MTV; former VJ, Channel V; former Miss India-Canada. Phone interview: April 2001.

Misra, Geetanjali. Program Officer, Sexuality and Reproductive Health, The Ford Foundation. Interview: July 2000.

Nidadavolu, Vijaya. Media Consultant, International Center for Research on Women; Documentary Film Assistant. Interviews: June and July 2000.

Oshidar, Cyrus. Vice President and Creative Director, MTV India. Interview: July 2000.

Phadke, Shilpa. Writer, Lecturer St. Xavier's College. Interview (and discussion group led by Phadke): July 2000.

Roy, Rahul. AAKAR, A Media Collective; Documentary Filmmaker (Masculinities project: "When Four Friends Meet."). Interview: June 2000.

Sen, Gargi. Filmmaker, Magic Lantern Foundation. Interviews: June and July 2000.

Sharma, Sharika. Product Manager, theindiaguide.com, Trisoft Design. Interview: June 2000.

Sivadas, Akhila. Coordinator, Media Advocacy Group. Interview: July 2000.

Sluggett, Cath. Sangini Project. Interview: June 2000.

To Have and to Hold
The Video Collector's Relationship with an Ethereal Medium

Kim Bjarkman

Television has prided itself on its liveness and nowness since its infancy. For audiences, television's transience stirs mixed feelings. Programs wash over us in a continuous ebb and flow, receding into the backwaters of our memories. When we wish to relive television past, we are "stuck with" current offerings, as lamented by the editor of the electronic television newsletter *This Week at the TV Barn*. The January 3, 2000, issue began by refusing to list the "greatest shows of the 1990s" because such an exercise is futile:

> The main problem with such lists is that they don't do anybody any good. You can't just go down to Blockbuster and pick out the first six episodes of *Nothing Sacred* or *I'll Fly Away* and take them home. Nor can you dial them up on pay-per-view. . . . For now . . . you're stuck with the reruns that TV stations or cable channels are willing to pay to put on the air, and that's not many. (http://www.tvbarn.com/2000/01/03.shtml)

With steady advances in video technology over the past two decades, more and more viewers refuse to accept that celebrated television moments are doomed to disappear forever. Programs we miss (in either sense) need not slip out of our grasp now that VCRs are a domestic staple. Video recorders seize texts out of the ether and give them material form so that they may be preserved, circulated, recollected, and relived. Beyond entertainment value, these recordings serve as exterior memory, cultural relic, and resource in the home.

This article surveys the diverse passions, practices, and priorities of fans who collect and trade video recordings of television broadcasts. Drawing on interviews with three collectors, I examine the measures these individuals take to contain, retain, and sustain an ephemeral medium. I hope to carry forward Uma Dinsmore's (1998) discussion of the value of videotape for collectors in her insightful ethnographic study "Chaos, Order and Plastic Boxes: The Significance of Videotapes for the People Who Collect Them," wherein she identified a meeting point for film and television studies to come together in a meaningful alliance: studying film spectators' relationship to the small screen. Examining the collecting habits of British film enthusiasts who purchase and record movies on video to transform the home into "domestic cinema,"[1] Dinsmore reported on collectors' gradual and reluctant "imposition" of rule-governed organizational systems as their collections grow unwieldy. We can deepen our understanding of videotape's significance for collectors by contrasting these findings with the methods and motives of television collectors. Focusing on film collectors, Dinsmore uncovered an ambivalent relationship with their videos. Some of her participants regard videotapes as eyesores to be hidden from sight or awkwardly navigated around in domestic space. Only begrudgingly and retroactively do they impose indexing and cataloguing systems, which threaten to detract from their experiences of the filmic text as an escape from the "mundane, everyday world of irritating domestic objects" (p. 319). As a video collector myself, I regularly encounter inversions of this attitude among collectors who prioritize television over film. Devotees and defenders of television—itself, like videotape, maligned as a mundane medium—tend to be fonder of videotape and more forgiving of its frailty and "ordinariness." Many celebrate video, along with orderly cataloguing systems. For these individuals, videotapes are not unsightly objects to be concealed and may even decorate and dominate domestic space. Furniture is shuffled to accommodate video libraries, not the other way around.

My interest in the activities of video collectors is deeply personal. This study grew out of my inability to recognize my own viewing/recording habits reflected in the pages of television studies' existing canon. David Morley's (1992) seminal ethnographic studies, along with Ann Gray's ([1987] 1997) influential "Behind Closed Doors: Video Recorders in the Home," examine the domestic politics underlying the British family unit's relationship to TV/video technology. Both report that men are the principal decision makers when it comes to family viewing, leaving women potentially alienated and disempowered by video technology.[2] My aim is to supplement these investigations into the domestic uses of video recorders by highlighting alternative uses of the VCR as domestic technology and viewing habits rivaling those of the traditionally conceived nuclear family (complete with technophobic women, who feature prominently in Morley's studies). As a single woman with more than two thousand videotapes, I am not a typical viewer; nor am I alone. A glimpse into television collectors' substantial subculture—seen by many as a "boy's club" but also thriving within predominantly female media fandoms—suggests ways in which changing uses of computer and video technologies are accommodating (and perhaps symptomatic of) gradual and widespread shifts in mind-sets when it comes to our television sets.

Morley (1992) rightly urged audience researchers to take into account television's growing commodity potential and shifting uses, considering its place within global as well as domestic and national contexts. While I share these goals, I am concerned that Morley's emphasis on the continuing symbolic centrality of the nuclear family eclipses certain audience contingents profoundly affected by the growing commodity potential of television texts, and integral to the formation of globally dispersed viewing communities: avid fan-collectors, more than casual viewers, demand the transformation of television texts from intangible images to concrete, exchangeable plastic keepsakes that can be arrayed on a shelf. They are also among those most invested in generating and sustaining transnational cyberspace "taste communities." Television enthusiasts who never meet face to face regularly interface in internet forums (web sites, newsgroups, and chat rooms) to discuss favorite programs or seek out potential traders. Increasingly, international videotape trading allows collectors to reach beyond current listings in their home towns. The VCR is no longer solely a tool for time-shifting; it has become a tool for *place*-shifting, swapping programs by mail for broadcasts from other regions and nations. The "greatest shows of the 1990s" may not all line rental shop shelves or syndication schedules, but collectors are increasingly looking online to establish a global trade in rare video and procure the programs they desire.[3]

Introductions

My interviewees demonstrate different levels of commitment to large-scale tape collecting and trading, their experiences spanning from five to sixteen years. All three are white, middle class, and unmarried (at the time of interview). John, a thirty-three-year-old public library cataloguer near Chicago, has accumulated three thousand tapes over sixteen years. He collects primarily comedy but also music, sports, science-fiction, and fantasy programs, regularly trading overseas for British broadcasts. He has also made contacts in Canada and Australia. John owns four TV sets and ten VCRs currently in use, including National Television System Committee (NTSC) and phase alternation line (PAL) decks for both VHS and Betamax, and a multistandard converter. Dave, twenty-six, is a computer software developer in northern England who first began dabbling in tape collecting at age seventeen. Trading with contacts in America and recording on average two dozen U.K. comedy and science-fiction series per season, plus miscellaneous documentaries and films, Dave amasses more than five hundred tapes per year. Because he shares a flat with two other collectors, Dave confines his own taping equipment to his bedroom, where tidy tape stacks lining his walls several layers deep are rapidly encroaching on his floor space. He plans to move soon to accommodate his collection's growth. Wendy, a linguistics graduate student in Wisconsin, collects on a more modest scale. At twenty-five, she has been taping seriously for five years, but her full library of four hundred tapes spans fifteen years. Wendy's living room is organized around a media center with three NTSC VHS VCRs, wired to record up to three programs while watching a fourth or a DVD. Her bedroom houses a multistandard TV/VCR for viewing British tapes. She archives up to ten series per season, primarily teen and children's science-fiction and fantasy shows, and so far has shipped tapes abroad to collectors in Canada, England, Australia, and Brazil.

John and Wendy have been regular trading contacts of mine since 1994, and Dave has been a contact since 1997. I selected this sample as my entry point into the video-collecting world for three reasons. First, I have had the opportunity to watch their collections mature for several years. Second, in a subculture given to discretion, I anticipated that close acquaintances would be more receptive to probing questions than randomly recruited participants.[4] Finally, all three trade across national borders and are prominent participants within larger trading circles. In college, Wendy and Dave founded "cult TV" clubs on their campuses, Dave's accruing more than three hundred student members. Since college, Wendy has been involved with several internet-based fan groups: she manages a web site, fan-fiction list, and discussion list (doubling as a video-trading loop) for the 1970s U.K. children's fantasy series *The Tomorrow People*, and she has comanaged and/or participated on similar lists for several U.S. and Canadian fantasy-dramas including *Sliders, Highlander: The Series, Forever Knight,* and *Buffy the Vampire Slayer.* John and Dave, meanwhile, network primarily with clusters of private collectors operating independently of specific fandoms.[5]

Communication with other collectors informs my interviewees' and my own observations about video-collecting culture, but it is not my intention to use interviewees' comments as springboards for launching unsound generalizations, nor to imply that this select sample is representative of all television collectors. What I do hope to suggest is that these collectors' unconventional but converging ideas about the role and relevance of video-recorded television challenge us to rethink the range of pleasures that VCRs provide beyond making "domestic cinema" or deferred viewing possible. These individuals suggest a range of personas, beyond viewer/spectator, that collectors adopt in tending their video libraries. The remaining pages survey seven (often simultaneous) positions assumed by these collectors, roles I dub the captor, chronicler, crusader, competitor, creator, curator, and cataloguer.

Exploring each collector persona in turn, I will necessarily speak in general terms when outlining operative discourses—the attendant codes, logics, ethics, and etiquettes—that constitute or circumscribe these identities (the collector qua captor, the collector qua curator, etc.). Clearly, not all television collectors occupy each of these hypothetical positions. The purpose of such a schematic approach is to encourage discussion of pleasures and identities that complement but at times also contradict those conceived by viewer-consumer models of audience analysis. Fans and collectors create their own disciplines and regimes, their own rule-bound systems, for the production of pleasures that are not necessarily in the service of hegemony or in sync with the logic of the market. If we continue to think of television audiences strictly in terms of disciplined and commodified viewership, we perpetuate the marginalization of the marginalized and overlook fascinating and flourishing sites of audience activity.

Locking Light in a Box: The Captor

For the collectors surveyed in this study, television archiving is more lifestyle than hobby—not a way to pass time but a ritual means of trapping time. Dave is adamant that career pressures "most certainly will not stop me from taping/archiving at any point in the future." He explains, "To me, setting the

VCR to catch programs I would not be around to record personally is just as much a part of my morning preparations as putting on a shirt and tie to go to the office." The VCR has a significance for Dave that takes precedence over the pleasures and conveniences of renting movies or time-shifting programming by several hours or days. He struggles against television's impermanence and intangibility, desiring to own, not merely watch, images that otherwise vanish with the moment of transmission.

What compels collectors to objectify pieces of ephemera, to capture electromagnetic waves and store them in a plastic shell? James Clifford (1985) argued that our possessions—knowledge, wealth, property—shape our identities, separating self from other. Exploring this relationship between subjectivity and objects, Clifford noted that as children we first begin to stake a claim in the world by fixating on objects and assigning them personal value:

> A boy's accumulation of miniature cars, a girl's dolls . . . in these small rituals we observe the channeling of obsession, an exercise in how to make the world one's own. . . . An excessive, sometimes even rapacious need to *have* is transformed into rule-governed, meaningful desire. Thus the self which must *possess*, but cannot have it all, teams to select, order, classify in hierarchies—to make "good" collections. (p. 238)

For the self who wants but cannot possess it all, the mere fact of desired objects that cannot be held within the corpus of the collection can cause considerable distress. Hence, John's cardinal rule about rare video: "If I can't have it, I don't want to know about it." Walter Benjamin's ([1955] 1978) famous essay on rare book collecting, "Unpacking My Library," describes the intense bond between a collector and his possessions. Ownership, insisted Benjamin, is "the most intimate relationship that one can have to objects. Not that they come alive in him [the collector]; it is he who lives in them" (p. 67). It is the will to own and not just enjoy that admits new items into the growing collection, wherein collectors build private worlds. "The most profound enchantment for the collector," said Benjamin, "is the locking of individual items within a magic circle in which they are fixed as the final thrill, the thrill of acquisition, passes over them" (p. 60). The collector's desire for this moment is never sated but renewed with each find. Between acquisitions, ambitions of discovery or recovery anticipate the pleasures of ownership. John relishes opportunities to sift through battered boxes of dusty, discarded tapes, since each unmarked black casing could conceal long-sought treasures. Among my own fondest collecting memories are hours spent roaming out-of-print video shops, combing car boot sales for another taper's castoffs, and browsing traders' inventories to select items to make my own.

Film collector Charles Tashiro (1996), in his essay "The Contradictions of Video Collecting," described his own collection as an extension of his personality, confessing that he found prolonged separation from it profoundly uncomfortable. Watching somebody else's copy of a favorite title does not hold the same appeal for Tashiro, since it is not "mine" (p. 17). A similar sentimented Benjamin ([1955] 1978) to conclude that for the book collector, "the most important fate of a copy is its encounter with him, with his own collection" (p. 61). The meanings the object holds for its owner after it is acquired are harder for Benjamin to unpack. He assured us that using (reading) the books in his collection is incidental, perhaps inessential to the collecting experience. The same can hold true for tape collecting. For bulk tapers, Tashiro (1996) pointed out, time spent recording new titles may preclude rewatching tapes or even watching some a first time (p. 11). They "tape against some future that never arrives," complained Tashiro, "fabricating a potential of limitless viewing pleasure" (p. 15). Video collectors thus stand accused of nursing an irrational habit, since those with ballooning collections seem to delight in "the march of tapes across the shelf" for its own sake, more than they savor the prospect of reviewing the contents (p. 15). This acquisition process can be as frustrating as it is fulfilling: the collector gains a sense of progress with each new tape but can never arrive at a sense of completion.

The desire to hold onto the new and all that came before may well defy our ability to see the trees for the forest, as Tashiro protested, and may be self-defeating where the goal is repeat viewing. However, the video collector's enthrallment with the expanding archive resonates not only with a materialist consciousness that marks our era but with Western culture's preoccupation with rule-bound systems of collection. As museums and libraries work to harbor history in material form, individuals in our consumer society are likewise compelled to hoard artifacts and may even feel a duty to collect—to record and preserve their past experiences. The next three sections explore variations on this compulsion in video collecting: the desire to build concrete memories (video deteriorates, but less rapidly than memory), to save doomed texts from the cultural dustbin, and to outcollect the competition.

Collecting Recollections and Recording Histories: The Chronicler

Marveling at the modern world's fetishization of archives, Pierre Nora (1989) observed that more than any society before us, we are preoccupied with documenting our own existence through physical traces. We dare not destroy any particle remains of our lives or culture that may hold some unforeseen value as historical evidence. As we perfect the means to produce the past on demand, conferring onto the archive the unending task of "remembering" for us, history and memory grow apart, and the latter comes to "rel[y] entirely on the materiality of the trace, the immediacy of the recording, the visibility of the image" (p. 13). "Hence the obsession with the archive that marks our age," wrote Nora, "attempting at once the complete conservation of the present as well as the total preservation of the past" (p. 13).

Archiving becomes as much an individual imperative as a societal one. We are self-appointed historians, whose private histories and memories intersect and take form, Nora (1989) suggested, in objects that serve as *"lieux de mémoire,"* or sites where "memory crystallizes and secretes itself" (p. 7). We strive "to stop time, to block the work of forgetting . . . to materialize the immaterial," to lock our experiences away as tangible records to be reaccessed at will—in journals, scrapbooks, and photo albums (p. 19). Video collectors treat tapes as one such site of memory. With vintage television, particularly, tapes serve as time capsules promising to store and restore memory. For this reason, strangers stumbling across Wendy's *Tomorrow People* web site, when requesting copies of the program, regularly confess a powerful desire for video verification of fading mental images. Mistrusting their own recollections, they seek external substitutes less susceptible to the ravages of time:

> They e-mail me with something that is so common it borders on a form let-ter. . . . Something along the lines of, " . . . I have never met anybody else who ever had even heard of this show! You have answered all of my dreams. I wasn't sure this show actually *existed*. How can I get tapes?" (Wendy)

Preoccupied with chronicling our passage through life, we each wager on which objects and signs will later be valuable to us, stowing these away in prepa-ration for a future occasion that (as Tashiro insisted) may never arise. This imper-ative intensifies when, like these *Tomorrow People* fans, we begin to pine for past moments we failed to ferret away in preparation for a present that has arisen. Wendy recalls her frustration as a teenager when her own fond childhood mem-ories of *The Tomorrow People* started slipping away, and all she had to remem-ber the show by were snippets of episodes lying around on tape. Today, per-ceiving that the price of memory is eternal vigilance, Wendy auditions programs based on informed predictions about which TV memories might compose her future "past." She dutifully records promising new shows every season on the gamble that those archived today may be tomorrow's favorite fading memories.

John and Dave, too, now archive everything they regularly watch. John decrees, "Don't watch TV; *tape* it." For him, the decision to archive a pro-gram is permanent. Dave agrees, "If it was interesting enough to be laid down in my archive to start with, then it is interesting enough to keep." Wendy's commitment to archived tapes is less absolute. When she tires of a show's fan-dom, she will consider purging those tapes from her collection—or, if she has no intention of joining that fandom to begin with, she may make low-grade, temporary recordings. Yet, like the others, Wendy finds the day-to-day acts of taping and viewing inextricably linked; watching no longer feels natural with-out a VCR remote close at hand. "To watch is to tape," she quips, recount-ing how several years ago she impulsively purchased a spare VCR to record a program while visiting relatives. When a bemused family friend asked why Wendy could not simply watch and enjoy the broadcast,

> my instant reaction was, "But I can't do that because there's no VCR here." And as soon as I said that, I realized that I had so thoroughly equated the recording and the viewing process that I couldn't. . . . I needed a VCR to watch the show. (Wendy)

The difference is like that between window shopping and going inside to make the purchase. Watching without taping would have made the experience feel incomplete. The subtext of "to watch is to tape" is that to watch is to save and savor whenever desired.

Marginal social groups, like individuals, are actively archiving their histories and memories, determining which texts deserve to be prized, preserved, and exchanged (cf. Nora 1989, 15). Media fandoms work toward this common end to the extent that members feel they have a "shared culture" to defend and preserve. By treating culturally derided texts as collectibles, fans attach value where dominant society may assign none, seeking legitimacy for texts dismissed as trivial, trashy, bizarre, or altogether forgettable by mainstream audiences (for more discussion, see Jenkins 1992, 17). By circulating programs in the concrete, exchangeable form video allows, fans claim the text not only as a narrative universe to colonize, by composing "fan fiction," but also as the material foundation of the fandom—its riches and its resources. Tapes become traces of a common cultural heritage that is "ours" to archive, and fan-collectors are guardians of the archive within their "imagined communities."[6]

To support communal acts of archiving, fan groups rely on industrious scribes and record keepers who annotate self-fashioned archives with historical records and documentation. Alongside fan fiction, fanzines, and newsletters, fan authors chronicle broadcast history with television-themed web sites and meticulous episode guides. Episode guide authors and compilers take the role of television chronicler-historian very seriously, publishing guides not only electronically (on sites such as epguides.com and tvtome.com) but in magazines and bound volumes. Alan Morton's (1997) self-published *The Complete Directory to Science Fiction, Fantasy and Horror Television Series,* for example, contains 336 episode guides spanning fifty years. Morton, a longtime trading acquaintance of John's, has spent years researching his guides in libraries and archives across the United States and United Kingdom. Designed as reference tools, his guides provide episode titles, synopses, air dates, cast and guest cast lists, and—with the collector in mind—lines to check off each episode as it is acquired. John himself has authored dozens of similar episode guides on the internet and is among the Internet Movie Database's fifty most prolific individual contributors of TV and movie data.

Trade lists circulated by collectors can be impressive chronicles in themselves. They present a strikingly different account of television's legacy than more official channels such as awards ceremonies or "picks and pans" pages in popular magazines, and they make their own case for what slices of television history deserve to be immortalized or condemned to obscurity. Fans and collectors build countercanons to rival the "classic" television canon, often conferring great value on failed series that were denied a chance to develop or find an audience, such as Fox's 2001–02 prime-time superhero spoof *The Tick.* A-list sitcoms such as *Seinfeld* and *Friends* look more out of place on a trade list than do riskier, more obscure, or fringe-appeal sitcoms such as *Get a Life, Parker Lewis Can't Lose,* and *Family Guy.* In trading transactions, quickly canceled comedies such as *Action* outperform long haulers with wide international circulation and strong syndication prospects, such as *Frasier.* By the same token, dramas discarded after or within a season, such as *American Gothic, EZ Streets, Nothing Sacred,* and *Profit,* carry more clout in trading circles than ratings success stories such as the *West Wing, Star Trek: The Next Generation,* and *The*

X-Files; even where the latter remain fan favorites and frequently appear on trade lists, copies are in low demand. Easy-to-obtain programs not only have less trade value but also fail to rouse the inner crusader—the collector persona who steps forward when a program's very right to exist is called into question by bet-hedging programmers, advertisers, and Nielsen's narrow notion of which audiences rate.

Solidarity and Civic Duty: The Crusader

Writing about historical archives, Michel-Rolph Trouillot (1995) observed that documents compete for their "right to existence" as they vie for ultimately limited spaces in the "historical landscape" (pp. 49–50). Media archives witness similar struggles, as processes of selection necessitate acts of deselection. Just as film scholars are still grieving the widespread disposal of early nitrate prints, and with them the erasure of much of Hollywood's history (cf. Allen and Gomery 1985, 29–30), British television collectors have never forgiven the British Broadcasting Corporation (BBC) for destroying broadcast masters throughout the 1970s. In the 1990s, the BBC again sought to purge portions of its holdings, including television and radio scripts, to reduce its storage burden. Alarmed fans wrote to the BBC, Dave recounts, volunteering to "give these valuable materials a good home where they would be respected." Thus, in creating private archives, fan-collectors sometimes see themselves picking up the slack for official archives. Indignant when beloved shows are effectively expunged from television history, collectors congregate to commiserate and to protest perceived archival exclusions. Dave ascribes "an element of civic duty" to archiving, with fans ensuring that copies continue to exist if stations cannot be trusted to retain their own master tapes. On the same logic, John records Chicago Cubs baseball games because "someone has to," since for the past fifty years Chicago's WGN has archived only highlights compilations.

For fans of unconventional television, favorite programs are not only subject to eventual archival extinction but more immediately are at the mercy of mass tastes. "The cancellation principle," as Wendy calls it, compels fans to record new series of interest faithfully from the outset, lest they be left with nothing if a promising show is dealt a swift death blow in the ratings (for further discussion of this mind-set in media fandom, see Jenkins 1992, 70). With video, collectors can effectively freeze the televisual text in time. Michel Foucault (1972) wrote that it is possible not only to increase a historical text's chances of survival by giving it material form but also "to snatch past discourse from its inertia." The text can be "reactivated," claimed Foucault, if it is revisited, read, interpreted, and remembered (p. 123). To this end, fandom groups coordinate their efforts to defend culturally devalued programs, save endangered programs, and breathe life back into ratings casualties. Wendy manages an online community bent on "resurrecting" *The Tomorrow People* from its grave at the Thames TV archive. She began distributing video sets of the program several years ago, as growing numbers of fans wandered onto her e-mail discussion list and web site with "*grand* memories [of the show] but not very *good* ones."[7] Wendy circulates the tapes not for profit (as I will discuss in a later section, this is a crucial distinction and point of pride for her) but to share the show she loves:

> I want people to have knowledge of the show, and to be able to talk about it and write fan fiction about it, and join me in my community. And I know they can't do it unless they have tangible copies to watch. (Wendy)

Wendy hopes that fans will gain the power to "remember the show so strongly they'll bring it back." In the meantime, she is grateful that the internet affords canceled shows such as *The Tomorrow People, Highlander: The Series,* and *Forever Knight* (the latter two, fittingly, being fantasies about immortality and the former being about rebirth) an afterlife in cyberspace.

Elitism, Completism, and the "True Fan": The Competitor

Although taping is largely an independent activity for my interviewees, the previous sections have suggested that it need not be a lonely or isolated one. This is true even for collectors outside of intimate fan communities. Some of Dave's most enduring friendships began as trading relationships:

> I do not see my lifestyle as being at all solitary in nature—there are a great many friends I have made through videotape archival. I stay in touch with friends from my home town . . . as well as people I've never met because of my activities. (Dave)

Dave and John are both networked into tightly knit trading loops of archivists who grant each other "free run" (in John's words) of their collections, instead of orchestrating trades on a one-for-one basis. Both describe a rapport and respect among "fellow archivists." Unacquainted fans, too, assist each other by posting VCR "alerts" on internet newsgroups and discussion lists when a popular performer, or a rare program or episode, surfaces in the schedule.

By no means is harmonious cooperation the glue that holds all trading circles together, however. Despite a communal sense of purpose among many fans and amateur archivists, much tape-collecting activity is fueled by the spirit of competition, even among longtime friends, as Dave attests:

> Every month . . . my friends gather round with their latest bound copy of a database printout, comparing sizes of archives, etc. In this technological age, there is also a lot of discussion about who has the best cataloguing system as well.

The existence of private archives does not level the playing field but rather redistributes archival power unevenly into the hands of particular fan contingents. Once fans liberate a text long buried in the official archives, the result is not a free-for-all; group dynamics impose limits on these resources, for both practical and interpersonal reasons. Video technology itself creates hierarchies: those closest to the trader with the "source" copy will obtain higher generation copies, while those who have to settle for a copy "from a friend of a friend of a friend" may barely be able to make out the images on their screens. In addition to technological guarantors of scarcity, group politics also work to ration rare video resources. The most exclusive trading circles admit only highly experienced collectors, by invitation or recommendation. While such barriers exist as a measure to ensure professionalism and quality control, erecting internal social hierarchies within fan communities also yields certain psychic rewards by shoring up a sense of privilege, authority, and insider identity.

Within fan communities, Wendy describes a series of concentric social "circles" with a core that can seem, for many, impenetrable. Media fandoms are microcosms unto themselves, complex communities united in allegiance to a common text or texts but often internally divided by factions, fractions, friction, and flaming. The innermost circles divvy up what power they wrest from "official" archival sources but may do so without wishing to throw open their doors to every newcomer ("newbie") who expresses an interest in their hard-won video valuables. Those who do penetrate a fandom's core community may earn a status, particularly among newer recruits to the fandom, as more authentic and authoritative fans. While the collecting cognoscenti at a fandom's hub win the respect of their peers, those on the periphery are more likely to be spurned should they boast about exhaustive video libraries, whether because they disturb that chain of privilege, disregard shared codes of courtesy and displays of community mindedness or, as is often the case, confirm their outsiderness by misapprehending the etiquette for soliciting trades. Describing how this insider-outsider dynamic impinges on video trading within fandoms, Wendy points to a particularly off-putting encounter with one fan at a media convention who alienated fellow convention-goers by approaching video trading as an illicit transaction. For Wendy and her friends, his exaggerated performance of secrecy, in-groupness, and specialized knowledge sealed his interloper status, calling to mind a shady back-alley figure trafficking merchandise under his *Highlander*-inspired trench coat: "Pssst. I have this episode, I have that episode! I have PAL, I have NTSC, I have SECAM [sequential color and memory]! I've got Beta! I've got VHS!"

Wendy perceives an "elitist mentality" within media fandoms, from which she does not exempt herself:

> Anybody can have every episode of *Buffy* [*the Vampire Slayer*] that's ever aired. All they have to do is tune in once a week for an hour. In order to be a "true" fan or to have the stuff that other fans might care about, you need to have the actors' appearances elsewhere—the ones from before they were famous, before they were on that show, or their appearance on an obscure channel or in another country . . . from ten years ago on some talk show that nobody's ever heard of, so that you can show that you were a *true* fan—not only that, but you were a true fan *way back when.*

Since trade lists are not judged on length but on their contents, newcomers labor to show they have the know-how to acquire earlier cast appearances on entering the fandom. This concern with thoroughness defines much of Wendy's own collection. Tucked beside her media center is a display case she jokingly calls her "shrine" to *Highlander: The Series* because it is artfully arranged and it has coffee mugs, and watch, and pendant, and videotapes and audiotapes.[8] It has recordings of one of the conventions I went to. Music videos, four copies of the first movie, including the American release, the pirated British release, the official British release—a.k.a. the director's cut—and the director's cut on DVD, which I bought three years before I had a DVD player.

The display case also contains various "clip" tapes compiling promotional blurbs, cast interviews, and guest appearances from other programs. By looking beyond a program to promotional clips and sideline work by its cast and creators, fan-collectors explode the boundaries of the self-contained television text.

Dave and John, who do not regularly participate in online fandoms, collect a comparable assortment of rare, obscure, and promotional clips. Both record favorite actors narrating children's cartoons, hosting nature documentaries, and advertising everything from beer to bank cards. They put this pre-disposition toward thoroughness down not to elitism but completism. Dave explains, "I am a completist and a perfectionist. If I see a program I like, I want the entire run of it at hand. I'll want other material from people in those programs." But both men agree with Wendy that the knack for forging productive alliances, as John comments, clearly delineates the "haves from the have-nots." Getting well connected can yield bootlegged blooper reels, unaired episodes, rough cuts,[9] or long-lost programs that predate the introduction of VCRs into most homes.

The preceding pages have examined videotape's significance to collectors as a means of holding onto television, in the form of memories but also in the more literal sense as an object to be held and possessed. The social and solitary dimensions of videotape trading, taken together, speak to the conflicted and at times contradictory relationship that collectors share not only with a transient medium but also with each other. Pulling against the pleasures of competitive archiving are the pleasures of solidarity and communal celebration that so regularly bring fans together to discuss, defend, rescue, or resurrect programs. In either case, pleasure is bound up with anxieties about television's resistance to the world of physical objects and must navigate the paradoxes of a medium that is at once pervasive and scarce. The remaining sections turn to the physical presence of the video collection within the home, factoring in fetishization of the videotape, the archive, and the catalogue. We rejoin the captor, chronicler, and competitor personae to introduce their alter egos, the creator, curator, and cataloguer.

Call It Art: The Creator

Clifford (1985) charged us to see archived objects for what they are, fetishes: "This tactic, necessarily personal, would accord to things in collections the power to fixate, rather than simply the capacity to edify or to inform" (p. 244). This section considers the videocassette as fetish object. Dinsmore's and Tashiro's film collectors focus on the film text itself and have little investment in the video copy, which can be happily discarded to upgrade to a superior print. TV collectors, in contrast, commonly attach meaning and symbolic value to the videotape itself.

Dinsmore's (1998, 319–21) film collectors perceive videotapes, especially "ordinary" tapes (i.e., recorded from television), as "dull or ugly objects" to be "dumped in a corner," though they speak with reverence when showing off prized items they have purchased: boxed sets and remastered, letter-boxed, or collector's edition releases, uncontaminated by commercials. Tashiro (1996), himself a film connoisseur, viewed video with undisguised contempt. Tapes enter his collection as "second-class citizens," pushed aside to make way for flawless, gleaming discs adorned with appealing sleeves. Tapes are merely a transitional stage; "worthy" films are eventually promoted to a more resilient medium that will grant them immortal life on his shelves:

> It is precisely *because* discs are permanent that they have the allure of the static, self-contained art work, the mystique of preservation, fragility that must be maintained, isolated, *revered*. Since the eventual destruction of a videotape is inevitable, it can be treated badly from the first. (p. 12)

Whereas neither John nor Dave would consider erasing or reusing an archived tape, Tashiro handled videotapes with "abusive indifference" on account of their relative fragility, "their cheap, shoddy availability, their ability to be erased and reused" (pp. 12–13). He touted the disc's visual and tactile superiority: "Discs fascinate as objects, their clear, cool surfaces promising technical perfection. While their *blankness* seems to offer limitless potential, a minimalist understatement in favor of the text, their silvery surfaces shimmer, refracting their surroundings into prismatic, kaleidoscopic fragments" (pp. 15–16).

For television collectors, it is not the gleaming simplicity of the disc but the literal blankness of the nonprerecorded videotape that holds this promise as a canvas for recording impressions of which images are worth revisiting or rescuing from television's unrelenting flow. Tashiro's disgust at tape's mundanity and malleability betrays a deeper disdain for the changeable, fleeting, and ultimately forgettable nature of television itself, in contrast to film's eternalness and legitimacy as "self-contained art work." This logic is inverted by the television collectors I spoke with, who take pains to distinguish themselves from consumers lining their shelves with store-bought merchandise. For them, favoring commercial tapes and discs is equivalent to preferring the perfection of the postcard to the personal touch of the photograph. As opposed to the mass-printed disc— a form, like the postcard or poster, denied any lingering claims to "originalness"—they see each off-air video recording as being in some sense unique. No two tapes will be identical in content and quality; even dubs never exactly duplicate the "original copy." Blank video, like camera film, allows television's consumers to hold onto some sense of their own creative participation, as they conjure images out of the air and capture them in small black boxes.[10]

Furthermore, given the well-established sites of institutional preservation for film, many video collectors feel no pressing need to collect or circulate these texts. For John and Wendy, professional releases of films, in their permanence and pervasiveness, pose little challenge and thus promise significantly less psychic pay-off. John rarely purchases prerecorded tapes or discs released in the United States "because I figure they're going to be available forever." Collector Philip Satterley (1995a), a longtime trading contact of John's and founder of an internet newsgroup devoted to videotape trading, captured this perspective succinctly and scathingly in the opening lines of his online manual, *The Beginner's Guide to Video Tape Collecting:*

> This guide is geared for a "non pre-recorded" video collecting. Sure it's really easy to skip on over to the local video retail outlet and plunk down tons of money on all the Tim Burton releases and put them on the shelf.

So, while Tashiro dismissed video and television as ephemeral media, television collectors may in turn view interchangeable, everlasting discs as their shelves' least worthy occupants, perhaps even handling them with the same "abusive indifference" Tashiro reserved for video. Accordingly, in an interesting reversal of the views voiced by Tashiro and by Dinsmore's interviewees, Wendy comments that she occasionally buys discs for their entertainment value but—with the exception of imported titles—does not count commercial-release movies among the contents of her video "collection." The dozen or more movie DVDs she owns are concealed in a cabinet, not proudly displayed on her main video shelves.

This stands in marked contrast to the attitudes of many media scholars I have talked to about their own media collections.[11] Colleagues who collect primarily film often comment on the counterintuitive logic of valuing videos over discs and "homemade" or "ordinary" recordings over "professional" ones. For my interviewees, the simplest explanation is that they see archiving as a labor of love (with as much emphasis on labor as love) and themselves as the captors, keepers, and, to some extent, creators and controllers of an elusive resource. Once that resource is readily available by conventional means, the urgency, and hence urge, to archive it vanishes. Thus, with *Buffy the Vampire Slayer*'s release on DVD, Wendy admits she no longer sees "any need" to archive the program. For television collectors, scarcity plays an important role in dictating which programs are the most "valuable" investments in the long term. In fact, John and Wendy both complain that the trade value of their off-air recordings diminishes the moment a program is released commercially on video or DVD.[12] For John, the mere fact of unavailability can make one program more tantalizing than another. He prefers *Doctor Who* to *Blake's 7,* for example, even though he sees the latter as a "technically superior" show. With the full run of *Blake's 7* widely available on commercially released video, there is, John feels, "nothing rare about it." The fact that some *Doctor Who* episodes no longer exist at all adds to this show's allure. John enjoys the communal quest to recover missing episodes and the way that lost episodes assume mythical proportions in the fandom's collective imaginings as individuals strain to reconstruct them from memory or by piecing together others' recollections with grainy screen-captured images in the pages of *Doctor Who Monthly*.

Although quasi-economic discourses of scarcity, supply and demand, and "trade value" are clearly operative in video-collecting culture, the symbolic or social value of rare recordings converts into actual monetary value less readily than one might expect. Video recordings turn television into exchangeable goods, yet traders conscientiously police their commodification. For John, Dave, and Wendy, video collecting is a creative pursuit, not an economic one. They regard tape collecting as a personal investment and form of self-expression that is not about the circulation of commodities but the circulation of symbols.[13] As new initiates to trading loops quickly learn, the preferred means of "payment" for items from others' collections is not cash but, if one has nothing else to offer, replacement blank cassettes or off-air recordings of programs currently running on local/regional channels that other traders may not receive. Wendy, unlike John and Dave, does regularly "distribute" tapes one way, as opposed to trading for other tapes, but on principle does not accept payment beyond reimbursement for shipping and cassette costs and, for large orders, a ¢25-per-dub contribution for VCR upkeep. John, Wendy, and Dave shun collectors who market copies of their tapes or, worse, trade to obtain rare items and subsequently sell copies at extortionate prices. They consider this practice an exploitation of fans and moreover of fellow traders' generosity, since this pseudo-commercial availability devalues the source trader's own copy. Furthermore, profiteering raises uncomfortable questions about the legality of tape trading and undermines trading culture's proud yet fragile self-construction as an outlaw enterprise—not criminal but literally operating outside the law or, as Wendy says, taking refuge in its "gray areas."[14] Tape-trading culture not only seeks to exempt itself from the strictures of copyright law but also positions its practices as outside of or adjacent to the laws of the commercial marketplace. Thus, traders who defend their activities in part through appeals to scarcity, necessity, devotion, civic duty, and perhaps even a Sherwood Forrest model of heroism (taking from the network archives, in a sense, to give to the fans) worry that their subculture's already tenuous camaraderie is compromised when trading gets collapsed into, and some argue demeaned by, commercial rules of exchange.

Although the bulk of their collecting consists of broadcast recordings, completism does lead John, Wendy, and Dave to purchase a fair number of prerecorded videos. When buying programs they have previously taped off air, they do so not for more legitimate copies or ornamental boxes but typically to obtain unbroadcast material or a higher quality copy. In the United Kingdom, where television programs are released commercially on video almost as routinely as films, prerecorded video has begun to trump broadcast by offering fans a "sneak peek" of yet- or never-to-be-aired "TV" footage. British comedy and quiz shows such as *Have I Got News for You* and *Never Mind the Buzzcocks* are releasing unaired episodes direct to video, and intriguingly, the box for a 2000 release of the BBC comedy sketch program *The Fast Show* boasts "brand new specials available before TV broadcast." While many U.K. comedy and science-fiction programs of interest to John and Dave are released on British video, they are typically deleted from commercial catalogues within several years, making prerecorded TV tapes as rare in the long term as off-air recordings. Both men point out that they do not consider such purchases necessary when they already have a complete off-air copy of a program, but Dave usually invests in the release if his existing broadcast copy is flawed. All three interviewees generally keep both copies/sets rather than purging their off-air recordings, which may still hold value for alternate cuts, bumpers, or commercials.

Commercials themselves are "prime hunting ground" for video collectors, Dave notes, especially those with early celebrity appearances that fans may not have "caught" at the time. He adds that advertisements give programs "some social context." Treating programs as temporally bounded events originating in a particular broadcast moment, television collectors commonly consult episode guides for original air dates even when their own copies may come from subsequent airings or alternate sources. Collectors recognize first runs, complete with original commercials, as somehow more authentic. John calls these recordings "the closest thing we have to time travel," pointing out that they turn vintage programs that are not "rare" (say, often repeated episodes of *I Love Lucy* or *M*A*S*H*) into high-demand items. Unlike movie collectors for whom video is merely a packaging, or a vehicle transporting the text from the big screen to the small, for the television collector video recordings are themselves objects of historical interest that seem to seal in traces of the televised "event."

While video collecting blurs notions of public broadcast and private property by transforming such events into personal possessions, the video archive also hybridizes public and private *space* in interesting ways. If film collectors strive to simulate cinema in domestic space, television collecting installs the preservationist mission and often the cultural codes (both democratic and disciplining) of the museum and library, public institutions that must negotiate dual roles as places of amusement and agencies for the conservation of precious relics. As such, these collectors not only archive their fetishes but in turn fetishize their archives. The remaining sections explore the TV collector's relationship to the archive as both physical entity and imagined domain.

Look but Do Not Touch: The Curator

While museums turn history into spectacle, video archives turn spectacle into history. To the extent that collectors envision themselves protecting valuable vestiges of television's legacy, video collecting is an act of cultural curating—a system for containing the past to recover and revivify it. Like museum specimens, the collector's spoils become yesterday's cultural curiosities lined up and labeled for tomorrow's eyes. With "the march of tapes across the shelf" (Tashiro 1996, 15), the collector guards the contents against the threat of erasure—from the tape, and thereby from memory, culture, and the collective imagination.

Like the rare book collector, the video collector cares for a fragile medium destined to degrade with time and exposure to the elements. For John and Wendy, a preoccupation with recording quality set in gradually, as they came to regard recording a long-term investment and experienced firsthand video's vulnerability as a storage format. To improve picture quality and prolong tape life span, both record only first- and second-generation copies, at the slowest recording speed on high-end tape stock.[15] As recommended by professional archivists, they store tapes vertically at a safe distance from magnetic fields and heating vents. Dave stores tapes horizontally and buys a less expensive brand, to save space and cut costs, but is equally mindful of environmental conditions; he closely monitors temperature, proximity to magnetic fields, and weight pressure from mounting stacks. Sensitive to the structural integrity of the archive, and the challenge it poses as an ever-expanding entity, my interviewees are hyperattentive to the physical presence of their collections as a whole, as well as the care and condition of individual recordings. Unlike Dinsmore's film collectors, none of them began collecting with a haphazard approach to tape storage. Each enthusiastically describes a rigorous, ritualized set of labeling and storage procedures, and Wendy takes the added precaution of storing tapes in sealed cases (as opposed to cardboard sleeves) and secure cabinets to fend off dust and prying hands.

Unlike the contemporary breed of cinephile to whom Barbara Klinger (2001, 141) attributed a "hardware aesthetic," or emphasis on the spectacular dimensions of film and technologies of home exhibition, my interviewees express little of the concern with fidelity and immersion common to "home theatre" enthusiasts. TV collecting culture values the excellence of recording technologies (which, for purposes of trading, are also the technologies of production and distribution) more than technologies of exhibition. Dave explains,

> Although the enjoyment factor enters consideration, I do feel that if I am laying down archive material, then it should be of the highest possible quality. Both for my benefit and for the benefit of others who may wish to have access to my archive.

As hobbyists and self-described tinkerers, my interviewees share the hardware aesthete's techno-centrism but subordinate spectacle to utility where the tools of home entertainment are concerned. If for the cinephile "form triumphs over content" (p. 141), with even a film's content being judged on how impressively its spectacular qualities complement superior home theatre equipment, the culture of television archiving prioritizes function over form in the final instance—and often in everyday practice. In place of a large-screen TV and surround-sound speakers to "mimic the conditions of the movie theatre within the home" (p. 136), my interviewees have unimposing, medium-sized TV sets. John and Dave do not eschew the technical discourses or aesthetic ambitions that afford film-collecting legitimacy; however, they are not interested in borrowing the cultural capital of cinema. They have made convenience and efficiency, not presentation or sensory envelopment, the organizing principle of the primary recording/viewing stations in their homes, which resemble workshops generously outfitted with cables, video boxes, labels, and printouts.

Television collecting culture is not without its own aesthetic sensibilities or logic of exhibition, however. Substituting for immersion in the text and technologies of the spectacular is immersion in the physical world of videotape. Specially designated shelving units are widely celebrated as a symbol of serious commitment to archiving. With an emphasis on taming chaos and maintaining order, prestige is attached to space management and, hence, to spare and efficient design rather than ornamental or showy display cases. While Dave's collection resides in stacks on the floor, masquerading as a jumble of ordinary objects invitingly assembled for visitors to sift through, it models a deceptive informality: what to outsiders may appear as an arbitrary arrangement of cassettes follows, on closer inspection or explanation, a meticulous logic. Like Dave's, Wendy's archive is at once an exercise in professionalizing and personalizing her living space; it is a closed, if not enclosed, space. Like patrons at a gallery, her guests are encouraged to browse freely but disciplined against handling tapes unsupervised. Commenting on her choice to shelve videos in plain view in her front room, Wendy explains,

> They are in immediate access to the equipment, and they are under strict protection from anybody who may be wandering in. They are not to be *touched*. Roommates are warned: "You are not to touch these. If you feel the need to touch these, you will ask first."

Even the elegant case displaying her *Highlander* tapes and memorabilia earned its prominent place in her living room through convenience—the shelf is simply too large to fit into a more private room. When arranging her tapes, Wendy is less concerned with the art of display than with routine issues of access to and retrieval of tapes from her collection. Though she concedes a curator's vigilance and protectiveness, Wendy is most comfortable in the role of video librarian.

Order, More Order, and (Tidy Rows of) Plastic Boxes: The Cataloguer

John, Dave, and Wendy find cataloguing not only a practical necessity but one of the central pleasures of archiving. All three maintain comprehensive inventories and, in fact, sidestepped the initial stages of "chaos" that Dinsmore described to implement labeling and cataloguing systems early on that would be refined as their collections took shape. John's preference for cataloguing actually predates his video-collecting habit. As a child, he filed the contents of his audiotapes of radio recordings on index cards in a Band-Aid box. Wendy also started with index cards, pasted onto cassettes as makeshift labels, before moving to a more sophisticated system of uniform laser-printed labels with eye-catching fonts and graphics.

For Wendy, a tape is satisfactorily "archived" when its proper label is applied and the tape is assigned to a spot on a shelf. To preserve her system, like many collectors, she asks traders not to mark or affix labels when sending her tapes. While she does not index her tapes in a database, Wendy's shelving arrangement is coherent and exact; episodes are archived chronologically by air date, so that tape spines read like a procession of bound journals across a bookshelf. She takes inventory in a notebook binder containing episode guide grids for every series she collects. Once a tape is labeled and shelved, Wendy checks off the episodes it contains on the appropriate grids.

John and Dave not only concern themselves with the state of their collections as they exist in domestic space but also fixate on their existence in virtual space. The computer database and printed catalogue are their indispensable archiving tools, the blueprints of their collections. "The confusion of the library," Walter Benjamin ([1955] 1978) wrote, is managed or disguised by "the order of its catalogue" (p. 60). To John and Dave, who manage rapidly growing collections, the key to a functioning storage and retrieval system is a database that facilitates cross-referencing and allows for title, artist, subject, or keyword field searches. John's archiving system suggests different priorities than Wendy's: "Actually putting it [a tape] on the shelf is just sort of a task that I have to do at some point. . . . The important step is getting it in the computer." Just as a public library's memory resides in its databases rather than its clerks or librarians, the large-scale video collector delegates the task of recollection to the computer. Dave, too, sees data entry as the vital link in his chain of archiving activities: "Until a given piece of information is in my catalogue, I do not officially count myself as having it in my archive." He catalogues immediately, labeling and logging a tape's contents within hours after recording. Like John, Dave has designed a sophisticated database capable of generating customized reports with a few key strokes, and he can locate the desired tape on his computer within a matter of seconds.[16]

For these collectors, then, sorting and list making are not "tiresome tasks" that tarnish the experience (cf. Dinsmore 1998, 319) but rewarding endeavors in themselves. Reducing television's overwhelming totality to a finite and manageable number of texts, the video catalogue defines the mental landscape of the archive. It affords a comforting sense of coherence, achievement, control, and authority (even authorship), as John and Dave pour proudly over the contents of their collections. As the collection grows, so does the catalogue, a by-product but increasingly a project in itself that presents its own managerial challenges and material pay-offs as missing episodes are obtained and slotted into the database like pieces in a jigsaw puzzle, cut from "want" lists and pasted into "have" lists. Benjamin ([1955] 1978, 60) has suggested that the collector's greatest satisfaction derives from the moment of acquisition. For John and Dave, this moment of relief and pleasure arrives once the tape's contents are inducted into the database, where they can be translated into tidy inventories and trade lists that further suspend television in time, defend against the deterioration of video with the permanence and conviction of print, and cement feelings of possession.[17]

Conclusions

In summary, ardent TV/video collectors are in many ways self-styled media historians, archivists dedicated to discovering and preserving remnants of television past and present. Some are focused on saving or resuscitating condemned texts, using the home video archive to aid in a media fandom's communal struggles to revive canceled shows and to subvert or supplement mainstream society's "classic TV" canon. But perhaps more important to individual collectors, video archiving also serves as a private means of resisting the impermanence of television and of memory by preserving physical records of cherished television moments. For the three collectors in this study, though, the rewards of video collecting extend beyond the pleasures of the televisual text itself. The VCR redefines the viewing experience, transforming it into a material act of consumption. TV's ethereal images and texts, snatched from the airwaves, become things that collectors can hold in their hands as well as in their memories—that they can possess, exchange, reexperience, and enjoy for years to come.

With a digital media "revolution" imminent, how are new domestic technologies likely to affect the lifestyles of these video collectors? Digital media is expected to force existing recording methods into retirement within a matter of years. Philips and Sony are hopeful that the "blue video" recorder, an optical disc medium, will replace VHS by 2005. Designed for compatibility with high-definition TV, this system uses a blue laser to burn recordings onto a CD-size disc with nearly five times the data capacity of a DVD (Ranada 2000, 38). Video collectors await these developments with anticipation but also anxiety. Video, like memory, deteriorates. New recording methods afford the media text an immortality inconceivable a decade ago. They promise to make degradation and storage space constraints worries of the past. On the other hand, the costs of bringing existing archives in line with new technology will be staggering. Collectively, my interviewees and I would need to transfer more than twelve thousand hours of footage (1.4 years of around-the-clock dubbing) with no guarantee that the newer medium will not itself be outmoded within the decade.

The internet, some argue, will eliminate the need for all this effort and expense. Downloadable audio and video data are expected to replace "physical data" in the music and film industries. Technology pundits and prognosticators wager that we will soon be using our modems to plug into incomprehensibly huge media servers from our homes. *Stereo Review's Sound & Vision*'s Ken Pohlmann (2000) predicted that this development will drive retail and rental shops out of the running and give the Hollywood star system a radical makeover, as narrow distribution channels are pried wide open. He raved that "the need to buy individual copies of movies or music recordings will vanish because it will be even more convenient to call up and access libraries infinitely larger than anyone's private collection" (p. 40). A similar fate, some speculate, awaits television. If a vast virtual archive can do our remembering for us, memory may begin to shed some of its material trappings—just as libraries and other institutional archives are gradually being rehoused bit by megabit into full-text databases. If television were to take up permanent residence on the internet, it is likely that fans would no longer feel an imperative to conserve new texts and preserve past ones. Residual texts would no longer take material form in our archives but linger where immaterial and ethereal discourse can in fact be reaccessed at will, as sources migrate from Trouillot's "historical landscape" to Pohlmann's digital mediascape.

There is much to be gained from these new video-on-demand technologies. What we are asked to sacrifice, however, are the pleasures of acquisition, ownership, guardianship, and membership. The internet has served the video collector well in building trading networks and fan communities, yet it ultimately runs counter to the TV collector's chief aim: to make the immaterial material. The blue-skies future forecasted by Pohlmann (2000) supposes that as tangible copies become irrelevant (indeed immaterial), we will gladly forfeit the personal copy as keepsake—and with it, our sentimental attachments to such materially constituted forms of memory. Pohlmann perceived a purely functional value to the private media library, discounting any personal or symbolic value. John confides that collecting will lose its allure and relevance for him if the all-inclusive media cyberarchive prophesied by Pohlmann becomes reality. When that day comes, John supposes, it will be time to look for a new hobby.

Notes

1. Since I originally wrote this article in winter 1999, I have come across two excellent articles on domestic cinema by Barbara Klinger. I suggest Klinger's (2001) newly revised account of the rise of "home theatre," in which she explored the pleasures of collecting for "cinephiles." Klinger focused on "high-end" collectors who seek to domesticate cinema or, more accurately, extend to home entertainment the sensory experience and legitimacy of cinema, with the aid of new media technologies in what she termed the "post-video era" (p. 136). See also Klinger (1998).

2. At the same time, Gray ([1987] 1997) revealed, VCRs grant these women a new range of pleasures and choices associated with TV viewing. Gray's housewives use video to sidestep spousal censure by time shifting or renting "women's genre" tapes in relative secrecy while husbands are at work.

3. Despite the internet's centrality today to media fandom, traders insist there is no real technological barrier to tape trading. Some international trading loops exist through paper correspondence alone, with members exchanging handwritten or typed lists and letters. Those without computer access can print requests in *The TV Collector* (a publication that also reproduces episode guides and trade lists) or join The TV Connection, a voicemail tape-exchange service based in California, which Philip Satterley's (1995b) *Tape Trading FAQ* describes as "by far the most immediate and personal way to find video and come in contact with other collectors." International trading has flourished in the past decade, with multistandard video-recording and conversion technology from Panasonic, Aiwa, Sharp, Sony, and other manufacturers becoming more widely available and affordable each year. Today, many European phase alternation line (PAL) VCRs play National Television System Committee (NTSC) recordings, eliminating for many traders the costs and complications of tape conversion. Even before such technology penetrated fandom communities, industrious traders were "converting" and circulating tapes from around the world through more primitive methods such as the "optical" or "camera transfer"—capturing the image from a PAL video, for instance, by pointing an NTSC camcorder at the screen (Satterley 1995a). Rare episodes or fragments of programs such as *Doctor Who,* lost when the British Broadcasting Corporation discarded much of its early programming, exist today because they have turned up in attics and private collections—that is, because fans have conferred the responsibilities, and privileges, of archiving onto themselves.

4. In exploring permutations of fandom, my intent is not to further pathologize fan culture or make a curiosity of "excessive" or "eccentric" TV consumption. Fandoms make their interactions public in a sense by congregating in internet forums and

convention centers, but they do not expressly invite analysis. A collector and trader myself, the interview process did not present the ethnographer's usual challenges of building rapport and minimizing my intrusion as academic "outsider"; instead, I faced the challenge of negotiating my dual role as participant and observer. Prior familiarity with my interviewees' recording habits and preferences informed my questions, which were broad and open ended to avoid soliciting "expected" answers. I encouraged interviewees to share their insights, introduce topics and themes not touched on by my prepared questions, and reflect freely on their own methods and motivations for viewing, recording, collecting, cataloguing, labeling, storing, and trading. Conscious that the critical/analytical gaze is inescapably a voyeuristic act, I will produce examples at points without naming specific groups, gatherings, or organizations, out of respect for participants' privacy.

5. The gender politics of video collecting are not the focus of the present study, but it is worth noting that my three sources all emphasize that tape collecting and trading can be a "boy's club." As a female collector, I do find myself in a minority. I have been taping comedy programs for fifteen years and trading since 1994. During that time, most of the tapers I have encountered with sprawling, eclectic collections and a proclivity for cataloguing have been male, while traders with narrower collections dedicated to select celebrities' works are often females affiliated with specific fandoms. These generalizations by no means hold true universally, however, and my own archiving activities are more commensurate with John's and Dave's than Wendy's. I would warn against artificial distinctions that posit a communal female tape-trading culture founded on principles of sharing and inclusion and a more reclusive and exclusive male one based in competition. As I will discuss, tape trading within female fan groups can be intensely competitive, and trading in more masculinized arenas can be highly cooperative. Nevertheless, distinguishing between fandom, nonfandom, and fandom-straddling strands within tape-trading culture may partially account for subtle and not-so-subtle differences exhibited by the one woman and two men in this study. Wendy is active in a largely female media fan subculture of the sort documented extensively by Henry Jenkins (1992), in which members compose interpretive fan fiction, produce fan videos, and convene in cyberspace and at media and gaming conventions to chat about the fictional worlds of their favorite programs. In contrast, John and Dave regard video collecting as a more individual than social enterprise, although both have peripheral contact with such fan communities on the internet and at media conventions, where John has regularly volunteered his services as a video room coordinator.

6. I borrow this term, coined by Benedict Anderson ([1983] 1991) in reference to the forging of national identity in the age of print media, for its wider application in the wake of new media technologies currently cultivating web-based or e-communities in virtual space.

7. Wendy's comment refers to vague recollections, though it also speaks to the power of memory to exaggerate the charms of programs that have passed into legend. John relates that "memory cheats" in *Doctor Who* fandom, as well, where fans—like adults returning to a childhood stomping ground to find everything smaller and less impressive than they remembered—have been disappointed when highly mythicized missing episodes, steeped in decades of romanticized memories, resurface to lay bare their technical and script flaws.

8. Wendy sees other fan memorabilia, such as photo stills, watches, and pendants, as "a side effect" of tape collecting, not an incentive. Most of her *Highlander: The Series* knickknacks came free as promotions with commercial-release box sets of the series. When Wendy does seek out nonvideo collectibles, it is not to announce her devotion

to "the world" but to affirm her insider identity. As a wink to fellow fans, she will purchase fan-made T-shirts or replica artifacts from the program's fictional universe:

> One fan on a list said something that I agree with very strongly. . . . Until they said it, I didn't realize that was my sentiment. They said they didn't want to own stuff that said, "Hey, I'm a *Highlander* fan." They wanted to own in-group stuff, stuff the characters on the show would have. . . . I don't care about owning the jacket that says "*Highlander* Hundredth Episode" in huge embroidered letters. I want to own the jacket that [the character] Joe Dawson wears on the show.

9. The Janurary 10, 2000, issue of "This Week at the TV Barn" reported on a recent must-have in *Buffy the Vampire Slayer*'s fandom. With rough cuts from *Buffy* and spin-off series *Angel*—early review copies released exclusively to critics—selling for upwards of $365.00 on eBay, "every TV critic in the country . . . is sitting on a potential video gold mine" (http://www.tvbarn.com/2000/01/10.shtml).

10. A paradox that torments video collectors, traders, and fan video makers is that their "originals" are always copies. Some fans take the "creator" role beyond recording/compiling programs onto designated or themed tapes. Fan video makers use editing decks or digital editing software to string clips of TV series into music-video tapestries, weaving new stories and teasing out narrative threads often unintended by programs' producers (see Jenkins 1992, 225–49, for discussion of fans' blurring of spectator/producers roles). Wendy, who makes fan videos to screen at media conventions, laments that generation loss and picture dropout betray her creations' use of borrowed parts that can never recapture the look of a broadcast master.

11. The pleasures of video archiving are, of course, not denied to academics. While I was researching this article, one colleague expressed that after he had begun recording TV in bulk for his dissertation research, his archiving rapidly took on more personal dimensions. Some scholars regard recording patterns/practices such as I am describing "excessive," for example, Graeme Turner's (1996) characterization of some of David Morley's ethnographic participants in *The "Nationwide" Audience,* who meticulously plan their evening viewing/taping schedules, as "ripe examples of real eccentricity" (pp. 135–36). On the other hand, given that media scholars, like fans, are to an extent "stuck with" limited reruns and dependent on "classic TV" channels such as TV Land and Nick at Night—which one media scholar informally remarked are furthering the "erosion of our television archive" by chopping scenes to squeeze in more advertisements—we can recognize many of our own concerns underlying fans' efforts to resist the disappearance, destruction, corruption, and erasure of television's heritage. Much pre-1980s television is today as elusive as the nineteenth-century live burlesque shows that Robert C. Allen (1991) painstakingly reconstructed from script fragments and secondary texts such as print programs, posters, and newspaper clippings. While TV historians have similar creative recourses for reconstructing the "missing" text, many are also forging productive alliances with private video archivists or going online to barter for rare broadcast material. Just as radio historians are indebted to private collectors of vintage radio, video collectors are also increasingly making their mark on television scholarship. The cassette recording remains for the time being our most direct link to historical broadcasts, and public and university archives do not necessarily have a monopoly on these relics and resources.

12. While Satterley and my interviewees associate movie collecting with widely available and mass-reproduced rather than "rare" artifacts, certainly film-collecting culture devises its own incentives for and means of marking—and the movie sales industry its own means of marketing—collectibles as "rare" and "scarce." Klinger (2001)

observed that "the language of scarcity permeates the discourses around film re-releases" (p. 138). Particularly limited-edition discs, she noted, along with "out-of-print, cult, non-commercial, letter-boxed, and other more marginal offerings help constitute the uncommon, sought-after media object, suggesting that the collector's trade has found a way to construct the categories of authenticity and rarity for mass-produced film arte-facts" (p. 139). Thus, exclusivity, friendly rivalry, and the logic of limited resources are hardly stripped out of the equation, since "the existence of these artefacts also helps to stimulate the competitive gamesmanship or 'sport' characteristic of this enterprise (i.e. to see who can procure the rarity)" (p. 139).

13. Nevertheless, a Marxist critique would likely argue that the activities being described throughout this article smack of commodity fetishism. Given my own empha-sis on collectors' desire to convert transitory broadcasts into exchangeable commodi-ties and their fetishization of videotapes and VCRs as objects, this criticism warrants attention. Certainly, my interviewees do express a deep-seated desire to consume and own mass culture in the form of texts and technologies. However, I aim to avoid the reductive equation of "willing consumers" with "dupes" by drawing attention to the diverse and personal pleasures and practices associated with video archiving. Further-more, I find the theoretical concept of commodity fetishism somewhat misses the mark here. Rather than averting their gaze from the material conditions of production, these collectors are transforming an industrial mode of manufacture into a more personal labor with the status of a skilled craft; they insinuate themselves into the act of cre-ation. At the same time, though, I would also caution against a hasty deduction that the obvious "activeness" of these audiences readily translates into an open resistance of capitalist ideology or of commercial media industries as purveyors of that ideology. This is not to say that strategies for resistance, as well as coping, are not integral to video archiving. Using domestic technology to time-shift or place-shift defies the quotidian ways in which power relentlessly organizes our lives by imposing schedules and limits— that is, the ways marketing systems as well as geographical barriers and time zones dic-tate when, where, and how we can consume what we want to consume. The VCR becomes a tool for struggle over access, not only to sites and moments of production (as with Henry Jenkin's [1992] "textual poachers") but moreover to sites and moments of consumption.

14. Wendy and John both make a point of emphasizing that they do not trade dubs of commercially available tapes, an illegal activity that denies profits to the pro-gram makers they admire but also, John stresses, is a poor use of time and video resources since that service is already provided by rental or retail operations such as Blockbuster, Suncoast, and Virgin Megastores.

15. Experienced tapers discern subtle grades of difference in the quality achievable with competing tape and equipment brands. Like the photographer comparing film or the painter testing canvas textures, many video collectors swear brand loyalty and can discuss at length tape abrasiveness, durability, sharpness of image, and fine distinctions in drop-out levels.

16. After locating the tape in a database or printout, locating it on a shelf is far less daunting with the aid of systematic storage and cassette indexing. John and Dave both assign two-part tape codes, similar to a library call number system. Their codes consist of an accession number (i.e., sequential) preceded by either the year or an abbre-viation denoting a title, actor's name, or generic category such as "miscellaneous." For example, Dave's 127th tape recorded in 1998 is coded "98/0127," *The Vicar of Dib-ley* would be coded "VoD3." Tapes are then stacked or shelved alphabetically/numer-ically. John demonstrated the efficiency of his system when I requested to see an obscure

thirty-second commercial buried within his collection of more than six thousand recorded hours. In less than two minutes, he had located the clip in his log book and pulled the tape from its shelf.

17. As touched on above (see "The Chronicler"), orderly list making is an indispensable practice of tape trading. A collection in chaos can be a serious setback, and the novice will not get far without the organizational tools of the trade—namely, user-friendly trade lists to circulate. For ease of access, traders may maintain multiple lists for different purposes. For instance, John keeps a "main list" for full series, a "clips list" of miscellaneous appearances sorted by actor or subject, a music videos list, and a want list. Beginners typically build on templates from other traders. Satterley (1995b) advised would-be collectors to begin an inventory list while their collections are in their infancy—day 1, tape 1. He recalled being teased by his family for logging his very first tape, heading the top page of an empty loose-leaf notebook "Tape 1." By 1994, his log had amassed more than five thousand pages.

References

Allen, Robert C. 1991. *Horrible Prettiness: Burlesque and American Culture*. Chapel Hill: University of North Carolina Press.

Allen, Robert C., and Douglas Gomery. 1985. *Film History: Theory and Practice*. New York: Knopf.

Anderson, Benedict. [1983] 1991. *Imagined Communities: Reflections on the Origin and Spread of Nationalism*. New York: Verso.

Benjamin, Walter. [1955] 1978. Unpacking My Library: A Talk about Book Collecting. In *Illuminations*, edited by Hannah Arendt, 59–67. New York: Schocken.

Clifford, James. 1985. Objects and Selves—An Afterword. In *Objects and Others: Essays on Museums and Material Culture: History of Anthropology*, vol. 3, edited by George W. Stocking Jr., 236–46. Madison: University of Wisconsin Press.

Dinsmore, Uma. 1998. Chaos, Order and Plastic Boxes: The Significance of Videotapes for the People Who Collect Them. In *The TV Studies Book*, edited by Christine Geraghty and David Lusted, 315–26. New York: Arnold.

Foucault, Michel. 1972. *The Archaeology of Knowledge and the Discourse on Language*. Translated by A. M. Sheridan Smith. New York: Pantheon.

Gray, Ann. [1987] 1997. Behind Closed Doors: Video Recorders in the Home. In *Feminist Television Criticism: A Reader*, edited by Charlotte Brunsdon, Julie D'Acci, and Lynn Spigel, 235–46. New York: Oxford University Press.

Jenkins, Henry. 1992. *Textual Poachers: Television Fans and Participatory Culture*. New York: Routledge.

Klinger, Barbara. 1998. The New Media Aristocrats: Home Theatre and the Domestic Film Experience. *Velvet Light Trap* 42 (fall): 4–19.

———. 2001. The Contemporary Cinephile: Film Collecting in the Post-video Era. In *Hollywood Spectatorship: Changing Perceptions of Cinema Audiences*, edited by Melvyn Stokes and Richard Maltby, 132–51. London: British Film Institute.

Morley, David. 1992. *Television, Audiences & Cultural Studies*. New York: Routledge.

Morton, Alan. 1997. *The Complete Directory to Science Fiction, Fantasy and Horror Television Series: A Comprehensive Guide to the First 50 Years 1946 to 1996*. Peoria, IL: Other Worlds Books.

Nora, Pierre. 1989. Between Memory and History: *Les Lieux de Mémoire*. *Representations* 26 (spring): 7–25.

Pohlmann, Ken C. 2000. Digital Horizons: Dot Com. *Stereo Review's Sound & Vision* (Collector's Issue), January, p. 40.

Ranada, David. 2000. Tech Talk: Let There Be Progress! *Stereo Review's Sound & Vision* (Collector's Issue), January, P. 38.

Satterley, Philip J. 1995a. The Beginner's Guide to Video Tape Collecting, Version 2.0. Retrieved from ftp: //src.doc.ic.ac.uk/public/media/tv/collections/tardis/trading/guide.gz.

———. 1995b. Tape Trading FAQ, Version 2.1. Retrieved from ftp://src.doc.ic.ac.uk/public/media/tv/collections/tardis/trading/faq.gz.

Tashiro, Charles. 1996. The Contradictions of Video Collecting. *Film Quarterly* 50 (2): 11–18.

Trouillot, Michel-Rolph. 1995. *Silencing the Past: Power and the Production of History.* Boston: Beacon.

Turner, Graeme. 1996. *British Cultural Studies: An Introduction.* 2nd ed. New York: Routledge.

PART 5

Considering Television

Essays in this section take up topics that expand general questions about television. It is certainly the case that many others in the collection do so as well, but here the issues are made more central.

I begin the section with an essay on *The Sopranos*. But the program is merely a beginning point for discussing substantial changes in some structures of the television industry, changes that I believe alter the fundamental place of the medium in contemporary society and culture. This essay replaces an earlier essay written with Paul M. Hirsch, "Television as a Cultural Forum." A key feature of that essay was its emphasis on the ways in which television, even in the limited version of the three-network era, provided cultural and political options to a degree greater than often acknowledged. If one considers today's television system as, for want of a better term, "five-hundred-channel television universe," I would argue that those options are far greater. Others would disagree. In any event, television's multiple offerings, combined with various recording devices, with varying means of access must be studied in new ways as well as old.

Deborah L. Jaramillo's essay on *The Sopranos* follows my own and fills gaps left open. Her focus on the economic and structural aspects of the integrated systems of television production and distribution uses the HBO series as a primary example of these complicated arrangements. In a sense, this essay takes the "production context" of part 2 to the corporate level. In doing so, Jaramillo again addresses key aspects of the "post-network" television environment. She shows how HBO managed to "brand" itself as the "outsider" creative force producing true "quality television," even though it is part and parcel of one of the largest, most dominant media conglomerates in history. What becomes clear is the strategic precision with which "content," marketing strategy, financial engagement, and sociocultural discourse are involved, perhaps manipulated, to become part of our understanding of television. Taken together, these first two essays suggest a range of questions that might be applied to almost any television program today, in almost any national, industrial context.

John Hartley's contribution here, taken from his book *Uses of Television,* could also be applied in any such context, but rather than focus on programs, schedules, industrial strategies, or economic power, he turns to the potential freedoms within television systems. His proposition is that television is engaged in "transmodern teaching," that it crosses the lines of "pre-modern, modern, and postmodern characteristics at once." Put another way, Hartley is arguing that we have almost always *misunderstood* television, its cultural and social roles. The chief suggestion embedded in his perspective is that television now and previously encourages a version of "democracy," a version he refers to as DIY (do-it-yourself) citizenship. It is a radical proposition filled out with "what ifs" that push even those who would disagree with him to consider (or reconsider) their own positions regarding the medium.

In the following essay Elizabeth Jacka agrees with Hartley—in almost all instances. One of the implications she draws from Hartley is that his view would call for rather staggering reassessments of one of the most hallowed aspects of television throughout the world, the notion of public service broadcasting (PSB) as best exemplified by the British Broadcasting Corporation (BBC). She, too, cites the multichannel environment, suggesting that the BBC, and by implication, the larger realm of various forms of public service television, have been marginalized. Without the monopoly assured by broadcast television, PSB becomes one among many offerings, with some others among them fulfilling some of the same purposes. Though Jacka notes some weaknesses in Hartley's position, she largely accepts the central point and suggests that the generalized defense of public service broadcasting no longer holds. In its place she suggests the importance of "situated microanalyses" of public broadcasters. She cites Nicholas Garnham as one of PSB's primary defenders.

In response Garnham will have little of her argument and even less of Hartley's. He dismisses the notion of DIY citizenship as ignoring real politics, hence having almost nothing to do with "democracy." Though he shares Jacka's concerns about the general state of public service broadcasting, he continues to point to the basic difference between that institution and television driven by the concerns of commercial, marketing aims. The three essays explore many of the basic issues facing television studies today—any general understanding of the medium, its social, political, and cultural organization, its uses by citizens. That these issues have been central to the study of television since its beginnings should not diminish them today.

These large problems lie at the core of Lynn Spigel's overview as well, an overview constructed in light of the events of September 11, 2001. Spigel explores the "circulation" of 9/11 in various forms of television, in dramatic programming, special events, talk shows, late-night comedy, even cartoons such as *South Park*. That all these sites and forms addressed the same topic in varying rhetorical, formal, and even ideological ways is yet another indication of the new television environment. As the discussions of *The Sopranos* suggest, Spigel points out that in this new context we have "both fragmentation and centralization at the same time." Moreover, she points to new media such as the Internet as adding still more layers to our recognition and understanding of current events. While such a morass of media could be seen as leading to cultural collapse or manipulation by powerful media managers, Spigel argues for a "materialist politics of hope" that treats the new global media environment as offering opportunities for richer communication.

The concluding essay here, Roger Silverstone's discussion of "Regulation, Media Literacy and Media Civics," barely mentions television, though it is implied in references to "mass media" and "broadcasting." Rather, the focus here is on deep notions of literacy—how we understand and use media, on ethics and morality—how the media lead us to treat others in varying manner. It also focuses on citizenship and must be read in light of concepts addressed by Hartley and debated by Jacka and Garnham. Like Hartley he believes in the self-reliance of individual media users: "Media are nothing if they do not convey meanings, and even if we can (and we can) negotiate those meanings for ourselves, and distance ourselves from those meanings we find unacceptable or unpalatable, in the absence of others [other users, other citizens] . . . our perceptions of the world cannot but be increasingly and consistently framed by what is seen and heard through screens and audio-speakers." Put another way, Silverstone is suggesting that we can't "do it ourselves" without the social connection, without what Lembo refers to as "sociality." This social necessity then requires moral, ethical, and political considerations of notions such as "regulation." What we do with public service broadcasting, what we do with commercial television, what we do with programs many might find objectionable, what we do with the politicians' uses of the medium—all these things must be considered in light of our understanding of the social roles of the media. This more fully developed understanding is what Silverstone means by "media literacy." This is the foundation of what he refers to as "media citizenship." Not coincidentally, these concepts are compared to previous understandings of literacy connected to books, and equally without coincidence, this essay concludes a collection that begins with Moses Hadas's admonition that "all who take education seriously in its larger sense" must come to "talk and write about television as they do about books."

"This Is Not Al Dente"
The Sopranos and the New Meaning of "Television"

Horace Newcomb

The catchphrase used to identify Home Box Office as a "premium" subscription cable television offering—"It's not TV; it's HBO"—is of course nothing more than a marketing strategy. *The Sopranos,* like all other original HBO series programming, is most assuredly produced for first screening on the home television set, and despite other venues such as restaurants and bars offering special "nights" for specific programs (another marketing ploy), or parties and group viewing in homes, it is personal television use that undergirds these series. Even the very significant ability of the organization to package the series on videotape and digital videodiscs is premised on home viewing on the (no matter how large) television screen.

For these reasons recognition has come to the series from every distinguished prize committee that recognizes "broadcasting" or "electronic media" or "television." It received Peabody Awards in two successive years, an unusual fact in itself. It has been nominated for Emmy Awards in almost every applicable category, from art direction to casting, directing, and editing, and has received the Emmy Awards in numerous categories, including prizes to the two central performers, Edie Falco and James Gandolfini. It has won Best Series from the Television Critics Association and has been recognized by the American Film Institute as among the ten best television programs available. Its cast, writers, and directors have been nominated for numerous awards. Fan groups and Web authors have repeatedly compared the program to the best on television. It has even won awards from technical groups, as with its receipt of the Cinema Audio Society Award for Sound Mixing in Television Series.

Still, the attempt by the Home Box Office organization to distinguish itself is important. It suggests a shared notion of what "TV" is—and is "not"—what the term means, how the medium is experienced, understood, how it is placed in the contexts of social and cultural life. Equally significant, it presumes certain economic and technological arrangements that are both adopted and altered by HBO. It also suggests that the "content" or the "style" or even the context of "HBO" can be distinguished from that of "TV." And indeed, there are some features that set this programming apart from what many viewers, through many years, had come to expect from "television" and what many producer/writer/creators and programmers had come to develop, create, and distribute.

In this way the phrase confirms, as the HBO marketers well know, that "television" has always carried meanings in and of itself. In many ways, these meanings bespoke invidious comparison to "culture" or "high culture," to "the arts" in general, to "film" in particular, to "quality" or "the serious." In short, "television" was identified as the inferior term in almost any comparative context. Now it must somehow be "re-marked," especially if it is to be marketed as remarkable. Modifiers such as "cable" or "broadcast," "basic" or "premium," "pay" or "free," or simply "something new," all suggest reasons to tune in or out, to subscribe or not. HBO, then, has attempted to link itself to the positive term in these long-running comparisons.

This attempt to further "brand" HBO, then, is not merely imprecise in suggesting a radical difference. Rather, these relationships, the connections to antecedent and the slide into alternative strategies for attracting viewers and, to some extent, telling stories, suggest that rather than evidencing that "it's *not*" TV, HBO's programming, as so intensely displayed in *The Sopranos,* is in fact exemplary of what television *is,* what it has steadily become in the past fifteen to twenty years. Here I address this shift and the implications embedded in a program such as *The Sopranos* under the heading of Post-Network Television, a formation also explored elsewhere in this volume, and one that signals changes in production and distribution strategies and in attitudes toward the medium. Most significantly, the term identifies a fundamental alteration in the cultural role of television. Within this truly significant change, HBO is merely a symptom.

Like all such major shifts, however, changes implied in the term "post-network" are deeply reliant on the comfortable, generalized familiarity with "TV" as experienced in the past. It is a past within easy memory of many viewer-users of the medium. Rather than exploring a program such as *The Sopranos* as a distinct "break" with that past, then, or considering HBO as somehow totally distinctive and new in its programming strategies or even in the "quality" of its program, other questions should be addressed. What, for example, could it mean that millions of viewers attending to this program also remember *Dragnet, Naked City, The Untouchables, The Fugitive, Police Story, Hill Street Blues,* or *NYPD Blue*? Equally significant, however, is a question such as this: What does it mean that these same viewers may remember *Father Knows Best* or *Eight Is Enough,* or, perhaps even more telling, *Roots* or *Dallas*? Such questions bring us to one of the most important approaches for understanding *The Sopranos* and HBO as "TV" and shed significant light on the meanings of post-network TV.

The Generic Heritage of *The Sopranos*

In some ways *The Sopranos'* link to television "crime drama" is its most tenuous among familiar genres. That the series is presented from the point of view of the criminal sets it apart and, as we shall see, partially defines its place in and its role in constructing, post-network television. Still, the presence of criminal activity treated in fiction is central to understanding the history of the medium. Drawing on film and radio presentations of similar material, television has long been the site of negotiated cultural significance of "law and order," "justice," "authority," and certainly "violence" or "crime."

The Untouchables (ABC, 1959–63; syndicated, 1992–94) became a controversial site for discussion and debate of a range of these social topics, as has *The Sopranos*. And while the earlier series is defined as a "Police Drama" (Brooks and Marsh 1999), fascination with the criminal characters whose lives were followed until their incarceration or violent end certainly provided enormous appeal to viewers. Indeed, as regular or recurring characters, many of these portrayals offered rather complex characterizations and foreshadowed deeper "psychological" exploration of criminals and more densely woven examinations of "mob life" than appeared in other programs. The police, either local or federal, play small but significant roles in *The Sopranos,* suggesting that other generic factors are at play here. But it would be a mistake to dismiss the influence of what catalog compilers designate as Crime Drama without realizing the resilience of that category.

While certain social and cultural topics, those named above as well as others, remain central to this genre, the treatment of these topics varies with the creation of new central characters and new professional contexts. Thus *Kojak* is both similar to yet different from *Columbo*. And thus, *The Sopranos* is both similar to and different from its most telling progenitors from this line, *Hill Street Blues* (NBC, 1981–87), *Homicide: Life on the Street* (NBC, 1993–99), and *NYPD Blue* (ABC, 1993–2005). These series have been as widely acclaimed as *The Sopranos* and equally credited as innovative, startling, and provocative. The connection, however, has more to do with the ways in which all three series modify their own "foundational genre."

While "action," "crime," "violence," and "justice" remain central to all these series, while those and similar topics generate story lines, and while they stand as devices related to the "goals" that must be evaluated and moved toward by central characters, they have now been relegated to a narrative space that forms only a portion of the plot in each instance. These topics are a part of the fictional worlds of the series, but no more and often less important than other aspects of those worlds, other devices demanding the attention of characters, other concerns that engage the sympathy and consideration of viewers, other elements forming the much larger process of cultural negotiation that is one function of any formation of "television."

The most powerful modification of the generic base, whether "crime story" told from the perspective of the criminal or "police drama" focused on the profession, is the expansion of three factors. The first is the move toward more complex characterization than was often found in earlier television programs (though this generalization itself bears more careful analysis than is presented here). Rather than presentation as character "types," such as the "policeman," the "detective," or the "mafioso," we have explorations of intense personal, individual psychological states and motivations of characters. An additional modified aspect of these series is their placement in social contexts that can best be described as beleaguered, social contexts in which "crime" is but one of a number of indicators of social decay or, at best, decline. Indeed, the central characters of the series in question are often presented as "besieged." Certainly this is a core factor in *Hill Street Blues, Homicide,* and *The Sopranos,* though somewhat less so in *NYPD Blue.*

And finally, perhaps most significantly, the exploration of all these states and motivations occurs in a context best described as "familial." The extension of a sense of the "biological family" to other groups is a strategy of long standing in television fiction, and often noted (see Feuer, Kerr, and Vahimagi 1984). Clearly, a primary purpose of this development is to use various characters as the locus of stories that can be added to the ongoing series. Each member of the family, or of the "family," can be developed with specific traits and in specific relation to other members of the group. Writers are able to focus on individuals and their traits and shuffle relationships among the group. The relationships, in turn, generate additional story material. In this way, conventional genres that concentrate on the professional activities of single, role-defined characters, sometimes described as centered on "the plot" of the series or the episode, are expanded in both production and narrative complexity.

The application of this strategy to professional groups is particularly telling in the crime/police drama context, where the roles of individuals, the depth of affection, the demands of loyalty are placed in settings rife with violence and death. That these are also "professional" settings, which are often, especially in American culture, specifically distinguished from "the home" or "the family," is equally significant.

As described by Thomas Schatz, these newer programs, derived in large measure from the MTM Studios ensemble comedies (e.g., *The Mary Tyler Moore Show,* CBS, 1970–77) and dramas (*Lou Grant,* CBS, 1977–82), exemplify a "domesticated workplace" in which "principal characters, all intelligent, well-educated professionals, eschew material rewards to work in under-funded social institutions where commitment outweighs income, where work is never finished nor the conflicts satisfactorily resolved, and where the work itself, finally, is its own reward" (Schatz 1997, 1872).

He goes on to say:

> The workplace in these series ultimately emerges as a character unto itself, and one which is both harrowing and oddly inspiring to those who work there. For the characters in *ER* and *N.Y.P.D. Blue* and the other ensemble workplace dramas, soul-searching comes with the territory, and they know the territory all too well. They are acutely aware not only of their own limitations and failings but of the inadequacies of their own professions to cure the ills of the modern world. Still, they maintain their commitment to one another and to a professional code which is the very life-blood of the workplace they share. (1873)

When applied to *The Sopranos,* terms such as "professional code" and "life-blood of the workplace" take on rather more powerful, richly layered significance.

Equally important, however, is the fact that the workplace, even when this setting is defined by violence, tension, and threat, can move into the domestic sphere where, again, notions of "life-blood" come to the fore. In this regard, another primary generic influence supporting development of a program such as *The Sopranos* is the prime-time family melodrama, best exemplified in U.S. television history by *Dallas*.

Dallas itself, of course, drew on powerful antecedents. Chief among them was the daytime "soap opera," and indeed, *Dallas, Dynasty, Falcon Crest, Knots Landing*, and other instances of the form were often referred to as "prime-time soaps." The denigration implied in the term derived from a sociocultural attitude central to "television," one that demeaned programming designed for women viewers working in the home, programming that highlighted emotional distress, that exaggerated events beyond the realm of verisimilitude, and that focused on private, individualized narrative constructions at the expense of social or otherwise "public" concerns. In soap opera, family is all, and as Robert Allen (1985) has shown, the peculiar narrative structure of soap opera depends on the dissemination of knowledge throughout the complex kinship patterns that map a given series. Thus, any particular alteration in relational connections—an affair, a divorce, a child planned, unplanned, unknown—ripples through pairs and triads of human binding ties, shifting power relations, accumulated knowledge, and emotional response. Clearly, the introduction, withholding, and circulation of information in *The Sopranos* is fraught with narrative possibility.

When this pattern arrived in prime time wedded, as it were, to social issues such as the workplace, accumulations of money and power, and international intrigue, and blending into politics, blackmail, and murder, the genre took on a new shape. The central character of *Dallas*, J.R. Ewing, was surely as villainous as Tony Soprano, but without the formal connection to "organized" crime he emerged merely as a "bad" son/brother/husband and committed, though mediocre and flawed, father. Moreover, throughout the series, he maintained a degree of, or at least proximity to, control—of events and therefore of the narrative—that all but eludes Tony. Insofar as *The Sopranos* is "about" Tony's grasp at control, he does provide a narrative center for the series. His desperation, however, results from familiar generic patterns. To the degree that control is always elusive, and that physical violence is so much more overtly possible in his worlds, the fictional world, the world it purports to depict, and the world "allowed" by production and presentation for HBO, his state and status are far more fragile than J.R.'s ever seemed to be.

The primary significance of the relationship between *The Sopranos* and *Dallas*, however, is not the villainous central character, as marvelous as the characters and the performances creating them are. Rather, it is that both must be generically defined as "family melodrama." This form of melodrama, like all others, bears a powerful social and cultural role as best defined by Peter Brooks in *The Melodramatic Imagination* (1984). There Brooks argues convincingly that melodrama, a nineteenth-century narrative invention, took on the social function previously secured by religion and religious belief—the marked distinction between good and evil and the attendant social forms of these categories. With transcendent power removed from comfortable and widespread general acceptance because of the analytical explorations of the Enlightenment, moral categorization had, in Brooks's view, become occluded, pushed beneath the veneer of society, only to emerge in the "excessive" possibilities afforded by melodrama.

Television, with its constant emphasis on family as both "content" and object (the viewing family), pushed toward melodrama in any number of generic patterns, from comedy to Westerns, medical drama to police procedural (see Thorburn 1976). The daytime soap opera was perhaps the most "excessive" form until the arrival of the prime-time melodramas of the 1970s. *Dallas,* then, leads easily into conjunction with other forms of "family."

Which brings us to one other significant generic foundation for *The Sopranos, The Godfather* series of films. This group of narratives, with numerous other "Mafia" films, doubtless prepared many viewers with a set of expectations and "knowledge" related to *The Sopranos. The Godfather* series provided a fully developed expressive linkage of the two meanings of "family," the social and the, perhaps fictional, "Mafia" sense of the term. As much family melodrama as crime drama, *The Godfather* series of three films generates sympathy and understanding as well as (perhaps more than) horror and disgust for criminal activity. Significantly, in preparation for a sequenced *television* broadcast of the three films, director Francis Ford Coppola reedited them into a more strict chronology, moving part of *The Godfather: Part II* to the preliminary or prologue position in the narrative. In this form the plight of Michael Corleone, already presented as tragedy rather than cautionary tale, takes on even more direct composition as a narrative of rise and fall and, significantly, becomes much more like "television."

As an "informational" source for media fictions related to the "Mafia," *The Godfather* films clearly instruct viewers regarding the world of *The Sopranos.* We know about the organizational hierarchies. We are familiar with some terminology. We know about degrees of initiation and participation. Most significantly, with regard to the work of *The Sopranos* as family melodrama, we know about degrees of status and rank. There is, finally, no way to compare the roles of Michael Corleone and Tony Soprano in terms of their relative positions within "this thing of ours." Yet, emotionally and psychologically, and hence narratively, both remain central to our understanding of what this fictional world is about and how it seems to relate to the worlds of lived experience. Tony's connection to "our" world is much more identifiable. Even if *The Godfather* is all about "family," *The Sopranos* are far more "familiar." And while it might be nice to think that Michael would himself benefit from visits to a shrink or use of psychopharmacological agents rather than in his failed attempts at confession in ecclesiastical settings, those actions will never be taken. For Tony and for viewers of *The Sopranos,* everything that happens happens in the context of Tony's frail psyche and resonates with multipage *Newsweek* spreads exploring the latest medical advance or social problem.

Tony's state of mind—the terribly troubled state of mind leading to panic attacks, consultation with a psychiatrist, a prescription for Prozac, as well as brutal murders—is made more pitiable than tragic because of his "professional" status. There are no princely postures here, no kisses of the ring. Not a "don," Tony is, rather, "middle management." The house is too big—post–*Father Knows Best* and pre-*Osbournes,* a gauche mini-mansion rather than a Long Island estate/compound. And the family is too typical, an exaggeration of varied aspects of the Corleones, as common as the viewers' latest meeting with the school principal.

For all these reasons, *The Sopranos* leans heavily on "television," the medium as it once was known and experienced, even as it moves toward post-network TV as we have come to use it. Consider the program as "TV," then, layered with negotiations exploring some of the issues inherent in the "crime drama": violence, obligation, justice, gender, as molded into "family melodrama." All this is clear from the first episode of the series.

In that strong introduction to the series, the major characters, focused on Tony Soprano's immediate family—his wife Carmella, his daughter Meadow, and his son A.J. (Anthony Jr.)—are introduced. A major element of the entire series begins as Tony faces the problems of his aging mother, Livia, whom he wishes to move into a retirement home rather than have remain alone in her own, lower-middle-class house. This "normalizing" problem, faced no doubt by many viewers at one time or another, is complicated by the fact that Tony, of course, has two "immediate families," the second being the proverbial "Mafia family" familiar in American popular culture and, presumably, part of America's social structure. Many members of this group are also introduced in the opening episode.

More significantly, we are introduced to the central conceit of the series—Tony Soprano's psychological distress. When he faints during a cookout, suffering what will later be diagnosed as a panic attack, the moment first seems more comic than serious. The irony of the "mob boss" succumbing to a disorder often associated (incorrectly) with mild-mannered and weak individuals is exaggerated by his physical stature, his tough language, and by the very role he portrays. It is understandable, then, when his discomfort in his first visits to his female psychiatrist also appears somewhat humorous. And in some ways, all the "normal"aspects of his life, such as dealing with his mother, his children, his wife, such as taking his prescribed Prozac, take on a strange and "edgy" quality. Are "these people," the middle-management Mafia bosses, more like "us" than the "dons" of *The Godfather* saga? The "humor" here derives in part from "our" discomfort, from experiencing an "incorrect" playing out of generic rules and expectations.

Still, in the midst of all the jarring explorations of contrasting and conflicting images, typologies, and behaviors, the episode remains true to its generic roots, drawing on "Mafia stories" filled with intrigue, suspicion, and violence. A key sequence involves Artie and Charmaine Bucco, friends of the Soprano families but not involved with the mob. Artie is a childhood friend of Tony's, and the Buccos have managed to open Vesuvio, a delightful Italian restaurant, a local eatery patronized by the community at large, including Tony and his group of associates, his "crew."

A problem develops when Tony's Uncle Junior, already jealous of Tony's rising position in the organization, plans a "hit" to take place in Vesuvio. Realizing this will destroy the Buccos, and unable to persuade Junior to have the hit made elsewhere, Tony offers Artie and Charmaine a free vacation. If the murder occurs in their absence, they cannot be implicated. Charmaine, however, is utterly unwilling to consider Tony's generosity. Her aim is to have her life and Artie's separated as much as possible from the crime family, and her anger at Tony and his offer is palpable.

Tony designs a creative alternative. He has Vesuvio burned down. The hit takes place elsewhere. Artie and Charmaine collect the insurance without knowing that Tony arranged to destroy the establishment they worked so hard to create.

Numerous other events occur in this episode, but a pattern is clearly established. Tony Soprano is enormously complicated. Able to destroy things and people in one scene, he is capable of great gentleness and concern in another. Whether this indicates an astounding ability to compartmentalize aspects of his life, a thoroughly convoluted moral structure, a schizophrenic stress culminating in his panic attacks, or merely a metaphorical commentary on human ability to behave and believe—to live, to survive—through contradiction, remains to be seen in subsequent episodes.

But these generic features, elaborately embroidered in an innovative fashion, explain only one aspect identifying *The Sopranos* as "TV." To fully understand its place in relation to that term, it is necessary to examine another identifying feature, television's capacity, its demand, for continuing stories.

The Power of Seriality

While the daytime soap opera clearly established the significance of continuing stories for the narrative and material economies of television, as they had in radio, by drawing loyal audiences back to the set day after day, programmers for prime-time TV first worked from a different logic. Associating prime time with a concept of the "male viewer" who wanted relaxation and excitement rather than involvement, programmers assumed that audiences would not be interested in stories without firm endings. Indeed, the genres prevalent in prime time, network television, the Western, the police drama, the medical and legal dramas, all "worked" toward closure. The bad gunfighter or other disruptive force would be removed, the case solved, the disease cured, the guilty identified and put away. While certain comedies reliant on real or fictional biological families had a sense of ongoing narrative caused by the aging of child actors, most episodes of these programs also exhibited a strong sense of ending.

By the mid-1970s, however, several related programming events forced television creators, programmers, and other network executives to consider alternative narrative strategies. Some comedies, notably those from the work of Norman Lear and, as Schatz (1997) suggested, from the MTM Studios, increasingly took on a sense of memory, the sense that events in one episode could have consequences in later episodes, that characters would change over time, relationships evolve. During this period several important "miniseries" were imported from England for programming on public television stations. These series, rather than turning viewers away from open-ended episodes, drew them in greater numbers. U.S.-produced miniseries such as *Rich Man, Poor Man* drew strong ratings. And in the winter of 1977, *Roots* became a national phenomenon. It was clear that the success of this program depended on more than the unusual programming strategy of playing all episodes in single week, or that that week happened to be one of the coldest on record. The "saga of an American family" also drew huge numbers of viewers because the narrative followed and developed a group of characters in ways far more complex than was the case for strictly "episodic" television programming.

These programs were followed by more calculated responses. The miniseries that was *Dallas* scored its own ratings success, was quickly developed for continuation, and became a story extended over hundreds of hours, with some narrative threads continued throughout the entire history of the series. Such successes made it possible for series such as *Hill Street Blues, St. Elsewhere,* or *L.A. Law* to experiment with varying degrees of seriality, responding to a host of economic pressures to expand or restrict the open-endedness of their stories.

Whatever the variation in form, however, viewers and critics, programmers and producers responded to the increasingly available complexities of serialized television. Characters could be developed more fully, less as "types" than as complicated individuals. As a result, *multiple* story lines could be drawn from any member of an ensemble cast, mixed with other ongoing stories, and moved toward partial closure—the solution to a crime, the dissolution of a marriage— without disrupting or closing off an episode. Indeed, these small closures opened other narrative possibilities. And one of the richest possibilities, explored in the best of these narratives, was the constant opening of the past, the discovery of why characters behaved as they now did and suggesting what could happen in the future. That actions have consequences was clearly a fact examined in serial television. To show that actions also have antecedents was a means to delight the "loyal viewer."

Consider, then, how the masterful use of serial narrative modifies *The Sopranos,* how it intensifies rather than dilutes its relation to "TV." Although any number of major narrative threads illustrate this narrative richness—continuing investigations by the FBI, Tony's relationship with his mother until her death (and after), the fragile nature of the Soprano marriage, the developing roles of the Soprano children, multiple story lines focused on internecine Mafia intrigues, and the effect of all these on Tony's continuing therapy—a far smaller topic also illustrates the power of the technique—the continuing roles of Artie and Charmaine Bucco in the world of *The Sopranos.*

The Buccos appear almost randomly throughout the series. Always, however, their participation is woven into larger aspects of the series in a manner that continues their own story, their own participation in the complicated universe that centers on Tony. And their presence always illuminates both Tony's character and the ever more complicated world of *The Sopranos*. In episode 3, for example, Carmella Soprano is charged with preparations for a substantial charity event. Concerned that the Buccos have not recovered financially from the loss of Vesuvio, and that they are the target of a second investigation of possible arson, Carmella arranges for them to cater the affair. Apparently without ill intention, Carmella treats Charmaine as "hired help" rather than as a friend of long standing. Angered, Charmaine retaliates, lashes out, informs Carmella that she slept with Tony while the two were in high school. Charmaine's fear of and anger at the Mafia world, the Mafia queens and princesses is a continuing commentary throughout the series. Unable to escape the smear potentially extending to all Italian Americans, she struggles to maintain a distance. The event also highlights the internal "class structure" of the Mafia society, with special attention to those who are aware of criminal activity and the "success" and power it entails, but who remain "straight." They remain outside that society, but their lives are inevitably entangled with its implications and actions. Tony can unilaterally decide to destroy Artie's restaurant, altering the Buccos' lives. Artie and Charmaine can only respond to events as they unfold.

In episode 13, for example, Vesuvio has been re-created with the help of insurance money and Tony's assistance and patronage. In hopes of demonstrating his gratitude, Artie visits Livia, who has been moved against her will into a retirement complex. While it is never clear whether Livia is addled or merely magnificently adept at manipulating all around her, she manages to inform Artie that Tony had Vesuvio torched. Outraged, Artie goes after Tony with a rifle. Tony easily manages the situation, relegating Artie to his own weak realities. When Tony later angrily confronts his mother, she denies even knowing anyone named Artie Bucco. This episode ends the first season with the Soprano family having dinner at Vesuvio. Artie and Charmaine can only serve and seethe.

In episode 18 Tony forces Artie to hire Furio, a new member of his crew, a recent immigrant from Italy. Charmaine is again annoyed that Artie must always accept Tony's demands. In episode 19 Artie attempts to help addicted gambler Davey Scatino. His actions annoy Tony, who insults him at a college night where the kids are exploring possible universities. In episode 23 Tony suffers nightmares. He blames them on "bad shellfish" Artie served him. (Artie checks with one of Tony's crew, who ate the same dish and had no problems. They agree it must have been the Indian food Tony ate later.) By episode 27 Artie is making a nuisance of himself. He gets drunk at Livia's funeral. He has become infatuated with Adriana, girlfriend of Tony's nephew, Christopher, and leaves Charmaine. He is the portrait of a pathetic attendant to power, a mob wannabe with no nerve.

In episode 34 Artie and Charmaine have separated, and Tony's crew is using Vesuvio as a hangout. In episode 35 Artie is overextending himself, having food shipped from Italy by Federal Express. Charmaine is back in episode 36, giving Tony grief for spending time in the restaurant. Carmella and Tony engage in one of their repeated arguments, and to needle him, Carmella throws out her knowledge of his high school escapades with Charmaine.

In episode 44 in the fourth season, Tony takes an interest in a racehorse owned by Ralphie Cifaretto. Not only does Tony's advice to the jockey lead to a winning race, but he seems to take inordinate comfort from his relationship with the horse. He's kinder, gentler, more at ease with himself. We relax a bit, pleased for him. In episode 45, however, he learns that Gloria, a woman with whom he recently had an affair, has committed suicide. When his therapist suggests the suicide resulted from Tony's abandonment of Gloria, guilt sets in. Tony's kindness and generosity, clearly erupting from this guilt, expand and extend to everyone around him, suggesting he feels this altered behavior will absolve him. At this time Artie is still attempting to expand Vesuvio and make it more elaborate. While Charmaine is still in the picture, Artie's wandering eye has settled now on Elodi Colbert, his lovely new hostess. She introduces him to her brother, Jean-Phillipe, who appeals to Artie's proximity to available mob money and persuades him to act as a broker, providing funds for a scheme to import Armagnac, "the new vodka." In yet another feature distinguishing him from his more elegant and ambitious criminal associates, Artie's motivation is that his take from interest on a loan will enable him to pay for the orthodontia his daughter needs. He tries to raise the money from Ralphie, who laughs him off. Tony wants to help his old friend, and in a grand "new-Tony" gesture, literally forces money on him.

When the deal disintegrates (Jean-Phillipe being more swindler than importer), Artie can't pay Tony what he owes. Patience wearing thin, Tony instructs him to collect on the debt and Artie, in yet another pathetic attempt to play tough, goes to Jean-Phillipe to demand repayment—after practicing his lines before a mirror. The outcome is predictable. Jean-Phillipe savagely beats Artie, who tries to assuage both guilt and humiliation in a suicide attempt. When Tony visits him in the hospital, a weeping Artie offers him ownership of Vesuvio. Tony derides the gesture (what would he do with a restaurant?) and requires instead that Artie forgive his six-thousand-dollar food and drink tab at Vesuvio (existence of which is already a very sore point with Charmaine). In a moment typical of this ongoing relationship, Artie spouts a bitter accusation indicative of just how much power Tony represents to people such as Artie. He suggests that Tony must have known all along of the outcome of all these complications—a strategy designed just so Tony could "eat free." In his therapy session the "old" Tony, tired of trying to assist the weak, emerges. "One suicide is bad enough. But two? They can go fuck themselves. I made a donation to the suicide hotline in her name. That's it."

Episode 52, the last in the fourth season, focuses on the Soprano marriage. Despite complex developments throughout the episode, it culminates in a harrowing argument between Tony and Carmella, who has discovered yet another of her husband's infidelities. Late in the episode, Tony, who has been thrown out of his house, eats alone at Vesuvio. Artie stops by the table and "sympathizes," his barely concealed smirk a reminder of his pleasure at Tony's plight. Tony's only reply, as he holds a fork of pasta above his plate and looks Artie in the eye: "This is not al dente." Artie turns and leaves. The small story of the Buccos, then, is constantly used to resonate with the moral and cultural aspects of this ongoing narrative. Everything that happens, as in any soap opera, affects them, yet their own actions also affect the story itself. They are both foil and victim of Tony Soprano and his families, caught in a web of fiction they neither direct nor escape.

What these various analyses of a few aspects of *The Sopranos* make clear is that the marketing slogan so prevalent on HBO, the attempt to distinguish this subscription channel from more available forms of "television," cannot diminish the fact that this series, like other "HBO Original Series," is fully grounded in "TV" as it has been known for almost half a century. This is not to say, however, that there are no differences between what is available on this "premium" cable/satellite offering and what is available to all audiences on broadcast television. The differences are first, economic. *The Sopranos,* via HBO, costs more and costs directly. But as with all television, material economy is relentlessly interwoven with cultural economy. It is not at all coincidental that when the producers of *The Sopranos* and other HBO series routinely accept the prizes mentioned at the beginning of this essay, they add an attendant phrase: "Thank God for HBO." What the material economy makes possible is a different relation to "content," to "audience," and to expressive culture, and these differences are at the heart of the new meanings of "TV" on which HBO depends—the meanings of post-network television.

HBO, *The Sopranos,* and the Economies of Post-Network Television

Clearly *The Sopranos'* serial is indicative of a continuing reliance on narrative strategies developed to a very high level in the fully mature network era of "television." These strategies were in themselves drawn from radio serials, and perhaps it is more accurate to speak of them as the narrative strategies of "broadcasting," which in any socio-cultural-economic-techno formation is afforded the opportunity to fill continuous regular time. While it is certainly the case that commercial, advertiser-supported systems have a stronger vested interest in compelling audiences to return to the same "time slot" in order to sell products, it is also the case that the aesthetic advantages of pursuing long-running, serialized narratives are appealing in any broad or narrowcasting system of electronic distribution to the home. The creation of miniseries, *tele-novelas,* and *teleroman* in varying systems attests to these benefits. The intensification of serialized aspects of television fiction has occurred in every setting.

The "It's Not TV" marketing strategy used by HBO to describe its premier fictional series, then, is hardly to be accepted at face value. A far better and more precise descriptor can be found in John Thornton Caldwell's discussion of varying forms of "televisuality" (1995). Caldwell uses the notion of televisuality to describe and define numerous aspects of television from the mid-1980s through the mid-1990s. His analysis addresses the industry, the audience, and the technologies used in production, but the concept of televisuality first defines a range of techniques by which programs and networks distinguish themselves from the welter of available content spread across multiple television offerings.

> Televisuality was a stylizing performance—an exhibitionism that utilized many different looks. . . . For example, the miniseries proved to be a quintessential televisual form, while the video-originated sitcom—at least with a few notable exceptions—resisted radical stylistic change. Conceived of as a presentational attitude, a display of knowing exhibitionism, any one of many specific visual looks and stylizations could be marshaled for the spectacle. The process of stylization rather than style—an activity rather than a static look—was the factor that defined televisual exhibitionism. (5)

One of the stronger of these techniques is "boutique television," which Caldwell describes in the following manner:

> Boutique programming constructs for itself an air of selectivity, refinement, uniqueness, and privilege. The televisual excess operative in boutique programming then, has less to do with an overload of visual form than with two other products: excessive intentionality and sensitivity. Programming's cult of sensitivity may involve the kind of spectacular cinematic spectacle more typical of loss-leader event programming, but it also may involve more restrained forms of drama, writing, and cinematography—subtle orchestrations of televisual form that create the defining illusion of a personal touch. (106–7)

This description could easily be applied to HBO's entire project of original series programming, and certainly to *The Sopranos,* so often identified as *David Chase's Sopranos.* So blatant is the claim ("It's Not TV"), that the plea for something intentional, something sensitive, something "personal," is all but written onto the surface of the slogan. Similarly, Caldwell's "boutique television" can also be equated in some ways with "quality television" as defined by Feuer, Kerr, and Vahimagi (1984) and explored in other essays. This notion of "quality" might result from critical acclaim, resting on an assessment of specific aesthetic features, and this is certainly the case with *The Sopranos,* evidenced by its many awards. It is also clearly the result of the economic value associated with "premium" or "subscription" channels within the larger universe of cable offerings. In the case of the HBO original series, this aspect is emphasized by association with a "movie" channel because for many critics, cultural commentators, viewers, and certainly producers, writers, directors, and actors, "film" still occupies higher cultural status than "television." Given the channel's freedom from restrictions imposed both by advertisers and by any concern for "free TV's" position as a central and centralizing medium bound by social conventions, and given the more substantial financial underwriting available to producers, some conventional notions of "quality" do accrue to programs created specifically for HBO. (That these programs are often filmed or edited in different versions, with a view toward later presentation on "non-premium" channels suggests that some of the significance of social and cultural boundaries is still in place.) As Caldwell suggests, however, all these definitions, strategies, tactics, slogans, and maneuvers resulting from fundamental alterations in the television context and the ways in which "quality" is positioned are hallmarks of the post-network, "televisual" formation.

It is not HBO that is "not TV"; rather, what once was known as "television" is no longer "TV." HBO's slogan is, in effect, dependent on a set of assumptions about the medium that no longer hold, a retro activation—and implicit denigration—of older general meanings and attitudes. Significantly, the marketing strategy "works" in that those older meanings, attitudes, and assumptions are still quite prevalent. They are sufficiently powerful to attract new audiences, looking for something "different," to HBO. Aesthetic conventions such as "irony," "character complexity," "realistic" depiction of extreme behaviors, exploration of "psychological states," and so on, often associated with "higher" forms of expressive culture, are more readily available here, as are relaxed restrictions on language and behavior. That these "freedoms" may result in mere self-indulgence by program creators (e.g., *Curb Your Enthusiasm*) is rarely cited as a detraction from the advantages offered by subscription channels.

The "premium" channels are not, however, the only locations of the search for "distinction." Equally significant are the ways in which the multichannel television environment has come to influence other television venues, notably the "lower" tiers of cable offerings and the founding networks themselves. The scramble for "televisual" strategies aimed at differentiating programs and channels from one another includes targeted programming for women (Lifetime, Oxygen, WE), for late teens/young adults (the WB), for fans of specific genres (the Sci-Fi Channel, Court TV), for aficionados of certain forms of cultural interaction such as sport (all the ESPN offerings), history (the History Channel), or animals (Animal Planet). Even the surge of offerings lumped under the heading of "reality television" can be linked to these developments. Like HBO's offerings, programming such as *Survivor, Big Brother, The Bachelorette, Fear Factor,* and *American Idol* (many of which, significantly, were U.S. adaptations or licensed versions of European "television") trades on "difference." And certainly the influences of programming such as *The Sopranos* can be discerned in programs such as FX's *The Shield,* a serialized narrative focused on the complex psychology and behavior of a "corrupt" policeman and his associates, replete with "strong language," "violence," and what would previously have been determined "unacceptable" depictions of sexuality. That this program and its central actor have been, like *The Sopranos,* distinguished with the receipt of major prizes again indicates the generalized shift in the historical definition of "television." From the perspective of HBO's "It's Not TV" slogan, none of these programs or channels would be "TV." In Caldwell's terms these programs could be seen as having merely developed relatively successful strategies of "distinction." No example of televisuality need be deemed "qualitatively" "better" or "worse" than another for having simply attracted attention.

Such a summary, of course, does insufficient service to Caldwell's analysis, which explores a range of alterations in the social role of the medium. But his analysis points toward an even more profound change, a fundamental shift in the cultural role of electronic mass media. The shift affects television's industrial base, the communities of those who create television programming, and the "uses" made of television by audiences. Yet these changes remain unevenly recognized or acknowledged within any of these groups.

I have previously argued that "traditional" network television—most familiar in the three-network system that flourished from the late 1940s through the mid-1980s—functioned for most of its existence as a "cultural forum" (Newcomb and Hirsch 1983). This role, defined and in part determined by television technology and the varying economic systems structuring its applications, affected and, again, in part determined the roles and positions of all who were in any way associated with the medium—creators, programmers, executives, regulators, advertisers, critics, scholars, and most importantly, viewers. It was also a role that defined and determined much of the general discourse surrounding television. Thus, schoolteachers, ministers, politicians, parents, and those in similar social roles could praise or blame "television" for any number of problems, any examples of excellence.

This was so in part because terrestrial broadcast television's limited channel capacity restricted far more than the amount of television available to audiences. Whether shaped by advertiser expectations and assumptions, by government fiat in state-controlled systems, or by cultural assumptions and commitments as in the BBC public service models, audiences were driven to shared viewing experiences. What they viewed was provided by creators and programmers who, in large measure, acknowledged this cultural role, defined it differently in different economic contexts, and made content that would appeal to and inform "mass" audiences or significant "segments" of that audience requiring special "service." Such central and centralizing media—providing information, telling stories, educating—exhibited far more commonality than distinction, even while offering a range, albeit limited, of ideological perspectives on the common topics and problems shared in the social settings. In this form, television was merely taking up the function of prior systems of mass communication and in so doing "permitting" or "forcing" those prior systems—print, cinema, radio—into new formations, in many ways newly fragmented in their appeals, marketing strategies, or political functions. While some of the "forum" function still defines aspects of "television," it does so in fewer and fewer cases. And when cable television surpassed "network" television in total number of viewers in 2002, the passing of "the network era" may have been completed.

If what we have known as television, then, is no longer definable in "forum-like" terms, I suggest it can now best be seen to operate under what sociologist Bernard Miege (1989) refers to as the logic of "publishing." In various forms, "television" now functions as a bookstore, a newsstand, or a library. Programs are available for purchase or on "loan for fee," as in subscription libraries that predated the modern "free public library." Whether the fee is paid directly as a license fee, a subscription fee, in taxes that support libraries, in the form of dollars added to products as payment for advertising, or in the more subtle form of attention "paid" to advertisements and programs depends on the specific socioeconomic contexts of media regulation. The point is that selections are now far more numerous, more tailored to specific interests as indicated above, and increasingly available on a more user-determined schedule.

Within the "bookstore" model, variations in television offerings are not limited to broad definitions of "the channel." Content varies within as well as among conventional demographic categories. Thus, on the Food Network, the styles and approaches of Emeril, Mario, the Iron Chef, or Martha Stewart represent different appeals and sets of meanings. While some viewers undoubtedly commit to the entire channel, others will pick and choose, follow favorites, or match some offerings found here with cooking programs found on other channels. Similarly, users of Court TV may watch "live" trials in progress, tapes of famous trials, fictional programs related to "law and order," or documentaries on specific topics—or move on to other channels for similar material. Those who would argue that such distinctions are meaningless should examine the programs more closely before making such general claims. All these offerings are better defined by comparison with materials available when browsing the shelves of libraries or the aisles of books and magazines for sale. The selection of a cookbook promising French cuisine is different from one focused on Italian or Pennsylvania Dutch cookery.

Indeed, in some cases the distinctions within channel offerings have led to splintering of channels into more precise categories. This has been the case with various music channels moving to "formats" similar to those used in radio. It has also been the case with sports programming, leading to offerings such as ESPNC, which offers sports contests played out and recorded years earlier. The Discovery Channel has proliferated into a number of distinct offerings. And channels such as Nickelodeon have expanded to include a range of offerings for fans of "nostalgia" television as well as offerings for children.

In such a context, HBO's "original series" programming is defined as much by a new set of meanings for "television" as by any other designation. The "quality" of these series is dependent in large measure on freedom from specific cultural conventions and often resembles works found on shelves of "adult" fiction monitored by traditional librarians who wished to prevent particular works from falling into the hands of immature readers. It is for this reason that some households refuse to subscribe to such offerings, worry over what "tier" of cable television will be most appropriate for their families, or remark with concern or alarm on the "relaxed" cultural and social sanctions applied to "network" television programming that is now also exploring this more relaxed cultural context. (Aware of these issues, HBO also offers a separate channel, HBO Family, to counter generalized criticism of its schedule. This channel, of course, requires purchase of a larger "package" from HBO or a separate fee, and is only available on certain cable systems.) What concerns regarding the availability of "inappropriate content" overlook or do not understand is that television, a term that once connoted precisely those cultural sanctions, no longer exists. In its place, using the same word, is "television," indicating a very different sort of cultural resource.

In a powerful and judicious commentary written more than forty years ago, classicist Moses Hadas (1962) argued that for television,

> [a] truer analogy than drama . . . is literature, which has traditionally held the general educational mandate television has now come to share. In literature, too, the scope is vast, the audience coextensive with literacy, and the benefits need not involve cash expenditure. In literature . . . there is a tangible critical climate, guided and made articulate by professional critics, perhaps, but shaped by all who take books seriously and write and talk about them. The critical climate, in turn, determines what books are made available; no writer who wishes to be heard and no sane publisher will fly in the face of it. A similar critical climate must be created for television; all who take education seriously in its larger sense—and not the professed critics alone—should talk and write about television as they do about books.

This perspective is more pertinent now than when first published. In the new model of post-network television programming, differences are meaningful not only to critics and reader-viewers but also, as Hadas's comment suggests, to the "authors," "illustrators," "editors," "publishers," and "archivists" of television. At present, few who work in television yet think of themselves as filling these roles. Nor do regulators, educators, religious leaders, parents, and students. They must begin to do so, however, if the social and cultural roles of the medium are to be clarified.

If television's political economy as well as the applied market economy must be seen as related to "publishing" rather than to "broadcasting" in the post-network era, so too must the moral and ideological economy be reconsidered. Concerns for the culture and society must be addressed as they are when individuals and communities create, distribute, and use books and magazines, newspapers, and libraries. *The Sopranos* illustrates HBO's ability to capitalize, in every way, on every aspect of post-network television, yet is still not evidence that HBO is "not TV." The success of this program and others merely establishes that some executives understand the newer model better than those in other organizations. It remains for all who share concern for the medium to do so as well.

Works Cited

Allen, Robert. 1985. *Speaking of Soap Operas*. Chapel Hill: University of North Carolina Press.

Brooks, Peter. 1984. *The Melodramatic Imagination: Balzac, Henry James, Melodrama and the Mode of Excess*. New York: Columbia University Press.

Brooks, Tim, and Earle Marsh. 1999. *The Complete Directory to Prime Time Network and Cable TV Shows: 1946–Present*. 7th ed. New York: Ballantine Books.

Caldwell, John Thornton. 1995. *Televisuality: Style, Crisis, and Authority in American Television*. New Brunswick, NJ: Rutgers University Press.

Feuer, Jane, Paul Kerr, and Tise Vahimagi, eds. 1984. *MTM: Quality Television*. London: British Film Institute.

Hadas, Moses. 1962. "Climates of Criticism." In *The Eighth Art: Twenty-three Views of Television Today*. Introduction by Robert Lewis Shayon. New York: Holt, Rinehart and Winston.

Miege, Bernard. 1989. *The Capitalization of Cultural Production*. New York: International General.

Newcomb, Horace, and Paul M. Hirsch. 1983. "Television as a Cultural Forum: Implications for Research." *Quarterly Review of Film Studies* 8/2.

Schatz, Thomas. 1997. "Workplace Programs." In *The Museum of Broadcast Communications Encyclopedia of Television*, ed. Horace Newcomb. Chicago: Fitzroy Dearborn.

Thorburn, David. 1976. "Television Melodrama." In *Television as a Cultural Force*, ed. Douglass Cater and Richard Adler. New York: Praeger.

The Family Racket
AOL Time Warner, HBO, *The Sopranos,* and the Construction of a Quality Brand

Deborah L. Jaramillo

The Sopranos, HBO's second original dramatic series, debuted in January 1999. HBO placed the gangster series on its schedule at a time when the press had declared broadcast network programming to be in a state of emergency.[1] Negative discourse surrounding television content is nothing new, but the idea that HBO had single-handedly saved television by beating it at its own game was new. Critical exuberance over *The Sopranos* overshadowed that surrounding its predecessor, *Oz,* essentially marking the distinction between the two series as a matter of accessibility. Prison violence is dark and disturbing; mob violence is sexy and presold. In *The Sopranos,* HBO had found a strong link to the cinematic gangster tradition—a generic showcase for violence legitimated by Academy Awards, Hollywood auteurs, and best-selling novels. The best part of the deal was that the broadcast networks had passed on series creator David Chase's pitch. HBO emerged as the savior, rescuing television from itself. The eagerness to play up competition between broadcast and cable through *The Sopranos* does everything to reinforce the methods by which HBO's parent company, AOL Time Warner (along with every other conglomerate), obscures its anticompetitive hold on media. *The Sopranos* as gangster television series stands as a significant link between programming strategies and corporate strategies, between winning approval and manufacturing it.

HBO positions *The Sopranos* in the marketplace in such a way that touts creativity, quality, and the auteur. The position that the series occupies in AOL Time Warner is what makes it an intriguing case study in the larger arena of competition. I will begin by exploring the ramifications of the generic inscription of the *The Sopranos.* To engage with the series on a marketing level, I will delve into the ways in which genre, coupled with HBO's distancing from broadcast television (evidenced even in its promotional slogan, "It's not TV. It's HBO.") culminates in a distinguishable brand name and a noticeable schism between pay cable and broadcast television. The carefully cultivated brand, hinging as it does on popular notions of "quality" television, perpetuates the idea of competition between broadcast network and cable television in spite of the evidence to the contrary. Such evidence is located most notably in the illegitimacy of the Nielsen ratings methodology and in the anticompetitive tiering strategies of AOL Time Warner.

Although the crux of this article is based on critical political economy, I will also rely on cinema and television genre study, auteur theory, and television industry history. The mix of disciplines, all leading to very specific ideas about ownership of media, illustrates the irrefutable connections between the textual craft and the commercial landscape. To begin to investigate the materialist rather than auteurist base for my case study, I begin by considering the industry.

Differentiating Pay Cable

Paying for television is nothing new. Subscription television, a service that required an extra fee in exchange for the privilege of viewing otherwise scrambled signals, was originally worked on by the Zenith Radio Corporation in the early 1930s (Gershon 1990, 3). The Federal Communications Commission (FCC), the federal regulatory body that selectively grants broadcast licenses and regulates visual and aural media, reluctantly gave its blessing to the subscription television ventures of the 1950s. Efforts to make subscription television the next best thing met with substantial opposition from theater owners and the three broadcast networks: ABC, NBC, and CBS (Gershon 1990, 8). The broadcasters vehemently argued that pay television would "'siphon' the quality and availability of free television" (Gershon 1990, 7). Two issues arise from this. The first is the highly publicized nature of the presumed siphoning effect, an issue underscored currently by the success of HBO and by the networks' so-called desperate attempt to lure audiences back (Weinraub 1999, 1E). The second issue is pay cable's history of unrest in relation to broadcast television.

Pay cable developed out of subscription television, and in the late 1950s and early 1960s, three separate efforts were launched to institute pay cable in the United States and Canada (Gershon 1990, 12). All three failed. In spite of these outcomes, the FCC authorized pay cable in 1968. In 1971, Charles D. Nolan, a Time Inc. cable company owner, developed HBO. By 1972, HBO was licensing films and covering major sports events for an extra fee (Wasko 1994, 75). In an effort to keep pay cable from siphoning broadcast network audiences, the FCC prohibited pay cable channels from running films and sports, HBO's bread and butter. Also prohibited was the inclusion of series programming on pay cable. These rules were put into place in March 1975. Not content to accept these restrictions, HBO took the FCC to court. In *Home Box Office v. Federal Communications Commission* (567 F.2d [1977]) the U.S. District Court found all of these regulations to be unconstitutional.

The lifting of these restrictions left HBO free to distribute films and sports via satellite, which had the added benefit of simultaneity—reaching cable systems across the country at the same time. Notwithstanding the difficult relationship between HBO and the major Hollywood studios regarding theatrical film releases, pay cable channels in general have had an easier time with programming content than broadcast television networks. In 1952, the U.S. House of Representatives held hearings to examine "objectionable television programming," the end result of which was a foray by the television industry into self-regulation: the Television Code (Boddy 1990, 246). This code operated much like Hollywood's Production Code, the independent system in place from 1934 to 1968 that enforced Christian ideas about decency in motion pictures. FCC regulation and industrial constraints have assured that although standards of decency have loosened over the years, broadcast television cannot abandon its roots in the public interest. One main reason for the maintenance of decency standards is advertising revenue. For instance, any program that offends the moral sensibilities of viewers-consumers might lose family-friendly advertisers.

For broadcast television, FCC regulations cover material that is not just obscene but simply indecent (Blumenthal and Goodenough 1998, 193). In 1992, Congress instituted a safe harbor block of time from midnight to 6 AM, which was eventually moved back to 10:00 PM from midnight (Blumenthal and Goodenough 1998, 193). Family viewing hour, an hour of programming suitable for consumption by both adults and children, has been dropped. Network standards and practices departments have met with a similar fate, since staff cutbacks have hit them the hardest (Lowry 1999c, 4). Despite earlier deregulation, the Telecommunications Act of 1996 prompted the television industry to self-regulate once more. Key to the industry's voluntary development of a ratings system was the underlying threat that failure would result in government intervention. The ratings system would be the basis for the government instituted V-chip, a device that allows parents, specifically, to selectively block programming from entering their homes.

In contrast to broadcast television, cable television is subject to laws that only prohibit the distribution of the slippery area of obscenity. Pay cable, in particular, has been a privileged party in the "tradition of greater latitude in the cable area" (Blumenthal and Goodenough 1998, 193). This tradition stems not only from legal aspects of cable control but also from the idea of private control. Cable and pay cable are extra services bought and paid for by the viewer-consumer directly as opposed to "free," over-the-air, broadcast television.[2] Broadcast television automatically enters the home with the aid of no special equipment (other than a television set and an antenna for better reception). Policy makers can therefore use such factors as automatic entry and the scarcity of the broadcast spectrum to guarantee more stringent regulation for broadcast television with little or no opposition.

HBO's unique position in a less regulated arena has been highly conducive to product differentiation on a massive scale. Although HBO began as a "program broker," buying up as many theatrical releases as possible, it quickly realized the necessity and potential of creating original programming (Mair 1988, 51). The impetus was twofold: original programming would mean some independence from movie studios and sports programming suppliers as well as more broadcast-type programming variety (Mair 1988, 51). As early as 1975, HBO launched *Standing Room Only* and *On Location* to fill time in its slate of feature films and sports programs. In 1985, another incentive prompted HBO to reinvigorate its programming: the VCR. The scheduling and monetary convenience of watching a movie on tape supposedly threatened HBO's ratings, prompting it to turn again to original programming. And, although earlier original programs served as fillers between movies, this time, the goal was to replace movies and to differentiate pay cable channels from one another (Garay 1988, 73).[3]

When viewed in retrospect, the reasons for the two initial thrusts toward original programming (noted as occurring a decade apart) reappear in much of the discourse surrounding HBO's original series lineup in the late 1990s. As in earlier times, HBO claims that competition from other channels and technologies as well as the need for programming diversity prompted the original programming of the 1990s. For much of the 1990s, *The Larry Sanders Show* was HBO's flagship series, but when the program concluded its six-year run in 1998, "HBO officials admit[ted] they were 'a little scared' . . . wondering what would qualify as an encore" (Lowry 1999a, 1F). HBO's first move was to ask Tom Fontana and Barry Levinson to create the channel's first dramatic series. The result was *Oz*, "the most brutal, vulgar show that's ever been on television" (Lieberman 1999, 3). But, this explicitness is precisely the point. In industry discourse, the future of pay-per-view television poses a threat to the exchange value of HBO's movie programming. HBO attracts subscribers by promising television premieres of Hollywood movies. If viewers can see their chosen movies on pay-per-view channels before they run on HBO, HBO cannot claim exclusivity. With movies premiering on television through pay-per-view channels, HBO could potentially become a second-run home theater rather than an exclusive home box office. Again, feeling vulnerable to the potential of another technology, HBO has taken broadcast programming a step further (Hamilton and Brown 1999, 68). This resurfacing of a winning strategy involves the systematic co-optation of traditional broadcast formats (hour-long dramas, half-hour-long sitcoms) through the addition of a pay cable sensibility—more leeway in the area of explicit content and no commercial interruptions.

The press sees in *Oz* and *The Sopranos* a combination of HBO's "inherent advantages" and creativity, amounting to a qualitative difference from broadcast television (Hamilton and Brown 1999, 68). Evaluative descriptors do nothing more than obscure the basic industrial factors behind HBO's strategies, though. HBO does not have to fill an entire weeklong primetime schedule with programming. Its movie library is always at its disposal. Similarly, HBO's original series producers are not bound by the broadcast standard of a season of twenty to twenty-five episodes; one season on HBO is thirteen episodes, approximately half that of broadcast networks. Fewer episodes ordered means more money to spend and more production time in which to spend it. Because of the calculated and self-perpetuating system of commerce that has supported broadcast television since its inception, the broadcast networks have neither the luxury nor the immunity from advertisers and ratings that HBO boasts. Without the financial constraints under which the networks function, HBO can target narrowly segmented niche markets, a concept essential to its branding.

Numbers, in the broadcast sense, are not key to HBO's survival. With its roughly 35 million subscribers (compared to the 100 million homes receiving the major networks), HBO has room to maneuver in terms of pleasing specific demographics (Lowry 1999a, 1F). To begin with, HBO has that already-privileged demographic base to work with: these viewers have the extra $10 per month to spend on HBO in addition to the $18 to $20 average for basic cable. Although ratings do not make or break HBO, the channel cannot "be content producing the TV equivalent of art-house films" without a sizable audience to support it (Lowry 1999a, 1F). The pressure is very real both to retain and lure subscribers.

HBO's decision to make series a significant portion of its lineup is indicative of three economic influences. The first, which some consider the primary influence, is to attract a substantial number of subscribers during the first run while accumulating episodes for subsequent runs on HBO's multiplex channels (HBO, HBO Plus, HBO Signature, HBO Family, HBO Comedy, and HBO Zone) and for digital video disc and video sales and rentals (Dempsey 1999, 3). Second, domestic syndication, once considered to be out of the question for *The Sopranos* because of explicit content, is now a viable option. David Chase shoots "HBO-lite" versions of every episode for the potential syndication market (Peyser 2001, 54). The third influence behind HBO's emphasis on original programming is the need to differentiate itself from uncut theatrical movies and made-for-TV movies: "glossy fare being presented by competing networks like Showtime and TNT" (Lowry 1999a, 1F). Consider a parallel scenario in the broadcast arena. The realism of programs such as *NYPD Blue* (1993 to 2005, ABC) and *Homicide* (1993 to 1999, NBC) has come as a response to explicit content in basic cable and pay cable programming as well as "declining network audiences and the almost desperate attempt to lure them back" (Weinraub 1999, 1E).[4] Product differentiation may come at least superficially in the form of a few programs, but the overriding agenda is far greater than its disparate parts. There is always a brand to be created.

The Brand Name

HBO works exhaustively to rope each of its original programs into the confines of flow and branding. *Flow,* the sequence of television programs, refers here to HBO's original programming lineup on Wednesdays in 1999: *Arli$$, Sex and the City, Oz,* and *The Sopranos* (Lieberman 1999, 3). Each program is introduced with a short, self-appreciating spot that declares HBO's original programming to be "refreshing, uncensored, groundbreaking." By asserting these values, HBO necessarily attributes the opposite to programming of its broadcast and basic cable "competitors": boring, constrained, routine. This eagerness to differentiate its product from that of broadcast television amounts to the creation of a brand.

Branding is a concept popularly associated with the field of marketing. It is not as widely discussed or written about in the field of television, either because it seems callous to apply a commercial aspect to the text or because it seems superfluous in a commercial medium. Because television is constructed as a profit-seeking business, it is not surprising that the literature on branding would translate well into the field of visual media. Branding is "the development and maintenance of sets of product attributes and values which are coherent, appropriate, distinctive, protectable, and appealing to consumers" (Murphy 1987, 3). HBO built its reputation on showing uncut theatrical films and boxing matches, products to which it held exclusive rights. The idea that subscribers can get products at HBO that they can get nowhere else has been a significant part of the channel's allure. In broadening its programming base to include original programs,

> HBO appears to have charted a new course in which series represent a primary component of its programming mix, hoping to distinguish the channel in a manner merely running uncut theatricals and even classy made-for-TV movies cannot, given the glossy fare being presented by competing networks like Showtime and TNT. (Lowry 1999a, 1F)

Inherent in the televisual branding process is channel differentiation, what is called "positioning" the brand (Marconi 1993, 38).

In this process, the brand's status or value is established in relation to other brands (Marconi 1993, 38). In the case of HBO's original programming branding strategies, the frame of reference for us is broadcast programming, and HBO is sure to incorporate that into its promotional slogan, "It's not TV. It's HBO." The implication is that TV is everything else. HBO's calculated effort to distance itself from television fare is also tied to niche marketing, the identification of "a segment of the market that has unique characteristics . . . not fully in agreement with the mainstream" (Marconi 1993, 101). Broadcast television programming is almost entirely synonymous with the mainstream, so there is no better way to appeal to a niche audience than to relocate a standard broadcast series format to a site that boasts its antitelevisuality. HBO has used its relative lack of FCC regulation to co-opt traditional broadcast series formats. In doing so, HBO has not only transformed industrial circumstances into an opportunity to brand but has also used its privileged position in pay cable (financially, legally, and demographically) to welcome the use of a very specific brand: "quality."

"Quality" Programming

The leeway that HBO has in terms of content relates to another facet of branding that involves "non-tangible factors" in the differentiation between products (Murphy 1987, 1). HBO's "refreshing, uncensored, [and] groundbreaking" programming uses its privileged position in pay cable to incorporate a greater degree of "realism" (read "sex and violence") (Littleton 1999, 1). Chris Albrecht, HBO's head of original programming (for both movies and series), has claimed that "the biggest single thing [HBO tries] to do is fulfill the purest form of the writer's creative vision" (Littleton and Torres 1999, 1). For HBO chairman and CEO Jeff Bewkes, this commitment to authorial freedom means that HBO's programs must "be judged to have a quality that is superior to what you can get on commercially-supported free TV" (Lowry 1999a, 1F). The channel's fostering of a pure, unfiltered "voice" led writer Larry Gelbart to conclude that *The Sopranos* is "chock-full of quality . . . point[ing] up the difference between what's possible in cable and in network" (Rochlin 1999, 25[2]). For Albrecht, Bewkes, and Gelbart, then, the nontangible factor at play in *The Sopranos* is what separates it from most broadcast programming: the fundamental, if elusive, notion of "quality."

The term *quality* is tossed about with great frequency but little regard for its disparate meanings among the popular press and interest groups on one hand and among television industry scholars on the other. "Quality" television is historically associated with Grant Tinker's independent production company, MTM Enterprises, Inc. MTM was responsible for such "quality" programs as *The Mary Tyler Moore Show* (1970 to 1977, CBS), *Hill Street Blues* (1981 to 1987, NBC), and *St. Elsewhere* (1982 to 1988, NBC). In her discussion of the MTM style, Jane Feuer noted the many uses of *quality* in the popular press. Innovative visual style, the use of film over video, actors with training in improvisational work rather than television, and a high degree of creative freedom all amount to how the press defines "quality" (Feuer, Kerr, and Vahimagi 1984, 32). In the industrial sense, though, Feuer took into account the fact that television programs are both text and commodity. The television industry's shift in 1970 to valuing upscale demographics over sheer ratings numbers is vital to the definition of "quality." "Quality" programs are those that appeal to young, urban adults from 18 to 34 years of age (Feuer, Kerr, and Vahimagi 1984, 3). If a series appeals to (and captures) decent numbers of an upscale demographic, large numbers of lower income viewers are secondary—quality over quantity.

To equate "quality" demographics with "quality" programming connotes a set of assumptions that link actively consuming urbanites to television programs that tackle "issues" in an insightful manner (Williams 1994, 143). If *The Sopranos* is "quality," as HBO and the press would have us believe, then the explicit violence is not problematic, as it would be on ABC, for instance. The critics who laud HBO for *The Sopranos* and bash FOX for its "bleep-heavy" 1999 sitcom *Action* fall back on "quality" and its attendant assumptions, barely concealing their "double standard for broadcast and cable TV" (Littleton 1999, A8). This pay cable chauvinism not only holds broadcast TV to a different standard but also implies that pay cable consumers can handle graphic language, sex, and violence in a more thoughtful and productive way than broadcast viewers. "Quality," then, is invoked to separate HBO from the masses.

"Authorial style," another important aspect of "quality," is essential to HBO's positioning of *The Sopranos* (Littleton 1999, A8). Key to the "quality" discussion is Feuer's assertion that Grant Tinker's involvement in achieving creative freedom for MTM's staff is "reminiscent of auteur historians' claims for certain film directors" (Feuer, Kerr, and Vahimagi 1984, 33). The television auteur is a controversial topic, but it is linked to cinema and therefore to a so-called higher brow entertainment medium than television. David Chase has fulfilled the roles of producer, director, and writer at various points in the three seasons of *The Sopranos,* and this solidifies his position as the auteur in the conventional sense. But, like Chase's broadcast TV colleagues Steven Bochco and David E. Kelley, it is in his role as producer that he maintains authorship. In spite of television's collaborative nature, scholars consider it to be a "producer's medium" (Newcomb and Alley 1983, xii). The producer is legally and financially responsible for the final product and oversees entire projects, whereas directors and writers may only work on a program for one episode (Newcomb and Alley 1983, xii). David Chase has filled all of these roles, and discursively, this lends an air of legitimacy to the series.

The notion of authorship links *The Sopranos* to cinema (and not just movies) and therefore to a more solidified notion of "quality" than that of television. The highest descriptor a television series can aspire to is "quality." But the "quality" of the cinema is called "art," a classification that supposedly negotiates no tension between economics and aesthetics. The belief that there is no appearance of commerce in art is a reflection fitting for *The Sopranos,* since the program is never interrupted by commercial breaks. Product placement is increasingly becoming a staple in each episode, but with the current state of Hollywood filmmaking, this only makes it more cinematic.[5] All comparisons of *The Sopranos* to cinema are not accidental. The fundamental link between *The Sopranos* and cinema is its generic inscription.

Generic Prestige

As mentioned before, *The Sopranos* is billed as a gangster drama or, as in a *Variety* article, an "unconventional Mafia drama" in which the criminals are clearly the sympathetic characters (Schneider 2000, 97). The use of the word *unconventional* in relation to genre speaks to a number of issues surrounding *The Sopranos* as a television text. There is no heritage of gangster dramas or even crime dramas on television. The common grouping is "police genre" (Kaminsky 1985, 53). Programs such as *The F.B.I.* (1965 to 1974, ABC) and *Ironside* (1967 to 1975, ABC) define the structure of the cop show and the inevitable capture of the criminal. The televisual Mafioso may be smarter than the cops, but he lacks the commitment to the people that the police have in abundance (Kaminsky 1985, 58). Throughout television's history, with the heavy influence of such cop shows as *Dragnet* (1951 to 1959 and 1967 to 1970, NBC) and *Hill Street Blues,* the emphasis has always been on getting the bad guy. *Wiseguy* (1987 to 1990, CBS) pushed boundaries a bit with an agent working undercover in various criminal organizations, but the program ultimately sided with the law. A decade later and following the success of *The Sopranos,* CBS in 2000 announced its own crime drama, *Falcone.* Postponed because of the violence at Columbine High School, the program follows an undercover policeman infiltrating a Mafia family in the style of the film *Don-*

nie Brasco (directed by Mike Newell, 1997). One could argue that the broadcast networks' commitment to the public interest plays into this privileging of the law and the justice system over the criminal, and for this reason, HBO is simply meeting a demand that could not be met on broadcast television. *The Sopranos* revels in siding with and even glorifying the criminal. Law enforcement is a very real, if secondary and annoying, threat to the stability and happiness of our hero, Tony Soprano (played by James Gandolfini).

For the aforementioned reasons, the placement of an actual gangster drama on television is unconventional. Equally unconventional is the structure of *The Sopranos*. The series lacks commercial breaks and therefore lacks the typical pacing strategies that broadcast hour-long dramas use to accommodate breaks. But although its form breaks with tradition, its content is not terribly radical. Yes, the gangster is the protagonist, but that atypical aspect is balanced with an ordinary family melodrama storyline. The program's tagline is "Family. Redefined." Publicity photos show Tony Soprano flanked on one side by his crime family and on the other by his biological family. A photo such as this combines the tropes of family programming and the "working 'family'" of the MTM "quality" tradition (Schatz 1987, 85). So, although *The Sopranos* deals with beating pregnant prostitutes to death in parking lots, it also deals with high school football games and empty nest syndrome. Likewise, the program's more melodramatic and serial elements recall conventions of the soap opera. Still, as connected to the series tradition of television as *The Sopranos* is, its tendency to "recombine" with other television genres is not acknowledged openly by the text (Feuer 1992, 158). A concession of that sort would negate the cachet already established through the careful combination of the auteur and the ancestral line.

The texts that *The Sopranos* references are not television texts. That would be impossible given the absence of a gangster heritage on television. *The Sopranos* owes its very existence to the cinematic gangster canon, and it advertises this through blatant and veiled intertextual references. The pilot episode contributed a small portion of screen time to a discussion of how Tony ranks *Goodfellas* (directed by Martin Scorsese, 1990) and each of the three installments of *The Godfather* (directed by Francis Ford Coppola, 1972, 1974, and 1990). Later, two characters relate their predicament to the "Luca Brasi situation," a direct but unnamed reference to *The Godfather*. Episode 2, "46 Long," concluded the teaser with Silvio (played by Steve Van Zandt) quoting Michael Corleone's famous line from *The Godfather: Part III:* "Just when I thought I was out, they pull me back in." Other instances of intertextual referencing include casting decisions (Dominic Chianese appeared in *The Godfather: Part II*, and several cast members are Scorsese alumni); borrowed storylines in "Legend of Tennessee Moltisanti" (episode 8), in which Christopher (played by Michael Imperioli) shoots a bakery clerk's foot, clearly referencing his character's fate in *Goodfellas;* camera work in "Proshai, Livushka" (episode 28), in which the elevator-ride shot of an undertaker mirrors the shot of Bonasera in *The Godfather,* general exuberance over gangster films in "D-Girl" (episode 20); and Freudian connections in "Proshai, Livushka" (episode 28), in which

Tony finally deals with the loss of his mother Livia (played by Nancy Marchand) by sobbing at the end of *The Public Enemy* (directed by William A. Wellman, 1931). This collapsing of maternal ties onto a classic Warner Bros, gangster film is the quintessential example of HBO's branding strategies.

These examples are integral to notions of niche marketing. Virtually anyone can appreciate an overt *Godfather* reference. But a special kind of viewer—a committed viewer with an involved, working knowledge of gangster films—can catch the covert references that persist throughout the three seasons of *The Sopranos*. These intertextual references of varying degrees of difficulty are interesting means of deconstructing the larger, paying audience into a more well-defined niche—that of the film buffs. But, these are not just any films. As Hollywood films go, these are royalty. They are what *The Sopranos* aspires to be and what HBO is betting *The Sopranos* will become, while the conglomerate behind it all carefully positions its product in the marketplace.

Time Warner Siphoning Itself

The earlier claim that HBO's programming strategies were directly affected by offerings from Showtime and TNT is telling, since both TNT and HBO share the same parent company. As Janet Wasko (1994, 96) noted, "industry lines have been blurred considerably since the formation of Time Warner," and this blurring has effectively obscured the basic illegitimacy of the rampant competition (which exists discursively, at least) in the television landscape.[6] The illegitimacy itself is rooted in Time Warner's status as the world's largest media company, a title the conglomerate earned when it swallowed Turner Broadcasting System in October 1997.[7]

HBO's parent was Time Inc. until the merger with Warner in 1989. Since then, HBO has become one in an increasingly long list of the conglomerate's entertainment holdings. Time Warner's television holdings currently include HBO, Cinemax, The WB, TBS Superstation, TNT, Turner Classic Movies, Cartoon Network, CNN, CNN Headline News, Comedy Central (of which it is a 50 percent owner), and Court TV (of which it is also a 50 percent owner). Time Warner's Warner Bros. Television currently produces such network programming as *ER* (1994 to present, NBC), *Friends* (1994 to 2004, NBC), and *The West Wing* (2000 to present, NBC). With the merger of Time Warner and America Online, the media conglomerate now maintains a large presence on the Internet, another so-called threat to HBO's interests.

If one examines the list of holdings more generally, one can clearly see that Time Warner has interests in three different tiers: over-the-air television, basic cable, and pay cable. In fact, Time Warner's position in television is so solidified that its networks and production companies received 42 percent of the 397 primetime Emmy nominations in 2000 (Time Warner Inc. 2000). HBO alone received 86 nominations, Warner Bros. Television received 54, TNT received 10, The WB received 5, and Cartoon Network and Comedy Central each received 1. The numbers only continue to rise, as evidenced by HBO's 94 nominations in 2001.

From publishing (*Time, Entertainment Weekly, People, Life,* and thirty other publications) to cyberspace, television, and feature films, it is not outrageous to argue that Time Warner has its bases covered. But, if one studies Time Warner's 2000 annual report of holdings and earnings, one can fully grasp the implications of the company line. The conglomerate claims to control more than its share of media in circulation, yet it also claims that it is in constant danger of being wiped out by competition (Time Warner Entertainment 2000). In its annual report, Time Warner simultaneously boasts its monopolistic might and attempts to persuade the reader and/or investor of the thriving, competitive atmosphere of media. These two ideas are in complete conflict with each other, yet they make the leap from Time Warner's annual report to the mouths of executives and the lines of the popular press.

In 1999, explaining a concentrated effort to return to movies after so much success with original series, Chris Albrecht cited competition from none other than TNT (Pursell 1999, 23). Given the above estimations about Time Warner's annual report, the attempt by an HBO executive to replace issues of ownership with free market ideas of competition is not surprising. In 1980, many consumers subscribed to both HBO and Cinemax, "which is exactly what the Time Inc. planners intended" (Mair 1988, 52). Time Inc. was after the appearance of competition between HBO and Cinemax, even going so far as to consider staggering the release of blockbuster movies onto the two channels (Mair 1988, 53). Twenty years later, the unwillingness to directly link ownership to the televisual landscape reinforces the status quo. Channels such as HBO are still seen as independent entities looming over broadcast networks rather than just cogs in a larger conglomerate's entertainment holdings. And, while HBO executives and employees of Time Warner publications are significant disseminators of this propaganda, much of the imaginary landscape is shaped by the allegedly impartial institution of audience measurement.

The Numbers Lie

One of the foundational campaigns of misinformation in the entertainment industry is the practice of counting radio listeners and television viewers. The Nielsen ratings amount to little more than a mutually agreed-on deception between the industry and the talent. Although the ratings are not a complete failure in terms of revealing general viewing patterns, their accuracy is highly questionable and industrially dangerous, especially since so much rides on what the numbers convey (Streeter 1996, 280). In the heyday of radio, the search for consumers propelled advertisers, who paid for programming, to measure radio's "productivity," or its skill in attracting the "commodity audience" (Meehan 1990, 121). Both advertisers and broadcasters were invested in determining if radio was indeed producing "an audience of consumers rather than of listeners," and to do this required a systematic mining of information about the audience (Meehan 1990, 121). Not content to rely on any research the radio networks produced, advertisers commissioned measurement for themselves. The same sort of bias evident in network research was also a problem for the advertisers' researcher, the Cooperative Analysis of Broadcasting (CAB). In 1930, the Hooper ratings subverted the CAB's dominance by manipulating methodology in such a way as to produce numbers that would please both the advertisers and the broadcasters (Meehan 1990, 123).

From this simple scenario, we can ascertain that if different methodologies can yield very different results, some selective tweaking can alter results in anyone's favor. This is even more evident in the ACNielsen company's entrance into the market in 1942. Because ACNielsen's advanced technological approach and minute-by-minute monitoring were more in keeping with America's postwar economic affluence and its attendant high-tech mind-set, by 1950, the audience measurement company was able to achieve monopoly status and buy out Hooper (Meehan 1990, 129). The ratings monopolist has remained relatively unshaken in a landscape that has seen cable and satellite superstations create fundamental shifts between networks and advertisers (Meehan 1990, 129). In this landscape, ACNielsen has honed its selectivity and definition of the commodity audience. In other words, of the entire lot of television watchers, ACNielsen's calculated selection of cable subscribers has drastically swayed the conception of the audience. The methodology behind this shift toward measuring the cable audience contributes directly to the popular conception of cable siphoning and the erosion of the broadcast audience.

To once again incorporate the company's creation of discourse into the equation, consider the ideology implicit in literature produced by Nielsen Media Research, a subsidiary of VNU, Inc.[8] As the "official national measurement service of the television industry for over 40 years," Nielsen (2000) maintains that "somebody has to count the viewers." In other words, to continue to operate as a monopolist for another 40 years, Nielsen has to count the viewers. Because the statement never clearly expresses why there is a necessity to count, it conceals its true mission: to construct a commodity audience for advertisers and networks. Nielsen maintains that its sample is representative and scientific and that its measurement is the "most democratic." However, advertiser interest in cable audiences has made broadcast households a minority. By equating larger audiences with successful audiences, Nielsen avoids any mention or discussion of prime demographics (inherent in its selection of cable households). Nielsen also relates its research process to the process of voting, further obscuring the selectivity of the sample. And, the statement neither differentiates between the cable and broadcast audiences used in its sample nor discusses the ramifications of including both.

As mentioned before, the proliferation of cable subscription rates prompted an advertiser interest in this audience. The abundance of cable channels also created an entirely new and untapped marketplace for ratings. Turner Broadcasting System persuaded Nielsen with monetary compensation to include cable subscribers in its sample. Turner's actions prompted the "official" downturn in network viewership (Meehan 1990, 131). The perception that the broadcast networks remain in severe decline depends on the number of broadcast households no longer included in Nielsen's sample and the number of cable households that have taken their place. The logic is simple: if the representation is not there, neither are the numbers.

But, this information has not found a place in a sea of publications and entertainment news magazine programs that tout the ratings as a weekly obsession. The excessive value (mis)placed on ratings is no longer just a staple of trade magazines such as *Variety* and *The Hollywood Reporter*. *Entertainment Weekly*, a fan magazine that dabbles in an easily consumed version of trade reporting, carries television ratings on a weekly basis (not in terms of rating points and shares but in terms of millions of households tuning in). When Chris Albrecht bases the success of *The Sopranos* on "ratings and critical acclaim," he escalates the power of Nielsen and the words of critics (Lowry 1999b, 1F). Nielsen is responsible for the numbers that convince the critics that the broadcast networks are "desperate" with "audiences and profits dwindling rapidly" (Sterngold 1999, 1E). The critics then blame the mass exodus to cable on "quality." As popular discourse moves from numbers of households to lofty intangibles such as "quality," the generative mechanisms are left behind. An instrument for determining monetary worth has become what many presume is an interactive game complete with democratic votes. An AOL Time Warner publication such as *Entertainment Weekly*, with its ratings reports and annual issue on ratings winners and losers, has solidified this presumption and naturalized the mere existence of ratings, just as Nielsen has worked to naturalize its methodology in its own publications.

Asking the Right Questions

The crux of the problem, then, is the saturation of the marketplace by conglomerates that seek to steer discourse in a direction that obscures ownership and questionable methods. The alleged competition that drove HBO to cultivate its original programming slate with *Oz, The Sopranos,* and *Sex and the City* is the very same that Time Warner insists exists in spite of its own admission of its gargantuan presence in the three televisual tiers: pay cable, basic cable, and broadcast television (not to mention pay-per-view television). So, HBO brands itself an outsider in the televisual terrain, a channel more akin to a grandiose cinematic heritage than a broadcast one. Its "quality" programming, the producers of which are wooed away from the networks, mimics this branding in content and form, while the complementary marketing obscures why this is so. No mention is made of the constraints under which broadcast television must operate, just as HBO officials omit the parentage that it and an alleged main competitor, TNT, share.

More profitable to Time Warner is the David-versus-Goliath, "quality"-versus-"trash" narrative surrounding *The Sopranos*. The telling and retelling of the narrative manifests in numbers posing as cardinal truth. Until less than a decade ago, ratings were strictly a trade constant. The skewed results on which the entertainment industry stakes careers have developed into a conversation piece for the populace. What better way to conceal the fact that Time Warner has its hands in every possible prized demographic in every possible tier than by creating a landscape in which the creativity of auteurs is compromised by such a crassly commercial tier as broadcast television? Meanwhile, HBO positions itself as the last bastion of creative freedom with uninterrupted programming. It would be interesting to research the supplementary income from product placement in *The Sopranos*. That is yet another aspect that is left out in discourse. But, it is not unusual for the channel that subsists entirely on a privileged, "quality" demographic to hide its commerce behind the brand of "quality" drama.

Notes

1. In writing this statement (and others like it), I do not intend to ascribe agency to HBO, the pay cable channel. When I use the term *HBO* as a subject in this sense (as in "HBO did this or that"), I mean HBO executives, officials, and general decision makers. These parties work in concert to serve the interest of HBO as a company, so I include them under the heading "HBO." Whenever possible, I refer to specific individuals who are responsible for certain statements or actions. At different points in the article, the term *HBO* will be used to represent its various incarnations. *HBO* will be synonymous with its decision-making employees, its status as a pay cable channel, the sum of its programming, and/or the company itself. Context will clarify usage.

2. I place the word *free* in quotation marks because the idea that over-the-air television programming is free is erroneous. Viewers pay for broadcast television by purchasing a television set, electrical services, and finally products advertised on television.

3. Although this move came in 1985, the pay cable market had more players by 1980. According to George Mair (1988, 56), between 1980 and 1981, HBO's (Time Inc.) share of the pay cable market had dropped from 60 percent to 49.3 percent. Showtime's (Viacom) share was up from 15.6 percent to 16.4 percent, and The Movie Channel's (Viacom) share was up from 5.4 percent to 8.8 percent.

4. *Oz* producers Tom Fontana and Barry Levinson also produced *Homicide*.

5. Among frequent and/or conspicuous products or manufacturers on *The Sopranos* are Coca-Cola products, Nintendo, Philips, Mercedes-Benz, Uncle Ben's rice, Marilyn Manson, Honeycomb, and Office Depot.

6. As of January 2001, Time Warner is AOL Time Warner.

7. October 1997 was the date of the merger's completion. The Federal Trade Commission gave its approval in February 1997.

8. VNU, Inc. is a publishing and information company based in the Netherlands.

References

Blumenthal, Howard J., and Oliver R. Goodenough. 1998. *This business of television.* 2d ed. New York: Billboard Books.

Boddy, William. 1990. *Fifties television: The industry and its critics.* Urbana: University of Illinois Press.

Dempsey, John. 1999. HBO renews three skeins. *Daily Variety,* 22 September, 3.

Feuer, Jane. 1992. Genre study and television. In *Channels of discourse, reassembled: Television and contemporary criticism,* 2d ed., edited by Robert C. Allen. Chapel Hill: University of North Carolina Press.

Feuer, Jane, Paul Kerr, and Tise Vahimagi, eds. 1984. *MTM "quality television."* London: British Film Institute.

Garay, Ronald. 1988. *Cable television: A reference guide to information.* New York: Greenwood.

Gershon, Richard A. 1990. Pay cable television: A regulatory history. *Communications and the Law* 12:3–26.

Graser, Marc. 1998. B-G names Baron biz veep. *Daily Variety,* 24 September, 8.

Hamilton, Kendall, and Corie Brown. 1999. HBO goes where the big networks fear to tread—And rules the summer. *Newsweek,* 21 June, 68.

Kaminsky, Stuart M. 1985. *American television genres.* Chicago: Nelson-Hall.

Lieberman, Paul. 1999. HBO's gritty prison drama *oz* finds its cast and writer-creator taking a hard look at the hard time known as life. *Los Angeles Times,* 8 August.

Littleton, Cynthia. 1999. Forged under fire: TB creativity flourishes amid criticism. *Daily Variety,* 27 July, 1.

———. 1999. Watchdogs howl at shows. *Daily Variety,* 31 August, A8.

Littleton, Cynthia, and Vanessa Torres. 1999. Vets react to Emmy nom fest. *Daily Variety,* 23 July, 1.

Lowry, Brian. 1999a. At HBO, life after *Larry* ain't so bad. *Los Angeles Times,* 15 May, 1F.

———. 1999b. Emmy nominations. *Los Angeles Times,* 23 July, 1F.

———. 1999c. Adjusting the off-color contrast. *Los Angeles Times,* 29 September, 4.

Mair, George. 1988. *Inside HBO: The billion dollar war between HBO, Hollywood, and the home video revolution.* New York: Dodd, Mead.

Marconi, Joe. 1993. *Beyond branding: How savvy marketers build brand equity to create products and open new markets.* Chicago: Probus.

Meehan, Eileen R. 1990. Why we don't count: The commodity audience. In *Logics of television: Essays in cultural criticism,* edited by Pat Mellencamp. Bloomington: Indiana University Press.

Murphy, John M., ed. 1987. *Branding: A key marketing tool.* New York: McGraw-Hill.

Newcomb, Horace, and Robert S. Alley. 1983. *The producer's medium: Conversations with creators of American TV.* New York: Oxford University Press.

Nielsen Media Research. 2000. *What TV ratings really mean* [Online]. Available: http://www.nielsenmedia.com/whatratingsmean.

Peyser, Marc. 2000. Why The *Sopranos* sing. *Newsweek,* 2 April, 48–57.

Pursell, Chris. 1999. HBO puts films to the fire. *Variety,* 25 October, 23.

Rochlin, Margy, comp. 1999. The new season/television and radio: Looking ahead; *Sopranos,* sex, and a Sunday standby. *New York Times,* 12 September, 25[2].

Schatz, Thomas. 1987. *St. Elsewhere* and the evolution of the ensemble series. In *Television: The critical view,* 4th ed., edited by Horace Newcomb. New York: Oxford University Press.

Schneider, Michael. 2000. TV's consolidation merges into 2000. *Variety,* 10 January, 97.

Sterngold, James. 1999. Faltering drama, heal thyself. *Los Angeles Times,* 25 August, 1E.

Streeter, Thomas. 1996. *Selling the air: A critique of the policy of commercial broadcasting in the United States.* Chicago: University of Chicago Press.

Time Warner Entertainment. 2000. *Form-type: 10-K* [Online]. Retrieved 30 March from LexisNexis (http://www.lexis-nexis.com).

Time Warner Inc. 2000. Time Warner companies lead this year's Emmy nominations.

Retrieved 20 July from the World Wide Web: http://cgi.timewarner.com/cgi-in/corp/news/index.cgi?template=article&article_id=200284.

Wasko, Janet. 1994. *Hollywood in the information age: Beyond the silver screen.* Austin: University of Texas Press.

Weinraub, Bernard. 1999. Pushing the bleeping envelope: Fox flirts with serious outrage. *The New York Times,* 12 August, 1E.

Williams, Betsy. 1994. "North to the future": *Northern Exposure* and quality television. In *Television: The critical view,* 5th ed., edited by Horace Newcomb. New York: Oxford University Press.

Television as Transmodern Teaching

John Hartley

This process to see other human beings as "one of us" rather than as "them" is a matter of detailed description of what unfamiliar people are like and of redescription of what we ourselves are like. This is the task not for theory but for genres such as ethnography, the journalist's report, the comic book, the docudrama, and ... the novel.... The novel, the movie, and the TV program have, gradually but steadily, replaced the sermon and the treatise as the principal vehicles of moral change and progress.

Richard Rorty, 1989: xiv

Pre-modernity, Modernity, Postmodernity, Transmodernity

I claim that television needs to be understood through the notion of trans-modern teaching. It is therefore worthwhile to clarify my usage of terms associated with "modern." There are both temporal and categorical issues to think about. Temporally, it seems obvious that a sequence can be found from pre-modern to modern, modern to postmodern. Categorically, however, there are well-known distinctions between modern and postmodern phenomena that are simply not time based—the modern and postmodern can and do coexist in time—and, perhaps they always have, at least in relation to media. Indeed, it is the argument of this book that not only can "postmodern" and "modern" characteristics be found side by side in many media contexts, but also that the "uses" of television continue social functions already present in pre-modern Europe (specifically, television is organizationally and socially a secularization of the medieval Catholic church, and also it connects with family and domestic contexts of sense-making that are largely oral and pre-modern). Hence I am anxious to characterize television as transmodern—partaking of pre-modern, modern and postmodern characteristics at once.

Modernity has been revitalized as an object of study in the period since postmodernity became a major debating topic in the humanities and social sci-

---

ences; indeed, John Frow sees "postmodernity" as a genre of theory-writing, rather than something which such writing describes in the world (see Frow, 1997: Chapter 1). Modernity can be understood approvingly as an era dedicated to founding knowledge on reason, truth, secularism and empirical or positive evidence; or disapprovingly as an era dominated by masculine knowledges, imperial powers and colonial exploitation. Similarly, postmodernity can be described approvingly as a retreat from myths of comprehensive, coherent truth, and a recognition of the need for self-reflexivity in the production of knowledge; or disapprovingly as an anything-goes relativism and the commodification of information, culture and communication.

It is not necessary for the cultural investigator to arbitrate such evaluative debates. Instead it is helpful to make some distinctions: moderniy is associated with specific historical developments.

- In **politics,** modernity began with the transfer of sovereignty from monarch to people; its inauguration can therefore appropriately be associated with the French Revolution.
- In **philosophy,** modernity began with the Enlightenment of the eighteenth century—again, centred on France.
- In **science,** modernity began with empiricism, positivism and pragmatism (the experimental method), associated with English writers like Francis Bacon and with the foundation of the Royal Society in the early seventeenth century.
- In **industrial** terms modernity is associated with the Industrial Revolution—again, centred on Britain in the late eighteenth and early nineteenth centuries.
- Meanwhile, what **historians** of Europe call the "early modern" period began much earlier, some time after the introduction of technologies like the plough, gunpowder and printing between the 1200s and 1400s, the invention of capitalist banking in Italy in the 1400s and 1500s, the market economy growing up within feudal societies throughout Europe (in Britain during the 1500s), and the expansion of both geographical and mental horizons attendant upon the Reformation and the Renaissance (late 1400s to early 1600s).

In recent social and political theory, however, the multi-origined and historically contingent nature of modernity has been underplayed in favour of categorical discussions centred not on the *condition* or period of modernity, but on the *ideology* of modernism—the militant promotion of modernist ideas about truth, progress, science, reason. Hence, debates about postmodernity have also tended towards the categorical—postmodernity is calculated from its implied opposition to and apparent temporal sequence after modernity, leading to modernist fears that if postmodernity is not contested it will destroy the modernist project. Looked at historically, it can be shown however that many of the conditions thought of as postmodern are not post- but coterminous with the modern.

Hence it may be proper to assert that there's a difference between modernity and postmodernity (understood as conditions in society requiring explanation), and modernism and postmodernism (understood as ideologies held by contending factions of the knowledge class). Similarly, just as modernity can be shown to be multi-origined and calculated from various starting dates spanning nearly half a millennium, so postmodernity can be traced back to the very beginnings of modernity, indeed as the necessary twin to modernity, in conditions that were always there but only recently resolved into analytical coherence. Hence histories of modernist media (such as the press) now have to recognize the extent to which the press was "postmodern" from the start: i.e. dedicated to the irrational and emotional as well as to reason and truth; to feminized, privatized, non-metropolitan knowledges as well as to public affairs; to questions of identity as well as power.

Modernist critics of "postmodern" media like television, conversely, need to understand that TV is a part of the modern world not despite but because of its blivitousness, its emphasis on entertainment not information, on surface not structure, on celebrity not power, on distribution not production, on audience not reality, on semiosis not reality. These "postmodern" features predate television in older media, and meanwhile television is also part of the modernist project of enlightenment, science, reason, progress, secularism, popular sovereignty, and the rest. And just as it follows that modernity was not a radical disruption of a pre-modern past to which it bore no resemblance (indeed there are those who think modernity has not yet occurred, certainly in its ideal form—see Frow, 1997: 1), so it follows that postmodernity is not a radical disruption of modernity, but a part of the same world. Hence it is now possible to argue that media such as television, far from being hyper-present-tense and postmodern, share in some semiotic, social, political and cultural characteristics and functions that are present in both modern and pre-modern conditions—indeed that television is a transmodern medium.

Meanwhile, if it is the case that modernity is multi-origined, it is therefore likely that it has not reached certain spheres of life and is still an "incomplete project." The late twentieth century has seen an unusually intense modernization of information, communication, culture and semiosis. But this very process, coming after the great political and industrial modernizations of the nineteenth century, looks to some commentators like the very opposite of modernity, namely postmodernity, since the cultural sphere was routinely ignored or discounted in modernist maps of social progress. But the shift of critical attention from the rational, scientific, progress-seeking, industrial conditions of "high" modernity to the cultural sphere of identity and semiosis does not mean that these things weren't there in previous times. Similarly, the very impressive monuments left to us by modernity in its most militant phase—from Manhattan and universal suffrage to the Soviet Union and science—don't obliterate previous realities entirely; whole areas of life, especially those connected with mothering and language-acquisition, are resistant to modernization and retain substantial pre-modern characteristics.

To summarize:

- Television is "**modern**"—it is organized as an advanced capitalist industry with divisions of labour and a commodified cultural form.

- Television is "**postmodern**"—its textuality is the ideal type of "po-mo" style: "the term refers to a broader cultural domain. . . . It is centred in the realm of the mass media rather than in high culture, and typically it refers to television (soap operas, advertisements, video clips, the 'real world of postmodernism') and to phenomena of style and fashion" (Frow, 1997: 19).
- Television is "**pre-modern**"—its cultural use is prefigured by socio-semiotic aspects of the first mass medium, the medieval Catholic church, and its phenomenal form exploits pre-modern (oral) modes of communication based on family and a domestic setting.
- Television is "**transmodern**"—it spans, transcends and conjoins modern, pre- and postmodern aspects of contemporary life; specifically by using oral, domestic discourses to teach vast, unknowable "lay" audiences modes of "citizenship" and self-knowledge based on culture and identity within a virtualized community of unparalleled size and diversity.

If Television Is Transmodern

It would be provocative and self-aggrandizing for a professional educator to claim that the most popular mass medium the world has ever seen is a branch of the teaching profession. I'm not doing that. My own experience accords with those among the producers and audiences of popular media for whom one of the main attractions of TV is that it is not like formal education. The pleasure of media is that they can be taken outside of the institutional confines of scholastic compulsion, tedium, control and conformism. Proof of TV's distance from schooling is that many teachers and professors are irrationally prejudiced against it. But I am nevertheless arguing that teaching is what TV does; and that this is the *use* of television. This is a social, historical view of television and of usage, seeking to interpret, after the event, what has in fact been done with television in modern/postmodern societies, rather than pretending to describe the intentions of its producers or consumers, much less the ostensible purpose of TV companies and channels. Television is a social institution of teaching in a "transmodern" (*longue durée;* see Braudel, 1958), anthropological perspective.

What constitutes the social function and practice of teaching? In pre-modern European society, a system lasting until the seventeenth century (at least in England and Wales), teaching was done by three social institutions: the family, the workplace and the church. There was no specific provision for social, political or civic education; persons were formed into *selves* by the family, into *roles* by apprenticeship into craft, professional or vocational mysteries—sometimes also performed within families, and into *souls* by the church. Obedience to apparently natural orders, themselves backed up by supernatural powers, was a high priority. Governance of the self was divided between family and church, each reinforcing the other's cosmological division of existence into hierarchies; obedience on the basis of the resemblance between different orders—e.g. natural father, "Father of the Nation" (monarch), "Holy Father" (pope) and God the Father. Secular law helped the same process, without ever intervening in individual education. In cities, people in different vocations were organized into guilds with different clothes (liveries); more generally the "vestimentary laws" ensured that people were what they appeared to be by forbidding anyone to dress outside their own rank and station. There were different legal systems for literate and non-literate people (clergy and laity); someone found guilty of a capital offence in secular law might save themselves from hanging if they could claim "benefit of clergy." Education in vocational skills was added to this mix both inside the family-system, for instance for women, craft workshops and rural workers, or in formal institutions outside the family, as in apprenticeships and military or religious training. It was only the military and religious training institutions—a small, specialist component of medieval teaching provision—that generated the formal school in the European context. The other functions of pre-modern teaching, the formation of *selves, souls* and most *roles,* were never included in formal school provision. They were catered for informally ("anthropologically" rather than "institutionally"—culturally rather than sociologically), although none the less systematically and effectively for that (see Ariès, 1962: part two; Duby, 1988; Hunter, 1994).

It is my view that the private, informal, but systematic teaching of "selfhood," belief-system ("soul") and social "role" remains with families, but that the part played in the medieval period by the church has been taken over in the modern era by the media, culminating in television. In this model, TV is not an extension of school, though it may be a competitor for hearts, minds and methods; historically it is devoted to teaching other things than those for which schooling was invented and is best suited.

Some of the previously private and informal aspects of education were also taken over by the state, and adopted within the curriculum of formal schooling, making the competition for hearts and minds active and militant. Since the nineteenth century especially schools have taken on responsibility for more and more areas of life. The basic requirements of literacy, numeracy, discipline and obedience have been augmented by physical training, and by "ideological" training in moral, sexual, social and cultural matters.

Meanwhile, the pre-modern assumption that the state enjoys a monopoly in communications has taken nearly 500 years to erode (still by no means completely), so the handover of functions from pre-modern family/church to modern family/media has been accompanied by an unceasing stream of interventionist legislation, regulation and persuasion designed not only to poach from the informal to the formal educational sectors many of these more "cultural" or "anthropological" teachings, but also to discipline and control the media's own educative tendencies, dictating what can be said, to whom, at what times of day, in what quantity and for what purpose. This practice has been progressively abandoned in publishing, but remains militantly in force in broadcasting. So in postmodern media, a pre-modern monarchical monopoly (control or "licensing" of communications) is joined by a modernist fear of "private" life; the result is that there's now a rather too militantly drawn line between education and media, with keep out! signs all round formal schooling.

One of the reasons schooling exploded into a much more important social institution with the coming of modernity remains its number-one function to this day, namely the teaching of print-literacy. Conversely, the medieval institutions of family and church were almost entirely oral in their modes of communication. Television has inherited this non-literate tradition of teaching, using song, story, sight and talk rather than "book-learning." There are very good historical reasons, going back to the Reformation and Counter-reformation in the sixteenth century, for those engaged in teaching to become very passionate indeed about these alternative technologies. As has been well-documented, protestantism was a religion based on print-literacy and individual practice (reading the Bible), while the medieval Catholic church relied on orality and collective practice (going to church). Some of the hostility to oral/visual modes of teaching, especially the hostility inherited by those working in formal institutions of print-literacy like schools, is based on the lethal antagonism between protestants and papists going back to the Renaissance. In other words, teaching became a ground upon which rival belief-systems competed for souls. This is still the case in the inherited antagonism that print/school people unthinkingly reproduce when they castigate television (Ong, 1958).

If TV Is Teaching

Rethinking television as an object of study through the concept of teaching allows for a critical reformulation of some very well-established but not very satisfactory theories of television. For instance, if television is thought of in terms of teaching not power, then the idea that TV programming and TV pervasion is best explained by reference to such cold-war concepts as ideology, propaganda and surveillance—power over some group or population—can be reformulated into a much less coercive, sinister and negative version based on teaching; "loving to influence others," in Richard Hoggart's throwaway phrase (Hoggart, 1970: 55).

- If TV is teaching, then accusations of "populism" can be dealt with and the whole debate re-argued, for "populism" and teaching are never entirely coterminous. One of the difficulties that has dogged those who write about television without critical pessimism is that this stance has too easily been dismissed as "populism." Populism is a "boo-word" in social theory, for good reason. Many political atrocities have been committed "in the name of the people," and politicians who veer from one position to another in order to follow popular opinion are universally derided. If cultural theory were to try to explain how society works by saying that whatever is popular is for that reason alone to be celebrated, then it would be wise to be cautious about the theory, for in certain circumstances crime, hanging and genocide have been "popular." Twentieth-century social and cultural theory has been powerfully influenced by émigrés from mid-century totalitarian regimes such as the Frankfurt School or Hannah Arendt, for whom "the popular" is by def-

inition populist and those who speak optimistically on behalf of the people are not democrats but demagogues; a reflex response has become
standard in social studies of the media. Anyone who *likes* "the popular," including television, is a populist and therefore to be criticized for
depoliticizing culture and endangering freedom. But if television is seen
as teaching, its institutional desire to influence its audiences doesn't have
to be seen as populism, or demagoguery, or tending towards totalitar-
ianism. Instead, television's love of influence can be interrogated along
different lines; as a positive form of "inter-generational" communication, perhaps, which is sometimes wonderful, sometimes woeful, but
neither inspired by a desire to rule the world nor transforming its unsus-
pecting viewers into fodder for fascism.

- If TV is teaching, terms like "market" and "consumer" can be put into
question; these do not describe the addresser/addressee relations of
teacher/taught, nor do they fully explain the relationship between television and its audiences. It is true that TV audiences are understood as
a market of consumers (increasingly so as TV moves towards non-
broadcast forms that people pay for directly). But in relation to individual television shows or even whole channels in the broadcast network, the concept of the consumer market is quite misleading. People
don't buy television shows, and those shows are not used up when they
are "consumed" by individual viewers. The only people who buy TV
shows are TV stations, and TV stations' own customers are not their
audiences but their advertisers (or regulatory authorities in the case of
public TV). The market for television is therefore not the public but
the industry; shows are not sold to the public; airtime is not sold to the
public; the public doesn't buy anything from TV. If TV is understood
as teaching, then the relations between TV and TV audiences can be
rethought.

- If TV is teaching, it is integrated with the great twentieth-century
institution of the three Ds—democracy, didactics and drama (Hartley,
1993); it is part of the convergent GEM-megalomerate (Government-
Education-Media), each institutional component of which employs
aspects of the other; government teaches via drama (politics as theatre);
media govern by education (entertainment is both ideological and
instructional); education dramatizes government (schooling instills
(self)-discipline)—but it's all "agoraphiliac" (Hartley, 1993); a love of
public space, of "the public" in the public sphere, teaching public virtues
by means of dramatic entertainment. It's the place of ancient, classical
citizenship.

- If TV is teaching, then arguments about quality are reformulated around
the notion of democratization, not decline. Popular and elite/high culture are integrated into one system, of which they are differentiated parts.
Here it is not a matter of some everlasting or absolute set of aesthetic
standards to which whole media, populations or epochs approximate (or
not, in the case of television and popular culture in the modern epoch),

but of a system of semiotic and textual productivity encompassing societies as a whole, within which it might make more sense to say that "high" culture is *a product of* popular culture—a necessary pole or antipode against which popular culture and media can set themselves in order to "count" *as* popular. If TV is teaching, in other words, it is teaching audiences about cultural distinction, the expansion of difference, and the segmentation of both cultural productivity itself and of the audience for it.

- If TV is teaching, there needs to be some reformulation of the concept of teaching itself. Let me make clear that by *teaching* I never mean *schooling*. Of course teaching may take place in schools, but schools operate to a narrow, specialist and institutionalized notion of teaching, which I take to be a general human or "anthropological" activity, taking place in societies that don't or didn't have schools, and in those societies that do have them, taking place in many contexts (such as the family, workplace and media) outside of school. Meanwhile, perhaps because of the associations with schooling, teaching-related concepts seem to enjoy rather low prestige ("pedantic," "academic," "sermonizing," "didactic," "school-marmish"). Professional teaching itself is undervalued both socially and in hierarchies of prestige. It is in stark contrast with philosophy, for instance, in the same way that TV is with the high arts—it is taken to be mere distribution or application, not creating original knowledge. School-teaching has of course both authoritarian and liberal internal philosophies and methods; it is both engineering and bricolage, profession and "sitting with Nellie." But while teaching in primary or secondary schools (a feminized and not wholly professionalized occupation) is undervalued, *theories* about the transfer of knowledge, culture, social structure and personal comportment are found at the very highest levels of educational prestige (departments of philosophy in ancient universities, or in social, political, cultural and anthropological theory). Some attention needs to be paid to the irony inherent in this; a rethinking of the importance of "distribution"—feeling the "width" of actual teacherly contact with people—and a less reverential attitude to the self-importance of "philosophy," which is only a theory of teaching that has lost its practice. TV is all distribution and no theory as well, but an astute "reading" of TV can yield important insights about how knowledge, beliefs, meanings and consciousness are actually communicated and transferred in the gigantic social systems of contemporary history.
- If TV is teaching, then concepts of entertainment, citizenship, life-long and distance learning, and domesticity need to be brought to bear on the understanding of teaching itself. Teaching and learning need to be seen as non-purposeful activities of a society, not outcome-oriented institutional practices.
- If TV is teaching, then we need to look at the producers of TV as part of the GEM "knowledge class"—they too are teachers, and they are thus "like us" (academics and critics)—converging with intellectuals and bringing popular culture and intellectual culture together.

- If TV is teaching, then we need to rethink the concept of the audience entirely—bringing together our understanding of TV audiences and that of students; where they are alike, where not. For instance, we do not formally examine TV audiences, nor do we knowingly entertain students. What is the use of TV for audiences; of school for students?
- If TV is teaching, then its international, commercial role can be rethought. Concepts such as "public service" and "education by stealth," even "nation shall speak peace unto nation" (the motto of the BBC), apply equally to commercial, global screen entertainment (and of course vice versa—commercial and public service media are in historic convergence). The pathologization of commercial media and the equal but opposite reverence for BBC-style media needs historical revaluation. Here's where we might return to early modern pedagogical institutions, and the struggle between the medieval Catholic church and protestant printing. . . . The Reformation is still being fought in adversarial rhetoric; we need to rethink this in the light of the convergence of technologies of teaching in transmodern media.
- If TV is teaching we need to re-interrogate the concept of the text: textual features are not seeking power over audiences but they are trying to influence them ("loving to influence" rather than "taking power over"). For instance, television violence is not a *behaviour* resulting from influence, but a *literacy* shared among users of the textual system—among the things that this literacy teaches is the differentiation of "good" from "bad" violence: the Gulf War from Ghaddafi; the cop from the villain; the justified defence from the unprovoked attack, etc. Similarly, television sex (see *Media International Australia,* 85, 1997, whole issue), bad-language (see Dening, 1992) and "dirt" (see Hartley, 1992a) are not symptoms of the decline of civilization but the necessary and inevitable appeal of communication. What is important is whether they are used well or not in each case, each context. And that is a question of what we used to call aesthetics (perhaps allied with notions of tact, respect, recognition of difference); it is not a question of power.
- If TV is teaching, then the questions of what is being taught, to whom, with what outcomes, are interesting to investigate. It is the argument of this book that television, via cross-demographic communication, visual culture, talk and narrative ("per sona" in fact), teaches the formation of identity and citizenship in a society characterized by the unknowability of its nevertheless sovereign populations. The outcome is both literacy in audio-visuality and citizenship of media (which I argue in later chapters of *Uses of Television* (1999) has evolved from "cultural citizenship" to "DIY citizenship" or "semiotic self-determination"), to be used who knows how, by populations whose purposes and actions are outside of the pedagogic relations used by TV.
- If TV is teaching, then it is a part of and "witness to" the transmodern, transnational democratization of culture.

References

Ariès, Philippe (1962) *Centuries of Childhood*. Trans. Robert Baldick. London: Jonathan Cape.

Braudel, Fernand (1958) "Histoire et science sociale, la longue durée." *Annales*, 725–53.

Dening, Greg (1992) *Mr. Bligh's Bad Language: Passion, Power and Theatre on the Bounty*. Cambridge: Cambridge University Press.

Duby, Georges (ed.) (1998) *A History of Private Life: Revelations of the Medieval World*. Trans. Arthur Goldhammer. Cambridge, MA: Harvard University Press.

Frow, John (1997) *Time and Commodity Culture: Essays in Cultural Theory and Postmodernity*. Oxford: Oxford University Press.

Hartley, John (1992) *Tele-ology: Studies in Television*. London and New York: Routledge.

Hartley, John (1993) *The Politics of Pictures: The Creation of the Public in the Age of Popular Media*. London and New York: Routledge.

Hoggart, Richard (1970) *Speaking to Each Other, Volume Two: About Literature*. Harmondsworth: Penguin.

Hunter, Ian (1994) *Rethinking the School: Subjectivity, Bureaucracy, Criticism*. Sydney: Allen & Unwin.

Media International Australia (1997) *Panic: Media, Morality, Culture* (themed issue), 85, November.

Ong, Walter J., S.J. (1958) *Ramus, Method, and the Decay of Dialogue: From the Art of Discourse to the Art of Reason*. Cambridge, MA: Harvard University Press.

"Democracy as Defeat"

The Impotence of Arguments for Public Service Broadcasting

Elizabeth Jacka

The analytical rhetoric which makes *democracy a defeat* is highly characteristic of the British left, Old and New.

Hartley (1999, 119)

John Hartley's (1999) book, *Uses of Television,* from which the above quotation is taken is the latest in a series of books he has published during the 1990s (Hartley 1992a, 1992b, 1996) in which he has taken issue (again) with the long tradition of left and right pessimism about television. What I find interesting (although often infuriating because of its highly polemical and aphoristic nature) about his work is his extended engagement with the question of democracy. In this article, I intend to examine what Hartley has to say about democracy and the media in some detail. However, my motivation for considering the concept of democracy is different from his.

My primary concern is with the current state of affairs with public service broadcasting (PSB), both the institution itself and the debate about the institution. There is no doubt that PSB is under threat around the world. The classic model, exemplified in the British Broadcasting Corporation and adapted to local conditions and histories in many different parts of the world, is under increasing strain. In various places and in various ways, public service broadcasters are struggling to respond to rapidly changing communication contexts. The sight of this venerable institution being attacked and starved of funds is distressing. And yet it must be admitted that much of what it does can justifiably be challenged and that the standard defenses of it sound more and more tired.

In most places where PSB is threatened, there is a veritable avalanche of discourse attempting to shore up its existence. Broadcasters, academics, "friends of PSB," community groups, special interest groups, and so forth clamor for its survival in various forums, such as submissions to government, letters to newspapers, e-mails to web sites, and so forth. In all this clamor, various key concepts are intoned like mantras—public service, public sphere, citizenship, democracy—as if by their repetition alone they had the power to persuade unwilling governments to continue to support the PSB.

In this article, I am going to challenge one of the orthodoxies that can be found in the literature on PSB, namely, its identification with the concept of democracy. This is one of those words whose very invocation tends to close off arguments but whose shifting meanings are complex and difficult to trace. It is a key concept among those defenders of PSB who resort to Habermasian-inspired defenses. It is also invoked by those opponents of PSB, from both the "right" (e.g., Rupert Murdoch) and the "left," who accuse the PSB of being elitist and thus inherently "antidemocratic." I attempt to thread my way through this conceptual mire by asking the following questions:

- What does the term *democracy* currently mean?
- Is it true that PSB makes a unique and indispensable contribution to it?

The Media, Democracy, and the Public Sphere

> "The public sphere": the phrase has ballooned into the God-term of democratic discourse theory. It represents the ideal: the unmoved mover and sacred sphere. . . . The notion of a sovereign public—both deliberative and rational—stands at the heart of the Enlightenment ideal of a democratic republic.
>
> (Gitlin 1998, 169)

An influential twentieth-century statement of the relationship between the media and democracy has been made by Nicholas Garnham in a number of frequently quoted articles (Garnham 1983, 1986, 1996). Heavily influenced by Habermas's notion of the public sphere, Garnham articulated an uncompromising modernist argument that combines a classic position on liberal democracy and an enlightenment view of the formation of public opinion.

> I take it as axiomatic that some version of communicative action lies at the heart of both the theory and practice of democracy. The rights and duties of a citizen are in large part defined in terms of freedom of assembly and freedom to impart and receive information. Without such freedoms it would be impossible for citizens to possess the knowledge of the views of others necessary to reach agreements between themselves, whether consensual or majoritarian, as to either social means or ends; to possess knowledge of the actions of those to whom executive responsibilities are delegated so as to make them accountable; to possess knowledge of the external environment necessary to arrive at appropriate judgment of both personal and societal interests. (Garnham 1996, 364)

His extended argument flies in the face of the "postmodernists" or "cultural relativists," as he called them, when he invoked a realm of universal rationality, a "single public sphere" (Garnham 1996, 371) with a "common normative dimension" (Garnham 1996, 369). This is generally tied to a view about the primacy of journalism in the media mix, and a particular variety of it, which James Carey (1993) called "high modern" journalism. This preference for high modern journalism in the media diet is accompanied by a disdain for low forms of media, such as talk shows and soap operas.

This kind of argument[1] has been used by Garnham and many others to make a case for the indispensability of PSB for the healthy functioning of democracy. Strong statements of support for PSB see it as being the most important or even the only vehicle for the fostering of democracy and citizenship.[2] James Curran (1992) exemplified such a position when he argued that whatever the defects in the public system (e.g., the potential for political manipulation), the private media system's democratic potential is fatally flawed by its commercial nature, even more so in these days of media concentration when media organizations are part of large, diversified multinational conglomerates. The arguments about the future of broadcasting are then carried on within the framework of a polarity between the "state and the market" (Garnham 1983; Tracey 1998), with the market side being lampooned for equating "democracy" with consumer sovereignty (Garnham 1996, 371). So far, so familiar.

There are, however, as John Keane (1995) pointed out, "major problems inherent in the argument that existing public service media are a bulwark of the public sphere" (p. 4). A serious one is the strange absence of any acknowledgment that the private media have fulfilled a great number of the aims seen as unique to PSB. Graham Murdock (1992), for example, saw PSB as having performed four key roles in the extension of citizenship rights in the first half of the twentieth century. These are, first, provision of a public space of information and debate; second, a mechanism of accountability of power holders; third, fostering national culture; and fourth, connecting the private (domestic) and the public (p. 33). It is not at all difficult to demonstrate that these are not unique to PSB and that privately owned media in Europe, the United States, Australia, and Canada certainly have achieved and continue to achieve all of them.

Of course, their success in doing so is far from guaranteed and rests on a complex set of factors, including regulatory arrangements and an intricate set of ethical protocols governing the practice of journalism. But nevertheless, it is the case that privately run media have an excellent record in the performance of Graham Murdock's list of public interest tasks.

Keane (1995) went on to argue that the decline of PSB in areas where it was hitherto strong must be seen as part of a wider

> political problem, evident in all the old democracies, in which political parties, professional associations, trades unions, churches, and other means of defining, projecting, and representing citizens' opinions to decision makers are either losing their vibrance [*sic*] or prompting new disputes about their own degree of "representativeness." (P. 5)

Another classic exponent of the "democracy as defeat" school of thought is Michael Tracey (1998). In his lament for the passing of the PSB era, *The*

Decline and Fall of Public Service Broadcasting, he saw the new media as simply exacerbating the already corrupted media environment in which we in the old democracies now live. For him, the pluralization of society is a loss for both democracy and public broadcasting, which depends on "coherent populations to which it could speak, and recognisable hierarchies of value within which that speech could be formed" (p. 263). He saw identity politics as a form of retribalization that is not "benign and munificent" but "troubled, unstable, alienated, and definitely not communal or caring" (p. 264).

This dissolution of a unitary "public" into incoherent tribes is accompanied, according to Tracey (1998), by a "dumbing down" of media, a "linguistic poverty and therefore a mental and moral poverty, daytime soaps, tabloid television, the trivialisation of public discourse, an evangelism of the ephemeral, the celebration of the insignificant, and the marginalisation of the important" (p. 264). This will only get worse with the advent of the broadband culture, which will see people meaninglessly grazing across multiple channels or even watching more than one at a time.

Democracy Now

Just about everyone seems to believe that representative and participatory democracy is in crisis.[3] The often cited evidence for political indifference is statistics about voter turnout (Coleman 2000, 67). For some commentators, the communications business is partly to blame. The "ideal" communication between elected and electors has been perverted, it is argued, by the rise of the public relations industry, the "spin doctors" and media managers, and the collusion between media professionals and party news managers, assisted by the present structure of the media as a "monological" broadcast culture with one-way communication. According to James Carey (1993), for example, a political system of "democracy without citizens" has evolved, one in which "journalism justifies itself in the public's name but in which the public plays no role, except as an audience: a receptacle to be informed by experts and an excuse for the practice of publicity" (p. 12). In such a situation, the public watches, as increasingly alienated and cynical spectators, and by the second half of the twentieth century, at least in the United States, the average citizen was no longer interested in politics (p. 13).[4]

However, I believe that we need to question the apparent obviousness of this frequently repeated analysis. It seems to me that underlying the large body of literature on the failures of both democracy and the media's role in fostering it is a notion of democracy as an essence—without seeing it as a changing and evolving phenomenon. Commentators seem locked into a vision of an "ideal democracy" that might be hyperrational or nostalgic, depending on which of the two dominant schools of thought is in play. One school of thought sees democracy as wanting, because it equates democracy with representative democracy; seeing a diminution in citizens' interest in the forms of representative government (parliaments, elections), it reads that as a decline in democracy itself. The second sees representative democracy, even if working effectively, as "thin democracy" in Benjamin Barber's (1994) terms, compared unfavorably with "strong democracy"—envisaged as a form of governance-in which citizens, rather than simply electing representatives according to their self-interests and then forgetting about politics for three or four years, participate at every level of decision making. Furthermore, through conversation they build a common vision about the common good—in short, the republican ideal.

Both of these visions of current democracy seem to be too limited. The first is deficient because it defines democracy very narrowly, namely as representative democracy (without explicitly saying so), and then bewails its apparent decline. The second—the ideal of communitarian democracy—is fatally flawed in a different way. Its effect in complex modern societies, if implemented on a large scale, would be conservative and coercive because it would involve imposing the "common good" on the whole of an extremely diverse society (Mouffe 1992, 227) (which is perhaps what fascism does).

How then can we get beyond these theories of contemporary democracy, which see it as inevitably wanting? A number of theorists have begun to articulate a more sophisticated theory of democracy that does justice to the actual complexity of (post)modern societies. Michael Schudson (1998), commenting on the "bowling alone–kicking in groups" debate,[5] saw the nature of citizenship changing in a pluralized society. For him, the blurring of the boundaries between public and private and the by now quite old recognition that the "personal is political" mean an expansion of our notions of citizenship and participation, not a shrinkage, as Tracey would see it.

Another contemporary commentator, Michael Walzer (1992), recognized that in modern societies, while admittedly citizens are rather passive (he described citizens as "spectators who vote"), it is also the case that "in the associational networks of civil society, in unions, parties, movements, interest groups and so on, these same people make many smaller decisions and shape to some degree the more distant determinations of state and economy" (p. 99).

Other theorists go further and point to the most significant change in modern democracy, namely that we now live in plural societies, societies in which it is impossible to imagine that there is a way to define the "general good." We might call this postmodern democracy. Some of the characteristics of the move from "modern" to "postmodern" democracy are an erosion of the boundary between public and private, a move from "politics" (in the narrow sense) to ethics, a shift from a single principle of social division (say "class") to plural definitions based on diverse identities, and a move from scientistic conceptions of truth to a pragmatics of persuasion (which is not irrationalism or subjectivism) (Yeatman 1994, 106).

Chantal Mouffe's (1992) conception of "radical democracy" begins to provide an account of how we can envisage democracy and citizenship in these postmodern, plural times. To build a political community under modern democratic conditions, we need, she argued, to go beyond the conceptions of citizenship of both the liberal and civic republican traditions (p. 225). She said that what we share and what makes us fellow citizens in a pluralized postmodern polity are not a substantive idea of the good—such a conception is impossible in a polity inevitably defined by difference—but an adherence to a "grammar of political conduct" (p. 231).

She invoked Michael Oakeshott's idea of the *res publica* or *societas*, which sees the political community as an ethical bond between citizens but that does not presuppose a substantive "common good." What binds people together is their common recognition of a set of ethical-political values. Citizenship is not one identity among others but an articulating principle that affects the different subject positions of the social agent while allowing for a plurality of specific allegiances and respect for individual liberty (Mouffe 1992, 235). Unlike liberal democracy, this "radical democracy" can recognize differential power relations, and via a principle of "democratic equivalence," democratic rights are thereby extended progressively to various identity groups (Mouffe 1992, 236). Radical democratic citizenship rejects the idea of an abstract universalist definition of "the public" opposed to the "private realm" of particularity and difference. The public-private binary is recast because private actions are carried out according to the public rules of the res publica (Mouffe 1992, 236).

This account has, I hope, the virtue of relativizing or historicizing our conceptions of democracy. It tries to recognize that democracy is not a fixed ideal type but something that is fluid and evolving. If you take an ideal type view of it, whether it is republican representative or republican communitarian, you inevitably see any departure from it as a crisis. If we impose an ideal type mode of communication—high modern journalism (Carey 1993) as republican representative and communication unmediated by big media interests as republican communitarian—one inevitably sees any departure from this also as a crisis.

If, however, we see democracy as pluralized, as marked by new kinds of communities of identity, as a system in which the traditional public-private divide does not apply, and as a system in which there are no universal visions of the "common good" but, rather, pragmatic and negotiated exchanges about ethical behavior and ethically inspired courses of action, then we will be able to countenance a plurality of communication media and modes in which such a diverse set of exchanges will occur. We will be open to the notion that ethical discourse can be present in many different kinds and genres of media texts and in many different forms of media organization. We will no longer privilege "high modern journalism," but nor will we mindlessly worship populist media. We will need a much more nuanced account of the connection between (various forms of) citizenship and the media,[6] something that is offered in the work of John Hartley, which I discuss in the next section.

Democracy and the Media Revisited

In *Uses of Television*, John Hartley (1999) referenced Chantal Mouffe, among others, to articulate a conception of media and democracy radically different from the one to be found in the work of the traditional proponents of PSB, such as Garnham and Tracey. Their arguments are founded, not always transparently, on a dichotomy between modernity (good) and postmodernity (bad).

Their binary conceptions can be captured as follows:

modernity	postmodernity
state	market
civil society	individualism
parliamentary democracy	community(ies)
citizen	consumer
national	global
class politics	identity politics
equality/fraternity	liberty
universal rationality	discursive particularity
public sphere	public sphericules
truth	plausibility/persuasion/seduction
information	entertainment
PSB	commercial media
real	virtual

I want to argue that John Hartley's work has the great advantage of breaking these binaries, which dog and limit the discussion of the media and democracy. It presents a complex and sophisticated argument against a narrowly modernist view of what democracy is and the claims of PSB to have a privileged relationship to it. In all the books he has published during the 1990s (Hartley 1992a, 1992b, 1996), and most recently and most synoptically in *Uses of Television* (Hartley 1999), Hartley developed an account of postmodern television (for him, television is quintessentially postmodern in its role in the formation of publics and of citizens) (Hartley 1999, 40).

Hartley's (1999) argument, in fact, is that television's strength is that it is both "premodern" and "postmodern"—what he called "transmodern." It is postmodern in that the boundaries dividing the fields of government, media, and education in modernity are blurred in postmodernity, where government and education are largely carried on within the field of media. And it is "premodern" because it is an oral medium and in it is re-created, at least virtually, the condition of the agora. In the agora, democracy (which belongs to the field of government), drama (which belongs to the field of media), and didactics (which belongs to the field of education) were "the same thing, practised in the same place by and for the same people, whose assembly in sight of each other *constituted* the audience" (p. 7). In television, these three fields are similarly merged.

Hartley (1999) went on to make a vigorous case for the preeminent role of the media, especially television, in what he called transmodern teaching and the formation of cultural citizenship. For him, PSB has no claims to a special role in relation to education or democracy. On the contrary, it is seen as a quintessentially "modern" and therefore partial institution, fixed in a period of history already surpassed. He went further and suggested that PSB is part of an "antidemocratic" left and right pessimism about television that predates the electronic media and has its origins in nineteenth-century fears about being swamped by the other (blacks, the poor, etc.) (pp. 104–5). Furthermore, in their desire to discipline the tastes of the "popular classes," the custodians of

PSB belong to the not-to-be-trusted "knowledge class." It is not to be trusted because it

> wants to take power over information media and cultural technologies like television, not only by running the business on behalf of the shareholders, but by regulating it, and controlling the literacies and discourses by means of which it is understood culturally. (P. 124)

This syndrome (or "habitus") is labeled by Hartley "democracy as defeat" (p. 119).

What does Hartley mean by "democracy" here? Sometimes, it seems he confused the concept of the democratic with the merely demotic. However, in *Uses of Television,* there is an elaborate theory of citizenship, building on the classic account of Thomas Marshall. Marshall described three historically succeeding but now coexisting types of citizenship: (1) civil, involving rights and freedoms; (2) political, involving representation; and (3) social, involving welfare. To this, Hartley added a fourth and a fifth: "cultural" citizenship and what he called do-it-yourself (DIY) citizenship. It is presumably clear what the first three have to do with democracy as it is usually understood, but what about cultural and DIY citizenship?

For Hartley (1999), cultural citizenship has to do with "identity" in the sense of identity politics—the "politics of the internally colonized demographics of modernity" (the poor, women, people of color) (p. 167). The second—DIY citizenship—supersedes (but continues to coexist with) the first. It is based on difference rather than identity and consists in the "practice of putting together an identity from the available choices, patterns and opportunities on offer in the semiosphere and the mediasphere" (p. 178). With DIY citizenship, " 'citizenship' is no longer simply a matter of a social contract between state and subject, no longer even a matter of acculturation to the heritage of a given community; DIY citizenship is a choice people can make for themselves" (p. 178).

It may seem that it is difficult to see the difference between Hartley's account of DIY citizenship and mere consumerism, that is, the freedom to choose products that will situate the buyer in a semiotic landscape of "style." However, I believe Hartley's views are motivated by a very different purpose than that of commerce, whether it be the commercial television industry or the advertising industry. For, even though he did not want to be lumped with the killjoy social improvers who haunt PSB or regulatory institutions, Hartley's arguments have a deeply ethical motivation. It might not be its explicit intention, but for Hartley (1999), popular television (that is, the television people love to watch) has the ethical effect of teaching cultural citizenship. It does this by "population-gathering," that is, by "gathering populations which might have little in common, and promoting among them a sense of common identity as television audiences" (p. 158); it teaches "cross-demographic communication" by providing a sense of intersubjectivity between various identity groups (pp. 31–32); it teaches audiences "cultural neighbourliness," that is, the ability to "stand back from insisting on their own rights and tolerate the peculiarities of those around them" (p. 172); it "ameliorates our manners" (p. 180).

But does this have much to do with democracy in the political sense? It would appear not. Hartley (1999) made constant reference to "post politics" (e.g., p. 120) without really explaining what he meant, although there are hints (p. 121) he was referring to the common observation that people now are less and less inclined to participate in electoral politics—witness low voter turnouts in places where voting is not compulsory. For Hartley, it appears, democracy and politics are antagonistic concepts; perhaps he would even see politics as the enemy of democracy—he spoke of the need for "democratization without politicization" (p. 161). We are indeed a far cry from the Habermasian conception of politics and the public sphere outlined by Garnham.

The kind of democracy Hartley (1999) had in mind is not political democracy but semiotic democracy—what Hartley called "semiotic self-determination," also known as DIY citizenship. Democratization of semiosis leads to a "truly sovereign community," a population "among whom relationships, decisions and ideas are negotiated and arbitrated." It is the "citizenship of the future; decentralized, post-adversarial, based on self-determination not state coercion" (p. 161): a truly panglossian vision.

A significant defect in the Hartley position is that even though he has an ostensibly reconciliatory purpose in trying to link the premodern and the postmodern in his conception of transmodern, he was too eager to discredit the fear-and-defeat critics of television. He established such an absolutely uncrossable divide between "modern" and "postmodern," between "discourse" and "politics" (the whole book is structured around various sets of binaries), that his argument ends up reinstating the eternal and undecidable wrangle between the Habermasian and the "postmodern," which does not advance matters much at all. He was so caught up in undermining the foundational high-culture/low-culture opposition that he saw in most of both left and right criticism of television and in celebrating television's delightful demotic messiness that he underplayed the way in which television, and in fact any form of public culture, is structured by a series of power-laden discourses that require interrogation. It is not that he was unaware of this—it is that he underplayed it.

However, for all its problems, I believe Hartley's work as a whole delivers some definite gains for the overall debate. There can be no doubt that he succeeded in deconstructing media pessimism of both the left and right and establishing once and for all that commercial/popular television does not need to be cast as a "bad object." I think he also made the case well that in the present environment, commercial television and public service television are on a course of convergence. He also made the point, predictable given his views on television, that new media are ideally suited for DIY citizenship because of enhanced interactivity and connectivity (Hartley 1999, 187). How then can we apply these insights to the issue of the role of PSB in a changing media environment?

Conclusion

The multichannel and digital environment changes profoundly the basis of the argument for the centrality of PSB in the media landscape. The argument made

sense as long as PSB existed in an atmosphere of relative spectrum scarcity—
a monopoly in Britain and the rest of Europe for so long and a situation of
controlled competition in Canada and Australia. In the passage from what we
can as a shorthand call the "welfare state" to neoliberalism (Rose and Miller
1992; Rose 1996), the political rationality of PSB (to educate, inform, and
influence taste) has been displaced by a new political rationality in which the
paternalistic state has no role. In such a situation, is PSB just one more item
of choice in a regime governed by individual consumer sovereignty? And, if
so, is its claim to a special status no longer valid?

I have argued already that the concept of democracy and the public sphere,
and its role in providing a defense of PSB, articulated in its classic form by
Nicholas Garnham but implicit in the work of other well-known proponents
of PSB such as Michael Tracey, fails. The critique of this position, which we
find in the work of John Hartley, provides a different view of the connection
between media and democracy—one that embraces a pluralization of society,
a pluralization of spaces for citizenly discourse, and a deconstruction of the
traditional hierarchies of value that have traditionally privileged the output of
public service broadcasters. Hartley argued that even old media (radio and television) have always done citizen-forming duty. This is even more evident in
the new media environment where some of the traditional arguments for the
special status of PSB, namely its ability to cater to minorities (the "market failure" argument), are undermined by the growth in channel availability. The
transnational reach of new media allows a greater diversity of channels catering to more and more specialized tastes and needs.

In my view, it is time to stop taking rhetorical positions in which PSB is
given some universal defense in terms of a list of unchanging principles, such
as those articulated by the United Kingdom's Broadcasting Review Unit in the
1980s and recirculated in a number of writings on PSB ever since.[7] The dominance of Europe, including the United Kingdom, in setting the agenda for
arguments in defense of PSB has obscured the great diversity of forms that
PSB takes at different sites. The failure of general arguments for the special-
ness of PSB has allowed free market–inspired arguments to gain purchase. PSB
needs to be looked at in each site where it exists and in the context of the particular media ecology in which it exists. Positions that give it an automatically
privileged position with respect to quality, democracy, and citizenship can no
longer be sustained. We need to provide very situated microanalyses of our
"public broadcasters" within their particular media and not endlessly regurgi-
tate tired and superseded general arguments about PSB's natural superiority.

In Australia right now, such an analysis would have to take into consideration, among other things, the following features of the media landscape, in
no particular order of importance. One, that thirty years of Australian content
regulation are looking very shaky in the face of the impossibility of imposing
local content rules on free-to-air broadcasters while exempting pay operators.
Two, it would have to pay attention to the complicated role of the Special
Broadcasting Service in both serving "ethnic" audiences and acting as the "cos-

mopolitan" broadcaster catering to taste elites. Three, it would need to analyze the role that broadcasting plays in mediating the troubled relationship between indigenous and nonindigenous Australians. Four, it would have to pay heed to the unevenness of population between the country and the city and the regional diversity of Australia. Five, it would have to be sensitive to the limitations of commercial media in providing independent news and comment.[8] Six, it would take into account the extreme concentration of media in Australia, with virtually only three big owners who carve up between them the press, free-to-air broadcasting, and much of the new media.

Quite different stories would be needed in other places. I would not presume to say how they should be told. However, I do believe that the "democracy as defeat" position, as Hartley called it, has absolutely no future, and we would all be better served if it were laid to rest. I must confess, I cannot see the future for publicly funded media; I am not sure it has one. But I do know that the nostalgic harking back to an earlier time when PSB provided a secure and predictable diet for a coherent national audience is fruitless. We need to move beyond it.

Notes

1. It might be more adequate to call this a "habitus" than an argument. To explore this fully would require another article, but what is notable about the debate about public service broadcasting (PSB) is, first of all, the passion with which it is conducted and, secondly, the sheer volume of endlessly repetitious restatements of the "mission" of PSB. A PSB attitude or attachment might qualify as a "habitus" in Bourdieu's (1990) sense, that is, "systems of durable, transposable dispositions, structured structures, predisposed to function as structuring structures, that is, as principles which generate and organise practices and representations" (p. 53). Thomas Streeter (1996) has another view on it:

> I argue that it [the debate over broadcasting] can be seen as an attempt, characteristic of twentieth century liberalism, to regain the footing lost in the shifting sands of one set of contradictions—the incoherence of atomistic individualism and of its industrial correlate, laissez-faire business principles—by shifting weight in the direction of another set of (equally contradictory) liberal principles—a faith in the power of expertise and objective scientific knowledge to make manifest a transcendent, reified "public interest." (P. 10)

2. This is really only true for the European tradition of media theory (which has deeply influenced thinking about broadcasting in Australia, New Zealand, Canada, etc.). Such a statement would be very odd in the context of the very different tradition of the United States, with its emphasis on a First Amendment approach to broadcasting policy and its very different broadcasting history (Streeter 1996, pass. and 188–89).

3. These generalizations, of course, only apply to the "advanced democracies," that is, the United States, United Kingdom, Canada, Australia, New Zealand, and Western Europe, although each of these cases is different, and a really detailed account of this problem would need to take account of variations. The connections between the media and democracy in places such as China, Thailand, Singapore, Indonesia, Russia, and so

forth obviously present a very different and interesting set of problems about which this article unfortunately has nothing to say.

4. Michael Schudson (1998) reminded us that the end of citizenship and public life has been proclaimed regularly since 1840, and as yet they do not seem to have quite disappeared (p. 295).

5. Robert Putnam's (1995) article, "Bowling Alone," argued that the erosion of social capital was reflected in the decline in the number of people who go bowling in bowling leagues (as against alone or in private groups). One of his critics, Nicholas Lemann (1996), riposted with an article called "Kicking in Groups," showing that in the same period, participation in soccer had increased astronomically.

6. One of the surprising things I discovered while researching this article is that there is remarkably little connection between political theorists and media theorists. I found that those theorists who are analyzing democracy now pay remarkably little attention to the role of the media (e.g., Barber 1994; Bauman 1999). Those who are analyzing the current role of the media in fostering democracy for the most part pay scant attention to recent work in political theory regarding the current nature of democracy, although there are honorable exceptions (e.g., Hacker 1996; Calabrese and Borchert 1996; Dahlgren 1998). For example, a leading proponent of such a model, Benjamin Barber (1994), was able to talk about the "conversations" citizens should be having in such an ideal democracy without discussing the role of the media—short sighted, to say the least.

7. These eight principles are (1) universality of availability, (2) universality of appeal, (3) provision for minorities, (4) a commitment to the education of the public, (5) distance from vested interests, (6) structured to encourage competition in programming standards not for audiences, (7) freedom for the program maker, and (8) fostering a public sphere (Tracey 1998, 26–32).

8. This was brought home to the Australian public (and the regulators) in 2000 by the biggest scandal to ever hit the Australian media scene. This was a set of events that has come to be known as the "cash-for-comment" affair, where it was revealed that a phenomenally popular and influential talk-back host had been bought by the major banks of Australia for several million dollars a year and was peddling their scripts as if they were his own political commentaries.

References

Barber, Benjamin. 1994. *Strong Democracy*. Berkeley: University of California Press.

Bauman, Zygmunt. 1999. *In Search of Politics*. Cambridge, UK: Polity.

Bourdieu, Pierre. 1990. *The Logic of Practice*. Cambridge, UK: Polity.

Calabrese, Andrew, and Mark Borchert. 1996. Prospects for Electronic Democracy in the United States: Rethinking Communication and Social Policy. *Media Culture and Society* 18 (2): 249–68.

Carey, James W. 1993. The Mass Media and Democracy: Between the Modern and the Postmodern. *Journal of International Affairs* 47 (1): 1–21. Available from http://web66.infotrac.galegroup.com/itw/onfomark/579/247/70224356w3/purl=rc2_EIM_2_the+).

Coleman, Stephen. 2000. The New Media and Democratic Politics. *New Media and Society* 1 (1):67–74.

Curran, James. 1992. Mass Media and Democracy: A Reappraisal. In *Mass Media and Society*, edited by James Curran and Michael Gurevitch, 82–117. London: Edward Arnold.

Dahlgren, Peter. 1998. *Public Service Media, Old and New: Vitalising a Civic Culture?* The 1998 Spry Memorial Lecture. Available from http://www.fas.umontreal.ca/com/spry/spry-pd-lec.html.

Garnham, Nicholas. 1983. Public Service versus the Market. *Screen* 24 (1): 6–27.

———. 1986. Media and the Public Sphere. In *Communicating Politics,* edited by P. Golding et al., 37–53. Leicester, UK: Leicester University Press.

———. 1996. The Media and the Public Sphere. In *Habermas and the Public Sphere,* edited by Craig Calhoun, 359–76. Cambridge, MA: MIT Press.

Gitlin, Todd. 1998. Public Sphere or Public Sphericules? In *Media, Ritual and Identity,* edited by Tamar Liebes and James Curran, 168–74. London: Routledge.

Hacker, Kenneth. 1996. Missing Links in the Evolution of Electronic Democratization. *Media, Culture and Society* 18 (2): 213–32.

Hartley, John. 1992a. *The Politics of Pictures: The Creation of the Public in the Age of Popular Media.* London: Routledge.

———. 1992b. *Tele-ology: Studies in Television.* London: Routledge.

———. 1996. *Popular Reality: Journalism, Modernity, Popular Culture.* London: Arnold.

———. 1999. *Uses of Television.* London: Routledge.

Keane, John. 1995. Structural Transformations of the Public Sphere. *Communication Review* 1 (1):1–22.

Lemann, Nicholas. 1996. Kicking in Groups. *Atlantic Monthly* 277:22–26.

Mouffe, Chantal. 1992. Democratic Citizenship and the Political Community. In *Dimensions of Radical Democracy: Pluralism, Citizenship, Community,* edited by Chantal Mouffe, 225–39. London: Verso.

Murdock, Graham. 1992. Citizens, Consumers and Public Culture. In *Media Cultures: Reappraising Transnational Media,* edited by Michael Skovmand and Kim Christian Schroder, 17–41. London: Routledge.

Putnam, Robert. 1995. Bowling Alone. *Journal of Democracy* 6:65–78.

Rose, Nikolas. 1996. Governing "Advanced" Liberal Democracies. In *Foucault and Political Reason: Liberalism, Neo-liberalism and Rationalities of Government,* edited by Andrew Barry, Thomas Osborne, and Nikolas Rose, 37–64. Chicago: University of Chicago Press.

Rose, Nikolas, and Peter Miller. 1992. Political Power beyond the State: Problematics of Government: *British Journal of Sociology* 43 (2): 172–205.

Schudson, Michael. 1998. *The Good Citizen: A History of American Civil Life.* New York: Free Press.

Streeter, Thomas. 1996. *Selling the Air: A Critique of the Policy of Commercial Broadcasting in the United States.* Chicago: University of Chicago Press.

Tracey, Michael. 1998. *The Decline and Fall of Public Service Broadcasting.* Oxford, UK: Oxford University Press.

Walzer, Michael. 1992. The Civil Society Argument. In *Dimensions of Radical Democracy: Pluralism, Citizenship, Community,* edited by Chantal Mouffe, 89–107. London: Verso.

Yeatman, Anna. 1994. *Postmodern Revisionings of the Political.* New York: Routledge.

A Response to Elizabeth Jacka's "Democracy as Defeat"

Nicholas Garnham

Professor Jacka, in this [volume], has done me the dubious honor of taking my work as representative of the position on democracy and public service broadcasting that she dubs "modernist." She argues that this position is no longer—if it ever was—a useful way to think about either democracy or the future of public service broadcasting. This is, she claims, because the modernist conception of democracy is ahistorical and no longer suited to "postmodern" societies and because it sees the impact of the media, and especially television, within a high- culture/low-culture optic and as part of the decline from modernity (good) to postmodernity (bad).

In its place, she argues for a concept of "radical democracy" (per Chantal Mouffe) linked to John Hartley's notion of postmodern television and semiotic democracy. And while she is clear that the old arguments for public service broadcasting, of which she takes me as an exemplar, have failed, she concludes rather uneasily that the new, improved postmodern positions have no need of either the concept or the practice. At least this is one less thing to worry about. But I say her conclusion is uneasy because she still seems to be concerned by regulatory questions relating to the structure and content of broadcasting in Australia. Such questions are close to the concerns of those wishing to defend public service broadcasting but that I think would be completely illegitimate from Hartley's perspective—attempts on the part of the dreaded "knowledge class" to police popular discourses and pleasures.

I do not want to waste space or the time of readers defending in any detail positions first articulated more than fifteen years ago and in the very specific context of British broadcasting policy debates. Suffice it to say that I do not recognize my position in Hartley's "democracy as defeat" description. I do not think television is either bad or part of a history of decline.

Indeed, it is hard to see how one could argue in favor of the British Broadcasting Corporation (BBC) if one thought TV was bad. Part of the case always was that democracy was an unfinished historical development and that while the BBC's record was clearly open to criticism from both democrats and libertarians on both political and cultural grounds, it was nonetheless a model to be improved rather than discarded. I do not think one can make any easy dichotomy between public and commercial broadcasting. Indeed, historically, it is clearly the case that many of the advances in the use of television as part of the public sphere in the United Kingdom were pioneered by commercial TV. But, crucially, it was public service regulated. I also agree with Jacka that public service broadcasting is not a universal ideal type but a set of historically concrete institutions and practices that require what she calls "situated microanalyses." To take only one obvious example, the practice of public service broadcasting has never been coterminous with the commercial-noncommercial divide. Indeed, many broadcasters who claim a public service remit are advertising financed. However, I do continue to believe—and, as it happens, opinion poll evidence shows that a significant proportion of the audience shares this view—that the presence or absence of advertising funding makes a difference.

I wish to focus on what Jacka rightly identifies as the key issues at stake—how we conceive of democracy, whether as actual practice or ideal type, and what role, if any, the media in general and public service broadcasting in particular might play within it. Jacka's argument is structured around two questions: What does the term *democracy* mean now? and Is it true that public service broadcasting makes a unique and indispensable contribution to it?

These questions are undoubtedly in the right order, and I will pay much greater attention to the question of democracy than to the question of public service broadcasting. For those who are interested, my wider, and most recently considered, views on theories of democracy and the role of the media can be found in Garnham (2000, chap. 8).

Jacka argues that the public sphere position, and my view in particular, is based on a liberal or representative/republican concept of democracy as its ideal type—that this concept is a historical and thus inevitably reads current developments as decline, hence the "democracy as defeat" label. Against this conception, which she calls "modernist," Jacka proposes a postmodernist democracy, which, following Mouffe, she refers to as "radical democracy." This is a version of democracy that "recognizes" we now live in plural societies, societies in which it is impossible to imagine that there is a way to define the "general good." In terms of the relation between this version of democracy and the media, she then turns to Hartley and his concept of postmodern television as the field within which government and education are largely carried on. This is supposedly where cultural and do-it-yourself (DIY) citizenship is created in a process of "democratization without politicization" and "democratization of semiosis." For me and my ilk, Jacka argues, media is at best a vehicle for democracy; for Hartley and others, it is democracy.

I agree that the public sphere position is based on a concept of representative republican democracy, but that is where my agreement ends. First, it is not true that it interprets the current position as one of defeat and decline. Inherent in the public sphere approach is a view of representative republicanism as unfinished business, as a historically developing form blocked and distorted by other social developments, including but not exclusively economic developments. It follows that public service broadcasting in its British form was never seen as an ideal type but as a historically developed form, worth defending certainly for its potential and in part on its record but as flawed in its actual performance as representative democracy itself. Second, Jacka claims that the supposedly superior postmodern concept of democracy is based on a "pragmatics of persuasion," when it is precisely such a pragmatics that lies at the heart of the public sphere. What then is at issue is the actual mechanics of this pragmatics and its relation to availability of and access to the media fields within which this process of persuasion is carried on. In terms of pragmatics, it certainly is true that the public sphere approach has placed too much emphasis on the "high journalism" model to the neglect of more effective forms of debate and persuasion. At the same time, it is, I think, entirely reasonable to argue that appeals to standards of scientificity and truth are more appropriate, and more socially beneficial, than appeals to emotion and prejudice in important areas of public democratic debate, perhaps particularly where ethical issues are involved. In terms of media fields, it is difficult, I think, to sustain the argument that structures of regulation and control have no influence on who is able to persuade whom of what.

But in the end, the core disagreement I have with Jacka's position is more fundamental. It concerns the nature and purpose of democratic politics. In brief, there has been a tendency among postmodern thinkers in their concern with discourse and identity and their understandable dissatisfaction with the ways in which existing representative politics has handled these issues to evacuate the central fields of political power, the exercise of the monopoly of force, and the distribution of resources. In the polities we all actually inhabit, we may want to agree philosophically that we cannot agree—indeed, that in the name of difference it is positively desirable not to agree about the common good—but in practice, either a version of the common good or the good of special interest groups will be imposed as a result of the political decisions of our representatives. In short, you can argue for as much pluralism as you like, but in the end, and necessarily, decisions will be taken that affect to a greater or lesser extent all citizens. Indeed, that is why we have politics at all and why democracy matters as a form of that politics.

In the end, politics is concerned not with discourse, that is at best the means to the end, but with rule. Forms of rule are inescapable because we live as social beings necessarily caught up in a common destiny. Politics thus concerns not our differences but those matters we unavoidably share in common. The unavoidability of this focus of politics on the common good is indeed well illustrated by Mouffe's vision of radical democracy. Citing Mouffe, Jacka argues that modern polities cannot share a vision of the common good but then argues that they must be based on a "grammar of political conduct" and a common recognition of a set of ethical-political values. What is this but a description of the common good and one indeed remarkably similar to that proposed by advocates of the public sphere approach. Where Mouffe's approach, and Jacka's in following her, comes unstuck is in proposing that this common good should be noninstrumental, as it is impossible to imagine a noninstrumental politics. To stress the key point once again, politics is about taking decisions that affect all citizens. Democracy is about ensuring that those decisions are, so far as possible, controlled by the people. The question then at issue is the process by which this is done. In polities of the size and complexity of modern polities, the best you can hope for, in my view, is that such decisions are taken within a structure of representative democracy informed by a widely accessible public debate.

It is within this context and vision of the core problem of democracy that I and others have argued for the potentially important role of public service broadcasting. To use Mouffe's language, we think that the "grammar of political conduct" must include a central place for the relatively uncoerced exercise of those investigatory, expositional, and debating functions that have been traditionally labeled journalism and that the exercise of those functions has been, is, and will continue to be threatened by the pressures of both state and commerce. This is not to argue that commercial media cannot and have not fulfilled some of these public sphere functions. Of course they have. Indeed, it would be hard for an advocate of the public sphere position to argue otherwise, since the founding model of the bourgeois public sphere was based on commercial print media. Nor is it to argue that the actual practice of public service broadcasting in its many different institutional forms has fulfilled its public sphere potential. It is clear that depending on the country concerned, it too often has been either too close to the interests of the state and the political class controlling the state or has allowed its agenda and definition of political issues to be defined too easily by an elite. Or it has pursued a broadly conservative, elite cultural policy and in so doing lost its necessary contact with the majority of the public.

Nor is it to close off the possibility that the public sphere potential of electronic media may be better delivered institutionally through regulated commercial media than through a classic stand-alone, license-financed broadcaster on the model of the BBC. That is a matter of pragmatic politics in each national or regional situation. But I do think that it is empirically demonstrable that the model of public service broadcasting in the United Kingdom (and here I include the total ecology of U.K. broadcasting, both the BBC and the highly regulated commercial sector and the very specific competitive interrelation between them) has played a more positive role in its relationship to democracy than has the commercially driven system in the United States. Thus, I also think—and this was the context of my original writings on this issue—that since we already had a broadcasting system with the BBC as the dominant player alongside highly regulated commercial operators, it was better to defend and build on the potential of that system in a public sphere direction than to simply give in to the forces of rampant deregulated commercialism.

All of this is to say nothing about public service broadcasting and culture in its wider sense. But in thinking through these problems, I do think that Hartley's approach, to which Jacka gives much weight, is less than helpful. First, as my remarks above have already hinted, I do not think it is either useful or legitimate to transfer the concept of democracy, and with it the concept of citizenship, to the cultural sphere en bloc. Its advantages as a rhetorical strategy are clear. Hartley identifies aspects of contemporary life and his view of the media's roles as "democratic" and as forms of "citizenship." Since no one wishes to be seen as undemocratic or against citizenship, this protects the position from critical examination. The dangers of this extension of the concept of democracy to what Hartley calls cultural and DIY citizenship become starkly apparent when he opposes democracy to politics and proposes replacing political democracy with "semiotic" democracy. In my view, once you separate democracy from politics, understood as the arena of common social decision making, the term loses its pertinence and changes its meaning.

The point about the historically successive attributes of citizenship analyzed by Thomas Marshall, which Hartley now wishes to extend, was that they pertained to attributes that were first fought for and then granted or attained as rights common to all citizens, whether to freedoms or resources. The problem with Hartley's concept of cultural citizenship is that it confuses two things. On one hand, cultural citizenship can be seen as an extension of civil rights, as the extension of the principle of religious toleration to cover all forms of identity formation. On the other, it can be seen as an extension of welfare rights to cover access to cultural resources. As the first case, and the example of religious toleration, indicates, the struggle for cultural citizenship in this sense is neither postmodern nor in any way particularly related to television. The issues raised are first the boundary between public and private—which forms of cultural practice and identity formation can we agree, democratically, should be left to the parties themselves outside the realm of both state regulation or support within what has classically been seen as civil society? And which, on the other hand, because of their impact on the lives of all citizens, deserve and require either state regulation or support? In no democratic polity can such matters be settled either easily, without conflict, or once and for all.

The second issue is the limits to toleration. In any democratic polity, there will be such boundary disputes, and there will be, if not theoretically legitimate at least pragmatic, limits to the range of identities and practices to which the polity, however democratic, can remain neutral if it is to remain a polity at all. The claim on cultural resources, on the other hand, raises a different, if related, set of issues. As I have said, one form of identity politics is a claim for toleration. But increasingly another form is a claim on scarce resources, whether access to broadcasting frequencies and production resources or other cultural subsidies. We find here one of the contradictions of identity politics. Too often there is an attempt to combine a request for "recognition" and a share of public resources that such recognition brings with it and, at the same time, to demonize the very common decision making, the politics, that must inevitably go with such resource distribution.

In the case of Hartley/Jacka, this general approach raises two issues. The first is whether there are ways alternative to and superior to the market for distributing common cultural resources. This is not a simple matter and is certainly not a simple either-or choice, if only because the market is itself not an homogeneous, unstructured, and unregulated entity. But it does seem to me that in approaching this debate, Hartley takes an excessively pollyannaish view of the practices, and identity-forming effects, of commercial media.

As I understand it, there are two arguments here. On one hand, we have semiotic democracy because people can freely construct their identities in a process of DIY citizenship by freely choosing from the available choices, patterns, and opportunities offered by the mediasphere—choices, patterns, and opportunities largely provided and expanded by commercial media. This is contrasted with bad old modern citizenship, which was apparently a contract between state and subject and a process of acculturation to the heritage of a given community. If you start with this rather strange view of the nature of modern democratic citizenship, it is easy to see how you can be seduced by the supposed liberating advantages of the contemporary commercialized mediasphere and can bracket public service broadcasting the ancien régime.

In my view, this position exaggerates both the freedoms that individual media consumers exercise (which is not the same as simply seeing commercial television as a bad object) and the role that media consumption plays, for better or worse, in the construction of personal identities. But perhaps more seriously, what lies behind Hartley's position is the old, noble, romantic, but discredited dream of anarchism, in which the enemy is the state and politics allied with the priests—now the knowledge class (of which, of course, Hartley is himself a member). And the ideal is precisely "democratization without politics" and a "citizenship of the future; decentralized, post-adversarial, based on self-determination not state coercion" (Hartley 1999, 161). There is much to be said about the problems facing contemporary democracies and the concept of citizenship in the modern world. But that they are becoming either postadversarial or more based on self-determination is not immediately obvious. As Jacka herself says, this is a truly panglossian view. It is thus difficult to see why she sees it as helpful in analyzing the future of public service broadcasting.

More useful to her is Hartley's view of popular television as a teacher of cultural citizenship, a pedagogic role it fulfills by "gathering populations which might have little in common, and promoting among them a sense of common identity as television audiences" (Hartley 1999, 158). By so doing, it is claimed it teaches "cultural neighbourliness" and thus "ameliorates our manners." This is a somewhat updated version of Elias (2000), and there is much to be said for it. However, it is largely incompatible with the previous notion of DIY citizenship and self-determination. Indeed, it is more usually mobilized as one of the key arguments for public service broadcasting, particularly in its generalist form in opposition to the increasingly themed and fragmented channel offerings of commercial TV. It is an argument also more usually attacked by the semiotic democrats of the Hartley type as smacking of cultural policing.

Why these common identities as television audiences should be in any way superior to or, from the point of view of their democratic potential, different from other identities supposedly fostered or promoted by public service television, such as belonging to a nation or cultural heritage, is not clear. Whether popular television has had this ameliorating effect on our manners is a matter for empirical investigation. But it is only by the sleight of hand of equating popular TV with commercial TV and equating public service with the unpopular, elitist, and killjoy that it is possible to sustain the argument that the audiences/publics built by commercial TV are in some way superior to, more liberated than, and less coerced than those constructed by public service. In my view, the opposite is, if anything, a more realistic position.

In conclusion, therefore, I wish to stress that the arguments between Jacka and myself turn on how we think about democracy. The issue of public service broadcasting is from this perspective very much secondary. While I share much of Jacka's pessimism about the future of public service broadcasting in its various forms, at least in the short term, I see this as no more than a minor setback for democracy—it faces much more serious problems and opponents than that. But it is interesting to note that the questions and problems that Jacka raises with regard to current Australian broadcasting policy have a distinctly familiar ring and can only be seen as problems, I would argue, from within a framework of thought broadly supportive of public service broadcasting and some notion of the public sphere as an important component of democratic politics. From a Hartleyan perspective, they are simply not problems but hangovers from the bad old modernist days of state coercion and killjoy cultural policing. I refuse to equate public service with elitism and the popular with the commercial. If the only alternatives are "democracy as defeat" and the pollyannaism of "democratization without politics," we really are in serious trouble.

References

Elias, Norbert. 2000. *The Civilizing Process.* Translated by Edmund Jephcott. London: Basil Blackwell.

Garnham, Nicholas. 2000. *Emancipation, the Media, and Modernity.* Oxford, UK: Oxford University Press.

Hartley, John. 1999. *Uses of Television.* London: Routledge.

Entertainment Wars
Television Culture After 9/11

Lynn Spigel

After the attacks of September 11, traditional forms of entertainment had to reinvent their place in U.S. life and culture. The de rigueur violence of mass media—both news and fiction—no longer seemed business as usual. While Hollywood usually defends its mass-destruction ethos with claims to "free speech," constitutional rights, and industry-wide discretion (à la ratings systems), in the weeks following September 11 the industry exhibited (whether for sincere or cynical reasons) a new will toward "tastefulness" as potentially trauma-inducing films like Warner's *Collateral Damage* were pulled from release. On television, violent movies also came under network scrutiny. USA canceled its prime-time run of *The Siege* (which deals with Arab terrorists who plot to bomb New York). At TBS violence-packed films like *Lethal Weapon* were replaced with family fare like *Look Who's Talking.* TNT replaced its 1970s retro lineup of *Superman, King Kong,* and *Carrie* with *Close Encounters of the Third Kind, Grease,* and *Jaws* (although exactly why the blood-sucking shark in Jaws seemed less disturbing than the menstruating teen in *Carrie* already begs questions about exactly what constitutes "terror" in the minds of Hollywood executives).[1]

But it wasn't just the "hard" realities of violence that came under self-imposed censorship. Light entertainment and "diversions" of all kinds also didn't feel right. Humorists Dave Letterman, Jay Leno, Craig Kilborn, Conan O'Brien, and Jon Stewart met the late-night audience with dead seriousness. While *Saturday Night Live* did return to humor, its jokes were officially sanctioned by an opening act that included a somber performance by Paul Simon, the entire New York Fire Department, and Mayor Giuliani himself. When producer Lorne Michaels asked the mayor if it was okay to be funny, Giuliani joked, "Why start now?" (implicitly informing viewers that it was, in fact, okay to laugh). In the midst of the new sincerity, numerous critics summarily declared that the attacks on the Pentagon and World Trade Center had brought about the "end of irony."[2]

Lynn Spigel, "Entertainment Wars: Television Culture After 9/11." From *American Quarterly,* 56:2 (June 2004), pp. 235–270. Copyright © The American Studies Association. Reprinted with permission of The Johns Hopkins University Press.

Despite such bombastic declarations, however, many industry leaders were actually in a profound state of confusion about just what it was that the public wanted. Even while industry leaders were eager to censor trauma-inducing images of any kind, video outlets reported that, when left to their own discretion, consumers were eagerly purchasing terrorist flicks like *The Siege* and *The Towering Inferno*. One video retailer noted an "uneasy" feeling about consumer desire for films like *The Towering Inferno*, and one store owner even "moved such videos so they were arranged with only the spines showing, obscuring the covers."[3] Meanwhile, Internet companies worried about the hundreds of vulgar domain names for which people applied in the hopes of setting up Web sites. One major domain name reseller halted auctions for several names it considered tasteless, including "NewYorkCarnage.com."[4] As these cases suggest, the media industries had to balance their own public image as discriminating custodians of culture with the vagaries of public taste.

Given its historical status as a regulated private industry ideally meant to operate in the "public interest," television was the medium hardest hit by this conflict between maintaining the image of "public servant" and the need to cater to the public taste (or at least to what advertisers think the public likes). Getting back to the normal balance between its public service and entertainment/commercial functions posed problems for broadcasters and cablers alike.[5] In the midst of the turmoil, the Academy of Television Arts and Sciences and CBS postponed the Emmy Award ceremonies twice.

To be sure, television executives' nervous confusion was rooted in the broader havoc that 9/11 wreaked on television—not just as an industry but also as "a whole way of life."[6] Most fundamentally, on September 11, the everydayness of television itself was suddenly disrupted by news of something completely "alien" to the usual patterns of domestic TV viewing.[7] The non-stop commercial-free coverage, which lasted for a full week on major broadcast networks and cable news networks, contributed to a sense of estrangement from ordinary life, not simply because of the unexpected nature of the attack itself but also because television's normal routines—its everyday schedule and ritualized flow—had been disordered. As Mary Ann Doane has argued about television catastrophes more generally, not only television's temporal flow, but also its central narrational agency breaks down in moments of catastrophe.[8] We are in a world where narrative comes undone and where the "real" seems to have no sense of meaning beyond repetition of the horrifying event itself. This, she claims, in turn threatens to expose the underlying catastrophe of all TV catastrophes—the breakdown of capitalism, the end of the cash flow, the end of the logic of consumption on which U.S. television is predicated.

By the weekend of September 15, television news anchors began to tell us that it was their national duty to return to the "normal" everyday schedule of television entertainment, a return meant to coincide with Washington's call for a return to normalcy (and, hopefully, normal levels of consumerism). Of course, for the television industry, resuming the normal TV schedule also meant a return to commercial breaks and, therefore, TV's very sustenance. Already besieged by declining ad revenues before the attacks, the television industry lost an estimated $320 million in advertising revenue in the week following the attacks.[9] So, even while the media industries initially positioned entertainment and commercials as being "in bad taste," just one week after the attacks the television networks discursively realigned commercial entertainment with the patriotic goals of the nation.[10] In short—and most paradoxically—entertainment and commercialism were rearticulated as television's "public service."

By September 27, Jack Valenti, president and CEO of the Motion Picture Association of America, gave this "commercialism as patriotism" ethos an official stamp of approval. In a column for *Variety,* he wrote: "Here in Hollywood we must continue making our movies and our TV programs. For a time, during this mourning period, we need to be sensitive to how we tell a story. But in time—and that time will surely come—life will go on, must go on. We in Hollywood have to get on with doing our creative work. . . . The country needs what we create."[11] Valenti's message was part of a much older myth of show business—a myth that ran through countless Depression-era and World War II musicals—a myth of transcendence in which showbiz folks put aside their petty differences and join together in patriotic song. If in the 1940s this myth of transcendence emboldened audiences for wartime sacrifice, now, in the twenty-first century, this transcendent myth of show business is oddly conjoined with national mandates for a return to "normal" consumer pleasures. In a bizarrely Baudrillardian moment, President Bush addressed the nation, begging us to return to normal life by getting on planes and taking our families to Disneyland.[12]

In fact, despite the initial tremors, American consumer culture and television in particular did return to normal (or at least a semblance of it) in a remarkably short span of time. Yet, while many people have noted this, the process by which this happened and the extent to which it was achieved beg further consideration. Media scholarship on 9/11 and the U.S. attacks in Afghanistan has focused primarily on print and television news coverage. This important scholarship focuses on the narrative and mythic "framing" of the events; the nationalistic jingoism (for example, the use of flag graphics on news shows); the relative paucity of alternative views in mainstream venues—at least in the immediate weeks following the attacks; the role of alternative news platforms, especially the Internet; competing global news outlets, particularly Al Jazeera; and the institutional and commercial pressure that has led to "infotainment."[13] Despite its significant achievements, however, the scholarly focus on news underestimates (indeed, it barely considers) the way the "reality" of 9/11 was communicated across the flow of television's genres, including its so-called entertainment genres.[14] The almost singular focus on news fails to capture the way television worked to process fear (even fear trumped up by the media) and return the public to "ordinary" life (including routine ways of watching TV). The return to normal has to be seen from this wider view, for it was enacted not just through the narrative frames of news stories but also through the repositioning of audiences back into television's fictive time and places—its familiar series, well-known stars, favorite characters, and ritualized annual events (such as the Emmy Awards).

In the following pages, I explore how an assortment of television genres—dramatic series, talk shows, documentaries, special "event" TV, and even cartoons—channeled the nation back to normalcy—or at least to the normal flows of television and consumer culture. I am particularly interested in how these genres relied on nationalist myths of the American past and the enemy/ "Orient." But I also question the degree to which nationalist myths can sustain the "narrowcast" logic of today's multichannel television systems (and the more general movement of audiences across multiple media platforms). In other words, I want to interrogate the limits of nationalist myths in the postnetwork, multichannel, and increasingly global media systems.

Admittedly, the fate of nationalism in contemporary media systems is a huge question that requires perspectives from more than one field of inquiry. (For example, we would need to explore the impact of deregulation and media conglomeration, the dispersal of audiences across media platforms, competition among global media news/entertainment outlets, relations between local and global media flows, audience and interpretive reception contexts, and larger issues of national identity and subjectivity.) My goal here is not to provide exhaustive answers to all of these questions (obviously no one essay could do so), but rather to open up some points of interrogation by looking at post-9/11 media industry strategies, the discourses of the entertainment trade journals, and especially at the textual and narrative logic of television programs that channeled the nation back to commercial TV "as usual."

History Lessons After 9/11

Numerous critics have commented on the way that the attacks of 9/11 were perceived as an event completely outside of and alien to any other horror that ever happened anywhere. As James Der Derian notes, as a consequence of this rhetoric of American exceptionalism, "9/11 quickly took on an *exceptional ahistoricity*" as even many of the most astute critics refused to place the events in a political or social context from which they might be understood. Der Derian argues that when history was evoked in nonstop news coverage of destruction and loss, it appeared as nostalgia and analog, "mainly in the sepia tones of the Second World War—to prepare America for the sacrifice and suffering that lay ahead."[15] But, at least after the initial news coverage of which Der Derian speaks, history was actually marshaled in a much more contradictory field of statements and images that filled the airwaves and ushered audiences back—not just toward nostalgic memories of World War II sacrifice—but also toward the mandates of contemporary consumer culture. On television these "contradictory" statements and images revolved around the paradox of the medium's twin roles as advertiser and public servant.

In the week following 9/11, television's transition back to normal consumer entertainment was enacted largely through recourse to historical pedagogy that ran through a number of television genres, from news to documentaries to daytime talk shows to prime-time drama. The histories evoked were both familiar and familiarizing tales of the "American experience" as newscasters provided a stream of references to classroom histories, including, for example, the history of U.S. immigration, Pearl Harbor, and Vietnam.[16] They mixed these analogies to historical events with allusions to the history of popular culture, recalling scenes from disaster film blockbusters, science fiction movies, and war films and even referencing previous media events, from the assassination of JFK to the death of Princess Diana. Following 24/7 "real time" news strategies that CNN developed in 1991's Gulf War, major news networks provided a host of "infotainment" techniques that have over the past decade become common to war reporting (i.e., fast-paced "MTV" editing, computerized/game-style images, slick graphics, digitized sound effects, banter among "experts," and catchy slogans).[17] On September 12, CNN titled its coverage "The Day After" (which was also the title of the well-known 1980s made-for-TV nuclear disaster movie). NBC sported the slogan "America Strikes Back"—based, of course, on the *Star Wars* trilogy. Meanwhile the FBI enlisted the television show *America's Most Wanted* to help in the hunt for terrorists.[18] As we searched for familiar scripts, the difference between real wars and "made-for-TV" wars hardly mattered. History had become, to use Michel de Certeau's formulation, a heterology of science and fiction.[19]

But what did this turn to familiar historical narratives provide? Why the sudden appeal of history? Numerous scholars, from Roland Barthes to Marita Sturken, have analyzed the ways in which history and memory serve to produce narratives of the nation. This work has shown how media (from advertising to film to television to music) play a central role in conjuring up a sense of national belonging and community.[20] Certainly, after 9/11, the media's will to remember was connected to the resuscitation of national culture in a country heretofore divided by culture wars and extreme political partisanship. For the culture industries, however, the turn to history was not only connected to the resuscitation of nationalism; history was also connected to the parallel urge to restore the business routines and marketing practices of contemporary consumer media culture.

At the most basic level, for television executives who were nervous about offending audiences, history was a solution to a programming dilemma. History, after all, occupies that most sought-after realm of "good taste." It is the stuff of PBS, the Discovery Channel, the History Channel—it signifies a "habitus" of educated populations, of "quality" TV, of public service generally. History's "quality" appeal was especially important in the context of numerous critical attacks on television's lack of integrity that ran through industry trade journals and the popular press after 9/11. For example, Louis Chunovic, a reporter for the trade journal *Television Week*, wrote: "In the wake of the terrorist attack on the United States, it's hard to believe Americans once cared who would win *Big Brother 2* or whether Anne Heche is crazy. And it's hard to believe that as recently as two weeks ago, that's exactly the kind of pabulum, along with the latest celebrity/politician sex/murder/kidnapping scandal, that dominated television news." Chunovic therefore argued, "We cannot afford to return to the way things were."[21] Ironically, however, the industry's post-9/11 upgrade to quality genres—especially historical documentaries—

actually facilitated the return to the way things were. Historical documentaries served a strategic role in the patriotic transition back to "normalcy"—that is, to commercial entertainment and consumer culture.

Let's take, for example, ABC's programming strategy on Saturday, September 15. On that day, ABC became the first major network to return to a semblance of normal televisual flow. Newscaster Peter Jennings presented a children's forum, which was followed by an afternoon lineup of historical documentaries about great moments of the twentieth century. The lineup included episodes on Charles Lindbergh, the Apollo crew and the moon landing, and a documentary on the U.S. press in Hitler's Europe. Interestingly, given the breakdown in surveillance, aviation, and communication technologies that enabled the attacks, all of the chosen histories were about great achievements of great men using great technologies, especially transportation and communications technologies.[22]

Meanwhile, from an economic point of view, these historical documentaries were first and foremost part of the contemporary network business strategy that industry people refer to as "repurposing." The documentaries were reruns repackaged from a previous ABC series narrated by Jennings and now "repurposed" for patriotism. This is not to say that Jennings or anyone else at ABC was intentionally trying to profit from disaster. Certainly, Jennings's forum for children provided a public service. But, as anyone who studies the history of U.S. television knows, the logic of capitalism always means that public service and public relations are flip sides of the same coin. In this case, the public service gesture of running historical documentaries also served to transition audiences from TV news discourse and live reportage back into prerecorded narrative series. Similarly, with an even more bizarre resonance, on the evening of September 15th NBC ran a special news report on *Dateline* followed by a rerun of the made-for-TV movie *Growing Up Brady*.

More generally, history was integral to the transition back to entertainment series programs. On October 3, 2001, NBC's *The West Wing*, one of television's leading quality series, preempted its scheduled season premiere to air a quickly drafted episode titled "Isaac and Ishmael." On the one hand, the episode (which teaches audiences about the situation in the Middle East) was clearly an earnest attempt by the cast and Creator/Executive Producer Aaron Sorkin (who wrote the script) to use television as a form of political and historical pedagogy.[23] On the other hand, the episode was also entirely consistent with contemporary business promotional strategies. Like the ABC strategy of repurposing, the NBC network followed the business strategy of "stunting"—or creating a stand-alone episode that attracts viewers by straying from the series architecture (the live *ER* is a classic example of the technique). In this case, *The West Wing* was in a particularly difficult position—for perhaps more than any other network series, it derives its "quality" appeal from its "timely relevance" and deep, if melodramatic, realism. (The series presents itself as a kind of parallel White House universe that runs simultaneously with everyday goings-on in Washington.)[24]

The credit sequence begins with successive headshots of cast members speaking to the audience in direct address (and in their celebrity personae). Martin Sheen welcomes viewers and announces that this episode is not the previously scheduled season premiere. In a subsequent headshot, another cast member even refers to the episode as "a storytelling aberration," signaling its utter discontinuity from the now routinely serialized/cumulative narrative structure of contemporary prime-time "quality" genres. Meanwhile, other cast members variously thank the New York Fire and Police Departments, while still others direct our attention to a phone number at the bottom of the screen that viewers can call to donate money to disaster relief and victim funds. In this sense, the episode immediately asks audiences to imagine themselves foremost as citizens engaged in an interactive public/media sphere. Nevertheless, this "public service" ethos is embroiled in the televisual logic of publicity. The opening credit sequence ends with cast members promoting the new fall season by telling audiences what kinds of plots to expect on upcoming episodes. The final "teaser" comes from a female cast member, Janel Moloney, who hypes the fall season by promising that her character will have a love interest in future shows.

After this promise of titillating White House sex, the episode transitions back to its public service discourse. Essentially structured as a teach-in, the script follows a group of high school students touring the White House and caught in the west wing after a terrorist bomb threat. Attempting to calm the nerves of the students, various cast members lecture this imaginary high school class about the history of U.S.–Middle East relations. In an early segment, Josh Lyman, a White House "spin doctor," teaches the frightened students about terrorism and Middle East animosity toward the West. After a wide-eyed female student asks, "Why is everyone trying to kill us?" Josh moves to the blackboard, where he begins his history lesson. While he admits that the United States is somewhat to blame (he mentions economic sanctions, occupation of Arab lands, and the U.S. abandonment of Afghanistan), he says all of this at such rapid-fire speed that there is no in-depth consideration of the issues. Instead, the scene derails itself from its "teaching" mission by resorting to the colonialist rhetoric of "curiosities." The scene ends with Josh telling the students of his outrage at the cultural customs of Islamic fundamentalists. The familiar list of horrors—from the fact that women are made to wear a veil to the fact that men can't cheer freely at soccer games—redirects the episode away from ethics toward an ethnocentric celebration of American cultural superiority.[25] Josh concludes by reminding the students that, unlike Islamic fundamentalists, Americans are free to cheer anything they like at football games, and American women can even be astronauts.

In this regard, the episode uses historical pedagogy to solidify American national unity *against* the "enemy" rather than to encourage any real engagement with Islam, the ethics of U.S. international policy, or the consequences of the then-impending U.S. bomb strikes. Moreover, because the episode's teach-in lectures are encompassed within a more overarching melodramatic rescue narrative (the terrorist bomb threat in the White House), all of the lessons the students (and by proxy, the audience) learn are contained within a narrative about U.S. public safety. In other words, according to the logic of this rescue narrative, we learn about the "other" only for instrumental reasons—our own national security.

In all of these ways, *The West Wing* performs some of the fundamental precepts of contemporary Orientalism. As Edward Said argues, in the United States—and in particular after World War II—Orientalism retains the racist histories of othering from the earlier European context but becomes increasingly less philological and more concerned with social-scientific policy and administration that is formulated in federal agencies, think tanks, and universities that want to "know" and thus police the Middle East. In this configuration, the production of knowledge about the Middle East is aimed at the maintenance of U.S. hegemony and national security, and it winds up producing an image of the Arab as "other"—the antithesis of Western humanity and progress.[26] Indeed, when Josh details the cultural wasteland of Islamic fundamentalism, he enacts one of the central rhetorical principles of Orientalism, for, as Said argues, the "net effect" of contemporary Orientalism is to erase any American awareness of the Arab world's culture and humanity (its poets, its novelists, its means of self-representation), replacing these with a dehumanizing social-scientific index of "attitudes, trends, statistics."[27]

The West Wing's fictional schoolroom performs this kind of social-scientific Orientalism in the name of liberal humanism. And it does so through a pedagogical form of enunciation that places viewers in the position of high school students—and particularly naive ones at that. The program speaks to viewers as if they were children or, at best, the innocent objects of historical events beyond their control. The "why does everyone want to kill us?" mantra espoused by *The West Wing*'s fictional students, becomes, to use Lauren Berlant's phrase, a form of "infantile citizenship"[28] that allows adult viewers comfortably to confront the horrors and guilt of war by donning the cloak of childhood innocence (epitomized, of course, by the wide-eyed figure of President Bush himself, who, in his first televised speech to Congress after the attacks, asked, "Why do they hate us?").

In the days following the attacks, the Bush administration spoke often of the eternal and "essential goodness" of the American people, creating a through-line for the American past that flattered a despairing public by making them the moral victims of a pure outside evil.[29] In a similar instance of denial, commentators spoke of "the end of innocence"[30] that the attacks ushered in as if America had been completely without knowledge and guilt before this day.[31] Not surprisingly, in this respect, the histories mobilized by the media after 9/11 were radically selective and simplified versions of the past that produced a kind of moral battlefield for "why we fight." As Justin Lewis shows in his survey of four leading U.S. newspapers, print journalists writing about 9/11 tended to evoke World War II and Nazi Germany while "other histories were, regardless of relevance, distinctly less prominent." Lewis claims that "the more significant absences [were] those histories that signify the West's disregard for democracy and human rights [such as] the U.S. government's support for the Saudi Arabian Theocracy."[32] He argues that the history of World War II and Nazi Germany was mobilized because of its compelling narrative dimensions—especially its good versus evil binary. While this creation of heroes and villains was also a primary aspect of television coverage, it seems likely that many viewers weren't really looking for "objective truth" so much as narrative itself. In the face of shock and uncertainty that seemed to make time stand still, these narratives offered people a sense of historical continuity with a shared, and above all moral, past.[33]

The need to make American audiences feel that they were in the moral position ran through a number of television's "reality" genres. One of the central ways that this moral position was promoted was through the depiction of women victims. According to Jayne Rodgers, journalists tended to frame news stories in "myths of gender," and, she claims, one of the central trajectories of these myths was a reversal of the gendered nature of heroism and victimization. Rodgers points out that even while "male deaths from the attacks outnumbered female deaths by a ratio of three to one," news narratives typically portrayed men as heroes (firemen, policemen, Giuliani) and women as victims (suffering and often pregnant widows). Despite the fact that there were thirty-three women firefighters and rescue workers on duty on September 11, the media portraits of heroism were mainly of men, which, as Rodgers aptly argues, worked to "restore gender, as well as social and political order."[34]

On television, these myths of gender were often connected to age-old Western fantasies of the East in which "Oriental" men assault (and even rape) Western women and, more symbolically, the West itself. (Cecil B. DeMille's *The Cheat* [1915] or Valentino in *The Sheik* [1921] demonstrate the longevity of this orientalized "rape" fantasy.) In the case of 9/11, the United States took its figural place as innocent victim in stories that interwove myths of gender and the Orient. Both daytime talk shows and nighttime news were filled with melodramatic tales of women's suffering that depicted women as the moral victims of Islamic extremism. And "women" here meant both the women of Afghanistan and American survivors (the widows) who lost their husbands during the attack. While of course these women are at one level real women who really suffered, on television they were fictionally rendered through melodramatic conventions that tended to elide the complexity of the historical causes of the tragic circumstances the women faced.

For example, in the weeks following the attacks, *Oprah!* ran episodes featuring pregnant survivors who had lost their husbands. These episodes intertwined personal memories (via home videos of the deceased) with therapy sessions featuring the traumatized women. In these episodes, the "talking cure" narrative logic of the talk show format was itself strangely derailed by the magnitude of events; the female guest was so traumatized that she was literally unable to speak. In one episode, for example, a young pregnant woman sits rigidly on stage while popular therapist Dr. Phil tells her about the twelve steps of trauma (and Oprah interjects with inspirational wisdom). The episode presents this woman as having lost not only her husband but also her voice and, with that, her ability to narrate her own story. In the process the program implicitly asks viewers to identify with this woman as the moral and innocent victim of *chance*. In other words, any causal agent (or any sense that her suffering is actually the result of complex political histories) is reduced to the "twist of fate" narrative fortunes of the daytime soap.

Writing about the history of American melodramas, Linda Williams demonstrates that this theme of the "suffering" moral victim (particularly women and African Americans) can be traced through cinematic and televisual media representations (including depictions of American historical events). Williams claims that victim characters elicit our identification through sentiment (not only with them but also, allegorically, with historical injustices they face). Following Lauren Berlant and Ann Douglas, she cautions that sentiment and vicarious identification with suffering—in both media texts and politics more generally—are often a stand-in for actual social justice, but, importantly, sentiment is not the same as justice. By offering audiences a structure of feeling (the identification with victims, their revealed goodness, and their pain), melodrama compensates for tragic injustices and human sacrifice. Or, as Williams puts it, "melodramatic climaxes that end in the death of a good person—Uncle Tom, Princess Charlotte, Jack Dawson (in *Titanic*) offer paroxysms of pathos and recognitions of virtue compensating for the loss of life."[35] In political melodramas (like the stories told of 9/11's female victims), pathos can often be an end in itself; the spectator emerges feeling a sense of righteousness even while justice has not been achieved in reality and even while many people feel completely alienated from and overwhelmed by the actual political sphere.

Addressing the public with the same kind of sentimental/compensatory citizenship, President Bush used the image of female suffering in his first televised address before Congress after the attacks. Harking back to Cold War paranoia films like Warner Bros.' *Red Nightmare* (which was made with the Defense Department and showed what a typical American town would look like if it were taken over by "commies"), President Bush painted a picture of the threat that terrorism posed to our freedom. "In Afghanistan," he claimed, "we see Al Qaeda's vision of the world," after which he listed a string of daily oppressions people might be forced to face should Al Qaeda's vision prevail. First on his list was the fact that "women are not allowed to go to school." The rhetorical construction here is important because by suggesting that Al Qaeda had a vision for the world, President Bush asked TV audiences literally to imagine themselves taken over by Al Qaeda and in the women's place—the place of suffering. Having thereby stirred up viewers' moral indignation and pathos, he then went on to justify his own plan for aggression, giving the Taliban a series of ultimatums. Whatever one thinks about Bush's speech, it is clear that the image of suffering female victims was a powerful emotional ploy through which he connected his own war plan to a sense of moral righteousness and virtue (and it is also clear that we had never heard him speak of these women in Afghanistan before that day).

A more complicated example is CNN's airing of the documentary *Beneath the Veil*, which depicts the abuses that women of Afghanistan suffered under the Taliban. Originally made in the spring of 2001 for Britain's Channel 4,

Beneath the Veil was produced "undercover" by Saira Shah (who grew up in Britain but whose father is from Afghanistan) and with considerable risk to the filmmaker (photography was outlawed by the Taliban, and the fact that Shah is a woman made the whole process doubly dangerous). *Beneath the Veil* outlines not only the Taliban's oppression and cruelty but also the history of global neglect of Afghan women, as well as the need for political action now. Shah is careful to reflect on her own Western assumptions about women, feminism, and Islam, and she shows that it is the Afghan women themselves—a group known as the Revolutionary Association of the Women of Afghanistan (RAWA)—who were the first to fight against the Taliban.

Beneath the Veil opens with footage shot (via hidden cameras) by RAWA. There are images of women huddled in a pickup truck and being brought to a football field turned public execution arena. They are killed for alleged adultery. Interspersed throughout the film are images of and dialogues about the women's oppression, RAWA's own efforts to liberate women, and Shah's documentary witnessing of the events. An accompanying Web site (still up) provides numerous links to information and zones of action and participation. The program and its Web site constitute an important political use of electronic media. While there are images of female suffering, the pathos elicited by the pictures is organized around the desire for action (which Williams reminds us can also be part of melodrama) rather than just sentiment as an end in itself.

When *Beneath the Veil* was rerun and repurposed by CNN in the context of the post-9/11 news coverage, however, its politics were significantly altered. In the two months following the attacks, CNN reran *Beneath the Veil* so many times that it became a kind of daily documentary ritual. Although it was certainly important for audiences to learn about this human rights disaster, we should nevertheless wonder why Western eyes were willing to look at this documentary with such fascination after 9/11 (as opposed to, say, on September 10). First, it should be noted that in the wake of 9/11 documentaries of all sorts (but especially ones about terrorism) were, according to *Variety*, a "hot property" in the television industry.[36] Second, whatever the original achievements of the program, in this new context audiences were led to make easy equivocations between the kind of oppression the women of Afghanistan faced and the loss of innocent life on American soil on September 11. In the context of CNN's programming flow, we saw *Beneath the Veil* adjacent to news footage depicting Ground Zero, stories of American victims and heroes, anthrax attacks, public safety warnings, mug shots of the FBI's most-wanted terrorists, and war footage depicting a bizarre mix of bombs and humanitarian aid being dropped on Afghanistan.[37] In this programming context, *Beneath the Veil* could easily be read as a cautionary tale (like *Red Nightmare*) and a justification for the U.S. bombings in Afghanistan. In other words, it might well have conjured up national unity for war as a moral position.

In the midst of the U.S. bombings, Shah produced a follow-up film, *The Unholy War*, which aired on CNN in mid-November 2001. This film documented the lives of women (especially three young Afghan girls) in the midst of the U.S. war against the Taliban. The film showed the destruction caused by bombings, the problems entailed in building a post-Taliban regime, and Shah's own failures in trying to help the three girls (she attempts to get them an education), whose father rejected her humanitarian efforts. *The Unholy War* disrupted the "flow" of CNN's rotation of *Beneath the Veil*. It also punctured President Bush's melodramatic rescue/war narrative and questioned (the usually unquestionable) ideologies of "humanitarianism" that legitimated the U.S. bombings. As Shah said in an interview with *Salon:* "I couldn't believe that we couldn't help them and that money wouldn't solve their problems. . . . That was a real revelation for me. I rather arrogantly, in a very Western way, assumed that I could solve their problems because I had good will and money. It taught me that their problems are more complex. It also taught me a lot about what's needed in Afghanistan, and how frustrating it is rebuilding a country that's been destroyed to the extent that Afghanistan has."[38]

Event TV and Celebrity Citizenship

While Shah's *Unholy War* suggests that there were indeed counterhistories and antiwar messages to be found on the airwaves and on Web sites like Salon.com, the news images of unfathomable destruction that aired on 9/11 resulted in industry attempts to match that spectacle with reparative images on a scale as great as the falling towers. In this respect, "event TV" (or television programs designed to take on the status and audience shares of media events) flourished after 9/11, allowing for another staging of national unity after the attacks. These staged events created a "meta-universe" of Hollywood stars enacting the role of patriotic publics.

The first of these events was the celebrity telethon *America: A Tribute to Heroes*. Telecast live from New York, Los Angeles, and London on September 21, 2001, at 9:00 PM, the two-hour program was simulcast on more than 320 national broadcast and cable networks. According to the Nielsen ratings, the telethon garnered a 65 share of U.S. households, making it one of the most-watched programs of the year, behind only the Super Bowl.[39]

America: A Tribute to Heroes featured an overwhelming community of stars recounting the stories of those who died or risked their lives in the struggle. These eulogies were interspersed with musical performances of popular hits from the baby-boom to post-boomer past (the assumed generations of donors). Like all televised funerals, this one deployed television's aesthetics of liveness to stave off the fear of death. In other words, not only the "live" feed but also the sense of unrehearsed spontaneity and intimate revelations gave viewers a way to feel that life goes on in the present. The ritualistic and funereal atmosphere resurrected the recently dead for the living, restoring faith not only in spiritual terms but also in terms of the medium itself (in other words, it was that most "degraded" of media—television—that brought us this powerful sense of healing and community).[40]

While certainly designed to be a global media event, this was a deliberately understated spectacle, achieved through a deliberate display of "star capital" minus the visual glitz and ego. Staged with "zero degree" style (just candles burning on an otherwise unadorned set), the program appealed to a desire to see Hollywood stars, singers, and sports heroes reduced to "real" people, unadorned, unrehearsed (or at least underrehearsed), and literally unnamed and unannounced (there was no variety host presiding over the entertainment, no identification of the stars, and no studio audience). This absence of style signified the authenticity of the staged event, thereby giving stars the authority to speak for the dead. So too, the actual mix of stars (for example, Muhammad Ali, Clint Eastwood, Paul Simon, Julia Roberts, Enrique Iglesias, Bruce Springsteen, Celine Dion, Chris Rock, Sylvester Stallone) combined what might otherwise have been a battle-of-star semiotics (given their often at-odds personas and historical associations) into a compelling and, for many people, moving site of mourning. The program's "interactive" aspect further strengthened the telethon's aura of community, as on-demand celebrity phone operators, from Goldie Hawn to Jack Nicholson, promised to reach out and touch us. In all of these ways, *America: A Tribute to Heroes* is a stunning example of how post-9/11 television has created not a public sphere per se, but rather a self-referential Hollywood public sphere of celebrities who stand in for real citizens and who somehow make us feel connected to a wider social fabric.

The Fifty-third Annual Emmy Awards ceremony, which was twice delayed because of the attacks, is another example. Jack Valenti's "show must go on" ethos was everywhere in the publicity leading up to and culminating in this yearly television event. Somehow the industry was convinced that the airing of the Emmys was so important to America that any sign of celebrity resistance to gather (whether for fear of being attacked or for fear of looking crassly self-absorbed) would somehow be tantamount to "letting the terrorists win." As Academy of Television Arts and Sciences Chairman Bryce Zabel told viewers, canceling the Emmys "would have been an admission of defeat. Like baseball and Broadway, we are an American tradition."[41]

It seems just as probable, however, that the Academy and CBS were also worrying about their own commercial viability in the post-9/11 climate. In other words, canceling the Emmys would not just be an admission of the defeat of the nation; it would also be an admission that the consumer logics of TV— its annual ceremonies and self-congratulations—had been defeated. In the wake of 9/11, the Emmys came to signify the degree to which the televisual and marketing scene could be revitalized. The broadcast, which took place on November 4 at Los Angeles's Shubert Theatre (almost two months after the originally scheduled broadcast), was carefully orchestrated in this regard. Although there were more "no-shows" than usual, and while the area outside the theater was reportedly a "surreal" scene of rooftop sharpshooters, the Emmy producers encouraged the stars to perform their roles in the usual fashion. Before the broadcast, Executive Producer Gary Smith coached the stars: "Don't be afraid to be excited. . . . That's what people are looking for."[42]

The Emmy Awards program was another self-referential celebrity public sphere, this time constructed through appeals to television and Hollywood history. The opening sequence begins with Christian trumpet player/singer Phil Driscoll doing a bluesy rendition of "America the Beautiful" with a backup choir of students from different colleges across the country. The national unity theme is underscored by a large screen display of video images (everything from images of the flag and the Statue of Liberty to historical footage of Charles Lindbergh's lift-off and civil rights protests to landscape images of prairies and cities, all spliced to together in a seamless quilt of meaning). This is followed by a female voiceover that announces: "Tonight television speaks to a global audience as we show the world images of an annual celebration. Our presence here tonight does more than honor an industry, it honors those cherished freedoms that set us apart as a nation and a people." After this, the scene cuts to veteran newscaster Walter Cronkite, who appears via satellite from Toronto. Cronkite directly addresses the camera and narrates a history of television's importance to American politics and culture. Evoking the words of the World War II broadcaster Edward R. Murrow, Cronkite says, "Television, the great common denominator, has lifted our common vision as never before, and television also reminds us that entertainment can help us heal."

The Driscoll performance, the video backdrop, the female voiceover, and finally the widely respected Cronkite provide a prelude to what will be the night's apologetic theme: the ritualistic honoring of stars is not narcissistic, commercialized self-indulgence, but instead a public service to America and its image in the world.[43] The opening sequence then transitions to host Ellen DeGeneres, who delivers her monologue as the cameras cut back and forth to a bevy of Hollywood stars seated in the audience. Significantly, among those singled out are stars associated with Hollywood liberalism, including the cast of *The West Wing* and Bill Maher (who had already been in trouble with his sponsors for what they perceived to be unpatriotic comments). In other words, like the telethon, the Emmy ceremony was not simply "right-wing" in its approach to patriotism; it presented well-known Hollywood liberals (including a grand finale by Barbra Streisand and, of course, DeGeneres herself) as part of a national community who leave their identity politics home to join together and defend the larger American cause. Drawing attention to the patriotic mission of this liberal constituency, DeGeneres humorously asks the audience, "What would bug the Taliban more than seeing a gay woman in a suit surrounded by Jews?"

While the opening act establishes television as its own historical reference and television stars as their own public, a sequence near the end of the broadcast is even more blatant in its self-referential memories of Hollywood nationalism and celebrity citizenship. And while the first act uses network-era "hard" newsman Cronkite (who is in Toronto and far removed from the pomp and pageantry), this later segment features the ultimate postnetwork celebrity journalist, Larry King (who is dressed in a tuxedo and obviously part of the Hollywood community). King introduces a montage of vintage footage portraying Hollywood's efforts in wartime (e.g., the Andrews Sisters; Betty Grable's legs; Bugs Bunny; Bob Hope and the USO; Marilyn Monroe posing for the boys and kissing a wounded GI; Frank Sinatra signing an autograph; Harpo Marx clowning on stage; Bob Hope and a bevy of sexy starlets in Vietnam; Bob Hope, Steve Martin, and Jay Leno in the Gulf interspersed with Vietnam footage of Hope and Phyllis Diller as well as black-and-white images of Nat King Cole and Milton Berle performing for the troops). The rapid, decontextualized series of star fetish icons and the musical accompaniment (from the Andrews Sisters' World War II hit "Boogie Woogie Bugle Boy," to a standard rock riff, to Lee Greenwood singing "I'm Proud to Be an American") establish a "commonsense" and highly sentimental history of Hollywood patriotism (or as Larry King put it while introducing the montage, "Over the years the beat of the music changes, but the heart beneath it never wavers"). This nostalgic display of stars, with its thesis of unchanging Hollywood sentiment, obscures the different historical contexts in which World War II, Korea, Vietnam, and the Gulf War were fought (and obviously also the very different levels of popular support these wars had).

The montage sequence ends with an overhead traveling shot picturing a vast audience of GIs applauding Bob Hope during the Gulf War. The sequence then dissolves back to an overhead traveling shot of the celebrity audience applauding in the Shubert Theatre. This dissolve from the GIs to the Emmy audience—and the fact that the shots are perfectly matched—establishes a visual rhetoric that asks viewers to imagine that soldiers and celebrities are contiguous publics, and perhaps even comparable public servants. Immediately after the dissolve, the show cuts back to Larry King (live) on stage, where he speaks into the camera: "Once again we're in a time when America's armed forces are being sent to defend our freedom, and once again the entertainment industry is giving what it can." The entire segment legitimates future wars through a sentimental journey through Hollywood's wartime past.

The segment is capped off by yet another invocation of Hollywood's self-referential public sphere. Larry King speaks directly into the camera but not, as is usually the case, in order to address the home audience. Instead, he addresses an ailing Bob Hope at home: "We know that Bob Hope is watching at home tonight. And you should know, dear Robert, that we are thinking of you. . . . From all of us here, thanks for the memories." King's direct address to Hope—intercut with stars applauding in the studio audiences—creates a completely enclosed universe of citizen celebrities, orchestrating a set of complex relays between popular memories of vintage Hollywood, military history since World War II, and the present-day meanings of nationalism and war. In this televised display of celebrity patriotism, public service and publicity find their ideal meeting ground.

Osama bin Laden Meets the *South Park* Kids

In the introductory pages of his essay "The Uncanny," Sigmund Freud discusses the intellectual uncertainty he faced during World War I when he found it impossible to keep up with the flow of international publications.[44] In the world of electronic "instant" histories, these problems of intellectual uncertainty are compounded in ways that Freud could never have imagined. The "uncanny" seems an especially appropriate trope for the current situation, as nothing seems to be what it was and everything is what it wasn't just minutes before it happened. In this context, the literate pursuit of history writing seems slow to the point of uselessness. This is, of course, compounded by the fact that the publishing industry is painfully behind the speed of both war and electronic media. So rather than partake of either historical "conclusions" or future "predictions," I want to open up some questions about television and nationalism vis-à-vis the changing economies of industrially produced culture.

Given the political divisions that have resurfaced since 2001, it seems likely that the grand narratives of national unity that sprang up after 9/11 were for many people more performative than sincere. In other words, it is likely that many viewers really did know that all the newfound patriotism was really just a public performance staged by cameras. Still, after 9/11 many people found it important to "perform" the role of citizen, which included the performance of belief in national myths of unity. And if you didn't perform this role, then somehow you were a bad American. In this respect, no matter what they thought of the situation, in the wake of 9/11 stars had to perform the role of "love it or leave it" citizen to remain popular (a lesson that Bill Maher learned with a vengeance when his TV show *Politically Incorrect* was canceled).[45]

But did the performance really work? Just days after the attacks, the limits of performative nationalism were revealed in the televised celebrity telethon *America: A Tribute to Heroes* when, in the final sequence, everyone gathered 'round Willie Nelson to sing "America the Beautiful." Now, this was certainly a bad performance. Most of the celebrities were either too embarrassed to sing, or else they just didn't know the words to this show tune turned national anthem.[46] Some stars were visibly squinting at teleprompters with consternation, hoping to sing a verse. Yet, because the telethon was foremost aimed at baby boom and post-baby boom generations, most audiences would have known the popular ballads that were directly aimed at these niche generations. Clearly pop songs like John Lennon's "Imagine" (sung by Neil Young), Bob Marley's "Redemption Song" (sung by Wyclef Jean), or Paul Simon's "Bridge over Troubled Waters" have more historical meaning to these taste publics than any national anthem does.

More generally, I think the post-9/11 performance of nationalism will fail because it really does not fit with the economic and cultural practices of twenty-first-century U.S. media society. The fact that there is no longer a three-network broadcast system means that citizens are not collected as aggregate audiences for national culture. As we all know, what we watch on TV no longer really is what other people watch—unless they happen to be in our demographic taste culture. The postnetwork system is precisely about fragmentation and narrowcasting. While the new five-hundred-channel cable systems may not provide true diversity in the sense of political or cultural pluralism, the postnetwork system does assume a culture that is deeply divided by taste, not one that is unified through national narratives.[47] In a multinational consumer culture it becomes difficult for media to do business without addressing the niche politics of style, taste, and especially youth subcultures that have become central to global capitalism. In the end, the new media environment does not lend itself to unifying narratives of patriotism, if only because these older forms of nationalism have nothing to do with the "return to normalcy" and normal levels of consumption. While nationalist popular culture does, of course, exist (and obviously rose in popularity after 9/11), it appears more as another niche market (those people who hang flags on their cars) than as a unifying cultural dominant.[48]

The actual cultural styles in these new narrowcast media markets are increasingly based on irony, parody, skepticism, and "TV-literate" critical reading protocols. For people who grew up watching *The Simpsons'* hilarious parodies of mass culture and national politics; for people who fell asleep to Dave Letterman or Conan O'Brien; and for viewers who regularly watched *Saturday Night Live, In Living Color, The Daily Show,* and *Mad TV*'s political/news parodies, a sudden return to blind patriotism (and blind consumerism) is probably not really likely.

In the first week after the September 11 attacks, the cable operators and networks all did cover the same story—and for a moment the nation returned to something very much like the old three-network system.[49] Yet, the case of 9/11 also demonstrates that in the current media landscape it is hard to sustain the fantasy of utopian collectivity that had been so central to previous media events. Comparing media coverage of 9/11 with the coverage of the Kennedy assassination, Fredric Jameson argues that back in 1963 a utopian fantasy of collectivity was in part constructed through news reporters' "clumsiness [and] the technological naiveté in which they sought to rise to the occasion." But, he claims, the media are now so full of orchestrated spectacle and public violence on a daily basis that many people had a hard time seeing media coverage of 9/11 as documents of anything sincere, much less as any kind of intersubjective, utopian communication. As Jameson puts it, despite the many claims that America lost its innocence on 9/11, it was "not America, but rather its media [that had] . . . definitively lost its innocence."[50]

Certainly, for industry executives who work in the competitive environment of narrowcasting, sentiments of national belonging and utopian collectivity quickly gave way to the "bottom line." In fact, even in the "good will" climate of September 2001, the industry was still widely aware of the competitive realities of the postnetwork marketplace. CNN, which then had an exclusive deal with the Al Jazeera network, tried to block other news outlets from broadcasting its satellite transmissions of bin Laden's video address.[51] Even the celebrity telethon was a source of industry dispute. Worried that cable telecasts would undercut audience shares for broadcasters, some network affiliates and network-owned-and-operated stations tried to stop a number of cable channels from simulcasting *America: A Tribute to Heroes.* According to *Variety,* upon hearing of possible cable competition, "some of the vocal managers at the Big Four TV stations . . . went bananas and threatened to cancel the telethon and schedule their own local programming."[52] So much for humanitarianism in the postnetwork age!

Given this competitive media marketplace, it comes as no surprise that industry insiders quickly revised their initial predictions about the fate of American popular culture. By October 4, the front page of the *New York Times* proclaimed, "In Little Time Pop Culture Is Back to Normal," stating that the industry was backtracking on its initial predictions that the events of September 11 would completely change culture. David Kissinger, president of the USA Television Production Group, told the *Times* that the industry's initial reaction to the attacks may have been overstated and that because most industry people were "terror stricken" on September 11, "we shouldn't be held accountable for much of what we said that week."[53]

In fact, within a month, even irony was back in vogue, especially on late-night TV, but increasingly also on entertainment programs. By early November, Comedy Central's *South Park*—a cartoon famous for its irreverence—ran an episode in which the *South Park* kids visit Afghanistan. Once there, Cartman (*South Park*'s leading bad boy) meets bin Laden, and the two engage in an extended homage to Warner Bros. cartoons. Bin Laden takes the roles of the wacky Daffy Duck, the dull-headed Elmer Fudd, and even the lovesick Pepe La Pew (he is shown romancing a camel much as Pepe romances a cat that he thinks is a skunk). Meanwhile, Cartman plays the ever-obnoxious Bugs Bunny (like Bugs, he even does a drag performance as a harem girl wooing a lovesick bin Laden, whose eyes, in classic Tex Avery cartoon style, pop out of his head).

Although the episode was the usual "libertarian" hodgepodge of mixed political messages (some seemingly critical of U.S. air strikes, others entirely Orientalist), its blank ironic sensibility did at least provide for some unexpected TV moments. In one scene, when the *South Park* kids meet Afghan children in a war-torn village, American claims of childish innocence (promoted, for example, in *The West Wing*'s fictional classroom) are opened up for comic interrogation. Dodging a U.S. bomb attack, the Afghan children tell the *South Park* kids, "Over a third of the world hates America." "But why?" ask the *South Park* kids, "Why does a third of the world hate us?" And the Afghan kids reply, "Because you don't realize that a third of the world hates you." While the episode ends with an over-the-top cartoon killing of bin Laden and an American flag waving to the tune of "America the Beautiful," the program establishes such a high degree of pastiche, blank irony, and recombinant imagery that it would be difficult to say that it encourages any particular "dominant" reading of the war. The laughter seems directed more at semiotic breakdowns, perhaps mimicking the way in which news coverage of the war seems to make people increasingly incapable of knowing what's going on—a point that one of the *South Park* characters underscores at the end of the show, when he says, "I'm confused."

To be sure, programs like *South Park* and the niche cable channels on which they appear might not translate into the old enlightenment dream of "public service" TV with a moral imperative for its national public. Television studies is, of course, riddled with debates over the question of whether these new forms of narrowcasting and multichannel media outlets will destroy what some critics call common culture. In response to the increasing commercialization and fragmentation of European electronic media, scholars like Jostein Gripsrud, Graham Murdock, and James Curran champion European public service broadcast models, and even while they do not advocate a simplistic return to paternalistic models of "cultivation" and taste, they seek a way to reformulate the ideal of an electronic democratic culture.[54] In the United States the situation is somewhat different. The "public interest" policy rhetoric on which the national broadcast system was founded has been woefully underachieved; broadcasters did not engage a democratic culture of diverse interests, but rather for the most part catered to the cultural tastes of their target consumers (which for many years meant white middle-class audiences). Moreover, the networks often interpreted public service requirements within the context of public relations and the strengthening of their own oligopoly power.[55] Meanwhile, the underfunded Public Broadcasting System grew increasingly dependent on corporate funding. And, as Laurie Ouellette argues, by relying on paternalistic notions of "cultivation" and catering to narrow-minded taste hierarchies, the network has alienated audiences.[56]

Still, I am not saying that the new multichannel and multiplatform system of niche culture is necessarily better. Instead, we need to ask exactly what the new fragmented niche networks, as well as the proliferation of Internet sites, provide. What do the new forms of multinational media outlets offer beyond the proliferation of products and styles? The question is even more complex when we consider the fact that cable and broadcast networks, Internet sites, search engines, television producers/distributors, movie studios, radio stations, newspapers, and publishing companies are increasingly part of global conglomerate media structures (Disney, Rupert Murdock's News Corp., Viacom, Time-Warner, etc.).[57] In the media industries, as in other postindustrial modes of capitalism, there is both fragmentation and centralization at the same time. Any attempt to consider the political effects of the multiplication of channels (and fragmentation of audiences) still has to be considered within the overall patterns of consolidation at the level of ownership.[58]

Perhaps I am a bit overly optimistic, but I do want to end by suggesting some alternative possibilities within the highly consolidated, yet also fragmented, global mediasphere. As Daniel Dayan and Elihu Katz argue, although media events may be hegemonically sponsored and often function to restore consensual values, they always also "invite reexamination of the status quo." Following Victor Turner, Dayan and Katz claim that media events put audiences in a "liminal" context, outside the norms of the everyday. Even if media events do not institutionalize new norms, they do "provoke . . . mental appraisal of alternative possibilities."[59] In this sense, although I have focused primarily on media myths of reunification and nationalism, it is also true that 9/11 provoked counternarratives and political dialogues. In particular, 9/11 made people aware of new prospects for communication in a rapidly changing media environment.

Certainly, the Internet allowed for a collective interrogation of mainstream media and discussions among various marginalized groups. According to Bruce A. Williams, while "mainstream media reiterated themes of national unity, the chat rooms allowed different groups of Americans to debate what the impact of the attacks was for them specifically."[60] Internet sites like Salon.com—as well as access to a host of international news outlets—provided alternative views and global discussions. Convergence platforms opened up venues for expression. For example, after 9/11 a chat room hosted by the Black Entertainment Television network included conversations about whether it was possible to reconcile black beliefs about racist police and fire departments with the heroic images of police and firefighters after 9/11. Resistance groups from around the globe used the Internet as a forum for antiwar e-mails, virtual marches, and group organizing. The Social Science Research Council's Web site allowed scholars to weigh in on the events at Internet speed. The "low-tech" medium of radio (especially National Public Radio) likewise provided alternative voices.

That said, my point here is not that "new" media or "alternative media" are categorically "better" than TV. Certainly, many Internet sites and talk radio stations were filled with right-wing war fever. As Williams suggests, because the Internet allows for insular conversations, some message boards (such as "Crosstar") discussed ways to draw clear ideological boundaries and to keep "dissident voices" (i.e., liberals) off the board.[61] In this respect, we should not embrace the Internet in some essentialist sense as a pure space of pluralism which is always already more democratic than "old" media. Instead, it seems more accurate to say that the presence of multiple media platforms holds out hopeful possibilities for increased expression, but what this will amount to in terms of democracy and citizenship remains a complex historical question.

In addition to the Internet, the presence of the Al Jazeera news network had a destabilizing effect on the status of information itself. Al Jazeera officials defy the democratic legacy of the "free press" that had been so crucial to U.S. Cold War politics. Whereas the United States used to claim that its so-called free press was a reigning example of "free world" democracy, Al Jazeera now has taken up the same public pose, claiming that it will present all sides of the story from a Middle Eastern vantage point. In their book on Al Jazeera, Mohammed El-Nawawy and Adel Iskandar discuss how the network's post-9/11 coverage—especially its graphic coverage of the U.S. bombings in Afghanistan and the circulation of bin Laden's videotapes—quickly became a public relations crisis for the Bush administration.[62] Troubled by the bad PR, the Bush administration formed a Hollywood summit to discuss the role the industry might play in the war on terrorism. The military also met with Hollywood talent at the University of Southern California's Institute for Creative Technologies, a military/Hollywood alliance that Jonathan Burston aptly terms "militainment."[63] By late November 2001 President Bush had signed an initiative to start the Middle East Radio network (which strives to counterbalance anti-Americanism in the Arab world and is aimed especially at youth audiences).[64] As such federally sponsored efforts suggest, the proliferation of news outlets, entertainment networks, and Internet sites, as well as the mounting synergy between Hollywood and the military, has changed the nature of semiotic warfare, and the United States is certainly keen to play by the new rules of the game.[65]

Back to Normal?

On the one hand, as I have suggested, much of the TV landscape looks like a continuation of the same kinds of programs that aired prior to 9/11, and for this reason it is tempting to say that television's "return to normal" transcended the events of 9/11 and that everything is as it was before. On the other hand, 9/11 haunts U.S. commercial television.[66] The memory of 9/11 now—in 2004—circulates in ways that disrupt the kind of historical narratives and nationalist logic that had been so central to the initial return to the normal TV schedule.

Since 2001 the history and memory of 9/11 have in fact become a national battleground—not only in the notorious fights over Ground Zero's reconstruction but also in the electronic spaces of television. By March of 2002 major networks had begun to feature commemorative documentaries that told the story of 9/11.[67] By March of 2004 President Bush launched a presidential campaign with TV ads that show historical footage of the firefighters, implicitly equating their heroism with his presidency. But whereas nationalist historical pedagogy initially served to solidify consent for the Bush administration, now the history and memory of 9/11 are not so simply marshaled. On March 5, 2004, just one day after the ads began to circulate, CNN interviewed a woman who had lost her husband on 9/11. Unlike the speechless pregnant widows on *Oprah!* back in 2001, this woman had regained her voice and spoke quite articulately of her disgust for the President's use of 9/11 footage for political ends.

In the end, I suspect that the current situation is ripe for new visions of apocalyptic techno-futures, with satellites, guided missiles, surveillance cameras, and communication media of all kinds at the core of an ongoing genre of techno-warfare criticism waged by Jean Baudrillard, Paul Virilio, and many others.[68] But it seems to me that, as forceful and perceptive as this kind of work has been, this is really just the easy way out. Instead of engaging in yet another stream of doom-and-gloom technological disaster criticism, it seems more useful to think about how cultural studies and media studies in particular might hold on to a politics of hope. What I have in mind is in no way the same as utopian claims to transcendence and unity (whether local, national, or global) through new media technologies. Rather, this politics of hope is situated in a confrontation with the actually existing historical divisions around us. This materialist politics of hope should embrace the new global media environment as an opportunity to listen to "the third of the world that hates us" rather than (to use Bush's formulation) clutter the globe with messages about "how good we are." The world has heard enough about America. Time now to tune in elsewhere.

Notes

Thank you to Marita Sturken, Jeffrey Sconce, Jan Olsson, Chris Berry, and four anonymous readers for their help with this essay.

1. "Disaster Programming," *Variety.com,* September 21, 2001, 1. For more on TV network cancellations of violent movies, see John Dempsey, "Cable Nets Nix Violent Pix in Wake of Tragedy," *Variety.com,* September 16, 2001, 1–2; Joe Flint and John Lippman, "Hollywood Revisits Terrorism-Related Projects," *Wall Street Journal,* Sep-

tember 13, 2001, B2; Joe Flint, "TV Programmers Avoid All Allusions to Attacks," *Wall Street Journal,* September 28, 2001, B6.

2. For speculations on the "end of irony" see Jeff Gordinier, "How We Saw It," *Entertainment Weekly,* September 28, 2001, 12; Peter Bart, "Where's the Snap and Crackle of Pop Culture?" *Variety.com,* September 30, 2001, 1–2. Note, however, that a counterdiscourse popped up immediately in venues like the Onion and Salon, which used irony early on. In an online essay, James Der Derian noted some of the inconsistencies in what he called the "protected zones of language" after 9/11, pointing out, for example, that irony was in some venues under attack: "President Bush was given room to joke in a morale-boosting visit to the CIA, saying he's 'spending a lot of quality time lately' with George Tenet, the director of the CIA." Der Derian also took on *New York Times* reporter Edward Rothstein for taking an "opportunist shot at postmodernists and postcolonialists" by "claiming that their irony and relativism is 'ethnically perverse' and produces 'guilty passivity.' " See Der Derian's "9/11: Before, After, and In Between," Social Science Research Council, After September 11 Archive, SSRC.org, 5 (the original posting date is no longer on the site).

3. Jennifer Netherby, "Renters Flock to Video Stores," *Videobusiness.com,* September 21, 2001, 1–2. *Video On Line* reported that "Wal-mart stores asked the studios for a list of their titles that contain scenes of the World Trade Center, presumably to take some merchandising action on those movies" (*VideoBusiness.com/news,* September 13, 2001, 1).

4. "Domain Names Grow after Attacks," *Variety.com,* September 25, 2001, 1.

5. Even while cable outlets are not regulated by the Federal Communications Commission to the extent that the broadcast networks are, they still are widely perceived as "service" industries and protectors of public safety in times of crisis (obviously, this is the platform of cable news outlets like CNN, which dramatically increased its viewership after 9/11).

6. I am borrowing Raymond Williams's phrase "a whole way of life," which he used to define culture. See his *Culture and Society, 1780–1950* (1958; New York: Columbia University Press, 1983), 325.

7. More generally, 9/11 disrupted the familiar/consumer uses of a host of communication technologies, from cell phones to television to satellites to video games, all of which now resonated in an uncanny sense with the militaristic/wartime uses for which their basic technology was developed.

8. Mary Anne Doane, "Information, Crisis, Catastrophe," in *Logics of Television: Essays in Cultural Criticism,* ed. Patricia Mellencamp (Bloomington: Indiana University Press, 1990), 222–39.

9. Venessa O'Connell, "TV Networks Cut $320 Million of Ads in Crisis," *Wall Street Journal,* September 19, 2001.

10. Variety reported that "commercial breaks were back across the board Monday [September 17]" (Rick Kissell, "TV Getting Back to Biz and Blurbs," *Variety.com,* September 17, 2001, 1).

11. Jack Valenti, "Hollywood, and Our Nation, Will Meet the Test," *Variety.com,* September 27, 2001, 1–2.

12. The President said this in a televised address he delivered at Chicago O'Hare Airport with the aim of convincing people to return to plane travel. Note, too, that in subsequent months various advertisers linked their promotional discourses to 9/11 and the idea of patriotic consumption. (For example, ads for United and American Airlines as well as financial corporations did this.)

13. For examples of literature on TV news, 9/11, and Afghanistan, see *Television*

and New Media 3 (May 2002); Daya Kishan Thussu and Des Freedman, eds., *War and the Media* (Thousand Oaks, Calif.: Sage, 2003); Stephen Hess and Marvin Kalb, eds., *The Media and the War on Terrorism* (Washington, D.C.: Brookings Institute, 2003); Barbie Zelizer and Stuart Allan, eds., *Journalism after September 11* (New York: Routledge, 2002).

14. As other scholars have argued, we should not accept at face value the information/entertainment binary that underpins the ideological logic of mainstream media systems. This binary—and the related binaries of important/trivial, private/ public, masculine/feminine, and high/low—not only elide the fact that news is also narrative (and increasingly entertaining) but also fail to acknowledge that entertainment also serves to provide audiences with particular ways of knowing about and seeing the world. See, for example, Richard Dyer, *Only Entertainment* (New York: Routledge, 1992); John Fiske, "Popular News," in *Reading Popular Culture* (Boston: Unwyn and Hyman, 1989); James Freedman, ed., *Reality Squared: Televisual Discourse on the Real* (New Brunswick, N.J.: Rutgers University Press, 2002).

15. Der Derian, "9.11," 2.

16. For an interesting discussion of media references to Pearl Harbor and the re-release of the film after 9/11, see Cynthia Weber, "The Media, the 'War on Terrorism' and the Circulation of Non-Knowledge," in Thussu and Freedman, eds., *War and the Media,* 190–99.

17. This kind of coverage is, of course, symptomatic of the general rise of "infotainment" in the climate of media conglomeration and a ratings-driven commercial ethos. For speculation on the social/political effects of the news coverage of 9/11 in terms of "infotainment," see Daya Kishan Thussu, "Live TV and Bloodless Deaths: War, Infotainment, and 24/7 News," in Thussu and Freedman, eds., *War and the Media,* 117–32. There is much additional literature on issues of infotainment. See, for example, Leonard Downie Jr. and Robert G. Kaiser, *The News about the News: American Journalism in Peril* (New York: Knopf, 2002); and Pierre Bourdieu, *On Television,* trans. Priscilla Parkhurst Ferguson (New York: New Press, 1998). For analysis of the effect that round-the-clock coverage of "real time" wars has on foreign policy, see Piers Robinson, *The CNN Effect: The Myth of News, Foreign Policy, and Intervention* (New York: Routledge, 2002).

18. Claude Brodesser, "Feds Seek H'wood Help," *Variety.com,* October 7, 2001; Michael Schneider, "Fox Salutes Request by Bush for 'Wanted' Spec," *Variety.com,* October 10, 2001.

19. Michel de Certeau, "History: Science and Fiction," in *Heterologies: Discourse on the Other,* trans. Brian Massumi (Minneapolis: University of Minnesota Press, 1986), 199–221.

20. Roland Barthes, *Mythologies,* trans. A. Lavers (London: Cape, 1972); Marita Sturken, *Tangled Memories: The Vietnam War, the AIDS Epidemic, and the Politics of Remembering* (Berkeley: University of California Press, 1997). For more on the role of memory/nostalgia in film, television, and other popular media, see, for example, the Cahiers du Cinéma interview with Michel Foucault, reprinted in *Edinburgh Magazine* 2 (1977): 19–25; Patrick Bommes and Richard Wright, "Charms of Residence," in *Making Histories: Studies in History Writing and Politics,* ed. Richard Johnson et al. (London: Hutchinson, 1982); George Lipsitz, *Time Passages: Collective Memory and American Popular Culture* (Minneapolis: University of Minnesota Press, 1989); Robert Rosenstone, *Visions of the Past: The Challenge of Film to Our Idea of History* (New York: Belknap Press, 1996); Robert Rosenstone, *Revisioning History: Film and the Construction of a New Past* (Princeton: Princeton University Press, 1994); Marcia Landy, ed., *The Historical Film:*

History and Memory in Media (New Brunswick, N.J.: Rutgers University Press, 2000); "Special Debate," *Screen* 42 (Summer 2001): 188–216 (this is a series of short essays on trauma and cinema); David Morley and Kevin Robins, "No Place Like Heimet: Images of Homeland," in *Spaces of Identity: Global Media, Electronic Landscapes, and Cultural Boundaries* (New York: Routledge, 1995), 85–104; Purnima Mankekar, *Screening Culture, Viewing Politics: An Ethnography of Television, Womanhood, and Nation in Postcolonial India* (Durham, N.C.: Duke University Press, 1999).

21. Louis Chunovic, "Will TV News—or Its Audience—Finally Grow Up?" *Television Week*, September 24, 2001, 15. Note that news executives responded to such criticism. For example, CBS's Mel Karmizan and Fox News Channel's Roger Ailes promised to upgrade news programs and to cover more international issues.

22. So, too, this ABC lineup followed the logic of what Daniel Dayan and Elihu Katz see as integral to media events more generally, namely, a "neo romantic desire for heroic action by great men followed by the spontaneity of mass action" (*Media Events: The Live Broadcasting of History* [Cambridge: Harvard University Press, 1992], 21).

23. Some people have told me that they found it a useful source of "modeling" for their own conversations with their children.

24. Several other series also created special episodes about the attacks or else planted references to 9/11 in preexisting episodes. NBC's *Third Watch* began its season on October 29 with a documentary in which real-life emergency workers recalled their experiences on 9/11. ABC's *N.Y.P.D. Blue* added two scenes acknowledging the attack into its season opener on November 6. As *New York Times* critic Caryn James pointed out, "The creators of 'Third Watch' and 'N.Y.P.D. Blue' have said they felt a responsibility to deal with the events, but the decision was practical, too. Their supposedly realistic characters would have seemed utterly unbelievable if they had ignored such an all-consuming tragedy" ("Dramatic Events That Rewrite the Script," *New York Times*, October 29, 2001 pg. E7).

25. Josh lists many of the same Taliban injustices that President Bush listed in his first televised speech to Congress after the attacks.

26. Edward W. Said, *Orientalism* (New York: Vintage Books, 1979), esp. 284–328.

27. Ibid., 291.

28. Lauren Berlant, *The Queen of America Goes to Washington City: Essays on Sex and Citizenship* (Durham, N.C.: Duke University Press, 1997).

29. As Slavoj Žižek wrote just days after the attacks, this sense of a pure "evil Outside" was the response of a public living in a fake "Matrix"-like existence, a public that had for so long considered itself immune to the suffering endured on a daily basis by other world populations and, in any case, in no way responsible for its own perpetuation of violence around the world. Slavoj Žižek, "Welcome to the Desert of the Real!" posted on Re: Constructions.mit.edu, September 24, 2001. The title is taken from a line in the film *The Matrix*. Žižek's short essay was later developed in a book. See his *Welcome to the Desert of the Real* (London: Verso, 2002). Der Derian's "9.11," 4–5, similarly evokes The Matrix.

30. Jack Lule, "Myth and Terror on the Editorial Page: *The New York Times* Responds to September 11, 2001," *Journalism and Mass Communication Quarterly* 29, no. 2 (2002): 275–93.

31. Yet, as Marita Sturken argues, this "end of innocence" theme is common to the stories spun around national disasters (for example, the same language was used after JFK's assassination). See Sturken, *Tangled Memories*, chap. 1.

32. Justin Lewis, "Speaking of Wars . . ." *Television and New Media* 3 (May 2002): 170.

33. In this sense, it is interesting to note how television created a continuous past, particularly with regard to World War II and Vietnam. In place of the grave generational divides these wars had previously come to signify, television presented unifying narratives that bridged the gap between the self-sacrificing "Greatest Generation" and baby-boomer draft dodgers. This was most vividly displayed when Vietnam POW/Senator John McCain met 1960s youth rebel Stephen Stills on the *Tonight Show*, reconciling their differences.

34. Jayne Rodgers, "Icons and Invisibility: Gender, Myth, and 9/11," in Thussu and Freedman, eds., *War and the Media*, 206, 207.

35. Linda Williams, *Playing the Race Card: Melodramas of Black and White: From Uncle Tom to O. J. Simpson* (Princeton: Princeton University Press, 2001), 24.

36. One month after the attacks, Variety reported, "A rash of documentaries—some put together in a hurry—that aim to explain terrorism is a hot property" (Andrea R. Vaucher, "Arab, Terror Docus Heat Up the Market," *Variety.com*, October 10, 2001, 1).

37. U.S. and British air strikes on Afghanistan began on October 7, 2001, and American warplanes attacked the Taliban in the field on October 10, 2001.

38. Saira Shah, cited in Janelle Brown, "Beneath the Veil' Redux," *Salon.com*, November 16, 2001, 1–2.

39. Rick Kissell, "Bush Speech, Telethon Both Draw Record Auds," *Variety.com*, September 23, 2001, 1–2.

40. As one of the readers for this article suggested, the telethon's aura of liveness might have also helped to stave off the fear that TV and commercial culture were themselves "dead." To be sure, live "call-in" donations to stars ensured that money was still circulating through the media wires (here, not through the crass commercialism of TV as usual, but through the exchange economies of charity).

41. He said this on the broadcast.

42. Gary Smith, cited in Joseph Adalian, "Show Finally Goes On and TV Biz Takes Heart," *Variety.com*, November 4, 2001, 1.

43. Underscoring the show's global impact, later in the ceremony there is a video montage of leaders from around the globe offering their condolences to the American public.

44. Sigmund Freud, "The Uncanny," in *Studies in Parapsychology* (1919; New York: Collier Books, 1963), 19–60. Freud discusses his lack of bibliographical references vis-à-vis the war in Europe on page 20.

45. When I delivered this paper at a conference at the University of California, Berkeley, Ratiba Hadj-Moussa pointed out that this dynamic of national performance doesn't necessarily suggest that people don't in some way believe in the performance. I want to thank her for this observation. Clearly, through the act of national performance, it is possible to actually to believe in the role you are playing—and even to believe in it more than ever!

46. Note, too, that "America the Beautiful" replaced the actual national anthem after 9/11 because no one seemed to be able to remember the words to the "Star-Spangled Banner."

47. Even news is now a matter of taste and "branded" by networks in ways that appeal to consumer profiles. For example, the news on Fox (especially its markedly conservative talk shows) attracts one of cable TV's most loyal publics, but many on the left mock its pretense of "Fair and Balanced" reporting. Al Franken's best-seller *Lies and the Lying Liars Who Tell Them: A Fair and Balanced Look at the Right* (New York: E. P. Dutton, 2003) and his lawsuit with Fox obviously drew on the more left-associated

taste publics that define themselves in distinction—in Bourdieu's sense—not only to Fox News but also to the viewers who (they imagine) watch it. For his discussion of taste as social distinction, see Pierre Bourdieu, *Distinction: A Social Critique of the Judgement of Taste*, trans. Richard Nice (Cambridge: Harvard University Press, 1984).

48. Even before the attacks, patriotic symbols were re-emerging as a fashion fad. Corporations such as Tommy Hilfiger, Polo Ralph Lauren, and the Gap Inc.'s Old Navy sported the flag trend, while European haute couture designer Catherine Malandrino unveiled her flag-motif fall collection in the summer of 2001 (which included a skirt that Madonna wore on her concert tour). See Teri Agins, "Flag Fashion's Surging Popularity Fits with Some Fall Collections," *Wall Street Journal*, September 19, 2001, B5. According to Agins, the post-9/11 flag fashions were an extension of this trend, not an invention of it.

49. In 1992 Dayan and Katz speculated on the fate of television, nationalism, and media events in what they saw to be an increasingly multichannel and segmented television system. They argued that while the old three-network or public broadcast systems "will disappear," television's previous functions of "national integration may devolve upon" media events. Their speculation now seems particularly apt. They also predicted that with new technologies and possible erosion of the nation state, "media events may then create and integrate communities larger than nations." See Dayan and Katz, *Media Events*, 23.

50. Fredric Jameson, "The Dialectics of Disaster," *South Atlantic Quarterly* 101 (Spring 2002): 300.

51. According to *Variety*, news organizations were "furious that CNN wouldn't forego competition" and "rallied against exclusives, saying that they don't serve the public's interest during a time of national crisis." ABC news spokesperson Jeffrey Schneider disputed any exclusivity deal by arguing fair use. He said, "There was no question in anybody's mind that these images from Al Jazeera were of compelling national interest," and "We felt we had a duty to broadcast them to the American people which far outweighed whatever commercial agenda CNN was attempting to pursue in this time of war." Meanwhile, Walter Isaacson, CEO of CNN News Group, told *Variety* that CNN had a "reciprocal affiliate deal" with Al Jazeera and that "it's Al Jazeera's material and we don't have a right to give it away." Isaacson did admit, however, that "in a time of war, we won't make a big deal about this sort of thing." See Paul Bernstein and Pamela McClintock, "Newsies Fight over Bin Laden Interview," *Variety.com*, October 7, 2001, 1–2.

52. John Dempsey, "Invite to Cablers to Join Telethon Irks Affils," *Variety.com*, September 20, 2001, 1. The underlying reasons for the broadcasters' concern had to do with issues of East Coast-West Coast transmission times. The big four networks—ABC, CBS, NBC, and Fox—aired the telethon at 9 PM eastern time, and because they wanted to make it seem like a simultaneous nationwide event, they also showed it taped via a dual feed at 9 PM on the West Coast. Some single-feed cable networks such as TBS and the National Geographic Channel, however, planned to show the telethon live at 6 PM on the West Coast, and thereby preempt the 9 PM taped West Coast network broadcast. Some network affiliates and owned and operated stations were simply unhappy that any cable networks were airing the telethon, even if cablers showed it simultaneously (at 9 PM) with the Big Four.

53. David Kessinger, cited in Rick Lyman with Bill Carter, "In Little Time Pop Culture Is Almost Back to Normal," *New York Times*, October 4, 2001.

54. See, for example, Jostein Gripsrud, ed., *Television and Common Knowledge* (New York: Routledge, 1999), esp. Graham Murdock, "Rights and Representations," 7–17; James Curran, "Mass Media and Democracy Revisited," in *Mass Media and Soci-*

ety, ed. James Curran and Michael Gurevitch, 2nd ed. (London: Arnold, 1996), 81–119.

55. See, for example, Vance Kepley Jr., "The Weaver Years at NBC," *Wide Angle* 12 (April 1990): 46–63, and "From 'Frontal Lobes' to the 'Bob and Bob Show': NBC Management and Programming Strategies, 1949–65," in *Hollywood in the Age of Television,* ed. Tino Balio (Boston: Unwin-Hyman, 1990), 41–62; Lynn Spigel, "The Making of a Television Literate Elite," in *The Television Studies Book,* ed. Christine Geraghty and David Lusted (London: Arnold, 1998), 63–85.

56. Laurie Ouellette, *Viewers Like You? How Public TV Failed the People* (New Brunswick, N.J.: Rutgers University Press, 2002).

57. ABC is now owned by Disney (which owns, for example, the Disney theme parks, radio stations, cable networks like ESPN and Lifetime, retail outlets, feature film companies, newspapers, and magazines); the multiple-system operator Comcast has recently bid for the now-struggling Walt Disney Company; CBS is owned by Viacom (which also owns, for example, Paramount Studios as well as cable networks like MTV and Nickelodeon, theme parks, and radio stations); NBC is owned by General Electric (which entered into a joint venture with Microsoft and owns MSNBC); and Fox is owned by Rupert Murdock's News Corp. (which owns, for example, Fox Broadcasting; Fox News Channel; Fox Sports Net; motion picture companies; magazines like *TV Guide, Elle,* and *Seventeen;* book publishers; and numerous newspapers and delivers entertainment and information to at least 75 percent of the globe). Meanwhile, media conglomerate Time-Warner owns a large number of cable channels, production companies, home video, magazines, music companies, and book publishers (for example, HBO, Cinemax, TNT, Comedy Central, E! Entertainment, Black Entertainment Television, Time-Life Video, Warner Bros. Television, Book of the Month Club, and its notorious deal with America Online). With telephone and cable operators acquiring and partnering with media corporations and moving into content, the synergy among these sectors is even more pronounced. These ownership structures make these media organizations more like vertically integrated movie studios of the classical period, as they have controlling stakes in all sectors of their industry—production, distribution, and exhibition—in addition to obvious benefits of owning multiple and related companies that reduce risk and increase opportunities for synergy between different companies in the umbrella corporation. Note, however, that the great instability of the technologies market (including, of course, the fate of AOL and the AOL–Time Warner merger) begs us to ask new questions regarding the future of media conglomeration and convergence.

58. Media conglomerates often say that consolidation of ownership leads to more choice (for example, some media conglomerates claim that consolidation of business holdings allows them to use income from their mainstream media outlets to launch minority channels). A variety of media activists, industry executives, media scholars, and government officials have, however, sharply attacked conglomeration and questioned the degree to which freedom of speech and diversity of representation can exist in a deregulated media system in which just a few major corporations own most of the media sources. See, for example, Patricia Aufderheide, *Communications Policy and the Public Interest: The Telecommunications Act of 1996* (New York: Guilford Press, 1999); Patricia Aufderheide, ed., *Conglomerates and the Media* (New York: New Press, 1997); Robert McChesney, *Corporate Media and the Threat to Democracy* (New York: Seven Stories Press, 1997); Ben H. Bagdikian, *The Media Monopoly,* 6th ed. (Beacon Press, 2000); Dean Alger, *Megamedia: How Giant Corporations Dominate Mass Media, Distort Competition, and Endanger Democracy* (New York: Rowman and Littlefield, 1998).

59. Dayan and Katz, *Media Events*, 20.

60. Bruce A. Williams, "The New Media Environment, Internet Chatrooms, and Public Discourse after 9/11," in Thussu and Freedman, eds., *War and the Media*, 183. It should be noted that the Pew Research Center found that nine out of ten Americans were getting their news primarily from television after the 9/11 attacks. See "Troubled Times for Network Evening News," *Washington Post*, March 10. Citing an ABC News poll, however, Williams claims that "almost half of all Americans now get news over the Internet, and over a third of them increased their reliance on online sources after September 11" ("New Media Environment," 176).

61. Williams, "New Media Environment," 182. Although Williams cites various online attempts to draw ideological boundaries, he doesn't necessary view this as a bad thing. While he admits that some such attempts were disturbing, he also argues that "insular conversations that are not easily accessible to the wider public play a positive role by allowing marginalized groups to clarify their distinct values in opposition to those of the society-at-large within the safety of a sympathetic and homogeneous group" (184). Despite his pointing to the insular nature of the Web and the desire of some groups to draw ideological boundaries, Williams also argues that there was a general air of civility on the Internet (188–89).

62. The administration viewed the presence of Al Jazeera's graphic war footage and bin Laden's videotapes (which were aired around the world) as a grave problem. On October 3, 2001 (a few days before the bombings began), Secretary of State Colin Powell asked the Qatari emir, Sheikh Hamad bin Khalifa, to "tone down" Al Jazeera's inflammatory rhetoric, and the Bush administration specifically requested that the tapes be taken off the network. The International Press Institute sent a letter to Colin Powell, stating that Powell's tactics had "serious consequences for press freedom" (176–77). Al Jazeera journalists defended their coverage of graphic images by stating that they were trying to cover the war objectively, from both sides (Mohammed El-Nawawy and Adel Iskandar, *Al Jazeera: The Story of the Network That Is Rattling Governments and Redefining Modern Journalism*, updated ed. [Cambridge, Mass.: Westview Press, 2002], 176–81). See also El-Nawawy and Iskandar's discussion of Europe's and Al Jazeera's coverage of Afghanistan (ibid., 186–89).

63. Jonathan Burston, "War and the Entertainment Industries: New Research Priorities in an Era of Cyber-Patriotism," in Thussu and Freedman, eds., *War and the Media*, 163–75. For more, see James Der Derian, *Virtuous War: Mapping the Military-Industrial Media Entertainment Network* (Boulder, Colo.: Westview, 2001). At ICT, technologies such as immersive simulation games are being developed simultaneously for entertainment and military uses.

64. A member of the Bush administration met with Hollywood studio chiefs and network executives in Beverly Hills on October 18 to discuss efforts to "enhance the perception of America around the world." See Peter Bart, "H'wood Enlists in War," *Variety.com*, October 17, 2001, 1–3. A few weeks later, they gathered in what was referred to as a "summit" to discuss more detailed plans for Hollywood's participation in the war effort. See Rick Lyman, "White House Sets Meeting with Film Executives to Discuss War on Terrorism," *Variety.com*, November 8, 2001, 1—3. See also Pamela McClintock, "Nets Rally Stars around Flag," *Variety.com*, December 3, 2001, 1–2.

65. Meanwhile, in a connected fashion, Al Jazeera's presence also threatens the hegemony of Western global news sources. Driven by fierce competition for Arab audiences, in January 2002 CNN officially launched its Arabic Web site, CNNArabic.com. See Noureddine Miladi, "Mapping the Al Jazeera Phenomenon," in Thussu and Freedman, eds., *War and the Media*, 159. Note that CNN launched the Web site at the same

time (January 2002) that Al Jazeera withdrew its exclusivity agreement with CNN because of the dispute over a tape CNN aired without its approval.

66. In a provocative thesis, Bret Maxwell Dawson argues that while TV returned to much of its previous content, television's temporal and narrational forms were "traumatized" by 9/11. He argues that the effects of this trauma can be seen in the way that elements of catastrophe television (e.g., live broadcasts, an aura of authenticity, and an obsession with time) have appeared with increasing popularity in reality TV and programs like Fox's *24*. See his "TV since 9/11" (master's thesis, University of New South Wales, Sydney, Australia, 2003). While I would not posit such deterministic notions of trauma, it does seem useful to think about how 9/11 relates to a particular historical conjuncture in aesthetic ideals of TV realism, and in particular TV's obsession with the reality genre and real time (which, as Dawson admits, began before 9/11).

67. This cycle of memorializing documentaries began with *CBS's 9/11* (aired March 10, 2002), which was followed by *Telling Nicholas* (HBO, May 12, 2002), *In Memoriam: New York City, 9.11* (HBO, May 26, 2002), and others. For a seminar I taught at UCLA, Sharon Sharp wrote a very interesting paper "Remembering 9/11: Memory, History, and the American Family," which considers how these documentaries used sentimental images of the family in crisis to tell histories of 9/11.

68. Baudrillard and Virilio both have published monographs on 9/11. See Jean Baudrillard, *The Spirit of Terrorism and Requiem for the Twin Towers,* trans. Chris Turner (London: Verso, 2002); Paul Virilio, *Ground Zero,* trans. Chris Turner (London: Verso, 2002).

Regulation, Media Literacy, and Media Civics

Roger Silverstone

The locus of our regulatory concerns needs to shift. In the new media world, a world that still includes old media and old yet resistant values driving institutional processes of mediation, the concern with markets, competition and content needs to be rethought. This is not only because of the decline of spectrum scarcity, or the incapacity of national governments to control international flows of information and communication, but because new media are challenging what it means to be human, through their increasing salience as both information and communication resources, and, as such, as crucial components of our relational infrastructure and our social life.

I want to suggest, in this short article, that an understanding of what it is to be human is, or certainly should be, the central question underlying, and in the final analysis regulating, the development of the mediated world in which more and more of us live, and by which almost all of us are affected. I intend to argue that existing forms of media regulation, at best operationalizations of what can be called applied ethics (Christians, 2000), at worst mindless enforcements of vested political or commercial interests, are not sufficient as guarantors of humanity or culture. Regulatory reform is still mostly a matter *for* governments and media industries, and a matter *of* establishing professional and commercial guidelines for practice (variously enforced) without conscious attention to first principles of social action or media representation, and without addressing other ways of enabling not just a responsible and an accountable media, but a responsible and accountable media culture. A responsible and accountable media can be encouraged and regulated, however imperfectly and however vulnerably. A responsible and accountable media culture is another matter entirely, for it depends on a critical and literate citizenry, and a citizenry, above all, which is critical with respect to, and literate in the ways of, mass mediation and media representation.

And I wish to suggest that at the core of such media literacy should be a moral agenda, always debated, never fixed, but permanently inscribed in public discourse and private practice, a moral discourse which recognizes our responsibility for the other person in a world of great conflict, tragedy, intolerance and indifference, and which critically engages with our media's incapacity (as well as its occasional capacity) to engage with the reality of that difference, responsibly and humanely. For it is in our understanding of the world, and our willingness and capability to act in it, that our humanity or inhumanity is defined.

Media as Environment

As Cees Hamelink has recently pointed out, the media are central in this increasingly urgent project of identifying what constitutes our humanity precisely because they are at the forefront in representing, through endless sequences of narratives and images, the "historical reality of dehumanization on a grand scale" (2000: 400).

And the media are indeed quite central to our capacity to be and to act in the world, as Marshall McLuhan (1964) once upon a time noted. It was he who most forcefully suggested that media, all media, are extensions of ourselves. They create and sustain an encompassing cultural environment which we all share. As we enter a digital age, one in which both the speed and range of communication seems to have been so intensified; as we shift from, at best, an active engagement with our singular media to an increasingly interactive engagement with our converging media, media which give us the world, access to the world and information about the world, we are confronted with this McLuhanistic vision even more insistently.

Of course McLuhan profoundly misrepresented the totality and homogeneity of media as providing a kind of cultural blanket over all peoples of the world. He persistently disregarded the significance of geography and society as in turn mediating power and access to material and symbolic resources. Nevertheless, and despite its political innocence, this mediated cultural environment is as significant, it might be said, for the human condition as the natural environment is. Though it is rarely so remarked upon. Indeed, both have holes in their ozone layers, chemical and moral in turn. Both are subject to the depredations and exploitations of the insensitive, the malicious and the self-interested. So although this environmental perspective makes, perhaps, more sense now than it ever did, it leaves untouched the thorny questions of who and what we are, and of how what we are in turn affects the ways in which media emerge and develop. And it still fails to register mediation as both a social and a political process. In other words, the humanity and inhumanity at the heart of the dynamics of mediation are left unexamined; they are presumed to be unproblematic.

Similarly, regulatory discourse rarely examines why regulation should take place in the first place. Its presumptions about public interest, freedom of expression, rights to privacy, competition policy, intellectual property and the like presume an ordered or at least an orderable world, and indeed a world that would benefit from deliberative, and presumably accountable, regulation. Yet at best regulatory procedures, focusing on producers but addressing consumers, are based on an acknowledgement and an acceptance of what I have already called applied ethics: sets of morally informed but rarely interrogated prescriptions for, or proscriptions of, practice. The main beneficiary of such regulatory impulses and practices is the putative citizen, in his or her public and private life. In such present regulatory discourse and practice such citizens need to be protected against the depredations of untrammelled vested interests, be they commercial or imperial. They need to be given freedoms to speak and to be heard; they need to be given freedoms of choice. They need to be consulted on how regulatory policies are formed and implemented (Collins and Murroni, 1996).

But who is the citizen these days? And how has his or her status as citizen been affected by the media, both old and new, both broadcast and interactive? In what ways do our media enable or disable our capacity to relate to each other as citizens, but also as human beings? In what ways do they enable or disable us as ethical beings in our relationship to the world? In what ways do the media both address us as, and enable us to be, global citizens, participants and actors in natural, commercial and cultural environments all of which extend beyond both the immediacy of neighbourhood and nation?

Home . . .

In an earlier work (Silverstone, 1999) I argued that almost all our regulatory impulses, those that engage with the ownership of media industries on the one hand and those that concern the welfare of the family on the other, are between them concerned with the protection of home. What links them is a preoccupation with *content:* with the images, sounds, narratives and meanings which are transmitted and communicated daily, and over which regulators increasingly feel they have little control. What appears on the page or on the screen, what is represented, especially in its consistency or inconsistency, its decency or indecency, its intrusiveness, is deemed to be important precisely because it has been allowed to cross this principal threshold, seeping into private spaces and private lives. This was, of course, the impetus for the earliest attempts at content regulation, in the Hays Code, for the cinema. But these anxieties and the regulatory attempts to manage them have become more insistent as 20th-century media migrated away from public to private screens, and from shared sitting rooms to solitary bedrooms.

Banal though it may seem, the media are seen to be important because of the power they are presumed to exercise over us, *at home,* a power that no amount of audience research can quite completely deny, and of course which most of us believe, one way or the other, naturally to be the case. Home, of course, needs to be understood in both literal and metaphorical senses. The defence of home is a defence of both the private spaces of intimate social relations and domestic security—the household; as well as of the larger symbolic spaces of neighbourhood and nation—the collective and the community. The two are complex in their interrelationship and do not always share common interests. Yet both are threatened by the media extension of cultural boundaries: both laterally, as it were, through the globalization of symbolic space, and vertically through the extension of accessible cultural into the forbidden or the threatening. In both cases home has to be defended against material breaches of symbolic security.

The liberalization of mainstream media and telecommunications in the 1980s and 1990s by a neo-liberal Conservative government brought with it an unexpected and unwelcome reduction in the capacity to control the flow of media content into the UK. Self-induced de-regulation in one context and for one set of dominating economic reasons produced, as it was bound to, a moral panic in another context, that of culture. The Broadcasting Standards Council was, as a consequence, created to protect both the vulnerable child at home and the vulnerable home-land as if it were a child. Current debates on the future of public service broadcasting in the UK rehearse the same dilemmas, for once again what is at stake is the moral integrity both of the home and the nation, in its citizens' capacity to exercise, both privately and publicly, meaningful choices (a precondition for a moral life) as well as a perceived need to protect that same citizen from the immorality of meaningless or threatening choices that unregulated commerce might be expected to bring in its train.

For every de-regulation there is a re-regulation, but not always in the same domain, and rarely for clearly defined or well-examined reasons. Competition policy is, therefore, as much about, and has consequences for, such breaches of personal security and domestic integrity—of the rights of the person and the personal—as it is about cross-media ownership and the future of public service broadcasting and the public sphere. Indeed it is precisely the private which is at stake in the discussions and deliberations on the latter.

And yet, while regulators struggle to control and direct, to label and to license content (as well as competition), parents and families struggle over a personal and private culture, shaping and protecting the domestic spaces where public and private moralities are supposed to coincide. This is a struggle for control, a struggle which propagandists, advertisers, television schedulers and portal designers well understand. And it is a struggle which parents understand too, as they argue with their children over time spent online. It is a struggle which, at least in part, defines, across lines of age and gender, the particular politics of individual households.

Regulation is, then, a private as well as a public matter. It takes place in front rooms as well as in debating chambers, in the cut and thrust of discussions over viewing habits, as well as in international debates over v-chips and trans-border media flows. In both these environments what is being fought over are the rights of, and control over, representation: of the availability of, and access to, the continuities and consistencies of both the immediacy, and the flow, of images and narratives. And in those representations what is at stake are the rights to define a relationship: between what is known and not known, between what is valued and not valued, between what one believes to be the truth and what one suspects as falsehood, and between what one lays claim to and what one can discard in one's relationship to the rest of the world. What is at stake, in these moments and mechanisms of regulation is, essentially, a moral order.

... and Away

As we become increasingly dependent on the mediated word and image for our understanding of what takes place beyond our front door; as everyday life, in its taken-for-granted ordinariness, becomes inseparable from the mediations that guide us through it, and connect or disconnect us from the everyday lives of others; how the media position us, or enable us to position ourselves, becomes crucial.

As citizens we are expected to take responsibility for, and to act responsibly in relation to, ourselves, our neighbours and also the strangers among us. Such expectations, arguably, have been undermined by (among other things) a century of electronic mediation, which has led to increasing privatization and individualization. The dominant trope in the analysis of 20th-century public life has been its erosion: the palpable lack of care, the paradoxical lack of communication, has been revealed in increasing alienation from the formal processes of politics and engagement in public life; perhaps not for all, but for many, especially in the wealthy and highly mediated democracies of industrial society.

These societies, equally, it goes without saying, are becoming increasingly connected to each other. What imperialism once enforced, globalization now enables, or indeed requires: a mutuality of increasingly highly stratified economic and financial structures and processes; a shared but still massively and unevenly discomforting physical environment; a political space that no longer knows, nor much cares about, national boundaries and territorial sovereignty; networks of information and communication that shrink social and cultural space and time to the size of a handset.

In this context, and taking the broadest sweep, problems of regulation become problems of governance, in which order and accountability are dreamed about on a global scale, and at the level of states and transnational non-governmental organizations. Foreign and domestic policy converges. Somehow even these dreams depend on a notion of citizenship, though a transcendent one, but they still require an engagement with the human—and they challenge it too. However they leave untouched and unexamined, for the most part, the individual in his or her humanity, in his or her sensibility. In what ways, if at all, can or should this humanity be affected by our regulatory impulses and institutions? In what ways should this humanity (or its lack) inform and affect our attempts at regulation and governance?

Early commentators, both utopian and dystopian, on the emerging late 19th-century wireless and telegraphic space recognized the implications of what has subsequently come to be known as the double life of media and communication: that they separate as well as connect. This paradox inevitably gives the lie to any contemporary notion of the media's role in what is called the death of distance. It raises the question of isolation and not just privatization—and isolation of both the individual and of the group. It also raises the question of the illusion of connection: that in our mediated innocence, in our mediated naïveté, we are unable to recognize how imprisoned we are, how easily blinded we are, by the mediations that apparently link us together. And it is somewhat ironic to observe that the supposed revolution in media culture occasioned by the arrival of digital and online technologies should be seen to be so singular and radical, above all in the capacity of these technologies to transcend the limits of electronic communication, limits perfectly well recognized (and feared) throughout the analogue 20th century (de Sola Pool, 1977; Marvin, 1988).

As I have argued elsewhere (Silverstone, 2003) there is often quite a fundamental confusion in much of the writing on the sociology and geography of new media. Time-space distanciation, or time-space compression, even ideas of the network society, suggest a profound and misleading elision between two kinds of distance: the spatial and the social. It is presumed in these discussions that the electronic mediation of physical or material connection provides at the same time, social, cultural or psychological connection. The technologically enabled transformation of time and space which marked the entry into the modern world certainly provided new conditions and possibilities for communication, communication that provided connection despite physical separation. Yet the contradictions at the heart of such communication become even more profound the more we insist that electronic mediation brings no penalty when it comes to understanding and caring for the other. Indeed, when we insist, on the contrary, that our world view is now global in its reach; that there is no escape; that nothing can be hidden, nothing can be, or is, ignored. But of course it can.

My point is that distance is not just a material, a geographical or even a social category, but it is, by virtue of all of these and as a product of their interrelation, a moral category. The overcoming of distance requires more than technology and indeed more than the creation of a public sphere. It requires what I have called proper distance (Silverstone, 2003). Proper distance is the critical notion that implies and involves a search for enough knowledge and understanding of the other person or the other culture to enable responsibility and care, as well as to enable the kind of action that, informed by that understanding, is in turn enabling. We need to be close but not too close, distant, but not too distant.

Proper Distance

The media have always fulfilled the function of creating some sense of proper distance, or at least they have tried, or claimed to be able, to do so. In the reporting of world events, the production of news, the fictional representation of the past, the critical interrogation of the private lives of public figures, the exploration of the ordinariness of everyday life, what is involved, in one way or another, is a negotiation between the familiar and the strange, as the media try, though always imperfectly, to resolve the essential ambiguities and ambivalences of contemporary life.

Yet such mediations have tended to produce, in practice, a kind of polarization in the determinations of such distance. The unfamiliar is either pushed to a point beyond strangeness, beyond humanity; or it is drawn so close as to become indistinguishable from ourselves. And, it should be said, there is also very little sense that we are the objects of the others' gaze, that how *we* are seen and understood by those far removed from us also matters; we need to see and understand that too. Perhaps this has never been more the case than now.

On the one hand we find ourselves being positioned by media representation as so removed from the lives and worlds of other people that they seem beyond the pale, beyond reach of care or compassion, and certainly beyond reach of any meaningful or productive action. Technology has a habit of creating such distance, and the bureaucracies that have been built around technologies have in the past, and with cataclysmic effects, reinforced this sense of separation and alienation, this immorality of distance (Bauman, 1993). This is certainly and obviously the case in times of conflict, but it is rarely far away even in peace.

Per contra, the representation, just as frequent and just as familiar, of the other as being just like us, as recoupable without disturbance into our own world and values has, though perhaps more benignly, the same consequence. We refuse to recognize not only that others are not like us, but that they can be made to be like us. What they have we share. What they are we know. They are as they appear in our documentaries and in our advertisements. Such cultural neo-imperialism represents the other side of the immorality of distance, in its refusal to accept difference, in its resistance to recognizing and valuing the stranger. Perhaps this could be called the immorality of identity.

In both cases we lose a sense of both the commonality and difference that should inform the ethics of how we live in the world. Either way we lose the capacity effectively to grasp both what we share and what we do not share as human beings. The irony of the electronically mediated century just passed, in which we have come to believe that the immediate and the visible is both necessary and sufficient to guarantee connection, is that this apparent closeness is only screen-deep.

Distance, therefore, can be proper (correct, distinctive and ethically appropriate) or it can be improper. If improper distance can be, and is, created, inter alia, through the mediations that electronic technologies provide for us, then it follows that we can use the notion of *proper* distance as a tool to measure and to repair the failures in our communication with and about other people and other cultures and in our reporting of the world, in such a way that our capacity to act in it is enabled and preserved (Boltanski, 1999; Silverstone, 2003). And it follows too that we can use the notion of proper distance as a way of interrogating those arguments, most recently in the analysis of the supposed miraculous capacity of the Internet, that mistake connection for closeness and closeness for commitment, and which confuse reciprocity for responsibility.

It is with the convergence between the public and the private, the personal and the social, that the notion of proper distance seeks to engage. And it is at this interface, perhaps increasingly confused and confusing, that social beings, citizens real or *manqué*, need both to confront a moral agenda that is appropriate to the conditions both of the mediation of the world and to the resulting mediated world, the world in which the other person appears to us— as through a glass darkly.

Media Literacy and Media Civics

Regulation has always been a technical activity. To suggest that it should also be a moral one has its dangers. Yet these dangers need to be confronted. What is missing so often in the regulatory discourse is the question: regulation for what, and for whom?

The focus on content, on media as representational technologies, is in many ways atavistic. It brings back concerns that many had thought long since buried in the analysis of mediation: concerns with ideology, effects, false consciousness even. On the other hand, our regulatory concern is still implicitly (and sometime explicitly) based on such assumptions as these: a political economy in which ownership determines content, and where content in turn determines meanings and effects.

Yet even if we can acknowledge, with recent media theory, that this linearity is misconceived and that receivers of communication, wherever they happen to be, and understood as audiences or users, are active interpreters and mediators of even the most consistent and dominant of media representations, it is still possible, reasonable and necessary to acknowledge the persistent power of our media's mediations. Media are nothing if they do not convey meanings, and even if we can (and we can) negotiate those meanings for ourselves, and distance ourselves from those meanings we find unacceptable or unpalatable, in the absence of others—both other meanings and other realities—our perceptions of the world cannot but be increasingly and consistently framed by what is seen and heard through screens and audio-speakers.

The multiple negatives of the last paragraph are intended, and intended to be, instructive. There is inevitably and necessarily a need for caution in any kind of moral position lest it be seen as, or become, moralistic. So it needs to be understood that the present argument is not for a new kind (or even an old kind) of censorship. On the contrary, at issue are the presumptions and preconditions for our understandable (perhaps even natural, at least sociologically speaking) concern for regulation. Perhaps it is time to recognize that regulation should not just be concerned with the protection of our own securities and of those we hold dear or for whom we have some formal, familial or even national, responsibility.

Regulation should address the wider and, I have suggested, the much deeper issue of our relationships to others, to those for whom we have no formal responsibility, to those who are distant in space or culture, the strangers amongst us, our neighbours abroad; but for whom our basic humanity requires that we should care. This is of course a tall order. However it suggests a shift, and one that—it might well be argued—is long overdue. It involves a shift away from regulation as narrowly conceived in the minds and practices of parliaments and councils, towards a more ethically oriented education, and towards a critical social and cultural practice which recognizes the particular characteristics of our mediated world. We once upon a time taught something called civics. It is perhaps time to think through what civics might be in our present intensely mediated century.

In one sense, perhaps, we could say that we have been here before, at least in part. The mid- and late 19th century saw, certainly in the UK but also in Western Europe and in the USA, the rise of a political project, broadly speaking, to incorporate disparate and displaced populations into civic culture. The displacement was for the most part internal: populations leaving the land and traditional cultures and finding themselves in cities and within urban and popular cultures. Industrialization was having profound social consequences, and the social consequences involved very significant and destabilizing shifts in the communicative infrastructures of everyday life. Such destabilization and the consequent danger of anomie among an increasingly concentrated population was clearly a source of anxiety among elites—both legitimate and paranoid. Nation states were being consolidated and any source of political resistance was clearly a focus of concern. At the same time democracies were maturing and working-class movements were themselves encouraging the displaced and disadvantaged—the still excluded—to generate the necessary social and cultural capital to participate increasingly fully and meaningfully in the public affairs of the strengthening state. There were both campaigns for, and political commitments to enable, mass literacy. Workers' educational movements engaged the mature; increasingly, universal primary and secondary education engaged the maturing.

All participation is double-edged. It is both enabling and constraining. The literacy of the book, the newspaper and the pamphlet brought with it both the means for incorporation into national culture and the means for the suppression of any alternative, but it also brought an increasingly informed, reflective and cultured citizenry. Vernacular literacy was a precondition of such participation and reflection. To pretend that this was not a regulatory project would be naïve. At the same time, however, it was also a liberating one—and in essence and in intent, very often, a genuinely moral one, whatever we might think about Victorian ethics. The focus of that first regulatory impulse was clearly that of the nation-state, a state enabled initially by the Gutenberg revolution (Eisenstein, 1979) and secured—at least for large slices of the 20th century—by Marconi's and Baird's (Scannell, 1989). The focus, now, arguably, is postnational, if by that can be meant the redrawing and puncturing of the boundaries around and between states in the face of globalizing culture.

Whereas the 19th-century civic project required the literacy of the written text, a literacy that was both literal and critical, the 21st century civic project requires a literacy of mass-mediated, electronic texts—and this too needs to be both literal and critical. But there the similarity ends. For the 21st century brings with it a different cultural and political challenge, in which the different media, both analogue and digital, are differently implicated in the structures and dynamics of everyday life.

For most, the literacy of the book was a literacy of decipherment: to be able to read, to follow, to understand, to appreciate. It required considerable application and the acquisition of sophisticated skills. Media literacy in an age of broadcasting was much less demanding, and the ease of access to complex audio-visual texts was seductive. The mass media were seen as more powerful, not just because they were mass, but because they dimmed critical skills, the skills of engagement and struggle with complexity (Rosenberg and White, 1957). It was not thought that literacy, at least in the terms where it was appropriately applied to the written text, was necessary. Indeed the mass media were seen to be destroying and undermining that kind of literacy. It is possible, of course, to argue that the Internet has created its own demands for a new kind of literacy, text-based but requiring new skills of organization and decipherment, and that this is already transforming the structured illiteracy of the age of broadcasting. I would suggest that, for the most part, the literacy required for the Internet is still seen to be essentially technical, and is rarely approached as requiring more sophisticated skills.

In both the new and the old media, therefore, very little attention has been given to media literacy as a critical activity. Very little attention has been given to media literacy as a civic activity. Very little critical attention has been given either to literacy or civics as an alternative to the blunderbuss of media regulation, or to the possibility of developing an ethical agenda which would inform such a project.

In a recent article Rüdiger Funiok (2000) has addressed some of these questions through an interrogation of audience ethics, that is, the responsibility that users of the media can, and should, develop for themselves. He cites Cees Hamelink's (2000: 400) conclusion that 'Media consumption should be viewed, like professional media performance, as a social practice which implies moral choices and the assumption of accountability for these choices.' This is a complex demand, of course, and extends way beyond the still limited framework that I am pursuing here. Yet the notion of responsibility is crucial, responsibility for oneself and for others; in the context of the family, of course, but also in the context of neighbourhood and nation (imagined communities both), and now in the context of a global culture and a global imaginary, which the world's media are daily creating.

Media literacy in this context is a political project, just as media civics is a "literary" one. The former is a prerequisite for full participation in late modern society, involving as it does the critical skills of analysis and appreciation of the social dynamics and social centrality of media as framing the cultures of the everyday. Media literacy above all requires an understanding of the non-transparency of media and of the moral implications of that non-transparency. And it requires an understanding of mediation as a social and political process. Media civics, correlatively, depends on media literacy. Media civics, crucial to citizenship in the 21st century, requires the development of a morality of responsibility and participation grounded in a critical engagement with mediation as a central component of the management both of state and global politics and that of everyday life: both of the system and the life-world.

There is very little that is surprising in these observations, at least from the point of view of the academic study of the media, but equally there is very little surprising in the observation that these fundamental critical principles have hitherto for the most part failed to inform both the deliberations of policy makers, and the judgements of citizens.

Conclusion

Our regulatory impulses need to be both informed and moderated by these concerns. Citizenship requires responsibility, and to exercise such responsibility well and thoroughly in turn requires the need to be able to see the world and to see through our media's limited and inadequate representations of it.

I have proposed the notion of proper distance as a framing device for such a project. Media civics has to burst the bounds both of the nation-state and the narcissistic limits of concern only with the individual and the self. Its regulatory embrace should bring the other into its ambit. A sense of proper distance is a moral sense, one in which the relationship between proximity and distance is mediated by an effective measure of understanding, care and responsibility. We need to know about each other in a way that can only involve a constant critical engagement with our media's representation of the other. Such engagement is as important to our relationships to our neighbours as to the strangers both amongst us and far away. The everyday, hitherto the site of a mostly unreflecting gaze, can, and should, be made more critically aware—for that is, after all, what our media can enable for us, if there is a mind to do so. Representational ethics, the ethics informing the production and reception of the images and stories of both old and new media, emerges from these discussions as a new and compelling concern.

Regulation is, therefore, not just a matter of production. And here as in other dimensions of media dynamics, production and consumption blur; the boundaries between them become indistinct. Equally the full responsibility for a moral agenda informing media practices should lie not with audiences and users only. It is the interests and understandings of audiences and users, the urgent requirements of citizenship, which should continue to constrain and increasingly determine the regulatory process. We are of course, responsible for ourselves. But, as Emmanuel Levinas insists, if we are to claim a full and proper humanity we must claim responsibility for the other. In this sense, as well as reading, we might need to regulate, against the grain.

References

Bauman, Zygmunt (1993) *Postmodern Ethics*. Cambridge: Polity Press.

Boltanski, Luc (1999) *Distant Suffering: Morality, Media, Politics*. Cambridge: Cambridge University Press.

Christians, Clifford (2000) "An Intellectual History of Media Ethics," pp. 15–46 in Bart Pattyn (ed.) *Media Ethics: Opening Social Dialogue*. Leuven: Peeters.

Collins, Richard and Cristina Murroni (1996) *New Media, New Policies*. Cambridge: Polity Press.

de Sola Pool, Ithiel (1977) *The Social Impact of the Telephone*. Cambridge, MA: MIT Press.

Eisenstein, Elizabeth (1979) *The Printing Press in an Age of Social Change*, 2 vols. Cambridge: Cambridge University Press.

Funiok, Rüdiger (2000) "Fundamental Questions of Audience Ethics," pp. 403–22 in Bart Pattyn (ed.) *Media Ethics: Opening Social Dialogue*. Leuven: Peeters.

Hamelink, Cees (2000) "Ethics for Media Users," pp. 393–401 in Bart Pattyn (ed.) *Media Ethics: Opening Social Dialogue*. Leuven: Peeters.

Marvin, Carolyn (1988) *When Old Technologies Were New: Thinking About Communications in the Late Nineteenth Century*. Oxford: Oxford University Press.

McLuhan, Marshall (1964) *Understanding Media*. London: Routledge and Kegan Paul.

Rosenberg, Bernard and David Manning White (eds.) (1957) *Mass Culture: The Popular Arts in America*. New York: The Free Press.

Scannell, Paddy (1989) "Public Service Broadcasting and Modern Public Life," *Media, Culture & Society* 11(2): 135–66.

Silverstone, Roger (1999) *Why Study the Media?* London: Sage.

Silverstone, Roger (2003) "Proper Distance: Towards an Ethics for Cyberspace," pp. 469–90 in Gunnar Liestøl, Andrew Morrison and Terje Rasmussen (eds.) *Digital Media Revisited: Theoretical and Conceptual Innovations in Digital Domains*. Cambridge, MA: MIT Press.

ABOUT THE AUTHORS

Mark Alvey is an exhibit developer/writer at The Field Museum in Chicago with interests in television and film. His work has appeared in *The Road Movie Book* (1997), *The Revolution Wasn't Televised: Sixties Television and Social Conflict* (1997), *Television: The Critical View* (2000), and *Screen.*

Jane Arthurs is Principal Lecturer in Cultural and Media Studies at the University of the West of England, Bristol. Her previous publications include *The Crash Controversy,* coauthored with Martin Barker and Ramaswami Harindranath (2001), *Women's Bodies: Discipline and Transgression,* coedited with Jean Grimshaw (1999), and *Television and Sexuality: Regulation and the Politics of Taste* (2004).

Sarah Banet-Weiser is Associate Professor in the Annenberg School for Communication at the University of Southern California. She is the author of *The Most Beautiful Girl in the World: Beauty Pageants and National Identity* (1999), which explores the interconnections of gender, race, and national identity within the Miss America pageant. She has published articles on sports and gender, children and technology, and children, media, and national identity.

Kim Bjarkman is a Ph.D. candidate in the Media and Cultural Studies Program in the Department of Communication Arts at the University of Wisconsin-Madison and a longtime collector of television comedy. Her research concentrates on humor and cultural hierarchies.

Aniko Bodroghkozy is Associate Professor and Interim Director of the Media Studies Program in the Department of English at the University of Virginia. She is the author of *Groove Tube: Sixties Television and the Youth Rebellion* (2001). Her current book project is *Negotiating Civil Rights in Prime-Time: Television Audiences and the Civil Rights Era.*

Caroline-Isabelle Caron is Assistant Professor of History at Queen's University, Kingston, Ontario, Canada. She specializes in the cultural history of Quebec and Acadian Francophones in Canada.

Marsha Cassidy teaches media studies and literature in the department of English at the University of Illinois at Chicago. She is the author of *What Women Watched: Daytime Television in the 1950s* (2005).

Christopher Castiglia is Associate Professor of English at Loyola University Chicago. He is the author of *Bound and Determined: Captivity, Culture-Crossing, and White Womanhood from Mary Rowlandson to Patty Hearst* (1996) and is currently completing *Interior States: The Romance of Reform and the Inner Life of a Nation.*

John Corner is Professor in the School of Politics and Communication at the University of Liverpool. He is author of numerous works on television, including *Critical Ideas in Television Studies* (1999). He is coeditor, with Alan Rosenthal, of *New Challenges for Documentary* (2005).

Jocelyn Cullity is a doctoral student in creative writing at Florida State University. She has recently published in *The Journal of Asian Studies, Journal of Communication Inquiry*, and *Passionfruit. Going to the Sea*, a television documentary about young women in China coproduced with Prakash Younger, won the Lester B. Pearson Award for International Development at the REEL Women's Film Festival.

Nicholas Garnham is Professor Emeritus of the University of Westminster, where he was Professor of Media Studies and Director of the Centre for Communication and Information Studies from 1976–2000. Since 1978 he has been an editor of *Media, Culture and Society*. He is the author of *Capitalism and Communication* (1990) and *Emancipation, the Media and Modernity: Arguments About the Media and Social Theory* (2000).

Nathan Godfried, Associate Professor of History at the University of Maine at Orono, is the author of *Bridging the Gap Between Rich and Poor: American Economic Development Policy Toward the Arab East, 1942–1949* (1987) and *WCFL: Chicago's Voice of Labor, 1926–1978* (1997).

John Hartley is Executive Research Director in the faculty of Creative Industries at Queensland University of Technology. He was recently named a Federation Fellow by the Australian government. Hartley is author of numerous books, articles, and essays dealing with television and new media, including *Uses of Television* (1999).

Annette Hill is a reader in communication at the Centre for Communication and Information Studies, University of Westminster. She is the author of *Shocking Entertainment: Viewer Response to Violent Movies* (1997) and the coauthor, with David Gauntlett, of *TV Living: Television, Culture, and Everyday Life* (1999). She is also the editor of *Framework: The Journal of Cinema and Media.*

Elizabeth Jacka is Professor of Communication Studies in the Faculty of the Humanities and Social Sciences at the University of Technology, Sydney. She has published several books on film and television history and policy including, most recently, *Australian Television and International Mediascapes*, with Stuart Cunningham (1996), and *New Patterns in Global Television: Peripheral Vision*, coedited with John Sinclair and Stuart Cunningham (1996).

Deborah L. Jaramillo received her Master of Arts in Media Arts from the University of Arizona in 2001. She is currently a doctoral student in the Department of Radio-Television-Film at the University of Texas at Austin.

Jeffrey P. Jones is Assistant Professor of Communication at Old Dominion University. He is the author of *Entertaining Politics: New Political Television and Civic Culture* (2005) and numerous articles dealing with the interactions of popular culture and politics.

Antonio C. La Pastina is Assistant Professor of Communication at Texas A&M University. He has conducted research in the Lower Rio Grande Valley, Central Texas, Northeast Brazil, and Central Italy. His work has appeared in *Journal of Broadcast and Electronic Media, International Journal of Cultural Studies, Communication Research,* and other journals.

Ron Lembo is Associate Professor Sociology at Amherst University. He is the author of *Thinking Through Television* (2000).

Elana Levine is a Ph.D. candidate in the Department of Communication Arts, University of Wisconsin-Madison. Her work has appeared in *Television & New Media*.

Amanda D. Lotz is Assistant Professor of Communication Studies at the University of Michigan. She has published articles in *Critical Studies in Media Communication, Feminist Media Studies, Television & New Media,* and other journals. She is the author of *Redesigning Women: Female-Centered Television After the Network Era* (forthcoming). The book explores the rise of female-centered dramas and cable networks targeted toward women in the late 1990s as the programs relate to changes in the U.S. television industry.

Sheldon H. Lu is Associate Professor of Chinese Literature and Film Studies at the University of Pittsburgh. He is the author of *From Historicity to Fictionality: The Chinese Poetics of Narrative* (1994) and *China, Transnational Visuality, Global Postmodernity* (2001); editor of *Transnational Chinese Cinemas: Identity, Nationhood, Gender* (1997); and coeditor, with Emilie Yeh, of *Chinese Language Film: Historiography, Poetics, Politics* (2005).

Jason Mittell is Assistant Professor of American Civilization and Film and Media Culture at Middlebury College. He is the author of *Genre and Television: From Cop Shows to Cartoons in American Culture* (2004) and is currently working on a book about narrative complexity in contemporary American television.

Susan Murray is Assistant Professor of Culture and Communication at New York University. She is the author of *Hitch Your Antenna to the Stars: Early Television and Broadcast Stardom* (2005) and coeditor of *Reality TV: Remaking Television Culture* (2004).

Horace Newcomb is Professor of Telecommunication in the Grady College of Journalism and Mass Communication, University of Georgia, where he holds the Lambdin Kay Chair for the Peabodys and is Director of the George Foster Peabody Awards. He is the editor of *Museum of Broadcast Communications Encyclopedia of Television* (2004).

Shawn J. Parry-Giles is Associate Professor of Communication, Affiliate Associate Professor of Women's Studies, and Director of the Center for Political Communication and Civic Leadership at the University of Maryland. She is the author of *The Rhetorical Presidency, Propaganda, and the Cold War, 1945–1955* (2002) and coauthor of *Constructing Clinton: Hyper-Reality and Presidential Image-Making in Postmodern Politics* (2002).

Trevor Parry-Giles is Assistant Professor of Communication at the University of Maryland. He is coauthor of *Constructing Clinton: Hyperreality and Presidential Image-Making in Postmodern Politics* (2002) and has published in *Quarterly Journal of Speech* and other journals.

Christopher Reed is Associate Professor and Chair of the Art Department at Lake Forest College in Illinois. He is the author of *Bloomsbury Rooms: Modernism, Subculture, and Domesticity* (2004) and editor of *A Roger Fry Reader* (1996) and *Not at Home: The Suppression of Domesticity in Modern Art and Architecture* (1996).

Yeidy M. Rivero is Assistant Professor in the Department of Communication and Culture at Indiana University, Bloomington. Her areas of interest include television studies, international communication, Latino/Latin American theater, and race and ethnic representations in media. She is author of *Tuning Out Blackness: Race and Nation in the History of Puerto Rican Television* (2005).

Greg Siegel is a Ph.D. candidate in the Department of Communication Studies at the University of North Carolina at Chapel Hill, where he is assistant editor of the journal of *Cultural Studies*. He has presented his work at the Society for Literature and Science Conference.

Roger Silverstone is Professor of Media and Communications at the London School of Economics. He is the author of numerous publications, including *Television and Everyday Life* (1994) and *Why Study the Media* (1999). His next book, *Screen Deep: Morality and Media in the 21st Century* is in preparation.

Lynn Spigel is Professor in the School of Communications at Northwestern University. She is author of *Welcome to the Dreamhouse: Popular Media and Postwar Suburbs* (2001) and *Make Room for TV: Television and the Family Ideal in Postwar America* (1992). She is coeditor, with Jan Olsson, of the anthology *Television After TV: Essays on a Medium in Transition* (2004).

David Thorburn is Professor of English and Media Studies at the Massachusetts Institute of Technology, where he is also Director of the MIT Communications Forum, sponsoring lectures, forums, and web-based activities, which compare the current experience of changing media with earlier periods of cultural and technological transformation.

Silvio Waisbord is Senior Officer at the Academy for Educational Development. Previously, he was an associate professor in the Department of Journalism and Media Studies at Rutgers University. He has written about media globalization, journalism, and development. He is coeditor of *Global Media, Latin Politics* (2002) and author of *Watchdog Journalism in South America: News, Accountability, and Democracy* (2000).

Mimi White is Professor of Radio/TV/Film at Northwestern University and in 2004–05 was the Bicentennial Fulbright Professor in North American Studies at the Renvall Institute, University of Helsinki. She is author of *Tele-Advising: Therapeutic Discourse in American Television* (1992) and coauthor with James Scwoch and Susan Reilly, of *Media Knowledge: Popular Culture, Pedagogy, and Critical Citizenship* (1992).

Prakash Younger is Assistant Professor in the Department of Film Studies at the University of Western Ontario. He recently served as program coordinator of the Persistence of Form Conference on Film and Literature at Florida State University. He has presented and published work on a variety of topics, including popular Indian cinema, classical film theory, and film as philosophy.